KU-774-259

VOLUME TWO

BÉRANGER—CHIMPANZEE

THE BRITISH ENCYCLOPEDIA

IN TEN VOLUMES

ILLUSTRATED

THE BRITISH ENCYCLOPEDIA

ILLUSTRATED

With an Introduction by
CYRIL NORWOOD, M.A., D. Litt.,
Headmaster of Harrow

Prepared under the general editorship of J. M. Parrish, M.A. (Oxon.), John R. Crossland, F.R.G.S., and Angelo S. Rappoport, Ph.D., B. ès L., with the specialist assistance and contributions of over 100 experts

VOLUME
TWO

ODHAMS PRESS LIMITED
LONDON, W.C. 2

KEY TO PRONUNCIATION

The method of marking pronunciations here employed is either (1) by marking the syllable on which the accent falls, or (2) by a simple system of transliteration, to which the following is the Key :

VOWELS

ā, as in f*a*te, or in b*a*re.

ä, as in *a*lms, Fr. *â*me, Ger. B*a*hn = á of Indian names.

ȧ, the same sound short or medium, as in Fr. b*a*l, Ger. M*a*nn.

a, as in f*a*t.

ạ, as in f*a*ll.

a, obscure, as in rur*a*l, similar to *u* in b*u*t, ė in her : common in Indian names.

ē, as in m*e* = *i* in mach*i*ne.

e, as in met.

ė, as in her.

ī, as in p*i*ne, or as *ei* in Ger. m*ei*n.

i, as in pin, also used for the short sound corresponding to ē, as in French and Italian words.

eu, a long sound as in Fr. jeûne = Ger. long *ö*, as in Söhne, Göthe (Goethe).

eu, corresponding sound short or medium, as in Fr. p*eu* = Ger. *ö* short.

ō, as in note, m*oa*n.

o, as in not, soft—that is, short or medium.

ö, as in m*o*ve, tw*o*.

ū, as in t*u*be.

u, as in t*u*b : similar to ė and also to *a*.

ụ, as in b*u*ll.

ü, as in Sc. ab*u*ne = Fr. *û* as in d*û*, Ger. *ü* long as in gr*ü*n, B*ü*hne.

u̇, the corresponding short or medium sound, as in Fr. b*u*t, Ger. M*ü*ller.

oi, as in *oi*l.

ou, as in p*ou*nd ; or as *au* in Ger. H*au*s.

CONSONANTS

Of the *consonants*, **b, d, f, h, j, k, l, m, n, ng, p, sh, t, v, z,** always have their common English sounds, when used to transliterate foreign words. The letter **c** is not used by itself in re-writing for pronunciation, **s** or **k** being used instead. The only consonantal symbols, therefore, that require explanation are the following :

ch is always as in ri*ch*.

d, nearly as *th* in *th*is = Sp. *d* in Ma*d*ri*d*, etc.

g is always hard, as in *g*o.

h represents the guttural in Scotch lo*ch*, Ger. na*ch*, also other similar gutturals.

ŋ, Fr. nasal *n* as in bo*n*.

r represents both English *r*, and *r* in foreign words, which is generally much more strongly trilled.

s, always as in *s*o.

th, as *th* in *th*in.

th, as *th* in *th*is.

w always consonantal, as in *w*e.

x = ks, which are used instead.

y always consonantal, as in *y*ea (Fr. *ligne* would be re-written lēny).

zh, as *s* in plea*s*ure = Fr. *j*.

THE BRITISH ENCYCLOPEDIA

VOLUME II

BÉRANGER (bā-rāṇ-zhā), **Pierre Jean de.** French lyric poet, born in Paris 19th Aug., 1780, in the house of his grandfather, a tailor, in the Rue Montorgueil. His father was a restless and scheming man, and young Béranger, after witnessing from the roof of his school the destruction of the Bastille, was placed under the charge of an aunt who kept a tavern at Peronne. At the age of fourteen he was apprenticed to a printer in Peronne, but was ultimately summoned to Paris to assist his father in his financing and plotting. After many hardships he withdrew in disgust from the atmosphere of chicanery and intrigue in which he found himself involved, betook himself to a garret, did what literary hack-work he could, and made many ambitious attempts in poetry and drama. Reduced to extremity, he applied in 1804 to Lucien Bonaparte for assistance, and succeeded in obtaining from him, first, a pension of 1000 francs, and five years later a university clerkship.

Although as yet unprinted, many of his songs had become extremely popular, and in 1815 the first collection of them was published. A second collection, published in 1821, made him obnoxious to the Bourbon Government, and, in addition to being dismissed from his office in the university, he was sentenced to three months' imprisonment and a fine of 500 francs. A third collection appeared in 1825, and in 1828 a fourth, which subjected him to a second State prosecution, an imprisonment of nine months, and a fine of 10,000 francs. In 1833 he published his fifth and last collection, thereafter remaining silent till his death. Shortly after the revolution of Feb., 1848, he was elected representative of the department of the Seine in the constituent Assembly, but sent in his resignation in the month of May of same year. He died at Paris on 16th July, 1857. From first to last he kept in sympathetic touch with the French people in all their humours, social and political, influencing men in the mass more than any lyric poet of modern times. Many of his pieces are inspired with a socialistic spirit of indignation and revolt. In private life he was the most amiable and benevolent of men, living unobtrusively with his old friend Judith Frère, who died a few months before him.—BIBLIOGRAPHY: Paul Boiteau, *Vie de Béranger*; A. Arnould, *Béranger, ses amis, ses ennemis, et ses critiques*; Jules Janin, *Béranger et son temps*; A. Boulle, *Béranger, sa vie, son œuvre.*

BERAR'. A province of British India, in the Deccan, till 1903 attached to Hyderabad, but now a commissionership in the Central Provinces and Berar (q.v.); area, 17,766 sq. miles, chiefly an elevated valley at the head of a chain of ghauts. It is watered by several affluents of the Godavari and by the Tapti, and has a fertile soil, producing some of the best cotton, millet, and wheat crops in India. The two principal towns of Berar are Amráoti (pop. 40,694) and Khamgaon (12,390). Coal and iron-ore are both found in the province, the pop. of which is 3,443,765. There are numerous cotton-mills at work. Berar was permanently leased by the Nizam to the British Government in 1853 in security of arrears due. *See* CENTRAL PROVINCES.

BERAT'. A fortified town in Albania; residence of a Greek archbishop. Captured by the Austrians during the European War, the town was retaken by the Italians on 3rd Oct., 1918. Pop. 10,403.

BERBER. A town on the right bank of the Nile, about 20 miles below the confluence of the Atbara, in the Anglo-Egyptian Sudan; it has risen greatly in importance through the Nile to Red Sea railway. Pop. 10,000.

BERBE'RA. A port and trading-place on the Somali coast, East Africa, on a bay affording convenient anchorage, in the Gulf of Aden. It was taken possession of by the British along with a strip of adjacent territory in 1885, and is now the chief place in British Somaliland. Trade is carried on with Aden and with the interior. Pop. 23,000, but it amounts to 30,000 during the annual fair.

BER'BERIS. *See* BARBERRY.

BER'BERS. A people spread over nearly the whole of Northern Africa, from whom the name *Barbary* is derived. The complex problem of the origin of the Berber race has not yet been solved. Sergi includes them in the "Mediterranean Race." Whatever opinion, however, may be held regarding their origin, they form a linguistic unity. The chief branches into which the Berbers are divided are, first, the Amazirgh or Amazigh, of Northern Morocco, numbering from 2,000,000 to 2,500,000. They are for the most part quite independent of the Sultan of Morocco, and live partly under chieftains and hereditary princes and partly in small republican communities. Second, the Shuluh, Shillooh, or Shellakah, who number about 1,450,000, and inhabit the south of Morocco. They are more highly civilised than the Amazirgh. Third, the Kabyles in Algeria and Tunis, who are said to number 960,000 souls; and fourth, the Berbers of the Sahara, who inhabit the oases. Among the Sahara Berbers the most remarkable are the Beni-Mzâb and the Tuaregs. To these we may also add the Guanches of the Canary Islands, now extinct, but undoubtedly of the same race.

The Berbers generally are about middle height; their complexion is brown, and sometimes almost black, with brown and glossy hair. They are sparely built, but robust and graceful; the features approach the European type. Their language has affinities to the Semitic group, but Arabic is spoken along the coast. They are believed to represent the ancient Mauritanians, Numidians, Gætulians, etc. The Berbers live in huts or houses, and practise various industries. Thus they smelt iron, copper, and lead, manufacture gun-barrels, implements of husbandry, etc., knives, swords, gunpowder, and a species of black soap. Some of the tribes breed mules, asses, and stock in considerable numbers, but many of the Berbers live by plunder.—BIBLIOGRAPHY: Jules Lionel, *Races Berbères*; Anthony Wilkin, *Among the Berbers of Algeria*; G. Sergi, *The Mediterranean Race*; R. Basset, *Contes populaires Berbères*; V. Piquet, *Les Civilisations de l'Afrique du Nord. Berbères.*

BERBICE (ber-bēs'). A district of British Guiana watered by the River Berbice, which is navigable for 175 miles, and has at its mouth the seaport Berbice or New Amsterdam, with a pop. of 8,000. *See* GUIANA.

BERCHTESGADEN (ber*h*'tes-gä-dėn). A town of Upper Bavaria, on the Achen or Alben in a beautiful situation, with a royal palace and villa, an ancient church, etc. There are important salt-mines in the neighbourhood, and the people are also renowned for artistic carvings in wood. Pop. 3740.

BERCK. A fishing-town of France, department Pas-de-Calais. A mile distant is Berck-Plage, a famous seaside resort. Pop. 13,890.

BER'DICHEV (Pol. *Berdyczew*). A city of the Ukraine, government of Kiev, with broad streets, well-built houses, numerous industrial establishments, and a very large trade, having largely-attended fairs. Pop. 55,613, including many Jews.

BERDYANSK'. A seaport of Southern Russia, government of Taurida, on the north shore of the Sea of Azof, with an important export and inland trade. Pop. 40,292.

BERE'ANS (or **BARCLAYANS,** from their founder, Barclay). An insignificant sect of dissenters from the Church of Scotland (originating in Edinburgh in 1773), who profess to follow the ancient Bereans (Acts, xvii. 10-13) in building their faith and practice upon the Scriptures alone, without regard to any human authority whatever. They hold that the majority of professed Christians err in admitting the doctrine of a natural religion, natural conscience, etc., not founded upon revelation or derived from it by tradition; and they regard saving faith as attended by assurance.

BERENGA'RIUS OF TOURS. Born about 1000 at Tours, a teacher in the philosophical school in that city, and in 1040 Archdeacon of Angers; renowned for his philosophical acuteness as one of the scholastic writers, and also for the boldness with which in 1050 he declared himself against the doctrine of transubstantiation, and for his consequent persecutions. He was several times compelled to recant, but always returned to the same opinions, until he was forced in 1080 by the opposition of Lanfranc to retire to St. Cosme, an island in the Loire, near Tours, where he died in 1088. This Berengarius must not be confounded with Peter Berenger of Poitiers, who wrote a defence of his instructor Abelard.

BERENICE (Macedonian form of Pherenice, "bringer of victory"). The name of several distinguished women of antiquity; in particular the wife of Ptolemy Euergĕtes, King of Egypt. When her husband went to war in Syria, she made a vow to devote her beautiful hair to the gods if he returned safe. She accordingly hung it in the temple of Venus, from which it disappeared, and was said to have been transferred to the skies as the constellation *Coma Berenices*. (*See* Catallus, *Carmen 66*.) Also the wife of Mithridates the Great, King of Pontus; put to death by her husband (about 71 B.C.) lest she should fall into the hands of Lucullus.

BERENICE (ber-e-nī'sē). Anciently a town on the Egyptian coast of the Red Sea, a place of great trade.

BER'ESFORD, Lord Charles W. de la Poer. Admiral, born in 1846, died 6th Sept., 1919, son of the fourth Marquess of Waterford; entered the navy in 1859, became commander in 1875, captain 1882, rear-admiral 1897, vice-admiral 1902, admiral 1906. He was in command of the Condor at the bombardment of Alexandria in 1882, subsequently rendering most valuable services on land at the head of the Naval Brigade and otherwise. He represented several constituencies in Parliament: Waterford, 1874-80; E. Marylebone, 1885-90; York, 1898-1900; Woolwich, 1902-3; Portsmouth, 1910-6, when he was created Baron Beresford of Metemmeh and of Curraghmore. He became commander of the Channel Fleet in 1903, of the Mediterranean Fleet in 1905, and of the Channel Fleet again in 1907. He retired (in 1911) owing to friction with the Naval Board, and criticised the policy of Lord Fisher in his famous book *The Betrayal* (1912), condemning the shipbuilding policy of Great Britain from 1902 to 1909. He was a Lord of the Admiralty from 1886 to 1888. His publications, besides essays and articles on naval matters, include a *Life of Nelson*, and *The Break-up of China*, which he published after a visit to China in 1898-9.

BER'ESFORD, William Carr, Viscount. A distinguished commander, a natural son of the first Marquess of Waterford, born 1768. He entered the army, lost an eye in Nova Scotia, served at Toulon, and in Corsica, the West Indies, and Egypt. In 1806, as brigadier-general, he commanded the land force in the expedition to Buenos Ayres; and in 1808 remodelled the Portuguese army, receiving in return the titles Marshal of Portugal, Duke of Elvas, and Marquess of Santo Campo. He was subsequently engaged at Badajoz, Salamanca, Vittoria, and Bayonne, and for his bravery at the battle of Toulouse was raised to the peerage with the title of Baron (Viscount, 1823) Beresford. He died in 1854.

BERET'TA. *See* BIRETTA.

BEREZ'INA. A tributary of the Dnieper, in the Russian province of Minsk, rendered famous by the disastrous passage of the French army under Napoleon during the retreat from Moscow, 27th-29th Nov., 1812.

BEREZOV'. A town in Western Siberia, government of Tobolsk, on a branch of the Obi, the entrepôt of a large fur and skin district. Pop., chiefly Cossack, 1900.

BERG. An ancient duchy of Germany, on the Rhine. After it had been long consolidated with the Prussian dominions, Napoleon revived the title, and conferred it, with an enlarged territory, on Murat (1806), and afterwards on his nephew, Louis Napoleon. At the Congress of Vienna, in 1815, the whole was given to Prussia, and it is now included in the governments of Arnsberg, Cologne and Düsseldorf.

BER'GAMA (ancient, **PERGAMOS**). A town of Turkey, north of Smyrna; contains fine ruins of a Roman palace, etc. Pop. about 13,223.

BER'GAMO. A town of North Italy, capital of the province of Bergamo (1076 sq. miles, 541,615 inhabitants), consisting of two parts, the old town situated on hills and having quite an ancient appearance, and the new town almost detached and on the plain. It has a cathedral, an interesting church of the twelfth century, a school of art, picture-gallery, etc. It trades largely in silk, silk goods, corn, etc., has the largest annual fair in N. Italy, and extensive manufactures. The comic characters in the Italian masked comedy are Bergamese, or affect the Bergamese dialect. Pop. 82,101.

BER'GAMOT. *See* CITRUS.

BER'GEDORF. A town of Germany, in the territory of Hamburg, and a short distance south-east of that city, on the Bille, a tributary of the Elbe. Pop. 18,320.

BERGEN (ber'gen). A seaport on the west coast of Norway, the second town of the kingdom, about 25 miles from the open sea, between which and this place several islands intervene. It is in the same latitude as Lerwick. It is situated on and about the heads of two creeks or inlets, one of which forms a deep and commodious harbour, a large part of the town being on the tongue of land between. Rocky hills from 800 to 2000 feet high encircle the town on the land side, and promote almost perpetual rains. The town is well built, but has many narrow and uneven streets, owing partly to the irregularity of the site, and the houses are mostly of wood. There are a number of squares or open places, including the market-place at the head of the harbour. There is a cathedral (built in 1537) and several other churches, one of them dating from the middle of the thirteenth century. Among educational and other institutions are a classical school, a "real-school," school of navigation, public library, museum, theatres, etc. Electric tramways have been introduced.

Trade. The trade is large, timber, tar, train-oil, cod-liver oil, hides, herrings and other fish, particularly cured cod-fish, being exported in return for coal, corn, wine, brandy, coffee, cotton, woollens, sugar, etc. The steam-vessels belonging to Bergen have a far larger tonnage than those belonging to any other Norwegian port, but sailing-vessels are comparatively few. There is now railway connection with Christiania, and a wireless-telegraph coast-station. The town was founded in the eleventh century, and soon became an important seat of trade. About 1340 a factory was established here by the Hanseatic cities of Germany. Bergen was devastated by fire on 15th Jan., 1916. Pop. 98,546.

BERGEN-OP-ZOOM (ber'gen-op-zōm). A town, Holland, in a marshy situation on the Schelde, 20 miles N.N.W. of Antwerp. It was formerly of great strength, both from the morasses surrounding it and from its fortifications (now demolished), and successfully resisted the attacks of the Duke of Parma in 1581 and 1588, and of Spinola in 1622, but was taken by the French in 1747 and 1794, and unsuccessfully attempted by the British in 1814. Pop. 21,618.

BERGERAC (bārzh-ràk). A town, France, department of the Dordogne, on the River Dordogne, over which is a fine bridge. It has ironworks, and manufactures paper, hosiery, earthenware, liqueurs, etc. Pop. 17,520.

BERGERAC (bārzh-ràk), **Savinien Cyrano de.** A French writer, born 1619; composed at college *Le Pédant Joué*, a comedy, which furnished hints for Molière's *Fourberies de Scapin*; entered the army and won a high reputation for bravery, but was disabled by wounds. Notwithstanding these, however, he was throughout life a notorious duellist and universally dreaded. His best-known works, which show a strong but eccentric intelligence, are his *Histoire Comique des États et Empires de la Lune*, and *Histoire Comique des États et Empires du Soleil*, describing visits to the moon and the sun; they find kinship with Lucian's *Veracious History*, certain portions of Rabelais, and Swift's *Voyage to Laputa*. He died in 1655 at Paris. The late French poet, Edmond Rostand, has made him the hero of his popular play, *Cyrano de Bergerac*, which had a remarkable success when produced in Paris in 1897, and in London in 1919.

BERGHAUS (ber*h*'hous), **Heinrich.** German geographer, born 1797, died 1884. He served in 1815 in the German army in France, and was from 1816 to 1821 employed in the great trigonometrical survey of Prussia under the War Department. From 1824 to 1855 he was professor of applied mathematics in the Berlin Academy of Architecture, and afterwards resided at Stettin. Besides his various maps and his great *Physical Atlas* (of which an English edition was brought out), he published *Allgemeine Länder-und-Völkerkunde* (6 vols., 1836-42); *Die Völker des Erdballs* (2 vols., 1852-3); *Grundlinien der physikalischen Erdbeschreibung* (1856); *Grundlinien der Ethnographie* (1856); *Deutschland seit hundert Jahren* (5 vols., 1859-62); *Was man von der Erde Weiss* (4 vols., 1856-60); *Sprachschatz der Sassen* (*Low German Dictionary*, 1878-82) (left incomplete), etc. *The Physical Atlas*, entirely remodelled, was published by his nephew, Hermann Berghaus (1828-90).

BERGHEM (ber*h*'hem), or **BERCHEM, Nicholas.** Dutch painter, born at Haarlem in 1620, was a pupil of his father, Peter Klaas or Claesz, and also of Van Goyen and the elder Weenix, and resided seven years in Italy. He produced a large number of works, chiefly landscapes with cattle, the finest of which are at the Amsterdam Museum, others in the Louvre, at Leningrad, in the Dresden Gallery, and in the National Gallery, London. His pictures are remarkable for their colouring, chiaroscuro, composition, and careful finish. He also produced a number of etched plates, now very rare. How he acquired the name Berghem is unknown. He died at Amsterdam, 1683. Dujardin was among his pupils.

BERGK (berk), **Theodor.** German classical scholar, born 1812, died 1881. He was successively professor at Marburg, Freiburg in Breisgau, and Halle, but resigned the last position in 1869, and afterwards resided at Bonn. He rendered most service in the criticism and explanation of Greek lyric poetry, his edition of the Greek lyric poets, *Poetæ Lyrici Græci* (first edition, 3 vols., 1843; fourth edition, 1878), being a standard work.

BERGMAN (ber*h*′màn), **Torbern Olof.** A Swedish physicist and chemist, born 1735, died in 1784. He studied under Linnæus at Upsala; in 1758 became doctor of philosophy and professor of physics there; and in 1767 became professor of chemistry. He succeeded in the preparation of artificial mineral waters, discovered the sulphuretted hydrogen gas of mineral springs, and published a classification of minerals on the basis of their chemical character and crystalline forms. His theory of chemical affinities greatly influenced the subsequent development of chemistry. His *Physical Description of the Earth* was published in 1766.

BERGMEHL (bèrg′māl). Mountain-meal or fossil farina, a geological deposit (freshwater) in the form of an extremely fine powder, consisting almost entirely of the siliceous cell-walls of diatoms. It has been eaten in Lapland in seasons of great scarcity, mixed with ground corn and bark. It is a variety of diatomite (q.v.).

BERGSON, Henri Louis. French philosopher, of Jewish extraction, born in Paris 18th Oct. 1859. He graduated from the École Normale in 1881, and, after teaching for some years at Angers, Clermont Ferrand, and at the Collège Rollin in Paris, was appointed to the chair of philosophy in the Collège de France in 1900. He was elected a member of the Institute in 1901, and of the Académie Française in 1914. He was Gifford lecturer at Edinburgh in 1912, and was very active in disseminating propaganda during the European War. He was awarded the Nobel Prize for Literature in 1927.

In philosophy Bergson represents the romantic idealism which has a great deal in common with the ideas of Fichte and Eucken. He neglects the forms of logical construction—endeavouring to explain by means of intuition the acting forces of the universe. These forces he considers, in opposition to mechanical materialism, as living and creative, constantly creating and in a process of evolution.

The fundamental idea of Bergson's philosophy is contained in his work *Essais sur les données immédiates de la conscience,* wherein he analyses the idea of duration and distinguishes between the real, psychological time, and the mathematical time, or its relation to space. Insisting on the distinction between our respective experiences of time and space, he regards everything as in a state of ceaseless change in which there is no repetition or recurrence. In his *Evolution Créatrice* he sets forth a theory of life based upon a new idea of evolution.

Bergson is not an intellectualist, for he teaches that intelligence alone cannot lead us to a complete knowledge of the material world. The intellect, according to him, is unable to do justice to the nature of life, because intellect is only a function of life which has developed to deal only with what is partial. Instinct, on the other hand, which would enable us to understand life, is directed only towards the concrete particular object and does not concern itself with understanding. Bergson, therefore, in opposition to all previous philosophies, and especially that of Kant, built upon and constructed by intellect, relies upon intuition, which is really instinct become self-conscious and disinterested. It is noteworthy that Bergson's works contain passages and ideas reminiscent of the Jewish cabbala and the *Zohar.*

His works include: *Essai sur les données immédiates de la conscience, Matière et Mémoire, L'Evolution créatrice, Le Rire, Essai sur la signification du Comique* (1912), *L'Energie Spirituelle* (1919), *Durée et Simultanéité* (1923), etc. Several of his works have been translated into English.

BIBLIOGRAPHY: William James, *A Pluralistic Universe*; A. Fouillée, *La Pensée et les Nouvelles Écoles anti-intellectualistes*; Gillouin, *La philosophie de M. Bergson*; A. Lindsay, *The Philosophy of Bergson*; Stewart, *Critical Exposition of Bergson's Philosophy*; W. H. Carr, *Henri Bergson: the Philosophy of Change*; Le Roy, *Une philosophie nouvelle, Henri Bergson*; Benda, *La Bergsonisme ou une philosophie de mobilité*; Kitchin, *Bergson for Beginners.* See also Bergson's work *Time and Free Will* (English translation of *Essai sur les données immédiates de la conscience*).

BERGUES (bārg). A fortified town, France, department Nord, in a marshy district 5 miles S. of Dunkirk; formerly a place of much more importance, with a large monastery (St. Winoc). It has an interesting belfry tower of the sixteenth century. Pop. 3880.

BER′GYLT (*Sebastes norvegicus*). A fish of the northern seas, belonging to the gurnard family, but resembling a perch, and of a beautiful reddish colour, sometimes found on the British coasts, especially those of eastern Scotland, and called Norway haddock and Norway carp. It may grow to the length of 2 feet, and is good eating.

BERHAMPORE. A municipal town and the administrative headquarters of Murshidábád district, Bengal; formerly a military station, and having still large barracks. It was the scene of the first overt act of mutiny in 1857. Pop. 26,670.

BERHAMPUR. A town and military station in the north-east portion of Madras Presidency, the headquarters of Genjám district, with a trade in sugar and manufactures of silks. Pop. 32,731.

BER'IBERI. A disease of some warm regions, endemic in parts of India, Indo-China, Ceylon, etc., characterised by paralysis, numbness, difficult breathing, and often other symptoms, attacking strangers as well as natives, and generally fatal. It has sometimes been carried by ships to England.

BE'RING. *See* BEHRING.

BERKELEY (bėrk'li). A small market town, England, Gloucestershire, on the right bank of the Little Avon, celebrated for its castle, where Edward II. was murdered. Pop. 790.

BERKELEY. A town in California, the seat of the State university, established in 1868. Pop. 80,000.

BERKELEY (bėrk'li), **Dr. George.** Bishop of Cloyne, in Ireland, celebrated as a philosopher for a theory which stamps him as a very original thinker. He was born at Dysert, in County Kilkenny, in 1685 (his father being an officer of customs), and became M.A. and Fellow of Trinity College, Dublin, in 1707. He went to England in 1713, and soon came to be on friendly terms with Steele, Addison, Arbuthnot, and Swift. In 1713 he went to the Continent as chaplain to Lord Peterborough, and travelled as far as Leghorn, but did not stay long. He went abroad again in 1716, this time as tutor to a young man, and his stay lasted four years, the greater part of the time being spent in Italy. In 1721 he was appointed chaplain to the Lord-Lieutenant of Ireland, the Duke of Grafton. By a legacy from Miss Vanhomrigh (Swift's Vanessa) in 1723 his fortune was considerably increased. In 1724 he became Dean of Derry. Between 1721 and 1724 he held several offices in Dublin University, and in 1721 had been made D.D. He now published his proposals for providing the American plantations with a better supply of religious teachers, and for the conversion of the American savages to Christianity by the establishment of a college in the Bermuda Islands; and subscriptions having been raised, he set sail for Rhode Island in 1728, proposing to wait there till a promised grant of £20,000 had been got from Government. The scheme, which was not particularly promising, never got a start, however, and in 1732 he returned to London, where he stayed about two years. In 1734 he obtained the bishopric of Cloyne, where he spent almost the whole of the remainder of his life. In 1752, giving up his bishopric, he went to England, and he died suddenly at Oxford on 14th Jan., 1753. Berkeley holds an important place in the history of philosophy. His three main doctrines are *nominalism, immaterialism,* and *acquired visual perception.* His new theory of vision was his first remarkable contribution to the subject of philosophy or psychology. In it he maintains that sight gives us nothing beyond sensations that are quite incomplete in themselves, and must be supplemented by tactual sensations, or sensations derived from the sense of touch, and that sight by itself can tell us nothing of distance.

By his idealistic metaphysical theory he maintains that the belief in the existence of an exterior material world is false and inconsistent with itself; that those things which are called *sensible material objects* are not external but exist in the mind, and are merely impressions made on our minds by the immediate act of God, according to certain rules termed *laws of nature*, from which He never deviates; and that the steady adherence of the Supreme Spirit to these rules is what constitutes the reality of things to His creatures, and so effectually distinguishes the ideas perceived by sense from such as are the work of the mind itself or of dreams; that there is no more danger of confounding them together on this hypothesis than on that of the existence of matter. Berkeley was admirable as a writer; as a man he was said by his friend Pope to be possessed of "every virtue under heaven." Among philosophers there is none who presents fewer vulnerable points than Bishop Berkeley.

His most celebrated philosophical works are: *Essay towards a new Theory of Vision* (1709); a *Treatise concerning the Principles of Human Knowledge* (1710), in which his philosophical theory is fully set forth; *Three Dialogues between Hylas and Philonous* (1713); *Alciphron, or the Minute Philosopher* (1732); and *Theory of Vision, vindicated and explained* (1733). Another publication of some note in its day was *Siris, Philosophical Reflections and Inquiries concerning the Virtues of Tar-water* (1744). Tar-water, the use of which he had learned in America, he regarded as a sort of panacea, good for man and beast, at all times and in all circumstances and all ailments. Other works of his are of a mathematical and theological order. The only complete collection is that of Prof. A. Campbell Fraser (1901).—BIBLIOGRAPHY: A. Campbell Fraser,

Berkeley: Works, Life, Letters, and Dissertation; Berkeley (in Philosophical Classics); Sir L. Stephen, *English Thought in the 18th Century*; James Hastings (editor), *Encyclopædia of Ethics and Religion* (article *Berkeley*); H. R. Mead, *Bibliography of Berkeley*; B. Rand, *Berkeley and Percival.*

BERKELEY, George Charles Grantley Fitzhardinge. Sixth son of the fifth Earl of Berkeley, but second son after the legally recognised marriage, born 1800. From 1832-52 he was Liberal member for West Gloucestershire. He became notorious in 1836 for his assault upon Fraser, the publisher (for which he had to pay damages), and his duel with Maginn for a hostile review in *Fraser's Magazine* of his first novel, *Berkeley Castle.* Besides other stories, poems, and works upon travel, sport, etc., he published in 1865-6 his *Life and Recollections,* in 4 vols., and in 1867 a volume of reminiscences entitled *Anecdotes of the Upper Ten Thousand.* Both gave rise to a considerable amount of disapproval. He died in 1881.

BERK'HAMPSTEAD, GREAT. A town in England, Hertfordshire, with fine old church (in part older than the Norman Conquest), grammar school, manufactures of wooden ware, etc. Birth-place of Cowper. Pop. (1931), 7295.

BERKSHIRE, or BERKS. A county of England, between Oxfordshire, Buckinghamshire, Surrey, Hampshire, and Wilts; area, 462,080 acres, of which eighth-ninths are cultivated or under timber. A range of chalk hills, entering from Oxfordshire, crosses Berkshire in a westerly direction, and forms a sort of continuation of the Chilterns. North of this is the fertile Vale of Whitchorse, so called from the gigantic figure of a horse scooped out on the side of a chalk hill (Whitehorse Hill, 856 feet), and conspicuous to all the county around. The western and central parts are the most productive in the county, which contains rich pasturage and excellent dairy farms, and is especially suited for barley and wheat crops. Berkshire pigs are famous. Timber abounds, particularly oak and beech, and Windsor Forest is in this county. The Thames skirts the county on the north, and connects the towns of Abingdon, Wallingford, Reading, Henley, Maidenhead, and Windsor with the metropolis. Other streams are the Kennet in the south, and the Ock in the Vale of Whitehorse, both tributaries of the Thames. Few manufactures are carried on, the principal being agricultural implements and machinery, artificial manures, flour, paper, and biscuits (at Reading). Malt is made in great quantities. The minerals are unimportant. Berkshire returns three members to the House of Commons, the county divisions being Abingdon, Newbury, and Windsor. The county town is Reading; others are Maidenhead, Newbury, Windsor, and Abingdon. Pop. (1931), 311,334.

BERKSHIRE REGIMENT, ROYAL (Princess Charlotte of Wales's). Raised in 1714, and once known as "Trelawny's," took part as marines in the bombardment of Copenhagen, fought in the Crimea, and earned the title "Royal" for services at Tofrek, Egypt (1885). In the European War the regiment was distinguished at Cambrai and Neuve Chapelle.

BER'LAD. A town of Rumania, on the Berlad, a navigable tributary of the Siret. Pop. 25,367.

BERLEN'GAS. A group of rocky islets off the coast of Portugal, with a lighthouse.

BERLICHINGEN (ber'li-*h*ing-ėn), **Götz** or **Godfrey von,** with the Iron Hand. Born at Jaxthausen, in Suabia, in 1480. He took part in various quarrels among the German princes; and having lost his right hand at the siege of Landshut, wore thereafter one made of iron. In constant feud with his baronial neighbours, and even with free cities like Nuremberg, he at last headed the insurgents in the Peasants' War of 1525, and suffered imprisonment on their defeat. After the dissolution of the Suabian League, he again fought against the Turks (1541) and the French (1544). He died in 1562. His autobiography, printed at Nuremberg in 1731, furnished Goethe with the subject of his drama *Goetz von Berlichingen.*

BERLIN'. The largest town in Germany; capital of the Prussian dominions and of the German Republic, in the province of Brandenburg, on a dreary sandy plain on both sides of the Spree, a sluggish stream, here about 200 feet broad. It has water communication to the North Sea by the Spree, which flows into the Havel, a tributary of the Elbe, and to the Baltic by canals connecting with the Oder. The original portion of the city, now a very small part of the whole, lies on the right bank of the river, and is irregularly built. The more modern portions are regular in plan, and the streets are lined with lofty and well-built edifices mostly of white freestone, or brick covered with a coating of plaster or cement. Of the numerous bridges the finest is the Palace (Schloss) Bridge, 104 feet wide, and having eight piers surmounted by colossal groups of sculpture in marble.

The principal and most frequented street, Unter den Linden (" under the lime trees,") is about two-thirds of a mile in length and 1600 feet wide, the centre being occupied by a double avenue of lime trees. At the east end of this street, and round the Lustgarten, a square with which it is connected by the Schloss Bridge, are clustered the principal public buildings of the city, such as the royal palace, the palace of the ex-Crown Prince, the arsenal, the university, the museums, Royal Academy, etc.; while at the west end is the Brandenburg Gate, regarded as one of the finest portals in existence. Immediately beyond this gate is the Tiergarten (zoological garden), an extensive and well-wooded park containing the palace of Bellevue and places of public amusement. From the south side of the Königsplatz, crossing the Tiergarten, runs the broad Siegesallee, adorned by thirty-two marble statues representing the rulers of the House of Hohenzollern, the gift of William II. to the city. There are also several other public parks. The palace or Schloss is a vast rectangular pile; the museum of painting and sculpture (opposite the Schloss) is a fine Grecian building; the cathedral is a grand new Renaissance structure; the theatre is a fine Grecian edifice. The library and palace of the ex-emperor are united; the former contains above 900,000 volumes and 15,500 manuscripts and charts. The arsenal (Zeughaus), besides arms and artillery, contains flags and other trophies of great antiquity. The university, the exchange, the Italian opera-house, the principal Jewish synagogue, the town hall, and the old architectural academy are all beautiful structures. The prevailing style of the newer buildings, both public and private, is Grecian, pure or Italianised. One of the most remarkable of modern monuments is that erected in 1851 to Frederick the Great in the Unter den Linden—the *chef d'œuvre* of Rauch and his pupils.

The literary institutions of the city are numerous and excellent; they include the university (founded in 1810), having an educational staff of over 500 professors and teachers, and attended by over 8000 students; the academy of sciences; the academy of fine arts; and the technical high school or academy of architecture and industry (occupying a large new building in the suburb of Charlottenburg).

Manufactures. The manufactures are various and extensive, including steam-engines and other machinery, brass-founding and various articles of metal, sewing-machines, paper, cigars, pottery and porcelain, pianos and harmoniums, artificial flowers, etc. In the iron-foundry, busts, statues, bas-reliefs, etc., are cast, together with a great variety of ornaments of unrivalled delicacy of workmanship. The oldest parts of the city were originally poor villages, and first rose to some importance under Markgraf Albert (1206-20), yet about two centuries ago Berlin was still a place of little consequence, the first important improvement being made by the great Elector Frederick William, who planted the Unter den Linden, and in whose time it already numbered 20,000 inhabitants. Under his successors, Frederick I. and Frederick the Great, the city was rapidly enlarged and improved, the population increasing fivefold in the hundred years preceding the death of Frederick the Great, and tenfold in the century succeeding it. The area of greater Berlin is 339 sq. miles, and the population within this area was, in 1925, 4,024,154.

BERLIN'. Former name of a town of Canada, province Ontario, about 60 miles W.S.W. of Toronto, with flourishing industries. At the request of the inhabitants the name of the town was changed to Kitchener in 1915. Pop. 30,793.

BERLIN', or BERLINE. A four-wheeled carriage consisting of an enclosed fore-portion for two occupants, and a back seat with a calash top for servants; invented in Berlin.

BERLIN BLUE. *See* BLUE.

BERLIN SPIRIT. A coarse spirit distilled from potatoes, beet, etc.

BERLIN, TREATY OF. The treaty, signed 13th July, 1878, at the close of the Berlin Congress, which was constituted by the representatives of the six Great Powers and Turkey. The Treaty of San Stefano, previously concluded between Turkey and Russia, was modified by the Berlin Treaty, which resulted in the division of Bulgaria into two parts, Bulgaria proper and Eastern Rumelia, the cession of parts of Armenia to Russia and Persia, the independence of Rumania, Serbia, and Montenegro, the transference of Bosnia and Herzegovina to Austrian administration, and the retrocession of Bessarabia to Russia. Greece was also to have an accession of territory. The British representatives were Beaconsfield, Salisbury, and Lord Odo Russell. By a separate arrangement previously made between Britain and Turkey, the former got Cyprus to administer.

BERLIOZ (ber-li-os), **Hector.** A French composer, born in 1803. He forsook medicine to study music at the Paris Conservatoire, where he gained the first prize in 1830 with his cantata *Sardanapale*. For about two years he studied in Italy, and when on his return he began to produce his larger works, he found himself compelled to take up the pen both in defence of his principles and for his own better maintenance. As critic of the *Journal des Débats* and feuilletonist he displayed scarcely less originality than in his music, his chief literary works being the *Traité d'Instrumentation* (1844), *Lettres Intimes* (1852), *Les Soirées d'Orchestre* (1853), and *A travers Chant* (1862). His musical works belong to the Romantic school, and are specially noteworthy for the resource they display in orchestral colouring. The more important are: *Harold en Italie*, *Episode de la Vie d'un Artiste*, and *Le Retour à la Vie*; *Roméo et Juliette* (1834), *Damnation de Faust* (1846); the operas *Benvenuto Cellini*, *Beatrice and Benedict*, and *Les Troyens*; *L'Enfance du Christ*, and the *Requiem*. He married an English actress, Miss Smithson, but afterwards lived apart from her. He died in 1869. Other literary works are *Voyage Musical en Allemagne et en Italie*, *Les Grotesques de la Musique*, etc. After his death appeared *Mémoires*, written by himself.—BIBLIOGRAPHY; A. Julien, *H. Berlioz: la vie, le combat, et les œuvres*; E. Hippeau, *Berlioz et son temps*; L. H. Berlioz, *Life of Berlioz* (in Everyman's Library).

BERM. In fortification, a level space a few feet wide between outside slope of a rampart and the scarp of the ditch.

BER'MONDSEY. A parliamentary and municipal borough of London, on the Surrey side of the Thames, between Southwark and Rotherhithe, with tanyards, wharfs, etc. It returns 2 members to Parliament. Pop. (1931), 111,526.

BERMU'DA, or SOMERS ISLANDS. A cluster of small islands in the Atlantic Ocean belonging to Britain and numbering about 360, set within a space of about 20 miles long and 6 wide; area, 19 sq. miles or 12,160 acres; about twenty inhabited. They were first discovered by Juan Bermudez, a Spaniard, in 1522; in 1609 Sir George Somers, an Englishman, was wrecked here, and, after his shipwreck, formed the first settlement. The most considerable are St. George, Bermuda or Long Island (with the chief town Hamilton, the seat of the Governor), Somerset, St. David's, and Ireland. They form an important British naval and military station. An immense iron floating-dock, capable of receiving a vessel of 17,500 tons, was towed from Britain to the Bermudas in 1902. The climate is generally healthy and delightful, but they have been sometimes visited by yellow fever. Numbers of persons from the United States and Canada now pass the colder months of the year in these islands. About 4000 acres are cultivated. The soil, though light, is in general rich and fertile; there is, however, little fresh water except rain-water, preserved in cisterns. The inhabitants cultivate and export potatoes, arrowroot, onions, bananas, tomatoes, etc. Oranges and other fruits are also cultivated. Bermuda is a British colony with representative government. The military stationed here usually number about 1500. Pop. (in 1921), 20,127 (including 7006 whites). Estimated pop. in 1926, 31,500.

BERMU'DA GRASS (*Cynodon dactylon*). A grass cultivated in the West Indies, United States, etc., a valuable fodder grass in warm climates. It is a perennial with erect branches on which flowers appear.

BERN. A town in Switzerland, capital of the canton Bern, and, since 1848, of the whole Swiss Confederation, standing on the declivity of a hill washed on three sides by the Aar. The principal street is wide and adorned with arcades and ornamented fountains; the houses generally are substantially built of stone. Among the public buildings are the great Gothic cathedral, built between 1421 and 1573; the Church of the Holy Spirit; the Federal Council buildings (or Parliament house), commanding a splendid view of the Alps; the university, founded in 1834; the town house, a Gothic edifice of the fifteenth century; the mint; several fine bridges; etc. Bern has an excellent public and other libraries, museum, etc. Trade and commerce good; manufactures: woollens, linens, silk stuffs, stockings, watches, clocks, toys, etc. Few cities have finer promenades, and the surroundings are very picturesque. Bern became a free city of the Empire in 1218. In 1353 it entered the Swiss Confederacy. Pop. 113,114.

The canton of Bern has an area of 2657 sq. miles. The northern part belongs to the Jura mountain system, the southern to the Alps; between these there is an elevated undulating region where the Emmenthal, one of the richest and most fertile valleys in Switzerland, is situated. The southern part of the canton forms the Bernese Oberland (Upperland). The lower valleys here are fertile and agreeable, higher up are excellent Alpine pastures, and above them rise the highest mountains of Switzerland (Finsteraarhorn, Schreckhorn, Wetterhorn, Eiger, and Jungfrau). The canton is drained by the Aar and its tributaries ; the chief lakes are those of Brienz, Thun, and Bienne. Of the surface over 58 per cent is under cultivation or pasture. Agriculture and cattle-rearing are the chief occupations ; manufactures embrace linen, cotton, silk, iron, watches, glass, pottery, etc. Bienne and Thun are the chief towns after Bern. Pop. 691,101, 87 per cent being Protestants, and nearly as many German-speaking.

BERNADOTTE (ber-nȧ-dot), **Jean Baptiste-Jules.** A French general, afterwards raised to the Swedish throne, the son of an advocate of Pau, born in 1764. He enlisted at seventeen, became sergeant-major in 1789, and subaltern in 1790. In 1794 he was appointed a general of division, and distinguished himself greatly in the campaign in Germany, and on the Rhine. In 1798 he married Mademoiselle Clary, sister-in-law of Joseph Bonaparte. The following year he became for a short time Minister of War, and on the establishment of the empire was raised to the dignity of Marshal of France, and the title of Prince of Ponte-Corvo. On the death of the Prince of Holstein-Augustenburg the heir apparency to the Swedish crown was offered to the Prince of Ponte-Corvo, who accepted with the consent of the emperor, went to Sweden, abjured Catholicism, and took the title of Prince Charles John.

In the maintenance of the interests of Sweden a serious rupture occurred between him and Bonaparte, followed by his accession in 1812 to the coalition of sovereigns against Napoleon. At the battle of Leipzig he contributed effectually to the victory of the Allies. At the close of the war strenuous attempts were made by the Emperor of Austria and other sovereigns to restore the family of Gustavus IV. to the crown ; but Bernadotte, retaining his position as Crown Prince, became King of Sweden on the death of Charles XIII. in 1818, under the title of Charles XIV. During his reign agriculture and commerce made great advances, and many important public works were completed. He died 8th March, 1844, and was succeeded by his son Oscar.—BIBLIOGRAPHY : Sarrans, *Histoire de Bernadotte* ; C. Schefer, *Bernadotte roi* ; L. Pinguad, *Bernadotte, Napoléon, et les Bourbons.*

BERNARD (ber-när), **Charles de.** A French novelist of the school of Balzac, born in 1804, died in 1850. His best works were : *Le Gerfaut* (1838), *Ailes d'Icare* (1839), *La Peau du Lion* (1841), *L'Homme Sérieux,* and *Le Gentilhomme Campagnard* (1847). Many of his earlier works, however, are also widely known, especially the *Femme de quarante ans* and the *Nœud Gordien.* He also wrote poems and dramatic pieces.

BERNARD (ber-när), **Claude.** French physiologist, born 1813 ; studied at Paris ; held in succession chairs of physiology in the Faculty of Sciences, the Collège de France, and the Museum, and died at Paris 1878. Amongst his many works may be cited his *Researches on the Functions of the Pancreas* (1849), *On the Sympathetic System* (1852), *Experimental Physiology in its Relation to Medicine* (1855-6), *On the Physiological Properties and Pathological Alterations of the various Liquids of the Organism* (1859), and his *Nutrition and Development* (1860).

BER'NARD, GREAT ST. A celebrated Alpine pass in Switzerland, canton of Valais, on the mountain-road leading from Martingy in Switzerland to Aosta in Piedmont, and rising to a height of 8150 feet. On the east side of the pass is Mount Velan, and on the west the Pointe de Dronaz. Almost on the very crest of the pass, near a small lake on which ice some-

St. Bernard Dog

times remains throughout the year, is the famous Hospice, next to Etna Observatory the highest inhabited spot in Europe. It is a massive stone building, capable of accommodating seventy or eighty travellers with beds, and of sheltering 300, and is tenanted by ten or fifteen brethren of the order of St. Augustine, who have devoted themselves by vow to the aid of travellers crossing the mountains. The institution is chiefly supported by subscription and donations. The severest cold recorded is 29° F. below zero, but it has often been 18° and 20° below zero ; and few of the monks survive the period of their vow.

The dogs kept at St. Bernard, to

assist the brethren in their humane labours, are well known. The true St. Bernard dog was a variety by itself, but this is now extinct, though there are still descendants of the last St. Bernard crossed with a Swiss shepherd's dog. The colour of these is yellowish, or white with yellow-grey or brown spots; head large and broad, muzzle short, lips somewhat pendulous, hanging ears. A pagan temple formerly stood on the pass, and classic remains are found in the vicinity. The Hospice was founded in 962 by St. Bernard of Menthon, an Italian ecclesiastic, for the benefit of pilgrims to Rome. In May, 1800, Napoleon led an army of 30,000 men, with its artillery and cavalry, into Italy by this pass.

BERNARD, LITTLE ST. A mountain, Italy, belonging to the Graian Alps, about 10 miles S. of Mont Blanc. The pass across it, one of the easiest in the Alps, is supposed to be that which Hannibal used. Elevation of Hospice, 7192 feet.

BERNARD (ber-när), **Pierre Joseph.** A French poet, to whom Voltaire gave the name Gentil-Bernard, born 1710. He was for some time the pet poet of the salons and of Madame de Pompadour's "petits soupers," reading there translations from Ovid's *Art of Love* and his own essays in erotic poetry. He was the librettist of Rameau's *Castor and Pollux.* Died 1775.

BER'NARD, SAINT, of Clairvaux. One of the most illustrious and influential ecclesiastics of the Middle Ages, born at Fontaines, Burgundy, near Dijon, 1090, of a noble family. In 1112 he became a monk at Citeaux; in 1115 first Abbot of Clairvaux, the great Cistercian monastery near Langres. His austerities, tact, courage, and eloquence speedily gave him a wide reputation; and when, on the death of Honorius II. (1130), two Popes, Innocent and Anaclete, were elected, the judgment of Bernard in favour of the former was accepted by nearly all Europe. In 1140 he secured the condemnation of Abelard for heresy; and after the election of his pupil, Eugenius III., to the papal chair, he may be said to have exercised supreme power in the Church. After the capture of Edessa by the Turks, he was induced to preach a new crusade, which he did (1146) with disastrous effectiveness, the large host raised by him being destroyed. He died 20th Aug., 1153. Seventy-two monasteries owed their foundation or enlargement to him; and he left no fewer than 440 epistles, 340 sermons, and 12 theological and moral treatises. St. Bernard has rightly been considered as the virtual Pope of his age, and for a few years the centre of Christendom was transferred from Rome to Clairvaux. The standard edition of his works is that of Mabillon. Many of St. Bernard's works have been translated into English by S. J. Eales. He was canonised in 1174 by Pope Alexander III. Dante's references to St. Bernard (*Paradiso,* xxxi.) show the regard in which he was universally held. *See* ABELARD.—BIBLIOGRAPHY: R. S. Storrs, *Bernard of Clairvaux*; J. C. Morison, *St. Bernard*; L. Janauschek, *Bibliographia Bernardina.*

BERNARD DE VENTADOUR. A troubadour of the twelfth century. The son of a domestic servant, he was detected in an amour with the wife of his master, the Comte de Ventadour, and took refuge at the Court of Raymond V., Comte de Toulouse. His songs, which were praised by Petrarch, are yet highly esteemed.

BER'NARDINE MONKS. A name given in France to the Cistercians, after St. Bernard. *See* CISTERCIANS.

BERNARDO DEL CARPIO. A half-legendary Spanish hero of the ninth century, son of Ximena, sister of Alphonso the Chaste, by Don Sancho of Saldagua. Alphonso put out the eyes of Don Sancho and imprisoned him, but spared Bernardo, who distinguished himself in the Moorish wars, and finally succeeded in obtaining from Alphonso the Great the promise that his father should be given up to him. At the appointed time his father's corpse was sent to him, and Bernardo in disgust quitted Spain for France, where he spent the remainder of his life as a knight-errant.

BERNARD OF MORLAIX. A monk of the abbey of Cluny under Peter the Venerable (1122-56). He wrote a Latin poem, *On the Contempt of the World,* in about 3000 leonine dactylic verses, from which are taken the popular hymns, *Jerusalem the Golden, Brief Life is Here Our Portion,* etc.

BERNARD OF TREVISO. A noted Italian alchemist, born at Padua 1406, died 1490. Most important work: *Tractatus de secretissimo philosophorum opere chemico* (1600).

BERNAUER (ber'nou-ėr), **Agnes.** The daughter of a poor Augsburg (or Biberach) citizen, whom Duke Albert of Bavaria, only son of the reigning prince, secretly married. He conducted her to his own castle of Vohburg; but his father wishing to marry him to Anne, daughter of the Duke of Brunswick, he was compelled to proclaim his marriage with Agnes, giving her for residence the castle of Straubing, on the Danube. The incensed Duke of Bavaria, however, caused her to be seized in her castle during the absence of his son, accused her of sorcery, and had her drowned in the Danube in 1435. Albert in revenge took arms against his father, but the Emperor Sigismund finally reconciled them. The Duke Ernest raised a chapel to the memory of Agnes, and Albert married the Princess of Brunswick.

BERNAY (ber-nā). A town, France, department of Eure, on the Charentonne, with some manufactures and a horse fair, held in the fifth week in Lent, one of the largest in France. Pop. 7883.

BERNBURG (bern'bụrh). A town, Germany, Free State of Anhalt, on both sides of the Saale, divided into the old, the new, and the high town, the first two communicating by a bridge with the last. It contains an oil-mill, breweries, distilleries; and manufactures paper, earthenware, copper and tin wares, etc. Pop. 34,305.

BERNE. *See* BERN.

BER'NERS, John Bourchier, Lord. An English baron, a descendant of the Duke of Gloucester, youngest son of Edward III., born 1474; member of Parliament, 1495-1529; aided in suppressing an insurrection in Cornwall, raised by Michael Joseph, a blacksmith, 1497; Chancellor of Exchequer, 1515; Ambassador to Spain, 1518; for many years Governor of Calais; died 1532. He translated Froissart's *Chronicles* (1523-5) and other works, his translation of the former being an English classic.

BER'NERS, or BARNES, Juliana, Lady. An English writer of the fifteenth century, of whom little more is known than that she was prioress of the nunnery of Sopewell, near St. Albans. The book attributed to her, and known as the *Boke of St. Albans*, is entitled, in the edition of Wynkyn de Worde (1496), *Treatyse perteynynge to Hawkynge, Huntynge and Fysshynge with an angle; also a right noble Treatyse on the Lygnage of Cot Armours*, etc. The treatise on fishing and on coat-armour did not appear in the first St. Albans edition of 1481. It was for a long time the popular sporting manual.—Cf. William Blades, *The Book of St. Albans* (1881).

BERNESE ALPS. The portion of the Alps which forms the northern side of the Rhone valley, and extends from the Lake of Geneva to that of Brienz, comprising the Finsteraarhorn, Schreckhorn, Jungfrau, Monk, etc.

BERNHARD (bern'härt), **Duke of Weimar.** General in the Thirty Years' War, born 1604, the fourth son of Duke John of Saxe-Weimar; entered the service of Holland, and afterwards the Danish army employed in Holstein. He then joined Gustavus Adolphus, and in the battle of Lützen, 1632, commanded the victorious left wing of the Swedish army. In 1633 he took Bamberg and other places, was made Duke of Franconia, and after the alliance of France with Sweden raised an army on the Rhine to act against Austria. After many brilliant exploits, he captured Breisach and other places of inferior importance, but showed no disposition to hand them over to the French, who began to find their ally undesirably formidable. He rejected a proposal that he should marry Richelieu's niece, the Duchesse d'Aiguillon, seeking instead the hand of the Princess of Rohan. This the French Court refused, lest the party of the Huguenots should become too powerful. He died somewhat suddenly in 1639 at Neuberg, the common opinion being that he was poisoned by Richelieu.

BERNHAR'DI, Friedrich von. German military author, born 22nd Nov., 1849, at St. Petersburg, died 1930. He entered the Prussian service in 1869, became professor at the Kriegsakademie in Berlin in 1898, commander of the 31st Cavalry Brigade at Strasburg in 1901, lieutenant-general in 1904, and commanded the 7th Army Corps in 1908. During the European War, Bernhardi became famous in England in consequence of an English translation of his work *Der nächste Krieg*, in which he predicted the course Germany would have to take should a great war break out. In 1921 he wrote a volume on Germany's struggle between 1914 and 1918. He died 10th July, 1930.

BERNHARDT (ber-när), **Rosine Sara.** French actress, born at Paris 1845. Of Jewish descent, her father French, her mother Dutch, her early life was spent largely in Amsterdam. In 1858 she entered the Paris Conservatoire, and gained prizes for tragedy and comedy in 1861 and 1862; but her début at the Théâtre Français in *Iphigénie* and Scribe's *Valérie* was not a success. After a brief retirement, she reappeared at the Gymnase and the Porte Saint-Martin in burlesque, and in 1867 at the Odéon in higher drama. Her success in Hugo's *Ruy Blas* led to her being recalled to the Théâtre Français, from which time she abundantly proved her dramatic genius. In 1879 she visited London, and again in 1880. In 1882 she married M. Damala, a Greek. Her tours both in Europe and America never failed to be successful, owing to the magnetism of her personality and her great histrionic talents, especially in acting scenes of pathos. In 1899 she established in Paris a theatre of her own, which she opened with a revival of *La Tosca*, and where she played the title part of *Hamlet*. In 1907 she published her autobiography. In 1913 she received the Cross of the Legion of Honour. She died in March, 1923.

BERN'HARDY, Gottfried. Classical scholar, born 1800; educated at Berlin; became professor at Halle in 1829; chief university librarian in 1844; died there 1875. Of his works the most valuable are his histories of the literature of Greece and Rome.

BER'NI, Francesco. Italian burlesque poet of the sixteenth century, born about 1497 in Tuscany. He took orders, and about 1530 became a canon of the Florence Cathedral, where he lived till his death in 1535. A vague story asserts that Berni, who was intimate with both Alessandro de' Medici and Ippolito de' Medici, was requested by each to poison the other, and that on his refusal he was poisoned himself by Alessandro. He takes the first place among the Italian comic poets. He wrote good Latin verses, and his *Rifacimento* of Boiardo's *Orlando Innamorato* is an admirable work of its class.

Another Berni (Count Francesco Berni, who was born in 1610 and died 1673) wrote eleven dramas and a number of lyrics.

BERNICIA. An ancient Anglian kingdom stretching from the Firth of Forth to the Tees, and extending inland to the borders of Strathclyde. It was united with Deira, and became part of the kingdom of Northumbria.

BERNICLE GOOSE. *See* BARNACLE GOOSE.

BERNIER (bern-yā), **Francois.** French physician and traveller, born at Angers about 1625; set out on his travels in 1654, and visited Egypt, Palestine, and India, where he remained for twelve years as physician to the Great Mogul Emperor Aurangzib. After his return to France he published his *Travels*, an abridgment of the philosophy of Gassendi, a *Treatise on Freedom and Will*, and other works. He died at Paris in 1688.

BERNINA (ber-nē'ná). A mountain of the Rhætian Alps, 13,300 feet high, in the Swiss canton of Grisons, remarkable for its extensive glaciers. The Bernina Pass attains an elevation of 7642 feet; a carriage-road over it, leading from Pontresina to Poschiavo, was completed in 1864. In 1910 an electric railway line, a continuation of the Albula line, and connecting the Upper Engadine with the Veltlin, was opened. The line starts at St. Moritz and runs over Celerina, Pontresina, and Poschiavo to Tirana.

BERNINI (ber-nē'nē), **Giovanni Lorenzo.** Italian painter, sculptor, and architect, born 1598. His marble group, *Apollo and Daphne*, secured him fame at the age of eighteen, and he was employed by Urban VIII. to prepare plans for the embellishment of the Basilica of St. Peter's. The belfry and bronze *baldachino* for the high altar of St. Peter's, the front of the College de Propaganda Fide, the church of St. Andrea à Monte Cavallo, the palace Barberini, the model of the monument of the Countess Matilda, and the monument of Urban VIII. are among his chief works. He declined Mazarin's invitation to France in 1644; and though for a short time neglected after the death of his patron, Urban, he speedily regained his position under Innocent X. and Alexander VII. In 1665 he accepted the king's invitation to Paris, travelling thither in princely state and with a numerous retinue. After his return to Rome he was charged with the decoration of the bridge of St. Angelo, the tomb of Alexander VII., etc. He died in 1680.

BERNIS (ber-nē), **François Joachim de Pierre de.** Cardinal and minister of Louis XV., born in 1715, died 1794. Madame de Pompadour presented him to Louis XV., who assigned him an apartment in the Tuileries, with a pension of 1500 livres. After winning credit in an embassy to Venice, he rose rapidly to the position of Minister of Foreign Affairs, and is possibly to be credited with the formation of the alliance between France and Austria which terminated the Seven Years' War. The misfortunes of France being ascribed to him, he was soon afterwards banished from Court, but was made Archbishop of Alby in 1764, and in 1769 Ambassador to Rome, where he remained till his death. When the aunts of Louis XVI. left France in 1791, they fled to him for refuge, and lived in his house. The Revolution reduced him to a state of poverty, from which he was relieved by a pension from the Spanish Court. His verse procured him a place in the French Academy. His *Mémoires et Lettres 1715-58* (Paris 1878), contains matter of interest.

BERNOUILLI, or **BERNOULLI** (ber-nö-yē). A family which produced eight distinguished men of science. The family fled from Antwerp during the Alva administration, going first to Frankfort, and afterwards to Bâle.—1. James, born at Bâle 1654, became professor of mathematics there 1687, and died 1705. He applied the differential calculus to difficult questions of geometry and mechanics; calculated the loxodromic and catenary curve, the logarithmic spirals, the evolutes of several curved lines, and discovered the so-called *numbers of Bernoulli.*—2. John, born at Bâle 1667, wrote with his brother James a treatise on the differential calculus; developed the integral calculus, and discovered, independently of Leibnitz, the exponential calculus. In 1694 he became doctor of medicine at Bâle, and in 1695 went, as professor of mathematics, to Groningen. After the death of his brother in 1705, he received the professorship of mathematics at Bâle, which he held until his death in 1748.—3. Nicholas, nephew of the former, born at Bâle in 1687; in 1705 went to Groningen to John Bernouilli, and, returning with him to Bâle, became there professor of mathematics. On the recommendation of Leibnitz he went as professor of mathematics to Padua in 1716, but returned to Bâle in 1722 as professor of logic, and in 1731 became professor of Roman and feudal law. He died in 1759. The three following were sons of the above-mentioned John Bernouilli:—4. Nicholas, born at Bâle 1695, became professor of law there in 1723, and died at Petrograd in 1726.—5. Daniel, born at Groningen 1700; studied medicine. At the age of twenty-five he went to Petrograd, returning in 1733 to Bâle, where he became professor of anatomy and botany, and in 1750 professor of natural philosophy. He retired in 1777, and died in 1782.—6. John, born at Bâle in 1710, went to Petrograd in 1732, became professor of rhetoric at Bâle in 1743, and in 1748 professor of mathematics. He died in 1790. The two following were his sons:—7. John, licentiate of law and Royal Astronomer in Berlin, born at Bâle in 1744. He lived after 1779 in Berlin as director of the mathematical department of the Academy. Died 1807.—8. James, born at Bâle in 1759; went to Petrograd, where he became professor of mathematics; married a granddaughter of Euler, but died in 1789 while bathing in the Neva.

BERNSTEIN, Eduard. German social democrat, born Berlin 6th Jan., 1859, the son of an engine-driver. He joined the Social Democratic party in 1872, and edited the *Sozialdemocrat* from 1881 to 1890, but the extreme vehemence of his attacks upon the government of Bismarck compelled him to leave Germany. He went to London in 1888, but returned in 1901 and became editor of the *Vorwärts*, the famous Socialist paper. Here he contended that every movement for the advancement of the people should be encouraged and taken advantage of by the common people, whom he urged to take an active part in politics. In 1902 he was elected a member of the German Reichstag, was re-elected in 1912 (but not in 1907), and played an important part in the German revolution in 1918; he was member for Breslau from 1920. He has been the subject of severe criticism on the part of his countrymen in consequence of a famous speech in which he maintained that Germany fully deserved nine-tenths of the conditions imposed upon her by the Treaty of Versailles. Among his works are: *Gesellschaftliches und Privateigentum* (1891), *Die Kommunistischen und demokratisch socialistischen Beweggungen in England während des 17 Zahrhunderts* (1895), *Zur Geschichte und Theorie des Sozialismus* (1900), *Die Arbeiterbewegung* (1910), *Die Internationale der Arbeiterklasse und die europäische Krieg* (1915), *Die deutsche Revolution* (1921), *Von 1850 bis 1872* (1926).

BERN'STORFF. The name of a German noble family, of whom the most distinguished was Johann Hartwig Ernst, Count von Bernstorff, Danish statesman under Frederick V. and Christian VII, born in Hanover 1712. He was the most influential member of the Government, which distinguished itself under his direction by a wise neutrality during the Seven Years' War, etc.; by measures for improving the condition of the Danish peasantry; by promoting science, and sending to Asia the expedition which Niebuhr accompanied. By his efforts Denmark acquired Holstein. He died 1772.

BERNY-EN-SANTERRE. A village of France, department of Somme. Fierce fighting took place around it in 1916.

BER'OË. A genus of small marine cœlenterate animals, ord. Ctenophora, transparent and gelatinous, globular in form, floating in the sea, and shining at night with phosphoric light.

BERO'SUS. A priest of the temple of Belus (Marduk) at Babylon early in the third century B.C., who wrote in Greek a *History of the Babylonian Chaldeans* founded on the ancient archives of the temple of Belus. It is known only by the quotations from it in Apollodorus, Eusebius, Josephus, etc.

BERQUIN (ber-kaŋ), **Arnaud.** French writer, born 1749, first attracted notice by his *Idylles*, and by several translations entitled *Tableaux Anglais.* He was best known by his *Ami des Enfants*, a series of narratives for children, for which, though plagiarised from Weisse's *Kinderfreund*, he received the prize of the French Academy in 1789. He was for some time the editor of the *Moniteur*. Died 1791.

BERRI, or BERRY. Formerly a province and dukedom, with Bourges as capital, almost in the centre of France. It is now mainly comprised in the departments of Indre and Cher.

BERRI, or BERRY, Charles Ferdinand, Duke of. Second son of the Count d'Artois (afterwards Charles X.), born at Versailles, 24th Jan., 1778. In 1792 he fled with his father to Turin and served under him and Condé on the Rhine. In 1801 he came to Britain, where he lived alternately in London and Scotland, occupied with plans for the restoration of the Bourbons. In 1814 he landed at Cherbourg, and passed on to Paris, gaining many adherents to the royal cause; but they melted away when Napoleon landed from Elba, and the count was compelled to retire with the household troops to Ghent and Alost. After the battle of Waterloo he returned to Paris, and in 1816 married. He was assassinated by Louvel, a political fanatic, on 14th Feb., 1820. The duke had by his wife, Carolina Ferdinanda Louisa, eldest daughter of Francis, afterwards King of the Two Sicilies, a daughter, Louise Marie Thérèse, afterwards Duchess of Parma, and a posthumous son subsequently known as Comte de Chambord.

BERRY. A fleshy fruit containing no hard parts except the seed, thus differing from the drupe (q.v.) in the absence of a hard endocarp. Examples are: (superior) grape, date, tomato, orange; (inferior) gooseberry, whortleberry, banana. Many fruits popularly termed "berries," such as strawberry, blackberry, and mulberry, are not berries in a botanical sense.

BERRY-AU-BAC. A village of France, department of Aisne. It was the scene of fierce fighting in 1914, 1915, and 1917.

BERRYER (ber-yā), **Antoine Pierre.** A French advocate and statesman, born in Paris 1790. In 1814 he proclaimed at Rennes the deposition of Napoleon, and remained till his death an avowed Legitimist. He assisted his father in the defence of Ney, secured the acquittal of General Cambronne, and defended Lamennais from a charge of atheism. His eloquence was compared with that of Mirabeau, and after the dethronement of Charles X. (1830) he remained in the Chamber as the sole Legitimist orator. His political services won for him a public subscription of 400,000 francs in 1836 to meet his pecuniary difficulties. In 1840 he was one of the counsel for the defence of Louis Napoleon after the Boulogne fiasco. In 1843 he did homage to the Comte de Chambord in London, adhering to him through the revolution of 1848, and voting for the deposition of the prince-president the morning after the *coup d'état*. He gained additional reputation in 1858 by his defence of Montalembert, and was counsel for the Patterson-Bonapartes in the suit for the recognition of the Baltimore marriage. In 1863 he was re-elected to the Chamber with Thiers, and in 1864 received a flattering reception in England. He died in 1868.

BERSAGLIERI (ber-säl-yä'rē). A corps of Italian sharpshooters organised early in the reign of Victor Emmanuel by General Alessandro della Marmora. Two battalions took part in the Crimean War and distinguished themselves at the battle of Tshernaya (16th Aug., 1855).

BERSERK'ER. A Scandinavian name for warriors who fought in a sort of frenzy or reckless fury, dashing themselves on the enemy in the most regardless manner. The first Berserker was said to have been Arngrim, the grandson of the eight-handed Starkadder and the fair Alfhilde. He wore no mail in battle, and had twelve sons, also called *Berserker*. The name is derived from the bearsark or bearskin shirt worn by early warriors.

BERTHA. An English Queen. She was a Frankish princess who married Ethelbert, King of Kent, about 560, and converted him to Christianity. As a result of her teaching, this religion spread widely among the Anglo-Saxons.

BERTHELOT, Pierre Eugène Marcellin. French chemist, born in Paris, 25th Oct., 1827, died in 1907. In 1860 he was appointed professor of organic chemistry at the École de Pharmacie in Paris, and in 1865 a new chair of organic chemistry was created for him at the Collège de France. In 1870, during the Franco-Prussian war, he was elected president of the Scientific Committee of Defence, and entrusted with the manufacture of dynamite and nitro-glycerine during the siege of Paris. He became president of the Committee on Explosives which introduced smokeless powder. In 1881 he was elected member of the Senate, and was Minister of Education in 1886. His discoveries and contributions to the knowledge of synthetical processes were most important, and he rendered valuable service with regard to explosives and thermo-chemistry, or the relations between the phenomena of heat and chemistry. He also discovered dyes extracted from coal-tar. In 1889 he was elected permanent secretary of the Academy of Sciences. Among his numerous works are: *Chimie organique fondée sur la Synthèse* (1860), *Leçons sur les méthodes générales de la Synthèse* (1864), *Leçons de Chimie sur l'isomérie* (1865), *Traité élémentaire de Chimie organique* (1872), *Sur la force de la poudre et la force des matières explosives* (1872), *Les origines de l'alchimie* (1885), *Collection des anciens alchimistes grecs* (1888), *La révolution chimique, Lavoisier* (1890), *Chimie des anciens* (1889), *La chimie au moyen âge* (1890), *Thermochimie, données et lois numériques* (1897), *Recherches expérimentales* (1901).

BERTHIER (bert-yā), **Louis Alexandre.** Prince of Neufchâtel and Wagram, Marshal, Vice-Constable of France, etc., born 1753; son of a distinguished officer. While yet young he served in America with Lafayette, and after some years' service in France he joined the army of Italy in 1795 as general of division and head of the general staff, receiving in 1798 the chief command. In this capacity he entered Rome, captured and carried off Pius VI., abolished the papal Government, and established a consular one. He followed Bonaparte to Egypt as chief of the general staff; was appointed by him Minister of War after the 18th Brumaire; accompanied him to Italy in 1800, and again in 1805, to be present at his coronation; and was appointed chief of the general staff of the grand army in Germany. In all Napoleon's expeditions he was one of his closest companions, on several occasions rendering valuable services, as at Wagram in 1809, when he gained the title of *Prince of Wagram.* After Napoleon's abdication, he was taken into the favour and confidence of Louis XVIII., and on Napoleon's return the difficulty of his position unhinged his mind, and he put an end to his life by throwing himself from a window in 1815. He left a son, Alexandre (born 1810, died 1887), one of the most zealous adherents of Napoleon III.

BERTHOLLET (ber-to-lā), **Claude Louis, Count.** An eminent French chemist, born 1748; studied medicine; became connected with Lavoisier; was admitted in 1780 member of the Academy of Sciences at Paris; in 1794 professor in the normal school there. He followed Bonaparte to Egypt, and returned with him in 1799. Notwithstanding the various honours conferred on him by Napoleon, he voted in 1814 for his dethronement, and was made a peer by Louis XVIII. His chief chemical discoveries were connected with the analysis of ammonia, the use of chlorine in bleaching, the artificial production of nitre, etc. His most important works were his *Essai de Statique Chimique* (1803), and the *Méthode de Nomenclature Chimique* (1787). He died in Paris 1822.

BERTHOLLE'TIA. The name given in honour of Berthollet to a genus of Myrtaceæ, of which only one species, *B. excelsa*, is known. This tree forms vast forests on the banks of the Amazon, Rio Negro, and Orinoco, averaging 100 feet in height, with a stem only 2 feet in diameter, and destitute of branches till near the top. It produces the well-known Brazil-nuts of commerce, which are contained in a round and strong seed-vessel, to the number of from fifteen to fifty or more, and contain a great deal of oil.

BERTILLON (bār-tē-yōn), **Alphonse.** French anthropologist and ethnographer, born in 1853, died in 1914. His name is well known in connection with a system for the identification of criminals, which is called after him. This consists in a regular series of accurate measurements to which the criminals are subjected; the length and breadth of the head and of the ear, the length of the middle finger, of the little finger, of the forearm, of the foot, of the body, of the span of the arms, etc., being taken, and the parts on the left side are those that are depended on rather than those on the right. The colour of the iris of the eye is also important. The system is employed in various countries with success; in some countries the finger-print system is preferred. The records are kept on cards which are so classified and arranged that any person who has been previously examined can be identified in a few minutes.

BERUKIN. A village of Palestine, 18 miles N.E. of Jaffa. It was the scene of a battle between the British and the Turks in April, 1918.

BERVIE, or INVERBERVIE. A royal burgh of Scotland, one of the Montrose district of burghs, on the coast of Kincardineshire at the mouth of the River Bervie, engaged in the flax manufacture. Pop. (1931), 1032.

BERWICK (ber'ik), or more fully, **BERWICK-ON-TWEED.** A seaport town of England, formerly a parliamentary borough and (with small adjoining district) a county by itself, but now incorporated with Northumberland, and giving name to a parliamentary division of the county. It stands on the north or Scottish side of the Tweed, within half a mile of its mouth. It is surrounded by walls of earth faced with stone, along which is an agreeable promenade; the streets are mostly narrow, straggling, and irregular. The Tweed is crossed by an old bridge of fifteen arches and by a fine railway viaduct.

Chief Industries. Iron-founding, the manufacture of engines and boilers, agricultural implements, feeding-cake, manures, ropes, twine, etc. In the beginning of the twelfth century, during the reign of Alexander I., Berwick was part of Scotland, and the capital of the district called Lothian. In 1216 the town and castle were stormed and taken by King John; Bruce retook them in 1318; but, after undergoing various sieges and vicissitudes, both were surrendered to Edward IV. in 1482, and have ever since remained English. Pop. (1931), 12,299.

The county of Berwick, the most eastern border-county of Scotland, is bounded by the North Sea, East Lothian, Roxburgh, Peebles, the River Tweed, and the English borders. It is nominally divided into the three districts of Lauderdale (the valley of the Leader), Lammermoor, and the Merse of March (the valley of the Tweed). Total area, 292,535 acres, of which two-thirds are productive. The principal rivers are the Tweed, the Leader, the Eye, the Whiteadder, and Blackadder. The minerals are unimportant, though freestone and marl are abundant. The county is famous for good agriculture, but has few manufactures, the principal being paper. Since 1918 Berwick unites with Haddington in returning one member to Parliament. The county town is now Duns. Pop. (1931), 26,601.

BERWICK, James Fitz-James, Duke of. Natural son of the Duke of York (afterwards James II.) and Arabella Churchill, sister of Marlborough, born at Moulins in the Bourbonnais in 1670, and first went by the name of Fitz-James. He received his education in France, served in Hungary, returned to England at the age of seventeen, and received from his father the title of duke. On the landing of the Prince of Orange he went to France with his father, and he was wounded at the battle of the Boyne, where he nominally commanded. He afterwards served under Luxembourg in Flanders; in 1702 and 1703 under the Duke of Burgundy; then under Marshal Villeroi. In 1706 he was made Marshal of France, and sent to Spain, where he gained the battle of Almanza, which rendered Philip V. again master of Valencia. In 1709 he held with honour the command in Dauphiné, displaying the highest strategic skill against the superior forces of the Duke of Savoy. He was killed at the siege of Philippsburg by a cannon-ball in 1734.

BERWICK, NORTH. A Royal burgh and seaport of Scotland, in Haddingtonshire, near the entrance of the Firth of Forth. It is now a popular holiday resort. Pop. (1931), 3473.

BERWYN. Mountains in Wales. The range borders Merionethshire, Montgomeryshire, and Denbighshire. Moelsoch (2716 feet) is the chief elevation.

BER'YL (Beryllium aluminium silicate). A colourless, yellowish, bluish, or less brilliant green variety of emerald, the prevailing hue being green of various shades, but always pale; chromium gives to the emerald its deep rich green. Its crystals are six-sided prisms, terminated by basal planes. The best beryls are found in Brazil, in Siberia, and Ceylon; but the mineral is widely distributed in granite rocks in all parts of the world. The bluish and transparent varieties are called *aquamarine*.

BERYLL'IUM (also called Glucinum). A metal occurring in beryl and other minerals, of a colour similar to zinc. Specific gravity, 2·1; malleable; does not oxidise in air or water. Atomic weight, 9·4; symbol, Be.

BERZE'LIUS, Johan Jacob, Baron. Swedish chemist, born in 1779; studied medicine at Upsala, and, after holding one or two medical appointments, was appointed lecturer in chemistry in the Stockholm Military Academy in 1806, and the following year professor of pharmacy and medicine. In 1808 he became a member of the Academy of Sciences at Stockholm, in 1810 director, and in 1818 its perpetual secretary. In 1818 the king made him a noble, and in 1835 a baron. He was also a Deputy to the National Assembly. He discovered selenium and thorium, first exhibited calcium, barium, strontium, tantalum, silicium, and zirconium in the elemental state, and investigated whole classes of compounds, as those of fluoric acid, the metals in the ores of platinum, tantalum, molybdenum, vanadium, sulphur salts, etc., and introduced a new nomenclature and classification of chemical compounds. In short, there was no branch of chemistry to which he did not render essential service. His writings comprise an important *Textbook of Chemistry*, *View of the Composition of Animal Fluids*, *New System of Mineralogy*, *Essay on the Theory of Chemical Proportions*, etc. He died in 1848.

BES. An Egyptian god, represented clad in a lion's skin, with the head and skull of the animal concealing his features, and with a dwarfish and altogether grotesque appearance.

BESANÇON (bė-sȧŋ-sōŋ). A town of Eastern France, capital of the department Doubs, situated on a rocky peninsula washed on three sides by the River Doubs, and surmounted by a strong citadel. It is further strengthened by an outlying system of forts on neighbouring eminences. The streets are spacious and well laid out, with fine cathedral and churches, public buildings and promenades. The manufactures comprise linen, cotton, woollen, and silk goods, ironmongery, etc.; but the principal industry is watch-making. Besançon is the ancient *Vesontio*, *Besontium*, or *Bisontium* described by Cæsar. In the fifth century it came into possession of the Burgundians; in the twelfth passed with Franche-Comté to the German Empire. In 1679 it was ceded to France along with the rest of Franche-Comté, of which it remained the capital till 1793, with a parliament, etc., of its own. Pop. 60,367.

BESANT, Annie. English theosophist. She became a secularist and was also a member of the Fabian Society and sat on the London School Board. For some years she lived in India. In 1917 her writings and speeches caused her arrest. In 1918 she was president of the national congress.

BESANT', Sir Walter. English novelist, born 1836, educated in London and at Christ's College, Cambridge, where he graduated as 18th Wrangler. He was for a time professor in the Royal College, Mauritius. His first work, *Studies in Early French Poetry*, appeared in 1868, and to the field of French literature also belong his *French Humorists* and his *Rabelais* (for the Foreign Classics Series). He was for years secretary to the Palestine Exploration Fund, and published a *History of Jerusalem* in connection with Professor Palmer, a life of whom he also wrote. He is best known by his novels, a number of which were written in partnership with James Rice, including *Ready-money Mortiboy*, *This Son of Vulcan*, *The Case of Mr. Lucraft*, *The Golden Butterfly*, *The Monks of Thelma*, etc. After Rice's death (1882), he wrote *All Sorts and Conditions of Men*, *All in a Garden Fair*, *The World Went very Well Then*, *The Rebel Queen*, etc. He died in 1901. His *Autobiography* was published in 1902.

BESH'LIK. A Turkish silver coin, value 5 piastres, or about 10*d.* sterling.

BESH'MET. A common article of food among tribes of the mountainous districts of Asia Minor, consisting of grapes boiled into the consistence of honey.

BESLERIA. A genus of Gesneraceæ, natives of tropical America. *B. lutea*, a common shade-plant in the mountains of Jamaica, has a water-calyx, the only instance so far recorded in this nat. ord.

BESSARA'BIA. A former government (or province) of Imperial Russia, stretching in a north-westerly direction from the Black Sea, between the Prut and Danube and the Dniester. It was conquered by the Turks 1474, taken by the Russians 1770, ceded to them by the Peace of Bucharest in 1812; the S.E. extremity was given to Turkey in 1856, but restored to Russia by the Treaty of Berlin, 1878, in exchange for the Dobrudsha. In the north the country is hilly, but in the south flat and low. It is fertile in grain, but is largely used for pasturage. Capital, Kishinev. A movement for self-government took definite form in May, 1917, which the Ukrainian Government at first opposed, but in November of that year admitted. Rumania, however, desired to retain possession of that portion of Russian Bessarabia given her by the Central Powers under the cancelled Treaty of Bucharest. After the defeat of the Central Powers in Nov., 1918, Bessarabia demanded to be united to Rumania. In March, 1920, the Supreme Council in Paris agreed to the reunion. Area, 17,146 sq. miles; pop. 2,865,506, chiefly Walachians, Gipsies, and Tartars.

BESSAR'ION, Johannes, titular patriarch of Constantinople and Greek scholar, born in Trebizond 1389, 1395, or 1403, died 1472. He was made Archbishop of Nicæa by John Palæologus, whose efforts to unite the Greek and Roman Churches he seconded in such a way as to lose the esteem of his countrymen and gain that of Pope Eugenius IV, who made him cardinal. He held various important posts, and was twice nearly elected Pope. The revival of letters in the fifteenth century owed not a little to his influence. He left translations of Aristotle and vindications of Plato, with valuable collections of books and MSS., presented by him to the Senate of Venice, and which formed the nucleus of the library of St. Mark.

BESSBOROUGH, Earl of. Irish title held since 1739 by the Ponsonby family. Bessborough is a small place in Co. Kilkenny, and in 1721 a landowner, then William Ponsonby, was made Baron Bessborough. In 1739 he was made an earl. The earl's eldest son is called Viscount Duncannon, and the 9th earl, when bearing this title, was M.P. for Dover, 1913-20. Later he became chairman of several undertakings. In 1931 he was appointed Governor-General of Canada.

BESSÉGES (bā-sāzh). A town, France, department of Gard, with important coal- and iron-mines and blast-furnaces. Pop. 7060.

BES'SEL, Friedrich Wilhelm. A German astronomer, born in 1784; appointed in 1810 director of the observatory at Königsberg. From 1824 to 1833 he completed a series of 75,011 observations on the celestial zone between 15° N. and 15° S. declination. In 1840 he called attention to the probable existence of a planetary mass beyond Uranus, resulting in the discovery of Neptune, a discovery due mainly to the calculations of Adams. He died in 1846. His principal works are the *Elements of Astronomy* (1818), and its continuations, the *Tabulæ Regiomontanæ* (1830) and *Astronomical Researches* (1841–2). His determination of the parallax of the star 61 Cygni was one of his most noteworthy practical achievements.

BES'SEMER. A town of the United States, in Alabama, named after the inventor, situated in the centre of coal- and iron-fields, and with numerous blast-furnaces. Pop. 20,271.

BES'SEMER, Sir Henry. English engineer and inventor, was born in Hertfordshire in 1813. He is celebrated for his new and cheap process or rapidly making steel from pig-iron by blowing a blast of air through it when in a state of fusion, so as to clear it of all carbon, and then adding just the requisite quantity of carbon to produce steel—a process which has introduced a revolution in the steel-making trade, cheap steel being made in vast quantities and used for many purposes in which its price prohibited its application. He was knighted in 1879, and died in 1898. *See* STEEL.

BEST, William Thomas. Musician, the greatest organist of his day, was born at Carlisle in 1826. Intended for a civil engineer, he took up music instead, and was practically self-taught. In 1847 he received his first appointment as organist, at Liverpool; some years after was an organist in London for a time, and in 1855 was appointed public organist of Liverpool on the completion of the great organ in St. George's Hall. This post he held for nearly forty years, being also a church organist and teacher. He was in particular request at the inauguration of new organs, and accordingly he inaugurated the great organ in the Albert Hall, London, in 1871, and the huge organ built for the Sydney town hall, Australia (9th Aug., 1890). He gave up his post as Liverpool organist in 1894, and died in 1897. He was an excellent pianist, a composer of music, and wrote an admirable work, *The Art of Organ-playing*.

BESTIAIRES (bes'ti-ārz), or **BESTIARIES.** A class of books very popular in the eleventh, twelfth, and thirteenth centuries, describing all sorts of animals, real and fabled, and forming a species of mediæval encyclopædia of zoology. The animals were treated as symbolic, and their peculiarities or supposed peculiarities spiritually applied. The volumes are to be found both in Latin and in the vernacular, in prose and in verse. The Bestiary appears in its complete development in Richard de Fournival's *Bestiaire d'Amour*, published in 1860.

BETA. See *Beet*.

BETANZOS (be-tȧn'thōs). A town of Northern Spain, province Coruña. Pop. 8122.

BET'EL, or BET'LE. A species of pepper, *Piper Betle*, a creeping or climbing plant, native of the East Indies, nat. ord. Piperaceæ. The leaves are employed to enclose a piece of the areca or betel-nut and a little lime into a pellet, which is extensively chewed in the East. The pellet is hot and acrid, but has aromatic and astringent properties. It tinges the saliva, gums, and lips a brick-red, and blackens the teeth.

BETEL-NUT. The kernel of the fruit of the beautiful palm *Arēca Catĕchu*, found in Southern India, Ceylon, Siam, and the Malay Archipelago, and named from being chewed along with betel-leaf. The tree begins to bear fruit when eight or ten years old. The fruit grows in bunches, each tree bearing from two to three bunches, and each bunch containing about 300 nuts. When ripe it is of the size of a cherry, conical in shape, brown externally, and mottled internally like a nutmeg. Ceylon alone exports 70,000 cwt. annually.

BETH'ANY (now called **EL' AZARIYEH** or **LAZARIEH**). A village of Palestine at the base of Mount Olivet, about 2 miles E. of Jerusalem, formerly the home of Martha, Mary, and Lazarus, and the place near which the ascension of Our Lord took place. The name means the "house of dates".

BETHES'DA ("house of mercy"). A pool in Jerusalem near St. Stephen's Gate and the Temple of Omar. It is 460 feet long, 130 broad, and 75 deep, and now known as Birket Israel (*see* John, v. 2-9).

BETHES'DA. An urban district or town of North Wales, Carnarvonshire, 5½ miles south-east of Bangor, famous for its great slate quarries, belonging to Lord Penrhyn, and giving employment to about 3000 men. Pop. (1931), 4476.

BETH-HORON. Two villages in Palestine. Beth-Horon, the upper, is 10½ miles N.W. of Jerusalem. It was one of the boundaries of the land given to the sons of Ephraim and was the scene of a great slaughter of the Amorites when pursued by Joshua.

BETH'LEHEM. The birth-place of Christ; a small town, in Palestine, 5 miles south from Jerusalem. Pop. 6658, chiefly Christians, who make rosaries, crucifixes, etc., for pilgrims. A richly-adorned grotto lighted with silver and crystal lamps, under the choir of the fine church built by Justinian, is shown as the actual spot where Jesus was born. There is a small village of the same name 7 miles N.W. of Nazareth.

BETHLEHEM. A town of the United States, founded by Moravians in 1741 in Pennsylvania, on the Lehigh, across which is a bridge connecting it with S. Bethlehem, the seat of Lehigh University. Pop. of both together, 57,892.

BETHLEHEM. A town and railway junction of the Orange Free State, 300 miles N.W. of Durban. Pop. 8689 (4856 white).

BETHLEHEMITES. A name applied (1) to the followers of John Huss, from Bethlehem Church, Prague, where he preached; (2) to an order of monks, established, according to Matthew Paris, in 1257, with a monastery at Cambridge; (3) to an order founded in Guatemala about 1655 by Fray Pedro de Betancourt, a Franciscan tertiary, a native of Teneriffe. It spread to Mexico, Peru, and the Canary Islands. An order of nuns founded in 1667 bore the same name.

BETHLEN, Count Stephen. Hungarian politician, born 8th Oct., 1874; he belonged to an old and rich family of Transylvania. In 1901 he was elected to the diet, or parliament, of Hungary and there for nearly 20 years he was one of the leaders of the opposition. After the Great War he assisted in driving Bela Kun from the country and in restoring order after the short Bolshevist régime. In 1921 he became Prime Minister, and for the next ten years he was responsible for the direction of affairs. He reformed the finances, the electoral system and the land laws, and foiled the attempts of the ex-Emperor Charles to recover the throne. In 1931 he resigned office.

BETHLEN-GABOR, that is, GABRIEL-BETHLEN. Born of a Protestant Magyar family in 1580; fought under Gabriel Bathory, and then joined the Turks, by whose aid he made himself Prince of Transylvania in 1613. In 1619 he assisted the Bohemians against Austria, and, marching into Hungary, was elected king by the nobles (1620). This title he surrendered in return for the cession to him by the Emperor Frederick II. of seven Hungarian counties and two Silesian principalities. After a brilliant reign, he died in 1629 without an heir.

BETHMANN HOLLWEG, Dr. Theobald von. Prussian politician, born at Hohenfinow, near Eberswalde, 29th Nov., 1856. In 1907 he was appointed Imperial Secretary of State for the Interior, and on 14th July, 1909, he succeeded Prince Bülow as Imperial Chancellor, and was in office at the outbreak of the European War. He became notorious for his utterance on the 4th of Aug., 1914. When Germany refused to evacuate Belgium, the British Ambassador, in accordance with instructions from his Government, demanded his passports. Bethmann Hollweg, on receiving the British Ambassador's farewell visit, complained that Great Britain was going to war, "just for a word, *neutrality*, which in war-time had so often been disregarded—just *for a scrap of paper*—on a kindred nation which desired nothing better than to be friends with her". Bethmann Hollweg remained in office eight years, but in 1917 he no longer found it possible to satisfy both the moderate and reactionary parties in the Reichstag, and consequently resigned on 14th July, 1917. The Kaiser then appointed Herr Georg Michaelis as Chancellor of the Empire. Bethmann Hollweg died 1st Jan., 1921. See GERMANY; EUROPEAN WAR.

BETHNAL GREEN. A municipal and parliamentary borough of eastern London, north-east of the city. The parliamentary borough has two divisions. Pop. (1931), 108,178.

BETHSAIDA. Village of Palestine, situated on the western shore of the Sea of Galilee. It was the birth-place of the Disciples, Andrew, Peter, and Philip. To-day, only a heap of ruins marks the spot. Another Bethsaida, at the other end of the Sea, is the place where Christ fed the 5000.

BÉTHUNE (bā-tün), an old town

of France, department of Pas-de-Calais, with various industries and a considerable trade. It suffered great damage during the European War. Pop. 19,956.—The family of Béthune (extinct since 1807) is celebrated, and a branch of it, to which Cardinal Beaton belonged, was established in Scotland about the end of the twelfth century.

BET'JUANS. *See* BECHUANAS.

BET'LIS, or BITLIS. A town of Turkey, not far from Lake Van, one of the most ancient cities of Kurdistan. Pop. (Turks, Kurds, and Armenians), about 40,000. The vilayet of Bitlis has a pop. of 398,700.

BETON. A concrete composed of sand, lime, and gravel, used to form artificial foundations on insecure sites. It is much used as a hydraulic cement in submarine works, and whole buildings have been constructed of it.

BET'ONY. The popular name of *Stachys Betonica* (or *Betonica officinālis*), a labiate British plant with purple flowers which grows in woods, formerly much employed in medicine, and sometimes used to dye wool of a fine dark-yellow colour.—**Water betony,** *Scrophularia aquatica,* is named from the resemblance of its leaf to that of betony.

BETROTH'MENT. A mutual promise or contract between two parties, by which they bind themselves to marry. It was anciently attended with the interchange of rings, joining hands, and kissing in presence of witnesses; and formal betrothment is still the custom on the continent of Europe—being either solemn (made in the face of the church) or private (made before witnesses out of the church)—but is no longer customary in England. As betrothments are contracts, they are valid only between persons whose capacity is recognised by law, and the breach of them may be the subject of litigation.

BETTERMENT. A term commonly used to mean an increase in the value of property arising not from any improvement effected on it by the owner, but from increase of population, general improvements carried out at the public expense, etc.

BET'TERTON, Thomas. English actor in the reign of Charles II., born in 1635; excelled in Shakespeare's characters of Hamlet, Othello, Brutus, and Hotspur, and was the means of introducing shifting scenes instead of tapestry upon the English stage. He died in 1710, and was buried in Westminster Abbey. He was the author of several adaptations: *The Woman made a Justice*, a comedy; *The Amorous Widow, or The Wanton Wife*; etc. Mrs. Saunderson, whom he married in 1670, was a celebrated actress.

BETTING. The staking or pledging of money or property upon a contingency or issue in which the person has no interest apart from the wager is the commonest example of a gaming or wagering contract. Such contracts while not illegal are void, in Scotland at common law, and in England under the Gaming Acts of 1845 and 1892, thus payment of a bet cannot be enforced in either country. A Bill of Exchange or Promissory Note given for a gaming debt can, however, be enforced by a subsequent holder who gave value for it without notice that it was given for such a debt. While betting is not in itself illegal, it is subject to many restrictions in the public interest. It is a criminal offence by statute to carry on betting as a business in any house, office, or other "place", i.e. a fixed address like a house or office. The leading statute is the Betting Act, 1853, extended to Scotland by the Betting Act, 1874. The former contains the main provisions for suppression of betting-houses; the latter imposes penalties on persons advertising or sending letters, circulars, or telegrams to induce betting.

An exception to the Betting Act, 1853, has been created by the Racecourse Betting Act, 1928, which legalises betting by means of a totalisator or similar machine on any racecourse approved by the Racecourse Betting Control Board (a body set up by this Act) on days when horse-races only take place on the racecourse. The Betting and Loans (Infants) Act, 1892, prohibits the incitement of minors to bet; the Racecourse Betting Act, 1928, forbids betting with persons apparently under the age of 17, and it is forbidden in Scotland by the Betting (Juvenile messengers) (Scotland) Act, 1928, to use persons under 16 to convey betting information. By the Finance Act, 1926, an excise duty was placed on bets, but this proved difficult to collect and in 1929 was replaced by an annual charge of £40 on each telephone in the book-maker's office. The extra charge for their telephones was abolished in 1930.

Since 1928 betting by means of a totalisator has also been legal in England, and to-day much betting is done in this way. The totalisators are under the Betting Control Board. In 1933 the totalisators on Greyhound Racing Courses were made illegal. The processes of betting may be usefully illustrated in connection with horse-racing.

Betters are divided into two classes: the backers of horses, and the book-maker, or professional betters, who form the betting-ring, and make a living by betting against horses according to a methodical plan, by which the element of chance is as far as possible eliminated. Thus the book-maker reckons with fair success on making more or less profit out of each season's engagements. Instead of backing any particular horse, the professional better lays the same sum against every horse that takes the field, or a certain number of them, and in doing so he has usually to give odds, which are greater or less according to the estimate formed of the chance of success which each of the horses has on which the odds are given. In this way, while in the event of the race being won (as is usually the case) by any of the horses entered in the betting-book of a professional better, the latter has always a certain fixed sum (say £1000) to pay, he receives from the backers of the losers sums which vary in proportion to the odds given. Thus, if a book-maker is making a £1000 book, and the odds against some horse are 4 to 1, he will, if that horse wins, have to pay £1000, while, if it loses, he will receive £250. It usually depends upon which horse it is that wins a race whether the book-maker gains or loses. If the first favourite wins, it is evidently the worst thing that could happen for the book-maker, for, as he is bound to receive the sum of the amounts to which all the horses except one have been backed, the largest deduction must be made from his total receipts on account of the first favourite. Very frequently the receipts of the book-maker are augmented by sums paid on account of horses which have been backed and never run at all. Sometimes, although not often, the odds are given upon and not against a particular horse. Books may also be made up on the principle of betting against any particular horse getting a place among the first three.

BETTWS-Y-COED (bet'ųs-i-kō-ed). A village of North Wales, on the eastern border of Carnarvonshire. It stands where the Thrwgy falls into the Conway, in the midst of some of the most beautiful scenery of Wales. Near are the famous Swallow Falls. It is 214¾ miles from London. Pop. 912.

BETWA. A river of India rising in the Vindhya Range in Bhopal, and, after a north-easterly course of 360 miles, joining the Jumna at Hamirpur.

BEUST (boist), **Friedrich Ferdinand, Count von.** Saxon and Austrian statesman, born at Dresden in 1809, died in 1886. He adopted the career of diplomacy, and as member of embassies or Ambassador for Saxony resided at Berlin, Paris, Munich, and London. He was successively Minister of Foreign Affairs and of the Interior for Saxony. At the London Conference regarding the Schleswig-Holstein difficulty he represented the German Bund. He lent his influence on the side of Austria against Prussia before the war of 1866, after which, finding his position in Saxony difficult, he entered the service of Austria as Minister of Foreign Affairs, became President of the Ministry, Imperial Chancellor, and in 1868 was created count. From 1871 to 1878 he was Ambassador in London, from 1878 to 1882 in Paris. In 1882 he retired from public life.

BEUTHEN (boi'tn). A town in Prussian Silesia near the S.E. frontier, in the government of Oppeln; the centre of a mining district, with various active industries. Pop. (including Rossberg), 86,881.

BEVELAND (bā've-lånt), **NORTH** and **SOUTH.** Two islands in the estuary of the Schelde, Netherlands, province of Zeeland; area of North Beveland, 15,200 acres, pop. 6000; area of South Beveland, 84,000 acres, pop. 23,000; chief town, Goes, 5000. It is very fertile, and has manufactures of salt, leather, beer, etc.

BEV'ERIDGE, William. An English divine, born in 1637, studied at Cambridge, and in his twenty-first year published a work on the study of Hebrew, Chaldee, Syriac, Arabic, and Samaritan, with a Syriac grammar. In 1660 he became vicar of Ealing, and was, after various ecclesiastical preferments, appointed Bishop of St. Asaph in 1704. He died at Westminster in 1708. His works include: *Institutiones Chronologicæ* (1669); *Synodicon*, containing the Apostolic Canons, etc. (1672); and minor devotional treatises on the Christian life, public prayer, etc.

BEV'ERLEY. A market town and municipal borough, E. Riding of Yorkshire, England, 8½ miles N.N.W. of Hull, and 1 from the River Hull, with which it has canal connection; has a fine Gothic minster, completed in the reign of Henry III., and in some respects unsurpassed. It is the seat of a suffragan bishop. Chief manufactures: iron castings, agricultural implements, manures, railway wagons, cement, etc. Pop. (1931), 14,011.

BEV'ERLEY, JOHN OF. An English prelate and saint, born about the middle of the seventh century at Harpham, Yorkshire; appointed

A Thomas Bewick Woodcut

abbot of St. Hilda; afterwards Bishop of Hexham in 685; and two years later Archbishop of York. He founded a college for secular priests at Beverley, where he retired in 717, and died in 721. Bede, who was his pupil, believed that he could work miracles, a power attributed to his remains for some centuries.

BEV'ERLY. A city of the United States, Massachusetts, on Massachusetts Bay, north-east of Boston. It manufactures shoes and is a summer resort. Pop. 25,086.

BEWDLEY ("Beaulieu"). A municipal borough, England, Worcestershire, on the Severn. Manufactures: combs, ropes, leather, and brasswork; some malting is also carried on. It gives name to one of the four parliamentary divisions of the county. Pop. (1931), 2868.

BEWICK (bu'ik), **Thomas.** A celebrated English wood-engraver, born in Northumberland in 1753. He was apprenticed to Beilby, an engraver in Newcastle, and executed the woodcuts in Hutton's *Mensuration* so admirably that his master advised him to turn his attention to wood-engraving. With this view he proceeded to London, and in 1775 received the Society of Arts' prize for the best wood-engraving. Returning in a short time to Newcastle, he entered into partnership with Beilby, and became known as a skilled wood-engraver and designer by his illustrations to *Gay's Fables*, *Æsop's Fables*, etc. He quite established his

Another Bewick Woodcut

fame by the issue in 1790 of his *History of Quadrupeds* (text compiled by Beilby), the illustrations of which were superior to anything hitherto produced in the art of wood-engraving. In 1797 appeared the first, and in 1804 the second volume of his *British Birds*, generally regarded as the finest of his works (text partly by Bewick). Enlarged and improved editions of both books soon followed. Among his other works may be cited the engravings for Goldsmith's *Traveller* and *Deserted Village*, Parnell's *Hermit*, and Somerville's *Chase*. He died in 1828. His younger brother, John, who gave promise of attaining equal eminence, died in 1795, aged thirty-five.

BEX (bā). A village of Switzerland, canton of Vaud, with salt-works and warm sulphur baths now much frequented. Pop. 4000.

BEXHILL. A municipal borough of England, on the coast of East Sussex, 5 miles to the south-west of Hastings, a watering-place. Pop. (1931), 21,229.

BEXLEY. An urban district in England, in Kent, south-east of Woolwich, comprising Bexley Heath and other places. The population in 1931 was 32,940.

BEY. *See* BEG.

BEYLE (bāl), **Marie-Henri.** A French author widely known by his pseudonym *de Stendhal*; born at Grenoble 1783; held civil and military appointments under the empire; took part in the Russian campaign of 1812, thence until 1821 lived at Milan, chiefly occupied with works on music and painting. After nine years' residence at Paris he became in 1830 Consul at Trieste, and in 1833 at Civita Vecchia. In 1841 he returned to Paris, and died in 1842. The distinguishing feature of his works was the application of acutely analytic faculties to sentiment in all its varieties, his best books being the *De l'Amour* (1822), *Le Rouge et le Noir* (1831), and *La Chartreuse de Parme* (1839). His posthumous works include: *Correspondance* (1855), *Journal 1801-14* (1888), *Lettres Intimes* (1892), etc.

BEYROUT (bī-röt'), or **BEIRUT** (ancient **BERYTUS**). The capital of Lebanon, 60 miles N.W. of Damascus (89 miles by railway); pop. 134,655, largely Christians. It stands on the north side of a tongue of land projecting into the Mediterranean and backed by the Lebanon Range, and the site partly consists of slopes facing the sea. The town has a beautiful situation, and has rapidly increased since 1835, mainly owing to the extension of the silk trade, of which it is the centre, silk being the most important export. Its other chief exports are barley, olive-oil, liquorice, sesame, fruit, tobacco, and wool. Cottons and iron goods are the chief imports. The chief manufactures are of silk and cotton. The old town has narrow, dirty streets, very different from the new with its modern houses, hotels, churches, colleges and schools, gardens and carriage drives.

There are here British, French, German, and American institutions, partly religious, partly educational. The American mission has a theological seminary, medical faculty, and training college, and numerous schools connected with it. The British mission has also a number of schools. The French institutions comprise a hospital, a Jesuit university, a large boarding-school for girls, monasteries, etc. There are many printing-offices in the town. There are gas-works, waterworks, electric tramways, and a railway runs to Damascus, with a branch to Homs and Hamah. The climate is healthy and agreeable, but in the hottest months large numbers of the inhabitants remove to temporary quarters on the heights of Lebanon. Ancient Beyrout was a Phœnician city. Under the Romans it was a place of importance, and it was an early seat of the silk manufacture. It afterwards declined, but it again rose to importance during the Crusades. In later times it was long in the possession of the Druses. It was bombarded and taken by the British in 1840. There was a massacre of Christians there in 1860. Its present flourishing condition is chiefly due to the large Christian and European element in the population. On 11th Oct., 1918, French and British warships entered the port of Beyrout and found the town evacuated. Ten days later the French troops took definite possession of Beyrout.

BE'ZA, or DE BÈSZE, Theodore. Next to Calvin the most distinguished man in the early reformed Church of Geneva; born of a noble family at Vezelay, Burgundy, 1519. Educated in Orleans under Melchior Volmar, a German scholar devoted to the Reformation, he became a licentiate of law in 1539, and went to reside at Paris. His habits at this time were dissipated, and his *Poemata Juvenilia*, Latin verses of a more than Ovidian freedom, were afterwards a frequent ground of attack upon him. The reforming influence of a severe illness led to marriage with his mistress, and to his retirement to Geneva in

1548, and his conversion to Protestantism. In 1549 he became professor of Greek at Lausanne, occupying himself with the completion of Marot's translation of the Psalms and the study of the New Testament, and corresponding frequently with Calvin. In 1558 he was sent by the Swiss Calvinists on an embassy to obtain the intercession of the Protestant princes of Germany for the release of Huguenots imprisoned in Paris. In the following year he went to Geneva as a preacher, and soon after became a professor of theology, and the most active assistant of Calvin. He also rendered admirable service to the cause of the reformers at the Court of the King of Navarre and in attendance upon Condé and Coligny.

In the conference at St. Germain in 1562 he spoke strongly against the veneration of images. At Calvin's death in 1564 the administration of the Genevese Church fell entirely to his care. He presided in the synods of the French Calvinists at La Rochelle (1571) and at Nîmes (1572); was sent by Condé (1574) to the Court of the Elector Palatine; and at the religious conference at Montpellier (1586) opposed James Andreas and the theologians of Würtemberg. At the age of sixty-nine he married his second wife (1588), and in 1597 wrote a lively poetical refutation of the rumour that he had recanted and was dead. In 1600 he resigned his official functions, and he died in retirement in 1605. Among his many works, his *Theological Treatises* and the *Histoire ecclésiastique des Églises réformées* (1580), sometimes ascribed to him, are still valuable; but he is most famous for his Latin translation of the New Testament.—BIBLIOGRAPHY: Article in Herzog-Hauck's *Real-encyclopædie*; H. M. Baird, *Th. Beza* (in Heroes of Reformation Series).

BEZ'ANT. A gold coin, believed to have been first struck at Byzantium, and long current in Europe, the value generally varying from a sovereign to half a sovereign. So-called bezants, representing coins without mark or device, are frequently employed as a heraldic charge.

BÉZIERS (bā-zyār; ancient, **BETERRÆ**). A town in Southern France, department Hérault, beautifully situated on a height and surrounded by old walls, its chief buildings being the cathedral, a Gothic structure crowning the height on which the town stands, and the old episcopal palace, now used for public offices. It has manufactures of woollens, hosiery, liqueurs, chemicals, etc., and a good trade in spirits, wool, grain, oil, and fruits. In 1209 Béziers was the scene of a horrible massacre of the Albigenses. Pop. 71,527.

BEZIQUE (be-zēk'). A simple game of cards most commonly played by two persons with two packs. It was a favourite game at the French Court in the eighteenth century. *Polish bezique* and *Rubicon bezique* differ from ordinary bezique.

BE'ZOAR. A concretion or calculus, of a roundish or ovate form, met with in the stomach or intestines of certain animals, especially ruminants. Nine varieties of bezoars have been enumerated, broadly divisible into those which consist mainly of mineral and those which consist of organic matter. The true Oriental bezoars, obtained from the gazelle, belong to the second class. They are formed by accretion of resin-like layers round some foreign substance, a bit of wood, straw, hair, etc., and burn with an agreeable odour. They were formerly regarded as efficacious in preventing infection and the effects of poison.

BEZWÂ'DÂ. A town of India, Madras, at the head of the Kistna delta, an important railway junction, with rock-cut temples, etc. Pop. 44,159.

BHAGALPUR (bhă-gal-pör'). A city in Bengal, capital of a district and division of the same name, on the right bank of the Ganges, here seven miles wide. There are several indigo-works in the neighbourhood. Pop. 68,878.—The division of Bhagalpur has an area of 19,776 sq. miles, and a pop. (chiefly Hindus and Mahommedans) of 8,145,000.—The district has an area of 4226 sq. miles; pop. 2,139,318.

BHAMO. A town of Burma, on the Upper Irrawaddy, about 40 miles from the Chinese frontier. It is the starting-point of caravans to Yunnan, and is in position to become one of the great emporia of the East in event of a regular overland trade being established between India and West China. Pop. 10,000.

BHANDARA (bhan-dā'ra). A town of India, Central Provinces, with manufactures of hardware and cottons. Pop. 13,468.

BHANG. *See* HASHISH.

BHARATPUR'. *See* BHURTPORE.

BHAR'TRIHARI. Indian poet, reputed author of a book of apophthegms, according to legend a dissolute brother of King Vikramâditya (first century B.C.), who became a hermit and ascetic. The collection of

300 apophthegms bearing his name is, however, probably an anthology. 200 of them were translated into English and published at Nuremberg by Abraham Roger as early as 1653, the first Indian writings known in Europe.

BHATGAON (bhát-gä'on). A town of Nepal, about 8 miles from Khatmandu. Pop. 25,000.

BHEELS, or BHILS. One of the non-Aryan races of India, usually included under the name Dravidic, and inhabiting the Vindhya, Satpura, and Satmala Hills. They are a relic of the Indian aborigines driven from the plains by the Aryan Rajputs. They appear to have been orderly and industrious under the Delhi emperors; but on the transfer of the power in the eighteenth century from the Moguls to the Mahrattas they asserted their independence, and being treated as outlaws took to the hills. Various attempts to subdue them were made by the Gaekwar and by the British in 1818 without success. A body of them was, however, subsequently reclaimed, and a Bheel corps formed, which stormed the retreats of the rest of the race and reduced them to comparative order. The hill Bheels wear little clothing, and live precariously on grain, wild roots, and fruits, vermin, etc., but the lowland Bheels are in many respects Hinduised. Their total numbers are upwards of a million (1,198,843 in 1901).—BIBLIOGRAPHY: Crooke, *Natives of Northern India*; G. Oppert, *The Original Inhabitants of India.*

BHEL. *See* BEL.

BHILSA, or BILSA. A town of India, in Gwalior State, on a trap rock, right bank of the Betwa. It has a fort and well-built suburb, but is chiefly interesting on account of the Buddist topes in the neighbourhood, those at Sanchi ($4\frac{1}{2}$ miles S.W.) being especially noteworthy. Pop. 9700.

BHIWÁ'NI. A town of India, Hissar district, Punjab, with trade in sugar, spices, salt, metals, cottons, etc. Pop. 33,270.

BHOLAN' PASS. *See* BOLAN PASS.

BHOOJ. *See* BHUJ.

BHOPAL (bho-päl'). A native State of Central India under British protection, on the Nerbudda, in Malwa. Area, 6902 sq. miles. The country is full of jungles, and is traversed by a part of the Vindhya Mountains. The soil is fertile, yielding wheat, maize, millet, pease, and the other vegetable productions of Central India. Chief exports: sugar, tobacco, ginger, and cotton. The district is well watered by the Nerbudda, Betwa, and minor streams. Pop. 730,000.—The capital of the above State, also called Bhopal, is on the boundary between Malwa and Gondwana. Pop. 45,094. There are fine artificial lakes east and west of the town.

BHÚJ (bhöj). Chief town of Cutch in India, Bombay Presidency, at the base of a fortified hill, with military cantonments, high school and school of art, mausoleums of the Raos or chiefs of Cutch, etc. Pop. 21,579.

BHURTPORE', or BHARATPUR'. A native State, India, in Rajputána, bounded E. by Agra, S. and W. by the Rajput States. Area, 1993 sq. miles. The surface is generally low, and the State is scantily supplied with water; soil generally light and sandy; chief productions: corn, cotton, and sugar. The country is also known as Brij, and is the only Ját State of any size in India. Under British protection since 1826. Pop. 496,437.—The capital, which has the same name, is a fortified place, and was formerly of great strength, Lord Lake being compelled to raise the siege in 1805 after losing 3100 men. It was taken by Lord Combermere in 1827. The rajah's palace is a large building of red and yellow freestone presenting a picturesque appearance. Pop. 33,495.

BHUTAN (bhụ-tän'). An independent State in the Eastern Himalayas, with an area of about 18,000 sq. miles, bordered by Tibet on the N. and E., by British India on the S., and by Sikkim on the W., and consisting of rugged and lofty mountains, abounding in sublime and picturesque scenery. Although mountainous and in many parts extremely cold, much of the country is productive and well cultivated, the mountain slopes being cut into terraces for this purpose. Streams are numerous and rain abundant, and there are extensive forests of fine timber, among the trees being beech, ash, oak, birch, maple, with pines and firs on the higher elevations. Wheat, barley, millet, and various kinds of vegetables are grown, including even potatoes. Irrigation is commonly employed. Wild animals are very numerous, including elephants, tigers, leopards, deer, wild hogs, etc. The chief domestic animal is a kind of pony peculiar to this region, strong and active, as well as handsome. The manufactures are confined to some common articles of home consumption: woollens, cottons, wooden ware, weapons, and implements of iron, etc.

The Bhutanese are a backward race,

and until 1907 were governed by a *Dharm Rajah*, regarded as an incarnation of deity, and by a *Deb Rajah*, with a council of eight. In 1907 the Deb Rajah, who was also Dharm Rajah, resigned his position, and the Tongsa Penlop, Sir Mgyen Wangchuk, was elected as the first hereditary Maharajah of Bhutan. They are nominally Buddhists, and priests and monks are numerous. After various aggressive incursions into the adjacent regions under British rule, and the capture and ill-treatment of Ashley Eden, the British envoy, in 1863, the Bhutias were compelled to cede to the British considerable portions of territory (in 1865) in return for a yearly allowance of £2500, to be raised to double the amount in case of good behaviour. In 1910 an amending treaty was concluded, under which the Bhutan Government surrendered the control of its foreign relations to the British Government, and the subsidy was raised to £6666 a year. The capital is Punakha, or Dosen, about 100 miles from Darjeeling, a place of great natural strength. Pop. 300,000. — Cf. J. C. White, *Sikkim and Bhutan*.

BIAF'RA, BIGHT OF. A bight or bay on the west coast of Africa running in from the Gulf of Guinea, having the Cameroon Mountains at its inner angle, and containing the Island of Fernando Po. The coast regions here now belong to Britain and France.

BIA'LA. A town in Galicia, formerly in the Austrian Empire, now in Poland, on the Biala (an affluent of the Vistula), here forming the boundary between Galicia and Silesia, and over which a bridge leads to the town of Bielitz, on the opposite side. Pop. 8257.

BIAL'YSTOK, or **BYELOSTOK.** Formerly a Russian town, now in Poland, province of Grodno, on the Biala. It has manufactures of woollens, silks, hats, etc., and is a railway centre of some note. Pop. 91,335.

BIA'NA. A town of India, Bhurtpore, an old place with many temples, venerated by Mohammedans. Pop. 8758.

BIANCAVIL'LA. A town of Sicily, on the southern side of Etna, in a fertile, well-watered district, where oranges, cotton, etc., are cultivated. Pop. 16,231.

BIANCHINI (-kē'nē), **Francesco.** Italian historian and astronomer, born 1662. Pope Alexander VIII. bestowed on him a rich benefice, with the appointment of tutor and librarian to his nephew Cardinal Pietro Ottoboni; and Clement XI. appointed him secretary to the commission for the correction of the calendar. He spent eight years in meridian measurement; left a portion of a *Universal History*, and works on the planet Venus, etc. He died in 1729.

BIARD (bē-är), **Auguste François.** A French genre painter, born in 1798, died in 1882. He travelled extensively, visiting Spain, Greece, Syria, Egypt, Mexico, Brazil, etc. Among his best-known pictures are: *The Babes in the Wood* (1828), *The Beggar's Family* (1836), *The Combat with Polar Bears* (1839), and *The Strolling Players*. A strong element of caricature runs through most of his works.

BIAR'RITZ. A small seaport, bathing-town, and winter resort, France, Basses-Pyrénées, about 5 miles from Bayonne, picturesquely situated on the rugged coast of the Bay of Biscay. It straggles along the coast for about 2 miles, and is well provided with hotels, and other accommodations for visitors. It is much frequented by English people, especially in winter and early in the year. It became a fashionable watering-place during the reign of Napoleon III., who had an autumn residence there. Pop. 22,955.

BI'AS. One of the seven sages of Greece, born at Priene, in Ionia; flourished about 570 B.C. He appears to have been in repute as a political and legal adviser, and many sayings of practical wisdom attributed to him are preserved by Diogenes Laertius.

BIAS (bi-äs'). One of the five large rivers of the Punjab, India, rising in the Himalayas (13,326 feet), and flowing first in a westerly and then in a southerly direction until it unites with the Sutlej after a course of 300 miles.

BIB. A fish of the cod family (*Morrhua lusca*), found in the British seas, about a foot long, the body very deep, esteemed as excellent eating. It is called also *pout* or *whiting pout*.

BIBERACH (bē'be-rȧh). A town of Germany, Würtemberg, on the Riss, formerly a free imperial city. The French, under Moreau, defeated the Austrians near Biberach in 1796. Pop. 10,070.

BIBI EIBAT. A rich oil-field in the Baku district. It is situated to the south of the town.

BIBLE (Gr. *biblia*, books, from *biblos*, the inner bark of the papyrus, on which the ancients wrote). A word which has come to mean substantially a sacred book. Thus the Koran is the bible of the Mohammedans. When we speak of *the* Bible, we mean the collection of the Sacred Writings or Holy Scriptures of the Christians. Its two main divisions, one received by both Jews and Christians, the other by Christians only, are improperly termed Testaments, owing to the confusion of two meanings of the Greek word *diathēkē*, which was applied indifferently to a covenant and to a last will or testament. The Jewish religion being represented as a compact between God and the Jews, the Christian religion was regarded as a new compact between God and the human race; and the Bible is therefore properly divisible into the Writings of the Old and New Covenants. The books of the Old Testament received by the Jews were divided by them into three classes: 1. *The Law*, contained in the *Pentateuch* or five books of Moses. 2. *The Prophets*, comprising Joshua, Judges, 1 and 2 Samuel, 1 and 2 Kings, Isaiah, Jeremiah, Ezekiel, and the twelve minor prophets. 3. *The Ketubim*, or *Hagiographa* (*holy writings*), containing the Psalms, the Proverbs, Job, in one division; Ruth, Lamentations, Ecclesiastes, Esther, the Song of Solomon, in another division; Daniel, Ezra, Nehemiah, 1 and 2 Chronicles, in a third. These books are extant in the Hebrew language; others, rejected from the canon as apocryphal by Protestants, are found only in Greek or Latin.

The books of Moses were deposited, according to the Bible, in the tabernacle, near the ark, the other sacred writings being similarly preserved. They were removed by Solomon to the temple, and on the capture of Jerusalem by Nebuchadnezzar probably perished. According to Jewish tradition, Ezra, with the assistance of the Great Synagogue, collected and compared as many copies as could be found, and from this collation an edition of the whole was prepared, with the exception of the writings of Ezra, Malachi, and Nehemiah, added subsequently, and certain obviously later insertions in other books. When Judas Maccabæus repaired the temple, which had been destroyed by Antiochus Epiphanes, he placed in it a correct copy of the Hebrew Scriptures, whether the recension of Ezra or not is not known. This copy was carried to Rome by Titus. The exact date of the determination of the Hebrew canon is uncertain, but no work known to be written later than about 100 years after the captivity was admitted into it by the Jews of Palestine. The Hellenistic or Alexandrian Jews, however, were less strict, and admitted many later writings, forming what is now known as the *Apocrypha*, in which they were followed by the Latin Church. The Protestant Churches at the Reformation gave in their adherence to the restricted Hebrew canon, though the *Apocrypha* was long included in the various editions of the Bible. The division into chapters and verses, as it now exists, is of comparatively modern origin, though divisions of some kind were early introduced. Cardinal Hugo de Sancto Caro, in the thirteenth century, divided the Latin translation known as the *Vulgate* into chapters for convenience of reference, and similar divisions were made in the Hebrew text by Rabbi Mordecai Nathan in the fifteenth century. About the middle of the sixteenth century the verses in Robert Stephanus's edition of the *Vulgate* were for the first time marked by numbers.

Old Testament. The earliest and most famous version of the Old Testament is the *Septuagint*, or Greek translation, executed by Alexandrian Greeks, and completed probably before 130 B.C., different portions being done at different times, some during the reign of Ptolemy Philadelphus (284-247 B.C.). This version was adopted by the early Christian Church and by the Jews themselves, and has always held an important place in regard to the interpretation and history of the Bible. The Syriac version, the *Peshito*, made early in the second century after Christ, is celebrated for its fidelity. The Coptic version was made from the *Septuagint* in the third or fourth century. The Gothic version, by Ulphilas, was made from the *Septuagint* in the fourth century, but mere insignificant fragments of it are extant. The most important Latin version is the *Vulgate*, executed by Jerome, partly on the basis of the original Hebrew, and completed in A.D. 405. For Aramaic paraphrases of the books of the Old Testament, *see* TARGUM; SAMARITANS.

The printed editions of the Hebrew Bible are very numerous. The first edition of the entire Hebrew Bible was printed at Soncino in 1488. The Brescian edition of 1494 was used by Luther in making his German translation. The editions of Athias (1661 and 1667) are much esteemed for their beauty and correctness. Van der Hooght followed the latter. Dr. Kennicott did more than any one of his predecessors to settle the Hebrew text. His Hebrew Bible appeared at Oxford during 1776-80, 2 vols. folio. The text is from that of Van der Hooght, with which 630 MSS. were collated. De Rossi, who published a supplement to Kennicott's edition (Parma, 1784-99, 5 vols. 4to), collated 958 MSS. The oldest-dated MS., the *Codex Babylonicus Petropolitanus*, goes back to the year A.D. 916, but it is probable that one or two MSS. of the Hebrew Bible belong to the ninth century. They present what is known as the Massoretic text, that is, the text provided with the vowel points and other markings which were inserted by Jewish scholars known as the *Massoretes*.—Cf. C. O. Ginsburg, *Introduction to the Massoretic Critical Edition of the Bible* (London, 1897).

New Testament. The books of the New Testament were all written in Greek, unless it be true, as some critics suppose, that the Gospel of St. Matthew was originally written in Hebrew. Most of these writings have always been received as canonical; but the Epistle to the Hebrews, commonly ascribed to St. Paul, that of St. Jude, the second of Peter, the second and third of John, and the Apocalypse, have been doubted. The three oldest MSS. are: (1) the Sinaitic MS. (at the Leningrad Library), discovered by Tischendorf in a convent on Mount Sinai, 1844, and acquired by the Czar in 1859, assigned to the middle of the fourth century; (2) the Vatican MS. at Rome, of similar date; (3) the Alexandrine MS. in the British Museum, assigned to the middle of the fifth century. It was given by Cyril Lucas, patriarch of Constantinople, to Prince Charles, afterwards Charles I., in 1621. (4) the Beza MS., given to the University of Cambridge in 1581, assigned to the sixth century, but probably older. Each MS. contains also the *Septuagint* Greek of the Old Testament in great part. The *Vulgate* of Jerome embraces a Latin translation of the New as well as of the Old Testament, based on an older Latin version. The division of the text of the New Testament into chapters and verses was introduced later than that of the Old Testament, but it is not precisely known when or by whom. The Greek text was first printed in the *Complutensian Polyglot*, in 1514; in 1516 an edition of it was published at Basel by Erasmus. Among later valuable editions are those of Lachmann, Tischendorf, Tregelles, Westcott and Hort, D. Weiss (1894-1900), and von Soden.

Translations. Of translations of the Bible into modern languages, the English and the German are the most celebrated. Considerable portions were translated into Anglo-Saxon, including the *Gospels* and the *Psalter*. Wycliffe's translation of the whole Bible (from the *Vulgate*), begun about 1356, was completed shortly before his death, which took place in 1384. The first printed version of the Bible in English was the translation of William Tindall or Tyndale, whose New Testament was printed in quarto at Cologne in 1525, a small octavo edition appearing at the same time at Worms. Tunstall, Bishop of London, caused the first edition to be bought up and burned. The *Pentateuch* was published by Tindall in 1530, and he also translated some of the prophetical books. Our translation of the New Testament is much indebted to Tindall's. A translation of the entire Bible was published by Miles Coverdale in 1535. It was undertaken at the instance of Thomas Cromwell, and, being made from German and Latin versions, was inferior to Tindall's. After the death of Tindall, John Rogers undertook the completion of his translation and the preparation of a new edition. In this edition the latter part of the Old Testament (after 2 Chronicles) was based on Coverdale's version. A revised edition was published in 1539 under the superintendence of Richard Taverner. In the same year as Taverner's another edition appeared, printed by authority, with a preface by Cranmer, and hence called Cranmer's Bible. This was the first Bible printed by authority in England, and a royal proclamation in 1540 ordered it to be placed in every parish church. This continued, with various revisions, to be the authorised version till 1568.

During 1557-60 an edition appeared at Geneva, based on Tindall's—the work of Whittington, Coverdale, Goodman, John Knox, and other exiles—and commonly called the Geneva or Breeches Bible (from "breeches" standing instead of "aprons" in Gen. iii. 7). This version, for sixty years the most popular in England, was allowed to be printed in England under a patent of monopoly in 1561. It was the first printed in Roman letters, and was also the first to adopt the plan previously adopted in the Hebrew of a division into verses. It omitted the Apocrypha, left the authorship of the Epistle to the Hebrews open, and put words not in the original in italics. The Bishops' Bible, published 1568 to 1572, was based on Cranmer's, and revised by Archbishop Parker and eight bishops. It succeeded Cranmer's as the authorised version, but did not commend itself to scholars or people. In 1582 an edition of the New Testament, translated from the Latin *Vulgate*, appeared at Rheims, and in 1609-10 the Old Testament was published at Douai. This is the version recognised by the Roman Catholic Church.

In the reign of James I a Hebrew scholar, Hugh Broughton, insisted on the necessity of a new translation, and at the Hampton Court Conference (1604) the suggestion was accepted by the king. The work was undertaken by forty-seven scholars divided into six companies, two meeting at Westminster, two at Oxford, and two at Cambridge, while a general committee meeting in London revised the portions of the translation finished by each. The revision was begun in 1607, and occupied three years, the completed work being published in folio in 1611. By the general accuracy of its translation and the purity of its style it superseded all other versions. In response, however, to a widely-spread desire for a translation even yet more free from errors, the Convocation of Canterbury in 1870 appointed a committee to consider the question of revising the English version. Their report being favourable, two companies were formed, one for the Old Testament and one for the New, consisting partly of members of Convocation and partly of outside scholars. Two similar companies were also organised in America to work along with the British scholars. The result was that the revised version of the New Testament was issued in 1881; that of the Old Testament in 1885. The revisers made few alterations but such as they deemed to be called for on the score of accuracy, clearness, and uniformity, as stated in the prefaces. A version with special corrections by the American revisers has also been published (1901).

Translations, independent of the Authorised Version, have been published by J. Moffat: *The New Testament* (1913); *The Old Testament* (1924).

In Germany some seventeen translations of the Bible, partly in the High German, partly in the Low German dialect, appeared between the invention of printing and the Reformation, but they had all to make way for Luther's great translation—the New Testament in 1522, and the whole Bible in 1534. The work of Bible-translation has been greatly stimulated by the Bible societies. Thus in the year 600 the Bible existed in about 8 languages; by 1500 it had been translated into 24; in 1600 the number had risen to quite 30. During the last 100 years the number has advanced to over 400.—BIBLIOGRAPHY: R. G. Moulton, *The Literary Study of the Bible*; A. S. Peake, *The Bible: its Origin, its Significance, and its Abiding Worth*; A. Blakiston, *The Bible of To-day*; T. K. Cheyne and J. S. Black, *Encyclopedia Biblica*; J. Orr, *The International Standard Bible Encyclopædia* (5 vols.).

BIBLE CHRISTIANS. A small sect founded by a Cornish Methodist preacher called O'Bryan, who profess to follow only the doctrines of the Bible and reject all human authority in religion. *See* METHODISM.

BIBLE COMMUNISTS. *See* PERFECTIONISTS.

BIBLE SOCIETIES. Societies formed for the distribution of the Bible or portions of it in various languages, either gratuitously or at a low rate. Efforts were made to provide a systematic dissemination of Bibles as early as the time of Charles I. of England, and a number of organisations already existed in the seventeenth century. Such were: The Society for the Propagation of the Gospel in Wales, The Society for Promoting Christian Knowledge, The Society for the Propagation of the Gospel in Foreign Parts, etc. The most famous and influential of all Bible societies, however, was founded in 1804, when a clergyman of Wales, whom the want of a Welsh Bible led to London, occasioned the establishment of the British and Foreign Bible Society. A great number of similar institutions were soon formed in all parts of Great Britain, and afterwards on the continent of Europe, in Asia, and in America, and connected with the British as a parent or kindred society. The British Society now controls about 8000 auxiliary societies, nearly 6000 of these in Great Britain, and spends each year £250,000.

Since its formation, the British and Foreign Bible Society has circulated versions of the whole or parts of the Scriptures in 665 languages or dialects. In more than thirty instances languages have for the first time been reduced to a written form in order to translate into them and circulate amongst the people the Bibles of this society. The total issues now amount to over 200,000,000 copies, of which nearly 80,000,000 are in English, while about 70,000,000 additional copies have been distributed by the kindred societies which have sprung out of it. The proceedings of the British and Foreign Bible Society gave rise to several controversies, one of which related to the neglecting to give the Prayer-book with the Bible.

Another controversy related to the circulation of the Apocrypha along with the canonical books. The Edinburgh Bible Society, established in 1809, and up to 1826 connected with the British and Foreign Bible Society, seceded on the occasion of the controversy regarding the circulation of the Apocrypha, and up to 1860 existed as a separate society. In 1861 this society was united with the National, the Glasgow, and other Bible societies, into a whole called the National Bible Society of Scotland, having its head-quarters in Edinburgh and Glasgow. Its total issue is now over 26,000,000 volumes. The Hibernian Bible Society, which has its head-quarters in Dublin, was established in 1806 to encourage a wider circulation of the Bible in Ireland. Total issue about 6,000,000 copies.

In Germany the principal Bible society is the "Prussian", established at Berlin in 1814 and having many auxiliaries. France has two principal Bible societies, whose head-quarters are at Paris, the one instituted in 1818, the other in 1833. Switzerland possesses various Bible societies, chief among which are those of Basel (1804), Bern, Lausanne, and Geneva. In the Netherlands there has existed since 1815 a fraternal union of different sects for the distribution of Bibles. The Swedish Bible Society was instituted in 1808, and the Norwegian Bible Society in 1816. The first Russian society in Leningrad printed the Bible in thirty-one languages and dialects spoken in the Russian dominions, and auxiliary societies were formed at Irkutsk, Tobolsk, among the Kirghises, Georgians, and Cossacks of the Don; but they were all suppressed by an imperial ukase in 1826. In 1831 a new Bible society was instituted at Leningrad —namely, the Russian Evangelical Bible Society. Italy, Spain, and Portugal have had as yet no Bible societies, but the British societies are energetic in providing them with Bibles in their own tongues. In the United States of America the great American Bible Society, formed in 1816, acts in concert with auxiliary societies in all parts of the Union. It has an annual expenditure of from £120,000 to £160,000, and an endowment that yields about £17,000. The number of Bibles issued from the Bible House was 2,301,847 in 1916, and 2,644,477 in 1917. Its total issue since its organisation has been about 80,000,000 volumes.

BIB'LIA PAU'PERUM ("Bible of the poor"). The name for block-books common in the Middle Ages, and consisting of a number of rude pictures of Biblical subjects with short explanatory text accompanying each picture.

BIBLICAL ANTIQUITIES. Under this term are included the manners, customs, events, remains, and records of Biblical, and more especially Old Testament, times. The practical aim of the study of Biblical antiquities, which may be conveniently pursued in such recent Bible dictionaries as those of Cheyne and Hastings, is to gain light upon the interpretation of the sacred text. The term Biblical antiquities is not much in use nowadays in designating a definite subsidiary branch of Bible study, but it corresponds most nearly to Biblical archæology among the generally-recognised Biblical sciences. So regarded, its special task is to interpret the remains of past phases of civilization that are to be found in the Bible, or which if found elsewhere may serve the purpose of Biblical exposition. A new interest in the antiquarian or archæological study of the Bible was awakened in 1873, when George Smith announced his discovery among the cuneiform tablets in the British Museum of close parallels to the Bible stories of the Creation and the Deluge. Since then the work of exploration in Bible lands has been diligently pursued, and the vital bearing of this work upon Old Testament study is amply illustrated in such an admirable handbook of Biblical archæology as Jeremias' *The Old Testament in the Light of the Ancient East.* Archæological material of great value for the textual interpretation of the New Testament is supplied by the vast quantity of Greek papyri discovered within the last generation in Egyptian rubbish-heaps. G. A. Deissman in Germany, and J. H. Moulton and G. Milligan in Great Britain have been pioneers in this interesting and fruitful branch of New Testament study. — BIBLIOGRAPHY: Keil, *Manual of Biblical Archæology*; A. Jeremias, *The Old Testament in the Light of the Ancient East.*

BIBLIOG'RAPHY (Gr. *biblion*, a book, and *graphō*, I describe). The knowledge of books, in reference to the subjects discussed in them, their different degrees of rarity, curiosity, reputed and real value, the materials of which they are composed, and the rank which they ought to hold in the classification of a library. The subject is sometimes divided into *general, national*, and *special* bibliography, according as it deals with books in general, with those of a particular country, or with those on special subjects or having a special character (as early printed books, anonymous books). A subdivision of each of these might be made into *material* and *literary*, according as books were viewed in regard to their mere externals or in regard to their contents.

Hardly any branch or department of bibliography has as yet been quite adequately treated. The reduction of bibliographic material to something like method and system was undoubtedly the work of France. Brunet's *Manuel du Libraire*, containing, in an alphabetical form, a list of the most valuable and costly books of all literatures; Barbier's *Dictionnaire des Ouvrages Anonymes*; Renouard's *Catalogue d'un Amateur*, for a long time the best guide of French collectors; and the *Bibliographie de la France*, recording the yearly accumulation of literary works, were all first works in their respective departments. The authors of anonymous and pseudonymous works are made known in Barbier's *Dictionnaire des Ouvrages Anonymes et Pseudonymes* (Paris, 1806-9), treating only of French and Latin works, Quérard's *Dictionnaire des Ouvrages Polyonymes et Anonymes de la Littérature Française* (Paris, 1854-6), and his *Supercheries Littéraires Dévoilées* (Literary Frauds Unveiled, Paris, 1845-56). Lorenz's *Catalogue Général de la Librairie Française* (1867, etc.) gives all books published in France since 1840.

The beginnings of English bibliography are to be found in Blount's *Censura Celebriorum Auctorum* (1690), and Oldys' *British Librarian* (1737). Among library catalogues are those of the Bodleian Library, the British Museum (with subject index of books added since 1880), and the Advocates' Library, Edinburgh. Catalogues compiled on a scientific system, by which the reader is assisted in his researches after books on a particular subject, are not uncommon on the European continent; but the only extensive one of the kind in Britain is that of the Signet Library, Edinburgh. Valuable classified catalogues are Sonnenschein's *The Best Books and Reader's Guide*, giving 100,000 modern works on all subjects.

Of other English bibliographical works we may mention the *Typographical Antiquities* of Ames, Herbert, and Dibdin; Brydges' *Censura Literaria* (1805); Didbin's *Bibliographical Decameron* (1817); Dr. Robert Watt's *Bibliotheca Britannica* (1824, 4 vols., two of subjects and two of authors); Lowndes' *Bibliographer's Manual* (edited by H. G. Bohn, 1869); S. A. Allibone's *Critical Dictionary of English Literature and British and American Authors* (1859-71); etc. The bulky booksellers' catalogues of Bohn and Quaritch; Low's *English Catalogue* of books published from 1835 onwards, in continuation of the *London Catalogue* giving all English books published from 1700; and the *Reference Catalogue of Current Literature* are also valuable bibliographical works. *The Dictionary of the Anonymous and Pseudonymous Literature of Great Britain* by Halkett and Laing (4 vols., 1882-8) is of high value. American literature has already given rise to a series of bibliographical works on both sides of the Atlantic, e.g. Ternaux-Compans, *Bibliothèque Américaine* (1837); Rich's *Bibliotheca Americana Nova*, giving books published between 1700 and 1844; *Bibliographical Catalogue of Books, Translations of the Scriptures, and other publications in the Indian Tongues of the United States* (1849); Duyckinck's *Cyclopædia of American Literature* (1856); Trübner's *Bibliographical Guide to American Literature* (1856); and the *General American Catalogue*, compiled by Lynds E. Jones and F. Leypoldt, 1880 (with later continuations).

Of German bibliographical works we shall only mention Heinius's *Allgemeines Bücherlexikon*, giving books published between 1700 and 1888, and Keyser's *Vollständiges Bücherlexikon* (1834, etc.), giving books published since 1750. German bibliography is particularly rich in the literature of separate sciences; and the bibliography of the classics and of ancient editions was founded by the Germans. *See* BIBLIOMANIA.—BIBLIOGRAPHY: W. P. Courtney, *A Register of National Bibliography* (London); Henri Stein, *Manuel de Bibliographie générale* (Paris); Ch. V. Langlois, *Manuel de Bibliographie historique* (Paris); Julius Petzholdt, *Bibliotheca Bibliographica*; Professor Ferguson, *Some Aspects of Bibliography*; A. G. S. Josephson, *Bibliographies of Bibliographies*; R. A. Peddie, *National Bibliographies*.

BIB'LIOMANCY. Divination performed by means of books, and especially of the Bible; also called *sortes biblicæ*, or *sortes sanctorum*. It consisted in taking passages at hazard, and drawing indications thence concerning things future, in the same way that the ancients drew prognostications from the works of Homer and Virgil. In 465 the Council of Vannes condemned the practice, as did the Councils of Agde and Auxerre. But in the twelfth century we find it employed as a mode of detecting heretics, and in the Galican Church it was long practised in the election of bishops, the installation of abbots, etc. *See* DIVINATION.

BIBLIOMA'NIA ("book-madness"). A passion for possessing curious books, which has reached its highest development in France and England, though originating in Holland towards the close of the seventeenth century. The true bibliomaniac is determined in the purchase of books, less by the value of their contents, than by certain accidental circumstances attending them, as that they belong to particular classes, are made of singular materials, or have something remarkable in their history. One of the most common forms of the passion is the desire to possess complete sets of works, as of the various editions of the Bible or of single classics; of the editions *in usum Delphini* and *cum notis variorum*; of the Italian classics printed by the Academia della Crusca; of the works printed by the Elzevirs or by Aldus.

Scarce books, prohibited books, and books distinguished for remarkable errors or mutilations have also been eagerly sought for, together with those printed in the infancy of typography, called *incunabula*, first printed editions (*editiones principes*), and the like. Other works are valued for their miniatures and illuminated initial letters, or as being printed upon vellum, upon paper of uncommon materials, upon various substitutes for paper, or upon coloured paper, in coloured inks, or in letters of gold or silver. In high esteem among bibliomaniacs are works printed on large paper, with very wide margins, especially if uncut, also works printed from copper plates, *éditions de luxe*, and limited issues generally. Bibliomania often extends to the binding. In France the bindings of Derome and Bozerian are most valued; in England those of Charles Lewis and Roger Payne. Many devices have been adopted to give a factitious value to bindings. Jeffrey, a London bookseller, had Fox's *History of King James II.* bound in foxskin; and books have been more than once bound in human skin. The edges of books are often ornamented with paintings, etc., and marginal decoration is frequently an element of considerable value. Another method of gratifying the bibliomaniac taste is that of enriching works by the addition of engravings—illustrative of the text of the book—and of preparing only single copies. —BIBLIOGRAPHY: F. S. Merryweather, *Bibliomania of the Middle Ages*; Fitzgerald, *The Book Fancier*.

BIBURY. A village of Gloucestershire, on the Coln, 7 miles from Cirencester. It is one of the most picturesque of the Cotswold villages. Several cottages, called Arlington Row, are the property of the National Trust.

BICANERE. *See* BIKANER.

BICARBONATE, or ACID CARBONATE. A salt of carbonic acid (H_2CO_3), obtained by replacing one hydrogen atom of the acid by a metal. Bicarbonate of soda ($NaHCO_3$) is used as an antacid, and effervescing liquors are usually produced by mixing it with acids such as tartaric acid. It is also the chief ingredient in baking-powder. Bicarbonates of calcium and magnesium are present in solution in many natural waters, and are the cause of what is known as temporary hardness in water.

BICE. The name of two colours used in painting, one blue the other green, and both native carbonates of copper, though inferior kinds are also prepared artificially.

BI'CEPS. *See* ARM.

BICESTER (bis'tėr). A town of England, in Oxfordshire; has an interesting old church, brewing, tanning, etc. Pop. (1931), 3109.

BICÊTRE (bē-sātr). A village of France, S.W. of Paris, with a famous hospital for old men and an asylum for lunatics, together forming one vast establishment. The neat little articles of wood and bone made by the inmates are known as *Bicêtre work*.

BICHAT (bē-shä), **Marie François Xavier.** French anatomist and physiologist, born at Thoirette, department of Ain, 1771, died 1802. He wrote *Traité des Membranes*, which was translated into almost all the languages of Europe; *Recherches sur la Vie et la Mort*; and *Anatomie Générale*—a complete treatise on anatomy and physiology. Bichat was the first who recognised the identity of the tissues in the different organs.

BICK'ERSTAFF, Isaac. Dramatic writer, born in Ireland about 1735, died in obscurity on the Continent about 1812. He wrote many successful pieces for the stage, some of which are still popular, and was a friend of Garrick, Boswell, etc.—In English literature the name *Isaac Bickerstaff* occurs as the name assumed by Swift in his controversy with Partridge, the almanac-maker, and also as the pseudonym of Steele as editor of *The Tatler*.

BICK'ERSTETH, Rev. Edward. Clergyman of the Church of England, born 1786, died 1850. He was in business as a solicitor in Norwich for a time, but took orders and went to Africa in 1816 to reorganise the stations of the Church Missionary Society. Returning to England, he was chosen secretary to that society. In 1830 he became rector of Watton in Hertford, and was one of the founders of the Evangelical Alliance. His publications, which had an immense circulation, included *The Christian Student*, *A Treatise on the Lord's Supper*, *A Treatise on Prayer*, *The Signs of the Times*, *The Restoration of the Jews*, *A Practical Guide to the Prophecies*, besides sermons and tracts without number.

BICYCLE. A light vehicle impelled by the rider. It consists of two wheels placed one before the other, and of connecting-bars or framework. A cog-wheel fixed on the back wheel is connected by a chain to a gear-wheel provided with two cranks and two pedals. The rider propels the machine by pressing the pedals with his feet. He sits upon a saddle generally placed above and between the two wheels, and steers the machine by a handle, which turns the front wheel in any required direction. It is kept in an upright position by the action of the rider's body and legs, by the steering power, and also by its own momentum. The speed of 50 miles an hour has been reached. Machines are usually provided with (1) *free wheels*, i.e. the cog-wheel on the back wheel is arranged so that it can rotate freely, relative to the wheel, in one direction of rotation; but is fixed, relative to the wheel, in the other direction. This permits the feet of the rider and the driving-cranks and pedals to remain at rest when descending hills. (2) *Three-speed gears*, i.e. the cog-wheel on the back wheel is attached to it through a mechanism so designed that the number of revolutions made by the cog-wheel, per revolution of the back wheel, can be varied by a small lever under the rider's control. This arrangement has the effect of giving the rider greater mechanical leverage if desired, and hills can be more easily ascended. Three ratios of speed are usually provided. (3) *Rim-brakes.* The brake blocks are applied to the metal rim and the wear of tyres is thus saved. For motor-bicycles, *see* MOTOR-VEHICLES.

BIDAR (bē'dar). A town of India, in the Nizam's Dominions, 75 miles N.W. of Hyderabad; noted for the metal ware to which it has given its name. *See* BIDERY.

BIDASSO'A. A river of North-Eastern Spain, forming for some distance the boundary between France and Spain. In 1813 Wellington effected the passage of the Bidassoa and entered France.

BIDDEFORD (bid'e-ford). A thriving town, United States, Maine, on the Saco, opposite to the town of Saco, with which it is connected by several bridges. The river falls, 42 feet high, afford valuable water-power. Pop. 17,633.

BID'DERY. *See* BIDERY.

BIDDING-PRAYER. An exhortation to prayer, which directly informs the congregation on the object for which the prayer is to be said, and ends with the Lord's Prayer. In England it is used in cathedrals, Inns of Court, and at University sermons.

BIDDLE, John. One of the pioneers of the modern Unitarians, born in 1615 at Wotton-under-Edge, in Gloucestershire, died in prison 1662. He was educated at Oxford, and became master of a free school at Gloucester. He was repeatedly imprisoned for his anti-Trinitarian views, and the Westminster Assembly of Divines, having got Parliament to decree the punishment of death against those who should impugn the established opinions respecting the Trinity, was eager for his execution, but the Act was not put in force. A general Act of Oblivion in 1652 restored him to liberty, when he immediately disseminated his opinions both by preaching and by the publication of his *Twofold Scripture Catechism*. He was again imprisoned, and the law of 1648 was to be put in operation against him when, to save his life, Cromwell banished him to St. Mary's Castle, Scilly, and assigned him a hundred crowns annually. Here he remained three years, until the Protector liberated him in 1658. He then continued to preach his opinions till the death of Cromwell, and also after the Restoration, when he was committed to jail in 1662, and died a few months after. He wrote *Twelve Arguments against the Deity of the Holy Spirit*, *Confession of Faith concerning the Holy Trinity*, etc.

BIDDULPH. An urban district of England, in the north-west of Staffordshire, 3½ miles south-east of Congleton, with collieries, ironworks, etc. Pop. (1931), 8346.

BIDEFORD (bid′e-ford). A municipal borough and seaport, England, County Devon, 44 miles N. of Plymouth, picturesquely situated on both sides of the Torridge, 4 miles from the sea. Its industries include rough earthenware, ropes, sails, etc. Its shipping trade was formerly large, but is not now of much importance. Pop. (1931), 8782.

BIDENS. A cosmopolitan genus of herbs, nat. ord. Compositæ. Two species are British marsh-plants; their fruits are animal-dispersed, the pappus consisting of 2-4 barbed bristles, hence the popular name Bur-marigold.

BID′ERY (from *Bidar*, a town in India). An alloy, primarily composed of copper, lead, tin, to every 3 ounces of which 16 ounces of spelter (zinc) are added. Many articles of Indian manufacture, remarkable for elegance of form and gracefully-engraved patterns, are made of it. It is said not to rust, to yield little to the hammer, and to break only when violently beaten. Articles formed from it are generally inlaid with silver or gold and polished.

BIDPAI (bid′pi), or **PILPAI** (pil′pi). The reputed author of a very ancient and popular collection of Eastern fables. The original source of these stories is the old Indian collection of fables called *Pancha Tantra*, which acquired its present form under Buddhist influences not earlier than the second century B.C. It was afterwards spread over all India, and handed down from age to age in various more or less different versions. An abridgment of this collection is known as the *Hitopadesa*. The *Pancha Tantra* was translated into Pehlevi in the sixth century of our era. This translation was itself the basis of a translation into Arabic made in the eighth century; and this latter translation (known as the *Book of Kalilah and Dimna*)—in which the author is first called Bidpai, the chief of Indian philosophers—is the medium by which these fables have been introduced into the languages of the West. The first English translation was published in 1570. *See* KALILAH AND DIMNA.

BIEBRICH (bē′bri*h*). A town of Prussia, district of Wiesbaden, on the right bank of the Rhine, with a fine castle, formerly the residence of the Dukes of Nassau. Pop. 21,250.

BIEL (bēl). *See* BIENNE.

BIELA'S (bē′la) **COMET.** Discovered by M. Biela (1782-1856), an Austrian officer, in 1826. Its periodic time was determined as 6 years 38 weeks. It returned in 1832, 1839, 1846, and 1852. On the latter two occasions it was in two parts, each having a distinct nucleus and tail. It has not since been seen as a comet; but in 1872, 1879, and 1885, when the earth passed through the comet's track, immense flights of meteors were seen, which have been connected with the broken-up and dispersed comet.

BIELEFELD (bē′le-felt). A town of Prussia, in the province of Westphalia, 38 miles E. from Münster; one of the chief places in Germany for flax-spinning and linen manufacture. Pop. 86,062.

BIELEV (bye-lev′). A town in Russia, government of Tula, with manufactures of soap, leather, etc., and a considerable trade. Pop. 8123.

BIELGOROD (byel′go-rod). A town, Russia, government of Kursk, and 76 miles S. from the town of Kursk, on the Donetz. It is an archbishop's see, and has important fairs. Pop. 30,570.

BIELITZ (bē′lits). A town of Poland, formerly in Austrian Silesia, 42 miles W.S.W. of Cracow, on the Biala, which divides Silesia from Galicia, with manufactures of woollens and linens, dye-works and print-fields Pop. 17,150.

BIELLA (bē-el′lȧ). A town of North Italy, province of Novara, 38 miles N.N.E. of Turin, the seat of a bishop. It has manufactures of woollen and linen cloth. Pop. 19,340.

BIELO-OZERO (byā-lo-o-zā′ro; "White Lake," from its white clay bottom). A Russian lake, government of Novgorod, 25 miles long by 20 broad. Its surplus waters are conveyed to the Volga by the River Sheksna.

BIELOPOL (byā′lo-pol). A town of the Ukraine, government of Kharkov. Pop. 15,000.

BIELOSTOK. *See* BIALYSTOK.

BIELSK (byelsk). A town of Poland, government of Grodno. Pop. 4780.

BIELZY (byel′tsi). A town in Bessarabia. Pop. 20,000.

BIENE, Auguste Van. Anglo-Dutch musician. He displayed his 'cello playing and acting to great effect in sentimental playlets very pleasing to the general public, a general favourite being a solo called

The Broken Melody. He died 23rd Jan., 1913.

BIENHOA (bi-en-hwä'). A town in Cochin-China, capital of a province of the same name, 20 miles N.W. of Saigon. It was taken by the French in 1861, and is now one of their fortified posts. Pop. 20,000.

BIENNE (bi-ān), or **BIEL.** A town, Switzerland, canton of Bern, 21 miles N.W. of Bern, beautifully situated at the N. end of the lake of same name, and at the foot of the Jura. Pop. 37,856.—The lake is about 7½ miles long by 2½ miles broad. It receives the waters of Lake Neufchâtel by the Thiel, and discharges itself into the Aar.

BIEN'NIAL. A plant that requires two seasons to come to maturity, bearing fruit and dying the second year, as the turnip, carrot, wall-flower, etc.

BIES-BOSCH (bēs'bosh). A marshy sheet of water, interspersed with islands, between the Dutch provinces of North Brabant and South Holland, formed in 1421 by an inundation which destroyed seventy-two villages and 100,000 people.

BIÈVRE (bi-ā-vr), **Marquis de.** Born 1747, died 1789; served in the corps of the French Musketeers, was in the body-guard of the King of France, and acquired much reputation by his puns and repartees. He is the author of several amusing publications, including *Le Séducteur*, a comedy in verse; an *Almanach des Calembours*, or collection of puns; and there is also a collection of his jests called *Bièvriana* (1800).

BIFFIN. A variety of excellent kitchen apple, often sold in a dry and flattened state.

BIFRÖST (bif'roust). In northern mythology, the name of the bridge represented as stretching between heaven and earth (Asgard and Midgard); really the rainbow.

BIG. *See* BIGG.

BIGA. An ancient Roman two-horse chariot.

BIG'AMY. The act or state of having two (or more) wives or husbands at once, an offence by the laws of most States. The present usage in criminal law of applying the term *bigamy* to what is practically *polygamy* is a corruption of the true meaning of *bigamy*. By the law of England—statute of 1604, repealed in 1828, but re-enacted in 1861—bigamy is a felony, punishable with penal servitude for any term not exceeding seven years and not less than three years, or imprisonment, with or without hard labour, not exceeding two years. If the party's wife or husband shall have been absent continuously for seven years, and is not known to be alive, the penalty is not incurred. In Scotland the punishment is less severe, being usually a short term of imprisonment. In other English-speaking communities the law resembles that of England. Bigamy is punishable on the continent of Europe and in the United States, the French "Code pénal" providing the punishment of "travaux forcés à temps."

BIG BERTHA. The long-range gun which began the fire on Paris on 23rd March, 1918. It is a slang term invented by the German soldiers, who applied it to the large Krupp cannon, the name of the owner of the Krupp works being Bertha von Bohlen. It was a naval gun, about 65 feet long, firing at an angle of 60°, and was located in the Forest of St. Gobain, about 75 miles from Paris. The original gun was blown up by an explosion, and another put out of action by French gun-fire, but there were others which continued to bombard the city till 5th Aug., 1918, when over twenty shells dropped in Paris. On Good Friday, 1918, a church was hit and about seventy worshippers killed and twice as many injured.

BIGG. A variety of barley, four-rowed, suitable for cultivation in more northerly localities.

BIGGLESWADE. A town in England, County Bedford, giving name to a parliamentary division of the county till 1918; manufactures of strawplait. Pop. (1931), 5844.

BIG HORN. A river of the United States, in Wyoming and Montana, the largest tributary of the Yellowstone.

BIG-HORN. The *Haplocĕrus montānus* or wild sheep of the Rocky Mountains, named from the size of its horns, which are 3½ feet long, the animal itself being of the same height at the shoulder. The Big-horns are gregarious, going in herds of twenty or thirty. They frequent the craggiest and most inaccessible rocks, and are wild and untamable. They are also called Rocky Mountain sheep.

BIGNO'NIA. A genus of plants of many species, inhabitants of hot climates, nat. ord. Bignoniaceæ, usually climbing shrubs furnished with tendrils; flowers mostly in terminal or axillary panicles; corolla trumpet-shaped, hence the name of *trumpet-flower* commonly given to these plants. All the species are splendid plants when in blossom, and many of them are cultivated in our gardens. *B. Leucoxȳlon*, a native of Jamaica, is a tree 40 feet high; the leaves of *B. Chica* yield a red colouring-matter, with which the Indians paint their bodies; *B. radicans*, or *Tecōma radicans*, is a much-admired species.

Big-horn or Rocky Mountain Sheep (*Haplocĕrus montānus*)

BIHACS (bē-hách′), or **BIHATCH.** A town and fortress in Yugo-Slavia, the scene of many battles during the Turkish wars. Pop. 6372.

BIHAR. *See* BEHAR.

BIJAPUR. *See* BEJAPOOR.

BIJÁYANAGUR. An ancient and celebrated city of India, now in ruins, in the Bombay Presidency, 30 miles N.W. of Bellary. It contains the remains of several magnificent temples, specimens of the purest style of Hindu architecture.

BIJNOR′. A town of India, in the United Provinces, 3 miles from the Ganges. Pop. 18,096.

BIKANER. A native State of Ráj-putána, India, under the superintendence of a political agent and the Governor-General's agent for Ráj-putána, lying between 27° 15′ and 30° 12′ N. lat., and 72° 15′ and 73° 50′ E. long. Area, 23,315 sq. miles; pop. 660,000.—*Bikaner*, the capital, is surrounded by a fine wall 3½ miles in circuit. It has a fort containing the rajah's palace, is irregularly built, but with many good houses, and manufactures blankets, sugar-candy, pottery, etc. Pop. (1931), 69,410.

BIK′ELAS, Dimitrios. One of the foremost writers of modern Greece, born in 1835. He published poems in 1862, and wrote much in prose, including tales and narratives—one of them *Lukis Laras*, translated into various tongues—essays and studies in history and politics, translations of several of Shakespeare's plays, etc. He died in 1908.

BIKH, or **BISH.** A famous Indian poison obtained from species of aconite, especially *Aconitum ferox*.

BI′LANDER. A small trading vessel with two masts, having a fore-and-aft mainsail (on the after mast) bent to a yard that is inclined at an angle of about 45 degrees, manageable by four or five men, and used chiefly in the canals of the Low Countries.

BILASPUR (bi-läs-pör′). A district in the governorship of the Central Provinces of India, lying between 21° 22′ and 23° 6′ N. lat., and between 80° 48′ and 83° 10′ E. long. Area, 7618 sq. miles; pop. 1,146,223. The administrative headquarters of the district are at Bilaspur, which is also the principal town. It is pleasantly situated on the south bank of the Arpa, and has a population of 24,295.

BILBA′O. A city in Northern Spain, capital of the province of Biscay or Bilbao, on the navigable Nervion, 8 miles from the sea. It has a cathedral and fine public buildings; flourishing industries: ironworks, steelworks, foundries, shipyards, etc. It is one of the principal seaports of Spain, and has a wireless station. Pop. (1931), 161,987.

BILBERRY. *See* WHORTLEBERRY.

BILBOES (bil′bōz). An apparatus for confining the feet of offenders, especially on board ships, consisting

Bilboes, from the Tower of London

of a long bar of iron with shackles sliding on it and a lock at one end to keep them from getting off, offenders being thus "put in irons."

BILDERDIJK (bil′dėr-dik) **Willem.** An eminent Dutch poet, born 1756, died 1831. He studied at Leyden, and cultivated poetry while practising as an advocate at the Hague. On the invasion of the Netherlands by the French, he left his country and lived abroad for many years, part of the time in London, where he delivered in the French language, lectures on literature and poetry. He returned to Holland in 1799, and soon afterwards published some of his principal works, many of which are translations or imitations. Of his own compositions the principal are: *Rural Life, The Love of Fatherland, The Maladies of Scholars, The Destruction of the First World*, etc. When Napoleon returned from Elba, Bilderdijk produced a number of war-songs, which are considered among the best in Dutch poetry. He also wrote a *Treatise on Geology*, a *History of Holland*, in 10 vols., etc.

BILE. A yellow bitter liquor, separated from the blood by the primary cells of the liver, and collected by the biliary ducts, which unite to form the hepatic duct, whence it passes into the duodenum, or by the cystic duct into the gall-bladder to be retained there till required for use. The most obvious use of the bile in the animal economy is to aid in the digestion of fatty substances and to convert the chyme into chyle. It appears also to aid in exciting the peristaltic action of the intestines. The natural colour of the fæces seems to be owing to the presence of bile. The chemical composition varies with the animal which yields it, but every kind contains two essential constituents, the bile salts and the bile colouring-matter associated with small quantities of cholesterine, fats, and certain mineral salts, chiefly chloride of sodium, phosphates, and iron. Some of the constituents of the bile return into the blood by absorption, the colouring-matters and cholesterine being the principal excrementitious substances. When bile is not secreted in due quantity from the blood, the unhealthy condition of biliousness results.

BILED-AL-JERID ("Land of Dates"). A track of North Africa lying between the south declivity of Atlas and the Sahara, noted (popularly but erroneously) for the production of date palms.

BILGE. The breadth of a ship's bottom, or that part of her floor which approaches to a horizontal direction, on which she would rest if aground. —**Bilge-water,** water which enters a ship and lies upon her bilge or bottom; when not drawn off, it becomes dirty and offensive.—**Bilge ways,** planks under a vessel's bilge to support her while launching.—**Bilge keels,** pieces like keels on either side of the bilge, on the outside.

BILHAR′ZIA. A parasite of the liver-fluke class, frequent in Africa, the best-known species being *B. hæmatobia*, which is often found in the portal veins and veins of the bladder of the human subject, and by the deposition of its masses of eggs in the ureter bladder, and great intestine may cause serious inflammation, hæmaturia (bloody urine), stone in the bladder, etc.

BIL′IARY CAL′CULUS. A concretion which forms in the gall-bladder or bile-ducts; gall-stone. It is generally composed of a peculiar crystalline fatty matter which has been called *cholesterine*.

BILIN′, or **BILINA.** A town, Bohemia, formerly in the Austrian Empire now in Czechoslovakia, 42 miles N.W. of Prague, prettily situated in the vale of the Bila, and celebrated for its mineral waters, which are drunk on the spot and largely exported, being useful in cases of rheumatism, stone, scrofula, Bright's disease, etc. Pop. 9700.

BILITON′. *See* BILLITON.

BILL. A cutting instrument, hook-shaped towards the point, or with a concave cutting edge, used by plumbers, basket-makers, gardeners, etc.; made in various forms and fitted with a handle. Such instruments, when used by gardeners for pruning hedges, trees, etc. are called *hedge-bills* or *bill-hooks*. Also an ancient military weapon, consisting of a broad hook-shaped blade, having a short pike at the back and another at the summit, attached to a long handle, used by the English infantry, especially in defending themselves against cavalry, down to the fifteenth century, and by civic guards or watchmen down to the end of the seventeenth.

BILL. A written or printed paper containing a statement of any particulars. In common use a tradesman's account, or a printed proclamation or advertisement, is thus called a bill. In legislation a bill is a draft of a proposed statute submitted to a legislative assembly for approval, but not yet enacted or passed and made law. When the Bill has passed and received the necessary assent, it becomes an Act. *See* PARLIAMENT.

Bill in Chancery. *See* PLEADING.

Bill of Attainder and **of Pains and Penalties** are forms of procedure in the British Parliament which were often resorted to in times of political agitation to procure the criminal condemnation of an individual. The person attainted lost all civil rights, he could have no heir, nor could he succeed to any ancestor, his estate falling to the Crown. These bills were promoted by the Crown, or the dominant party in Parliament, when any individual obnoxious to them could not readily be reached by the ordinary forms of procedure. Parliament, being the highest court of the kingdom, could dispense with the ordinary laws of evidence, and even if actuated by passion or servilely devoted to the authorities, condemn the accused in the most arbitrary manner. They were very common under the Tudors, and as late as 1820 the trial of Queen Caroline took place under a bill of pains and penalties. Bills of attainder are prohibited by the constitution of the United States.

Bill of Costs is an account rendered by an attorney or solicitor of his charges and disbursements in an action, or in the conduct of his client's business.

Bill of Entry, a written account of goods entered at the custom-house.

Bill of Exceptions. *See* TRIAL.

Bill of Exchange (including *promissory notes* and *inland bills* or *acceptances*). A bill of exchange is defined as an order in writing addressed by one person to another, signed by the person giving it, requiring the person to whom it is addressed to pay on demand or at a fixed or determinable future time a certain sum of money to or to the order of a specified person or to bearer. Bills of exchange are divided into foreign and inland bills, but in mercantile usage the term bill of exchange is seldom applied to other than foreign bills. An inland bill of exchange, generally called a bill of acceptance, has more in common with a promissory note than with a foreign bill of exchange. We give the common forms of the three documents.

(1) *Promissory Note*

£100 : 0 : 0.

Liverpool, 2nd November, 1932.

Three months after date I promise to pay to the order of W. S. [or 'to W. S. or his order'] the sum of One Hundred Pounds sterling, for value received. (Signed) J. D.

(2) *Inland Bill or Acceptance*

£100 : 0 : 0.

Liverpool, 2nd November, 1932.

Three months after date pay to our order [or 'to the order of W. S.'] the sum of One Hundred Pounds sterling, for value received.

(Signed) F. G. & Co.

To Messrs. A. B. & Co., London.

This form is accepted by writing across the body of the bill:—

'Accepted,
A. B. & Co.'

(3) *Foreign Bill of Exchange*

£100 : 0 : 0.

Lima, 2nd November, 1932.

At sixty days' sight of this first of exchange (second and third of same tenor and date unpaid) pay to the order of W. S. the sum of One Hundred Pounds sterling, value as advised [or, 'which charge to our account', or 'to account of ——— as advised']. (Signed) F. & Co.

To F. B. & Co., Liverpool.

(Second and third drawn in same form as the first, one only of the set being negotiable. Instead of three copies being used, which is called drawing a bill in parts, one only may be drawn, the form then used being 'this sola of exchange'.)

The acceptor of this bill writes across it the date on which it is presented, together with his signature, thus:—

'Accepted, 4th December, 1932,
F. B. & Co.'

The person who makes or draws the bill is called the *drawer*; he to whom it is addressed is, before acceptance, the *drawee*, and after accepting it, the *accepter*; the person in whose favour it is drawn is the *payee*; if he endorse the bill to another, he is called the *endorser*, and the person to whom it is thus assigned is the *endorsee* or *holder*. A bill when properly stamped is negotiable, and may be discounted at a bank, or may pass from hand to hand by the process of endorsement, many names being frequently attached to one bill as endorsers, each of whom is liable to be sued upon the bill if it be not paid in due time. The value of the stamp required in Britain is 2*d*. for £5, rising at fixed stages with the value of the bill at the rate of 1*s*. per £100. The last phase in the negotiation of a bill is usually its being discounted with a banker. The merchant may either discount it with a bill-broker, who re-discounts it with the banker, or he may take it direct to the banker. The broker or banker deducts (as do also the previous negotiators of a bill) a discount, or equivalent for the use of the money he pays until the due date of the bill, when he expects it will be repaid him. There is usually a current rate of discount for first-class bills, which is determined in Great Britain by the rates of the Bank of England.

When a bill reached the date of payment, and was not duly paid, it used to be *noted* or *protested*, but this is now only done with foreign bills. Protesting is a legal form, in which the payee is declared responsible for all consequences of the non-payment of the bill. Noting is a temporary form, used as a preliminary to protesting. It consists in a record by a notary-public of the presentation of the bill, and of the refusal of the payee to honour it. Unless a bill is noted for non-payment on the due date, the endorsers are freed from responsibility to pay it. In determining the due date of a bill, a legal allowance, varying in different countries, called *days of grace*, has to be taken into account. In Great Britain three days of grace are allowed on all bills indiscriminately, except bills drawn on demand. A bill of exchange drawn and accepted merely to raise money on, and not given, like a genuine bill of exchange, in payment of a debt, is called an *accommodation bill*.

Bill of Exchequer. *See* EXCHEQUER.

Bill of Health, a certificate or instrument signed by consuls or other proper authorities, delivered to the masters of ships at the time of their clearing out from all ports or places suspected of being particularly subject to infectious disorders, certifying the state of health at the time that such ships sailed.

Bill of Indictment, a written accusation submitted to a grand-jury. If the grand-jury think that the accusation is supported by probable evidence, they return it to the proper officer of the court endorsed with the words "a true bill," and thereupon the prisoner is said to stand indicted of the crime and bound to make answer to it. If the grand-jury do not think the accusation supported by probable evidence, they return it with the words "no bill," whereupon the prisoner may claim his discharge. *See* INDICTMENT.

Bill of Lading, a memorandum of goods shipped on board a vessel, signed by the master of the vessel, who acknowledges the receipt of the goods and promises to deliver them in good condition at the place directed, dangers of the sea excepted. Bills of lading can be transferred by endorsement; the endorsement transfers all rights and liabilities under the bill of lading of the original holder or consignee. *See* AFFREIGHTMENT.

Bill of Mortality. *See* MORTALITY.

Bill of Particulars. *See* PLEADING.

Bill of Rights and Declaration of Rights, two documents which constituted the convention by which the Prince and Princess of Orange were called to the throne of England, and are the basis of the conditions on which the crown of England is still held.

The Declaration of Rights, afterwards embodied in the bill, first recited the illegal acts of King James; secondly, declared these acts to be illegal; and, thirdly, declared that the throne should be filled by the Prince and Princess of Orange in accordance with the limitations of the prerogative thus prescribed. It contains the following specific declarations: "That the pretended power of suspending laws and the execution of laws, by regal authority without consent of Parliament, is illegal; That levying of money for or to the use of the Crown by pretence of prerogative without grant of Parliament, is illegal; That it is the right of the subjects to petition the king; That the raising or keeping a standing army within the kingdom in time of peace, unless it be with consent of Parliament, is illegal; That elections of members of Parliament ought to be free; That the freedom of speech or debates on proceedings in Parliament ought not to be impeached or questioned in any court or place out of Parliament; And that, for redress of all grievances, and for the amending, strengthening, and preserving of the laws, parliaments ought to be held frequently." The Bill of Rights, passed in 1689, confirmed these declarations, settled the crown upon Protestants, and declared that any king or queen of England who should marry a Papist would be incapable of reigning in England, and the subjects absolved from allegiance.

Bill of Sale, a formal instrument for the conveyance or transfer of personal chattels, as household furniture, stock in a shop, shares of a ship. It is also given to a creditor in security for money borrowed, or obligation otherwise incurred, empowering the receiver to sell the goods if the money is not repaid with interest at the appointed time, or the obligation not otherwise discharged. The former is called an *absolute bill of sale*, and is governed by the Act of 1878; the latter is called a *bill by way of security*, and is governed by Acts of 1878 and 1882. *See* POSSESSION.—BIBLIOGRAPHY: Sir I. Pitman, *Bills, Cheques, and Notes*; H. P. Read, *The Bills of Sale Acts*; Sir J. B. Byles, *Treatise on the Law of Bills of Exchange*; E. T. Baldwin, *The Law of Bankruptcy and Bills of Sale*; W. V. Ball, *Deeds of Arrangement, and Bills of Sale*.

BILLAUD - VARENNE (bi-yō-vâ-rān), **Jacques-Nicholas.** A noted French revolutionist, born at Rochelle, 1756, died in Haiti 1819. He bore a principal part in the murders and massacres which followed the destruction of the Bastille; voted immediate death to Louis XVI.; and officiated as president of the Convention in Oct., 1793. In 1795, on a reaction having taken place against the ultra party, he was arrested and banished to Cayenne.

BILL-BROKER. A financial agent

or money-dealer, who discounts or negotiates bills of exchange, promissory notes, etc. *See* BROKER.

BILL-CHAMBER. A department of the Court of Session in Scotland, in which one of the judges officiates at all times during session and vacation. All proceedings for summary remedies, or for protection against impending proceedings, commence in the bill-chamber, such as interdicts. The process of sequestration or bankruptcy also issues from this department of the court.

BILLET. Log of firewood. In metallurgy billet denotes a gold ingot or steel bar. It is also a heraldic term, and in Romanesque and Norman architecture denotes an ornamental moulding.

BIL'LETING. A mode of feeding and lodging soldiers, when they are not in camp or barracks, by quartering them on the inhabitants of a town. The necessity for billeting occurs chiefly during movements of the troops or when any accidental occasion arises for quartering soldiers in a town which has not sufficient barrack accommodation. The billeting of soldiers on private householders is now abandoned in Britain, but all keepers of inns, livery-stables, ale-houses, victualling-houses, and similar establishments, are liable to receive officers and soldiers billeted on them. The provisions by which billeting is now regulated are contained in the Army Act, 1881, renewed annually. The Army (Annual) Act, 1909, provided for the billeting of Territorial forces in case of national emergency. In 1917 the Billeting of Civilians Act came into force.

BILLET-MOULDING. An ornament common in Norman architecture, consisting of an imitation of billets, or round pieces of wood, placed in a hollow moulding with an interval between each usually equal to their own length.

BILL-FISH. The gar-pike or long-nosed gar (*Lepidostĕus ossĕus*), a fish common in the lakes and rivers of the United States; but the name is also given to other fishes.

BILL-HOOK. *See* BILL (cutting instrument).

BILLIARDS (bil'yėrdz). A well-known game, probably (like its name) of French origin, played with ivory balls on a flat table. Various modes of play, constituting many distinct games, are adopted, according to the tastes of the players, some being more in favour in one country, some in another. The common English billiard-table is an oblong, about 12 feet by 6, covered with fine and very smooth green cloth, on a perfectly level bed of slate, and having a raised edge all round lined with cushions which are made tolerably firm and elastic, much of the skill of the game consisting in calculating the rebound of the balls in various directions from the cushions. Along the edges of the tables are six semicircular holes arranged at regular intervals in the cushion, through which the balls are allowed to drop into small nets called pockets, under the sides of the table. The pockets are placed one at each corner of the table, and two opposite each other in the middle of the long sides. Each player is provided with a *cue* to strike the balls. The cue is a wooden rod from 4 or 5 to 6 or 8 feet long, rounded in form, and tapering gradually from 1½ inches in diameter at the butt to ⅜ inch or less at the point, which is tipped with leather and rubbed with chalk to prevent the cue from slipping.

Instructions. In the common game two players engage. Each has a white ball, and a red ball is common to the two. In beginning the game the red ball is placed on a spot near one end of the table, and equidistant from the corner pockets. A line drawn across the table at the other end marks off a space called *baulk*. In this space a semicircle is described, out of which the player, in commencing, must send his ball, either striking the red or giving his opponent a "miss", that is, playing without striking the red ball, which scores one against him. When the game has commenced, the player is at liberty to strike at either his opponent's ball or the red, and continues to play as long as he succeeds in scoring. The whole of an uninterrupted run of play is called a *break*. There are various modes of scoring. When a player strikes both balls with his own, it is called a *cannon*, and counts two; when he pockets his own ball, after striking another, it is called a *losing hazard*, and counts two if made off his opponent's ball, three if off the red; when he pockets his opponent's ball it counts two; when he pockets the red, three. When the player fails to strike either ball, it scores one against him; if he goes into a pocket without striking, it scores three against him.

After the ordinary game the most favourite varieties are *pyramids* and *pool*. The former is so called from the position in which the balls are placed at the beginning of the game. It is played with fifteen balls; and the object of the players is to try who will pocket, or "pot," the greatest number of balls. Pool is also a game of "potting," but is played somewhat differently It is a favourite game with those who play for stakes, insomuch that it may be considered almost exclusively a gambling game. It embraces an indefinite number of players, each of whom is provided with a ball of a different colour from any of the others. They play in succession, and each tries to pot his opponent's ball. If he succeeds with one, he goes on to the next; if he fails, another player takes his turn, playing first on the ball of the last player. There are thus two points which a pool-player has to aim at: to pot as many balls as possible, and to keep his ball in a safe position relatively to that of the following player, as the player whose ball is potted has to pay the penalty prescribed by the game.

The common billiard-table used in France is smaller than the English, and has no pockets, the game being entirely a cannon game. This kind of table is now very common in America, and there a four-pocket table is also in use. The American term for cannon is "carom," and in American play two red balls (or a red and a pink) and two white ones are commonly employed.

BILLINGHAM. An urban district of Durham, which stands on the Tees nearly opposite Middlesborough. During the Great War the government had large factories here, which are now part of the works of Imperial Chemical Industries. Shipbuilding is another industry. Pop. (1931), 17,972.

BIL'LINGSGATE. The principal fish-market of London, on the left bank of the Thames, a little below London Bridge. It has been frequently improved, and was rebuilt in 1852 and again during 1874-6. From the character, real or supposed, of the Billingsgate fish-dealers, the term *Billingsgate* is applied generally to coarse and violent language.

BIL'LINGTON, Elizabeth. The most distinguished female singer of her day in England, born about 1768 in London, died in Italy in 1818. Her mother was an English vocalist, her father a Saxon musician named Weichsel. She appeared as a singer at the age of fourteen, and at sixteen married James Billington, a double-bass player. She made her debut as an operatic singer in Dublin, and afterwards appeared at Covent Garden. She visited France and Italy, and Bianchi composed the opera of *Inez de Castro* expressly for her performance at Naples. From 1802 to 1811 she sang in Italian opera in London, when, having amassed a handsome fortune, she retired from the stage.

BILLITON'. A Dutch East Indian island between Banca and the S.W. of Borneo, of an irregular subquadrangular form, about 40 miles across. It produces iron and tin, and exports sago, coco-nuts, pepper, tortoise-shell, trepang, edible birds'-nests, etc. It was ceded to the British in 1812 by the Sultan of Palembang, but in 1824 it was given up to the Dutch. Area, 1860 sq. miles; pop. 73,409.

BIL'LON. An alloy of copper and silver, in which the former predominates, used in some countries for coins of low value, the object being to avoid the bulkiness of pure copper coin.

BILLY-BOY. A flat-bottomed, bluff-bowed vessel, rigged as a sloop, with a mast that can be lowered so as to admit of passing under bridges.

BILMA. An oasis of the Sahara, about half-way between Fezzan and Bornu, producing much salt. *See* SAHARA.

BILSA. *See* BHILSA.

BILSTHORPE. Village of Nottinghamshire, in Sherwood Forest. In 1929 a coal-mine was opened here and 400 houses built for the miners.

BIL'STON. A town, England, in Staffordshire, since 1918 giving name to a parliamentary division of Wolverhampton; it has manufactories of hardware. Pop. (1931), 31,248.

BIL'TONG. A name in South Africa for strips of lean meat dried in the sun and used as food, resembling the jerked beef of South America.

BI'MANA. Animals having two hands: a term applied by Cuvier to the highest order of Mammalia, of which man is the type and sole genus. By some naturalists man is classified as a sub-division of the ord. Primates, which includes also the apes, monkeys, and lemurs.

BIMET'ALLISM. That system of coinage which recognises coins of two metals (silver and gold) as legal tender to any amount; or in other words, the concurrent use of coins of two metals as a circulating medium, the ratio of value between the two being arbitrarily fixed by law. It is contended by advocates of the system that by fixing a legal ratio between the value of gold and silver, and using both as legal tender, fluctuations in the value of the metals are avoided, whilst the prices of commodities are rendered steadier. In England the bimetallic system was abandoned, and the single gold standard legalised in 1870, although the latter had been in operation since

1699. France, Belgium, Switzerland, Italy, Greece, and Rumania, who had formed the Latin Union in 1865, unanimously adopted the single gold standard in 1867, and finally abandoned the bimetallic system in 1877. In the United States bimetallism as a popular cause disappeared from view after 1900. *See* GRESHAM'S LAW; MONEY.—BIBLIOGRAPHY: Prof. W. S. Jevons, *Investigations in Currency and Finance*; Sir D. Barbour, *Theory of Bimetallism*; article in *Dictionary of Political Economy*.

BIM'LIPATAM. A seaport of India, Madras Presidency, with a brisk trade. Pop. 10,000.

BINAB'. A town, Persia, pleasantly situated in the midst of orchards and vineyards, 55 miles S.S.W. from Tabriz, and 8 miles E. of Lake Urumiya. Pop. about 7500.

BINARY. Twofold; double.—**Binary compound,** in chemistry, a compound of two elements, or of an element and a compound performing the function of an element, or of two compounds performing the function of elements, according to the laws of combination. The term is now little used.—**Binary theory of salts,** the theory which regarded all salts as being made up of two oxides, an acid oxide and a basic oxide; thus sodium carbonate as made up of soda (Na_2O) and carbon dioxide (CO_2).—**Binary star,** a double star whose members revolve round a common centre of gravity.

BINCHE (banৃsh). A town of Belgium, province of Hainaut, with manufactures of lace, pottery, etc. During the European War it was occupied by the Germans, who held it until the end of 1918. Pop. 11,690.

BINDRABUND. *See Brindaban.*

BIND-WEED. The common name of plants of the genus Convolvŭlus, especially of *C. arvensis*, and also of plants of the allied genus Calystegia, especially *C. Soldanella* and *C. sepium*. The black bryony is called *black bind-weed*; Smilax is called *rough bind-weed*; *Solānum Dulcamāra* (the bitter-sweet) is the *blue bind-weed* of Ben Jonson.

BING'EN. A town of Germany, in Hesse-Darmstadt, on the left bank of the Rhine, in a district producing excellent wines. The Mäusethurm or Mouse-tower in the middle of the river is the scene of the well-known legend of Bishop Hatto. Pop. 10,186.

BINGHAM. Market-town of Nottinghamshire. It is 8 miles from Nottingham on the L.N.E. Rly. Pop. 1576.

BING'HAM, Joseph. English writer, born in 1668, died 1723; distinguished himself as a student at Oxford, and devoted his attention particularly to ecclesiastical antiquities. He was compelled to leave the university for alleged heterodoxy, but was presented to the living of Headbourn-Worthy, near Winchester, and afterwards to that of Havant, near Portsmouth. His great work, *Origines Ecclesiasticæ*, or Antiquities of the Christian Church, in 10 vols., was published 1708-22.

BING'HAMTON. A town, United States, State of New York, at the junction of the Chenango and Susquehanna Rivers, with numerous manufactures and an extensive flour and lumber trade. Pop. 76,662.

BING'LEY. A market town, W. Riding of Yorkshire, 15 miles W.N.W. of Leeds, with considerable manufactures of worsted, cotton, paper, and iron. Pop. (1931) 20,553.

BINGLEY, Ward. Dutch actor, born at Rotterdam in 1755, of English parents, died at the Hague, 1818. In 1799 he made his debut on the stage of Amsterdam, and almost from the first took his place at the head of his profession, not only in the Dutch theatres, but also in those which performed French plays in Amsterdam and the Hague.

BIN'NACLE or **BITTACLE.** A case or box on the deck of a vessel near the steering-apparatus, containing the compass and lights by which it can be read at night. See illustration p. 54.

BIN'NEY, Rev. Thomas, D.D., LL.D. Popular Independent preacher, theologian, and controversialist, born at Newcastle-on-Tyne, 1798, died 1874. He was pastor of Weigh House Chapel, London, for forty years; was a voluminous writer on polemical subjects, his most successful venture as an author being *Is it Possible to make the Best of Both Worlds?*—a work for young men.

BINOCULAR. Instrument for aiding simultaneous vision with both eyes. In its simplest form it is a pair of spectacles. It may also be in the form of a telescope, microscope or stereoscope.

BINO'MIAL. In algebra, an expression consisting of two terms or members, connected by the sign + or – The *binomial theorem* is the celebrated theorem given by Sir Isaac Newton for raising a binomial to any power, or for extracting any root of it by a converging infinite series.

BIN'TANG. An island of the Dutch East Indies, at the southern extremity of the Malay Peninsula; area, 454 sq. miles; pop. 18,500; yields catechu and pepper.

BIN'TURONG (*Arctictis binturong*), a carnivorous animal of the civet family, with a prehensile tail, a native of the Eastern Archipelago.

BINUE (bin'ų-e). *See* BENUE.

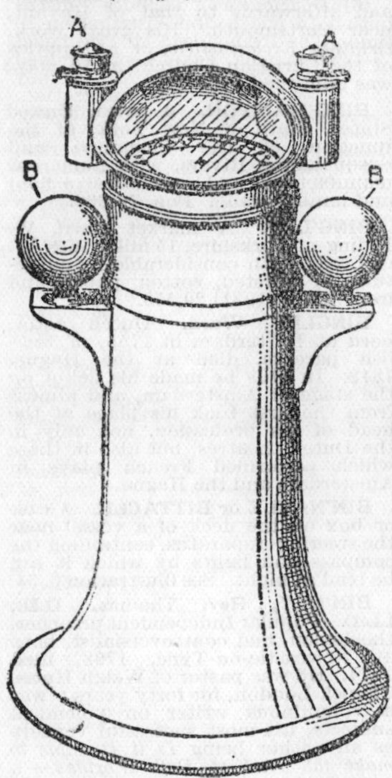

Binnacle
AA, Lamps. BB, Soft iron balls for correcting the quadrantal deviation

BINYON, Robert Lawrence. English poet, born in 1869. He won the Newdigate Prize for English verse at Trinity College, Oxford. He became an assistant in the British Museum. He has published several volumes of poems, written plays, and edited catalogues of drawings in the British Museum. In 1932 he was made a Companion of Honour.

BI'OBIO. A Chilian river, rises in Lake Huchueltui, flows in a N.W. direction for 180 miles, and falls into the Pacific at the city of Concepción. It gives its name to a province of the country, with over 110,000 inhabitants; area, 5353 sq. miles.

BIO-CHEMISTRY. Study of the chemical aspects of animal and plant psychology.

BIOGEN'ESIS. The history of life-development generally; specifically, that department of biological science which speculates on the mode by which new species have been introduced; often restricted to that view which holds that living organisms can spring only from living parents. *See* EMBRYOLOGY; VARIATION AND SELECTION.

BIOG'RAPHY. That department of literature which treats of the individual lives of men or women; and also, a prose narrative detailing the history and unfolding the character of an individual written by another. When written by the individual whose history is told, it is called an *autobiography*. This species of writing is as old as literature itself. In the first century after Christ, Plutarch wrote his *Parallel Lives*; Cornelius Nepos, *The Lives of Military Commanders*; and Suetonius, *The Lives of the Twelve Cæsars*. Modern biographical literature may be considered to date from the seventeenth century, since which time individual biographies have multiplied enormously. By common consent Boswell's *Life of Johnson* is the most famous biography ever written in spite of its lack of form. Other notable biographies are Southey's *Life of Nelson*, Morley's *Life of Gladstone* and Winston Churchill's *Life of Lord Randolph Churchill*. Lives of most of the celebrities of the nineteenth century have been written, but these are usually far too long and too laudatory. Lytton Strachey's *Life of Queen Victoria*, which set a new fashion in biography, is an exception, being thoroughly critical. Dictionaries of biography have proved extremely useful, Moréri's *Dictionnaire Historique et Critique* (1671) being perhaps the first of this class. During the nineteenth century and the beginning of the twentieth have been published the *Biographie Universelle* (85 vols., 1811-62), *Nouvelle Biographie Générale* (46 vols., 1852-66), Chalmers's *General Biographical Dictionary* (32 vols., 1812-7), Rose's *Biographical Dictionary* (12 vols., 1848-50), the admirable *Dictionary of National Biography* (63 vols., the first published in 1885, the last in 1900, with two Supplements of 4 vols., 1901 and 1912), Appleton's *Cyclopædia of American Biography* (7 vols., 1887-1900), J. Vapereau's *Dictionnaire*

Universel des Contemporains, V. Plarr's *Men and Women of the Time*, A. M. Hyamson's *Dictionary of Universal Biography*. An American *Dictionary of National Biography* was planned after the Great War, the second volume of which appeared in 1932.

BIOLOGY (Gr. *bios*, life, *logos*, discourse), the science of life and living things, and broadly divided into Botany and Zoology, which deal respectively with plants and animals. The study of Man, however, is only partly included in the latter, for his mind and the results of its activity are treated of by other sciences, such as Psychology, Sociology, Philosophy, and Theology.

The chief branches of Biology are seven in number: (1) Morphology, (2) Physiology, (3) Embryology (Development), (4) Classification (Taxonomy), (5) Ecology (Bionomics), (6) Distribution in space and time, (7) Philosophical Biology.

(1) *Morphology* (Gr. *morphē*, form, *logos*, discourse) is concerned with the external form and structure of organisms; the study of the latter by dissection is termed Anatomy; while Histology (Gr. *histos*, a tissue, *logos*, discourse) carries structural analysis a step farther by use of the compound microscope. This demonstrates that the materials (tissues) composing the bodies of all but the lowest forms are made up of *cells*, i.e., unit masses of living substance (protoplasm) and the products of their activity. The lowest plants (Protophyta) and the lowest animals (Protozoa) are unicellular, i.e. possess one-celled bodies.

(2) *Physiology* (Gr. *physis*, nature, *logos*, discourse) deals with the actions or functions of organisms, most of these having to do with the preservation of the individual, while propagation or reproduction enables the continuance of the species.

(3) *Embryology* or *Development* embraces the morphology and physiology of immature organisms, from the earliest to the adult stage.

(4) *Classification* or *Taxonomy* (Gr. *taxis*, order, *nomos*, law) endeavours to arrange organisms in subordinated groups according to their likenesses and differences. Modern classifications aim at expressing actual blood-relationship, and take the form of genealogical trees.

(5) *Ecology* (Gr. *oikos*, home, *logos*, discourse) or *Bionomics* (Gr. *bios*, life, *nomos*, law) considers organisms with reference to their surroundings and environment (including other organisms), and deals with the various adaptations to such surroundings. There are, for example, numerous adaptations between flowers and insects, securing crossing of the former by the unconscious agency of the latter, which benefit in their turn by the food (nectar and pollen) placed at their disposal.

(6) *Distribution* includes distribution in space and distribution in time. The former leads to the belief that organisms have been evolved in various centres, from which they have afterwards spread by migration. Sometimes distribution is discontinuous, e.g., tapirs are found in the Malay region and tropical America, but nowhere else. The explanation is that they formerly existed in intervening regions, where they have since become extinct. Distribution in *time* is worked out from the study of the fossil remains of different geological ages. The gradual advance from lower to higher forms has thus been demonstrated, and the actual pedigrees of some species, e.g. the horse, worked out in detail.

(7) *Philosophical Biology* uses the data provided by other branches in the endeavour to solve general problems regarding life. The two chief problems concern the origin of species and the origin of life itself. As to the former, it is generally conceded that there has been a process of evolution, but the details are still obscure. We know scarcely anything about the origin of life.

BI'ON. Born in Smyrna, or in its neighbourhood; an ancient Greek pastoral poet, flourished about 100 B.C. He wrote bucolic and erotic poems, fragments of which are extant. He is supposed to have spent the last years of his life in Sicily, where he was poisoned.

BION, of Borysthenes, in Sarmatia, a Greek philosopher, flourished in the first half of the third century B.C.

BI'OPLASM. *See* PROTOPLASM.

BIOT (bē-ō), **Jean Baptiste.** French mathematician and physicist, born at Paris 1774, and died there 1862. He became professor of physics in the Collège de France in 1800; in 1803 member of the Academy of Sciences; in 1804 was appointed to the Observatory of Paris; in 1806 was made member of the Bureau des Longitudes; in 1809 became also professor of physical astronomy in the University of Paris. In connection with the measurement of a degree of the meridian he visited Britain in 1817. He is especially celebrated as the discoverer of the circular polarisation of light. Besides numerous memoirs contributed to the Academy and to scientific journals, he wrote

Essai sur l'histoire générale des sciences pendant la Révolution, Précis élémentaire de physique expérimentale, Traité de physique expérimentale et mathematique, Mémoire sur la vraie constitution de l'atmosphère terrestre, as well as works on the astronomy of the ancient Egyptians, Indians, and Chinese.—His son, Edouard Constant (born 1803, died 1850), was an eminent Chinese scholar.

BIOTITE. *See* MICAS.

BI'PED. An animal having two feet, applied to man and birds, indicating their mode of progression rather than the mere possession of two limbs.

BIPEN'NIS. A double-headed axe, the weapon usually depicted in the hands of the Amazons in ancient works of art.

BIPLANE. *See* AEROPLANE.

BI'PONT (or **BIPONTINE**) **EDITIONS.** Famous editions of the classic authors, printed at Zweibrücken (Fr. *Deux Ponts,* Lat. *Bipontium*), in the Rhenish Palatinate. The collection forms 50 vols. 8vo., begun in 1779 and finished at Strasbourg.

BIQUADRAT'IC EQUATION. In algebra, a rational integral equation in one variable, the highest power of the variable which occurs being the fourth. An equation of this kind, when complete, is of the form $x^4 + Ax^3 + Bx^2 + Cx + D = 0$, where A, B, C, and D denote any known quantities whatever.

BIR, or Bireh-jik. A town of Mesopotamia, 62 miles N.E. of Aleppo, on the Euphrates, at the point where the great caravan-route from Syria to Bagdad crosses the river. Pop. about 10,000.

BIRAGUE (bē-räg), **René de.** Born at Milan 1506 or 1507, died 1583. He sought an asylum in France from the hostility of Louis Sforza, and became a cardinal and chancellor of France. He was a party in the secret council at which the massacre of St. Bartholomew was organised ; and he was generally believed to have repeatedly employed poison to rid himself and his patroness, Catherine de' Medici, of persons who stood in their way.

BIRBHÚM, or BEERBHOOM. A district of British India, in the Bardwán division, governorship of Bengal; area, 1753 sq. miles; pop. 847,000. Chief manufactures: silk and lacquered wares.

BIRCH (Betŭla). A genus of tree, ord. Betulaceæ, comprising only the birches and alders, which inhabit Europe, Northern Asia, and North America. The common birch (*Betŭla alba*) is indigenous throughout the north, and on high situations in the south of Europe. It is extremely hardy, and only one or two other species of trees approach so near to the north pole or ascend to such levels. The wood of the birch, which is light in colour, and firm and tough in texture, is used for chairs, tables, bedsteads, and the woodwork of furniture generally, also for fish-casks and hoops, and for smoking hams and herrings, as well as for many small articles. In France wooden shoes are made of it. The bark is whitish in colour, smooth and shining, separable in thin sheets or layers. Fishing-nets and sails are steeped with it to preserve them.

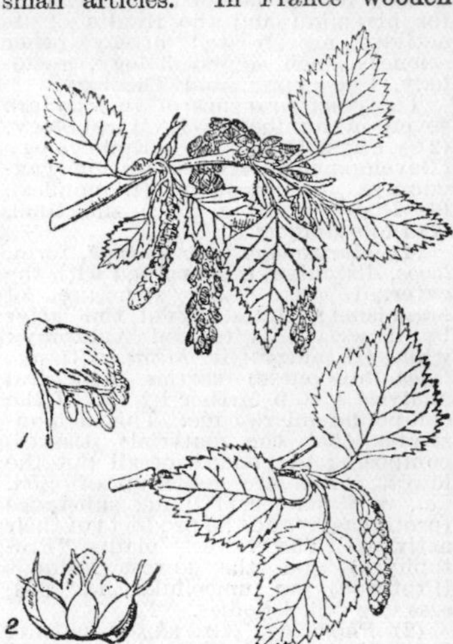

Birch (*Betŭla alba*)

1, Male flower. 2, Female flowers

In some countries it is made into hats, shoes, boxes, etc. In Russia the oil extracted from it is used in the preparation of Russian leather, and imparts the well-known scent to it. In Lapland bread has been made from it. The sap, from the amount of sugar it contains, affords a kind of agreeable wine, which is produced by the tree being tapped during warm weather in the end of spring or beginning of summer, when the sap runs most copiously. The dwarf birch (*B. nana*), a low shrub, 2 or 3 feet high at most, is a native of all the most northerly regions. *B. lenta,* the cherry birch of America, and the black birch (*B. nigra*) of the same country, produce valuable timber, as do other American species. The paper birch of America (*B. papyracĕa*) has a bark that may be readily divided into thin sheets almost like paper. From it the Indian bark canoes are made. Both the *B. lutĕa* and *papyracĕa* were introduced from Canada, the former in 1750, the latter in 1767.

BIRCH, Samuel, D.C.L., LL.D. Orientalist, born in London, 1813, died 1885. He entered the British Museum as assistant keeper of antiquities in 1836, and ultimately became keeper of the Egyptian and Assyrian antiquities. He was specially famed for his capacity and skill in Egyptology, and was associated with Baron Bunsen in his work on Egypt, contributing the philological portions relating to hieroglyphics. His principal works, besides numerous contributions to the transactions of learned societies, to encyclopædias, etc., include: *Gallery of Antiquities* (1842), *Catalogue of Greek Vases* (1851), *Introduction to the Study of Hieroglyphics* (1857), *Ancient Pottery* (1858), *Egypt from the Earliest Times* (1875). He edited *Records of the Past*, from 1873 to 1880. He had the LL.D. degree from St. Andrews and Cambridge, D.C.L. from Oxford, besides many foreign academical distinctions.

BIRCH, Thomas. An industrious historian and biographer, born in London in 1705, killed by a fall from his horse 1766. He took orders in the Church in 1730, and obtained in 1732 a living in Essex. In 1734 he engaged with others in writing the *General Historical and Critical Dictionary*, founded on that of Bayle, and completed, in 10 vols. fol., in 1741. He subsequently obtained various preferments in the Church. Among his numerous works are: *Life of the Right Hon. Robert Boyle* (1744), *Life of Archbishop Tillotson* (1752), *Memoirs of the Reign of Queen Elizabeth* (1754), *History of the Royal Society* (1757), etc. He was a friend and correspondent of Dr. Johnson.

BIRCHINGTON. A watering-place in Kent, which has become a popular holiday resort. It is 4 miles from Margate. Pop. 3503.

BIRCH-PFEIFFER (bir*h*-pfī'fr), **Charlotte.** German dramatist and actress, born in Stuttgart 1800, died at Berlin 1868. She married Dr. Birch of Copenhagen in 1825, and obtained great success as a performer and an author. She was for some years manager of the Zurich theatre, and afterwards of the Hoftheater in Berlin. She wrote several novels and some seventy plays.

BIRD, Edward, R.A. An English painter, born at Wolverhampton 1772, died at Bristol 1819. He became an academician in 1815. He excelled in historical and genre subjects. Among his chief pictures are: *The Surrender of Calais, Death of Eli*, and *Field of Chevy Chase*.

BIRD, Isabella (Mrs. Bishop). English traveller, born in Yorkshire in 1832, and educated privately; owing to infirmities of health began to travel about 1854, and continued her wanderings almost to the close of her life, dying in 1904. She was married to Dr. John Bishop in 1881, but he died four years afterwards. Among her many popular narratives of travel are: *The Englishwoman in America* (1856), *A Lady's Life in the Rocky Mountains, The Hawaiian Archipelago, Unbeaten Tracks in Japan, The Golden Chersonese and the Way Thither, Journeys in Persia and Kurdistan, Among the Tibetans, Korea and her Neighbours* (1898). She was the first lady to be elected a Fellow of the Royal Geographical Society.

BIRD-BOLT. A short, thick, blunt arrow, fired from a cross-bow, for shooting birds.

BIRD-CALL. An instrument for imitating the cry of birds in order to attract them so that they may be caught.

BIRD-CATCHING SPIDER. A name applied to gigantic spiders of the genera Mygăle and Epeira, more especially to the *Mygăle avicularia*, a native of Surinam and elsewhere, which preys upon insects and small birds, which it hunts for and pounces on. It is about 2 inches long, very hairy, and almost black; its feet when spread out cover an area nearly a foot in diameter.

BIRD-CHERRY. A species of cherry (*Prunus Padus*), a very ornamental tree in shrubberies owing to its purple bark, its bunches of white flowers, and its berries, which are successively green, red, and black. Its fruit is nauseous to the taste, but is greedily eaten by birds. The wood is much used for cabinet-work. It is common in the native woods of Sweden and Scotland.

BIRD-LICE. A name given to a number of wingless insects parasitic on birds, belonging to various genera and families, and forming a common annoyance to cage-birds, pigeons, etc.

BIRD-LIME. A viscous substance used for entangling birds so as to make them easily caught, twigs being for this purpose smeared with it at places where birds resort. It is prepared from holly-bark, being extracted by boiling; also from the viscid berries of the mistletoe.

BIRD OF PARADISE. The name for members of a family of birds of splendid plumage, allied to the crows, inhabiting New Guinea and the adjacent islands. The family includes eleven or twelve genera and a number of species, some of them remarkably beautiful. The largest species is over 2 feet in length. The king bird of paradise (*Paradisĕa regia*) is possibly the most beautiful species, but is rare. The great bird of paradise has a magnificent plume of feathers, of a delicate yellow colour, coming up from under the wings, and falling over the back like a jet of water. The feathers of the *P. major* and *P. minor* are those chiefly worn in plumes. These splendid ornaments are confined to the male bird.

Great Bird of Paradise (*Paradisĕa apoda*)

BIRDOSWALD. Site of the Roman-British station of Amboglanna. It is the largest fort on Hadrian's Wall.

BIRD PEPPER. *See* CAPSICUM.

BIRDS. *See* ORNITHOLOGY.

BIRD-SEED. Seed for feeding cage-birds, especially the seed of *Phalăris canariensis*, or canary-grass.

BIRD'S EYE. Name for various flowers with central spots or eyes. The mealy primula, with its yellow-centred, purple flowers, is bird's eye primrose; the germander speedwell, with bright blue flowers, is called bird's eye; so is corn adonis, preferably called pheasant's eye. Herb robert is red bird's eye. It denotes also cut-tobacco containing sections of mottled stalks.

BIRD'S-EYE MAPLE. Curled maple, the wood of the sugar-maple when full of little knotty spots somewhat resembling birds' eyes; much used in cabinet-work.

BIRD'S-EYE VIEW. The representation of any scene as it would appear if seen from a considerable elevation right above.

BIRD'S-FOOT. A common name for several plants, especially papilionaceous plants of the genus Ornithŏpus, their legumes being articulated, cylindrical, and bent in like a claw.

King Bird of Paradise (*Paradisĕa regia*)

BIRD'S-FOOT TREFOIL. The popular name of *Lotus corniculātus*, a common British plant, also found in most parts of Europe as well as in Asia, North Africa, and Australia, a useful pasture-plant.

BIRD'S-NEST. A name popularly given to several plants, as *Neottia nidus-avis*, a British orchid found in beech woods, so called because of the mass of stout interlaced fibres which form its roots; *Monotrŏpa Hypopitys*, a parasitic ericaceous plant growing on the roots of trees in fir woods, the leafless stalks of which resemble a nest of sticks; and *Asplenium Nidus*, a common epiphyte in the Eastern Tropics, from the manner in which the fronds grow, leaving a nest-like hollow in the centre.

BIRDS'-NESTS, Edible. The nests of the salangane (*Colloc ılia fuciphăga*) and other species of swifts (or swiftlets) found in the Indian seas. They are particularly abundant in the larger islands of the Eastern Archipelago. The nest has the shape of a common swallow's nest, is found in caves, particularly on the sea-shore, and has the appearance of fibrous, imperfectly-concocted isinglass. When procured before the eggs are laid, the nests are of a waxy whiteness, and are then esteemed most valuable; when the bird has laid her eggs, they are of second quality; when the young are fledged and flown, of third quality. They appear to be composed of a mucilaginous substance secreted by special glands, and not, as was formerly thought, made from a glutinous marine fucus or seaweed. The Chinese consider the nests as a great stimulant and tonic, and it is said that about 8½ millions of them are annually imported into Canton.

BIRDS OF PASSAGE. Birds which migrate with the season from a colder to a warmer, or from a warmer to a colder climate, divided into *summer birds of passage* and *winter birds of passage*. Such birds always breed in the country to which they resort in summer, i.e. in the colder of their homes. Among British summer birds of passage are the cuckoo, swallow, etc., which depart in autumn for a warmer climate; while in winter woodcock, fieldfares, redwings, with many aquatic birds, as swans, geese, etc., regularly flock to Britain from the north. In America the robin is a familiar example. *See* MIGRATION OF ANIMALS.

BIRDS OF PREY. The Accipitres or Raptores, including vultures, eagles, hawks or falcons, buzzards, and owls. See illustration p. 60.

BIRD-SPIDER. *See* BIRD-CATCHING SPIDER.

BIRDWOOD, Field-Marshal Sir William Riddell, Bart., G.C.B., G.C.M.G., K.C.S.I., C.I.E., D.S.O. Born in 1865, and educated at Clifton and Sandhurst. He served in command of detached landings of the Australian and New Zealand army corps above Gaba Tepe, and commanded the Dardanelles army during the evacuation. In France he commanded the Australian troops and the Fifth Army. He was created a baronet in 1919. In March, 1925, he was created Field-Marshal, and in August of the same year he was appointed Commander-in-Chief in India. He has been Master of Peterhouse, Cambridge, since 1931.

BI'REN, or BI'RON, Ernest John von, Duke of Courland. Born in 1690, died 1772, the son of a landed proprietor. He gained the favour of Anna, Duchess of Courland and niece of Czar Peter the Great, and when she ascended the Russian throne (1730),

BIRDS OF PREY

1. Golden Eagle. 2. Peregrine Falcon. 3. Common Buzzard. 4. Tawny Owl. 5. Condor.

Biren was loaded by her with honours and introduced at the Russian Court. He was made Duke of Courland in 1737, and continued a powerful favourite during her reign, freely indulging his hatred against the rivals of his ambition. He caused 11,000 persons to be put to death, and double that number to be exiled. On the death of Anna he became regent, but he was exiled to Siberia in 1741. On the accession of Elizabeth to the throne she permitted his return to Russia, and in 1763 the duchy of Courland was restored to him.

BIRET'TA, BIRRETTA, or **BE-RET'TA.** An ecclesiastical cap of a square shape with stiff sides and a tassel at top, usually black for priests, violet for bishops, and scarlet for cardinals. The form of the biretta, devised in the seventeenth century, is peculiar to the Roman Church, but it is after all only a variant of the original *biretum,* which developed into head-coverings of different shapes and significance. The use of the *biretum* as a symbol of office or dignity was not confined to the clergy, and it still survives as official head-gear in many European countries, such as the *barette* of French barristers and judges, the *black cap* of the English judge, etc.

BIRIA. A town of India, United Provinces; famous for sugar-refineries. Pop. 9160.

BIRKBECK, George. The founder of mechanics' institutes, born at Settle, Yorkshire, in 1776, died in London in 1841. He studied medicine at Edinburgh; was appointed to the chair of natural and experimental philosophy in the Andersonian Institute at Glasgow in 1799, where he successfully established a class for mechanics. In 1806 he settled as a physician in London, and founded the London Mechanics' Institute in 1822, now known as the Birkbeck College.

The **Birkbeck Building Society,** also named after him, became one of the largest in the country. From it emerged the **Birkbeck Bank,** which failed in 1911. Its liabilities were nearly £11,000,000, but 16*s.* 9*d.* in the £ was returned to the shareholders and depositors.

BIRKDALE. A former urban district of England, on the south-west coast of Lancashire, now within the borough of Southport.

BIR'KENFELD (-felt). A principality belonging to Oldenburg, surrounded by the Rhenish districts of Coblenz and Trier; area, 194 sq. miles; pop. 51,263. It has a market town of the same name. *See* OLDENBURG.

BIR'KENHEAD. A parliamentary, county, and municipal borough of England, in Cheshire, on the estuary of the Mersey, opposite Liverpool. It has commodious docks with a lineal quay space of over 9 miles, and a complete system of railway communication for the shipment of goods and direct coaling of steamers. The principal industries are ship-building and engineering. Its commerce is in all respects a branch of that of Liverpool. The communication with Liverpool is by large steam-boats, and by a railway tunnel under the bed of the Mersey 4½ miles long including the approaches. In 1925 work was commenced on a tunnel for vehicular traffic, and boring was completed in 1928. The town returns two members to Parliament. Pop. (1931), 147,946.

BIRKENHEAD, First Earl of. *See* SMITH, FREDERICK EDWIN.

BIRKET-EL-KEROON ("Lake of the Horn"). An Egyptian lake in the Faiyum, about 30 miles in length by 6 miles in breadth. It communicates with the Nile, and had connection formerly with the artificial Lake Mœris, with which it has been confounded. It is situated 141 feet below sea-level, and is about 60 feet deep in its deepest parts.

BIRKETT, William Norman. English lawyer, born at Ulverston, 6th Sept., 1883, he passed a few years in business and then went to Cambridge, where he was president of the union. In 1913 he became a barrister and in 1921 a K.C. In 1923 he entered Parliament as Liberal M.P. for East Nottingham. Birkett was defeated at the election of 1924, but regained his seat in 1929, only to lose it in 1931.

BIR'MINGHAM. A great manufacturing city of England, situated on the small River Rea near its confluence with the Tame, in the N.W. of Warwickshire, with suburbs extending into Staffordshire and Worcestershire; 109¾ miles N.W. of London, and 97 miles S.E. of Liverpool. It is the principal seat of the hardware manufacture in Britain, producing metal articles of all kinds from pins to steam-engines. It manufactures fire-arms in great quantities, swords, jewellery, buttons, tools, steel-pens, locks, lamps, bed-steads, gas-fittings, sewing-machines, articles of papier-mâché, railway-carriages, etc. The quantity of solid gold and silver plate manufactured is large, and the consumption of these metals in electro-plating is very great. Japanning, glass manufacturing, and glass-staining or painting

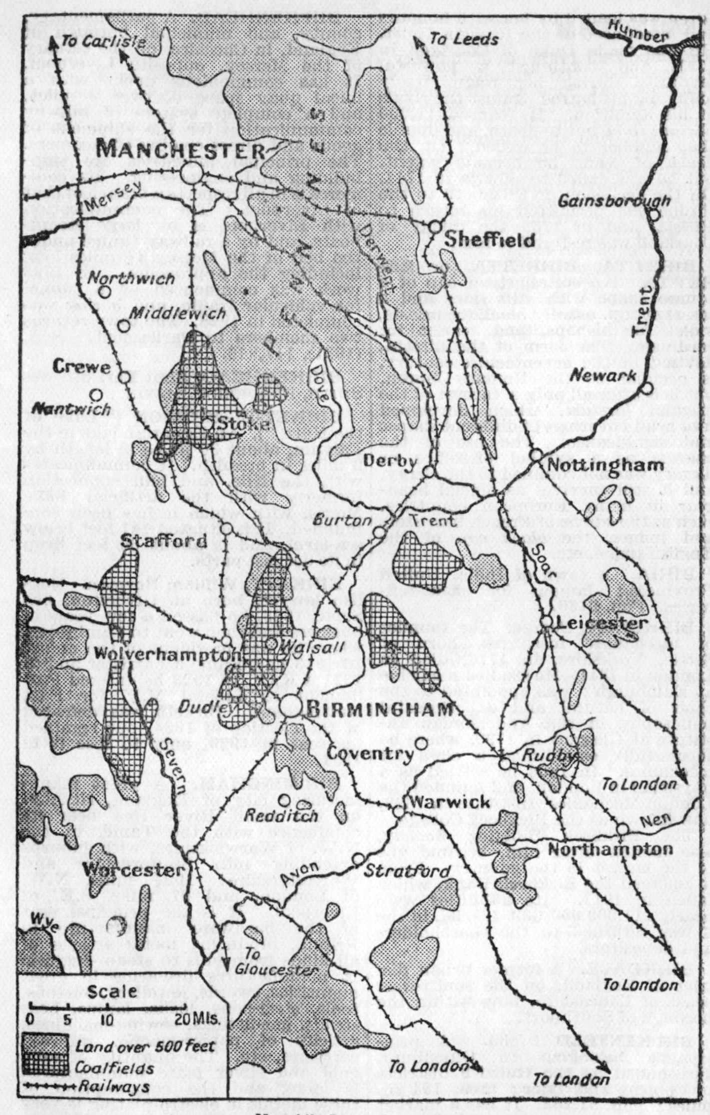

Map of the Birmingham District

form important branches of industry, as also does the manufacture of chemicals. At Soho and Smethwick in the vicinity of the town were the famous works founded by Boulton and Watt, who there manufactured their first steam-engines, where gas was first used, plating perfected, and numerous novel applications tried and experiments made.

Among the public buildings are the town hall, a handsome building of the classic style, the Council House or Municipal Buildings, the new general hospital, the municipal technical school, the new law courts, the new post office, the Birmingham and Midland Institute, the Art Gallery, the free library, the exchange buildings, etc. There are statues of the Prince Consort, James Watt, Sir Robert Peel, Lord Nelson, Dr. Priestley, Rowland Hill, Sir Josiah Mason, and others. There are various fine churches, and perhaps the finest ecclesiastical building of all is the Roman Catholic cathedral, a noble Gothic structure. The principal educational institutions are: The University (opened in 1900), which has developed from the Mason University College, founded by Sir Josiah Mason in 1875, opened in 1880, and united with Queen's College (as the medical department) in 1892; a Roman Catholic college at Oscott; (King Edward's) Grammar School; and a school of art and design. The Reform Act of 1832 made Birmingham a parliamentary borough with two members; the Act of 1867 gave it a third; the Redistribution Act of 1885 divided it into seven divisions, and the Representation of the People Act of 1918 into twelve, each sending one member to Parliament. Birmingham is known to have existed in the reign of Alfred, in 872, and is mentioned in the *Domesday Book* (1086) by the name of *Bermengeham*. Another old name of the town is *Bromwycham*, a form still preserved very nearly in the local pronunciation *Brummagem*. It became a city by royal grant in 1888. In 1801 the pop. was 73,670; in 1911, 840,202; and was returned in 1931 as 1,002,413.

BIRMINGHAM. A town of the United States, near the centre of Alabama, a great seat of the iron trade, having iron-ore, coal, and limestone in abundance at hand, so that its blast-furnaces, foundries, and other works are readily supplied. It has grown up since 1880. Pop. 259,678.

BIRMINGHAM, George A. *See* HANNAY, JAMES OWEN.

BIR'NAM. A hill in Perthshire, Scotland, 1324 feet high, once covered by the royal forest immortalised by Shakespeare in *Macbeth*. The village of Birnam lies at the foot of the hill in the Tay valley, and is ¾ mile distant from Dunkeld, which is on the left bank of the river.

BIRON (bē-rōn), **Charles de Gontaut, Duke of.** Born about 1562. He was a great favourite with Henry IV., who raised him to the rank of Admiral of France in 1592, and in 1598 made him a peer and duke. He was sent to England in 1601 to announce Henry's marriage with Mary de' Medici, but about the same time he was found guilty of forming a treasonable plot with the Duke of Savoy, and executed 1602. Shakespeare introduced him into *Love's Labour's Lost*, and Chapman wrote a play about his conspiracy.

BIRRELL, Augustine. Author and politician, born in 1850. He was educated at Amersham and Trinity Hall, Cambridge. He entered Parliament in 1889, and was President of the Board of Education 1905-7, and Chief Secretary to the Lord-Lieutenant of Ireland 1907-16. His publications include: *Life of Charlotte Brontë* (1885); *Obiter Dicta* (1887); *Men, Women, and Books* (1894); *Collected Essays* (1900); *Some Early Recollections of Liverpool* (1924); and in 1930 *Et Cetera*, a volume of reflections.

BIRS NIMRUD. A famous mound in Babylonia, on the west side of the Euphrates, 6 miles S.W. of Hillah, generally identified as the remains of the Tower of Babel.

BIRSTALL. A mining town of England, Yorkshire (W. Riding). Pop. (1931), 7205.

BIRTH, or LABOUR. In physiology, the act by which a female of the class mammalia brings one of her own species into the world. The period of gestation is very different in different animals, but in each particular species it is fixed with much precision. At the end of the thirty-ninth or the beginning of the fortieth week the human child has grown within the womb and reached the state in which it is capable of living separate from the mother, hence follows the birth. Contractions of the womb come on, called from the pain accompanying them *labour-pains*. The upper part of the womb contracts first, the lower part connecting with the passage of the vagina becomes thin and expanded, and the child, usually head first, is pressed downwards into the vagina, and then out of it and out of the mother's body. First labours are often protracted to eighteen hours—

average twelve hours—later labours are more rapid.

After the birth of the child there is usually a short rest, and then the placenta or after-birth, a large soft fleshy mass, is expelled. Premature birth is one which happens some weeks before the usual time, namely, after the seventh and before the end of the ninth month. Late birth is a birth after the usual period of forty weeks, but English law allows a longer time under special circumstances. In Scotland a child born after the tenth month from the father's death is accounted illegitimate. Abortion and miscarriage take place when the fœtus is brought forth so immature that it cannot live. A common cause is syphilis. The commonest time is at the third month, but they occur up to seven months. In order that a child may be born healthy, the parents must be healthy, and the greatest care should be taken of the mother, particularly in the three months immediately preceding the date of the labour or confinement.

BIRTH - CONTROL. Individual control of birth, by artificial means. In recent years, the ideal of quality in population rather than quantity has become general; and birth-control, usually by artificial contraceptive methods, has been a keenly discussed subject, affecting as it does ethics, biology, medicine, psychology, religion, and economics. Dr. Marie Stopes is its chief exponent. A medical committee has recommended that no married person should be hindered from obtaining knowledge of contraceptive methods; while, on the other hand, the Roman Catholic Church denounces all such practices as definitely sinful.

BIRTH MARK. *See* NŒVUS.

BIRTH'RIGHT. *See* PRIMOGENITURE.

BIRTH'WORT (*Aristolochia clematītis*). A European shrub, so called from the supposed services of its root when used medically in parturition.

BIRTLEY. District of Durham. It is 4½ miles from Gateshead, on the L.N.E. Rly., and is a mining centre. During the Great War a huge factory for making ammunition was built here.

BISACCIA (bē-sȧch'ȧ). An Italian town, province of Avellino (Principato Ultra), 30 miles E.N.E. of Avellino in the Apennines. Pop. 8020.

BISACQUINO (bis-ak-kwē'nō). A town of Sicily, province of Palermo. Pop. 9160.

BISALNAG'AR. A town of India, in Baroda, Bombay Presidency; manufactures of cotton; transit trade. Pop. 21,376.

BISALPUR'. A town of India, United Provinces, 24 miles east of Bareli. Pop. 9400.

BIS'CAY (Sp. *Vizcaya*). A province of Spain near its north-east corner, one of the three Basque provinces (the other two being Alava and Guipuzcoa); area, 836 sq. miles. The surface is generally mountainous; the most important mineral is iron, which is extensively worked; capital, Bilbao. Pop. 415,513.

BISCAY, BAY OF. That part of the Atlantic which lies between the projecting coasts of France and Spain, extending from Ushant to Cape Finisterre, celebrated for its dangerous navigation.

BISCEGLIE (bē-shel'yā). A seaport of Italy, province of Bari, on the west shore of the Adriatic, surrounded by walls, and in general badly built. The neighbourhood produces good wine and excellent currants. Pop. 32,000.

BISCHOF (bish'of), **Karl Gustav.** German chemist and geologist, born at Nuremberg 1792, died at Bonn 1870. He was appointed professor of chemistry at Bonn in 1822. He published in London, 1841, *Researches on the Internal Heat of the Globe* (in English); but his chief work is the *Lehrbuch der Chemischen und Physikalischen Geologie* (1847-54).

BISCHOFF (bish'of), **Theodor Ludwig Wilhelm.** German anatomist and physiologist, born in Hanover 1807, died at Munich 1882. He became professor of comparative and pathological anatomy at Bonn in 1836; of anatomy at Giessen in 1844; and from 1855 to 1878 he occupied a chair at Munich. He was the author of several treatises, and gained distinction by his researches in embryology.

BISCHWEILER (bish'vī-lėr). A town of Alsace, 12 miles N. of Strasburg, on the Moder, with flourishing manufactures of cloth. Pop. 8150.

BISCUIT (bis'kėt; Fr., "twice-baked"). A kind of hard, dry bread which is not liable to spoil when kept. Biscuits are either fermented or unfermented, the kinds in ordinary use being generally fermented, while the unfermented biscuit is much used at sea, and hence called sea-biscuit. More than a hundred different sorts of biscuit are manufactured, and, owing to the immense demand, manual labour has long since been superseded in the larger works by machinery. In making sea-biscuit the flour is mixed with water, converted into dough by a revolving shaft armed with knives, kneaded with rollers, cut, stamped, conveyed on a framework drawn by chains through an oven open at both ends, and thence passed to a drying-room, all without being touched by hand. Two thousand pounds weight of biscuits can thus be turned out of a single oven in a day of ten hours. In many fancy biscuits the process is of course more elaborate, but, even in these, machinery plays an important part. Sea-biscuit should continue sound for eighteen months or two years; its nutritive properties are to those of bread as eighteen to twenty-four. *Meat biscuits* are made of flour mixed with the soluble elements of meat.

BISCUIT. In pottery, a term applied to porcelain and other earthenware after the first firing and before glazing. At this stage it is porous and used for wine-coolers, etc. See POTTERY.

BISE (bēz). A keen northerly wind prevalent in the north of the Mediterranean. *See* BREEZE.

BISEGLIE. *See* BISCEGLIE.

BISHARIN (bi-shä-rēn′). A race inhabiting Nubia, between the Nile and the Red Sea, somewhat resembling the Bedouins, and living by pasturage. They are Mahommedans by religion; in character they are said to be cruel and treacherous. Personal property does not exist among them, the family or the tribe having the ownership.

BISHNUPUR′. Town of India, Bankurá district of Bengal, with manufactures of cottons and fine silk cloth and a brisk trade. Pop. 19,000.

BISHOP. The highest of the three orders in the Christian ministry—bishops, priests, and deacons—in such Churches as recognise three grades. The name is derived from the Greek *episkopos*, meaning literally an overseer, through the A.Sax. *biscop*, *bisceop*. Originally, in the Christian Church, the name was used interchangeably with *presbyter* or *elder* for the overseer or pastor of a congregation; but at a comparatively early period a position of special authority was held by the pastors of the Christian communities belonging to certain places, and the name of bishop became limited to these by way of distinction. There is much that is doubtful or disputed in regard to the history of the episcopal office. Roman Catholics and many others hold that it is of divine ordination and existed already in apostolic times; and they maintain the doctrine of the apostolical succession, that is to say, the doctrine of the transmission of the ministerial authority in uninterrupted succession from Christ to the apostles, and through these from one bishop to another. Presbyterians deny that the office was of divine or apostolic origin, and hold that it was a growth of subsequent times easily accounted for, certain of the presbyters or pastors acquiring precedence as

Bishop of the Early Christian Church

From a mosaic in St. Sophia, Constantinople

bishops over others, just as the bishops of the chief cities (Jerusalem, Antioch, Alexandria, Constantinople, Rome) obtained precedence among the bishops and received the title of metropolitan bishops, while the Bishop of Rome came to be regarded as the head of the Church and the true successor of Peter.

Already in the fifth century the Popes had begun to send to the newly-elected metropolitan bishops (now called archbishops) the pallium, a kind of official mantle, as a token of their sanction of the choice. Two centuries later it became the custom to consecrate bishops by investing them with the ring and crosier, the former as a token of marriage with the Church, the latter as a symbol of the pastoral office. This investiture, as giving validity to the election of the bishops, became the source of long-continued contests between the Popes and the temporal sovereigns in the Middle Ages. At present in the Roman Catholic Church the bishop is usually elected by the presbyters of the diocese, subject to the approbation of the Pope and of the secular power. When the monarch is Roman Catholic, a bishopric may be in the royal gift, subject to papal approval. The bishop comes next in rank to the cardinal; he is styled *reverendissimus*, *sanctissimus*, or *beatissimus*. His special insignia are the mitre and crosier or pastoral staff, a gold ring, the pallium, dalmatica, etc. He guards the purity of doctrine in his diocese, appoints professors in the clerical colleges, licenses books on religious subjects, ordains and appoints the clergy, consecrates churches, takes charge of the management of funds for ecclesiastical or pious purposes, etc. The bishops of the Greek Church have similar functions but on the whole less authority. They are always selected from the monastic orders.

In the Church of England bishops are nominated by the sovereign, who, upon request of the dean and chapter for leave to elect a bishop, sends a *congé d'élire*, or licence to elect, with a letter missive, nominating the person whom he would have chosen. The election, by the chapter, must be made within twelve days, or the sovereign has a right to appoint whom he pleases. A bishop, as well as an archbishop, has his consistory court to hear ecclesiastical causes, and makes visits to the clergy, etc. He consecrates churches, ordains, admits, and institutes priests; confirms, suspends, excommunicates, grants licences for marriage, etc. He has his archdeacon, dean, and chapter, chancellor, and vicar-general to assist him. Bishops of the Church of England rank in order of precedency immediately above barons. Their wives as such enjoy no title or precedence. Bishops are addressed as "Right Reverend," and have legally the style of "Lord." In all the bishops of England and Wales now number forty-one; and of these twenty-six sit in the House of Lords—the Archbishops and the Bishops of London, Durham, and Winchester by perpetual right, the others in order of seniority. In the Protestant Episcopal Church of Ireland there are thirteen bishops, including the metropolitans of Armagh and of Dublin. In the Scottish Episcopal Church there are seven bishops. There are also about 120 British colonial and missionary bishops belonging to the Anglican Church. Of Roman Catholic bishops there are 56 in Great Britain and about 150 in the British dominions. In the United States the Protestant Episcopal Church has over sixty bishops, the Roman Catholic Church over a hundred. In the United States there are also the bishops of the Methodist Episcopal Church, thirteen in number.

Bishops in partibus infidelium (in parts occupied by the infidels), in the Roman Catholic Church, are bishops consecrated under the fiction that they are bishops in succession to those who were the actual bishops in places where Christianity has become extinct, or almost so, through the spread of Mohammedanism, as in Syria, Asia Minor, and the northern coast of Africa. Such titles are given to missionary bishops in countries imperfectly Christianised, and were formerly given to the Roman Catholic bishops in Britain, the bishop of the northern district of Scotland, for instance, up to 1878 having the title of Bishop of Nicopolis.

Suffragan bishops are bishops consecrated to assist other bishops in performing the duties of their dioceses, though any bishop is a suffragan in relation to his archbishop.

BIBLIOGRAPHY: E. Hatch, *Organisation of the Early Christian Churches*; Réville, *Les origines de l'épiscopat*; R. C. Moberly, *Ministerial Priesthood*; T. M. Lindsay, *The Church and the Ministry in the Early Centuries*; L. Duchesne, *Christian Worship: its Origin and Evolution* (English translation).

BISHOP. A beverage made by pouring hot or cold red wine upon the pulp and peel of oranges, and spicing and sugaring to taste. If white wine is employed, it is known as *Cardinal*; if Tokay, it is termed *Pope*.

BISHOP, Mrs. *See* BIRD, ISABELLA.

BISHOP, Sir Henry Rowley. Musical composer, born in London in 1780, and trained under Bianchi, composer to the London Opera House. From 1809, when his first opera, *The Circassian Bride*, was produced at Drury Lane, until his masque *The Fortunate Isles*, written to celebrate Queen Victoria's marriage, he composed about a hundred works for the stage—among others the music of *Guy Mannering*, *The Slave*, *The Miller and his Men*, *Maid Marian*, *The Virgin of the Sun*, *Aladdin*, *Hamlet*, versions of operas by Rossini,

Meyerbeer, and others, *Waverley, Manfred,* etc. From 1810 to 1824 he acted as musical composer and director to Covent Garden Theatre. He also arranged several volumes of the *National Melodies,* and completed the arrangement of the music for Moore's *Irish Melodies,* commenced by Stevenson. Shortly after the accession of Queen Victoria he was knighted. He was elected Reid professor of music in Edinburgh University in 1841, and in 1848 professor of music in the University of Oxford. He died in 1855.

Bishop-weed (*Ægopodium Podagraria*)

1, Flower. 2, Fruit. 3, Cross section of fruit

BISHOP-AUCKLAND. A town, England, County Durham (giving name to one of the eleven parliamentary divisions of the county), with engineering works, and important coal-mines in the neighbourhood. The palace of the Bishop of Durham, with a fine park, is here (whence the name). Pop. (1931), 12,269.

BISHOP BARNABY. The may-bug or lady-bird.

BISHOP'S CASTLE. Borough and market-town of Shropshire. It is 22½ miles from Shrewsbury. The Bishops of Hereford had a castle here. Pop. (1931), 1352.

BISHOP'S RING. Name applied to a halo extending 20° to 30° from the sun. It is caused by diffraction of solar light through minute dust-particles in the air. First observed at Honolulu on 5th Sept., 1883, ten days after the eruption of Krakotoa, it was observable in various localities three years afterward.

BISHOP'S STAFF. *See* CROSIER.

BISHOP-STORTFORD. A town of England, County Hertford, on the River Stort; trade chiefly in grain and malt. Pop. (1931), 9509.

BISHOP'S WALTHAM. Village of Hampshire. It is 10½ miles from Winchester, on the S. Rly. The name is due to the fact that the Bishop of Winchester had here a castle, of which some ruins remain. It was once a market-town.

BISHOP-WEARMOUTH. *See* SUNDERLAND.

BISHOP-WEED (*Ægopodium Podagraria*). An umbelliferous plant of Europe, with thrice-ternate leaves and creeping roots or underground stems, a great pest in gardens from its vigorous growth and the difficulty of getting rid of it: called also *Gout-wort, Herb Gerard,* etc.

BISIGNANO (bē-sē-nyä′nō). A town of S. Italy, province of Cosenza, seat of a bishop; destroyed by earthquake in 1887.

BISKRA. A town, health resort, and oasis of Algeria, department of Constantine. Pop. 11,690.

BIS′LEY. A parish of England, in W. Surrey, where the annual meetings of the National Rifle Association (founded in 1860) are now held.

BIS′LEY. A town of England, Gloucestershire, with cloth manufactures. Pop. 1151.

BISMARCK ARCHIPELAGO. The name formerly given by the Germans to New Britain, New Ireland, and the Admiralty Islands, which adjoin their portion of New Guinea. Area, about 15,570 sq. miles; pop. about 190,000.—The Archipelago, acquired by Germany in 1884, was occupied by an Australian force on 12th Sept., 1914. *See* NEW GUINEA, TERRITORY OF; NEW HANOVER; etc.

BISMARCK-SCHÖNHAUSEN (bis′-märk-sheun′-hou-zėn), **Otto Eduard Leopold, Prince.** Born of a noble family of the "Mark" (Brandenburg), at Schönhausen, 1st April, 1815; studied at Göttingen, Berlin, and Greifswald; entered the army and became lieutenant in the Landwehr. After a brief interval devoted to his estates and to the office of Inspector of Dikes, he became in 1846 a member of the Provincial diet of Saxony, and in 1847 of the Prussian Diet. In 1851 he was appointed representative of Prussia in the Diet of the German Federation at Frankfort, where with brief interruptions he remained till 1859, exhibiting the highest ability in his efforts to checkmate Austria and place Prussia at the head of the German States. From 1859-62 he was Ambassador at St. Petersburg, and in the latter year, after an embassy to Paris of five months' duration, was appointed First Minister of the Prussian Crown. The Lower House persistently refusing to pass the Bill for the reorganisation of the army, Bismarck at once dissolved it (Oct., 1862), closing it for four successive sessions until the work of reorganisation was complete.

When popular feeling had reached its most strained point the Schleswig-Holstein question acted as a diversion, and Bismarck—by the skilful manner in which he added the duchies to Prussian territory, checkmated Austria, and excluded her from the new German Confederation, in which Prussia held the first place—became the most popular man in Germany. As Chancellor and President of the Federal Council he secured the neutralisation of Luxembourg in place of its cession by Holland to France; and though in 1868 he withdrew for a few months into private life, he resumed office before the close of the year. A struggle between Germany and France appearing to be sooner or later inevitable, Bismarck, having made full preparations, brought matters to a head on the question of the Hohenzollern candidature for the Spanish throne. Having carried the war to a successful issue, he became Chancellor and Prince of the new German Empire. Subsequently, in 1872, he alienated the Roman Catholic party by promoting adverse legal measures and expelling the Jesuits. He then resigned his presidency for a year, though still continuing to advise the emperor.

Towards the close of 1873 he returned to power, retaining his position until, in March, 1890, he disagreed with the emperor and tendered his resignation. In 1878 he presided at the Berlin Congress, in 1880 at the Berlin Conference, and in 1884 at the Congo Conference. His life was twice attempted—at Berlin in 1866, and at Kissingen in 1874. He died 31st July, 1898.—BIBLIOGRAPHY: Horst Kohl, *Fürst Bismarck, Regesten zu einer Wissenschaftlichen Biographie*; H. Blum, *Bismarck und Seine Zeit*; P. Schulze and O. Koller, *Bismarck-Literatur*; Charles Lowe, *Bismarck: a Political Biography*; M. Busch, *Bismarck: Some Secret Pages of his History*; P. Matter, *Bismarck et son Temps*; C. G. Robertson, *Bismarck.*

BIS'MUTH. A metal of a faint reddish-white colour, and a lamellar texture. Chemical symbol, Bi; atomic weight, 208; specific gravity, 9·8. It is somewhat harder than lead, not malleable, and when cold is very brittle and may be easily powdered. Its internal fracture exhibits large shining plates variously disposed. It fuses at 268° C., and expands as it solidifies. It is often found native in a crystalline state investing the ores of other metals, particularly cobalt. The oxide and sulphide are also found in nature. Bismuth is much used in the manufacture of fusible alloys, as it has the remarkable property of lowering the fusion-point of the alloys, and expands on cooling. It is a constituent of pewter, printers' types, etc. Eight parts of bismuth, 5 of lead, and 3 of tin constitute the fusible metal Newton's alloy, which melts at 94·5° C. Similar alloys are Rose's metal and Wood's metal, the latter containing bismuth, lead, tin, and cadmium, and melting at 68° C. These fusible alloys are used in the preparation of safety-valves for boilers, etc. Various compounds of bismuth are used medicinally and in the arts. For example, basic bismuth nitrate is largely used in medicine and in the preparation of cosmetics and paints, although for the latter purpose it is being replaced by zinc oxide, which is not darkened by sulphuretted hydrogen. Bismuth oxychloride is used in the preparation of pearl powders.

BI'SON. The name applied to two species of ox. One of these, the European bison or aurochs (*Bos bison* or *Bison europæus*), is now nearly extinct, being found only in the forests of Lithuania and the Caucasus. The other, or American bison, improperly termed buffalo (*Bison americanus*), was formerly found over a wide region in the United States and Western Canada, where it was wont to wander in immense herds, but may now be considered as extinct in the wild state, having been ruthlessly slaughtered, especially after the building of the transcontinental railway in 1867. The two species closely resemble each other, the American bison, however, being for the most part smaller, and with shorter and weaker hind-quarters. The bison is remarkable for the great hump or projection over its fore-shoulders, at which point the adult is almost six feet in height; and for the long, shaggy, rust-coloured hair over the head, neck, and fore-part of the body. In summer, from the shoulders backwards, the surface is covered with a very short fine hair, smooth and soft as velvet. The tail is short and tufted at the end. The American bison used to be much hunted for sport as well as for its flesh and skin. Its flesh is rather coarser grained than that of the domestic ox, but was considered by hunters and travellers as superior in tenderness and flavour. The hump is highly

Bison (*Bison americanus*)

celebrated for its richness and delicacy. Their skins, especially that of the cow, dressed in the Indian fashion, with the hair on, make admirable defences against the cold, and are known as *buffalo robes*; the wool has been manufactured into hats and a coarse cloth. The American bison has been found to breed readily with the common ox, the issue being fertile among themselves.

BISQUE (bisk). A kind of unglazed white porcelain used for statuettes and ornaments.

BISQUE. A rich soup made from cray-fish, etc.

BISQUE. Odds given by a stronger to a weaker player in tennis, golf, or croquet.

BISSA'GOS. A group of about thirty islands near the west coast of Africa, opposite the mouth of the Rio Grande, between lat. 10° and 12° N. The largest, Orango, is about 25 miles in length, and most of them are inhabited by a rude negro race, with whom some trade is carried on. Most of the islands are under native chiefs nominally vassals of Portugal. At Bolama, or Bulama, once a British settlement, but abandoned as unhealthy in 1793, there is a Portuguese town, a thriving and pleasant place, the seat of Government for the Portuguese possessions in this quarter.

BISSEN, Wilhelm. A Danish sculptor, born in 1798, died 1868. He studied at Rome under Thorwaldsen, who in his will appointed Bissen to complete his unfinished works and take charge of his museum. Bissen's own works include a classic frieze of several hundred feet for the palace-hall at Copenhagen, an *Atalanta Hunting, Cupid sharpening his Arrows,* etc.

BISSEXTILE. A term denoting a calendar year containing 366 days. It is commonly called a leap year. It gained its name because it contains a day intercalated every fourth year in February by the Julian calendar. This was called bissext because the sixth day before the March calends, that followed February 24th, was reckoned twice.

BISSING, Baron von. Born in 1844. He took part in the wars of 1866 and 1870, when he was attached to the staff of the Crown Prince Frederick. In 1914 he was called from retirement and given command at the depot of the army corps at Münster. At the end of Nov., 1914, he became second military German Governor-General of Belgium in succession to von Beseler. During his tenure of office he showed great severity and ruthlessness, and was responsible for the death of Nurse Cavell (q.v.). He died, while still holding office, on 19th April, 1917.

BIS'TORT (*Polygŏnum Bistorta*). A perennial plant of the buckwheat family (Polygonaceæ), found in Britain, and from its astringent properties (it contains much tannin) sometimes used medicinally. In the north of England the plant is called "Easter Giant," and near Manchester "Patience Dock."

BISTRE, or BISTER. A warm-brown pigment, a burned oil extracted from the soot of wood, especially beech. It furnishes a fine transparent wash, but is chiefly employed in the same fashion as sepia and indian ink for monochrome sketches.

BIS'TRITSA. A town of Rumania, in Transylvania, formerly a free town of Hungary. It is situated on the River Bistritsa, an affluent of the Szamos. Pop. 13,251.

BISULNUGGUR. *See* BISALNAGAR.

BIT. The part of a bridle which goes into the mouth of a horse, and to which the reins are attached. There is a great variety of forms, to which special names are given, such as the "Pelham bit," the "Weymouth bit," the "Liverpool bit," etc., the last being the most popular.—Also one of the movable boring-tools used by means of the carpenter's brace.

BITE. Wound made by the teeth. Hydrophobia may be caused by the bite of a dog if bacterial infection is present. The bite of certain snakes, such as vipers and cobras, may cause death.

BITHNOOR (bit-hör'), or **BITTOOR.** A town, India, United Provinces, 12 miles N.W. of Cawnpore, on the Ganges, long the abode of a line of Mahratta chiefs, the last of whom died without issue in 1851. His adopted son, Nana Sahib, who claimed the succession, was the instigator of the massacre of Cawnpore. Pop. 4386.

BITHYN'IA. An ancient territory in the N.W. of Asia Minor, on the Black Sea and Sea of Marmora, at one time an independent kingdom, afterwards a Roman province. The cities of Chalcedon, Heraclea, Nicomedia, Nicæa, and Prusa were in Bithynia. In the eleventh century it was conquered by the Seljuks, and in 1298 a new kingdom was founded there by the Ottoman Turks, of which, prior to the capture of Constantinople, Brusa (Broussa) was the capital.

BITLIS. *See* BETLIS.

BITON'TO. A town, Italy, province of Bari, the seat of a bishop, with a handsome cathedral. The environs produce excellent wine. Pop. 31,000.

BITSCH (bich). A town in the north of Alsace-Lorraine, in a pass of the Vosges, and having a strong citadel on a hill. Pop. 3640.

BITTER-ALMOND. The bitter variety of *Amygdălus communis*, or common almond.

BITTER-ASH. A tree, *Simarūba amāra*, a native of the West Indies, the root-bark of which is used as a tonic.

BIT'TERFELD (-felt). A town in Prussian Saxony, on the Mulde, with manufactures of cloth, pottery, etc. Pop. 19,384.

BITTER-GOURD. *See* COLOCYNTH.

BITTER - KING. The *Soulamĕa amāra*, a tree of the quassia order peculiar to the Moluccas and Fiji Islands, the root and bark of which, bruised and macerated, are used in the East as an emetic and tonic.

BITTER LAKES. Salt lakes on the line of the Suez Canal.

BIT'TERN. The name of several grallatorial birds, family Ardeidæ or herons, genus Botaurus. There are two British species, the common bittern (*Botaurus stellāris*), and the little bittern (*B. minūtus*), a native of the south, and only a summer visitor to Britain. Both, however, are becoming rare from the reclamation of the marshy grounds that form their favourite haunt. The common bittern is about 28 inches in length, about 44 in extent of wing; general colour, dull yellowish-brown, with spots and bars of black or dark-brown; feathers on the breast long and loose; tail short; bill about 4 inches long. It is remarkable for its curious booming or bellowing cry, from which come

Bittern (*Botaurus stellāris*)

the provincial names of *miredrum* and *butterbump*, etc. The eggs (greenish-brown) are four or five in number. The little bittern is not more than 15 inches in length. The American bittern (*B. lentiginōsus*) has some resemblance to the common European bittern, but is smaller.

BIT'TERN. The syrupy residue from evaporated sea-water after the common salt has been taken out of it. It is used in the preparation of Epsom-salts (sulphate of magnesia), or Glauber's salts (sulphate of soda), and contains also chloride of magnesium, iodine, and bromine.

BITTER-NUT. *See* CARYA.

BITTER-ROOT (*Lewisia rediviva*). A plant of Canada and part of the United States, ord. Portulacaceæ, so called from its root being bitter though edible, and indeed esteemed as an article of food by whites as well as Indians. From the root, which is long, fleshy, and tapering, grow clusters of succulent green leaves, with a fleshy stalk bearing a solitary rose-coloured flower rising in the centre, and remaining open only in sunshine. Flower and leaves together, the plant appears above ground for only about six weeks; it can live through long periods of drought, and has been known to live for nearly two years without water.

BITTERS. A liquor (frequently spirituous) in which bitter herbs or roots have been steeped. Gentian, quassia, angelica, bog-bean, chamomile, hops, centuary, etc., are all used for preparations of this kind. The well-known Angostura bitters have aromatic as well as bitter properties. Bitters are employed as stomachics, anthelmintics, etc.

BITTER-SALT. Epsom-salts, sulphate of magnesia.

BITTER-SPAR. Rhomb-spar, the crystallised form of dolomite or magnesian limestone.

BITTER - SWEET. *See* NIGHTSHADE.

BITTER VETCH. A name given to the species of Orŏbus, e.g. the common bitter vetch of Britain, *O. tuberosus*, a perennial herbaceous plant with racemes of purple flowers and sweet edible tubers.

BITTER-WORT. *See* GENTIAN.

BITU'MEN. A mineral substance of a resinous nature, composed principally of hydrogen and carbon, and appearing in a variety of forms which pass into each other and are known by different names, from *naphtha*, the most fluid, to *petroleum* and *mineral tar*, which are less so, thence to *maltha* or *mineral pitch*, which is more or less cohesive, and lastly to *asphaltum* and *elastic bitumen* (or *elaterite*), which are solid. It burns like pitch, with much smoke and flame. It consists of 84 to 88 of carbon and 12 to 16 of hydrogen, and is found in the earth, occurring principally in the secondary, tertiary, and alluvial formations. It is a very widely-spread mineral, and is now largely employed in various ways. As the binding substance in mastics and cements it is used for making roofs, arches, walls, cellar-floors, etc., water-tight, for street and other pavements, and in some of its forms for fuel and for illuminating purposes. The bricks of which the walls of Babylon were built are said to have been cemented with bitumen, which gave them unusual solidity.

BITUMINOUS SHALE, or SCHIST. An argillaceous shale impregnated with bitumen and very common in the coal-measures. It is largely worked for the production of paraffin, etc.

BIT'ZIUS, Albert. A popular Swiss author, better known by his pseudonym of Jeremias Gotthelf, born 1797, died 1854. His chief works were his *Scenes and Traditions of the Swiss* (1842-6); *Grandmother Katy* (1848); *Uli the Farm-servant*, and *Uli the Farmer* (1850); *Stories and Pictures of Popular Life in Switzerland* (1851).

BI'VALVES. Molluscous animals having a shell consisting of two halves or valves that open by an elastic hinge and are closed by muscles; as the oyster, mussel, cockle, etc.

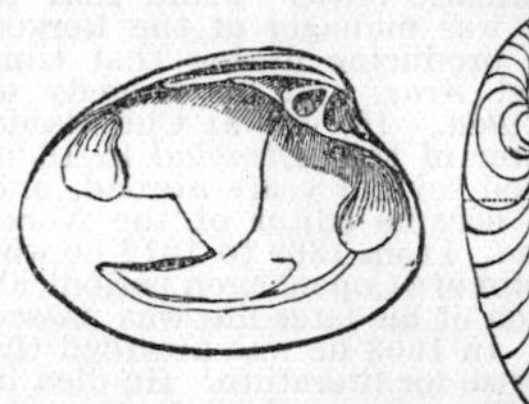
Bivalve Shell

BIVOUAC (biv'ụ-ak). The encampment of soldiers in the open air without tents or huts, but with temporary shelters improvised out of whatever materials may be at hand.

BIXA. *See* ANNATTO.

BIXSHOOTE. A village of Belgium, in Flanders, the scene of fighting during the European War. *See* YPRES, BATTLES OF.

BIZER'TA, or BENZERT'. A seaport of Tunis, the most northern town of Africa, on a bay of the Mediterranean, at the entrance of a narrow channel, nearly a mile long, communicating with the Lake of Bizerta, a fine, deep salt-water lagoon teeming with fish. The French have deepened the channel and constructed harbour works here; next to Toulon, Bizerta is now the most important naval port of France in the Mediterranean. The country around is beautiful and fertile. Pop., chiefly Arabians, 20,503.

BIZET (bē-zā), **Georges.** French composer, born 1838, died 1875; studied with brilliant success at the Paris Conservatoire, and gained the Grand Prix de Rome in 1857. He had several operas put on the stage, with indifferent success, but his chief work, *Carmen*, brought out shortly before his death, has had as great a vogue as perhaps any modern opera. His opera *The Fair Maid of Perth* was performed for the first time in Manchester on 4th May, 1912.

BJELBOG (byel'bog). In Slavonic mythology, the pale or white god, as opposed to Tshernybog, the black god, or god of darkness.

BJÖRNEBÖRG (by*eur*'ne-borg). A seaport of Finland, in the Gulf of Bothnia. Pop. 18,400.

BJÖRNSON, Bjornstjerne (by*eur*n'-styer-ne by*eur*n'son). Norwegian novelist, poet, and dramatist, born in

1832. He entered the University of Christiania in 1852, and speedily became known as a contributor of articles and stories to newspapers and as a dramatic critic. From 1857 to 1859 he was manager of the Bergen theatre, producing during that time his novel *Arne*, and his tragedy of *Halte Hulda*. He was at Christiania part-editor of the *Aftenblad* in 1860, then lived several years abroad, and in 1866 became editor of the *Norsk Folkeblad*. From 1869 to 1872 he was co-director of a Copenhagen periodical, and much of his later life was passed abroad. In 1903 he was awarded the Nobel prize for literature. He died in 1910. The strong democratic tendencies of his novels found a practical outcome in the active part taken by him in political questions bearing upon the Norwegian peasantry and popular representation. Among his Tales and novels are: *Synnœve Solbakken, Arne, The Fisher-maiden, A Happy Boy, Railways and Churchyards, In God's Way*. Among his dramatic pieces are: *The Newly-married Couple, Mary Stuart in Scotland, A Bankruptcy, Beyond Our Powers, Laboremus, Daglannet*, etc. Björnson was an eloquent advocate of Pan-Germanism.—BIBLIOGRAPHY: G. Brandes, *Critical Studies*; Chr. Collin, *B. Björnson*; Payne, *B. Björnson*; *The Novels of B. Björnson* (London, 1894, etc.), edited by E. Gosse.

BJÖRNSTJERNA (by*eurn*'sher-nȧ), **Magnus Frederick Ferdinand, Count.** Swedish statesman and author, born 1779, died 1847. Having entered the Swedish army and risen to be colonel, he went with the Swedish troops to Germany in 1813 and took part in the battles of Grossbeeren, Dennewitz, the passage of the Elbe, the storming of Dessau, and the battle of Leipzig. He also received the surrender of Lübeck and of Maestricht. After the capitulation of Paris, he fought in Holstein and in Norway, at length concluding with Prince Christian Frederick at Moss the convention uniting Norway and Sweden. In 1826 he was made a count, and in 1828 plenipotentiary to Great Britain, where he continued till 1846. He published works on *British Rule in the East Indies*, on the *Theogony, Philosophy, and Cosmogony of the Hindus*, etc.

BLACK. The negation of all colour, the opposite of white. There are several black pigments, such as *ivory-black*, made from burnt ivory or bones; *lamp-black*, from the smoke of resinous substances; *Spanish-black*, or *cork-black*, from burnt cork, etc.

BLACK, John. Author and editor, the son of a Berwickshire shepherd, and born in 1783. After being employed in a lawyer's office, first in Duns and then in Edinburgh, he removed in 1810 to London, where he became engaged as parliamentary reporter for the *Morning Chronicle*, ultimately rising to be its editor. He retired in 1843, and died in 1855. Amongst other works he was the author of a *Life of Tasso*, and translator of the lectures of the brothers Schlegel on *Dramatic Art and Literature*, and on the *History of Literature*.

BLACK, Joseph. A distinguished chemist, born at Bordeaux, of Scottish parents, in 1728; entered Glasgow University and studied chemistry under Dr. Cullen. In 1754 he was made Doctor of Medicine at Edinburgh, his thesis being on the nature of the causticity of lime and the alkalies, which he demonstrated to be due to the absence of the carbonic acid present in limestone, etc. In 1756 he extended and republished this thesis, and was appointed professor of medicine and lecturer on chemistry at Glasgow in succession to Dr. Cullen, whom he succeeded also in the Edinburgh chair in 1766. The discovery of carbonic acid is of interest not only as having preceded that of the other gases made by Priestley, Cavendish, and others, but as having preceded in its method the explanation given by Lavoisier of the part played by oxygen in combustion. His fame, however, chiefly rests on his theory of "latent heat." He died in 1799.

BLACK, William. Novelist, born in Glasgow in 1841, first studied art, but eventually became connected with the Glasgow press. In 1864 he went to London, and in the following year joined the staff of the *Morning Star*, for which he was special correspondent during the Austro-Prussian war of 1866. His first novel, *Love or Marriage* (1867), was only moderately successful, but his *In Silk Attire, Kilmeny*, and especially *A Daughter of Heth* (1871), gained him an increasingly wide circle of readers. For a few years he was assistant editor of the *Daily News*. He died in 1898. Other works: *The Strange Adventures of a Phaeton* (1872), *A Princess of Thule* (1873), *The Maid of Killeena* (1874), *Three Feathers* (1875), *Madcap Violet* (1876), *Green Pastures and Piccadilly* (1877), *Macleod of Dare* (1878), *White Wings* (1880), *Sunrise* (1881), *The Beautiful Wretch* (1882), *Shandon Bells* (1883), *Judith Shakespeare* (1884), *White Heather* (1885), *The Strange Adventures of a House-boat* (1888), *In Far Lochaber* (1889), *The New Prince Fortunatus* (1890), *Highland Cousins* (1894), and *Wild Eelin* (1898).

BLACK ACTS. The Acts of the Scottish Parliaments of the Jameses I.-V., of Queen Mary, and of James VI.; so called from their being printed in black letter.

In English law, the Act passed under George I. with reference to the "Blacks," a body of armed deer-stealers, etc., who infested Epping Forest.

BLACK'ADDER, John. A Scottish Covenanter, born in 1615. Having been obliged to demit his charge at Troqueer in favour of an Episcopal incumbent, he went with his wife and family to Caitloch, in the parish of Glencairn, and became one of the most popular of the itinerant preachers, successfully eluding the numerous warrants issued against him. In 1674 he was outlawed and a large reward offered for his body. In 1678 he went to Holland, and again in 1680, but on his return to Edinburgh in 1681 he was apprehended and imprisoned upon the Bass, where he died in 1685.

BLACK AND TAN. Name given to a force raised in 1920 by the British Government for service in Ireland. Recruited from men who had served in the Great War, they were sent to put down the disorders then prevalent, but their presence was signalised by increased violence which was answered by reprisals. They were withdrawn when peace was made in 1922. A branch of the Royal Irish Constabulary, the men wore khaki uniforms with a black hat and armband, hence the name black and tan.

BLACK-BAND. A mineral carbonate of iron occurring in beds in the coal-measures, and containing coaly matter sometimes sufficient in quantity for its calcination. Most of the Scottish iron was at one time obtained from it. It is now almost completely worked out. *See* IRON.

BLACK BASS. A species of spiny-finned fish of the sea perch and bass family. They are dark fresh-water fish, weighing up to 5 lb.

BLACK-BEETLE. A popular name for the cockroach. *See also* BLAPSIDÆ.

BLACK'BERRY. A popular name of the brambleberry or the plant itself.

BLACK'BIRD (*Turdus merŭla*). Called also the *merle*, a well-known species of thrush, common in Britain and throughout Europe. It is larger than the common thrush, its length being about 11 inches. The colour of the male is a uniform deep black, the bill being an orange-yellow; the female is of a brown colour, with blackish-brown bill. The nest is usually in a thick bush, and is built of grass, roots, twigs, etc., strengthened with clay. The eggs, generally four or five in number, are of a greenish-blue, spotted with various shades of brown. The song is rich, mellow, and flute-like, but of no great variety or compass. It feeds on insects, worms, snails, fruits, etc. The blackbirds or crow-blackbirds of America are quite different from the European blackbird, and are more nearly allied to the starlings and crows. *See* CROW-BLACKBIRD. The red-winged blackbird (*Agelaius phœnicĕus*), belonging to the starling family, is a familiar American bird that congregates in great flocks.

BLACK-BOY. A name for the grass trees (*Xanthorrhœa*, nat. ord. Tiliaceæ) of Australia yielding black-boy gum and akaroid or Botany Bay resin.

BLACK'BURN. A municipal, county, and parliamentary borough of England, Lancashire, 2½ miles N.N.W. of Manchester. It is pleasantly situated in a sheltered valley, and has rapidly improved since 1850, the town hall, exchange, and other buildings being of recent erection. It has a free grammar-school, founded by Queen Elizabeth in 1557, a free school for girls, founded in 1765, and many other schools; and a free library, a public park of 50 acres, etc. Blackburn is one of the chief seats of the cotton manufacture, there being upwards of 140 mills, as well as works for making cotton machinery and steam-engines. The cottons made in the town and vicinity have an annual value of about £5,000,000. It returns two members to Parliament. Pop. (1931), 122,695.

BLACKBURN ROVERS. Association football club. It was founded in 1874 and was one of the first to adopt professionalism, which it did about 1882. Since then it has been continually in the front rank. Six times, 1884, 1885, 1886, 1890, 1891, and 1928, it has won the Association Cup, and twice, 1912 and 1914, the championship of the League.

BLACK-CAP (*Sylvia atricapilla*). A European passerine bird of the warbler family, 6 inches long, upper part of the head black, upper parts of the body dark-grey with a greenish tinge, under parts more or less silvery white. The female has its hood of a dull rust colour. The black-cap is met with in England from April to September. Its nest is built near the ground; the eggs, from five to six, are reddish-brown, mottled with a deeper colour. The sweetness of its song is only surpassed by that of the nightingale. The American black-cap is a species of tit-mouse (*Parus atri-*

capillus), so called from the colouring of the head.

Black-cap (*Sylvia atricapilla*)

BLACK CHALK. A soft variety of argillaceous slate, containing 10 to 15 per cent of carbon, and used for drawing.

BLACK-COCK. *See* GROUSE.

BLACK COUNTRY. A popular name for the district of coal-mines and ironworks in South Staffordshire, and extending into Warwick and Worcestershire.

BLACK DEATH. *See* PLAGUE.

BLACK DRAUGHT. Sulphate of magnesia and infusion of senna, with aromatics to make it palatable.

BLACKFEET INDIANS. A tribe of American Indians, partly inhabiting the United States, partly Canada, from the Yellowstone to Hudson's Bay.

BLACKFISH (*Tautŏga americāna*). A fish caught on the American coast, especially in the vicinity of Long Island. whence large supplies are obtained for the New York market. Its back and sides are of a bluish or crow black; the under parts, especially in the males, are white. It is plump in appearance, and much esteemed for the table, varying in size from 2 to 12 lb. Another fish, the *Zentrolŏphus morio*, found in the Mediterranean and on the coas of Western Europe, is also called blackfish. It belongs to the mackerel family. In Scotland the term is applied to foul or newly-spawned fish. In America two species of small whale of the genus Globiocephălus also get this name.

BLACK FLY. The name of two flies (*Simulium molestum* and *S. nocīvum*) whose bite is very troublesome to man and beast in the Northern United States and Canada.

BLACK FOREST (Ger. *Schwarzwald*). A chain of European mountains in Baden and Würtemberg, running almost parallel with the Rhine for about 85 miles. The Danube, Neckar, Kinzig, and other streams rise in the Black Forest, which is rather a chain of elevated plains than of isolated peaks; highest summit, Feldberg, 4900 feet. The skeleton of the chain is granite, its higher points covered with sandstone. The principal mineral is iron, and there are numerous mineral springs. The forests are extensive, chiefly of pines and similar species, and yield much timber. The manufacture of wooden clocks, toys, etc., is the most important industry, and employed, in 1914, 40,000 persons. The inhabitants of the forest are quaint and simple in their habits, and the whole district preserves its old legendary associations.

BLACK FRIARS. Friars of the Dominican order: so called from their habit. *See* DOMINICANS.

BLACK FRIDAY. Name given to Friday, 6th Dec., 1745, and Friday, 11th May, 1866. On the former day, Charles Edward and his Highlanders were at Derby, and this caused a financial panic in London. The second panic was due to the failure of the banking firm of Overend, Gurney & Co., which had liabilities of £11,200,000.

BLACK GUM, TUPELO, or PEPPERIDGE (*Nyssa multiflōra*, ord. Cornaceæ). A North American tree, yielding a close-grained wood, difficult to split, and hence used for the hubs of wheels, hatters' blocks, etc.

BLACKHEATH. An open common of 70 acres, Kent, England, about 6 miles S.E. of London Bridge, much resorted to by pleasure parties. It has been the scene of many remarkable events, such as the insurrectionary gatherings of Wat Tyler (1381) and Jack Cade (1450), and the exploits of various highwaymen. Blackheath gives its name to a residential district belonging to the metropolitan borough of Lewisham.

BLACK HILLS. A hilly region of the United States, S. Dakota, and partly Wyoming, rich in timber, but especially in gold, as well as other minerals. The highest point, Harney Peak, is 7216 feet above the sea.

BLACK HOLE OF CALCUTTA. A small chamber, 20 feet square, in the old fort of Calcutta, in which, after their capture by Surajah Dowlah, the whole garrison of 146 men were confined during the night of 21st June, 1756. Only twenty-three survived. The spot is now marked by a monument.

BLACKIE, John Stuart. Scottish writer, long professor of Greek in the University of Edinburgh, born at Glasgow in 1809; educated at Aberdeen, Edinburgh, Göttingen, and Berlin. He passed as advocate at the Edinburgh bar in 1834, in which year appeared his metrical translation of *Faust*. In 1841 he was appointed to the chair of Latin literature in Marischal College, Aberdeen—a post held by him until his appointment to the Greek chair at Edinburgh in 1852, from which he retired in 1882. Both in writing and upon the platform his name has been associated with various educational, social, and political movements. Among his more important works are his *Metrical Translation of Æschylus* (1850); *Lays and Legends of Ancient Greece, etc.* (1857); *Discourse on Beauty* (1860); *Lyrical Poems* (1860); *Metrical Version of the Iliad* (1866); *Musa Burschicosa* (1869); *Four Phases of Morals* (1871); *Self-culture* (1873); *The Wise Men of Greece* (1877); *Natural History of Atheism* (1877); *Lay Sermons* (1881); *Altavona, Fact and Fiction from my life in the Highlands* (1882); *Burns* (1887); *Christianity and the Ideal of Humanity* (1893). He died in 1895.—Cf. A. M. Stoddart, *John Stuart Blackie*.

BLACKING. For boots and shoes, etc., usually contains for its principal ingredients oil, vinegar, ivory or bone black, sugar or molasses, strong sulphuric acid, and sometimes caoutchouc and gum-arabic. It is used either liquid or in the form of paste, the only difference being that in making the paste a portion of the vinegar is withheld.

BLACK ISLE. The peninsula in the east of the Scottish county of Ross and Cromarty, between the Moray Firth, Inverness Firth, and Beauly Firth on one side, and the Cromarty Firth on the other, generally well cultivated and fertile. The town of Cromarty is at its seaward extremity.

BLACK-JACK. *See* BLENDE.

BLACK LEAD. *See* GRAPHITE.

BLACK-LETTER. The name commonly given to the Gothic characters which began to supersede the Roman characters in the writings of Western Europe towards the close of the twelfth century. The first types were in black-letter, but these were gradually modified in Italy until they took the later Roman shape introduced into most European states during the sixteenth century. *See* PRINTING.

BLACKLEY. A parliamentary division of Manchester.

BLACK LIST. A list of bankrupts or other parties whose names are officially known as failing to meet pecuniary engagements.

BLACK'LOCK, Thomas. A Scottish poet, born at Annan in 1721. At the age of six months he lost his sight by smallpox; and as he grew up, his father—who was a bricklayer—and other friends read to him the English classics. At the age of nineteen he lost his father, and was supported by Dr. Stephenson, a physician in Edinburgh, who sent him to school and to the university. In 1746 he brought out a volume of poems, and soon gained a wide circle of friends, amongst whom were David Hume and Joseph Spence, who wrote an account of his life, prefixed to the third edition of his poems in 1756. After passing through the usual theological course, he was licensed in 1759; he married in 1762, and was soon after appointed minister of Kirkcudbright. Being opposed by his parishioners, he resigned his living, and retired to Edinburgh, where he received students of the university as boarders, and assisted them in their studies. In 1766 he was created D.D. A letter written by him to a friend of Burns in 1786 is said by the poet to have induced him to give up his intended emigration and go to Edinburgh. Blacklock wrote, besides his poems, several prose works, and died in 1791. An edition of his poems was published in 1793, with a life by Henry Mackenzie.

BLACK-MAIL. A certain rate of money, corn, cattle, or the like, anciently paid, in the north of England and in Scotland, to certain men who were allied to robbers, to be protected by them from pillage. Blackmail was levied in the districts bordering the Highlands of Scotland till the middle of the eighteenth century.

BLACK'MORE, Sir Richard. Physician and writer in verse and prose, the son of an attorney in the county of Wilts; entered the University of Oxford in 1668; became a schoolmaster; then travelled on the Continent, took the degree of M.D. at Padua, and was admitted Fellow of the Royal College of Physicians in 1687. In 1695 he published his heroic poem *Prince Arthur*, and two years later was knighted and appointed physician to William III. A ponderously worthy man, though very middling poet, he became the common butt of the day, no amount of ridicule, however, being sufficient to restrain his desire for literary distinction. His *Paraphrases on Job* (1700) was followed by *Eliza, an Epic in Ten Books* (1705) and by *The Nature of Man* (1711). His poem *The Creation* (1712) received the praise of Addison and Johnson; but his *Redemption*, in six books (1722), and his *Alfred*, in twelve (1723), reverted to the unrelieved monotony of his earlier style. He left several prose works on theology and medicine, and died in 1729.

BLACKMORE, Richard Doddridge. Novelist, born at Longworth, Berkshire, 1825; educated at Tiverton School and Exeter College, Oxford, where he graduated in 1847. In 1852 he was called to the Bar at the Middle Temple, and afterwards practised. He died in 1900. His greatest success was *Lorna Doone, a Romance of Exmoor* (1869), one of the best of modern romances. Other novels by him are: *Clara Vaughan* (1864); *Cradock Nowell, a Tale of the New Forest* (1866); *The Maid of Sker* (1872); *Alice Lorraine, a Tale of the South Downs* (1875); *Cripps the Carrier* (1876); *Erema* (1877); *Mary Anerley* (1880); *Christowell* (1882); *Tommy Upmore* (1884); *Springhaven* (1887); *Perlycross* (1894); *Tales from the Telling House* (1896); *Dariel* (1897), etc. He also published a translation of Virgil's *Georgics* (1862 and 1871).

BLACK MOUNTAINS. The group which contains the highest summits of the Appalachian system, Clingman's Peak being 6707 feet, Guyot's Peak, 6661. *See* APPALACHIAN MOUNTAINS.

BLACKPOOL. A municipal, county, and parliamentary borough, and a much-frequented watering-place of England, on the coast of Lancashire, between the estuaries of the Ribble and Wyre. It consists of lofty houses ranging along the shore for about 3 miles; has an excellent promenade, three splendid piers, a lofty tower (not unlike the Eiffel Tower) which can accommodate 10,000 people, a large aquarium, fine winter-gardens, etc. Since 1918 it returns one member to Parliament. Pop. (1931), 101,543.

BLACK PRINCE. *See* EDWARD.

BLACK QUARTER (Quarter Evil, Black Leg, or Anthrax). A fatal infectious disease which attacks cattle. Extreme lameness and formation of gas under the skin are characteristic features. Carcasses must be burnt. Cure is rarely effected, but preventive inoculation has proved successful.

BLACK'ROCK. A town of Ireland, on Dublin Bay, about 5 miles from the capital; sea-bathing and residential locality. Pop. (1926), 9931.

BLACKROD. A town of England, in Lancashire, about 3½ miles north-east of Wigan, with coal-mines, bleaching and other works. Pop. 3599.

BLACK-ROD. In England, the usher belonging to the Order of the Garter, so called from the black rod which he carries. His full title is Gentleman-usher of the Black Rod, and his deputy is styled the Yeoman-usher. They are the official messengers of the House of Lords; and either the gentleman- or the yeoman-usher summons the Commons to the House of Lords when the royal assent is given to Bills or royal speeches read, and takes into custody parties guilty of breach of privilege and contempt.

BLACK SCAB. Disease occurring on potatoes. It produces on the surface of the tuber large irregular warts, which are caused by a parasitic fungus.

BLACK SEA (ancient **Pontus Euxinus**). A sea situated between Europe and Asia, and connected with the Mediterranean by the Bosporus, Sea of Marmara, and Dardanelles, and by the Strait of Kertch with the Sea of Azov, which is, in fact, only a bay of the Black Sea. It is bounded by Russia, Caucasia, Asia Minor, Bulgaria, and Rumania. Area of the Black Sea with the Sea of Azov, about 175,000 sq. miles, with a depth in the centre of 1000-1200 fathoms and few shoals along its shores. The water is not so clear as that of the Mediterranean, and is less salt on account of the many large rivers which fall into it—the Danube, Dniester, Dnieper, Don, etc.

Though not tidal, there are strong currents. It is subject to violent tempests, especially in winter, and the elevation of the land often gives to them a kind of whirling motion. During January and February the shores from Odessa to the Crimea are ice-bound. It contains few islands, and those of small extent. The most important ports are those of Odessa, Kherson, Nicolaiev, Kertch, Novorossysk, Batum, Trebizond, Samsun, Sinope, Kustendji, and Varna. The fisheries are of some value. After the capture of Constantinople, the Turks excluded all but their own ships from the Black Sea until 1774, when, by the Treaty of Kainarji, they ceded to Russia the right also to trade in it. The same right was accorded to Austria in 1784, and by the Peace of Amiens to Britain and France in 1802. The preponderance thereafter gained by Russia was one of the causes of the Crimean War, in which she was compelled to cede her right to keep armed

BLACKPOOL TOWER

vessels in it, the sea being declared neutral by the Treaty of Paris, 1856. In 1871, however, the sea was de-neutralised by the European Powers assembled at London. *See* DARDANELLES; EUROPEAN WAR.

BLACK-SNAKE (*Zamenis constrictor*). A common non-venomous snake of the United States, reaching a length of 5 or 6 feet, and so agile and swift as to have been named the Racer. It feeds on small quadrupeds, birds, etc., and is useful in killing rats.

BLACKSOD. Bay on the western coast of Ireland. It is in Co. Mayo, and makes a very fine harbour. Its length is 10 miles.

BLACK'STONE, Sir William. An eminent jurist, born in London in 1723; was educated at the Charterhouse and Pembroke College, Oxford, and became Fellow of All Souls. He entered the Middle Temple in 1741, and in 1746 was called to the Bar, but made little progress in the courts, though he became recorder of Wallingford. At Oxford he gave lectures on law, which suggested to Charles Viner the idea of founding a professorship of common law at Oxford; and Blackstone was in 1758 chosen the first Vinerian professor. In 1759 he published a new edition of the Great Charter and Charter of the Forest; and during the same year resumed his attendance at Westminster Hall with abundant success. In 1761 he was elected member of Parliament for Hindon, made King's Counsel and Solicitor-General to the queen. He was also appointed principal of New Inn Hall; which office, with the Vinerian professorship, he soon resigned. In 1765 he published the first volume of his famous *Commentaries on the Laws of England*, the other three volumes being produced at intervals during the next four years. Its merits as an exposition made it for a long period the principal textbook of English law. In 1770 he was offered the post of Solicitor-General, and, declining it, was knighted and made one of the justices of Common Pleas, continuing in office until his death in 1780.

BLACKTHORN. *See* SLOE.

BLACK TIN. Tin ore when dressed, stamped, and washed ready for smelting, forming a black powder.

BLACK VOMIT. The contents of the stomach vomited during the later stages of yellow fever. The dark colour is due to the presence of altered blood, and, though not necessarily a fatal symptom, it is only present in the severer forms of the disease.

BLACK WAD. An ore of manganese, used as a drying ingredient in paints.

BLACK WATCH (Royal Highlanders), **THE.** Raised in 1739 for the defence of the Highlands, it was not incorporated in the regular army until 1740, when it paraded for that purpose at a spot near Aberfeldy, now marked by a memorial stone. This famous regiment saw service at Fontenoy, and was engaged in the West Indies, India, the Peninsula, Egypt, and South Africa (1846-7, 1851-3, 1899-1902). During the European War the Black Watch exhibited its old quality at the Aisne and Givenchy, at Gheluvelt, where it routed the Prussian Guard, and at Neuve Chapelle and Loos.

BLACKWATER. The name of a number of streams in different parts of the United Kingdom, the chief being a fine river in the south of Ireland, which enters the sea at Youghal after a course of 106 miles, the last ten of which are navigable, the next largest Irish river after the Shannon.

BLACKWATER FEVER. A fever, often fatal, occurring in West Africa and Central America, and specially prone to attack Europeans in those regions. It is characterised by high fever, dark-coloured urine (hence the name), and delirium with great prostration, and frequently ends in coma and death. Those attacked by it have previously been the subjects of repeated attacks of malaria. No special organism has been found, and the general opinion at present is that it is the result of malarial infection.

BLACKWELL, Elizabeth. The first woman to obtain the degree of M.D. She was born in England in 1821, and settled in America with her parents in 1831, where from 1838 to 1847 she was engaged in teaching. After numerous difficulties, she was admitted into the College of Geneva, N.Y., and graduated M.D. in 1849. She afterwards studied in Paris, and commenced practice in New York in 1851, where, in 1854, with her sister Emily, she opened a hospital for women and children. From 1868 she resided in England, and died there in 1910. Her works include: *Counsels of Parents on the Moral Education of their Children in Relation to Sex* (1879), *Pioneer Work in Opening the Medical Profession to Women* (1895), etc.

BLACK-WOOD, or INDIAN ROSEWOOD. A leguminous tree of Hindustan (*Dalbergia latifolia*), the timber of which is highly valued and much used in the manufacture of fine furniture. The Australian Black-wood is the *Acacia melanoxȳlon*.

BLACK'WOOD, William. An Edinburgh publisher, born at Edinburgh 1776, died 1834. He started as a bookseller in 1804, and soon became also a publisher. The first number of *Blackwood's Magazine* appeared 1st April, 1817, and it has always been conducted in the Tory interest. He secured as contributors most of the leading writers belonging to the Tory party, among them Sir Walter Scott, Lockhart, Hogg, Professor Wilson, De Quincey, and others. The work of editor he performed himself. After his death the business, which had developed into a large publishing concern, was carried on by his sons, and the magazine still keeps its place among the leading periodicals.

BLADDER, URINARY. A muscular sac, lined inside with mucous membrane, acting as a reservoir for the urine. Its size and position vary with the amount of fluid it contains. It occupies the anterior and median portion of the pelvis—in the male situated behind the pubic bone and above and in front of the rectum; in the female above and in front of the vagina and uterus. The urine, which is excreted in the kidneys, is conveyed into the bladder by two tubes, the ureters, which enter on each side at the base of the bladder in an oblique direction to prevent regurgitation of urine. The urine is passed out of the bladder through the urethra, the internal orifice of which is also at the base in the middle line. When the bladder gradually fills with urine, it distends in all directions except in front and at the base.

BLADDER CAMPION. *See* SILENE.

BLADDER-FERN. *See* CYSTOPTERIS.

BLADDER-NUT. A name of shrubs or small trees of the genus Staphylēa, ord. Sapindaceæ, natives of Europe, Asia, and North America, the fruits of which consist of an inflated bladdery capsule containing the seeds.

BLADDER SENNA (*Colutea arborescens*). A leguminous shrub of S. Europe, with bladder-like pods and purgative properties.

BLADDER-WORM. The encysted or quiescent stage in the life-history of a tapeworm. It consists of a vesicle filled with fluid, on the inner side of which is developed a head or scolex (or more than one). If swallowed by the final host, the head becomes everted, fixes itself by hooks or suckers (or both) to the lining of the intestine, and becomes the adult tapeworm by producing a chain of flattened buds (*proglottides*), each provided with a double set of sexual organs. A Cysticercus is a simple bladder-worm with only one head, e.g. *C. cellulosæ*, found in the flesh of pigs and becoming the tapeworm of man (*Tænia solium*). A larger bladder-worm with numerous heads is a Cœnurus, e.g. *C. cerebralis*, living on the outside of the sheep's brain, and becoming the tapeworm *T. cœnurus* in the sheep-dog. Echinococcus is a very large bladder-worm, within which are secondary cysts, each resembling a Cœnurus. *E. veterinorum* is found in the liver or other abdominal organs in various hoofed mammals (and in man), and the adult tapeworm (*T. echinococcus*) is a minute form living within the dog.

BLADDERWORT. The common name of plants of the genus Utricularia, nat. ord. Lentibulariaceæ. There are over 200 species found in tropical and temperate zones, many of them being submerged water-plants, others growing in moss or as epiphytes. All bear numerous tiny pitchers or bladders on their leaves, which serve to entrap water-fleas, tadpoles, and other small animals. The structure of these bladders is remarkable, one of the most striking features being the inwardly-opening flap at the entrance which acts as a trap-door. Three species grow in Britain in pools and ditches, especially where the water is peaty; *U. vulgaris* is the commonest of these, but all are somewhat rare.

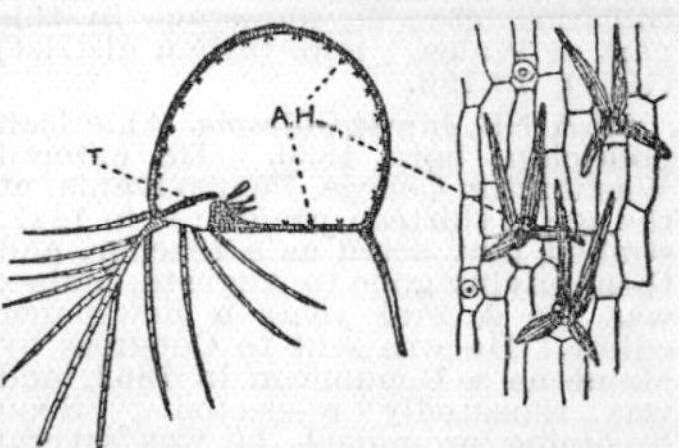

Bladderwort

Magnified section of bladder, and portion of inner surface (highly magnified). T, Trap-door. AH, Absorbing hairs.

BLADDER-WRACK (*Fucus vesiculōsus*). A seaweed so named from the floating vesicles in its fronds. *See* BROWN ALGÆ.

BLADUD′. In legendary British history, the father of King Lear, said to have founded Bath, having been cured by its waters.

BLAEBERRY. *See* WHORTLEBERRY.

BLAENAVON. A town of Monmouthshire, on the Avon, with coal-mines. Pop. (1931), 11,075.

BLAES. A miner's term for the rock known to the geologist as shale. It is a laminated indurated mud, often containing considerable quantities of carbonaceous matter.

BLAEU, BLAEUW, or **BLAUW** (blä'u̥). A Dutch family celebrated as publishers of maps and books. William (1571-1638) established the business at Amsterdam, constructed celestial and terrestrial globes, and published *Novus Atlas* (6 vols.) and *Theatrum Urbium et Munimentorum.* His son John (died 1673) published the *Atlas Magnus* (11 vols.) and various topographical plates and views of towns. The works of this family are still highly valued.

BLAGOVYESHCHENSK (blà-go-vyes'chensk). A Russian town of Eastern Siberia, capital of the province of the Amur, on the River Amur where the Zeya enters it; now an important place. Pop. 61,000.

BLAINA. A village in W. Monmouthshire, which joins with Nantyglo in forming an urban district, where are some of the tin-plate works, collieries, etc., so numerous in this part of Wales. Pop. (urban district) (1931), 13,190.

BLAINE, James Gillespie. American politician, born 1830. He entered Washington College, Pennsylvania, at the age of thirteen, graduated in 1847, studied law, acted as a teacher, and then, having gone to Augusta, Maine, was for several years a newspaper editor. He was sent to Congress by Maine as a Republican in 1862, and was repeatedly re-elected. Soon becoming prominent, he was several times Speaker of the House of Representatives. In 1876 he entered the Senate, and the same year he was second in his candidature for presidential nomination by the Republican National Convention; he was also unsuccessful in his candidature in 1880; but in 1884 he was nominated by a large majority, though the presidency went to Cleveland. In 1888, though again a candidate for nomination, he was defeated. In 1884 appeared the first volume of his *Twenty Years of Congress.* He was an advocate for protection as against free trade. He died in Jan., 1893.—Bibliography: J. E. Crawford, *James G. Blaine*; C. E. Stanwood, *James G. Blaine*; H. T. Peck, *American Party Leaders.*

BLAINVILLE (blaṇ - vēl), **Henri Marie Ducrotay de.** French naturalist, born 1777, died 1850. After attending a military school, and also studying art, his interest in Cuvier's lectures led him to the study of medicine and natural history. Cuvier chose him for his assistant in the Collège de France and the Museum of Natural History, and in 1812 secured for him the chair of anatomy and zoology in the Faculty of Sciences at Paris. In 1825 he was admitted to the Academy of Sciences; in 1829 he became professor in the Museum of Natural History, lecturing on the mollusca, zoophytes, and worms; and in 1832 he succeeded Cuvier in the chair of comparative anatomy there. His chief works are: *L'Organisation des Animaux ou Principes d'Anatomie Comparée* (1822); *Manuel de Malacologie et de Conchyliologie* (1825); *Cours de Physiologie Générale* (1833); *Manuel d'Actinologie* (1834); *Ostéographie* (1839-64), a work on the vertebrate skeleton.

BLAIR, Hugh, D.D. Scottish divine and author, born at Edinburgh 1718, died 1800. He was minister successively of Collessie in Fifeshire, Canongate Church, Edinburgh, Lady Yester's Church, and the High Church. In 1762 he was made professor of rhetoric and belles-lettres in the University of Edinburgh, being the first to occupy this chair. He is author of a *Dissertation on the Poems of Ossian*; *Lectures on Rhetoric and Belles Lettres*; and *Sermons,* which were long greatly esteemed, and which, attracting the attention of George III., procured for the author a pension of £200 a year.

BLAIR, Robert. Author of *The Grave,* born in Edinburgh 1699, died 1746. He was ordained, in 1731, minister of Athelstaneford, where he spent the remainder of his life. His famous work *The Grave* (1743) was once esteemed as one of the standard classics of English poetical literature. His third son, Robert (1741-1811), rose to be president of the Court of Session.

BLAIR-ATH'OLL. A village of Scotland, Perthshire, 34½ miles N.N.W. of Perth. Near it is Blair Castle, the seat of the Duke of Atholl. Pop. 1557.

BLAIRGOW'RIE. A burgh in Perthshire, Scotland, on the Ericht, united with Rattray in 1929. It has linen manufactures and cultivation of small fruits. Pop. (1931), 4676.

BLAKE, Edward. Canadian lawyer and statesman, born in 1833, died in 1912. He was educated at Toronto, graduating from University College in 1857. He was called to the Bar in 1859, and speedily gained a high position in his profession. In 1867 he became a member of the Ontario, as well as of the Canadian, Parliament, and in the former took the position of leader of the Liberal opposition. On his party coming into power in 1871, he became Premier of the Ontario legislature, but after one session resigned. In 1873 he became a member of the Canadian Cabinet, and soon after President of the Council and Minister of Justice under the Mackenzie administration, which lost office in 1878. He was afterwards leader of the Liberal party in the Canadian legislature, but resigned the position in 1887. In 1892 he was elected member for an Irish constituency (S. Longford) in the British Parliament, and became an active member of the Home Rule party, but retired in 1907.

BLAKE, Robert. A celebrated British admiral, born at Bridgewater in 1599, died at the entrance of Plymouth Sound, 1657. On finishing his education at Oxford, he lived for some time in a private manner on the fortune left him by his father. He was elected member for Bridgewater in the Parliament of 1640. This being soon dissolved, he lost his election for the next, and sought to advance the Parliamentary cause in a military capacity in the war which then broke out. He soon distinguished himself, and in 1649 he was sent to command the fleet with Colonels Deane and Popham. He attempted to block up Prince Rupert in Kinsale, but the prince, contriving to get his fleet out, escaped to Lisbon, where Blake followed him. Being refused permission to attack him in the Tagus by the King of Portugal, he took several rich prizes from the Portuguese, and followed Rupert to Malaga, where, without asking permission of Spain, he attacked him and nearly destroyed the whole of his fleet.

His greatest achievements were, however, in the Dutch war which broke out in 1652. On the 19th of May he was attacked in the Downs by Van Tromp with a fleet of forty-five sail, the force of Blake amounting only to twenty-three, but Van Tromp was obliged to retreat. On 29th May he was again attacked by Van Tromp, whose fleet was now increased to eighty sail. Blake had a very inferior force, and after every possible exertion was obliged to retreat into the Thames. In February following he put to sea with sixty sail, and soon after met the Dutch admiral, who had seventy sail and 300 merchantmen under convoy. During three days a running fight up the Channel was maintained with obstinate valour on both sides, the result of which was the loss of eleven men-of-war and thirty merchant ships by the Dutch, while that of the English was only one man-of-war. In this action Blake was severely wounded.

On 3rd June he again engaged Van Tromp, and forced the Dutch to retire with considerable loss into their own harbours. In Nov., 1654, he was sent with a strong fleet to enforce a due respect to the British flag in the Mediterranean. He sailed first to Algiers, which submitted, and then demolished the castles of Goletta and Porto Ferino, at Tunis, because the dey refused to deliver up the British captives. A squadron of his ships also blocked up Cadiz, and intercepted a Spanish Plate fleet. In April, 1657, he sailed with twenty-four ships to Santa Cruz, in Teneriffe; and, notwithstanding the strength of the place, burned the ships of another Spanish Plate fleet which had taken shelter there, and by a fortunate change of wind came out without loss. He died before landing on English soil, and was buried in Westminster Abbey, whence his body was removed at the Restoration and buried in St. Margaret's Churchyard.—BIBLIOGRAPHY: Doctor Johnson, *Life of Blake*; Hepworth Dixon, *Robert Blake, Admiral and General at Sea.*

BLAKE, William. Mystic artist and poet, author of much poetry, and of designs mainly allegorical or symbolical. He was the son of a London hosier, and was born in 1757. He was apprenticed to an engraver at the age of fourteen. After completing his apprenticeship, he was for a short time a student in the Royal Academy, and for years supported himself mainly by engraving for the booksellers. In 1782 he married Catherine Boucher, who proved an invaluable help to him in his work. Next year he published *Poetical Sketches* without illustrations. *Poetical Sketches* was printed and published in the ordinary way, but, failing to find a publisher for his next work, *Songs of Innocence,* he invented a process by which he was both printer and illustrator of his own poems. He engraved upon copper both the text of his poems and the surrounding decorative design and to the pages printed from the plates an appropriate colouring was afterwards added by hand. In this way the whole of his future work was produced.

Some of his other best-known works are: *Gates of Paradise, Book of Thel, Marriage of Heaven and Hell, Songs of Experience, Book of Urizen, Song of Los, Book of Ahania,* etc. He also illustrated Young's *Night Thoughts,* Blair's *Grave,* and *The Book of Job.* The distinguishing feature of his genius was the faculty of seeing the creations of his imagination with such vividness that they were as real to him as objects of sense. He died in 1828. Lives of Blake have been written by Alex.

Gilchrist (1863) and William Rossetti (1874); and a critical essay on his life and works by A. C. Swinburne was published in 1868. His complete poetical works were collected in 1874, and a volume of etchings from his works, with descriptive text by W. B. Scott, was published in 1878. In 1893 appeared *The Works of W. Blake*, edited by E. J. Ellis and W. B. Yeats; and in 1905 *Poetical Works* edited by John Sampson.—BIBLIOGRAPHY: A. Symons, *William Blake*; E. J. Ellis, *The Real Blake*; B. de Selincourt, *William Blake*; G. K. Chesterton, *William Blake*; A. G. R. Russell, *Engravings of William Blake*; C. Gardner, *W. Blake: the Man*.

BLAKENEY. Village on the Norfolk coast, 5 miles from Holt. At Blakeney Point is a bird sanctuary covering 1100 acres.

BLANC (bläṇ), **Auguste Alexandre Philippe Charles.** Younger brother of Louis Blanc, born 1813, died 1882. An eminent art-critic, he was elected a member of the French Academy in 1878, and filled the chair of æsthetics and art-history in the Collège de France. He wrote *Grammaire des Arts du Dessin*, *L'Art dans la Parure et dans le Vêtement*, *Observations sur les Arts Egyptien et Arabe*, etc.

BLANC (bläṇ), **Jean Joseph Charles Louis.** French historian, publicist, and politician, born at Madrid 1811, died at Paris 1882. He was educated at Rhodez and Paris, and early devoted himself to the career of journalism. In 1839 he founded the *Revue du Progrès*, in which first appeared his *De l'Organization du Travail.* Between 1841 and 1844 appeared his *Histoire de Dix Ans: 1830-1840.* On the outbreak of the revolution of 1848 Blanc was elected a member of the Provisional Government, and appointed president for the discussion of the labour question. After the closing of the Ateliers Nationaux, a scheme which he strenuously opposed, and the June insurrection of 1848, he was prosecuted for conspiracy, but escaped to England. During his residence there, he wrote the bulk of his *Histoire de la Révolution Française.* His other works of note are: *Lettres sur l'Angleterre* (1865-7), *Histoire de la Révolution de 1848* (1870), *Questions d'Aujourd'hui et de Demain* (1873-4). On the downfall of the Second Empire, Blanc returned to Paris, and became a member of the National Assembly. His ideas have had a great influence on the development of Socialism in France.

BLANC, MONT. *See* MONT BLANC.

BLANCHARD (bläṇ-shär), **François.** French aeronaut, born 1753, died 1809. In 1785 he crossed the Channel in a balloon, for which feat he received a pension from the French king. He made many remarkable ascents in various parts of the world. His wife, born 1778, was his companion in many of his voyages, and was killed by her balloon taking fire, 1819.

BLANCHARD (blan'shärd), **Laman.** English miscellaneous writer, born in 1804, died 1845. In 1828 he published a volume of poetry, entitled *Lyrical Offerings.* In 1831 he became editor of the *Monthly Magazine*, and was afterwards connected with several magazines and newspapers. The death of his wife affected him so deeply that in a moment of temporary insanity he committed suicide. His tales and essays, entitled *Sketches from Life*, were published with a memoir by Lord Lytton in 1849; his poetical works in 1876.

BLANCHE OF CASTILE. Daughter of Alphonso IX., queen of Louis VIII., King of France, and mother of St. Louis, born 1187, died 1252. On the death of Louis VIII. she procured the coronation of her son, and during his minority held the reins of government in his name with distinguished success. In 1244, when St. Louis left for the Holy Land, she again became regent, and gave new proofs of her abilities and firmness as a ruler.

BLANCH-HOLDING. A mode of tenure not infrequent in Scotland by which the tenant is bound to pay only a nominal, or trifling, yearly duty to his superior, as an acknowledgment of his right, and only if demanded.

BLANCHING. *See* ETIOLATION.

BLANC-MANGE (blė-mäṇzh'). In cookery, a name of different preparations of the consistency of a jelly, variously composed of dissolved isinglass, arrow-root, maize-flour, etc., with milk and flavouring substances.

BLANCO, CAPE (literally, "White Cape"). An African cape, on the west coast of the Sahara, discovered by the Portuguese in 1441.

BLANDFORD FORUM. A municipal borough, England, County Dorset, giving the title of marquess to the Duke of Marlborough. Pop. (1931), 3371.

BLANE, Sir Gilbert. Scottish physician, born in Ayrshire 1749, died 1834. He was educated at Edinburgh University, but took the degree of M.D. at Glasgow. He became private physician to Admiral Rodney, and then physician to the fleet in the W. Indies, in which position he introduced the use of lime-juice and other means of preventing scurvy into the navy. From 1783 to 1795 he was physician in St. Thomas's Hospital. He was physician-in-ordinary to George IV, both before and after he became king. His chief publication is *Elements of Medical Logic* (1819).

BLANESBURGH, Lord. British lawyer. Born 12th Sept., 1861, Robert Younger went to Edinburgh Academy and Balliol College, Oxford. He became a barrister and in 1915 was made a judge. In 1919 he joined the Court of Appeal, and in 1923 was made a Lord of Appeal and a life peer. He presided over the committee that inquired into the subject of unemployment insurance. Lord Blanesburgh was appointed chief British delegate on the Reparations Commission in Paris in 1925.

BLANGY. A village in France, department Pas-de-Calais. It was the scene of fierce fighting in the European War.

BLAN'KENBERGHE (-berg). A much-frequented seaside resort on the coast of Belgium. Pop. 6053; in summer, 60,000.

BLAN'KENBURG. A town of Germany, in the former duchy of Brunswick, on the northern slope of the Hartz Mountains, a favourite resort of tourists. On the summit of a height is the ducal palace. Pop. 11,490.

BLAN'KENESE (-nā-ze). A town on the right bank of the Elbe, 5 miles W. of Altona; a pleasure-resort of the Altonese and Hamburgers. Pop. 4736.

BLANKETEERS. Nickname given to some Manchester operatives in 1817. About 5000 men assembled on 10th March in St. Peter's Field, each carrying provisions and a blanket, purposing to walk to London to lay their grievances before the Prince Regent. The gathering caused some consternation and the Habeas Corpus Act was suspended. The leaders were taken and imprisoned, and the project frustrated.

BLANKNEY. Village of Lincolnshire. It is 8 miles from Sleaford, on the L.N.E. Rly. The hall was long the seat of Viscount Chaplin and here are the kennels of the Blankney Hunt, one of the most famous in England.

BLANK VERSE. Verse without rhyme, first introduced into English poetry (from the Italian) by the Earl of Surrey, who was beheaded in 1547. Blank verse was first employed in the English drama by Sackville in *Gorboduc* (1561). The most common form of English blank verse is the decasyllabic; such as that of Milton's *Paradise Lost*, or of the plays of Shakespeare. From Shakespeare's time it has been the kind of verse almost universally used by dramatic writers, who often employ an additional syllable, making the lines not strictly decasyllabic. One of the earliest appearances of the term blank verse is in *Hamlet*, ii., 2: "The lady shall say her mind freely, or the blank verse shall halt for't", though Nash used the phrase in 1589. The term is not applied to the Anglo-Saxon and Early English alliterative unrhymed verse.

BLANQUI (blän-kē), **Jerome Adolphe** French economist, born at Nice 1798, died at Paris 1854. While studying medicine at Paris, he made acquaintance with Jean Baptiste Say, and was induced to devote himself to the study of economics. He succeeded Say in the Conservatoire des Arts et Métiers as professor of industrial economy. Blanqui, who favoured a free-trade policy, published, among other works, *Précis Elémentaire d'Economie Politique* and *Histoire de l'Economie Politique en Europe*.

BLANQUI, Louis Auguste. Brother of the above, born 1805, died 1881, was early engaged as a socialistic revolutionist and conspirator, and spent much of his life in prison for his extreme opinions and actions. In 1870 he established a club and journal, *La Patrie en Danger*. His writings were collected in 1885 under the title of *Critique Sociale*. *See* COMMUNISM.

BLANTYRE (-tīr'). A populous mining parish in Lanarkshire, Scotland, containing the town of Stonefield (pop. 7288), and several villages, at one of which (Low Blantyre) Dr. Livingstone was born. Pop. 17,015. The name has been given to an African mission station founded in 1876 by the Established Church of Scotland, between the Upper Shiré River and Lake Shirwa, now a centre of settlement and trade.

BLAP'SIDÆ. A family of nocturnal black beetles, whose wings are generally obsolete and their elytra soldered together. They frequent gloomy damp places, and when seized discharge, in self-defence, a liquid of a peculiar penetrating odour. *Blaps mortisāga*, or church-yard beetle, is the most familiar British specimen.

BLAR'NEY. A village, Ireland,

5 miles N.W. of the city of Cork, with Blarney Castle in its vicinity. A stone called the *Blarney Stone*, near the top of the castle, is said to confer on those who kiss it the peculiar kind of persuasive eloquence alleged to be characteristic of the natives of Ireland. The "groves of Blarney" are extensive and interesting. Pop. 778.

BLASCO IBAÑEZ. *See* IBAÑEZ.

BLA'SIUS, or **BLAISE, ST.** Bishop of Sebaste, in Armenia, is said to have suffered martyrdom about 316. He is said to have been tortured with a wool-comb, hence he is claimed as the patron-saint of the wool-combers.

BLAS'PHEMY is the denying of the existence of God, assigning to Him false attributes, or denying His true attributes; contumelious reproaches of our Saviour; profane scoffing at the Holy Scriptures, or exposing them to ridicule and contempt. In Catholic countries it also includes the speaking contemptuously or disrespectfully of the Holy Virgin or the saints. By the common law of England blasphemies of God, as denying His being and providence, all contumelious reproaches of Jesus Christ, etc., are punishable by fine and imprisonment, or corporal punishment. According to a celebrated judgment of Lord Hales, "Christianity being parcel of the law of England, to reproach the Christian religion is to speak in subversion of the law"; but in a case decided in 1883 it was held that a person may attack the fundamentals of religion without being guilty of a blasphemous libel "if the decencies of controversy are observed". Thus, although the English law still embodies the tradition which treats blasphemy as a sin, in practice it treats it as an offence against the peace and good order of society. Police court proceedings are frequently taken against persons for blasphemy. In Scotland the punishment for blasphemy was death, but by the Acts of 1825 and 1837 this was changed to a fine or imprisonment. Profane swearing and cursing is punishable by the Profane Oaths Act, 1745. Similar laws are in force in other countries.

BLAST, HOT. *See* BLAST-FURNACE.

BLAST-FURNACE. The name given to the smelting-furnace used for obtaining metal or matte from ore mixed with suitable fuel and flux with the aid of a blast of air. It may be circular, elliptical, or rectangular in cross-section, and the height is considerably greater than the width. It is largely used for the extraction of iron, copper, and lead from their ores, and to some extent in the extraction of tin, antimony, and nickel. The blast-furnace used for the smelting of iron-ores is a tall cylindrical structure, 80 to 100 feet high, consisting of a shell of iron or mild-steel plates lined with fire-bricks. The widest part of the furnace, situated

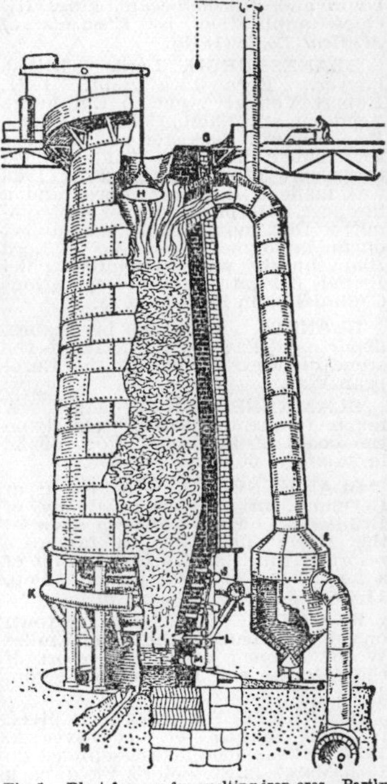

Fig. 1.—Blast furnace for smelting iron-ores. Partly in section to show construction

K, Hot-blast pipe from blast-heating stove. L, Tuyeres (see fig. 2). J, Water-pipes. M, Slag-notch. N, Molten iron from tap-hole. H, Bell for closing mouth of furnace. G, Charging platform. F, Down-comer, carrying off gases from furnace. E, Dust-catcher. O, Gas-main.

a little less than half-way up, is known as the *bose*, above this is known as the shaft or body, and below it as the *boshes*, which taper to the hearth in which the molten iron collects. The opening at the top, where the ore, fuel (usually coke), and flux (usually limestone) are admitted, is the throat, which is closed by a cup-and-cone arrangement for the admission of the charge and the prevention of the escape of the waste gases which are largely used for burning under boilers, or for driving gas-engines.

The air-blast, which is propelled by a powerful blowing-engine, is heated to a temperature of 1000° to 1500° F., and injected into the furnace through tuyeres situated near the top of the hearth of the furnace. The use of hot blast in iron-smelting was due to James B. Neilson, of Glasgow, and was introduced in 1828. It has been the means of great economies in fuel-consumption and large increases in the output of furnaces. Further economies in fuel have been more recently effected by drying the air previous to its use. In 1905 Gayley published the first results obtained by drying the air used in the Isabella blast-furnace near Pittsburg, which showed an increase in output of 25 per cent, and a decrease in fuel consumption of 20 per cent. The charging of the furnace goes on day and night, the charge being kept within a few feet of the top. The molten iron, which collects at the bottom, is run from time to time into pigs in sand-moulds or into special moulds carried on an endless chain, whilst the slag formed from the extraneous matter in the ore, the flux, and the ash of the fuel is run into slag-bogies for disposal.

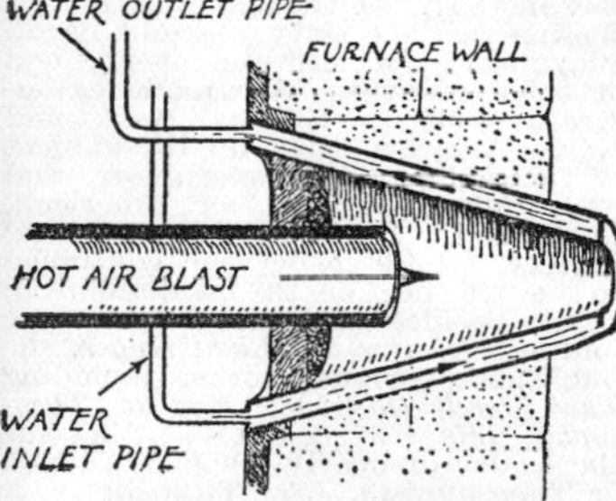

Fig. 2.—Section of furnace wall, showing a Tuyere in section

Blast-furnaces produce up to 500 tons of pig-iron per 24 hours, 5 to 6 tons of air are required, and, on an average, 1 ton of coke per ton of iron produced. In the smelting of copper-ores, the blast-furnace is mainly used for the treatment of sulphide-ores with the object of producing a matte which consists of sulphides of copper and iron in various proportions, and from which the copper is subsequently extracted. For example, a copper-ore containing 3 to 5 per cent of copper may be smelted to a matte containing 30 to 40 per cent copper. The furnaces used are not so tall as iron blast-furnaces, are usually rectangular in cross-section, up to 54 inches wide, and may be over 100 feet long. The walls generally consist of a double casing of iron or mild steel, and in the space between the two casings a stream of water is caused to flow, thus constituting a water-jacketed furnace. No lining of fire-brick is required, as a thin deposit of slag solidifies on the lining and protects it from the action of the charge. A lower pressure of blast is used, and the matte and slag are allowed to run from the furnace into a settler, where they are separated. The furnaces used for lead-smelting are generally smaller than copper-matting furnaces but wider. Water-jackets are used round the boshes of the furnace, but the shaft is lined with fire-brick, and the hearth or crucible is fitted with a siphon arrangement for the withdrawal of the lead.—BIBLIOGRAPHY: Carl Schnabel, *Handbook of Metallurgy*, translated by Henry Louis; Sir W. C. Roberts-Austen, *Introduction to the Study of Metallurgy*; A. H. Hiorns, *Principles of Metallurgy*.

BLASTINE. *See* EXPLOSIVES.

BLASTING. The operation of breaking up masses of stone or rock by means of explosives, as in quarrying, mining, tunnelling, etc. In ordinary operations holes are bored into the rock of from 1 to 3 inches in diameter, by means of a steel-pointed drill, by striking it with hand-hammers or by means of a pneumatic hammer-drill. After the hole is bored to the requisite depth, it is cleaned out, the explosive is introduced, the hole is "tamped" or filled up above with clay or sand, and the charge exploded by means of a fuse or by electricity. In larger operations mines or shafts of considerable diameter take the place of such holes. Shafts are sunk to depths sometimes of more than 60 feet, and from the main shaft, or shafts, galleries or headings are driven some distance in various directions, with headings at intervals, terminating in chambers for the charges. Enormous charges are frequently made use of, upwards of 20 tons of gunpowder having been fired in a single blast.

One of the greatest blasting operations ever attempted was the removal of the reefs in the East River, near New York, known as Hellgate. An entrance-shaft was first sunk, from which a number of galleries or tunnels were bored in various directions, connected by numerous intersecting galleries, all pierced with a vast number of holes for charges. Upwards of 100 tons of rend-rock, besides dynamite and powder, were used, and millions of tons of rock were dislodged. The blowing up of the Vimy Ridge during the late war is another example of a huge blast. Numerous important improvements have been made in blasting by the substitution of rock-boring machines for hand-labour. Of such machines in which the "jumper" or drill is repeatedly driven against the rock by compressed air or steam, being also made to rotate slightly at each blow, there are many varieties.

Improvements in blasting-agents and drilling have been important factors in the recent development of mining. The explosives now used belong usually to the nitro-glycerine class, and are fired by detonators containing fulminate of mercury. In placing the holes for blasting, the nature and inclination of the strata, and the position of the holes relatively to each other, have to be carefully considered to obtain the best results. The charge is usually ignited by electricity, and delay-action fuses may be used to fire several charges in proper rotation. The charges may be connected to the exploder in series, in parallel, or in series parallel. Low-tension fuses are the safest to use, as they can be tested before use. Great advances have been made in the manufacture of so-called flameless explosives for use in gassy mines during recent years. The Mines Act prohibits the use of other than permitted explosives in all coal-mines.—BIBLIOGRAPHY: Drinker, *Tunnelling, Explosive Compounds and Rock Drills*; C. Prelini, *Earth and Rock Excavation*; C. le Neve Foster, *A Treatise on Ore and Stone-Mining*; Spon's *Dictionary of Engineering*, article *Boring and Blasting*.

BLASTING GELATINE. A powerful explosive which consists of a solution of gun-cotton in a far larger quantity of nitro-glycerine, forming a yellowish jelly-like mass that is exploded by means of a detonator.

BLAS'TODERM (Gr. *blastŏs*, a germ; *dĕrma*, skin). In biology, the external cellular part of a very young embryo, from which the body and embryonic membranes are formed. *See* EMBRYOLOGY.

BLASTOGEN'ESIS. In biology, Weismann's theory of origin from germ plasma. *See* EMBRYOLOGY.

BLASTOI'DEA. An entirely extinct group of Echinodermata, allied to the crinoids, are found in Palæozoic rocks. The animal was enclosed in a case formed of calcareous plates, and had not free arms; but appendages like those on crinoid arms have been found on the pore-bearing areas, which are five in number, and run from the summit almost to the base of the bud-like case. There is a short stem for attachment to the sea-floor.

BLAS'TOMERE (Gr. *blastŏs*, a germ; *mĕrŏs*, a part). In biology, the term applied to each cell into which the ovum divides after fertilisation.

BLAT'TIDÆ. A family of insects of the ord. Orthoptera. They are extremely voracious, some species apparently eating almost everything that comes in their way. The type of the family is the well-known cockroach (*Periplaneta orientālis*).

BLAVAT'SKY, Helen. A Russian theosophist, was born in Ekaterinoslav in 1831. At the age of seventeen she married the sixty-year-old Baron Blavatsky, but left him at the end of three months. She made extensive travels in Europe, Asia, and North America, took up the subject of theosophy and Eastern lore, and with Colonel Olcott, an American, founded in 1875 the Theosophical Society, whose leader she continued to be till her death in London in 1891. Besides editing a theosophistic journal, *Lucifer the Lightbringer*, she published various works, including *The Secret Doctrine*, *Key to Theosophy*, *Isis Unveiled*, etc. She was the leader of nearly 100,000 Adepts, or Theosophists. *See* THEOSOPHY.

BLAYDON. A town of England, County Durham, on the south bank of the Tyne, about 4 miles west of Newcastle, near a bridge across the river. It has bottle-works, foundries, collieries, manufactures of sanitary earthenware, fire-bricks, chemical manures, etc. Since 1918 Blaydon gives its name to a parliamentary division of the county. Pop. (1931), 32,259.

BLAYE (blā). A fortified port of France on the Gironde, covering with other forts the approach to Bordeaux. Pop. 4250.

BLA'ZONRY. In heraldry, the art of describing coats-of-arms in proper technical terms and method.

BLEACHING. The technical term which denotes various processes by means of which fibres, yarns, and cloth are made to appear much lighter in colour than they were before being subjected to the chemical actions involved in the processes. Several substances are used for bleaching, e.g. calcium hypochlorite, sodium hypochlorite, sodium peroxide, hydrogen peroxide, the choice of which depends upon the particular substance to be treated. Bleaching is practised extensively in connection with cotton and linen goods, the more extended process being applied to linen, because the flax fibre is more difficult to bleach than the cotton fibre; the latter contains a higher percentage of cellulose than does the former. The methods adopted for bleaching yarns differ naturally from those for bleaching cloth, although the agents used may be the same; in both cases it is usually essential to perform the operation with a view to economic production.

The degrees of whiteness to which yarns are brought by the process are known in general as "half-bleach", "three-quarter-bleach", and "full-bleach", or their equivalents "duck", "house-duck", and "high-house-duck", the symbols for which are respectively D., H.D., and H.H.D. There are other stages besides these, such as boiled, soured, creamed, and changed. The colour of cloth is distinguished by the same names, and to facilitate the operations it is usual to sew several pieces end to end, after each has been marked for identification, and to draw the length of cloth through a porcelain guide, over a guide-roller in the liming-machine, under rollers immersed in the milk of lime, between squeezing-rollers and again under the immersed rollers. This method of threading the cloth is repeated until several rounds are formed, the cloth being guided by successive pegs, so that a long length of cloth may be accommodated in the machine, and each part of the cloth passes in and out of the milk of lime in its journey from one end of the machine to the other, and thus becomes impregnated with the solution.

The length of cloth is drawn from the liming-machine over a winch, and arranged in folds over the perforated plate at the bottom of the lime-pot or boiling "kier." When all the cloth is in the kier, the lid is clamped down and steam admitted. The condensed steam and the milk of lime in the cloth provide the solution, and the boiling is continued for six to ten hours. The liquid is forced up a central pipe, impinges against a concave plate, from which it rebounds, to be deposited on the cloth and to percolate through the folds. When the boiling is completed, the liquid is run off and fresh water flushed into the kier; then the cloth is removed to the washing-machine. High-pressure kiers are often used for the above lime-boiling process.

After a thorough washing, the cloth is immersed in a tank of hydrochloric acid of about 2½° Twaddell. This operation is termed the "lime sour," and any lime which has not been removed by washing reacts with the hydrochloric acid. Thus: $Ca(OH)_2 + 2HCl \rightarrow CaCl_2 + 2H_2O$. The calcium chloride, being soluble in water, may be removed by washing. The second boil or "lye-boil" follows, and for this soda-ash or a mixture of soda-ash and caustic soda is made into solution, in which the cloth is boiled for six to eight hours. The "chemicking" process in the chemic system comes next, the cloth being immersed for three or four hours in a solution of bleaching-powder (calcium hypochlorite or sodium hypochlorite of about ¾° Twaddell, often the former substance). The hypochlorite reacts with the hydrochloric acid as follows: $CaOCl_2 + 2HCl \rightarrow CaCl_2 + HCl + HOCl$; and $HOCl \rightarrow HCl + O$, and the colouring-matter of the cloth is oxidised by the free oxygen.

A second or even a third immersion in the chemic cistern takes place. The cloth now passes to the "scald," a boiling process after chemicking, as distinct from the "lye-boil," which preceded chemicking. Soda-ash is again used, the scalding is continued from three to six hours. Then follows a second chemick and a second scald, a third chemick, and then an immersion for two hours in hydrochloric acid. The bleaching is now complete, and it only remains to wash the cloth thoroughly. In some cases the cloth, when not urgently wanted, is spread in the fields. One, two, or three "works," as the cycle of operations is termed, are conducted according to the degree of whiteness desired.

The long length of cloth is in a more or less twisted or compressed condition during the whole of the bleaching operations, but it is necessary to open it out to its full width for the finishing operations. As the cloth is drawn from the last washing-machine, the creases or folds are removed by the scrolls and beaters of a scutching- and expanding-machine, and delivered in full width by the plaiting-down apparatus. The cloth may be fed mechanically from the scutcher or by hand to the starch-box of a mangle, led through the starch-mixture, and then guided by expanders to a number of steam-heated pans or cylinders in order that it may be dried to the desired degree. Damasks and similar elaborate cloths are also starched in the same way, but guided, stretched and partially dried in what is known as a stentering-machine, some of which for plain cloth are provided with jigging and weft-straightening mechanism. The automatic guiding apparatus ensures that the selvages shall be at their proper position with regard to the stenter-clips, and the latter are so constructed that they are incapable of gripping any part of the cloth except the selvage, but as soon as the two selvages are gripped the stretching action commences. Several types of plain cloth are stretched by belt-stretching machines, and other plain cloths are beetled either by a wood faller-bettle or by a spring beetle. They are then examined and again sewn end to end for calendering, after which the finished goods are made up into parcels suitable for the various markets. — BIBLIOGRAPHY: M. Bottler, *Modern Bleaching Agents and Detergents*; S. R. Trotman (and E. L. Thorp), *The Principles of Bleaching and Finishing of Cotton*; J. Huebner, *Bleaching and Dyeing of Vegetable Fibrous Materials*.

BLEACHING-POWDER, or Chloride of lime. Is made by exposing slaked lime to the action of chlorine. It is generally regarded as chloro-hypochlorite of calcium ($CaOC_2$). It is soft white powder with a distinct odour of chlorine, partly soluble in water, yielding a solution which is alkaline in reaction. It liberates chlorine on the addition of acids, and is much used as a disinfectant, an oxidiser, and a bleaching agent.

BLEAK. A small river fish, 6 or 7 inches long, the *Leuciscus alburnus*, of the Carp family. It somewhat resembles the dace, and is found in many European and British rivers. Its back is greenish, otherwise it is of a silvery colour, and its silvery scales are used in the manufacture of artificial pearls, an industry introduced from China about the middle of the seventeenth century. It is good eating.

BLECHNUM. *See* HARD-FERN.

BLEEDING. *See* HEMORRHAGE and PHLEBOTOMY.

BLEEDING HEART. *See* DIELYTRA.

BLEEDING OF PLANTS. The name given to the flow of sap which takes place from cut stems under certain conditions. The amount exuded varies in different plants, from a few drops to several gallons in a day. The pressure under which the liquid is forced out is likewise very variable, as is the duration of the bleeding, which may continue for months in the Century-plant, and even for years in the palm *Arenga saccharifera*. According to Humboldt, a single individual of the Century-plant may yield as much as 250 gallons of sap in this way. The bleeding-sap of the Vine is almost pure water, but that of the Sugar Maple contains over 3 per cent, and that of the Century-plant nearly 9 per cent of sugar. The exact cause of bleeding is not clear; doubtless it often has some connection with root-pressure, but this explanation does not apply to some of the most striking instances, such as the Toddy-palms, in which the effect of the wounds inflicted on the living tissues seems to have a share in producing the active flow of sap.

BLEEK (blāk), **Friedrich.** German biblical scholar and critic, born 1793, appointed professor of theology at Bonn 1829, died 1859. He was the author of expository books, *Introductions to the Old and New Testaments* (1860-2), etc.

BLEEK, Wilhelm Heinrich Immanuel. Son of the above, an able linguist, especially in the South African languages, born in Berlin 1827, died at Cape Town 1875. In 1855 he went to South Africa and devoted himself to the study of the language, manners, and customs of the natives. In 1860 he was appointed public librarian at Cape Town, and his researches were rewarded with a pension from the civil list. He was principal author of the *Handbook of African, Australian, and Polynesian Philology* (1858-63), his other chief productions being *Vocabulary of the Mozambique Languages* (1856), *Comparative Grammar of South African Languages* (1862), *Hottentot Fables and Tales* (1864), and *The Origin of Language* (1868).

BLEIBTREU, Karl. German poet and dramatist, born in 1859. He was educated in Berlin and London, and in 1886 he proclaimed in his famous work *Die Revolution der Litteratur* modern naturalistic tendencies. In 1889 he was one of the originators of the *Freie Bühne* which was founded in Berlin. Among his works, which show power and individuality, are: *Geschichte der deutschen Litteratur*, *Lord Byron* (a drama), *Kosmische Lieder*, *Grössenwahn* (a novel), *Zur Geschichte der Taktik und Strategie*, etc.

BLENDE (Ger. *blenden*, to blind). A term applied by mineralogists to several minerals having a peculiar lustre, as ruby-blende, horneblende, and zinc-blende. The term is now chiefly applied to the sulphide of zinc (ZnS) frequently called black-jack by the miner. Zinc-blende when pure contains 67 per cent of zinc, but iron is usually present to the extent of 1 or 2 per cent or more. It occurs in veins usually associated with galena, calcite, and fluor-spar. Its colour ranges from yellow to deep brown or black. When scratched it yields a brown powder. It is the most abundant of the zinc-bearing minerals, and the most important ore of the metal.

BLENHEIM (blen'im ; Ger. blen'-hīm). A village in Bavaria, on the Danube. Near it was fought, 13th Aug., 1704, during the War of the Spanish Succession, the famous battle of Blenheim (or *Höchstädt*, from another village in the vicinity), in which Marlborough and Prince Eugene, commanding the allied forces of England and Germany (52,000 men), gained a brilliant victory over the French and Bavarians (56,000). The victors lost some 12,000 in killed and wounded ; the vanquished 40,000, including prisoners, of whom Villars was one.—The palatial residence of the Dukes of Marlborough at Woodstock, Oxfordshire, was named from this victory. The estate of Woodstock, which belonged to the Crown, having been conferred by Queen Anne on the great Commander, Parliament granted a perpetual pension of £4000 a year, and half a million sterling to erect a suitable family seat. Sir John Vanburgh was the architect.

BLENHEIM DOG. A variety of spaniel, bearing a close resemblance to the King Charles breed, but somewhat smaller, so named from having been originally bred by one of the Dukes of Marlborough. It has a short muzzle, long silky hair without any curl, and long pendulous ears.

BLENNORHŒ'A. In medicine, a copious discharge from a mucous membrane.

BLENNY. A genus of acanthopterygious fishes (Blennius) distinguished by a short rounded head and a long compressed smooth body. Owing to the smallness of their gill openings, they can exist for some time without water. Several species frequent the British coasts, as the *B. Montagui*, or Montagu's blenny ; *B. ocellaris*, the ocellated blenny or butterfly-fish ; *B. pholis*, the shanny. Many of the genus hatch their young within the body of the female and produce them alive.

BLÉRÉ (blā-rā). A French town, department of Indre-et-Loire, on the Cher, 15 miles E.S.E. of Tours. Pop. 2043. In the vicinity is the Château Chénonceaux (q.v.).

BLÉRIOT. A type of monoplane built by Louis Blériot, the French airman, who was the first to fly across the English Channel (1909), employing a machine of this type.

BLESBOK (*Alcelăphus albifrons*). An antelope of South Africa with a white-marked face, a general purplish-chocolate colour, and a "saddle" of a bluish colour ; found in great numbers in the Transvaal and elsewhere, and much hunted.

BLESSED THISTLE (*Carduus benedictus*). A native of the south of Europe, formerly in great repute as a medicinal plant.—Cf. *Much Ado about Nothing*, iii., 4, 72.

BLESSING, or BENEDICTION. A prayer or solemn wish imploring happiness upon another ; a certain holy action which, combined with prayer, seeks for God's grace for persons, and, in a lower degree, a blessing upon things, with a view either to their efficiency or safety. The lifting up of hands is practised in the act of ceremonial blessing. In the Roman Catholic Church the sign of the cross is made, and the thumb and the two first fingers of the right hand are extended, the two remaining fingers turned down. In the Greek Church the thumb and the third finger of the same hand are conjoined, the other fingers being stretched out. Some see in this position a representation of the sacred monogram in Greek letters of our Lord's name.—In the English liturgy there are two blessings or benedictions ; in the service of the Scottish Episcopal Church there is only one.

BLESSINGTON, Marguerite, Countess of, was born near Clonmel, Ireland, 1789, died at Paris 1849. She was the daughter of Mr. Edmund Power, an improvident man of good family, and at the age of fifteen was married to a Captain Farmer, who died in 1817 ; and a few months after his death his widow married Charles John Gardiner, Earl of Blessington. In 1822 they went abroad, and continued to reside on the Continent till the earl's death in 1829, when Lady Blessington took up her abode in Gore House, Kensington. Her residence became the fashionable resort for all the celebrities of the time ; and that notwithstanding a doubtful connection which she formed with Count d'Orsay, with whom she lived till her death. In 1834 she published her *Conversations with Lord Byron.* She wrote numerous novels, including *The Belle* *of a Season, The Two Friends, Strathern*, and *The Victims of Society*; and acted as editress for several years of Heath's *Book of Beauty, The Keepsake*, and the *Gems of Beauty*.

BLETCHLEY. Village of Buckinghamshire. It is 46½ miles from London, and is an important junction on the L.M.S. system. Pop. 6169.

BLICHER (blē'*h*er), **Steen Steensen,** Danish lyrical poet and novelist born 1782, died 1848. His collected poems, which are national and spirited, were published 1835-6, and his novels, which give admirable pictures of country life in Jutland, in 1846-7. He also translated Ossian, and Goldsmith's *Vicar of Wakefield.*

BLICKLING. Village of Norfolk. It is on the Bure near Aylesham, and is famous for its hall. The property of the Marquis of Lothian, this stands in a fine park. Earlier the estate belonged to the Boleyn family. In 1932 the fine library was sold in New York.

BLIDA (blē'dä). A fortified town of Algeria 32 miles inland by rail from Algiers, well-built, with modern houses and public edifices, the centre of a flourishing district, and having a good trade. Pop. 39,371.

BLIDWORTH. Village of Nottinghamshire. It is 4 miles from Mansfield, and has coal-mines in the neighbourhood. It is famed for the custom called the rocking which dates from the thirteenth century. Here in St. Mary's Church, on Candlemas Day, the latest baptised boy in the parish is rocked in a cradle by the vicar.

BLIGH (blī), **William.** The commander of the ship *Bounty* when the crew mutinied in the South Seas and carried her off. He was born at Plymouth in 1753, died at London 1817. The *Bounty* had been fitted out for the purpose of procuring plants of the bread-fruit tree, and introducing these into the West Indies. Bligh left Tahiti in 1789, and was proceeding on his voyage for Jamaica when he was seized, and, with eighteen men supposed to be well affected to him, forced into the launch, sparingly provisioned, and cast adrift not far from the Island of Tofoa (Tonga Islands), in lat. 19° S. and long. 184° E. By admirable skill and perseverance, though not without enduring fearful hardships, they managed to reach the Island of Timor in forty-one days, after running nearly 4000 miles. Bligh, with twelve of his companions, arrived in England in 1790, while the mutineers settled on Pitcairn Island, where their descendants still exist. Bligh became Governor of New South Wales in 1806, but his harsh and despotic conduct caused him to be deposed and sent back to England. He afterwards rose to the rank of admiral.

BLIGHT. A name commonly employed to denote the effects of disease or any other circumstance which causes plants to wither or decay. It has been vaguely applied to almost every disease of plants, whether caused by the condition of the atmosphere or of the soil, the attacks of insects, parasitic fungi, etc. *See* PLANT-PATHOLOGY.

BLIM'BING (called also **Cucumber Tree**). The indian name of the fruit of *Averrhoa Bilimbi*, a small tree, family Oxalidaceæ, the fruit being acid and resembling a small cucumber. The carambola (q.v.) belongs to the same genus.

BLIND. A screen of some sort to prevent too strong a light from shining in at a window, or to keep people from seeing in. *Venetian blinds* are made of slats of wood, so connected as to overlap each other when closed, and to show a series of open spaces for the admission of light and air when in the other position.

BLIND (blint), **Karl.** German political agitator and writer on history, mythology, and Germanic literature, born in 1826, died in 1907. He was educated at Heidelberg and Bonn, and from his student days till he settled in England in 1852 he was continually engaged in agitating or in heading risings in the cause of German freedom and union. He was frequently imprisoned. The democratic propaganda was strongly supported by his pen; and he wrote *Fire-burial among our Germanic Forefathers*; *Teutonic Cremation*; *Yggdrasil, or The Teutonic Tree of Existence*; etc.

BLIND, THE. The modern definition of the expression "blind," according to the Education, Employment, and Maintenance Bill for the Blind, the second reading of which was passed on 12th March, 1920, is given as "being too blind to perform work for which sight is ordinarily required."

There are, of course, a great number of causes for loss of sight (see *Colour blindness, Hemeralopia, Nyctalopia*), and the latest statistics show that there are in Great Britain some 30,000 dependent blind persons.

Of late years much has been achieved in the education and industrial equipment of the blind, and there are now comparatively few large cities in the world that do not possess a school or institution of some kind for the blind. The occupations in which the blind are found capable of engaging can be divided into two heads: firstly, professional occupations; secondly, industrial. Under the first head come such occupations as massage, secretarial work, telephony, and poultry-farming while under the second head come basket-making, mat-making, boot-repairing, netting, brush-making, fancy work of various kinds, sewing of sacks and bags, carving of articles of wood, under which heading can also be included general carpentry and picture-frame making, while the Great War has given an impetus, especially in foreign countries, to metal-working, and to a certain extent to the management of machinery.

In late years a great impetus has been given, in Britain, to the higher education of the blind by the foundation of the National Institute for the Blind in 1914, which sprang from the British and Foreign Blind Association (founded by Dr. Armitage in 1868). The National Institute has done useful pioneer work in the higher education of the blind; while a long-felt need has been filled by the establishment of "Sunshine House," Chorley Wood, Herts, as a school and kindergarten for blind babies, who are received there and cared for until they reach the age of five years, when they can be admitted to one or other of the schools for the blind throughout the country. The Royal Normal College and Academy of Music for the Blind at Upper Norwood is also an institute that is doing good work.

Braille. Various systems have been devised for the purpose of teaching the blind to read. Louis Braille was born in 1809. He was a pupil and afterwards a professor of the Institut National des Jeunes Aveugles, Paris, and in 1834 he perfected the system which is now recognised all the world over as being the best and most complete method devised for enabling blind people to read by means of embossed type. The Braille system for literature and music was introduced into general use in England by Dr. T. R. Armitage in 1868. There is also another form of embossed printing; this type is known as Moon type, invented in 1847 by William Moon of Brighton. This type has been adapted to numerous languages and dialects. In 1855 the first Home Teaching Society was founded in London, and its committee decided that William Moon's system was the best for the use of the blind residing in their homes, that they might learn to read and be provided with books. Most of the characters in Moon type are either unaltered or slightly-modified forms of the Roman letters; the complete alphabet consists of only nine distinct characters of the simplest form utilised in various positions.

Since the Great War many more occupations have been thrown open to blind men, on account of the nation's debt to the soldiers and sailors blinded in battle. This led to the establishment of St. Dunstan's Hostel for Blinded Soldiers and Sailors in March, 1915, when fourteen blinded soldiers entered the Hostel. By the end of 1919 over 1500 men had been trained there. The success of the Hostel was due primarily to the fact that Sir Arthur Pearson was himself blind, and yet had overcome his difficulties with exceptional vigour and courage. Thanks to the splendidly-equipped workshops and offices, combined with up-to-date business methods, not only were the recognised industries rapidly taught, but a highly-successful School of Massage was established for the men of St. Dunstan's by the National Institute for the Blind, and men were also trained as telephonists, shorthand-typists, and poultry-farmers. The men were also, practically without exception, taught Braille and type-writing. The work is now being carried on by the St. Dunstan's After-Care Branch for Blinded Soldiers and Sailors, which is now affiliated to the National Institute for the Blind.—BIBLIOGRAPHY: T. R. Armitage, *Education and Employment of the Blind*; W. Moon, *Light for the Blind*; Emile Javal, *The Blind Man's World*; P. Villey, *Le Monde des Aveugles*.

BLIND-FISH. The name of several species of fish, family Amblyopsidæ, inhabiting the American cave-streams. They are all small, the largest not exceeding 5 inches. In the typical species (*Amblyopsis spelæus*) of the Mammoth Cave of Kentucky the eyes are reduced to a useless vestige hidden under the skin, the body is translucent and colourless, and the head and body are covered with numerous rows of sensitive papillæ, which form very delicate organs of touch.

BLIND HARRY. *See* HARRY THE MINSTREL.

BLIND SPOT. Optic disc in the retina where the optic nerve enters the eye. It is a circle with raised margins, insensible to light and colours.

BLIND STORY. *See* TRIFORIUM.

BLIND-WORM, or SLOW-WORM (*Anguis fragilis*). A snake-like lizard devoid of external limbs, though the bones of the shoulders and pelvis exist in a rudimentary form; length about a foot, and of nearly equal thickness throughout. There is a giant of 17 inches in the British Museum. Its eyes, though brilliant, are small, and hence its common name. An interesting feature is the possession of an unpaired functional eye on the top of the head, as in some other lizards, and also in the Tuatara (Hatteria or Splenodon), an archaic lizard-like reptile native to New Zealand. (*See* PINEAL GLAND.) It is common in Great Britain, and is spread over almost the whole of Europe, Western Asia, and Northern Africa. It is perfectly harmless, living upon worms, insects, and snails, and hibernating during the winter. It receives its specific name of *fragilis* from the fact that when frightened it stiffens its muscles to such an extent, and becomes so rigid, that its tail may be snapped off by a slight blow.

BLISTER. A thin vesicle on the skin, containing watery matter or serum, whether occasioned by a burn or other injury. The term is also used of the application of some substance to the skin to produce a vesicle filled with serous fluid. Blistering a part of the skin is done to produce counter-irritation for the relief of pain, to lessen congestion in internal organs, etc. Cantharides (q.v.) or Spanish fly is the most commonly used and most effective. It is applied to the chest in pleurisy and pericarditis, over nerves in neuritis, over the mastoid region in ear trouble, and over joints in chronic synovitis. Many other substances are also used.

BLISTER-BEETLE. *See* CANTHARIDES.

BLISTER-STEEL. Iron bars which, when converted into steel, have their surfaces covered with blisters, probably from the expansion of minute bubbles of air. Steel is used in the blister state for welding to iron for certain pieces of mechanism, but is not employed for making edge-tools. It requires for this purpose to be converted into cast or shear steel.

BLIZZARD. A name, probably onomatopœic and akin to *blast* and *bluster*, for a violent storm of wind, accompanied by fine snow, such as occurs in the western United States. Blizzards sometimes cause heavy loss of life, as in 1836, 1866, and 1888. The word is often used in Britain to describe a violent snow-squall.

BLOCH, Jean de. Polish financier of Jewish descent, economist and writer on military history; born in 1836. He was administrator of the railway system connecting the Black Sea and the Baltic, and promoted an industrial movement in Poland. He became famous, however, as a propagandist of universal peace, a subject on which he wrote numerous articles and to which he devoted his great work entitled *La Guerre* (1898), translated into English in 1899 under the title *Is War now Impossible?* The author endeavoured to prove that under modern conditions war would not pay even for the victorious nation, as it would necessarily be trench warfare and of such length as to result in economic failure, bankruptcy, and revolution. This work is supposed to have inspired Czar Nicholas II. to issue his famous peace declaration, resulting in the Hague Conference in 1899. He died in 1902.

BLOCH (blo*h*), **Marcus Eliezer.** A naturalist of Jewish descent, born at Ansbach in 1723, died 1799. His principal work is *Die Naturgeschichte der Fische* (Natural History of Fishes), folio 1785-99, with 432 coloured plates.

BLOCK. A mechanical contrivance consisting of one or more grooved pulleys mounted in a casing or shell which is furnished with a hook, eye, or strap by which it may be attached to an object, the function of the apparatus being to transmit power or change the direction of motion by means of a rope or chain passing round the movable pulleys. Blocks are single, double, treble, or fourfold, according as the number of sheaves or pulleys is one, two, three, or four. A *running block* is attached to the object to be raised or moved; a *standing block* is fixed to some permanent support. Blocks also receive different denominations from their shape, purpose, and mode of application. They are sometimes made of iron as well as of wood. Blocks to which the name of *dead-eyes* has been given are not pulleys, being unprovided with sheaves.

BLOCKADE′. The rendering of intercourse with the seaports of an enemy unlawful on the part of neutrals, and consisting essentially in the presence of a sufficient naval force to make such intercourse difficult. Blockade is universally admitted to be a belligerent right to which under International Law neutrals are obliged to submit. It must be declared or made public, so that neutrals may have notice of it. If a blockade is instituted by a sufficient authority, and maintained by a sufficient force, a neutral is so far affected by it that an attempt to trade with the place invested subjects vessel and cargo to confiscation by the blockading Power. The rules of blockade in time of war were fixed by the "Declaration of London," 4th Dec., 1908-26th Feb., 1909.

Great Britain, however, it must be remembered, had not been bound in International Law by the Declaration of London, that declaration never having been ratified by Parliament. The British Government, however, announced, on 20th Aug., 1914, that they proposed to abide by the rules of the declaration, subject to certain minor modifications. In Feb., 1916, a Minister of Blockade, with Cabinet rank, was appointed, and in July, 1916, important emendations were made in the rules according to which the blockade of the Central Empires was being enforced. This was effected in a drastic manner by formally withdrawing the "Declaration of London," by means of an Order in Council, known as the "Maritime Rights Order" of 8th July, 1916. The term is also used to describe the state of matters when hostile forces sit down around a place and keep possession of all the means of access to it, so as to cut off its communication with the outside world, and so compel surrender from want of supplies. *See* CONTINENTAL BLOCKADE; DECLARATION OF LONDON; PRIZE-COURT.—Cf. Paul Fauchille, *Du Blocus Maritime*.

BLOCK-BOOKS. Before and for a short time after the invention of printing, books printed from wooden blocks each the size of a page and having the matter to be reproduced, whether text or picture, cut in relief on the surface.

BLOCKHOUSE. A defensible post, usually rectangular, constructed to give shelter and protection to its garrison, consisting of possibly thirty men. In a general way, locally available materials enter largely into the construction of such a post, and it gives no protection against artillery-fire. The walls are provided with loopholes for all-round fire, and good trenches and earthworks outside the house materially add to its strength. Efficient obstacles should also be provided. In the South African War blockhouses were found so useful that they practically became an article of store, in that they were prepared and fitted at convenient depots and sent in sections to the required spots to be erected. Such blockhouses consisted of a wooden framework with shell walls of corrugated iron filled with earth, stones, or rubble. On extended lines of communication, where economy of man-power is imperative, blockhouses are useful as a protection against raids, and, so used, they combine many of the desiderata for a defensive position, e.g. they afford good cover, the garrison is actually on the position to be defended, and they possess many advantages for the storage of ammunition and supplies.

It is to be expected that in the future blockhouses will be used only in warfare against an enemy unprovided with modern means of destruction; they were so used in the late war in both East and West Africa. In suitable country a blockhouse may be partly underground, the excavated earth being used to form a strong bullet-proof parapet sufficient to carry the beams and roofing-material, while, on the north-west frontier of India, the local "sangar," or circular wall of loose stones, is to all intents and purposes a blockhouse without a roof. The "pill-boxes" of reinforced concrete were hardly blockhouses in the usually accepted sense of the term, being constructed merely for fighting purposes in the battle-line.

BLOCK-PRINTING. *See* TYPOGRAPHY; CALICO PRINTING.

BLOCKS AND TACKLE. *See* PULLEY.

BLOCKSBERG. *See* BROCKEN.

BLOCKSHIP. A vessel used to close a harbour by sinking it in the channel. Any vessel can be used provided it is filled with concrete or some heavy material. In former days a blockship was a storeship.

BLOCK-SYSTEM. A system of working or controlling the traffic on railways, in which the line is divided into sections of varying length, with signal and telegraphic connection at the end of each section. The actual length of each section is fixed, in the first instance, upon the particular conditions and requirements of the line; they may be as short as half a mile and up to 4 miles long. The essential principle of the system is that no train is allowed to enter upon any one section till that section is signalled to be wholly clear, so that there is always the equivalent of a section between successive train.

BLOCK-TIN. Tin of a certain

state of purity, not quite equal to the better quality known as grain tin.

BLOEMAART (blö'märt), **Abraham.** A Dutch painter, born 1564, died in 1657. He was the son of an architect and sculptor, who sent him to Paris, where he studied for three years, subsequently returning to Amsterdam and Utrecht, where he settled and painted all sorts of subjects, his landscapes being the most esteemed. He had four sons, of whom Cornelis (born 1603, died 1680) was sent by his father as an art student to Paris, and afterwards lived and worked in Rome as a distinguished engraver.

BLOEMFONTEIN (blöm'fon-tīn). The chief town and seat of the Provincial Government of the Orange Free State, 680 miles N.E. of Cape Town, in a high but healthy region, having railway connection with the Cape Province and Transvaal and the Natal lines. It stands on a plain surrounded by low hills, and is regularly laid out, with a large market square in the centre. It has some fine buildings, including the cathedral and other places of worship, Government house, town hall, post office, legislative buildings, two colleges, library, museum, etc. Pop. 40,000 (28,503 white in 1926).

BLOIS (blwä). Capital of the French department of Loir-et-Cher, 100 miles S.S.W. of Paris, on the Loire. It consists of an upper town, a lower town, and several suburbs, with one of which it communicates by a stone bridge of eleven arches. The old castle, which played an important part in French history, has been restored and kept up by the Government. There is also a cathedral of late date, the Church of St. Nicholas (twelfth century), a bishop's palace, Roman aqueduct, etc. The castle was long occupied by the counts of the name, and became a favourite residence of the kings of France. Louis XII. was born there; and Francis I., Henry II., Charles IX., and Henry III. held their Courts in it. Pop. 24,607.

BLOMFIELD, Charles James. Bishop of London, born at Bury-St.-Edmunds in 1786, died at Fulham in 1857. He was at Trinity College, Cambridge, where he took high honours and was elected Fellow. He was ordained in 1810, and, after filling successively several curacies, and acting for a time as chaplain to the Bishop of London, was presented to the rectory of St. Botolph's, Bishopsgate. In 1822 he became Archdeacon of Colchester, in 1824 he was made Bishop of Chester, and in 1828 Bishop of London. He was a distinguished classical scholar, and published editions of several of the dramas of Æschylus, writing also on kindred subjects for the *Edinburgh* and *Quarterly Review*. He also published an edition of Euripides, and one of Callimachus. He edited a translation of the *Greek Grammar* of Matthiæ, executed by a younger brother, Edward (1788-1816). His chief distinction was gained by his energy in the management of his diocese, and his success in the cause of church extension in the metropolis. By his exertion many churches were built and schools started, and the colonies benefited by his efforts as well as London. In regard to the Tractarian movement, his attempts to lead his clergy to take a middle course gave rise to a good deal of discussion in his diocese.

BLOMFIELD, Sir Arthur William. English architect, born 6th March, 1829, he was a younger son of Charles James Blomfield (1786-1857) who was Bishop of Chester, 1824-28, and Bishop of London, 1828-56. He was educated at Rugby and Trinity College, Cambridge, and became an architect. As an ecclesiastical architect he was in the first rank. His works include the restoration of Southwark Cathedral and the erection of many churches, including St. Barnabas, Oxford, and St. Mary's, Portsea. Knighted in 1897, he died 30th Oct., 1899.

Blomfield's nephew, **Sir Reginald Theodore Blomfield,** also became a noted architect. Born 20th Dec., 1856, he was educated at Haileybury and Exeter College, Oxford. He became A.R.A. in 1905 and R.A. in 1914, and was President of the Royal Institute of British Architects, 1912-14. He has written several works on architecture, chiefly from the historical point of view, and became a specialist in garden design. In 1919 he was knighted.

BLOND, Jacques Christophe le. Miniature-painter and originator of colour-printing, born at Frankfort-on-the-Main, 1670, died in a hospital in Paris 1741. He spent most of his life and all his means in comparatively unsuccessful experiments in printing engravings in colour, and in attempts to reproduce the cartoons of Raphael in tapestry.

BLON'DEL. A French minstrel and poet of the twelfth century, a confidential servant and instructor in music of Richard Cœur de Lion. While his master was the prisoner of the Duke of Austria, Blondel, according to the story, went through Palestine and all parts of Germany in search of him. He sang the king's own favourite lays before each keep and fortress till the song was at length taken up and answered from the windows of the castle of Loewenstein, where Richard was imprisoned. This story is preserved in the Chronicles of Rheims, of the thirteenth century. The poems of Blondel, with all the legendary and historical data relating to him, were published by Prosper Tarbé (Rheims, 1862).

BLONDIN, Charles. Stage-name of **Jean François Gravelet.** French acrobat, born at St. Omer, 24th Feb., 1824, he early specialised in tight-rope walking, especially with spectacular incidents. His celebrity was established in 1859 by crossing Niagara Falls on a rope 160 feet above the water. He performed at the Crystal Palace, 1861, and made occasional reappearances, once from mast to mast on a liner at sea. He died at Ealing, London, 19th Feb., 1897.

BLOOD. The fluid which circulates through the arteries and veins of the

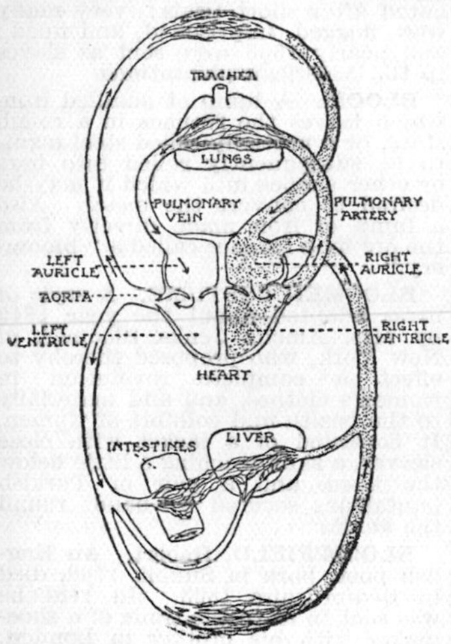

human body and that of other animals. This circulation is necessary to life, as blood acts as a nutritive medium by conveying food materials from digestive organs, and also by carrying oxygen from the lungs to all parts of the body, receiving in exchange waste products, which are taken to the excretory organs. The central organ of the blood circulation is the heart (q.v.). Blood is an opaque fluid, scarlet from arteries, purplish from veins—the change in the latter is due to the loss of oxygen. It is composed of plasma and corpuscles, and possesses the property of coagulation shortly after it leaves the blood-vessels. If left in a receptacle for ten minutes, the red fluid is changed into a dark, solid mass of clot suspended in a yellowish fluid—the serum. This is due to the action of a substance in the blood called fibrin.

Corpuscles.—There are two kinds of blood corpuscles, red and white. The former, which are always disc-shaped, are much more numerous. In man and mammals they are round; in lower vertebrates oval. They measure $\frac{1}{3200}$th inch in diameter, and act as oxygen carriers and nutritive medium. The latter are slightly larger, colourless, and of various shapes and sizes. They have the power of eating up foreign matter—phagocytosis—and are closely connected with the phenomena of inflammation and immunity. For every white corpuscle there are five hundred red. The specific gravity of human blood at all times only varies between 1·050 and 1·066. Blood is always alkaline in reaction, and is composed of from 70-75 per cent water to 20-25 per cent solids. The chief solid constituent is hæmoglobin ($\frac{9}{10}$ths of the whole solids); it is found in the red corpuscles. The others are nucleo-protein, lecithin, cholestrin, and small quantities of many inorganic salts, the two chief being sodium chloride and sodium carbonate. It has been estimated lately that the average amount of blood in man is about $\frac{1}{20}$th of the total weight of the body.—BIBLIOGRAPHY: A. C. Coles, *The Blood*; R. J. M'L. Buchanan, *The Blood in Health and Disease* (Oxford Medical Publications); P. J. A. Bechamp, *The Blood and its Third Anatomical Element*; O. C. Gruner, *Biology of the Blood-cells.*

BLOOD, AVENGER OF. In Scripture, the nearest relation of anyone that had died by manslaughter or murder, so called because it fell to him to punish the person who was guilty of the deed.

BLOOD, Thomas (commonly called Colonel Blood). Born in Ireland about 1618, died in London 1680, was a disbanded officer of Oliver Cromwell, and lost some estates in Ireland at the Restoration. His whole life was one of plotting and adventure, though it is probable that he acted a double part, keeping the Government informed of so much as might secure his own safety. His most daring exploit was an attempt to steal the crown jewels (9th May, 1671) from the Tower. He was seized with the crown in his possession, but was not only pardoned by Charles, but obtained forfeited Irish estates of £500 annual value.

BLOOD-BIRD (*Myzomēla sanguinolenta*). An Australian species of honey-sucker, so called from the rich scarlet colour of the head, breast, and back of the male.

BLOOD-HOUND. A variety of dog with long, smooth, and pendulous ears, remarkable for the acuteness of its smell, and employed to recover game or prey which has escaped wounded from the hunter, by tracing the lost animal by the blood it has spilt: whence the name of the dog. There are several varieties of this animal, as the Cuban, the African, and the English blood-hound, a descendant, no doubt, of the famous St. Hubert hound of France. In some places blood-hounds have not only been trained to the pursuit of game, but also to the chase of man. In America they used to be employed in hunting fugitive slaves, and have been employed more recently for police and military purposes.

BLOOD - LETTING. *See* PHLEBOTOMY.

BLOOD-MONEY. The compensation by a homicide to the next of kin of the person slain, securing the offender and his relatives against subsequent retaliation; once common in Scandinavian and Teutonic countries, and still a custom among the Arabs. The term is also applied to money earned by laying or supporting a charge implying peril to the life of an accused person.

BLOOD-POISONING. *See* PYÆMIA.

BLOOD-RAIN. A phenomenon of Southern Europe, the Canary Islands, and elsewhere, consists of rain with which is mingled grey or reddish dust. Chemical and microscopical analysis has shown this dust to be largely minute organisms, including fragments of the shells of diatoms, the whole coloured by red oxide of iron. These, drawn up into the air from the African deserts by whirlwinds, subsequently fall with rain.

BLOOD-ROOT, or **BLOOD-WORT** (*Sanguinaria canadensis*). A plant of Canada and the United States, belonging to the poppy order, and so named from its root-stock yielding a sap of a deep orange colour. It has heart-shaped deeply-lobed leaves and a white or pink flower, borne on a scape. The rhizome contains sanguinarine and other alkaloids, and has been used as an expectorant and anti-asthmatic.

BLOOD-STONE. *See* HELIOTROPE.

BLOOD TRANSFUSION. Transferring of blood from one body to another. Human blood has been classified into four different groups, and it is important that the blood of the donor should belong to the same group as that of the patient.

BLOOD-VESSELS. *See* ARTERIES; VEINS; HEART.

BLOOD-WOOD. A name of several trees. Indian blood-wood (*Lagerstrœmia regīnæ*) is a large tree (nat. ord. Lythraceæ) with wood of a blood-red colour, used for many purposes. It is called also *jarool.*

BLOOD-WORM. The blood-red larva of a midge (genus Chironŏmus) found in water; also a small red worm used as bait by anglers.

BLOODY ASSIZES. Those held by Judge Jeffreys in 1685, after the suppression of Monmouth's rebellion. Upwards of 300 persons were executed after short trials; very many were flogged, imprisoned, and fined; and nearly 1000 were sent as slaves to the American plantations.

BLOOM. A lump of puddled iron, which leaves the furnace in a rough state, or a partially-rolled steel ingot, to be subsequently rolled into bars or other shapes into which it may be desired to convert the metal. Also a lump of iron made directly from the ore by a furnace called a "bloomery."

BLOOMER COSTUME. A style of dress adopted about the year 1849 by Mrs. Amelia Jenks Bloomer, of New York, who proposed thereby to effect a complete revolution in women's clothes, and add materially to the health and comfort of women. It consisted of a jacket with close sleeves, a skirt reaching a little below the knee, and a pair of Turkish pantaloons secured by bands round the ankles.

BLOOM'FIELD, Robert. An English poet, born in Suffolk 1766, died in Bedfordshire 1823. In 1781 he was sent to learn the trade of a shoemaker with his brother in London. In the country, where he resided for a short time in 1786, he first conceived the idea of his poem *The Farmer's Boy*, which was written under the most unfavourable circumstances in a London garret. It was published in 1800, and had a great popularity. He subsequently published *Rural Tales, Wild Flowers, The Banks of the Wye, May Day with the Muses*, etc. Several efforts were made to place him in comfortable circumstances, but he became hypochondriacal, and died in poverty.

BLOOM'INGTON. A thriving city, State of Illinois, United States, 60 miles N.N.E. of Springfield. It has several important educational institutions, including the Illinois Wesleyan University, a college for women, and the State Normal University, in the vicinity. Has coal-mines, iron industries, railway works, etc., and a large trade. Pop. 30,930.

BLOOM'INGTON. A town of the United States, in Indiana, seat of the State university. Pop. 18,277.

BLOOMSBURY. A district of London, bounded by Holborn and New Oxford Street on the S., Tottenham Court Road on the W., Euston Road on the N., and Southampton Row on the E.

BLOUNT (blunt), **Charles.** Son of of Sir H. Blount, born 1654; a deistical writer, is said to have had the assistance of his father in writing a work called *Anima Mundi, or An Historical Account of the Opinions of the Ancients concerning the Human Soul after this Life, etc.* (1679). He wrote various other works of the same nature, and also an excellent treatise on the liberty of the press. He shot himself in 1693, in consequence of the refusal of his deceased wife's sister to marry him.

BLOUNT, Sir Henry. English traveller, born 1602, died 1682. He travelled through various parts of the south of Europe and Egypt, and published an account of his travels, called *Voyage to the Levant.* He was knighted by Charles I., and during the Civil War took part with the Royalists. After the king's death he came to London, and was employed by Cromwell and the Parliament in several important affairs.

BLOUSE (blouz, Fr. blöz). A loose upper garment, generally of linen or cotton, worn by men; a blue linen blouse being commonly worn by French workmen. From this is derived the garment of various materials now so commonly worn by women.

BLOW, John. A musical composer, born in 1648, died 1708. He became organist of Westminster Abbey, and was afterwards appointed composer to the Royal Chapel. His secular compositions were published under the name of *Amphion Anglicus* in 1700.

BLOWERS. In mining, fire-damp is frequently liberated from joints and fissures in the coal, and may escape with a hissing sound. Such an escape is described as a blower. These discharges are often emitted with considerable force, and may continue for some time before the pressure of the gas falls sufficiently to render further emission inaudible.

BLOW-FLY. A name for *Musca vomitoria, Sarcophaga carnaria,* and other species of two-winged flies that deposit their eggs on flesh, and thus taint it.

BLOWING-MACHINE. Any contrivance for supplying a current of air, as for smelting ores in blast-furnaces, renewing the air in confined spaces, etc. This may consist of a single pair of bellows, but more generally two pairs are combined to secure continuity of current. When large quantities of air are required at a pressure of less than 1 lb., a centrifugal fan is used, which consists of a spiral-shaped metal casing with central inlets, a peripheral outlet, and a central horizontal shaft with blades which revolve at a high speed. Turbo-blowers, in which from four to six centrifugal pressure-blowers on a single shaft are connected in series, the discharge from one fan-wheel forming the feed of the next following, are being largely used for supplying the blast to metallurgical furnaces. Rotary blowers, in which two impellers attached to parallel shafts revolve in opposite directions in a casing having an inlet and an outlet, are used when large quantities of air are required at a pressure up to 3 lb. per sq. inch. To this class belongs the well-known Roots blower. When high pressures, such as 10 to 16 lb. for iron blast-furnaces, or 25 to 30 lb. per sq. inch for Bessemer converters, are required, double-acting piston-blowers are generally used, worked by steam-engines, or in modern ironworks by gas-engines driven by the waste gases from the blast-furnaces. Rotary-blowers and fans, actuated by power, are also largely used.

BLOWITZ, Henri Georges Stephan Adolphe Opper de. French journalist, born at Blowitz, Pilsen, Bohemia, in 1825. He went to France, where he taught languages and contributed to the *Gazette du Midi* and other journals. In 1870 he became a naturalised French subject and a warm supporter of Thiers. In July, 1871, he became Paris correspondent of *The Times,* to which he contributed over 4000 columns. De Blowitz was one of the first correspondents to appreciate the value of the "interview." He published the entire text of the Treaty of Berlin before it was issued, and in 1875 he revealed the plans of the German military party for another invasion of France. He also published

Midi à quatorze Heures, a comedy; *Une course à Constantinople*; and his *Memoirs* (1903). He died in 1903.

BLOW-PIPE. An instrument used for the production of high temperatures. In its simplest form it consists of a straight tube of brass, glass, or other material about 7 inches long, half an inch in diameter at one end, and tapering to a fine point at the other. About 2 inches from the narrow end the tube is bent at right angles. By means of this a stream of air may be directed into a jet of flame. The size of the flame, which is non-luminous, is diminished, and as the combination is concentrated in a much smaller area, the temperature of the flame is considerably higher.

The blow-pipe flame consists of three distinct cones. Cone A is filled with a cool mixture of air and combustible gas. Cone B is termed the *reducing* zone, and the best reducing position is at the point. In zone B there is not sufficient air to burn all the carbon to carbon dioxide; hence the zone is rich in carbon *monoxide*, which reacts by removing oxygen from the substance containing it. Cone C is the *oxidising* zone, and here the supply of oxygen from the surrounding air is unlimited. The blow-pipe is much used in mineral analysis, as, by its means, metallic compounds may be reduced to the metallic state or transformed into characteristic oxides. By passing a stream of oxygen under pressure into a flame, an extremely high temperature may be attained. The blow-pipe in a modified form is made use of in glass-blowing and in autogenous welding. By using an oxyhydrogen blow-pipe, by means of which compressed oxygen and compressed hydrogen pass through a narrow orifice and are ignited, a high temperature is produced suitable for autogenous welding of iron and for filling up blow-holes in molten steel castings. The oxyhydrogen flame is now largely superseded by the oxy-acetylene flame, as a higher temperature is thus produced by the use of a smaller quantity of acetylene. Large steel plates may be cut with great ease, holes bored in blocks of metal, and the soldering of iron, aluminium, and copper accomplished. The principle of the blow-pipe is used in various blow-lamps and in oil-stoves, when oil and vapour are burned as they escape from small holes under pressure.

The name is also given to the pipe or tube through which poisoned arrows are blown by the breath, used by South American Indians and natives of Borneo. The tube or blow-pipe is 8 to 12 feet long, with a bore scarcely large enough to admit the little finger, and the arrow is forced through by a sudden expulsion of air from the lungs (like a pea from a boy's pea-shooter), being sometimes propelled to a distance of 140 yards.

BLUBBER. The fat of whales and other large sea animals, from which train-oil is obtained. The blubber lies under the skin and over the muscular flesh. It is eaten by the Eskimo and the sea-coast races of the Japanese Islands, the Kuriles, etc. The whole quantity yielded by one whale ordinarily amounts to 40 or 50, but sometimes to 80 or more cwts. *See* WHALE.

BLÜCHER (blü'*h*er), **Gebhard Leberecht von.** Distinguished Prussian general, born at Rostock 1742, died at Krieblowitz, in Silesia, 1819. He entered the Swedish service when fourteen years of age and fought against the Prussians, but was taken prisoner in his first campaign, and was induced to enter the Prussian service. Discontented at the promotion of another officer over his head, he left the army, devoted himself to agriculture, and by industry and prudence acquired an estate. After the death of Frederick II. he became a major in his former regiment, which he commanded with distinction on the Rhine in 1793 and 1794. After the battle of Kirrweiler, in 1794, he was appointed major-general of the army of observation stationed on the Lower Rhine. In 1802, in the name of the King of Prussia, he took possession of Erfurt and Mühlhausen. On 14th Oct., 1806, he fought at the battle of Auerstädt. After the Peace of Tilsit, he laboured in the department of war at Königsberg and Berlin. He then received the chief military command in Pomerania, but at the instigation of Napoleon was afterwards, with several other distinguished men, dismissed from the service.

In the campaign of 1812, when the Prussians assisted the French he took no part; but no sooner did Prussia rise against her oppressors than Blücher, then seventy years old, engaged in the cause with all his former activity, and was appointed commander-in-chief of the Prussians and the Russian corps under General Winzingerode. His heroism in the battle of Lützen (2nd May, 1813) was rewarded by the Emperor Alexander with the Order of St. George. The battles of Bautzen and Hanau, those at the Katzbach and Leipzig, added to his glory. He was now raised to the rank of field-marshal, and led the Prussian army which invaded France early in 1814. After a period of obstinate conflict, the day of Montmartre crowned this campaign, and, 31st March, Blücher entered the capital of France. His king, in remembrance of the victory which he had gained at the Katzbach, created him Prince of Wahlstadt, and gave him an estate in Silesia.

On the renewal of the war in 1815 the chief command was again committed to him, and he led his army into the Netherlands. On 15th June Napoleon threw himself upon him, and Blücher, on the 16th, was defeated at Ligny. In this engagement his horse was killed, and he was thrown under its body. In the battle of the 18th Blücher arrived upon the ground at the most decisive moment, and, taking Napoleon in the rear and flank, assisted materially in completing the great victory of Belle Alliance or Waterloo. He was a rough and fearless soldier, noted for his energy and rapid movements, which had procured him the name of "Marshal Vorwärts" (Forward).—BIBLIOGRAPHY: Varnhagen van Ense, *Fürst Blücher von Wahlstadt*; B. Scherr, *Blücher, seine Zeit und sein Leben*; E. F. Henderson, *Blücher and the Uprising of Prussia against Napoleon.*

BLUE. One of the seven colours into which the rays of light divide themselves when refracted through a glass prism, seen in nature in the clear expanse of the heavens; also a dye or pigment of this hue. The substances used as blue pigments are of very different natures, and derived from various sources; they are all compound bodies, some being natural and others artificial. They are derived almost entirely from the vegetable and mineral kingdoms. The principal blues used in painting are *ultramarine*, which was originally prepared from lapis-lazuli or azurestone—a mineral found in China and other Oriental countries—but, as now prepared, it is an artificial compound of china-clay, carbonate of soda, sulphur, and charcoal; *Prussian* or *Berlin blue*, which is a compound of cyanogen and iron; *blue bice*, prepared from carbonate of copper; *indigo blue*, from the indigo plant, or prepared synthetically. Besides these, there are numerous other blues used in art, as *blue-verditer*, *smalt-* and *cobalt-blue*, from cobalt, *lacmus*, or *litmus*, etc. Before the discovery of aniline or coal-tar colours, dyers chiefly depended for their blues on *woad*, *archil*, *indigo*, and *Prussian blue*, but now a series of brilliant blues are obtained from coal-tar, possessing great tinctorial power and various degrees of durability.

True blue meant originally "a staunch Presbyterian," as *blue* was the favourite colour of the Scottish Covenanters of the seventeenth century. After the Revolution of 1688, it was combined with orange or yellow as the Whig colours. These were adopted on the cover of the Whig periodical, the *Edinburgh Review*, first published in 1802.

BLUEBEARD. The hero of a well-known French tale, *Barbe Bleue*, by Charles Perrault, originally French, founded, it is believed, on the enormities of a real personage, Gilles de Rais (or Retz), a great nobleman of Brittany, whom Michelet called *la bête d'extermination*, and who was put to death for his crimes in 1440. Others connect the story with Comorre, a Breton chief of the sixth century.

BLUE-BELL. A name given in England to the wild hyacinth (*Scilla nutans*), and in Scotland to the harebell (*Campanula rotundifolia*).

BLUE-BERRY. An American species of whortleberry (*Vaccinium pennsylvanicum*).

BLUE-BIRD. A small dentirostral, insessorial bird, the *Erythăca*, or *Sialia Wilsoni*, very common in the United States. The upper part of the body is blue, and the throat and breast of a dirty red. It makes its nest in the hole of a tree or in the box that is so commonly provided for its use by the friendly farmer. The blue-bird is the harbinger of spring to the Americans; its song is cheerful, continuing with little interruption from March to October, but is most frequently heard in the serene days of the spring. It is also called *blue robin* or *blue redbreast*.

BLUE-BOOKS. The general name for many official publications in book or pamphlet form, printed for the British Government, laid before the Houses of Parliament, and sold to the public. The printing of its proceedings was adopted by the House of Commons in 1681, and in 1836 the practice of selling the papers to the public was commenced. They are so called simply from being stitched up in dark-blue paper wrappers, and include all reports and papers moved for by members or granted by Government on particular subjects; the reports of committees; statistics of the trade, etc., of the country and of the colonies; and ambassadorial and consular reports from foreign countries and ports. The official publications of foreign countries are distinguished by the colour of their respective bindings. Austrian and Spanish are bound in red, Chinese and French in yellow, Italian and Mexican in green, German and Portuguese in white, Belgian and Japanese in grey.

BLUE-BOTTLE (*Centaurĕa Cyănnus*). A British composite plant, rather tall and slender, with blue flowers, growing in cornfields.

BLUE-BOTTLE FLY. A large blue species of blow-fly (*Musca vomitoria*).

BLUE-BREAST. *See* BLUE-THROAT.

BLUE - COAT SCHOOL. *See* CHRIST'S HOSPITAL.

BLUE CROSS. The name given to a British organization, founded in 1912, for the care of dogs and horses in warfare. It is run on the lines of the Red Cross.

BLUE ENSIGN. Flag composed of a blue field with the union flag in the upper corner next the staff. It distinguishes the Royal Naval Reserve as well as the consular service.

BLUE-EYE. The blue-faced honey-eater of Australia (*Entomyza cyanōtis*).

BLUEFIELDS. *See* MOSQUITO TERRITORY.

BLUE-FISH (*Temnŏdon* or *Pomatŏmus saltātor*). A fish common on the eastern coasts of America, allied to the mackerel, but larger, growing to the length of 3 feet or more, and much esteemed for the table. It is very destructive to other fishes. It is also called horse-mackerel, green-fish, skip-jack, etc.

BLUE-GOWNS. An order of paupers in Scotland, called also the *King's Bedesmen*, to whom the kings annually distributed certain alms on condition of their praying for the royal welfare. Their number was equal to the number of years the king had lived. The alms consisted of a blue gown or cloak, a purse containing as many shillings Scots (pennies sterling) as the years of the king's age, and a badge bearing the words "*Pass and repass*," which protected them from all laws against mendicity. Edie Ochiltree, in Sir Walter Scott's novel *The Antiquary*, is a type of the class. The practice of appointing bedesmen was discontinued in 1833, and the last of them drew his last allowance from the exchequer in Edinburgh in 1863.

BLUE-GRASS (*Poa pratensis*). An American pasture grass of great excellence, especially abundant in Kentucky.

BLUE - GREEN ALGÆ (Cyanophyceæ, Myxophyceæ, or Schizophyceæ), the coloured section of the Schizophyta or Fission-plants, of which group the Bacteria (Schizomycetes) form the colourless section. Like the Bacteria, they are very minute and extremely simple in structure, unicellular (Glœocapsa) or filamentous (Oscillatoria), without definite nuclei, devoid of sexuality, multiplying chiefly by ordinary cell-division; photosynthetic pigments, ranging from blue-green to red, are always present in their cells. Blue-green algæ live in water or on damp soil, most rocks and walls, etc. They are among the first plants to take possession of newly-formed soil (e.g. on the Island of Krakatoa, after all life had been exterminated by the great volcanic eruption of 1886), which they help to prepare for larger and more exacting plants. Great masses of some species accumulate at certain seasons on the surface of lakes ("breaking of the meres"); the Red Sea owes its name to a similar phenomenon. Several Cyanophyceæ are constituents of Lichens (q.v.).

BLUE JOHN. A miner's name for purple fluorspar.

BLUE LAWS. A name for certain laws said to have been made in the early government of New Haven. Connecticut, anent breaches of manners and morality, but most of which probably never existed.

BLUE LIGHT. *See* BENGAL LIGHT.

BLUE-MANTLE. One of the English pursuivants-at-arms, connected with the Herald's College.

BLUE MOUNTAINS. The central mountain range of Jamaica, the main ridges of which are from 6000 to 8000 feet high. Also a mountain chain of New South Wales, part of the great Dividing Range. The highest peaks rise over 4000 feet above the sea. The range is now traversed by a railway, which attains a maximum height of 3494 feet.

BLUE NILE. *See* NILE.

BLUE PETER. a blue flag having a white square in the centre, used to signify that the ship on which it is hoisted is about to sail.

BLUE-PILL. A preparation of mercury for medicinal use. It consists of mercury 1, confection of roses $1\frac{1}{2}$, liquorice $\frac{1}{2}$; strength, 1 in 3 of mercury. It is widely used as a purgative, and usually followed by a dose of salts twelve hours later.

BLUE PRINTS. A method of copying plans or working drawings. The finished drawing is first traced in dense-black ink on tracing-cloth, which is then placed on a glass-fronted frame. A sheet of sensitized white paper is then placed behind the tracing-cloth and glass, the whole clamped together, and exposed to daylight. On completion, the print is then placed in water, which turns the whole surface blue, with the exception of those parts which were under the black lines in the tracing and which remain white. This method is now being superseded by a process which gives black lines on a white ground, enabling the print to be afterwards coloured.

BLUE RIBBON. A term for a high distinction of any kind. It owes its origin to the fact that the ribbon of the Order of the Garter is dark blue. The Lord Chancellorship is called the lawyer's blue ribbon.

BLUE RIDGE. The most easterly ridge of the Alleghany or Appalachian Mountains. The most elevated summits are the peaks of Otter (4001 feet) in Virginia.

BLUES. Light blue is the colour of Cambridge University and of Eton College, while dark blue is the colour of Oxford University and of Harrow School. So " to be a Blue " means to represent either of these universities or either of these schools at rowing, cricket, etc. To win a Blue at Oxford or Cambridge, it is necessary to take part in an inter-university contest. The Blue for rowing is the oldest and most coveted of these distinctions. Full Blues are given for rowing, cricket, athletics, and both kinds of Football. Cambridge also gives a full Blue for hockey, but Oxford does not. Half Blues are awarded for tennis, swimming, boxing, shooting, and various other forms of recreation, including chess.

BLUE-STOCKING. A literary lady: applied usually with the imputation of pedantry. The term arose in connection with certain meetings held by ladies in the days of Dr. Johnson for conversation with distinguished literary men. One of these literati was a Mr. Benjamin Stillingfleet, who always wore blue stockings, and whose conversation at these meetings was so much prized that his absence at any time was felt to be a great loss, so that the remark became common: " We can do nothing without the *blue-stockings* "; hence these meetings were sportively called *blue-stocking clubs*, and the ladies who attended them *blue-stockings*.

BLUE-STONE, or BLUE-VITRIOL. Sulphate of copper, a dark-blue crystalline salt used in dyeing and for other purposes, $CuSO_4$, $5H_2O$.

BLUE-THROAT. A bird (*Sylvia suecica*) with a tawny breast marked with a sky-blue crescent, inhabiting the northern parts of Europe and Asia. It is a bird of passage, and is taken in great numbers in France for the table.

BLUE-VITRIOL. *See* BLUE-STONE.

BLUE-WING. A genus of American ducks, so called from the colour of the wing-coverts. One species (*Querquedŭla discors*) is brought in great quantities to market, the flesh being highly esteemed for its flavour.

BLUFFS. An American name for such high, steep banks of a stream or lake as form prominent headlands. Bluffs frequently extend some distance inland as plateaus.

BLUMENBACH (blö′men-bä*h*), **Johann Friedrich.** Celebrated German naturalist, born 1752, died 1840. He studied at Jena and Göttingen, and wrote on the occasion of his graduation as M.D. a remarkable thesis on the varieties of the human race. He became professor of medicine, librarian, and keeper of the museum at Göttingen in 1778, where he lectured for fifty years. His principal works are the *Institutiones Physiologicæ*, long a common textbook; *Handbuch der vergleichenden Anatomie* (Handbook of Comparative Anatomy), the best treatise that had appeared up to its date; and *Collectio Craniorum Diversarum Gentium.* The last work, published between 1790 and 1828, gives descriptions and figures of his extensive collection of skulls, still preserved at Göttingen. He advocated the doctrine of the unity of the human species, which he divided into five varieties, Caucasian, Mongolian, Negro, American, and Malay.

BLUNDELLSANDS. Watering-place of Lancashire. It stands on the Mersey, 6½ miles from Liverpool, of which it is practically a suburb. It is reached by the L.M.S. Rly.

BLUNDELL'S SCHOOL. Public school of Devonshire. Just outside Tiverton, it was founded in 1604 by Peter Blundell, a Tiverton tradesman. The present buildings, which hold about 350 boys, were built in 1882; the old building mentioned in *Lorna Doone* was in the town itself.

BLUN′DERBUSS. A short gun with a very wide bore and a bell-shaped muzzle, capable of holding a number of slugs or bullets, and intended to do execution at a limited range without exact aim. This type of gun is now quite obsolete.

BLUNT, John Henry. English theological writer, born 1823, died 1884. He held various curacies, and afterwards was appointed to the living of Beverston, Gloucestershire. He wrote much; among his chief works are the *Dictionary of Doctrinal and Historical Theology*; *Dictionary of Sects, Heresies, etc.*; *History of the English Reformation*; *Household Theology*; *Annotated Book of Common Prayer*.

BLUNT, John James. English divine, born 1794, died 1855; from 1839 Lady Margaret professor of divinity at Cambridge. His works include: *Sketch of the Reformation in England*; *Undesigned Coincidences in the Old and New Testament*, an argument for their veracity; *On the Right Use of the Early Fathers*; *History of the Church during the First Three Centuries*; *Sermons*; etc.

BLYTH (blith). A seaport, market town, and urban district of England, Northumberland, on the south side of the River Blyth at its mouth, this river here forming a small estuary after a course of about 20 miles. The town is well built, the harbour is safe and convenient, and there are fine docks, and a pier a mile in length. Shipbuilding, engineering, brick-making, etc., are carried on, as also fishing; there are many collieries in the neighbourhood, and much coal is exported. There is a good beach, and Blyth is famous for sea-bathing. Pop. (1931), 31,808.

BOA. A genus of serpents, family Boidæ, having the jaws so constructed that they can dilate the mouth sufficiently to swallow bodies thicker than themselves. They are also distinguished by having a hook (vestigial hind-limb) on each side of the vent; the tail prehensile; the body compressed and largest in the middle, and with small scales, at least on the posterior part of the head. The genus includes some of the largest species of serpents, reptiles endowed with immense muscular power. They seize sheep, deer, etc., and crush them in their folds, after which they swallow the animal whole. The boas are peculiar to the hot parts of South America. The *Boa constrictor* is not one of the largest members of the genus, rarely exceeding 20 feet in length; but the name boa or boa constrictor is often given popularly to any of the large serpents of similar habits, so as to include the Pythons of the Old World and the Anaconda and other large serpents of America.

BOAB'DIL, Abu-Abdullah. Last Moorish King of Granada; gained the throne in 1481 by expelling his father, Mulei Hassan, and became the vassal of Ferdinand of Aragon. By his tyranny he provoked the hostility of his own subjects, and Ferdinand, taking advantage of the dissensions which prevailed, laid siege to Granada. The Moors made a valiant defence, but Boabdil capitulated in 1492, and retired to a domain of the Alpujarras assigned to him by the victor. He afterwards passed into Africa, and fell in battle while assisting the King of Fez in an attempt to dethrone the King of Morocco.

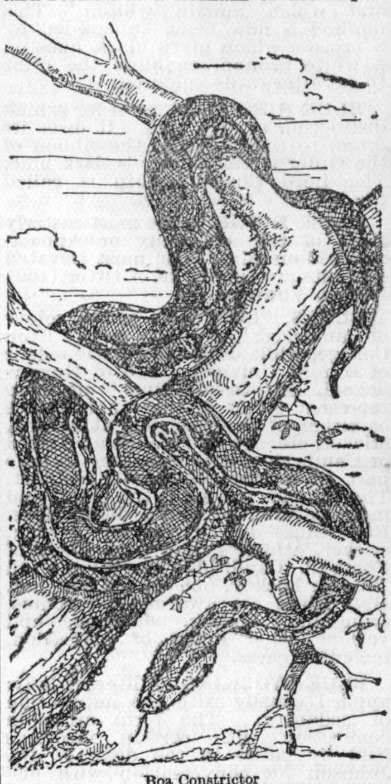
Boa Constrictor

BOADICE'A. Queen of the Iceni, in Britain, during the reign of Nero. Having been treated in the most ignominious manner by the Romans, she headed a general insurrection of the Britons, attacked the Roman settlements, reduced London to ashes, and put to the sword all strangers to the number of 70,000. Suetonius, the Roman general, defeated her in a decisive battle (A.D.

62), and Boadicea, rather than fall into the hands of her enemies, put an end to her own life by poison.

BOANERGES. Descriptive surname given by Jesus to two prominent disciples, James and John. In modern usage it sometimes describes vehement orators.

BOAR (wild hog). Domestic breeds of pig are derived from the European wild boar (*sus scrofa*), which was hunted in Britain in the sixteenth century, is still found in France and other parts of Europe. The Indian wild boar (*S. cristatus*) furnishes the sport called pig-sticking. In some localities domestic swine turned loose have become wild again.

BOAR'S HILL. District near Oxford. Across the Thames in Berkshire, it is about 4 miles from the city. It has become a favourite residential area. Owing to its beautiful situation, it was decided in 1929 to take steps to protect its amenities. There John Masefield lives, and has his private theatre.

BOARD. A number of persons having the management, direction, or superintendence of some public or private office or trust; often an office under the control of an executive government, the business of which is conducted by officers specially appointed.

BOARD OF ADMIRALTY. *See* ADMIRALTY.

BOARD OF EDUCATION. A department of the British Government constituted on 1st April, 1900, in place of the former Educational Department of the Privy Council (including the Science and Art Department). It has supreme control of primary, secondary, and technical education in England, and is assisted by a consultative committee.

BOARD OF TRADE. A department of the British Government, having wide and important functions respecting the trade and navigation of the kingdom. It is presided over by a member of the Cabinet as president, there being also permanent secretary, a parliamentary secretary, etc. Its various permanent departments include: Overseas Trade (Development and intelligence), Mercantile Marine, Mines, Commercial Relations and Treaties, Companies, Industrial Property (including Patent Office), Statistics, and many others dealing with such matters as Finance, Bankruptcy, etc. The Board of Trade issues a weekly paper, *The Board of Trade Journal*, the Overseas Trade Department publishes annual reports, and there are many reports from all departments. The *Railway Department* has the supervision of railways and railway companies, and must be supplied with notices of application for railway Acts and with plans before the relative Bill can be brought before Parliament. Before a line is opened for traffic the permission of the board on the report of an inspector must be got; and on the occurrence of an accident, notice must be sent to the department, which is then empowered to take any measures it may deem necessary for the public safety or interest. It also takes under its supervision tramways, subways, canals, gas- and waterworks.

The *Harbour Department* exercises a supervision over harbours, lighthouses, pilotage, electric supply, gas, etc. The *Marine Department* administers the Merchant Shipping Act of 1894. It has to see to the registration, condition, and discipline of merchant ships; to watch over the mercantile marine offices, and to see that the regulations with regard to the engagement of seamen and apprentices are carried out; to examine officers, and make investigations into misconduct and wrecks; and conjointly with the Admiralty it deals with the Royal Naval Reserve. The *Financial Department* has to keep the accounts of the board, controlling the receipts and expenditure. It also deals with Greenwich pensions, seamen's savings-banks, the distribution of the effects of seamen dying abroad, and the like. The *Bankruptcy Department* appoints official receivers and generally administers the Bankruptcy Acts. The Patent Office is under the Board of Trade, as well as the standards of weights and measures, the registration of joint-stock companies, the administration of the Electric Lighting Acts, etc. The *Commercial Intelligence Department*, founded in 1899, became in 1917 the *Department of Overseas Trade*.

BOAT. A small open vessel or water-craft usually moved by oars or rowing. The forms, dimensions, and uses of boats are very various, and some of them carry a light sail. Large vessels, whether ships of war or merchantmen, carry with them a number of boats; and since steam has become so common as a propelling power, it has also been employed in ships' boats. A ship of war has now usually several large boats propelled by steam, with others that are rowed, as a barge, pinnace, yawl, cutter, jolly-boat, and gig. Every British passenger ship is required to carry a number of boats sufficient to convey all the persons on board, one of such boats being a properly-fitted life-boat. *See* Barge; Pinnace; Rowing; etc.

BOAT-BILL (*Cancrōma cochlearia*). A South American bird of the family Ardeidæ or herons, about the size of a common fowl, with a bill not unlike a boat with the keel uppermost; its chief food is fish.

BOAT-FLY, or **WATER BOATMAN** (*Notonecta glauca*). An aquatic hemipterous insect which swims on its back; the hind-legs resembling oars, the body representing a boat: hence the name; common in Britain.

BOAT'SWAIN (commonly pronounced bō'sn). A warrant-officer in the navy who has charge of the sails, rigging, colours, anchors, cables, and cordage. His office is also to summon the crew to their duty, to relieve the watch, etc. In the merchant service one of the crew who has charge of the rigging and oversees the men.

BOAZ. Biblical character, who, by his marriage to Ruth became the great-grandfather of David.

BOB'BIN. A reel or other similar contrivance for holding thread. It is often a cylindrical piece of wood with a head, on which thread is wound for making lace; or a spool with a head at one or both ends, intended to have thread or yarn wound on it, and used in spinning-machinery (when it is slipped on a spindle and revolves therewith) and in sewing-machines (applied within the shuttle).

BOBBINITE. *See* Explosives.

BOBBIN-NET. A machine-made cotton net, originally imitated from the lace made by means of a pillow and bobbins.

BOB'BIO. A small town of N. Italy, province of Pavia, the seat of a bishop, with an old cathedral, and formerly a celebrated abbey founded by St. Columbanus. Pop. 5200.

BOB-O-LINK. *See* Rice-bird.

BOBRUISK. A fortified town of Russia, government of Minsk. Pop. 42,309.

BOCCACCIO (bok-kat'chō), **Giovanni.** Italian novelist and poet, son of a Florentine banker. He was born, 1313, in Certaldo, a small town in the valley of the Elsa, 20 miles from Florence; died there 1375. He spent some years unprofitably in literary pursuits and the study of the canon law, but in the end devoted himself entirely to literature. He found a congenial atmosphere in Naples, where many men of letters frequented the Court of King Robert, among the number being the great Petrarch. In 134[illegible] Boccaccio fell in love with Maria, an illegitimate daughter of King Robert, who returned his passion with equal ardour, and was immortalized as Fiammetta in many of his best creations. His first work, a romantic love-tale in prose, *Filocopo*, was written at her command; as was also the *Teseide*, the first heroic epic in the Italian language, and the first example of the *ottava rima.* In 1341 he returned to Florence at his father's command, and during a three years' stay produced three important works, *Ameto, L'amorosa Visione* and *L'amorosa Fiammetta,* all of them connected with his mistress in Naples.

In 1344 he returned to Naples, where Giovanna, the granddaughter of Robert, who had succeeded to the throne, received him as became a distinguished man. Between 1344 and 1350 most of the stories of the *Decameron* were composed at her desire or at that of Maria Fiammetta. This work, on which his fame rests, consists of 100 tales represented to have been related in equal portions in ten days by a party of ladies and gentlemen at a country house near Florence while the plague was raging in that city. The stories in this wonderful collection range from the highest pathos to the coarsest licentiousness. They are partly the invention of the author, and partly derived from the fabliaux of mediæval French poets and other sources. On the death of his father Boccaccio returned to Florence, where he was greatly honoured, and was sent on several public embassies. He also went to Padua to communicate to Petrarch the tidings of his recall from exile and the restoration of his property. From this time an intimate friendship grew up between them which continued for life. They both contributed greatly to the revival of the study of classical literature, Boccaccio spending much time and money collecting ancient manuscripts.

In 1373 he was chosen by the Florentines to occupy the chair which was established for the exposition of Dante's *Divina Commedia.* His lectures continued till his death. Among his other works may be mentioned *Filostrato,* a narrative poem; *Il Ninfale Fiesolano,* a love story; *Il Corbaccio, Laborrinto d'Amore,* a coarse satire on a Florentine widow; and several Latin works. The first edition of the *Decameron* appeared without date or place, but is believed to have been printed at Florence in 1469 or 1470. The first edition with a date is that of Valdarfer, Venice, 1471; what is, perhaps, the only existing perfect copy of this was sold in London in 1812 for £2260.—Cf. E. Hutton, *Giovanni Boccaccio: a Biographical Study.*

BOCCAGE (bok-äzh), **Marie Anne du.** A French poetess, much admired and extravagantly praised by Voltaire, Fontenelle, Clairaut, and others, born 1710, died 1802. Her writings comprise an imitation of *Paradise Lost*; *The Death of Abel*; *The Amazons*, a tragedy; and a poem called *The Columbiad.*

BOCCA TIGRIS, or **BOGUE.** The embouchure of the principal branch of the Chu Kiang, or Canton River, China.

BOCCHERINI (bok-ker-ē′nē), **Luigi.** Italian composer of instrumental music. He was born in 1740 at Lucca, and died at Madrid 1805. His compositions consist of symphonies, sestets, quintets, quartets, trios, duets, and sonatas for the violin, violoncello, and pianoforte. He never composed anything for the theatre; and of church compositions we find but one, his *Stabat Mater.*

BOCHART (bo-shär), **Samuel.** French theologian and Oriental scholar, born at Rouen 1599, died at Caen 1667, where he was Protestant clergyman. His chief works are his *Geographia Sacra* (1646), and his *Hierozoicon*, or treatise on the animals of the Bible (London, 1663).

BOCHNIA (bo*h*′ni-a). A town of Poland, formerly in Austrian Galicia, 25 miles E.S.E. of Cracow; extensive mines yielding gypsum, zinc, and rock-salt. Pop. 10,000.

BOCHOLT (bo*h*′olt). A town of Germany, province of Westphalia, on the Aa; cotton-spinning and weaving, etc. Pop. 30,268.

BOCHUM (bo*h*′ųm). A German town, province of Westphalia, 5 miles E.N.E. of Essen; manufactures iron, steel, hardwares, etc. Pop. 313,480.

BOCK, or **BOCKBIER.** A variety of German beer made with more malt and less hops than ordinary German beer, and therefore sweeter and stronger.

BOCK′ENHEIM (-hīm). A town of Germany, Wiesbaden, now included in Frankfurt-on-the-Main; with flourishing manufactures of machinery, etc.

BÖCKH (beuk), **Philipp August.** An eminent German classical antiquary, born at Karlsruhe 1785, died at Berlin 1867. He was educated at Karlsruhe and Halle, and obtained in 1811 the chair of ancient literature in the University of Berlin, where he remained for the rest of his life. He opened a new era in philology and archæology by setting forth the principle that their study ought to be an historical method intended to reproduce the whole social and political life of any given people during a given period. Among his chief works are an edition of Pindar (1811-22); *The Public Economy of the Athenians* (1817), translated into English and French; *Investigations into the Weights, Coins, and Measures of Antiquity* (1836); and *Documents concerning the Maritime Affairs of Attica* (1840). The great *Corpus Inscriptionum Græcarum* was begun by him with the intention of giving in it every Greek inscription known in print or manuscript.

BOCLAND, BOCKLAND, or **BOOKLAND.** One of the original English modes of tenure of manor-land which was held by a short and simple deed under certain rents and free services. This species of tenure has given rise to the modern freeholds.

BODE (bo′de), **John Elert.** German astronomer, born 1747, died 1826. His best works are his *Astronomical Almanac* and his large *Celestial Atlas* (Himmelsatlas), giving a catalogue of 17,240 stars (12,000 more than in any former chart).

BODE'S LAW is the name given to an arithmetical formula, previously made known by Kepler and Titius of Wittenberg, expressing approximately the distances of the planets from the sun. It assumes the series 0, 3, 6, 12, 24, 48, 96, etc., each term after the second being double the preceding term; to each term 4 is added, producing the series 4, 7, 10, 16, 28, 52, 100, etc. These numbers are, with the exception of 28, roughly proportional to the distances between the planets and the sun. The law has no theoretical foundation.

BODENBACH. A town of Czechoslovakia, formerly belonging to Austria. Pop. 15,100.

BODEN-SEE. *See* CONSTANCE, LAKE OF.

BO′DENSTEDT (-stet), **Friedrich Martin.** German poet and miscellaneous writer, born in 1819. Having obtained an educational appointment at Tiflis, he published a work on the peoples of the Caucasus (1848), and *A Thousand and One Days in the East*, which were very successful. In 1854 he was appointed professor of Slavonic at Munich, and in 1858 was transferred to the chair of Old English. He was afterwards a theatrical director at Meiningen, and travelled in the United States, etc. Among the best of his poetical works are the *Songs of Mirza-Schaffy*, purporting to be translations from the Persian, but really original, which have passed through more than 100 editions. He translated Shakespeare's *Sonnets*, and with other writers issued a new translation of Shakespeare's works. He died in 1892.

BODIN (bo-daṇ), **Jean.** A French political writer, born in 1530, died 1596. He studied law at Toulouse, delivered lectures on jurisprudence there, and afterwards went to Paris and practised. His great work *De la République* (1576) has been characterised as the ablest and most remarkable treatise on the philosophy of government and legislation produced from the time of Aristotle to that of Montesquieu.

BODLE. A copper coin formerly current in Scotland, of the value of two pennies Scots, or the sixth part of an English penny. The name is said to have been derived from a mint-master of the name of Bothwell.

BODLEIAN LIBRARY at Oxford, founded by Sir Thomas Bodley in 1598, opened 1602. It claims a copy of all works published in Britain, and for rare works and MSS. it is second only to the Vatican. It contains about 500,000 books. *See* LIBRARIES.

BODLEY, Sir Thomas. The founder of the Bodleian Library at Oxford, born at Exeter in 1544, died in London 1612. He was educated partly at Geneva, whither his parents, who were Protestants, had retired in the reign of Queen Mary. On the accession of Elizabeth they returned home, and he completed his studies at Magdalen College, Oxford. He travelled much on the Continent, and was employed in various embassies to Denmark, Germany, France, and Holland. In 1597 he returned home, and dedicated the remainder of his life to the re-establishment and augmentation of the public library at Oxford. He expended a very large sum in collecting rare and valuable books, besides leaving an estate for the support of the library. He was knighted at the accession of James I.

BOD'MER, Johann Jakob. German poet and scholar, born 1698, died at Zürich 1783, where he had been professor of history for fifty years. He did great service by republishing the old German poets and by his numerous critical writings.

BOD'MIN. County town of Cornwall, England, nearly in its centre, well built, with a fine church, erected about the middle of the fifteenth century. It gives name to a parliamentary division of the county. Pop. (1931), 5526.

BODO'NI, Giambattista. Celebrated Italian printer, born at Saluzzo 1740, died at Parma 1813. In 1758 he went to Rome, and was employed in the printing-office of the Propaganda. He was afterwards at the head of the ducal printing-house in Parma, where he produced works of great beauty. His editions of Greek, Latin, Italian, and French classics are highly prized.

BODY-SNATCHING. A practice of secret exhumation of dead bodies for sale as subjects for dissection. Watch-towers, some of which can still be seen, were built near churchyards, so that the resurrectionists could be overlooked. The practice of body-snatching gave inspiration to the "Burke and Hare" murders.

BOECE (bois), or **BOYCE, Hector.** Scottish historian, born at Dundee about 1465. He studied first at Dundee, and then at the University of Paris, where he became professor of philosophy in the College of Montaigu, and made the acquaintance of Erasmus. About 1500 he quitted Paris to assume the principalship of the newly-founded university of King's College, Aberdeen. In 1522 he published in Paris a history in Latin of the prelates of Mortlach and Aberdeen. Five years afterwards appeared the work on which his fame chiefly rests, the *History of Scotland* in Latin—*Scotorum Historiæ a prima gentis origine*, etc. It abounds in fable, but the narrative seems to have been skilfully adjusted to the conditions of belief in his own time. In 1536 a translation of the history was published, made by John Ballentyne or Bellenden for James V. It was used by Holinshed and thus indirectly by Shakespeare. He died in 1536.

BOEHM (bām), **Sir Joseph Edgar, R.A.** Sculptor, born at Vienna, 1834, of Hungarian parents. He studied art in Italy and Paris, and settled in England in 1862. He executed many statues for public monuments, including those to Bunyan at Bedford, Carlyle and Tyndall on the Thames Embankment, Beaconsfield and Stanley at Westminster, etc., besides many portrait-busts. He died 12th Dec., 1890.

BOEHME (beu'me) or **BOEHM, Jakob.** German mystical writer, called the "Teutonic Theosopher", born in 1575, died in 1624. He was apprenticed to a shoemaker in his fourteenth year, and ten years later he was settled at Görlitz as a master-tradesman, and married to the daughter of a thriving butcher of the town. He was much persecuted by the religious authorities, and at his death the rites of the Church were but grudgingly administered to him. Raised by contemplation above his circumstances, a strong sense of the spiritual, particularly of the mysterious, was constantly present with him, and he saw in all the workings of nature upon his mind a revelation of God, and even imagined himself favoured by divine inspirations.

His first work appeared in 1616, and was called *Aurora*. It contains his revelations on God, man, and nature. Among his other works are: *De tribus Principiis*, *De Signatura Rerum*, *Mysterium Magnum*, etc. His writings all aim at religious edification, but his philosophy is very obscure and often fantastic. The philosophical value of Boehme lies in his suggestion that in all "things" as cognised by human apprehension there must exist a hidden and a manifested element. The first collection of his works was made in Holland in 1675 by Henry Betke; a more complete one in 1682 by Gichtel (10 vols., Amsterdam). William Law published an English translation of them, 2 vols. 4to. In England, Sir Isaac Newton, William Law, William Blake, and others have been students of Boehme. *See* MYSTICISM.—BIBLIOGRAPHY: H. A. Fechner, *Jacob Böhme, sein Leben und seine Schriften*; J. Claassen, *J. Boehme, sein Leben und seine theosophischen Werke*; E. Boutroux, *Le philosophe allemand Jacob Boehm*; A. J. Penny, *Studies in Jacob Boehme*.

BŒHMERIA (bē-mē´ri-a). A genus of plants, ord. Urticaceæ or Nettles, closely resembling our stinging nettle. A number of the species yield tenacious fibres, used for making ropes, twine, net, sewing-thread, and gas mantles. *B. nivĕa* is the Chinese grass, the Malay *ramie*, which is shrubby and 3 or 4 feet high. It is a native of China, South-Eastern Asia, and the Asiatic Archipelago, where, and in India, it has long been cultivated. The plant has been introduced into cultivation in several British colonies and in parts of the United States, Algeria, etc. *See* RAMIE.

BŒO´TIA. A division of ancient Greece, lying between Attica and Phocis, and bounded E. and W. by the Eubœan Sea and the Corinthian Gulf respectively, had an area of 1119 square miles. The whole country is surrounded by mountains, on the S. Mounts Cithaeron and Parnes, on the W. Mount Helicon, on the N. Mount Parnassus and the Opuntian Mountains, which also closed it in on the E. The northern part is drained by the Cephissus, the waters of which formed Lake Copais; the southern by the Asopus, which flows into the Eubœan Sea.

The country originally had a superabundance of water, but artificial drainage works made it one of the most fertile districts of Greece. The inhabitants were of the Æolian race; most of the towns formed a kind of republic, of which Thebes was the chief city. Epaminondas and Pelopidas raised Thebes for a time to the highest rank among Grecian States. Refinement and cultivation of mind never made such progress in Bœotia as in Attica, and the term Bœotian was used by the Athenians as a synonym for dullness, but somewhat unjustly, since Hesiod, Pindar, the poetess Corinna, and Plutarch were Bœotians. Bœotia now forms with Attica a nome or department of the kingdom of Greece, with a pop. of 407,063; capital Livadia.

BOERHAAVE (bör´hä-ve), **Hermann.** Celebrated Dutch physician, born 1668, died 1738. Destined for the clerical profession, in 1682 he was sent to Leyden to study theology. In 1689 he received the degree of Doctor of Philosophy; soon after he began the study of medicine, and in 1693 was made Doctor of Medicine at Harderwyck. In 1701 the University of Leyden chose him to deliver lectures on the theory of medicine; and in 1709 he was appointed to the chair of medicine and botany. He now published his *Institutiones Medicæ in Usus Annuæ Exercitationis*, and *Aphorismi de Cognoscendis et Curandis Morbis in Usum Doctrinæ Medicinæ*, the former expounding his medical system, the latter classifying diseases and treating of their cause and cure. In 1714 he was made rector of the university, and soon after appointed to the chair of practical medicine. He was also appointed professor of chemistry. His fame brought people from all parts of Europe to ask his advice.

BOERS (börz; Du. *boer*, a farmer). The farmers of Dutch origin in South Africa. In 1836-7 many Boers, being dissatisfied with the British government in Cape Colony, migrated beyond the Orange River, and a number found their way to what is now Natal. Here there had been British settlements for some years, and the British formally annexed the country in 1843. Subsequently the Boers were allowed to establish the Orange Free State as an independent republic, and several other small republics, which finally were combined into one—the South African Republic, or Transvaal.

In 1877 the Transvaal was annexed by Britain, according to the wish of many of the people, but war broke out in 1880, British forces suffered more than one defeat, and in 1881 the country was accorded a modified independence. Henceforth it was a common feeling among the Boers that they and not the British must be predominant in South Africa, and in Oct., 1899, after an insolent ultimatum, the united forces of the Transvaal and Orange State invaded Natal. The war which followed with Britain was concluded by the final surrender of the Boers in May, 1902; the two States having been declared British territory in 1900. *See* SOUTH AFRICA; TRANSVAAL.—BIBLIOGRAPHY: D. Livingstone, *The Transvaal Boers*; Lucas, *The History of South Africa to the Jameson Raid*; Keane, *The Boer States, land and people.*

BOETHIUS. A Latinised form of *Boece. See* BOECE.

BOETHIUS (bo-ē'thi-us), **Anicius Manlius Severinus.** A celebrated Roman statesman and philosopher, born about A.D. 470 in Rome or Milan, of a rich and ancient family; executed 525. Theodoric, King of the Ostrogoths, then master of Italy, loaded him with marks of favour and esteem, and raised him to the first offices in the empire. He was three times consul, and received the greatest possible honour from people, Senate, and king. But Theodoric, as he grew old, became irritable, jealous, and distrustful of those about him, and was worked upon by some whom Boethius had made enemies by his strict integrity and vigilant justice. These at last succeeded in prejudicing the king against him, and he was accused of a treasonable correspondence with the Court of Constantinople, imprisoned for a time, and then put to death.

He made translations of the Greek philosophers, particularly Aristotle, which, in the Middle Ages, caused him to be regarded as the highest authority in philosophy. There is no evidence that he was a Christian. His fame now chiefly rests on his *Consolation of Philosophy*, written in prison, partly in prose and partly in verse, a work of elevated thought and diction. We have an Anglo-Saxon translation of it by King Alfred, and it was early translated into other languages. His influence may be traced in Beowulf and in Chaucer, in Provençal popular poetry, and in the *Divina Commedia.*—Cf. H. F. Stewart, *Boethius: an Essay.*

BOETTGER WARE. *See* DRESDEN CHINA.

BOG. A tract of soft, wet, spongy land, in which the soil is, sometimes to a depth of more than 40 feet, composed of decaying and decayed vegetation. The usual origin is the formation of a shallow pool, which induces the growth of aquatic plants. These gradually extend from the edges towards the centre; mud gathers round them, and a semi-liquid mass is formed, which promotes the growth of moss, particularly of the Sphagnum variety. This flourishes, absorbs water, and produces a new growth on the upper part; the older growth below rots, and, owing to pressure, gradually solidifies, displacing the water. A clay subsoil, frequently occurring over gravel, is very favourable to the formation of bogs, owing to its retentive character. In such circumstances, heavy rains, causing an excess of water, may lead to the bursting of a bog and to the flooding of the adjacent country with a mass of peat and water; such a disaster occurred near Killarney in 1896, resulting in the loss of several lives. In addition to this danger, bogs have a prejudicial effect upon the climate in their neighbourhood.

The reclamation of shallow bogs may be effected at comparatively small cost by drainage, and the reclaimed soil is often highly productive. This is more generally possible in the case of black bogs or "mountain mosses", formed by rapid decomposition of vegetable matter. The deeper red bogs or peat mosses, light in consistency, full of filaments, and formed by slow decay, are less easily dealt with, being very retentive of water. The latter variety generally occur in extensive plains, and are usually level, though frequently slightly elevated towards their centre. In the reclamation of a bog, the drainage must be thorough and permanent; mineral matter must be mingled with the bog-soil to consolidate and fertilise it; and carefully considered rotation of crops must be followed.

The most satisfactory additions to bog-soil include calcareous earths, limestone gravel, shell-sand and shell-marl. Among the many bogs found in Ireland, the great Bog of Allen, lying east of the Shannon and containing 150,000 acres, is the chief, exceeding in size any other in the British Isles. Chat Moss, in Lancashire, over which George Stephenson successfully carried the Liverpool and Manchester Railway in 1829, has an area of 10 sq. miles. In Solway Moss a troop of horse is said to have been lost in 1542.

BOGAR'DUS, James. An American inventor, born in 1800, died in 1874. Among his inventions were the "ring-flyer" or "ring-spinner" used in cotton manufacture (1828), the eccentric mill (1829), an engraving-machine (1831), and the first dry gas-meter (1832). In 1839 he gained the reward offered for the best plan for carrying out the penny postage system by the use of stamps. In 1847 he built the first complete cast-iron structure in the world, and the first wrought-iron beams were made from his design. His delicate pyrometer and deep-sea sounding-machine were valuable additions to scientific instruments.

BOG ASPHODEL (*Narthecium ossifrăgum*). A British plant of the lily family, with pretty starlike flowers, growing in elevated moory and boggy grounds.

BOGATZ'KY, Karl Heinrich von. German Protestant theological writer, born 1690, died 1774. His principal works are: *Güldenes Schatz-Kästlein der Kinder Gottes* (1718), *Geistliche Gedichte* (1749). The English translation of the former is well known by the title of Bogatzky's *Golden Treasury*.

BOG-BEAN. *See* BUCK-BEAN.

BOG-BUTTER. A fatty spermaceti-like mineral resin found in masses in Irish peat-bogs, and sometimes at least representing actual butter which had been placed there for preservation.

BOGHEAD COAL. A brownish coal, found at Boghead, near Bathgate, Linlithgowshire; it is rich in volatile hydrocarbons, and is used for the production of mineral oil and gas. With the material known as Torbanite, from Torbanehill, Fifeshire, it may be taken as the type of several coals accumulated in swampy lakes, and composed of algæ, excreta of organisms, and particularly of the resins left on the decay of plants and spores drifted from the land. Coals of this type have been called "sapropelic", and are also popularly known as "bogheads".

BOG IRON-ORE. A loose, porous, earthy ore (iron hydroxide) found at the bottom of peat-bogs and swamps. It is formed by the decomposition and precipitation of carbonates and oxides of iron held in solution by the waters of the morass; it is used for the removal of sulphur in the manufacture of gas. It frequently forms a pan that interferes with the drainage of arable lands, since the soluble salts of iron oxidise at the surface of the water-table in the sub-soil. This process is greatly aided in swamps by the "iron bacteria" (q.v.), which deposit iron hydroxide in or on their cell-walls and cause extensive accumulations.

BOG MOSS. *See* SPHAGNUM.

BOG MYRTLE. *See* MYRICA.

BOGNOR REGIS. An English coast town and health resort in Sussex, about 6½ miles south-east of Chichester, with convalescent homes, esplanade and pier, assembly-rooms and theatre, etc. Pop. (1931), 13,510.

BOG-OAK. Trunks and large branches of oak found imbedded in bogs and preserved by the antiseptic properties of peat, so that the grain of the wood is little affected by the many ages during which it has lain interred. It is of a shining black or ebony colour, derived from its impregnation with iron, and is frequently converted into ornamental pieces of furniture and smaller ornaments, as brooches, ear-rings, etc.

BOGODUKHOFF (-*hof'*). A town of the Ukraine, in the government of Kharkov, with a considerable trade. Pop. 11,500.

BOGOMILI (bō-gō-mē'lē). An ascetic and mystical sect of the Greek Church. The origin of the name has been found in the frequent use by them of the two Slavonic words *Bog milui*, "Lord, have mercy". It may, however, be derived from *Bogumil*, "Beloved of God". They were a sect of dualistic heretics, and flourished particularly among the Bulgarians. They developed from the Paulicians and Enchites or Messalians, and came into prominence in the twelfth century, if not in the tenth. They held that God had two sons, Sathaniel and Logos, the former of whom rebelled and created the material world, but was finally subdued by the Logos or Christ. The sect was powerful in Bulgaria for about five centuries, and by its method of teaching did much to preserve and circulate old legends and folk-lore, including many early versions of Oriental fictions.

BOG-ORE. *See* BOG IRON-ORE.

BOGOS. A pastoral Hamitic people of Northern Abyssinia, occupying a fine plateau and mountain district, and numbering about 10,000, almost entirely engaged in cattle-rearing, though there is some tillage and a trade in corn, butter, ivory, skins, buffalo-horns, and ostrich feathers. The men are well built and fairly handsome, the women of a lower type. They have peculiar patriarchal institutions with regularly established laws. Their religion is officially Christian, but Mahommedanism has a considerable number of adherents. Their chief village is Keren.

BOGOSLOV. A small volcanic island on the north-west coast of Unalaska, in the Aleutian Islands; it is a haunt of sea-lions.

BOGOTÁ (formerly **Santa Fé de Bogotá**). A city of South America, capital of Colombia and of the State or department of Cundinamarca, and seat of an archbishop, situated on an elevated plain 8600 feet above the sea, at the foot of two lofty mountains, with a healthy though moist climate, and a temperature rarely exceeding 59° F. Bogotá being subject to earthquakes, the houses are low, and strongly built of sun-dried brick. The principal street, *Calle Real*, is very handsome, terminating at one end in a square, formed by the palace of the president, the cathedral, the custom-house, etc. There are a university, four colleges, a library, national museum, observatory, botanic garden, theatre, mint, etc. The inhabitants are mostly Creoles. Bogotá is an emporium of internal trade, and has breweries and flour-mills. Its manufactures of soap, cloth, leather, glass, etc., are not of great importance. It was founded in 1538. Pop. 235,000.—The plateau of Bogotá seems to be the basin of a dried-up lake. It is drained by the River Bogotá or Funza, which forms the Fall of Tequendama, about 475 feet high.

BOG-TROTTER, a term originally applied contemptuously to the Irish peasantry from the ability shown by them in crossing their native bogs by leaping from tussock to tussock—a frequent means of escape from police and soldiery.

BOGUE (bōg). An acanthopterygian fish (*Boöps* or *Box vulgaris*), family Sparidæ, or giltheads, found in the Mediterranean, and sometimes on the coasts of Britain. The eyes are large, and the general colouring brilliant.

BOGUE (bōg), **David.** The originator of the London Missionary Society, born in Berwickshire in 1750, died 1825. He studied at Edinburgh, and was licensed as a preacher of the Church of Scotland. In 1771 he was employed as usher in London, and afterwards became minister of an Independent chapel at Gosport, where he formed an institution for the education of young men for the Independent ministry. He then began the formation of the grand missionary scheme which afterwards resulted in the London Missionary Society, and took an active part in the foundation of the British and Foreign Bible Society and the Religious Tract Society. He wrote an *Essay on the Divine Authority of the New Testament* (1802); *Discourses on the Millennium* (1813-6); and, in conjunction with Dr. Bennet, a *History of Dissenters* (1809-12).

BO'GUS. An Americanism meaning counterfeit, and applied to any spurious or counterfeit object; as, a *bogus* government, a *bogus* law. The origin of the term is uncertain.

BOHAIN (bō-aŋ). A town of North-Eastern France, department of Aisne, district of St. Quentin, on the railway from that town to Lille, with manufactures of woollen goods. It was the scene of severe fighting during the Great War, in Oct., 1918. Pop. 6899.

BOHEA (bo-hē'). An inferior kind of black tea. The name is sometimes applied to black teas in general, comprehending Souchong, Pekoe, Congou, and common Bohea.

BOHE'MIA (Ger. *Böhmen*). The western portion of the Republic of Czechoslovakia, till the break-up of the Dual Monarchy in 1918 a Crown land and titular kingdom belonging to Austria, bounded by Bavaria, Saxony, the Prussian province of Silesia, Moravia, and the archduchy of Austria; area, 20,102 sq. miles; pop. 7,106,766, of whom more than 2,000,000 were Germans, the rest mostly Czechs. The language of the country is the Czech dialect of the Slavonic (see *Czech Language*); in some districts, and in most of the cities, German is spoken.

Bohemia is surrounded on all sides by mountains, and has many large forests. Its plains are remarkably fertile. The chief rivers are the Elbe and its tributary the Moldau, which is even larger. All sorts of grain are produced in abundance, as also large quantities of potatoes, pulse, sugar-beet, flax, hops (the best in Europe), and fruits. Wine is not abundant, but in some parts is of good quality. The raising of sheep, horses, swine, and poultry is carried on to a considerable extent. The mines yield silver, copper, lead, tin, zinc, iron, cobalt, arsenic, uranium, antimony, alum, sulphur, plumbago, and coal. There are numerous mineral springs, but little salt. Spinning and weaving of linen, cotton, and woollen goods are extensively carried on; manufactures of lace, metal, and wood work, machinery, chemical products, beet-root sugar, pottery, porcelain, etc., are also largely developed. Large quantities of beer (Pilsener) are exported. The glassware of Bohemia, which is known all over Europe, employs 50,000 workers. The trade, partly transit, is extensive, Prague, the capital, being the centre of it. The largest towns are Prague, Pilsen, Liberec, Budejovice, Teplice, Usti nad Labem, and Cheb. The educational establishments include the Prague University and upwards of 4000 ordinary schools. Till 1918 Bohemia was governed locally by a single chamber of 242 members and was represented in the Lower House of the Reichsrath by 130 members.

Literature. Bohemia possesses a literature of considerable bulk, including in it also works written in Czech by Moravian and Hungarian writers. The earliest fragments, such as the MSS. of Kralodvür and of Zelena Hora, referred to the tenth century, are forgeries of the nineteenth century. It was not till after the thirteenth century that Bohemian literature attained to any development. The next century was a period of great activity, and to it belong versified legends, allegorical and didactic poems, historical and theological works, etc. The most flourishing period of the older literature falls within 1409-1620, John Huss (1369-1415) having initiated a new era, which, however, is more fertile in prose works than in poetry. The following period, up to the beginning of the nineteenth century, was one of decline, but in recent times there has been a great revival, and in almost all departments Bohemian writers have produced works of merit.

History. Bohemia was named after a tribe of Gallic origin, the Boii, who were expelled from this region by the Marcomanni at the commencement of the Christian era. The latter were in turn obliged to give place to the Germans, and these to the Czechs, a Slavonic race who had established themselves in Bohemia by the middle of the fifth century, and still form the bulk of the population. Before the close of the sixth century this Slavonic people came under the domination of the Avars of Hungary. But early in the seventh century they regained their freedom with the aid of their ruler Samo, whom the Czechs elected as their king. The country was at first divided into numerous principalities. Christianity was introduced about 878.

In 1092 Bohemia was finally recognised as a kingdom under Wratislas II. In 1230 the monarchy, hitherto elective, became hereditary. The monarchs received investiture from the German Emperor, held one of the great offices in the Imperial Court, and were recognised as among the seven Electors of the empire. Frequently at strife with its neighbours, Bohemia was successively united with and disunited from Hungary, Silesia, Moravia, etc., according to the course of wars and alliances. Ottokar II. (1253-78) had extended his conquests almost from the Adriatic to the Baltic, when he lost them and his life in contest with Rudolph, the founder of the House of Hapsburg.

After the close of the Przemysl dynasty (which had held sway for about six centuries) by the assassination of Ottokar's grandson, Wenceslas III. the House of Luxemburg succeeded in 1310, and governed Bohemia till 1437, the reign of Charles II. (1346-78) being especially prosperous. Towards the close of this second dynasty civil wars were excited by the spread of the Hussite movement, the central figure of the struggle being John Ziska, the leader of the Taborites. A temporary union between the moderate Hussites and the Catholics having proved a failure, the reformed party elected as king, in 1433, the Protestant noble, George Podibrad. On his death in 1471 they chose Wladislas, son of Casimir, King of Poland, who also obtained the crown of Hungary. His son Louis was killed in the battle of Mohacz against the Turks, and Ferdinand of Austria became in 1527 sovereign of both kingdoms.

Bohemia then lost its separate existence, being declared a hereditary possession of the House of Austria; and its subsequent history pertains to that of the Austrian Empire. In 1848 an attempt was made to assert its ancient independence against the Austrian dominion; a conflict took place, Prague was bombarded, and the insurrection suppressed. *See* CZECHO-SLOVAKIA. The latter half of last century and the beginning of the present witnessed a revival of the national spirit among the Czechs. This and the strong desire for local self-government which at the outbreak of the Great War changed to a desire for absolute independence finally led in 1919 to the formation of the state of Czecho-Slovakia.—BIBLIOGRAPHY: Count F. Luetzow, *Bohemia*; Ernest Denis, *La Bohème depuis la Montagne Blanche*; T. Capek, *Bohemia under Hapsburg Misrule*; Count F. Luetzow, *A History of Bohemian Literature*; H. Jellinek, *La Littérature Tchèque Contemporaine.*

BOHEMIAN BRETHREN (**Moravian Brethren,** or **Unitas Fratrum**). A Christian sect of Bohemia, formed from the remains of the stricter sort of Hussites, in the latter half of the fifteenth century. The Bohemian Brethren are a link in a chain of sects beginning with Wycliffe (1324-84). The ideas of the Englishman found favour with Huss, and Bohemia proved a better soil for their growth than England. They took the Scriptures as the ground of their doctrines throughout, and sought to frame the constitution of their churches on the apostolic model. They had a rigid system of mutual supervision extending even to the minute details of domestic life. Being persecuted, numbers retired into Poland and Prussia. Those who remained in Moravia and Bohemia, and who had their chief residence at Fulneck, in Moravia, were hence called *Moravian Brethren.*

BOHEMIAN FOREST (*Böhmerwald*). A mountain ridge extending from the Fichtelgebirge southward towards the confluence of the Ilz and the Danube, and separating Bavaria from Bohemia. The highest peaks are the Arber (4790 ft.) and the Rachel.

BOHEMIANISM. Phrase used for the unconventional way of living adopted by artists, literary men and students in Paris, London and elsewhere. It comes from the fact that the gypsies who lived this kind of life were believed to have come from Bohemia. Paris was the original home of Bohemianism, and it still flourishes there.

BO'HEMOND, Marc. Son of the Norman adventurer Robert Guiscard, who rose to be Duke of Apulia and Calabria. Born about 1056. After distinguishing himself in Greece and Illyria against Alexius Comnenus, he returned to find that in his absence his younger brother Roger had seized upon the paternal inheritance (1085). War ensued, but Bohemond, contenting himself with the principality of Tarentum, ultimately threw his energy into the Crusades. He took a leading part in the campaign in Asia Minor, captured Antioch (1098), and assumed the principality; but was taken prisoner in 1101 and held captive for two years. In 1106 he married Constance, daughter of Philip I. of France, and, after an unsuccessful renewal of war with Alexius, died at Canossa in 1111. Five of his descendants held in succession the principality of Antioch for over a century and a half.

BOHLEN (bō'len), **Peter von.** German Orientalist, born in 1796, died in 1840. Having devoted himself to the Oriental languages, he obtained an appointment at Königsberg in 1825 as extraordinary, and in 1830 as ordinary, professor of Oriental literature. The most important of his writings is a work entitled *Das alte Indien* (Ancient India).

BÖHME. *See* Böehme.

BÖHMISCH-LEIPA (b*eu*'mish-lī-på). *See* Leipa.

BOHN (bōn), **Henry George.** English bookseller, born at London, of a German family, in 1796, died 1884. He was the publisher of the well-known *Libraries*, or collection of standard works at moderate prices, to which he contributed some translations and works edited by himself; and he prepared an edition of **Lowndes's** *Bibliographer's Manual*, etc.

BOHOL (bo-*h*ol'). One of the Philippine Islands, north of Mindanao. It is woody and mountainous. Area, 1534 sq. miles. Pop. 460,800.

BÖHTLINGK (b*eu*t'lingk), **Otto.** German Sanskrit scholar, born at Petrograd in 1815; chief work, a *Sanskrit-German Dictionary*, in 7 vols. (1853-75), prepared in conjunction with Prof. Roth of Tübingen. He died in 1904.

BOHUN. Name of a famous Norman family. Having settled in England, its members became rich and powerful landowners. In 1199 Henry Bohun was made Earl of Hereford and was one of the barons associated with the signing of Magna Carta. Another Bohun opposed Edward I. The male line died out in 1373.

BOIAR'DO, Matteo Maria, Count of Scandiano. Italian poet, scholar, knight, and courtier, born near Ferrara in 1434. From 1488 to 1494, the year of his death, he was commander of the city and castle of Reggio, in the service of Ercole d'Este, Duke of Modena. His chief poem was his uncompleted *Orlando Innamorato* (1495), a romantic epic, the principal Italian poem before the *Orlando Furioso* of Ariosto, though now chiefly known by the *rifacimento* of Berni. His other works include a comedy, *Il Timone*; *Sonnetti e Canzoni*; *Carmen Boucolicon*; *Cinque Capitoli in terza rima*; and translations from Lucian, Apuleius, and Herodotus.

BOI'ARS, or BOY'ARS. An order of the old Russian aristocracy next in rank to the ruling princes, and bearing much the same relation to them as the lesser barons of England and Scotland did to the greater in the feudal ages. The boiars enjoyed many exclusive privileges, held all the highest military and civil offices, and were so powerful that the ancient imperial ukases contained the clause: "The emperor has willed it, the boiars have approved it." The order was abolished by Peter the Great, who gave its members a place in the Russian nobility.

BO'IDÆ. A family of large non-venomous serpents, with two mobile hooks or spurs, the vestiges of hind-legs, near the vent. The type genus is Boa.

BOIELDIEU (bwäl-dy*eu*), **Adrien François.** A celebrated French composer, born at Rouen in 1775. He early displayed great musical talent, his first opera, *La Famille Suisse*, being well received in 1795 at Rouen. In 1795 he repaired to Paris, and rose rapidly in reputation, producing several operas, of which the best was *Le Calife de Bagdad* (1799). Domestic difficulties drove him in 1802 to Russia, where he became musical director to the emperor. On his return to Paris in 1811 he produced, among other works, his two masterpieces, *Jean de Paris* (1812) and *La Dame Blanche* (1825), which place him in the first rank of composers of French comic opera. For some years he was professor of composition and pianoforte at the Conservatoire. He died in 1834.

BOI'I. A Celtic people, whose original seat is supposed to have been the Upper Saône and the higher parts of the Seine and Marne. They migrated to Cisalpine Gaul, crossed the Po, and established themselves between it and the Apennines, in the country previously occupied by the Umbrians. After a more or less constant strife with the inhabitants of Southern Italy, they attacked the Romans in support of Hannibal in 218 B.C., and though defeated, maintained the war until their subjugation by Scipio Nasica, 191 B.C. The remnant of the tribe sought refuge among the Tauriscans in the territory since called after them Bohemia, from which there was a later migration, about 58 B.C., to Bavaria, to which also they gave their name.

BOIL. A boil appears as a conical swelling on the surface, hard around the margin and soft at the apex. It is very painful and exquisitely tender. The infection enters through a hair follicle, and this becomes the centre or "core" of the boil, really a small area of gangrene, but the extent of skin involved is always limited, and a single boil never becomes very large or widespread. The appearance of a "crop" of boils indicates that the patient's general condition is lowered and he is more susceptible to the infection.

Treatment. The popular treatment by poultices and fomentations is very apt to lead to the spread of the infection, and a more satisfactory method is to cover the part with a piece of Unna's plaster, making a small opening for the apex of the boil to come through. A pad of lint should be placed on top to protect from pressure and irritation. The best treatment for "crops" of boils is by vaccines.

BOILEAU-DESPREAUX (bwä-lō-dā-prō-ō), **Nicholas** (commonly called **Boileau**). A French poet, born in 1636 at Paris. He studied in the Collège d'Harcourt and in the Collège de Beauvais, and entered the legal profession, but soon left it to devote himself entirely to belles-letters. In 1660 appeared his first satire, *Adieux d'un Poète à la Ville de Paris*, followed rapidly by eight others, and ultimately by three more, to complete the series. They attacked with much critical acumen, and in vigorous but finely-finished verse, the poets and writers of the older school. In 1664 he wrote his prose *Dialogue des Heros de Roman*, which sounded the knell of the artificial romances of the period. His *Epistles*, written in a more serious vein, appeared at various times from 1669 onwards; but his masterpieces were *L'Art Poétique* and *Le Lutrin*, published in 1674. The former is an imitation of the *Ars Poetica* of Horace with reference to French verse, the latter a mock-heroic poem which furnished Pope with a model for *The Rape of the Lock*.

In many respects his writings determined the trend of all subsequent French poetry, and he left, through his influence upon Dryden, Pope, and their contemporaries, a permanent mark upon English literature. For some time he held the post of historiographer in connection with Racine, and was elected academician in 1684, though only after the interference of the king in his favour. He died in 1711 of dropsy.—BIBLIOGRAPHY: G. Lanson, *Boileau*; Dreyfus-Brissac, *Un faux classique: Boileau*; F. Brunetière, article *Boileau* in *La grande Encyclopédie*.

BOILER. The name applied to any vessel for boiling large quantities of liquor in, but most commonly used as the designation of a metallic vessel in which water is converted into steam by the agency of fire, the steam being intended by its expansive force to give motion to a steam-engine, or to be used for a variety of manufacturing purposes. Boilers are now generally constructed of mild steel, having a tensile strength of about 30 tons per sq. inch. In locomotive boilers the fire-boxes are almost always constructed of copper, but in some cases, especially in America, mild steel is used here also. The tubes of locomotive boilers are of brass; those of water-tube boilers mostly of mild steel. The tubes of ordinary marine boilers are usually of wrought iron or mild steel.

Boilers may be grouped in two classes, namely, *shell or tank boilers* and *tubular boilers*. The latter class may be again subdivided into *fire-tube* and *water-tube boilers*. A boiler of the former class consists of a large shell or tank, usually cylindrical, with flat ends. This shell contains the water and steam, so that the whole shell is exposed to the full pressure of the steam. In some cases the furnaces are external, but generally they are contained within the shell. In fire-tube boilers the products of combustion pass through tubes of small diameter, whereas in water-tube boilers the water flows through the tubes, and the products of combustion flow over the outsides of the tubes.

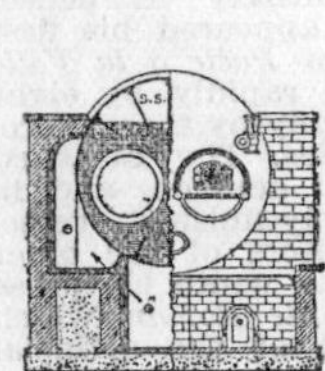

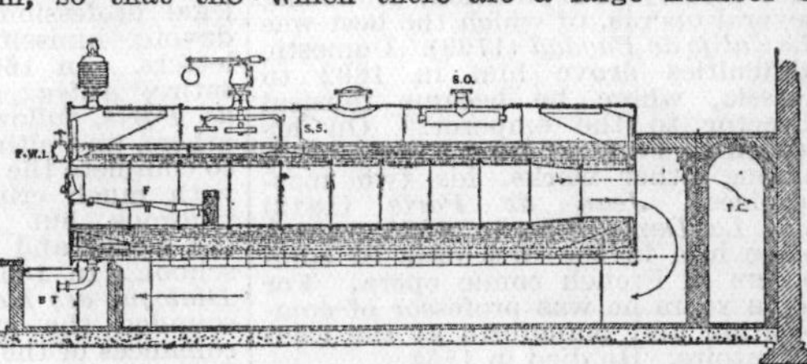

Cross-section Front elevation Longitudinal section

Fig. 1.—Lancashire Boiler

S.S., Steam space. F.W.I., Feed-water inlet. F., Furnace. S.O., Steam outlet. B.T., Blow-out trench. T.C., To chimney.

Cornish and Lancashire Boilers are examples of shell boilers of the flue type. The *Lancashire boiler* (see fig. 1) is 20 to 30 feet long, and 7 to 9 feet in diameter. Within it are two cylindrical flues, at the front ends of which are the two furnaces. Conical "Galloway tubes" are usually fitted into the internal flues for the purpose of improving the circulation of the water. At the rear end of the fire-grate is a fire-brick bridge, which serves to prevent the fuel from falling over the end of the grate, but its main object is to cause the gases to mix more rapidly in order to facilitate rapid and complete combustion. The boiler is cased in brickwork, so built as to form external flues at the sides and beneath. The products of combustion, after leaving the internal flues, pass down to the bottom flue, along which they flow to near the front end of the boiler. They then flow through the side flues to the rear end, and thence into the flue leading to the chimney. *Marine* and *locomotive boilers* are examples of the tubular class of boiler. They are multi-tubular fire-tube boilers. A marine boiler—a cylindrical shell-boiler with two furnaces—is shown in fig. 2. Marine boilers, also called Scotch boilers, may be single-ended or double-ended; that is, they may have furnaces at one end only or at both ends. The furnaces are in cylindrical flues communicating with internal combustion-chambers, from which there are a large number of return tubes above the flues leading to the uptake. In a locomotive boiler it is usual to have a fire-brick arch dividing the fire-box into two compartments, the upper of which serves as a combustion-chamber. The gases flow from the fire-box through the small tubes to the smoke-box at the front end. As a high chimney cannot be used, there must be an artificial or forced draught, and this is always obtained by means of a steam blast. The exhaust steam from the engine cylinders is used for the purpose.

Water-tube Boilers, as distinct from fire-tube boilers, have been arranged in three classes, namely: (1) those with *limited circulation*; (2) those with *free circulation*; (3) those with *accelerated circulation*. The special feature of the first class, of which the Belleville boiler is the type, is the use of tubes rising in successive coils or folds, each receiving water at the lower end and discharging steam and water at the upper. The circulation is limited to what is necessary to replace the water evaporated, and there is no water-reservoir. Boilers of the second class have horizontal or slightly-inclined generating tubes connecting

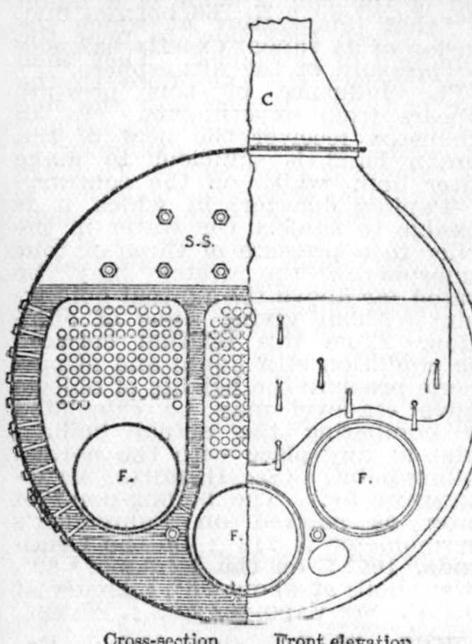

Cross-section Front elevation

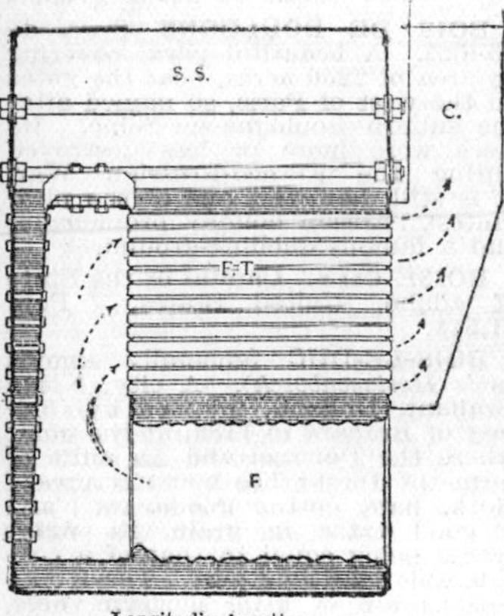

Longitudinal section

Fig. 2.—Marine Cylindrical Boiler

S.S., Steam space. F.T., Fire-tubes. F., Furnace. C., Chimney.

vertical or inclined water-spaces. The principal kinds in use are the Niclausse and the Babcock & Wilcox (see fig. 3), which is of sectional construction. In boilers of accelerated circulation there are vertical tubes of various shapes connecting horizontal reservoirs, generally of a cylindrical shape. The water is returned from the top steam-drum to the water-drum at the bottom by large down-take tubes. The principal examples of this type of boiler are the Thornycroft (see fig. 4), the Yarrow, the Normand, the Normand-Sigaudy, and the Stirling. Water-tube boilers of the second and third classes are used exclusively in war-vessels and in large electric-power stations; while Scotch boilers

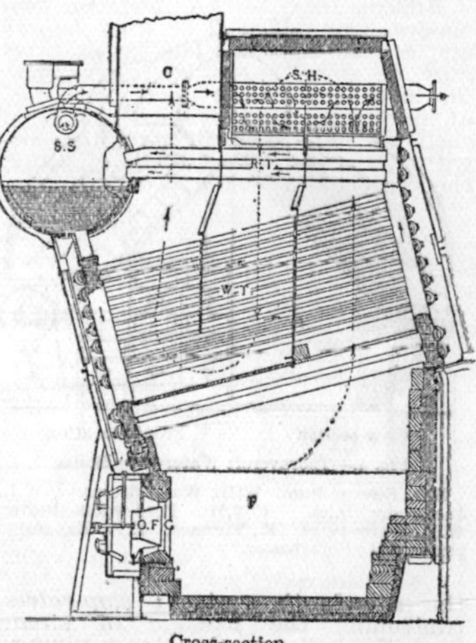

Cross-section

Fig. 3.—Babcock & Wilcox Boiler, with superheater fitted for oil-firing, for mail and passenger vessels

S.S., Steam space. W.T., Water-tubes. F., Furnace. R.T., Return tubes. S.H., Superheater. C., Chimney. O.F.G., Oil-firing gear.

are still prevalent in the mercantile marine. Water-tube boilers are less liable to explosion, and can be built in much larger units and for higher working-pressures than are practicable with Lancashire or Scotch boilers. Babcock boilers are now built to supply steam at a temperature of 700° F., at a working-pressure of 475 lb. per sq. inch.

A *Green's economiser* is an arrangement of cast-iron tubes, usually vertical, which is generally inserted in the flues leading from boilers. Its function is to heat the feed-water by means of the hot products of combustion after they leave the boiler. The products of combustion flow round the outsides of these tubes, and the tubes are kept clean by automatic scrapers, which continuously remove the soot from them. The advantages of superheated steam for land plants are now generally recognised, and *superheaters*, for supplying heat to the steam after it leaves the boiler, are usually added to land boilers. Successful *mechanical stokers* have also been devised.

Boiler Fittings. The principal *boiler fittings* are as follows: *pressure-gauges*, to show the pressure of steam; *safety-valves*, of which there should be two on each boiler, one beyond

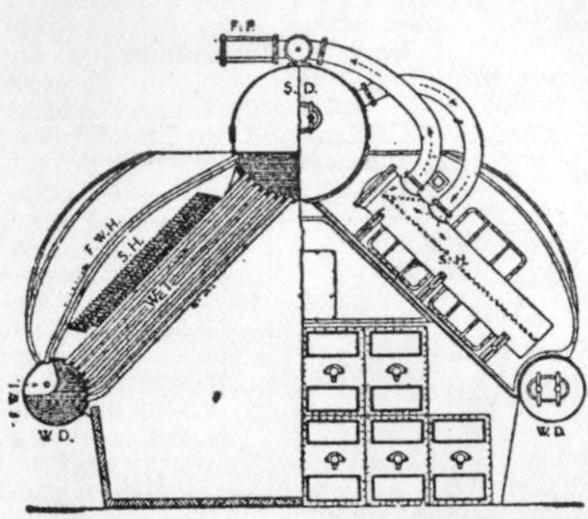

Cross-section Front elevation

Fig. 4.—Thornycroft Water-tube Boiler

S.D., Stream drum. W.D., Water drums. F.W.I., Feed-water inlet. F.W.H., Feed-water heater. W.T., Water-tubes. F., Furnace. E.P., Expansion piece. S.H., Superheater.

the attendant's control; *stop-valves*, controlling the passage of steam from the boiler to the steam-piping; *separators*, for drying the steam if it is not superheated; *water-gauges* showing the water-level; *feed check-valves*, for regulating the supply of water; also *automatic feed-water regulators*, *injectors*, and *feed-pumps*.—BIBLIOGRAPHY: W. H. Fowler, *Steam Boilers*; F. B. Kleinhaus, *Boiler Construction*; W. Inchley, *Steam Boilers and Accessories*; W. W. F. Pullen, *Testing of Engines, Boilers, and Auxiliary Machinery*; E. M. Shealy, *Steam Boilers* (Engineering Education Series).

BOILING-POINT. The temperature at which a heated-up fluid is converted into vapour. The conversion takes place chiefly at the point of contact with the source of heat, and the bubbles of vapour rising to the surface, and breaking there, produce the commotion called *ebullition*. At the ordinary atmospheric pressure ebullition commences at a temperature which is definite for each liquid. The escape of the heated fluid in the form of vapour prevents any further rise of temperature in an open vessel when the *boiling-point* has been reached. The exact definition of the boiling-point of a liquid is "that temperature at which the tension of its vapour exactly balances the pressure of the atmosphere."

The influence of this pressure appears from experiments. In an exhausted receiver the heat of the human hand is sufficient to make water boil; while, on the contrary, in Papin's digester, in which it is possible to subject the water in the boiler to a pressure of three or four atmospheres, the water may be heated far above the normal boiling-point without giving signs of ebullition. From this relation between the ebullition of a liquid and atmospheric pressure the heights of objects above sea-level may be calculated by comparing the actual boiling-point at any place with the normal boiling-point. (*See* HEIGHTS, MEASUREMENT OF.) The boiling-point of water as marked on Fahrenheit's thermometer is 212°; on the Centigrade, 100°; on the Réaumer, 80°. Ether boils at about 96°, mercury at 662° F. *See* VAPORISATION; WATER.

BOIS D'ARC (bwȧ-därk; Fr., bow-wood). Same as *Osage Orange*.

BOIS DE BOULOGNE (bwä dė bö-lōn). A beautiful park, covering an area of 2250 acres, near the gates on the west of Paris, so named after the suburb Boulogne-sur-Seine. Its trees were more or less destroyed during the Franco-Prussian War. It is still, however, one of the pleasantest Parisian holiday promenades and a famous duelling-ground.

BOISÉ CITY. Capital of the State of Idaho, United States. Pop. 21,544.

BOIS-LE-DUC (generally known as *'s Hertogenbosch*). A city, North Brabant, Holland, founded by Godfrey of Brabant in 1184, at the point where the Dommel and Aa unite to form the Diest; has manufactures of cloth, hats, cotton goods, etc., and a good trade in grain, its water traffic being equal to that of a considerable maritime port. The fortifications are of little modern value, but the surrounding country can be readily inundated at need. The cathedral, dedicated to St. John the Evangelist, is one of the finest in the Netherlands; it was almost entirely rebuilt between 1458-98. The Duke of York was defeated here by the French in 1794. Pop. 41,371.

BOISSERÉE (bwäs-rā) **GALLERY.** A celebrated gallery of pictures in the Pinakothek or picture gallery at

Munich, collected by the brothers Sulpice (1783-1854) and Melchior Boisserée. In 1827 King Ludwig of Bavaria purchased it for 120,000 thalers.

BOISSONADE (bwă-so-näd), **Jean François.** A French classical scholar, born 1774, died 1857. He became in 1809 assistant of Larcher as Greek professor of the Faculty of Letters in Paris, and four years afterwards he succeeded him both in the Faculty and in the Institute. In 1816 he was elected academician, and in 1828 was called to the chair of Greek literature in the Collège de France. Besides editing many of the minor classics, he issued *Vitæ Sophistarum* (1822). *Syllogæ Poetarum Græcorum* (1823-6), *Anecdota Græca* (1829-33), *Anecdota Nova* (1844).

BOISSY D'ANGLAS (bwă-sē dāṇ-lä), **François Antoine, Comte de.** A French statesman of the revolutionary period, born 1756, died 1826. In 1789 he was elected at Annonay to the States-General, and in 1792 to the Convention. He voted against the death of Louis XVI., and after the fall of Robespierre was appointed secretary of the Convention, and entrusted with the provisioning of Paris at a time of famine. He was made a member of the Council of Five Hundred in 1795, president of the Tribunate in 1803, senator and commander of the Legion of Honour in 1805, and a peer by Louis XVIII. in 1814. Besides many brochures, he wrote an *Essai sur la vie et les opinions de M. de Malesherbes* (1819-21), *Études Littéraires et Poétiques d'un Vieillard* (1825).

BOITO, Arrigo. Italian composer and poet, born at Padua in 1842. In his early days he devoted much time to the study of the classics, and studied music at the Conservatoire at Milan. He served as a volunteer under Garibaldi in 1866, during the war with Austria, and in 1867 settled in Paris as a journalist. His first opera, *Mefistofele*, was produced at the Scala, Milan, on 5th March, 1868, but his chief musical work consisted of his operatic libretti, wherein he was greatly influenced by Wagner. In 1877 he published a volume of poems (with the anagram *Tobio Garrio* as the author's name) which exhibit his remarkable lyrical gifts and also his love for the uncanny. In 1892 he was appointed inspector-general of technical instruction in the Conservatori of Italy. He was elected a Senator in his own country, and in 1893 received the honorary degree of Mus.D. from the University of Cambridge. He died 10th June, 1918.—Cf. Grove's *Dictionary of Music.*

BOJADOR'. A cape on the west coast of Africa, one of the projecting points of the Sahara; till the fifteenth century the southern limit of African navigation. The coast of the Sahara from Cape Blanco to this cape and a considerable portion of the interior has been proclaimed Spanish territory.

BOJAR (bo'yär). *See* BOIAR.

BOJARDO (bo-yär'dō). *See* BOIARDO.

BOKHARA, or **BUKHARA** (bo-ä'rȧ). A former Soviet republic of Central Asia, till 1919 a vassal to Russia, and since 1924 part of the Uzbek Republic, bounded by the Russian provinces of Sir Darya, Samarqand, and Ferghana, by Afghanistan, by Transcapia, and by Khiva; area, 79,440 sq. miles. The country in the west is to a great extent occupied by deserts; in the east are numerous ranges of mountains. Cultivation is mainly confined to the valleys of the rivers, the chief of which is the Oxus or Amu Darya. The climate is warm in summer, but severe in winter; there is very little rain, and artificial irrigation is necessary. Chief minerals are gold, salt, alum, and sulphur. Besides cereals, cotton, silk, and tobacco are cultivated, and also a good deal of fruit.

The total population, about 3,000,000, consists of the Uzbek Tatars, the former ruling race, to whom the emir belonged; the Tajiks, who form the majority; Kirghiz, with Turcomans, Arabians, Persians, etc. The only two towns of importance are the capital, Bokhara (pop. 75,000), Karshi (pop. 25,000). The capital, according to Vambéry the centre of Tatar civilization, is behind the large towns of Western Asia in general luxury and comfort, though the country is distinguished from other countries of Central Asia by its numerous schools. Till 1917 Bokhara was a khanate with an emir who was theoretically absolute. The manufactures are unimportant, but there is a very considerable caravan trade, cotton, rice, silk, and indigo being exported, and woven goods, sugar, iron, etc., being imported. The trade is chiefly with Russia. The Russian Transcaspian Railway now crosses the country and reaches Samarqand. Since 1925 Bokhara has been in Tajikstan Republic, which is a constituent part of the Uzbek Republic.

History. Bokhara was the ancient Sogdiana or Maracanda, capital Samarqand; was conquered by the Arabs in the eighth century, by Genghis Khan in 1220, and by Timur in 1370, and finally seized by the Uzbeks in 1505. From 1826-60 it was governed by a restless and tyrannous ruler, with whom both the British and the Russians sought to stand on good terms. His successor, the Emir Mozaffar-ed-din, came into conflict with the latter, who, in 1868, compelled the cession of Samarqand and important tracts of territory, and the emir then became practically a vassal of Russia.

After the Russian expedition to Khiva in 1873, an agreement was come to between Russia and Bokhara by which Bokhara received a portion of the territory ceded by Khiva to Russia, while the Russians received various privileges in return. Bokhara became practically a Russian dependency. Mozaffar died in 1885, and was succeeded by his son, Abdul-Ahad, who was guided by a Russian agent. Abdul-Ahad was succeeded by his son, Sayid-mir-Alim Khan, in 1911.

Bokhara. The capital of the khanate; it is 8 or 9 miles in circuit, and is surrounded by a mud wall. The streets are narrow and the houses poorly built; principal edifices: the palace of the khan, crowning a height near the centre of the town and surrounded by a brick wall 70 feet high; and numerous mosques, schools, bazaars, and caravanserais. The trade was formerly large with India, but has been almost completely absorbed by Russia. Pop. 75,000.—BIBLIOGRAPHY: Vambéry, *History of Bokhara*; A. le Messurier, *From London to Bokhara*; E. O'Donovan, *The Merv Oasis*; O. Olafson, *The Emir of Bokhara and his Country*.

BOKHARA-CLOVER. *See* MELILOT.

BOLA'MA. *See* BISSAGOS.

BOLAN' PASS. A celebrated defile in the Hala Mountains, N.E. of Beluchistan, on the route between the Lower Indus and Beluchistan and Afghanistan. It is about 60 miles long, hemmed in by lofty precipices, and in parts so narrow as to be very easily defended. It is traversed by a military road and military railway (partly of the cog-wheel type). The entrance of the pass next India is 800 feet high, the outlet 5800 feet, the latter being about 35 miles S.E. of Quetta.

BOLAS (that is, "balls"). A form of missile used especially by the Indians in the southern parts of South America. It consists of a rope or line having at either end a stone, ball of metal, or lump of hardened clay. When used it is swung round the head by one hand, and then hurled at an animal so as to entangle it by twisting round its legs or otherwise.

BOLBEC. A town, France, department of Seine-Inférieure, on the Bolbec, a tributary of the Seine. It has a Roman Catholic and a Protestant church, and manufactures of printed cottons and handkerchiefs, linen and woollen stuffs, lace, etc. Pop. 11,080

BOLCHOW (bol'*h*of). *See* BOLKHOFF.

BOLE. An earthy product of the decay of rocks rich in iron, especially of basaltic lavas under ordinary processes of weathering. It is a compact red or yellowish clay, rich in iron hydroxide, with a conchoidal fracture, and has been used as a pigment (Berlin or English red). A soft red ochre, probably a bole, was known to the ancients as *Lemnian Earth*.

BOLER'O. A popular Spanish dance of the ballet class for couples, or for a single female dancer. The music, which is in triple measure, is generally marked by rapid changes of time, and the dancers mostly accompany the music with castanets.

BOLE'TUS. A genus of fungi, ord. Hymenomycetes, family Polyporineæ. The characters of the genus are: broad, hemispherical cap, the lower surface formed of open tubes, cylindrical in form, and adhering to one another, but separable from the cap. The basidia are borne on the inner surface of the tubes. *Boletus edulis* and several other species are edible, but many are poisonous.

South American Indian with Bolas

BOLEYN (bul'in), **Anne.** Second wife of Henry VIII. of England, eldest daughter of Sir Thomas Boleyn and Elizabeth Howard, daughter of the Duke of Norfolk. The exact date of her birth is uncertain, but was probably 1501. She attended Mary, sister of Henry, on her marriage with

Louis XII., to France, as lady of honour, returning to England about 1522, and becoming lady of honour to Queen Catherine. The king, who soon fell passionately in love with her, without waiting for the official completion of his divorce from Catherine, married Anne in Jan., 1533, having previously created her Marchioness of Pembroke. When her pregnancy revealed the secret, Cranmer declared the first marriage void and the second valid, and Anne was crowned at Westminster with unparalleled splendour.

On 7th Sept., 1533, she became the mother of Elizabeth. She was speedily, however, in turn supplanted by her own lady of honour, Jane Seymour. Suspicions of infidelity were alleged against her, and in 1536 the queen was brought before a jury of peers on a charge of treason and adultery. Smeaton, a musician, who was arrested with others, confessed that he had enjoyed her favours, and on 17th May she was condemned to death. The clemency of Henry went no further than the substitution of the scaffold for the stake, and she was beheaded on 19th May, 1536. Whether she was guilty or not has never been decided; that she was exceedingly indiscreet is certain.—BIBLIOGRAPHY: P. Friedmann, *Anne Boleyn*; Blaze de Bury, *Un Divorce Royal*; J. A. Froude, *The Divorce of Catherine of Aragon*; M. A. S. Hume, *The Wives of Henry VIII.*

BOLGRAD. A town of Bessarabia, at the north end of Lake Jalpusch, with an important trade in grain. Pop. 12,821.

BOLI. A town in the north-west of Asia Minor, 130 miles east by south of the Bosporus, on the River Boli, with warm springs in the neighbourhood. Pop. 11,000.

BOLIDE (bō-lid). A name applied to a meteor seen to explode in the atmosphere. When fragments reach the earth, the designation of "meteor" or "aerolite" is given, though no necessary difference of constitution is implied.

BO'LINGBROKE, Henry St. John, Viscount. English statesman and political writer, born in 1678 at Battersea, London. He was educated at Eton and at Oxford, where he had a reputation both for ability and libertinism. In 1700 he married a considerable heiress, the daughter of Sir Henry Winchcomb, but they speedily separated. In 1701 he obtained a seat in the House of Commons, attaching himself to Harley and the Tories. He at once gained influence and became Secretary of War in 1706, though he retired with the ministry in 1708. He continued, however, to maintain a constant intercourse with the queen, who preferred him to her other counsellors, and on the overthrow of the Whig ministry in 1710, after the Sacheverell episode, he became one of the Secretaries of State.

In 1712 he was called to the House of Lords by the title of Viscount Bolingbroke, and in 1713, against much popular opposition, concluded the Peace of Utrecht. At this period the Tory leaders were intriguing to counteract the inevitable accession of power which the Whigs would receive under the House of Hanover; but shortly after the conclusion of the peace a contention fatal to the party broke out between the Lord High Treasurer (Harley, Earl of Oxford) and Bolingbroke. Queen Anne, provoked by Oxford, dismissed him, and made Bolingbroke Prime Minister, but died herself four days later. The Whig dukes at once assumed the power and proclaimed the Elector king. Bolingbroke, dismissed by King George while yet in Germany, fled to France in March, 1715, to escape the inevitable impeachment by which, in the autumn of that year, he was deprived of his peerage and banished. James III., the Pretender, invited him to Lorraine and made him his Secretary of State, but dismissed him in 1716 on a suspicion of treachery. He remained for some years longer in France, where (his first wife having died) he married the Marquise de Villette, niece of Madame de Maintenon, occupying himself with various studies. In 1723 he was permitted to return to England, living at first retired in the country in correspondence with Swift and Pope. He then joined the opposition to the Walpole ministry, which he attacked during eight years in the *Craftsman* and in pamphlets with such vigour and skill that in 1735 a return to France became prudent, if not necessary. In 1742, on the fall of Walpole, he came back in the expectation that his allies would admit him to some share of power; but, being disappointed in this respect, he withdrew entirely from politics and spent the last nine years of his life in quietude at Battersea, dying in 1751.

He wrote an excellent and forcible style, his chief works being *A Dissertation upon Parties*, *Letters on the Spirit of Patriotism*, on *The Idea of a Patriot King*, and on *The State of Parties at the Accession of George I.*, *Letters on the Study of History* (containing attacks on Christianity), and other works. Pope was indebted to him for suggestions for his *Essay on Man*. He was clever and versatile, but unscrupulous and insincere.—BIBLIOGRAPHY: Goldsmith, *Life of Bolingbroke*; W. E. H. Lecky, *England in the Eighteenth Century*; Walter Sichel, *Bolingbroke and his Times*; A. Hassall, *Life of Viscount Bolingbroke.*

BOLIVAR. Standard monetary unit of Venezuela. Silver coins of 5, 2·5, and one bolivar are current. It is composed of 100 centavos, and at par is worth about 9½*d*.

BOLIVAR (bo-lē'vär), **Simon** (*El Libertador*). The liberator of Spanish South America, born at Caracas, 24th July, 1783. He finished his education in Europe, and, having then joined the patriotic party among his countrymen, he shared in the first unsuccessful efforts to throw off the Spanish yoke. In 1812 he joined the patriots of New Granada in their struggle, and, having defeated the Spaniards in several actions, he led a small force into his own country (Venezuela), and entered the capital, Caracas, as victor and liberator, 4th Aug., 1813. But the success of the revolutionary party did not last long. Bolivar was beaten by General Boves, and before the end of the year the Royalists were again masters of Venezuela.

Bolivar next received from the Congress of New Granada the command of an expedition against Bogotá, and, after the successful transfer of the seat of government to that city, retired to Jamaica. Having again returned to Venezuela, he was able to rout the Royalists under Morillo, and, after a brilliant campaign, effected in 1819 a junction with the forces of the New Granada Republic. The battle of Bojaca, which followed, gave him possession of Santa Fé and all New Granada, of which he was appointed President and Captain-General. A law was now passed by which the Republics of Venezuela and New Granada were to be united in a single State, as the *Republic of Colombia*, and Bolivar was elected the first President.

In 1822 he went to the aid of Peru, and was made Dictator, an office held by him till 1825, by which time the country had been completely freed from Spanish rule. In 1825 he visited Upper Peru, which formed itself into an independent republic named *Bolivia*, in honour of Bolivar. In Colombia a civil war arose between his adherents and the faction opposed to him, but Bolivar was confirmed in the presidency in 1826, and again in 1828, and continued to exercise the chief authority until May, 1830, when he resigned. He died at Carthagena on the 17th Dec., 1830.

One of the departments of Colombia is named after him, as are also a state of the Republic Venezuela, and the town *Ciudad Bolivar*.—BIBLIOGRAPHY: Larrazabal, *Life of Simon Bolivar*; Ducoudray-Holstein, *Histoire de S. Bolivar*; F. L. Petre, *Simon Bolivar*.

BOLIVIA (formerly called **Upper Peru**). A republic of South America, bounded N. and E. by Brazil, S. by the Argentine Republic and Paraguay, and W. by Peru and Chile. The boundary disputes of Bolivia with Brazil and with Chile were settled by treaties of Nov., 1903, and Oct., 1904. That with Peru was settled in 1911-2; that with Paraguay is as yet without result. The area is estimated at 550,000 sq. miles. As a result of the war with Chile, Bolivia lost her coast territory, about 29,000 sq. miles. The population was estimated in 1927 at 3,464,945. A large proportion of the inhabitants belong to aboriginal races (the Aymaras and the Quichuas), the larger portion of the remainder being Mestizos or descendants of the original settlers by native women. Sucre or Chuquisaca (pop. 16,194) is the nominal capital, but the largest town and seat of government is La Paz; other towns are Potosi, Oruro, and Cochabamba.

Physical Features. The broadest part of the Andes, where they take in Lakes Titicaca and Aullagas, and divide into two chains, the Eastern and Western Cordilleras, lies in the western portion of the State. Here are some of the highest summits of the Andes, as Sorata, Illimani, and Sajama. The two chains enclose an extensive table-land, the general elevation of which is about 12,500 feet, much of it being saline and barren, especially in the south. The ramifications of the eastern branch extend a long way from the Cordillera, forming numerous valleys which pour their waters into the Pilcomayo, a tributary of the Paraguay, and into the Mamoré, Beni, and other great tributaries of the Amazon. These tributaries, many of which are navigable, traverse a region of great plains. A new line from La Paz to the province of Yungas will eventually establish communication with the steamers on the Rivers Beni, Mamoré, and other tributaries. It will thus render accessible to the outer world (by small steamers) a vast and fertile tract. In the south-east there is an extensive barren region with salt marshes. Titicaca, the chief S. American lake, is only partly in Bolivia.

Climate and Trade. The climate, though ranging between extremes of heat and cold, is very healthy, and cholera and yellow fever are unknown. The elevated regions are cold and dry, the middle temperate and delightful, the lower valleys and plains quite tropical. Among animals are the llama, alpaca, vicuña, chinchilla, etc.; the largest bird is the condor. Bolivia has long been famed for its mineral wealth, especially silver and gold, the total value of these metals produced between 1545 and 1875 being estimated at nearly £400,000,000. Potosi was once famous for its silver. The value of the tin produced (a quarter of the total tin output of the world) is now greater than that of silver, and little gold is obtained. The country is capable of producing every product known to South America, and it is estimated that about 4,940,000 acres are under cultivation; but agriculture is in a backward condition. Coffee, coca, cacao, tobacco, maize, and sugar-cane are grown, and there is an immense yield of india-rubber.

The imports and exports were estimated at £5,666,517 and £9,814,502 respectively for 1926. The chief exports are tin, silver, copper, rubber, cinchona bark, cocoa, coffee, apalca wool, etc. Roads are few and bad, but with these improved and extended, more railways, and advantage taken of the Amazon and its tributaries, trade would soon increase. With the sea it has connection by a railway from Mollendo in Peru to Lake Titicaca, and by another from the Chilian seaport Antofagasta. A new line was opened in July, 1917, from Oruro to Cochambamba. In 1927 the republic had 1302 miles of railway in operation, and a large mileage under construction. Accounts are kept in *bolivianos*, about twelve and a half = one British sovereign.

Government. By its Constitution Bolivia is a democratic republic. The executive power is in the hands of a president elected for four years, and the legislative belongs to a Congress of two chambers, both elected by universal suffrage. The revenue and expenditure for 1927 amounted to £3,685,135 and £3,698,035 respectively. The former is derived mainly from custom duties, spirit duties, minerals, rubber export, patents, and stamps. The public debt of Bolivia on 30th June, 1927, amounted to £12,940,857. The State religion is Roman Catholicism, but public worship according to the rites of other religions is permitted. By a law of 19th March, 1912, all marriages must be celebrated by the civil authorities. Primary instruction is free and compulsory, and the State spent about £300,000 in 1916 for educational purposes.

History. Bolivia under the Spaniards long formed part of the viceroyalty of Peru; afterwards it was joined to that of La Plata or Buenos Ayres. Its independent history commences with the year 1825, when the republic was founded. The Constitution was drawn up by Bolivar, in whose honour the State was named Bolivia; and was adopted by Congress in 1826. It has since undergone important modifications. But the country has been almost continually distracted by internal and external troubles, and can scarcely be said to have had any definite Constitution. It suffered severely in the war which, with Peru, it waged against Chile in 1879 and subsequent years, and which ended in the loss of territory already mentioned. The beginning of this century witnessed a decided increase in the value of Bolivia's exports; a further impetus was given during the World War by the great demand for minerals. This increase in prosperity gave rise to a short period of peace, which was broken in 1928 by a border dispute with Paraguay. A peaceful settlement was made, however, in 1929.

The autocratic government set up in 1926 by Dr. Hernando Siles was responsible for the withdrawal of certain civil rights granted to the people by the Constitution. Dr. Siles assumed the powers of a dictator, revised the Constitution, and filled the Government with his own followers, in order to ensure his own re-election. A revolution broke out in 1930, and was supported by the army. The president fled and the government was taken over by General Blanco Galindo.—BIBLIOGRAPHY: L. H. de Bonelli, *Travels in Bolivia*; Charles Wiener, *Bolivie et Pérou*; Child, *The Spanish American Republics*; Paul Walle, *Bolivia*; W. A. Reid, *Bolivia: the Heart of a Continent*.

BOLKHOFF (bol'*h*of). An ancient town of Russia, government of Orel; the industries embrace leather and hemp, hosiery, tallow, gloves, soap. Pop. 27,105.

BOLL (bōl). A Scotch measure for corn, still in use, but not a legal one, varying in different districts and for different articles. A boll of wheat or beans is equal to 4 bushels, a boll of oats, barley, and potatoes to 6 bushels.

BOL'LANDISTS. The Society of

Jesuits which published the *Acta Sanctorum*, a collection of lives of the saints of the Roman Catholic Church. They received this name from John van Bolland (born 1596, died 1665), who edited the first five volumes from materials already accumulated by Heribert Rosweyd, a Flemish Jesuit (died 1629). The society was first established at Antwerp, removed to Brussels on the abolition of the Society of Jesuits in 1773, and dispersed in 1794. A new association was formed in 1837 under the patronage of the Belgian Government, and the publication of the *Acta Sanctorum* has been continued. *See* ACTA SANCTORUM.

BOLLINGTON. An urban district or town of England, Cheshire, 2½ miles north-east of Macclesfield, with silk and cotton factories, etc. Pop. (1931), 5027.

BOLL WORM. Caterpillar which pierces the flower buds and pods or bolls of the cotton plant. It is the larva of the owl moth, *Heliothis armigera*, and is a destructive American pest. In India cotton is attacked not by this but by the caterpillar of another genus, Earias, which also supplies the Egyptian boll worm.

BOLOGNA (bo-lōn′yȧ). One of the oldest, largest, and richest cities of Italy, capital of the province of the same name, in a fertile plain at the foot of the Apennines, between the Rivers Reno and Savena, surrounded by an unfortified brick wall. It is the see of an archbishop, and has extensive manufactures of silk goods, velvet, artificial flowers, etc. The older quarters are poorly, and the modern handsomely built. There are colonnades along the sides of the streets affording shade and shelter to the foot-passengers.

Buildings. Among the principal buildings are the Palazzo Pubblico, which contains some magnificent halls adorned with statues and paintings; the Palazzo del Podestà; and the church or basilica of St. Petronio. Among the hundred other churches, S. Pietro, S. Salvatore, S. Domenico, S. Giovanni in Monte, S. Giacomo Maggiore, all possess rich treasures of art. The leaning towers Degli Asinelli and Garisenda, dating from the twelfth century, are among the most remarkable objects in the city; and the market is adorned with the colossal bronze *Neptune* of Giovanni da Bologna. An arcade of 640 arches leads to the church of Madonna di S. Lucca, situated at the foot of the Apennines, near Bologna, and the resort of pilgrims from all parts of Italy. Bologna has long been renowned for its university, claiming to have been founded by Theodosius II. in 433 (but in reality dating from the eleventh century), and having a library, founded in 1605 by Aldrovandi, which numbers 250,000 volumes and 9000 MSS. In the thirteenth century the number of students is said to have amounted to 10,000. The Instituto delle Scienze, established in 1690, has a library which numbers about 160,000 volumes, with 6000 MSS. The church of San Domenico has a library of 120,000 volumes. The Academy of Fine Arts has a rich collection of paintings by native artists, such as Francia, and the later Bolognese school, of which the Caraccis, Guido Reni, Domenichino, and Albano were the founders.

History. Bologna was founded by the Etruscans under the name of *Felsina*; became in 189 B.C. the Roman colony *Bononia*; was taken by the Longobards about A.D. 728; passed into the hands of the Franks, and was made a free city by Charlemagne. In the twelfth and thirteenth centuries it was one of the most flourishing of the Italian republics; but the feuds between the different parties of the nobles led to its submission to the papal see in 1513. Several attempts were made to throw off the papal yoke, one of which, in 1831, was for a time successful. In 1849 the Austrians obtained possession of it. In 1860 it was annexed to the dominions of King Victor Emmanuel. Pop. 245,647.—The province of *Bologna*, formerly included in the papal territories, forms a rich and beautiful tract; area, 1465 sq. miles; pop. 642,200.

BOLOGNA, Giovanni (properly Jean Boulogne). Sculptor and architect, born at Douai 1524, studied at Rome, and passed most of his life at Florence, where he died in 1608. Chief works: a marble *Rape of the Sabines*, and a bronze *Mercury*.

BOLOGNA PHIAL. A small flask of unannealed glass, which flies into pieces when its surface is scratched by a hard body.

BOLOGNA STONE. A name for a variety of heavy-spar or sulphate of barytes.

BOLOM′ETER. A most sensitive electrical instrument, invented by Professor S. P. Langley, for the measurement of radiant heat. *See* THERMOMETRY.

BOLO PASHA. A French financial adventurer, born at Marseilles in 1867. A remarkable though wholly unscrupulous man, he had lived by his wits from his earliest years. For some time he exercised the profession of dental surgeon, and afterwards was a grocer and a restaurant-keeper. He carried out several ingenious swindles, escaping, however, for the most part without punishment. In 1894 he married at Buenos Ayres a lady named Henriette Soumaille, whom he soon abandoned. He came to Bordeaux in 1902, where he was an agent for champagne. In 1905 he committed bigamy by marrying a very wealthy widow named Müller, with whose money he engaged in business on a large scale.

Bolo's financial schemes were very ambitious, and although none of them were successful, he lived extravagantly, was received in the best circles of society, and counted among his friends the late Judge Monier and Joseph Caillaux. At the beginning of the European War (1914-8) he was again in serious financial difficulties, and therefore quite ready to listen to proposals from agents of the German Government. He entered into communication with the enemy through the ex-Khedive of Egypt, and received large sums, totalling over £336,000, from the emissaries of Count Bernstorff, German Ambassador to the United States.

Bolo was tried before a court martial in 1918 (4th-14th Feb.), the charge against him being that of conspiring to create a defeatist movement in France, by purchasing and attempting to obtain control of several influential daily papers. Found guilty, he was condemned to death, and shot at Vincennes on 17th April.

BOLOR-TAGH, also **BILAUR,** or **BELUT TAGH.** A mountain range formerly imagined to exist in Central Asia between Eastern and Western Turkestan as the axis of the continent. At that point, however, there is really a lofty table-land called the Pamir.

BOLSE'NA (ancient **Volsinii,** one of the twelve Etruscan cities). A walled town, Italy, province of Rome, on the north side of a lake of the same name. The district yields a good wine. Pop. 3700.—The lake (ancient **Lacus Volsiniensis**) is 10 miles long, 7 miles broad, and is well stocked with fish.

BOLSHEVISM. Social and political movement that arose in Russia during the Great War. The word means great, and was given to those who formed the majority in the Communist Party. After 1917, under Lenin and Trotsky, its principles were carried out ruthlessly. They included nationalisation of the means of production, disestablishment of the church, and in general the abolition of the capitalist system. The organisation that replaced the old order proved extremely efficient, but economic laws were too strong for it in several directions.

The leaders set up an organisation for conducting propaganda in foreign countries; but, except for a short time in Hungary, the results were not very tangible. What is called the Five Year Plan was launched in 1928 with the object of rivalling the industrial and agricultural output of other nations. In 1929 a Bolshevik calendar was introduced.

BOLSOVER. An urban district or town of England, in the north-east of Derbyshire, 5 miles east of Chesterfield. Bolsover Castle, belonging to the Duke of Portland, is partly ancient. Coal-mining and quarrying are carried on. Pop. (1931), 11,811.

BOLT HEAD. Cape of Devonshire. It is on the south coast, just west of the estuary of the Salcombe river. A fine natural feature, over 400 feet high, it was acquired in 1928 by the National Trust.

BOLTON, or **BOLTON-LE-MOORS.** A large manufacturing town and municipal, parliamentary, and county borough of Lancashire, England, lying 11 miles N.W. of Manchester, and consisting mainly of two divisions, Great Bolton and Little Bolton, separated from each other by the River Croal. The town, which is of considerable antiquity, received its charter in 1256, and became a manufacturing town as early as 1337, when there was an immigration of Flemings; but its main growth has been of comparatively recent date, and in large part due to the inventions of its sometime residents Arkwright and Crompton.

In manufacturing industries it is now surpassed by few places in Britain, and it contains some of the largest and finest cotton-mills in the world, the yarns spun being generally fine, and a great variety of fancy goods being produced, besides plain calicoes; while bleaching is also carried on. There are large engineering works, besides collieries, paper-mills, foundries, chemical works, etc.

Among the public buildings is one of the finest market-halls in England; a mechanics' institution, a noble building in the Romanesque style; the Chadwick Museum; and a town hall, in the Grecian style, with a tower 220 feet high, fronting the spacious market square. The free grammar-school of the town, founded in 1641, has two university exhibitions of £60 a year each. The Bolton Free Public Library, opened in 1853, contains about 50,000 vols. There are two parks and three recreation grounds. Bolton returns two members to Parliament. Pop. (county borough), 177,253 (1931).

BOLTON ABBEY. Village of Yorkshire (W.R.). It is 22 miles from Leeds on the River Wharfe, on the L.M.S. Rly. There are ruins of a priory, the church of which is now the parish church. Here is a modern residence of the Duke of Devonshire.

BOLTON-ON-DEARNE. Urban district of Yorkshire (W.R.). It is a coal-mining centre on the Dearne, 7 miles from Rotherham, and stands on the L.M.S. Rly. Pop. (1931), 14,242.

BOLT-ROPES. Ropes used to strengthen the sails of a ship, the edges of the sails being sewn to them. Those on the sides are called *leech-ropes*, the others *head* and *foot ropes*.

BO'LUS. 1. A pill-like mass of some medicinal substance larger than the ordinary pill. It is used in the same manner as the pill. 2. A mass of masticated food ready to be swallowed.

BOLZANO. *See* BOTZEN.

BOMA. A trading station on the lower Congo, seat of government of the Congo State.

BOMARSUND'. A former Russian fortress on the Aland Islands at the entrance of the Gulf of Bothnia, bombarded and forced to capitulate to the allied French and English in 1854 during the Crimean War, and then destroyed.

BOMB. A missile thrown by hand, propelled by other means, or dropped, filled with some form of powerful explosive and constructed to detonate on impact, or fitted with a time-fuse.

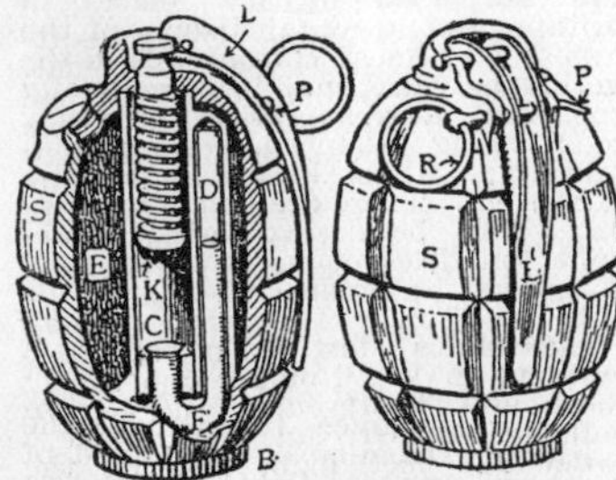

Hand Bomb or Grenade

S, Grooved cast-iron shell. K, Spring-impelled firing-pin, adapted to operate on percussion cap C in communication with time fuse F leading to detonator D, which fires the explosive E. L, External lever held at "safety" by safety-pin P. R, Ring attached to safety-pin. B, Base which unscrews for insertion of fuse and detonator.

The word is also sometimes used to describe an infernal machine arranged to explode at a given time. Under its original meaning the word "bomb" was applied to the earlier forms of explosive missiles used in mortars or

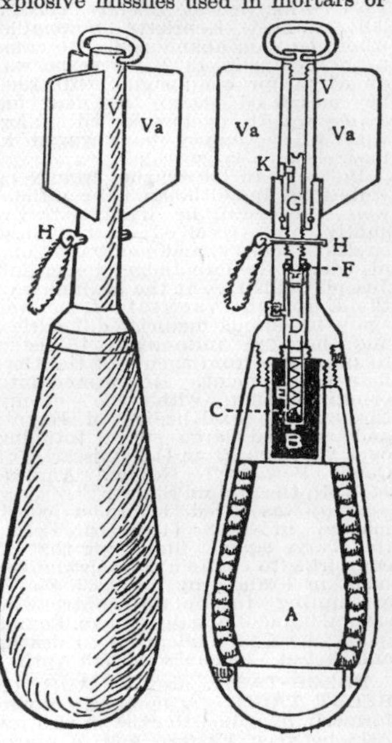

Air-craft Bomb

A, High-explosive surrounded by shrapnel bullets. B, Primer. C, Cylinder with striker at its base. D, Detonator case. E, Light spring between detonator and striker. F, Holes through detonator case for metal balls which fit into a recess in the tail-piece. These carry the weight of the detonator so long as the spindle holds them apart. G, Spindle. H, Safety-pin. Va, Vanes. When the safety-pin is withdrawn, and the bomb is released, the vanes revolve as the bomb falls, causing the spindle to become unscrewed from the tail-piece, when the balls fall inward, and so leave the full weight of the detonator case resting on the light spring. K, Stop fixed to vane spindle V, preventing it going back after release of balls and thus locking the tail-piece to the vane spindle, causing the bomb to revolve during the remainder of its flight. On impact the momentum carries the detonator downwards against the spring until it reaches the striker and explodes the bomb.

guns at a time when the usual projectile was a solid iron ball. The meaning is now restricted to those forms of destructive missiles which have been evolved during war for use from air-craft or trench-mortars. The name is also applied to small grenades which are thrown by individuals by hand. These grenades are a revival of an older form of missile (grenadier, one who uses a grenade).

The modern bomb is of all sizes, from the hand-grenade capable of being thrown by a man, to the largest and most complicated bomb carried one or two at a time by powerful air-craft. Every bomb is arranged to explode on impact, and is provided with a detonator to ensure the explosion. Most kinds have a tail or other guiding arrangement to keep them point foremost in flight. For convenience and security of handling, all bombs are provided with a safety arrangement, which before use requires to be adjusted to the action position. In the hand-grenade this takes the form of making certain adjustments and of removing the safety-pin.

In the air-craft bomb the arrangement is more complicated though practically automatic; i.e. the firing mechanism, after a preliminary adjustment at the time the bomb is placed in the carrying position, is set in motion by the action of the air on a valve at the nose of the falling bomb, bringing the striker into the necessary position to act on the detonating arrangement. This action takes place on the bomb striking the ground or any obstacle. Such a bomb is attached to a carrier, point or nose foremost and parallel to the body of the air-craft. It is released by an arrangement operated from the car or pilot's seat, and, when so released, performs the first part of its journey in the same time of flight as the parent air-craft, finally assuming the vertical position, in which it is kept by its fins or guiding arrangement. Bombs may be filled either with high-explosive, inflammatory material, or a smoke-producing composition, according to the purpose for which they are designed.—In geology the term is applied to certain masses of lava, hurled forth from a volcanic vent by explosive action.

BOMBA. *See* FERDINAND II OF NAPLES.

BOM'BARD. A kind of cannon or mortar formerly in use, generally loaded with stone instead of iron balls. Hence the term *bombardier*.

BOMBARDIER (-dĕr'). An artillery soldier whose duties were connected with mortars, howitzers, etc.; now the lowest grade of non-commissioned officer in the artillery.

BOMBARDIER BEETLE. A name given to beetles of the genera Brachinus and Aptinus, family Carabidæ, because of the remarkable power they possess of being able to defend themselves by expelling from the anus a pungent acrid fluid, which explodes with a loud report on coming in contact with the air.

BOMBARD'MENT. An attack on a locality by explosive missiles from land, sea, or air. A bombardment is one of the recognised and legitimate methods of making war, but by the Laws and Customs of War, as laid down by The Hague Convention of 1907, its use is confined to the case of defended localities. Fortifications are not necessary to constitute a defended locality; the mere presence of troops is sufficient. A bombardment of an undefended town or locality *by any means whatever* is forbidden. The only apparent exception to this is the case of a naval bombardment, which may be resorted to to coerce an undefended town if such town refuses to comply with requisitions for supplies legitimately made under the Laws and Customs of War. In all bombardments it is customary, but not obligatory, for the commander of an invading force to give notice of his intention to bombard, and all hospitals, churches, and historic buildings, if duly marked and not used for military purposes, must be spared as far as possible.

BOMBAR'DON. A large musical instrument of the saxhorn family, in tone not unlike a euphonium. Its compass is from F on the fourth ledger-line below the bass-staff to the lower D of the treble-staff.

BOMBASINE (Fr. *bombasin*, silk, or cotton). A mixed tissue of silk and worsted, the first forming the warp and the second the weft. It is fine and light in the make, and may be of any colour, though black is now most in use.

BOMBAX. A genus of large, soft-wooded, palmate-leaved trees, nat. ord. Sterculiaceæ, natives of tropical countries. The flowers are borne singly, or in groups, on the trunk or old branches. The large woody fruits contain numerous seeds enveloped in a mass of silky hairs, which forms one source of the substance known as silk-cotton. *See* SILK-COTTON TREE.

BOMBAY' (Port., "good harbour"). Chief seaport on the west coast of India, and capital of the Presidency of the same name. It stands at the southern extremity of the Island of Bombay, and is divided into two portions, one known as the Fort, and formerly surrounded with fortifications, on a narrow point of land with the harbour on the east side and Back Bay on the west; the other known as the City, a little to the north-west.

In the Fort are Bombay Castle, the Government offices, and almost all the merchants' warehouses and offices; but most of the European residents live outside of the mercantile and native quarters of the town in villas or bungalows.

Bombay has many handsome buildings, both public and private, as the cathedral, the university, the secretariat, the high court, town hall, great railway terminus, etc. Various industries, such as dyeing, tanning, and metal working, are carried on, and there are large cotton-factories. The commerce is very extensive, exports and imports of merchandise reaching a total value of over £80,000,000 annually. The harbour is one of the largest and safest in India, and there are commodious docks. There is a large traffic with steam-vessels between Bombay and Great Britain, and regular steam communication with China, Australia, Singapore, Mauritius, etc.

The Island of Bombay, which is about 11 miles long and 3 miles broad, was formerly liable to be overflowed by the sea, to prevent which substantial walls and embankments have been constructed. The harbour is protected by formidable rock-batteries. After Madras, Bombay is the oldest of the British possessions in the East, having been ceded by the Portuguese in 1661. Pop. 1,157,851.

BOMBAY'. One of the three Presidencies of British India, between lat. 14° and 29° N., and long. 66° and 77° E. It stretches along the west of the Indian Peninsula, and is irregular in its outline and surface, presenting mountainous tracts, low barren hills, valleys, and high tablelands. It is divided into a northern, a central, and a southern division, the Sind division, and the town and island of Bombay. The northern division contains the districts of Ahmedabad, Kaira, Panch Mahals, Broach, Surat, Thana, Kolába; the central, Khandesh, Nasik, Ahmednagar, Poona, Sholapur, Satara; the southern, Belgaum, Dharwar, Kaladgi, Kanara, Ratnagiri. Total area, 187,074 sq. miles; pop. 22,259,977, including the city and territory of Aden in Arabia, 80 sq. miles (pop. 56,500).

The native or feudatory States connected with the Presidency (the chief being Kathiawar) have an area of 63,453 sq. miles and a pop. of 7,411,675. The Portuguese possessions Goa, Damán, and Diu geographically belong to it. Many parts, the valleys in particular, are fertile and highly cultivated; other districts are being gradually developed by the construction of roads and railroads. The southern portions are well supplied with moisture, but a great part of Sind is the most arid portion of India. The climate varies greatly, parts being very unhealthy, while other places, such as Poona, are very favourable to Europeans.

The chief productions of the soil are cotton, rice, millet, wheat, barley, dates, and the coco palm. The manufactures are cotton, silk, leather, etc. The great export is cotton, which is also the chief manufactured article. The administration is in the hands of a governor and council. The revenue usually exceeds the expenditure. The chief source of revenue is the land, which is largely held on the ryotwar system. — BIBLIOGRPAHY: The annual *Administration Report*; G. Keatinge, *Agricultural Progress in Western India.*

BOMBAY DUCK. *See* BUMMALO.

BOMB-KETCH. A kind of vessel formerly built for the use of mortars at sea in a bombardment. Bomb-ketches were usually of 100 to 150 tons burden, about 70 feet long, and had two masts. They were built very strong to sustain the violent shock produced by the discharge of the mortars, of which they generally carried two.

BOM'BYX. *See* SILK-WORM.

BONA, or BONE. A seaport and fortified city of Algeria, with manufactures of burnooses, tapestry, and saddles, and a considerable trade. Pop. 45,171.

BONA FIDES, or BONA FIDE (fi'dēz, fi'dē; Lat., "good faith," "in good faith"). A term derived from the Roman jurists, implying the absence of all fraud or unfair dealing. A *bona fide* traveller in England and Scotland is one who is actually travelling at some distance from home on Sunday and is thus legally entitled to demand and obtain wine or spirits at an hotel. In the law of Scotland a *bona fide* possessor is a person who holds property upon a title which he honestly believes to be good.

BONAPARTE (bon'a-pärt). The French form which the great Napoleon was the first to give to the original Italian name *Buonaparte,* borne by his family in Corsica. As early as the twelfth and thirteenth centuries there were families of this name in Northern Italy, members of which reached some distinction as governors of cities (*podestà*), envoys, etc. But the connection between the Corsican Bonapartes and these Italian families is not clearly established, though probably the former descended from a Genoese branch of the family, which transplanted itself about the beginning of the sixteenth century to Corsica, an island then under the jurisdiction of Genoa. From that time the Buonapartes ranked as a distinguished patrician family of Ajaccio.

About the middle of the eighteenth century there remained three male representatives of this family at Ajaccio, viz. the Archdeacon Luciano Buonaparte, his brother Napoleon, and the nephew of both, Carlo, the father of the Emperor Napoleon I. Carlo or Charles Buonaparte, born 1746, studied law at Pisa University, and on his return to Corsica married Letizia Ramolino. He fought under Paoli for the independence of Corsica, but when further resistance was useless he went over to the side of the French, and was included by Louis XV. amongst the 400 Corsican families who were to have rights in France as noble. In 1777 he went to Paris, where he resided for several years, procuring a free admission for his second son Napoleon to the military school of Brienne. He died in 1785 at Montpellier.

By his marriage with Letizia Ramolino he left eight children: Giuseppe, or Joseph, King of Spain; Napoleon I., Emperor of the French (*see* NAPOLEON I.); Lucien, Prince of Canino; Maria Anna, afterwards called Élise, Princess of Lucca and Piombino, and wife of Prince Bacciocchi (*see* BACCIOCCHI); Luigi, or Louis, King of Holland; Carlotta, afterwards named Marie Pauline, Princess Borghese (*see* BORGHESE); Annunciata, afterwards called Caroline, wife of Murat (*see* MURAT), King of Naples; and Girolamo, or Jerome, King of Westphalia.—BIBLIOGRAPHY: Williams and Lester, *The Napoleonic Dynasty*; C. Leynadier, *Histoire de la famille de Bonaparte, de l'an 1050 à l'an 1848*; D. A. Bingham, *The Marriages of the Bonapartes*; F. Masson, *Napoléon et sa famille.*

BONAPARTE, Jerome. Youngest brother of Napoleon I., was born at Ajaccio in 1784, and at an early age entered the French navy as a midshipman. In 1801 he was sent out on an expedition to the West Indies, but the vessel, being chased by English cruisers, was obliged to put in to New York. During his sojourn in America, Jerome Bonaparte became acquainted with Miss Elizabeth Patterson, the daughter of the president of the Bank of Baltimore, and, though still a minor, married her, in spite of the protests of the French consul, on 24th Dec., 1803. The emperor, his brother, whose ambitious views were thwarted by this marriage, after an ineffectual application to Pope Pius VII. to have it dissolved, issued a decree declaring it to be null and void.

After considerable services both in the army and navy, in 1807 Jerome was created King of Westphalia, and married Catherine Sophia, Princess of Würtemberg. His government was not wise or prudent, and his extravagance and his brother's increasing exactions nearly brought the State to financial ruin. The battle of Leipzig put an end to Jerome's reign, and he was obliged to take flight to Paris. He remained faithful to his brother through all the events that followed till the final overthrow at Waterloo. After that, under the title of the Comte de Montfort, he resided in different cities of Europe, but eventually chiefly at Florence. After the election of his nephew, Louis Napoleon, to the presidentship of the French Republic, in 1848, he became successively governor-general of Les Invalides, a marshal of France, and president of the Senate. He died in 1860.

From his union with Miss Patterson only one son was born, Jerome, who was brought up in America, and married a lady of that country, by whom he had a son, who served as an officer in the French army during the Crimean War. The offspring of this marriage was not, however, recognised as legitimate by the French tribunals. Of the three children that were born to Jerome Bonaparte from his second marriage one was Prince Napoleon Joseph, who assumed the name of Jerome, and was well known by the nickname "Plon-Plon." He died in 1891, having married Clotilde, daughter of King Victor Emmanuel of Italy. He had three children—Victor (born 18th July, 1862), who married Princess Clementine, a daughter of Leopold II., King of the Belgians; Louis; and Marie Letizia. The first of these, since the death of Napoleon III.'s son, the Prince Imperial, is generally recognised by the Bonapartist party as the heir to the traditions of the dynasty. He had to leave France in 1886, a law being passed expelling pretenders to the French throne and their eldest sons.

BONAPARTE, Joseph. The eldest brother of Napoleon I., was born in Corsica in 1768, educated in France at the College of Autun, returned to Corsica in 1785, on his father's death, studied law, and in 1792 became a member of the new administration of Corsica under Paoli. In 1793 he emigrated to Marseilles, and married the daughter of a wealthy banker named Clari. In 1796, with the rise of his brother to fame after the brilliant campaign in Italy, Joseph began a varied diplomatic and military career.

At length, in 1806, Napoleon, having himself assumed the imperial title in 1804, made Joseph King of Naples, and two years afterwards transferred him to Madrid as King of Spain. His position here, entirely dependent on the support of French armies, became almost intolerable. He was twice driven from his capital by the approach of hostile armies, and the third time, in 1813, he fled, not to return. After Waterloo he went to the United States, and lived for a time near Philadelphia, assuming the title of Count de Survilliers. He subsequently came to England, finally repaired to Italy, and died at Florence in 1844.

BONAPARTE, Letizia Ramolino. The mother of Napoleon I., and, after Napoleon's assumption of the imperial crown, dignified with the title of *Madame Mère*. Born at Ajaccio in 1750, she was married in 1767 to Charles Buonaparte. She was a woman of much beauty, intellect, and force of character. Left a widow in 1785, she resided in Corsica till her son became First Consul, when an establishment was assigned to her at Paris. On the fall of Napoleon she retired to Rome, where she died in 1836.

BONAPARTE, Louis. Second younger brother of the Emperor Napoleon I., and father of Napoleon III., was born in Corsica in 1778. He was educated in the artillery school at Châlons, accompanied Napoleon to Italy and Egypt, and subsequently rose to the rank of brigadier-general. In 1802 he married Hortense Beauharnais, Josephine's daughter, and in 1806 was compelled by his brother to accept, very reluctantly, the Dutch crown. He exerted himself in promoting the welfare of his new subjects, and resisted as far as in him lay the tyrannical interference and arbitrary procedure of France ; but, disagreeing with his brother in regard to some measures of the latter, he abdicated in 1810 and retired to Grätz, under the title of the Count of St. Leu. He died at Leghorn in 1846. He was the author of several works which show considerable literary ability.

BONAPARTE, Lucien. Prince of Canino, next younger brother of Napoleon I., was born at Ajaccio in 1775. He emigrated to Marseilles in 1793, and having been appointed to a situation in the commissariat at the small town of St. Maximin in Provence, he married the innkeeper's daughter. Here he distinguished himself as a Republican orator and politician, and was so active on this side that after Robespierre's fall he was in some danger of suffering as a partisan. His brother's influence, however, operated in his favour, and in 1798 we find him settled in Paris and a member of the newly-elected Council of Five Hundred. Shortly after Napoleon's return from Egypt in 1799 he was elected President of the Council, in which position he contributed greatly to the fall of the Directory and the establishment of his brother's power, on the famous 18th Brumaire (9th Nov.). Next year, as Napoleon began to develop his system of military despotism, Lucien, who still held to his Republican principles and candidly expressed his disapproval of his brother's conduct, fell into disfavour and was sent out of the way as Ambassador to Spain.

Eventually, when Napoleon had the consulate declared hereditary, Lucien withdrew to Italy, settling finally at Rome, where he devoted himself to the arts and sciences, and lived in apparent indifference to the growth of his brother's power. In vain Napoleon offered him the crown, first of Italy and then of Spain ; but he came to France, and exerted himself on his brother's behalf, both before and after Waterloo. Returning to Italy, he spent the rest of his life in literary and scientific researches, dying in 1840. Pope Pius VII. made him Prince of Canino. He was the author of several works, amongst which are two long poems. His eldest son, Charles Lucien Laurent Bonaparte, born in 1803, achieved a considerable reputation as a naturalist, chiefly in ornithology. He published a continuation of Wilson's *Ornithology, Iconografia della Fauna Italica, Conspectus Generum Avium*, etc. He died in 1857. Another son, Pierre (1815-81), led an unsettled and disreputable life, and became notorious in 1870 by killing, in his own house at Paris, the journalist Victor Noir, who had brought him a challenge. He got off on the plea of self-defence, but had to leave France.

BONAR, Horatius. Scottish divine and hymn-writer, born 1808, died 1889. Educated at Edinburgh High School and University, he became a minister of the Scottish Church, but left it for the Free Church in 1843, and, after being nearly thirty years a minister at Kelso, was from 1866 till his death minister of Chalmers Memorial Church, Edinburgh. He wrote many religious tracts, sermons, and other works, including *Songs for* *the Wilderness, The Bible Hymnbook, Hymns Original and Selected, The Desert of Sinai, Hymns of Faith and Hope, Days and Nights in the East, Hymns of the Nativity and other Pieces*, etc. Some of his hymns, such as *I heard the voice of Jesus say*, have been extremely popular.

BONAS'SUS. *See* AUROCHS.

BONAVENTURA, ST. (otherwise **JOHN OF FIDANZA**). One of the most renowned scholastic philosophers, born in 1221 in the Papal States; became in 1243 a Franciscan monk; in 1253 teacher of theology at Paris, where he had studied; in 1256 general of his order, which he ruled with a prudent mixture of gentleness and firmness. In 1273 Gregory X. made him a cardinal, and he died in 1274 while papal legate at the Council of Lyons. He was canonised in 1482 by Sixtus IV. His writings are elevated in thought and full of a fine mysticism, a combination which procured him the name of *Doctor Seraphicus*. This title seems to have been first given to him in 1333. While teaching in Paris he had already received the name of *Doctor Devotus*. He wrote on all the philosophical and theological topics of the time with authority, but best, perhaps, on those that touch the heart and imagination. Among his writings are: *Itinerarium Mentis in Deum, Reductio Artium in Theologiam, Centiloquium*, and *Breviloquium*. Thomas Aquinas and Bonaventura were the two greatest theologians of Scholasticism, but their philosophies differ considerably. "The former extended the Kingdom of God by the love of theology, the latter by the theology of love."

BONAVISTA. A seaport and fishing centre of Newfoundland, on the east coast of the island, at the entrance of the bay of same name. Pop. 4052.

BON'CHURCH. Village of the Isle of Wight. About a mile from Ventnor, it stands beneath St. Boniface's Down and is a famous beauty spot. It has an interesting old church and farther up the hill is a new one with the tomb of A. C. Swinburne in the churchyard.

BOND. An obligation in writing to pay a sum of money, or to do or not to do some particular thing specified in the bond. The person who gives the bond is called the obligor, the person receiving the bond is called the obligee. A bond stipulating either to do something wrong in itself or forbidden by law, or to omit the doing of something which is a duty, is void. No person who cannot legally enter into a contract, such as an infant or a lunatic, can become an obligor, though such a person may become an obligee. No particular form of words is essential to the validity of a bond. A common form of bond is that on which money is lent to some company or corporation, and by which the borrowers are bound to pay the lender a certain rate of interest for the money.

BOND STREET. London street, famous as a shopping centre. It runs from Piccadilly to Oxford Street and is divided into Old Bond Street at the Piccadilly end and New Bond Street. It is named after Sir John Bond, a member of the household of Queen Henrietta Maria.

BONDAGE. *See* SERFS.

BONDED WAREHOUSES are vaults or warehouses in which articles are lodged under bond for the payment of any revenue duties chargeable thereon. Goods liable to customs or excise duties are said to be *in bond* when they are temporarily placed in such vaults or warehouses under a bond by the importer or owner that they will not be removed till the duty is paid on them.

BOND'FIELD, Margaret Grace. English politician. Born 17th March, 1873, in Somerset, she spent some years as a shop assistant. In 1898 she became assistant secretary to the shop assistants union and was soon a prominent trade unionist; also lecturing and writing for the Labour Party. In 1923 she was elected M.P. for Northampton. She lost her seat in 1924 but in 1926 was returned for Wallsend. In 1924 she was Secretary to the Ministry of Labour, and in 1929 was made Minister for Labour, being the first woman to sit in a British Cabinet. In Aug., 1931, she resigned office and in Oct. lost her seat in Parliament.

BONDING. *See* BRICKWORK; MASONRY.

BONDOU, or BONDU. A district of Senegal, French West Africa, the centre being in about lat. 14° N., long. 12° 30′ W. It has a luxuriant vegetation, magnificent forests, and is in many parts under good culture, producing large crops of cotton, millet, maize, indigo, tobacco, etc. The inhabitants are Fulahs. It is governed by a king, but is now under French control.

BONE, Muirhead. British artist, born in Glasgow in 1876, he studied art there and soon began to draw for the press. In 1901 he settled in London where his etchings attracted attention. They were mainly scenes of commercial life and activity, but during the Great War he was equally successful in his etchings of the battlefields. He was an official artist on the western front and with the Fleet. He is trustee of the Imperial War Museum and the National Gallery.

BONE. A hard material constituting the framework of mammalia, birds, fishes, and reptiles, and thus protecting vital organs such as the heart and lungs from external pressure and injury. In the fetus the bones are formed of cartilaginous (gristly) substance, in different points of which earthy matter—phosphates and carbonates of lime—is gradually deposited till at the time of birth the bone is partially formed. After birth the formation of bone continues, and in the temperate zones they reach their perfection in men between the ages of twenty and twenty-five. From this age till fifty they change but slightly; after that period they grow thinner, lighter, and more brittle. Bones are densest at the surface, which is covered by a firm membrane called the *periosteum*; the internal parts are more cellular, the spaces being filled with marrow, a fatty tissue, yellow or red, supporting fine blood-vessels.

Bone consists of nearly 34 per cent. organic material and of 66 per cent. inorganic substances, chiefly phosphate, carbonate, and fluoride of lime, and phosphate of magnesium. The organic material is converted into gelatine by boiling. It is this which makes bones useful for yielding stock for soup. The inorganic substances may be dissolved out by steeping the bone in dilute hydrochloric acid. Bones, from the quantity of phosphates they contain, make excellent manure. *See* BONE MANURE.—Bones play an important part in religious ceremonies and beliefs, and in folk-tales dealing with the renewal of life in dismembered dead. *See* BURIAL.

Broken Bones. *Symptoms*—Inability to move, severe pain, swelling; in a compound fracture the bone is sticking through the skin. *Treatment*—An amateur must interfere as little as possible. Place the limb in a position as near the normal as can be, protect the patient from exposure and shock (q.v.) and summon skilled assistance immediately.

Bone Implements appeared first in the Stone Age. Awls, eyed needles, harpoons, and engraved spear throwers were followed by combs, spoons and axe-handles. They still abound among primitive peoples.

BONE-ASH, or BONE-EARTH The earthy or mineral residue of bones that have been calcined so as to destroy the animal matter and carbon. It is composed chiefly of phosphate of lime, and is used for making cupels in assaying, etc.

BONE-BED. In geology, a bed containing numerous fragments of fossil bones, teeth, etc., as in the Rhætic formation in the south-west of England and the Ludlow bone-bed in the Silurian formation.

BONE BLACK, IVORY BLACK, or **ANIMAL CHARCOAL** is obtained by heating bones in close retorts till they are reduced to small coarse grains of a black carbonaceous substance. This possesses the valuable property of arresting and absorbing into itself the colouring-matter of liquids which are passed through it. Early in the nineteenth century it was discovered that it is much more effective as an absorbent of organic colouring-matters than wood charcoal. Hence it is extensively used in the process of sugar-refining, when cylinders of large dimensions filled with this substance are used as filters. After a certain amount of absorption the charcoal becomes saturated and ceases to act. It has then to be restored by reheating, or may be used to make bone-ash. Bone black has also the property of absorbing odours, and so may serve as a disinfectant of clothing, rooms, etc.

BONE-BRECCIA (-brech'i-a). In geology, an agglomeration of bones and irregular rock-fragments, often cemented by Calcium carbonate, found in the floors or in pockets and solution-hollows of limestone rocks.

BONE-CAVES. Caverns containing deposits in which are embedded large quantities of the bones of animals (many of them extinct), dating from the Pliocene or later geologic periods.

BONE MANURE. One of the most important fertilizers in agriculture. The value of bones as manure arises chiefly from the phosphates and nitrogenous organic matters they contain; and where the soil is already rich in phosphates bone is of little use as manure. It is of most service, therefore, where the soil is deficient in this respect, or in the case of crops whose rapid growth or small roots do not enable them to extract a sufficient supply of phosphate from the earth—turnips, for instance, or late-sown oats and barley. There are several methods for increasing the value of bones as manure, by boiling out the fat and gelatine, for instance, the removal of which makes the bones more readily acted on by the weather and hastens the decay anddistribution of their parts, or by grinding them to dust or dissolving them in sulphuric acid, by which latter course the phosphates are rendered soluble in water.

Bones have long been used as manure in some parts of England, but only in a rude, unscientific way. It was in 1814 or 1815 that machinery was first used for crushing them in Yorkshire and Lincolnshire, and bone-dust and dissolved bones are now largely employed as manures, great quantities of bones being now imported into Great Britain for this purpose, chiefly from the Indies and Argentine. Considerable quantities are also imported from Morocco, Egypt, and Brazil, the total consumption of bones as manure being estimated at about 100,000 tons per annum. Before being utilized in agriculture they are often boiled for the oil or fat they contain, which is used in the manufacture of soap and lubricants.

BONFIRE. A large fire lighted out of doors in celebration of some event; originally a fire in which bones were burned.

BONHEUR (bo-*neur*), **Rosa.** A distinguished French artist and painter of animals, born at Bordeaux, 22nd March, 1822. When only eighteen years old she exhibited two pictures, *Goats and Sheep* and *Two Rabbits*, which gave clear indications of talent. Since that time a long list of pictures, *Tillage in Nivernais* (1849), *The Horse Fair* (1853), *Haymaking* (1865), etc., have made her name famous. In 1867 she exhibited *Ponies from the Isle of Skye*. A small replica by her own hands of *The Horse Fair* is in the National Gallery, the original being in New York. She was the first woman to be made an officer of the Legion of Honour. She died in 1899.

BONIFACCIO (bō-nē-fách'ō). A seaport in Corsica, on the strait of the same name, which separates Corsica from Sardinia. Wine and oil are exported, and a coral fishery is carried on. Pop. 3594. The Strait of Bonifaccio is 7 miles broad, and contains several small islands.

BON'IFACE. The name of nine Popes.—**Boniface I.,** elected 418. He was the first to assume the title of the First Bishop of Christendom. He died 422.—**Boniface II.,** elected 530, died in 532. He acknowledged the supremacy of the secular sovereign in a council held at Rome.—**Boniface III.,** chosen 607, died nine months after his election.—**Boniface IV.,** elected 608, died 615. He converted the Pantheon at Rome into a Christian church.—**Boniface V.,** 619 to 625. He endeavoured to diffuse Christianity among the English.—**Boniface VI.,** elected 896, died a fortnight after.—**Boniface VII.,** elected 947, during the lifetime of Benedict VI., and therefore styled Antipope. Expelled from Rome in 984, he returned and deposed and put to death Pope John XIV. He died 985.

Boniface VIII. (1294-1303), Benedict Cajetan, one of the ablest and most ambitious of the Popes. His idea was, like that of Gregory VII., to raise the papal chair to a sort of universal monarchy in temporal as well as spiritual things. In pursuit of this design he engaged in incessant quarrels with the German emperors and King Philip of France. He was not, however, very successful. The excommunication which he launched against Philip of France was ignored, and he was proceeding to lay all France under interdict when he was seized at Anagni by an agent of Philip and a member of the great Colonna family which Boniface had banished from Rome. After three days' captivity the people of Anagni rose and delivered him; but he died a month later, probably from the privations and agitation he had undergone. In 1300 Boniface instituted the jubilees of the Church, which, at first centennial, afterwards every twenty-five years, became a great source of revenue to the papal treasury.—**Boniface IX.** (1389-1404), elected during the schism in the Church while Clement VII. resided at Avignon. He made a shameless traffic of ecclesiastical offices, dispensations, etc., and lavished the treasures thus procured on his relations or on costly buildings—the fortification of the castle of St. Angelo, for instance, and the Capitol. He died in 1404.—Cf. A. E. McKilliam, *A Chronicle of the Popes*.

BONIFACE, ST. The apostle of Germany, whose original name was Winfrid. He was born in Devonshire in 680, of a noble Anglo-Saxon family. In his thirtieth year he took orders as a priest, and in 718 he went to Rome and was authorized by Gregory II. to preach the gospel to the pagans of Germany. His labours were carried on in Thuringia, Bavaria, Friesland, Hesse, and Saxony, through all of which he travelled, baptizing thousands and consecrating churches. He erected bishoprics and organised provincial synods. In 723 he was made a bishop, and in 732 an archbishop and primate of all Germany. Many bishoprics of Germany, as Ratisbon, Erfurt, Paderborn, Würzburg, and others, and also the famous abbey of Fulda, owe their foundation to him. He was slain in West Friesland by some heathen tribes in 755, and was buried in the abbey of Fulda.

BONIN', or **ARCHBISHOP ISLANDS.** Several groups of small islands, North Pacific Ocean, belonging to Japan, and lying to the south of it. The largest is Peel Island, which is inhabited by Japanese and Polynesians, who cultivate maize, vegetables, tobacco, and the sugar-cane, and engage in fishing. It is frequently visited by vessels engaged in whale-fishing, which obtain here water and fresh provisions.

BONINGTON, Richard Parkes. English painter, born 1801, died 1828. He spent the greater part of his life in France, was solely a water-colourist up till 1824, and then began to paint in oil. In 1826 he first exhibited in England, but never lived long there. His subjects are chiefly landscapes, views in cities, and historical genre pictures ; and his position as an artist, notwithstanding his early death, is extraordinarily high. He excelled especially in water-colours. Among his works are : *Francis I. and the Queen of Navarre, Henry III. receiving the Spanish Ambassador,* and *The Fish Market, Boulogne.*

BONITO (bo-nē'tō). A name applied to several fishes of the mackerel family, one of which, the bonito of the tropics, or stripe-bellied tunny (*Thynnus pelamys*), is well known to voyagers from its persistent pursuit of the flying-fish. It is a beautiful fish, steel-blue on the back and sides, silvery on the belly, with four brown longitudinal bands on each side. It is good eating, though rather dry. The *Auxis vulgāris* and *Pelămys sarda* also go under this name.

BONN. An important German town in the Rhenish province of Prussia, beautifully situated on the left bank of the Rhine, with magnificent promenades and prospects in the environs. It has some trade and manufactures, but is chiefly important for its famous university, founded in 1777 by Elector Maximilian Frederick of Cologne. Enlarged and amply endowed by the King of Prussia in 1818, it is now one of the chief seats of learning in Europe, with a library of about 350,000 volumes, an anatomical hall, mineralogical and zoological collections, museum of antiquities, a botanical garden, etc. The teachers in the five faculties are about 200, and the students number about 4000. Lange, Niebuhr, Schlegel, Ritschl, Brandis, and other names famous in science or literature are connected with Bonn, and Beethoven was born there. Bonn was long the residence of the Electors of Cologne, and finally passed into the hands of Prussia by the arrangements of the Congress of Vienna in 1815. Pop. 90,249.

BONNER, Edmund. Bishop of London, infamous for burning Protestants. He was born about 1495 of obscure parentage. He took a doctor's degree at Oxford in 1525, and, attracting the notice of Cardinal Wolsey, received from him several offices in the Church. On the death of Wolsey he acquired the favour of Henry VIII., who made him one of his chaplains, and sent him to Rome to advocate his divorce from Queen Catherine. In 1540 he was consecrated Bishop of London, but on the death of Henry (1547), having refused to take the oath of supremacy, he was deprived of his see and thrown into prison. On the accession of Mary he was restored to his bishopric, and he distinguished himself during this reign by a persecution of the Protestants, 200 of whom he caused to be put to death. After Elizabeth succeeded he remained unmolested until his refusal to take the oath of supremacy, on which he was committed to the Marshalsea (1560), where he remained a prisoner until his death in 1569.

BON'NET. A covering for the head, now especially applied to one worn by women. In England the bonnet was superseded by the hat as a head-dress two or three centuries ago, but it continued to be distinctive of Scotland to a later period. The term is also applied to various protective devices in mining and engineering. It also means a decoy, one whose business it is to lure others to play or buy.

BONNET-PIECE. A Scottish coin, so called from the king's head on it being decorated with a bonnet instead of a crown. It was struck by James V., and is dated 1539. Bonnet-pieces are very rare, and in high estimation amongst antiquaries.

BONNET-ROUGE (bo-nā-rözh ; Fr. "red-cap"), the emblem of liberty during the French Revolution, and then worn as a head-dress by all who wished to mark themselves as sufficiently advanced in democratic principles : also called *liberty cap.*

BONNEVAL (bon-vål), **Claude Alexandre, Count.** An adventurer, born in 1675 of an illustrious French family. In the War of the Spanish Succession he obtained a regiment, and distinguished himself by his valour as well as by his excesses.

On his return to France he was obliged to fly in consequence of some expressions against the minister and Madame de Maintenon. Received into the service of Prince Eugene, he now fought against his native country, and, after performing many signal services, he was raised in 1716 to the rank of lieutenant field-marshal in the Austrian service, and distinguished himself against the Turks at Peterwardein.

But his reckless and impatient spirit brought him into conflict with the superior authorities, and he finally took refuge in Constantinople, where he was well received. He was now converted to Mohammedanism, submitted to circumcision, received the name of *Achmet*, was made a pasha of three tails, and as general of a division of the army achieved some considerable successes against Russians and Austrians. He died in 1747. The memoirs of his life published under his name (in 1750) are not genuine.—Cf. A. Vandal, *Le Pacha Bonneval.*

BONNIVARD (bon-ē-vär), **François de.** The "prisoner of Chillon," born in 1496, made famous by Byron and Delacroix. An ardent republican, he took the side of the Genoese against the pretensions of the Dukes of Savoy. In 1530 he fell into the hands of the duke, and was imprisoned till 1536 in the castle of Chillon, when the united forces of the Genevese and the Bernese took Chillon. One of his most important works is *Chronique de St. Victor*, the MS. of which was only published in 1831. He died at Geneva 1570.

BONNY. A town and a river of W. Africa, in the delta of the Niger, where a considerable trade is done in palm-oil, etc. Pop. 6500.

BONPLAND (bōṇ-pläṇ), **Aimé.** A distinguished French botanist, born at Rochelle 1773. While pursuing his studies at Paris, he made the acquaintance of Alexander von Humboldt, and agreed to accompany him in his celebrated expedition to the New World. During this expedition he collected upwards of 6000 plants, previously unknown, and on his return to France in 1804 was made director of the gardens at Navarre and Malmaison, and published *Description des plantes rares de Navarre* (1813). On the Restoration he proceeded to South America, and became professor of natural history at Buenos Ayres. Subsequently, while on a scientific expedition up the River Paraná, he was arrested by Dr. Francia, the Dictator of Paraguay, as a spy, and detained for eight years. He afterwards settled in Brazil, where he died in 1858.

BON'TEBOK. The pied antelope (*Alcelăphus pygarga*), an antelope of S. Africa, with white markings on the face, allied to the blesbok.

BO'NUS. Something given over and above what is required to be given, especially an extra dividend to the shareholders of a joint-stock company, holders of insurance policies, etc., out of accrued profits.

BONY PIKE, or **GAR-FISH** (*Lepidosteus*). A remarkable genus of fishes inhabiting North American lakes and rivers, and one of the few living forms that now represent the order of ganoid fishes so largely developed in previous geological epochs. The body is covered with smooth enamelled scales, so hard that it is impossible to pierce them with a spear. The common gar-fish (*L. osseus*) attains the length of 5 feet, and is easily distinguished by the great length of its jaws.

BONZES. The name given by Europeans to the priests of the religion of Fo or Buddha in Eastern Asia, particularly in China and Japan. They do not marry, but live together in monasteries. There are also female bonzes, whose position is analogous to that of nuns in the Roman Catholic Church.

BOOBY (*Sula fusca*). A swimming bird nearly allied to the gannet, and so named from the extraordinary stupidity with which, as the older voyagers tell, it would allow itself to be knocked on the head without attempting to fly. The booby lives on fish, which it takes, like the gannet, by darting down upon them when swimming near the surface of the water.

BOODHA. *See* BUDDHA.

BOODROOM. A seaport near the south-west of Asia Minor, close by the site of ancient Halicarnassus. Pop. 6000.

BOOK. The general name applied to a printed volume. In early times books were made of the bark of trees; hence the Latin *liber* means bark and book, as in English the words *book* and *beech* may be connected. The materials of ancient books were largely derived from the papyrus, a plant which gave its name to paper. The use of parchment, prepared from skins, next followed, until it was supplanted in Europe by paper in the twelfth century, though paper was made in Asia long before this. *See* BIBLIOGRAPHY; BOOKBINDING.

Bookselling is now a large and flourishing business, with its own trade organisations, trade papers, benevolent funds, etc. The selling of books, usually in sets, direct to the public on the hire purchase system is a separate branch. An associated industry is that of bookbinding.

Book collecting is a popular hobby, and enormous prices have been paid for certain old books, e.g. first folios of Shakespeare. First editions of other writers, including some modern ones, also fetch high prices. The world's chief saleroom for books is Sotheby's in London. One of the finest collections outside the British Museum and other national libraries, is that possessed by J. Pierpont Morgan.

BOOK'BINDING. The art of arranging and making up the sheets of a book

Embossed Leather Bookbinding. The cover of a seventeenth-century copy of the Gospel of St. John

into a volume. In the Middle Ages the work of binding the manuscripts then used was done by the monks, in a heavy and excessively solid style. With the invention of printing, and the consequent multiplication of books, binding became a great mechanical art, in which the Italians of the fifteenth and sixteenth centuries took the lead. Later on the French binders enjoyed a well-deserved supremacy for delicate and elegant work, and it was not till almost the opening of the nineteenth century that English bookbinding began to take the foremost place.

The first operation in bookbinding is to fold the sheets. The printed sheets usually contain eight or sixteen pages. On the first page of each sheet is a letter or figure called a signature. After the sheets are folded and arranged in consecutive order, the book is pressed in a screw or hydraulic press, and is then sawed on the back in several places in order to admit the cords on which it is to be sewed. It should now have double papers put in at front and back to act as end-papers. When the book has been sewed and papered, it is secured by a coating of glue on the back, and, when the glue is dry, the back is rounded with a hammer. It is then screwed up very tight in the press between hardwood boards.

The back of the book is now beaten smooth ; and the edge of the back being beaten on the edge of the boards that compress it, a groove is formed for the board to rest in. The paste boards are now laced to the book by the ends of the cords on which it is sewed, and the superfluous parts cut away. The book is again pressed for several hours to make it solid for cutting, which operation is performed by a device called a *plough.* The book has now reached the stage of edging ; edges may be either gilt, marbled, or sprinkled. In gilding, it is screwed tightly in the press, the white of an egg diluted with water is spread on with a camel's-hair brush and the gold leaf fixed. When dry it is burnished with an agate stone.

Marbling is done by dipping the edges slightly into the colouring-mixture as it floats on the surface of gum-water. Sprinkling is performed with a brush, which the workman dips in colour and shakes in small drops on the edge. After the headband has been added the book is lined, ready for the leather cover. The cover, after being damped with water and smeared with paste on its rough side, is now pulled on and doubled over the edges of the boards, and the sides and edges are neatly squared and smoothed. The book is put in the press for some hours, and is then ready for ornaments and lettering. The letters or ornaments on books are made with brass tools engraved in relief. A book is called *half bound* when only the back and corners are leather.

The above description applies chiefly to the binding of books in leather and in the strongest manner ; but many books are now bound entirely in cloth, a style of binding which, though less strong, is cheaper and more expeditious. The cloth covers or " cases " are made up complete, embossed, gilt, and lettered before being attached to the book, the ornaments being stamped upon them by presses acting on metal dies. The covers are usually attached by thin canvas glued to the backs, as well as by the back-cords, or tapes used instead.—BIBLIOGRAPHY: J. W. Zaehnsdorf, *The Art of Bookbinding*; S. T. Prideaux, *Historical Sketch of Bookbinding*; Brassington, *History of the Art of Bookbinding*; C. J. Davenport, *The Book: its History and Development*; H. T. Coutts and G. A. Stephen, *Manual of Library Bookbinding*.

BOOK-KEEPING. Is the art or method of recording mercantile or pecuniary transactions, so that at any time a person may be able to ascertain the details and the extent of his business. It is divided, according to the general method pursued, into book-keeping by *single* or by *double entry*.

Single Entry. Book-keeping by single entry is comparatively little used, except in retail businesses of small extent, where only the simplest record is required. In its simplest form debts due to the trader are entered in the day-book at the time of the transaction to the debit of the party who owes them; and debts incurred by the trader to the credit of the party who gave the goods. From this book the accounts in a summarized form are transferred to the ledger, where one is opened for each different person, one side being for Debtor, and the other for Creditor. When a balance-sheet of the debts owing and owed is made, this, together with stock and cash in hand, shows the state of the business.

Double Entry. A system first adopted in the great trading cities of Italy, gives a fuller and more accurate record of the movement of a business, and is necessary in all extensive mercantile concerns. The chief feature of double entry is its system of checks, by which each transaction is twice entered, to the Dr. side of one account and then to the Cr. side of another. An important feature of the system consists in adopting, in addition to the personal accounts of debtors and creditors contained in the ledger, a series of what are called *book accounts*, which are systematic records in the form of debtor and creditor of particular classes of transactions. For every debt incurred some consideration is received. This consideration is represented under a particular class or name in the ledger, as the debtor in the transaction in which the party from which the consideration is received is the creditor.

Thus A buys goods to the value of £100 from B. He enters these in his journal—Stock Account. Dr. £100 (for goods purchased) To B, £100. The first £100 appears in the Dr. column of the journal, and is posted in the ledger to the debit of Stock Account; the second appears in the Cr. column, and is posted in the ledger to the Cr. of B. In like manner, when the goods are paid, Cash, for which an account is opened in the ledger, is credited with £100, and B is debited with the same. When the goods are sold (for cash) Stock is credited and Cash is debited. If the amount for which they sell is greater than that for which they were bought, there will be a balance at the debit of Cash, and a balance at the credit of Stock. The one balance represents the cash actually on hand (from this transaction), the other the cause of its being on hand. If there is a loss on the transaction, the balance will be on the other side of these accounts. Ultimately the balance thus arising at Dr. or Cr. of Stock is transferred to an account called Profit and Loss, which makes the stock account represent the present value of goods on hand, and the profit and loss account, when complete, the result of the business.

In this system the risk of omitting any entry, which is a very common occurrence in single-entry book-keeping, is reduced to its smallest, as unless a particular transaction is omitted in every step of its history, the system will inexorably require that its whole history should be given to bring the different accounts into harmony with each other.

In keeping books by double entry, the books composing the set may be divided into two classes, called principal and subordinate books. The subordinate books are those in which the transactions are first recorded, and vary both in number and arrangement with the nature of the business and the manner of recording the facts. The most important of these (all of which are not necessarily to be found in the same set) are Stock Book, Cash Book, Bill Book, Invoice Book, Account Sales Book. The principal books are made up exclusively from the subordinate books and classified documents of the business. In the most perfect system of double entry they consist of two, the Journal and Ledger. The journal contains a periodical abstract of all the transactions contained in the subordinate books, or in documents not entered in books, classified into debits and credits. The ledger contains an abstract of all the entries made in journal classified under the heads of their respective accounts. It is an index to the information contained in the journal, and also a complete abstract of the actual state of all accounts, but gives no further information; while the journal gives the reason of each debit and credit, with a reference to the source where the details of the transaction are to be found. There is an Institute of Book-keepers at 133 Moorgate, London, E.C., and instruction in the subject is given in all colleges where business methods are taught. *See* ACCOUNTANTS.—BIBLIOGRAPHY: *Encyclopædia of Accounting* (6 vols.); J. W. Heaps, *The Antiquity of Book-keeping*; T. H. Russell and W. J. Jackman, *Book-keeping, Accounting, and Auditing*; R. J. Porters, *Pitman's Dictionary of Book-keeping*.

BOOKMAKER. Name given to a man through whom betting is done. Bookmakers are found on racecourses, including greyhound racing tracks, and also in their offices, where they call themselves turf accountants. By taking bets on the various horses in a race they make a book on that race; hence the name.

Before 1926 in Great Britain betting was illegal and bookmakers were liable to prosecution. In that year a licensing scheme was introduced, the licence costing £10 a year. When in 1929 the betting tax was abolished, a charge of £40 a year for each telephone was made, but this and the licence were abolished in 1930.

BOOK OF THE DEAD. Ancient Egyptian work. It is a collection of exorcisms, funerary texts and directions for the soul's journey through the underworld. Based upon a predynastic nucleus it grew by the Ptolemaic Age into a substantial work in at least 165 chapters. It was frequently inscribed on papyrus, sometimes with magnificent illustrations.

BOOK-PLATES. Plates bearing a person's name, and often the Latin words *ex libris* ("from among the books"—of), used to attest the ownership of books, one of them being usually pasted inside the front cover of each book. Such plates are generally more or less of an artistic character, and may bear some heraldic, emblematic, or other device. They were first employed about the end of the fifteenth century (1480). Albrecht Dürer was the first to give his attention to the designing and engraving of book-plates. The first book-plates in England were made towards the end of the sixteenth century.—BIBLIOGRAPHY: J. Leicester Warren (Lord de Tabley), *A Guide to the Study of Book-plates*; Egerton Castle, *English Book-plates*; H. W. Fincham, *Artists and Engravers of British and American Book-plates*.

BOOKS, CENSORSHIP OF. The supervision of books by some authority so as to settle what may be published. After the invention of printing the rapid diffusion of opinions by means of books induced the Governments in all countries to assume certain powers of supervision and regulation with regard to printed matter. The Popes were the first to institute a regular censorship. By a bull of Leo X. in 1515, the bishops and inquisitors were required to examine all works before they were printed, with a view to prevent the publication of heretical opinions. As this decree could not be carried out in countries which had accepted the reformed religion, they prepared a list of prohibited books (*Index Librorum Prohibitorum*), books, that is, which nobody was allowed to read under penalty of the censure of the Church. This index continues to be reprinted and revised down to date, as well as another index commonly called the *Index Expurgatorius*, containing the works which may be read if certain expurgations have been made.

In England the censorship was established by Act of Parliament in 1662, but before that both the well-known Star-chamber and the Parliament itself had virtually performed the functions. In 1694 the censorship of books in England ceased entirely. In France the censorship, like so many other institutions, was annihilated by the Revolution. During the Republic there was no formal censorship, but the supervision of the Directory virtually took its place, and at length in 1810 Napoleon openly restored it under another name (Direction de l'Imprimerie). After the Restoration it underwent various changes, and was re-established by Napoleon III., but again abolished. Censorship, however, has been exercised over pamphlets and journals at different periods. In the old German Empire the Diet of 1530 instituted a severe superintendence of the press, but in the particular German States the censure was very differently applied, and in Protestant States especially it has never been difficult for individual authors to obtain exemption.

In 1849 the censorial laws were repealed, but were again gradually introduced, and existed in a modified form in most of the German States until 1918. The censorship was abolished in Denmark in 1770, in Sweden in 1809, in the Netherlands in 1815. In the United States of America it has never existed. In Russia and Austria a despotic censorship existed until the revolutions of 1917 and 1918. *See* PRESS, FREEDOM OF THE; THEATRE.

BOOK-TRADE. The production and distribution of books commercially. Even in ancient times, before the invention of printing, this trade had attained a high degree of importance, at Alexandria and later at Rome, where Horace mentions the brothers Sosii as the chief booksellers of his time. Copies of books were readily multiplied in those times, as we hear of as many as a thousand slaves being employed at one time in writing to dictation. After the fall of Rome, down to the twelfth century, the trade in books was almost entirely confined to the monasteries, and consisted chiefly in the copying of manuscripts and the barter or sale of the copies, generally at a very high price. But with the rise of the universities the trade received a new development, and in all university towns booksellers and book-agents became numerous.

The invention of printing had a powerful effect on the trade of bookselling, as was first manifested in the commercial towns and free cities of the German Empire. The printers were originally at the same time publishers and booksellers, and they were in the habit of disposing of their books at the chief market towns and places frequented by pilgrims. It was only in the sixteenth century that these two branches of trade began generally to be carried on independently.

The two chief departments of the book-trade now are publishing and bookselling by retail in all its branches, printing being regarded as a separate business. For the most part these two departments of the trade are carried on separately, but it is not uncommon for them to be united. The publisher of a book is the one who brings it before the public in a printed form, often purchasing the copyright, with the condition of publishing the work at his own risk ; or the risk (profit or loss) may be shared between the author and publisher. Very frequently books are printed at the cost of the author or some learned society, and published on commission. In order to secure as large a sale as possible, the publisher brings himself into connection with the retail booksellers, who are the direct means of distributing the book to the public. Second-hand booksellers belong to a special department of the retail book-trade. Many of the books they deal in are long ago out of print.

In Britain the chief seat of the book-trade is London, Edinburgh coming next (after a long interval) ; but publishing is also carried on to a considerable extent in Dublin, Manchester, Glasgow, and some other places. In France the centre of the book-trade is Paris. The book-trade of the United States, the chief seats of which are New York, Philadelphia, and Boston, is now very large. The manner in which it is conducted is almost the same as in Britain. Canada and Australia are also developing a considerable business of this kind. The great centre of the German book-trade is at Leipzig, and the fair held in this city at Easter is the occasion on which all the accounts made in the book-trade during the past year ar settled.

The common practice is for the booksellers to receive supplies of new books from the publishers on commission, with liberty to send back to the publisher all the copies that are not sold before the time of settlement at the Easter Fair (Ostermesse), or to carry over a part of them to next year's account if the sale has so far been unsuccessful. All business between the publishers and retail booksellers is carried on indirectly by means of commission-agents, especially in Leipzig, but also in Berlin, Vienna, Frankfort, and other towns. Every bookseller out of Leipzig has his agent there, who conducts all his business, and is in constant communication with the other booksellers. A large number of the publishers deposit with their agents at Leipzig a stock of the works which they have published, and commission them to carry out all orders on their account. The retail bookseller sends all his orders to his agent, who communicates them to the Leipzig publishers and the agents of the other publishers. In Italy there is no central point either for the production of books or for the conduct of the trade by means of agents. Florence, Milan, and Turin hold nearly the same position.

In publishing new books, besides the expense of copyright, paper, press work, etc., the publisher has to consider the number of presentation copies required for reviews, the percentage off the price allowed to the retail booksellers, in many cases also to the commission-agent, and the expenses of advertising and making the work known to the public. This last is a very important department of a publishing office, and it is nothing uncommon for a publisher to spend £2000 or £3000 on advertising an important work.

The total number of works (including new editions) annually published in Britain is usually between 9000 and 10,000 ; the annual number of French publications is stated at about 14,000, and of Italian at about 12,000. — BIBLIOGRAPHY: Charles Knight, *Shadows of the Old Booksellers* ; Henry Curwen, *History of Booksellers* ; W. Besant, *The Pen and the Book*; F. A. Mumby, *Romance of Bookselling: a History from the Earliest Times to the Twentieth Century*; S. Unwin, *The Truth about Publishing*.

BOOKWORM. Term denoting the larval form of several species of small beetles (*anobium* and *ptinus*) which injure old books. They gnaw the bindings and riddle the leaves. Other wingless insects resembling neuroptera (*atropos*), which infest old, damp books, are preferably called book lice.

BOOLAC′. *See* BOULAK.

BOOLE, George. English mathematician and logician, born in 1815, died in 1864. A native of Lincoln and educated there, he opened a school in his twentieth year, and by private study gained such efficiency in mathematics that in 1849 he was appointed to the mathematical chair in Queen's College, Cork, where the rest of his life was spent. In 1857 the Universities of Dublin and Oxford conferred on him the degrees of LL.D. and D.C.L. respectively. In mathematics he wrote on *Differential Equations, General Method in Analysis, The Comparison of Transcendents*, etc. In logic he wrote *An Investigation of the Laws of Thought*, and *The Mathematical Analysis of Logic*, a profound and original work, in which a symbolic language and notation were employed in regard to logical processes.

BOOLUNDSHUHUR. *See* BULANDSHAHR.

BOOM. A long pole or spar run out from various parts of a ship or other vessel for the purpose of extending the bottom of particular sails. Also a strong beam, or an iron chain or cable, fastened to spars extended across a river or the mouth of a harbour, to prevent an enemy's ships from passing.

BOOM (bōm). A town in Belgium, about 12 miles south of Antwerp. Pop. 19,288.

BOO′MERANG. A missile instrument used by the natives of Australia, and by some peoples of India, made of hard wood, about the size of a common reaping-hook, and of a peculiar curved shape, sometimes resembling a rude and very open V. The boomerang, when thrown as if to hit some object in advance, instead of going directly forward, slowly ascends in the air, whirling round and round to a considerable height, and returns to the position of the thrower. If it hits an object, of course, it falls. The Australians are very dexterous with this weapon, and can make it go in almost any direction, sometimes making it rebound before striking.

BOONDEE′, or BUNDI. A principality, India, in Rajputana, under British protection; area, 2220 sq. miles. Although small, Boondee is important as lying in a central position. Pop. 187,068.

Boondee, the capital, is picturesquely situated, and its antiquity, numerous temples, and magnificent fountains give it a very interesting appearance. Pop. 19,000.

BOONE, Daniel. An American pioneer and backwoodsman, born 1735, died 1820. In 1769, with five companions, he went to explore the little-known region of Kentucky, and was taken prisoner by the Indians. In 1775 he built a fort on the Kentucky River, where Boonesborough now is, and settled there. In 1778 he was taken prisoner by the Indians, and was retained and adopted into the family of a Shawanese chief, but at length he effected his escape. In the end of the century he removed from Kentucky into Missouri. From him a number of places in the United States take the name of Boone, Booneville, etc., all of small importance.

BOONE. A town of the United States, near the centre of Iowa, on the Des Moines River, a railway and industrial centre, with coal-mines, etc. Pop. 11,886.

BOORHANPOOR′. *See* BURHANPUR.

BOOSTER. Electrical apparatus. *See* DYNAMO.

BOOT. An article of dress, generally of leather, covering the foot and extending to a greater or less distance up the leg. (*See* SHOE.) Hence the name boot, or *bootikin*, was given to an instrument of torture made of iron, or a combination of iron and wood, fastened on to the leg, between which and the boot wedges were introduced and driven in by repeated blows of a

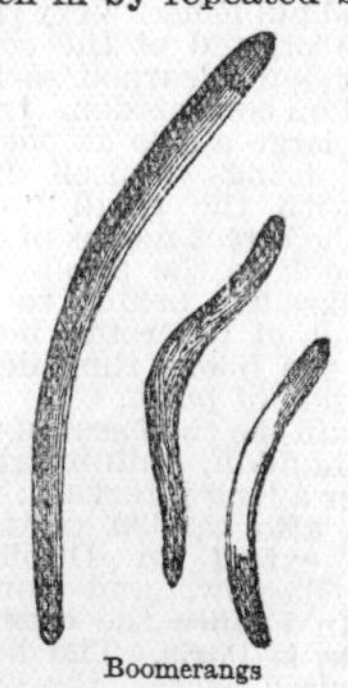

Boomerangs

mallet, with such violence as to crush both muscles and bones. The special object of this form of torture was to extort a confession of guilt from an accused person. The last recorded case of its use in Great Britain was during the latter half of the seventeenth century.

BOOTAN'. *See* BHUTAN.

BOOTES (bo-ō'tēz; that is, ox-driver, ploughman). The Greek name of a northern constellation, called also by the Greeks *Arctophylax*. It contains Arcturus, a star of the first magnitude.

BOOTH, Barton. An English actor of celebrity in the reigns of Queen Anne and George I. He was born in 1681, and placed under Dr. Busby, at Westminster School, but he ran away from school at the age of seventeen, and joined a company of strolling players. After performing in Dublin with great applause, he returned in 1701 to London, where, having joined the Drury Lane Company, his reputation reached its height with the performance of the title part of Addison's famous tragedy *Cato*. He died in May, 1733, and was buried in Westminster Abbey.

BOOTH, Charles. A writer on sociology, born at Liverpool in 1840; long member of a Liverpool mercantile firm; made a Privy Councillor in 1904. His chief work, in which he was assisted by a number of coadjutors, is entitled *Life and Labour of the People in London*. It extends over several volumes, and gives a vast amount of statistical and other information, throwing light upon all the different phases of the subject. His works, specially devoted to the aged poor, include: *The Endowment of Old Age* (1892), *The Aged Poor: Condition* (1894); *Old Age Pensions* (1899); *The Religious Influences of London*. He died in 1916.

BOOTH, Edwin Thomas. An American actor, son of the distinguished English actor, Junius Brutus Booth (1796-1852; spent most of his life in the United States). He was born in 1833 near Baltimore, and made his first appearance at Boston in 1849. He was eminent for his personation of Shakespearian characters, Othello, Richard III., Iago, Shylock, etc., and was the leading American tragedian. In 1882 he made a tour in Europe, and was well received. He died in 1893. His brother, John Wilkes (born 1839), also an actor, was the murderer of President Lincoln, 14th April, 1865. He was shot by those who sought to bring him to justice.

BOOTH, William. "General" or head of the Salvation Army. Born at Nottingham in 1829, died 20th August, 1912. He was educated privately, was for some time a preacher among the Wesleyan Methodists, and afterwards a minister of the Methodist New Connexion, but left the latter body to devote himself to general evangelistic work. In 1865 he began a mission in the East End of London, which in 1878 assumed the name of the Salvation Army, and has become an organisation carrying on its labours all the world over. (*See* SALVATION ARMY.) In 1890 his scheme for ameliorating the condition of the more degraded and vicious classes in England was propounded in his book *In Darkest England and the Way Out*, and led to a liberal subscription of funds. He established several weekly and monthly publications, and his travels in connection with his great organisation were very extensive. He was an honorary D.C.L. of Oxford, and a freeman of London. His works include: *Love, Marriage and the Home*; *The Training of Children*; *Religion for Every Day*; *Salvation Soldiers*; *Visions*; and others.—BIBLIOGRAPHY: Charles T. Bateman, *Everybody's Life of General Booth*; A. M. Nicol, *General Booth and the Salvation Army*.

BOOTH, William Bramwell. Son of the preceding. He was General of the Salvation Army from 1912 to 1929. He died in June, 1929, the year in which he was made a Companion of Honour. His works include: *Social Reparation* (1899); *Bible Battleaxes* (1901); *Papers on Life and Religion* (1920); *These Fifty Years* (1929).

BOO'THIA FELIX. A peninsula of British North America, stretching northwards from the Arctic Circle, discovered by Captain Ross in 1830. In the west coast of this country, Ross was able to localise the north magnetic pole.

BOOT'IKIN. *See* BOOT.

BOO'TLE. A municipal, county, and parliamentary borough of England, in Lancashire, adjoining Liverpool, the docks of which great seaport extend into the borough, so that Bootle is almost a Liverpool suburb. Pop. (1931), 76,799.

BOOTLEGGER. Man who sells intoxicating liquor in countries where the sale is prohibited, chiefly the United States. It came from the practice adopted by traders in remote districts of carrying bottles of liquor in the tops or legs of their boots. After the introduction of prohibition in 1919, bootlegging flourished in the United States on an enormous scale.

BOPAL'. *See* BHOPAL.

BOPP, Franz. A distinguished German Sanskrit and philologist, born at Mainz in 1791, died at Berlin in 1867. In 1812 he went to Paris for the study of Sanskrit and Oriental literature, and remained there five years. After living for some time in London and Göttingen, he settled in Berlin, where he eventually became ordinary professor of Oriental literature. He contributed much to the study of Sanskrit in Europe, and he may be said to have been one of the first who raised philology to the rank of a science. His most important work in this field was his *Comparative Grammar of Sanskrit, Zend, Greek, Latin, Gothic, old Slavonic, and German*, of which an English translation appeared in 1845, and a French by Bréal in 1866.

BOPPARD (bop'ärt). An ancient walled town of Rhenish Prussia, district of Coblentz, on the left bank of the Rhine, formerly an imperial city. Pop. 6396.

BO'RA, Katharina von. Wife of Luther, born in 1499. She took the the veil early; but feeling unhappy in her situation, applied, with eight other nuns, to Luther. The nuns were released from their convent, and in 1525 Luther married her, having himself by this time laid aside the cowl. After Luther's death she kept boarders for her support. She died at Torgau in 1552.

BORACIC ACID, or BORIC ACID. A compound of the element *boron* with hydrogen and oxygen (H_3BO_3). It is found in some volcanic regions contained in the steam issuing from fissures in the soil, notably the volcanic districts of Tuscany, and much of the boric acid used is derived from this source. Steam and other gases issue from the so-called *suffioni*, and are condensed in lagoons round the jets. The amount of boric acid volatilised in the steam is small, but if it is directed into the lagoons the water becomes gradually saturated, and the acid is obtained by the concentration of this solution. It is also manufactured from minerals, such as boracite, borocalcite, and borax, occurring at Stassfurt, in the United States, and in South America.

Boric acid crystallises in white shining crystals, which melt on heating to a glassy mass. It is soluble in water, has an acid reaction, and turns the colouring-matter turmeric from yellow to brown. Boric acid is largely used as a mild antiseptic in medicine and as a food-preservative for butter, milk, cream, and vegetables; for the last purpose it acts better when mixed with borax. Its use as a preservative is very carefully restricted. It is also used in the glazing of porcelain, in the preparation of glass, and the treatment of wicks for stearine candles.

BO'RAGE (Borāgo). A genus of plants belonging to the nat. ord. Boraginaceæ, having rough hairy foliage and blue, panicled, drooping flowers, and characterised by mucilaginous and emollient properties. *Borago officinalis*, a British plant, gives a coolness to beverages in which its leaves are steeped, and is used for making claret-cups and in the manufacture of cordials. The flowers are used for garnishing salads.

BORAGINA'CEÆ. The Borage family, a natural order of regular-flowered gamopetalous dicotyledons, containing a large number of herbs or shrubs chiefly found in the northern temperate regions, among them being

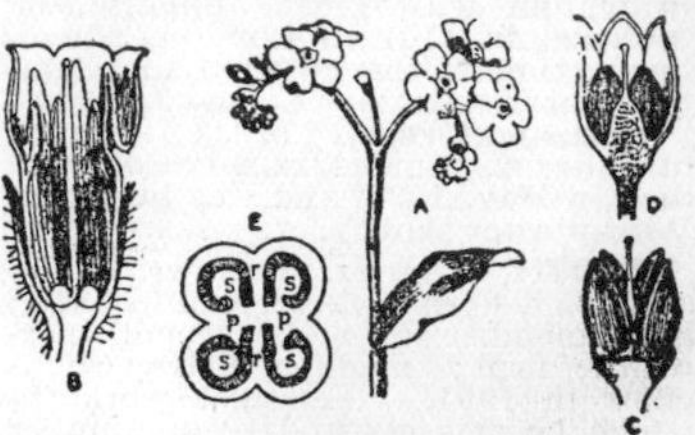

Boraginaceæ

A, Inflorescence of Forget-me-not. B, Flower of Comfrey in vertical section. C, Nutlets of Forget-me-not. D, Same in vertical section. E, Diagrammatic section of ovary. *s*, Ovules. *r*, Midribs of carpels. *pp*, Lines along which carpels are joined.

borage, alkanet, comfrey, and forget-me-not. Characteristic features are the rough hairs, alternate exstipulate leaves, the inflorescence (a scorpioid cyme), and the fruit consisting of four nutlets.

BORAH, William Edgar. American politician, born 29th June, 1865, he was sent to the Senate in 1906 as representative of Illinois. There he became prominent as the leading advocate of the policy of keeping clear of all European alliances, opposing any connection with the League of Nations and the World Court. He was equally insistent that the debts owing to the United States by European nations should be paid in full. He refused nomination for the vice-presidency in 1924.

BORAS (bụ'rōz). A town of Southern Sweden, 45 miles east of Gothenburg by rail, an important seat of the cotton manufacture. It was founded by Gustavus Adolphus in 1632. Pop. (in 1927), 38,236.

BORAS'SUS. *See* PALMYRA PALM.

BORAX, sodium tetraborate ($Na_2B_4O_7$, $10H_2O$). Native borax was originally obtained from a series of salt lakes in Thibet and sent to Europe under the name of Tincal, and this was at one time the only source of borax. The most important deposits of borax are found in the desert regions of California, where there are very thick surface deposits. Borax is also prepared from other mineral borates, such as colemanite and borocalcite, naturally-occurring calcium salts of boric acid, boracite ($Mg_3B_8O_{15}$-$MgCl_2$), the double salt of magnesium borate and magnesium chloride occurring in Germany, and boronatrocalcite, the double sodium calcium salt of boric acid ($Na_2B_4O_7 2CaB_4O_7 18H_2O$) in Chile and Peru. Pure borax is the sodium salt of pyroboric acid, and forms large transparent six-sided prisms, which dissolve readily in water, have an alkaline reaction, effloresce in air, and when heated swell up, lose water of crystallisation, and melt to a transparent glass.

Industrial Uses. Borax is much used in the industrial world. It is used in the manufacture of glazes for bricks and tiles, in the making of cements which require to be polished, in the manufacture of enamel-ware, and in glass. Being a good detergent, it is also used in the manufacture of soap and laundry starch. Along with boric acid it is employed as a preservative for meat, fish, and other foods, and in the curing of bacon. It is used also in the preparation of hard from soft wood, in textile industry as a mordant, in soldering as it dissolves oxides of metals and renders the surface of the metal clean, in the dressing of leather, and in medicine on account of its antiseptic properties.

BOR'DA, Jean Charles. A French mathematician and physicist, born in 1733, died 1799. He served in the army and navy, and distinguished himself by the introduction of new methods and instruments connected with navigation, geodesy, astronomy, etc., being in particular the inventor of the reflecting circle. He was one of the men of science who framed the new system of weights and measures adopted in France.

BORD-AND-PILLAR SYSTEM. *See* MINING.

BORDEAUX (bor-dō). One of the most important cities and ports of France, capital of the department of Gironde, on the left bank of the Garonne, about 70 miles from the sea. It is built in a crescent form round a bend of the river, which is here lined with fine quays and crossed by a magnificent stone bridge, leading to the suburb La Bastide, also by a railway bridge. It consists of an old and a new town, the former mostly composed of irregular squares and narrow crooked streets; while the latter is laid out with great regularity, and on a scale of magnificence hardly surpassed by any provincial town in Europe, with fine wide streets, handsome squares, and extensive and finely-planted promenades.

Buildings. The finest square is the Place des Quinconces, containing monuments and statues of Montaigne and Montesquieu, and two rostral columns. There is also a fine Jardin Public, comprising a botanic garden. Important buildings are the Cathedral of St. André, mostly of the eleventh, twelfth, and fourteenth centuries, with fine detached bell-tower; the old church or cathedral of St. Seurin; St. Michael's Church, with grand front of florid Gothic; Ste. Croix, in basilica form, dating from the tenth century; archi-episcopal palace, Palais de Justice, hotel de ville, exchange, grand hospital, custom-house, etc. Among institutions are a university, founded in 1441 during the English domination, with four faculties, academy of science and art, public library, founded in 1768 (over 200,000 vols.), picture-gallery, containing works by Rembrandt, Rubens, Titian, etc.

Trade. Its position gives Bordeaux admirable facilities for trade, and enables it to rank next after Marseilles and Havre in respect of tonnage employed. Large vessels sail up to the town, and there is ready communication by railway or river with the Mediterranean, Spain, and the manufacturing centres of France. Pauillac, nearer the sea, forms an out-port for the largest class of vessels. Graving and other docks have recently been provided. The chief exports are wine and brandy; sugar and other colonial produce and wood are the chief imports. The foreign trade has very wide ramifications. Shipbuilding is the chief industry, and there are sugar-refineries, woollen and cotton mills, potteries, soapworks, distilleries, etc.

History. Bordeaux is the *Burdigala* of the Romans. By the marriage of Eleanor, daughter of the last Duke of Aquitaine, to Henry II. of England, Bordeaux was transferred to the English Crown. Under Charles VII., in 1451, it was restored again to France. In Revolution times it was the chief seat of the Girondists, and suffered severely from the Terrorists. In 1870-1, and again in Aug., 1914, it was the temporary seat of Government. Montaigne and Montesquieu were born in the neighbourhood; the latter is buried in the church of St. Bernard. Pop. 262,990.

BORDELAIS WINES. The wines of Bordeaux and district, especially the red wines made in the eleven departments of the south-west of France, Gironde, Landes, Lot, Tarn et Garonne, etc., though it is in the Gironde alone that the famous growths are found. The soil of Médoc produces such famous wines as Château-Margaux, Château-Lafitte, and Château-Latour. Their characteristics are fine bouquet, velvety softness on the palate, and the faculty of acting beneficially on the stomach without mounting too readily to the head. Besides the red wines, known as *claret*, there are also white wines, of which the finest are Sauterne, Barsac, Preignac and Bommes.

BORDEN. Village of Kent. It is 2 miles from Sittingbourne. Here is a farm institute, opened in 1930, and controlled by the Kent County Council.

BORDEN, Mary. Anglo-American novelist. Daughter of William Borden of Chicago, she was married in 1918 to Brig.-Gen. Edward Louis Spears. Her first book, *Jane, Our Stranger*, gained immediate popularity, and her later works established her name as a writer. They include *Three Pilgrims and a Tinker*, *The Romantic Woman*, *Four O'Clock*, *Jericho Sands*, *The Forbidden Zone*, *Flamingo*, and *A Woman with White Eyes*.

BORDEN, Sir Robert Laird. Canadian statesman, born at Grand Pré, Nova Scotia, in 1854. In 1872 he became instructor in the Glenwood Institute, but returned to Nova Scotia and studied law at Halifax. He practised law, soon became notable in his profession, and appeared as counsel in important cases. In 1896 he was elected a Conservative member of the House of Commons, and in 1901 became leader of the Conservative opposition. He lost his seat in 1904, but was re-elected in 1905, and after the Liberal defeat in 1911 he became Premier. He visited England in 1912 to confer with the British Government on the naval situation. After his return to Canada, he tried to introduce a measure for a contribution of 35 million dollars for the construction of three Dreadnought battleships for the home country, but the Bill was rejected. He was made a member of the Imperial Privy Council in 1912. He attended a meeting of the British Cabinet on 14th July, 1915, being the first overseas minister to do so, and was the representative of Canada at the Imperial War Conference in 1918.

BOR'DENTOWN. A town in New Jersey, United States, on the Delaware, 28 miles N.E. of Philadelphia. Pop. 4232.

BORDER, or BORDERS, THE. The territory adjacent to the frontier line between England and Scotland, the scene of frequent fights and forays among neighbouring clans and families from the eleventh till the end of the seventeenth century. The dividing line varied at different times, shifting according to the surging of the tide of war or diplomacy. At present the boundary is marked mostly by natural features, but is partly an imaginary line, the chief natural boundaries being the Tweed, the Cheviots, the Kershope, Liddel, and Sark. At one time Lothian belonged to England, or at least to the English kingdom of Northumbria, but was transferred to the Scottish kingdom in 1018. Cumberland, again, belonged at one time to Scotland, but finally became part of England, being annexed by William Rufus (1092). Many important events in the wars between the two countries naturally took place in the district of the Borders, such as the battles of Halidon Hill (near Berwick, 1333), Otterburn (1388), Homildon Hill (near Wooler, 1402), Flodden (1513), Solway Moss (1542), Ancrum Moor (1544). Invasions of territory from either side were often terribly destructive, not even churches and monasteries being spared. Some of the most famous religious houses of Scotland, of which noble ruins still exist, were on the Scottish side—Melrose, Kelso, Dryburgh, Jedburgh—hardly matched by similar houses on the English side.

With a view to put down lawlessness, officials with special powers were appointed by both the English and the Scottish kings, the frontier districts being divided into the East, the West, and the Middle Marches, with their respective wardens. Many fine ballads and songs belong to this once lawless region, to the Scottish border in particular, in which are innumerable spots memorable in poetry and romance. Many of them have been collected by Sir Walter Scott in *Minstrelsy of the Scottish Border* (1802 and 1803).—BIBLIOGRAPHY: G. Ridpath, *Border History of England and Scotland*; J. M. Wilson, *Tales of the Borders*; John Veitch, *History and Poetry of the Scottish Border*; W. S. Crockett, *The Scott Country*; J. Lang, *A Land of Romance: the Border, its History and Legend*.

BORDER REGIMENT, THE. Chiefly recruited from Norfolk and Essex in 1702, was long engaged under Hill in the Peninsula, and holds honours for the Crimea, Mutiny, and South Africa (1899-1902). During the European War it was engaged in the first battle of Ypres.

BORDESLEY. A suburb of Birmingham, England. It formerly gave its name to a parliamentary division of Birmingham.

BORDIGHERA (bor-dē-gā'rȧ). Town of N.W. Italy, on the Mediterranean coast, district of San Remo, a favourite winter residence for invalids. Pop. 6160.

BORDONE (bor-dō'nā), **Paris.** Italian painter of the Venetian school, born at Treviso in 1500, died at Venice 1570. He was a pupil of Titian, and was invited to France by Francis I., whose portrait he painted, as also those of the Duke of Guise, the Cardinal of Lorraine, and others. His works are not rare in the public and private collections of Europe, his most famous picture being *The Old Gondolier Presenting the Ring of St. Mark to the Doge* in the Academy at Venice; *Vertumnus and Pomona* is in the Louvre; *Daphnis and Chloe* in the National Gallery.

BORE, or EAGRE (derived most probably from the Scand. *bāra*, wave, billow). A natural phenomenon caused when an exceptionally high tide, as a "spring" tide, flows up a river which possesses a swift current, a funnel-shaped estuary and a large bar of sand. The rapid influx of the tide, unable to spread laterally, raises a wave which may be several feet in height. Bores occur on the Rivers Ganges, Indus, and Brahmaputra, that on the last named sometimes being 12 feet high; at Hang-choo-foo, and in the Bay of Fundy; and in Britain on the Solway, Trent, and Severn. The Severn bore is well seen at Newnham, and causes a rise of 50 feet at Chepstow, 2 miles up the Wye; the eagre, or ægir, of the Trent is at its best near Gainsborough.

BO'REAS. The name of the north wind as personified by the Greeks and Romans.

BORECOLE (bōr'kōl). A variety of *Brassica olerăcea*, a cabbage with the leaves curled or wrinkled, and having no disposition to form into a hard head.

BOREL. A French type of monoplane, produced by the firm of Borel, designed by Léon Morane, and used by Jules Védrines in 1911.

BORER. A name given to the larvæ of certain insects which bore holes in trees and thus injure them.

BORGERHOUT (bor'ger-hout). A Belgian town, forming a suburb of Antwerp, with bleaching and dyeing works, and woollen manufactories, etc. Pop. 54,200.

BORGHESE (bor-gā'ze). A Roman family, originally of Sienna, where it held the highest offices from the middle of the fifteenth century. Pope Paul V., who belonged to this family, and ascended the papal chair in 1605, loaded his relations with honours and riches. He bestowed, among other gifts, the principality of Sulmone on Marco Antonio Borghese, the son of his brother Giovanni Battista, from which is descended the present Borghese family.

BORGHESE, Camillo, Prince. Born in 1775, died in 1832. When the French invaded Italy, he entered their service, and in 1803 he married Marie Pauline, the sister of Napoleon (born at Ajaccio 1780, died at Florence 1825). In 1806 he was created Duke of Guastalla, and was appointed Governor-General of the provinces beyond the Alps. He fixed his Court at Turin, and became very popular among the Piedmontese. After the abdication of Napoleon, he broke off all connection with the Bonaparte family, and separated from his wife.

The *Borghese Palace* at Rome, partly the work of Paul V., contained one of the richest collections of art in the city, most of which has been transferred to the *Villa Borghese*. The latter, which, since 1903, has been called Villa Umberto I., lies just outside the Porta del Popolo. It formerly belonged to the Borghese family, but it is now public property.

BORGIA, Cesare (che'zȧ-re bor'jȧ). The natural son of Pope Alexander VI. and of a Roman lady named Vanozza, born in 1478. He was raised to the rank of cardinal in 1492, but afterwards divested himself of the office, and was made Duc de Valentinois by Louis XII. In 1499 he married a daughter of King John of Navarre, and accompanied Louis XII. to Italy. He then, at the head of a body of mercenaries, carried on a series of petty wars, made himself master of the Romagna, endeavoured to make himself Duke of Bologna and Florence, and had seized Urbino when Alexander VI. died, 1503.

He was now attacked by a severe disease, at a moment when his whole activity and presence of mind were needed. He found means, indeed, to get the treasures of his father into his possession, and assembled his troops in Rome; but enemies rose against him on all sides, one of the most bitter of whom was the new Pope, Julius II. Borgia was arrested and carried to Spain. He at length made his escape to his brother-in-law the King of Navarre, and was killed before the castle of Viana, 12th March, 1507. He was charged with the murder of his elder brother, of the husband of his sister Lucretia, and the stiletto or secret poisoning was freely used against those who stood in his way. With all his crimes he was a patron of art and literature.—BIBLIOGRAPHY: M. Creighton, *History of the Papacy*; R. Sabatini, *The Life of Cesare Borgia*; J. Fyvie, *The Story of the Borgias.*

BORGIA, Lucretia. Daughter of Pope Alexander VI., and sister of Cesare Borgia, born 1480, died 1523. In 1493 she was married to Giovanni Sforza, Lord of Pesaro, but after she had lived with him for four years, Alexander dissolved the marriage, and gave her to Alphonso, nephew of Alphonso II. of Naples. Two years after, this new husband was assassinated by the hired ruffians of Cesare Borgia. Her third husband was Alphonso d'Este, son of the Duke of Ferrara. She was accused by contemporaries of incest, poisoning, and almost every species of enormous crime; but several modern writers defend her, maintaining that the charges which have been made against her are false or much exaggerated. She was a patroness of art and literature.

BORGO. Akin to borough, Italian for "town" or "castle," the name for several towns built on or round a castellated rock; as Borgo San Donnino, a cathedral city of Parma (pop. 15,480); Borgo, the northern district of Rome.

BOR'GU. A district of Africa, in the Western Sudan, lying about lat. 10° N., and on the west of the Niger, partly in Northern Nigeria, partly in Dahomey (French). *See* NIGERIA.

BORING. The process of perforating wood, iron, rocks, or other hard substances by means of instruments adapted for the purpose. For boring wood the tools used are *awls, gimlets, augers,* and *bits* of various kinds, the latter being applied by means of a crank-shaped instrument called a *brace,* or else by a lathe, transverse-handle, or drilling-machine. Boring in metal is done by *drills* or *boring-bars* revolved by boring-machines. Boring in the earth or rock for mining, geological, or engineering purposes is effected by means of augers, drills, or jumpers, sometimes wrought by hand, but now usually by machinery driven by steam or by compressed air. In ordinary mining practice a bore-hole is usually commenced by digging a small pit about 6 feet deep, over which is set up a shear-legs with pulley, etc. The boring-rods are from 10 to 20 feet in length, capable of being jointed together by box and screw, and having a chisel inserted at the lower end. A lever is employed to raise the bore-rods, to which a slight twisting motion

Boring with rigid rods can, up to a depth of about 120 feet, be done by hand; between this and 300 feet by lever; but beyond 300 feet steam power must be utilized.

is given at each stroke, when the rock at the bottom of the hole is cut by the repeated percussion of the cutting-tool. A sludge-pump is used to clear out the triturated rock. The work is much quickened by the substitution of mechanical power for manual labour.

Of the many forms of boring-machines now in use may be mentioned the diamond boring-machine, invented by Leschot, a French engineer. In this the cutting-tool is of a tubular form, and receives a uniform rotatory motion, the result being the production of a cylindrical core from the rock, of the same size as the inner periphery of the tube. The boring-bit is a steel thimble, about 4 inches in length, having two rows of Brazilian black diamonds firmly embedded therein, the edges projecting slightly. The diamond teeth are the only parts which come in contact with the rock, and their hardness is such that an enormous length can be bored with but little appreciable wear.

The Davis calyx drill is similar in action to the diamond drill, except that saw-teeth of hard steel are formed on the crown and replace the diamonds. Another type of core-drill which is now largely used consists of a boring-crown formed from a steel cylinder which is slotted at several points. Chilled-steel shot are passed down the hollow rods, and pass through the slots and get between the head and the rock. The rolling action abrades the rock, and an annular space is cut round a core as in diamond boring. Rope boring, where a wire rope raises the cutting-chisel instead of rods, is largely used in prospecting for oil, or where definite information of the strata passed through is not essential. *See* TOOLS.—Cf. *Dictionary of Engineering*, article *Boring and Blasting*.

BORIS. King of Bulgaria. A son of King Ferdinand, he was born at Sofia, 30th Jan., 1894. When his father abdicated in Oct., 1918, he succeeded to the throne, and after he came of age proved himself a good ruler. In Oct., 1930, he married Giovanna, a daughter of the King of Italy.

BORISSOGLYEBSK. A town of Russia, government of Tambov; active trade. It was captured by the Bolshevik Government in 1919. Pop. 22,600.

BORISSOV. A Russian town, government of Minsk. Not far from it took place the disastrous passage of the Berezina by the French in 1812. Pop. 15,250.

BOR'KUM. A flat sandy island in the North Sea, near the coast of Hanover, off the estuary of the Ems, belonging to Prussia, a favourite resort for sea-bathing. Pop. 600.

BORLASE, William. English writer, born in Cornwall 1695; died 1772; studied at Oxford, took holy orders, and became successively rector of Ludgvan and vicar of St. Just. In 1754 he published *Antiquities of Cornwall*, and in 1758 *Natural History of Cornwall*.

BORMIO. A small town of N. Italy, province Sondrio, with celebrated warm mineral springs. Pop. 2170.

BORN, Bertrand de. French troubadour and warrior, born about the middle of the twelfth century in the castle of Born, Périgord, died about 1209. He dispossessed his brother of his estate. This brother was supported by Richard Cœur de Lion in revenge for de Born's satirical lays. Dante (*Inferno*, Canto 28) places him in hell on account of his verses intensifying the quarrel between Henry II. and his sons. He compares him to Achitophel, who incited the sons of David against their father.

BORNA. An old town of Germany, in Saxony, 17 miles S.E. of Leipzig. It manufactures iron, felt, and shoes. Pop. 10,980.

BORNEO (corrupted from *Bruni* or *Brunei*, the name of a State on its north-west coast). One of the islands of the Malay Archipelago, and the third largest in the world. It is nearly bisected by the equator, and extends from lat. 7° 4′ N. to 4° 10′ S., and from long. 108° 50′ to 119° 20′ E.; greatest length, 850 miles, greatest breadth, 600 miles; area, 285,000 sq. miles. It is not yet well known, though our knowledge of it has been greatly increased in recent years. There are several chains of mountains ramifying through the interior, the culminating summit (13,455 feet) being Kini-Balu, near the northern extremity. The rivers are very numerous, and several of them are navigable for a considerable distance by large vessels. There are a few small lakes.

Productions. Borneo contains immense forests of teak and other trees, besides producing various dye-woods, camphor, rattans and other canes, gutta-percha and india-rubber, honey and wax, etc. Its fauna comprises the elephant, rhinoceros, tapir, leopard, buffalo, deer, monkeys (including the orang-outang), and a great variety of birds. The mineral productions consist of gold, antimony, iron, tin, quicksilver, zinc, and coal, besides diamonds. It is only portions of the land on the coast which are well cultivated. Among cultivated products are sago, gambier, pepper, rice, tobacco, etc. Edible birds'-nests and trepang are important articles of trade. The climate is not considered unhealthy. The population is estimated at about 2,165,015 comprising Dyaks (the majority of the inhabitants), Malays,

Chinese, and Bugis. The south-western, southern, and eastern portions, more than two-thirds of the island, are possessed by the Dutch, under whom are a number of semi-independent princes.

On the N.W. coast is the Malay kingdom of Brunei or Bruni. Its chief town is Brunei, on the river of the same name, a place of considerable trade, and the residence of the Sultan. Since 1841 there has been a State under English rule (though not under the British Crown) on the W. coast of the island, namely, Sarawak (q.v.), founded by Sir James Brooke; while Labuan, an island off the N.W. coast, is a British colony. In 1881 an English commercial company, with a charter from the British Government, acquired sovereign rights over the northern portion of the island, extending northwards from about lat. 5° 6′ N. on the west, and lat. 4° 5′ on the east, and including some adjacent islands. On 12th May, 1888, the British Government proclaimed a formal protectorate over the State of North Borneo, and in 1898 certain borderlands were acquired from the Sultan of Brunei. British North Borneo has an area of 31,106 sq. miles, several splendid harbours, a fertile soil, and a good climate.

The soil is believed to be well adapted for all tropical products, especially tobacco, coffee, sugar, sago, tapioca, coco-nuts, rubber, pepper. Gold, coal, and other minerals have been found. The chief settlement is Sandakan, the capital, on Sandakan Bay. The revenue, which amounted to £434,336 in 1926, is from customs and excise dues, licences, forests, etc. Tobacco and cigars, birds'-nests, rattans, rubber, gutta-percha, timber, copra, etc., are exported, the trade being chiefly with Singapore and Hong-Kong. The imports and exports (including gold) for 1926 amounted to £970,319 and £1,987,233 respectively. Pop. (census 1921), 257,804. North Borneo, Brunei, and Sarawak are all under British protection.—BIBLIOGRAPHY: F. Hatton, *North Borneo*; C. Hose and W. MacDougall, *The Pagan Tribes of Borneo*; L. W. W. Gudgeon, *British North Borneo*.

BORN'HOLM. A Danish island in the Baltic Sea, 24 miles long and 19 broad; pop. 44,000. It is rather rocky, and better suited for pasture than tillage. The people are chiefly engaged in agriculture and fishing; pottery-ware and clocks are made. Rönne is the chief town.

BOR'NU. Formerly a negro kingdom of the Central Sudan, on the W. and S.W. side of Lake Chad, now mainly in the north-east of Northern Nigeria, and thus in British territory; area, 57,000 sq. miles, with pop. estimated at 5,000,000. It is a pleasant and fruitful land, intersected by streams that enter Lake Chad, and presents a favourable example of negro civilisation. The people practise agriculture and various arts and manufactures, and are mostly Mahommedans. The *Mai*, or Sultan, had an army of 30,000 men, many armed with fire-arms. Kuka, or Kukawa, near the western shore of Lake Chad, is a place of some trade, and another large town is Maidugari. Previous to the advent of the British, Bornu, which once had a stable government, had fallen into a state of chaos and bloodshed. *See* CAMEROONS; NIGERIA.—Cf. A. Schultze, *The Sultanate of Bornu*.

BORO BU'DOR. The ruin of a splendid Buddhist temple in Java, situated near the junction of the Rivers Ello and Progo. It is a pyramid, each side measuring 600 feet at the base, and is supposed to belong to the seventh century of our era.

BORODINO', BATTLE OF (called also **Battle of the Moskwa**). A sanguinary battle fought near a village of this name on the River Moskwa, 7th Sept., 1812, between the French under Napoleon and the Russians under Kutusov. Each party claimed the victory. At the end of the day the Russians retreated in good order, no pursuit taking place. The French force amounted to about 150,000 men; the Russian was somewhat less; 50,000 dead and dying covered the field.

BORO-GLYCERINE. A compound of boracic acid with glycerine, represented by the formula $C_3H_5BO_3$. It is a powerful antiseptic, and, being perfectly harmless, is useful in the preservation of food and in surgery.

BORON (symbol, B; atomic weight, 11. An element resembling carbon in some respects. It is not found free, but occurs fairly abundantly in its compounds. (*See* BORAX.) It is a dark-brown amorphous powder, infusible, and a poor conductor of heat. It combines directly with oxygen, chlorine, nitrogen, etc., at high temperatures, and burns in air with a bright-green flame if heated to 700° C. It may be obtained in a crystalline impure state, and is then nearly as hard as diamond, and in the form of dust is used for polishing. Boron is used in the preparation of Boron steel, a high-grade steel of great hardness.

BOROTRA, Jean. French tennis player, born in 1898. Borotra, a very versatile tennis player, noted for the speed of his game, first came into prominence in 1921. He has twice won the men's singles at Wimbledon, in 1924 and 1926, and has won many Hard and Covered Court championships.

BOROUGH (bu'rō). A corporate town; a town with an organised municipal government. If it sends a representative or representatives to Parliament, it is a *parliamentary borough*; if not, it is a *municipal borough*. The qualifications for voters in both are the same. Many large boroughs are also *county boroughs*. In all boroughs a mayor is chosen annually, and a certain number of aldermen and councillors periodically, the burgesses or voters electing the councillors, and the councillors electing the mayor and aldermen. Mayor, aldermen, and councillors form the council. The corresponding term in Scotland is spelled *burgh*.

BOROUGHBRIDGE. Market-town of Yorkshire (W.R.). It is on the Ure, 18 miles from York and 207½ from London, on the L.N.E. Rly. Near are the Devil's Arrows, three stones nearly 20 feet high. Pop. 600.

BOROUGH - ENGLISH. In law, a mode of descent in some ancient boroughs and manors, in which the owner's youngest son, or his youngest brother (if he has no issue), is the heir. This mode of descent has been abolished by the Administration of Estates Act, 1925.

BOROVICHI (-vich'ē). A Russian town, government of Novgorod, on the great canal and river water-way which connects the Volga with Lake Ladoga. Pop. 11,000.

BORROME'AN ISLANDS. Four small islands in Lago Maggiore, N. Italy, taking their name from the family of Borromeo. Vitelliano Borromeo in 1671 caused garden soil to be spread over them, and converted them from barren rocks into gardens. Isola Bella, the most celebrated of the group, contains a handsome palace, with gardens laid out upon terraces rising above each other.

BORROME'O, Carlo, Count. A celebrated Roman Catholic saint and cardinal, born 1538 at Arona, on Lago Maggiore, died at Milan 1584. In 1560 he was successively appointed by his uncle, Pius IV (1559-66), apostolical prothonotary, refendary, cardinal, and Archbishop of Milan. The reopening and the results of the Council of Trent, so advantageous to the papal authority, were chiefly effected by the great influence of Borromeo, which was felt during the whole sitting of the Council. He improved the discipline of the clergy, founded schools, libraries, hospitals, and was indefatigable in doing good. Immediately after his death miracles were said to be wrought at his tomb, and his canonisation took place in 1610. His feast is celebrated on 4th Nov.—His nephew, Count Federigo Borromeo, also cardinal and Archbishop of Milan, equally distinguished for the sanctity of his life and the benevolence of his character, was born at Milan in 1564, and died in 1631. He is celebrated as the founder of the Ambrosian Library (q.v.).

BOR'ROW, George Henry. Born in 1803 at East Dereham, in Norfolk. His father was a captain in the army, and moved about from place to place, taking his family with him. Borrow's education was therefore extremely unconventional. He was for a time at Edinburgh High School, but he picked up most of his learning at odd moments. After spending some years in a lawyer's office, Borrow went to London and worked as a literary hack; afterwards his health broke down, and he adopted a wandering life for some time, associating much with gipsies, of whom he was always fond. He afterwards went to Spain as an agent of the Bible Society; he relates his experiences in *The Bible in Spain* (1843). His other works include *Lavengro* (1851), and its sequel, *The Romany Rye* (1857), both curious autobiographical books, and *Wild Wales* (1862). Borrow died at Oulton in 1881.—BIBLIOGRAPHY: Walling, *George Borrow, the Man and his Work*; C. K. Shorter, *George Borrow and his Circle*; W. I. Knapp, *Life of George Borrow*.

BOR'ROWDALE. A beautiful valley in the lake district of England, in Cumberland, at the head of the Derwent.

BORROWING DAYS. The last three days of March; the popular notion being, in Scotland and some parts of England, that they were borrowed by March from April. The fiction is of great antiquity, and probably arose in the observation of a frequent wintery relapse about the end of March.

BORROWSTOUNNESS (popularly **BO'NESS'**). A burgh in Linlithgowshire, Scotland, with good docks and a large trade in coal, iron, timber, etc. The wall of Antoninus ran through the parish of Borrowstounness, and traces of it, called Graham's Dyke, are visible. Pop. (1931), 10,095.

BORSAD. A town of India, Bombay Presidency, about midway between Baroda and Ahmedabad, and distant from each about 40 miles. Pop. 12,228.

BORSIP'PA. A very ancient city of Babylonia, the site of which is marked by the ruins Birs Nimrud.

BORSTAL. Village of Kent. It is near Chatham, and gives its name to a system by which offenders, between the ages of 16 and 21, instead of being sent to prison, go to a Borstal Institution, where they are trained to earn an honest living. The system was introduced in 1902, and there is a Borstal Association to further it, but it only became possible in its present form after the passing of the Prevention of Crimes Act, 1908. Males are sent to Borstal and females to Aylesbury, where they are looked after by the Aylesbury Association.

BORSTAL SYSTEM. A method of dealing with juvenile or adolescent offenders. *See* CRIMINOLOGY; PRISONS.

BORT, or CARBONADO. A massive form of diamond found in the State of Bahia, Brazil. Having no continuous cleavage, it is useful for setting in the crowns of the diamond-drills used for rock-boring. A mass found in 1895 weighed 631·9 grammes (22½ ounces).

BORY DE SAINT VINCENT (bō-rē dė saṉ vaṉ-sàṉ), **Jean Baptiste George Marie.** French naturalist, born 1780, died 1846. About 1800-2 he visited the Canaries, Mauritius, and other African islands. He afterwards served for a time in the army, and conducted scientific expeditions to Greece and to Algiers. Chief works: *Voyage dans les quatre principales Îles des Mers d'Afrique*; *Expedition Scientifique de Morée*; *L'Homme, Essai zoologique sur le Genre Humain.* He also contributed numerous articles to scientific publications, and edited the *Dictionnaire classique d'Histoire naturelle.*

BORYSTHENES (bo-ris'the-nēz). The ancient name of the Dnieper.

BORZOI. Russian wolfhound. It is used for hunting wolves. It ranks as a long-haired greyhound, slower but more powerful than the English type, with longish jaws, narrow but deep chest, and silky, white coat.

BOSA. A seaport, west coast of Sardinia, in an unhealthy district, with a cathedral and a theological seminary. Pop. 6910.

BOSANQUET, Bernard. British philosopher, born in 1848. Educated at Harrow and Balliol College, Oxford, he was professor of Moral Philosophy at St. Andrews from 1903 to 1908. His works include: *Knowledge and Reality* and *The Philosophical Theory of the State.* He died 1923.

BOSCAN-ALMOGAVER', Juan. A Spanish poet, born towards the close of the fifteenth century, died about 1540. He was the creator of the Spanish sonnet, and introduced Italian forms into Spanish poetry.

BOSCASTLE. Village of Cornwall. It is 5½ miles from Camelford, and has a small harbour. The magnificent scenery in the neighbourhood has made it a centre for holiday-makers.

BOSCAW'EN, Hon. Edward. British admiral, son of the first Viscount Falmouth, born in 1711, died 1761. He distinguished himself at Porto Bello and Cartagena, and in 1747 took part, under Anson, in the battle of Cape Finisterre. His chief exploit was a great victory in 1759 over the Toulon fleet, near the entrance of the Straits of Gibraltar.

BOSCH-BOK (bosh'bok). *See* BUSH-BUCK.

BOS'COBEL. A locality in Shropshire, remarkable historically as the hiding-place of Charles II. for some days after the battle of Worcester, 3rd Sept., 1651. At one time Charles was compelled to conceal himself among the branches of an oak in Boscobel Wood, where it is related that he could actually see the men who were in pursuit of him and hear their voices. The "royal oak," which now stands at Boscobel, is said to have grown from an acorn of this very tree.

BOSCOMBE. District of Bournemouth. To the east of the town, and on the S. Rly., it is noted for its beautiful chine and woods. *See* BOURNEMOUTH.

BOSCOVICH (bos'ko-vich), **Roger Joseph.** Astronomer and geometrician, born at Ragusa 1711, died at Milan 1787. He was educated among the Jesuits, and entered into their order. He was employed by Pope Benedict XIV. in various undertakings, and about 1750 measured a degree of the meridian in the Ecclesiastical States. He afterwards became mathematical professor in the University of Pavia, whence, in 1770, he removed to Milan, and there erected the celebrated observatory at the College of Brera.

BOSE, Sir Jagadis Chandra. Indian physicist, born 30th Nov., 1858. He was educated at Calcutta and Cambridge, and in 1885 became professor of physics in Calcutta. In 1896 he devised a coherer of the type since developed in wireless communication, together with delicate instruments for generating and studying electrical waves. After laborious researches with his crescograph, which multiplies the incidents of plant growth ten million times, he demonstrated the essential identity of the vital mechanism of animals and plants. Knighted in 1917, he became F.R.S. 1920. His works include: *Plant Response, Life Movements in Plants,* and *The Nervous Mechanism of Plants.*

BO'SIO, François Joseph, Baron. Sculptor, born at Monaco 1768, died at Paris 1845. He was much employed by Napoleon and by the successive Bourbon and Orleans dynasties. His works are well known in France and Italy.

BOSNA-SERAI. *See* SERAJEVO.

BOS'NIA. Till 1918 an Austrian province in the north-west of the Balkan Peninsula, west of Serbia, placed by the Treaty of Berlin (13th July, 1878) under Austrian administration for an undefined future period; definitely acquired by Austria in 1909; area (including Herzegovina), 19,768 sq. miles (of which Bosnia Proper occupies 16,200), with 1,889,929 inhabitants, mostly of Slavonian origin, and speaking the Serb tongue. They are partly Mohammedans, partly Roman and Greek Catholics. By autograph letter, dated 5th Oct., 1908, and addressed to the Premier of the two States, the sovereignty of the Austrian Emperor was extended over these two provinces.

The country is level towards the north, in the south mountainous. Its chief rivers are the Sava, the Verbas, the Bosna, Rama, and Drina. About half the area is covered with forests. Tillage is carried on in the valleys and low grounds, maize, wheat, barley, rye, buckwheat, hemp, tobacco, etc., being grown. Fruits are produced in abundance. Sheep, goats, and swine are numerous. The minerals include coal, which is worked in several places, manganese, antimony, iron, etc. Among the manufactures are iron goods, arms, leather, linens, and woollens. Bosnia had been subject to Turkey from the beginning of the fifteenth century till 1875, when an insurrection of the inhabitants led indirectly to the Russo-Turkish war of 1877-8 and the subsequent dismemberment of the Turkish Empire. In 1919, after the fall of the Austrian Empire, Bosnia and Herzegovina became part of Yugoslavia, the new State of the Serbs, Croats, and Slovenes.—Cf. A. Bordeaux, *La Bosnie Populaire.*

BOSPORUS, or **BOSPHORUS.** The strait, 18 miles long, joining the Black Sea with the Sea of Marmara, called also the Strait of Constantinople. It is defended by a series of strong forts; and by treaty of the European Powers (1841), confirmed by the Treaty of Berlin (1878), no ship of war belonging to any nation could pass the Bosporus without the permission of Turkey. One of the clauses, however, of the armistice, accepted by Turkey on 30th Oct., 1918, was that the Dardanelles, Bosporus, and Black Sea were to be opened to the Allies. Over this channel (about 3000 feet wide) Darius constructed a bridge of boats on his Scythian expedition. The *Cimmerian Bosporus* was the name given by the ancients to the strait that leads from the Black Sea into the Sea of Azov. There was also anciently a kingdom of the name of Bosporus, so called from this strait, on both sides of which it was situated.

BOSS. In architecture, an ornament placed at the intersection of

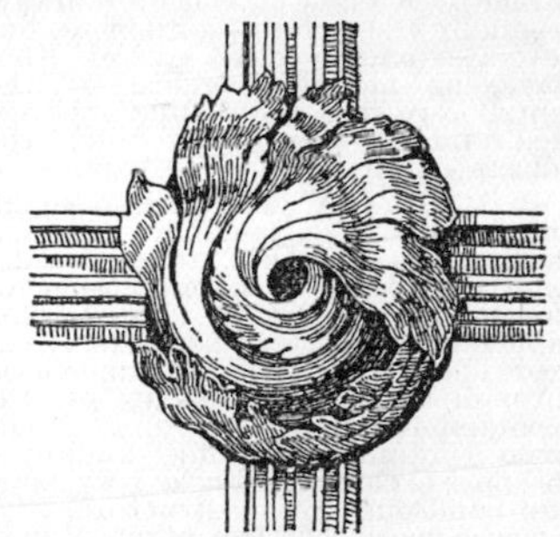

Boss. York Cathedral

the ribs or groins in vaulted or flat roofs; it is frequently richly sculptured with armorial bearings or other devices.

BOSS (and **BOSSISM**). "A political leader gone wrong," a term derived from the Du. *baas*, master, overseer. It has come largely into use among American negroes. In American politics the term is applied to such politicians as have secured control of certain offices, and are often able to direct the course of legislation to their own advantage. *See* TAMMANY HALL.

BOSSUET (bos-ü-ā), **Jacques Bénigne.** Illustrious French preacher and theologian, born in 1627, died in 1704. At the age of fifteen he entered the College of Navarre, where he studied Greek and the Holy Scriptures, read the ancient classics, and investigated the Cartesian philosophy. In 1652 he was ordained priest, and made a canon of Metz, where his piety, acquirements, and eloquence gained him a great reputation. In 1670 he was appointed preceptor to the Dauphin, and in 1681 he was given the see of Meaux. He drew up the famous propositions adopted by the assembly of French clergy, which secured the freedom of the Gallican Church against the aggressions of the Pope. (*See* GALLICAN CHURCH.) In his latter years he opposed Quietism, and prosecuted Madame Guyon; and when his old friend Fénelon defended her, he caused him to be exiled. He was unrivalled as a pulpit orator, and greatly distinguished for his strength and acumen as a controversialist. The great occupation of his life was controversy with the Protestants. A complete edition of his works appeared in 31 vols. (Paris, 1862-4).

BOSTAN'JI (Turk., from *bostan*, a garden). A class of men in Turkey, originally the Sultan's gardeners, but now also employed in several other ways, as mounting guard at the seraglio, rowing the Sultan's barge, etc., and likewise in attending the officers of the royal household.

BOS'TON. A municipal borough and port of England, in Lincolnshire, on the Witham, about 5 miles from the sea. The name stands for Botolph's town, St. Botolph having founded a monastery here about the year 650. The trade has increased through the improvement of the accommodation for shipping. The town contains some fine buildings, the parish church being a very large and handsome Gothic structure, with a tower nearly 300 feet high. Ropes, sails, agricultural implements, etc., are made. A parliamentary borough till 1918, Boston now unites with Holland in returning one member to Parliament. Pop. of municipal borough (1931), 16,597.

BOSTON. In the United States, the capital of Massachusetts, and the largest city in New England. It lies 234 miles by rail N.E. of New York, on Massachusetts Bay, at the mouth of Charles River. It has a capacious harbour, covering 144 sq. miles, protected from storms by a great number of islands, on several of which are fortifications. The scenery is varied and picturesque; the site partly consists of peninsulas, East Boston being on an island. The streets are mostly narrow and irregular in the older parts of the town, but in the newer parts are many fine spacious streets. There are many small parks, and a series of connecting parks is in process of formation; at present the Common and the Public Garden in the heart of the city are the chief pleasure-grounds.

Buildings. Among the principal buildings are the State-house, the county court-house, the post office, Faneuil Hall (from Peter Faneuil, who presented it to the city in 1742), famous historically as the meeting-place of the revolutionary patriots; the city hall or old State-house, now used as public offices; the splendid granite custom-house, of Grecian architecture; public halls, theatres, etc. Harvard University, situated at Cambridge, which may be regarded as a Boston suburb, was founded in 1636. The medical branch of this institution is in Boston. The Boston Athenæum has two large buildings—one containing a library, and the other a picture-gallery, a hall for public lectures, and other rooms for scientific purposes. The library consists of about 250,000 vols. Boston University, founded principally by Isaac Rich, and incorporated in 1869, consists of the college of liberal arts, college of music, college of agriculture, school of theology, school of laws, school of medicine, and the school of all sciences. It is open to women as well as men: average number of students, 2000. A prominent feature in Boston is the number of good libraries. Besides those already mentioned, there is the Public Library, founded in 1854, which maintains 250 agencies and already contains over 1,000,000 vols.; the State Library, with 300,000 books and pamphlets; and others.

Trade. Boston carries on an extensive home and foreign trade, and is also largely engaged in the fisheries. Many manufactures are carried on, one of the principal being that of boots and shoes. The first American newspaper was set up here in 1704. The book-trade of the city is important, and some of the periodicals are extensively circulated.

History. Boston was founded in 1630 by English emigrants, and received its name from Boston in Lincolnshire, whence several of the settlers had come. Notwithstanding its increasing size and importance, the affairs of Boston for nearly two hundred years were administered by the town's-people assembled in "town's meeting". In the War of Independence it played an important part. It was here that the opposition to the British measures of colonial taxation was strongest. The defiance reached its height when the Stamp Act was repealed, and the Tea Act denounced by three cargoes being thrown into the harbour. Here the battle of Bunker Hill was fought, 17th July, 1755. Pop. 781,188.

BOSTON, Thomas. A Scottish divine, born at Dunse 1676, died 1732. He was educated at Edinburgh University, received licence to preach in 1697, and in 1707 was appointed to the parish of Ettrick in Selkirkshire, where he remained all his life. Besides engaging hotly in the ecclesiastical controversies of his time, Boston published a volume of sermons, several theological treatises, and his two well-known works, *The Crook in the Lot* and *Human Nature in its Fourfold State.*

BOS'WELL, James. The friend and biographer of Dr. Johnson. Eldest son of Lord Auchinleck, one of the judges of the supreme court in Scotland. He was born at Edinburgh in 1740, and died in London in 1795. He was educated at Edinburgh, and became a member of the Scottish Bar, but never devoted himself with earnestness to his profession. In 1763 he became acquainted with Johnson—a circumstance which he himself calls the most important event of his life. He afterwards visited Voltaire at Ferney, Rousseau at Neufchâtel, and Paoli in Corsica; with the last-named he became intimate. In 1768, when Corsica attracted so much attention, he published his *Account of Corsica, with Memoirs of Paoli.* In 1785 he settled at London, and was called to the English bar. Being on terms of the closest intimacy with Johnson, he at all times diligently noted and recorded his sayings, opinions, and actions, for future use in his contemplated biography. In 1773 he accompanied him on a tour to the Scottish Highlands and the Hebrides, and he published an account of the excursion in the spring of 1786. His *Life of Samuel Johnson,* one of the best pieces of biography in the English language, was published in 1791. His son Alexander, born in 1775, created a baronet in 1821, killed in a duel in 1822, excelled as a writer of Scottish humorous songs, and was also a literary antiquary of no inconsiderable erudition.

BOSWEL'LIA. A genus of balsamic plants belonging to the myrrh family (Amyridaceæ), several species of which furnish the frankincense of commerce, known as olibanum. Indian olibanum is got from *Boswellia thurifĕra,* a large timber tree found in the mountainous parts of India.

BOS'WORTH. A small town in the county of Leicester, England, about 3 miles from which is Bosworth Field, where was fought, in 1485, the battle between Richard III. and the Earl of Richmond, afterwards Henry VII. This battle, in which Richard lost his life, put an end to the Wars of the Roses. Bosworth gives its name to a parliamentary division of the county.

BOSWORTH, Joseph. English philologist, born in Derbyshire 1790, died 1876. He was ordained deacon in 1814, and after filling several livings in England was British chaplain at Amsterdam and Rotterdam for twelve years. He devoted much time to researches in Anglo-Saxon and its cognate dialects, the result of his studies appearing from time to time. His chief works are his *Anglo-Saxon Grammar, Dictionary of the Anglo-Saxon Language,* and *Compendious Anglo-Saxon and English Dictionary.* In 1857 he was presented to the rectory of Water Shelford, Buckingham, and next year was appointed Rawlinson professor of Anglo-Saxon at Oxford. He was M.A. and LL.D. of Aberdeen, Ph.D. of Leyden, and D.D. of Cambridge. In 1867 he gave £10,000 to establish a professorship of Anglo-Saxon at Cambridge.

BOTAN'IC GARDENS. Establishments in which plants from all climates are cultivated for the purpose of illustrating the science of botany, and also for introducing and diffusing useful or beautiful plants from all parts of the world. In Britain the chief gardens are those of Kew (q.v.), Edinburgh, and Dublin. The most famous on the continent are the *Jardin des Plantes* at Paris, founded 1634; and those of Berlin, Copenhagen, Florence, etc. In America the chief are those of New York, Philadelphia, and Cambridge. Important exotic gardens are those of Calcutta, Peradeniya, Rio de Janeiro.

BOTANY (Gr. *botanē,* herb, plant), or **PHYTOLOGY** (Gr. *phyton,* plant, and *logos,* discourse). The science which treats of the vegetable kingdom.

Plants may be studied from several different points of view. The consideration of their general form and structure, and the comparison of these in the various groups from the lowest to the highest, constitutes *morphology. Anatomy* and *histology* treat respectively of the bulkier and the more minute internal structure of the parts, and *physiology* of their functions. *Systematic botany* considers the arrangement of plants in groups and sub-groups according to the greater or less degree of resemblance between them. *Geographical botany* tells of their distribution on the earth's surface, and strives to account for the facts observed, while *palæo-botany* bears the same relation to distribution in the successive geological strata which make up the earth's crust. *Economic botany* comprises the study of the products of the vegetable kingdom as regards their use to man.

Protococci. The simplest plants are very minute, and can only be studied by use of the compound microscope. A little rain-water which has been standing some time when thus examined is found to contain a number of roundish green objects, each of which is an individual plant, consisting of one cell only, with an external limiting membrane or cell-wall of a substance known as *cellulose,* within which is granular, viscid *protoplasm.* The protoplasm, or living substance, has embedded in it an oval more solid body, the *nucleus,* and a lobed chloroplast, which is permeated by a green pigment, chlorophyll. *Protococcus,* as this little plant is called, though so simple, is yet able, by virtue of the living protoplasm, to take up food from the water around it, to work that food up into more cellulose and protoplasm so as to increase in size, and, finally, to produce new individuals, more Protococci.

If we imagine Protococcus to elongate considerably and be repeatedly divided across by cell-walls, we get a row or filament of cells, a very common form among the low orders of plants: the masses of green threads seen floating in ditches in the spring and summer consist of such a filamentous plant called *Spirogyra.* Or we may have a thin flat sheet of cells, as in the delicate green seaweed *Ulva.* Increased complexity of structure is exemplified in many of the ordinary seaweeds, the stalk and more or less flattened expansions of which are several to many cells thick, the external cell-layers differing somewhat in structure from the internal. But we cannot distinguish in any of these between a stem, leaf, or root, as we can for instance in the more highly-differentiated fern. Plants in which such a distinction cannot be drawn are called *Thallophytes,* and their whole body a *thallus.*

Thallophytes can be divided into two classes: *Algæ* and *Fungi.* The former are distinguished by the presence of the green colouring-matter chlorophyll, which is of vital importance in the physiology of the plant; sometimes the green colour is obscured by the presence of a brown or red compound, as in the brown and red seaweeds. The Fungi contain no chlorophyll, and also differ in being composed, not of expansions or masses of cells like the algæ, but of numbers of delicate interlacing tubes or *hyphæ,* often forming, as in the mushroom, quite large and complicated structures. *Lichens* are an interesting class between Algæ and Fungi, inasmuch as they are built up of an alga and a fungus, which live together and are mutually dependent on each other.

Mosses and Ferns. Going a step higher we reach the *Mosses,* where, for the first time, we distinguish a clear differentiation of the part of the plant above ground into a stem and leaves borne upon it. The stem is attached to the soil by delicate colourless hairs—*rhizoids.* Its structure is, however, very simple, and the leaves are merely thin plates of cells.

Rising still higher to the fern-like plants, including *Equisetums* (Horsetails) and *Lycopods* (Club-mosses), we notice a great advance in complexity both of external form and internal structure. The leaves are large, often much branched, the stem stout and firm, while instead of the few simple hairs which was all the indication of a root-system to be found in the moss, there are well-developed true roots. Microscopic examination of sections of stem, leaf, or root, shows great differences in structure between various groups of cells; there is, in fact, marked *differentiation of tissues.* A tissue is a layer, row, or group of cells which have all undergone a similar development; by *differentiation of tissues* we mean that various layers, rows, or groups have developed in different ways, so that we can make out and mark by distinctive names the elements of which a stem or leaf is built up. The different cells and tissues are specialised for various functions, so that physiological division of labour goes hand in hand with structural differentiation.

The structure of thallophytes and mosses is very simple, but in the ferns, besides other well-marked tissues, we meet with one of so great importance in the higher plants, and so constantly present, that it is used as a distinctive characteristic of all the plants above the mosses. Ferns and flowering-plants which contain this *vascular tissue* are known as *vascular plants,* in contrast to the thallophytes and mosses, or *cellular plants,* where it is not found.

Microscopical examination of a very thin longitudinal slice of the stem, root, or leaf-stalk of a vascular plant shows bundles of long cells running lengthwise, the walls of which are not so uniformly thin as

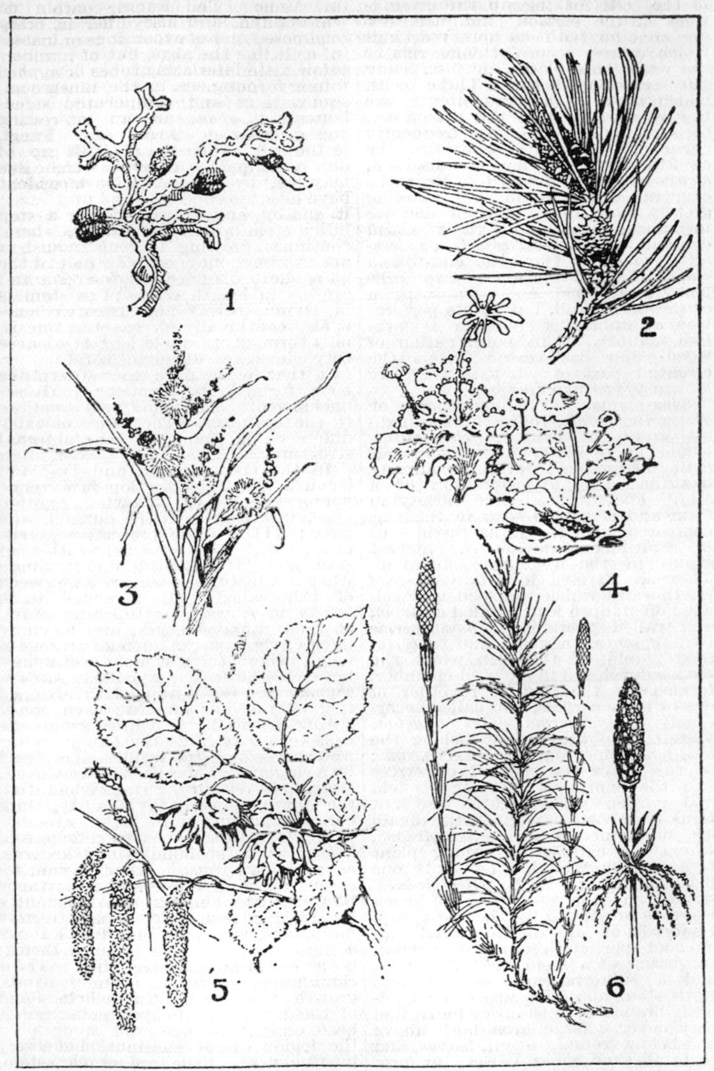

BOTANY

1. Thallophyte. Algæ. 2. Gymnosperm. Pine, male and female cones. 3. Monocotyledon. Bur reed. 4. Bryophytes. Liverworts. 5. Dicotyledon. Male and female catkin and fruit of hazel. 6. Pteridophytes. Horsetail.

in the cells making up the groundwork of the portion examined, but are covered with curious markings which represent local thickenings of the walls, thin places, or *pits*, being left between them. These cells, which have no living contents, are the wood-cells; they are placed end to end, and when, as frequently occurs, the end-walls separating the cavities of two cells become absorbed, a *wood-vessel* is formed. Near the elements of the wood, but differing greatly from them in their delicate unchanged walls and thick viscid contents, are the *bast-vessels*, or *sieve-tubes*, so called from the end-to-end communication between two cells being established, not by absorption of the whole wall, but by its perforation at numerous spots in a sieve-like manner. This combination of wood- and bast-vessels forms the essential part of what is therefore known as vascular tissue.

Seed-plants. *Phanerogams*, or *Flowering-plants*, represent the highest group of plants: *Seed-plants* would be a better name, as their main distinction from those already described is the production of a *seed*. The much greater variety in form and structure seen in them as compared with the ferns justifies us in regarding them as the highest group in the vegetable kingdom. They are divided into two classes: (1) those in which the seed is developed on an open leaf, termed a carpel, and called therefore *Gymnosperms* (Gr. *gymnos*, naked, and *sperma*, seed); and (2) those in which the seed is developed in a closed chamber, formed by the folding together of one or more carpels, and called accordingly *Angiosperms* (Gr. *angeion*, vessel). To the former belong the *Conifers*—pines and firs—and *Cycads*; to the latter the rest of our trees and the enormous number of field and garden plants which are not ferns or mosses. Angiosperms again are subdivided into *Monocotyledons*, where the embryo or young plant contained in the seed has only one primary leaf; and *Dicotyledons*, where an opposite pair of such leaves is present. Like the last group, Phanerogams are differentiated into a shoot portion above the ground, consisting of a stem bearing leaves, and a subterranean root portion. Both stem and root are often copiously branched, so that one individual may cover a large area both above and below ground. Stem, leaves, and roots all show great variety in form and adaptation.

The embryo, or rudimentary plant contained in the seed, consists of a very short axis or stem, bearing one (in Monocotyledons) or two (in Dicotyledons) primary leaves, the *cotyledons*, above which it terminates in a little bud or *plumule*, while below them the axis passes into the primary root or *radicle*. When the seed germinates, the radicle protrudes between the separating seed-coats, and growing downwards fixes itself in the soil. Then the plumule grows out, accompanied or not, as the case may be, by the cotyledons, which have hitherto concealed and protected it, and by rapid growth soon develops into a stem bearing leaves. The stem continues growing in length at its apex throughout the life of the plant; at a short distance below the apex growth in length ceases; but while in Gymnosperms and Dicotyledons it also continually increases in thickness through its whole length, Monocotyledons are distinguished by the fact that when once the stem has been formed its diameter remains unchanged. The same rule applies to the branches. The cause of this difference is found in the internal structure.

In the Gymnosperm and Dicotyledon a transverse section in a very young stage has the following appearance. Starting from the outside, we have: (1) a single protective layer of cells with thick external walls, the *epidermis*. (2) Inside this, and forming what is called the *cortex*, are a number of thin-walled cells arranged like bricks in a wall, or touching only at their rounded edges, and leaving intercellular spaces. Such an arrangement, where there is no dovetailing between the cells, is called *parenchymatous*. (3) Within the cortex a ring of vascular bundles, each consisting essentially of a little group of bast-vessels towards the outside and wood-vessels on the inside, separated by a single layer of cells, the *cambium-layer*. (4) Within the ring of bundles the *pith*, of parenchyma like the cortex, and united to it by strands of similar parenchymatous cells passing between the bundles and known as *medullary rays*. As the young stem grows, however, the spaces between the bundles are filled up by development of fresh bast, cambium, and wood, so that instead of a number of separate bundles there is a *complete* vascular ring. The cambium-ring remains in active growth throughout the whole life of the plant, and by producing new bast on the outside and wood on the inside causes continual increase in thickness. The epidermis soon gives way beneath the strain of the growth inside, and is replaced as a protective layer by the *bark*, development of which keeps pace with increase in diameter. Now in the young monocotyledonous stem, instead of a few bundles arranged in a ring separating pith from cortex, a great number are scattered through the whole internal parenchymatous tissue. The bundles, moreover, have no cambium-layer, so that when once formed their development is complete, and there is no increase in thickness.

Stems. Stems, which may be *simple* or *branched*, are either *aerial* or *subterranean*. *Aerial* forms are (1) *erect*, as the trunks of trees, or the more slender stems of most herbaceous plants, or the hollow *culms* of grasses; (2) *prostrate*, as the creeping *runners* of the strawberry; or (3) *climbing*, in which case they may either twine round a support, like the hop; or hold on by means of *prickles*, like the bramble; or more usually by *tendrils*, as in the vine; or, finally, by roots given off from the stem, as in the ivy.

Examples of subterranean stems are (1) the *rhizome*, a horizontal stem sending forth aerial shoots from its upper and roots from its lower surface; (2) the *tuber*, a much-swollen fleshy stem, like the potato, the eyes of which are buds; (3) the *bulb*, a very short undeveloped stem with crowded overlapping leaves, as the onion.

Branches. *Branches* proceed from buds which are formed in the autumn in the axils of the leaves, that is, at the point where the leaf or leaf-stalk is joined on to the stem; they remain dormant through the winter, and grow out into new shoots in the spring.

Leaves. The *leaf* is borne on the stem; its tissues are similar to and continuous with those of the stem, but their arrangement is somewhat different, in accordance with the thin flattened character of the leaf. The growth and duration of leaves are limited. The places where leaves come off from the stem are called *nodes*.

There is great variety both in the position and form of leaves. Their *position* is said to be *radical* when they are all borne close together at the base of the stem, as in the dandelion; or *cauline*, when they are borne on the upper parts; in the latter case they may have a *whorled* arrangement, where several come off at the same level in a circle round the stem, as in Herb Paris; or *opposite*, where two stand on opposite sides at each node, as in the gentians; or *alternate*, where only one comes off at any given level. A leaf may be *stalked* or *sessile*; if sessile, the blade is joined directly on to the stem. The stalk is known as the *petiole*, the flattened expanded blade as the *lamina*.

The leaf may be *simple* or *compound*. A simple leaf cannot be divided without tearing the lamina; while a compound leaf is made up of independent leaflets, which may all come off from the same point, as in the horse-chestnut, which is the *digitate* form; or may be arranged along a continuation of the petiole, as in the ash, which is the *pinnate* form of a compound leaf. The tissue of the lamina is traversed by vascular bundles, which are continuous through the petiole with those of the stem. The infinite variety of their ramifications is the cause of the often very characteristic *venation* of the leaves.

Leaves are said to be *deciduous* when they fall annually, as they do in the most common forest trees; or *evergreen* when they last longer, as in the firs, laurels, etc. Leaves of phanerogams are often very much modified or *metamorphosed*, e.g. those curious leaf-growths known as pitchers, and many tendrils, such as those of the pea tribe. When we consider the flower we shall find that its various members are all more or less modified leaves.

Roots. In Dicotyledons and Gymnosperms the primary *root* or radicle after emerging from the seed continues to grow vigorously, often with copious lateral branching, forming an extensive root-system; but in Monocotyledons it soon perishes, and its place is taken by roots developed from the base of the stem; such roots are called *adventitious*. Adventitious roots occur also in Dicotyledons, as in creeping stems like the strawberry. The clinging roots of the ivy are also adventitious. There are many forms of roots: some are large and woody, as those of trees; others fibrous, as in grasses; or they may be greatly swollen, forming the fleshy globose root of the turnip, or the conical one of the carrot. Such fleshy developments are due to the plant storing up a quantity of reserve food-material in the first year, on which to draw in the second, when it expends all its energy in flowering and fruiting. The potato, which is a swollen stem, answers the same purpose. The mistletoe and other parasites give off sucker-like roots which penetrate into the tissues of their host.

Reproduction. As to their *reproduction*, plants may be *asexual*, that is, not requiring the co-operation of two distinct (male and female) elements to produce a new individual; or *sexual*, when two such elements are necessary, and a process of fertilisation takes place in which the female cell is impregnated (fertilised) by a male cell, and the cell resulting from the fusion of the two gives rise by very extensive growth and division to a new individual.

In the very lowest plants, like Protococcus, only asexual reproduction is known, but in most Thallophytes both forms occur. In the asexual method numbers of small cells called *spores* are produced which on germination give rise to a plant similar to that which bore them. In the sexual process the contents of a male organ escape and impregnate the *oösphere* (*ovum*), or female cell contained in the female organ. The fertilised oosphere is termed an *oöspore*, and by growth and division gives rise to a plant like that on which it was produced. In mosses and fern-like plants both sexual and asexual reproduction occur; but here the history of the life of the plant is divided into two stages, one in which it exists as an asexual individual, another in which it is sexual. In the fern, for instance, brown marks are seen on the back of some of the leaves; these are little cases containing spores; the fern as we know it is an asexual individual producing spores. The spores when set free germinate on a damp surface and produce *not* a new fern-plant, but a tiny green heart-shaped cellular expansion, called a *prothallus*, attached to the substratum by delicate *rhizoids*. Microscopical examination of its under surface reveals the sexual organs, a male organ producing motile male cells, which escape, pass into the female organ, and fertilise the oosphere, which then becomes the oospore. The oospore does not produce a new prothallus, but a fern-plant like the one with which we originally started. The cycle is thus complete.

Flower. The *flower* of a seed-plant is a shoot modified for purposes of reproduction. A buttercup, for instance, consists of a number of modified leaves borne in several whorls on the somewhat expanded top of the stalk, the *receptacle* or *thalamus*. Dissection of the flower shows (1) an outer whorl of five green leaves, very like ordinary foliage leaves; these are the *sepals*, and together make up the *calyx*. (2) An inner whorl of five yellow leaves, composing the *corolla*, each leaf being a *petal*. (3) More or less protected by the petals are a great number of *stamens*, each consisting of a slender stalk or *filament* capped by an *anther*, a little case containing the dry powdery *pollen*. The stamens are really much-modified leaves; collectively they form the *andrœcium*. (4) The rest of the receptacle right up to the apex is also covered by very much modified leaves, the *carpels*, forming the *pistil* or *gynœcium*. Each carpel consists of a basal portion, the *ovary*, in which is contained an *ovule*, and of a terminal beak-like portion, the *style*.

The andrœcium and gynæcium, being the parts directly concerned in reproduction, are distinguished, as the *essential* organs of the flower, from the calyx and corolla, which are only indirectly so concerned, though of great importance in the process. The ovule contained in the ovary is equivalent to the spore-case produced by the fern, but instead of liberating the spore and producing an independent sexual individual it remains in the ovary, where processes go on *within* it corresponding to those resulting in the formation of the free and independent prothallium of the fern, and finally an oosphere is produced.

Pollen from the stamen of the same or another plant has meanwhile been brought on to the special receptive portion of the style known as the *stigma*, where it protrudes a long tube which reaches right down through the style to the ovule. This tube contains the male element; it comes into close contact with the oosphere and fertilisation ensues. The oosphere then becomes an oospore, which by growth and division forms the *embryo*, or new plant, while still included in the coats of the ovule. The ovule thus becomes the seed, which ultimately leaves the mother plant, bearing with it the embryo.

In the buttercup the members of each whorl of leaves composing the flower spring from the receptacle quite independently of each other, and of those of adjoining whorls. In many flowers, however, *cohesion* takes place between the similar members of a whorl; thus the petals frequently cohere to a greater or less distance from their base, and two great divisions of the Dicotyledons depend on this condition, namely, *Polypetalœ*, where the petals are free, as in the buttercup and poppy; and *Gamopetalœ*, with more or less coherent petals, as in the harebell and primrose. Similarly the gynæcium, instead of being composed of free carpels as in the buttercup, the *apocarpous* condition, may be formed by the cohesion of several carpels into a one- to several-chambered *compound* ovary, as in the snap-dragon, when it is said to be *syncarpous*. *Adhesion* also occurs between members of different whorls; thus the stamens are frequently inserted on the base of the petals, so that if we pull off a petal a stamen comes with it; and sometimes, as in orchids, the andrœcium and gynæcium are adherent. If the other floral whorls are inserted on the receptacle beneath the pistil they are said to be *hypogynous* and the pistil *superior*, as for instance in the poppy; if, on the other hand, as in the fuchsia, they spring from the top of the ovary, they are said to be *epigynous* and the pistil *inferior*.

An important characteristic is the *fruit*, which results after fertilisation from the ovary. While the changes are going on by which the ovule becomes the seed the ovary also grows, often enormously, and forms the *pericarp*, which surrounds and protects the seed or seeds. The pericarp consists of an outer layer or *epicarp*, a middle layer or *mesocarp*, and an inner layer or *endocarp*. The outer usually forms the skin of the fruit; the two others may be succulent, as in the *berry*, or the mesocarp only may be succulent and the endocarp hard and stony, as in the drupe. Besides the embryo the seed contains a store of food-material on which the young plant feeds during the first stages of its growth. This consists of albuminous, starchy, or fatty matter. In what are called *albuminous* seeds, as those of palms, the seed is chiefly composed of food-tissue in which is embedded a small embryo; the edible part of a coconut is the storage-tissue. In other seeds, like the bean, the fleshy cotyledons have already absorbed this food-material into themselves, and the seedling draws on its own cotyledons for support; these seeds are known as *exalbuminous*.

It was stated above that the ovule might be fertilised by pollen from the same flower or from another plant; experiment has shown that the latter produces better results, both as regards quality and quantity of seed, and the vigour of the seedlings. That is, *cross-fertilisation* is preferable to *self-fertilisation*, and the various, often extremely curious, shapes of a flower and its parts are mainly for the purpose of ensuring the former and preventing the latter.

Many flowers contain both stamens and pistil, these are termed *bisexual* or *hermaphrodite* (☿); while others contain stamens or pistil only, such are said to be *unisexual*. When both male (♂) and female (♀) flowers occur on the same plant the species is *monœcious*, like the hazel; while it is *diœcious* if the separate sexes are borne on different individuals, as is the case in the hop.

Plants which, like the sunflower, pass through all the stages from germination to production of fruit and seed in one season, and then perish, are called *annuals*; if two years are required, as with the turnip and onion, they are *biennials*; while *perennials* last several to many years, during which they may flower and seed many times.

Physiology. A plant is built up chiefly of four elements: carbon, hydrogen, oxygen, and nitrogen, with small quantities of sulphur and phosphorus and some mineral matter. Substances containing these must therefore form the food. A green plant can take up its carbonaceous food in a very simple form by means of the green *chloroplasts* contained especially in its leaves. These absorb some of the sun's rays, and by virtue of the energy represented by the light so absorbed obtain the carbon from the carbonic acid gas present in the atmosphere. An animal, having no chlorophyll, has to use more complex carbon-containing compounds, in fact those which have already been worked up in the vegetable kingdom. The other items of the food are obtained from the water and mineral salts in the soil, the salts being brought into solution and absorbed with large quantities of water by the roots. The leaves are the laboratory where the food is worked up into the complex compounds which form the plant substance, and to raise the crude material from the absorbing roots to the leaves there is an upward current of liquid through the stem. This is known as the *transpiration current*; it travels in the wood. A much larger quantity of water is absorbed than is required as food; this is got rid of by *transpiration*, that is, by the giving off of water-vapour from the leaves. This is evident if a plant be placed under a glass shade in the sunlight, the vapour given off becoming condensed on the glass. The complex compounds elaborated in the leaves are returned to all parts of the plant where growth, or storage of reserve-material, is taking place, by means of the other constituent of the vascular bundle, the bast tissue.

Fungi and a few seed-plants contain no chlorophyll, and cannot therefore get their carbonaceous food from the carbonic acid gas of the atmosphere, but have to live on decaying vegetable or animal matter, when they are termed *saprophytes* (Gr. *sapros*, rotten), like mushrooms, or on living plants or animals, when they are *parasites*; such are the fungi which cause diseases in these organisms. Plants, like animals, breathe; respiration goes on both day and night, and is represented by the absorption of oxygen from, and the return of carbonic acid gas to, the atmosphere. If we prevent a plant from breathing, that is, keep it in an atmosphere containing no free oxygen, it will sooner or later die.

Growth implies an increase in size, and involves a redistribution of the available material. It is well illustrated by the germination of a seed at the expense of its store of food-materials under suitable conditions of water-supply, aëration, and temperature.

Movement of one kind or another is a universal property of plants. Among the higher types, it most frequently consists in unequal growth induced by some external agency, as in the *heliotropic* curvatures of a stem towards light.

Systematic Botany. In botany, as in zoology, individuals which closely resemble each other form collectively a *species*. Species which, though having each some distinctive peculiarity, yet on the whole resemble each other, constitute a genus. Assemblages of genera agreeing in certain marked characters form *families* or *natural orders*. The names of the orders are generally formed on the type of *Rosaceæ*, the rose order, *Ulmaceæ*, the elm order, etc. *Classes*, such as *Monocotyledons* and *Dicotyledons*, contain a large number of natural orders, The older systems of classification were based largely on the uses of plants, for they were studied simply from a medicinal or generally economic point of view. In 1682, however, John Ray discovered the difference between Monocotyledons and Dicotyledons, and published an arrangement of plants founded on their structural forms, especially on the characters afforded by the seed ; this formed the basis of the *natural* system of classification, one, that is, which brings together those genera and families which a careful comparative study of the whole structure and development shows to be most nearly related. Linnæus did not recognise Ray's great primary divisions, and his system (1735) is a purely *artificial* one, since it only takes account of a few marked characters afforded by the essential organs of the flower, and does not propose to unite plants by their natural affinities. Owing to the exclusive part played by the essential organs this arrangement is known as the *sexual system*. The great value of Linnæus's work was his careful scientific revision and adjustment of all the known genera, and his introduction of the binomial system of nomenclature, in which every species has a double name, that of the genus to which it belongs coming first, then that of the species; thus *Bellis perennis*, *L.* is the daisy, and the name shows that the species *perennis* of the genus *Bellis* is the plant in question. The *L.* which follows indicates that we mean the plant so named by *Linnæus*. The sexual system is now only of historic interest. By the sagacity of the Jussieus the genera of Linnæus were more or less naturally grouped under Ray's primary divisions ; and by the subsequent labours of De Candolle, Robert Brown, Lindley, and many others we have attained to a fairly natural system, according to which all our great collections are arranged.

Bentham and Hooker (*Genera Plantarum*) subdivide Angiosperms as follows :—

Class I. *Monocotyledons*. — Contains thirty-four natural orders arranged in seven series.

Class II. *Dicotyledons*.

Sub-class 1. Polypetalæ (petals free).

Series i. Thalamifloræ.—Stamens inserted on the thalamus. Contains thirty-three natural orders.

Series ii. Disciflorae.—Thalamus expanded within the calyx into a cup-like disc, from which the stamens spring. Contains twenty-two natural orders.

Series iii. Calycifloræ.—Stamens epigynous, or inserted on the edge of the cup-like receptacle. Contains twenty-seven natural orders.

Sub-class 2. Gamopetalæ (petals united).—Contains forty-five natural orders.

Sub-class 3. Apetalæ (petals absent).—Contains thirty-six natural orders.

The system of Engler, which recognises only two sub-classes of Dicotyledons, viz. Archichamydeæ and Metachlamydeæ (Sympetalæ), though not so convenient in practice, is probably more in accordance with natural affinity.—BIBLIOGRAPHY : F. O. Bower, *Botany of the Living Plant*; F. O. Bower and D. T. Gwynne-Vaughan, *Practical Botany for Beginners* ; J. M. F. Drummond, *Botany*, in *Science in Modern Life* ; J. R. Green, *Vegetable Physiology* ; *History of Botany in the United Kingdom* ; Sir J. D. Hooker, *Students' Flora of the British Islands* ; T. Horwood, *British Wildflowers in their Natural Haunts* ; A. Kerner von Marilaun and F. W. Oliver, *Natural History of Plants* ; A. F. W. Schimper, *Plant Geography* ; D. H. Scott, *Structural Botany* ; G. F. Scott Elliot, *A First Course in Practical Botany*; *Botany of To-day* ; H. M. Ward, *Diseases of Plants* ; J. C. Willis, *Flowering Plants and Ferns* ; T. W. Woodhead, *The Study of Plants* ; R. C. Punnett, *Mendelism* ; Sir J. C. Bose, *Nervous Mechanism of Plants* ; *Plant Autographs* ; *Motor Mechanism of Plants* ; *Growth and Tropic Movements of Plants*.

BOTANY BAY. A bay in New South Wales, so called by Captain Cook on account of the great number of new plants collected in its vicinity. The English penal settlement, founded in 1788, and popularly known as Botany Bay, was established on Port Jackson, some miles to the northward, near where Sydney now stands.

BOTANY BAY OAK. *See* BEEFWOOD.

BOTANY BAY RESIN. *See* BLACKBOY.

BOTAR'GO. A relish made of the salted roe of the mullet or tunny, used on the Mediterranean coasts. *See* CAVIARE.

BOTAU'RUS. *See* BITTERN.

BOT-FLY, or **BOTT-FLY.** One of a family of flies (Œstridæ) of which the larvæ (bots) are parasitic in the bodies of hoofed mammals. The larvæ of the Horse Bot-fly (*Gastrophilus equi*) live in the stomach of the horse; those of the Ox Bot-fly or Warble-fly (*Hypoderma bovis*) under the skin of the back in cattle; and those of the Sheep Bot-fly (*Œstrus ovis*) in the nasal cavities of the sheep.

BOTH (bōt), **John** and **Andrew.** Two Flemish painters, born about 1610. John painted landscapes, Andrew filling in figures in so careful a manner that their picture looked like the work of one hand. Their works are in great repute. Andrew was drowned at Venice in 1650. John died at Utrecht shortly after.

BOTHA, Louis. Boer statesman, born in 1863 at Greytown, Natal, died Sept., 1919. In his earlier days he took part with the Boers who seized a portion of the territory of the Zulus afterwards incorporated in the Transvaal, and subsequently was cornet in the Vryheid district, and a member of the Transvaal Volksraad. On the outbreak of the South African War he took an active part in the invasion of Natal and the operations against Ladysmith, and when General Joubert fell ill he succeeded to his position, and was in chief command when the affairs of Colenso and Spion Kop took place. On Joubert's death (March, 1900) he became Boer commander-in-chief, and after Cronje's surrender he concentrated the Boer troops in the Lydenburg district, still determined on resistance, but at last agreed to the terms of peace (1902). He became the first Prime Minister of the Transvaal in 1907. He was in favour of the union of the S. African colonies in 1909. He visited England in 1907, representing his country at the Colonial Conference held in London, and again in 1911, when he received honorary degrees from Oxford, Cambridge, and Glasgow. He was made an honorary general in the British army in 1912. In 1910, upon the formation of the Union of South Africa, he became Prime Minister and Minister of Native Affairs, a post which he retained till his death. During the European War he commanded the Union forces in South-West Africa (1914-5), and achieved complete success, all the German forces in South-West Africa surrendering in July, 1915.

BOTH'IE (Gael, *bothag*, a cot). A house, usually of one room, for the accommodation of a number of work-people engaged in the same employment; especially, a house of this kind in parts of Scotland, in which a number of unmarried male or female farm servants or labourers are lodged in connection with a farm. Bothies are most common in the north-east of Scotland (but practically unknown in the Lothians), and are chiefly for the accommodation of unmarried male farm servants engaged on the larger farms, who as a rule have to do their cooking and keep the bothie in order for themselves. The bothie system has often been condemned, although it has its advantages. In no other way would it be possible for young men engaged in farm labour to live so cheaply.

BOTH'NIA, GULF OF. The northern part of the Baltic Sea, which separates Sweden from Finland. Length about 450 miles, breadth 90 to 130 miles, depth from 20 to 50 fathoms. Its water is but slightly salt, and it freezes so severely in winter that sledges and carriages can be driven over it.

BOTHRIOCEPH'ALUS. A genus of worms belonging to the tapeworm family, one species of which (*B. latus*) is found in the intestines of man in Russia, Switzerland, North America, and Japan. The bladder-worm stage infests the muscles of pike and some other freshwater fishes.

BOTHRODENDRON. A genus of extinct Lycopodiales, found in the lower Carboniferous and upper Devonian. The so-called "paper-coal" of Toula, in Russia, consists of layers of cuticle from the stem-epidermis of these plants, scarcely differing from cuticle of living plants in respect of appearance, power of swelling in water, and behaviour towards aniline dyes; a unique instance of preservation of vegetable matter almost unchanged through millions of years.

BOTH'WELL. A village of Lanarkshire, Scotland, on the Clyde, 8 miles east of Glasgow. Here is Bothwell Bridge, where a decisive battle was fought in 1679 between the Scottish Covenanters and the royal forces commanded by the Duke of Monmouth, in which the former were totally routed. Near by are the fine ruins of Bothwell Castle, once a stronghold of the Douglases. The population of the parish at the census of 1931 was 60,660.

BOTH'WELL, James Hepburn, Earl of. Known in Scottish history by his marriage to Queen Mary, born about 1526. It is believed that he was deeply implicated in the murder of Darnley, Mary's husband, and that he was even supported by the queen. He was charged with the crime and tried, but, appearing along with 4000 followers, was readily acquitted. He was now in high favour with the queen, and with or without her consent he seized her at Edinburgh, and, carrying her a prisoner to Dunbar Castle, prevailed upon her to marry him after he had divorced his own wife. But by this time the mind of the nation was roused on the subject of Bothwell's character and actions. A confederacy was formed against him, and in a short time Mary was a prisoner in Edinburgh, and Bothwell had been forced to flee to Denmark, where he died in 1576.

BOTLEY HILL. Hill of Surrey. It is near Tatsfield, close to the main road from Croydon to Westerham, and is 850 feet high, being, next to Leith Hill, the highest point in the county. In 1929 the B.B.C. decided to erect a receiving and research station here.

BOTOCU'DOS. A Brazilian race of savages who live 70 to 90 miles from the Atlantic, in the virgin forests of the coast range. They receive their name from the custom which they have of cutting a slit in their under lip and in the lobes of their ears, and inserting in these, by way of ornament, pieces of wood shaped like the bung of a barrel (Port. *botoque*). They are very skilful with the bow and arrow, and live chiefly by hunting. They number only a few thousands, and are decreasing.

BOTOLPH. English saint. Little is known of his life beyond the fact that he became a monk and founded a monastery somewhere in England. His festival is kept on 17th June in England, and on 25th June in Scotland.

BOTOSA'NI. A town of Rumania, in the north of Moldavia. Pop. 32,874.

BO-TREE. The *Ficus religiōsa*, pipal, or sacred fig tree of India and Ceylon, venerated by the Buddhists and planted near their temples. One specimen at Anuradhapoora in Ceylon is said to have been planted in 288 B.C. It was greatly damaged by a storm in 1887.

BOTRYCHIUM (bo-trik'i-um). A genus of ferns, family Ophioglossaceæ, one species of which (*B. lunaria*, or common moonwort) is a native of Britain, growing on elevated heaths and pastures where other ferns are seldom found. *B. virginianum*, the largest species, is a native of North America, New Zealand, the Himalayas, etc.

BOTRYOP'TERIS. The type of the Botryoptereæ, a family of fossil (Palæozoic) ferns, forming, together with the Zygoptereæ, the group of Cœnopterideæ (q.v.), the most primitive of known genuine ferns. Remains of several species of Botryopteris, with the internal structure well preserved, have been found in the coal-measures of Britain and France.

BOTRY'TIS. A genus of Fungi Imperfecti, section Hyphomycetes. *B. cinerea* and *B. vulgaris* are very common on decaying vegetable matter, and may become dangerous parasites on cultivated plants, such as the potato ; the former has been regarded as the conidial stage of an Ascomycete (*Sclerotinia Fuckeliana*). *B. bassiana* causes the destructive disease of silk-worms known as " muscardine ".

BOTTA, Paul Émile. French traveller and archæologist, born about 1805. In 1833 he was appointed French consul at Alexandria. He undertook a journey to Arabia in 1837, described in his *Relation d'un Voyage dans l'Yémen*. He discovered the ruins of ancient Nineveh in 1843 while acting as consular agent for the French Government at Mosul. As the result of his investigations he published two important works—one on the cuneiform writing of the Assyrians, *Mémoire de l'Écriture Cunéiforme Assyrienne*, and the other upon the monuments of Nineveh, *Monuments de Ninive* (five vols. folio, with drawings by Flandin, Paris, 1846-50)—the latter of which is a work of great splendour, and marks an era in the study of Assyrian antiquities. He died in 1870.

BÖTTGER, or **BÖTTIGER** (beut'gėr, beu'ti-gėr), **Johann Friedrich.** German alchemist, the inventor of the celebrated Meissen porcelain, born in 1682. His search for the philosopher's stone, or secret of making gold, led him into many difficulties. At last he found refuge at the Court of Saxony, where the Elector erected a laboratory for him, and forced him to turn his attention to the manufacture of porcelain, resulting in the invention associated with his name. He died in 1719.

BOTTICELLI (bot - tē - chel ′lē), **Sandro** (*Alessandro Filipepi*). An Italian painter of the Florentine school, born in 1444, died 1510. Working at first in the shop of the goldsmith Botticello, from whom he takes his name, he showed such talent that he was removed to the studio of the distinguished painter Fra Lippo Lippi. From him he learnt his vigorous style, to which he added a gracefulness of his own. He painted flowers, especially roses, with incomparable skill. In his later years Botticelli became an ardent disciple of Savonarola, and is said by Vasari to have neglected his painting for the study of mystical theology. His pictures *Adoration of the Magi*, *Nativity*, *Venus and Mars*, and *Madonna with Child* are in the National Gallery, London. — BIBLIOGRAPHY: A. P. Oppé, *Sandro Botticelli*; A. J. Anderson, *The Romance of Sandro Botticelli*; L. Binyon, *The Art of Botticelli*.

BÖTTIGER (beu ′ ti - ger), **Karl August.** A German archæologist, born in 1760, died in 1835. After studying at Leipzig, he became director of the gymnasium at Weimar, and it was here that, while he enjoyed the society of Goethe, Schiller, Wieland, and other distinguished men, he began his literary career. In 1814 he was appointed chief inspector of the Museum of Antiquities in Dresden, where he lived till his death. Among his most important works are: *Sabina, oder Morgenscenen einer reichen Römerin* (Sabina, or Morning Scenes of a Wealthy Roman Lady); *Griechische Vasengemalde* (Paintings on Greek Vases); *Ideen zur Archæologie der Malerei* (Thoughts on the Archæology of Painting).

BOTTLE (Fr. *bouteille*, dim. from L. *butta*, flask, wine-skin). A vessel of moderate or small size, and with a neck, for holding liquor. By the ancients they were made of skins or leather; they are now chiefly made of glass or earthenware. The common black bottles of the cheapest kind are formed of the most ordinary materials, sand with lime, and sometimes clay and alkaline ashes of any kind, such as kelp, barilla, or even wood ashes. This glass is strong, hard, and less subject to corrosion by acids than flint-glass.

BOTTLE-BRUSH. The common name of shrubs or trees of the genus Callistemon, nat. ord. Myrtaceæ, natives of Australia. The stamens are very long and brightly coloured, and as the flowers are massed together in dense spikes, a flowering branch somewhat resembles the kind of brush used for cleaning bottles, test-tubes, etc.

BOTTLE-FLOWER. *See* BLUE-BOTTLE.

BOTTLE-GOURD. A kind of gourd, genus Lagenaria, the dried fruits of which, when the pulp is removed, are used in warm countries for holding liquids.

BOTTLE-NOSE. A kind of whale, of the dolphin family, genus Hyperoödon, 20 to 28 feet long, with a beaked snout and a dorsal fin, a native of northern seas. The caaing-whale is also called bottle-nose.

BOTTLE-TREE (*Sterculia rupestris*). A tree of North-Eastern Australia, ord. Sterculiaceæ, with a stem that bulges out into a huge rounded mass. It abounds in a nutritious

Bottle-tree (*Sterculia rupestris*)

mucilaginous substance, and contains a large reserve of water. Similar trees of the genus Cavanillesia are found in the thorn-forests (Catingas) of Brazil.

BOTTOMLEY, Horatio William. English journalist, born 23rd March, 1860; after some business experiences he became a journalist and founded *The Financial Times*. Later he established *John Bull*, which, under his direction, had an enormous circulation. He was the defendant in many libel actions, usually conducting his own defence, and was a popular speaker and writer during the war period. From 1906-12, and again 1918-

22, he was M.P. for S. Hackney, being a Liberal, but with independent tendencies. In May, 1922, he was sentenced to penal servitude for fraud. He was released in 1927.

BOT'TOMRY. A contract by which a ship is pledged by the owner or master, when he cannot communicate with the owner, for the money necessary for repairs to enable her to complete her voyage. The freight and even the cargo may be pledged as well as the ship. A loan secured on the cargo alone is said to be taken up at *respondentia*. The conditions of such a contract usually are that the debt is repayable only if the ship arrives at her destination. As the lender thus runs the risk of her loss, he is entitled to a high premium or interest on the money lent. The latest bottomry bond takes precedence of all previous ones.

BOTULISM. A form of food-poisoning caused by the bacillus *Botulinus*, discovered by Van Ermengen. It is much less frequent than food-poisoning due to putrefaction, and is caused by eating tainted liver, blood-ham, smoked meat, and game birds, especially grouse; but other food-stuffs have been the agents in some outbreaks. The chief symptoms are dryness of throat, dilated pupils, deafness, facial and cardio-respiratory paralysis. Obscure nervous symptoms were observed in the patients who suffered in the outbreak in London in 1918. In contrast to other forms of food-poisoning, gastro-intestinal symptoms are not prominent.

BOT'ZEN, or **BOLZA'NO.** An old town of Italy, formerly in the Austrian province of Tirol, well built, at the junction of roads from Switzerland, Germany, and Italy, which makes it one of the busiest and most important places in the Italian Trentino. It has silk and cotton manufactures, tanneries, dyeworks, and largely attended annual fairs. Pop. 40,590.

BOUCHES-DU-RHÔNE (bösh-dü-rōn; "Mouths of the Rhone"). A department in the S. of France, in ancient Provence. Chief town, Marseille. Area, 2025 sq. miles, of which about one-half is under cultivation. The Rhone is the principal river. The climate is generally very warm; but the department is liable to the *mistral*, a cold and violent N.E. wind from the Cevennes ranges. Much of the soil is unfruitful, but the fine climate makes the cultivation of figs, olives, nuts, almonds, etc., very successful. The manufactures are principally soap, brandy, olive-oil, chemicals, vinegar, scent, leather, glass, etc. The fisheries are numerous and productive. Pop. 1,101,672.

BOUCICAULT (bō'si-kō), **Dion.** Dramatic author and actor, born at Dublin, 20th Dec., 1822, and educated partly at London University. He was intended for an architect, but the success of a comedy, the well-known *London Assurance*, which he wrote when only nineteen years old, made him decide to be a playwright. Boucicault, being a remarkably facile writer, in a few years had produced quite a lengthy list of pieces, both in comedy and melodrama, and all more or less successful. We may mention *Old Heads and Young Hearts, Love in a Maze, Used Up, The Corsican Brothers*. In 1853 he went to America, where he was scarcely less popular than in England. On his return in 1860 he produced a new style of drama, dealing largely in sensation but with more heart in it than his earlier work. *The Colleen Bawn* and *Arrah-na-Pogue* are the best examples. Indeed the best Boucicault could do was such pictures of Irish life and manners. His last appearance in London was in his play *The Jilt* in 1886. As an actor he was clever, although, perhaps, not highly gifted. His dramatic pieces are said to number more than 150. He died in 1890. His son Dion and his daughter Nina have also distinguished themselves on the stage.

BOUDOIR (bö'dwär). A small room, furnished comfortably, where a lady may retire to be alone (from Fr. *bouder*, to pout, to be sulky). The boudoir is the peculiar property of the lady, where only her most intimate friends are admitted.

BOUFFLERS, or **BOUFLERS** (bö-flär), **Louis François, Duc de.** Marshal of France, one of the most celebrated generals of his age, born in 1644, died 1711. He learned the art of war under such renowned generals as Condé, Turenne, and Catinat. His defence of Namur against King William of England and of Lille against Prince Eugene are famous, and he conducted the retreat of the French at Malplaquet with such admirable skill as quite to cover the appearance of defeat.

BOUGAINVILLÆA. A genus of spinous climbing shrubs or small trees, nat. ord. Nyctaginaceæ, natives of S. America. The apparent flower is really a small group of rather inconspicuous flowers almost hidden by three large brilliantly-coloured bracts; these are deep magenta or brick-red in *B. spectabilis*, a very handsome plant widely cultivated in warm countries, where it is very useful for covering walls, outhouses, etc. Owing to its rank growth, it is suitable for greenhouses only where plenty of space is available.

BOUGAINVILLE (bö - gan - vēl), **Louis Antoine de.** A famous French navigator, born at Paris in 1729. At first a lawyer, he afterwards entered the army and fought bravely in Canada under the Marquis of Montcalm, and it was principally owing to his exertions, in 1758, that a body of 5000 French withstood successfully a British army of 16,000 men. After the battle of 13th Sept., 1759, in which Montcalm was killed and the fate of the colony decided, Bougainville returned to France, and served with distinction in the campaign of 1761 in Germany. After the peace he entered the navy, and became a distinguished naval officer. In 1763 he undertook the command of a colonising expedition to the Falkland Islands; but as the Spaniards had a prior claim the project was abandoned. Bougainville then made a voyage round the world, which enriched geography with a number of new discoveries. The expedition returned to St. Malo in 1768, and he published an account of his voyage (*Description d'un Voyage autour du Monde*, Paris, 1771-2). In the American War of Independence he distinguished himself at sea, but withdrew from the service after the Revolution, and died in 1811.

BOUGAINVILLE ISLAND (see above). An island in the Pacific Ocean belonging to the Solomon group (area, 3500 sq. miles), formerly under German protection, but occupied by the Australian troops on 31st Dec., 1914. It is separated from Choiseul Island by **Bougainville Strait.**

BOUGH, Samuel (generally "Sam"). Artist, born near Carlisle 1822, died 1878; was a self-taught painter, first of theatrical scenery at Manchester and Glasgow, spent the last twenty years of his life at Edinburgh, becoming A.R.S.A. 1856, and R.S.A. 1875. His works are mostly landscapes, and the best of them are in water-colour, his style being marked by breadth, freedom, boldness, and command of atmospheric effect.

BOUGHTON. Village of Northamptonshire. It is 2 miles from Kettering. Boughton Park, a seat of the Duke of Buccleuch, was built by a duke of Montagu and stands in a large park. The gardens are notable. Another Boughton is 3 miles from Northampton.

BOUGHTON, George Henry. English artist, born in Norfolk, 4th Nov., 1833; he passed his youth in New York. He studied art in Paris, and about 1863 his pictures became known in London, where he had settled. In 1879 he was made A.R.A., and in 1898 R.A. He died 19th Jan., 1905. Boughton's paintings are mainly subject pictures, such as "The Return of the Mayflower" and those dealing with country life in Holland, New England and Brittany. He is represented in the Tate Gallery.

BOUGHTON, Rutland. British composer, born 1878, and educated at Aylesbury and the Royal College of Music. The Glastonbury Festival School of Music Drama was founded by him in 1904.

Among his works *The Immortal Hour* is outstanding. He also wrote *The Queen of Cornwall*, a music drama, *The Moon Maiden*, a choral ballet, *Agincourt*, for male voices, etc.

BOUGIE (bö - zhē). A fortified seaport on the coast of Algeria, well situated for trade, which it carried on in the Middle Ages to a greater extent than now, though under French rule it is again prosperous, exporting wax, honey, grain, etc. Pop. 25,261.

BOUGIES (bö'zhēz; the French word for tapers). In surgery, applied to certain smooth cylindrical rods which are introduced into the canals of the human body (the rectum, urethra, and œsophagus) in order to widen them, or more rarely to apply medicaments to a particular part in the interior of the body. They are distinguished from catheters by being quite solid. They are made sometimes of linen dipped in wax and then rolled up, sometimes of a kind of plaster and linen, also of caoutchouc or gutta-percha, or of metal, such as lead, silver, or German silver.

BOUGUER (bö - gā), **Pierre.** A French mathematician and astronomer, born in 1698. He was associated with Godin and La Condamine in an expedition to the South American equatorial regions to measure the length of a degree of the meridian. The main burden of the task fell upon Bouguer, who performed it with great ability, and published the results in his *Théorie de la Figure de la Terre* (1749). He also invented the heliometer, perfected by Fraunhofer, and his researches on light laid the foundation of photometry. He died in 1758.

BOUGUEREAU (bö-grō), **Adolphe William.** French painter, born in 1825, died 1905. He studied for seven years at the École des Beaux

Arts (1843-50), and for five years at Rome (1850-5), and in 1855 made a name for himself by his *Martyr's Triumph*, a picture representing the body of St. Cecilia borne to the Catacombs. His works are very numerous, and are generally marked by refinement and elegance. Many of them deal with subjects connected with classical mythology, *The Triumph of Venus* being the chief. Some are religious or ecclesiastical in subject, a certain number being frescoes, and others portraits, etc.

BOUILLON (bö-yōn̦). Originally a German duchy, now a district in Belgium, 9 miles wide and 18 long, on the borders of Luxembourg and Liège, a woody and mountainous tract, with some 21,000 inhabitants. The small town of Bouillon was once the capital of the duchy, which belonged to the famous Crusader, Godfrey of Bouillon.

BOUILLON, GODFREY OF. *See* GODFREY OF BOUILLON.

BOULAK′. A town of Lower Egypt, a suburb and port of Cairo. It has cotton, sugar, and paper factories, and till recently had a famous museum of antiquities. Pop. 10,000.

BOULANGER (bö-län̦-zhā), **Georges Ernest Jean Marie.** French general, born in 1837, died in 1891. He entered the army; served with credit in the Italian war, in Cochin China, and China; was for a time an instructor in the military school of St. Cyr; fought in the Franco-German War and against the Commune, holding in the end the rank of colonel. He rendered useful service in the organisation of the army, became general of brigade in 1880, and in 1882 became director-in-chief of infantry in the Ministry of War. In 1884 he became general of division and took command of the troops in Tunis, where he made himself highly popular. In 1886 he became War Minister under M. Freycinet, in which position he managed to have himself looked upon as the man destined to give France her revenge upon Germany. But Boulanger's vanity led him too far, and he was removed from the army on the charge of insubordination in 1888. He was immediately elected a member of the Chamber of Deputies, and for a time continued to embarrass the rulers of France; but on a prosecution being brought against him he fled from France. He was found guilty in absence of maladministration of public funds, and the Boulangist movement died away. In 1891, while residing at Brussels with his mistress, the lady died, and Boulanger committed suicide.—BIBLIOGRAPHY: Verly, *Le General Boulanger et la Conspiration Monarchique*; Guyot, *Le Boulangisme.*

BOULDER (bōl′dėr). A rounded stone of some size, worn by atmospheric weathering, torrent action, or by glacial drag and movement, from a rock mass, and in some cases carried for a long distance from its source.

BOULDER (bōl′dėr). A town of the United States, in Colorada, at the eastern base of the Rocky Mountains, at the height of 5300 feet, 24 miles north-west of Denver, with good railway connections. It is the seat of the State university. Pop. 11,223.

BOULDER-CLAY (*Till* in Scotland). A loamy or clayey deposit containing abundant boulders which have often been transported from a long distance and are foreign to the place where they now lie. The frequent occurrence of boulders and pebbles irregularly scratched, and the fact that the rock-floor below the boulder-clay is commonly polished and also scratched, indicate that the transporting agent was glacier-ice. The occurrence of marine shells in boulder-clay is no proof that the deposit took place beneath the sea, since glaciers are known to gather into themselves the loose matter over which they move and to carry it to unexpected positions before melting finally sets in.

Boulder-clay covers a large part of Scotland, Ireland, and Northern and Central England, the chalky boulder-clay of England extending as far south as London. The loams of the great North German lowland, of Finland, and of a large area in Russia are boulder-clays deposited as the great ice-sheets from Scandinavia melted away. In Spitsbergen and Greenland the mode of formation can be easily seen at the foot of shrinking glaciers, the lower layer of glaciers of the broad "continental" type being largely composed of mixed gathered-up material in a cement of ice. The presence of boulder-clay has provided arable land over wide areas where the underlying rocks would have yielded poor and insufficient soil. The most familiar boulder-clay is that formed over wide areas of Europe and North America by the ice of the Glacial Epoch at the opening of Quaternary times. *See* DRIFT; GLACIER.

BOULEVARD (böl-vär). A French word formerly applied to the ramparts of a fortified town, but when these were levelled, and the whole planted with trees and laid out as promenades, the name boulevard was still retained. Modern usage applies it also to many streets which are broad and planted with trees, although they were not originally ramparts. The most famous boulevards are those of Paris.

BOULOGNE (bö-lon-yė or bö-lōn), or **BOULOGNE-SUR-MER.** A fortified seaport of France, department of Pas de Calais, at the mouth of the Liane. It consists of the upper and lower town. The former is surrounded by lofty walls, and has thirteenth-century ramparts; the latter, which is the business part of the town, has straight and well-built streets, and is semi-English in character, many of the signboards being in English, the shops having an English air, and much English being spoken. In the castle, which dates from 1231, Louis Napoleon was imprisoned in 1840. Boulogne has manufactories of soap, earthenware, linen and woollen cloths; wines, coal, corn, butter, fish, linen and woollen stuffs, etc., are the articles of export. Steamers run daily between Boulogne and England, crossing over in two hours. Napoleon, after deepening and fortifying the harbour, encamped 180,000 men here with the intention of invading Britain at a favourable moment; but upon the breaking out of hostilities with Austria, 1805, they were called to other places. Pop. 51,854.

BOULOGNE, BOIS DE. *See* BOIS DE BOULOGNE.

BOULOGNE-SUR-SEINE. A town of France, department of Seine, south-west of Paris, of which it is a suburb. It is from this place that the celebrated Bois de Boulogne gets its name. Pop. (1926), 75,559.

BOULT, Adrian Cedric. English musician, born at Chester, 8th April, 1889. He was educated at Westminster School and Christ Church, Oxford. Afterwards he studied music at Leipzig, and after the World War became known as a conductor, not only in London and Liverpool, but also in New York, Vienna, and elsewhere abroad. From 1924-30 he was in Birmingham as director of the city orchestra, and in 1930 he became musical director to the B.B.C.

BOULTON (bōl'ton), **Matthew.** A celebrated mechanician, born at Birmingham in 1728, died there 1809. He was a manufacturer of hardware, and invented and greatly improved the making of inlaid steel buckles, buttons, watch-chains, etc. In 1762 he added to his premises by the purchase of the Soho, a barren heath near Birmingham, where he established an extensive manufactory and school of the mechanical arts. The introduction of the steam-engine at Soho led to a connection between Boulton and James Watt, who became partners in trade in 1769.

BOUNTY. In political economy, a reward or premium granted for the encouragement of a particular species of trade or production, the idea being that the development of such trade or production will be of national benefit. In Britain the idea of the inefficacy of bounties to sustain or develop commerce or manufactures is in general pretty well established, the usual argument being that it is nothing less than taxing the general community in order to encourage individuals to engage in businesses which, in the existing state of markets and competition, it would be better to leave alone. Hence the British Government has long given up the system of bounties, except in such peculiar cases as the subsidies granted for carrying the oceanic mails, and recently to assist in the sugar-beet industry.—The same name is given to a premium offered by Government to induce men to enlist in the public service, especially to the sum of money given in some States to recruits in the army and navy. The highest bounty offered in Britain was during the wars with Napoleon, when it rose to about £24. During the Civil War in America the bounty was at one time so high as $900 (£180). The bounty given to army recruits in Britain was abolished by the Army Enlistment Act of 1870, but they are still allowed a free kit.—King's bounty is a grant made by the sovereign to those of his subjects whose wives are delivered of three or more children at one birth.

BOUNTY, MUTINY OF THE. On 28th April, 1789, owing to the harsh and tyrannical conduct of their commander (Lieut. Wm. Bligh), the crew of H.M.S. *Bounty* mutinied when a few days out from Tahiti. Bligh and the loyal members of the ship's company were turned adrift in the launch, but succeeded in reaching Batavia.

The mutineers put back into Tahiti, where most of them settled. Nine, however, sailed for Pitcairn Island, accompanied by some native women. Next year, Captain Edwards of H.M.S. *Pandora* captured twelve of the mutineers at Tahiti and hanged three of them. The fate of those who sailed for Pitcairn Island remained unknown until 1808, when an American vessel touching there found the island inhabited by a half-caste community, the children of the *Bounty* mutineers and their native wives, ruled by John Adams, the last surviving British sailor. Adams lived until 1829. Pitcairn Island is still inhabited by descendants of the *Bounty* mutineers.

BOUQUETIN (bö'ke-tin). *See* IBEX.

BOURBON (bör-bõn). An ancient French family which has given three dynasties to Europe, the Bourbons of France, Spain, and Naples. The first of the line known in history is Adhemar, who, at the beginning of the tenth century, was lord of the Bourbonnais (now the department of Allier). The power and possessions of the family increased steadily through a long series of Archambaulds of Bourbon till in 1272 Beatrix, daughter of Agnes of Bourbon and John of Burgundy, married Robert, sixth son of Louis IX. of France, and thus connected the Bourbons with the royal line of the Capets. Their son Louis had the barony converted into a dukedom and became the first Duc de Bourbon.

Two branches took their origin from the two sons of this Louis, Duke of Bourbon, who died in 1341. The elder line was that of the Dukes of Bourbon, which became extinct at the death of the Constable of Bourbon in 1527, in the assault of the city of Rome. The younger was that of the Counts of La Marche, afterwards Counts and Dukes of Vendôme. From these descended Anthony of Bourbon, Duke of Vendôme, who by marriage acquired the kingdom of Navarre, and whose son, Henry of Navarre, became Henry IV. of France. Anthony's younger brother, Louis, Prince of Condé, was the founder of the line of Condé.

There were, therefore, two chief branches of the Bourbons—the royal, and that of Condé. The royal branch was divided by the two sons of Louis XIII., the elder of whom, Louis XIV., continued the chief branch, whilst Philip, the younger son, founded the House of Orleans as the first duke of that name. The kings of the *elder French royal line* of the House of Bourbon run in this way: Henry IV., Louis XIII., XIV., XV., XVI., XVII., XVIII., and Charles X. The last sovereigns of this line, Louis XVI., Louis XVIII., and Charles X. (Louis XVII., son of Louis XVI., never obtained the crown), were brothers, all of them being grandsons of Louis XV. Louis XVIII. had no children, but Charles X. had two sons, viz. Louis Antoine de Bourbon, Duke of Angoulême, who was dauphin till the revolution of 1830, and died without issue in 1844, and Charles Ferdinand, Duke of Berry, who died, 14th Feb., 1820, of a wound given him by a political fanatic. The Duke of Berry had two children: (1) Louise Marie Thérèse, called Mademoiselle d'Artois; and (2) Henri Charles Ferdinand Marie Dieudonné, born in 1820, and at first called Duke of Bordeaux, but afterwards Count de Chambord, who was looked upon by his party until his death (in 1883) as the legitimate heir to the crown of France.

The branch of the Bourbons known as the *House of Orleans* was raised to the throne of France by the revolution of 1830, and deprived of it by that of 1848. It derives its origin from Duke Philip I. of Orleans (died 1701), second son of Louis XIII., and only brother of Louis XIV. A regular succession of princes leads us to the notorious Égalité Orléans, who in 1793 died on the scaffold, and whose son, Louis Philippe, was King of France from 1830 to the revolution of 1848. His grandson Louis Philippe, Count de Paris (born in 1838, died in 1894), after the death of Count de Chambord, the last male representative of the elder Bourbons, united in himself the claims of both branches, now vested in his nephew Jean, son of the late Duke of Chartres.

The *Spanish-Bourbon dynasty* originated when in 1700 Louis XIV. placed his grandson Philip, Duke of Anjou, on the Spanish throne, who became Philip V. of Spain. From him descends Alphonso XIII., born in 1886, who occupied the throne of Spain until 1931.

The royal line of *Naples*, or the Two Sicilies, took its rise when in 1735 Don Carlos, the younger son of Philip V. of Spain, obtained the crown of Sicily and Naples (then attached to the Spanish monarchy), and reigned as Charles III. In 1759, however, he succeeded his brother, Ferdinand VI., on the Spanish throne, when he transferred the Two Sicilies to his third son, Fernando (Ferdinand IV.), on the express condition that this crown should not be again united with Spain. Ferdinand IV. had to leave Naples in 1806; but after the fall of Napoleon he again became king of both Sicilies under the title of Ferdinand I., and the succession remained to his descendants till 1860, when Naples was incorporated into the new kingdom of Italy.—BIBLIOGRAPHY: Achaintre, *Histoire chronologique et généalogique de la maison royale de Bourbon*; L. Dussieux, *Généalogie de la maison de Bourbon de 1256 à 1869*; D. A. Bingham, *The Marriages of the Bourbons*.

BOURBON, Charles, Duke of, or **CONSTABLE OF BOURBON.** Son of Gilbert, Count of Montpensier, born in 1490, and by his marriage with the heiress of the elder Bourbon line acquired immense estates. He received from Francis I., in the twenty-sixth year of his age, the sword of Constable, and in the war in Italy rendered important services by the victory of Marignano and the capture of Milan. After occupying for years the position of the most powerful and highly-honoured subject in the realm, he suddenly fell into disgrace, his wealth and influence having aroused a feeling of resentment in the king. The intrigues, too, of the Court party, headed by the king's mother and the Duke of Alençon, were threatening to deprive him both of honours and estates.

The Constable, embittered by this return for his services, entered into treasonable negotiations with the Emperor Charles V. and the King of England (Henry VIII.), and eventually fled from France to put his sword at the service of the former. He was received with honour by Charles, who knew his ability, and, being made general of a division of the imperial army, contributed greatly to the overwhelming defeat of Francis at Pavia. But the Bourbon found that Charles V. was readier to make promises to him than to fulfil them, and he returned disappointed and desperate to the command of his army in Italy, an army nominally belonging to the emperor, but composed mostly of mercenaries, adventurers, and desperadoes from all the countries of Europe. Supplies falling short, and the emperor refusing to grant him more, the Constable formed the daring resolve of leading his soldiers to Rome and paying them with the plunder. On 6th May, 1527, his troops took Rome by storm, and the sacking and plundering continued for months. But the Bourbon himself was shot as he mounted the breach at the head of his soldiers. He was but thirty-eight years of age.

BOURBON, ISLE OF. *See* Reunion.

BOURBONNAIS (bŏr - bon - ā). A former province of France, with the title first of a county, and afterwards of a duchy, lying between Nivernais, Berry, and Burgundy, and now forming the department of the Allier.

BOURBON-VENDÉE (bör-bōn-vān-dā), **Napoléon - Vendée.** A French town, now **La Roche-sur-Yon.**

BOURCHIER, John, Lord Berners. *See* Berners.

BOURDALOUE (bör-dá-lö), **Louis.** One of the great Church orators of France, was born at Bourges in 1632, and entered the Order of the Jesuits, becoming teacher of rhetoric, philosophy, and morals in the Jesuit college of his native place. In 1669 he was selected to occupy the pulpit of the Church of St. Louis, and he preached for a series of years at the Court of Louis XIV. with great success. The lofty and dignified eloquence with which he assailed the vices of contemporary society brought him fame even at a time when Paris was ablaze with the feasts of Versailles, the glory of Turenne's victories, and the masterpieces of Corneille and Racine. After the repeal of the Edict of Nantes (1686) he was sent to Languedoc in order to convert the Protestants, a task in which he was not unsuccessful. His sermons are amongst the classics of France. He died in 1704. His works were published between 1707 and 1734.

BOURDON (bör′don). A bass stop in an organ or harmonium having a droning quality of tone.

BOURG (börg), or **BOURG-EN-BRESSE.** A town of Eastern France, capital of the department of Ain, well built, with a handsome parish church, public library, museum, monuments to Bichat, Joubert, and Edgar Quinet, and near the town the beautiful Gothic church of Brou, built in the early sixteenth century; some manufactures and a considerable trade. Pop. 23,117.

BOURGELAT (börzh-lä), **Claude.** Creator of the art of veterinary surgery in France, born in 1712, died 1779. He established the first veterinary school in his native town in 1762, and his works on the art furnished a complete course of veterinary instruction.

BOURGEOIS (bur-jō′). A size of printing type larger than brevier and smaller than long primer, used in books and newspapers.

BOURGEOIS (börzh-wȧ), **Léon Victor Auguste.** French statesman, born in Paris in 1851. He studied at the Lycée Charlemagne, and in 1880 became sub-prefect of Rheims. He was prefect of Tarn in 1882, director of the Ministry of the Interior in 1886, and Prefect of Police in 1887. He entered the Chamber of Deputies in 1888, and became Minister of the Interior in 1889. In 1895 he became Premier, but resigned in the following year. He was Minister of Public Instruction in 1898, and at the head of the French delegation to The Hague Peace Conference in 1899. He was president of the Chamber of Deputies from 1902 to

1904, Minister for Foreign Affairs in 1906, and Minister of Labour in 1917. He was a great advocate of the League of Nations, the plan for which was adopted on 25th Jan., 1919, Bourgeois becoming the French Delegate. He was elected president of the Senate in 1920, and after the resignation of Paul Deschanel, President of the French Republic, in September of the same year, he was invited to stand for the Presidency, but refused. His works include: *L'Éducation de la Démocratie Française, Essai d'une Philosophie de la Solidarité.* He was awarded the Nobel Peace Prize in 1921. He died in 1925.

BOURGEOISIE (börzh-wȧ-zē). A name applied to a certain class in France, in contradistinction to the nobility and clergy as well as to the working classes and proletariat. It thus includes all those who do not belong to the nobility or clergy, and yet occupy an independent position, from financiers and heads of great mercantile establishments at the one end to master tradesmen at the other. It corresponds to the English term "middle classes." Etymologically the word refers to the old class of freemen or burgesses residing in towns.

BOURGES (börzh). An ancient city of France, capital of the department of Cher, situated at the junction of the Auron and Yèvre, 144 miles S. of Paris, formerly surrounded by ramparts, now laid out as promenades. It has crooked and gloomy streets, and houses built in the old style. The most noteworthy building is the cathedral (an archbishop's) of the thirteenth century, and one of the finest examples of Gothic architecture in France. Bourges is a military centre and has an arsenal, cannon-foundry, etc.; manufactures of cloth, leather, etc. Pop. 45,067.

BOURGET (bör-zhā), **Paul.** French novelist, poet, essayist, and critic, born at Amiens in 1852, educated at Clermont-Ferrand and Paris. It was as a poet that he first made his appearance, and he has published several collections of verse, but it is as a novelist and critic that he has chiefly distinguished himself. Among his works are: *L'Irréparable, Cruelle Enigme, Un Crime d'Amour, André Cornelis, Mensonges, Le Disciple, Un Cœur de Femme, La Terre Promise, Un Scrupule, Un Saint Steeple-chase, Une Idylle Tragique, La Duchesse Bleue, Le Fantôme, L'Etape, Un Divorce, L'Emigré, La Barricade, Le Tribun, La Crise, Le Démon de Midi* (1914), *Le Sens de la Mort* (1915), *Lazarine* (1917), *Nemesis* (1918), *Laurence Albane* (1920), *Un Drame dans le Monde* (1921), *Conflicts Intimes* (1925), *Le Danseur Mondaine* (1926), *Nos Actes nous Suivent* (1927), etc. Among essays and studies are *Essais de Psychologie Contemporaine, Nouveaux Essais, Etudes et Portraits*; other prose works being *Sensations d'Italie* and *Outre-Mer*, the last the result of a visit to the United States. Bourget has also stayed for some time in England and Ireland, and has a wider knowledge of life and literature than many French writers.

BOURGET. Lake of France, near Aix les Bains; it is 11 miles long and about 2 broad and, with the mountains in the background, it is famed for its beauty. Its waters are carried to the Rhône.

BOURGET, LE. Village of France, really a suburb of Paris. It is 6 miles to the N.E. of the city, and the site of the aerodrome at which travellers to and from Paris alight and depart.

BOURKE (bėrk). A town of New South Wales, 503 miles north-west of Sydney by rail, in a district rich in copper-ore. Pop. 3000.

BOURLON WOOD. 3½ miles west of Cambrai, the scene of much fierce fighting in November and December, 1917. *See* EUROPEAN WAR.

BOURMONT (bör-mōṇ), **Louis Auguste Victor de Ghaisne, Comte de, Marshal of France.** Born in 1773, died in 1846. Entering the Republican army, he distinguished himself under Napoleon, who made him a general of division. After the Restoration, he readily took service with the new dynasty, and in 1830 commanded the troops which conquered Algiers, for which success he was made a marshal. After the revolution of 1830 he followed the banished Charles X. into exile, but at the amnesty of 1840 retired to his estate in Anjou, where he died.

BOURNE (bōrn), **Vincent.** An English scholar, born 1695, died 1747. In 1721, after graduating as M.A. at Cambridge, he became a master in Westminster School, where he remained, so far as is known, to the end of his life. He is one of the few who have attained fame for writing Latin verse. His poems in Latin, which include original compositions and versions of English pieces, were first published in 1734. Cowper and Lamb translated poems of his.

BOURNE (bōrn). An ancient market town of England, in Lincolnshire, 35 miles south by east of Lincoln, consisting mainly of four streets meeting in the market-place. There is an old church in the Norman and subsequent styles of architecture; and the Old Red House, formerly the residence of Sir Everard Digby of the Gunpowder Plot, an Elizabethan mansion, is now used as a railway station. Pop. (1931), 4889.

BOURNEMOUTH (bōrn'-). An English county and parliamentary borough and watering-place in Hampshire, with one of the best beaches in England. It has many handsome buildings, a fine climate, and beautiful scenery, and has risen with great rapidity. Pop. (1931), 116,780.

BOURNOUSE. *See* BURNOOSE.

BOURNVILLE. A model village, founded in 1879 as a garden city by George Cadbury of the celebrated cocoa firm, in Worcestershire, about 3 miles south-west of Birmingham. It was the first "garden city" to be built in England, the aim being to put the working people inhabiting it in thoroughly healthy conditions.

BOURRIENNE (bö-rē-ān), **Fauvelet de.** A French diplomatist, born in 1769, and educated along with Bonaparte at the school of Brienne, where a close intimacy sprang up between them. Bourrienne went to Germany to study law and languages, but, returning to Paris in 1792, renewed his friendship with Napoleon, from whom he obtained various appointments, including that of Minister Plenipotentiary at Hamburg. Notwithstanding that his character suffered from his being involved in several dishonourable monetary transactions, he continued to fill high State offices, and in 1814 was made Prefect of Police. On the abdication of Napoleon he paid his court to Louis XVIII., and was nominated a Minister of State. The revolution of July, 1830, and the loss of his wealth affected him so much that he lost his reason, and died in a lunatic asylum in 1834. His *Mémoires sur Napoléon, le Directoire, le Consulat, l'Empire et la Restauration* (published in 10 vols. in 1829) are valuable.

BOURSE. A French word used in a special sense for an exchange, particularly Stock Exchange (q.v.).

BOUSSA (bös'a), or **BUSSANG.** A town of West Africa, in Northern Nigeria, province of Borgu, on the Niger, near where are rapids. It was here that Mungo Park met his death in 1805. Pop. estimated at 12,000 to 18,000.

BOUSSINGAULT (bö-saŋ-gō), **Jean Baptiste Joseph Dieudonné.** French chemist, born at Paris in 1802, died 1887. He went to S. America in the employment of a mining company, and made extensive travels and valuable scientific researches there. Returning to France, he became professor of chemistry at Lyons in 1839, was elected a member of the Institute, and then made Paris his chief residence. His works deal chiefly with agricultural chemistry, and include: *Economie Rurale* (translated into English in 1845); *Mémoires de Chimie agricole et de Physiologie*; *Agronomie, Chimie agricole, et Physiologie* (7 vols., published between 1860 and 1884).

BOUSTROPHE'DON. A kind of writing which is found on Greek inscriptions of great antiquity. The lines do not commence uniformly at one side, but run on alternately from left to right and from right to left. It is called *boustrophēdon* (turning like oxen) because in this way oxen ploughed a field.

BOUTERWEK (bö'ter-vek), **Friedrich.** German writer on philosophical and literary subjects, born in 1766, died in 1828. After applying himself to many departments of learning, jurisprudence, poetry, etc., he at last devoted himself entirely to philosophy and literary history. His best title to remembrance is his *History of Modern Poetry and Eloquence*, published 1801-19, which is the fruit of wide study and matured judgment. In particular the part which treats of Spanish poetry and eloquence has been highly valued, and has been translated into Spanish, English, and French.

BOUTROUX, Étienne Émile Marie. French philosopher, born at Montrouge (Seine) in 1845; studied in Paris and at the University of Heidelberg. He was appointed director of the Institut (Fondation) Thiers in 1902, and elected a member of the Académie Française in 1912. Boutroux's philosophical doctrine rests upon analysis of logical and of causal necessity, and in the distinction between the point of view of quality and that of quantity. The former permits us to perceive only permanency, immobility, and fatality; while the latter enables us to distinguish motion, finality, contingency, and progress. Among his works are: *De la Contingence des Lois de la Nature* (1874 and 1907); *De l'Idée de Loi naturelle dans la Science et la Philosophie contemporaines* (1895, English translation, 1911); *Questions de Morale et d'Éducation* (1905), English translation as *Education and Ethics* (1913); *William James* (1912). He died in Nov., 1921.

BOUTS RIMÉS (bö rē-mā; Fr., "rhymed ends"). Words or syllables given as the ends of the verses, the other parts of the lines to be supplied by the ingenuity of the poet. In the seventeenth century the composition of *bouts rimés* was a fashionable amusement. Alexandre Dumas tried to revive this futile amusement in 1865, and Dante Gabriel Rossetti frequently wrote sonnets with *bouts rimés* for practice.

BOUVAR'DIA. A genus of Rubiaceæ, natives of Tropical America; several species are cultivated for their handsome flowers, which are generally red or white and, in some cases, sweet-scented.

BOUVET ISLAND. An isolated island in the South Atlantic, about 2500 miles east of South Georgia. In 1825 it was occupied by the British, but in 1922 Norway occupied the island (it is a suitable whaling base) and claimed sovereignty. The claim was not admitted, but in 1928 Britain ceded Bouvet Island to Norway as an act of grace. Britain retained the adjacent Thomson Island.

BOUVINES. Village of France. Not far from Lille, it was formerly in Flanders, and is famous for the battle fought here 27th July, 1214. On this occasion the French under Philip Augustus defeated the forces of John of England and the Emperor Otto IV.

BOVEY TRACEY. Village of Devon. It is 7 miles from Moreton Hampstead on the G.W. Railway, and stands amid beautiful scenery on the edge of Dartmoor. The church, dedicated to S. Thomas à Becket, was built by one of his murderers, William de Tracey. Pottery is made here, as a suitable clay is found in the **Bovey Tracey beds.** These are geological formations in the valley of the Teign which contain sand, clay, and lignite.

BOV'IDÆ. The ox family of animals, including the ox, the bison, buffalo, yak, zebu, etc.

BOW. The name of one of the most ancient and universal weapons of offence. It is made of steel, wood, horn, or other elastic substance. The shape of the bow is nearly the same in all countries. The ancient Grecian bow was somewhat in the form of the letter Σ: in drawing it, the hand was brought back to the right breast, and not to the ear. The Scythian bow was nearly semicircular. The long-bow was the favourite national weapon in England. The battles of Crécy (1346), Poictiers (1356), and Agincourt (1415) were won by this weapon. It was made of yew, ash, etc., of the height of the archer, or about 6 feet long, the arrow being usually half the length of the bow. The arbalist, or cross-bow, was a popular weapon with the Italians, and was introduced into England in the thirteenth century, but never was so popular as the long-bow. In England the strictest regulations were made to encourage and facilitate the use of the bow. Merchants were obliged to import a certain proportion of bow-staves with every cargo; town councils had to provide public shooting-butts near the town. Of the power of the bow, and the distance to which it will carry, some remarkable anecdotes are related. Thus Stuart (*Athenian Antiquities*, i.) mentions a random shot of a Turk, which he found to be 584 yards. In the journal of King Edward VI. it is mentioned that 100 archers of the king's guard shot at a 1-inch board, and that some of the arrows passed through this and into another board behind it, although the wood was extremely solid and firm. *See* ARCHERY.

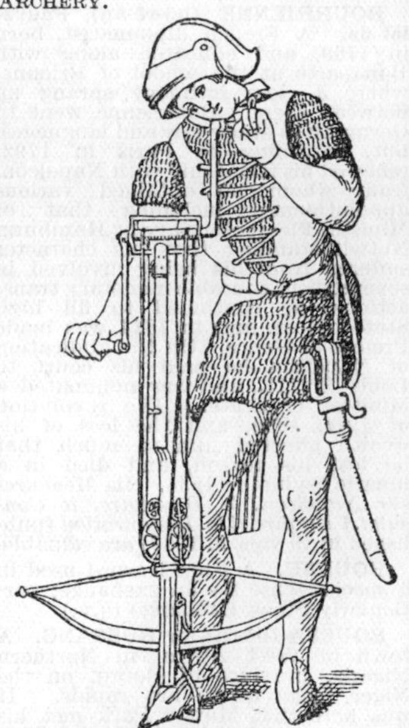

Bow. Archer winding up his Cross-bow. (Fourteenth Century)

BOW. In music, the name of that well-known implement by means of which the tone is produced from violins, and other instruments of that kind. It is made of a thin staff of elastic wood, tapering slightly till it reaches the lower end, to which the hairs (about 80 or 100 horse-hairs) are fastened, and with which the bow is strung. At the upper end is an ornamental piece of wood or ivory called the *nut*, and fastened with a screw, which serves to regulate the tension of the hairs. François Tourte brought the art of bow-making to perfection towards the end of the eighteenth century.

BOW BELLS. The peal of bells belonging to the church of St. Mary-le-Bow, Cheapside, London, and celebrated for centuries. One who is born "within the sound of Bow Bells" is considered a genuine Cockney.

BOWDICH (bou'dich), **Thomas Edward.** African traveller, born in 1790. In 1816 he led an embassy to the King of Ashanti, and afterwards published an account of his mission (1819). Having undertaken a second African expedition, he arrived in the River Gambia, where he died of disease, 1824.

BOWDLER, Thomas. English author, born near Bath, 11th July, 1754. He was educated at Scottish universities and became a doctor. He practised in London, but is known for an edition of Shakespeare which he prepared. Called *The Family Shakespeare*, this appeared in 1818, all phrases which might be considered coarse or indecent having been removed. Bowdler also issued an expurgated edition of Gibbon's *Decline and Fall*, and his method gave rise to the verb "to bowdlerise," meaning to alter. He died 24th Feb., 1825.

BOWDOIN (bō'dn), **James.** American politician, born 1727 at Boston, New England, died 1790. He distinguished himself as an opponent of the policy of Britain; in 1785 was appointed Governor of Massachusetts, and he was a member of the convention assembled to deliberate on the adoption of the constitution of the United States. He was a friend and correspondent of Franklin.—*Bowdoin College*, Brunswick, Maine, was named after him. It is a flourishing institution, and has had among its students Longfellow and Hawthorne.

BOWEL. An animal's intestines. In man it consists of the small and large intestine. The small one is about 20 feet long and the large one only about 5 feet long but much wider. It is also called the colon, and is subject to a severe inflammatory complaint called colitis. The failure of the bowel to function is called constipation. The bowels serve to complete the digestion of food and to allow of its absorption into the blood-stream. The useless food remains are gradually moved onwards, remaining in a liquid state until they become, except in time of illness, a semi-solid mass and ready to be voided.

BOWEN, Lord. English lawyer, born at Woolaston, Mon., 1st Jan., 1835, a son of a clergyman, Charles Synge Christopher Bowen. He was educated at Rugby and Balliol College, Oxford. He became a barrister in 1861, and after some very successful years was made a judge in 1879. In 1893 he became a Lord of Appeal and a life peer. A great classical scholar and translator of Virgil's *Aeneid*, he died 10th April, 1894.

BOWER (bou'ėr). An anchor: so named from being carried at the *bow* of a ship. *See* ANCHOR.

BOWER, Archibald. A Scottish writer, born in 1686, of Catholic parents. He was employed by the booksellers in conducting the *Historia Literaria*, a monthly review of books, and in writing a part of the *Universal History*, in 60 vols. 8vo. He also published a *History of the Popes*, characterised by the utmost zeal against Popery. He died a Protestant in 1766.

BOWER-BIRD. A name given to certain Australian birds of the starling family from a remarkable habit they have of building bowers to serve as places of resort. The bowers are constructed on the ground, and usually under overhanging branches in the most retired parts of the forest. They are decorated with variegated feathers, shells, small pebbles, bones, etc. At each end there is an entrance left open. These bowers do not serve as nests at all, but seem to be places of amusement and resort, especially during the breeding season. —*The Satin Bower-bird* (*Ptilonorhynchus holosericĕus*) is so called from its beautiful glossy plumage, which is of a black colour. Another common species is the *Spotted Bower-bird* (*Chlamydēra maculāta*), which is about 11 inches long, or rather smaller than the first-mentioned and less gay in colour, but is the most lavish of all in decorating its bowers.

BOWIE-KNIFE. A sheath-knife or hunting-dagger with a broad curved blade from 10 to 15 inches long, much used by hunters of the Western United States. It is named after Colonel James Bowie (1790-1835), who in a fight near Natchez (1827) killed an opponent with a knife made from a blacksmith's file.

BOW INSTRUMENTS are all the instruments strung with catgut from which the tones are produced by means of the bow. The most usual are the double-bass (*violono* or *contrabasso*), the small bass, or *violoncello*, the tenor (*viola di braccio*), and the violin proper (*violino*). In reference to their construction the several parts are alike ; the difference is in the size.

BOWLAND. Forest area in Lancashire. It is a hilly and moorland district on the borders of Yorkshire, between Blackburn and Lancaster. Part of the Pennine region, it covers some 300 sq. miles. A proposal has been made to make it a national park.

BOW LEG. Malformation of the legs of a human being. It means that the legs, instead of being straight are bowed or bandy. It is often the result of rickets, and can be cured by wearing splints or in other ways, if the child is treated early.

BOWLES (bōlz), **William Lisle.** An English poet. He was born in 1762 at King's Sutton, Northamptonshire, where his father was vicar, died in 1850. He was educated at Winchester and Oxford, where he gained high honours. In 1789 he composed a series of sonnets, by which the young minds of Coleridge and Wordsworth, then seeking for new and more natural chords in poetry, were powerfully affected. Having taken holy orders, Bowles was, in 1805, presented to the living of Bremhill, in Wiltshire, where he continued to reside for the rest of his life. Besides the sonnets he published several poems, *The Spirit of Discovery, The Missionary of the Andes, St. John in Patmos*, etc., which are characterised by graceful diction and tender sentiment rather than by any higher qualities.

BOWLINE (bō'-). In ships, a rope leading forward, which is fastened by bridles to loops in the ropes on the perpendicular edge of the square sails. It is used to keep the weather-edge of the sail tight forward and steady when the ship is close-hauled to the wind.

BOWLS. An outdoor game highly popular in Scotland and many parts of England. If it did not originate in England, the game must have been introduced not long after the Norman Conquest. It was established in England before its introduction into Scotland, where the practice of it has been modified in many respects. The game is not much played in Ireland. At various times the game was prohibited on account of its use threatening to bring about the decay of archery. It is played on a smooth level piece of turf, about 40 yards long and surrounded by a shallow ditch. A small white ball, the *jack*, is placed at one end of the *green*, and the object of the players, ranged in sides at the other end, is to roll the large lignum-vitæ *bowls* so that these may come to rest as near as possible to the jack. The bowls, formerly biased by the insertion of lead, are now made very slightly conical, and thus travel in a curvilinear direction. The skill and attraction of the game consist chiefly in making correct allowance for this bias. The game is won by the side which owns the greater number of bowls near the jack after all have been played. The bowling-green, often enclosed within a thick yew hedge, is an attractive feature of many old-world gardens.

BOWMAN, Sir William. English anatomist and surgeon, born in 1816. He was surgeon to King's College Hospital, London, professor of physiology and anatomy in King's College, and was especially distinguished as an opthalmic surgeon. He gained the Royal Society's royal medal for physiology in 1842. He was collaborator with Todd in the great work on the *Physiological Anatomy and Physiology of Man*, and wrote on ophthalmology. He was created a baronet in 1884, and died in 1892.

BOWNESS-ON-WINDERMERE. A small town of England, in Westmorland, on the east side of Windermere, a resort of tourists, with a quay and pier, and ample hotel accommodation. Pop. 1107.

BOWRING (bou'ring), **Sir John.** An English statesman and linguist, born at Exeter 1792, being the son of a cloth manufacturer. While still very young he was taken by his father into his own business, and employed by him to travel in different parts of Europe. Having an extraordinary linguistic faculty, he made use of his residence in foreign countries to acquire the different languages, and his first publications consisted of translations of poems and songs from the Russian, Serbian, Polish, Magyar, Swedish, Frisian, Esthonian, Spanish, and other languages. He is well known also by his translations from Goethe, Schiller, and Heine. He was an ardent Radical and supporter of Jeremy Bentham, and edited the *Westminster Review* from 1825 to 1830. He held various Government appointments, one of them being the governorship of Hong-Kong, and the last being in 1861, when he was sent to Italy to report on British commercial relations with the new kingdom. He died 23rd Nov., 1872.

BOWSPRIT (bō′-). The large boom or spar which projects over the stem of a vessel, having the foremast and foretop-mast stays and staysails attached to it, while extending beyond it is the jib-boom.

BOWSTRING-HEMP. The fibre of the leaves of an East Indian plant, or the plant itself, *Sanseviera zeylanica* ord. Liliaceæ, so named from being made by the natives into bow-strings.

BOW-WINDOW. A kind of bay-window (q.v.); a window constructed so as to project from a wall, properly one that forms a segment of a circle.

BOWYER (bō′yėr), **William.** An English printer and classical scholar, born 1699, a native of London, where his father, also a printer, carried on business. In 1729 he became printer of the votes of the House of Commons, and subsequently printer to the Society of Antiquarians and to the Royal Society. In 1767 he was nominated printer of the journals of the House of Lords and the rolls of the House of Commons. He died in 1777.

BOX DAY. In Scotland a day when, the courts of law being closed, lawyers and litigants can hand in papers.

BOX-ELDER. The ash-leaved maple (*Negundo aceroides*), a small but beautiful tree of the United States, from which sugar is sometimes made.

BOXERS. Members of a Chinese secret society professing fervent nationalism and hatred of foreigners. *See* CHINA.

BOXING and **PUGILISM.** The art of self-defence by fighting with the fists, looked on as pre-eminently a national accomplishment of Britain. It first came into note about 1719, was exceedingly popular from twenty to thirty years later, and, after a temporary decline, reached its full glory in the early portion of the nineteenth century, when such professionals as Spring, Mendoza, Jackson, Belcher, and Gully were prominent. Men of the highest rank were often present at pugilistic combats; the leading boxers were the heroes of the day; and Byron tells how he took lessons in the art from Jackson. Prize-fighting gradually fell into disrepute, and boxing with the *gloves*, invented by Jack Broughton, is the only form allowed by law since 1863. Boxing formed an item in the sports of ancient Greece and Rome, additional danger being given to the encounters by the boxers' fists being armed with a specie of "knuckle-duster" (called a *cæstus*), consisting of leather bands loaded with iron or lead. Boxing, therefore, consisting in the skill of striking with the closed hand, or fist, protected by padded gloves, is distinguished from *pugilism*, in which bare fists, or very light gloves, are employed.—BIBLIOGRAPHY: *Encyclopædia of Sport and Games*; Spalding's *Athletic Library* (published annually); F. P. D. Radcliffe, *The Noble Science*; J. G. B. Lynch, *The Complete Amateur Boxer*; G. Carpentier, *My Methods: or Boxing as a Fine Art.*

BOXING-DAY. The day after Christmas, which has long been held as a holiday in England. It is so called from the practice of giving Christmas *boxes* as presents on that day.

BOXING THE COMPASS. In seaman's phrase, the repetition of all the points of the compass in their proper order—an accomplishment required to be attained by all sailors.

BOXMOOR. Residential district in Hertfordshire. It is 24 miles from London and 2½ from Hemel Hempstead on the L.M.S. Railway.

BOX-THORN. A name for straggling, thorny, flowering shrubs, genus Lycium, ord. Solanaceæ, often cultivated as hedge-plants, several being European.

BOX-TORTOISE. A name given to one or two North American tortoises, genus Cistūdo, that can completely shut themselves into their shell.

BOX-TREE (*Buxus sempervīrens*). A shrubby evergreen tree, 12 or 15 feet high, ord. Euphorbiaceæ, a native of England, Southern Europe, and parts of Asia, with small oval and opposite leaves, and greenish, inconspicuous flowers, male and female on the same tree. It was formerly so common in England as to have given its name to several places—Boxhill, in Surrey, for instance, and Boxley, in Kent. It is not known, however, whether it is really indigenous or only introduced, perhaps by the Romans. The wood is of a yellowish colour, close-grained, very hard and heavy, and admits of a beautiful polish. On these accounts it is much used by turners, wood-carvers, engravers on wood (no wood surpassing it in this respect), and mathematical-instrument makers. Flutes and other wind-instruments are formed of it, as are white chessmen. The box of commerce comes mostly from the regions adjoining the Black Sea and Caspian, and is diminishing in quantity. In gardens and shrubberies box trees may often be seen clipped into various formal shapes. There is also a dwarf variety reared as an edging for garden walks and the like.

BOYACA′. In South America, one of the departments or provinces of Colombia. On the west side the country is traversed by a chain of the Andes, from which it slopes towards the east into immense plains or *llanos*, mostly uncultivated, and watered by the tributaries of the Orinoco. Area, 16,460 sq. miles. Pop. 657,167. Capital, Tunja.

BOY′ARS. *See* BOIARS

BOY-BISHOP. Formerly, in England, a boy chosen by cathedral choirs or pupils in grammar-schools as a mock-bishop to take leading parts in certain mummeries or festivities in the month of December (6th-28th) annually. The custom was abolished by Henry VIII. in 1542, restored by Queen Mary, and again abolished by Elizabeth. On the Continent it was suppressed by the Council of Basel in 1431, but was revived in some places, and lingered on as late as the end of the eighteenth century.

BOYCE, William. English musical composer, born 1710, a native of London, and a pupil of Dr. Maurice Greene, organist of St. Paul's. He was subsequently organist to the Chapel Royal, and wrote many pieces for the theatre and other places of entertainment, but his principal compositions are church services. One of his anthems, "Blessed is he that considereth the poor," is sung every year at the festival given for the sons of the clergy. He died in 1779. He published a splendid collection of church music in 3 vols. folio.

BOY′COTTING. A name given to an organised system of social and commercial ostracism employed in Ireland in connection with the Land League and the land agitation of 1880 and 1881 and subsequently. Landlords, tenants, or other persons who are subjected to boycotting find it difficult or impossible to get anyone to work for them, to supply them with the necessaries of life, or to associate with them in any way. It took its name from Captain C. C. *Boycott*, Lord Erne's agent, against whom it was first put in force. Although the name is modern, the practice of boycotting is as ancient as civilisation itself. The outlaw or outcast from primitive society was subjected to a severe form of boycotting. Ostracism in the Greek world and excommunication by the Church in the Middle Ages are other forms of boycott. The boycott is now being extensively used in the economic world, notably by trade unionists.

BOYD, Andrew Kennedy Hutchison. Scottish clerical writer, born 1825, died 1899; studied at King's College, London, and entered the Middle Temple; afterwards graduated at Glasgow University and entered the Scottish Church. He was parish minister from 1865 till his death, at St. Andrews. He early made his name familiar, especially through his *Recreations of a County Parson*, contributed to *Fraser's Magazine*, with his initials A. K. H. B. attached; and besides three series of these he wrote various collections of essays and papers, such as *Graver Thoughts of a Country Parson*, *Leisure hours in Town*, *Autumn Holidays of a Country Parson*, *Critical Essays of a Country Parson*, etc. He also wrote rather full reminiscences in successive portions entitled *Twenty-five Years of St. Andrews and Elsewhere*, and *Last Years of St. Andrews*.

BOYD, Zachary. An eminent Scottish divine of the seventeenth century, born about 1585 in Ayrshire. After studying at Glasgow University, he went to the College of Saumur, in France, and in 1611 he was made a regent in this university. In consequence of the persecution of the Protestants, he was obliged in 1621 to return to his native country, and two years later was appointed minister of the Barony parish, Glasgow, and was thrice elected rector of the university there. He wrote many works, amongst which the principal is the *Last Battell of the Soule in Death*. His *Zion's Flowers*, a collection of metrical translations of Scripture history, often called *Zachary Boyd's Bible*, was bequeathed, along with many other manuscripts and a large sum of money, to the University of Glasgow. It is a quaint specimen of the devotional culture of the time. He died in 1653 or 1654.

BOY′DELL, John. An English engraver, born in 1719. He is chiefly distinguished as an encourager of the fine arts. With the profits of a volume of engravings executed by himself, and published in 1746, he set up as a print-seller, and soon established a high reputation as a liberal patron of good artists, with the result that for the first time English prints began to be exported to the Continent. He engaged Reynolds, Opie, West, and other celebrated painters to illustrate Shakespeare's works, and from their pictures was produced a magnificent volume of plates, *The Shakespeare Gallery* (London, Boydell, 1803). In 1790 Boydell had been made Lord Mayor; but the outbreak of war consequent on the French revolution injured his foreign trade and brought him into difficulties. He died in 1804.

BOY-ED, Karl. Captain in the German navy, and naval attaché of the German Embassy in Washington. He was dismissed by the United States Government on 4th Dec., 1915, for improper activity in naval matters.

BOYER (bwä-yā), **Alexis.** French surgeon, born 1757, died 1833. He had a brilliant career as a student, and was appointed first surgeon to Napoleon, receiving at the same time the title of Baron of the Empire. His chief works are: *Traité d'Anatomie* (Paris, 1797-9); *Traité des Maladies Chirurgicales et des Opérations qui leur conviennent* (11 vols. 1814-26).

BOYER (bwä-yā), **Jean Pierre.** President of the Republic of Haiti, born in 1776 at Port-au-Prince, died at Paris 1850. He was a mulatto by birth, but was educated in France. In 1792 he entered the French army, and fought with distinction against the English in San Domingo. It was largely by his efforts that in 1821 all parts of Haiti were brought under one republican Government, of which he was chosen President. His administration in its earlier years was wise and energetic; but afterwards financial difficulties and other causes made the Haitians dissatisfied with his rule, and a revolt drove him into exile in 1843.

BOYLE. A town of Ireland, County Roscommon, with a large trade in corn and butter. Boyle Abbey, now in ruins, dates from the twelfth century. Pop. 5655.

BOYLE, Charles. Earl of Orrery, born 1676, died 1731. He was nominally the editor of the edition of the *Epistles of Phalaris* which led to a famous controversy with Bentley (*see* BENTLEY), and to Swift's *Battle of the Books.* He served in the army and as a diplomatist, and wrote a comedy and some worthless verse. The astronomical apparatus called the orrery took its name from him.

BOYLE, Richard. Earl of Cork, English statesman. Born in 1566. In 1588 he went to Dublin with little or no money, but with good recommendations, and by prudence and ability he managed to acquire considerable estates. As clerk of the Council of Munster he distinguished himself by his talents and activity, and became successively a knight and Privy Councillor, Baron Boyle of Youghal, and finally, in 1620, Viscount Dungarvan and Earl of Cork. He was an able and energetic ruler, introducing many useful arts and manufactures amongst the people. Disaffection and rebellion he put down with a strong and vigorous hand. He died in 1643.

BOYLE, Robert. A celebrated natural philosopher. He was born at Lismore, Ireland, 1626, and was the seventh son of Richard, the first Earl of Cork. After finishing his studies at Eton, he travelled for some years on the Continent till in 1644 he settled in the manor of Stalbridge, Dorsetshire, which his father had left him. Here he devoted himself to scientific studies, to chemistry and natural philosophy in particular. He was one of the first members of the society founded in 1645, afterwards known as the Royal Society. At Oxford, to which he had gone in 1652, he occupied himself in making improvements on the air-pump, by means of which he demonstrated the elasticity of air.

Although his scientific work shows an accurate, minute, and methodical intellect, in religious matters he was subject to melancholy and fanciful terrors. He began to study Hebrew and Greek, and formed connections with such eminent scholars as Pococke, Clarke, Barlow, etc. He also instituted public lectures, known as the Boyle, Lectures "for proving the Christian religion against Atheists, Deists, Pagans, Jews, and Mohammedans, not descending to any controversies amongst Christians themselves." The first series was delivered by Richard Bentley. Samuel Clarke, Whiston, F. D. Maurice, C. Merivale, H. Wace, and W. C. E. Newbolt have been amongst succeeding Boyle lecturers. Boyle died in 1691, and was interred in Westminster Abbey.

BOYLE, Roger. Earl of Orrery, brother of Robert Boyle, born in 1621, died 1679. In Ireland he zealously supported the cause of Charles I., but after the death of the king he retired for a time from public life. At length he accepted a commission from Cromwell, whom he served with zeal and fidelity, and by whom he was highly esteemed. On the death of Cromwell he exerted himself with such dexterity to bring about the royal restoration that Charles II. rewarded him with the title of Earl of Orrery.

BOYLE'S LAW (otherwise called Mariotte's Law). A law in physics to the effect that the volume of a gas will vary inversely as the pressure to which it is subjected if its temperature is kept constant. *See* THERMODYNAMICS.

BOYNE. A river in Ireland, which rises in the Bog of Allen, and after a course of 60 miles falls into the Irish Sea 4 miles from Drogheda. On its banks was fought (1st July, 1690) the battle between the adherents of James II. and William II. in which the latter proved victorious, James being obliged to flee to the Continent. The anniversary of the victory (held on 12th July) is still celebrated by Irish Protestants. Large numbers of Orangemen assemble throughout Ulster, marching in their Lodges with banners and standards, and with fife and drum bands playing such tunes as *The Protestant Boys, The Boyne Water*, and *The Orange Lily*. Loyal speeches are made, and the anti-British faction in Ireland is denounced.

BOYS' BRIGADE, THE. The Boys' Brigade is the pioneer organisation for training boys on the now familiar system, combining physical, mental, moral, and religious instruction. It was started by Sir William A. Smith in 1883, when he raised the 1st Glasgow Company, and has since spread all over the British Empire, the United States of America, and even to some Continental countries, such as Denmark and Sweden.

The original object of the movement, as described in the words of the Constitution, was " The advancement of Christ's Kingdom amongst Boys, and the promotion of habits of Obedience, Reverence, Discipline, Self-respect, and all that tends towards a true Christian Manliness," and to this it has strictly adhered. Military organisation and drill are used as a means of securing the interest of boys, banding them together in the work of the Brigade, and promoting among them such habits as the Brigade is designed to form.

Its activities are designed to give the boy who has not had the advantage of a public school education a real sense of honour and esprit de corps, and as the services in the school chapel supply the spiritual influences in a public school, so the Company Bible Class occupies the most important position in the work of the Boys' Brigade. The boy may be attracted by the uniform—it is of the simplest possible character—the drill, gymnastics, the football club, or the camp, but is ultimately held by the two forces, religion and discipline, until at the age of seventeen he leaves the Brigade to become a man of character and a more useful citizen. Each Company is self-supporting, and must be connected with a Church or Christian organisation of some kind.

No person can be nominated for a commission unless his nomination is supported by the head of the organisation with which the Company is connected. A junior organisation was started in 1918, for boys between the ages of nine and twelve, under the name of The Boy Reserves.

The Boys' Brigade is entirely interdenominational. His Majesty the King is the patron of the Brigade, the Archbishop of Canterbury and the Archbishop of York are vice-presidents, and amongst the honorary vice-presidents are many of the bishops of the Church of England and the presidents and moderators of practically all the other Churches in England, Scotland, and Ireland. The Boys' Life Brigade, founded in 1899, is now united with it. The strength is about 100,000. The Junior Organisation, which has about 50,000 members, is known as the Life Boys. The headquarters are at Abbey House, Westminster, London, S.W.

BOYS' CLUBS. The number of Boys' Clubs in existence has been greatly increased during the last twenty-five years. This has been the case particularly in Manchester, where some of the Clubs have over a thousand members. The Clubs, which are intended for working boys past school age, organise outdoor activities for their members, giving them facilities for playing games in the evenings and half-holidays. They also organise educational work, holding classes in the club-rooms, and arranging for their members to attend night-schools and polytechnics. Moreover, they guide their members in their employment, and usually have an employment bureau. The Club thus supplies to working boys the help, care, and guidance which in the case of other boys are supplied by the secondary school. Some clubs, though not all, have junior sections for schoolboys.

Boys' Clubs have in recent years become more useful and more attractive. This is partly due to the rise of other organisations for boys, such as the Boy Scouts. In some cases a Troop of Scouts is run in connection with the Club. In consequence it is a common practice for Boys' Clubs to organise not only a summer camp, but also a week-end one.—BIBLIOGRAPHY: B. P. Neuman, *Boys' Clubs in Theory and Practice*; Russell and Rigby, *Working Lads' Clubs*; C. W. Steffens, *Clubs and Clubwork amongst Working Lads and Men*.

BOY SCOUT MOVEMENT, THE. The Boy Scout Movement provides boys with a subsidiary form of education which tends to make them good citizens. It was started in

England in 1908 by General Sir Robert (later Lord) Baden-Powell, and in less than a dozen years it spread to every part of the British Empire and has been taken up by almost every civilised country in the world. The Boy Scouts throughout the world number several millions. The training aims at developing character and intelligence, as well as physical health and self-care. Handicrafts of various kinds are taught, and proficiency badges are awarded to those who pass tests in different subjects. Nature-study and woodcraft are considered of the greatest importance, and out-of-door life in camp is a great feature of the Boy Scout training.

The principle and spirit of the whole training are contained in the Scout Promise: I promise on my honour (1) To do my duty to God and the King; (2) To help other people at all times; (3) To obey the Scout Law. And the Scout Law: (1) A Scout's honour is to be trusted; (2) A Scout is loyal; (3) A Scout's duty is to be useful and to help others; (4) A Scout is a friend to all, and a brother to every other Scout; (5) A Scout is courteous; (6) A Scout obeys orders; (7) A Scout is a friend to animals; (8) A Scout smiles and whistles under all difficulties; (9) A Scout is thrifty; (10) A Scout is clean in Thought, Word, and Deed.

Scouts are graded in three classes—wolf cubs, aged 8 to 11; scouts, aged 11 and upwards; and rover scouts, aged 17 and upwards. Each boy belongs to a patrol, and a number of patrols form a group. Scout-masters are in command of the boys. Badges are given for proficiency in various handicrafts and other useful activities. In 1929 a world jamboree was held at Birkenhead. The headquarters are at 25 Buckingham Palace Road, London, S.W. 1. — BIBLIOGRAPHY: Lord Baden-Powell, *Scouting for Boys*; M. Adams, *The Boy Scouts' Companion*; N. E. Richardson and O. E. Loomis, *The Boy Scout Movement applied by the Church*; E. Wood, *The Boy Scouts' Roll of Honour*.

BOZ. Pen-name adopted by Charles Dickens. Under it he wrote a series of literary sketches for the *Morning Chronicle* (London), published afterwards in book form, as *Sketches by Boz*, in 1836. *The Pickwick Papers* first appeared under this pseudonym, which is a corruption of Moses, a name jocularly given to the novelist's youngest brother.

BOZEN. *See* BOTZEN.

BOZRAH. The name of several places mentioned in the Bible, and difficult to identify with modern localities. One Bozrah was an ancient city of Edom. Another was a city of Moab, by many identified with Bosrah, about 80 miles south of Damascus, and now little but a scene of ruins.

BOZZARIS (bot-sä′ris), **Marko.** A hero of the Greek War of Independence against the Turks, born in the end of the eighteenth century. After the fall of Suli he retired to the Ionian Islands, from whence he made a vain attempt to deliver his native country. In 1820, when the Turks were trying to reduce their overgrown vassal, Ali Pasha of Janina, to submission, the latter sought aid from the exiled Suliotes, and Marko Bozzaris returned to Epirus. On the outbreak of the War of Independence he at once joined the Greek cause, and distinguished himself as much by his patriotism and disinterestedness as by his military skill and personal bravery. In the summer of 1823, when he held the command-in-chief of the Greek forces at Missolonghi, he made a daring night attack on the camp of the Pasha of Scutări, near Karpenisi. The attack was successful; but the triumph of the Greeks was clouded by the fall of the heroic Bozzaris. His deeds are celebrated in the popular songs of Greece.

BRA. A town in North Italy, province of Cuneo, with a trade in cattle, grain, wine, and silk. Pop. 15,990.

BRABANÇONNE (brȧ-băṅ-son′). The national song of the Belgians, written during the revolution of 1830 by Jenneval, an actor at the theatre of Brussels, and set to music by Campenhout. *See* NATIONAL ANTHEMS.

BRABANT′. The central district of the lowlands of Holland and Belgium, extending from the Waal to the sources of the Dyle, and from the Meuse and Limburg plains to the Lower Schelde. It is divided between the kingdoms of Holland and Belgium, into three provinces: (1) Dutch or North Brabant, area, 1920 sq. miles, pop. 763,016; (2) the Belgian province of Antwerp, area, 1093 sq. miles, pop 1,173,363; and (3) the Belgian province of South Brabant, area, 1268 sq. miles, pop. 1,680,065. The country is generally a plain, gently sloping to the N.W., and is mostly fertile and well cultivated, agriculture and the rearing of cattle being the principal employments of the inhabitants. In the north the inhabitants are Dutch; in the middle district, Flemings; in the south Walloons. Southward of Brussels the language is French; northward, Dutch and Flemish.

History. In the fifth century Brabant came into possession of the Franks, and after being alternately included in and separated from Lorraine, it emerges at length in 1190 as a duchy under a Duke of Brabant. It eventually came by marriage into possession of the Dukes of Burgundy, and passed with the last representative of that line, Mary of Burgundy, to the House of Austria, and finally to Philip II. of Spain. In the famous revolt of the Netherlands, caused by the cruelties of King Philip and his agent, the Duke of Alva, North Brabant succeeded in asserting its independence, and in 1648 it was incorporated with the United Provinces. South Brabant remained, however, in possession of the Spaniards, and at the Peace of Utrecht in 1714 passed again, along with the other southern provinces of the Netherlands, to the Imperial House of Austria. *See* BELGIUM.

BRACEGIRDLE, Anne. English actress. She was born about 1674, and introduced to London by the Bettertons. In 1688 she played Lucia in Shadwell's *Squire of Alsatia*, and was later successful in Congreve's plays. Her Shakespearean favourites were Isabella, Cordelia, and Portia. A rivalry between her and Mrs. Oldfield led to her leaving the stage in 1707. She died in Sept., 1748, and was buried in Westminster Abbey.

BRACELET. A kind of ornament usually worn on the wrist, the use of which extends from the most ancient times down to the present, and belongs to all countries, civilised as well as uncivilized. Bracelets were in use in Egypt and amongst the Medes and Persians at a very remote period, and in the Bible the bracelet is frequently mentioned as an ornament in use among the Jews, both men and women. Among the ancient Greeks bracelets seem to have been worn only by the women. The spiral form was preferred, and very often made to assume the appearance of snakes, which went round the arm twice or thrice. Among the Romans it was a frequent practice for a general to bestow bracelets on soldiers who had distinguished themselves by their valour. Roman ladies of high rank frequently wore them both on the wrist and on the upper arm. Among the ancient heathen Germanic tribes they formed the chief and almost only ornament, as is shown by their being so often found in old graves. They seem to have been used by the men even more than by the women, and were the gifts by which an ancient German chief attached his followers to himself. So, in old Anglo-Saxon poems, "ring-giver," is a common name for the lord or ruler.

Bracken (*Pteris aquilina*). A, Rhizome

BRACES. In ships, ropes passing through blocks at the ends of the yards, used for swinging the latter round so as to meet the wind in any desired direction.

BRACHIOPODA (bra-ki-op'o-da), A group of shell-bearing animals, so named from the development of a long spirally-coiled, fringed appendage or arm on either side of the mouth (Gr. *brachiōn*, an arm, and *pous*, *podos*, a foot), serving as respiratory organs. They are bivalves, and in this respect they resemble the Lamellibranchiata. They have no proper power of locomotion, and remain fixed to submarine bodies, in some cases by a peduncle passing through an aperture at the "beak." They are widely diffused, and in the fossil state are interesting to the geologist by enabling him to identify certain strata. The chief living genera are Lingula, Terebratula, and Rhynchonella.

BRACHYCEPHALIC (bra-ki-se-fal'-ik; Gr. *brachys*, short, *kephalē*, the head). A term applied in ethnology to heads whose diameter from side to side is not much less than from front to back, as in the Bavarian type: opposed to *dolichocephalic*.

BRACHYPTERÆ (bra-kip'te-rē; "short-winged"). A name given to a family of web-footed birds, penguins, auks, divers, guillemots, etc., in which the wings are short and the legs placed far back in the body. They are all strong divers and swimmers.

BRACHYURA (bra-ki-ō'ra; "short-tailed"). A section of the ten-footed crustaceans or crabs (Decapoda), having a very short jointed tail folded closely under the thorax, as in the common crab.

BRACKEN, or **BRAKE** (*Pteris aquilina*). A species of fern very common in Britain and Europe generally, and often covering large areas on hill-sides and waste grounds. It has a black creeping rhizome, with branched pinnate fronds growing to the height often of several feet, and it forms an excellent covert for game. The plant is astringent and anthelmintic ; when burned it yields a good deal of alkali. The rhizome is bitter, but has been eaten in times of famine. It was formerly a staple article of food among the Maoris.

BRACKET. A short piece or combination of pieces, generally more or less triangular in outline, and projecting from a wall or other surface. They may be either of an ornamental

Bracket, Harlestone Church, Northamptonshire

order, as when designed to support a statue, a bust, or such like, or plain forms of carpentry, such as support shelves, etc. Brackets may also be used in connection with machinery, being attached to walls, beams, etc., to support a line of shafting.

BRACKLEY. A market town and municipal borough of England, in the south of Northamptonshire, said to have been a place of importance before the Conquest. Lace is manufactured. Pop. (1931), 2181.

BRACQUEMOND, Félix. French painter and etcher, born in 1833. He began to exhibit in 1852, but won his reputation by his original etchings, represented by over 1000 plates. In 1867 he introduced a new mode of decoration on china, and in 1872 became connected with the painting department of the famous porcelain factory at Sèvres. He also established a studio for ceramic decoration, where he did a great deal of work for several factories. He died in 1914.

BRACT. A leaf, from the axil of which a flower or flower-stalk proceeds, and thus distinguished from the ordinary leaf, from the axil of which the leaf-bud proceeds. It often differs from other leaves in shape or colour, but sometimes the distinction is not clearly defined. Bracteoles are bractlets borne on the flower-stalk itself. See illus. p. 180.

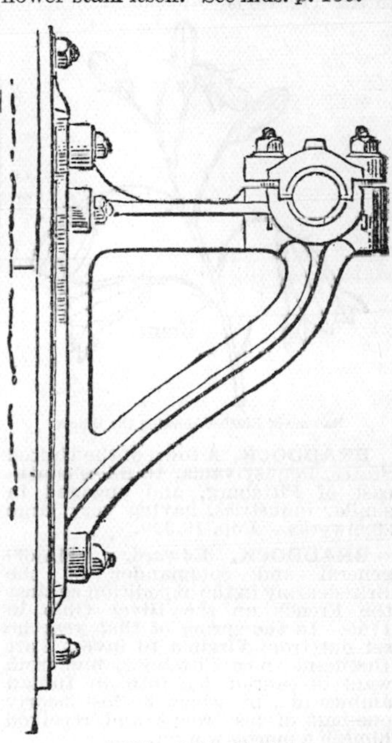
Wall-bracket for Shafting

BRAC'TEATES (-āts). Old thin coins of gold or silver, with irregular figures on them, stamped upon one surface only, so that the impression appears raised on one side while the other appears hollow.—*Bracteated* coins, coins of iron, copper, or brass, covered over with a thin plate of some richer metal such as gold or silver. They derive their name from *bractea*, leaf of gold or other metals. See NUMISMATICS.

BRACTON, Henry de. One of the earliest writers on English law, flourished in the thirteenth century. He studied law at Oxford, became a judge, and afterwards Chief Justice of England, but is chiefly remembered now for his treatise *De Legibus et Consuetudinibus Angliæ* (On the Laws and Customs of England).

BRADBURY. Colloquial name for the treasury notes for £1 and 10*s*., first issued in 1914. They were so called because they were signed by Sir John Bradbury (afterwards Lord Bradbury), then permanent Secretary to the Treasury.

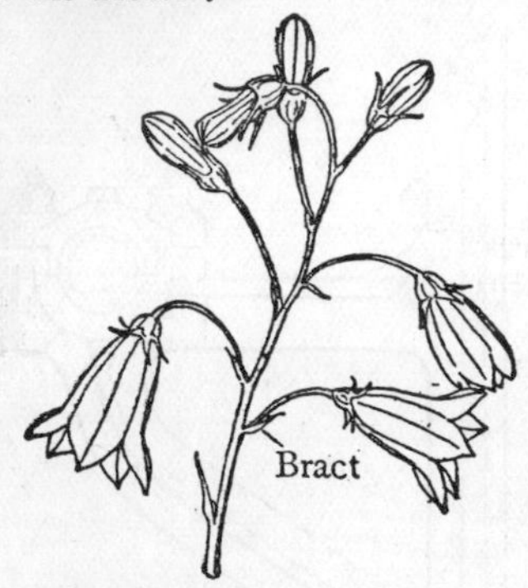

Raceme of Bluebell showing the Bracts

BRADDOCK. A town of the United States, Pennsylvania, 10 miles south-east of Pittsburg, and engaged in similar industries, having very large steelworks. Pop. 19,329.

BRADDOCK, Edward. Major-general and commander of the British army in the expedition against the French on the River Ohio in 1755. In the spring of that year he set out from Virginia to invest Fort Duquesne, now Pittsburg, but from want of caution fell into an Indian ambuscade, by which he lost nearly one-half of his troops and received himself a mortal wound.

BRADDON, Mary Elizabeth (Mrs. Maxwell). Novelist, born in London in 1837, died 4th Feb., 1915. After publishing some poems and tales, in 1862 she brought out *Lady Audley's Secret*, the first of a series of clever sensational novels. She long edited the magazine *Belgravia*. Her son, Mr. W. B. Maxwell, is a well-known novelist.

BRADFIELD. Village of Berkshire. It is 8 miles from Reading, and is known for its public school, which owes much to the inspired work of Dr. H. B. Gray, who was head master from 1880-1910. In the grounds is a theatre on the Greek model, in which Greek plays are given. Another Bradfield is a village 7 miles from Sheffield.

BRAD'FORD. A municipal, parliamentary, and county borough and important manufacturing town in W. Riding of Yorkshire, England. The more modern portion has well-built streets, and since 1861 most extensive street improvements have been carried out at great cost. There are some fine buildings (such as the town hall), and among institutions are the technical college, public library, theological college for Congregationalists, free grammar-school endowed by Charles II., fever hospital, and other hospitals. There are several fine public parks, besides Baildon Moor (over 600 acres), and an extensive system of waterworks. Bradford is the chief seat in England of the spinning and weaving of worsted yarn and woollens, and has also manufactures of alpaca, mixed goods, silk, plush, velvet, machine-works, foundries, etc. It was incorporated in 1847, was accorded the rank of a city in 1897, and in 1907 the chief magistrate received the title of lord mayor. Since 1918 it returns four members to Parliament. It became a bishopric in 1919. Pop. (county borough) (1931), 298,041.

BRADFORD. A town of the United States, in the north of Pennsylvania, in a region rich in mineral oil, thus giving employment to many of the inhabitants. Pop. 19,306.

BRADFORD, William. Leader of the Pilgrim Fathers. Of Yorkshire birth, he was born in 1589. Embracing Puritan opinions, he migrated to Holland and carried on business as a weaver at Leyden for some years. When the emigration of the English refugees to America was projected, he became one of its most active promoters, and was one of the party that sailed in the *Mayflower*. From 1621 until his death, with only a few short intervals, he served as Governor of Plymouth Colony. He wrote a valuable *History of Plymouth Colony*. Bradford died 9th May, 1657.

BRADFORD-ON-AVON, or **GREAT BRADFORD.** An ancient town of England, in Wiltshire, beautifully situated 32½ miles N.W. of Salisbury, on the banks of the Lower Avon, with manufactures of woollen cloth. Pop. (1931), 4735.

BRADING. An ancient town, once a parliamentary borough, in the east of the Isle of Wight, on the Yar. Pop. 1500. Legh Richmond, the author of *Annals of the Poor*, was curate at Brading, and the heroine of his *Dairyman's Daughter*, Elizabeth Wallbridge, lies buried in the churchyard of Arreton. In 1880 the remains of a Roman villa were discovered near the town.

BRADLAUGH (brad'la̤), **Charles.** English secularist, atheist, and advocate of republicanism, born in London in 1833. He was well known by his writings and lectures, and more especially by his efforts to gain admission to Parliament. In 1874 he became acquainted with Mrs. Annie Besant, and this partnership lasted until 1886. Jointly they published and circulated in 1876 a famous pamphlet called *Fruits of Philosophy*. Being elected for Northampton in 1880, Bradlaugh claimed the right to make affirmation simply instead of taking the oath which members of Parliament take before they can sit and vote, but being a professed atheist this right was denied him. Though he was repeatedly re-elected by the same constituency, the majority of the House of Commons continued to declare him disqualified for taking the oath or affirming; and it was only after the election of a new parliament in 1885 that he was allowed to take his seat without opposition as a representative of Northampton. He was editor of the *National Reformer*. He died in 1891.

BRAD'LEY, James. English astronomer, born at Sherborne in 1692. He studied theology at Oxford, and took orders; but devoting himself to astronomy, he was appointed in 1721 professor of that science at Oxford. Six years afterwards he made known his discovery of the aberration of light, and his researches for many years were chiefly directed towards finding out methods for determining precisely that aberration. It is largely owing to Bradley's discoveries that astronomers have since been able to make up astronomical tables with the necessary accuracy. In 1741 Bradley was made Astronomer Royal, and removed to Greenwich. He died in 1762. His *Astronomical Observations* were published at Oxford, 1805.

BRADMAN, Donald George. Australian cricketer. Born at Cortamundra, New South Wales, 27th Aug., 1908, he was educated there, and became famous as a cricketer. Having played for the state, he was chosen to play for Australia in 1928 against the English team. His scoring powers placed him in the front rank of batsmen, and he more than maintained his high reputation when he visited England in 1930 as a member of the Australian team. In the test match at Leeds he scored 324 runs, a record for these matches, and he finished the tour with the remarkable average of 98·66.

BRADSHAW, John. President of the "High Court of Justice" which tried and condemned Charles I. Born in 1602. He studied law at Gray's Inn, and attained a fair practice. When the king's trial was determined upon, Bradshaw was appointed president of the court; and his stern and unbending deportment at the trial did not disappoint expectation. Afterwards he opposed Cromwell and the Protectorate, and was in consequence deprived of the chief justiceship of Chester. On the death of Cromwell he became Lord President of the Council, and died in 1659. At the Restoration his body was exhumed and hung on a gibbet with those of Cromwell and Ireton.

BRADSHAW'S RAILWAY GUIDE. A well-known English manual for travellers, first issued by George Bradshaw, a printer and engraver of Manchester in 1839. It is now published on the 1st of each month, and contains the latest arrangements of railway and steamboat companies, besides other useful information. There are now many such handbooks in the field.

BRADWAR'DINE, Thomas. "Doctor Profundus," Archbishop of Canterbury, born about 1290, died 1349. He was distinguished for his varied learning, and more particularly for his treatise *De Causa Dei contra Pelagium*, an extensive work against the Pelagian heresy, for centuries a standard authority. He was chaplain and confessor to Edward III., whom he accompanied to France, being present at Crécy and the capture of Calais. Being appointed archbishop, he hastened to England, but died of the Black Death on reaching London.

BRA'DY, Nicholas. Born in 1659 at Bandon, in Ireland. He was rector of the church of St. Catherine Cree, London, and afterwards of Richmond, Surrey. He made a translation of the *Æneid*; but is only remembered now as the collaborator of Nahum Tate in that version of the Psalms which is used in the Episcopal Church. He died in 1726.

BRAD'YPUS. *See* SLOTH.

BRADYSEISM (from the Gr. *bradus*, slow, *seismos*, an earthquake). A term used by J. Milne and others for movements of the earth's crust that take place slowly, unaccompanied by noticeable earthquake shocks. Beaches have thus been raised and shores depressed, and the relative heights of mountain ridges have been altered, without disturbance to human occupations in the district.

BRAEMAR′. A Highland district in the S.W. corner of Aberdeenshire. It contains part of the Grampian range with the heights of Ben Macdhui, Cairntoul, Lochnagar, etc. The district has some fine scenery, valleys and hill-sides covered with birch and fir, but consists mostly of deer forest. Balmoral Castle, a favourite residence of Queen Victoria, is here, on the banks of the Dee.

BRAGA. An ancient town in Northern Portugal, the seat of an archbishop who is Primate of Portugal, charmingly situated on a rising ground and surrounded by walls flanked with towers, and with suburbs outside. It contains an archiepiscopal palace, and a richly-ornamented Gothic cathedral of the thirteenth century, and is a place of considerable trade and manufactures. There still exist remains of a Roman temple, amphitheatre, and aqueduct. Pop. 21,970.

BRAGA, Theophilo. Portuguese statesman, born in 1843. He studied law at Coimbra and became professor of modern languages at Lisbon in 1872. He was president of the Portuguese Republic from October 1910 to August 1911, and from May to October, 1915. He was also a poet of distinction. He died in 1924.

BRAGAN′ZA, or BRAGAN′ÇA. A town of Portugal, capital of the former province of Trasos-montes, with a castle, the ancient seat of the Dukes of Braganza, from whom the last reigning family of Portugal was descended. Pop. 5480.

BRAGG, Sir William Henry. English scientist, born at Wigton, Cumberland, 2nd July, 1862. He was educated at King William's College, Isle of Man, and Trinity College, Cambridge. Having been third wrangler, he was Professor of Physics at Adelaide, 1886-1908; at Leeds 1909-15, and in London 1915-23. In 1923 he was appointed Fullerian Professor of Chemistry at the Royal Institution, and Director of the Davy-Faraday Research Laboratory. His work in physical chemistry has been concerned with the study of the minute structure of crystals, radioactivity, and X-rays. In this he has been assisted by his son, William Lawrence Bragg, who was, like his father, a Fellow of Trinity College, Cambridge, and was, in 1919, appointed Professor of Physics at Manchester. Both father and son have received many honours, including the F.R.S., and in 1915 jointly a Nobel prize. Sir W. H. Bragg was knighted in 1920, President of the British Association in 1928, and awarded the Order of Merit in 1931.

BRAHAM (brā′am), **John.** A celebrated tenor singer, of Jewish extraction. He was born in London in 1774. He appeared with the greatest success on the leading stages of France, Italy, and the United States, as well as in his own country. He excelled mainly in national songs, such as *The Bay of Biscay O*, and *The Death of Nelson*, and continued to attract large audiences even when eighty years old. He died in 1856.

BRAHE (brä′ā), **Tycho.** Danish astronomer, born in 1546 of a noble family, died 1601. He studied law at Copenhagen and Leipzig, but from 1565 gave himself up to astronomy, and in 1580 built an observatory on the Island of Hveen in the Sound, providing it with the best instruments then procurable. Here he thought out the planetary system associated with his name, the earth, by his theory, being regarded as the centre of the heavenly bodies. After the death of his patron, Frederick II. of Denmark, he left his native country in 1597 and went to Germany. Here he was patronised by the Emperor Rudolph, who gave him a yearly allowance and a residence at Prague, where he died. His astronomical works were all written in Latin, the principal of which, *Astronomiæ Instauratæ Progymnasmata*, was edited by Kepler (Prague, 1602-3). He is chiefly remarkable for his services to practical astronomy, his observations being superior in accuracy to those of his predecessors.

BRAHILOW. *See* BRAÏLA.

BRAHMA. Showy, fluffy domestic fowl. It was produced in America by crossing two Asiatic breeds, and won popularity as a table bird and a good layer, but over-cultivation of its decorative appearance caused its deterioration for practical purposes.

BRAH′MA. A Sanskrit word signifying (in its neuter form) the Universal Power or ground of all existence, and also (in its masculine form with long final syllable) a particular god, the first person in the Triad (Brahmā, Vishnu, and Siva) of the Hindus. The personal god Brahmā is represented as a red or golden-coloured figure with four heads and as many arms, and he is often accompanied by the swan or goose. He is the god of the fates, master of life and death, yet he is himself created, and is merely the agent of Brahma, the Universal Power.

BRAH'MANISM. A religious and social system prevalent amongst the Hindus, and so called because developed and expounded by the sacerdotal caste known as the Brahmans (from *brahman*, devotion, or, more correctly, magic; from root *brih* or *vrih*, to speak; the word may be compared to the ancient Irish *bricht*, magical spell). Popularly, Brahmanism is still understood to denote the religion of those inhabitants of India who worshipped Brahma as their supreme god, in contradistinction to those who professed Buddhism,

Brahma

and, in more recent times, Mahommedanism. This interpretation, however, is founded upon a misconception. The characteristic mark of Brahmanism is the acknowledgment of the Veda as the divine revelation, of which the Brahmans as a body became custodians and interpreters, being also the officiating priests and the general directors of sacrifices and religious rites. As the priestly caste increased in numbers and power they went on elaborating the ceremonies, and added to the Vedas other writings tending to confirm the excessive pretensions of this now predominant caste, and give them the sanction of a revelation.

The earliest supplements to the Vedas are the Brahmanas, more fully explaining the functions of the officiating priests. Both together form the revealed Scriptures of the Hindus. In time the caste of Brahmans came to be accepted as a divine institution, and an elaborate system of rules defining and enforcing by the severest penalties its place as well as that of the inferior castes was promulgated. Other early castes were the Kshattriyas or warriors, and the Vaisyas or cultivators, and it was not without a struggle that the former recognised the superiority of the Brahmans. It was by the Brahmans that the Sanskrit literature was developed; and they were not only the priests, theologians, and philosophers, but also the poets, men of science, lawgivers, administrators, and statesmen of the Aryans of India.

The sanctity and inviolability of a Brahman are maintained by severe penalties. The murder of one of the order, robbing him, etc., are inexpiable sins; even the killing of his cow can only be expiated by a painful penance. A Brahman should pass through four states: First, as Brahmachari, or novice, he begins the study of the sacred Vedas, and is initiated into the privileges and the duties of his caste. He has a right to alms, to exemption from taxes, and from capital and even corporal punishment. Flesh and eggs he is not allowed to eat. Leather, skins of animals, and most animals themselves are impure and not to be touched by him. When manhood comes he ought to marry, and as Grihastha enter the second state, which requires more numerous and minute observances. When he has begotten a son and trained him up for the holy calling, he ought to enter the third state, and as Vanaprastha, or inhabitant of the forest, retire from the world for solitary praying and meditation, with severe penances to purify the spirit; but this and the fourth or last state of a Sannyasi, requiring a cruel degree of asceticism, are now seldom reached, and the whole scheme is to be regarded as representing rather the Brahmanical ideal of life than the actual facts. This division of the religious life of the Hindus into four stages, or *asramas*, clearly shows that asceticism was one of the factors which greatly influenced religious life in India, and contributed in a high degree to give it its peculiar character.

The worship represented in the oldest Vedic literature is that of natural objects: the sky, personified in the god Indra; the dawn, in Ushas; the various attributes of the sun, in Vishnu, Surya, Agni, etc. These gods were invoked for assistance in the common affairs of life, and were propitiated by offerings which, at first few and simple, afterwards became more complicated and included animal sacrifices. In the later

Vedic hymns a philosophical conception of religion and the problems of being and creation appears struggling into existence; and this tendency is systematically developed by the supplements and commentaries known as the Brahmanas and the Upanishads. In some of the Upanishads the deities of the old Vedic creed are treated as symbolical. Brahma, the supreme soul, is the only reality, the world is regarded as an emanation from him, and the highest good of the soul is to become united with the divine. The necessity for the purification of the soul in order to ensure its reunion with the divine nature gave rise to the doctrine of metempsychosis or transmigration.

This philosophical development of Brahmanism caused a distinct separation between the educated and the vulgar creeds. Whilst from the fifth to the first century B.C. the higher thinkers amongst the Brahmans were developing a philosophy which recognised that there was but one god, the popular creed had concentrated its ideas of worship round three great deities—Brahmā, Vishnu, and Siva—who now took the place of the confused old Vedic Pantheon. Brahmā, the creator, though considered the most exalted of the three, was too abstract an idea to become a popular god, and soon sank almost out of notice. Thus the Brahmans became divided between Vishnu, the preserver, and Siva, the destroyer and reproducer, and the worshippers of these two deities now form the two great religious sects of India. Siva, in his philosophical significance, is the deity mostly worshipped by the conventional Brahman, while in his aspect of the Destroyer, or in one of his female manifestations, he is the god of the low castes, and often worshipped with degrading rites. But the highly-cultivated Brahman is still a pure theist, and the educated Hindu in general professes to regard the special deity he chooses for worship as merely a form under which the One First Cause may be approached.

The sharp division of the people of India into civilised Aryans and rude non-Aryans has had a great influence upon Brahmanism, and thus the spiritual conceptions of the old Vedic creed have been mixed in modern Hinduism with degrading superstitions and customs belonging to the so-called aboriginal races. Suttee, for example, or the burning of widows, has no authority in the Veda, but like most of the darker features of Hinduism is the result of a compromise which the Brahmanical teachers had to make with the barbarous conceptions of non-Aryan races in India. The Buddhist religion has also had an important influence on the Brahmanic.

The system of caste originally no doubt represented distinctions of race. The early classification of the people was that of "twice-born" Aryans (priests, warriors, husbandmen) and once-born non-Aryan (serfs); but inter-marriages, giving rise to a mixed progeny, and the variety of employments in modern times, have profoundly modified this simple classification. Innumerable minor distinctions have grown up, so that amongst the Brahmans alone there are several hundred castes who cannot intermarry or eat food cooked by each other.

The Brahmans represent the highest culture of India, and as the result of centuries of education and self-restraint have evolved a type of man distinctly superior to the castes around them. They have still great influence, and occupy the highest places at the courts of princes. Many, however, are driven by need or other motives into trades and employments inconsistent with the original character of their caste. *See* BUDDHISM; HINDUISM.—BIBLIOGRAPHY: A. Barth, *The Religions of India*; Monier Williams, *Brahmanism and Hinduism*; John Dowson, *A Classical Dictionary of Hindu Mythology and Religion*; F. Max Müller, *Six Systems of Indian Philosophy*; L. Milloué, *Le Brahmanisme*; V. Fausböll, *Indian Mythology according to the Mahābāhrata in Outline*; D. A. Mackenzie, *Indian Myth and Legend.*

BRAHMANS. The Brahman caste heads the list in the Hindu theory of social economy. Brahmans are the hereditary priests of Hinduism, claiming a mythical origin from the supreme soul through the mouth of Brahma, the father of all men. The Brahman having been born from the mouth of Brahma, the next three main divisions of mankind, the soldiers, the traders, and the servants, proceeded in their turn from the arms, legs, and feet. The life of the Brahman is governed entirely by ceremonious observances: though born a Brahman he does not become one by religion until he has assumed the sacred thread, the hall mark of each of the three highest castes of Hindus, that of the Brahmans being longer than those of the others. The sacred thread once assumed—probably at the age of ten—the rules of caste descend with their full weight on to the newly created Brahman. Among these rules are the following: he must prepare, cook, and eat his own food, on his own special cooking-place, and during the combined operation must not leave the prepared spot; nor must so much as the shadow of another man fall on his food. He may not take water from anyone but a Brahman (which would defile him), though he may drink from any foul pond or tank. He must be to all intents and purposes a vegetarian, and he may not cross the ocean or leave India. These are but a few of the caste rules, but are sufficient to show that the real advantages of a Brahman as a soldier are to seek. However, there are two regiments of Brahmans—the 1st and 3rd—in the Indian army, and it is only fair to say that the Brahman on service does to some small extent waive some of his caste rules.

The Brahman physically is a big upstanding man, and in pre-mutiny days was very largely enlisted for that reason; but in those days enlistment was only for the service in India, and when required to serve outside the country the Brahman objected. For many years now such an absurdity has been impossible, and all sepoys, Brahmans or others, have to agree to forgo caste prejudices so far as they affect their military service, as a condition of being enlisted. On return to India an expensive purification is necessary.

BRAHMAPU'TRA. A large river of Asia, whose main source is in a great glacier mass of the Himalayas, and which receives various tributaries separating its basin from the eastern affluents of Lake Manasarowar, in Tibet. At first called the Sanpo, it flows eastwards north of the Himalayas, and, after taking a sharp bend and passing through these mountains, it emerges in the north-east of Assam as the Dihong; a little farther on it is joined by the Dibong and the Lohit, when the united stream takes the name of Brahmaputra. The total length is 1800 miles. After entering Bengal it joins the Ganges at Goalanda, and farther on the Meghna, and their united waters flow into the Bay of Bengal. The Brahmaputra is navigable by steamers for about 800 miles from the sea, and it is commercially most important.

BRAHMA-SAMAJ, or the **THEISTIC CHURCH OF INDIA.** Founded in 1830 by an enlightened Brahman, Ram Mohan Ray, who sought to purify his religion from impurities and idolatries. The name is a Bengali phrase which may be translated "Society of Brahman." This Church, while accepting what religious truth the Vedas may contain, rejects the idea of their special infallibility, and founds its faith on principles of reason. The members do not in principle recognise the distinction of caste, and have made great efforts to weaken this as well as other prejudices amongst their countrymen. The Samaj has exercised a very great influence on religious opinion all over India, and its work has also had a good deal of weight, especially in Bengal, in the matter of social reform.

BRAHMS (brämz), **Johannes.** German composer, son of a musician, born at Hamburg 1833, died at Vienna 1897. He made a position for himself as composer and pianist at an early age, and his musical compositions received the approval of Liszt and Schumann. The greater part of his life was spent at Vienna, and was entirely devoted to composition. His works are very numerous, and belong to several different classes, but include no operas, though two overtures are among them. They comprise three hundred solo songs, a number of sacred and secular choral works, concerted vocal works, orchestral works, chamber music, pianoforte solos, Hungarian dances arranged as duets for the piano, etc. Brahms ranks among musicians as a classicist, and is now admitted to be one of the great musicians of Germany.—BIBLIOGRAPHY: W. J. Baltzell, *Dictionary of Musicians*; Grove's *Dictionary of Music.*

BRAILA. A town in Rumania, formerly a fortress, on the left bank of the Danube, which divides itself here into a number of arms, one of them forming the harbour of the town. The export of grain and the sturgeon fisheries are amongst the principal industries in Brăila. Pop. 68,310.

BRAILS. On ships, a name given to all the ropes employed to haul up the bottoms, lower corners, and skirts of the great sails in general.

BRAIN. The dominant organ of the nervous system, and the seat of consciousness and volition in man and the higher animals. The nerves of smell, sight, hearing, and taste carry to the brain impulses from the organs of special sense which awaken a consciousness of events happening in the outside world, and the special sensations and feelings excited by such stimulation as it affects the nose, eyes, ears, and tongue; and the brain also provides the mechanism whereby the effects of such sensory stimulation can be expressed in appropriate action. But the brain also receives impulses coming from the skin and from all parts of the body which excite a consciousness of touch and temperature, of pressure, position in space, and movement, i.e. information concerning the body itself.

The greater part of the human brain is formed by the cerebral hemispheres,

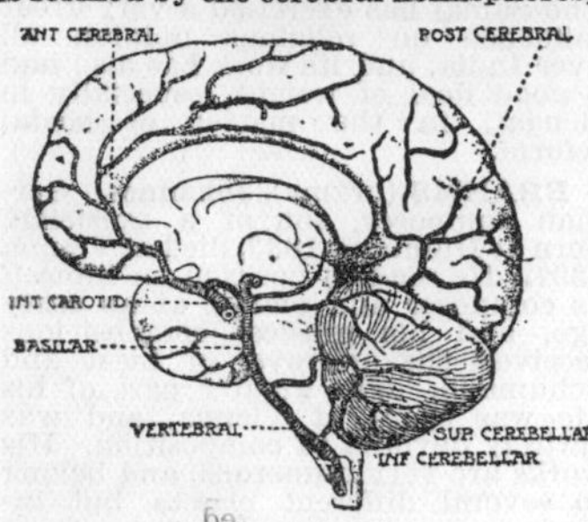

How the Brain is Fed

which occupy the upper part of the head. The surface of these structures consists of a layer of grey substance, the *cerebral cortex*, which is the recording apparatus and the organ of memory and discrimination, the

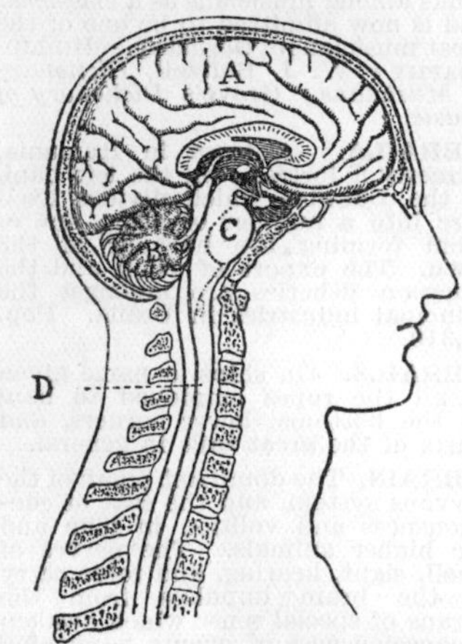

Section of Human Head, showing the Brain
A, Cerebrum. B, Cerebellum. C, Pons varolii. D, Spinal cord

instrument by means of which an individual can learn by experience, and modify his actions and behaviour in the light of acquired knowledge. The cerebral cortex of one side controls the movements of all the muscles of the other side of the body, and it renders possible the acquisition of the power of learning skilled movements. After injury to a certain part of the cerebral hemispheres of, say, the right side of the brain, or the fibres that connect it with the spinal cord, the muscles of the left side of the body would become paralysed, as in cases of apoplectic "stroke"; and, vice versa, injury to the left side of the brain causes paralysis of the right side of the body. Underneath the back part of the cerebral hemispheres there is a large organ, about half as big as the clenched fist, called the *cerebellum* or lesser brain, which occupies the lower back part of the skull. It regulates the balance of the activities of the scores of muscles that must act harmoniously together to effect any orderly movement of the body. It does the "staff work" in organising the actions which the dominant organ—the *cerebral cortex*—orders to be performed. The brain is also concerned with the performance of vast numbers of instinctive actions which are not due to deliberate volition, even though they may be consciously controlled or restrained. The brain is enclosed in three membranes called *mengines*.—BIBLIOGRAPHY: L. B. Rawling, *The Surgery of the Skull and Brain*; J. S. Bolton, *The Brain in Health and Disease*; A. Binet, *The Mind and the Brain*; H. E. Santee, *Anatomy of the Brain and Spinal Cord*.

BRAIN-CORAL. Coral of the genus Meandrīna, so called from its rounded shape and surface markings resembling the convolutions of the brain.

BRAINE-LE-COMTE (brān-lė-kont). An ancient town in Belgium, province of Hainaut, about 20 miles S.S.W. of Brussels, with a handsome church of the thirteenth century; and breweries, dyeworks, oil and cotton mills, etc. Pop. 9700.

BRAIN'TREE. A town of England, in Essex, about 40½ miles from London, with crape and silk manufactures. Pop. 8912.

BRAKE. A contrivance for retarding or arresting motion by means of friction. In machinery it generally consists of a brake-block, actuated by simple or compound levers, which may be forcibly pressed upon the periphery of a wheel, rotating on, or fixed upon, a shaft or axis. In its application to railway trains, brakes are fitted to each wheel of the train, connected throughout by means of a train-pipe, and operated by air, either by the *compression* or *vacuum* method. They are controlled by the driver, but can be applied in emergency by the guard, and operate automatically in the event of a breakage of the coupling causing a rupture of the train-pipe. In the

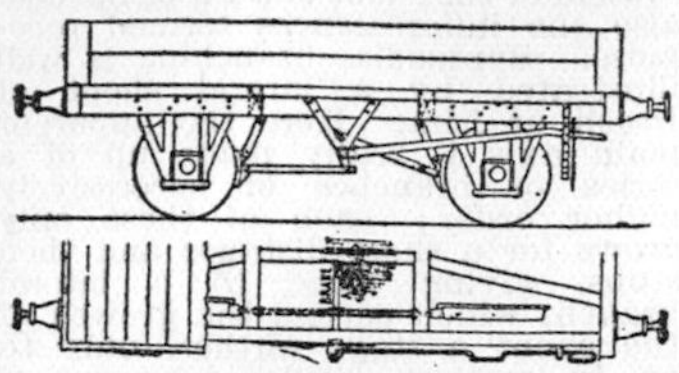

Brake (Morton's Patent). For operating by hand This hand-brake operates on all four wheels from either side of the truck

compression method, of which the Westinghouse brake is an example, the air is compressed by a pump on the locomotive, and conveyed by means of the train-pipe to a cylinder under each coach, the pistons of which act on the brake-

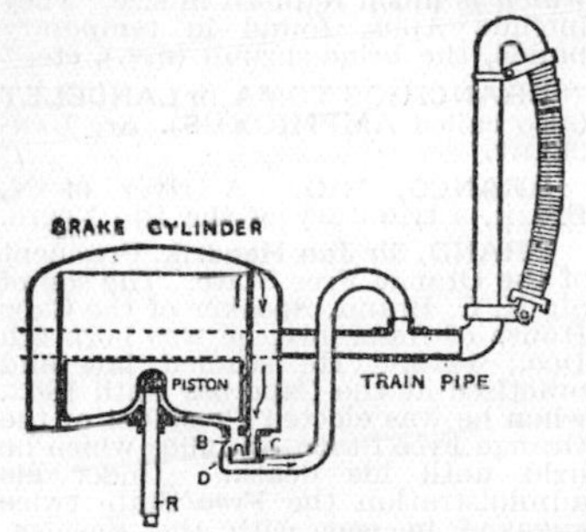

Brake. Vacuum Railway Brake

Continuation of train pipe omitted on left-hand side. The train-pipe is made continuous by coupling the flexible parts to the corresponding parts on the adjacent carriages. To release the brakes the driver turns a handle and the air in each brake cylinder is sucked out from both sides of the piston by the passages B and C. The air from the upper side lifts the little ball D on its way out. When the train is to be stopped, air is admitted to the train-pipe. It then rushes under the piston, but it cannot get into the space above, for the ball closes the passage. So the pressure of the atmosphere forces the piston, and the rod R which is connected to the brake blocks on the wheels, upwards, and then the brakes are applied.

levers. In the *vacuum* method, exemplified in the Longbridge brake, the brakes are held off by exhausting the air from the cylinders beneath the coaches, and the admission of air at atmospheric pressure operates the brakes. *See* AIR-BRAKE.—Cf. Kempe's *Engineer's Year Book.*

BRAKE (vehicle). *See* BREAK.

BRAM'AH, Joseph. The inventor of the Bramah lock, the Bramah press, etc., born in Yorkshire in 1748, died in 1814. He set up business in London as manufacturer of various small articles in metalwork, and distinguished himself by a long series of inventions, such as improvements in paper-making, fire-engines, printing-machines, etc. He is especially known for an ingeniously-constructed lock, and for the hydraulic press (q.v.). He also patented several plans for fountain-pens.

BRAMAH'S PRESS. *See* HYDRAULIC PRESS.

BRAMANTE (brá-mán'tā), **Francesco Lazzari.** A great Italian architect, born in 1444. He applied himself first to painting, in which he acquired considerable renown, but at length devoted himself to architecture. He was patronised by the Popes, and his first great work at Rome was the union of the straggling buildings of the Vatican with the Belvedere gardens, so as to form one fine whole. But his greatest work was the part he had in the building of the new church of St. Peter at Rome, of which he was the first architect. He died, however, in 1514, while the building was still in an early stage of construction, and his designs were much altered by succeeding architects, among others Fra Giocondo and Raphael, until Michael Angelo returned to the fundamental ideas of Bramante.

BRAM'BLE (*Rubus fruticōsus*). The name commonly applied to the bush with trailing prickly stems which bears the well-known berries usually called in Scotland brambles, and in England blackberries. It is similar to the raspberry, and belongs to the same genus, nat. ord. Rosaceæ. It is rarely cultivated, but as a wild plant it grows in great abundance. The flowers do not appear till late in the summer, and the fruit, which is deep purple or almost black in colour, does not ripen till autumn.

BRAM'BLING, or BRAMBLE-FINCH. The mountain-finch (*Fringilla montifringilla*). Larger than the chaffinch, and very like it. It breeds in the north of Scandinavia, and visits Britain and the south of Europe in winter.

BRAMLEY, Frank. English artist. Born in Lincolnshire, 6th May, 1857, he studied in Antwerp and Paris. In 1884 his first painting was accepted by the Academy. In 1894 he was elected A.R.A. and in 1911 R.A. He died 10th Aug., 1915. Bramley's most famous picture is *The Hopeless Dawn* in the Tate Gallery, London.

BRAMPTON. An ancient town, England, Cumberlandshire, formerly with tweed manufactures. Pop. 2590.

BRAN. The husky part of any kind of grain separated by the bolter from the flour. Its composition is as follows: water, 13; gluten, 19·5; fatty matter, 5; husk with starch, 55; and ashes, 7·5; but the results of different analyses vary considerably. It is the coarsest of the offals, the others, less coarse, being pollards, sharps, and middlings. It is employed in feeding cattle, and has also been found useful as a manure. It is a favourite food for horses, and when made into a *mash* has a slightly laxative effect.

BRANCHIÆ (brang'ki-ē). *See* GILLS.

BRANCHING. A plant-organ is said to branch when it forks or gives off a lateral outgrowth like itself. Leaves differ fundamentally in structure from the stems on which they are borne, and are thus regarded not as branches but as *appendages* of the stem. Leaves, however, may

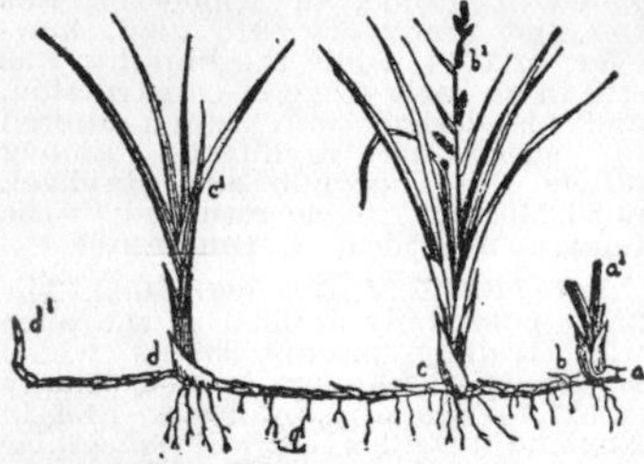

Branching. Sympodial Rhizome of Carex

themselves branch, in which case they are said to be *compound.* In the lower groups of plants, forking (*dichotomy* or *dichotomous branching*) is common; among seed-plants *lateral branching* is the rule, and the stem-branches are most often axillary, i.e. a branch arises at the base of each leaf and between it and the parent stem. The branches of stems arise from superficial tissues (*exogenously*), the surface layer or epidermis being continuous over branch and parent stem; root-branches (rootlets) are *endogenous*, i.e. they originate in the internal tissues, and bore their way out, breaking through the surface of the parent root.

Branching may be *monopodial* or *sympodial*. In the former case there is a permanent main axis, from which lateral branches arise in succession without overtopping it; each of these may, in its turn, act as a main axis for branches of higher order. Examples are any tap root system or the shoot of a Fir or Spruce; also the inflorescences termed racemose. Sympodial branching is well illustrated by a lateral shoot of Beech or Elm. Here the apparent main axis is really made up of a series of branches of successively higher order; each of these only grows for a short distance and then stops, giving place to a lateral branch, which carries the growth of the shoot a stage farther, only to be, in its turn, displaced by one of its own lateral branches, and so on. Many creeping shoots (e.g. Carex, Iris) are also sympodial, as are the inflorescences termed cymose.

BRANCHIOP'ODA (brang-ki-). A group of crustaceous animals, so called because their branchiæ, or gills, are situated on the feet. They have three pairs of jaws, and the head is not distinct from the thorax, which is much reduced in size. They include Apus, found in temporary ponds, the brine-shrimp (q.v.), etc.

BRANCHIOS'TOMA, or **LANCELET** (also called **AMPHIOXUS**). *See* LANCELET.

BRANCO, RIO. A river of N. Brazil, a tributary of the Rio Negro.

BRAND, Sir Jan Hendrik. President of the Orange Free State. The son of Sir H. C. Brand, Speaker of the Cape House of Assembly, he was born 6th Dec., 1823. He studied law and practised at the Cape bar until 1863, when he was elected President of the Orange Free State, an office which he held until his death. Under his administration the Free State twice engaged in war with the Basutos. He was invited to become President of the Transvaal and thus unite the two Dutch republics, but declined to be a party to a manœuvre which he regarded as hostile to Great Britain. He was knighted in 1882, and died 14th July, 1888.

BRAN'DENBURG. A province of Prussia, surrounded mainly by Mecklenburg and the provinces of Pomerania, Posen, Silesia, and Prussian Saxony. The soil consists in many parts of barren sands, heaths, and moors; yet the province produces much grain, as well as fruits, hemp, flax, tobacco, etc., and supports many sheep. The forests are very extensive. The principal streams are the Elbe, the Oder, the Havel, and the Spree. Berlin is in Brandenburg. Area, 15,071 sq. miles; population (not including Berlin, q.v.),

2,592,430. The Old Mark of Brandenburg was bestowed by the Emperor Charles IV. on Frederick of Hohenzollern, and is the centre round which the present extensive kingdom of Prussia has grown up.—The town *Brandenburg* is on the Havel, 36 miles W.S.W. of Berlin. It is divided into three parts—an old town, a new town, and a cathedral town—by the river, and has considerable manufactures, including silk, woollens, leather, etc. Pop. 60,953.

BRANDENBURG, NEW. A town of Germany, in Mecklenburg-Strelitz, with what used to be a grand-ducal palace. Pop. 12,348.

BRANDES, Georg Morris Cohen. Danish critic, of Jewish extraction, born in 1842. He studied at the University of Copenhagen, travelled for several years, lived for five years in Berlin, and from 1882 resided at Copenhagen. A disciple of Comte, Taine, Mill, and Spencer, Brandes is considered, perhaps rightly, not only as the first of Danish critics but also as one of the greatest systematic critics of literature in modern times. He concerns himself with the currents of European thought rather than with national achievements, and his works display cosmopolitan sympathies. Among his works, which are numerous, are: *Æsthetic Studies*, *French Æsthetics*, *Criticisms and Portraits*, *The Main Literary Currents of the Nineteenth Century*, *Eminent Authors of the Nineteenth Century*, *Men and Works in European Literature*, *Impressions of Poland*, *Shakespeare*, *Recollections of my Childhood and my Youth*, and *Jesus, a Myth*. He died on 19th February, 1927.

BRAND'ING. A form of punishment once in use in England for various crimes, but abolished in 1822. It was performed by means of a red-hot iron, and the part which was branded was the cheek, the hand, or some other part of the body. Even after branding had been abolished in all other cases, a milder form of it was for a long time retained in the army as a punishment for desertion, the letter D being marked with ink or gunpowder on the left side of a deserter 2 inches below the armpit. This also has been abolished.

BRAN'DIS, Christian August. German scholar, born in 1790, died in 1867. After studying at Kiel and Göttingen, he was induced by Niebuhr to accompany him to Rome as secretary to the Prussian embassy. In 1822 he was made professor of philosophy at the University of Bonn. From this date his name became well known as that of a contributor to the learned journals of Germany, till in 1835 the appearance of the first part of his great work on the *History of Greek and Roman Philosophy* acquired for him a European reputation.

BRAND'LING. A small red worm used for bait by anglers, and found in dung-heaps. The name is sometimes applied to parr or young of salmon.

BRANDON. An old English market town in N.W. Suffolk, on the Little Ouse; flint implements were made here in neolithic times. Pop. 2462.

BRAN'DON. A rising town of Canada, in Manitoba, 132 miles west of Winnipeg, a railway centre on the Assiniboine. Pop. 17,082.

BRANDON AND BYSHOTTLES. An urban district of England, 3 miles south-west of Durham, in a district of collieries. Pop. (1931), 17,099.

BRANDT (brånt), or **BRANT, Sebastian.** Author of a famous German satire, the *Narrenschiff*, or Ship of Fools. He was born at Strasburg in 1458, and studied law at Basel, dying in 1521. The *Narrenschiff* is written in verse, and is a bold and vigorous satire on the vices and follies of the age. It took the popular taste of its time, and was translated into all the languages of Europe. *The Ship of Fools*, by Alexander Barclay (1509), is partly an imitation, partly a translation of it.

BRANDY. The liquor obtained by the distillation of wine, or of the refuse of the wine-press. It is colourless at first, but usually derives a brownish colour from the casks in which it is kept or from colouring-matters added to it. The best brandy is made in France, particularly in the Cognac district in the department of Charente. Much of the so-called brandy sold in Britain and America is made there from more or less coarse whisky, flavoured and coloured to resemble the real article; and France itself also exports quantities of this stuff. Nearly all wine-growing countries make brandy. The brandy imported into the United Kingdom varies in different years from about two million to three million gallons, almost all from France. In Great Britain there is a duty of £3, 15*s.* 4*d.* per proof gallon on all brandy imported. Brandy is often used medicinally as a stimulant, stomachic, and restorative, or in mild diarrhœa. In America various distilled liquors get the name of brandy, as cider brandy, peach brandy.

BRANDYWINE CREEK. A small

river which rises in the State of Pennsylvania, passes into the State of Delaware, and joins Christiana Creek near Wilmington. It gives its name to a battle fought near it, 11th Sept., 1777, between the British and Americans, in which the latter were defeated.

BRANGWYN, Frank. An English painter, born at Bruges in 1867. He received his first instructions in art from his father, and worked for some time in the studio of William Morris (q.v.). He has travelled in the East on several occasions, and his work bears obvious traces of Oriental influences. His pictures include: *Modern Commerce* (which is in the Royal Exchange, London), *Trade on the Beach* (in the Luxembourg, Paris), *St. Simon Stylites* (in Venice), and *Turkish Boatmen* (in the Prague gallery). He was elected A.R.A. in 1904, and R.A. in 1919. During the European War he designed several striking posters intended to stimulate recruiting and the purchase of war bonds. Cf. Shaw-Sparrow, *Frank Brangwyn and his Work.*

BRANK, or BRANKS. An instrument formerly in use in Scotland, and to some extent also in England, as a punishment for scolds. It consisted of an iron frame which went

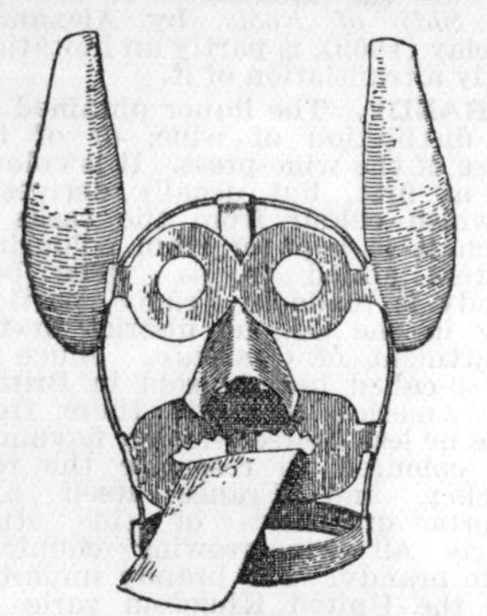

Branks

over the head of the offender, and had in front an iron plate which was inserted in the mouth, where it was fixed above the tongue, and kept it perfectly quiet.

BRANKSOME. A former urban district of England, in Dorsetshire, west of Bournemouth and south-east of Poole, of which it now forms part.

BRANK'URSINE. *See* ACANTHUS.

BRANT. *See* BRANDT.

BRANT'FORD. A flourishing town of Canada, province of Ontario, on the Grand River (which is navigable), 24 miles W.S.W. of Hamilton; it has railway machine-shops, foundries, and an active trade. Pop. 30,107.

BRANTÔME (brąn-tōm), **Pierre de Bourdeilles, Seigneur de.** French writer, born in Perigord about 1540, died in 1614. He was of an old and noble family, and became a soldier when quite young. After a brilliant life in courts and camps he withdrew to his estate in Perigord, and spent his time in writing memoirs, which give an admirable picture of his age, with particulars which a chaster and more fastidious pen could hardly have set down. He left France in the suite of Mary Stuart when she went to Scotland to take possession of her kingdom, and he has left a touching account of this journey of the unfortunate queen. His memoirs consist of *Vies des Hommes illustres et des grands Capitaines Français, Vies des grands Capitaines Etrangers, Vies des Dames illustres, Vies des Dames galantes.* All his MSS. were collected by the École des Chartes in 1904.

BRASENOSE. One of the colleges of Oxford University, founded by William Smith, Bishop of Lincoln, and Sir Richard Sutton, in 1509. The origin of the name is doubtful, but there is a large nose of brass over the entrance. The college is well endowed, and contributes over £2000 per annum to university purposes.

BRAS'IDAS. A Spartan general who in the Peloponnesian War overthrew the Athenian army under Cleon at Amphipolis, but was himself mortally wounded, 422 B.C.

BRASOV. *See* CRONSTADT.

BRASS. An alloy of copper and zinc, of a bright-yellow colour, and hard, ductile, and malleable. English standard brass consists of two parts by weight of copper to one of zinc. It casts well, and is capable of being hammered, rolled, and even drawn into wire. As a rule these properties are not required in brass castings, and large quantities of scrap brass are often used in their manufacture, causing the introduction of certain impurities such as tin, iron, and lead. Brasses suitable for hot rolling contain from 55 to 60 per cent copper, the remainder being zinc; the best-known alloy of this type being Muntz metal, containing 60 per cent copper, 40 per cent zinc, largely used as a sheathing for ships. Brasses for cold rolling contain over 60 per cent copper, the best alloy for tubes and wire-drawing containing 70 per cent copper, 30 per cent zinc. Brass which is to be turned is made more easily workable by the addition of about 2 per cent of lead. Naval brass contains 1 per cent tin. Tombac and pinchbeck are varieties of brass containing 86 and 83 per cent copper respectively.

BRASS. A river and town of the Niger delta, near the chief mouth.

BRAS'SARTS. Pieces of ancient plate armour which united the armour-plates on the shoulder and elbow. Demi-brassarts shielded only the front.

BRASSES, Sepulchral or Monumental. Large plates of brass inlaid in polished slabs of stone, and usually exhibiting the figure of the person

An Example of Brass Work

intended to be commemorated, either in a carved outline on the plate or in the form of the plate itself. In place of the figure we sometimes find an ornamented cross. The earliest example of these monumental slabs now existing in England is that on the tomb of Sir John D'Abernon (died 1277) at Stoke D'Abernon in Surrey. Among the examples known in Scotland are the memorials of the Regent Murray (1569) in St. Giles Cathedral, Edinburgh; and of the Minto family (1605) in the Cathedral of Glasgow. These brasses are of great value in giving us an exact picture of the costume of the time to which they belong. Haines's *Manual of Monumental Brasses* is invaluable to the student.

BRASSEUR DE BOURBOURG (bräseur dė bör-bör), **Charles Étienne.** French writer on American history, archæology, and ethnology, born 1814, died 1874. He entered the priesthood, was sent to North America by the Propaganda, and lived and travelled here and in Central America for a number of years, partly in the performance of ecclesiastical functions. Among his works are: *Histoire du Canada* (1851); *Histoire des Nations civilisées du Mexique et de l'Amérique Centrale*; *Popol Vuh, le Livre sacré des Quichés*; *Monuments anciens du Mexique*; *Études sur le Système graphique et la Langue des Mayas*; etc.

BRASSEY, Thomas. An English railway contractor, born 1805, died 1870. His operations were on an immense scale, and extended to most of the European countries, as well as to America, India, and Australia, one of his greatest works being the Grand Trunk Railway of Canada, with the great bridge over the St. Lawrence at Montreal. He left a very large fortune.

BRASSEY, Thomas. Son of above, born 1836, died Feb., 1918, created Baron Brassey in 1886, and earl in 1911; was Secretary to the Admiralty and Civil Lord, Governor of Victoria, and wrote on naval matters (*British Navy*, 5 vols., 1881). His first wife (died 1887) wrote *Voyage of the Sunbeam* and other books. He founded and first edited the *Naval Annual* (1886). He covered 400,000 knots in his yacht *Sunbeam*, which he presented to the Government of India as a hospital ship in 1916. His titles passed to his only son, Thomas Allnutt Brassey, but became extinct when he died 11th Nov., 1919.

BRAS'SICA. An important genus of cruciferous plants, including among its numerous species many of great economical value, as the cabbage, turnip, rape, etc. Owing to the numerous crossed races which have been produced in modern times, the limits of the species have been broken down, and often cannot easily be recognised.

BRATISLAVA. City and river port

of Czecho-Slovakia. It was formerly in Hungary and was called Pressburg; the Magyars called it Pozsony. It stands on the Danube, about 50 miles from Vienna, and is the centre of a considerable trade by rail and river. There are also some manufactures. The cathedral is a Gothic edifice. The castle on the Schlossberg is in ruins. Pressburg was the capital of Hungary from 1541 to 1784, but in 1919 it was given to Czecho-Slovakia. Slovak university was founded here in 1919. The city has an important broadcasting station. Pop. 123,852.

BRAT'TICE. In mines, a partition of light wood boards or canvas which divides a shaft or underground roadway into two, and furnishes a means of conducting the ventilation into the working face. *See* MINING.

BRAUNAU (broun'ou). A town of Czechoslovakia, formerly in Austria, near the Prussian frontier, with an old Benedictine abbey and an important woollen industry. In 1618 the attempt to build a Protestant church here gave rise to the Thirty Years' War. Pop. 6820.

BRAUNSBERG (brounz'berg). A town, Prussia, government of Königsberg, on the Passarge, about 4 miles from its junction with the Frische Haff. Pop. 13,893.

BRAUWER (brou'ver), **Adrian.** *See* BROUWER.

BRAVI (brä'vē). The name formerly given in Italy, and particularly in Venice, to those who were ready to hire themselves out to perform any desperate undertaking. The word had the same signification in Spain, and both the word and the persons designated by it were found in France in the reign of Louis XIII. and during the minority of Louis XIV.

BRAVO (brä'vō). An Italian adjective used as exclamation of praise in theatres, meaning "well done! excellent!" The correct usage is to say *bravo* to a man, *brava* to a woman, *bravi* to several persons.

BRAVU'RA AIR. An air so composed as to enable the singer to show his skill in execution by the addition of embellishments, striking cadences, etc.

BRAWN. A preparation made from the flesh of swine freed from all bones, formed into a roll, boiled, and pressed. In times past it was a very favourite dish in the country districts during the autumn or early spring, when the annual pig-killings took place. Wiltshire brawn is in much repute.

BRAXY. A disease of sheep, being a plethora of the blood resulting from a change from poor to rich pasturage usually fatal in a few hours. In the United Kingdom it is specially prevalent throughout the west coast of Scotland, the north of England, and the west coast of Ireland. There are various forms of braxy, each representing a distinct and separate diseased condition.

BRAY (Irish *Bré*). A seaside resort in Ireland, Wicklow, picturesquely situated between the Bray and Bray Head, 12 miles S.E. of Dublin. Pop 7691.

BRAY. Town of Berkshire. On the right bank of the Thames, near Maidenhead, its name is celebrated owing to the ballad of *The Vicar of Bray*. The identity of the accommodating vicar is uncertain. The dates of the song indicate Francis Carswell, vicar from 1667 to 1709, but there appears to have been an earlier incumbent, Simon Aleyn, vicar from 1540 to 1588, whose principles were equally elastic. Pop. 3803.

BRAY. A village of France, department of Somme, the scene of fighting during the European War.

BRAZIL', United States of. A republic in South America, occupying nearly one-half of that continent; greatest length, E. to W., 2690 miles; greatest length, N. to S., 2600 miles; area estimated at 3,275,510 sq. miles, or about one-sixth smaller than Europe. It is bounded S.E., E., and N.E. by the Atlantic Ocean, N. by French, Dutch, and British Guiana, and Venezuela; W. and S.W. by Ecuador, Peru, Bolivia, Paraguay, the Argentine Republic, and the Republic of Uruguay. Brazil is divided into a federal district, twenty States, many of them larger than Great Britain, and a "territory." The population by official census in 1920 was 30,635,605, but is estimated now at 40,272,650. Capital, Rio de Janeiro; pop. 1,468,621.

Physical Features. The coast has few indentations of importance—the chief being the estuaries of the Amazon and Pará in the north—and good harbours are comparatively few. As a whole the country may be regarded as having three natural divisions, namely, one belonging to the basin of the Amazon, another belonging to the La Plata basin, and a third consisting of the eastern portion watered by a number of streams directly entering the Atlantic. The Amazon valley is bounded by elevated table-lands which, in the lower course of the river, approach within a comparatively short distance of each other. The characteristic feature of this region is its immense low-lying, forest-covered plains, intersected by innumerable watercourses, and in many parts subject to annual inundation, the vegetation being of the most luxuriant character, from the heat and frequent rains. The greater part of this vast region is unpopulated except by Indians, and as yet of little commercial importance. The climate, notwithstanding the tropical heat and moisture, is comparatively healthy, and the facility for commerce given by thousands of miles of great navigable streams must in time attract numerous settlers. To some extent this has already taken place in the region of the Lower Amazon. Here the development of a trade in the juice of the india-rubber trees, which grow in vast quantities, has attracted thousands of Brazilians from the adjoining provinces, and thus has covered thousands of miles of rivers with steamers, and spread a population over vast areas that otherwise would have remained dormant for many years.

This northern part of Brazil is unequalled in the number and magnitude of the streams which compose its river system and connect it with Venezuela, Colombia, Ecuador, Peru, and Bolivia. On the north side the chief affluents of the Amazon are the Rio Negro and the Japura, the former giving through the Cassiquiare continuous water communication with the Orinoco. Amongst the southern affluents which are important as water highways into the interior of Brazil are the Xingu, the Tapajos, the Madeira, the Purus, and the Jurua; the Madeira being the most important, and forming a navigable water-way into Bolivia, except that it is interrupted by falls about 200 miles below where it enters Brazil. The Tocantins is another large stream from the south, which enters the Pará estuary and hardly belongs to the Amazon basin. The forest region of the Amazon occupies about one-fourth of the country; the rest is made up of undulating tablelands 1000 to 3000 feet above the sea, mountain ranges rising to 10,000 feet, and river valleys.

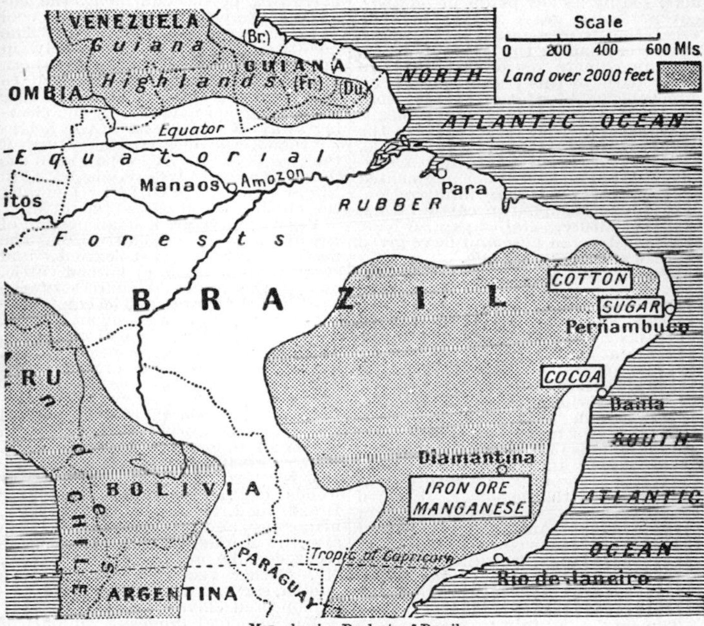

Map, showing Products of Brazil

The great streams belonging to the La Plata basin, in the south, are the Paraguay and Paraná. The watershed between this and the Amazonian basin, near the western boundary of Brazil, is only about 500 feet above sea-level, and here a canoe can be hauled across from a headstream of the Madeira to be launched on one belonging to the Paraguay. It would thus be easy to connect the one system with the other by means of a canal, and so connect the La Plata with the Orinoco. The water-shed rises gradually from west to east.

The southern part of Brazil is characterised by its low plains or *pampas*, covered with grass or scrub. Its vegetation is of a much less tropical character than in the Amazon basin, and its climate more variable. In many parts of this region there is an admirable field for future colonisation, though it is as yet defective in means of transport. Near the coast, in the provinces of S. Paulo, Rio Grande, and Paraná, there is already a considerable population, much augmented by German and Italian immigration, and mostly occupied in cattle-raising and agriculture. Railways also have been constructed here and have given a great stimulus to trade.

The most important river in Eastern Brazil is the San Francisco, which is the great water-way into its interior, and after a course of 1800 miles discharges its waters into the Atlantic at San Antonio. The three greatest cities of Brazil, Rio de Janeiro, Pernambuco, and Bahia, are all endeavouring to develop a traffic in connection with this river. A State line has now been constructed round the falls of Pedro Affonso on its lower course, and thus has brought the traffic of the upper river into communication with the lower. Eastern Brazil exhibits a great variety in surface, climate, and productions, and though large tracts consist of arid and sandy table-lands, it contains within itself the greater part of the population, wealth, and industry of the country.

The chief mountain ranges are near the south-eastern coast. The Serra do Mar or Maritime range commences in the far south, and travels close to the coast-line in a north-easterly direction till it reaches Rio de Janeiro and Cape Frio, where it culminates in the Serra dos Orgãos, or Organ Mountains, from 7000 to 8000 feet above the sea, and forming the noblest element in the marvellous scenery of the bay of Rio de Janeiro. West of the Serra do Mar lies the Serra Mantequeira, which farther north is known as the Serra do Espinhaço. Here are the loftiest summits in Brazil, Itatiaia-Assu, the highest of all, being 9823 feet above the sea. Between the sources of the Tocantins and Paraná are the Montes Pyreneos, the second most elevated ridge in Brazil, some of its heights being estimated at nearly 8000 and 10,000 feet above the level of the sea.

Climate. As almost the whole of Brazil lies south of the equator, and in a hemisphere where there is a greater proportion of sea than land, its climate is generally more cool and moist than that of countries in corresponding latitudes in the northern hemispheres. In the southern parts of Brazil, in consequence of the gradual narrowing of the continent, the climate is of an insular character—cool summers and mild winters. The quantity of rain differs widely in different localities. The northern provinces generally are subject to heavy rains. At Rio, where the climate has been much modified by the clearing away of the forests in the neighbourhood, the mean temperature of the year is 74° F. At Pernambuco the temperature rarely exceeds 82°; in winter it descends to 68°. Generally the climate of Brazil is delightful.

Vegetation. Only a small portion of Brazil is as yet under cultivation. The pastures are of vast extent, and support great herds of horned cattle, one of the principal sources of the wealth of the country. The chief food-supplying plants are sugar, coffee, cocoa, rice, tobacco, maize, wheat, manioc (or cassava), beans, bananas, ginger, yams, lemons, oranges, figs, etc.—coffee being the staple product of the country. As much coffee, indeed, is produced in Brazil as in all the rest of the world together. Cotton is also an important crop and export. Besides great supplies of rubber, the forests yield dyewoods and fancy woods of various kinds, including Brazil-wood, rosewood, fustic, cedar, mahogany, and a variety of others, as also Brazil-nuts, coco-nuts, vegetable ivory, copaiba, arnotto, piassava fibre, etc. Other vegetable products are vanilla, sarsaparilla, ipecacuanha, cinnamon, and cloves.

The principal domestic animals of Brazil are horned cattle and horses. Sheep are kept only in some parts, chiefly in the south. Goats and hogs are abundant. The wild animals comprise the puma, jaguar, sloth, porcupine, etc. Monkeys are numerous. Amongst the feathered tribes are the smallest—the humming-bird—and one of the largest—the rhea—parrots in great variety, tanagers, toucans, and the harpy eagle. The reptiles consist of the boa-constrictor and other species of serpents, some of them venomous, alligators, and freshwater turtles, the eggs of which yield a valuable oil. The insects are, many of them, remarkable for the beauty of their colours and their size, especially the butterflies. Amongst the most notable are the white ant, very numerous and very destructive, and the scorpion, which attains a length of 6 inches. Among minerals the diamonds and other precious stones of Brazil—emeralds, sapphires, rubies, beryls, etc.—are well known. Gold also is procured in considerable quantities. Other minerals are quicksilver, copper, manganese, iron, lead, tin, antimony, and bismuth. The shores and rivers abound with fish.

Population. The population of Brazil consists of whites, Indians, negroes, and people of mixed blood, and is estimated at 40,272,650. The native Brazilians, mostly descendants of the Portuguese settlers, but often with a mixture of Indian or African blood, are greatly wanting in energy. The white population, which is, perhaps, a third of the whole has in recent years been increased by Italian, Portuguese, and German immigration. The negroes are over 2,000,000 in number, and till 1888 were partly slaves. Of the Indians some are semi-civilised, but others (estimated at 600,000) roam about in a wild state, and are divided into a great many tribes speaking different languages. The State language is Portuguese. Primary education is gratuitous, but not compulsory. In recent years public instruction has made great progress. Brazil has many public libraries. The National Library in Rio contains more than 400,000 books and MSS.

Trade. The principal imports are cottons, linens, woollens, machinery, hardware and cutlery, wheat, flour, wine, coals, etc., the manufactured articles and coals being largely from Britain. The exports consist of coffee, rubber, sugar, cotton, hides, skins, maté, cacao, tobacco, Brazil-nuts, wax, drugs, etc. The main export is coffee, the total value exported annually being over £60,000,000 (£69,582,000 in 1926, and £62,689,000 in 1927); total exports in 1927, £88,689,000; imports £79,641,000: imports from Britain in 1927, £14,391,004; exports, £4,466,357. The chief money of account is the milreis (1000 reis), nominal value 2*s.* 3*d.*; the paper milreis has a par value of 1*s.* 4*d.* The English sovereign is legal tender at 8889 reis each. The length of telegraph lines in Brazil is about 54,526 miles, and of railways about 19,026, but these are being extended.

The prevailing religion of Brazil is Roman Catholic, but all religions are now on an equal footing. Previous to 1889 the government was monarchical, but in that year a revolution took place and a republic was established. By the new constitution of 1891 each of the old provinces forms a State, having its own local Government, with representation in a Congress appointed by popular vote, and consisting of a Senate and a Chamber of Deputies. By the military law of 1923 military service is obligatory on every Brazilian from 21 years of age to 44. The total peace strength of the army is 43,015, and there is a gendarmerie of 26,000.

History. Brazil was discovered in 1499 by Vincente Yanez Pinçon, one of the companions of Columbus in the service of Spain, and next year was taken possession of by Pedro Alvares de Cabral on behalf of Portugal. The first Governor-General was Thome de Sousa, who in 1549 arrived in the Bay of Bahia and established the new city of that name, making it the seat of his Government. The usurpation of the crown of Portugal by Philip II. left Brazil in a defenceless and neglected condition, and the English, French, and Dutch made successive attempts to obtain a footing. The Dutch were the most persevering, and for a time almost divided the Brazilian territory with the Portuguese. The tyranny of the Dutch governors, however, incited their native and Portuguese subjects to revolt, and after a sanguinary war, in 1654 the Dutch were driven out and the Portuguese remained masters of an undivided Brazil. The value of Brazil to Portugal continued steadily to increase after the discovery of the gold-mines in 1698 and the discovery of the diamond-mines in 1728.

The vigorous policy of the Portuguese Government under the administration of the Marquis de Pombal (1760-77) did much to open up the interior of Brazil, though his high-handed modes of procedure left amongst the Brazilians a discontent with the home Government which took shape in the abortive revolt of 1789. On the invasion of Portugal in 1807 by the French, the sovereign of that kingdom, John VI., sailed for Brazil, accompanied by his Court and a large body of emigrants. He raised Brazil to the rank of a kingdom (in 1813), and assumed the title of King of Portugal and Brazil. But on his return to Portugal in 1821 he found the Portuguese Cortes unwilling to grant civil and political equality to the Brazilians—a fact which raised such violent convulsions in Rio Janeiro and other parts of Brazil that Dom Pedro, the king's son, was forced to head the party resolved to make Brazil independent, and in 1822 a National Assembly declared the separation of Brazil from Portugal, and appointed Dom Pedro the constitutional emperor.

In 1864 began a severe struggle between Brazil and Paraguay, caused principally by the arbitrary conduct of Lopez, the Dictator of Paraguay. Brazil, though joined by Uruguay and the Argentine Confederation, had to bear the brunt of the war, which terminated only with the death of Lopez in 1870. This struggle entailed upon Brazil an immense expenditure of men and money, but it established her reputation as a Great Power, and secured the freedom of the navigation of the La Plata river-system. In 1853 the importation of slaves was prohibited, in 1871 an Act was passed for the gradual emancipation of slaves, and in 1888 slavery was finally abolished.

In 1889 Dom Pedro II., who had reigned since 1831, was dethroned by a revolution. Brazil was declared a republic under the title of United States of Brazil. The proceedings of the President, Fonseca, led to a revolutionary movement in 1891, and there was civil war in 1893-4. Boundary treaties were signed respectively with Colombia (1907), Peru (1909), and Uruguay (1913). In 1914 Wenceslao Braz became President. Brazil broke off diplomatic relations with Germany on 10th April, 1917. Until 1926 Brazil was a member of the League of Nations. In 1930 there was serious trouble in the republic, and a dictatorship was established. This lasted until 1932 when there was a return to normal forms of government. An economic crisis, caused by the poor prices paid for the coffee crop, followed, and in 1931 the country suspended payment on its foreign loans.—BIBLIOGRAPHY: E. Levasseur, *e Brésil*; N. O. Winter, *Brazil and her People of To-day*; J. Burnichon, *Le Brésil d'aujourd'hui*; G. J. Bruce, *Brazil and the Brazilians*; J. D. M'Ewan, *Brazil*; J. C. Oakenfull, *Brazil, Past, Present, and Future.*

BRAZIL. A town of the United States, capital of Clay County, Indiana, between Terre Haute and Indianapolis; a railway centre and coal-mining place. Pop. 8744.

BRAZILET'TO. The wood of *Cæsalpinia crista*, an inferior Brazil-wood brought from Jamaica, or of *C. bijuga.*

BRAZIL - NUTS. *See* BERTHOLLETIA.

BRAZIL-TEA. A name for maté.

BRAZIL-WOOD. A kind of wood yielding a red dye (brasiline), obtained from several trees of the genus Cæsalpinia, ord. Leguminosæ, natives of the West Indies and Central and South America. The wood is hard and heavy, and as it takes on a fine polish it is used by cabinet-makers for various purposes, but its principal use is in dyeing red.

BRA'ZING, or BRASS - SOLDERING. *See* SOLDERING.

BRAZOS (brä'zōs). A large river, United States, Texas, rising in the N.W. part of the State, and flowing into the Gulf of Mexico, after a course of 950 miles, 40 miles W.S.W. of Galveston. During the rainy season, from February to May inclusive, it is navigable by steamboats for about 300 miles.

BRAZZA (brȧt'sȧ). An island in the Adriatic, formerly belonging to Austria, now to Yugoslavia. It is 24 miles long and from 5 to 7 broad, mountainous and well wooded. It produces good wines and oil, almonds, silk, etc. Pop. 19,330.

BRAZZAVILLE. The capital of the French Congo territory on the north or right bank of the River Congo at Stanley Pool, on a site ceded to the French explorer Savorgnan de Brazza in 1880. Pop. 6300.

BREACH. The aperture or passage made in the wall of any fortified place by the ordnance of the besiegers for the purpose of entering the fortress.—*Breaching batteries* are batteries of heavy guns intended to make a breach.

BREACH. In law, any violation of a law, or the non-performance of a duty imposed by law. Breaches are of various kinds:—

Breach of Close. In English law, any entry upon another man's property which is not warranted by being made in the exercise of a right.

Breach of Covenant. The act of violating an agreement in a deed either to do or not to do something.

Breach of Peace. An offence against the public safety or tranquillity either personally or by inciting others. Breaches of peace are such as affrays, riots, routs, and unlawful assemblies, forcible entry or detainer by violently taking or keeping possession of lands or tenements with menaces, force, and arms; riding, or going, armed with dangerous or unusual weapons, terrifying people; challenging another to fight, or bearing such a challenge, besides certain other offences.

Breach of Promise (of marriage). The failure to implement one's promise to marry a particular person, in consequence of which that person may raise an action for damages, though it is only the woman as a rule that gains damages. It is the only action in contract where *exemplary* damages may be awarded, and then only when the breach of promise has been aggravated by seduction. A promise to marry given by a person who, to the knowledge of the other party, is married is void as against public policy, and no action will lie if, on becoming free to marry, the promiser refuses to fulfil it.

Breach of Trust. A violation of duty by a trustee, executor, or any other person in a fiduciary position, as, for instance, when a trustee manages an estate intrusted to him for his own advantage rather than for that of the trust.

BREAD. The flour or meal of grain kneaded with water into a tough and consistent paste and baked. There are numerous kinds of bread, according to materials and methods of preparation; but all may be divided into two classes: *fermented, leavened,* or *raised,* and *unfermented, unleavened, not raised.* The latter is the simplest, and no doubt was the original kind, and is still exemplified by biscuits, the oat-cakes of Scotland, the corn-bread of America, the *dampers* of the Australian colonies, and the still ruder bread of savage races. It was probably by accident that the method of bringing the paste into a state of fermentation was found out, by which its toughness is almost entirely destroyed, and it becomes porous, palatable, and digestible.

All the cereals are used in making bread, each zone using those which are native to it. Thus maize, millet, and rice are used for the purpose in the hotter countries, rye, barley, and oats in the colder, and wheat in the intermediate or more temperate regions. In the most advanced countries bread is made from wheat, which makes the lightest and most spongy bread.

The fermentation necessary for the ordinary loaf-bread is generally produced by means of leaven or yeast, and the first thing to be done towards the manufacture of a batch of bread is, in the language of the baker, *to stir a ferment.* For this purpose water, yeast, flour, and some potatoes mashed and strained through a cullender, are mixed together and worked up into a thin paste, in which, on being left at rest for a time, an active fermentation sets in, the carbonic acid generated causing the mixture to rise and fall. In about three hours the fermenting action is at rest, and the mixture may now be used, but it is not generally used till at the end of four or five hours.

The next operation is called *setting the sponge.* This consists in stirring up the above ferment well, adding some lukewarm water, and mixing in as much flour as will make the whole into a pretty stiff dough, which receives the name of the *sponge.* The sponge, being kept in a warm place, begins to ferment in the course of an hour or so, heaving and swelling up till at last the imprisoned carbonic acid bursts from the mass, which then sinks or collapses. This is called *the first sponge,* and from it the bread may be made; but the fermentation is often allowed to proceed, and the rising and falling to go on a second time, producing what the bakers call *the second sponge.*

The next process is called *breaking the sponge,* and consists in adding to it the requisite quantity of water and salt, the sponge being thoroughly mixed up with the water. The remainder of the total quantity of flour intended to be employed is gradually added, and the whole is kneaded into a dough of the due consistency. The dough, being allowed to remain in the trough till it rise or *give proof,* is then weighed off into lumps, which are shaped into loaves and placed in the oven. In the process of baking they swell to about double their original size.

The chemical changes which have been taking place during this process may be explained in the following way: An average quality of flour consists of gluten 12 parts, starch 70, sugar 5, gum 3, water 10; total, 100. When water is added to the flour, in the first operation of baking, it unites with the gluten and starch, and dissolves the gum and sugar. The yeast or barm added acts now upon the dissolved sugar, especially at an elevated temperature, and produces the vinous fermentation, forming alcohol and setting free carbonic acid as a consequence of the transformation of the elements of the sugar. The gaseous carbonic acid is prevented from escaping by the gluten of the mass, and if the mixing or kneading has been properly performed it remains very equally diffused through every part of the dough. The alcohol and carbonic acid are carried into the oven with the dough, and the former partially escapes, while the latter gas, being expanded by the heat, produces the lightness and sponginess of the loaf. It may be produced in bread-making by other means than fermentation, as by some of those well-known preparations called "baking powders," which usually contain bicarbonate of potash or of soda, with tartaric acid.

In the country districts of France and Switzerland leaven is made by saving a little of the dough used in baking, mixing it with flour and water added in several portions, and then allowing it to stand so as to encourage fermentation. Leavened bread is considered by some as more healthful than yeast-bread, because the acids it contains help digestion.

Aerated Bread. So called because made with aerated water—that is, water strongly impregnated with carbonic acid under pressure, the dough being also worked up under pressure and caused to expand by the carbonic acid when the pressure is removed.

The several qualities of flour used for bread-making are known by the names of *firsts* or *whites, seconds* or *households,* and *thirds,* according to the degree of fineness resulting from the process of bolting or dressing. The last two contain a certain proportion of the bran. *Brown* or *whole-flour* bread is considered to be very wholesome. It is made from undressed wheat, and consequently contains the bran as well as the flour.

Various adulterations are found in bread, such as chalk, starch, potatoes, etc.; but the commonest is alum, which enables the baker to give to bread of inferior flavour the whiteness of the best bread, and also to keep in the loaf an undue quantity of water, which, of course, increases its weight. Boiled rice is also used for the same purpose. In Britain bakers adulterating bread are liable to a penalty of not more than £10 and not less than £5 for every offence, and to have their names advertised in the newspapers. In the making of bread the flour or meal of wheat, barley, rye, oats, buckwheat, Indian corn, rice, beans, pease, and potatoes may be used, along with salt, eggs, water, milk, and leaven or yeast of any kind; but any other ingredient is regarded as an adulteration.

All bread except French or fancy bread and rolls must be sold by weight (avoirdupois), and bakers must provide a beam and scales with weights for the purpose of weighing it if required. Bread made wholly or partially of any other flour or grain than that of wheat must be stamped with the letter M. The penalty of adulterating flour or meal is not more than £20 nor less than £5.—BIBLIOGRAPHY: Jago, *The Science and Art of Bread-making*; Boutroux, *Le Pain et la Panification*; Rorer, *Bread and Bread-making*.

BREADAL'BANE. A Highland district in the western part of Perthshire, in the centre of the Grampians. The Marquess of Breadalbane, head of a branch of the Campbell family, is the chief proprietor, and takes his title from it.

BREAD-FRUIT. A large globular fruit of a pale-green colour, about the size of a child's head, marked on the surface with irregular six-sided depressions, and containing a white and somewhat fibrous pulp, which when ripe becomes juicy and yellow. The tree that produces it (*Artocarpus incisa*) belongs to the ord. Moraceæ (nearly allied to the Urticaceæ or nettle tribe), and grows wild in Otaheite and other islands of the South Seas, whence it was introduced into the West Indies and S. America. It is about 40 feet high, with large and spreading branches, and has large bright-green leaves deeply divided into seven or nine spear-shaped lobes.

The fruit is generally eaten immediately after being gathered, but is also often prepared so as to keep for some time either by baking it whole in close underground pits or by beating it into paste and storing it underground, when a slight fermentation takes place. The eatable part lies between the skin and the core, and is somewhat of the consistence of new bread. Mixed with coco-nut milk it makes an excellent pudding. The inner bark of the tree is made into a kind of cloth. The wood is used for the building of boats and for furniture. The jack (*Artocarpus integrifolia*), much used in India and Ceylon, is another member of this genus.

BREAD-NUTS. The seeds of the *Brosimum Alicastrum*, a tree of the same order as the bread-fruit. The bread-nut tree is a native of Jamaica. Its wood, which resembles mahogany, is useful to cabinet-makers, and its nuts make a pleasant food, in taste not unlike hazel-nuts.

BREAD-ROOT, or **PRAIRIE TURNIP** (*Psoralĕa esculenta*). A leguminous plant of the United States, with edible farinaceous tubers.

BREAD-TREE. *See* KAFFIR-BREAD.

BREAK, or **BRAKE.** A large four-wheeled vehicle with a straight body and a raised seat in front for the driver, and containing seats for six, eight, or more persons.

BREAKING BULK. The act of beginning to unlade a ship, or of discharging the first part of the cargo.

BREAK'WATER. A work constructed in front of a harbour to serve as a protection against the violence of the waves. The name may also be given to any structure which is erected in the sea with the object of breaking the force of the waves without and producing a calm within. Breakwaters are usually constructed by sinking loads of unwrought stone along the line where they are to be laid, and allowing them to find their angle of repose under the action of the waves. When the mass rises to the surface, or near it, it is surmounted with a pile of masonry, sloped outwards in such a manner as will best enable it to resist the action of the waves. The great breakwaters are those of Cherbourg and Marseilles in France, Plymouth, Portland, and Holyhead in Great Britain, Alexandria in Egypt, and Delaware Bay in N. America.

In less important localities floating breakwaters are occasionally used. These are built of strong open woodwork, partly above and partly under water, divided into several sections, and secured by chains attached to fixed bodies. The breakers lose nearly all their force in passing through the beams of such a structure. A breakwater of this kind may last for twenty-

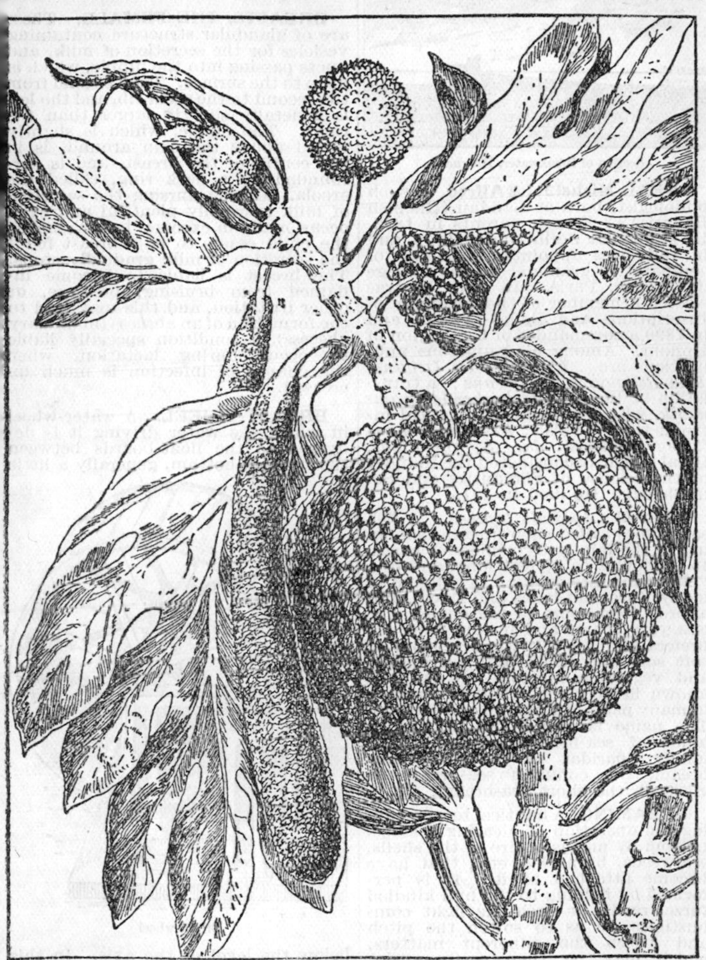

Fruit and Foliage of Bread-fruit Tree (*Artocarpus incisa*)

five years. — BIBLIOGRAPHY: Cunningham, *Harbour Engineering*; De Cardemoy, *Les Ports modernes*.

Section of Breakwater, Holyhead

BRÉAL, Michel Jules Alfred. French philologist, born at Landau (Rhenish Bavaria) of French parents in 1832. He studied at Berlin under Bopp, and in 1864 was appointed professor of comparative grammar at the Collège de France, Paris. In 1875 he was elected a member of the Academy of Inscriptions and Belles-Lettres, and in 1890 a commander of the Legion of Honour. Among his numerous publications are: *L'Etudes des Origines de la Religion Zoroastrienne*; a translation of Bopp's *Vergleichende Grammatik*, with historical and critical introductions (5 vols.); *Essai de Sémantique: Science des Significations.* Bréal is rightly considered the founder of the science of Semantics and Semasiology. He died in 1915.

BREAM (*Abrămis brama*). A fish sometimes called carp-bream, belonging to the family Cyprinidæ or carps. It is about 2 to 2½ feet long, and of a yellowish-white colour. It is found in many European lakes and rivers, and affords good sport to the angler, but is a very coarse and insipid food. It prefers still water with a bottom of soft soil, and feeds both on animal and vegetable matter. It is little known in Scotland, though common in many parts of England and Ireland. The name is also given to various kinds of sea-fishes, mostly of the family Sparidæ, as the black sea-bream, the common sea-bream or gilthead, the short sea-bream, etc.

BREAMING. A nautical term meaning the operation of clearing a ship's bottom by means of fire of the shells, sea-weeds, barnacles, etc., that have become attached to it. It is performed by holding to the hull kindled furze, reeds, or such-like light combustibles, so as to soften the pitch and loosen the adherent matters, which may be then easily swept off.

BREASTPLATE. A piece of defensive armour covering the breast, made of leather, brass, iron, steel, or other metals. Among the ancient Jews the name was given to a folded piece of rich, embroidered stuff worn by the high-priest. It was set with twelve precious stones bearing the names of the tribes.

BREASTS, THE FEMALE. These are of glandular structure containing vesicles for the secretion of milk, and ducts passing into the nipple, which is open to the surface. They extend from the second to the sixth rib, and the left is generally slightly larger than the right. The nipple, which is slightly raised above the skin around, is in the centre of the breast, and is surrounded by a dark ring, called the areola. During nursing the secretion of milk is usually plentiful and even occasionally in excess; but whenever the child ceases to be "breast fed" the secretion of milk gradually stops. The breast is liable to become inflamed from bruising, pressure, or other irritation, and this may lead to the formation of an abscess (mammary abscess), a condition specially liable to occur during lactation, when the chance of infection is much increased.

BREAST-WHEEL. A water-wheel in which the water driving it is delivered to the float-boards between the top and bottom, generally a little

Breast-wheel

below the level of the axis. In this kind of wheel the water acts partly by impulse, partly by weight.

BREASTWORK. A fieldwork, usually made of earth, built up for protection. Many of the so-called "trenches," especially in the wet parts of Flanders, were actually breastworks.

BREATH. The air which issues from the lungs during respiration through the mouth and nose. This expired air contains less oxygen than the air taken in during respiration (inspired air), and a very much larger proportion of carbonic acid gas (carbon dioxide), and also a larger amount of aqueous vapour. Further, it contains a varying amount of other substances owing their origin to secretions in the mouth, nose, throat, and lungs. These may be present as a result of disease, causing the breath to be offensive ("bad breath"), as from ulcers in the nose, carious teeth, septic infections of the mouth, throat, or lungs. Frequent mouth-washes and gargles should be used for the minor mouth and throat troubles, and further treatment according to the site of the disease.

BREATHING. *See* RESPIRATION.

BRECCIA (brech'i-a). A rocky mass composed of angular fragments of the same rock or of different rocks united by a matrix or cement. Sometimes a few of the fragments are a little rounded; but an aggregate of rounded stones is styled conglomerate. *Osseous breccia* is, as its name implies, a mass of fragmental bones in a cement, which is often rich in calcium phosphate. Many breccias, such as the limestone examples from the Alps, which are used with striking effect as ornamental marbles, result from fracturing processes during the stress of mountain-building.

BRÈCHE-DE-ROLAND (brāsh-dė-rō-lāṉ). That is, "the breach of Roland," a mountain pass in the Pyrenees, between France and Spain, which, according to a well-known legend, was opened up by Roland, one of the paladins of Charlemagne, with one blow of his sword Durandal, in order to afford a passage to his army. It is an immense gap in the rocky mountain barrier 43 miles to the north of Huesca.

BRECHIN (brē'*h*in). A royal, municipal, and police burgh of Scotland, in Forfarshire, finely situated on the South Esk. It has considerable linen manufactures, two distilleries, a paper-mill, etc. It is an old town; was the seat of a Culdee college, and from the twelfth century that of a bishop. There is a cathedral dating back to the thirteenth century, and now the parish church, and near it is the tall round tower which, with the exception of the one at Abernethy, is the only example of this kind of structure in Scotland. Almost in the town, and overlooking the river, stands Brechin Castle, the ancient seat of the Maules of Panmure (Earls of Dalhousie). Pop. (1931), 6838.

BRECKLAND. District near Thetford, Norfolk. After the Great War the land was bought by the State and trees were planted, thus making it into a large forest which is supervised by the Forestry Commission.

BREC'ON, or BRECK'NOCK. A county of South Wales; area, 744 sq. miles; pop. (1931), 57,771. It is mountainous, and is watered by the Wye, the Usk, the Taf, etc. Though rugged in its surface, nearly half of it is under cultivation or in pasture; and wool, butter, and cattle are sent into the English markets. There are extensive ironworks in the S.E., but it contains only a small part of the coal-field which extends into the adjacent counties of Monmouth and Glamorgan. Half the inhabitants still speak Welsh. Since 1918 Brecon unites with Radnor in returning one member to Parliament.

Brecon, or Brecknock. The capital of the above county, previous to 1885 a parliamentary borough, stands near its centre, in an open valley at the confluence of the Honddu and Usk, and in the midst of the grandest scenery of South Wales. The chief trade is in connection with agriculture and the manufacture of iron. Mrs. Siddons and Charles Kemble were natives of Brecon. Pop. (1931), 5334.

BREDA (brā-dä'). A town in Holland, province of North Brabant, at the confluence of the Merk and the Aa. Breda was once a strong fortress and of great military importance as a strategical position. From the sixteenth to the end of the eighteenth century Breda has an interesting military history of sieges, assaults, and captures, with which the names of the most famous generals of their time, the Duke of Parma, Maurice of Orange, the Marquis Spinola, Dumouriez, and Pichegru, are connected. It was the residence for a time of the exiled Charles II. of England, and it was in the Declaration of Breda that he promised liberty of conscience, a general amnesty, etc., on his restoration. Pop. 44,868.

BREE (brā), **Matthæus Ignazius van.** A Flemish painter, born 1773, died 1839. He painted the *Death of Cato*, and other classical subjects, as well as scenes pertaining to modern history, especially the grand picture representing Van der Werff, Burgomaster of Leyden, addressing the famishing populace in 1576, and telling them that they might share his body among them.

BREECH, BREECH-LOADING. All modern guns and fire-arms, with the exception of certain forms of mortars, are breech-loading, i.e. the cartridge is inserted into the cartridge-chamber at the breech end of the arm instead of being forced down the barrel from the muzzle by means of a ramrod. In muzzle-loading days the breech was a solid mass of metal designed to receive the shock of discharge consequent on the ignition of the powder through the touch-hole or vent. (Guns were "spiked" and rendered temporarily useless by hammering a nail into this hole in the breech.) The introduction of rifling made some sort of breech-loading essential, as it was found impossible to get satisfactory results from forcing a bullet down a rifled barrel. This fact led to many attempts being made to solve the problem, which was considerably complicated by the difficulty of preventing the escape of gas and flame from the breech; and it was finally recognised that no breech action for small arms would be entirely satisfactory unless a fixed cartridge with a metal or non-inflammable case were used.

In the first half of the nineteenth century the Germans invented the needle-gun—a breech-loading arm on the bolt principle. In our army the first breech-loader—the Snider—was introduced in 1867. In this weapon the breech was operated by a block hinged to the right of the barrel. This was followed in 1871 by the Martini-Henry on the falling-block and lever system; with this rifle brass cartridge-cases were also used. Finally we accepted the bolt system of the Lee-Metford, which, with improvements, is the system now in use.

Breech actions for guns of all calibres are necessarily more complicated. They are of various patterns, among them being those known as the "interrupted screw," the "eccentric screw," and the "wedge." The first works as a single-motion swinging block, the second with a half turn which exposes or covers the cartridge-chamber, and the last slides in a slot.

BREECHES. An article of clothing for the legs and lower part of the body in use among the Babylonians and other ancient peoples as well as among the moderns. In Europe we find them first used among the Gauls; hence the Romans called a part of Gaul *breeched Gaul* (*Gallia braccāta*).

BREECHING. A rope used to secure a ship's gun and prevent it from recoiling too much in battle.

BREEDE (brā'de). A river in the south-west of Cape Province, entering the sea at Port Beaufort, and navigable for a few miles.

BREEDING. The art of improving races or *breeds* of domestic animals or modifying them in certain directions, by continuous attention to their pairing, in conjunction with a similar attention to their feeding and general treatment. Animals (and plants no less) show great susceptibility of modification under systematic cultivation; and there can be no doubt that by such cultivation the sum of desirable qualities in particular races has been greatly increased, and that in two ways.

Individual specimens are produced possessing more good qualities than can be found in any one specimen of the original stock; and from the same stock many varieties are taken characterized by different perfections, the germs of all of which may have been in the original stock but could not have been simultaneously developed in a single specimen. But when an effort is made to develop rapidly, or to its extreme limit, any particular quality, it is always made at the expense of some other quality, or of other qualities generally, by which the intrinsic value of the result is necessarily affected. High speed in horses, for example, is only attained at the expense of a sacrifice of strength and power of endurance. So the celebrated merino sheep are the result of a system of breeding which reduces the general size and vigour of the animal, and diminishes the value of the carcass. Much care and judgment, therefore, are needed in breeding, not only in order to produce a particular effect, but also to produce it with the least sacrifice of other qualities.

Breeding, as a means of improving domestic animals, has been practised more or less systematically wherever any attention has been paid to the care of live stock, and nowhere have more satisfactory results been obtained than in Britain. One of the earliest improvers in Britain was Robert Bakewell, of Dishley, in Leicestershire, who commenced his experiments about 1745, and was very successful, especially with sheep, the celebrated Dishley breed of Leicestershire sheep having since maintained a high reputation. Quantity of meat, smallness of bone, lightness of offal; in cows, yield and quality of milk; in sheep, weight of fleece and fineness of wool, have all been studied with remarkable effects by modern breeders.

Plant-breeding is now extensively practised for a great variety of species. Crossing was first introduced (for wheat) by Knight, late in the eighteenth century, while Shirreff in 1819 initiated the method of selection. In recent years Biffen and others have applied Mendelian principles with much success. *See* ATAVISM, HEREDITY, MENDELISM.—BIBLIOGRAPHY: Darwin, *Variations of Plants and Animals under Domestication*; Wilson, *Principles of Stockbreeding*.

BREEZE, or **BREEZE-FLY.** *See* GADFLY.

BREEZES, SEA AND LAND. *See* WIND.

BREGENZ (brā'gents). Chief town of Vorarlberg, Austria, 77 miles W. by N. of Innsbruck, beautifully situated on a slope which rises from the Lake of Constance. It is the ancient *Brigantium*, and was once of importance as a fortified place. Pop. 7750; district, 34,743.

BRE'HONS. Ancient magistrates among the Irish. It is derived from the Irish word *Breitheamh*, which means a judge. They were hereditary, had lands assigned for their maintenance, and administered justice to their respective tribes—each tribe had one brehon—seated in the open air upon some hill or eminence.

Brehon law was reduced to writing at a very early period, as is evident from the antiquity of the language in which it is written, and in the earliest manuscripts we find allusions to a revision of it said to have been made in the fifth century by St. Patrick and other learned men, who are said to have expunged from it the traces of heathenism, and formed it into a code called the *Senchus Mor*, or *Great Immemorial Custom*. Another volume contains the document known as the *Book of Aicill*, which is a compilation of the dicta and judgments of King Cormac Mac Airt and of the famous warrior and renowned jurist Cennfaeladh who lived in the seventh century.

The Brehon law was exclusively in force in Ireland until the year 1170. It was finally abolished by James I. in 1605. The Brehon Law Commission, appointed in 1852, published 6 vols. of the *Ancient Laws of Ireland* (1865-1901).

BREISACH. A small but ancient town of Southern Germany, on the Rhine, in Baden, formerly a free imperial city, and a fortress of importance down to the middle of the eighteenth century, being frequently besieged. It is often called Old Breisach, in opposition to New Breisach, a fortress on the opposite side of the river, in Alsace. Pop. 3130.

BREISGAU (brīs'gou). One of the most fertile and picturesque districts of Germany, in the south of Baden, in the Rhine valley, containing part of the Black Forest. Chief town, Freiburg.

BREITENFELD (brī'tn-felt). A village in Saxony, 5½ miles N. of Leipzig, notable as the scene of two battles of the Thirty Years' War, the first gained by Gustavus Adolphus over Tilly and Pappenheim in 1631; the second by the Swedish general Torstenson over the Imperialists commanded by Archduke Leopold and Piccolomini in 1642.

BREMEN. State of Germany. It includes the city of Bremen, the port of Bremerhaven, and some other districts, altogether covering 99 sq. miles. It belongs to the German republic, and before 1918 was a state of the German Empire. Its affairs are managed by a Senate of 12 members, two of whom are burgomasters. They are chosen by the House of Burgesses, which has 120 members elected by all citizens. Pop. 338,846.

BREMEN (brā'men). A free city of Germany, capital of the State of Bremen, one of the three Hanse towns, on the Weser, about 46 miles from its mouth, in its own small territory of 99 sq. miles, besides which it possesses the port of Bremerhaven at the mouth of the river. The town is partly on the right, partly on the left bank of the Weser, the larger portion being on the former. Here is the old and business section of the town, the streets of which are narrow and crooked, and lined with antique houses, and which contains the cathedral, founded about 1050, the old Gothic council house, with the famous wine-cellar below it, the town hall, the merchants' house, and the old and the new exchange. The Vorstadt, or suburbs lying on the right bank outside the ramparts of the old town, are now very extensive. The manufacturing establishments consist of tobacco and cigar factories, sugar-refineries, rice-mills, iron-foundries, machine-works, rope and sail works, and shipbuilding yards.

Its situation renders Bremen the emporium for Hanover, Brunswick, Hesse, and other countries traversed by the Weser, and next to Hamburg it is the principal seat of the export and import and emigration trade of Germany. Vessels drawing 17½ feet can now come up to the town itself; but the bulk of the shipping trade centres in Bremerhaven. It has docks capable of receiving the largest vessels, and is connected by railway with Bremen, where the chief merchants and brokers have their offices.

The chief imports are tobacco, cotton and cotton goods, wool and woollen goods, rice, coffee, grain, petroleum, etc., which are chiefly re-exported to other parts of Germany and the Continent. After Hamburg Bremen is the greatest port for the international trade of Germany. Pop. (1925), (state) 338,846; (town) 294,966.

History. Bremen was made a bishopric by Charlemagne about 788, was afterwards made an archbishopric, and by the end of the fourteenth century had become virtually a free imperial city. The constitution is republican. Up to Nov., 1918, the State and free city of Bremen formed a republic, governed by a Senate of sixteen members, chosen for life, forming the executive, and the Burgerschaft (or Convent of Burgesses) of 150 members, invested with the power of legislation. The Convent was elected for six years.

With the outbreak of the German Revolution, in Nov., 1918, Bremen became a more democratic republic. The Senate and the Convent were abolished, and the Workers' and Soldiers' Council took over the government. By the constitution of 1920, however, the Burgerschaft was re-established. It elects a Senate of 14 members from whom two Burgermeister are elected.

BREMEN. Name of a German liner launched in 1928 by the North German Lloyd Co. In July, 1929, it made a record passage across the Atlantic, Europe to New York, which stood as a record until beaten by the *Europa* in 1930. The ship displaces 49,800 tons. Another *Bremen* was a German cruiser that was sunk in the Baltic by a British submarine in Dec., 1915.

BREMER (brā'mer), **Frederika.** A Swedish novelist, born near Åbo, in Finland, in 1802, died 1865. She early visited Paris, and at subsequent periods of her life, up to 1861, she travelled in America, England, Switzerland, Italy, Turkey, Greece, and Palestine. She also resided for some time in Norway. She wrote an account of her travels; but her fame chiefly rests on her novels, which were translated into German and French, and into English by Mary Howitt. Among the chief of these are: *Neighbours, The President's Daughters, Nina,* and *Strife and Peace.*

BRENDON HILLS. Range of limestone hills in Somerset. They are about 6 miles south of Watchet and attain a height of about 1400 feet.

BREMERHAVEN (brā'mer-hä-vn). *See* BREMEN.

BRENNER. A mountain in the Tirolese Alps between Innsbruck and Botzen; height, 6777 feet. The road from Germany to Italy, traversing this mountain, reaches the elevation of 4495 feet, and is one of the lowest roads practicable for carriages over the main chain of the Alps. A railway through this route was opened in 1867.

BRENNUS. The name or title of several princes of the ancient Gauls, of whom the most famous was the leader of the Senones, who invaded the Roman territory about the year 390 B.C. He conquered Etruria from Ravenna to Picenum, besieged Clusium, defeated the Romans near the Allia, sacked Rome, and besieged the capitol for six months, but ultimately retired on payment of a large amount of gold.

Connected with this invasion are the well-known stories of the massacre of about eighty venerable Senators who awaited the Gauls in their chairs of office in the Forum; of the salvation of the capitol by the cackling of geese; and of the throwing of the sword of Brennus into the scales when the Romans complained that the weights used by the Gauls were false. According to Polybius, the Gauls returned home in safety with their booty; but according to Livy, Brennus was disastrously defeated by Camillus, a distinguished Roman exile, who arrived with succour in time to save the capitol.

BRENTA. A river in North Italy, falling, after a winding course of 112 miles, into the Adriatic. Formerly its mouth was at Fusina, opposite Venice; but a new course was made for it.

BREN'TANO, Clemens. A German poet and romancer, born in 1778, died in 1842. He studied at Jena, and resided successively at Frankfort, Heidelberg, Vienna, and Berlin. In 1818 he retired to the convent of Dülmen, in Münster, and the latter years of his eccentric life were spent at Ratisbon, Munich, and Frankfort-on-the-Main. He had a powerful imagination, and his works display an elaborate satirical humour, but a curious vein of mysticism and misanthropy runs through them. He was the brother of Elizabeth von Arnim, Goethe's "Bettina."

Among his principal works are: *Satires and Poetical Fancies* (1800); *The Mother's Statue* (1801); *The Joyous Musicians*, drama (1803); *Ponce de Léon*, drama (1804); *The Foundling of Prague*, drama (1816); *History of the Brave Caspar and the Fair Annerl*, an admirable novelette (1817); and *Gokel, Hinkel, und Gakeleia* (1838), a satire on the times. *Die Romanzen vom Rosenkranz* (Romances of the Rosary) was published posthumously in 1852. He was also the author of a work (*Nachtwachen des Bonaventura*) long attributed to Schelling.

BRENTFORD, Viscount. English politician. William Hicks, a son of Henry Hicks, was born in Kent, 23rd June, 1865. He became a solicitor and, having married the daughter of R. H. Joynson of Bowdon, took the name of Joynson-Hicks. As a Conservative in 1908 he defeated Mr. Winston Churchill at N. W. Manchester, lost his seat in 1910, was returned for Brentford in 1911, and represented Twickenham from 1918 till his elevation to the peerage.

In the Lloyd-George administration (1918-20) he was Parliamentary Secretary to the Overseas Trade Department, and was created a baronet in 1919. In the first Baldwin administration (1922-3) he was successively Postmaster-General, Financial Secretary to the Treasury, and Minister of Health. Throughout the second Baldwin ministry (1924-9) he was Home Secretary, and on going out of office was raised to the peerage as Viscount Brentford of Newick. As a recognised lay leader of the evangelical party in the Church of England, Joynson-Hicks was instrumental in procuring the rejection by Parliament of the revised Prayer Book. He died 8th June, 1932.

BRENT'FORD AND CHISWICK. An urban district of Middlesex, England, 7 miles W. of London, with saw-mills, pottery-works, foundries, etc. Here Edmund Ironside defeated Canute in 1016; and Prince Rupert defeated Colonel Hollis in 1642. Pop. (1931), 62,617. Brentford and Chiswick forms a parliamentary division of the county.

BRENT GOOSE (*Bernicla Brenta*). A wild goose, smaller than the common barnacle goose and of much darker plumage, remarkable for length of wing and extent of migratory power, being a winter bird of passage in France, Germany, Holland, Great Britain, the United States, Canada, etc. It breeds in high northern latitudes; it feeds on drifting seaweeds and saline plants, and is considered the most delicate for the table of all the goose tribe.

BRENTWOOD. A market town and urban district of England, in Essex, 11 miles south-west of Chelmsford, with training, industrial, and other schools, and the county lunatic asylum. Pop. (1931), 7209.

BRESCIA (brā'shi-à; Lat. *Brixia*). A city of North Italy, capital of the province of the same name; it is beautifully situated at the foot of the Alps, and is of a quadrilateral form, about 4 miles in circuit. Its public buildings, particularly its churches, are remarkable for the number and value of their frescoes and pictures. Among its chief edifices are the new cathedral, a handsome structure of white marble, begun in 1604, the Rotonda, or old cathedral, the town hall (La Loggia), and the Broletto, or courts. The city contains a museum of antiquities, picture-gallery, botanic garden, a fine public library, a theatre, hospital, etc. An aqueduct supplies water to its numerous fountains.

Near the town are large ironworks, and its fire-arms are esteemed the best that are made in Italy. It has also silk, linen, and paper factories, tan-yards, and oil-mills, and is an important mart for raw silk. Brescia was the seat of a school of painting of great merit, including Alessandro Bonvicino, commonly called "Il Moretto," who flourished in the sixteenth century.

History. The city was originally the chief town of the Cenomanni, and became the seat of a Roman colony under Augustus about 15 B.C. It was burned by the Goths in 412, was again destroyed by Attila, was taken by Charlemagne in 774, and was declared a free city by Otho I. of Saxony in 936. In 1426 it put itself under the protection of Venice. In 1796 it was taken by the French, and was assigned to Austria by the Vienna Treaty of 1815. In 1849 its streets were barricaded by insurgents, but were carried by the Austrians under General Haynau. It was ceded to Sardinia by the Treaty of Zürich, 1859. Pop. 118,861. The province has an area of 1645 sq. miles; pop. 660,198.

BRESLAU (bres'lou). An important city in Germany, the third largest in the Prussian dominions (Berlin and Cologne have larger populations), is the capital of the province of Silesia, and is situated on both sides of the Oder. The public squares and buildings are handsome, and the fortifications have been converted into fine promenades. The cathedral, built in the twelfth century, and the Rathhaus, or town hall, a Gothic structure of about the fourteenth century, are among the most remarkable buildings. There is a flourishing university, founded in 1702 and extended in 1810, with a museum, library of 400,000 volumes, observatory, etc.

Breslau has manufactures of machinery, railway carriages, furniture, and cabinet ware, cigars, spirits and liqueurs, cotton and woollen yarn, musical instruments, porcelain, glass, etc., and carries on an extensive trade. Breslau was the seat of a bishop by the year 1000; an independent duchy from 1163 to 1335; then belonged to Bohemia; and was ceded to Austria in 1527. In 1741 it was conquered by Frederick II. of Prussia. Pop. 599,770.

BRES'SAY. One of the Shetland Isles, E. of Mainland, from which it is separated by Bressay Sound, about 6 miles long and 1½ in breadth. Its line of coast is rocky and deeply indented; its interior is hilly and largely covered with peat-moss. Sea-fishing is the principal occupation, kelp and hosiery are manufactured, and quarries of slate are wrought. Pop. (1931), 583.

BREST. A seaport in the N.W. of France, department of Finistère. It has one of the best harbours in France, and is the chief French naval base, having safe roads capable of containing 500 men-of-war in from 8 to 15 fathoms at low water. The entrance is narrow and rocky, and the coast on both sides is well fortified. The design to make it a naval arsenal originated with Richelieu, and was carried out by Duquesne and Vauban in the reign of Louis XIV., with the result that the town was made almost impregnable.

Brest stands on the summit and sides of a projecting ridge, many of the streets being exceedingly steep. Several of the docks have been cut out of the solid rock, and a breakwater extends far into the roadstead. The manufactures of Brest are inconsiderable, but it has an extensive trade in cereals, wine, brandy, sardines, mackerel, and colonial goods. It is connected with America by a cable terminating near Duxbury, Massachusetts. The English and Dutch were repulsed at Brest in 1694. In 1794 it was blockaded by Howe, who won a great victory off the coast over the French. Pop. (1926), 69,481.

BREST-LITOVSK. A fortified town of Poland, on the Bug, formerly belonging to Russia, province of Grodno, an important railway centre, and with a large trade. Two fairs are held annually. The fortress was captured by the Germans on 25th Aug., 1915. Pop. 54,000. The peace of Brest-Litovsk, between the Bolshevik Government and Germany, was signed 3rd March, 1918. *See* EUROPEAN WAR.

BREST-SUMMER, BREAST-SUMMER, or **BRESSOMER.** In building, a beam or summer placed horizontally to support an upper wall or partition, as the beam over shop windows; a lintel.

BRETAGNE (brė - tȧn - yė). *See* BRITTANY.

BRETÈCHE, or **BRETESCHE** (bre-tesh'). A name common to several wooden, crenellated, and roofed erections, used in the Middle Ages in sieges by the assailants to afford protection while they were undermining the walls, and by the besieged to form defences behind breaches. Later, the name was given to a sort of roofed wooden balcony or cage, crenellated and machicolated, attached by corbels, sometimes immediately over a gateway.

BRETIGNY (brė-tēn-yē). A village of France, department of Eure-et-Loire. By the Treaty of Bretigny (8th of May, 1360), between Edward III. of England and John II. of France, the latter, who had been taken prisoner at Poitiers, recovered his liberty for a ransom of 3,000,000 crowns, while Edward renounced his claim to the crown of France, and relinquished Anjou and Maine, and the greater part of Normandy, in return for Aquitaine, Gascony, Poitou, Saintonge, Périgord, Limousin, etc.

BRETON (brė-tōn̦), **Jules.** French painter, born in 1827, died 1905; studied at Ghent, Antwerp, and Paris, and made his mark chiefly as a painter of rustic life, including rural and religious festivals. He was elected a member of the Institute in 1866, was made commander of the Legion of Honour in 1889, and chosen a foreign member of the Royal Academy in 1899. Among his works are: *Return of the Harvesters* (1853), *Women Gleaning, Blessing the Fields, The Return of the Gleaners, The Close of Day, Potato Gatherers, Washerwomen on the Breton Coast, The Song of the Lark*, etc. He published poems and an autobiographic work —*La Vie d'un Artiste*.

BRETON. Language of Lower Brittany. A Celtic language, allied to Cornish and Welsh, it is one of the Indo-European group. Because of its regularity of grammar and idiomatic structure, it is not a patois. Breton literature is best exemplified in the old ballads of the story-tellers, for until comparatively recent times, French was the aristocratic and Breton the popular language. The recent growth of national feeling has done much to arouse a literary interest in Breton.

BRETON DE LOS HERREROS (bre-ton' de los er-er'ōs), **Don Manuel.** A popular Spanish poet, born in 1796, died in 1873. He furnished the Spanish stage with more than 300 pieces, original and adapted, besides writing lyrical and satirical poems, etc.

BRET'ONS. The inhabitants of Brittany.

BRETTS AND SCOTS, LAWS OF. The name given in the thirteenth century to a code of laws in use among the Celtic tribes in Scotland, the Scots being the Celts north of the Forth and Clyde, and the Bretts being the remains of the British inhabitants of the kingdom of Cambria, Cumbria, or Strathclyde, and Reged. Edward I. issued in 1305 an ordinance abolishing the usages of the Scots and Bretts. Only a fragment of them has been preserved.

BRETWAL'DA. A title applied to one of the Anglo-Saxon tribe-chiefs or kings, who it is supposed was from time to time chosen by the other chiefs, nobility, and ealdormen to be a sort of dictator in their wars with the Britons.

BREUGHEL (brœu'hel). The name of a celebrated Dutch family of painters, the first of whom adopted this name from a village not far from Breda. This was Pieter Breughel, born 1525 or 1530, died 1569 or 1590, also called, from the character and subject of most of his representations, the Droll or the Peasants' Breughel. He left two sons—Pieter and Jan. The former (1564-1637) is commonly known as the Younger Breughel, though he also obtained the name of Hell Breughel, from the many scenes painted by him in which devils and witches appear. His *Orpheus playing on his Lyre before the Infernal Deities*, and *Temptation of St. Anthony*, are specially noteworthy in the history of grotesque art. The former picture hangs in the gallery of Florence.

The second son, Jan (1568-1625 or 1642), known as Velvet Breughel, or Flower Breughel, was distinguished for his landscapes and small figures. He also painted in co-operation with other masters, his *Four Elements* and other pictures being the joint work of Rubens and himself. Later, members of this family are Ambrose, director of the Antwerp Academy of Painting between 1635 and 1670; Abraham, who for a time resided in Italy, and died in 1690; the brother of the latter, John Baptist, who died in Rome; and Abraham's son, Caspar Breughel, known as a painter of flowers and fruits.

BREVE (brēv). In music, a note formerly square, as |⊏⊐|; but now of an oval shape, with a line perpendicular to the stave on each of its sides: |⊖|. For nearly two centuries it was the musical unit of duration, but has since been supplanted by the semibreve, the breve being of comparatively rare occurrence.

BREV'ET. In Britain and the United States applied to a commission to an officer, giving him higher nominal rank than that for which he receives pay. In the British army brevet rank is only conferred upon Field Officers.

BREV'IARY. The book which contains prayers or offices to be used at the seven canonical hours of matins, prime, tierce, sext, nones, vespers, and compline by all in the orders of the Church of Rome or in the enjoyment of any Roman Catholic benefice. It is not known at what time the use of the Breviary was first enjoined, but the early offices were exhaustive from their great length, and under Gregory VII. (1073-85) their abridgment was considered necessary, hence the origin of the Breviary (Lat. *brevis*, short). In 1568 Pius V. published that which has remained, with few modifications, to the present day. The Roman Breviary, however, was never fully accepted by the Gallican Church until after the strenuous efforts made by the Ultramontanes from 1840 to 1864.

The Psalms occupy a large place in the Breviary; passages from the Old and New Testament and from the fathers have the next place. All the services are in Latin, and their arrangement is very complex. In 1902 Pope Leo XIII. appointed a commission to study historico-liturgical questions and to consider the Breviary, the Missal, the Pontifical, and the Ritual. The English *Book of Common Prayer* is based on the Roman Breviary.

BREVIER. *See* TYPE.

BREWING. The process of extracting a saccharine solution from malted grain and converting the solution into a fermented and sound alchoholic beverage called *ale* or *beer*. The preliminary process of *malting* (often a distinct business from that of brewing) consists in promoting the germination of the grain for the sake of the saccharine matter into which the starch of the seed is thus converted. The barley or other grain is steeped for about two days in a cistern and then piled in a heap, or *couch*, which is turned and re-turned until the radicle or root, and acrospire or rudimentary stem, have uniformly developed to some little extent in all the heap of grain. The wort diminishes in density owing to its fermentation; this diminution is technically known as *attenuation*. This treatment lasts from seven to ten days, by which time the grain has acquired a sweet taste, the life of the grain being then destroyed by spreading the whole upon the floor of a kiln to be thoroughly dried.

At this point begins the brewing process proper, which in breweries is generally as follows: The malt is crushed or roughly ground in a malt-mill, whence it is carried to the mashing-machine, and there thoroughly mixed with hot water. The mixture is now received by the mash-tun—a cylindrical vessel with a false perforated bottom held about an inch from the true one. In the mash-tun the useful elements are extracted from the malt in the form of the sweet liquor known as wort, and the tun, therefore, is fitted with an elaborate system of revolving rakes for thoroughly mixing the malt with hot water. The mixing completed, the mash-tun is covered up and allowed to stand for about three hours, when the taps in the true bottom are opened and the wort or malt extract run off. The wort being drained into a copper, the hops are now added, and the whole is boiled for about two hours, the boiling, like the addition of hops, tending to prevent acetous and putrefactive fermentation.

When sufficiently boiled, the contents of the copper are run into the hop-back—a long, rectangular vessel with a false bottom 8 or 9 inches from the true bottom. The hot wort, leaving the spent hops in the hop-back, runs through the perforations in the false bottom and thence into the cooler—a large flat vessel—where the worts are cooled to about 100° F. From the cooler the liquor is admitted to the refrigerator, generally a shallow rectangular vessel, which reduces the temperature almost to that of the cold water, or about 58°. The worts are next led by pipes into the large wooden fermenting-tuns, where yeast or barm is added as soon as the wort begins to run in from the refrigerator.

During the operation of fermentation, by which a portion of the saccharine matter is converted into alcohol, the temperature rises considerably, and requires to be kept in check by means of a coil of copper piping with cold water running through it lowered into the beer. When the fermentation has gone far enough, and the liquor has been allowed to settle, the beer becomes comparatively clear and bright, and may be run off and filled into the trade casks or into vats.

Kinds. The various beers manufactured from grain have sometimes been classified under the heads of *beer*, *ale*, and *porter* or *stout*; but at the present day this classification will not hold, as *beer*, though it occasionally may have a specific meaning, is often used as the general name for all malt liquors. Both terms belong to the early or Anglo-Saxon period of the English language, but in more modern times the term *beer* seems to have been applied more especially to malt liquor flavoured with hops, wormwood, or other bitters. Ale was originally made from barley malt and yeast alone, and the use of hops was first introduced in Germany, which is still a great brewing country.

One of the kinds of German beer now widely known and consumed is *lager beer*—that is, *store* beer, the name being given to it because it is usually kept for four to six months before being used. In brewing it the fermentation is made to go on rather slowly and at a low temperature. A special kind of yeast is used, which ferments at the bottom of the tuns instead of on the surface.

Among the most celebrated beers are the English pale ales brewed at Burton-on-Trent. The excellence of the Burton ale depends partly on the water used, which is all drawn from wells, and contains carbonates and sulphates of lime and magnesia in large quantities, and partly on the method of brewing.

The English bitter beer made for home consumption is less bitter than that which is sent abroad, at least as brewed by the best brewers; but a good part of the beer sold under this name is of poor quality, and would have little flavour were it not for the hops. Porter, which is very largely made in London, as also in Dublin, is of a very dark colour, this colour being obtained by the use of a certain proportion of malt subjected to a heat sufficient to scorch or blacken it.

History of Manufacture. The manufacture of ale or beer is of great antiquity. Herodotus ascribes the invention of brewing to Isis, and it was certainly practised in Egypt. Xenophon mentions beer as being used in Armenia, and the Gauls were early acquainted with it. Pliny mentions an intoxicating liquor made of corn and water as common to all the nations of the west of Europe, and in England ale-booths were regulated by law as early as the eighth century. The London brewers received a charter from Henry VI. in 1445. Until the eighteenth century the wealthier classes of this country generally brewed their own beer. The industry is now becoming more and more centralised. A rude process of brewing is carried on by many uncivilised races; thus *chica* or maize beer is made by the South American Indians, and millet beer by various African tribes.

BREW'STER, Sir David. Natural philosopher, born at Jedburgh 1781, died in 1868. He studied at Edinburgh University for the Church, but was attracted by the lectures of Robison and Playfair to science. In 1807 he was an unsuccessful candidate for the mathematical chair at St. Andrews, but became in the same year M.A. of Cambridge, LL.D. of Aberdeen, and member of the Royal Society of Edinburgh, to the *Transactions* of which he contributed important papers on the polarisation of light. In 1808 he became editor of the *Edinburgh Encyclopædia*, and in 1819, in conjunction with Jameson, founded the *Edinburgh Philosophical Journal*, of which he was sole editor from 1824 to 1832.

Brewster was one of the founders of the British Association, and its president in 1850. In 1832 he was knighted and pensioned, and both before and after this time his services to science obtained throughout Europe the most honourable recognition. From 1838 to 1859 he was principal of the united colleges of St. Leonard's and St. Salvator at St. Andrews, and in the latter year was chosen principal of the University of Edinburgh—an office which he held till his death. Among his inventions were the " polyzonal lens " (introduced into British lighthouses in 1835), the kaleidoscope, and the improved stereoscope.

His chief works are a *Treatise on the Kaleidoscope* (1829); *Letters on Natural Magic*, addressed to Sir Walter Scott (1831); *Treatise on Optics* (1831); *More Worlds than One* (1854); and *Lives of Euler, Newton, Galileo, Tycho Brahe, and Kepler* (1841).

BREWSTER SESSIONS. Special statutory sessions of the justices which are held in August and September of every year for the granting of new licences for the sale of excisable liquor.

BRIALMONT (brē-àl-mōŋ, **Henri Alexis.** Belgian military writer, born in 1821; entered the army in 1843 as lieutenant of engineers; became head of this branch; retired 1886. Among his works are: *Considérations Politiques et Militaires sur la Belgique*; *Histoire du Duc de Wellington*, translated into English by Gleig; *Étude sur la Défense des États et sur la Fortification*; and many works about fortification. He died in 1903.

BRI'AN (surnamed *Boroimhé* or *Boru*). A famous chieftain of the early Irish annals, who became King of Munster in 978, defeated the Danes of Limerick and Waterford, attacked Malachi, nominal king of the whole island, and became king in his stead (1002). He was slain at the close of the battle of Clontarf, near Dublin, in 1014, after gaining a signal victory over the revolted Maelmora and his Danish allies.

BRIANÇON (brē-àŋ-sōŋ; ancient, **BRIGENTIUM**). A town and fortress of France, department of Hautes Alpes, on the right bank of the Durance. It occupies an eminence 4284 feet above sea-level, and has been called the Gibraltar of the Alps. The town itself is of little importance, but has manufactures of silks, woollens, and cottons, and a good trade, and there are coal-mines in the neighbourhood. Pop. 7888.

BRIAND, Aristide. French politician, born at Nantes in 1862. Educated at the College of St. Nazaire, he became a barrister and political editor of the Socialist paper *La Lanterne*. Elected to the Chamber in 1902, he was expelled from the Socialist party when he took office in 1906 as Minister of Public Instruction. He was Premier several times (1909-1911, 1915-1917, 1921-1922, 1925-1926), was Minister of Justice in 1914, and was notably successful as Foreign Minister, taking a leading part in the Locarno negotiations. He died in 1932. Outstanding events in Briand's earlier career were his share in the separation of Church and State, and his action in fighting the great strike of 1910. After the Great War he signed the Treaty of Locarno and the Peace Pact of 1928, and took part in the European negotiations of those years. In 1930 he put forward the idea of a United States of Europe.

BRIANSK'. A town, Russia, government of Orel, on the Desna, with a considerable trade and various industries (ironworks, hemp-weaving, etc.), and near it are a cannon-foundry and a manufactory of small-arms. Pop. 32,100.

BRIAR, or BRIER. The wild rose. The well-known *briar-root* tobacco-pipes are made from the root of a large kind of heath (Fr. *bruyère*, heath), a native of S. Europe, Corsica, Sardinia, Algeria, etc.

BRIAREUS (brī-ā'rē-us). In Greek fable, a giant with 100 arms and 50 heads, who aided Jupiter (Zeus) in the great war waged with the Titans.

BRIBE. A reward given to a person, especially to some public officer or functionary who has a duty to perform towards others, to induce him to violate his official duty, or not to act simply as his duty requires, but so as to suit the person bribing; very commonly a corrupt payment of money for the votes of electors in the choice of persons to places of trust under Government.

Bribery is in most countries regarded as a crime deserving severe punishment. In Britain Acts amending and consolidating previous Acts against bribery at elections were passed in 1854 and in 1868, when it was enacted that election petitions should be tried by a specially-constituted court. Bribery at municipal elections was dealt with by an Act passed in 1872, in which year the passing of the Ballot Act introduced a new safe-guard; but bribery in parliamentary elections was more directly aimed at by the Corrupt Practices Act of 1883, which renders a person convicted of treating, bribery, etc., liable to fine or imprisonment with hard labour. Money, or almost any valuable consideration given or promised to electors, before, during, or after an election, may be construed into bribery, and the legal expenditure of candidates is brought within fixed limits. A candidate found guilty may thus be debarred from sitting in the House of Commons for seven years, and all guilty persons may be declared incapable of holding a public office or exercising any franchise. An Act of 1884 brings bribery at municipal elections under similar punishments and disabilities.

Special laws exist against the corruption of jurymen (*embracery*) and of revenue officers. A person offering a bribe to an excise officer is liable to a fine of £500, the officer receiving the bribe being similarly liable. The most celebrated case of judicial bribery in England is that of Francis Bacon, Lord St. Albans, who was sentenced to pay a fine of £40,000, to be imprisoned, to be incapable of holding office, and to be excluded from Parliament. By the Extradition Act of 1906, bribery is an extraditable offence.

BRICK. A sort of artificial stone, made principally of argillaceous earth, formed in moulds, dried in the sun, and baked by burning, or, as in many Eastern countries, by exposure to the sun. Sun-dried bricks of great antiquity have been found in Egypt, Assyria, and Babylonia, and in the mud walls of old Indian towns. Under the Romans the art of making and building with bricks was brought to great perfection, and the impressions on Roman bricks, like those on the bricks of Babylonia over 6000 years old, have been of considerable historic value. The Roman brick was afterwards superseded in England by the smaller Flemish make.

Of the various clays used in brick-making, the simplest, consisting chiefly of silicates of alumina, are almost infusible, and are known as fire-clays, the Stourbridge clay being specially famous. Of such clays fire-bricks are made. Clays containing lime and no iron burn white, the colours of others being due to the presence in varying proportions of ferric oxide, which also adds to the hardness of bricks. The clay should be dug in autumn and exposed to the influence of frost and rain. It should be worked over repeatedly with the spade and tempered to a ductile homogeneous paste, and should not be made into bricks until the ensuing spring.

The making of bricks by hand in moulds is a simple process. After being made and dried for about nine or ten days they are ready for the burning, for which purpose they are formed into *kilns*, having flues or cavities at the bottom for the insertion of the fuel, and interstices between them for the fire and hot air to penetrate. Much care is necessary in regulating the fire, since too much heat vitrifies the bricks and too little leaves them soft and friable.

Bricks are now largely made by machines of various construction. In one the clay is mixed and comminuted in a cylindrical pug-mill by means of rotatory knives or cutters working spirally and pressing the clay down to the bottom of the cylinder. From this it is conveyed by rollers and forced through an opening of the required size in a solid rectangular stream, which is cut into bricks by wires working transversely. Machine-made bricks are heavier, being less porous than hand-made bricks, and are more liable to crack in drying; but they are smoother, and, when carefully dried, stronger than the hand-made.

BRICKLAYING. The art of building with bricks and of uniting them by means of cement or mortar into various forms. Bricklaying in ordinary circumstances is a simple operation, but it requires thoroughness and care to ensure that the joints between bricks are even and of the right thickness and that the facework is flush.

In ordinary bricklaying, a layer of mortar is spread over the preceding course of brickwork by means of a trowel, which tool is also used to cut and trim bricks when necessary. Smaller trowels are also used for pointing. The mortar having been carefully spread so as to fill up all empty spaces and joints, each brick is put in position and, if necessary, tapped with the trowel in order to press out the excess mortar and secure a joint of the required thickness, though the brick should not be pressed down until it touches the brick beneath, as then the joints become so thin that they lose strength. All but the exposed surfaces of the bricks should be properly surrounded with mortar, and it is well to remember that though bricks may be made to unite by means of a dab of mortar, and may be pointed up outside, such work, though far too common, does not make good brickwork.

When the brick is tapped, the superfluous mortar which is squeezed out is removed by the trowel and scraped off on to the edge of the brick being laid, and helps to form the vertical joint of the next brick. When the brick used is made with a frog on one side, the frog is laid uppermost, and when filled with mortar forms a joint which keys the brick into the wall.

Bricks should be used wet, as a dry brick in summer will evaporate the water from mortar and will prevent proper adhesion. During frost, bricklaying should be discontinued, as the action of frost prevents the proper setting of mortar.

Bricklaying has been very much speeded up in America by means of labour-saving devices, such as travelling cradles for bringing bricks to the workmen at the required height and in the right position, and hand machines for spreading mortar of the right consistency.—BIBLIOGRAPHY: F. B. Gilbreth, *Bricklaying Systems*; C. F. Mitchell, *Brickwork and Masonry*; F. Malepeyre, *Nouveau Manuel du Briquetier* (Manuels Boret).

BRIDE, ST. *See* BRIDGET.

BRIDEWELL. Originally a famous house of correction in Blackfriars, London, subsequently used as a general term for houses of this kind. The building took its name from a well once existing between Fleet Street and the Thames, and dedicated to St. Bride. Henry VIII. built on this site, in 1522, a palace for the accommodation of the Emperor Charles V., which was afterwards converted by Edward VI. into an hospital to serve as a workhouse for the poor and a house of correction for the idle and vicious. The greater part of the building was destroyed in the great fire of 1666. New Bridewell, built in 1829, was pulled down in 1864.

BRIDGE. A structure of stone, brick, wood, or iron, affording a

Cantilever: Forth Bridge

passage over a stream, valley, or the like. The earliest bridges were no doubt trunks of trees. The arch seems to have been unknown amongst most of the nations of antiquity. Even the Greeks had not sufficient acquaintance with it to apply it to bridge-building. The Romans were the first to employ the principle of the arch in this direction, and after the construction of such a work as the great arched sewer at Rome,

Suspension and Bascule: Tower Bridge, London

the *Cloaca Maxima,* a bridge over the Tiber would be of comparatively easy execution. One of the finest examples of the Roman bridge was the bridge built by Augustus over the Nera at Narni, the vestiges of which still remain. It consisted of four arches, the longest of 142 feet span. The most celebrated bridges of ancient Rome were not generally, however, distinguished by the extraordinary size of their arches, nor by the lightness of their piers, but by their excellence and durability. The

Suspension: Brooklyn, U.S.A.

span of their arches seldom exceeded 70 or 80 feet, and they were mostly semicircular, or nearly so.

The Romans built bridges wherever their conquests extended, and in Britain there are still a number of bridges dating from Roman times. One of the most ancient post-Roman bridges in England is the Gothic triangular bridge at Crowland, in Lincolnshire, said to have been built in 860, having three archways meeting in a common centre at their apex, and three roadways. The longest old bridge in England was that over the Trent at Burton, in Staffordshire, built in the twelfth century, of squared freestone, and recently pulled down. It consisted of thirty-six arches, and was 1545 feet long. Old London Bridge was commenced in 1176, and finished in 1209. It had houses on each side like a regular street till 1756-8. In 1831 it was altogether removed, the new bridge, which had been begun in 1824, having then been finished.

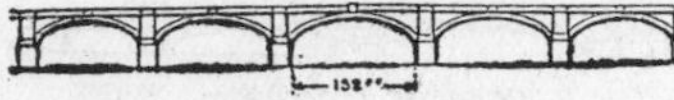

Stone: London Bridge

The art of bridge-building made no progress, after the destruction of the Roman Empire, till the eighteenth century, when the French architects began to introduce improvements, and the constructions of Perronet (Nogent-sur-Seine; Neuilly; Louis XVI. bridge at Paris) are masterpieces. Some of the stone bridges built in modern times far surpass those of older times in width of span, the widest being at Plauen, Saxony, of 295 feet span, Luxemburg, 236 feet, and Cabin John (Washington aqueduct), 220.

Stone Bridges. Stone bridges consist of an arch or series of arches, and in building them the properties

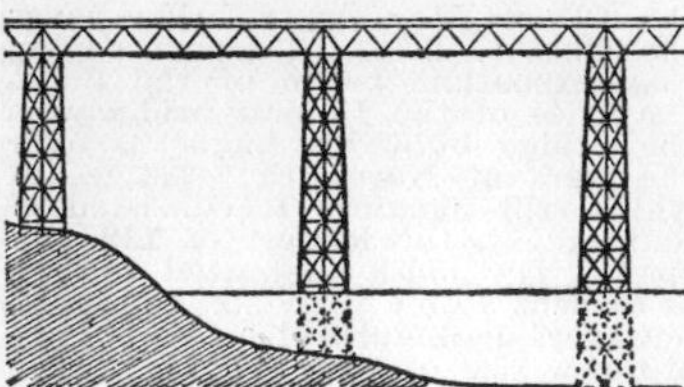

Lattice Girder: Crumlin Viaduct, Wales

of the arch, the nature of the materials, and many other matters have to be carefully considered. It has been found that in the construction of an arch the slipping of the stones upon one another is prevented by their mutual pressure and the friction of their surfaces; the use of cement is thus subordinate to the principle of construction in contributing to the strength and maintenance of the fabric. The masonry or rock which receives the lateral thrust of an arch is called the *abutment*, the perpendicular supports are the *piers*. The width of an arch is its *span*; the greatest span in any stone bridge is about 250 feet.

A one-span bridge has, of course, no piers. In constructing a bridge across a deep stream it is desirable to have the smallest possible number of points of support. Piers in the waterway are not only expensive to form, but obstruct the navigation of the river, and by the very extent of resisting surface they expose the structure to shocks and the wearing action of the water. In building an arch, a timber framework is used called the *centre*, or *centering*. The *centering* has to keep the stones or *voussoirs* in position till they are keyed in, that is, all fixed in their places by the insertion of the keystone.

Iron Bridges. The first iron bridges were erected from about 1777 to 1790. The same general principles apply to the construction of iron as of stone bridges, but the greater cohesion and adaptability of the material give more liberty to the architect, and much greater width of span is possible. At first iron bridges were erected in the form of arches, and the material employed was cast iron; but the arch has now been generally superseded by the beam or *girder*, with its numerous modifications; and wrought iron or steel is likewise found to be much better adapted for resisting a great tensile strain than cast metal.

Numerous modifications exist of the beam or girder, as the *lattice girder*, *bow-string girder*, etc.; but of these none is more interesting than the *tubular* or hollow girder, first rendered famous from its employment by Robert Stephenson in the construction of the railway bridge across the Menai Strait, and connecting Anglesey with the mainland of North Wales. This is known as the Britannia Tubular Bridge. The tubes are of a rectangular form, and constructed of riveted plates of wrought iron, with rows of rectangular tubes or cells for the floor and roof respectively. The bridge consists of two of these enormous tubes or hollow beams laid side by side, one for the up and the other for the down traffic of the railway, and extending each to about a quarter of a mile in length.

Victoria Bridge. The Victoria Bridge over the St. Lawrence at Montreal, originally tubular, is no longer so, the upper portion having been reconstructed with an open track. It is nearly 2 miles in length, or about five and a half times as long as the bridge across the Menai Strait.

Tay Bridge. A girder railway bridge across the Firth of Tay at Dundee was opened in 1887, being the second built at the same place, after the first had given way in a great storm. It is 2 miles 73 yards long, has 85 spans, is 77 feet high, and carries two lines of rails.

Forth Bridge. The bridge over the

Firth of Forth at Queensferry, completed in 1889, is built on the cantilever principle, of which it was the first very notable example. It has two chief spans of 1710 feet, two others of 680 feet, fifteen of 168 feet, and seven small arches, and the bridge gives a clear headway for navigation purposes of 150 feet above high-water of spring-tides. The great spans consist of a cantilever at either end, 680 feet long, and a central girder of 350 feet. Both the above bridges carry the lines of the London and North-Eastern Railway. (*See* FORTH BRIDGE.) The cantilever has also been adopted in some other great bridges, one of the most remarkable being the one opened in 1905 over the Zambesi just below the celebrated Victoria Falls, which has a span of 650 feet, carries a double line of rails, and is said to be the highest bridge in the world.

But all earlier bridges are surpassed in magnitude and boldness of design by the new cantilever bridge over the St. Lawrence at Quebec. The successful completion of the Forth Bridge encouraged Canadian engineers to attempt a similar design. The first attempt failed, owing to the collapse of the south cantilever arm in 1907. A fresh start was made, but even with improved plans and the instructive experience gained by the previous effort the work did not proceed without interruptions. It had been hoped to finish the erection of the bridge by the end of 1916. In September of that year the centre span, which had been erected three miles lower down the river, was completed and was towed upon scows to its position in the bridge site. Hydraulic hoists were employed in lifting it, but a single faulty casting in the hoisting apparatus gave way, and the span fell and sank to the bottom of the river.

By September of the following year a new span was ready for hoisting into place, and on the second attempt the difficult and delicate task was carried through without accident. The following figures show the colossal size of the structure: total length of bridge 3240 feet, length of main span, 1800 feet; length of suspended span, 640 feet; length of cantilever arm, 1160 feet; length of anchor arms, 1030 feet; depth of trusses at main pier, 310 feet; depth of trusses at end of cantilever and anchor arms, 70 feet; depth of suspended span at centre, 110 feet; width of bridge centre to centre trusses, 88 feet; clear height of steelwork above high water, 150 feet; weight of steel in bridge, 66,000 tons; quantity of masonry, 106,000 cu. yards; depth of main piers below high water, 101 feet; height of anchor piers above high water, 136 feet. Estimated total cost, 15,000,000 dollars.

The importance of this link between the northern and southern shores of the St. Lawrence can hardly be calculated. It shortens the railway journey by 200 miles, and connects ten of the largest railway systems of the Dominions, and, to mention only one great industry, it provides a clear road for transport of the produce of the pulp forests and mills of Northern Quebec to the Eastern States. The bridge was formally opened by the Prince of Wales in July, 1919.

A cantilever is a structure the main feature of which is a projecting arm jutting out over the space to be spanned and supporting the roadway; and two cantilevers may be made to meet directly, or the space between may be bridged over by a girder connected with both. The cantilever principle has the advantage that it may be employed where there might be great difficulties in the way of a bridge otherwise constructed, since the projecting arm may be built out from either side of the river or other opening to be crossed, and at a great height if necessary. In some cases a bridge with an arch or arches of wrought iron or steel is preferred chiefly or solely because such a structure has a more handsome appearance than some other bridges.

Kaiser Wilhelm Bridge. A notable example of the built-up arched steel-girder bridge is the Kaiser Wilhelm Bridge carrying the railway over the gorge of the River Wupper near Solingen, Germany. The span is 560 feet, and the rail level is 350 feet above the river; its total length is 1657 feet. Another bridge of this kind is the Washington Bridge over the Harlem River, New York, 2375 feet long, roadway 133 feet above the river, the two chief arches 510 feet span. Two notable single-span arched bridges are the bridge joining Newcastle-on-Tyne and Gateshead and the great bridge across Sydney Harbour (New South Wales). The arch of the Sydney Bridge has a span of 1050 feet.

Suspension Bridges. Suspension bridges, being entirely independent of central supports, do not interfere with the river, and may be erected where it is impracticable to build bridges of any other kind. The entire weight of a suspension bridge rests upon the piers at either end, from which it is suspended, all the weight being below the points of support.

Such bridges always swing a little, giving a vibratory movement which imparts a peculiar sensation to the passenger.

The modes of constructing these bridges are various. The roadway is suspended either from chains or from wire-ropes, the ends of which require to be *anchored*, that is, attached to the solid rock or masses of masonry or iron. One of the earlier of the great suspension bridges is that constructed by Telford over the Menai Strait near the Britannia Tubular Bridge, finished in 1825; the opening between the points of suspension is 580 feet. The Union Suspension Bridge, near Berwick, and the suspension bridge over the Avon at Clifton are other British examples.

Sydney Bridge

On the European continent the Fribourg Suspension Bridge in Switzerland, span 870 feet, erected 1834, is a celebrated work; as is that over the Danube at Budapest, 1250 feet.

In North America, where, as above indicated, some notable developments in the art of bridge-construction have been introduced, the enormous railway system, traversing a country of great rivers, has given an exceptional stimulus, and the greatest suspension bridges have been erected in America. For a number of years the most notable was the suspension bridge spanning the East River and connecting the city of New York with Brooklyn, opened in 1883. The central or main span is 1595½ feet from tower to tower, and the land spans between the towers and the anchorages 930 feet each; the approach on the New York side is 2492 feet long, and that on the Brooklyn side 1901 feet, making the total length 5989 feet. A similar great bridge has been constructed at no great distance, and was opened in 1903, having been begun in 1897. It has a total length of 7264 feet, the main span being 1600 feet, the supporting towers 335 feet in height, and the clear height above the water 135 feet; the width is 118 feet, and besides carriage-ways and paths for foot-passengers and cycles, there are four tracks for electric cars and two for railways on the elevated system.

Movable Bridges. Certain kinds of bridges are known as *movable bridges*. The *bascule*, or drawbridge—in which the roadway may be raised and lowered in one or two pieces—is a common form; and there are also *swing bridges*—opening horizontally to let shipping pass; bridges constructed so as to roll horizontally on wheels or otherwise; bridges in which the movable part, carrying the traffic, is suspended from a high iron framework or cables, under which shipping passes; these forming *transporter bridges*, as the bridge across the Mersey between Runcorn and Widnes, etc.

Pontoon or *floating* bridges are formed of pontoons or boats over which the roadway is laid, there being often the means of making an opening for shipping. A *flying bridge* is simply a kind of ferry. The Tower Bridge, London, crossing the Thames, is a unique structure, a combined suspension and bascule bridge, opening in the centre to admit ships, and having an elevated footway for passengers, with lifts and stairs in two towers.—BIBLIOGRAPHY: M. W. Davies, *Theory and Practice of Bridge Construction*; T. C. Fidler, *Practical Treatise on Bridge Con-*

struction; C. E. Fowler, *Practical Treatise on Subaqueous Foundations*; Jacoby and Davis, *Foundations of Bridges and Buildings*; W. S. Sparrow, *A Book of Bridges.*

BRIDGE, Sir John Frederick. English organist; he was born at Oldbury, 5th Dec., 1844, becoming a chorister at Rochester Cathedral when a boy. Study and success in two minor posts led to his appointment as organist of Manchester Cathedral in 1869. In 1875 he became deputy, and in 1882 chief organist at Westminster Abbey. He officiated at two coronations and retired in 1918. Knighted in 1897, Bridge was professor at the London University, the Royal College of Music, and Gresham College. He wrote cantatas, oratorios, and other kinds of church music as well as a book, *A Westminster Pilgrim.* Bridge died 18th March, 1924.

BRIDGE, AUCTION. The leading British card-game, introduced (in a modified form) into the Portland Club by Lord Brougham in 1894. The preliminaries of the game are as in whist (q.v.), except that the last card is not exposed. The dealer, after scrutinising his hand, makes the first "call", that is, he states that with a certain suit as trumps he will take a certain number of tricks above "book" (six)—thus "one club", "two spades", "three no-trumps". The player next on the left now calls, but his bid must exceed in value that of the previous caller.

In calculating this value one club counts 6, two clubs 12, one diamond 7, one heart 8, one spade 9, and one no-trump 10. So the calling goes on till a limit is reached. If a player does not wish to call, he passes. When a call is "doubled", it means that one of the opposing players doubts the ability of the caller to make his contract. The player who makes the final call plays the hand. The opponent on his left leads, declarer's partner exposes his hand, and the game proceeds as in whist.

The scoring-card has two vertical columns, one for each of the opposing sides, and is also divided by a horizontal line. Below this line the value of tricks taken is entered—only those above six counting, and then only if the contract has been made. Thirty points below the line make a game, on the completion of which both sides commence a new game.

A rubber is two games. All other scores, such as 100 for *grand slam* (thirteen tricks), 50 for *little slam* (twelve tricks), and points for honours, are entered above the line and do not count towards game. The five honours are the ace, king, queen, knave, and ten of the trump suit. A rubber counts 250 points above the line; the other scores are detailed on the back of every bridge scoring block.

Contract Bridge. Contract Bridge is a variation of Auction Bridge, the main differences being in values and in scoring. The fundamental principles of both games are the same.

BRIDGE-HEAD. A position commanding the crossing of a river, but not necessarily at an actual bridge. It may be a long way away from the river itself. Its function is to prevent the enemy from interfering with the crossing army, and to enable the army behind to form in security.

BRIDGEMAN, Viscount. English politician. Born 31st Dec., 1864, William Clive Bridgeman was a grandson of the Earl of Bradford. He had a brilliant career at Eton and Trinity College, Cambridge, and was in the cricket eleven at both. In 1904 he was elected to the L.C.C., and in 1906 became M.P. for the Oswestry division. He was made a Lord of the Treasury in 1915, and remained a member of the Coalition ministry as Secretary to the Ministry of Labour and afterwards to the Board of Trade. From 1920-22 Bridgeman was Secretary for Mines, from 1922-24 Home Secretary in the Unionist Cabinet, and from 1924-29 First Lord of the Admiralty. On his retirement he was made a viscount. In 1932 he was elected President of the M.C.C.

BRIDGEND. A market town and urban district of S. Wales, Glamorganshire, 19½ miles from Cardiff, 3 miles from the sea. Pop. (1931), 10,033.

BRIDGE'NORTH or BRIDGNORTH. A municipal borough, England, Shropshire, 20½ miles S.E. of Shrewsbury, on the Severn, which divides it into two portions, called the High Town and the Low Town, connected by a handsome bridge of six arches. The principal manufactures are carpeting and worsteds. Pop. (1931), 5151.

BRIDGE OF ALLAN. A town of Scotland, in Stirlingshire, on the border of Perthshire, on the Allan; a favourite resort for invalids on account of its exceptionally mild climate and its saline mineral waters. It has baths, a hydropathic, and several industrial works. Pop. (1931), 2897.

BRIDGE'PORT. A seaport of Connecticut, United States, 58 miles

N.E. of New York, on an arm of Long Island Sound, with a large coasting trade, but chiefly supported by its manufactures, including the large sewing-machine factories of Wheeler, Wilson, & Co., Elias Howe, etc. Pop. 146,716.

BRIDGES, Robert Seymour. English poet, born 23rd Oct., 1844. Educated at Eton and Corpus Christi College, Oxford, he afterwards studied medicine at St. Bartholomew's Hospital, London. He practised for some time, holding several hospital appointments, but retired in 1882. His works include: *Nero: a Tragedy* (1885); *The Return of Ulysses* (1890); *Shorter Poems* (1890); *The Humours of the Court* (1893), modelled upon Calderon; *Milton's Prosody* (1893); *Essay on John Keats* (1895); *Demeter: a Masque*; *The Spirit of Man*; *The Testament of Beauty* (1929), etc. He was appointed Poet Laureate in 1913 on the death of Alfred Austin. He died in 1930, and was succeeded as Laureate by John Masefield.

BRIDGET. The name of two saints of the Roman Catholic Church.—The first, more correctly Brigid, better known as **St. Bride,** was born in Ireland about 451 or 452, died in 525 at Kildare. She was exceedingly beautiful, and to avoid offers of marriage and other temptations implored God to render her ugly, which prayer was granted. An order of nuns of St. Bride was established, which continued to flourish for centuries. St. Bride was held in great reverence in Scotland as well as in Ireland.

The second **St. Bridget**, or more properly Birgit or Brigitte, was the daughter of Birger Persson, governor and provincial judge (*lagman*) of Uppland, and one of the wealthiest landowners of the country. Birgit was born about 1303, and died at Rome in 1373, on her return from a pilgrimage to Palestine. She left some mystic writings, and was the originator of a new religious order, at one time numerous. She was canonised by Pope Boniface IX. in 1391. Her youngest daughter, Catherine, was also canonised, and became the patron saint of Sweden.

BRIDGE'TON. A port of entry in New Jersey, United States, situated on both sides of Cohansey Creek, 20 miles above its entrance into Delaware Bay. Pop. 15,699.

BRIDGETOWN. Capital of the Island of Barbados, West Indies, extending along the shore of Carlisle Bay, on the S.W. coast of the island, for nearly 2 miles. Vessels anchor in the bay, and there is also an inner harbour. Its appearance is very pleasing, the houses being surrounded by trees, while hills of moderate height rise behind, studded with villas. Bridgetown is the starting-point of a railway (28 miles). It has a college, grammar-school, town hall, hospital, etc. Pop. 13,500.

BRIDGEWATER, Francis Egerton, Duke of. English nobleman, born in 1736. His estate of Worsley contained valuable coal-mines, and with the view of establishing a communication between these and the town of Manchester, at 7 miles' distance, he employed Brindley to construct a navigable canal, which, after having encountered much opposition and ridicule, was triumphantly carried through. He was the chief promoter of other excellent works of the same kind. He died in 1803. *See* BRINDLEY.

BRIDGEWATER TREATISES. A series of books, the outcome of the will of the Rev. Henry Francis, Earl of Bridgewater, who died in 1829, bequeathing a sum of £8000, which should be paid to the person or persons chosen to write and publish 1000 copies of a work on the power, wisdom, and goodness of God as manifested in the creation. The result was eight works on animal and vegetable physiology, astronomy, geology, the history, habits, and instincts of animals, etc., which at one time enjoyed great popularity. The names of the writers are Dr. Chalmers, Dr. Kidd, Dr. Whewell, Sir Charles Bell, Dr. Roget, Dr. Buckland, Rev. William Kirby, and Dr. Prout. The best known of the treatises are those by Bell, Buckland, and Whewell.

BRIDGMAN, Laura. A blind deaf-mute, born in Hanover, New Hampshire, in 1829. Till the age of two years she was a bright, active child, when a severe illness deprived her of the senses of sight, hearing, and smell, and partly also of that of taste. She was put under the care of Dr. Howe of Boston, and the history of the methods by which she was gradually taught to read, write, and eventually perform most of the ordinary duties, and even some of the accomplishments, of life, is a very interesting one. She became herself a teacher of persons similarly afflicted, and led an active and useful life, dying in 1889.

BRIDGNORTH. Borough and market town of Shropshire. It stands on the Severn, 20½ miles from Shrewsbury and 133¾ from London, on the G.W. Railway. It is divided by the river into an upper and lower town. There are some half-timbered houses, and on a hill the ruins of the castle. Pop. (1931), 5151.

BRIDGWATER, or BRIDGE-WATER. A municipal borough and port, Somerset, England, on the Parret, which is navigable as far up as the town for small vessels. A considerable shipping trade is carried on, chiefly coastwise. Bricks are made here in great quantities, especially bath-bricks—which are made nowhere else. Up till 1870, when it was disfranchised for bribery, Bridgwater returned two members to Parliament; it now gives its name to a parliamentary division. Pop. (1931), 17,139.

BRIDLE. The head-stall and bit by which, and by the reins, a horse is governed. The bridle is a very ancient piece of harness, and very early bridles differed little from those still in use. Harness-bridles differ from riding-bridles in being stouter and having blinders or blinkers upon them.

BRID'LINGTON, or BURLINGTON. A municipal borough of Yorkshire, England, agreeably situated about 40½ miles N.E. from York, comprising the Old Town, a mile inland, and *Bridlington Quay*, a favourite sea-bathing resort, having fine sands, chalk cliffs, grand views, esplanades, public gardens, etc.; also mineral waters resembling those of Scarborough and Cheltenham. There is a good harbour. Pop. (1931), 19,704.

BRID'PORT. A municipal borough and seaport in Dorsetshire, England, between the Rivers Bride and Asker, which unite a little below the town, and form a safe harbour for small vessels. There are manufactures of shoe-thread, twine, lines, sail-cloth, fishing-nets, etc. Pop. (1931), 5917.

BRIDPORT, Viscount. English admiral. The son of a clergyman, Alexander Hood was born in 1727, and entered the navy in 1741. He served with distinction under Hawke at Quiberon and under Keppel at Ushant. He was promoted rear-admiral of the white in 1780, and vice-admiral in 1787, in which year he was also knighted. In 1793 he served as Howe's second-in-command on the "Glorious First of June," and for his services was created Baron Bridport in the peerage of Ireland. In 1795 he fought the action of Belle-Ile, which, though indecisive, made him a popular hero. He was given a British peerage and appointed vice-admiral of England. For some time he was practically supreme in the direction of the naval operations against France, and personally conducted the blockade of Brest from 1798 until 1800. On his retirement he was created viscount. He died 2nd May, 1814.

BRIEF, which comes from the Lat. *brevis*, short, denotes a brief or short statement or summary, particularly the summary of a client's case which the solicitor draws up for the instruction of counsel. A brief may also mean, in law, an order emanating from the superior courts. A *papal brief* is a sort of pastoral letter in which the Pope gives his decision on some matter which concerns the party to whom it is addressed. The brief is an official document, but of a less public character than the bull. *See* BULL.

BRIEG (brēh). A town, Prussia, province of Silesia, on the left bank of the Oder, which is here crossed by a long wooden bridge, 27 miles S.E. of Breslau, with a considerable transit trade and some manufactures, chiefly linens, woollens, cottons, leather, etc. Pop. 27,344.

BRIEG, BRIGUE, or BRIG (brēg). A town of Switzerland, canton Valais, in the Rhone valley, at the foot of the road passing over the Simplon, and near the Swiss entrance of the Simplon Tunnel. Pop. 2500.

BRIEL (brēl), or **BRIELLE** (brē-el'). Sometimes called the *Brill*, a fortified seaport of Holland, near the mouth of the Maas, province of South Holland. The taking of Briel in 1572 was the first success of the revolted Netherlanders in their struggle with Philip II. of Spain. The famous Admiral Van Tromp was born here. Pop. 3810.

BRIENNE (brē-ān). A small town of France, department of Aube. In the military academy which formerly existed here Napoleon received his early military training. Brienne was also the scene of a fierce battle between Blücher and Napoleon (29th Feb., 1814).

BRIENNE, JOHN OF. A celebrated Crusader, born 1148, died 1237, the son of Erard II., Count of Brienne. He was present at the siege of Constantinople in 1204, and afterwards, in 1209, married the granddaughter and heiress of Amaury, King of Jerusalem. Brienne thus obtained an empty title, which he afterwards ceded to the Emperor Frederick II. Later on he was again formally associated with Baldwin II., as joint emperor of the Latin Empire in the East. After a series of heroic exploits in defence of his dominions, in 1237 he resigned his crown to retire into a monastery, where he died.

BRIENZ (brē'ents). A town, Switzerland, canton of Bern, beautifully situated on the N.E. shore of the Lake of Brienz. It is notable for its wood-carving. Pop. 2518.

BRIER. *See* BRIAR.

BRIERFIELD. An urban district of England, in Lancashire, 2½ miles north-east of Burnley, and near Nelson. Pop. (1931), 7696.

BRI'ERLY HILL. A town in Staffordshire, England, on the Stour. It lies in a rich mineral district, and carries on considerable industry in coal-mines, brickworks, ironworks, etc. Pop. (1931), 14,344.

BRIEUC, ST. (saŋ brē-*eu*). A seaport town, France, department of Côtes du Nord, about a mile above the mouth of the Gouët. It is the seat of a bishop and has a very ancient cathedral. It manufactures cottons, woollen stuffs, and paper. Pop. 28,000.

BRIEUX, Eugène. French dramatist, born 1858. He was editor of the *Nouvelliste de Rouen*, and was afterwards on the staff of the *Figaro* and the *Gaulois*. His first play, *Bernard Palissy* (1880), he wrote in collaboration with Salandri, but it was his *Ménage d'Artistes* (1890) which met with considerable success at the Théâtre Libre, and established his reputation as a playwright. Among his other plays are: *Blanchette* (1892); *Les Trois Filles de M. Dupont* (1897); *L'Engrenage* (1894); *La Robe Rouge* (1900); *L'Evasion* (1896); *Petite Amie* (1902); *Maternité* (1904); *Les Hannetons* (1906); *Les Avariés* (1901); *Les Remplaçantes* (1901); *La Foi* (1912); *La Femme Seule* (1912); *L'Avocat* (1922); *La Famille Lavolette* (1926).

Brieux introduced philosophical discussions into his plays, criticising and throwing ridicule on the many social evils of the time. *Maternité*, *Les Avariés* (Damaged Goods), and *Les Trois Filles de M. Dupont* have been translated into English, the first-named by Mrs. Bernard Shaw. He was elected a member of the Académie Française in 1909.

BRIEY. A town of France, department of Meurthe-et-Moselle, 14 miles north-west of Metz. The rich iron district around it was occupied by the Germans in 1914, and liberated in Nov., 1918. Pop. 2500.

BRIG. A sailing vessel with two masts rigged like the foremast and mizzen-mast of a full-rigged ship. *See* BRIGANTINE.

BRIGADE'. A brigade is a higher formation of troops, whether cavalry, artillery, or infantry, consisting of an indeterminate but small number of regiments, batteries, or battalions. A cavalry brigade consists of three regiments. A brigade of artillery before the European War consisted of two batteries of horse artillery or three batteries of field artillery, in either case with an ammunition column. During the war an extra battery was added to both of these formations. An infantry brigade before the war and up to Jan., 1918, consisted of four battalions; since then it has consisted of three. A brigade is commanded by a brigadier;

Brig

a brigade-major (often a captain in rank) is the chief staff-officer of a brigade.

BRIGADIER-GENERAL. Temporary rank in the British Army, the lowest for a general officer. He commands a brigade of infantry or cavalry. The rank was abolished in 1920, in favour of that of colonel commandant, but was revived in 1928. The equivalent rank in the navy is commodore.

BRIG'ANDINE. A piece of defensive armour worn in the Middle Ages, consisting of thin jointed scales of plate, generally sewed upon linen or leather, the whole forming a coat or tunic.

BRIG'ANTINE. A sailing vessel with two masts, the foremast rigged like a brig's, the mainmast rigged like a schooner's. Called also *hermaphrodite brig*.

BRIGG. A town of Lincolnshire, England, giving name to a parliamentary division. Pop. (1931), 4019.

BRIGGS, Henry. A celebrated mathematician, born in 1561. When

Gresham College was founded in London, he became professor of geometry there. In 1619 he was appointed first Savilian professor of astronomy at Oxford. In 1616 he visited Napier, the inventor of logarithms, and afterwards published his work on logarithms, which suggested an important improvement upon Napier's system. He died in 1631 at Oxford.

BRIGHOUSE. A municipal borough of England, W. Riding of Yorkshire, 4 miles north of Huddersfield and 4½ south-east of Halifax, on the Calder. It has a technical school, and manufactures of woollens, worsted, carpets, cottons, silks, machinery, etc. Pop. (1931), 19,756.

BRIGHT, John. English orator and politician, born at Greenbank, near Rochdale, Lancashire, 16th Nov., 1811. His father, Jacob Bright, carried on a cotton-spinning and manufacturing business of which the son became the head. He first became known as a leading spirit along with Cobden in the Anti-Corn-Law League. In 1843 he was chosen member of Parliament for Durham, and distinguished himself as a strenuous advocate of free trade and reform. In 1847 he sat for the first time for Manchester, but in 1857 his opposition to the Crimean War had made him so unpopular in the constituency that he lost his seat by a large majority. He was, however, returned for Birmingham, and soon after made speeches against the policy of great military establishments and wars of annexation.

In 1865 he took a leading part in the movement for the extension of the franchise, and strongly advocated the necessity of reform in Ireland. In the Gladstone ministry formed in 1868 he was President of the Board of Trade and afterwards Chancellor of the Duchy of Lancaster, and he held the latter office again under Gladstone from 1880 to 1882. In 1886 he joined the Liberals who opposed Gladstone's schemes for Ireland, and contributed by his letters and influence to the overthrow of the Gladstone party. He was a member of the Society of Friends. He died 27th March, 1889.—BIBLIOGRAPHY: G. B. Smith, *The Life and Speeches of the Right Hon. John Bright*; C. A. Vince, *John Bright*; Robertson, *Life and Times of John Bright*; G. M. Trevelyan, *The Life of John Bright.*

BRIGHTLINGSEA. A seaport of England, in north-east Essex, near the mouth of the Colne, 10 miles south-east of Colchester; a yacht station, and engaged in the oyster fishery and boat-building. Pop. (1931) 4145.

BRIGHTON (bri'tun; formerly **BRIGHTHELMSTONE**). A county borough and favourite watering-place in England, county of Sussex, 51½ miles from London. It is situated on a gentle slope, protected from the north winds by the high ground of the South Downs immediately behind the town, and is well built, with handsome streets, terraces, squares, etc. In front of the town is a massive sea-wall, with a promenade and drive over 3 miles in length, one of the finest in Europe. Amongst the remarkable buildings, all of modern date, is the Pavilion, built by George IV., which cost upwards of £1,000,000. It is in the Oriental style, with numerous cupolas, spires, etc. The building and its gardens, which are open to the public as pleasure-grounds, cover 9 acres. There is a very large and complete aquarium, and two fine piers.

Brighton has no manufactures, and is resorted to chiefly as a watering-place. It was about the middle of the eighteenth century that Dr. Russell, an eminent physician, drew attention to Brighton, which subsequently was patronised by George IV., then Prince of Wales; in this way a fishing village rose to be a fashionable and populous watering-place. It sends two members to Parliament. Pop. (1931), 147,427.

BRIGHTON. A town and popular seaside resort of Australia, Victoria, on the east shore of Port Phillip Bay, 7½ miles south-east of Melbourne, of which it is practically a suburb, many of the citizens of Melbourne having residences here. Pop. 21,235.

BRIGHT'S DISEASE. A name given to various forms of kidney disease and so called from Dr. Bright of London, who first described the condition. It is a diffuse nephritis, and appears in an acute and a chronic form. The acute form is due to the action of cold or toxic agents on the kidneys, and is characterised by inflammatory changes in the epithelial, vascular, or intertubular tissues of the kidneys, respectively varying in intensity—hence different forms are recognised.

Symptoms. The most characteristic symptoms are found in the urine, which is of high specific gravity, scanty, high coloured, and contains blood and albumin. In chronic Bright's disease several varieties are also recognised. It usually follows an acute attack, and the changes that occur in the kidney tissues are permanent. The outstanding symptoms are back pain, anæmia, cachexia, disturbed digestion, dropsy, and increased output of urine of low specific gravity and containing a small amount of albumin. There is a close association between chronic Bright's disease and disease of the heart and arteries, while cerebral disturbances are frequently the cause of death.

BRIGNOLES (brin-yōl). A town in Southern France, department of Var, in a fertile valley celebrated for its salubrity. Pop. 5120.

BRIHUEGA (brē-wā'gȧ). A town of Spain, in New Castile, on the Tajuna. Here in 1710 the allies under Lord Stanhope were defeated by the Duke of Vendôme in the Spanish Succession War. Pop. 3300.

BRIL. The name of two brothers who distinguished themselves as landscape-painters.—Matthew, born at Antwerp in 1550, died in 1584; repaired when a very young man to Rome, and was employed on the galleries and saloons of the Vatican.—Paul, born about 1554, died about 1626, and of much superior talent, joined his brother in Rome, and amongst other labours executed a large fresco, *Martyrdom of St. Clement* (his greatest work, 68 feet long), in the Sala Clementina of the Vatican. Paul is memorable as having done much to develop landscape-painting as an independent branch of the art. His best pictures do not fall much short of those of Claude Lorraine, his great successor.

BRILL (*Rhombus lævis*). A fish resembling the turbot, but inferior in quality, and distinguished from it by its inferior breadth and by the perfect smoothness of its skin. The brill is of a pale-brown colour above, marked by scattered yellowish or reddish spots. It is abundant in the English Channel, and is esteemed for the table.

BRILLAT-SAVARIN (brē-yä-sȧ-vȧ-raṇ). A French author, who, although he wrote works on political economy, archæology, and duelling, is now known only by his famous book on gastronomy, the *Physiologie du Goût*, published in 1825 (English translation under the title *Gastronomy as a Fine Art*). He was born at Bellay in 1755, and after holding several honourable positions as a magistrate, died in Paris, 1826.

BRIM'STONE. Roll sulphur. Sulphur is purified by distillation, the vapour being led into brickwork chambers. Part of the vapour liquefies, falls to the bottom, and can be run off and cast in cylindrical moulds, and when solid is known as brimstone. See SULPHUR.

BRINDABAN (brin-dä-ban'). A town of India, United Provinces, Muttra District, right bank of the Jumna, one of the holiest cities of the Hindus, as being the scene of many adventures in the life of Krishna, with one thousand temples, shrines, and sacred sites. Pop. 18,443.

BRINDISI (brēn'di-sē; ancient, **BRUNDUSIUM**). A seaport and fortified town, province of Lecce, Southern Italy, on the Adriatic, 45 miles E.N.E. of Taranto. In ancient times Brundusium was an important city, and with its excellent port became a considerable naval station of the Romans. Its importance as a seaport declined in the Middle Ages, and was subsequently completely lost, and its harbour blocked, until in 1870 the Peninsular and Oriental Steam Navigation Company put on a weekly line of steamers between Brindisi and Alexandria for the conveyance of mails and passengers by railway and steamer between Europe and the East. Brindisi has since risen into considerable importance. It is also one of the principal Italian torpedo-stations. Pop. 38,985.

BRIND'LEY, James. An English engineer and mechanic, born in 1716, died in 1772. When the Duke of Bridgewater was occupied in planning a communication between his estate at Worsley and the towns of Manchester and Liverpool by water, Brindley undertook the work, and by means of aqueducts over valleys, rivers, etc., he completed the Bridgewater Canal between 1781 and 1761, so as to form a junction with the Mersey. The other great works of this kind undertaken by him were the Grand Trunk Canal uniting the Trent and Mersey, and a canal uniting that with the Severn.

BRINE. Water saturated with common salt. It is naturally produced in many places beneath the surface of the earth, and is also made artificially, for preserving meat, a little saltpetre being generally added to the solution.

BRINE-SHRIMP. A branchiopodus crustacean, the *Artemia salīna*, about ½ inch in length, and commonly found in the brine of salt-pans previous to boiling.

BRINJAL. An Asiatic name for the egg-plant or its fruit.

BRINVILLIERS (braṇ-vēl-yā), **Marie Marguerite d'Aubray, Marchioness of.** Born about 1630, executed 1676. She was married in 1651 to the Marquis of Brinvilliers, but after some seven or eight years of married life a young cavalry officer named Sainte-Croix inspired her with a violent passion, and being instructed by him in the art of preparing poisons, she poisoned in succession her father, her two brothers, and her sisters, chiefly, it is thought, in order to procure the means for living extravagantly with her paramour. The sudden death of Sainte-Croix caused, it is said, by the falling off of a glass mask which he used to protect himself in preparing poisons, led to the discovery of letters incriminating Madame de Brinvilliers. It is thought that she fled to England, and she afterwards went to Liège, where she was captured, conveyed to Paris, and condemned to death.

BRIO (brē′ō). An Italian word signifying vivacity, but now much used also in other languages to express a very catching, spirited, or even fiery manner of doing a thing, particularly in reference to artistic execution, as in singing, piano-playing, etc.

BRIONI. Small group of islands in the Adriatic, off the coast of Istria and north-west of Pola. The largest of them, Brioni Maggiore, is a favourite holiday resort.

BRIQUETTES. Masses of fuel in the shape of bricks or small ovoids, consisting mainly of coal-dust and some binding-material, such as pitch, tar, or asphalt, the materials being mixed together and then heated, the briquettes being pressed in moulds. Briquettes serve as a useful household fuel, and have the property of burning very slowly, remaining alight for a long time. They are also used in heating the furnaces of boilers and for other purposes. They were first made in France, and are still largely made there, though quite common in Britain also, being made chiefly in South Wales from anthracite coal-dust. They are for the most part exported to the Continent. Finely-divided iron-ore is now pressed into briquettes, which are heated until they consolidate. In this form the small ore particles which would otherwise choke the blast-furnace can be used up and smelted.

BRISACH. *See* Breisach.

BRISANCE. *See* Explosives.

BRIS′BANE. The capital of Queensland, about 25 miles by water from the mouth of the River Brisbane, which intersects the town. Brisbane was originally settled, in 1825, as a penal station by Sir Thomas Brisbane (whence the name of the town). In 1842 the district was opened to free settlers, and on the erection of Queensland into a separate colony in 1859, Brisbane became the capital. Since then it has made great progress, and now possesses many fine public buildings, such as the Houses of Legislature, erected at a cost of over £100,000, the town hall and the Albert Hall, the vice-regal lodge, the post and telegraph offices, etc. There are also botanical gardens, several parks, etc. The climate is tropical, the annual rainfall about 55 inches. The town is the terminus of the western and southern railway system, and the port is the principal one in the colony. Pop. (with suburbs) 313,251.

BRIS′BANE, General Sir Thomas MacDougall. A Scottish soldier and astronomer, born in 1773. After serving in Flanders and the West Indies, he commanded a brigade under the Duke of Wellington during the Peninsular War, and took part in the battles of Vittoria, Orthes, and Toulouse. In 1821 he was appointed governor of New South Wales, where his administration tended greatly to promote the prosperity of the colony. At the same time he devoted himself to astronomy, and from his observatory at Paramatta catalogued 7385 stars, until then scarcely known. (*Brisbane Catalogue*, printed in 1835.) On his return to Scotland he continued his astronomical pursuits, and died in 1860.

BRISGAU. *See* Breisgau.

BRISSON, Eugène Henri. French statesman, born in 1835. He was elected to the National Assembly in 1871, and became President of the Chamber of Deputies in 1881, an office which he held with several interruptions for many years. Among his publications are: *La Congregation, Aperçu historique* (1902); *Souvenirs: Affaire Dreyfus* (1908). He also established, in conjunction with Challemel-Lacour, the *Revue politique*. He died in 1912.

BRISSOT (brē-sō), **Jean Pierre** (also called **BRISSOT DE WARVILLE**). A French political writer, born in 1754, executed 30th Oct., 1793. He early turned his attention to public affairs, associating himself with such men as Pétion, Robespierre, Marat, etc. In 1780 he published his *Théories des Lois Criminelles*, and two years afterwards an important collection called the *Bibliothèque des Lois Criminelles*. During the Revolution he made himself known as a politician and one of the leaders of the Girondist party. The extreme views of the men of the "Mountain" having prevailed over more moderate counsels, Brissot, like most of his party, suffered death by the guillotine.

BRISTLE-FERN (*Trichomanes radicans*). The only representative in the British Isles of the large genus of filmy ferns, Trichomanes. It is a rare plant, being confined to the South of Ireland and Wales, where it grows among damp, shaded rocks near waterfalls, etc. The name is sometimes applied to the genus as a whole; it refers to the characteristic bristle-like receptacles on which the sporangia are borne. *See* FILMY FERNS.

BRISTLES. The stiff, coarse, glossy hairs of the hog and the wild boar, especially of the hair growing on the back; extensively used by brushmakers, shoemakers, saddlers, etc., and chiefly imported from Russia and Germany.

BRIS'TOL. A cathedral city of England, a municipal, county, and parliamentary borough, situated partly in Gloucestershire, partly in Somersetshire, but forming a county in itself. It stands at the confluence of the Rivers Avon and Frome, which unite within the city, whence the combined stream (the Avon) pursues a course of nearly 7 miles to the Bristol Channel. The Avon is a navigable river, and the tides rise in it to a great height. The town is built partly on low grounds, partly on eminences, and has some fine suburban districts, such as Clifton, where the celebrated suspension-bridge across the Avon, 703 feet long and 245 feet above high-water mark, unites the two counties.

The public buildings are numerous and handsome, and the number of places of worship very great. The most notable of these are the cathedral, founded in 1142, exhibiting various styles of architecture, and recently restored and enlarged; St. Mary Redcliff, said to have been founded in 1293, and perhaps the finest parish church in the kingdom. Among modern buildings are the exchange, the guild hall, the council house, the post office, the new grammar-school, the fine arts academy, the West of England and other banks, insurance offices, etc.

The charities are exceedingly numerous, the most important being Ashley Down Orphanage, for the orphans of Protestant parents, founded and long managed by the Rev. George Müller, which may almost be described as a village of orphans. Bristol has a number of endowed schools, the principal of which are the grammar-school, Queen Elizabeth's hospital, the Red Maids' School (which educates and provides for 80 girls, and gives them marriage portions), Colston's Hospital, the trade school, and the cathedral school.

Amongst the educational institutions are the University College, the Theological Colleges of the Baptists and Independents, Clifton College, and the Philosophical Institute. The University of Bristol, founded in 1909, has a staff of 210 teachers, and about 1000 students. The university unites with the universities of Durham, Manchester, Liverpool, Leeds, Sheffield, and Birmingham in returning two members to Parliament. There is a school of art, and also a public library.

Trade. Bristol has glass-works, potteries, soap-works, tanneries sugar-refineries, and chemical-works, shipbuilding and machinery yards. Coal is worked extensively within the limits of the borough. The export and import trade is large and varied. Bristol is among the oldest seaports in Great Britain, and occupies a leading place among the great ports of the country. There is a harbour in the city itself, and the construction of new docks at Avonmouth and Portishead has given a fresh impetus to the port. Bristol is one of the healthiest of the large towns of the kingdom. It has an excellent water-supply chiefly obtained from the Mendip Hills.

History. In old Celtic chronicles we find the name *Caer Oder*, or "the City of the Chasm," given to a place in this neighbourhood, a name peculiarly appropriate to the situation of Bristol, or rather of its suburb Clifton. The Saxons called it *Bricgstow*, "bridge-place." In 1373 it was constituted a county of itself by Edward III. It was made the seat of a bishopric by Henry VIII. in 1542 (long united with Gloucester). In 1831 the Reform agitation gave origin to riots that lasted for several days. The rioters destroyed a number of public and private buildings, and had to be dispersed by the military. Sebastian Cabot, Chatterton, and Southey were natives of Bristol. Since 1918 Bristol returns five members to Parliament. Pop. (1931), 396,918.

BRISTOL. A seaport in Rhode Island, United States. It has a pleasant situation, is a favourite place of summer resort, and has a considerable trade. Pop. 12,000.

BRISTOL. A town of the United States, partly in Virginia, partly in Tennessee. It is the seat of two colleges. Pop. 20,849.

BRISTOL-BOARD. A fine kind of pasteboard, smooth, and sometimes glazed, on the surface.

BRISTOL-CHANNEL. An arm of

the Atlantic, extending between the southern shores of Wales and the south-western peninsula of England, and forming the continuation of the estuary of the Severn. It is remarkable for its high tides.

BRISTOL-STONE. Rock-crystal, or Bristol-diamond, small, round crystals of quartz, found in the Clifton limestone, near the city of Bristol, in England.

BRITAIN, or GREAT BRITAIN. The island consisting of the three countries, England, Scotland, Wales, the name being also used as equivalent to the British Islands collectively, or to the British Empire. Great Britain and Northern Ireland, with their connected islands, form the United Kingdom of Great Britain and Northern Ireland.

The British Islands form a kind of archipelago in the north-west of Europe. The principal islands are Great Britain and Ireland, separated from each other by the Irish Sea, which near the centre attains its greatest width of about 140 miles; but between Holyhead, in Wales, and Howth Head, in Ireland, is not wider than 60 miles; while the distance between the Mull of Kintyre, in Scotland, and Fair Head, in Ireland, is only about 12 miles.

Great Britain is the largest island in Europe, and the seventh largest in the world. Its nearest approach to the continent of Europe is at its S.E. extremity, where the Straits of Dover, separating it from France, are only 21 miles broad. Its length, measured on a line bearing N. by W. from Rye to Dunnet Head, is 608 miles. The breadth varies exceedingly; between St. David's Head, in Pembrokeshire, and the Naze, in Essex, it is 280 miles; between the Clyde at Dumbarton and the Forth at Alloa it is only 32 miles. The shape of Ireland is more regular than that of Great Britain, and bears a considerable resemblance to a rhomboid. Its greatest length going straight north and south is 280 miles, and its greatest breadth from west to east is 180 miles.

Area of Great Britain and Northern Ireland

	Sq. Miles (with Inland Water).	Acres (without Inland Water).
England	50,875	32,559,868
Wales	7,469	4,780,470
Scotland	30,406	19,070,466
Channel Islands ..	75	48,083
Isle of Man	227	145,325
Northern Ireland ..	5,237	3,351,970
Totals ..	94,289	59,956,182

The British Isles rise from a submarine plateau connecting them geologically with the rest of Europe, of which at a remote period they must have actually formed a part. This is evidenced, too, by the similarity of the British fauna and flora to the continental.

Surface. The N. part of Britain is, for the most part, rugged, mountainous, and barren, this being the character of much of Scotland. To the N. of a line drawn from the Firth of Clyde on the W. to Stonehaven on the E. coast is the region generally known as the Highlands, divided into a northern and a southern portion by the great hollow of Glenmore through which runs the Caledonian Canal. The chief feature of the southern portion is the mountain mass of the Grampians, the culminating points of which, Ben Nevis and Ben Macdhui, are the highest British summits, being respectively 4406 and 4296 feet.

South of the Highlands lies the plain of the Forth and Clyde, a region of coal and iron, in which the chief manufacturing industries of Scotland are carried on. South of this again is the elevated region of the Southern Highlands or Southern Uplands, less rugged and more pastoral than the Highlands proper. Towards the S.E. are the Cheviot Hills, on the borders of England and Scotland. Here commences the long Pennine chain running south into England, branching off into the mountains of Cumberland and the Lake District (Cumbrian Mountains), and terminating beyond the Peak of Derby, in the heart of England.

The highest summit of the English mountains is in the north-west (Lake District), namely, Scawfell, 3210 feet. Further south and west is the Cambrian range, spread over the greater part of Wales, and containing, among others, the highest mountain of S. Britain—Snowdon, 3560 feet. Over great parts of England the elevations are mostly insignificant, and the general character of the country is that of undulating plains.

In Ireland the most marked feature is the dreary expanse of bogs which stretches over its interior. This flatness of the interior is caused by the fact that most of the mountain masses attain their greatest elevation near the coast, and rapidly decline as they recede from it. Carn Tual, in the south-west, the culminating point of the island, is 3414 feet high.

Rivers and Lakes. The mountains which constitute the principal watersheds of Great Britain being generally at no great distance from the W. coast, the rivers which descend from them in that direction have generally a short course, and are comparatively unimportant. The two great exceptions to this rule are the Clyde and the Severn, which owe both their volume and the length of their course to a series of longitudinal valleys, which, instead of opening directly to the coast, take a somewhat parallel direction. The chief rivers entering the sea on the E. coast, proceeding from N. to S., are the Spey, Don, Dee, Tay, Forth, Tweed, Tyne, Ouse, Trent, and Thames, the last named in navigable importance the greatest river of the world. No river of importance empties itself either on the N. or S. coast.

Owing to the great central flat of Ireland, its rivers usually flow on in a gently winding course in different directions to the sea. Those of importance are not very numerous; but one of them, the Shannon, is the longest river of the British Isles, its length being 224 miles; while the Thames is 210 miles. The Tay (length 120 miles) is said to have the largest volume of water.

The lakes of the British Isles are distinguished for beauty rather than size; the largest, but among the least interesting, is Lough Neagh, in the north of Ireland. While both Great Britain and Ireland are provided with numerous streams which are either themselves navigable or act as the feeders of canals, the coasts supply a number of excellent harbours invaluable to the commerce of the country.

Climate. Their maritime situation has a favourable effect on the climate of the British Isles, making it milder and more equable than that of continental countries in the same latitude. The temperature of the Atlantic, raised by the influx of the Gulf Stream, is communicated to the winds and vapours which are wafted along its surface, and the prevailing winds in Britain being from the south-west, the country is kept constantly at a relatively high temperature. The south-west winds, too, are charged with vapour, and often bring rain, thus supplying the country with abundant moisture. Ireland, from its more westerly position, has these characteristics in the most marked degree, the warmth and moisture of the west winds making it markedly a "green isle."

For the same reason the western shores of the islands have a milder and more equable temperature than the eastern shores, the former being on an average one or two degrees cooler in summer and several degrees warmer in winter. The range of temperature between the coldest and the warmest months is at London 26°, in England generally 24½°, while at Paris it is 30°. The range at Edinburgh is 25°, while at Petrograd it is 55°. The mean winter temperature at Dublin is 39°, or 3 degrees higher than that of Milan, Pavia, Padua, or the whole of Lombardy.

Agriculture. In almost every district in Great Britain where the plough can move, farming of a superior description may be seen, and, according to Professor Thorold Rogers, "it may be confidently averred that owing to improvements in stock and seeds, agriculture in the United Kingdom is at a higher level than in any other country." Thorough and systematic draining, the extensive use of artificial manures, and the employment of the newest implements are among the chief features of modern British agriculture, the skilled farmer having always been ready to take advantage of any useful results and discoveries arrived at by modern science.

A peculiar feature of English as distinguished from Scottish husbandry is the large amount of arable land forming permanent hayfields. These are kept fertile by heavy doses of farmyard manure, and yield grass of admirable feeding qualities. Much of the land thus employed is naturally of poor quality, but by the careful management of perhaps a century has become covered with a close sward of the richest green, furnishing admirable food for stock. The great extent of the permanent pasture is also a feature of Irish agriculture.

In the rearing and fattening of stock there is no country in the world that can be compared to several districts of Great Britain. It is sufficient to mention, among horses, the race-horse, the "shire-horse", the Suffolk punch, and the Clydesdale; among cattle, the shorthorn, the Hereford, the Aberdeen-Angus, and the Ayrshire; among sheep, the South Downs and Leicesters.

The principal cereal crops grown in England are wheat, barley, and oats, oats now covering the largest area; the principal green crops are turnips, potatoes, mangolds, vetches, etc. In Ireland and Scotland oats are by far the principal grain crop; by far the chief green crop being in Ireland potatoes, in Scotland turnips. Hops are grown to a large extent in Kent, and less extensively in some other parts of southern England.

The most marked feature in the agriculture of Great Britain during recent years is the gradual increase in the proportion which the amount of land in grass bears to that under corn and green crops; an increase without doubt attributable to the increased facility with which cereals can be obtained from foreign countries,

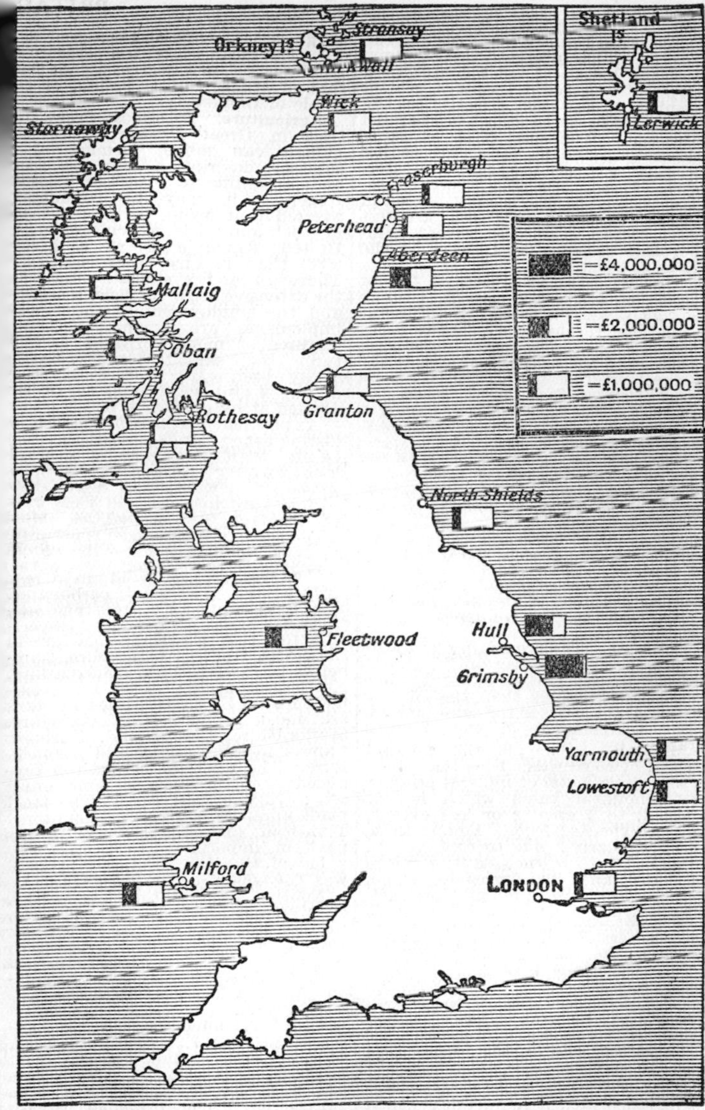

Map showing the chief fishing centres of the British Isles, and the value of the fish landed at each port making it more profitable for British farmers to devote themselves to the rearing of live stock. Of the whole area of Great Britain less than 60 per cent is under the plough or in pasture; but in England the proportion is about 75 per cent, and in Wales above 60 per cent, while in Scotland it is under 25 per cent (so much of Scotland being barren). In Ireland the proportion is about 75 per cent. The agriculture of Ireland, though the soil itself offers every advantage to the farmer, is in a very different condition from that of Great Britain, being in a very backward state on the whole, mainly owing to the subdivision of holdings and to over-cropping, combined with the ignorance and unskilfulness of the people.

The following table shows the distribution of crops in Great Britain in 1927:

	Acres.
Under corn crops	5,992,075
Under green crops and flax	2,784,008
Grasses under rotation, clover, &c.	3,957,255
In permanent pasture	16,792,840

The total in crops or grass amounted in 1927 to nearly 26,000,000 acres. Fully 6,000,000 acres are under cereal crops. The total number of agricultural holdings in Great Britain in 1926 was 478,655.

The following table shows the number of horses used in or connected with agriculture, and of cattle, sheep, and pigs in 1927.

	Great Britain.
Horses	1,249,323
Cattle	7,485,690
Sheep	24,607,752
Pigs	2,888,127

Minerals. Such is the mineral wealth of the British Isles that there is scarcely a metal or mineral product of economical value which is not worked, to a greater or less extent, beneath their surface. Among these the first place is due to *coal*, which, in regard both to the quantity raised annually and its aggregate value, surpasses any other mineral product. The coal-fields are not confined to one particular district, but extend as a series of basins in an irregular curve from central Scotland through northern and middle England to the Bristol Channel. On the east side of Scotland there are coal-fields both north and south of the Forth; farther west lie the coal-basins of Lanark, Renfrew, and Ayrshire; the first famous throughout the world for the immense manufacturing establishments which it mainly has called into existence and made prosperous.

In the north of England is the great coal-field centring near Newcastle, which gives it its name. The proximity of this field to the sea and the excellence of the coal, unrivalled for domestic use, early made it a great theatre of mining operations. The next coal-field to the south includes a large central space comprising parts of Yorkshire, Derbyshire, Nottinghamshire, and Lancashire, and divided by a separating belt of the lower strata of the Carboniferous system into a kind of twin fields, the one of which extends from Leeds to Nottingham, while the other has its greatest length from S.W. to N.E., and borders, at its E. and W. extremities respectively, on Manchester and Liverpool. The only other coal-field of a magnitude similar to those already mentioned is that of South Wales. There are several minor fields, as the North Staffordshire, the Shropshire, the Warwickshire, and the South Staffordshire. Coal is also worked in Kent.

The output of coal in the United Kingdom in the year 1925 was fully 243,176,231 tons; in 1927 it was 260,000,000 tons. Of the whole output, about a sixth is exported annually. The estimated value of the total output in 1925 was about £198,978,154.

The *iron*-ores smelted in Great Britain are principally carbonates. The most important ironstone districts are those of Yorkshire (especially the rich Cleveland district in the North Riding), Lancashire, Cumberland, Staffordshire, Lincolnshire, Northamptonshire, and the coal-measures of Scotland. Blast-furnaces are most numerous in Yorkshire, Staffordshire, Cumberland, Durham, Lancashire, S. Wales, and Lanarkshire. The quantity of pig-iron produced is about 7,000,000 tons annually; 7,350,000 in 1927. The steel made annually is over 7,000,000 tons. Tin, lead, and zinc are the metals next in importance to iron. The value of the lead produced in 1926 was £368,000; of the tin £571,000.

Another important article is salt, chiefly from rock-salt and brine-pits, the quantity produced in 1926 being valued at £1,378,000. Quarries, which furnish granite, freestone, and roofing-slates, are numerous throughout the kingdom, except in the S.E. of England. The total estimated value of the minerals raised in 1899 was nearly £117,310,000; in 1902, £107,134,800; in 1907, £135,279,000; in 1916, £214,034,524; in 1917, £223,933,989; in 1925, £221,385,931.

Fisheries. The principal British fisheries are those of herring, haddock, ling and cod, turbot, soles, and other

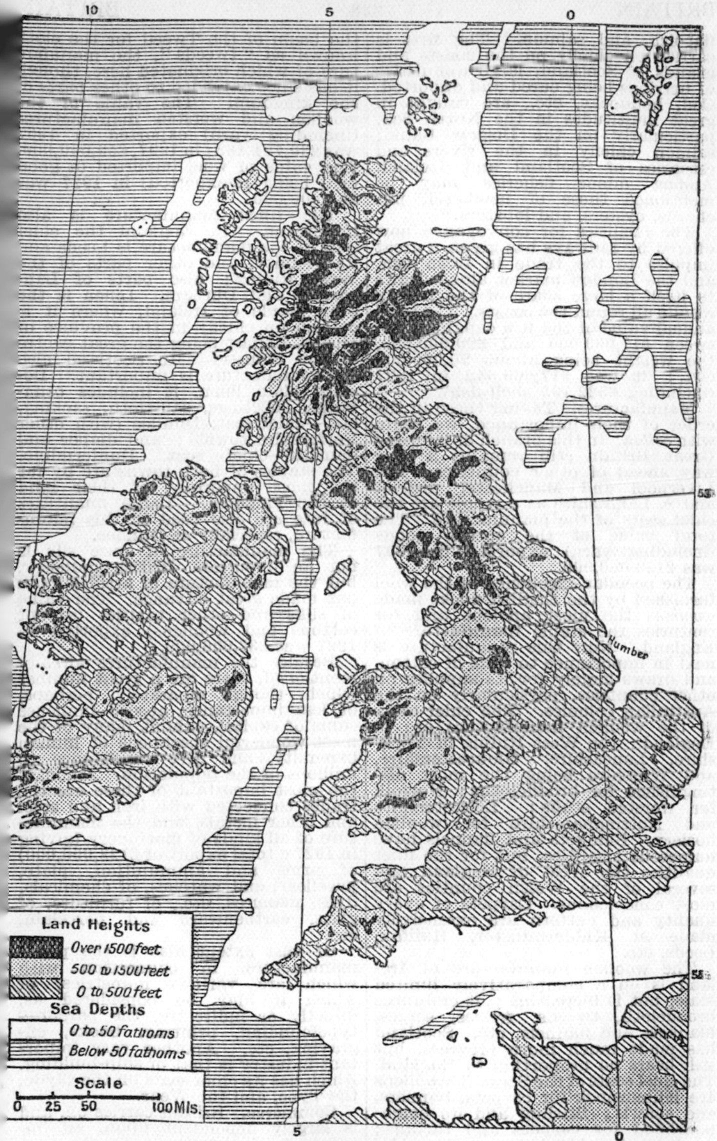

Map showing Physical Features of British Isles

flat-fish, and salmon. The first is carried on chiefly on the coasts and islands of Scotland, large quantities of herrings being cured and exported. Cod, haddocks, etc., are caught in great multitudes in the North Sea, particularly on the Dogger Bank; salmon chiefly in the rivers and estuaries of Scotland and Ireland. Among minor fisheries may be mentioned those of mackerel, pilchards, oysters, and lobsters.

The facilities for conveyance now offered by railways has given a great impulse to the trade in fresh fish, and the London market alone draws to itself a large share of the fishing results all round the coasts. The total annual value of the fish caught is between £17,000,000 and £20,000,000, the weight being about 20,000,000 cwt.; it was £17,660,542 in 1927 (including £522,705 shell-fish).

Manufactures. Taking these in the order of their importance, we begin with *cotton.* In this branch of industry Great Britain still remains a long way ahead of other countries. The Liverpool and Manchester district and S. Lancashire as a whole are the chief seats of the manufacture. The total value of the cotton goods (including yarn) exported in 1927 was £150,000,000.

The peculiar excellence of the wool furnished by the English flocks made *woollens* the most ancient and for centuries the staple manufacture of England. Now this manufacture is next in importance to that of cotton, and draws largely for its supplies on other countries, particularly on the Australian colonies. The chief seats of the woollen manufacture are in England: the West Riding of Yorkshire, Lancashire, Gloucestershire, and Wiltshire being the most distinguished for broadcloths; Norfolk for worsted stuffs; Leicestershire and Nottinghamshire for woollen hosiery. Blankets and flannels have numerous localities, but for the finer qualities the West of England and several of the Welsh counties are most conspicuous. Carpets of every quality and pattern are extensively made at Kidderminster, Halifax, Leeds, etc.

The woollen manufacture of Ireland is on a comparatively limited scale, but is increasing; it embraces broadcloth, tweeds, friezes, serges, blankets and flannels, etc. Scotland has made much more progress, but still bears no proportion to England. The chief seats of the Scottish woollens are Kilmarnock for carpets, bonnets, and shawls; Stirling and its neighbourhood for carpets and tartans; Ayrshire for blankets, etc.; Galashiels, Selkirk, and other places in the basin of the Tweed for the cloth known as "tweeds", the manufacture of which originated here, though it has since extended to other parts of the kingdom. The value of the woollen and worsted manufactures (including yarn) exported in 1907 was £30,721,168; in 1927, £59,000,000. The value of wool imported (a good deal being re-exported) in 1927 was £64,000,000.

The *linen* manufacture is also important. In England the chief seat of the manufacture is Leeds and its vicinity, and other parts of the West Riding; also parts of Lancashire and Durham. Linen is the only staple of Ireland, where it is carried on chiefly in the province of Ulster, Belfast being the great centre of the industry. In Scotland also the manufacture is important. Besides plain linen, it includes osnaburgs, sheetings, sail-cloth, sacking, etc.—chief seat, Dundee (with other Forfarshire towns); and diaper and damask—chief seat, Dunfermline. The staples of both towns are by far the most important of their kind in the kingdom. Large quantities of jute are also used in this manufacture, especially at Dundee.

The manufacture of pure silk is not an important British industry, but the manufacture of artificial silk has made great advance. The value of silks and other textiles (except cottons and woollens) exported in 1927 was £32,000,000.

Besides the manufactures already mentioned, there are a great number which, though separately, perhaps, of less importance, absorb immense sums of capital, exhibit many of the most wonderful specimens of human ingenuity, and give subsistence to millions of the population. Amongst the most important of these are the trades connected with iron and steel and other metals, and the manufacture of all kinds of machinery (giving in 1927 a total export of £128,000,000) of arms and ammunition, plate, jewellery, and watches, of chemicals, dyes, manures, etc., of furniture, of glass, earthenware and porcelain, etc.

Of vast extent also is the paper manufacture, in connection with which are various industries, of which it may be considered as, directly or indirectly, the parent—typefounding, printing, books, engraving, etc. Another very important industry is that of ship-building, which has its chief seats on the Clyde, the Tyne, and the Wear.

Commerce. Britain carries on, and is largely dependent upon, an immense foreign trade. As she is a manufacturing country with a popu-

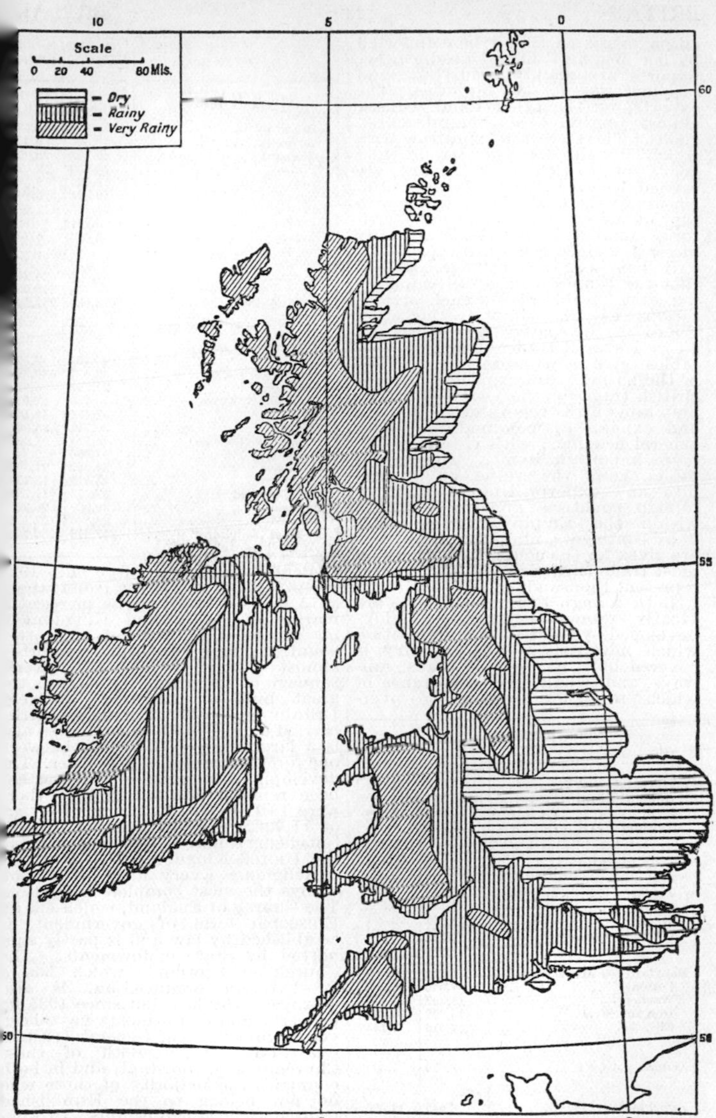

The British Isles, showing how the rainfall varies in different places

lation larger than can be supported by her own agricultural produce, her imports are mainly foodstuffs, and raw materials for the factories. The exports, on the other hand, consist almost entirely of manufactured goods. There are few countries with which Britain does not trade, and goods of British manufacture are carried to every part of the world. Naturally there is a large trade with the dominions and overseas territories, and this has been steadily increasing since the European War.

It has been generally recognised that the Empire can be self-supporting, and for this reason such organisations as the Empire Marketing Board have spared no efforts to foster Imperial trade. The following tables give a comprehensive view of the nature, value, and direction of British trade for the year 1927. The first table gives the value of imports and exports by commodities under general headings, with details of the more important items. The second table shows the value of imports into and exports from Britain to foreign countries and to countries within the Empire—the grouping is by continents, and separate figures are given for the countries with which most trade is carried on. The figures represent thousands of pounds.

Both foreign and inland trade are greatly promoted by the highly-developed systems of communication which now exist. The country is covered by a network of roads, railways, and canals, the importance of which to trade cannot be over-

	Imports	Exports
Food, Drink, and Tobacco ..	416,722	55,655
Grain and flour	55,818	4,338
Meat	93,905	3,859
Tobacco	11,376	5,823
Raw Materials	173,038	72,749
Coal	34	34,653
Timber	29,140	518
Cotton	27,182	1,521
Wool	34,544	12,591
Oil seeds, oils, &c. ..	24,964	3,333
Manufactured Articles ..	261,718	309,439
Cottons	8,942	56,943
Woollens	13,447	26,176
Iron and Steel	19,622	30,535
Oils, &c.	29,415	7,145
Animals not for food ..	3,329	1,698
Parcel post	6,445	14,936
Totals	**861,253**	**454,489**

	Imports	Expor
Foreign Countries		
Europe	369,645	171,39
Belgium	33,190	15,57
Denmark	46,696	9,21
Germany	64,163	32,00
France	40,922	32,02
Africa	11,109	8,28
Egypt	10,841	6,80
Asia	21,755	17,62
Persia	5,791	78
Japan	6,952	6,33
China	7,773	7,97
America	194,473	55,47
U.S.A.	104,009	26,21
Argentine	52,744	15,05
Total (foreign)	**613,836**	**267,75**
Empire		
Europe	40,495	45,36
Irish Free State	36,547	39,04
Africa	25,773	36,87
Union of S. Africa ..	13,120	22,93
Asia	57,401	48,18
India	36,711	33,09
Straits Settlements ..	5,391	4,965
Ceylon	11,996	2,820
Australasia	84,032	27,307
Australia	45,679	15,153
New Zealand	37,775	11,731
America	39,960	28,985
Canada	32,840	22,151
Total (Empire)	**247,416**	**186,736**

estimated. There were in 193 20,402¾ miles of railway, and abou 4673 miles of canal. The mercantil marine of the United Kingdom far greater than that of any othe country, and, indeed, comprise almost one-half of the total worl tonnage of shipping. Not only is th great bulk of the trade betwee Britain and other foreign countrie carried on in British ships, but so als is a large part of the trade betwee one foreign country and another. Th development of British shipping ha been remarkable, and in 1927 ther were 18,110 ships with a net tonnag of 11,906,528 (5678 ships of 516,99 tons being sailing vessels) registered i the United Kingdom.

Religion. Every form of religio enjoys the most complete toleration The Church of England, which has a Episcopal form of government, i established by law and is partly sup ported by State endowments. Th Church of Scotland, which has a Presbyterian organisation, is als established by law, but since 1925 it property and endowments have bee vested in a body of General Trustee (*see* SCOTLAND). Both of these Churches are Protestant, and in both countries the majority of those who do not belong to the Established Church are also Protestants. In England, however, these all belong to Churches having a different organisation from that of the Anglican Church

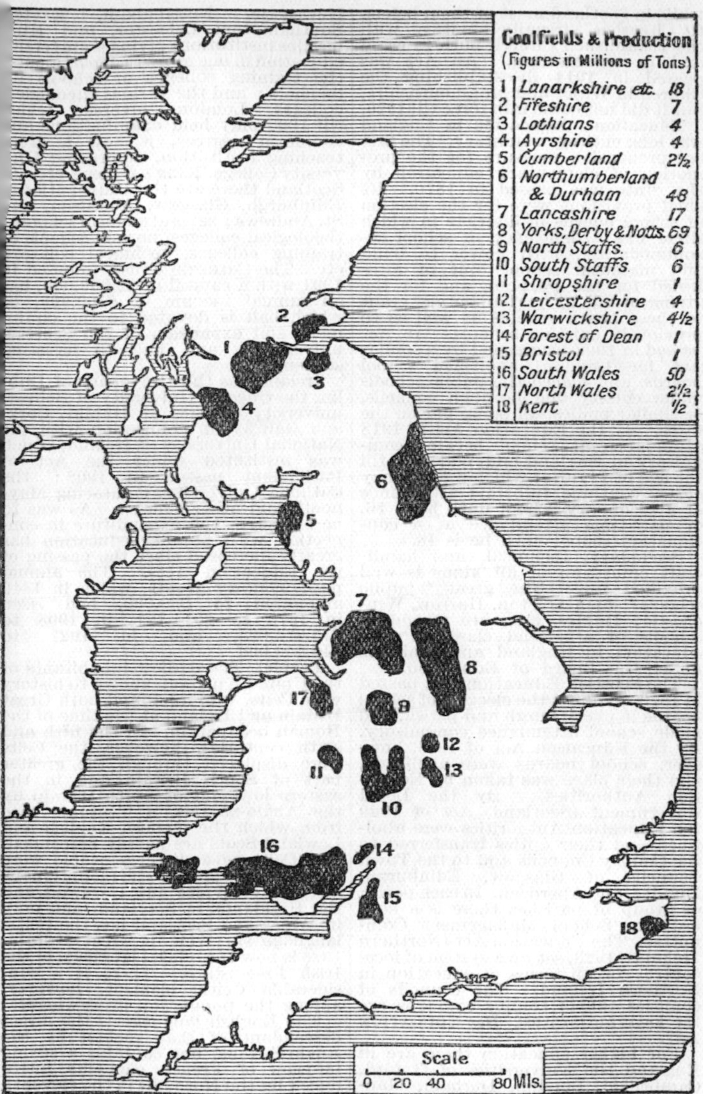

Coalfields and Productions

while in Scotland most of them belong to Churches virtually identical with the Established Church both in creed and in organisation. An Act was passed in 1914 disestablishing the Church in Wales and Monmouthshire, but it did not come into force till 1920.

Education. Education in England was long entirely voluntary. The first comprehensive measure for the promotion of elementary education by the State was passed in 1870. Its chief provisions were for the election of school boards in districts in which there was a deficiency of school accommodation, with power to build and maintain schools out of rates levied for the purpose, and for the giving of aid by parliamentary grant to these board schools as well as to previously existing schools. An Act passed in 1902 (succeeded by a similar Act for London) abolished school boards, and placed the public schools under county and borough councils, or similar bodies, all being put on the rates. By the Education Act of 1918 attendance at school became compulsory in England and Wales up till the age of 14, after which a pupil may either continue full-time attendance at a secondary school until he is 16, or part-time attendance at a continuation school until he is 18.

Secondary, technical, and handicraft education of all kinds is well provided for. The great " public schools " such as Eton, Harrow, Winchester, Rugby, etc., are secondary schools of a special class. Public education in England and Wales is under the Board of Education.

The Scottish Education Act, passed in 1872, required the election of school boards in every burgh and parish, and made school attendance compulsory. By the Education Act of 1918, however, school boards were abolished, and their place was taken by Education Authorities. By the Local Government (Scotland) Act of 1929 the Education Authorities were abolished and their duties transferred to the County Councils and to the Town Councils of Glasgow, Edinburgh, Dundee, and Aberdeen. In each parish or group of parishes there is a subordinate School Management Committee. The Education Act (Northern Ireland), 1923, set up a system of local control for all forms of education in Northern Ireland. The councils of counties and of county boroughs are the local authorities. *See* EDUCATION ACT.

For higher education there are in England the Universities of Oxford, Cambridge, London, Durham, Manchester, Birmingham, Liverpool, Leeds, Sheffield, Wales, Bristol, and Reading, also university colleges at Newcastle, Nottingham, Exeter, Southampton, Leicester, and Hull, besides institutions giving a university education in one or more departments; the training colleges or schools for teachers ; and the various theological colleges. London University, which till 1900 only held examinations and conferred degrees, is now a great teaching institution, embracing University College, King's College, etc. In Scotland there are the Universities of Edinburgh, Glasgow, Aberdeen, and St. Andrews ; several medical schools, theological colleges, normal schools or training colleges, technical colleges, etc. The Carnegie Trust, founded in 1901 with a capital of £2,000,000, has an annual income of £100,000, of which half is devoted to the equipment and expansion of the Scottish universities, and half to assisting students.

Ireland has the University of Dublin, the Queen's University of Belfast, university colleges at Dublin, Cork, and Galway, in connection with the National University of Ireland, which was instituted under the Act of Parliament passed in 1908 ; the Catholic University, embracing Maynooth and other colleges. As was to be expected, the expenditure in connection with popular education has greatly increased since the passing of the Education Acts. The annual parliamentary grants, which in 1840 amounted to £30,000, had risen in 1870 to £914,721, in 1908 to £13,272,625, and in 1927 to £46,450,000.

People. The earliest inhabitants of the United Kingdom known to history were Celts, who inhabited both Great Britain and Ireland at the time of the Roman occupation. In the fifth and sixth centuries, however, the Celts were displaced through the greater part of South Britain and in the eastern lowlands of North Britain by the Anglo-Saxons, a Teutonic race from which the modern English and Lowland Scots are mainly descended. The Celts as a distinct people were gradually confined to the mountainous districts of Wales and Cornwall and the Highlands of Scotland, and only in Wales and Scotland has the Celtic language survived in Great Britain. Erse is now the official language of the Irish Free State. There is a considerable Celtic element, however, among the population everywhere.

The English language is the direct descendant of that spoken by the Anglo-Saxons, but contains a strong infusion of French elements introduced by the Normans in the eleventh and following centuries, as well as other elements, chiefly of Latin and Greek origin, introduced in later

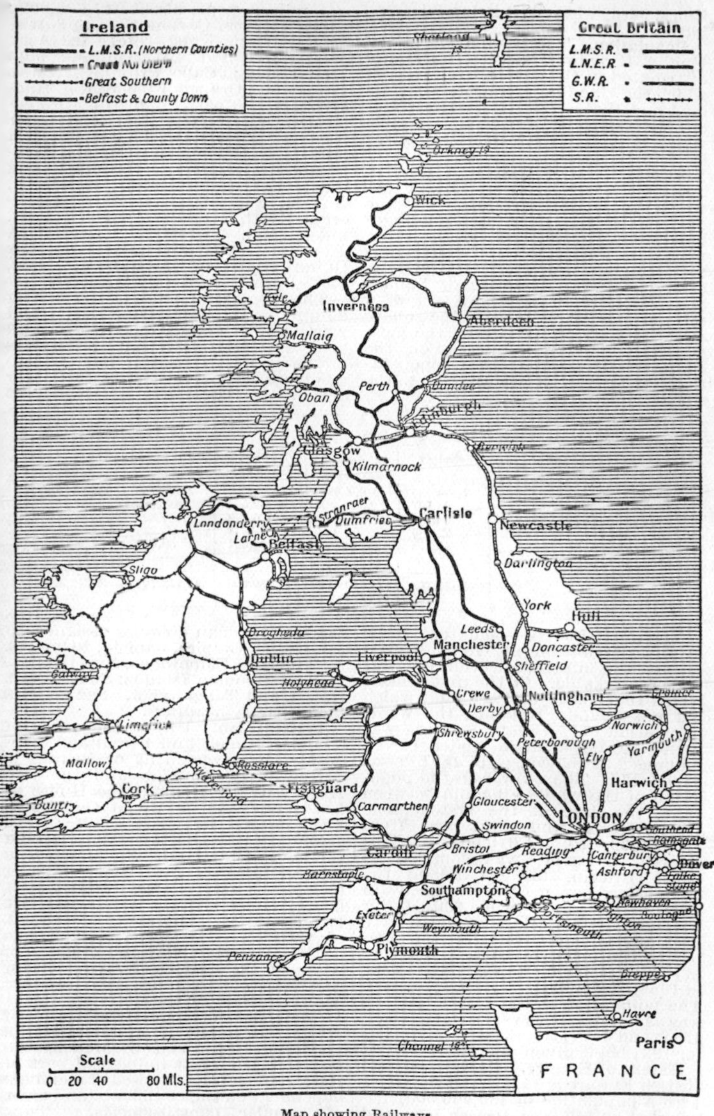

Map showing Railways

times, many of the last being scientific terms.

Population. The population of the United Kingdom is very unequally distributed in the several countries of which the kingdom is composed. England and Wales had, in 1931, a population equal to 685 to the square mile, which is denser than in any country in Europe, except Saxony; that of Northern Ireland 238, and that of Scotland 159. Except Middlesex, which is largely occupied by the metropolis, the most densely-populated county in England is Lancashire, which has a population of above 2680 to the square mile; and the population of the two counties of Lanark and Renfrew in Scotland shows a ratio of more than 1670 to the square mile. Saxony and Belgium, the most densely-populated countries on the continent of Europe, have a population respectively of 830 and 665 to the square mile.

sq. miles, pop. about 47,600,000; India, Cyprus, Ceylon, Straits Settlements, Hong-Kong, etc., in Asia, area, 2,126,121 sq. miles, pop. 333,000,000; Cape Province, Natal, Transvaal, Orange Free State, Rhodesia, Gold Coast, Mauritius, protectorates, Egypt, Zanzibar and other African possessions, 3,822,667 sq. miles, pop. 50,600,000; Canada, Newfoundland, Jamaica, Trinidad and other West India islands, Honduras, Guiana, and all possessions in America North or South, 4,008,214 sq. miles, pop. 11,142,000; Australia, Tasmania, New Zealand, Fiji, New Guinea, islands in the Pacific, etc., area, 3,278,917 sq. miles, pop. 7,795,000.

The increase of some of the British dominions, especially of Canada and Australia, in population, wealth, and trade has been something prodigious in the present century. Self-government has been conceded to the larger dominions. The above figures include

Divisions	Males	Females	Total, 1931	Total, 1921	Total, 1911
England	17,844,709	19,510,208	37,354,917	35,678,530	34,045,290
Wales	1,294,135	1,298,879	2,593,014	2,206,712	2,025,202
Scotland	2,325,867	2,516,687	4,842,554	4,882,288	4,760,904
Northern Ireland (1926) ..	608,205	648,117	1,256,322	1,256,322	1,250,531
Isle of Man	22,489	26,849	49,338	60,238	52,016
Channel Islands	43,958	49,103	93,061	89,614	96,899
Army and Navy abroad ..	—	—	—	—	145,729
Total	22,139,363	24,049,843	46,189,206	44,173,704	42,376,571

The great increase that took place in the population of Great Britain during the nineteenth century was very remarkable. At the first census, which took place in 1801 (and which did not include Ireland), the whole population of Great Britain was found to be a little under eleven millions; at the census of 1891 it was 33,028,172. The growth in the population of the whole kingdom between 1831, the date of the first reliable Irish census, and 1901 was from 24,400,000 to 41,610,000. This growth, however, was confined to Great Britain, for in Ireland the population has greatly declined (in 1841 it was fully 8,000,000). For England the following estimates have been made for periods before the nineteenth century: in 1086, 1,500,000; in 1377, 2,500,000; in 1583, 4,500,000; in 1688, 5,000,000; in 1750, 6,400,000. The population of the British Islands was as follows by the censuses of 1931, 1921, and 1911, the males and females for 1931 being given separately :—

Extent of Empire. The area of the British Empire is 13,356,759 sq. miles, with a population of 450,000,000, distributed as follows: British Isles and possessions in Europe, area, 120,840

the late German colonies assigned to the British Empire, namely, Bismarck Archipelago, Cameroons, New Guinea, Samoa, Solomon Islands, South West Africa, and Tanganyika. See articles under these headings.

Constitution. Under the name of a constitutional and hereditary monarchy the government of Britain is vested in a sovereign and the two Houses of Parliament—the House of Lords and the House of Commons. Laws passed by these Houses, and assented to by the sovereign, become the laws of the land. But under this general fixity of form the centre of real power may change greatly, as it has in Great Britain within the last two centuries. The sovereign's right of veto on Acts of Parliament has practically passed into desuetude, while of the two legislative Houses, the House of Commons, from its being the expression of the national will as a whole, has become the real centre of power and influence. Popular rights and liberties are thus secured by the fact that the most influential part of the legislature is composed of members dependent on the confidence and trust of popular constituencies. Thus though the powers of the Parliament may be regarded as unlimited, yet it must always in the end give way before a decided and clear expression of public opinion. It is often said, therefore, that the constitution of Great Britain is in great part an unwritten law, and this unwritten law is continually receiving additions and adapting itself to the new forces and needs of the time.

This natural flexibility of the British constitution is one of its greatest merits, and what most distinguishes it from the more rigid systems of other countries. One of the best examples of this quiet growth of unwritten law is the position occupied by such a body as the Cabinet, a body never officially recognised by any Act of Parliament, and wholly unknown to the written law, yet practically the highest executive body in the kingdom, though nominally the executive government is vested in the sovereign. On this subject Walter Bagehot remarks: "The efficient secret of the English constitution may be described as the close union, the nearly complete fusion of the executive and legislative powers. According to the traditional theory as it exists in all the books, the goodness of our constitution consists in the entire separation of the legislative and executive authorities, but in truth its merit consists in their singular approximation. The connecting-link is the Cabinet."

The Sovereign. By an Act of Parliament of 1927 the sovereign's title is "by the Grace of God, of Great Britain, Ireland, and the British Dominions beyond the Seas, King, Defender of the Faith, Emperor of India." The fundamental maxim upon which the right of succession to the throne depends is, that the crown is, by common law and constitutional custom, hereditary, and that the right of inheritance may from time to time be changed or limited by Parliament; under which limitations the crown still continues hereditary in the English House of Windsor, the name adopted by the royal family in 1917. The crown descends to the males in preference to the females, strictly adhering to the rule of primogeniture. The sovereign is of age at eighteen years.

The heir to the crown has, since the time of Edward III., inherited the title of Duke of Cornwall, and receives that of Prince of Wales by letters patent. By letters patent of 30th Nov., 1917, the titles of royal highness and prince or princess are to be restricted in future to the sovereign's children, the children of the sovereign's sons, and the eldest living son of the eldest son of the Prince of Wales.

The power of the sovereign is limited by the laws. The divine right, so obstinately maintained by the Stuarts, was never recognised by the nation, and William III., Mary, and Anne ascended the throne, according to express declarations, only by virtue of a transmission of the crown to them by the nation. But the maxim has been acknowledged, particularly since the Restoration, that there is no power in the State superior to the royal prerogatives; the acts of the king are therefore subject to no examination, and the king is not personally responsible to any tribunal: hence the maxim, The king can do no wrong.

Yet there is sufficient provision for confining the exercise of the royal power within the legal limits. 1. All royal acts are construed in accordance with the laws, and it is taken for granted that the king can never intend anything contrary to law. 2. The counsellors of the king are responsible for the royal acts, and, as well as all those who are concerned in the execution of them, are liable to impeachment and examination, without the right of defending themselves by pleading the royal commands. 3. The Parliament and the judicial tribunals have also the right to discuss freely such royal acts, and, in particular, Parliament and each individual member of the Upper House has the right to make remonstrances to the Crown. 4. Individuals are protected from any abuses of the royal power by the Habeas Corpus Act, the liability of the agents to prosecution, the right of complaining to Parliament, and the liberty of the Press.

The king is the supreme head of the State in peace and war, the lord paramount of the soil, the fountain of justice and honour, and the supreme head of the Church. He has the prerogative of rejecting Bills in Parliament, which, however, has not been exercised since the year 1692. As the generalissimo, or the first in military command within the kingdom, he has the sole power of raising and regulating fleets and armies, which, however, is virtually controlled by the necessity he is under of obtaining supplies from Parliament. As the fountain of justice, and general conservator of the peace of the kingdom, he alone has the right of erecting courts of judicature, and all jurisdictions of courts are derived from the Crown. As the fountain of honour, of office, and of privilege, he has the power of conferring dignities, privileges, offices, etc. In the foreign relations of the nation he is considered the nation's representative, and makes treaties, declares war, etc. As advisers he has the Privy Council and the Cabinet.

The Parliament. The origin of the British Parliament has been sought, rightly enough, in the *witenagemôts* or national assemblies of the Anglo-Saxons. In a somewhat different form these were continued in the Norman times, and as early at least as the reign of Henry III. we find not only the barons and the high ecclesiastics, but also the knights of the shire, with the burgesses, summoned to attend. These formed the *three estates*, now known as the lords spiritual, the lords temporal, and the commons.

In the reign of Edward III. (1327-77) the separation of the estates into two Houses—the House of Lords, consisting of the lords spiritual and the lords temporal, and the House of Commons, consisting of the knights, citizens, and burgesses — became settled. All the peers were not originally entitled to a seat as a matter of right, but only those who were expressly summoned by the king. Every hereditary peerage of the United Kingdom now entitles its holder to a seat in the House of Lords. The number is indefinite, and may be increased at the pleasure of the Crown, which, however, cannot deprive a peer of the dignity once bestowed. The Upper House at present comprises about 740 members, but the voting strength was about 720 in 1931. By the Act of Union with Scotland, 16 representatives of the Scottish peerage are elected by the Scottish nobility for each Parliament's duration. Ireland used to send 28 peers elected for life, but vacancies are not now filled.

The Parliament is not permanent, and it is the royal prerogative to summon and dissolve it. The first business of the Commons is to elect a Speaker. The members then take the oath of allegiance, and when this is done the king's speech is read, being answered by an address from each House. In the Upper House the Lord Chancellor presides, holding the position of the Speaker in the Commons. All grants of subsidies or parliamentary aids must originate with the House of Commons, and the Lords have not the right to amend, but only to accept or reject, a money Bill.

The powers, however, of the House of Lords have been much restricted by the Parliament Act, 1911. This Act enables the Commons to pass certain Bills without the consent of the other Chamber. Thus, if a money Bill is not passed unamended by the House of Lords within a month of its being sent up, it becomes law upon the royal assent being signified, without the consent of the Upper House. The Speaker of the Commons decides what is a money Bill within the meaning of the Act.

As the Parliament is summoned, so it is prorogued by the royal authority. A dissolution of the Parliament is effected either by the authority of the Crown, or by length of time. The House of Commons being chosen but for five years, at the expiration of that time Parliament is dissolved *ipso facto*.

The Lower House of Parliament has the direction of all financial concerns; and there is no subject which may not be brought before it by petition, complaint, or motion of a member.

The Upper House is the supreme court of judicature in the nation. In civil cases it (now represented by the Lords of Appeal in Ordinary) is the supreme court of appeal from the superior tribunals of the three kingdoms. In indictments for treason or felony, or misprision thereof, where the accused is a peer of the realm, the House of Lords are the judges of the law and the fact. In cases of impeachment by the House of Commons the House of Lords are also the judges. All the forms of a criminal trial are then observed, and the verdict must be by a majority of at least twelve votes.

The House of Commons previous to the Reform Bill of 1832 consisted of 658 members, of whom 513 were for England and Wales, 45 for Scotland, and 100 for Ireland. In this representation there were great injustices and anomalies. Many of the boroughs had quite fallen into decay, so that a place like the famous Old Sarum, which consisted only of the ruins of an old castle, sent two members to Parliament, while great manufacturing towns like Manchester and Birmingham were absolutely without representation. Not only the *rotten boroughs*, as these decayed constituencies were called, but also in many cases the towns, where the right of suffrage belonged to a small number of freeholders, were practically in the hands of a single family, and in this way a few great houses—Norfolk, Bedford, Devonshire, and the Pelhams—commanded more than 100 seats in Parliament. For the few places that were in the hands of independent voters a shameless system of bribery existed, in spite of the prohibitory laws, and the prices of votes were generally well known: a seat for a small place cost about £5000.

The Reform Bill of 1832 brought great changes. Occupiers of lands or tenements in counties at a yearly rent of not less than £50, and occupiers as owner or tenant of a house or shop in a borough of a yearly value of £10, now received the franchise. Fifty-six rotten boroughs were wholly disfranchised; thirty boroughs were deprived of one member; and one borough (Melcombe-Regis cum Weymouth, which had four) of two members; twenty-two boroughs were created in England to return two members each, and nineteen boroughs to return one member each. Besides taking away the right of election from many insignificant places, and vesting it in large, or at least in tolerably numerous constituencies in new boroughs, the Act introduced something like uniformity in the qualifications of the voters of the old boroughs and cities, and extended the elective franchise from close corporations, or privileged bodies, to the citizens at large.

After several unsuccessful attempts by Lord John Russell, Lord Palmerston, and Gladstone to pass Bills for further reform, in 1867 Disraeli, then Chancellor of the Exchequer, succeeded in carrying through a Bill which conferred the borough franchise on all householders who had resided in the borough for twelve months previous to the last day of July in any year, and had been assessed for and paid poor-rates, and on all lodgers who had occupied for a like period lodgings of the yearly value of £10 unfurnished. In counties the franchise was bestowed on occupiers as owners or tenants of subjects of £12 rateable value, and the copyhold and leasehold franchise was reduced from £10 to £5.

This Bill related only to England and Wales, but Bills of a similar character were passed for Scotland and Ireland in the following year. In this way the electorate, which was 1,352,970 in 1867, rose to 2,243,259 in 1870. The total number of members still remained at 658. To Manchester, Liverpool, Birmingham, and Leeds were assigned three members each, and to London University one. Populous counties were further divided, and to many of the divisions two members each were given.

From the union of Scotland with England in 1707 till 1832 the former returned forty-five members to the House of Commons, thirty for the thirty-three counties, and fifteen for fifteen districts or burghs. Superiors, or persons holding directly from the Crown, alone voted in the counties. In two counties there were only three real voters in each. The number of persons who actually voted at the elections of the burghs was very inconsiderable, consisting, in general, of the magistrates and town council, amounting only to twenty in each burgh, or in all the sixty-six burghs to 1320.

By the Scottish Reform Act of 1832 eight members were added to the representation: Edinburgh and Glasgow receiving two each, and Aberdeen, Dundee, Greenock, Perth, and Paisley one each. The right of voting was also placed as near as possible on the same footing as in England; but the number of members, though increased, was not in proportion with the constituency of England or even Ireland. By the Scottish Reform Act of 1868 the burgh franchise was assimilated to that of England, being conferred on householders, but in counties the occupation tenure was £14 or upwards. Seven additional seats were given: one to the Universities of Aberdeen and Glasgow, one to those of Edinburgh and St. Andrews, one to Glasgow city (which now had three), one to Dundee (which now had two), and one each to the counties of Lanark, Ayr, and Aberdeen, which were divided into two divisions, each returning a member.

Since the legislative union with Britain in 1801 Ireland had sent 100 members to the House of Commons. By the Reform Act of 1832 five members were added, and £10 copyholders, etc., admitted amongst the classes of county voters. In 1850 occupiers of land rated at £12 a year were admitted to vote. In the borough franchise the £10 qualification for owner or occupant was adopted in the reform of 1832, much the same as in England; and by the Act of 1850 the franchise was further extended to £8 occupiers. By the Reform Bill of 1868 the occupation franchise in towns was reduced from £8 to £4, and for lodgers it was fixed at the same as in England and Scotland.

The Representation of the People Act of 6th Dec., 1884, established a uniform householder and a uniform lodger franchise throughout the kingdom. Equally important changes were effected by the Redistribution Act passed in June, 1885. By it 79 small boroughs in England and Wales (including four districts of boroughs in the latter) and 24 in Ireland ceased to return members separately, while in Scotland the Haddington and Wigtown districts of burghs lost the burgh franchise. In England 36 small boroughs, and in Ireland 3, lost one member each. The members for Liverpool were increased to 9, for Birmingham, the Tower Hamlets, and Glasgow to 7 each, for Manchester to 6, for Leeds and Sheffield to 5 each, and other important centres in proportion. Thirty-three new boroughs, chiefly in the London Metropolitan district were created. Many of the larger boroughs were divided and a member given to each division; large counties were dealt with in a similar way. The numerical strength of the House was also raised, the gross number of members being 670, of which England got 465 (2 additional), Wales 30 (as before), Scotland 72 (12 additional), and Ireland 103 (2 less).

Under the Representation of the People Act, 1918, the franchise was revised and extended, about 2 million new male voters and 6 million women being enfranchised. Under the same Act the seats in Great Britain were redistributed on the basis of one member of the House of Commons for every 70,000 of the population. By the Representation of the People (Equal Franchise) Act, 1928, the franchise was extended to women on the same terms as to men.

The following is a summary of the distribution of members according to the Act of 1918. On 10th Aug., 1911,

	Counties	Boroughs	Univ.	Tot.
England and Wales	254	266	8	528
Scotland ..	38	33	3	74
N. Ireland ..	8	4	1	13
	300	303	12	615

provision was made for the payment of a salary of £400 a year to every member of the House, excluding those who are already in receipt of salaries as officers of the House, as ministers, or as officers of His Majesty's household. There were 128 members in 1914 who declined to receive a salary in war-time.

Ranks and Titles. The laws acknowledge only two distinctions of rank or civil status, the nobility and the commonalty. The distinction is by no means like that between the patricians and plebeians in ancient Rome, nor that between the nobles and citizens of France in the eighteenth century, and the peculiar privileges of the nobility are few and insignificant. Intermarriages with commoners are usual, and the sons of peers mingle with commoners in the House of Commons, where wealth, talent, and industry are at least as well represented as birth. Moreover, the House of Lords is continually recruited from the House of Commons by the conferring of peerages on its more distinguished members. The peers are exempted from the performance of a few little public services, such as sitting on juries, etc. They have also a right to be tried by the House of Lords on indictments for treason, or felony, or misprision thereof; but the administration of justice before this tribunal is as strict as in the ordinary courts. Their persons cannot be arrested in civil cases.

The titles borne by those who form the peerage are, in a descending scale, duke, marquess, earl, viscount, baron. Of these earl is the oldest, this title dating from the Anglo-Saxon period, when it was equivalent to that of *ealdorman* or governor of a shire. The other ranks at this early period were those of the *athlings*, or princes of royal blood; *thanes*, who were royal officers or considerable landowners; and the *ceorls*, or husband-men, below, whom were the serfs or slaves.

After the Conquest the title of *baron* came into use. The *barons* formed an inferior class of nobles to the earls, though the term might also be used to include all the peers. The title of *duke* arose under Edward III., who created his eldest son Duke of Cornwall (1337). The title of marquess was introduced in the time of Richard II.; that of viscount during the reign of Henry VI. It is only the actual holders of these titles who are, strictly speaking, the nobility; their families are only noble by courtesy.

The chief privilege that the titles confer is a seat in the House of Peers or—since the term *lord* is often used as equivalent to *peer*—the House of Lords. The Scottish and Irish peers sit in the House only by deputation; but many Scottish and Irish peers have also titles belonging to the peerage of Great Britain or the United Kingdom, in virtue of which they sit; thus the Earl of Moray sits as Baron Stuart.

The titles of nobility above mentioned are inherited by the eldest son, who, during the life of the father, bears by courtesy his next highest title if he is a duke, marquess, or earl; if the father be a viscount or baron the son is only an "honourable"; the heir apparent to a Scottish peerage (below the rank of earl) is, however, in many instances known as "The Master of ——." (*See* ADDRESS, FORMS OF.) The younger sons of a duke or marquess are by courtesy entitled to be called "Lord John ——," or whatever their Christian names may be. The younger sons of an earl, however, are like all the sons of a viscount or baron, "The Hon. John ——." The daughters of dukes, marquesses, and earls are "Lady Jane ——," "Lady Mary ——," and the daughters of viscounts and barons are "The Hon. Jane ——," "The Hon. Mary ——."

Next below the rank of the nobility are the *baronets*. This dignity was created by James I. in 1611, and descends to the eldest son. There are no privileges annexed to the baronetcy, but the title is considered as an honour, and is often bestowed on men who have distinguished themselves in a civil or military capacity.

Below the baronets are *knights* (who also have *Sir* before their names) and esquires, and all others that may be classed among the gentry. This last term is sufficiently vague, but may be said to include the richer landed proprietors, and all to whom wealth, office, or talents have secured a certain respect and standing in society. All these may be said to have a claim to be considered as of the rank of esquires, which, however, by law is somewhat restricted in its application.

Army and Navy. The British army is raised on the authority of the sovereign, who is looked on as its head; but the number of troops and the cost of the different branches are regulated annually by a vote of the House of Commons. Till 1908 the army consisted of the regular army and auxiliary forces, this latter including militia and volunteers; from 1908 till 1914 it consisted of the regular army and territorial force. The total number of men in the estimates for 1908-9 was 799,610, including reserves, territorial force (314,063), regular troops in India, and an expeditionary force of 160,000. The annual cost, formerly £17,000,000 or £18,000,000, was £73,000,000 for 1900-1, £27,459,000 for 1908-9.

No citizen was obliged to bear arms except for the defence of his country. The militia, while it existed, could be raised, when required, by ballot. Conscription was introduced into Great Britain by the Military Service Act, 1916, covering men from 18 to 40 years of age. Under the Military Service Act, 1918, the age for compulsory service was raised to 50 for men in general, and to 55 years for duly-qualified medical practitioners.

At the end of 1917 the strength of the British army (exclusive of the army in India) was over 4,000,000 men. In 1927-8 the total establishment of the Regular Army was 210,436, and the Army Estimates for the year were £41,565,000. The head of military affairs is the Secretary of State for War, who is responsible to Parliament. *See* ARMY.

The administration of the navy is carried on by the Board of Admiralty, consisting of seven members, and having at its head the First Lord, who has supreme authority. A reorganisation of the Admiralty took place in May, 1917, and in Jan., 1918. The estimates for 1914-5 made provision for a total of 151,000 men and boys in the naval service, of whom 118,078 were officers and seamen serving afloat, 18,585 marines, 3130 were men belonging to the coastguard, and 7875 boys in training, besides reserves 51,836. The total number in Dec., 1917, was 430,000, including 42,000 of the Royal Naval Air Service, whilst the estimates for 1926-7 made provision for a total of 102,675 men and boys to be employed in the naval service. The estimated pre-war expenditure for 1914-5 was £51,550,000, whilst the naval estimates for 1926-7 amounted to £58,100,000.

The British navy is very powerful and formidable; it consisted, at the end of 1928, of 20 battleships and battle-cruisers, 50 cruisers (other 13 building), 17 flotilla leaders, 150 destroyers, 55 submarines, 8 aircraft carriers, and numerous other craft.

Finance, Revenue, Expenditure. The practice of borrowing money in order to defray a part of the war expenditure began in the reign of William III. At first it was customary to borrow upon the security of some tax, or portion of a tax, set apart as a fund for discharging the principal and the interest of the sum borrowed. This discharge was, however, very rarely effected, and at length the practice of borrowing for a fixed period was almost entirely abandoned, and most loans were made upon *interminable* annuities, or until such time as it might be convenient for Government to pay off the principal.

Originally the interest paid by the Government on these loans was comparatively high and subject to considerable variation. But in the reign of George II. a different practice was adopted. Instead of varying the interest upon the loan, the rate of interest was generally fixed at three or three and a half per cent, the necessary variation being made in the principal funded. Thus, if Government were anxious to borrow in a three per cent stock, and could not negotiate a loan for less than four and a half per cent, they effected their object by giving the lender, in return for every £100 advanced, £150 three per cent stock—that is, they bound the country to pay him or his assignees £4, 10*s*. a year in all time to come, or, otherwise, to extinguish the debt by a payment of £150. In consequence of this practice the principal of the debt now amounts to far more than the sum actually advanced by the lenders.

At the death of William III. the public debt, partly by reason of the long wars, amounted to £16,394,702, the public income being £3,895,205. By far the greater part of the next reign also was a time of war, and on the death of Queen Anne the national debt amounted to £54,145,363. The reign of George I. was undisturbed by war, which enabled the Government of the time to reduce the debt by £2,053,125, so that at the accession of George II. the whole amount of the debt was £52,092,238. At the conclusion of the Peace of Paris after the Seven Years' War it was £138,865,430, and at the end of the American War, £239,350,148. During the French War £601,500,334 of new debt was contracted, and on the 1st of Feb., 1817, when the English and Irish exchequers were consolidated, the total debt was £840,850,491. Since then the debt has been greatly reduced, with temporary increases owing to the Crimean and S. African Wars.

At the commencement of the European War, Aug., 1914, the whole amount of it was £708,000,000. This included both a funded and an unfunded debt. The latter species is that for which no fixed provision has been made, and consists partly of exchequer bonds and treasury bills running for short periods at a definite rate of interest. In 1927 the total debt amounted to £7,653,900,000, of which amount £2,065,000,000 represented advances to allies and dominions.

There is besides this an immense local debt. The public revenue and expenditure have greatly increased in recent times; thus in 1886-7 they were respectively £90,772,758 and £89,996,752; in 1890-1, £89,489,112 and £87,732,855; while in the year 1899-1900 the revenue was £119,839,905, and the expenditure £133,722,407; in 1908-9, £154,350,000 and £154,109,000; and in 1913-4, £198,243,000 and £197,493,000 respectively. In 1919 the revenue was £889,020,825, and the expenditure £2,579,301,188; in 1920 they were £1,339,571,381 and £1,665,772,928; in 1927, £805,701,000 and £842,395,027; and in 1932-3, £766,800,000 and £766,004,000 respectively.

History. The island in the remotest times bore the name of *Albion*. From a very early period it was visited by Phœnicians, Carthaginians, and Greeks, for the purpose of obtaining tin. Cæsar's two expeditions, 55 and 54 B.C., made it known to the Romans, by whom it was generally called *Britannia*; but it was not till the time of Claudius, nearly a hundred years after, that the Romans made a serious attempt to convert Britain into a Roman province.

Some forty years later, under Agricola, the ablest of the Roman generals in Britain, they had extended the limits of the Provincia Romana as far as the line of the Forth and the Clyde. Here the Roman armies came into contact with the Caledonians of the interior, described by Tacitus as large-limbed, red-haired men. After defeating the Caledonians under Galgacus at "Mons Graupius," Agricola marched victoriously northwards as far as the Moray Firth, establishing stations and camps, remains of which are still to be seen.

But the Romans were unable to retain their conquests in the northern part of the island, and were finally forced to abandon their northern wall and forts between the Clyde and the Forth and retire behind their second wall, built in A.D. 120 by Hadrian, between the Solway and the Tyne. Thus the southern part of the island alone remained Roman, and became specially known as Britannia, while the northern portion was distinctively called Caledonia. The capital of Roman Britain was York (Eboracum).

Under the rule of the Romans many flourishing towns arose. Great roads were made, traversing the whole country and helping very much to develop its industries. Christianity was also introduced, and took the place of the Druidism of the native British. Under the tuition of the Romans the useful arts and even many of the refinements of life found their way into the southern part of the island.

Thus from the time of the Roman conquest, and still more decidedly after the Saxon invasions in the fifth century, the history of Britain branches off into a history of the southern part of the island, afterwards known as England, and a history of the northern part of the island, afterwards named Scotland. It was not till the union of the crowns in 1603 that the destinies of England and Scotland began again to unite; and it was not till the final union of the Parliaments in 1707 that the histories of the two countries may be said to merge into one. From this latter period accordingly we shall give an outline of the history of the United Kingdom. *See also the articles* ENGLAND, SCOTLAND, and IRELAND.

The measure which declared the Parliaments of England and Scotland united, and the two countries one kingdom, known as the United Kingdom of Great Britain, was passed, after violent opposition, in the reign of Queen Anne, 1st of May, 1707. This union, however much it was opposed by the prejudices and interests of particular men or classes at the time, has contributed very much to the prosperity of both countries.

The Grand Alliance, which it had been the aim of William's later years to form between Holland, Austria, and England against the threatening growth of French power, now held the field against the armies of France, and the victories of Marlborough at Blenheim and Ramillies, and the taking of Gibraltar and Barcelona, ended in the Treaty of Utrecht in 1713, by which the British right of sovereignty over Hudson's Bay, Newfoundland, Nova Scotia, Minorca, and Gibraltar was acknowledged, and the foundation of Britain's imperial and colonial power securely laid. The remainder of Anne's reign was distracted by the never-ending altercations of domestic parties. She died on the 1st of Aug., 1714; and with her ended the line of the Stuarts, who had held the sceptre of England 112, and that of Scotland 343 years.

At her death George I., Elector of Hanover, maternally descended from Elizabeth, daughter of James I., according to the Act of Settlement, ascended the throne of Britain. The Whigs under this prince regained that superiority in the national councils of which they had long been deprived, and this, along with the suspension of the Habeas Corpus Act and some other extreme precautionary measures, increased the irritation of the Tory and Stuart party.

The '15 Rebellion. In 1715 the Earl of Mar in Scotland and the Earl of Derwentwater in England raised the standard of rebellion and proclaimed the Chevalier St. George (the Old Pretender) king. But the insurrection, feebly supported by the people, was soon suppressed. In 1716 the Septennial Act was passed, making Parliament of seven instead of three years' duration. In 1720 occurred the extraordinary growth and collapse of the South Sea Company.

From this date till 1742 the government was virtually in the hands of Sir Robert Walpole, the first, we might say, of modern premiers, governing the Cabinet and chiefly responsible for its doings. Walpole had great sagacity, prudence, and business ability, and could manage dexterously the king, the Parliament, and the people alike. It is true that in the case of the Parliament he achieved this by undue influence in elections and a scandalous use of bribery. But the power he thus acquired was generally wisely used. The failure of the war with Spain, into which he had reluctantly entered, drove him from office, and in 1742 his long ministry came to an end.

In 1743 George II., frightened at the dangers to Hanover, dragged Britain into the wars between France, Prussia, and Austria, regarding the succession of the Emperor Charles. George himself fought at the head of his troops at Dettingen (1743), where he obtained a complete victory over the French, which was balanced, however, later on by the defeat at Fontenoy (1745).

The '45 Rebellion. A fresh attempt was now made to restore the Stuart family to the throne of Britain. Charles Edward, son of the Old Pretender, having been furnished by France with a small supply of money and arms, landed on the coast of Lochaber, in the Western Highlands, in 1745, and was joined by a considerable number of the people. Marching southwards with 1500 Highlanders, his forces increasing as he advanced, he entered Edinburgh without opposition; and having defeated Sir John Cope near Prestonpans he marched into England. He now took Carlisle, and advanced, through Lancaster, Preston, and Manchester, to Derby, within 100 miles of London; but finding himself disappointed of expected succours from France, and the English Tories, contrary to his expectations, keeping aloof, he commenced his retreat into Scotland, closely pursued by the king's troops, whom he again defeated at Falkirk. With this victory his good fortune terminated. The Duke of Cumberland, having arrived from the Continent, put himself at the head of the forces which were destined to check the rebels; and the armies having met at Culloden, near Inverness, Charles was completely defeated. After lurking for six months amidst the wilds of Inverness-shire, he at length, with much difficulty, escaped to France.

The War of the Austrian Succession, which still continued, and which was the cause of hostilities between the French and British in India as well as elsewhere, was terminated by the Treaty of Aix-la-Chapelle in 1748. During most of this period Pelham and his brother, the Duke of Newcastle, had been the ruling ministers, and in their hands the art of government had reached a low level both as regards morality and ability. In 1752 the *New Style* of reckoning time was introduced, and, the *Old Style* being eleven days behind, the 3rd of September, 1752, was called the 14th. At the same time the 1st of January was fixed as the opening day of the year, instead of the 25th of March.

Seven Years' War. Soon after, the French, uneasy at the growing colonial power of Britain, made a determined effort against the British colonies and possessions in North America and the East Indies, and at first the British met with several disasters in America. In 1756 the Seven Years' War broke out, Austria and France being allied on the one side, and Prussia and

Britain on the other, and ill success attended the British arms in Europe also.

Fortunately, a great war minister, William Pitt, now took the helm of the State. In 1758 the British made themselves masters of several French settlements in North America, while the attack made by Wolfe on Quebec in 1759 was completely successful, and gave Britain the whole of Canada. The same year the British and their allies defeated the French at Minden in Prussia. In the East Indies the French were even less successful than in America. Clive's victory at Plassey (1757) and Coote's at Wandewash (1760) secured the British Empire in the East, and together with the naval feats of Hawke and Boscawen made Britain the greatest of maritime and colonial powers.

On the accession of George III. in 1760 hostilities were still carried on, generally to the advantage of the French as far as the theatre of war in Germany was concerned, but still more to their loss in the other quarters of the world where they were engaged with the British in a struggle for supremacy, and this notwithstanding that Spain had now joined her forces to those of France. At length the success of the British arms induced France and Spain to accede to terms, and the war ended by the Treaty of Paris in 1763. The French relinquished nearly all their possessions in North America; Minorca was restored to Britain; in the East Indies they got back their factories and settlements, on condition that they should maintain neither forts nor troops in Bengal; Cuba and Manilla were resigned to the Spaniards. In Europe everything was restored to the *status quo*.

American War of Independence. The expenses of this war, which had been undertaken partly for the defence of the American colonies, had added upwards of £72,000,000 to the national debt. It seemed to the British people to be just that the Americans should be taxed to assist in payment of the interest. The Americans did not deny the justice, but replied that if they were to be taxed they had a right to be represented in Parliament, in order that, like other British subjects, they might be taxed only in consequence of their own consent. Grenville, then the Prime Minister, stood to his purpose, however, and introduced a Bill for imposing certain stamp duties on the American colonies. The Americans protested and resisted, and partly by the influence of the great Pitt, who had steadily opposed the measure, the Bill was withdrawn.

On the illness of Pitt, now Lord Chatham, in 1767, Townshend became Premier, and again revived the project of taxing the Americans by imposing duties on tea; and in 1770 Lord North, as his successor, set himself to carry it out. The result was that in 1775 America had to be declared in a state of rebellion, and a war began, in which both France and Spain joined the revolted colonies, and of which the result was the recognition of the independence of the United States. On the American side of this struggle the great name is that of George Washington. On the British side the war was unskilfully conducted, and though they gained some successes these were more than counterbalanced by such blows as the capitulation of Burgoyne with nearly 6000 men at Saratoga (1777), and of Cornwallis at Yorktown with 7000 (1781). Against their European foes the British could show such successes as that of Admiral Rodney off Cape St. Vincent (1780); the brilliant defence of Gibraltar by General Eliott (1779-82); and Admiral Rodney's victory over the French fleet in the West Indies (1782).

The war closed with the Peace of Versailles in 1783. Britain finally acquired several West Indian islands; Spain got Florida and Minorca, France Pondicherry and Chandernagore in India. The struggle had added over £100,000,000 to the British national debt.

From 1783 to 1801 the government of Britain was directed by William Pitt, the younger son of Lord Chatham, who when only twenty-four years of age was appointed First Lord of the Treasury and Chancellor of the Exchequer. The affairs of Ireland and India, and the impeachment of Warren Hastings, were among the first subjects which occupied the attention of Pitt's ministry.

In 1782 the Irish had been able to extort from Britain, then engaged in her struggle with the American colonies, the right to establish an independent Parliament, so that from this year there were two independent Governments in the British Isles till 1800, when Pitt, who had in the interval had some experience of the difficulties arising out of two coordinate legislatures, contrived once more to unite them.

French Revolution. In 1789 the French Revolution was begun. For a time there was considerable sympathy in England with this movement; but as the revolutionaries proceeded to extreme measures there was a reaction in English feeling, of which Edmund Burke became the great exponent, and the execution of Louis XVI. gave rise to diplomatic measures which finally terminated in the National Convention declaring war against Britain, on 1st Feb., 1793.

At first Britain co-operated with Prussia, Austria, etc., against France, and successes were gained both by sea and land; but afterwards on the Continent the armies of the French Republic were everywhere triumphant, and in 1797 Britain stood alone in the conflict, and indeed soon found a European coalition formed against her. The war was now largely maritime, and the naval successes of Jervis off St. Vincent and of Duncan off Camperdown were followed, when Bonaparte led an expedition to Egypt, having India as its ultimate object, by the victories of Nelson in Aboukir Bay, and Abercromby at Alexandria. In 1798 a rebellion in Ireland had to be crushed.

Napoleon Bonaparte. Peace was made in 1802 by the Treaty of Amiens, only to be broken by another declaration of war in 1803, as the ambitious projects of Napoleon became evident.

In spite of the efforts of Pitt (who died in 1806) in the way of forming and supporting with funds a new coalition against France, the military genius of Napoleon swept away all opposition on land, though the naval victory of Trafalgar (1805) established Britain's supremacy on the seas. Napoleon, who had assumed the title of Emperor of the French in 1805, and was now virtually the ruler of Europe, put forth his Berlin decrees (1807) prohibiting all commerce with Britain wherever his power reached, set his brother Joseph on the throne of Spain, and occupied Portugal.

Peninsular War. But the spirit of resistance had now taken deep root in the British people, and in 1808 troops were sent into Spain under Sir John Moore, and a year later Wellington, at that time General Sir Arthur Wellesley, landed in Portugal. Then began that famous series of successful operations (the Peninsular War) which drove back the French into their own country, and powerfully contributed to undermine the immense fabric of Napoleon's conquests. The other chief European Powers having united, Paris was occupied in 1814, Napoleon was deposed and exiled to Elba, and Louis XVIII. placed on the throne of France. Escaping in 1815, Napoleon appeared once more in the field with a large army. Wellington and Blücher hastened to oppose him, and at Waterloo Napoleon's long career of conquest ended in a crushing defeat. The restoration of Louis followed, and Napoleon was sent to the prison of St. Helena.

Of her conquests Britain retained Tobago, St. Lucia, Mauritius, the Cape of Good Hope, Demerara, Essequibo, Berbice, Heligoland, and Malta; Ceylon and Trinidad had been gained in 1802. So that Britain emerged from this long struggle with a very great increase of territorial possessions and political importance.

Home Administration. After the termination of the wars with Napoleon many things concurred to make a troublous era in the home administration. The new burden of debt which the wars had left on the nation, the bad harvests of 1816 and 1817, a succession of Governments which had no idea but that of absolute resistance to all reforms, etc.; all these contributed to increase discontent. The result was a strong Radical agitation, accompanied often by serious riots throughout the country, more especially in the large towns, and loud demands for reform in Parliament and the system of representation. The death of George III. and accession of George IV. in 1820 made little change in this respect.

From 1822 a succession of able statesmen, Canning, Peel, and Lord Grey, gave the Government a more liberal turn, and did much to satisfy the popular demands. The Catholics were admitted to Parliament; the severity of the old restrictions on commerce was relaxed; and in the face of a determined opposition Earl Grey carried the Reform Bill of 1832 (two years after the accession of William IV.), which gave large manufacturing towns a voting power in some proportion to their importance, and practically transferred the centre of political power from the aristocratic to the middle classes. The next great public measure was the abolition of negro slavery in every British possession in 1834.

William IV. died 20th June, 1837, and was succeeded by Victoria. The year following is notable as that in which the Chartists began their movement for reform, which continued more or less active, with popular assemblies, presentations of monster petitions, and occasional tumults, till 1848, when it was without much trouble suppressed.

The same years saw the struggle of the Anti-Corn-Law League, of which Cobden and Bright were the chiefs, and which was finally successful, Sir Robert Peel, the leader of the Tory party, himself proposing the repeal of the corn duties (1846). The principle of free trade had further victories in the repeal of the navigation laws, and in the large abolition of duties made during Lord Aberdeen's ministry (1853).

Crimean War. In 1852-3 dissension arose between Russia and Turkey regarding the rights of the Latin and Greek Churches to preferable access to the "holy places" in Palestine. The Emperor of Russia, resenting concessions made to French devotees, sent Prince Menschikov to Constantinople to demand redress, and, not being satisfied, war was declared, 26th June, 1853. On the plea that it was impossible to leave Russia a free hand in dealing with Turkey, France and Britain formed an alliance against Russia, 28th March, 1854. The invasion of the Crimea followed; several important battles (Alma, Balaclava, Inkerman) took place, resulting in favour of the Allies, till at length Sebastopol fell (1855), and peace was signed the following year at Paris. Russia ceded a part of Bessarabia to Turkey, and consented to the free navigation of the Danube and the neutrality of the Black Sea. (*See* CRIMEAN WAR.)

Indian Mutiny. Scarcely was the Crimean War over when Britain was threatened with the loss of her possessions in India through the mutiny of the Sepoys. For a time the authority of Government was entirely suspended throughout the greater part of Bengal, the whole of Oude, and a large portion of Central India; but in a comparatively short time 70,000 British troops, poured in from Burmah, Mauritius, the Cape, and elsewhere, entirely suppressed the rebellion. (*See* INDIAN MUTINY.) One result of the mutiny was that, by a Bill passed 2nd Aug., 1858, the sovereignty hitherto exercised over the British possessions in India by the East India Company was transferred to the British Crown.

Two wars with China (1858 and 1860), during which Canton was bombarded and Pekin taken by united forces of Britain and France, opened up five new Chinese ports to trade, with other advantages. The great civil war in America occurred between 1861 and 1866, and had for a time a disastrous effect on the cotton trade in Lancashire, causing widespread distress. (*See* COTTON FAMINE.) Between 1861 and 1867 the Fenian movement, which had for its object the separation of Ireland from the United Kingdom, occasioned some excitement. *See* FENIANS.

Parliamentary reform was attempted by several Governments without success, until the Government of the Earl of Derby in 1867 passed a measure establishing the principle of household suffrage. This year also saw the passing of the Act by which the Dominion of Canada was constituted. In 1867 the Abyssinian expedition set out, and effected its object—the relief of English captives—in the spring of 1868. In the same year Lord Derby was succeeded by Disraeli as leader of the Conservative party, then in office. Before the end of the year a general election put the Liberals in power.

Gladstone's Administration. In 1869 Gladstone's administration passed a Bill for the disestablishment of the Irish Church. In 1870 an Irish Land Law Bill, having for its object the regulation of the relations between landlord and tenant, became law; and during the same session the Act of Parliament establishing a national system of education for England was passed. In 1871 the purchase of commissions in the army was abolished. Next followed the Ballot Act and the Scotch Education Act. Early in 1874 Gladstone dissolved Parliament, and, a large Conservative majority being returned, Disraeli (afterwards Earl of Beaconsfield) again became Premier.

Disraeli's Administration. The Ashanti War, begun the previous year, was brought to a successful termination early in 1874. In 1876 the title of Empress of India was added to the titles of the queen. During the Russo-Turkish War of 1877-8 Britain remained neutral, but took an important part in the settlement effected by the Berlin Congress, and acquired from Turkey the right to occupy and administer Cyprus.

The Afghan War of 1878-9 and the Zulu War of 1879 belong to the closing years of Disraeli's administration. The general election of 1880 gave the Liberals a large majority, and Gladstone again became Premier. Ireland now called for special attention, and an Irish Land Act, establishing fair rent, fixity of tenure, and free sale, was passed in 1881; but this did not abate the demand for Home Rule, which under Parnell and subsequently has been a dominating factor in politics.

Boer War. The annexation of the Transvaal, carried out in 1877, led to war with the Transvaal Boers in 1880-1. A British force was defeated at Majuba Hill early in 1881, and peace was concluded on the basis of a limited independence for the Transvaal, the limitations being largely removed in 1884.

The rebellion of Arabi Pasha in Egypt in 1882 led to the bombardment of Alexandria by the British fleet and to military operations in Egypt; and the revolt in the Egyptian Sudan under the Mahdi resulted in its temporary separation. The failure to relieve Khartoum and save General Gordon helped to make the ministry unpopular. The Reform Act of 1884, extending household suffrage to the counties, was followed by a Redistribution Act in 1885. The general election of 1885 left the Parnellites masters of the political situation, and early in 1886 Lord Salisbury, who had been a short time Premier, made way for Gladstone.

Gladstone, the Liberal leader, now determined to adopt a plan of Home Rule for Ireland, and in 1886 he introduced a Home Rule Bill which failed to pass. Gladstone appealed to the country, which declared against Home Rule by a large majority, and Lord Salisbury again became Prime Minister.

Salisbury's Administration. The most important Acts passed under the second Salisbury administration (1886-92), which received independent support from the Liberal Unionists, were the Local Government (England and Wales) Act (1888) and the Local Government (Scotland) Act (1889), which established county councils; and the Free Education Act (1891). The majority obtained by the Liberals at the general election of 1892 was small.

Gladstone as Prime Minister introduced his second Home Rule Bill in 1893. It passed through the House of Commons, but was rejected in the Upper House by an overwhelming majority. Of the measures which became law under this administration, the most notable were the Local Government Act of 1894, under which parish and district councils were created; and the Finance Act of 1894, which made important changes in the death duties.

Lord Rosebery. Gladstone resigned the premiership in 1894, and Lord Rosebery then became head of the Government; but defeat on a petty War Office question next year led to the resignation of the ministry.

Salisbury's Third Administration. Lord Salisbury formed his third administration, and at the general election of 1895 secured a majority of 152. The new ministry included several Liberal Unionists, notably the Duke of Devonshire and Joseph Chamberlain, the latter as Secretary for the Colonies.

The principal Acts passed by the Unionist ministry of 1895-1900 were the following: The Agricultural Rates Act (1896), a temporary measure relieving farmers of half their local rates, twice renewed since; the Education Act (1897), giving greater financial assistance to voluntary or denominational schools; the Workmen's Compensation Act (1897), an important measure due chiefly to the Liberal Unionist part of the ministry; the Vaccination Act (1898), a partial concession to the opponents of compulsory vaccination; the Local Government (Ireland) Acts (1898 and 1900), extending to Ireland the system of local government enjoyed by England and Scotland; and the Commonwealth of Australia Constitution Act (1900), by which the federation of the Australian colonies was accomplished.

An expedition under Sir Herbert (afterwards Earl) Kitchener succeeded in 1898 in recapturing Khartoum and the Egyptian Sudan for Egypt. At a place called Fashoda, Kitchener met a French expedition from the west, and for a time the relations between Britain and France were strained, but France ultimately agreed to withdraw and recognise the Egyptian Sudan as within the British sphere. The boundary dispute with Venezuela, which at one time nearly caused war with the United States, was settled by arbitration in 1899. Early in Oct., 1899, war broke out with the Boer republics of South Africa. (*See* SOUTH AFRICA, UNION OF.) Fighting also took place in 1900 in Ashanti and China. (*See* CHINA.) Towards the end of 1900 Lord Salisbury appealed to the country, and obtained a fresh lease of office with a majority of 134.

On 22nd Jan., 1901, Queen Victoria died in her eighty-third year. Her jubilee (1887) and diamond jubilee (1897) had been celebrated with great pomp and rejoicing, and her reign of sixty-three and a half years is the longest in the history of England. She was succeeded by her eldest son, Edward VII., who showed himself an active promoter of peaceful relations with other countries.

The Boer War was concluded in the middle of 1902 by the Treaty of Vereeniging, and almost immediately afterwards Lord Salisbury retired from office, being succeeded in the premiership by his nephew, A. J. Balfour.

The Education Act of 1902 did away with school boards where they existed, bringing the voluntary and former board schools alike under education committees in England and Wales, and the same change was made in London in 1903. The Irish Land Act of 1903 was a measure of the first importance, its object being to transfer practically all the agricultural land of Ireland to farmers or peasant proprietors. In the autumn of 1903 Chamberlain resigned office in order to be free to advocate a change in the country's fiscal policy, intended to unite the colonies more closely with the mother country—a change which many have regarded as meaning a return to protection.

Balfour's Administration. Balfour had endeavoured to steer a middle course in regard to tariff reform, being in favour of preferential tariffs and so-called "retaliation." The introduction of indentured Chinese labour into the Transvaal gold-mines in 1904 aroused much controversy in Parliament and the country. The Licensing Act of 1904 for England and Wales made fundamental alterations in the tenure of licences. The question of unemployment having compelled attention, the Balfour ministry passed an Act (1905) creating machinery for dealing with distress from this cause. The Aliens Act of 1905 should here be mentioned, as also the Anglo-French agreement (1904), and the Anglo-Japanese Treaty (1905).

Campbell-Bannerman's Administration. Balfour's ministry having resigned in Dec., 1905, a new Government was formed by Sir Henry Campbell-Bannerman, and a general election took place in Jan.-Feb., 1906, the result being overwhelmingly in favour of the new ministry. A Labour party has since been prominent in Parliament.

Asquith's Administration. In 1908 Mr. Asquith became Premier, on the death of Sir Henry. Measures in favour of labour were passed, such as the Eight Hours Act for coal-miners and the Old Age Pensions Act. A national scheme of insurance against unemployment and sickness was brought forward in 1911. On 6th May, 1910, Edward VII. died, and his son became king as George V. (q.v.). In 1911 the Parliament Bill, depriving the Lords of all power over money bills, was introduced and carried. The Bill passed the Lords with difficulty, and only because new peers would have been created to form a majority, if necessary. The Act also provided that a bill passed in three successive sessions by the Commons might be presented for the Royal Assent without the approval of the Lords. Thus the Irish Home Rule Bill and the Welsh Disestablishment Bill, both rejected by the Lords, received the Royal Assent and were placed on the statute book on 18th Sept., 1914. Both these Acts, however, were definitely suspended in 1915 until the close of the European War.

The National Insurance Bill was passed in 1912. In the summer of 1914, owing to the resuscitation of Home Rule, Ireland was on the verge of civil war, and a disagreement existed between the United Kingdom and the self-governing colonies on the question of naval policy, and in August the European War (q.v.) broke out. In May, 1915, Mr. Asquith formed a Coalition Government in which Mr. Lloyd George became Minister of Munitions. The year was also made memorable by the Derby Recruiting Campaign.

The great problems which the British Government had to face in 1915 were the recruiting of the army, finances, and supply of munitions. It was soon evident that Kitchener's army was not sufficient to carry on the war, and conscription, as opposed to voluntary enlistment, was proposed. The Derby Recruiting Campaign was consequently started. In Jan., 1916, the Military Service Bill was introduced into Parliament, and became law in May of the same year. In April a revolution, organised by the Sinn Feiners, broke out in Ireland. Towards the end of the year Mr. Asquith resigned the Premiership; Mr. Bonar Law, the leader of the Unionist party, having refused to become Premier, Mr. Lloyd George was invited to form a ministry.

Lloyd George's Ministry. In 1917 the National Service Bill, from which Ireland was excluded, was introduced and passed. In June of the same year the Commons granted votes to women, and in 1918 made women eligible as Members of Parliament. The most important measure of 1918 was the Electoral Reform Act, by which 8 million people (including 6 million women) were granted a vote (see p. 238).

The Armistice was signed in November, and in December a new general election took place, and the Coalition Government was returned. In 1922 the Coalition Government resigned and, an election taking place, Bonar Law became Premier. He resigned in May, 1923, and was succeeded by Mr. Stanley Baldwin. Mr. Baldwin went to the country in Dec., 1923, on the issue of Protection for Trade. The Conservatives were returned the largest party in the House, but without a clear majority. Thus Mr. Ramsay MacDonald, on the defeat of the Government, became the first Labour Premier. In Oct., 1924, however, Mr. MacDonald appealed to the country and was defeated.

Baldwin's Ministry. In Nov., 1924, Mr. Baldwin formed a Conservative Government. He held office till June, 1929, when as the result of a general election Mr. Ramsay MacDonald formed a second Socialist Government, though his party had not a clear majority in the House.

MacDonald's Ministry. This Labour Government remained in power till Aug., 1931, when, in view of the economic crisis, it resigned. Mr. Ramsay MacDonald then formed a National Government. A general election was held in Oct., and the National Government was returned with an overwhelming majority. *See* COLONY; IRELAND; LOCARNO; RUHR; ETC.

BRITANNIA. Name given to Britain by the Romans. It is used to-day for the female figure that appears on some of the British coins, and is used in other ways to represent Britain, for instance on medals. The figure on the copper coins was introduced in the time of Charles II., the Duchess of Richmond serving as the artist's model.

BRITANNIA. Formerly a training ship for officers of the British Navy. The early naval cadets were trained on warships, one of which was the *Britannia,* which was put to this service in 1859. It was replaced by another vessel, also named *Britannia,* which was stationed at Portsmouth and then at Dartmouth. In 1903 the cadets were transferred to a college at Dartmouth.

BRITANNIA METAL (also called **White Metal**). A metallic alloy consisting of 85 to 94 per cent tin, 5 to 10 per cent antimony, 1 to 3 per cent copper, and about 1 per cent zinc or bismuth. This last addition is made to increase the fusibility of the metal, which is used for teapots, spoons, and other household utensils. For a time it was used as a substitute for pewter, but is now itself giving way to nickel-silver.

BRITAN'NICUS. Son of the Roman Emperor Claudius, by Messalina, born A.D. 42, poisoned A.D. 56. He was passed over by his father for the son of his new wife Agrippina. This son became the Emperor Nero, whose fears that he might be displaced by the natural successor of the late emperor caused him to murder Britannicus.

BRITISH ACADEMY. An academy or association of learned men incorporated by royal charter in 1902, its main object being to promote the study of literature, mental and moral science. The maximum number of fellows is 100, distributed under four main sectional committees, devoted respectively to history and archæology, philology, philosophy, economics, and jurisprudence.

BRITISH ASSOCIATION FOR THE ADVANCEMENT OF SCIENCE. A society first organised in 1831, mainly through the exertions of Sir David Brewster, whose object is to assist the progress of discovery, and to disseminate the latest results of scientific research, by bringing together men eminent in all the several departments of science. Its first meeting was held at York on 26th Sept., 1831, under the presidency of Lord Milton; and all the principal towns of the United Kingdom have on different occasions formed the place of rendezvous, a different locality being chosen every year. The sittings extend generally over about a week.

The society is divided into sections, which, after the president's address, meet separately during the séances for the reading of papers and conference. Soirées, conversaziones, lectures, and other general meetings are usually held each evening during the meeting of the association. As the funds which the society annually collects are more than sufficient to cover its expenses, it is enabled to make money grants for the pursuit of particular scientific inquiries, which otherwise might not be conducted so efficiently, if at all.

In 1884 the association held its meeting at Montreal, in 1897 at Toronto, in 1905 in S. Africa, in 1909 at Winnipeg, while in 1914 it met in Australia. For the first time since the foundation of the association, no annual meetings were held in 1917 and 1918. The meeting in 1930 was held at London, and that of 1932 was held at York. The headquarters are at Burlington House, London, W.1.

BRITISH BROADCASTING CORPORATION. *See* WIRELESS.

BRITISH CENTRAL AFRICA. *See* CENTRAL AFRICA.

BRITISH COLUMBIA. A British colony forming, with Vancouver Island, a province of the Dominion of Canada. It is situated partly between the Rocky Mountains and the sea, partly between Alaska and the meridian of 120° W., and extends from the United States boundary north to the 60th parallel N. lat.; area, 355,855 sq. miles, of which 353,416 are land area, and 2439 water area. Till 1858 it was part of the Hudson Bay Territory; in that year gold discoveries brought settlers, and it became a colony. Vancouver Island, 16,000 sq. miles, became a colony at the same time, but was afterwards joined to British Columbia; it became part of the Dominion in 1871.

Physical Features. The coast-line is much indented, and is flanked by numerous island, the Queen Charlotte Islands being the chief after Vancouver. The interior is mountainous, being traversed by the Cascade Mountains near the coast, and by the Rocky Mountains farther east. There are numerous lakes, generally long and narrow, and lying in the deep ravines that form a feature of the surface, and are traversed by numerous rivers. Of these the Fraser, with its tributary the Thomson, belongs entirely to the colony, as does also the Skeena; while the upper courses of the Peace River and of the Columbia also belong to it. All except the Peace flow into the Pacific. The mountain ranges (highest summit: Robson Peak, 12,972 feet) afford magnificent timber (including the Douglas pine and many other trees); and between the ranges are wide grassy prairies.

Part of the interior is so dry in summer as to render irrigation necessary, and the arable land is comparatively limited in area, but there is a vast extent of splendid pasture land. The climate is mild in the lower valleys, but severe in the higher levels; it is very healthy.

Products and Industries. The chief products of the colony are gold, coal, silver, iron, copper, galena, mercury, and other metals; timber, furs, and fish, the last, particularly salmon, being very abundant in the streams and on the coasts. Gold exists almost everywhere, but has been obtained chiefly in the Cariboo and Kootenay districts. The coal is mined chiefly in Vancouver Island, and large quantities are now raised at Nanaimo. Mining, cattle-rearing, agriculture, dairying, fruit-growing, salmon-canning, and lumbering are the chief industries.

Victoria, on the S.E. coast of Vancouver Island, is the capital (pop. 66,600). New Westminster, near the mouth of the Fraser River, is a place of some importance (pop. 17,524); but Vancouver, the seaport at the terminus of the Canadian Pacific Railway, is the largest town (pop. 246,593). Besides this railway and branches there is one between Nanaimo and Victoria, with others. Steamers run to China, Japan, and Australia in connection with the Canadian Pacific Railway. British Columbia has a separate Parliament and administration, with a lieutenant-governor of its own. (*See* CANADA.)

Pop. in 1901, 178,657; in 1911, 392,480; in 1921 the census population was 524,582, and the census bureau estimate for 1927 was 575,000. The present population is 694,263. There are about 29,000 Indians and 15,000 Chinese. The revenue and expenditure for 1926-7 were 20,258,915 and 17,846,690 dollars respectively; and for 1930, 25,498,409 and 25,066,980.—BIBLIOGRAPHY: A. G. Brown, *British Columbia, its History, People, etc.*; F. Fairford, *British Columbia.*

BRITISH EMPIRE LEAGUE. An association founded in London in 1895 for the promotion of closer commercial intercourse between the United Kingdom and other parts of the British Empire.

BRITISH GUM. *See* DEXTRINE.

BRITISH HONDURAS. *See* HONDURAS, BRITISH.

BRITISH ISLES. The name sometimes applied to Great Britain, Ireland, and the neighbouring islands. It consists of Scotland, England, Wales, North Ireland, Irish Free State, Isle of Man, and the Channel Islands. Total area, 121,633 sq. miles. Pop., approximately, 49,000,000.

BRITISH LEGION, THE. A corps raised in Britain in 1835, numbering 10,000 men, under the command of General De Lacy Evans, to assist Queen Isabella of Spain in the war with Don Carlos.

BRITISH MUSEUM. The great national museum in London. It owes its foundation to Sir Hans Sloane, who, in 1753, bequeathed his various collections, including 50,000 books and MSS., to the nation, on the condition of £20,000—less by £30,000 than the original cost—being paid to his heirs. Montague House, which was bought for the purpose for £10,250, was appropriated for the museum, which was first opened on the 15th Jan., 1759. The original edifice having become inadequate, a new building in Great Russell Street was resolved upon in 1823, the architect being Sir R. Smirke, whose building was not completed till 1847.

In 1857 a new library building was completed and opened at a cost of £150,000. It contains a circular reading-room 140 feet in diameter, with a dome 106 feet in height. This room contains accommodation for 300 readers comfortably seated at separate desks, which are provided with all necessary conveniences. Subsequently, the accommodation having become again inadequate, it was resolved to separate the objects belonging to the natural history department from the rest, and to lodge them in a building by themselves. Accordingly a large natural history museum was erected at South Kensington, and the specimens pertaining to natural history (including geology and mineralogy) were transferred thither, but they still form part of the British Museum.

Further additions to the Great Russell Street buildings were made in 1910 and 1911. The Edward VII. Galleries were opened on 7th May, 1914.

The British Museum is under the management of 48 trustees. It is open daily, free of charge. Admission to the reading-room as a regular reader is by ticket, procurable on application to the chief librarian, there being certain simple conditions attached. The library, which is now one of the largest and most valuable in the world, has been enriched by numerous bequests and gifts, among others the splendid library collected by George III. during his long reign. A copy of every book, pamphlet, newspaper, piece of music, etc., published anywhere in British territory, must be conveyed free of charge to the British Museum within one month after the publication. It has a building at Colindale, near Hendon, where newspapers are stored.

The museum contains eight principal departments, namely, the department of printed books, maps, charts, plans, etc.; the department of manuscripts; the department of natural history; the department of Oriental antiquities; the department of Greek and Roman antiquities; the department of coins and medals; the department of British and mediæval antiquities and ethnography; and the department of prints and drawings.

BRITISH NORTH AMERICA. A name under which are included the Dominion of Canada and the colony of Newfoundland, comprising all the mainland north of the United States (except Alaska) and a great many islands.

BRITISH THERMAL UNIT (B.T.U.). The amount of heat required to raise by one degree F. the temperature of one pound of water at or near its temperature of maximum density, or 39·1°.

BRITON FERRY. A seaport town (urban district) of S. Wales, Glamorganshire, at the mouth of the River Neath, a few miles east of Swansea, with coal-mines, iron and steelworks, tin-plate works, etc. Pop. 9176.

BRITONITE. *See* EXPLOSIVES.

BRIT'TANY, or BRETAGNE. An ancient duchy and province of France, corresponding nearly to the modern departments of Finistère, Côtes du Nord, Morbihan, Ille et Vilaine, Loire Inférieure. It is supposed to have received its name from the Britons who were expelled from England and took refuge here in the fifth century. Along the coast and towards its seaward extremity the country is remarkably rugged, but elsewhere there are many beautiful and fertile tracts. Fisheries employ many of the inhabitants. The people still retain their ancient language, which is closely allied to Welsh, and is exclusively used by the peasantry in the western part of the province.

BRITTON, John. An English writer on architectural antiquities, born in 1771, died in 1857. In 1801 appeared the *Beauties of Wiltshire*, in 2 vols., by J. Britton and E. W. Brayley. These collaborateurs, with others, subsequently completed a similar work for all the other counties of England (London, 1801-16, 18 vols.; 1825, 26 vols.; etc.). In 1805 Britton published his *Architectural Antiquities of England*, in five 4to vols., which was followed by his *Cathedral Antiquities*, in 14 vols., 1814-35, and *Dictionary of the Architecture and Archæology of the Middle Ages*, 1832-8. A large number of works of a similar character bear his name as joint or sole author or editor.

BRITZ'KA, or BRITZS'KA. A kind of small carriage, the head of which is always a movable calash, and having a place in front for the driver, and a seat behind for servants.

BRIVE-LA-GAILLARDE (brēv-lá-gā-yärd). A town of South-Western France, department of Corrèze, surrounded by fine boulevards planted with elms. Manufactures: woollens, cottons, candles, brandy, etc. Pop. 26,718. The Romano-Gallic name was *Briva-Curretia*.

BRIXEN. An old town of Italy, formerly in the Austrian province of Tirol, 104 miles from Vienna by rail, with a cathedral. Pop. 6670.

BRIX'HAM. A seaport and sea-bathing resort, England, Devonshire, on the south of Torbay. Brixham was the place where William III. landed, 5th Nov., 1688. Pop. (1931), 8147.

BRIXTON. A commercial district of S.W. London. It is in the metropolitan borough of Lambeth.

BRI'ZA. A genus of grasses, commonly called quaking grass, maiden's hair, or lady's tresses. There are about thirty species, chiefly found in South America. Two (*B. media* and *B. minor*) are natives of Britain; these and other species are found in gardens as ornamental plants.

BRNO. *See* BRÜNN.

BROACH, or BAROACH (brōch, ba-rōch'). A town in Guzerat (Gujerat), Hindustan, on the Nerbudda, one of the oldest seaports of Western India, with a considerable coasting trade. The town was taken by storm by the British in 1772, and, with the district, ceded to them by treaty with Sindhia in 1803. Pop. 42,648.

BROACH (brōch; Fr. *broche*, a spit). A term sometimes applied to a spire that springs directly from a tower, there being no intermediate parapet.

BROAD ARROW. A Government mark placed on British stores of every description (as well as on some other things), to distinguish them as public or Crown property, and to obliterate or deface which is felony. Persons in possession of goods marked with the broad arrow forfeit the goods and are subject to a penalty. The mark is alluded to in a charter of James II. in 1687. The common explanation of it, therefore, as being derived from the cognisance of Henry Sidney, Earl of Romney, who was Master-General of the Ordnance (1693-1702), is not supported by the dates.

BROAD CHURCH. A name given originally to a party in the Church of England, assuming to be midway between the Low Church or Evangelical section and the High Church or Ritualistic; now widely applied to the more tolerant and liberal section of any denomination.

BROAD PIECE. A name sometimes given to English gold pieces broader than a guinea, particularly Caroluses and Jacobuses.

BROADS. A number of sheets of water in Norfolk, now a great resort of holiday-makers.

BROAD'SIDE. In a naval engagement, the whole discharge of the artillery on one side of a ship of war. The term is also applied to any large page printed on one side of a sheet of paper, and, strictly, not divided into columns.

BROAD'STAIRS. An English watering-place, east of Kent. Pop. (with St. Peter's) (1931), 12,748.

BROAD'SWORD. A sword with a broad blade, designed chiefly for cutting, formerly used by some regiments of cavalry and Highland infantry in the British service. The claymore or broadsword was the national weapon of the Highlanders.

BROCA, Paul. French surgeon and anthropologist, born 1824, died 1880. In 1849 he became professor of surgical anatomy in Paris, and in 1859 he founded, in spite of the opposition of the Government, the Anthropological Society. In 1861 he made the discovery of the seat of articulate speech in the third convolution of the left frontal lobe of the brain, called *Broca's convolution*.

BROCADE'. A stuff of silk, enriched with raised flowers, foliage, or other ornaments. The term is applied to silks figured in the loom, distinguished from those which are embroidered after being woven. Brocade is in silk what damask is in linen or wool.

BROCC'OLI. A late variety of the cauliflower, hardier and with more colour in the flower and leaves. The part used is the succulent flower-stalks. Broccoli is inferior in flavour to cauliflower, but serves as a substitute for it when the latter cannot be obtained.

BROCH (bro*h*). A name for certain prehistoric structures in Scotland resembling low, circular, roofless towers with walls of great thickness, built of unhewn stones and without lime or cement, and entered by a narrow passage. There are small chambers in the thickness of the wall accessible only from the interior. These structures were evidently built for defence. They are most numerous in Orkney, Shetland, and the northern counties.

BROCK, Sir Thomas. English sculptor. A native of Worcester, he was born in 1847, and settled in London in 1866. His *Eve* and *The Moment of Peril*, two magnificent pieces of statuary, are in the Tate gallery, London. He designed the memorial to Queen Victoria, near Buckingham Palace, and was responsible for the designs on the coinage first issued in 1893. In 1891 he was elected R.A., and he was knighted in 1911. He died on Aug. 22, 1922.

BROCKDORFF-RANTZAU, Count Ulrich von. German diplomatist, born 1869, died 1928. He became Consul-General at Budapest in 1909, and Minister at Copenhagen in 1912. He was German Foreign Secretary in 1918, and came to Paris in 1919 as head of the delegation to receive the Peace Treaty. Brockdorff refused to sign the treaty, returned to Germany, and resigned.

BROCK'EN, or BLOCKSBERG. The highest summit of the Hartz Mountains (3745 feet), in Saxony, celebrated for the atmospheric conditions which produce the appearance of gigantic spectral figures in the clouds, being shadows of the spectators projected by the sun.

BROCKHAUS (brok'hous), **Friedrich Arnold.** Founder of the eminent German publishing house still carried on by his descendants, born 1772, died in 1823. In 1811 he settled at Altenberg, where the first edition of the *Conversations-Lexikon* was completed, 1810-1 (14th edition, 1901-4). The business rapidly extended, and he removed to Leipzig in 1817. The chief branches of the firm are in Berlin and Vienna, and among the literary undertakings of the house have been several important critical periodicals and some large historical and bibliographical works.

BROCKHAUS, Hermann. Son of F. A. Brockhaus, Orientalist, born at Amsterdam 1806, died 1877. From 1848 till his death he was professor of Sanskrit at Leipzig, and published many works on Oriental literature. He edited the great *Allgemeine Encyklopädie* of Ersch und Gruber, published by his father's firm.

BROCKTON. A town of the United States, Massachusetts, a flourishing place, with large manufactures of boots and shoes, etc. Pop. 63,797.

BROCK'VILLE. A town of Canada, province of Ontario, on the left bank of the St. Lawrence, about 40 miles below Kingston and 160 above Montreal. It is a divisional point on the Canadian National Railway. In the immediate vicinity are the Thousand Islands and other resorts on the St. Lawrence River. Pop. 9736.

BRODIE, Sir Benjamin Collins, Bart, D.C.L., F.R.S. An English surgeon, born 1783, died 1862. He was the leading surgeon of his day, and attended George IV., and was sergeant-surgeon to William IV. and to Victoria. He was made a baronet in 1834, and from 1858 to 1861 was president of the Royal Society. He published a number of works all connected with his profession.—His eldest son, **Sir Benjamin Collins Brodie,** a celebrated chemist, was born in London 1817, died 1880. In 1855 he was appointed professor of chemistry at Oxford.

BRO'DY. A town in the Ukraine (formerly in Austrian Galicia), near the Russian frontier, 50 miles E.N.E. of Lemberg. It was captured by the Russians in July, 1916, after a battle, and was reoccupied by Austrian troops in Feb., 1918. It has 17,750 inhabitants, about two-thirds of whom are Jews. The commerce with Russia and Turkey is important.

BROGLIE (brol-yē). A family of Italian origin distinguished in the annals of French wars and diplomacy.

1. François Marie, Duc de, Marshal of France, born in 1671, died in 1745; was highly distinguished in the field, and also in diplomacy.

2. Victor François, Duc de, eldest son of preceding, likewise Marshal of France, born in 1718, died 1804; served in Italy, Bohemia, Bavaria, and Flanders. He was Minister of War for a short time in 1789, and took part in the invasion of Champagne, 1792.

3. Claude Victor, Prince de, born in 1757, guillotined 27th June, 1794, was the third son of Victor François. He joined the revolutionary party, and was appointed field-marshal in the army of the Rhine, but upon his refusal to acknowledge the decree of the 10th of Aug., suspending the royal authority, was deprived of his command, and afterwards summoned before the revolutionary tribunal, and led to the guillotine.

4. Achille Léonce Victor Charles, Duc de, peer of France, son of Claude Victor, born 1785, died 1870. In 1816 he married a daughter of Madame de Staël, and was made a member of the chamber of peers. After the revolution of 1830, the Duc de Broglie and Guizot were the chiefs of the party called *Doctrinaires*. He was Minister of Public Instruction for a short time in 1830, and Minister of Foreign Affairs from Oct., 1832, to April, 1834. In 1849 he was a Conservative member of the Legislative Assembly, and after the *coup d'état* he continued a bitter enemy of the imperial régime. His later years were devoted to philosophical and literary pursuits, and in 1856 he was elected a member of the French Academy.—Cf. Guizot, *Le Duc de Broglie* (1870).

5. Albert, Duc de, son of the preceding, statesman and author, born 1821. His principal work, *The Church and the Roman Empire in the Fourth Century*, has passed through many editions. He died in 1901. He had been Ambassador at London, Minister of Foreign Affairs, and head of a short-lived Royalist ministry in 1877.

BROGUE (brōg; Ir. and Gael. *brog*). A coarse and light kind of shoe made of raw or half-tanned leather, of one entire piece, and gathered round the foot by a thong, formerly worn in Ireland and the Highlands of Scotland. The term is also used of the mode of pronunciation peculiar to the Irish.

BROKE, Sir Philip Bowes Vere. A British admiral, born in 1776, died in 1841; distinguished himself, particularly in 1813, as commander of the *Shannon*, in the memorable action which that vessel, in answer to a regular challenge, fought with the United States vessel *Chesapeake* off the American coast, and in which the latter was captured.

BROKEN HILL. A great silver- and lead-mining centre in New South Wales, 925 miles west of Sydney, with which it has railway connection. Pop. 22,990.

BROKEN-WIND. A disease in horses (and dogs) which disables them from bearing fatigue. The condition is regarded as hereditary. In this disease the expiration of the air from the lungs occupies double the time that the inspiration of it does; it requires also two efforts rapidly succeeding to each other, attended by a slight spasmodic action, in order fully to accomplish it. It is attended by a deep cough, and the affected animal suffers from indigestion. Careful dieting and rest after meals are the best palliatives.

BROKER. An agent who is employed to conclude bargains or transact business for others in consideration of a charge or compensation, which is usually in proportion to the extent or value of the transaction completed by him, and is called *brokerage*. The broker effects his clients' business with a *dealer* or *jobber*.

In large mercantile communities the business of each broker is usually limited to a particular class of transactions, and thus there are brokers with several distinctive names, as *bill-brokers*, who buy and sell bills of exchange for others; *insurance-brokers*, who negotiate between underwriters and the owners of vessels and shippers of goods; *passage-brokers*, who are concerned in the selling or letting of steerage passages in a ship proceeding from any place in Europe, not within the Mediterranean Sea; *ship-brokers*, who are the agents of owners of vessels in chartering them to merchants or procuring freights for them from one port to another; their contracts generally provide that if the ship does not arrive the loan and interest shall not be recoverable; *stock-brokers*, the agents of dealers in shares of joint-stock companies, Government securities, and other monetary investments. *See* STOCK EXCHANGE.

BROM'BERG. A town of Poland, formerly in the Prussian province of Posen, on the Brahe, near its confluence with the Vistula. Among its industries are machinery, iron-founding, tanning, paper, tobacco, chicory, pottery, distilling, and brewing. The Bromberg Canal connects the Brahe with the Netz, and thus establishes communication between the Vistula, the Oder, and the Elbe. Pop. 117,519.

BROME, Alexander. Minor English poet and dramatist, born 1620, died 1666. He was the author of many royalist songs and epigrams. He published *The Cunning Lovers*, a comedy, 1654; *Fancy's Festivals*, 1657; *Songs*, etc., 1660; *Translation of Horace*, 1666.

BROME, Richard. Poet and dramatist, died 1652. He wrote *The Jovial Crew, or The Merry Beggars*; *The Northern Lass*; *The Antipodes*; and many other plays, ten of which were edited and published by Alexander Brome soon after his death. He was originally a servant of Ben Jonson's, on whose style he endeavoured to mould his own.

BROME-GRASS. The name given to grasses of the genus Bromus. There are about 70 species (8 British), occurring both in the Old and the New World, known by having their spikelets many-flowered, two awnless glumes to each floret, two paleæ or valves, the lowermost of which has a rough, straight, rigid awn proceeding from below the tip of the valve. They are of little value as forage.

BROMELIA'CEÆ. The pineapple family, a natural order of monocotyledons, taking its name from the genus Bromelia (so called after a Swedish botanist, Olaus *Bromel*), to which the pineapple was once incorrectly referred, and consisting of herbaceous plants remarkable for the hardness and dryness of their grey foliage. They abound in tropical America, commonly growing epiphytically on the branches of trees.

With the exception of the pineapple (*Ananassa sativa*) the Bromeliaceæ are of little value, but some species are cultivated in hot-houses for the beauty of their flowers. Owing to the presence of water-absorbing hairs of remarkable structure, they can exist in dry hot air without contact with the earth, and in hot-houses are often kept hung in moist moss.

BROMIDES. The name given to the salts of hydrogen bromide or hydrobromic acid (HBr). Bromides occur as potassium, sodium, or magnesium salts in sea-water. Magnesium bromide ($MgBr_2$) occurs associated with carnallite in Stassfurt deposits, and in the United States is associated with rock-salt. These deposits form the chief source of the bromides. The metallic bromides are crystalline salts mostly soluble in water; the non-metallic bromides are decomposed by water.

Silver bromide is used in the preparation of photographic plates and printing-paper. Potassium bromide is used medicinally as a sedative, also in photography; cadmium bromide in photography; and crude magnesium bromide for the preparation of the element bromine.

BROMINE (Gr. *bromos*, a fetid odour). A non-metallic element discovered in 1826; chemical symbol, Br.; atomic weight, 80. In general chemical properties it resembles chlorine and iodine, and is generally associated with them. At ordinary temperatures bromine is a heavy, dark-reddish liquid of powerful and suffocating odour and emitting a red vapour. It has bleaching properties like chlorine, is very poisonous, and is much used as an oxidising agent and in the preparation of many organic compounds.

Bromine is never found free, but as bromides it occurs in small quantities in sea-water and in some salt springs. It is prepared from crude magnesium and sodium bromides, occurring in Germany, and in the United States, by taking advantage of the fact that chlorine displaces bromine from its compounds. Thus in manufacture, when a dilute solution of magnesium bromide is allowed to trickle down towers up which chlorine gas is passing, the following reaction takes place ($MgBr_2 + Cl_2 = MgCl_2 + Br_2$); the bromine vapour, evolved at the top of the tower, is obtained as a red liquid by passing through condensers. It unites with hydrogen, forming hydrobromic acid, and with many of the elements in forming bromides.

BROM'LEY. A municipal and parliamentary borough of England, County Kent, 9¾ miles S.S.E. of London, with a hospital, founded by Bishop Warner in 1666 for forty widows of clergymen, and a palace formerly belonging to the Bishop of Rochester. A mineral spring, St. Blaize's Well, has been famous since before the Reformation. Since 1918 Bromley sends one member to Parliament. Pop. (1931), 45,348.

BROMS'GROVE. A town of England, in the county of Worcester, 13 miles S.W. of Birmingham, on the left bank of the Salwarp. Nail-making is the chief industry, and chemicals, buttons, wagons, railway carriages, etc., are made. Pop. (1931), 9520.

BRON'CHI (-kī). The two branches into which the trachea (windpipe) divides in the chest. The right bronchus is wider, shorter, and more vertically directed than the left. Each bronchus ramifies into innumerable smaller tubes—the bronchial tubes—in the substance of the lung.

BRONCHITIS (bron-kī'tis). An inflammation of the mucous membrane of the bronchial tubes (air-passages) leading into the interior of the lungs. It is a widespread and common disease, both in its acute and chronic forms, and, though rarely serious in healthy adults, is often fatal to infants and the aged, as bronchopneumonia frequently supervenes. Acute bronchitis is the common sequel of "catching cold," and is nothing more than the extension downward of an ordinary coryza ("cold in the head"). It occurs most frequently in the changeable weather of early spring and late autumn, and its association with cold is well indicated by the popular expression "cold on the chest."

Bronchitis is associated with many other affections—with measles, influenza, whooping-cough, typhoid fever, and malaria in its acute form, while in kidney disease, gout, and heart disease it is found in its chronic form.

Symptoms. The symptoms are those of a feverish cold, headache, languor, and pains, with slight fever, varying according to the intensity of the attack. Most characteristic are the typical bronchial symptoms—tightness and rawness of the chest, with a rough paroxysmal cough, causing intense pain under the sternum. The cough, dry at first, later becomes loose, with abundant muco-purulent spit. Great relief is experienced when this latter occurs.

Treatment. In mild cases household remedies are sufficient. Hot foot-bath, warm bath, hot drinks, and mustard plasters on the chest are all useful. In severe cases the patient should be in bed and have suitable medicinal treatment for the early "tight" stage, and, along with this, saturation of the air of the room with moisture (bronchitis kettle) gives great relief. The later stages, with loose cough, should be treated with expectorant mixtures. Vaccine treatment has not been successful.

Chronic bronchitis is not very amenable to any form of treatment, and once established recurs each winter, usually with increasing severity, hence the well-known "winter cough" of the chronic bronchitic. Exposure to cold and wet aggravates the condition much, while warmth and comfort, especially along with residence in warm climates during the winter months, can ward off the far-reaching ill-effects for many years.

BRONCHOCELE (bron'ko-sēl). *See* GOITRE.

BRONGNIART (broŋ-nyär), **Alexandre.** French geologist and mineralogist, born in 1770, died in 1847. He was appointed in 1800 director of the porcelain manufactory at Sèvres. In 1807 appeared his *Traité Elémentaire de Minéralogie*; and along with Cuvier he wrote *Description Géologique des Environs de Paris*. He also wrote other works on mineralogy and geology, and in 1844 appeared his *Traité des Arts Céramiques*. He was a member of the Academy of Sciences, and in 1822 succeeded Haüy as professor of mineralogy in the

Museum of Natural History.—His son **Adolphe Théodore Brongniart,** born 1801, died 1876, became professor of botany at the Jardin des Plantes, Paris, 1833, and was the author of several botanical works.

BRON'TE. A town of Sicily, 24 miles N.N.W. of Catania, in a picturesque situation at the W. base of Mount Etna. Lord Nelson was created Duke of Bronte by the Neapolitan Government in 1799. Pop. 20,280.

BRON'TË, Charlotte (afterwards **Mrs. Nicholls**). English novelist, born at Thornton, in Yorkshire, 21st April, 1816, died at Haworth, 31st March, 1855. She was the third daughter of the Rev. Patrick Brontë,

Charlotte Brontë

rector of Thornton, from which he removed, in 1820, on becoming incumbent of Haworth, a moorland village in the West Riding of Yorkshire, about 3 miles from Keighley. Her mother died soon after this removal, and her father, an able though eccentric man, brought up Charlotte and her sisters in quite a Spartan fashion, inuring them to every kind of industry and fatigue.

After an education received partly at home and partly at neighbouring schools, Miss Brontë became a teacher, and then a governess in a family. In 1842 she went with her sister Emily to Brussels, with the view of acquiring a knowledge of the French and German languages, and she subsequently taught for a year in the school she had attended there. In 1844 arrangements were made by her and her sisters Emily and Anne to open a school at Haworth, but no progress was ever made with their scheme.

They resolved now to turn their attention to literary composition; and in 1846 a volume of poems by the three sisters was published, under the names of Currer, Ellis, and Acton Bell. It was issued at their own risk, and attracted little attention, so they quitted poetry for prose fiction, and produced each a novel. Charlotte (Currer Bell) tried to publish *The Professor*, but it was everywhere refused, and was not given to the world till after her death. Emily (Ellis Bell), with her tale of *Wuthering Heights*, and Anne (Acton Bell), with *Agnes Grey*, were more successful.

Charlotte's failure, however, did not discourage her, and she wrote *Jane Eyre*, which was published in Oct., 1847. Its success was immediate and decided. Her second novel, *Shirley*, appeared in 1849. Previous to this she had lost her two sisters, Emily dying on 19th Dec., 1848, and Anne on 28th May, 1849 (after publishing a second novel, *The Tenant of Wildfell Hall*). In the autumn of 1852 appeared Charlotte's third novel, *Villette*. Shortly after, she married her father's curate, the Rev. Arthur Bell Nicholls, but in nine months died of consumption. Her originally rejected tale of *The Professor* was published after her death in 1857. On the 29th July, 1913, *The Times* published four letters written by Charlotte Brontë in 1844 and 1845, throwing some light on the matter of her *Villette*. In 1908 the parsonage at Haworth was opened as a Brontë Museum.

BIBLIOGRAPHY: Elizabeth Gaskell, *Life of Charlotte Brontë*; A. Birrell, *Life of Charlotte Brontë*; C. K. Shorter, *The Brontës: Life and Letters*; *idem*, *Charlotte Brontë and her Circle*; May Sinclair, *The Three Brontës*; Frederika Macdonald, *The Secret of Charlotte Brontë*.

BRONTOMETER (Gr. *brontē*, thunder, and *metron*, measure). An instrument devised in 1890, by G. J. Symons, for recording barometric oscillations and other phenomena of thunderstorms. For further particulars *see* PROCEEDINGS OF THE ROYAL SOCIETY, Vol. xlviii., p. 59.

BRONTOSAU'RUS. A gigantic reptile of the ord. Dinosauria, known from the Upper Jurassic strata of Wyoming. The diameter of its skull is smaller than that of the fourth neck-vertebra, but the animal was some 70 feet long; its ally, *Atlantosaurus*, attaining a length of 115 feet. It was herbivorous and lived in swampy localities.

BRONX. Part of the city of New York, containing the University buildings. It stands north of Manhattan, from which it is separated by the Bronx River. In 1897 it became a borough of New York City.

BRONZE. An alloy of copper and tin with small quantities of other metals. It is a fine-grained metal which takes a good polish and is harder and more fusible than copper. In various parts of the world weapons and implements were made of this alloy before iron came into use, and hence the *Bronze Age* is regarded as the one coming between the *Stone Age* and the *Iron Age* of archæology. (*See* ARCHÆOLOGY.)

Both in ancient and modern times it has been much used in making casts of all kinds, medals, bas-reliefs, statues, and other works of art; and varieties of it are also used for bells, guns, etc. Its colour is reddish-brown or olive-green, and is darkened by exposure to the atmosphere.

Ancient bronze generally contains from 4 to 15 per cent of tin. The alloy of the British coinage consists of 95 per cent copper, 4 per cent tin, and 1 per cent zinc. Statuary bronze consists of 85 parts copper, 11 parts zinc, and 4 parts tin. An alloy known as phosphor bronze, consisting of about 90 per cent copper, 9 per cent tin, and 0·5-0·75 per cent phosphorus has been found to have peculiar advantages for certain purposes. It is harder than ordinary bronze, and is suitable for electric conduits.

Aluminium bronze contains copper and aluminium in different proportions, depending on the use to which it is put. One variety is of a golden colour, and is made into watch-chains and ornaments. Manganese bronze contains a varying amount of manganese, up to 30 per cent. It is very hard and tenacious, and is used in the construction of machinery such as the screws of ships. Silico bronze contains small amounts of silicon in place of phosphorus, and has much the same properties as phosphor bronze; it is a very good conductor, and is used for telephone wires.

BRONZE-WING. A name for certain species of Australian pigeons, chiefly of the genus Phaps, distinguished by the bronze colour of their plumage. The common bronze-winged ground-dove (*P. chalcoptĕra*) abounds in all the Australian colonies, and is a plump bird, often weighing a pound, much esteemed for the table.

BRONZING. The operation of covering articles with a wash or coating to give them the appearance of bronze. Two kinds are common, the yellow and the red. The yellow is made of fine copper dust, the red of copper dust with a little pulverised red ochre. The fine green tint which bronze acquires by oxidisation, called *patĭna antīqua*, is imitated by an application of salammoniac and salt of sorrel dissolved in vinegar. Bronze may also be deposited on small statues and other articles with good effect by means of the electro-plate process.

BROOCH (brōch). A kind of ornament worn on the dress, to which it is attached by a pin stuck through the fabric. They are usually of gold or silver, often worked in highly-artistic patterns and set with precious stones. Brooches are of great antiquity, and were formerly worn by men as well as women, especially among the Celtic races. Among the Highlanders of Scotland there are preserved in several families ancient brooches of rich workmanship and highly ornamented. Some of them seem to have been used as a sort of amulet or talisman.

BROOKE, Henry. Dramatist and novelist, the son of an Irish clergyman, born in 1703, died 1783. He was educated at Dublin University, and numbered Swift, Pope, and Garrick among his friends. In 1745 he was made barrack-master at Mullingar, and spent the rest of his life in literary work. He wrote many plays and novels, his chief novel being *The Fool of Quality, or, The History of Henry, Earl of Moreland* (1765-70).

BROOKE, Sir James. Celebrated as the Rajah of Sarawak, born in Bengal in 1803, and died in Devonshire 1868. In 1838, having gone to Borneo, he assisted Rajah Muda Hassim, uncle of the Sultan of Brunei, in suppressing a revolt. For his services he was made Rajah and Governor of Sarawak, a district on the N.W. coast of the island, and being established in the Government he endeavoured to induce the Dyak natives to abandon their irregular and piratical mode of life and to turn themselves to agriculture and commerce; and his efforts to introduce civilisation were crowned with wonderful success. He was made a K.C.B. in 1847, and was appointed Governor of Labuan. In 1863 he finally returned to England. He was succeeded by his nephew, Sir Charles Brooke.

BROOKE, Rupert. British poet, born in 1888 at Rugby, where his father was a housemaster. He was educated at Rugby and at King's College, Cambridge (B.A. 1909).

His first poems appeared in 1911. When the Great War broke out he arrived from America, received a commission, and was with the Naval Brigade at Antwerp. In Feb., 1915, he was sent with the Royal Naval Division to the Dardanelles, but he fell ill after a sunstroke at Lemnos and succumbed to blood-poisoning, dying at Scyros on Friday, 23rd April, 1915, "the day of England's Saint and England's Poet."

Brooke was a poet of extraordinary charm, and his poems reveal both an epicurean joy in life and an intense passion, as well as a sense of melancholy at the vanity of human pleasures.

BROOKE, Rev. Stopford Augustus. Writer, born in Ireland in 1832, died 18th March, 1916. He took the degrees of B.A. and M.A. at Trinity College, Dublin, and was ordained in 1857. He was minister of Bedford Chapel, London, from 1876 till 1894, up till 1880 as a clergyman of the Church of England, from which he then seceded, though continuing to occupy the same pulpit. From this time he became a Unitarian. In 1872 he was appointed a chaplain-in-ordinary to the queen. He was well known as a preacher and writer on religious subjects, but especially as a critic and historian of English literature.

Besides sermons and poems, his works include: *Life and Letters of F. W. Robertson of Brighton*; *Christ in Modern Life*; *Theology in the English Poets*; *Primer of English Literature*; *Early Life of Jesus*; *History of Early English Literature*; *Tennyson: His Art and Relations to Modern Life*; *The English Poets from Blake to Tennyson*; *Jesus and Modern Thought*; *The Old Testament and Modern Life*; *The Gospel of Joy*; *The Poetry of Robert Browning*; *The Life Superlative*; etc.

BROOK FARM. A socialistic experiment, which grew out of the philosophical movement represented by the Transcendental Club, of which Ripley, Emerson, Hawthorne, and Margaret Fuller were leading members. As an attempt to solve the social problem through the institution of equality in rewards, the Brook Farm Association of Education and Agriculture was founded at Roxbury, Massachusetts, in 1841. The leading spirit was George Ripley.

In 1844 the Brook Farm Community was reorganised as a Fourieristic Community, and began to attract wide attention. The enthusiasm, however, soon began to wane, and in 1847 the society was dissolved. *See* FOURIER.—BIBLIOGRAPHY: Russell, *Home Life of the Brook Farm Association* (1900); Sears, *My Friends at Brook Farm* (1912); also Hawthorne, *The Blithedale Romance*.

BROOK'LIME (*Veronica Beccabunga*). A European plant, with blue flowers, common in ditches and wet places in Britain, a species of speedwell.

BROOKLINE. A town of the United States, forming a suburb of Boston. Pop. 47,490.

BROOK'LYN. Since 1898 a portion of New York city, on the W. end of Long Island, separated from New York proper by East River, a strait about three-quarters of a mile broad, crossed by steam-ferries, and by two suspension bridges, the most remarkable of such structures yet erected. (*See* BRIDGE.)

Brooklyn is one of the finest cities in the United States, with broad, straight streets, many of them planted with rows of trees. It has a waterfront of 33 miles, and covers an area of 47,450 acres. Pop. (1900), 1,166,582; (1910), 1,634,351; (1920), 2,018,356; present pop. 2,560,401. It is popularly known as the "city of churches," having about 500 of all denominations. Among the public buildings are the city hall, of white marble, the jail, the county court-house, the academy of music, etc. The literary and charitable institutions are very numerous. The Atlantic Dock is one of the largest in the States, covering 40 acres. The United States navy-yard, on Wallabout Bay, occupies 45 acres. Brooklyn is a favourite residence of wealthy New Yorkers. It has a large trade. It was founded in 1625, and was the scene of several memorable events of the revolution.

BROOKS, Charles Shirley. English novelist, dramatist, and journalist, born 1816, died 1874. He was for several years on the staff of the *Morning Chronicle*, and undertook a special mission to Russia, Syria, and Egypt. He wrote many plays and novels, among the latter being *Aspen Court*, *The Silver Cord*, *The Gordian Knot*, etc. His drama, *The Creole, or, Love's Fetters*, was produced at the Lyceum on 8th April, 1847, with considerable success. He succeeded Mark Lemon as editor of *Punch* in 1870, and retained the position until his death.

BROOM. A popular name which includes several allied genera of plants of the nat. ord. Leguminosæ and of the sub-ord. Papilionaceæ, plants distinguished by a leguminous fruit and papilionaceous flowers. The common broom of Europe (*Cystĭsus scopārius*) is a bushy shrub ith straight angular branches, of a rk-green colour, deciduous leaves, id flowers of a deep golden yellow. s twigs are often made into brooms, id are used as thatch for houses and rnstacks. They have also been sed for tanning. The whole plant as a very bitter taste, and a decocon of it is diuretic, in strong doses metic.

White Broom or **Portugal Broom** (*C. albus*) has beautiful white owers.

Spanish Broom or **Spart** (*Spartium unceum*) is an ornamental flowering hrub growing in Africa, Spain, Italy, nd the south of France, and often ultivated in English gardens. It has pright, round branches that flower t the top, and spear-shaped leaves. ts fibre is made into various textile abrics, and is also used in papermaking.

Dyer's Broom (*Genista tinctoria*) ields a yellow colour used in dyeing.

Butcher's Broom is *Ruscus aculeatus*, an evergreen shrub of the ord. Liliaceæ, therefore entirely different rom the brooms proper. Wherever broom occurs (or also furze), the land s almost sure to be suitable for timber-planting, as it is generally loamy and well drained.

BROOM-CORN, or **BROOM-GRASS** (*Sorghum vulgāre*, millet or guineacorn). A plant of the order of grasses, with a jointed stem, rising to the height of 8 or 10 feet, extensively cultivated in warm countries as a cereal, and for feeding cattle and poultry. The branched panicles are made into carpet brooms and brushes.

BROOM-RAPE. *See* OROBANCHACEÆ.

BROSE'LEY. A town, Shropshire, England, 13 miles S.E. of Shrewsbury. It has manufactures of tobacco-pipes, tiles, and fire-bricks. Pop. 3663.

BROS'IMUM. *See* BREAD-NUTS.

BROTH. The liquid in which some kind of flesh is boiled or macerated. Beef-tea is a kind of broth. Scotch broth is a kind of soup to which vegetables of all kinds and pearl barley or rice have been added.

BROTHERS. A term applied to the members of monastic and military orders as being united in one family. *Lay brothers* were an inferior class of monks employed in monasteries as servants. Though not in holy orders, they were bound by monastic rules.

BROTHERS, Richard. English fanatic and self-styled prophet, born in 1757, died in 1824. He served as a lieutenant in the army, which he quitted in 1789, refusing from conscientious scruples to take the oath necessary to entitle him to his half-pay. He announced himself in 1793 as the apostle of a new religion, dating his call from 1790. He styled himself the "Nephew of the Almighty, and Prince of the Hebrews, appointed to lead them to the land of Canaan." He published in 1794 *A Revealed Knowledge of the Prophecies and Times*, in two books. He was committed to Newgate for prophesying the death of the king, and subsequently to Bedlam as a dangerous lunatic, but was released in 1806. The believers in Brothers are not yet extinct, and the supporters of the Anglo-Israel theory regard him as the first writer on their side.

BROTTON. A town of England, in the north-east of Yorkshire, not far from the sea, in Skelton and Brotton urban district, where ironstone is worked. Pop. (urban district), 13,654 (1931).

BROUGHAM (bröm or brō'em). A close four-wheeled carriage, with a single inside seat for two persons, glazed in front and with a raised driver's seat, named after and apparently invented by Lord Brougham.

BROUGHAM (bröm or brō'em), **Henry, Baron Brougham and Vaux.** Born at Edinburgh, 19th Sept., 1778, died at Cannes, 7th May, 1868. He was educated at Edinburgh, studied law there, and was admitted a member of the Society of Advocates in 1800. Along with Jeffrey, Horner, and Sydney Smith he bore a chief part in the starting of the *Edinburgh Review* in 1802, to which he contributed a great number of articles.

Finding too circumscribed a field for his abilities in Edinburgh, he removed to London, and in 1808 was called to the English Bar. In 1810 he entered Parliament as member for the borough of Camelford, joined the Whig party, which was in opposition, and soon after obtained the passing of a measure making the slave-trade felony. From 1812 until 1816 he remained without a seat, when he was returned for Winchelsea. He represented this borough up to 1830. On his return to Parliament he at once began an agitation for social, political, and especially educational reform. In 1825 he was elected Lord Rector of Glasgow University, and also introduced a Bill into Parliament for the incorporation of London University, of which he may be considered one of the chief founders. He also bore an active part in establishing the Society for the Diffusion of Useful Knowledge in 1827.

Meantime his reputation as a

brilliant speaker and able barrister had been gradually increasing, and his fearless and successful defence of Queen Caroline in 1820 and 1821 placed him on the pinnacle of popular favour. At the general election of 1830 he was returned for the large and important county of York. In the ministry of Earl Grey he accepted the post of Lord Chancellor, and was raised to the peerage in 1830, with the title of Baron Brougham and Vaux. In this post he distinguished himself as a law reformer, and aided greatly in the passing of the Reform Bill of 1832. In 1834 the Whig ministry was dismissed, and this proved the end of his official life. Though for years he continued an active member of the House of Lords, he was never afterwards a member of any ministry.

In connection with his later years we may mention his presidency of the Law Amendment Society and of the Social Science Association. In legal procedure he was the means of introducing various reforms. Lord Brougham accomplished a large amount of literary work, contributing to newspapers, reviews, and encyclopædias, besides writing several independent works; and he had no mean reputation in mathematics and physical science. His works, collected by himself, and published in 11 vols. (1857-60), include biographical, political, and literary writings. He also wrote an autobiography, published posthumously, under the title *Life and Times of Henry, Lord Brougham.*—BIBLIOGRAPHY: J. B. Atlay, *Victorian Chancellors*; R. H. M. Buddle Atkinson and G. A. Jackson, *Brougham and his Early Friends: Letters to James Loch.*

BROUGHAM, John. Actor and dramatist, born in Dublin 1814, died in New York 1880. He wrote upwards of a hundred pieces, including *The Game of Life, Romance and Reality, Love's Livery, The Duke's Motto*, etc., and contributed largely to periodicals. He was well known as an actor both in England and in America.

BROUGHTON (bra̧'tun), **John Cam Hobhouse, Lord.** English writer and statesman, born 1786, died 1869. He was the son of Sir Benjamin Hobhouse, and was an intimate friend of Lord Byron, whom he accompanied in his travels to Greece and Turkey in 1809. He published in 1812 *Journey into Albania and other Provinces of the Turkish Empire.* He also accompanied Byron to Italy in 1816-7, and wrote *Historical Illustrations of the Fourth Canto of Childe Harold.* In 1816 he published *Letters on the Hundred Days, or Last Reign* . *Napoleon.*

He entered Parliament in 1819 a member for Westminster. In 18 he entered Earl Grey's ministry a Secretary for War, and became Privy Councillor. In 1833 he wa made Chief Secretary for Irelan and in 1835 he was appointed Pres dent of the Board of Control i Lord Melbourne's Government. H held this office till Sept., 1841, an in Lord Russell's administratio 1846-52. He was raised to th peerage as Baron Broughton in 185

BROUGHTON (bra̧'tun), **Rhod** English novelist, born in 1840, th daughter of a clergyman. She wa much less prolific than some Englis lady novelists, and her early work attracted much more attention tha her later. Among the chief are *Cometh up as a Flower* (1867) *Not Wisely but too Well* (1869); *Re as a Rose is She* (1870); *Good-bye Sweetheart, Good-bye* (1872); *Nanc* (1873); *Joan* (1876); *Belinda* (1883 *Scylla or Charybdis?* (1895); *Dea Faustina* (1897); *Lavinia* (1902) *The Devil and the Deep Sea* (1910) *Between Two Stools* (1912). He earlier novels show a cleverness vigour, and originality of plot an characterisation hardly maintaine in her more recent ones. She die 5th June, 1920.

BROUGHTY FERRY (bra̧'ti). A town of Scotland, County Angus, N shore of the estuary of the Tay, 4 miles E. of Dundee, so called from a ferry across the Tay to Ferry-port on-Craig (Tayport), in Fifeshire. It is a popular residental town for the prosperous business people of Dundee At the east end of the town is the old castle of Broughty, still kept up for the defence of the Tay. Pop. 11,058 (1911); united to Dundee 1913.

BROUSSA (brös'à). *See* BRUSA.

BROUSSAIS (brö - sā), **François Joseph Victor.** French physician, born 1772, died 1838. He is regarded as the founder of what was called the physiological system of medicine. According to his theory, irritability was the fundamental property of all living animal tissues, and every malady proceeded from an undue increase or diminution of that property.

BROUSSONET (brö-so-nā), **Pierre Marie Auguste.** French naturalist, born 1761, died 1807. He lived for some time in England, and was a friend of Sir Joseph Banks. He published *Ichthyologia*, and *Memoirs towards the History of the Respiration of Fishes.* He was professor of

›tany at Montpellier, and a member the Academy of Sciences.

BROUSSONETIA (brö-so-nē'ti-a). ›e MULBERRY.

BROUWER (brou'ver), or **BRAU-** **'ER, Adriaan.** A Dutch painter, born 1608, died in 1640. He was a pupil Franz Hals, and was patronised by ubens; but was of very dissipated abits. His works are chiefly tavern ›enes and other delineations of low fe, and rank among the best of their ind.

BROWN. A colour which may be ›garded as a mixture of red and lack, or of red, black, and yellow. here are various brown pigments, ıany of mineral origin, as bistre, mber, and cappagh brown.

BROWN, Charles Brockden. An minent American novelist, born ı Philadelphia in 1771, died 1810. Ie was destined for law, but the term ıtended for preparatory legal study 'as principally occupied with literary ›ursuits. His novel *Wieland, or the Transformation*, was published in 798; *Ormond, or the Secret Witness*, ı 1799; and *Arthur Mervyn* in 800. In the last-named work the avages of the yellow fever, which he author had witnessed in New York and Philadelphia, are painted vith great realism. He was origi- ıator of the *Monthly Magazine* and *American Review* (1799-1800). He lso founded in 1805 the *Literary Magazine and American Register*, vhich he edited for five years. Among is other works are *Clara Howard* 1801) and *Jane Talbot* (1804).

BROWN, Ford Madox. English ›ainter, grandson of Dr. John Brown of Edinburgh, the author of he Brunonian system of medicine, ›orn in 1821, died in 1893. In 1844 nd 1845 he contributed (unsuccess- ully) cartoons of *The Finding of he Body of Harold*, *Justice*, and ›ther subjects to the competitive xhibition for the frescoes of the Houses of Parliament. Among his principal works are: *King Lear*, *Chaucer at the Court of Edward III.*, *The Last of England*, *Work*, *Cordelia's Portion*, the Manchester town hall frescoes, etc. He is generally rated as a Pre-Raphaelite, but though a close intimacy existed between him and the brotherhood, he never actually joined them.

His son, **Oliver Madox Brown**, born 1855, died 1874, from early boyhood showed remarkable capacity both in painting and literature, especially prose fiction and poetry. His *Literary Remains* were published in 1876.

BROWN, George. Canadian journalist and politician, born in Edinburgh, Scotland, 1818, and educated at the High School there. He emigrated to the United States with his father, and assisted in the management of a newspaper at New York; but in 1843 removed to Toronto, Canada, where he founded a newspaper, *The Globe*, which was very successful. In 1852 he was returned to Parliament, and rapidly rose to the first rank as a debater and advocate of reforms. In 1858 he became Premier, and formed an administration, which, however, owing to an adverse vote of the Assembly, lasted only three days. In 1862, while on a visit to Scotland, he married Miss Annie Nelson, daughter of the well-known Edinburgh publisher.

On his return to Canada he joined, in 1864, the Coalition Government as leader of the reform section, and took an active part in the conferences held at Charlottetown and Quebec on the subject of the federation of the North American colonies; but resigned his office as minister in Dec., 1865. He was called to the Senate in 1873, and the year after went to Washington along with Sir Edward Thornton to negotiate a commercial treaty with the United States. He died on 9th May, 1880, of a gunshot wound inflicted by a discharged employee. Brown was a great personal force in Canadian politics, and contributed powerfully to the cause of reform.

BROWN, Sir George. Distinguished British general, born near Elgin 1790, died 1865; served in the Peninsular War, and in the American campaign of 1814. He became lieutenant-general in 1851; and distinguished himself in the Crimean War at Alma, Inkerman, and Sebastopol. He was made K.C.B. in 1855.

BROWN, John. Scottish covenanting martyr, born about 1627, killed 1685. He is said to have fought against the Government at Bothwell Bridge in 1679, and to have been on intimate terms with the leaders of the persecuted party. He was shot by Claverhouse and a party of his dragoons at Priestfield or Priesthill in the upland parish of Muirkirk, Ayrshire, where he cultivated a small piece of ground and acted as a carrier.

BROWN, John. Scottish divine, minister in the Burgher dissenting body at Haddington, born in 1722, died 1787. By intense application to study he learned French, Italian, German, Arabic, Persian, Syriac, and Ethiopic, as well as Greek and Hebrew. His most important works are: *The Self-interpreting Bible*; *Dic-*

tionary of the Bible; *Explication of the Assembly's Catechism*; *The Christian Journal*; *Explication of Scripture Metaphors*; *System of Divinity*; *General History of the Church*; *Particular History of the Churches of England, Scotland, and Ireland*; and *Harmony of Scripture Prophecies*.

BROWN, John, M.D. Author of the Brunonian system in medicine, born in Berwickshire 1735, died in London 1788. After studying medicine at Edinburgh University he took the degree of Doctor of Medicine at St. Andrew's, and after practising and teaching in Edinburgh he published his *Elements of Medicine* (in Latin). He maintained that the majority of diseases were proofs of weakness and not of excessive strength or excitement, and therefore contended that indiscriminate lowering of the system, as by bleeding, was erroneous, and that supporting treatment was required. His system gave rise to much opposition, but his opinions materially influenced the practice of his professional successors. Having fallen into difficulties, he removed to London in 1786.

BROWN, John, D.D. Scottish divine, grandson of the Rev. John Brown of Haddington, born 1784, died 1858. He was ordained pastor of the Burgher congregation at Biggar in 1806. In 1821 he removed to Edinburgh; and in 1834 became professor of theology in connection with the body to which he belonged, afterwards merged in the United Presbyterian Church. He was author of numerous works, chiefly in Biblical criticism (such as his *Exposition of the Discourses and Sayings of our Lord*), some of which were very popular.

BROWN, John. An American opponent of slavery, born 1800, hanged 1859. He early conceived a hatred for slavery, and, having removed to Osawatomie, Kansas, in 1855, he took an active part against the pro-slavery party, the slavery question there giving rise already almost to a civil war. In the summer of 1859 he rented a farm-house about 6 miles from Harper's Ferry, and organised a plot to liberate the slaves of Virginia. On 16th Oct. he, with the aid of about twenty friends, surprised and captured the arsenal at Harper's Ferry, but was wounded and taken prisoner by the Virginia militia next day, tried, and executed at Charlestown, 2nd Dec.

BROWN, John. Physician and essayist, son of John Brown, D.D., born at Biggar 1810, died at Edinburgh 1882. He graduated M.D. in 1833 and began practice as a phys cian. His leisure hours were devote to literature, many of his contrib tions appearing in the *North Britis Review, Good Words,* and oth periodicals. His collected writing were published under the title *Horæ Subsecivæ* (Leisure Hours), an embrace papers bearing on medicin art, poetry, and human life generally Several of his sketches (such as *Ra and his Friends, Our Dogs, P Marjorie, Jeems the Doorkeeper*), o which his fame chiefly rests, hav been published separately. Humour tenderness, and pathos are his chie characteristics.

BROWN, or BROWNE, Robert Founder of an English religious sec first called *Brownists*, and afterward *Independents*, born about 1550, an studied at Cambridge, where, i 1580, he began openly to attac the government and liturgy of th Church of England as anti-Christian After attacking the Establishe Church for years he was excom municated, but was reinstated, an held a Church living for over fort years, dying in 1633. The sect o Brownists, far from expiring wit their founder, soon spread, and a Bill was brought into Parliamen which inflicted on them very sever pains and penalties. In process o time, however, the name of Brownist was merged in that of Congrega tionalists or Independents.

BROWN, Robert. Botanist, born at Montrose, 21st Dec., 1773, died in London 10th June, 1858, the son of a Scotch Episcopalian clergyman. He received his education at Marischal College, Aberdeen, and afterwards studied medicine at Edinburgh. In 1800 he was appointed naturalist to Flinder's surveying expedition to Australia. He returned with nearly 4000 species of plants, and was shortly after appointed librarian to the Linnæan Society.

In 1810 he published the first volume of his great work *Prodromus Floræ Novæ Hollandiæ et Insulæ Van Diemen.* No second volume of it ever appeared. He was the first English writer on botany who adopted the natural system of classification, which has since entirely superseded that of Linnæus. In 1814 he published a botanical appendix to Flinder's account of his voyage, and in 1828 *A Brief Account of Microscopical Observations on the Particles contained in the Pollen of Plants, and on the General Existence of Active Molecules in Organic and Inorganic Bodies*.

He also wrote botanical appendices for the voyages of Ross and arry, the African exploration of Denham and Clapperton and others, and described, with Dr. Bennet, the plants collected by Dr. Horsfield in Java. In 1810 he took charge of the collections and library of Sir Joseph Banks. He transferred them in 1827 to the British Museum, and was appointed keeper of botany in that institution.

He became a Fellow of the Royal Society in 1811, D.C.L. Oxford in 1832, a foreign associate of the French Academy of Sciences in 1833. He received the Copley medal in 1839, and was appointed president of the Linnæan Society in 1849. As a naturalist Brown occupied the very highest rank among men of science. A collection of his miscellaneous writings was published by the Ray Society (1866-7).

BROWN, Thomas. Poet and miscellaneous writer, described by Addison as "of facetious memory," born at Shifnal, Shropshire, 1663, died in London 1704. He is the author of numerous dialogues, letters, poems, etc., witty, coarse, and indelicate, first collected in 1707.

BROWN, Thomas Edward. Manx poet, born 1830, died 1897. Educated at King William's College, Isle of Man, and Christ Church, Oxford, he was a Fellow of Oriel 1854-8, vice-principal of King William's College 1858-61, and second master at Clifton College, Bristol, 1863-92. His chief poems are of a narrative class, but he had also a decided lyric gift. His best-known volume is entitled *Fo'c's'le Yarns*, others being *The Doctor and Other Poems*, *The Manx Witch and Other Poems*, and *Old John and Other Poems*. A collective edition of his poems appeared in 1900, and his letters have also been published, with a memoir.

BROWN, Dr. Thomas. Scottish metaphysician, born at Kirkmabreck, Kirkcudbright, in 1778, died at Brompton, London, 1820. He was educated at the High School, and subsequently at the University of Edinburgh, where he obtained the professorship of moral philosophy. He distinguished himself, at a very early age, by an acute review of the medical and physiological theories of Erasmus Darwin, in a work entitled *Observations on Darwin's Zoonamia*. He published some indifferent poems, which were collected in 1820.

But he chiefly deserves notice on account of his metaphysical speculations, his chief work being *Lectures on the Philosophy of the Human Mind* (1822). His system reduces the intellectual faculties to three great classes—perception, simple suggestion, and relative suggestion; employing the term suggestion as nearly synonymous with association. He held original views in regard to the part played by touch and the muscular sense in relation to belief in an external world. His development of the theory of cause and effect was first suggested by Hume.

BROWN ALGÆ, or PHÆOPHYCEÆ. An extensive and varied phylum of marine Algæ, easily distinguished by their brown or olive-green colour, due to the presence of phycophæin in the chromatophores in addition to chlorophyll, which is masked thereby. They form the bulk of the seaweeds of the shore and of comparatively shallow water, and grow most luxuriantly in the colder seas, where the Giant Kelps (Macrocystis and Nereocystis) attain to huge dimensions.

The simplest forms, e.g. Ectocarpus, are small filamentous plants, but the majority are larger and of more massive construction, the common Wracks (Fucus), with their flattened, dichotomously-branched, leathery thallus attached to a rock or similar object by a holdfast, being good examples of the average degree of vegetative complexity in the group. The Kelps (Laminariaceæ) are bigger again, and still more elaborate in structure, including among their tissue-forms sieve-tubes precisely like those of Angiosperms, a striking instance of parallel evolution. The principal subdivisions of this great phylum, with representative genera, are shown below:—

A. Phæosporeæ. Asexual reproduction by zoospores; sexual reproduction never oögamous.

1. Ectocarpaceæ. Thallus of branched or variously-interwoven filaments; growth usually intercalary. Ectocarpus, Chorda, Leathesia.

2. Sphacelariaceæ. Thallus as in 1; growth by very prominent apical cells. Sphacelaria, Cladostephus.

3. Cutleriaceæ. Thallus flattened; growth trichothallic. Cutleria.

4. Laminariaceæ (Kelps). Thallus large, massive, and highly differentiated; growth intercalary. Laminaria, Alaria, Lessonia, Macrocystis, Nereocystis.

B. Cyclosporeæ. Asexual reproduction by tetraspores, or wanting; sexual reproduction oögamous.

5. Dictyotaceæ. Sexual organs superficial; asexual reproduction by tetraspores. Dictyota, Padina.

6. Fucaceæ (Wracks). Sexual organs contained in conceptacles; asexual reproduction nil. Fucus,

Pelvetia, Ascophyllum, Himanthalia, Sargassum.

Interesting stages in the evolution of dissimilar male and female gametes from isogametes are seen in the genus Ectocarpus; in Cutleria, not only the gametes, but also the organs in which they are produced (gametangia), differ greatly in size. Alternation of generations exists in Cutleria and Dictyota.

As in the case of the Green Algæ, the ancestors of the Phæophyceæ are to be sought among the coloured Flagellates—in this case among the types with brown or yellow chromatophores—a whole series of probable connecting-links being already known. The Brown Algæ have not given rise to any of the groups of higher plants; the existence of a number of endophytic forms, on the other hand, suggests a possible evolution of Fungoid types from this group, though the evidence for this is far less strong than in the case of the Green Algæ. *See* HETEROGAMY; GENERATIONS, ALTERNATION OF; and articles on genera mentioned.

BROWN BESS. A name familiarly given to the old Government regulation bronzed flint-lock musket formerly used in the British army.

BROWN COAL. A term sometimes used as synonymous with Lignite (q.v.), but more properly applied to the dark, compact deposits arising from finely-divided woody matter accumulated in ancient swamps or even in lagoons. The percentage of carbon is about 60, and the ash, as in peat, may be 12; but brown coal in places passes into mere carbonaceous shale, which is of much less value as fuel. Stems of trees are often embedded in it. Important beds occur in Oligocene and Miocene strata in North Germany and Bohemia.

BROWNE, Charles Farrar. An American humorist, best known as "Artemus Ward," born at Waterford, Maine, 1836, died at Southampton, England, 1867. Originally a printer, he became editor of papers in Ohio, where his humorous letters became very popular. He subsequently lectured on California and Utah in the States and in England, where he contributed to *Punch*. His writings consist of letters and papers by "Artemus Ward," a pretended exhibitor of wax figures and wild beasts, and are full of drollery and eccentricity.

BROWNE, Hablot Knight. An English designer of humorous and satirical subjects, and an etcher of considerable skill, better known by the pseudonym of "Phiz," born a[t] Kennington, Surrey, 1815, died a[t] Brighton 1882. In 1835 he succeeded Seymour as the illustrator o[f] Dickens's *Pickwick*, and was afterwards engaged to illustrate *Nicholas Nickleby*, *Dombey & Son*, *Martin Chuzzlewit*, *David Copperfield*, and other works of that author. He also illustrated the novels of Lever, Ainsworth, etc., besides sending many comic sketches to the illustrated serials of the time.

BROWNE, Isaac Hawkins. English poet, born at Burton-on-Trent 1706, died 1760. Author of *Design and Beauty*; *The Pipe of Tobacco* (in which he imitates Pope, Young, Swift, and others); and a Latin poem, *De Animi Immortalitate*, modelled on Lucretius and Virgil.

BROWNE, Sir Thomas. An English physician and writer, born in London 1605, died at Norwich 1682. He was educated at Winchester School and Oxford, where he took the degree of M.A. He practised as a physician for some time in Oxfordshire. He subsequently visited the continent of Europe and received the degree of M.D. at Leyden. On his return to England he settled as a physician at Norwich, where he married and acquired extensive practice and reputation. In 1642 was published his *Religio Medici* (A Physician's Religion), which excited the attention of the learned, not only in England but throughout Europe, gave rise to doubts of the author's orthodoxy, and was translated into various languages.

In 1646 his literary reputation was still further heightened by the appearance of his *Pseudodoxia Epidemica, or Treatise on Vulgar Errors*, a work of extraordinary learning, and accounted the most solid and useful of his literary labours. In 1658 his *Hydriotaphia, or Treatise on Urn-Burial*, appeared conjointly with his *Garden of Cyrus*, a work treating of horticulture from Adam's time to that of Cyrus. These works ranked him very high as an antiquary; and he maintained a wide correspondence with the learned both at home and abroad.

In 1665 he was made an honorary member of the College of Physicians, and in 1671 Charles II., visiting Norwich, conferred on him the honour of knighthood. Of a most amiable private character, he was happy in the affection of his large family and numerous friends; and passed through a remarkably tranquil and prosperous literary and professional life. Though he wrote xposing vulgar errors, he was himself believer in alchemy, astrology, and itchcraft. Sir Thomas Browne's *Vorks, including his Life and Correspondence,* were edited by Simon Vilkin in 1835.—BIBLIOGRAPHY: E. osse, *Sir Thomas Browne*; C. Vhibley, *Essays in Biography.*

BROWNE, William. An English oet, born at Tavistock, in Devonhire, in 1591, died about 1645. In is twenty-third year he published is *Britannia's Pastorals,* which met ith great approbation; and in the ollowing year appeared his *Shepherd's Pipe,* a collection of seven clogues. In 1616 he published the econd part of his *Britannia's Pastorals,* which was as successful as the ormer. Browne was tutor to Robert Dormer, Earl of Carnarvon, who was illed at the battle of Newbury, and lled a similar office in the family of he Earl of Pembroke.

BROWNE, William G. English raveller in Africa and Asia, born n London 1768, killed by robbers n Persia 1813. He visited the African kingdoms of Darfur and Bornu in 1791, and was the first to nake those countries known to Europeans. He published in 1799 *Travels in Africa, Egypt, and Syria, rom 1792 to 1798.*

BROWNHILLS. A town (urban listrict) of England, Staffordshire, 6 miles south-west of Lichfield, in a listrict where are extensive coalnines. Pop. (1931), 18,368.

BROWN HOLLAND. An unbleached linen used for various articles of clothing and upholstery.

BROWNIE. In Scotland, an imaginary spirit formerly believed to haunt houses, particularly farmhouses. Instead of doing any injury, he was believed to be very useful to the family, particularly to the servants if they treated him well, for whom he was wont to do many pieces of drudgery while they slept. The brownie bears a close resemblance to the Robin Goodfellow of England, and the *Kobold* of Germany.

BROWNING, Elizabeth Barrett. English poetess, born at Burn Hall, Durham, in 1809, died at Florence 1861. Her father, Edward Moulton, took the name of Barrett on succeeding to some property. She grew up at Hope End, near Ledbury, Herefordshire, where her father possessed a large estate. Her bodily frame was from the first extremely delicate, and she had been injured by a fall from her pony when a girl, but her mind was sound and vigorous, and disciplined by a course of severe study of the classics. When only seventeen she published *An Essay on Mind,* with other poems.

A money catastrophe compelled her father to settle in London, and her continued delicacy received a severe shock by the accidental drowning of her brother, causing her to pass years in the confinement of a sick-room. Her health was at length partially restored, and in 1846 she was married to Robert Browning, soon after which they settled in Italy, and continued to reside for the most part in the city of Florence.

Elizabeth Barrett Browning

Her *Prometheus Bound* (from the Greek of Æschylus) *and Miscellaneous Poems* appeared in 1833; *The Seraphim* and other poems in 1838. In 1856 a collected edition of Mrs. Browning's works appeared, including several new poems, and among others *Lady Geraldine's Courtship. Casa Guidi Windows,* a poem on the struggles of the Italians for liberty in 1848-9, appeared in 1851.

The longest and most finished of all her works, *Aurora Leigh,* a narrative and didactic poem in nine books, was published in 1857. *Poems before Congress* appeared in 1860, and two posthumous volumes, *Last Poems,* 1862, and *The Greek Christian Poets and the English Poets* (prose essays and translations), 1863, were edited by her husband.

The love letters of Robert and Elizabeth Barrett Browning were sold at Sotheby's on 2nd May, 1913, for £6501; the autograph MS. of Mrs.

Browning's *Sonnets from the Portuguese* for £1130; and the autograph MS. of her *Aurora Leigh* for £920.—BIBLIOGRAPHY: J. H. Ingram, *Elizabeth Barrett Browning* (Eminent Women Series); F. G. Kenyon, *The Letters of Elizabeth Barrett Browning*; G. M. Merlette, *La vie et l'œuvre d'Elizabeth Browning*; L. Whiting, *The Brownings: Their Life and Art.*

BROWNING, Robert. Poet, born at Camberwell, 7th May, 1812, died 12th Dec., 1889. After completing his education at University College, London, he went to Italy, where he made diligent study of its mediæval history and the life of the people. In 1846 he married Elizabeth Barrett and thereafter resided chiefly in Italy, making occasional visits to England.

His first poem, *Pauline*, was published in 1833; followed by *Paracelsus* in 1835; *Strafford, a Tragedy* (1837), produced at Covent Garden, Macready and Helen Faucit playing the chief parts. *Sordello* appeared in 1840, followed by the series called *Bells and Pomegranates*, including the three plays *Pippa Passes*, *King Victor and King Charles*, and *Colombe's Birthday*; four tragedies: *The Return of the Druses*, *A Blot on the Scutcheon*, *Luria*, and *A Soul's Tragedy*; and a number of dramatic lyrics, among them the well-known *Pied Piper of Hamelin*, and *How they Brought the Good News from Ghent to Aix* (1841-46).

Between 1846 and 1868 appeared *Men and Women*, *Christmas Eve and Easter Day*, *Dramatis Personæ*, and some shorter poems. *The Ring and the Book* (1869), his longest poem, was followed by *Balaustion's Adventure* and *Prince Hohenstiel-Schwangau* (1871), *Fifine at the Fair* (1872), *Red Cotton Nightcap Country* (1873), *Aristophanes' Apology*, *Inn Album* (1875), *Pacchiarotto* (1876), *La Saisiaz* (1878), *Dramatic Idylls* (1879-80), *Jocoseria* (1883), *Ferishtah's Fancies* (1884), *Parleyings with certain People of Importance in their Day* (1887), *Asolando* (1889). He received the degree of D.C.L. from Oxford in 1882.

A Browning Society for the study of his works was formed in 1881, under whose auspices several of his dramas have been performed. His poems are often difficult to understand from the quick transitions of thought, and they are not infrequently rugged and harsh in expression, yet they are among the chief poetic utterances of last century.

BIBLIOGRAPHY: Mrs. Sutherland Orr, *The Life and Letters of Browning*; *Browning Society Paper*; Arthur Symons, *An Introduction the Study of Browning*; Stopfo Brooke, *The Poetry of Robert Brow ing*; G. K. Chesterton, *Browning* English Men of Letters Series).

BROWNISM and **BROWNIST** *See* BROWN, ROBERT.

BROWN SPAR. A name f ferriferous varieties of dolomite a magnesite, and also for the calciu magnesium iron carbonate ankerit and the iron carbonate siderite.

BROWNSVILLE. A town of t United States, near the southe point of Texas, 15 miles above t mouth of the Rio Grande, opposi Matamoros, Mexico. Pop. 22,021.

BROWN UNIVERSITY. An Ame can institution at Providence, Rho Island, founded 1764. It is und Baptist control, has about 90 pr fessors and teachers and 1000 student and a library of about 240,0 volumes.

BROXBURN. A town of Scotlan West Lothian, with paraffin-oil wor and coal-mines. Pop. 8315.

BRUCE. A family name disti guished in the history of Scotlan The family of Bruce (or *de Brus*) w of Norman descent, its found having obtained from William t Conqueror large grants of land Northumberland. After being fr quently involved in border warfa with the Scots, the House of Bru received a grant of the lands Annandale from David I., while st Earl of Cumbria and Lothian. Th granting of lands to Norman noble of which this is merely one exampl is a very important factor in Scottis history.

BRUCE, David. *See* DAVID II.

BRUCE, Edward. A brother Robert I., who, after distinguishin himself in the War of Independenc crossed in 1315 to Ireland to aid th native *septs* or clans against th English. After many successes h was crowned King of Ireland a Carrickfergus, but fell in battle nea Dundalk in 1318.

BRUCE, James. African traveller born at Kinnaird House, Stirling shire, in 1730. He received hi education at Harrow and at th University of Edinburgh, and entere the wine trade, but having inherite his father's estate in 1758 he soo gave up business. From 1763 t 1765 he held the consulship of Algiers and in 1765 he visited successivel Tunis, Tripoli, Rhodes, Cyprus, Syria and several parts of Asia Minor where he made drawings of the ruin of Palmyra, Baalbec, etc.

In 1768 he set out for Cairo, navigated the Nile to Syene, crossed the desert to the Red Sea, passed some months in Arabia Felix, and reached Gondar, the capital of Abyssinia, in 1770. In that country he ingratiated himself with the sovereign and succeeded in reaching the sources of the Abai, then considered the main stream of the Nile. On his return to Gondar he found the country engaged in a civil war, and more than three years elapsed before he was able to return to Cairo. After visiting France and Italy he returned to Scotland in 1774.

His long-expected *Travels* did not appear until 1790, and were received with some incredulity, though succeeding travellers have proved them in large part accurate. Bruce lost his life by an accidental fall down stairs in 1794.

BRUCE, Michael. A Scottish poet, born at Kinnesswood, Kinross-shire, in 1746. At first a herd-boy, he succeeded in attending Edinburgh University, occupying himself in the intervals as a village schoolmaster. The struggle against poverty brought on consumption, and he died in 1767. His poems, of which the best known is the *Elegy* on his own approaching death, were published by the Rev. John Logan in 1770. This volume contained a well-known *Ode to the Cuckoo* which Logan afterwards claimed as his own, though he really seems only to have somewhat improved Bruce's poem.

BRUCE, Robert (Robert de Brus). Fifth lord of Annandale, born 1210, died at Lochmaben Castle 1295. He was possessed of extensive estates in Cumberland, of which he was made sheriff in 1255. He was one of the fifteen regents of Scotland during the minority of Alexander III.; and was one of the competitors for the Scottish crown on the death of Margaret, the Maid of Norway, in 1290—Bruce being the grandson of David, Earl of Huntingdon, by his second daughter Isobel, while Baliol claimed as the great-grandson by the eldest daughter Margaret. On the decision of Edward being given in 1292 in favour of Baliol, Bruce resigned the estate of Annandale to his eldest son to avoid doing homage to his rival.

BRUCE, Robert, Earl of Carrick. Eldest son of the preceding, accompanied Edward I. to Palestine in 1269; married, in 1271, Martha Margaret, Countess of Carrick. Like his father he resigned the lordship of Annandale to his eldest son to avoid acknowledging the supremacy of Baliol. On the revolt of the latter Bruce fought on the English side, and after the battle of Dunbar made an unsuccessful application to Edward for the crown. He died in 1304.

BRUCE, Robert. The greatest of the kings of Scotland, born 1274. He was the son of the preceding. In 1296, as Earl of Carrick, he swore fealty to Edward I., and in 1297 fought on the English side against Wallace. He then joined the Scottish army, but in the same year returned to his allegiance to Edward until 1298, when he again joined the national party, and became in 1299 one of the four regents of the kingdom.

Robert Bruce

In the three final campaigns, however, he resumed fidelity to Edward, and resided for some time at his Court; but, learning that the king meditated putting him to death on information given by the traitor Comyn, he fled in Feb., 1306, to Scotland, stabbed Comyn in a quarrel at Dumfries, assembled his vassals at Lochmaben Castle, and claimed the crown, which he received at Scone on the 27th March.

Being twice defeated, he dismissed his troops, retired to Rathlin Island, and was supposed to be dead, when, in the spring of 1307, he landed on the Carrick coast, defeated the Earl of Pembroke at Loudon Hill, and in two years had wrested nearly the whole country from the English. He then in successive years advanced into England, laying waste the country; and on 24th June, 1314, defeated at Bannockburn the English forces advancing under Edward II. to the relief of the garrison at Stirling.

In 1316 he went to Ireland to the aid of his brother Edward, and on his return in 1318, in retaliation for inroads made during his absence, he took Berwick and harried Northumberland and Yorkshire. Hostilities continued until the defeat of Edward near Byland Abbey in 1323, and though in that year a truce was concluded for thirteen years, it was speedily broken. Not until 4th March, 1328, was the treaty concluded by which the independence of Scotland was fully recognised.

Bruce did not long survive the completion of his work, dying at Cardross Castle on 7th June, 1329. He was twice married; first to a daughter of the Earl of Mar, Isabella, by whom he had a daughter, Marjory, mother of Robert II.; and then to a daughter of Aymer de Burgh, Earl of Ulster, Elizabeth, by whom he had a son, David, who succeeded him.—BIBLIOGRAPHY: John Barbour, *The Brus* (edited by W. W. Skeat in 1894); John of Fordun, *Chronica Gentis Scotorum* (edited by W. F. Skene in 1871); Kerr, *Life and Reign of Robert the Bruce* (1811); A. Lang, *History of Scotland*.

BRUCE, Stanley Melbourne. Australian politician. Born at Melbourne, 15th April, 1883, he was educated at the grammar school there and at Trinity Hall, Cambridge. He rowed in the boat race of 1904 and returning home became managing director of the firm of Patterson, Laing & Bruce. He served in Europe during the Great War, won the M.C., and was twice wounded. In 1918 Bruce entered the House of Representatives, and in 1921 was made Treasurer of the Commonwealth in the nationalist ministry. In 1923 he succeeded Mr. Hughes as Prime Minister, became also Minister for External Affairs and attended the Imperial Conferences of 1923 and 1926. In Sept., 1929, his Government was defeated and he left office. In 1932 he joined the Coalition ministry under Mr. Lyons, and was sent to represent Australia in London, as resident minister, a new departure.

BRUCE, William Spiers. Scottish explorer and scientist. He was born in Edinburgh, 1st Aug., 1867, and had a brilliant career in natural science at Edinburgh University. In 1892 he made his first voyage to polar regions as naturalist to the Scottish Antarctic Expedition. In that capacity he subsequently took part in the Jackson-Harmsworth Arctic Expedition (1896-7); the Coats Nova Zembla Expedition (1898) and the Prince of Monaco's Spitsbergen Expeditions of 1898 and 1899. As leader of the Scottish National Antarctic Expedition (1902-4) he discovered 150 miles of the coast-line of Antarctica. Later he made several further visits to Spitsbergen, the last in the year before his death, which occurred on 28th Oct., 1921.

BRUCH, Max. German musical composer, born at Cologne, Jan., 1838. He showed his musical genius at a very early age, and produced his first operetta, *Scherz, List und Rache*, when he was twenty. He was musical director at Coblentz, and in 1878 settled for a time in England, where he was offered the direction of the Liverpool Philharmonic Society in 1880. In 1883 he went to the United States, where he conducted his own oratorio, *Arminius*, in Boston. In 1893 he returned to Berlin to take up his post as director of the Hochschule. His real field was concert music for chorus and orchestra.

His musical productions include: *Scherz, List und Rache* (1858); *Lorelei* (1863); *Die Flucht der heiligen Familie*; *Frithjof* (1864); *Flucht nach Egypten*; *Odysseus* (1871); *Arminius*; *Kol Nidrei*; *Moses*; *Gustav Adolf*; etc., besides two collections of arrangements, one a book of *Hebraische Gesänge*, and the other a set of Scottish songs. He died at Berlin, Oct., 1920.

BRUCHSAL (brü*h*'zal). A town of Baden, 25 miles south of Heidelberg. It was the residence of the prince-bishops of Spires from the eleventh century, but lost its importance until it became a considerable railway centre. The palace, the principal building of the town, erected in the eighteenth century and restored in the twentieth, was the residence of the Dukes of Baden until 1918. Pop. 16,469.

BRUCINE. An alkaloid accompanying strychnia in nux vomica. Its taste is exceedingly bitter and acrid, and its action on the animal economy is entirely analogous to that of strychnia, but much less powerful.

BRUCITE. A mineral composed of magnesium hydroxide, found at Texas. Its colour is white, tinged grey, green, or blue, and it is used for sugar-refining.

BRUEYS-D'AIGALLIERS (brü-ā-dā-gāl-yā), **François-Paul.** A French admiral, born at Uzés 1753, became captain in 1792, and vice-admiral in 1798. He successfully conveyed Bonaparte and his army to Egypt in

1798, but was killed in the subsequent naval battle in the Bay of Aboukir shortly before his ship, the *Orient*, blew up.

BRUGES (brüzh; Fl. *Brugge*, that is, Bridges). An old walled city of Belgium, capital of West Flanders, 57 miles N.W. of Brussels, an important railway and canal centre, the chief canal being the new ship canal connecting it with the North Sea at Zeebrugge (6½ miles); canals connect also with Ghent and Ostend. Bruges has over fifty bridges, all opening for the passage of ships.

In the thirteenth and fourteenth centuries it was one of the chief commercial places in Europe, and an important member of the Hanseatic League. Towards the end of the fifteenth century it began to decline, but still carries on a considerable trade with the north of Europe, and is by its canals an entrepôt of Belgian commerce.

Among its more noteworthy buildings are the Halles, a fine old building, with a tower 354 feet high, in which is a numerous set of chimes; the hôtel de ville, the bourse, and the palace of justice; the church of Notre-Dame, with its elevated spire and splendid tombs of Charles the Bold and Mary of Burgundy; etc. The town possesses interesting works of art by Jan Van Eyck, Memling, the Van Oosts, etc. Textile goods, lace, etc., are manufactured. The town was captured by the Germans on 14th Oct., 1914, and re-occupied by Belgian troops on 18th Oct., 1918. Pop. 52,976.

BRUGSCH (brügsh), **Heinrich Karl.** German Egyptologist, born in 1827. He early devoted himself to the study of Egyptian antiquities, and resided a number of years in Egypt, being for some time in the employment of the Egyptian Government, by which he was created a bey, and subsequently a pasha. He also travelled in Persia. His works are very numerous, and include an autobiography. His *History of Egypt from the Monuments* has been translated into English. He died in 1894.

BRÜHL (brül), **Heinrich Count von.** Minister and favourite of Augustus III., King of Poland, born in 1700, died 1763. In 1747 he became the Prime Minister of Augustus, to gratify whose wishes he exhausted the State, plunged the country into debt, and greatly reduced the army. He acquired great wealth and lived in greater state than the king himself. His profusion was often beneficial to the arts and sciences, and his library of 62,000 vols. forms a chief part of the Royal Library at Dresden.

BRUISE. Injury to the body. It is caused by a violent blow resulting in the rupture of the smaller blood-vessels and usually a swelling of the parts affected. The swelling is caused by the exudation of blood and effusion of lymph into the tissues. In some cases the bruise shows at some distance from the place where the blow was received, owing to the effused blood having flowed through the tissues before reaching the skin. Severe bruises may be relieved by applying lint soaked in cold water of a mixture of equal parts of methylated spirits and water. If the skin is broken, bathe with warm water containing tincture of iodine (½ teaspoonful to 1 pint) and apply lint spread with boracic ointment.

BRUMAIRE (bru-mār; L. *bruma*, winter). The second month in the calendar adopted by the first French Republic, beginning on the 23rd Oct., and ending 21st Nov. The 18th Brumaire of the year VIII. of the French Revolution (9th Nov., 1799) witnessed the overthrow of the Directory by Bonaparte. The next day he dispersed at the point of the bayonet the Council of Five Hundred, and was elected Consul.

BRUMMELL, George Bryan (*Beau Brummell*). Son of a clerk in the Treasury, born in London in 1778. He was educated at Eton and at Oxford, and at the age of sixteen made the acquaintance of the Prince of Wales, afterwards George IV., who made him a cornet in his own regiment of the 10th Hussars, and secured his rapid promotion.

The death of his father in 1794 brought him a fortune of £30,000, which he expended in a course of sumptuous living, extending over twenty-one years, during which his *dicta* on matters of etiquette and dress were received in the beau-monde as indisputable. His creditors at length became clamorous, and in 1816 he took refuge in Calais, where he resided for many years, partly supported by the remains of his own fortune and partly by remittances from friends in England. Subsequently (1830) he was appointed Consul at Caen, but on the abolition of the post was reduced to absolute poverty, and died in a lunatic asylum at Caen in 1840.—BIBLIOGRAPHY: W. Jesse, *Life of G. Brummell*; R. Boutet de Monval, *Beau Brummell and his Times*.

BRUN'ANBURGH. The scene of a battle in which Athelstan and the Anglo-Saxons defeated a force of Scots, Danes, etc., in 937. Its locality is somewhat doubtful, but is supposed to be somewhere in the north of England or in Cheshire.

BRUNCK (brunk), **Richard François Philippe.** Classical commentator, born at Strasburg in 1729, died there in 1803. He published valuable editions of Virgil, Apollonius Rhodius, Aristophanes, the Gnomic poets, Plautus, Terence, and Sophocles—the last his masterpiece.

BRUNDUSIUM. *See* BRINDISI.

BRUNE (brün), **Guillaume Marie Anne.** Marshal of France, son of a lawyer at Brive-la-Gaillarde, born 1763. In 1793 he joined the army, and afterwards distinguished himself at Arcola and Verona as general of brigade in the Italian army. In 1799 he compelled the British and Russians to evacuate the north of Holland. In 1800 he pacified La Vendée, and, replacing Masséna as commander of the Italian army, led his troops over the mincio, conquered the Austrians, passed the Adige, took possession of Vicenza and Roderevo, and hastened the conclusion of peace. From 1802-4 he was ambassador at Constantinople, and in the latter year was made a marshal.

Losing the favour of Napoleon, he remained without employment for some years, but on the return of Napoleon from Elba he received an important command in the south of France, which he was shortly compelled to surrender at the second Restoration. He then set out for Paris, but was attacked and brutally killed by the populace at Avignon.

BRUNEHILDA. A Visigothic princess, married to Siegebert I., King of Austrasia, in A.D. 568. To avenge her sister (assassinated at the instigation of Fredegonde) she involved her husband in a war with his brother Chilperic, in the course of which Siegebert was murdered, 575, and she herself taken prisoner. She induced Meroveus, one of Chilperic's sons, to marry her, effected her escape, recovered her authority and maintained it till 613, when she was captured by Fredegonde's son, Clothaire II. of Soissons, who had her torn to pieces by wild horses as the murderess of ten kings and royal princes.

BRUNEI (brö'nī), or **BRUNI.** A Malayan sultanate on the N.W. coast of Borneo, between Sarawak and British North Borneo, exporting sago, gutta-percha, rubber, etc.; pop. 25,444. Its capital, also called Brunei, is situated on the river of the same name, about 14 miles from its mouth, the houses being mostly raised above the water on posts. It has a considerable trade, its population being about 15,000. Brunei has been under British protection since 1888. In 1906 the Sultan handed over the general administration to the British Resident.

BRUNEL', **Isambard Kingdom.** English engineer, son of Sir Mark Isambard Brunel, born in 1806, died in 1859. He was educated at the Henri IV. College, Paris, and commenced practical engineering under his father, acting at twenty as resident engineer at the Thames Tunnel. Among his best-known works were the *Great Western, Great Britain*, and *Great Eastern* steamships; the entire works on the Great Western Railway, to which he was appointed engineer in 1833, the Hungerford Suspension Bridge, docks at Plymouth, Milford Haven, etc.

BRUNEL', Sir Mark Isambard. A distinguished engineer, was the son of a Normandy farmer, and born near Rouen in 1769. He was educated in Rouen, his mechanical genius early displaying itself. In 1786 he entered the French naval service, and in 1793 only escaped proscription by a hasty flight to America, where he joined a French expedition to explore the regions around Lake Ontario. He was afterwards employed as engineer and architect in the city of New York, erecting forts for its defence, and establishing an arsenal and foundry.

In 1799 he proceeded to England and settled at Plymouth, rapidly winning reputation by the invention of an important machine for making the block-pulleys for the rigging of ships. Among his other inventions were a machine for making seamless shoes, machines for making nails and wooden boxes, for ruling paper and twisting cotton into hanks, and a machine for producing locomotion by means of carbonic acid gas; but his greatest engineering triumph was the Thames Tunnel, commenced March, 1825, and opened in 1843. In 1841 he was knighted. He died in Dec., 1849.

BRUNELLESCHI (brö-nel-es'kē), **Filippo.** Italian architect, born in 1377 at Florence. He won some reputation as an inventor and sculptor, and made special studies in the then little-known science of perspective, but devoted himself particularly to architecture. When at Rome with Donatello he conceived the idea of bringing architecture back to Græco-Roman principles as opposed to the dominant Gothic. In this he was successful, his work opening the way for Alberti, Bramante, Vignola, and Palladio.

His great achievement was the dome of the cathedral of Santa Maria at Florence, the possibility of which was denied by other architects. It has remained unsurpassed, the dome of St. Peter's, though it excels it in height, being inferior to it in massiveness of effect. Other important works by him were the Pitti Palace at Florence, the churches of San Lorenzo and Spirito Santo, and the Capella dei Pazza. He died in 1446.

BRUNET (brü-nā), **Jacques Charles.** French bibliographer and bookseller at Paris, born 1780, died 1867. He began his bibliographical career by the preparation of several auction catalogues, and of a supplementary volume to the *Dictionnaire Bibliographique* of Cailleau and Duclos (Paris, 1802). In 1810 was published the first edition of his valuable *Manuel du Librarie, et de l'amateur de livres*, which has gone through many editions and extensions, and is still perhaps the best book of its class.

BRUNETIÈRE, Ferdinand. French literary critic, born in 1849. He came into prominence in 1875 by his contributions to the *Revue des Deux Mondes*, a periodical of which he became editor in 1895. Brunetière was perhaps one of the greatest systematic critics of Modern French literature. Like Taine, he saw a natural evolution in literary tradition, although he accorded greater play to individuality.

His philosophical ideas may be summed up as "idealistic pessimism." He manifested great zeal for Roman Catholicism as opposed to the doctrines of the French intellectuals. He found materialism repellent and proclaimed the bankruptcy of science.

Among his numerous works are: *Manuel de l'Histoire de la Littérature Française* (1897); *Evolution des Genres dans l'Histoire de la Littérature* (1890); *Le Roman Naturaliste* (1883); *Discours académiques* (1901); *Nouveaux Essais sur la Littérature contemporaine* (1904); *Histoire de la Littérature Française classique* (1905); *Sur les Chemins de la Croyance* (1905). He died in 1906.—BIBLIOGRAPHY: J. Sargeret, *Les grands Convertis*; Babbitt, *The Masters of Modern Criticism.*

BRUNHILDA. In Norse mythology, the chief of the Valkyries, or warrior maidens. She is best known through Wagner's opera cycle, *The Ring of the Nibelungs*, as she is the heroine of the second opera, *The Valkyrie.*

BRUNI. An oddly-shaped island on the south coast of Tasmania, consisting of N. Bruni and S. Bruni, united by a narrow slip of land.

BRUNI. *See* BRUNEI.

BRUNI, Leonardo. *See* BRUNO.

BRUNINGS (brö'ningz), **Christian.** A great hydraulic architect of Holland, born in 1736; appointed general inspector of rivers by the States of Holland in 1769; died 1805.

BRÜNN, or **BRNO.** A city in Czechoslovakia (till 1918 in Austria), capital of Moravia, on the railway from Vienna to Prague, nearly encircled by the Rivers Schwarzawa and Zwittawa. It contains a cathedral and other handsome churches; a landhaus, where the provincial assembly meets, and several palaces; and has extensive manufactures of woollens. It is the centre of Moravian commerce, a great part of which is carried on by fairs. Near it is the fortress of Spielberg, in which Trenck and Silvio Pellico were confined. Pop. 263,646.

BRUNO, Giordano (jor-dä'nō). An Italian philosopher of the Renaissance born at Nola in 1548. He entered the order of Dominicans, but was accused of impiety, and, after enduring much persecution, fled from Rome about 1577 and reached Geneva in 1579. Here he was soon persecuted in turn by the Calvinists, and travelled slowly through southern France to Paris, where he was offered a chair of philosophy, but declined to fulfil its conditions of attendance at mass. He lectured for some time, however, but in opposition to the antiquated Aristotelianism of the time and in exposition of a logical system based on the *Ars Magna* of Raymond Lully.

In 1583 he went to London, where he published several of his works, and to Oxford, where his reception was not at all cordial. In 1585 he went by way of Paris and Marburg to Wittenberg, and from 1586 to 1588 taught his philosophy there. He next went to Prague and to Helmstedt, where he remained till 1589; thence to Frankfort until 1592; and finally to Padua, where he remained until the Inquisition of Venice arrested him and transferred him to Rome. After an imprisonment of seven years, during which he steadfastly refused to retract his doctrines, he was burned, 16th Feb., 1600, for apostasy, heresy, and violation of his monastic vows.

Most of his works were published between 1584 and 1591, the chief being the *Cena de la Ceneri* (Ash Wednesday Table-talk, dialogues giving an exposition of the Copernican theory; the *Spaccio della*

Bastia Trionfante (Expulsion of the Triumphant Beast, a moral allegory); the *Della Causa, Principio ed Uno*; and the *Dell' Infinito, Universo, e Mondi*—all in 1584; the *Cabala del Cavallo Pegaseo* in 1585; and the three metaphysical works, *De triplici Minimo et Mensura*; *De Monade, Numero et Figura*, and *De Immenso et Innumerabilibus*—all in 1591. His doctrines, however, forming a more complete Pantheistical system than had been previously exhibited, represent the highest level of the thought of the period.

Bruno has been called the "Philosopher of Astronomy." He adopted the theory of the universe foreshadowed by Copernicus. Neo-Platonism and Scholasticism were some of the influences which determined Bruno's thought, and gave his philosophy a strange confusion of old and new ideas. His efforts to establish a unitary concept of nature commanded the admiration of Spinoza, Jacobi, and Hegel.—BIBLIOGRAPHY: Chr. Bartholmess, *Jordano Bruno*; T. Frith, *Life of Giordano Bruno*; A. Riehl, *Giordano Bruno*; J. L. M'Intyre, *Giordano Bruno*.

BRUNO, BRUNI, or **BRUNUS, Leonardo.** An Italian scholar, born in 1370 at Arezzo, whence his name *Aretino*. He was secretary to the papal chancery under Innocent VII., Gregory XII., Alexander V., and John XXIII. On the deposition of Pope John he escaped to Florence, where he wrote his history of Florence, received in consequence the rights of citizenship, and afterwards, by the favour of the Medici, became Secretary to the Republic till his death in 1444. He did much to advance the study of Greek literature by his literal Latin translations from Aristotle, Demosthenes, Plutarch, etc., and was the author of biographies of Dante and Petrarca.

BRUNO, ST.—1. The Benedictine apostle of Prussia who accompanied St. Adalbert to Prussia, was appointed chaplain to the Emperor Henry II., and who, having been taken by the pagans of Lithuania, had his hands and feet cut off, and was beheaded in 1009.

St. Bruno,—2. The founder of the order of Carthusian monks, born at Cologne about 1030 of an old and noble family; appointed by Bishop Gervais superintendent of all the schools of the Rheims district, whether he attracted many distinguished scholars, among others Odo, afterwards Pope Urban II. Subsequently he was offered the bishopric of Rheims, but, declining it, repaired with six friends to Hugo, Bishop of Grenoble, who, in 1084 or 1086 led them to the Chartreuse, the spot from which the order of monks received its name. Here, in a bleak and narrow valley, Bruno and his companions built an oratory, and small separate cells for residence.

In 1089 he reluctantly accepted the invitation of Urban II. to Rome, but refused every spiritual dignity, and in 1094 founded a second Carthusian establishment in Della Torre, Calabria. Here he died in 1101. He was beatified by Leo X. and canonised by Gregory XV.

BRUNO, THE GREAT, Archbishop of Cologne and Duke of Lorraine. Third son of Henry the Fowler, and brother of the Emperor Otho I. He was employed in various important negotiations, and was a great patron of learning. Commentaries on the Pentateuch, and some biographies of saints, are ascribed to him. He died in A.D. 965, at Rheims.

BRUNONIAN THEORY (in medicine). *See* BROWN, JOHN, M.D.

BRUNSBÜTTEL' (brụnz'bu̇t-l). A small Prussian seaport at the western extremity of the Kaiser-Wilhelm or North Sea and Baltic Canal.

BRUNS'WICK (Ger. *Braunschweig*). Till 1918 a duchy and sovereign State in the north-west of Germany, area 1420 sq. miles. It is divided into several detached portions, surrounded by the Prussian provinces of Hanover, Saxony, and Westphalia. A good portion of it is hilly or undulating, and it partly belongs to the Hartz mountain system.

Mining is carried on chiefly in the Hartz, and the minerals include iron, lead, copper, brown coal, etc. About half the surface is arable, and the chief cultivated products are grain, flax, hops, tobacco, potatoes, and fruit. Brewing, distilling, the manufacture of linens, woollens, and leather, the preparation of paper, soap, tobacco, beet-sugar, with agriculture and mining, afford the principal employment of the people.

History. On the death of the Duke of Brunswick without issue, in 1884 the Duke of Cumberland claimed the succession. Bismarck, however, interfered, and the Brunswick Diet decided to place the duchy under a regent—Prince Albrecht of Prussia being elected to the post. He died in Sept., 1906, and the Brunswick Diet chose as regent John Albert, Duke of Mecklenburg-Schwerin.

On 24th May, 1913, Prince Ernest Augustus, son of the Duke of Cumberland, was married to Princess Victoria Louisa, only daughter of the ex-Emperor William II. This was a preliminary to the reconciliation of the Houses of Hanover and Hohenzollern, and the succession of the prince to the throne of Brunswick. He actually ascended the throne of Brunswick as reigning duke on 3rd Nov., 1913. On 8th Nov., 1918, the Duke of Brunswick was deposed, and the duchy was proclaimed a republic (Räterepublik Braunschweig).

For 1930-1 the revenue was 62,339,010 marks, and the expenditure was 65,251,060 marks. Pop. is 501,875, mostly Lutherans by religion. Brunswick, the capital, is on the Oker, and on the railway from Hanover to Berlin.

The older streets are narrow, tortuous, and antiquated. The principal buildings of note are the ducal palace, the cathedral of St. Blaise (1173), St. Catherine's Church (dating from 1172), and St. Magnus's (1031), the Gewandhaus, and the fine old Gothic council house. The educational institutions include the polytechnic school, a gymnasium, etc., and there are a city museum, a ducal museum, and a public library.

The principal manufactures are wool, linen, jute, machinery, sewing-machines, gloves, lacquered wares, etc., chemicals, and the town is famous for beer. Pop. 146,725.

BRUNSWICK. A town of Maine, United States, on the Androscoggin, 26 miles N.E. of Portland. At Bowdoin College, in this town, Hawthorne and Longfellow graduated in 1825, and the latter filled the chair of modern languages for several years. Pop. 6621.

BRUNSWICK. A seaport of the United States, Georgia, on St. Simon's Sound, a few miles from the open sea, with a trade in cotton, yellow-pine lumber, etc. Pop. 14,000.

BRUNSWICK, FAMILY OF. A distinguished family founded by Albert Azo II., Marquis of Reggio and Modena, a descendant, by the female line, of Charlemagne. In 1047 he married Cunigunda, heiress of the Counts of Altorf, thus uniting the two Houses of Este and Guelph. From his son, Guelph, who was created Duke of Bavaria in 1071, and married Judith of Flanders, a descendant of Alfred of England, descended Henry the Proud, who succeeded in 1125, and by marriage acquired Brunswick and Saxony. Otho, the great-grandson of Henry by a younger branch of his family, was the first who bore the title of Duke of Brunswick (1235).

By the two sons of Ernest of Zell, who became duke in 1532, the family was divided into the two branches of Brunswick-Wolfenbüttel and Brunswick-Hanover, from the latter of which comes the present royal family of Britain. The former was the German family in possession of the duchy of Brunswick until the death of the last duke in 1884.

George Louis, son of Ernest Augustus and Sophia, granddaughter of James I. of England, succeeded his father as Elector of Hanover in 1698, and was called to the throne of Great Britain, in 1714, as George I.

BRUNSWICK, Ferdinand, Duke of. Fourth son of Duke Ferdinand Albert, was born at Brunswick in 1721. In 1739 he entered the Prussian service, was engaged in the Silesian wars, and in the Seven Years' War commanded the Allied army in Westphalia. He drove the French from Lower Saxony, Hesse, and Westphalia, and was victorious at Crefeld and Minden. After the peace he retired to Brunswick, and died in 1792.

BRUNSWICK, Friedrich Wilhelm, Duke of. Fourth and youngest son of Duke Karl Wilhelm Ferdinand of Brunswick, born in 1771. During the war against France, in 1792 and subsequently, he fought in the Prussian armies, was twice wounded, and once made prisoner with Blücher at Lubeck.

For the campaign of 1809 he raised a free corps in Bohemia, but was compelled to embark his troops for England, where he was received with enthusiasm. His corps immediately entered the British service, and was afterwards employed in Portugal and Spain, the Parliament granting him a pension of £6000, until he returned to his hereditary dominions, 1813. The events of 1815 called him again to arms, and he fell at Quatre Bras, 1815. Caroline, wife of George IV., was a sister of this prince.

BRUNSWICK, Karl Wilhelm Ferdinand, Duke of. Born in 1735; entered upon the government in 1780. He received the chief command of the Austrian and Prussian army against France in 1792, and designed to press forward from Lorraine to Paris, but, after taking Longwy and Verdun, was baffled in Champagne by Dumouriez, defeated at Valmy by Kellerman, and obliged to evacuate the province. In 1793 the duke, in conjunction with the Austrians, opened the campaign on the Upper Rhine, took Königstein and Mentz, and prepared to attack Landau. After a long and doubtful struggle, the Austrian lines were broken by Pichegru, and the duke was obliged to follow their retreat across the Rhine. At Auerstadt he was mortally wounded in 1806.—Cf. Lord Fitzmaurice, *Charles W. F., Duke of Brunswick.*

BRUNSWICK, NEW. *See* NEW BRUNSWICK.

BRUNSWICK BLACK. A varnish composed chiefly of lamp-black and turpentine, and applied to cast-iron goods. Asphalt and oil of turpentine are also ingredients in some kinds of it.

BRUNSWICK GREEN. A green pigment, usually prepared from copper filings.

BRUSA, BROUSSA (brö'så), or **BURSA.** A city in Asia Minor, south of the Sea of Marmora, connected by railway with its port Mudania, with a pop. of about 65,000 Turks, Greeks, Armenians, and Jews, engaged in commerce, and the manufacture of satins, silk stuffs, carpets, gauze, etc. The town is situated in a fertile plain which is enclosed by the ridges of Olympus, and abounds in hot springs. Brusa represents the ancient Prusa, long capital of Bithynia, and one of the most flourishing towns in the Greek Empire of Constantinople. It was the residence of the Turkish sovereigns from 1329 until the transference of the seat of empire to Adrianople in 1365.

BRUSH. (1) A well-known implement of bristles, hair, or wire, set in wood, etc., and used for scrubbing, sweeping, and many other purposes. There are two chief varieties, those with stiff hair or fibres, and those with flexible. The former are made of hogs' bristles, whalebone fibres, vegetable fibres of various kinds (brush-grass, palms, etc.), and sometimes wire is made to serve the same purpose. The latter are made of hogs' bristles, or of the hair of the camel, badger, squirrel, sable, goat, etc., and are chiefly used for painting, the smallest kinds being called *pencils*, and consisting of a single tuft only.

(2) A device for conducting the current into or out of the rotary armature in a dynamo.

BRUSH, Charles Francis. American inventor, born 17th March, 1849, he studied chemistry and began his business life as a consulting chemist in Cleveland, near his birthplace, in Ohio. He became known by his inventions, the chief of which were an arc lamp and a storage battery for electricity, then just coming into use. To manufacture these and other electrical apparatus he founded the Brush Electric Co., which soon became one of the largest of its kind. Brush died 15th June, 1929.

BRUSH-TURKEY. *See* TALLEGALLA.

BRUSH-WHEEL. A toothless wheel sometimes used in light machinery to turn a similar wheel by means of bristles or some brush-like or soft substance, as cloth, buff-leather, india-rubber, or the like.

BRUSILOV, Alexis. Russian soldier, born in 1861. He served in the Russo-Turkish War (1877-8), and when the European War broke out was Commander-in-Chief of the Russian Eighth Army. In 1916 he conquered nearly the whole of Bukovina. He became Commander-in-Chief of the Russian army in 1917, but was soon superseded by Kornilov. He was arrested by the Bolshevik Government in Sept., 1918, but was eventually released and joined the Bolsheviks, commanding a Russian army against the Poles in 1920. He died in 1926.

BRUSSA. *See* BRUSA.

BRUS'SELS (Fl. *Brussel*; Fr. *Bruxelles*). The capital of Belgium and of the province of Brabant, is situated on the small River Senne, which is not navigable, but serves as a canal-feeder. The city consists of a north-western or lower portion and a south-eastern or upper portion. The older part is surrounded with fine boulevards on the site of its fortifications, and in many places presents a congeries of twisted streets.

The upper town, which is partly inside the boulevards and partly outside, is the finest part of the city, and contains the king's palace, the palace of the chambers, the palace of justice (a magnificent new building ranking among the finest in Europe), the palace of the fine arts, the public library and museum, etc.; and has also a fine park of 17 acres, around which most of the principal buildings are situated.

The lower town retains much of its ancient appearance. The hôtel de ville (1401-55) is an imposing Gothic structure, with a spire 364 feet in height, the square in front of it being perhaps the most striking of all the public places of Brussels. The cathedral of Saint Gudule (dating in part from the thirteenth century) is the finest of many fine churches, richly adorned with sculptures and paintings.

The whole town is rich in monuments and works of art. The institutions comprise a university, an academy of science and the fine arts and polytechnic school; one of the finest observatories in Europe; a conservatorium of music; a public library, containing 400,000 volumes and 30,000 MSS.; a picture-gallery, with the finest specimens of Flemish art; and many learned societies and educational organisations.

Manufactures. The manufactures and trade are greatly promoted by canal communications with Charleroi, Mechlin, Antwerp, and the ocean, and by the network of Belgian railways. The industries are varied and important. Lace was an ancient manufacture, and is still of great importance; the manufacture of cotton and woollen fabrics, paper, carriages, and many minor manufactories are carried on. There are breweries, distilleries, sugar-refineries, foundries, etc.

Language. The language spoken by the upper classes is French, and Flemish is that of the lower; but German, Dutch, and English are also a good deal spoken.

History. During the Middle Ages Brussels did not attain great importance. It was walled by Baldric of Louvain in 1044, was more completely fortified in 1380, and was twice burned and once ravaged by the plague during the fifteenth century. It was bombarded and burned by the French in 1695, and was again taken by the French in 1794, and retained till 1814, when it became the chief town of the department of the Dyle.

From 1815 to 1830 it was one of the capitals of the kingdom of the Netherlands, and in 1830 was the chief centre of the revolt which separated Belgium from Holland. Brussels was occupied by the Germans on 20th Aug., 1914, and re-entered by King Albert of Belgium on 23rd Nov., 1918. Pop. (with suburbs) in 1914, 720,347; in 1926, 808,664.

BRUSSELS CARPET. *See* CARPET.

BRUSSELS SPROUTS. One of the cultivated varieties of cabbage (*Brassica oleracea*), having an elongated stem 4 or 5 feet high, with small clustering green heads like miniature cabbages. They are cultivated in great quantities near Brussels, where they were grown in 1213.

BRUTUS, or BRUT. The first king of Britain; a purely mythical personage, said to have been the son of Sylvius, and grandson of Ascanius, the son of Æneas. He landed in Devonshire, destroyed the giants then inhabiting Albion, and named the island after himself. At his death the island was divided among his sons; Locrine, Cumber, and Albanact. The legend is found in Geoffrey of Monmouth, Wace, and Layamon.

BRUTUS, Decimus Junius. Served under Julius Cæsar in Gaul, and was afterwards commander of his fleet, but, like his relative, Marcus Junius Brutus, joined in the assassination of Cæsar. He was afterwards for a short time successful in opposing Antony, but was deserted by his soldiers in Gaul and betrayed into the hands of his opponent, who put him to death in 43 B.C.

BRUTUS, Lucius Junius. One of the first two consuls, son of Marcus Junius, by the daughter of the elder Tarquin. He saved his life from the persecutions of Tarquin the Proud by feigning himself insane, whence his name *Brutus* (stupid). On the suicide of Lucretia (*see* LUCRETIA), however, he threw off the mask, and headed the revolt against the Tarquins. Having secured their banishment, he proposed to abolish the regal dignity and introduce a free government, with the result that he was elected to the consulship, in which capacity he condemned his own sons to death for conspiring to restore the monarchy. He fell in battle 509 B.C.

BRUTUS, Marcus Junius. A distinguished Roman, born 85 B.C.; was at first an enemy of Pompey, but joined him on the outbreak of civil war, and remained with him until

Marcus Junius Brutus
From the statue in the Museo Capitolino, Rome

the battle of Pharsalia. He then surrendered to Cæsar, who made him in the following year Governor of Cisalpine Gaul, and afterwards of Macedonia. He soon, however, joined the conspiracy against Cæsar, and by his influence ensured its success.

After the assassination he took refuge in the East, made himself master of Greece and Macedonia, and with a powerful army joined Cassius in the subjugation of the Lycians and Rhodians. In the meantime the triumvirs, Octavianus, Antony, and Lepidus, had been successful at Rome, and were prepared to encounter the army of the conspirators, which, crossing the Hellespont, assembled at Philippi in Macedonia. Cassius appears to have been beaten at once by Antony; and Brutus, though temporarily successful against Octavianus, was totally defeated twenty days later. He escaped with a few friends; but, seeing that his cause was hopelessly ruined, fell upon the sword held for him by his confidant Strato, and died (42 B.C.).—BIBLIOGRAPHY: G. Boissier, *Cicero and his Friends*; J. L. Strachan-Davidson, *Cicero*.

BRUX (brüks). A town of Czechoslovakia, on the Biela, in the neighbourhood of which are extensive coalfields, and the famous mineral springs of Seidlitz and Püllna. Pop. 26,000.

BRUYÈRE (brü-yār), **Jean de la.** A French writer, born at Paris in 1645. He purchased the place of treasurer of Caen; but for a short time after, through the influence of Bossuet, he was employed in the education of the Duke of Bourbon, grandson of the great Condé, with a pension of 3000 livres, and was attached to his person during the remainder of his life. In 1688 he published a translation of the *Characters* of Theophrastus into French, and accompanied it with a succession of characters, in which he represented the manners, and frequently the leading personages, of his time in an ingenious and piquant style. In 1695 he was elected a member of the French Academy. He died in 1696.

BRYA. A genus of leguminous trees, sub-ord. Papilionaceæ, natives of Central America and West Indies. The heart-wood of *B. Ebenus* is Jamaica ebony or cocos-wood.

BRYAN, William Jennings. American politician, born Salem, Illinois, 19th March, 1860. He studied at the Union College of Law, Chicago, and practised law till 1890, when he was elected to Congress. Although he had gained a reputation as a speaker, he failed in his attempts to enter the Senate in 1893 and 1894. He then took up the question of free silver, which he discussed in public speeches and in the *Omaha World Herald*, which he edited from 1894 to 1896. Bryan severely criticised the gold standard, and, as a result of a speech delivered at the Democratic National Convention, he was nominated for President. He was, however, defeated by M'Kinley in the elections of 1896 and 1900, and by Taft in 1908.

In 1912 he supported Dr. Woodrow Wilson. He became Secretary of State in President Wilson's Cabinet on 4th March, 1913, but resigned on 9th June, 1915. In 1900 he founded *The Commoner*, a political weekly. His works include: *Under Other Flags* (1894), *The First Battle* (1897), *The Old World and Its Ways* (1907), *A Tale of Two Conventions* (1912). He died in 1925.

BRYANSK, or **BRJANSK.** *See* BRIANSK.

BRY'ANT, Jacob. English philologist and antiquary, born in 1715, died in 1804. He studied at Eton and Cambridge, became tutor of the sons of the famous Duke of Marlborough, the eldest of whom he accompanied to the Continent as secretary, and after his return received a lucrative post in the Ordnance, which gave him leisure for researches into Biblical, Roman, and Grecian antiquities. His most important work was the *New System of Ancient Mythology*, 1774-6. Amongst other things he endeavoured to prove the purely fictional nature of the *Iliad*, and that Melita, on which St. Paul was wrecked, was not Malta, but an island in the Adriatic.

BRY'ANT, William Cullen. An American poet and journalist, born in Hampshire, Massachusetts, in 1794. At ten years of age he published translations from Latin poets; at thirteen wrote *The Embargo*; and at eighteen *The Thanatopsis*. In 1815 he was admitted to the Bar, and practised with success till 1825, when he established the *New York Review*. In 1826 he became assistant editor of the *Evening Post*, a leading organ of the New York Democrats, of which he was long chief editor.

His poems, first collected in 1832, took rank as the best America had up to that time produced. In 1842 he issued *The Fountain and other poems*; and a new edition of his poems in 1858 was followed by metrical translations of the *Iliad* in 1869 and of the *Odyssey* in 1871. His *Letters of a Traveller* record his visits to Europe in 1834 and subsequently. He died in 1878.

BRYCE, James, first Viscount. Born in 1838, and educated at Glasgow High School, Glasgow University, and Trinity College, Oxford. He was Regius Professor of Civil Law at Oxford from 1870 to 1893, member of Parliament for Tower Hamlets 1880, Under Secretary of State for Foreign Affairs 1886, Chancellor of the Duchy of Lancaster 1892, President of the Board of Trade 1894, Chief Secretary for Ireland

1905-6, and Ambassador Extraordinary at Washington 1907-13.

His publications include: *The Holy Roman Empire* (1862), *The American Commonwealth* (1888), *Studies in Contemporary Biography* (1903), and *South America: Observations and Impressions*. He received the Order of Merit in 1907, was created a viscount in 1914, and a G.C.V.O. in 1917. He died 22nd Jan., 1922.

BRYCE REPORT, THE. In Dec., 1914, the British Government appointed a committee to consider and advise on the evidence as to outrages alleged to have been committed by German troops during the European War. The Committee, which consisted of Lord Bryce (chairman), Sir Frederick Pollock, Sir Edward Clark, Sir Kenelm Digby, Sir Alfred Hopkinson, Mr. H. A. L. Fisher, and Mr. Harold Cox, collected their evidence mainly from Belgian refugees, wounded Belgian soldiers, and British officers and soldiers. The report was issued in May, 1915, and conclusively proved that "there were in many parts of Belgium deliberate and systematically organised massacres of the civil population, that the rules and usages of the war were frequently broken, and the red cross and white flag abused."

BRYNMAWR. A market town and urban district of S. Wales, Brecknock, in the extreme south-east of the county, not far from Tredegar, Nantyglo, and other important places in Monmouthshire, with ironworks, etc. Pop. (1931), 7247.

BRY'ONY (Bryonia). A genus of plants, nat. ord. Cucurbitaceæ (gourds). The only British species, the Common Bryony (*B. dioica*), a climbing plant common in hedges, has cordate palmate leaves and axillary bunches of flowers, and red berries which are highly poisonous. The thick long fleshy root has acrid emetic and purgative properties, and has been used medicinally. The so-called Black Bryony (*Tamus commūnis*) belongs to a different natural order, the Dioscoreaceæ or yams. It has cordate undivided leaves, greenish flowers, red berries, and a black fleshy root.

BRYOPHYLLUM. A genus of plants of the house-leek family. *B. calycinum*, grown in hot-houses, readily produces buds on the edges of the leaves.

BRYOPHYTA, or BRYOPHYTES. The lowest group of the Cormophytes or higher plants, comprising the two classes of Liverworts (Hepaticæ) and Mosses (Musci). They have a well-marked alternation of generations; the gametophyte is the dominant phase or "plant", the sporophyte being a mere spore-producing structure, the *sporogonium*, which may be elaborate in structure, but never becomes entirely self-supporting and independent. The mosses have leafy shoots; the liverworts may be either leafy or thalloid. True roots are never formed, the functions of these organs being to some extent performed by *rhizoids*. Conducting tissues, if present, are rudimentary in comparison with the vascular strands of the Pteridophyta and seed-plants.

Though land-plants, Bryophyta are relatively dependent on water—which they absorb over their whole surface—and flourish best in moist surroundings (especially humid mountain forests of the tropics); nevertheless, xerophytic forms are not unknown amongst them.

It is in the Bryophyta that the *archegonium* first appears in the evolutionary history of green plants; this characteristic flask-shaped receptacle enclosing the egg-cell is found in all Bryophytes and Pteridophytes and in most Gymnosperms. Nothing like it exists among green Algæ, and its origin is quite obscure. For this reason alone, the break between Algæ and Bryophyta must be regarded as one of the most serious gaps in the family tree of green plants. The cleavage between Bryophyta and the groups above them is almost as sharp, although the recent discovery of small rootless, and perhaps leafless, Devonian Pteridophytes of very primitive construction (Rhynia) has brought these two groups into closer relation to one another.

It is doubtful whether liverworts or mosses should be regarded as the more primitive; Liverworts display the wider range of structure, while the average level of organisation is rather higher in mosses. See Generations, Alternation of; Liverworts; Mosses.

BRYOZO'A (Gr. *bryon*, moss, and *zōon*, an animal). See Polyzoa.

BUANSU'AH (*Cyon primævus*). A wild dog of Northern India, supposed by some to be the original type of the dog tribe.

BU'BALINE ANTELOPE (*Bubălis mauretanica*). An ox-like antelope of N. Africa, of a yellowish-brown colour, with horns at first pointing forward and outward, and then turning backward. It inhabits the desert tracts.

BU'BALUS. The genus to which the buffalo belongs.

BUBAS'TIS. An ancient Egyptian

town, so named from the goddess Bast, sometimes identified with the Greek Artĕmis or Diana. The cat was sacred to her, and the Bubasteia or festivals of the goddess were the largest and most important of the Egyptian festivals.

BUBO. An inflammatory swelling of the lymphatic glands, acute or indolent in type, usually in reference to the groin, but occasionally to other parts, e.g. parotid bubo. Bubonic plague is so named on account of the appearance of buboes.

BUBO. A genus of owls, including the great horned or eagle owl (*B. ignavus*), and the Virginian horned owl (*B. virginianus*).

BUBONIC PLAGUE. An epidemic disease of extreme virulence, marked by fever, delirium, and the appearance of buboes. There are various types of different severity, but on the whole the mortality is high, and it may appear in a very malignant form. It occurs throughout the East, where it is always present, and, though found in the east of Europe, is not common in the west. Small outbreaks of late years have arisen in this country at seaports, owing to the infection having been brought by shipping from the East.

The bacillus of plague, which was discovered in 1894, lives inside the fleas which are found in large numbers on both black and grey rats. The infection may be conveyed through cracks and abrasions of the skin, but the common mode of infection is now recognised to be by the bites of fleas which are carrying the bacillus.

BUCARAMANGA. A town of Colombia, S. America, capital of department of Santander, 185 miles N.N.E. of Bogotá; an important coffee centre, with mines of gold, copper, and iron in the neighbourhood. Pop. 25,000.

BUCCANEERS′. A name derived from Carib *boucan*, a place for smoking meat, first given to European settlers in Hayti or Hispaniola, whose business was to hunt wild cattle and swine and smoke their flesh. In an extended sense it was applied to English and French adventurers, mostly seafaring people, who, combining for mutual defence against the arrogant pretensions of the Spaniards to the dominion of the whole of America, frequented the W. Indies in the seventeenth century, acquired predatory and lawless habits, and became ultimately, in many cases, little better than pirates.

The earliest association of these adventurers began about 1625, but they afterwards became much more formidable, and continued to be a terror, until the opening of the eighteenth century, inflicting heavy losses upon the shipping trade of Spain, and even attacking large towns. Among their chief leaders were Montbars (Il Exterminador), Peter the Great of Dieppe, L'Olonnas, de Busco, Van Horn, and the Welshman Henry Morgan, who, in 1670, marched across the isthmus, plundered Panama, and, after being knighted by Charles II., became Deputy-Governor of Jamaica. The last great exploit of the buccaneers

Buccaneer

was the capture of Carthagena in 1697, after which they are lost sight of in the annals of vulgar piracy.

BIBLIOGRAPHY: Captain James Burney, *History of the Buccaneers of America*; G. W. Thornbury, *Monarchs of the Main*; C. H. Haring, *The Buccaneers in the West Indies in the Seventeenth Century*; Johnston, *Famous Privateersmen and Adventurers of the Sea*; J. Exquemelin, *The Buccaneers of America*.

BUCCINATOR ("a trumpeter", from Lat. *buccina*, a trumpet). A flat thin muscle of the cheek. It compresses the cheeks and retracts the angle of the mouth, thereby assists in mastication and in regulating the expulsion of air in whistling or playing a wind-instrument.

BUCCLEUCH (bu-klö′). The title (now a dukedom) of one of the oldest families in Scotland, tracing descent from Sir Richard le Scott in the reign of Alexander III. (latter half of the thirteenth century), and first becoming conspicuous in the person of the border chieftain Sir Walter Scott of Branxholm and Buccleuch—the latter an estate in Selkirkshire. The son of Sir Walter, bearing the same name, was for his valour and services raised to the peerage in 1606 as Lord Scott of Buccleuch, and his successor was made an earl in 1619.

In 1663 the titles and estates devolved upon Anne, daughter of the second earl, who married the Duke of Monmouth, illegitimate son of Charles II., the pair in 1673 being created Duke and Duchess of Buccleuch, etc. Subsequently the Dukedom of Queensberry passed by marriage into the family.

BUCCON'IDÆ. *See* BARBETS.

BUCEN'TAUR. The name of the splendid galley in which the doge of Venice annually wedded the Adriatic. This name, actually derived from the Italian *buzino d'oro*, golden bark, has often been incorrectly derived from Lat. *bucentaurus*, a mythical monster, half man and half ox, invented for the purpose of this derivation.

BUCEPH'ALUS (" Ox-head "). The horse of Alexander the Great. On its death from a wound Alexander built over its grave, near the Hydaspes, a city called *Bucephala*.

BUCER (bụ'tser), **Martin.** A sixteenth-century reformer, whose real name was Kuhhorn (cowhorn), of which *Bucer* is meant to be the Greek equivalent, born 1491 at Schlettstadt, in Alsace. In 1521 he left the Dominican order and became preacher at the Court of the Elector Frederick, and afterwards in Strasburg, where he was professor in the university for twenty years. In 1548 Edward VI. invited him to Cambridge, where he held the office of professor of theology, and died in 1551. In 1557 Queen Mary caused his bones to be burned. Cardinal Contarini called him the most learned divine among the heretics. He wrote a commentary on the *Psalms* under the name of Aretius Filinus, a work *De regno Christi*, and many treatises.

BU'CEROS. *See* HORN-BILL.

BUCH (bụ*h*), **Leopold von.** A German geologist, born in 1774, died in 1853. He made extensive geological excursions on the continent of Europe, and also visited the Canary Islands, the Hebrides, and the coasts of Scotland and Ireland. He was the author of various important works; and compiled a magnificent geological map of Germany.

BUCHAN (bu*h*'an). A district of Scotland, lying in the N.E. of Aberdeenshire, between the mouths of the Deveron and the Ythan.

BUCHAN, Alexander. Scottish meteorologist, born 11th April, 1829, of humble parents; he was educated at Edinburgh. He studied science and in 1860 was appointed Secretary of the Scottish Meteorological Society. He devoted his time to observing weather conditions from the Society's observatory on Ben Nevis and made certain forecasts about the weather, known as Buchan's periods, three warm and six cold in the year. These attracted renewed attention about 1925 and were found remarkably correct in succeeding years. Buchan died 13th May, 1907.

BUCHAN, John. Scottish novelist, born in Peebleshire, 26th August, 1875, the son of a minister; he had a brilliant career at Glasgow and Oxford Universities. He became a barrister and was for a time in South Africa under Lord Milner. He then joined the publishing firm of Thos. Nelson & Sons and wrote a number of stories, and one or two other works. Perhaps the best of his many romances are *Prester John*, *The Thirty-Nine Steps*, *Greenmantle*, *Huntingtower*, *The Dancing Floor* and *Witch Wood*, but there are many others, including *The Runagates Club*, *The Courts of the Morning*, and *The Blanket of the Dark*. He wrote a *History of the War* and *Lives* of Montrose and Raleigh. In 1932 he published the centenary *Life* of Sir Walter Scott. During the Great War he went to the front for *The Times* and served in the Ministry of Information. In 1927 Buchan was elected Unionist M.P. for the Scottish Universities. In 1931 he was made a Companion of Honour.

Under the name of O. Douglas, Buchan's sister Anna is the authoress of *The Setons*, *Penny Plain*, and other novels.

BUCHAN (buk'an or bu*h*'an), **William.** A Scottish medical writer, born in 1729; studied at Edinburgh, and commenced practice there where also he published in 1769 his work entitled *Domestic Medicine: or, the Family Physician*—the first work of the kind published in Britain. Before his death, in 1805, nineteen large editions had been sold. It was translated into French, and became even more popular on the Continent and in America than at home. Buchan was induced by its success to remove to London, where for many years he enjoyed a lucrative practice.

BUCHANAN (bu-kan'an), **Claudius,**

D.D. A distinguished missionary in India, born at Cambuslang, Scotland, in 1766. He was educated at the Universities of Glasgow and Cambridge; became chaplain to the East India Company in 1795; and in 1800 was appointed professor of Greek, Latin, and English, and vice-provost in the college at Fort William. He returned to Europe in 1808, and published his *Christian Researches in Asia* (1811), and *Colonial Ecclesiastical Establishment* (1813). He died in 1815.

BUCHANAN, George. Scottish reformer, historian, scholar, and Latin poet, born in the parish of Killearn, Stirlingshire, in 1506. An uncle sent him in 1520 to the University of Paris, but the death of his uncle compelled him to return, and in 1523 he joined the French auxiliaries employed by the Regent Albany, serving as a private soldier in one campaign against the English. He was then sent to the University of St. Andrews, where he took the Arts degree in Oct., 1525.

Following his tutor, Mair or Major, to France, he became in 1526 a student in the Scots College of Paris; took his degrees; in 1529 was elected professor in the College of St. Barbe; and in 1532 was engaged as friend and tutor to Gilbert Kennedy, Earl of Cassillis, with whom he resided for five years, and to whom he inscribed his first published work, a translation of Linacre's *Rudiments of Latin Grammar*, printed in 1533.

In 1536 Cassillis and Buchanan returned to Scotland, where the latter published his *Somnium*, a satire against the Franciscans. To shield him from the hostility of the Roman Catholic party, James V. retained him as preceptor to his natural son James Stuart, encouraging him to write the *Franciscanus*, one of the most pungent satires to be found in any language. By the Catholic influence he was arrested in 1539, but escaped to London and thence to France, where he became professor of Latin at Bordeaux, wrote his tragedies *Jephthes* and *Baptistes*, and translated the *Medea* and *Alcestis* of Euripides. Among his pupils was Montaigne, and he was on intimate terms with the elder Scaliger.

From Bordeaux Buchanan removed to Paris, and thence to Portugal to take a chair in the University of Coimbra. Here he was sentenced by the Inquisition to be confined in a monastery, but at length received permission to depart, and was shortly afterwards appointed to a regency in the College of Boncourt at Paris, an office held by him till 1555, when he was engaged as tutor to the son of the Comte de Brissac. During this period a portion of his version of the Psalms in Latin verse was published.

About 1560 he returned to Scotland, and for some time acted as tutor to the young Queen Mary, to whom he dedicated his version of the Psalms. He had now openly joined the leaders of the Reformation. In 1566 he was nominated principal of St. Leonard's College, St. Andrews, and in the following year was chosen moderator of the General Assembly, the only instance of the chair being held by a layman. When Elizabeth called witnesses from Scotland to substantiate the charges against Mary, Buchanan accompanied the Regent Moray into England, and his evidence against her was highly important. In 1570 he was selected to superintend the education of King James, whom he made an excellent scholar. He was also appointed Keeper of the Privy-Seal, a post which he held till 1578.

In 1579 he published his *De Jure Regni apud Scotos*, a work in which he defended the rights of the people to judge of and control the conduct of their governors, and which subsequently had much influence on political thought. The dedication of his *Rerum Scoticarum Historia* (History of Scotland) to the king is dated 29th Aug., 1582, and on the 28th Sept. following Buchanan died.

As a Latin writer both of prose and verse he was perhaps the best of his day, as evidenced by his history and his version of the Psalms. As regards its matter, the former is uncritical, the earlier part being based on the legendary history of Boece, but it is of great value for matters belonging to his own time.—BIBLIOGRAPHY: P. H. Brown, *George Buchanan, Humanist and Reformer*; D. Macmillan, *Life of George Buchanan*; Sir J. E. Sandys, *A History of Classical Scholarship*.

BUCHANAN, James. Fifteenth President of the United States, born in Pennsylvania, 1791; son of an Irishman who had quitted Europe in 1783. James Buchanan was educated at Dickinson College, Carlisle; was admitted to the Bar in 1812; was elected to the legislature of Pennsylvania in 1814; and in 1820 was sent to Congress, of which he continued a member till 1831. After having been sent to Russia to conclude a commercial treaty he was in 1833 elected to the Senate, and under the presidency of Polk (1845-9) was appointed Secretary of State.

During the presidency of General Taylor he retired from public life, but in 1853 General Pierce, on being elected President, named him Ambassador of the United States at London. He returned to America in 1856 as Democratic candidate for the presidency, and was elected by a large majority over Fremont, the Republican candidate, and inaugurated in March, 1857. By his pro-slavery views Buchanan succeeded in delaying the storm which burst out on the election of his successor Lincoln.

He lived in retirement after the close of his administration (1860), of which he published an account two years before his death in 1868.

BUCHANAN, Robert. An English poet, born in 1841. His earliest volumes of verse, *Undertones* (1863), *Idylls and Legends of Inverburn* (1865), and *London Poems* (1866), gained him a reputation for truth, simplicity, humour, and pathos, and he afterwards produced various volumes of poetry which have been no less well received; such as *Wayside Poesies* (1860); *North Coast and other Poems* (1867); *The Drama of Kings* (1871); *Ballads of Life, Love, and Humour* (1882); *The City of Dream* (1888); *The Wandering Jew* (1893). He also wrote novels, *The Shadow of the Sword, God and the Man, The Child of Nature*, etc., and plays. He died in 1901.

BUCHANITES. An extraordinary sect of Scottish fanatics which sprang up in 1783 in a dissenting church at Irvine, Ayrshire, under the leadership of a Mrs. (more commonly known as "Lucky") Buchan. She declared herself to be the woman of Rev. xii., and Mr. White, the clergyman of the congregation to which she belonged, her "man-child", and taught her followers they would be translated to heaven without tasting of death. The sect was always small, and became extinct soon after the death of Mrs. Buchan in 1792. They are said to have lived in promiscuous intercourse, and to have despised marriage. The last survivor of the Buchanite sect died in 1848.

BUCHAN NESS. The easternmost promontory of Scotland, near Peterhead, Aberdeenshire.

BUCHAREST. *See* BUKAREST.

BUCHARIA. *See* BOKHARA.

BUCHEZ (bü-shā), **Philippe Joseph Benjamin.** French physician and writer, born in 1796. He wrote *Introduction à la Science de l'Histoire* (1833) and *Essai d'un Traité Complet de Philosophie* (1839). Between 1833 and 1838 he published, in concert with M. Roux-Lavergne, a *Histoire Parlementaire de la Révolution Française* (40 vols.). After the revolution of 1848 he was elected to the constituent National Assembly, and was for a brief period its wholly incompetent President. Retiring from public life he confined himself to literature, his chief subsequent work being the *Histoire de la Formation de la Nationalité Française* (1859). He died in 1865.

BUCHHOLZ (bu̥*h*'hōlts). A town of Saxony, with extensive manufactures of laces, trimmings, etc. Pop. 9307.

BÜCHNER, Friedrich Karl. German philosopher and physician, born at Darmstadt in 1824. He studied at Giessen, Strasburg, and Vienna, and in 1852 became lecturer at Tübingen, a post which he was compelled to resign in consequence of the controversy raised by his famous work *Kraft und Stoff* (1855). In this work Büchner maintained the indestructibility of matter and denied the existence of either deity or plan in nature. He subsequently practised medicine in Darmstadt, where he died in 1899.

His other works include: *Aus Natur und Wissenschaft* (1862-84), *Der Mensch und seine Stellung in der Natur* (1870), *Licht und Leben* (1881), *Darwinismus und Socialismus* (1894), *Im Dienste der Wahrheit* (1899).

BUCHON (bü-shōn̥), **Jean Alexandre.** A French historical writer, born 1791, died in 1846. After a period of European travel for the collection of documents he published his *Collection des Chroniques Nationales Françaises, écrites en Langue Vulgaire de XIIIme au XVIme Siècle* (47 vols., 1824-9), commencing with the *Chroniques de Froissart.* For a short time (1828-9) he was inspector of the archives and libraries of France. Among other works may be noted his *Histoire Populaire des Français* (1832), *La Grèce Continentale et la Morée* (1843).

BUCHU (bu̥k'u̥). The name of several plants belonging to the Cape Province, genus Barosma, ord. Rutaceæ, used in medicine, in the form of a powder or tincture, in disorders of the urinogenital organs.

BUCKAU (bu̥k'ou). A town of Prussian Saxony, close to Magdeburg, in which it was incorporated in 1887, the seat of flourishing manufactures, especially of machinery and iron goods.

BUCK-BEAN, BOG-BEAN, or **MARSH-TREFOIL** (*Menyanthes trifoliāta*). A beautiful plant of the ord.

Gentianaceæ, common in spongy, boggy soils, and found in Britain, throughout Europe, in Siberia, and in North America. It is from 6 to 12 inches in height, and blossoms in Britain about the second half of

Buck-bean (*Menyanthes trifoliāta*)

a, Section of capsule showing seeds; *b*, Ovary and style, with calyx-teeth below

June. The flowers are heterostyled, and the white and pink corolla has a coating of dense fleshy hairs. The whole plant, the root especially, has an intensely bitter taste, and formerly ranked highly as a tonic.

BÜCKEBURG (bük'e-bu̦rh). A town of Germany, capital of the Republic of Schaumburg-Lippe (a principality till 1918). Pop. 5800.

BUCKFASTLEIGH. An ancient town (and urban district) of England, in the south of Devonshire, on the Dart, 5½ miles north-west of Totnes, with manufactures of woollens, especially serges, and other industries. A Benedictine house is here, an old abbey church being partially restored. Pop. (1931), 2406.

BUCKHAVEN. An old fishing town of Scotland, in Fifeshire, on the Firth of Forth, now forming with Methil and Innerleven a police burgh. Buckhaven has a harbour of its own, and at Methil, where large quantities of coal are shipped from neighbouring collieries, the harbour is of recent construction. Pop. (1931), 17,643.

BUCK-HOUND. A kind of hound similar to but smaller than a stag-hound, once commonly used in Britain for hunting bucks. The Master of the Buck-hounds was until quite recently the title of an officer of the royal household in England.

BUCKHURST HILL. A town of England, Essex, about 10 miles from London, finely situated on the summit of a hill near Epping Forest; attracts many visitors. Pop. (1931), 5486.

BUCKIE. An important fishing-town on the coast of Banffshire, Scotland. Pop. (1931), 8688.

BUCK'INGHAM, or BUCKS. An inland county, England, bounded by Northampton, Bedford, Hertford, Middlesex, Berks, and Oxford; area about 730 sq. miles, or 479,360 acres, of which over 400,000 are under crops or permanent pasture. The rich vale of Aylesbury stretches through the centre, and a portion of the Chiltern range across the south of the county, which is watered by the Ouse, the Thame, and the Thames.

The breeding and fattening of cattle and pigs are largely carried on, also the breeding of horses, and much butter is made. The manufactures are unimportant, among them being straw-plaiting, thread lace, and the making of wooden articles, such as beechen chairs, turnery, etc. There are also paper-mills, silk-mills, etc. The mineral productions are of no great importance.

The county comprises eight hundreds, those of Stoke, Burnham, and Desborough being known as "the Chiltern Hundreds." Buckingham is nominally the county town, but Aylesbury is the assize town. The county returns three members to the House of Commons for Aylesbury, Buckingham, and Wycombe districts. The pop., according to the census of 1931, is 271,565.

Buckingham. A municipal and, until 1885, a parliamentary borough, is pleasantly situated on a peninsula formed by the Ouse. Malting and tanning are carried on, and some lace is made. Pop. (1931), 3082.

BUCKINGHAM, George Villiers, Duke of. Favourite of James I. and Charles I. of England, born in 1592, his father being George Villiers, knight. At eighteen he was sent to France, where he resided three years, and on his return made so great an impression on James I. that in two years he was made a knight, a gentleman of the bedchamber, baron, viscount, Marquess of Buckingham, Lord High-Admiral, etc., and at last dispenser of all the honours and offices of the three kingdoms.

In 1623, when the Earl of Bristol was negotiating a marriage for Prince Charles with the Infanta of Spain, Buckingham went with the prince incognito to Madrid to carry on the suit in person in the hope of securing the Palatinate as dowry. The result, however, was the breaking off of the marriage, and the declaration of war with Spain. During his absence Buckingham was created duke.

Buckingham Palace

After the death of James in 1625 he was sent to France as proxy for Charles I. to marry the Princess Henrietta Maria. In 1626, after the failure of the Cadiz expedition, he was impeached, but saved by the favour of the king. Despite the difficulty in obtaining supplies Buckingham took upon himself the conduct of a war with France, but his expedition in aid of the Rochellese proved an entire failure. In the meantime the spirit of revolt was becoming more formidable; the Petition of Right was carried despite the duke's exertions; and he was again protected from impeachment only by the king's prorogation of Parliament. He then went to Portsmouth to lead another expedition to Rochelle, but was stabbed on 24th Aug., 1628, by John Felton, an ex-lieutenant who had been disappointed of promotion. —BIBLIOGRAPHY: A. T. Thompson, *Life and Times of George Villiers, Duke of Buckingham*; Philip Gibbs, *The Romance of George Villiers.*

BUCKINGHAM, George Villiers, Duke of. Son of the preceding, born at Westminster 1627; studied at Trinity College, Cambridge; served in the royal army under Rupert and then went abroad. In 1648 he returned to England, was with Charles II. in Scotland and at the battle of Worcester, and afterwards served as a volunteer in the French army in Flanders. He then returned to England, and in 1657 married the daughter of Lord Fairfax.

At the Restoration he became Master of the Horse and one of the king's confidential *cabal* (1667-73). In 1666 he engaged in a conspiracy, and in 1676 was committed to the Tower for contempt by order of the House of Lords; but on each occasion he recovered the king's favour. On the death of Charles he retired to his seat in Yorkshire, where he died in 1688. Among his literary compositions the comedy of *The Rehearsal* (1671) takes the first place.

BUCKINGHAM, James Silk. English traveller, writer, and lecturer, born near Falmouth, 1786. After trying several professions, and wandering over a great part of the world, he came to London, where he established the *Athenæum*, well known as a literary journal. He also published his *Travels in Palestine* (1822), *Travels among the Arab Tribes* (1825), *Travels in Mesopotamia* (1827), and *Travels in Assyria, Media, and Persia* (1830).

In 1832 he was chosen member of Parliament for Sheffield, and retained his seat till 1837. Subsequently he made a tour of three years in America. In 1843 he became secretary to the British and Foreign Institute. He also published volumes on his Continental tours and an autobiography. He died in 1855.

BUCKINGHAM PALACE. A royal palace in London, facing St. James's Park, built in the reign of George IV., and forming one of the residences of the sovereign.

BUCK'LAND, Francis Trevelyan. English naturalist, son of Dr. W. Buckland, born in 1826; studied at Winchester and Christ Church, Oxford. From 1848 to 1851 he was student, and from 1852 to 1853 house-surgeon, at St. George's Hospital. He became assistant-surgeon in the 2nd Life Guards in 1854. On the establishment of the *Field* newspaper in 1856 he joined the staff, writing for it until 1865. In 1866 he commenced a weekly journal of his own, *Land and Water*, and in 1867 was appointed an inspector of salmon fisheries. He died in 1880.

His best-known books are his *Curiosities of Natural History* (4 vols., 1857-72), *The Logbook of a Fisherman and Zoologist* (1875), and *The Natural History of Fishes* (1881); but there was also a large mass of desultory work showing much natural sagacity.

BUCKLAND, Rev. William, D.D. English geologist, born at Axminster, Devon, in 1784; educated at Winchester and at Corpus Christi College, Oxford, where he held a fellowship from 1808 to 1825. In 1813 he was appointed reader in mineralogy at Oxford; and in 1818 a readership of geology was expressly instituted for him. A paper contributed by him to the *Philosophical Transactions* in 1822, entitled *Account of an Assemblage of Fossil Teeth and Bones discovered in a Cave at Kirkdale, Yorkshire, in the Year 1821*, procured for him the Copley Medal; and on this was founded his *Reliquiæ Diluvianæ*, published in 1823. To him belongs the honour of having first discovered the coprolites in Cambridgeshire and their manurial value for agricultural purposes. He was also one of the first to investigate the cause of potato disease.

In 1825 he was presented by his college to the living of Stoke Charity, Hants, and the same year became one of the canons of Christ Church Cathedral, Oxford. In 1832 he acted as president of the British Association. In 1836 his Bridgewater Treatise was published, under the title of *Geology and Mineralogy considered with Reference to Natural Theology*. In 1845 he was made Dean of Westminster, and in 1847 one of the trustees of the British Museum. He died in 1856.

BUCKLE, Henry Thomas. English historical writer, born 1821, the son of a wealthy London merchant. At an early age he entered his father's counting-house, but at the age of eighteen, on inheriting his father's fortune, he devoted himself entirely to study. The only thing he allowed to distract him from his more serious pursuits was chess, in which he held a foremost place amongst contemporary players.

His chief work, a philosophic *History of Civilisation*, of which only two volumes (1858 and 1861) were completed, was characterised by much novel and suggestive thought, and by the bold co-ordination of a vast store of materials drawn from the most varied sources. Three volumes of his *Miscellaneous and Posthumous Works* were edited by Helen Taylor in 1872. He died, while travelling, at Damascus, 1862.

BUCKLER. A kind of small shield formerly worn on the left arm, and varying in form and material, among the latter being wicker-work, wood covered with leather, a combination of wood and metal, etc.

BUCKLEY. A town of N. Wales, Flintshire, situated between Mold and Hawarden, with manufactures of coarse earthenware, drain-pipes, bricks, etc. Pop. (1931), 6900.

BUCKMASTER, Stanley Owen, Viscount. British politician, born 1861. He was educated at Christ Church, Oxford, was called to the Bar in 1884, and became a K.C. in 1902. He sat as member of Parliament (Liberal) for Cambridge Borough, 1906-10, and for Keighley Division of W. Riding of Yorkshire, 1911-5. He was knighted in 1913 on becoming Solicitor-General, and was appointed Lord High Chancellor of England in May, 1915. He resigned in Dec., 1916, on the fall of the Asquith Ministry.

BUCK'RAM. A coarse textile fabric stiffened with glue and used in garments to give them or keep them in the form intended. The term was formerly applied to fine linen or cotton cloth.

BUCKROSE. One of the three parliamentary divisions of the East Riding of Yorkshire.

BUCK-SHOT. A large-sized leaden shot, employed by sportsmen for killing deer and other large game. It was issued to the Irish constabulary in place of ball cartridge during the chief secretaryship of W. E. Forster (1880-2). For Buckshot-war, *see* PENNSYLVANIA.

BUCK'SKIN. A kind of soft leather of a yellowish or greyish colour, made originally from deer-skins, but now usually from sheep-skins. The softness which is its chief characteristic is imparted by using oil or brains in dressing it. The name is also given to a kind of twilled woollen cloth without a pile or "face."

BUCK'THORN (Rhamnus). The name of an extensive genus of trees and shrubs, ord. Rhamnaceæ. There are two British species, the common buckthorn, and the alder or breaking buckthorn. Both are comparatively rare in Scotland and Ireland, but occur more frequently in England. The common buckthorn (*Rhamnus cathartica*), a British and North American shrub, grows to 7 or 8 feet, has strong spines on its branches, elliptical and serrated leaves, male and female flowers on different plants, a greenish-yellow calyx, no corolla, and a round black berry. It flowers in May.

The berries are purgative, but harsh in action. The bark yields a yellow dye, the berries sap green. Dyer's buckthorn (*R. infectorius*) yields French or yellow berries. The bark of several species, especially *R. Purshiana* (cascara sagrada), has cathartic properties.

BUCK'WHEAT, or **BRANK** (*Fagopȳrum esculentum* or *Polygŏnum Fagopȳrum*). A plant of the ord. Polygonaceæ, with branched herba-

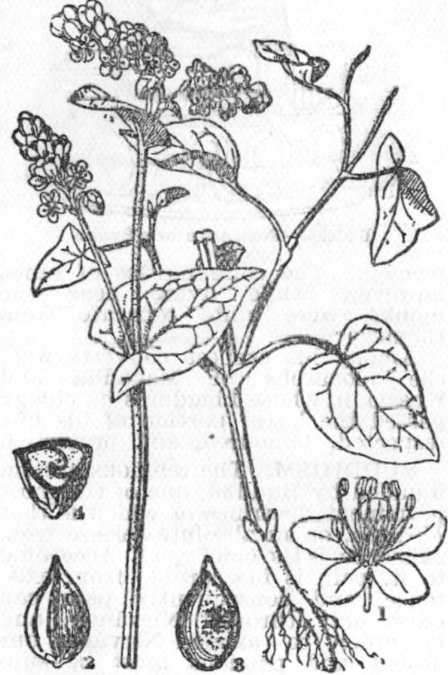

Buckwheat or Brank (*Polygonum Fagopyrum*)
1, Flower. 2, Fruit. 3, 4, Sections of fruit.

ceous stem, somewhat arrow-shaped leaves, and purplish-white flowers, growing to the height of about 30 inches, and bearing a small triangular grain of a brownish-black hue without and white within. The shape of its seeds gives it its German name *Buchweizen*, "beech-wheat," whence the English name. The plant was first brought to Europe from Asia by the Crusaders, and hence in France is often called Saracen corn. It grows on the poorest soils. It is cultivated in China and other eastern countries as a bread-corn.

In Europe buckwheat has been principally cultivated as food for oxen, swine, and poultry; but in Germany it serves as an ingredient in pottage, puddings, and other food, and in America buckwheat cakes are common.

BUCZACZ (bö'chàch). A town of Ukraine (till 1918 of Austria), in Galicia, on the Stripa. In 1872 a treaty of peace was signed here between the Poles and the Turks. The town was taken by the Russians in Brusilov's advance in June, 1916. Pop. 13,000.

BUD. The name of bodies of various form and structure, which develop upon vegetables, and contain the rudiments of future organs, as stems, branches, leaves, and organs of fructification. Upon exogenous plants they are in their commencement cellular prolongations from the medullary rays, which force their way through the bark. In general, a single bud is developed each year in the axil of each leaf, and there is one terminating the branch called a terminal bud. The life of the plant during winter is stored up in the bud as in an embryo, and it is by its vital action that on the return of spring the flow of sap from the roots is stimulated to renewed activity.

Buds are distinguished into leaf-buds and flower-buds. The latter are produced in the axil of leaves called floral leaves or bracts. The terminal bud of a branch is usually a flower-bud, and as cultivation is capable of producing flower-buds in place of leaf-buds, the one is probably a modification of the other.

BUDAPEST (-pesht'). The official name of the united towns of Pest and Buda or Ofen, the one on the left, the other on the right of the Danube, forming the capital of Hungary.

Buda. Buda, which is the smaller of the two, and lies on the west bank of the river, consists of the fortified Upper Town on a hill; the Lower Town or Wasserstadt at the foot of the hill, and several other districts. Among the chief buildings are the castle and several palaces, the arsenal, town hall, Government offices, etc., and a beautiful Jewish synagogue in the Moorish style, erected in 1861, and two others built in 1872 and 1901. The mineral baths of Buda have long been famous, the Bruckbad and Kaiserbad having both been used by the Romans.

Pest. Pest, or the portion of Budapest on the left or east bank of the river, is formed by the inner town of Old Pest on the Danube, about which has grown a semicircle of districts—Leopoldstadt, Theresienstadt, Elizabethstadt, etc. The river is at this point somewhat wider than the Thames at London, and the broad quays of Pest extend along it for from two to three miles. Pest retains, on the whole, fewer signs of antiquity than many less venerable towns. Its fine frontage on the Danube is modern, and includes the new Houses of Parliament, the academy, and other important buildings.

The oldest church in Buda dates from the thirteenth century (completed in the fifteenth century and restored in 1896); the oldest church in Pest was built in 1500; the largest building is a huge pile used as barracks and arsenal. There is a well-attended university. Its chief manufactures are machinery, iron wares, china, chemicals, silk, leather, tobacco, etc. A large trade is carried on in grain, wine, wool, cattle, etc.

Budapest is strongly Magyar, and as a factor in the national life may almost be regarded as equivalent to the rest of Hungary. It was not until 1799 that the population of Pest began to outdistance that of Buda; but from that date its growth was very rapid and out of all proportion to the increase of Buda. In 1799 the joint population of the two towns was little more than 50,000; in 1900 it was 732,322; in 1910 it was 880,371; and in 1920, 1,217,325.

BUDA'UN. A town of India, United Provinces, consisting of an old and a new town, the former partly surrounded by ancient ramparts; there is a handsome mosque, American mission, etc. Pop. 38,230. The district of Budaun has an area of 2017 sq. miles, and a pop. of 1,024,000.

BUDDHA (bụd'ha; "the Wise" or "the Enlightened"). The sacred name of the founder of Buddhism, an Indian sage who appears to have lived in the fifth century B.C., the approximate date of his birth being 560 B.C. and of his death 480 B.C. His personal name was Siddhartha, and his family name Gautama; and he is often called also Sakya-muni (from *Sakya*, the name of his tribe, and *muni*, a Sanskrit word meaning a sage). He was born in the Lumbini Grove, near Kapilavastu, a few days' journey north of Benares, where his father was king.

Siddhartha, filled with a deep compassion for the human race, left his father's Court, and lived for years in solitude till he had penetrated the mysteries of life, and become the Buddha. He then began to teach his new faith, in opposition to the prevailing Brahmanism, commencing at Benares. In his mildness, his readiness to overlook insults, his zeal, chastity, and simplicity of life, he is not unlike St. Francis of Assisi.

His order was composed of those who renounced the world to live a life of contemplation as monks and nuns, for in course of time he extended his monastic system to include

Buddha.—From a Burmese Bronze

women. The communities of nuns, however, while living near the monks, were quite separate from them.

Among his earliest converts were the monarchs of Magadha and Kosala, in whose kingdoms he chiefly passed the latter portion of his life, respected, honoured, and protected.

BUDDHISM. The religious system founded by Buddha, one of the most prominent doctrines of which is that *Nirvâna*, or an absolute release from existence, is the chief good. According to it, pain is inseparable from existence, and consequently pain can cease only through Nirvâna; and in order to attain Nirvâna our desires and passions must be suppressed, the most extreme self-renunciation practised, and we must, as far as possible, forget our own personality.

In order to attain Nirvâna eight conditions must be kept or practised. The first is in Buddhistic language *right view*; the second is *right judgment*; the third is *right language*; the fourth is *right purpose*; the fifth is *right profession*; the sixth is *right application*; the seventh is *right memory*; the eighth is *right meditation.*

The five fundamental precepts of the Buddhist moral code are: not to kill, not to steal, not to commit adultery, not to lie, and not to give way to drunkenness. To these there are added five others of less importance, and binding more particularly on the religious class, such as to abstain from repasts taken out of season, from theatrical representations, etc.

There are six fundamental virtues to be practised by all men alike, viz. charity, purity, patience, courage, contemplation, and knowledge. These are the virtues that are said to "conduct a man to the other shore." The devotee who strictly practises them has not yet attained Nirvâna, but is on the road to it. The Buddhist virtue of charity is universal in its application, extending to all creatures, and demanding sometimes the greatest self-denial and sacrifice. There is a legend that the Buddha in one of his stages of existence (for he had passed through innumerable transmigrations before becoming "the enlightened") gave himself up to be devoured by a famishing lioness which was unable to suckle her young ones.

There are other virtues, less important, indeed, than the six cardinal ones, but still binding on believers. Thus not only is lying forbidden, but evil-speaking, coarseness of language, and even vain and frivolous talk, must be avoided.

Buddhist metaphysics are comprised in three theories—the theory of transmigration (borrowed from Brahmanism), the theory of the mutual connection of causes, and the theory of Nirvâna. The first requires no explanation. According to the second, life is the result of twelve conditions, which are by turns causes and effects. Thus there would be no death were it nor for birth; it is therefore the effect of which birth is the cause. Again, there would be no birth were there not a continuation of existence. Existence has for its cause our attachment to things, which again has its origin in desire; and so on through sensation, contact, the organs of sensation and the heart, name and form, ideas, etc., up to ignorance. This ignorance, however, is not ordinary ignorance, but the fundamental error which causes us to attribute permanence and reality to things. This, then, is the primary origin of existence and all its attendant evils.

Nirvâna or extinction is eternal salvation from the evils of existence, and the end which every Buddhist is supposed to seek. In this respect Nirvâna was practically one with the ideal of the pantheistic Brahmin. The pantheistic Brahmin, however, said: "Recognise your identity with the great impersonal god Brahma; at death you lose your individuality, your conscious existence, to become absorbed in the all-god Brahma."

In Buddha's system the all-god Brahma was ignored. And as prayers and offerings to the traditional gods were held to be of no avail for the attainment of the negative state of bliss, Buddha, more consistent than the pantheistic Brahmin, rejected both the Vedas and the Vedic rites.

One of the most striking contrasts between Brahmanism and Buddhism was the latter's "religious democracy." Brahmanism was intertwined with class distinction, whilst Buddha considered virtue, not blood, to be the test of superiority. He welcomed men of low as well as high birth and station. Sakya-muni did not leave his doctrines in writing; he declared them orally, and they were carefully treasured up by his disciples, and written down after his death.

The determination of the canon of the Buddhist scriptures as we now possess them was the work of three successive councils, and was finished two centuries at least before Christ. Since Buddhism involved a protest against caste distinctions it was eagerly adopted by the Dasyus or non-Aryan inhabitants of Hindustan. It was pure, moral, and humane in its origin, but it came subsequently to be mixed up with idolatrous worship of its founder and other deities.

Although now long banished from Hindustan by the persecutions of the Brahmins, Buddhism prevails in Ceylon, Burmah, Siam, Annam, Tibet, Mongolia, China, Java, and Japan, and its adherents are said to comprise about a third of the human race, although recent authorities maintain that the Buddhists in the whole world are not more than one hundred millions.

BIBLIOGRAPHY: R. Spence-Hardy, *Manual of Buddhism*; Sir E. Arnold, *Light of Asia*; P. Bigandet, *Life or Legend of Gautama, the Buddha of the Burmese*; Sir Monier Monier-Williams, *Buddhism*; H. Baynes, *Way of Buddha*; T. W. Rhys-Davids, *Buddhism*; Mrs. Rhys-Davids, *Buddhism*.

BUDDHIST ARCHITECTURE. *See* ARCHITECTURE (INDIAN).

BUDDING. The art of multiplying plants by causing the leaf-bud of one species or variety to grow upon the branch of another. The operation is known as Shield Budding, and consists in shaving off a leaf-bud, with a portion of the wood beneath it, which portion is afterwards removed by a sudden jerk of the operator's finger and thumb, aided by the budding-knife. An incision in the bark of the stock is then made in the form of a **T**; the two side lips are pushed aside, the bud is thrust between the bark and the wood, the upper end of its bark is cut to a level with the cross arm of the **T**, and the whole is bound up with worsted or other soft fastening, the point of the bud being left exposed.

In performing the operation, a knife with a thin flat handle and a blade with a peculiar edge is required. The bud must be fully formed; the bark of the stock must separate readily from the wood below it; and young branches should always be chosen, as having beneath the bark the largest quantity of *cambium* or layer out of which new tissue is formed. The maturer shoots of the year in which the operation is performed are the best. The autumn is the best time for budding, though it may also be practised in the spring. *See* HORTICULTURE.

BUDDLEIA. A genus of Loganiaceæ, native of America, India, and S. Africa. Several species are half-hardy shrubs, grown for their flowers, which are showy and very rich in honey.

BUDE, or BUDEHAVEN. A small seaport and watering-place of England, on the north-west coast of Cornwall, at the mouth of the River Bude, 15 miles N.W. of Launceston. The cliff scenery is fine, and the climate is bracing in summer and mild in winter. Pop. (urban district), 3836 (1931).

BUDÉ (bü-dā), or **BUDÆUS, Guillaume.** A French scholar, born at Paris in 1467, and died in 1540. After a lawless youth he devoted himself to the study of literature. Among his philosophical, philological, and juridical works, his treatise *De Asse et Partibus ejus* (1514) and his *Commentarii Græcæ Linguæ* (1529) are of the greatest importance. By his influence the Collège Royal de France and the Bibliothèque de Fontainebleau were founded.

BUDEJOVICE. *See* BUDWEIS.

BUDG'ELL, Eustace. English man of letters, author of about three dozen papers, signed "X," in the *Spectator*, born 1686, died 1737. He was first cousin, once removed, to Addison, and went with him to Dublin in 1709 as secretary. On the accession of George I., Budgell obtained several valuable Irish appointments, from which he was removed for an attack on the Lord-Lieutenant, the Duke of Bolton. He lost three-fourths of his fortune in the South Sea Bubble in 1720, and spent the rest in a fruitless attempt to get into Parliament. Disgraced by an attempted fraud in connection with Dr. Matthew Tindal's will, he committed suicide by drowning himself in the Thames.

BUDGERIGAR (*Melopsittacus undulatus*). The small warbling or grass parakeet of Australia. *See* PARAKEET.

BUDG'ET. The annual financial statement which the British Chancellor of the Exchequer makes in the House of Commons, usually in April. It contains a view of the general financial policy of the Government, and at the same time presents an estimate of the probable income and expenditure for the following twelve months, and a statement of what taxes it is intended to reduce, increase, or abolish, or what new ones it may be necessary to impose. The term first came into use in England about 1760. The British Budget estimate for 1928-9 was for £812,262,000 revenue and for £805,195,000 expenditure.

BUDHA'NA. A town of India, in the United Provinces. Pop. 6000.

BUDIS'SIN. *See* BAUTZEN.

BUDLEIGH SALTERTON. An English watering-place and health-resort on the south coast of Devonshire, at the mouth of the Otter, 5 miles east of Exmouth. Pop. (1931), 3162.

BUDWEIS (bụd'vīs). A city of Czechoslovakia, 75 miles S. of Prague, well built, with a cathedral and episcopal palace, a flourishing trade, and manufactures of earthenware, cloth, machinery, etc. Pop. 44,022.

BUEN AYRE (bụ-en ī'rā), or **BONAIR.** A small island off the coast of Venezuela, belonging to the Dutch, 50 miles in circumference; produces cattle, goats, poultry, and salt. Pop. 5050.

BUENOS AIRES (bụ-en'ōs ī'rās). A city of South America, capital of the Argentine Republic, on the S.W. side of the La Plata, 150 miles from its mouth. It was founded in 1535 by Don Pedro de Mendoza, and is built with great regularity, the streets uniformly crossing each other at right angles. It contains the palace of the President, the House of Representatives, a town hall, a number of hospitals and asylums, a cathedral, several monasteries, nunneries, and

Catholic and Protestant churches, several theatres, a university, and a custom house. The university, founded in 1821, is attended by over 4000 students. There are also a medical school, normal and other schools, besides literary and scientific societies.

Formerly large vessels could only come within 8 or 9 miles of the town, but they can now come up to it and enter the extensive docks that have been constructed, about £5,000,000 having been spent on harbour works and channels. La Plata (capital of the province), a new town 30 miles lower down the estuary, serves as a sub-port.

Buenos Aires is one of the leading commercial centres of South America, its exports and imports together annually amounting to over £100,000,000. Chief exports are wool, wheat, maize, meat, hides and skins, tallow, etc. There are six railways running from the city, and 100 miles of tramway in the city and suburbs. About one-fourth of the inhabitants are white; the rest are of mixed blood or Indians, negroes, etc. Pop. in 1927, 1,972,823.

The province of Buenos Aires has an area of 117,777 sq. miles, and consists mostly of level or slightly-undulating plains (*pampas*), which afford pasture to vast numbers of cattle, sheep, and horses. Pop. (1927), 2,814,601.

BUFF'ALO. An ungulate or hoofed ruminant mammal, family Bovidæ or oxen, the best-known species of which is the common or Indian buffalo (*Bos bubălus*), larger than the ox and with stouter limbs. Unlike the African species, Indian buffaloes have been domesticated in their native country from time immemorial, and have been introduced into many of the warmer countries of the Old World, notably into Italy in the sixth century, and also into Hungary, Rumania, Egypt, Syria, and Java.

A full-grown male is a bold and powerful animal, quite a match for any tiger. The buffalo is less docile than the common ox, and is fond of marshy places and rivers. It is, however, used in tillage, draught, and carriage in India, Italy, etc. The female gives much more milk than the cow, and from the milk the *ghee* or clarified butter of India is made. The hide is exceedingly tough, and a valuable leather is prepared from it, but the flesh is not very highly esteemed. Another Indian species is the arnee (*B. arni*), the largest of the ox family.

Cape Buffalo. The Cape buffalo (*B. Caffer*) is distinguished by the size of its horns, which are united at their bases, forming a great bony mass on the front of the head. It attains a greater size than an ordinary ox.

1, Head of Cape Buffalo (*Bubalus Caffer*)
2, Head of Indian Buffalo (*Bubalus Buffelus*)

The name is also applied to wild oxen in general, and particularly to the bison of North America. *See* Bison.

BUFF'ALO. A town, United States, New York, at the E. extremity of Lake Erie, the mouth of the Buffalo River, and the head of the Niagara River. It has a water front of 2½ miles on the lake and of the same extent on the Niagara River, which is here crossed by an iron bridge.

The position of Buffalo on the great water and railway channels of communication between the west and the east makes it the centre of a vast trade in grain, live stock, and other commodities. The harbour is capacious, and is protected by extensive breakwaters. The Erie Canal, which connects with the Hudson, has its western terminus here.

The whole site is a plain with a gentle descent towards the lake, well covered with houses, except where open spaces or squares have been left for ornament and ventilation. There is a splendid public park.

The principal buildings are the city and county hall, the custom-house and post office, the arsenal, and the Ellicott Square building (one of the largest office structures in the world); other buildings and institutions of note are: a young men's literary association, an orphan asylum, a general hospital, and a fine cemetery covering about 76 acres.

Manufactures are numerous and varied. At the Pan-American Exposition held here in 1901 President M'Kinley was assassinated by an anarchist. Population, 506,775.

BUFFALO-BERRY (*Shepherdia argentĕa*). A shrub of the oleaster family, a native of the States and Canada, with lanceolate silvery leaves and close clusters of bright-red edible berries about the size of currants.

BUFFALO-GRASS (*Buchloe dactyloides*). A strong-growing N. American grass, so called from forming a large part of the food of the buffalo, and said to have excellent fattening properties.

BUFFER. Any apparatus for deadening the concussion between a moving body and the one on which it strikes. In railway carriages they are usually placed in pairs at each end, and are fitted to indiarubber buffing springs. *Hydraulic buffers* are now employed for various purposes, in gun-carriages for instance (*see* CANNON).

BUFFET. A cupboard, sideboard, or closet to hold china, crystal, plate, and the like. The word is also very commonly applied to the spaces set apart for refreshments in public places.

BUFF LEATHER. A sort of dull, pale-yellowish chamois leather prepared from the skin of the buffalo and other kinds of oxen, dressed with oil, like chamois. It is used for making bandoliers, belts, pouches, gloves, and other articles.

BUFFON (bü-fōn), **George Louis Leclerc, Count de.** Celebrated French naturalist, born at Montbard, in Burgundy, 1707, died in Paris 1788. Being the son of a rich man he was able to travel, and he visited Italy and England. In 1739 he was appointed superintendent of the Royal Garden at Paris (now the Jardin des Plantes), and devoted himself to the great work, *Natural History*, which occupied most of his life. It is now obsolete and of small scientific value, but for long it had an extraordinary popularity, and was the means of diffusing a taste for the study of nature throughout Europe.

After an assiduous labour of ten years the three first volumes were published, and between 1749 and 1767 twelve others, which comprehend the theory of the earth, the nature of animals, and the history of man and the mammalia. In these Buffon was assisted by Daubenton in the purely anatomical portions. The next nine volumes, which appeared from 1770 to 1783, contain the history of birds, from which Daubenton withdrew his assistance, the author being now aided by Guéneau de Montbelliard, and afterwards by the Abbé Bexon. Buffon published alone the five volumes on minerals, from 1783 to 1788. Of the seven supplementary volumes, of which the last did not appear until after his death in 1789, the fifth formed an independent whole, the most celebrated of all his works. It contains his *Epochs of Nature*, in which the author gives a second theory of the earth, very different from that which he had traced in the first volumes, though he assumes at the commencement the air of merely defending and developing the former.

Buffon was raised to the rank of count by Louis XV., whose favour, as also that of Louis XVI., he enjoyed. His works were translated into almost every European language.—BIBLIOGRAPHY: M. J. P. Flourens, *Histoire des Travaux et des Idées de Buffon*; A. S. Packard, *Lamarck*.

BUFFOON′. A merry-andrew, a clown, a jester; from the It. *buffone*, from *buffare*, to jest, to sport. *Buffo*, in Italian, is the name given to a comic actor; a burlesque play is called a *comedia buffa*, and a comic opera *opera buffa*. The Italians, however, distinguish the *buffo cantante*, which requires good singing, from the *buffo comico*, in which there is more acting.

BUFFS, THE (East Kent Regiment). Raised during the reign of Elizabeth, and received the privilege of marching through the city of London with drums beating. They distinguished themselves greatly under Marlborough, as later in the Peninsula and in South Africa (1879 and 1900-2). Sent to the front in 1914, the regiment took an active part in the "great push" of 1916.—**The Ross-shire Buffs,** the old 78th regiment, now the Second Battalion of Seaforth Highlanders.

BUFON′IDÆ. A family of tailless amphibia, comprehending the toads.

BUG, or **BOG.** A river of the Ukraine, which falls into the estuary of the Dnieper near Kherson, after a course of about 500 miles. Another river of the same name, the Western Bug, rises in Galicia, and falls into the Vistula about 20 miles N.N.W. of Warsaw. Both are navigable for considerable distances. Severe fighting took place along the banks of the Western Bug during the European War (q.v.).

BUG. A name given to the *Cimex lectularius*, otherwise known as the house-bug or bed-bug, is a member of the ord. Hemiptera. The common bug is about $\frac{3}{16}$ inch long, wingless, of a roundish depressed body, dirty rust colour, and emits an offensive smell when touched. The female lays her eggs in summer in the crevices of edsteads, furniture, and walls of ooms. Its larvæ are small, white, nd semi-transparent. They attain ill size in eleven weeks. The mouth f the bug has a three-jointed pro-oscis, which forms a sheath for a ucker. It is fond of human blood, ut eats various other substances. 'he name was formerly applied loosely o insects of various kinds, and in he United States it is generally used vhere *beetle* would be used in England.

BUGEAUD (bü-zhō), **Thomas Robert, Duke d'Isly.** A Marshal of France, born in 1784, died at Paris 1849. He entered the army in 1804 as a simple grenadier, but rose to be colonel before the fall of Napoleon. After the revolution of 1830 he obtained a seat in the Chamber of Deputies. He was afterwards sent to Algeria, where he carried out successfully many minor operations against the Arabs, by means of his system of flying columns. On the revolution of 1848 he adhered to Louis Philippe to the last. Under the presidency of Louis Napoleon he was appointed commander-in-chief of the army of the Alps.

BUGENHAGEN (bö'gen-hä-gen), **Johann.** German reformer, friend and helper of Luther in preparing his translation of the Bible. He was born in 1485, and died in 1558. He fled from his Catholic superiors to Wittenberg in 1521, where he was made, in 1522, professor of theology. He effected the union of the Protestant free cities with the Saxons, and introduced into Brunswick, Hamburg, Lübeck, Pomerania, Denmark, and many other places, the Lutheran service and church discipline. He translated the Bible into Low German (Lübeck, 1533); wrote an *Exposition of the Book of Psalms* (Interpretatio in Librum Psalmorum) and a *History of Pomerania.*

BUGGY. A name given to several species of carriages or gigs: in England, a light one-horse two-wheeled vehicle without a hood; in the United States, a light one-horse four-wheeled vehicle, with or without a hood or top; in India, a gig with a large hood to screen those who travel in it from the sun's rays.

Buggy

BUGIS (bö'giz), or **BUGHIS.** A people of the Indian Archipelago, chiefly inhabiting the eastern coast and a good deal of the interior of the southern peninsula of the Island of Celebes, their chief town being Boni. They are described as peaceable, orderly, and well-behaved, are the chief carriers and factors of the Indian seas, and are engaged in the manufacture of iron, copper, cotton, etc., and in trepang, pearl, and other fisheries. Large communities of them have also been formed in Borneo, in Sumatra, and in many small islands of the archipelago.

BU'GLE. A military musical brass wind-instrument of the horn kind, sometimes furnished with keys or valves. It is used in the British and other armies to sound signal calls. The name is an abbreviation of *bugle-horn,* that is, buffalo-horn, from the obsolete English word *bugle,* a wild ox (Lat. *buculus,* a small ox). (See illustration on p. 290.)

BUGLE. The common name for Ajŭga, a genus of labiate plants.

Two of the species are British, *A. reptans*, a woodland plant with dark leaves and blue flowers, formerly held in high esteem as an application to wounds; and *A. chamæpitys*, yellow bugle, a plant which grows in chalky fields.

BUGLE. A shining elongated glass-bead, usually black, used in decorating women's dresses and also in trafficking with savage tribes.

BU'GLOSS. *See* BORAGINACEÆ.

BUHL-WORK (böl-). A description of inlaid work, said to have been invented by André Charles Boulle (1642-1732), a French cabinet-maker, whom Colbert described as "le plus habile ébéniste de Paris." It consisted at first of unburnished gold, brass, enamel, or mother-of-pearl worked into complicated and ornamental patterns, and inserted in a ground of dark-coloured metal, wood, or tortoise-shell; but at a later period the use of wood of a different colour was introduced by Reisner, and to his process the modern practice of buhl-work is chiefly confined.

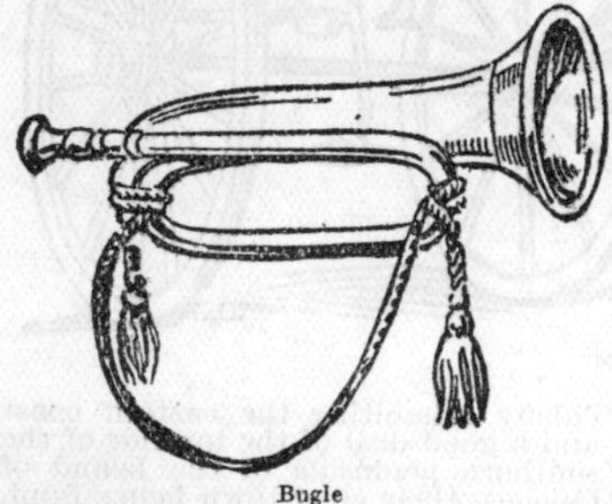

Bugle

BUHRSTONE (bör'-), or **BURRSTONE.** A name given to certain siliceous or siliceo-calcareous stones, whose dressed surfaces present a burr or keen-cutting texture, whence they are much used for millstones. The most esteemed varieties are obtained from the upper freshwater beds of the Paris basin, and from the Eocene strata of South America.

BUILDING LEASE. A lease of land for a long term of years, usually 99 years, at a rent called a ground-rent, the lessee covenanting to erect certain edifices thereon, and to maintain the same during the term. At the expiration of the lease the houses built become the absolute property of the landlord. In Scotland it is called a *feu*, and the price assumes the shape of an annual feu-duty.

BUILDING SOCIETIES. Join stock benefit societies for the purpo of raising by periodical subscriptio a fund to assist members in obtaini small portions of landed propert and houses, which are mortgaged t the society till the amount of th shares drawn on shall be fully repai with interest. These societies may b divided into two sections: the pr prietary and the mutual societie The former class takes money o deposit, paying a somewhat highe rate of interest than can generally b had on money available at call, an gives loans for building purposes, o the like, repayable by instalments The profit of the company lies in th difference between the rate charge to borrowers and the rate paid t depositors.

The mutual societies are of tw chief kinds, either limited to a certai term of years and confined to a certai number of members, or permanent and not confined to any definit number of members, but ready t receive new members as long as th society exists. A favourite form of th terminating society is to allot it capital among the members, according to the number of shares they hold by ballot. The subscriptions are paid weekly or monthly, and on securing an "appropriation" the member repays this sum very much as he would pay his rent, over a term of years, at the end of which the house or land becomes his own. He also maintains his small subscription, and at the winding-up of the society he is entitled to a share of the profits.

Terminable societies are giving place to the permanent kind. These, by the constant admission of new members, have a constant supply of funds at their disposal, and are thus able to supply the demands of all the borrowers; while the security offered to investors induces many people to enter the society merely with the view of having a convenient means of depositing their savings, and not with the intention of acquiring any real property for themselves.

The first building society in England was organised in Birmingham in 1781, a second was established at Greenwich in 1809, and another was founded at Kirkcudbright, in Scotland, in 1825. They became numerous during the nineteenth century, and in 1930 there were in Great Britain 1026 societies with over 1,400,000 members and investors. Their total funds were over £370,000,000. There is a national union of building societies, and in their interests a paper, *The Building Societies Gazette*, is published.—BIBLIOGRAPHY: E. Rigley, *How to Manage Building*

Associations; Charles N. Thompson, Treatise on Building Associations.

BUILTH WELLS. A town of Wales, in the north-east of Brecknock, with saline, sulphurous, and chalybeate springs that attract numbers of invalids. Pop. (1931), 1663.

BUITENZORG (boi′ten-zorg; "without care"). A favourite residential town in the Island of Java, about 40 miles south of Batavia, with which it is connected by rail. It contains a fine palace of the Governor-General, celebrated botanic gardens, etc. Pop. 34,000.

BUJALANCE (bö-*h*à-lån′thā). A city of Spain, in the province of Andalusia, 21 miles E. by N. of Cordova; manufactures cloth and woollen fabrics, earthenware, and glass. Pop. 11,281.

BUKAREST′, or BUCHAREST. The capital of Rumania, situated on the Dimbovitza about 33 miles north of the Danube, in a fertile plain. It is in general poorly built, among the chief buildings being the royal palace, the National Theatre, the university buildings, the National Bank, the Mint, and the archiepiscopal church. There are handsome public gardens.

Manufactures are varied but unimportant; the trade is considerable, the chief articles being grain, wool, honey, wax, wine, and hides. The mercantile portion of the community is mostly foreign, and the whole population presents a curious blending of nationalities.

History. Bukarest became the capital of Wallachia in 1665, in 1862 that of the united principalities of Wallachia and Moldavia. A treaty was concluded here in 1812 between Turkey and Russia by which the former ceded Bessarabia and part of Moldavia. The Treaty of Bukarest between Germany and Rumania was signed in May, 1918, but annulled by the Armistice of 11th Nov., 1918. Pop. 308,987.

BUKOVINA (bö-ko-vē′nà). Formerly an Austrian duchy, forming the south-eastern corner of Galicia, and bordering on Russia, Rumania, and Hungary. Area, 4033 sq. miles; pop. 800,098. It is traversed by ramifications of the Carpathians, and much of the surface is occupied by swamps and forests. There are few industries except those connected with the land. Education is in a backward state. Chief town, Czernowitz. Bukovina now forms part of Greater Rumania (q.v.).

BULAC′, or BULAK′. *See* BOULAK.

BULACAN′. A town in the Philippines, Island of Luzon, about 22 miles N.W. of Manila; chief industries: sugar-boiling and the manufacture of silken mats. Pop. 15,000.

BULA′MA, or BOLA′MA. An island on the west coast of Africa, one of the Bissagos.

BULANDSHAHR (bu̥-*l*and-shär′). A district of India, United Provinces, in the alluvial plain between the Ganges and the Jumna; producing cotton, indigo, sugar, etc. Area, 1911 sq. miles; pop. 1,138,101.—Bulandshahr, the capital, has a pop. of 17,500.

BU′LAU, or TIKUS (*Gymnura Rafflesii*). An insectivorous mammal of the hedgehog kind, but belonging to a distinct family native to Sumatra and Malacca. The muzzle is much prolonged, the fur interspersed with long hairs or bristles, the tail naked, and it has glands which secrete musk.

BULAWAY′O, or BULUWAYO. A town of South Africa, in Southern Rhodesia, in a grazing region with gold and coal adjacent, 4470 feet above sea-level, 1360 miles by rail from Cape Town. It is built round a large market-square, has churches, schools, various public buildings, banks, hotels, hospital, newspapers, etc., and is making rapid progress. It is on the railway from Cape Town to the Victoria Falls, and is connected similarly with Salisbury and the Portuguese port of Beira. Lobengula, king of the Matabele, had his kraal or capital not far from this site. White pop. (1926), 7650.

BULB. A modified leaf-bud, formed on a plant upon or beneath the surface of the ground, emitting roots from its base, and producing a stem from its centre. It is formed of imbricated fleshy scales or of concentric coats or layers. It encloses the rudiments of the future plant and a store of food to nourish it. The bulb contains sufficient nutriment to give the plant a good start in spring, and part of its development consists in producing a fresh bulb or bulbs for the following season.

Examples of bulbs are the onion, lily, hyacinth, etc. Many such plants are objects of cultivation, either for use or beauty, and give rise to a large traffic. In Holland they are grown in enormous quantities, forming a staple industry, and in Japan millions of lily bulbs alone are annually exported to Europe and the United States.

BULBUL (bu̥l′bu̥l). The Persian name for the nightingale, or a species of nightingale, rendered familiar in English poetry by Moore, Byron, and

HUNGARY
ROUMANIA
YUGOSLAVIA
BULGARIA
ALBANIA
GREECE
TURKEY
ITALY
ASIA MINOR
BLACK SEA
ADRIATIC SEA
AEGEAN SEA
IONIAN SEA
TYRRHENIAN SEA
MEDITERRANEAN SEA
Sea of Marmora
Odessa
Pruth
Constantza
Varna
Burgas
Bucharest
Danube
Ruschuk
Iron Gate
Transylvanian Mts
Balkan Mts
Rhodope Mts
Maritsa
Philippopolis
Adrianople
Constantinople
Bosporus
Angora
SOFIA
Nish
Morava
BELGRADE
Tisa
Drave
Save
Dinaric Alps
Trieste
Po
Vardar
Salonika
Tirana
Durazzo
Pindus
Mt Olympus
Mts Parnassus
Corfu
Ionian Is
G. of Corinth
Patras
Corinth
Morea
ATHENS
Piraeus
G. of Aegina
Rhodes
Str. of Messina
Sicily
CRETE
Candia
on same scale
Scale
0 50 100 150 Mls.
Railways
Land over 1000 ft.
12
20
24
28
32
44
40
36

:hers. The same name is also given Asia to sundry other birds.

BULGA'RIA. A European king-om (a principality from 1878 to 908), formerly part of the Turkish ominions, and under the Treaty of Berlin (1878) a principality tributary o Turkey, the Sultan being suzerain. Until 1919 it was bounded north by Rumania, east by the Black Sea, outh by Turkey and the Ægean Sea, and west by Serbia and Greece. By he Treaty of Neuilly, signed 27th Nov., 1919, Bulgaria ceded Thrace o Greece, and a strip of territory on he north-west frontier to Yugoslavia. It was also deprived of its Ægean ittoral. The principal towns are Sofia, Philippopolis, Varna, and Ruschuk. Varna and Burgas are the chief ports.

The country belongs to the Balkan system, and is intersected by streams carrying the drainage to the Danube and Ægean. Southern Bulgaria or Eastern Rumelia is the region south of the Balkans.

Agriculture and Trade. Bulgaria possesses much good land and a good climate; agriculture is the chief occupation of the people, most of the population being engaged in it. Large crops of wheat, maize, barley, oats, and rye are grown. The rearing of cattle and horses is carried on. Many of the farmers own their holdings. Agricultural produce is exported, manufactured goods imported, the total imports and exports for 1931 amounting to £6,917,530 and £8,808,856 respectively.

Education. Education is now improving; it is free and nominally compulsory for a period of 4 years (8-12). The State religion is that of the Greek Church. In 1916 the Gregorian was substituted for the Eastern Calendar. The revenue, which was a little over £7,000,000 in 1911, rose to £9,555,265 in 1931, the expenditure being about the same. The revenue and expenditure for 1918 were £19,244,000 and £19,176,560 respectively. Obligatory military service was abolished by the Treaty of Nevilly, 1919; the war strength of the army must not exceed 20,000.

Constitution. Under the Treaty of Berlin a constitution was drawn up by an assembly of Bulgarian notables in 1879, being amended in 1893 and 1911. The legislative authority is vested in a single chamber, called the Sobranje or National Assembly, elected by universal suffrage for four years. The capital is Sofia.

History. On the 29th April, 1879, Prince Alexander of Battenberg, cousin of the Grand-Duke of Hesse, was elected prince by unanimous vote of the constituent assembly. In 1885 a national rising took place in Eastern Rumelia, the Turkish governor was expelled, and union with Bulgaria was proclaimed. In consequence, Serbia demanded an addition to her own territory, and began a war against Bulgaria (Nov., 1885), in which she was severely defeated. By the treaty which followed, the Prince of Bulgaria was appointed Governor-General of Eastern Rumelia for a term of five years, to be renominated at the end of that time by sanction of the Great Powers.

These events greatly irritated Russia, whose agents managed to seduce certain regiments of Bulgarians; and in Aug., 1886, the prince was seized and carried off, while it was proclaimed that he had abdicated. The people were still with him, but the danger of Russian interference led to his formal abdication. In 1887 Prince Ferdinand of Saxe-Coburg accepted an invitation to occupy the throne, and at last Turkey and the six Great Powers sanctioned this.

In 1908, taking advantage of what seemed a favourable state of matters in Turkey, Bulgaria declared its full independence; and next year, after lengthy negotiations, this was conceded, Turkey receiving compensation. The ruler had the title of King or "Tsar." On 30th Sept., 1912, Bulgaria, allied with Serbia, Greece, and Montenegro, commenced war on Turkey (First Balkan War), which was ended by the Treaty of London, 30th May, 1913, by which the size of Bulgaria was increased considerably. The Balkan League against Turkey, however, soon broke up, and a war among the Allies was the result (Second Balkan War). Rumania intervened, and peace was concluded on 10th Aug., 1913, by the Treaty of Bukarest, by which Bulgaria had to surrender about 2000 sq. miles to Rumania.

In Oct., 1915, Bulgaria decided to participate in the European conflict, siding with Germany, Austria, and Turkey. On 29th Sept., 1918, Bulgaria signed an armistice, and on 5th Oct., Tsar Ferdinand abdicated in favour of his son Boris, who now reigns, as King Boris III., over a kingdom, however, which has been deprived of a considerable amount of valuable territory. The area since 1919 has been 39,814 sq. miles. The total census population in 1931 was 6,006,000.

BIBLIOGRAPHY: G. Bousquet, *Histoire du peuple Bulgare*; L. Delaunay, *La Bulgarie d'hier et de demain*; F. Fox, *Bulgaria*; N. Mikhoff; *La Bulgarie et son Peuple*; G. C. Logio, *Bulgaria: Problems and Politics.*

BULGARIA. A genus of Fungi, group Discomycetes. *B. polymorpha* is not uncommon on dead trunks, especially of beech. The apothecia are shining black discs, as much as an inch across and of the consistency of india-rubber. Of the 8 spores in each ascus, 4 are black and 4 colourless. The fungus may behave as a parasite on oak.

BULGARIANS. A race of Finnish origin, whose original seat was on the banks of the Volga, and who subdued the old Mœsian population and established a kingdom in the present Bulgaria in the seventh century. They soon became blended with the conquered Slavs, whose language they adopted. In the ninth century Kroum, king of the Paonian Bulgars, created the unity of Bulgaria. Boris adopted Christianity in 864. The real creator, however, of Bulgaria was Simeon the Great. After the fall of Tirnovo in 1393 the country was conquered by the Turks. Towards the end of the eighteenth century the national idea began to revive among the Bulgarians, but all attempts to shake off the Turkish yoke failed until the Russo-Turkish War. *See* BULGARIA.

The Bulgarian language is divided into two dialects, the old and the new; the former is the richest and best of the Slavonic tongues, and although extinct as a living tongue is still used as the sacred language of the Greek Church. The Bulgarians are now spread over many parts of the Balkan Peninsula.

BULIM'IA. Abnormal excessive hunger, often coming on in paroxysmal attacks, and causing the patient to commit extraordinary excesses in eating. It may occur in diabetes and some gastric disorders, but more commonly in hysteria and in psychoses. Some of the ten thousand Greeks under Xenophon were affected with this disease when on the march near the Euphrates (cf. *Anabasis*, book iv., chap. 5).

BULKHEAD. Name given to the partitions in a ship which divide it into watertight compartments. They are found especially in battleships, when they are numbered. The word is also used for similar partitions in tunnelling operations.

BULL (Lat. *bulla*, a boss, later a leaden seal). A letter, edict, or rescript of the Pope, published or transmitted to the churches over which he is head, containing some decree, order, or decision, and in many cases having a leaden seal attached (although a golden seal was used on exceptional occasions), impressed on one side with the hea of St. Peter and St. Paul, on the oth with the name of the Pope.

In modern times the leaden bul has given way to a stamp in red in In its superscription the Pope invar ably takes the title of "episcopu servus servorum Dei." The docu ment is in Latin and on parchmen *See* CURIA; PAPACY.

BULL. The name given to th male of any bovine quadruped. Fo stock exchange terms, *see* BULL AND BEARS.

BULL, John. The English natio personified, and hence any typica Englishman: first used in Arbuth not's satire, *The History of John Bull* designed to ridicule the Duke o Marlborough; and in which th French are personified as *Lewis Ba boon*, the Dutch as *Nicholas Frog* etc.

BULL, Ole Bornemann. Famous violinist, born at Bergen, in Norway 1810, died 1880. He secured great triumphs both throughout Europe and in America by his wonderful playing. He lost all his money in a scheme to found a colony of his countrymen in Pennsylvania, and had to take again to his violin to repair his broken fortunes. He afterwards settled down at Cambridge, Massachusetts, and had also a summer residence in Norway, where he died.

BULLACE (bụl'ās). A kind of wild plum (*Prunus insititia*) common in many parts of England but rare in Scotland, used for making jam, etc.

BULL-BAITING. A barbarous pastime popular in England during many centuries, approved by Pepys and Dr. Parr, and not finally suppressed by law till 1835. It consisted in tying a bull to a stake and setting dogs to worry the animal.

BULL-DOG. A variety of the common dog, remarkable for its short, broad muzzle, and the projection of its lower jaw, which causes the lower front teeth to protrude beyond the upper. The head is massive and broad; the lips are thick and pendulous; the ears pendent at the extremity; the neck robust and short; the body long and stout; and the legs short and thick.

The bull-dog is a slow-motioned ferocious animal, and for this reason is often employed as a watch-dog. It was formerly used—as its name implies—for the barbarous sport of bull-baiting. The twentieth-century bull-dog, however, is little more than a genially dispositioned lap-dog.

The **bull-terrier** was originally from a cross between the bull-dog and the terrier. It is smaller than the bull-dog, lively, docile, and very courageous.

BULLEN, Anne. *See* BOLEYN.

BULLER, Sir Redvers Henry. English general, born in Devonshire in 1839, died in 1908; joined the army in 1858, served in China in 1860, in the Red River Expedition (Canada) in 1870, in the Ashanti War (1874), the Zulu War of 1878-79, in which he gained the Victoria Cross, having been made lieutenant-colonel in 1878. In the Boer War of 1881 he was chief of staff to Sir Evelyn Wood, and in the war in Egypt next year he won special distinction at Tel-el-Kebir and elsewhere. In the Sudan campaign of 1884-5 he was chief of staff to Lord Wolseley, and at the battle of Abu-Klea he took command when Sir Herbert Stewart was wounded. From 1887-90 he was quartermaster-general, from 1890-7 adjutant-general; K.C.B. in 1885, lieutenant-general in 1891, G.C.B. in 1894.

In 1899 he went to Natal as commander in the war with the Boer republics. His great task was the relief of Ladysmith, in which, however, he was foiled for a time (especially at Colenso and Spion Kop), though he was ultimately successful (after Lord Roberts had arrived to take the chief command in South Africa), and rendered valuable services in clearing the Boers out of Natal and subsequently. He held the Aldershot command (1st Army Corps) in 1901, but was relieved from this post on account of public utterances that were held to be a breach of military discipline and regulations.

BULLERS OF BUCHAN (bụl'ėrs). A natural curiosity on the coast of Aberdeenshire, 5¾ miles S.S.W. of Peterhead, consisting of a series of huge granite cliffs, with a large rocky caldron into which the sea rushes through a natural archway in the top of which is an opening locally called "the pot."

BULLET. (1) A solid elongated projectile forming the missile portion of the cartridge used in a rifle, pistol, or machine-gun of small calibre; (2) a spherical ball forming part of the contents of a shrapnel shell.

In its earlier form a bullet was invariably a solid sphere of lead which was loaded independently of the charge of gunpowder; small-arms were then muzzle-loading smooth bores, and had no great range or accuracy. With the introduction of rifling various attempts were made to adapt the spherical bullet to the new arm, but with scant success till the invention of the breech-loading system made it possible to use an elongated bullet as large as, or even slightly larger than, the bore of the rifles; this bullet, being forced by the explosion of the charge into the grooves of the rifling, leaves the barrel with a rotary motion, giving a considerable measure of stability, and keeping the point foremost during the subsequent flight. During this flight three distinct forces act on the bullet, i.e. the explosion, which drives it forward; gravity, which draws it down; and the resistance of the air, which lessens its speed. The elongated form of the modern bullet largely discounts this resistance of the air by affording great weight in proportion to the surface exposed to the air. The muzzle-velocity of such a bullet is from 2000 to 2500 feet per second.

The bullet in use in the British service has a length of 1¼ inches, and tapers to a comparatively sharp point. It is of compound construction, and consists of a core of lead tipped with aluminium and an envelope of cupro-nickel. A bullet which has a proportion of its envelope removed or cut so as to expose the soft core "sets up" or "mushrooms" on impact, and causes a much more severe wound than would be caused by the same bullet with its core completely covered; the use of such a bullet is, therefore, forbidden among civilised nations by the laws and usages of war exemplified in The Hague Convention.

BULLETIN (bụl'e-tin). An authenticated official report concerning some public event, such as military operations, the health of the sovereign or other distinguished personage, issued for the information of the public. The name is also given to some periodical publications recording the proceedings of learned societies.

BULLET-TREE, or BULLY-TREE (*Mimūsops balāta*). A forest tree of Guiana and neighbouring regions, ord. Sapotaceæ, yielding an excellent latex known as *balata*, having properties giving it in some respects an intermediate position between gutta-percha and india-rubber, and making it for certain industrial purposes more useful than either. In the United States it is used as a chewing material. The timber of the tree also is valuable. *See* GUTTA-PERCHA.

BULL-FIGHTS. The favourite popular diversion of Spain and Spanish America. They are held in open amphitheatres, or bull-rings, in which the spectators occupy circular tiers of seats; the great bull-ring of Madrid accommodates 12,000 people. The combatants, almost always professionals, enter the arena in procession.

They include: *picadores,* who fight on horseback, dressed in old Spanish costume; *chulos,* or *banderilleros,* foot-combatants, clad in gay garb, wearing coloured cloaks and carrying banners; and, finally, the *matador,* who deals the animal the *coup de grâce.*

At a given signal the bull is admitted to the arena. Bulls for the purpose are carefully bred and usually of proved temper and courage. The *picadores,* stationing themselves near the animal, commence the attack with lances, soon goading the creature to fury. The horses, always old and worthless animals, and usually blindfolded, are frequently killed and almost invariably badly wounded, and the rider often has to fly on foot. The *chulos* assist him by drawing the bull's attention with their cloaks, saving themselves from imminent danger by vaulting the wooden fence enclosing the arena. In due course the *banderilleros* take their part by endeavouring to transfix the bull with their *banderillas*—barbed darts adorned with coloured paper and sometimes carrying attached squibs or crackers. Finally the *matador,* or *espada,* the popular hero of the fight, advances with a naked sword and a red flag. Attracting the bull's attention with the latter, he gives the fatal blow. The slaughtered animal being dragged from the arena, another is introduced, and the exhibition frequently continues until several bulls have been thus killed.

In spite of occasional papal interference and other attempts to put down the practice, bull-fights maintain their popularity in Spain, though their introduction into Southern France has fortunately met with small success.

An interesting and less brutal, though apparently dangerous, variety of "bull-fighting" is sometimes exhibited by men who allow a bull to charge them, the animal turning aside at the last moment if the man maintains a rigid and perfectly motionless position.

In Portugal a milder form of bull-fighting is practised. The bull's horns are truncated and padded, so that the men and horses are not seriously injured. The bull himself is never killed.

BULLFINCH. An insessorial bird, *Pyrrhŭla Europœa,* family Fringillidæ or finches, with short thick rounded bill, beak and crown of the head black, body bluish-grey above and bright tile-red below. It occurs in Britain, in the middle and south of Europe and in Asia, and when tamed may be taught to sing musical airs. *P. synoica* is an Asiatic species, and *P. cineriola* an inhabitant of Brazil.

Bull-fight

BULL-FROG. The *Rana pipiens,* a large species of frog found in North America, 8 to 12 inches long, of a dusky-brown colour mixed with a yellowish-green, and spotted with black. These frogs live in stagnant water, and utter a low croaking sound resembling the lowing of cattle, whence the name.

BULL-HEAD. The popular name of certain fishes. One of these, the *Cottus gobio,* a British fish, is about 4 inches long, with head very large and broader than the body. It is often called also *Miller's-thumb.* Several closely-related marine species are common on our coasts. The six-horned bull-head (*C. hexacornis*) is a North American species. In America this name is given to a species of Pimelōdus, called also *Cat-fish* and *Horned-pout.*

BULLINGER (bụl'ing-ėr), **Henry.** A celebrated Swiss reformer, born in 1504, died at Zurich 1575. He was the intimate friend of Zuinglius, whom he succeeded in 1531 as pastor of Zurich. He kept up a close correspondence with the principal English reformers. The *Zurich Letters*, published by the Parker Society, contains part of this correspondence, and, among others, letters addressed to him by Lady Jane Grey. He wrote numerous theological works.

BULL'ION. Uncoined gold or silver, in bars, plate, or other masses, but the term is frequently employed to signify the precious metals coined and uncoined. The imports and exports of bullion to and from the United Kingdom in 1915 amounted to £21,388,527 and £46,578,689 respectively. In 1919 they were £68,969,083 and £17,344,631.

Bullfinch

BULL-ROARER. An instrument consisting of a small flat strip of wood, or sometimes bone, through a hole in one end of which a piece of string is passed. When whirled rapidly round, a loud moaning hum or "roar" is produced. Though known in Europe merely as a toy, it plays an important part among many primitive peoples, being credited with magic powers, and in some cases even worshipped as a god. This is especially the case in Australia, where the aborigines use deep-toned "man *tunduns*" and shriller "woman *tunduns*," both of which are employed in religious ceremonies.

The bull-roarer is also known in Sumatra and among the N. American Indians, while it is believed to be identical with the *rhombos* of the ancient Greeks.

BULL RUN. A stream in the N.E. of Virginia, flowing into the Occoquan River, 14 miles from the Potomac; the scene of two great battles, during the American Civil War, in which the Federals were defeated. The first battle was fought 21st July, 1861; and the second on 30th Aug., 1862.

BULLS AND BEARS. In stock-exchange slang, manipulators of stocks; the former operating in order to effect a rise in price, the latter doing all they can to bring prices of stock down for some special deal in stock.

BULL'S-EYE. (1) A round piece of thick glass, convex on one side, inserted into the decks, ports, scuttle-hatches, or skylight-covers of a vessel for the purpose of admitting light.

(2) A small lantern with a lens in one side of it to concentrate the light in any desired direction.

(3) In *rifle-shooting*, the centre of a target, of a different colour from the rest of it and usually round.

Since the South African War (1899-1902) changes have been made in the targets used for the General Musketry Course. The old-fashioned white target with black bull's-eye is now only used for the preliminary grouping practices; application and rapid practices are fired at targets consisting of a brown figure and a green background. These targets are supposed to be like the figures of soldiers in service-dress. The figure upon them is still, however, loosely spoken of as the bull's-eye.

BULL'S HORN THORN. A name of certain tropical American species of Acacia (e.g. *A. sphærocephala*) which furnish one of the longest-known and best-established instances of myrmecophily (q.v.). The large stipular thorns which are common in the genus are in these plants hollow and thin-walled, and are inhabited by ferocious ants, which gain access by boring a hole near the tip of each thorn. At the ends of the leaflets are small pear-shaped bodies (called Belt's corpuscles, after the traveller and naturalist Thomas Belt, who first described this remarkable association of ants with plants) rich in protein and oil, which serve as food for the ants. Drink is provided by a large nectary situated at the base of the leaf-stalk. As in other cases of myrmecophily, the ants are not mere intruders, but act as "police," keeping off marauders of their own kind and other animal foes.

BULL-TROUT. A large species of fish of the salmon family, the *Salmo eriox*, thicker and clumsier in form than the salmon, but so like it as sometimes to be mistaken for it by fishers. It attains a weight of 15 to 20 lb., and lives chiefly in the sea, ascending rivers to spawn. Its scales are smaller than those of the salmon, and its colour less bright.

BULLY-TREE. *See* BULLET-TREE.

BÜLOW (bü'lō), **Bernhard, Prince von.** German statesman, born in 1849. He served in the Franco-Prussian War and entered the Foreign Office in 1874. During the Russo-Turkish War he was Chargé d'Affaires at Athens. In 1897 he was appointed Foreign Secretary, and in 1900 became Chancellor of the German Empire and Prime Minister of Prussia. His diplomacy was in accordance with the ideas of the Kaiser William II. The meeting of the Algeciras Conference in 1906 was the result of his efforts.

He was raised to princely rank on 9th June, 1905. The failure of his Budget proposals in 1909 led to his resignation. His work *Imperial Germany* was published in 1914. He died in 1929.

BÜLOW (bü'lō), **Friedrich Wilhelm von.** Prussian general, born in 1755, died 1816. He was actively engaged against the French at the earliest periods of the revolutionary war; and his services in 1813 and 1814, especially at Grosbeeren and Dennewitz, were rewarded with the Grand Cross of the order of the Iron Cross and the title Count Bülow von Dennewitz. As commander of the fourth division of the Allied army he contributed to the victorious close of the battle of Waterloo.

BÜLOW (bü'lō), **Hans Guido von.** Pianist and composer, born at Dresden 1830; was intended for a lawyer, but adopted music as a profession. He studied the piano under Liszt, and made his first public appearance in 1852. In 1855 he became leading professor in the Conservatory at Berlin; in 1858 was appointed court pianist; and in 1867 he became musical director to the King of Bavaria.

His compositions include overture and music to *Julius Cæsar*, *The Minstrel's Curse*, and *Nirwana*; songs, choruses, and pianoforte pieces. He was considered one of the first of pianists and orchestral conductors. He died in 1894.

BULOZ (bü-loz), **François.** Born near Geneva, Switzerland, 1803, died at Paris 1877; founder and editor of the *Revue des Deux Mondes*, the celebrated French fortnightly literary magazine.

BULRAMPUR (bal-räm'pu̧r). A town of Oudh, India; the largest town in the Gonda district, and the residence of the Maharaja of Bulrampur. Pop. 14,800.

BULRUSH (bu̧l'-). The popular name for large rush-like plants growing in marshes, not very definitely applied. Some writers apply the name to *Typha latifolia* and *T. angustifolia* (cat's-tail or reed-mace). But it is more generally restricted to *Scirpus lacustris*, a tall rush-like plant from which the bottoms of chairs, mats, etc., are manufactured.

BULSAR'. A port and town of India, in Surat district, Bombay, on the estuary of the Auranga. It exports timber, and manufactures cloth, bricks, tiles, and pottery. Pop. 16,000.

BULUWAYO. *See* BULAWAYO.

BULWARK. Rampart of protection. This word is applied to walls and similar structures raised for defence, and is specially applied to the plating of a ship above the upper deck. It is figuratively used to denote anything that wards off danger.

The *Bulwark* was the name of a battleship of 15,000 tons completed in 1902. On 26th Nov., 1914, she was blown up when at anchor in the Medway, only 12 men being saved out of a crew of nearly 800. An earlier *Bulwark* is now used as a training ship.

BULWER (bu̧l'-), **Henry Lytton.** Lord Dalling and Bulwer, diplomatist and author, elder brother of Lord Lytton, born 1804, died 1872. He was attached to the British embassies at Berlin, Brussels, and The Hague from 1827 to 1830, when he entered Parliament. In 1837 he was sent as Secretary of Legation to Constantinople; subsequently he was minister at Madrid and Washington, and he succeeded Lord Stratford de Redcliffe as ambassador at the Porte (1858-65). Among his writings are *France, Social, Literary, and Political*; *Life of Byron*; *Life of Palmerston*; and *Historical Characters*. He was raised to the peerage in 1871.

BULWER LYTTON. *See* LYTTON, LORD.

BUM-BOAT. A small boat used to sell vegetables, etc., to ships lying at a distance from shore.

BUM'MALO, or **BUMMALO'TI.** The Indian name for a small glutinous, transparent fish, about the size of a smelt, found on the coasts of Southern Asia, which, when dried, is much used as a relish by both Europeans and Indians, and facetiously called *Bombay-duck*. It is the *Saurus ophiŏdon*, family Scopelidæ.

BUMPING RACE. *See* ROWING.

BUMPING TABLE. *See* METALLURGY.

BUNBURY. A seaport of Western Australia, on the south-west coast, connected by railway with Perth and other towns. Pop. 2750.

BUNCOMBE, or BUNKUM. A county in North Carolina; area, 624 sq. miles. Pop. 49,795. The term *Bunkum*, meaning talking for talking's sake, bombastic speech-making, originated with a congressional member for this county, who declared, during a debate in Congress in 1820, that he was only talking for *Buncombe*, when attempts were made to cut his oratory short.

BUNCRA'NA. A small market town of Ireland, County Donegal, on Lough Swilly, watering-place and tourist resort. Pop. (1926), 2309.

BUNDABERG. A port of Queensland, on the River Burnett, about 8 miles above its mouth, serving as the outlet of a district in which there are sugar-plantations and factories. It exports sugar and timber. Pop. 10,000.

BUNDELKHAND, or BUNDELCUND. A tract of country in India, partly included in the United Provinces, partly in Central India; area, 20,500 sq. miles. It includes the British districts of Hamirpur, Jalaun, Jhánsi, Lalitpur, and Banda, and thirty-one native States. The Bundelkhand Agency (area, 9851 sq. miles) comprises States belonging to Central India. Pop. 1,750,000.

BUNDER-ABBAS. *See* BENDER-ABBAS.

BUNDESRATH (bun'des-rät). *See* GERMANY; SWITZERLAND.

BUNDI. *See* BOONDEE.

BUNDO'RAN. A village of Ireland, County Donegal, on Donegal Bay, a favourite seaside resort. Pop. (1931), 1337.

BUN'GALOW. In India, a house or residence, generally of a single floor. Native bungalows are constructed of wood, bamboos, etc.; but those erected by Europeans are generally built of sun-dried bricks, and thatched or tiled, and are of all styles and sizes, but invariably surrounded by a veranda.

BUN'GAY. A market town, England, County Suffolk, on the right bank of the Waveney, 30 miles N.E. of Ipswich. It contains the ruins of an ancient castle, a stronghold of the Bigods, Earls of Norfolk. Pop. (1931), 3098.

BUNHILL FIELDS. Cemetery and public garden in Finsbury, London. It is in City Road, opposite Wesley's Chapel, and covers about six acres. It was used as a burial ground in the seventeenth century, especially for Nonconformists, and here are the graves of John Bunyan, Daniel Defoe, Isaac Watts, and others. It was made a public garden in 1869.

BUN'ION. The formation of a membranous sac, called a bursa, over the head of the bone at the base of the great toe. This bursa may become inflamed and even suppurate, causing much pain and discomfort. A bony outgrowth is usually found under the bursa, and this, along with the displacement of the toe with which a bunion is so often associated, increases the deformity of the foot.

BU'NIUM. *See* EARTH-NUT.

BUNK. A wooden box or case serving as a seat during the day and a bed at night; also one of a series of sleeping-berths arranged above each other.

Bungalow in Malaya

BUNKER HILL. A small eminence in Charlestown, now a portion of Boston, Massachusetts; scene of the first important battle in the revolutionary war, fought 17th June, 1775. A considerable body of Americans having been sent to occupy the peninsula on which Charlestown stands, a British force was sent to dislodge them. This was not effected till after three assaults on their entrenched position, with a loss of 1000 men, while the Americans did not lose half that number.

BUNKUM. *See* BUNCOMBE.

BUNSEN (bun'sen), **Christian Karl Josias, Chevalier.** A distinguished German diplomatist and scholar, born at Korbach, in the principality of Waldeck, 1791, died 1860. In 1815 he made the acquaintance of Niebuhr, who shortly after procured for him the post of secretary to the Prussian embassy at Rome. In 1824 he was appointed Chargé d'Affaires, and afterwards minister. After a stay of twelve years in Rome he was sent, as Prussian minister, first to Switzerland, and then to England, where he remained till the breaking out of the Eastern difficulty in 1854. In his official capacity he won the esteem of all, and with Britain especially he was connected by many ties. His later years were spent at Heidelberg and at Bonn exclusively in literary pursuits.

Among his best-known works are : *Die Verfassung der Kirche der Zukunft* (The Constitution of the Church of the Future), Hamburg, 1845 ; *Aegyptens Stelle in der Weltgeschichte* (Egypt's Place in the World's History), Hamburg, 1845 ; *Hippolytus und seine Zeit* (Hippolytus and his Time), London, 1851 ; and lastly, his greatest work, *Bibelwerk für die Gemeinde* (Bible Commentary for the Community), the publication of which was unfinished at his death. His *Memoirs*, by his widow, were published in 1868.

BUNSEN, Robert Wilhelm Eberard. Eminent German chemist, born at Göttingen 1811. He studied at Göttingen University, and at Paris, Berlin, and Vienna ; was appointed professor at the Polytechnic Institute of Cassel, 1836 ; at the University of Marburg in 1838, at Breslau in 1851, and finally professor of experimental chemistry at Heidelberg in 1852. Among his many discoveries and inventions are the production of magnesium in quantities, magnesium light, spectrum analysis, the Bunsen burner, etc. He died in 1899.

BUNSEN BATTERY. A form of galvanic battery, the cells of which consist of cleft cylinders of zinc immersed in dilute sulphuric acid, and rectangular prisms of carbon

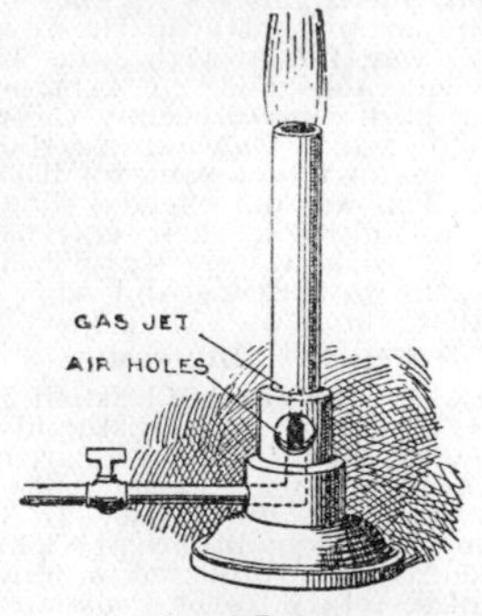

Bunsen Burner

in nitric acid, with an intervening porous cell of unglazed earthenware.

BUNSEN BURNER. A form of gasburner especially adapted for heating, consisting of a tube, in which, by means of holes in the side, the gas becomes mixed with air before ignition, so that it gives a non-luminous smokeless flame of high temperature.

BUNT. Sometimes called *Pepper Brand*, or *Stinking Smut*, a fungoid disease incidental to cultivated corn, consisting of a black powdery matter, having a disagreeable odour, occupying the interior of the grain of wheat

John Bunyan

and a few other Gramineæ. This powdery matter consists of innumerable minute chlamydospores belonging to one of the smut-fungi (Ustilagineæ of the genus Tilletia), caused by the attack of *Tilletia caries*, a kind of mould. The disease may be prevented by pickling the seed-corn before sowing it with diluted copper sulphate or formalin, or immersing for five minutes in hot water (127° to 133° F.). *See* FUNGI.

BUNTER. In geology, a name for the lower series of the Triassic system, generalised from the German term *Bunter Sandstein*. It is a brightly-coloured variegated sandstone prevalent in the lower part of the beds laid down in fresh water or on an arid continental surface. Hence the corresponding sandstones and pebble-beds of the " New Red Sandstone " (Triassic) system in the British Isles are commonly styled the Bunter Beds. In France it is known as the *grès bigarré*.

BUNT'ING. The popular name of a number of insessorial birds, family Emberizidæ, chiefly included in the genus Emberiza ; such as the English or common bunting ; the rice-bunting ; the Lapland, snow, black-headed, yellow, cirl, and ortolan buntings. The yellow-bunting or yellow-hammer (*E. citrinella*) is one of the most common British birds. The common or corn-bunting (*E. miliaria*) is also common in cultivated districts. The snow-bunting (*Plectrophenax nivālis*) is one of the few birds which inhabit the solitudes of the polar regions.

BUNT'ING. A thin woollen stuff, of which the colours and signals of a ship are usually made; hence, a vessel's flags collectively.

Conical-buoy

BUNYA-BUNYA. The native Australian name of the *Araucaria Bidwillii*, a fine Queensland tree with cones larger than a man's head, containing seeds that are eagerly eaten by the blacks.

BUN'YAN, John. Author of the *Pilgrim's Progress*, the son of a tinker, and born at the village of Elstow, near Bedford, in 1628, died in London, 1688. He followed his father's employment, but during the Civil War he served as a soldier. Returning to Elstow, after much mental conflict his mind became impressed with a deep sense of the truth and importance of religion. He joined a society of Anabaptists at Bedford, and at length undertook the office of a public teacher among them.

Can buoy

Acting in defiance of the severe laws against dissenters, Bunyan was detained in prison for twelve years (1660-72), but was at last liberated, and became pastor of the community with which he had previously been connected. During his imprisonment he wrote *Profitable Meditations*, *The Holy City*, etc., and also the curious piece of autobiography entitled *Grace Abounding to the Chief of Sinners*.

In 1675 he was sent to prison for six months under the Conventicle Act. To this confinement he owes his chief literary fame, for in the solitude of his cell he produced the first part of that admired religious allegory the *Pilgrim's Progress*. In 1909 the Religious Tract Society announced that versions of this book had been published in 112 different languages and dialects. His *Holy War*, his other religious parables, and his devotional tracts, which are numerous, are also remarkable, and many of them valuable.

On obtaining his liberty Bunyan resumed his functions as a minister at Bedford, and became extremely popular. He died when on a visit to London.—BIBLIOGRAPHY: Rev. J. Brown, *John Bunyan: His Life, Times, and Work*; J. A. Froude, *John Bunyan* (in English Men of Letters); W. H. White, *Life of John Bunyan*.

Cage-buoy with light

BUNZLAU (bunts'lou). A town, Prussia, province of Silesia, 28 miles W. of Liegnitz. Industries: woollen and linen, pottery. Pop. 14,700.—*Jung-Bunzlau* is a town of Czechoslovakia, 31 miles N.E. of Prague, with 16,000 inhabitants.

BUONAPARTE. *See* BONAPARTE.

Spherical-buoy with Staff and Globe

BUONAROTTI (bu-o-nȧ-rot'tē), **Michael Angelo.** *See* MICHAEL ANGELO.

BUOY (boi). Any floating body employed to point out the particular situation of a ship's anchor, a shoal, the direction of a navigable channel, etc. They are made of wood, or now more commonly of wrought-iron plates riveted together and forming hollow chambers. They are generally moored by chains to the bed of the channel, etc. They are of various shapes, and receive corresponding names; thus there are the *can*-buoy, the *nun*-buoy, the *bell*-buoy, the *mooring*-buoy. *Gas*-buoys are filled with compressed gas and fitted with a suitable burner, and the gas being lighted burns continuously, thus giving guidance at night.

BU'PHAGA. *See* BEEF-EATERS.

BUPRES'TIDÆ. A family of beetles, distinguished by the uncommon brilliancy and highly-metallic splendour of their colours.

BUR, or **BURR.** A term applied to fruits provided with hooks for dispersal by fur-bearing animals. *See* BURDOCK; GEUM; ENCHANTER'S NIGHTSHADE; etc.

BUR'BAGE, Richard. Famous actor and contemporary of Shakespeare, the son of James Burbage (died 1597), also an actor, and the first builder of a theatre in England. He was born about 1567, died 1619. He was a member of the same company as Shakespeare, Fletcher, Hemming, Condell, and others, and filled all the greatest parts of the contemporary stage in turn. He was the original Hamlet, Lear, Othello, and Richard III., and played the leading parts in the plays of Beaumont and Fletcher, Ben Jonson, Webster, Marston, etc. Besides being an eminent actor, he seems to have been also a successful painter in oil-colours.

BUR'BOT, or **BURBOLT.** A fish of the cod family, genus Lota (*L. vulgaris*), shaped somewhat like an eel, but shorter, with a flat head. It has two small barbs on the nose and another on the chin. It is called also *Eel-pout* or *Coney-fish,* and is found in several of the English rivers and lakes of the northern counties; but it is said to arrive at its greatest perfection in the Lake of Geneva. It is delicate food.

BURCKHARDT (bu̧rk'hàrt), **Johann Ludwig.** A celebrated traveller, born at Lausanne in 1784, died at Cairo 1817. He came to England in 1806, and undertook a journey of exploration to the interior of Africa for the African Association. He started in 1809, assuming an Oriental name and costume; spent some time in Syria, thence visited Egypt and Nubia; spent several months at Mecca, and visited Medina; and, after a short stay in Egypt, died at Cairo while preparing for his African journey.

His works are: *Travels in Nubia* (1819), *Travels in Syria and the Holy Land* (1822), *Travels in Arabia* (1829), *Notes on the Bedouins and Wahabys* (1830), and *Arabic Proverbs* (1831).

BUR'DEKIN. A river of the N.E. of Queensland, with a course of about 350 miles. With its affluents it waters a large extent of country, but it is useless for navigation.

BUR'DETT, Sir Francis. English politician, born 1770, died 1844. In 1796 he entered Parliament as member for Boroughbridge, and advocated parliamentary reform and various Liberal measures. He afterwards sat for Middlesex and from 1807 to 1837 for Westminster. In 1810 he was convicted of breach of privilege, and after a struggle between the police and the populace, in which some lives were lost, he was imprisoned in the Tower. In 1819 he was again imprisoned, and fined £2000 for a libel. In his later years he became a Tory, and represented North Wilts. In 1793 he married the youngest daughter of Thomas Coutts, the banker.

BURDETT-COUTTS (köts), **Angela Georgina.** Daughter of the above, born 1814; became deservedly popular for the liberal use she made in public and private charities of the wealth that came to her from her grandfather (Thomas Coutts). In 1871 she was created a baroness, and in 1881 married W. L. Ashmead-Bartlett, who assumed her surname. She died in Dec., 1906.

BUR'DOCK. The popular name of the composite plant *Arctium Lappa,* a coarse-looking weed with globose flower-heads, each of the scales of the involucre being furnished with a hook. Though a weed in Britain, the plant is cultivated as a vegetable in Japan.

BURDWAN'. *See* BARDWAN.

BUREAU (bū-rō'). A writing-table; also the chamber of an officer of Government and the body of subordinate officers who labour under the direction of a chief.

BUREAUCRACY. A term often applied to those Governments in which the business of administration is carried on in departments, each under the control of a chief; or more broadly, the system of centralising the administration of a country through regularly-graded series of Government officials. Bureaucracy also implies a Government characterised by observance of petty details and an adherence to official tradition and "red tape."

BUREN, Martin van. Eighth President of the United States, born at Kinderhook, N.Y., 5th Dec., 1782. The term of his presidency was 1837-41. He died 24th July, 1862.

BURETTE (bū-ret′). A graduated glass tube occasionally used for dividing a given portion of any liquid into small quantities of a definite amount.

BURG. A town, Prussia, province of Saxony, 12 miles N.E. of Magdeburg. It has cloth manufactures, spinning-mills, iron-foundries, etc. Pop. 24,074.

BUR′GAGE TENURE. In England, a tenure in socage, whereby burgesses, citizens, or townsmen hold their lands or tenements of the king or other lord for a certain yearly rent. In Scotland the term indicates that tenure by which the property in royal burghs is held under the Crown, proprietors being liable to the (nominal) service of watching and warding, or, as it is commonly termed, "service of burgh, used and wont."

BURGAS (bur′gäs), or **BOURGAS.** A Bulgarian seaport on the Black Sea, in Southern Bulgaria. Pop. (1926), 31,363.

BURGDORF, or **BERTHOUD.** A Swiss town, canton of Bern, on the Emmen, a railway centre, with manufactures of textiles, etc., and a trade in cheese. There is an old castle here in which Pestalozzi held his famous school for six years (1798-1804). Pop. 9381.

BURGEE. Small penant used by yachts and pointed or swallow-tailed, according to the owner's status. Club flags are always pointed; those of a commodore or vice-commodore are swallow-tailed. Only the Royal Yacht Squadron may fly the white ensign, but other royal clubs may bear a crown on the burgee.

BURGENLAND. A German-speaking district detached from Hungary and given to Austria in 1921-2. Area, 1552 sq. miles; pop. 286,299. Oedenburg remained Hungarian.

BÜRGER (bür′gėr), **Gottfried August.** A celebrated German poet, born 1st Jan., 1748. He studied at Halle and Göttingen; and his attention being drawn towards literature, especially the ballad literature of England and Scotland, he was inspired with the idea of winning a reputation in this department where Uhland and Schiller had already preceded him. In 1773 appeared his *Lenore*, which took the German public by storm, and his poems have continued to be very popular with his countrymen. Scott translated his *William and Helen* and *The Wild Huntsman*. Though he wrote odes, elegies, etc., he was more at home in ballads and simple songs than in higher poetry. His life was not a successful or a happy one. He died 8th June, 1794.

BURGESS. Form of burgher, one who lives in a borough. It is sometimes used for the men sent to Parliament by the boroughs and universities, although its early meaning was for the voters. In some of the American colonies, e.g. Virginia, the elected representatives were known as the House of Burgesses, and the term is still in use.

BURGH (bur′ė). The Scottish term corresponding to the English "borough," and applied to several different kinds of town corporations. A *royal burgh* is a corporate body erected by a charter from the Crown. The corporation consists of the magistrates and burgesses of the territory erected into the burgh. The magistrates are generally a provost and bailies, dean of guild, treasurer, and common council.

With regard to the method of electing councils, the old constitutions of the burghs exhibited an almost endless variety in their details, but all of them agreed in the essential principle of the "close system," by which the old councils had the privilege of electing their successors. An Act in the reign of William IV. abolished this system and substituted for it a popular mode of election, and now the municipal and parliamentary franchise have been assimilated. The royal burghs now number sixty-six, most of them singly or in groups electing parliamentary representatives, though others have lost this privilege.

Burghs of Barony. Corporations analogous to royal burghs, the magistrates of which are elected either by the superior of the barony, or by the inhabitants themselves, according to the terms of the charter of erection.

Burghs of Regality. Kind of burghs of barony which had regal or exclusive jurisdiction within their own territory till the abolition of hereditary jurisdictions.

Parliamentary Burghs. Such as, not being royal burghs, send representatives to Parliament. There are fifteen of these, namely, Airdrie, Coatbridge, Cromarty, Falkirk, Galashiels, Greenock, Hamilton, Hawick, Kilmarnock, Leith, Musselburgh, Oban, Paisley, Peterhead, and Port-Glasgow. The mode of election of councillors and magistrates of parliamentary burghs is the same as in royal burghs.

Police Burghs. Populous places, the boundaries of which are settled in terms of the Police Act of 1862, and the affairs of which are managed by commissioners elected under the Act by the inhabitants. *See* BOROUGH.

BURGH ACRES. Small patches of land lying in the neighbourhood of royal burghs in Scotland, usually feued out to and occupied by persons resident within the burgh.

BURGHERS (bur'gėrz). A body of Presbyterians in Scotland, constituting the majority of the early Secession Church, which was split into two in 1747 on the lawfulness of accepting the oath then required to be taken by the burgesses in certain burghs. The Burghers accepted the oath, while the Antiburghers did not deem it lawful. *See* UNITED PRESBYTERIAN CHURCH.

BURGHLEY, or BURLEIGH. *See* CECIL.

BURGKMAIR (burk'mīr). A family of German artists in the fifteenth and sixteenth centuries, the best known of whom is Hans, born at Augsburg in 1473. Several of his paintings are to be seen at Augsburg, Munich, Nürnberg, etc., but these have contributed far less to his fame than his woodcuts, which are not inferior to those of his friend Albert Dürer. The most celebrated is the series of 135 cuts representing the triumphs of the Emperor Maximilian. He died in 1531.

BURG'LARY (derived from the Fr. *bourg*, a town, and O.Fr. *laire*, Lat. *latro*, a thief). Defined in English law to be a breaking and entering the dwelling-house of another, in the night, with intent to commit some felony within the same, whether such felonious intent be executed or not. Both breaking and entering are considered necessary to constitute the offence. The opening a door or window, picking a lock, etc., constitutes a *breaking*. Likewise, knocking at the door, and, on its being opened, rushing in, has been so considered. So, if a lodger in the same house open and enter another's room. The breaking and entering must, however, be in the night to make it burglary, and the duration of night is from 9 o'clock p.m. to 6 o'clock a.m. Burglary is made punishable by penal servitude for life, or for any period not less than three years, or by imprisonment. Similar laws are prevalent in the United States and elsewhere. *See* FELONY; HOUSE-BREAKING.

BÜRGLEN (bür'glen). A village in the canton of Uri, Switzerland, celebrated as the birth-place of William Tell.

BUR'GOMASTER. The chief magistrate of a municipal town in Holland, Belgium, and Germany. The title is equivalent to the English *mayor* and the Scottish *provost*.

BURGON, John William. English divine, born in 1813, educated at private schools and classes connected with London University; was for some ten years in his father's counting-house, and then went to Oxford University, where he graduated in 1845, winning the Newdigate prize and also obtaining other honours, as well as a fellowship of Oriel (1846). Having entered the Church, he held several curacies in succession, and in 1863 was presented to the vicarage of St. Mary's, Oxford. This charge he held till his appointment to the deanery of Chichester (1875), where he died in 1888. He was a strong opponent of the revised version of the New Testament, and in general was a "champion of lost causes and impossible beliefs." Among his writings, besides sermons, are: *Oxford Reformers, The Revision Revised, The Traditional Text of the Holy Gospels Vindicated, Causes of the Corruption of the Traditional Text,* and *Lives of Twelve Good Men* (a popular compilation).

BURGOS (bur'gos). A city of Northern Spain, once the capital of the kingdom of Old Castile, and now the chief town of the province of Burgos. It stands on the declivity of a hill on the right bank of the Arlanzon, and has dark narrow streets full of ancient architecture, but there are also fine modern promenades. The cathedral, commenced in 1221, is one of the finest examples of Gothic architecture in Spain. It contains the tombs of the famous Cid, and of Don Fernando, both natives of Burgos, and celebrated throughout Spain for their heroic achievements in the wars with the Moors. Before the removal of the Court to Madrid, in the sixteenth century, Burgos was in a very flourishing condition, and contained thrice its present population. It has some manufactures in woollens and linens. Pop. 32,755.—The province has an area of 5480 sq. miles, largely hilly or mountainous, but with good agricultural and pastoral land. Pop. 341,197.

BURGOYNE (bur-goin'), **John.** An English general officer and dramatist, born 1722, died 1792. After serving in various parts of the world, he was in 1777 appointed commander of an army against the revolted Americans, and took Ticonderoga, but had at last to surrender with his whole army at Saratoga to a greatly superior American force. He was ill received on his return to England, and deprived of his command of the 76th Light Dragoons and the governorship of Fort William, but Fox and Sheridan took his part and received his parliamentary support. Burgoyne wrote several comedies, including *The Maid of the Oaks*, produced by Garrick in 1775, and *The Heiress*, a play that held the stage for over a century.

BURGOYNE, Sir John Fox. Son of the above, an eminent officer of engineers, born 1782. Entering the Royal Engineers, he served in Malta, Sicily, Egypt, and, with Sir John Moore and Wellington, in the Peninsula from 1809 to 1814, and was present at all the sieges generally as first or second in command of the engineers. In 1851 he was made a lieutenant-general, and was principal engineer adviser to Lord Raglan at Sebastopol till recalled in 1855. In the following year he was created a baronet, and in 1868 a field-marshal. He died 7th Oct., 1871.

BURGUNDY. A region of Western Europe, so named from the Burgundians, a Teutonic or Germanic people originally from the country between the Oder and the Vistula. They migrated first to the region of the Upper Rhine, and in the beginning of the fifth century passed into Gaul and obtained possession of the south-eastern part of this country, where they founded a kingdom having its seat of government sometimes at Lyons and sometimes at Geneva. They were at last wholly subdued by the Franks.

In 879 Boson, Count of Autun, succeeded in establishing the royal dignity again in part of this kingdom. He styled himself King of Provence, and had his residence at Arles. His son Louis added the country beyond the Jura, and thus established *Cis-Juran Burgundy*. A second kingdom arose when Rudolph of Strettlingen formed *Upper or Trans-Juran Burgundy* out of part of Switzerland and Savoy. Both those Burgundian kingdoms were afterwards united, and finally, on the extinction of Rudolph's line, were incorporated with Germany.

But a third State, the historical *Duchy of Burgundy*, consisting principally of the French province of Bourgogne or Burgundy—the region with which the name is most familiarly associated—had been formed as a great feudal and almost independent province of France in the ninth century. This first ducal line died out with a Duke Philip, in 1361, and the duchy, reverting to the Crown, was, in 1363, granted by King John of France to his son Philip the Bold, who thus became the founder of a new line of Dukes of Burgundy. A marriage with Margaret, daughter of Louis III., Count of Flanders, brought him Flanders, Mechlin, Antwerp, and Franche-Comté. He was succeeded by his son Duke John the Fearless, whose son and successor, Philip the Good, so greatly extended his dominions that on his death in 1467 his son Charles, surnamed the Bold, though possessing only the title of duke, was in reality one of the richest and most powerful sovereigns of Europe. *See* CHARLES THE BOLD.

Charles left a daughter, Mary of Burgundy, the sole heiress of his States, who by her marriage to Maximilian of Austria transferred a large part of her dominions to that prince, while Louis XI. of France acquired Burgundy proper as a male fief of France. Burgundy then formed a province, and is now represented by the four departments of Yonne, Côte-d'Or, Saône-et-Loire, and Ain. It is watered by a number of navigable rivers, and is one of the most productive provinces in France, especially of wines.—BIBLIOGRAPHY: E. Petit de Vausse, *Histoire des ducs de Bourgogne de la race Capétienne*; Percy Allen, *Burgundy, the Splendid Duchy*.

BURGUNDY PITCH. A resin got from the Norway spruce (*Picea excelsa*) and several other pines. It is used in medicine as a stimulating plaster. It takes its name from Burgundy in France, where it was first prepared.

BURHAMPUR. *See* BERHAMPUR.

BURHÁNPUR. A town of India, Central Provinces, formerly the capital of Kandeish, and famous for its muslin and flowered-silk manufactures, which still exist to some extent though the town has long been declining. Pop. 22,777.

BURIAL (be'ri-al). The mode of disposing of the dead, a practice which varies amongst different peoples. Amongst savage races, and even amongst some cultured peoples of the East, exposure to wild animals or birds of prey is not uncommon. The careful embalmment of their dead by the ancient Egyptians may be regarded as a special form of burial. The Jews and most of the nations of antiquity buried their dead. Amongst the Greeks and Romans both cremation and interment were practised, though amongst the latter burning became common only in the later times of the republic. In this form of burial the corpse, after being borne in procession through the streets, was placed upon a pyre built of wood, and profusely sprinkled with oils and perfumes. Fire was set to the wood, and after the process of cremation was complete the bones and ashes were carefully gathered together by the relatives and placed in an urn.

With the introduction of the Christian religion, consecrated places were appropriated for the purpose of general burial, and the Roman custom of providing the sepulchre with a stone and inscription was continued by the Christians. The practice of cremation then declined and finally disappeared, but has recently to no small extent been revived. In England every person has a right to be buried in the churchyard of the parish where he dies, and such burial may take place either with the service of any Christian Church or without any service. It is the duty of the incumbent of a parish to perform funeral services for the parishioners, but not if cremated. Cf. W. H. F. Basevi, *The Burial of the Dead.*

Burial, Law regarding. Among points of law relating to burials and burial-grounds the following may be mentioned. While parishioners have a right to be buried in the churchyard of their parish, the particular locality is at the discretion of the incumbent and churchwardens. It is the duty of a person's executors to see that his body is buried in a suitable manner; or the body may be cremated, this being quite lawful. The expense of the burial of a pauper falls upon the parish to which he was chargeable, but by the common law the person liable to bury a dead body is the householder in whose premises it lies. The popular notion that a corpse may be arrested for debt is erroneous.

In regard to burying-places or cemeteries various Acts have been passed, the main objects of which have been to provide for the closing of crowded burying-grounds, to establish burying-boards, and to confer on the central authority larger powers of control over burial-places. Burial-boards were first established for London in 1852, and soon after an Act was passed for extending them to the country generally. They may now be appointed by parish or urban councils for individual parishes or districts; or several parishes may unite to form a joint burial-board. It is the duty of such a board to provide a cemetery for their own special area, and this may be either within or without the area. The cemetery is to be divided into a consecrated and an unconsecrated portion, the former for burials according to the rites of the Church of England. The expenses form a charge upon the poor-rates, but the board is empowered to charge fees.

In 1879 general powers for providing cemeteries were conferred on all sanitary authorities, rural and urban, and the Local Government Board may compel them to provide a cemetery where necessary, the land to be obtained compulsorily if not otherwise obtainable. The Local Government Board has an extensive supervision and jurisdiction in regard to burials. It may order burials to cease wholly or partially in any existing burial-ground, and may prohibit the opening of a new burial-ground, if deemed in an unsuitable locality. Many cemeteries are now owned by private persons or companies. A special Act regulating cremation was passed in 1900, by which burial authorities may now provide crematories for public use.

BU'RIATS. A nomadic Tartar people, a branch of the Eastern Mongols, inhabiting the southern part of the government of Irkutsk and Transbaikalia. Their number is about 250,000. Their language is a Mongolian dialect, distinct from the Kalmuck. With regard to religion the Buriats are either Buddhists or Shamanists. They live in huts called *yurts*, which in summer are covered with leather, in winter with felt. They support themselves by their flocks, by hunting, and the mechanical arts, particularly the forging of iron.

BURIDAN (bü-rē-däṇ), **Jean.** A French scholastic philosopher of the fourteenth century, born at Béthune in Artois towards the end of the thirteenth century. He was a disciple of Occam at Paris, and has attained a kind of fame from an illustration he is said to have used in favour of his theory of determinism (that is, the doctrine that every act of volition is determined by some motive external to the will itself), and which still goes under the name of "Buridan's ass." He is said to have supposed the case of a hungry ass placed at an equal distance from two equally-attractive bundles of hay, and to have asserted that in the supposed case the ass must inevitably have perished from hunger, there being nothing to determine him to prefer the one bundle to the other. The nature of the illustration, however, makes it more likely that it was invented by Buridan's opponents to ridicule his views than by himself. Buridan died after 1385 at the age of sixty.

BU'RIN, or GRAVER. An instrument of tempered steel, used for engraving on copper, steel, etc. It is of a prismatic form, having one end attached to a short wooden handle, and the other ground off obliquely, so as to produce a sharp triangular point. In working, the burin is held in the palm of the hand, and pushed forward so as to cut a portion of the metal.

BURITI (bụ-rē'tē). A South American palm (*Mauritia vinifĕra*) growing to the height of 100-150 feet, preferring marshy situations, and bearing an imposing crown of fan-shaped leaves. A sweet vinous liquor is prepared from the juice of the stem, as also from the fruits.

BURKE, Edmund. A writer, orator, and statesman of great eminence, born in Dublin, 12th Jan., 1729. After studying at Trinity College, Dublin, where he took a bachelor's degree, he went to London in 1750, and became a law student at the Temple. He applied himself more to literature than to law, and in 1756 published his *Essay on the Sublime and the Beautiful*, which attracted considerable attention, and procured him the friendship of some of the most notable men of the time.

The political career for which he had been arduously preparing himself all along at length opened up to him on his appointment as private secretary to W. G. Hamilton, Secretary for Ireland, in 1761. On his return he was

Burke

rewarded with a pension of £300 per annum, and obtained the appointment of private secretary to the Marquess of Rockingham, then First Lord of the Treasury. Through the same interest he entered Parliament as member for Wendover (1765). The great question of the right of taxing the American colonies was then occupying Parliament, and the Rockingham ministry, having taken, mainly through Burke's advice, a middle and undecided course, was soon dissolved (1766).

From 1770 to 1782 Lord North was in power, and Burke held no office. From 1774-80 he was member for Bristol. In several magnificent speeches he criticised the ministerial measures with regard to the colonies, and advocated a policy of justice and conciliation. In 1782, when the Rockingham party returned to power, Burke obtained the lucrative post of Paymaster-General of the Forces, and shortly after introduced his famous Bill for economical reform, which passed after considerable amendments had been made to it. On the fall of the Duke of Portland's Coalition ministry, 1783, of which Burke had also been part, Pitt again succeeded to power, and it was during this administration that the impeachment of Hastings, in which Burke was the prime mover, took place. The lucidity, eloquence, and mastery of detail which Burke showed on this occasion have never been surpassed.

The chief feature in the latter part of Burke's life was his resolute struggle against the ideas and doctrines of the French revolution. His attitude on this question separated him from his old friend Fox, and the Liberals who followed Fox. His famous *Reflections on the Revolution in France*, a pamphlet which appeared in 1790, had an unprecedented sale, and gave enormous impetus to the reaction which had commenced in England. From this time most of his writings are powerful pleadings on the same side. We may mention *An Appeal from the New to the Old Whigs*, *Letter to a Noble Lord*, *Letters on a Regicide Peace*, etc. In 1794 he withdrew from Parliament. Three years after, on 8th July, 1797, he died, his end being hastened by grief for the loss of his only son.—BIBLIOGRAPHY: Sir James Prior, *Memoir of the Life and Character of Edmund Burke*; T. MacKnight, *History of the Life and Times of Burke*; Viscount Morley, *Edmund Burke* (in English Men of Letters Series); John MacCunn, *The Political Philosophy of Burke*.

BURKE, Robert O'Hara. An Australian explorer, born in County Galway, Ireland, in 1820, died in Australia 1861. After serving in the Austrian army he went to Australia, and after seven years' service as inspector of police was appointed commander of an expedition to cross the continent of Australia from south to north. He and his associate Wills reached the tidal waters of the Flinders River, but both perished of starvation on the return journey.

BURKE, Sir John Bernard. British scholar, born in London, 5th Jan., 1814, his father, John Burke (1787-1848) was the founder of the *Peerage and Baronetage* and the *Landed Gentry* which still bears the family name. The son took over the work of editing these volumes in 1847 and did other work of a similar kind. In 1853 he was made Ulster king-at-arms and in 1854 he was knighted. He died 12th Dec., 1892.

BURKING. A species of murder by suffocation, which derives its name from William Burke, a native of Ireland, who, in 1828-9, was detected, tried, and executed at Edinburgh, for the murder of numerous individuals. The vigilance with which the burying-grounds throughout the country were watched rendered a supply of subjects for anatomical schools almost altogether impracticable, and the demand for dead bodies consequently became great. This led the above-mentioned individual, in conjunction with another wretch named Hare, to decoy into their lodging-house and murder by strangulation many obscure wayfarers, whose bodies they sold to a school of anatomy at prices averaging from £8 to £14.

BURLAP. *See* HESSIAN.

BURLEIGH, Bennet. British war correspondent, born at Glasgow in 1844, died 1914. He took part in the American Civil War, fighting on the Confederate side, and was twice sentenced to be shot. He was *Central News* correspondent during the bombardment of Alexandria, and in 1892 joined the staff of the *Daily Telegraph*, for which paper he acted as correspondent in Egypt, Madagascar, South Africa, Morocco, Manchuria, Tripoli, and the Balkans. He wrote *The Empire of the East.*

BURLEIGH, Lord. *See* CECIL.

BURLESQUE (bur-lesk′). Signifies a low form of the comic, arising generally from a ludicrous mixture of things high and low. High thoughts, for instance, are clothed in low expressions, noble subjects described in a familiar manner, or vice versa. The true comic shows us an instructive, if laughable, side of things; the burlesque travesties and caricatures them in order to excite laughter or ridicule. H. J. Byron and W. S. Gilbert wrote many burlesques for the stage. Thackeray's burlesques are unsurpassed, especially *The Rose and the Ring*, and *Novels by eminent hands. See* PARODY; CARICATURE.

BURLET′TA. A light, comic species of musical drama, which derives its name from the Italian *burlare*, to jest. It originated in Italy, from whence it passed to the Transalpine countries.

BURLEY-IN-WHARFEDALE. A town of England, W. Riding of Yorkshire, on the Wharfe, 8 miles north of Bradford, a seat of the woollen manufacture. Pop. (1931), 3960.

BURLINGTON. A town in England. *See* BRIDLINGTON.

BURLINGTON. The name of several towns in the United States.—1. A city in Vermont, on Lake Champlain, the chief commercial centre of the State, with a considerable trade in timber; woollen, cotton, and flour mills, etc. The University of Vermont (founded in 1791) is here. Pop. 22,779. 2. A city in Iowa, on the Mississippi, with a Baptist college, and manufactures of agricultural implements, etc. Pop. 24,057. 3. A city of New Jersey, on the Delaware, 7 miles above Philadelphia. Pop. 8336.

BURLINGTON HOUSE. Public building in Piccadilly, London. It is the headquarters of several learned societies and here each year the Royal Academy holds its annual exhibition of pictures. It consists of Old Burlington House, built by the Earl of Burlington and bought by the State in 1854 and New Burlington House built after that date. The societies here include the Royal Society, the British Academy, the British Association, the Chemical Society and others.

The title of **Earl of Burlington** is borne by the Duke of Devonshire. It was given to a member of the Cavendish family in 1831 and in 1858 William, the 2nd earl, succeeded his cousin as 7th Duke of Devonshire.

BURMA. A country of South-Eastern Asia, bounded on the north by Assam and Tibet, on the east by Chinese territory and Siam, elsewhere mainly by the Bay of Bengal; area nearly 233,710 sq. miles. It is traversed by great mountain ranges branching off from those of Northern India and running parallel to each other southwards to the sea. Between these ranges and in the plains or valleys here situated the four great rivers of Burma—the Irrawaddy, its tributary the Chindwin, the Sittang, and the Salween—flow in a southerly direction to the sea, watering the rich alluvial tracts of Lower Burma, and having at their mouths all the great seaports of the country—Rangoon, Bassein, Moulmein, Akyab, etc. The Irrawaddy is of great value as a highway of communication and traffic, being navigable beyond Bhamo, near the Chinese frontier, or over 800 miles. In their lower courses the rivers overflow their banks in the rainy season.

Products. Though its resources are almost entirely undeveloped, the country, as a whole, is productive, especially in the lower portions. Here grow rice, sugar-cane, tobacco, cotton, indigo, etc. Cotton is grown almost everywhere; tea is cultivated in many of the more elevated parts. The forests produce timber of many sorts, including teak, which grows most luxuriantly, and is largely exported. Ironwood is another valuable timber; and among forest products are also the bamboo, cutch, stick-lac, and rubber.

Minerals. Burma has great mineral wealth—gold, silver, precious stones, iron, marble, lead, tin, coal, petroleum, wolfram, etc.; but these resources have not yet been much developed. The chief precious stone is the ruby, and the mines of this gem belong to the Crown. Sapphire, amber, and jade are also obtained.

Animals. Among wild animals are the elephant, rhinoceros, tiger, leopard, deer of various kinds, and the wild hog. Among domestic animals are the ox, buffalo, horse, and elephant. The rivers abound with fish.

Fruits. The most common fruits are the guava, custard-apple, tamarind, pine, orange, banana, jack, and mango. The yam and sweet-potato are cultivated, and in some parts the common potato.

Climate. The climate as a whole is warm, though not unhealthy, except in low jungly districts. The rainfall among the mountains is as much as 190 inches per annum.

People. The natives all belong to the Mongolian type of mankind, but are made up of a great variety of races besides the Burmese proper, as Talaings, Shans, Karens, etc. The Burmese proper are of a brown colour, with lank black hair (seldom any on the face), and have active, vigorous, well-proportioned frames. They are a cheerful, lively people, fond of amusement, averse to continuous exertion, free from prejudice of caste or creed, temperate and hardy. The predominant religion is Buddhism. Missionaries are active in their efforts, but the Christian faith has not yet made much progress in the country. Polygamy is permitted by Buddhist law, but is rare, and is considered as not altogether respectable. Divorce is easily obtained. Women in Burma occupy a much freer and happier position than they do in Indian social life. They go about freely, manage the household, and make successful women of business, conducting not merely retail trades but also large wholesale concerns.

Education is very general, one of the chief occupations of the monks in the numerous monasteries being the teaching of boys to read and write. Many of these monastic schools are under Government inspection. The province has about 7000 public and over 17,000 private institutions, with 412,000 and 205,000 scholars respectively.

The Burmese are skilful weavers, smiths, sculptors, workers in gold and silver, joiners, etc. The ordinary buildings are of a very slight construction, chiefly of timber or bamboo raised on posts; but the religious edifices are in many cases imposing, though the material is but brick. Carving and gilding are features of their architecture. The Burmese language is monosyllabic, like Chinese, and is written with an alphabet the characters of which (derived from India) are more or less circular. There is a considerable literature.

Lower Burma and Upper Burma. Burma is now divided into *Lower Burma* and *Upper Burma*, the former till 1886 being called British Burma, while the latter till that date was an independent kingdom or empire. Lower Burma (comprising Aracan, Pegu, Irrawaddy, Tenasserim) was acquired from Independent Burma in 1826 and 1852 as the result of two wars terminating in favour of Britain. The country now forms a single province (the largest of the Indian Empire), the official area being 233,710 sq. miles, the population 13,212,192. Under British rule it has prospered greatly, the population and trade having increased immensely. Roads, canals, railways, and other public works have been carried out. Exports and imports together are valued at over £50,000,000 per annum, a large share of the trade being with Britain, to which great quantities of rice and teak are sent, the export of the former amounting to over 2,000,000 tons. The chief city and port is Rangoon (345,505), which is connected by railway with Mandalay (148,917), Moulmein, etc.

Under its native kings the form of government in Upper Burma was absolute monarchy, the seat of government being at Mandalay. The king was assisted in governing by a Council of State known as the *Hloot-daw*, to which belonged the functions of a house of legislature, a cabinet, and a supreme court. The king had power to punish at his pleasure anyone, even the great officers of State. The revenue was derived from taxes levied in a very irregular and capricious manner, and official corruption was rampant. The criminal laws were barbarously severe. Capital punishment was commonly inflicted by decapitation, but crucifixion and disembowelling were also practised. After the loss of the maritime provinces the influence of Independent Burma greatly declined, as did also its Asiatic and foreign trade.

History. The Burmese empire is of little note in ancient or general history. Since the sixteenth century the Burmese proper have mostly been the predominant race, and ruled the Peguans, Karens, etc., throughout the country. The capital has at different times been at Ava, Pegu, Prome, or elsewhere. In the latter half of the eighteenth century the Burmese emperors began a series of wars of conquest with China, Siam, Assam, through which they greatly enlarged the empire. This brought them into contact with the British, and in 1824 war was declared against them on account of their encroachments on British territory and their seizure of British subjects. The war terminated in the cession of the provinces of Aracan and Tenasserim to the British. Peace continued for some years, but various acts of hostility having been committed by the Burmese, the maltreatment of British subjects in 1852 occasioned a second war, at the end of which the British possessions were extended to include the whole of Pegu.

The third and last war occurred in 1885 in consequence of the arrogance and arbitrary conduct of King Theebaw. The result was that Upper Burma was annexed to the British Empire by proclamation of the Viceroy of India, 1st Jan., 1886. The area thus annexed was about 200,000 sq. miles, of which half belonged to the kingdom proper, half to the semi-independent Shan States. Since 1923 the province has been under a governor. There are seven administrative divisions (four in Lower Burma, three in Upper Burma) under Commissioners. The Shan States are governed by their own chiefs through British political officers. Bands of *dacoits* or robbers still cause some trouble in the country, which as a whole, however, is peaceful enough.—BIBLIOGRAPHY: Sir Arthur Phayre, *History of Burma*; J. Nisbet, *Burmah under British Rule—and Before*; J. Dautremer, *Burma under British Rule*.

BURMANNIACEÆ. A small nat. ord. of monocotyledonous herbs, shade-plants of tropical forests, mostly colourless saprophytes; allied to Orchidaceæ.

BUR′NABY, Frederick Gustavus. English soldier and traveller, born 1842, son of the Rev. G. Burnaby. He was educated at Harrow, and entered the Royal Horse Guards in his eighteenth year. In 1875 he made his famous ride to Khiva—a journey that presented great difficulties. In 1876 he rode through Asiatic Turkey and Persia. Of both these journeys he published narratives. In 1885 (17th Jan.), while serving as lieutenant-colonel of the Royal Horse Guards in the Egyptian campaign, he was killed at the battle of Abu-Klea.

BURNAND, Sir Francis Cowley. Editor of *Punch*, born in 1836, died 21st April, 1917. He was educated at Eton and Cambridge, was called to the Bar, but took to literature as a profession, joined the *Punch* staff about 1862, and became editor of the paper in 1880. He wrote a number of plays, mostly of the nature of burlesques and light comedies (his *Black-eyed Susan*, a burlesque of Jerrold's drama of same name, had an extraordinary success), various works of the nature of caricatures or parodies of other works, such as *New Light on Darkest Africa* and *Ride to Khiva*, making fun out of H. M. Stanley and Colonel Burnaby respectively, and *Strapmore*, a sort of travesty of Ouida's novel *Strathmore*. *Happy Thoughts*, first published in *Punch*, is another of his successful books. He was knighted in 1902. In 1904 he published his *Reminiscences*, an entertaining work. Early in 1906 he resigned the editorship of *Punch*.

BURNE-JONES, Sir Edward. English painter, born in 1833, at Birmingham, where and at Exeter College, Oxford, he was educated. He early adopted the profession of artist, and came under the influence of D. G. Rossetti. He painted in water-colour and in oil, and his works are marked by richness of colouring, and by poetical, ideal, and mediæval characteristics. He was created a baronet in 1884, and died in 1898. Among his pictures are: *The Merciful Knight*, *The Beguiling of Merlin*, *The Mirror of Venus*, *King Cophetua and the Beggar-maid*, etc.

BURNES (bèrnz), **Sir Alexander.** Born at Montrose in 1805. Studied at the academy there, and having obtained a cadetship in the Indian army, arrived at Bombay in 1821. His promotion was rapid, and in 1832 he was sent on a mission to Central Asia, and visited Afghanistan, Bokhara, Merv, etc., returning by way of Persia. He was then sent to England, and published his travels, which were well received. In 1839 he was appointed political agent at Cabul. Here, in 1841, he was murdered on the breaking out of an insurrection, as, thirty-eight years later, Sir Louis Cavagnari, with his staff was murdered.

BUR′NET. The popular name of the genus Sanguisorba, nat. ord. Rosaceæ. There are two British species: Lesser Burnet (*S. minor*), which grows to the height of about 2 feet, with smooth alternate imparipinnate leaves, and flowers arranged in rounded heads of a purplish colour. Greater Burnet (*S. officinālis*), also a perennial plant with imparipinnate leaves; flowers red, arranged on oval spikes at the extremity of long peduncles. Both kinds make very wholesome food for cattle. *S. canadensis* is a Canadian species.

BUR'NET, Gilbert. A celebrated prelate and historian, born at Edinburgh in 1643. Having studied at Aberdeen, he travelled into Holland in 1664. He was ordained in 1665, was for some years minister of Saltoun parish, and became professor of divinity at Glasgow in 1669. Here he resided more than four years and wrote several works, one of them his *Vindication of the Church and State of Scotland.* In 1675 he became chaplain to the Rolls Chapel, London.

He was long in great favour at Court, but the Court favour did not continue, for Burnet, dreading the machinations of the Catholic party, joined the opposition, and wrote his *History of the Reformation in England,* the first volume of which appeared in 1679 (the other two in 1681 and 1714 respectively). His connection with the opposition party afterwards became very intimate, and he published several works in favour of liberty and Protestantism. Eventually he was invited to the Hague by the Prince and Princess of Orange, and had a great share in the councils relative to Britain. He accompanied the Prince of Orange to England as chaplain, and was rewarded for his services with the bishopric of Salisbury. As a prelate Bishop Burnet distinguished himself by fervour, assiduity, and charity. He died in March 1715, leaving behind him his well-known *History of his own Times* (2 vols. fol., 1723-34).

BURNETT, Frances Hodgson. Novelist, born in Manchester in 1849. Went with her parents to the United States in 1865, long resided there, being married to Dr. S. M. Burnett in 1873—a union dissolved in 1898—afterwards returned to reside in England, and married there in 1900, her second husband being the late Stephen Townesend (died 1914), surgeon, actor, and author. Her first conspicuous success was with *That Lass o' Lowrie's*, a story of collier life in her native county, which, after coming out in *Scribner's Magazine,* appeared in book form in 1877; but the best known of all her writings is *Little Lord Fauntleroy* (1886), a story of child life, which has had remarkable success both as a book and as a drama. Among other of her stories are: *Haworth's, A Fair Barbarian, His Grace of Ormonde, The Shuttle, The Making of a Marchioness, The Dawn of a To-morrow, T. Tembarom.* She died in 1924.

BUR'NETT, James, Lord Monboddo. Judge of the Court of Session in Scotland, born in 1714 at the family seat of Monboddo, in Kincardineshire. After studying at Aberdeen he went to the University of Groningen, whence he returned in 1738, and commenced practice as an advocate at the Scottish Bar. In 1767 he was made one of the Lords of Session. He distinguished himself by some voluminous and learned works, having published a *Dissertation on the Origin and Progress of Language* (1771-76, 3 vols. 4to), and *Ancient Metaphysics* (1778, etc., 3 vols. 4to). His works contain a strange mixture of paradox and acute observation. He died at Edinburgh, 26th May, 1799.

BURNETT'S DISINFECTING LIQUID. A strong solution of zinc chloride with a little iron chloride. It is an antiseptic and deodorising liquid, largely used for crude disinfection, e.g. sewage, bilge-water, etc.

BURNEY, Charles. An English composer and writer on music, born 1726, died 1814. He studied under Dr. Arne, and soon obtained a reputation for his musical pieces. While organist at Lynn Regis he commenced his *General History of Music* (1776-89). He wrote also several other valuable works. His second daughter, Frances Burney (Madame d'Arblay), published a memoir of her father.

BURNEY, Frances. *See* D'ARBLAY.

BURNHAM. An English watering-place on the Somerset coast, Bridgewater Bay, with a fine sandy beach. Pop. (1931), 5120.

BURNHAM BEECHES. A fine tract of forest land, about 600 acres in area, in Buckinghamshire, near the village of Burnham, and some 3 miles north-west of Slough, belonging to the Corporation of London, and kept up as a public recreation ground. Some of the beeches are very large and old.

BURNHAM - ON - CROUCH. An English seaport in the south-east of Essex, on the north shore of the Crouch, a centre of oyster-culture, herring-fishing, etc. Pop. (1931), 3395.

BURNING-GLASS. A lens which, by bringing the sun's rays rapidly to a focus, produces a heat strong enough to kindle combustible matter. The lenses commonly used are convex on both sides, and have a small focal length. That such a glass may produce its greatest effect it is necessary that the rays of the sun should fall upon it in a perpendicular direction. The effect may be greatly augmented by the use of a second lens, of a smaller focal length, placed between the first and its focus. Some immense burning-glasses have been made, producing surprising effects. Concave *burning-mirrors* produce the same kind of results, and have decidedly greater power than burning-glasses of equal extent and curvature. The concavity must present a surface of high reflecting power (polished silver or other metal, or silvered glass), and is usually spherical or parabolic. Plane mirrors may also be employed like concave ones, if several of them are combined in a proper manner. The ancients were acquainted with such mirrors, and Archimedes is said to have set the Roman fleet on fire at the siege of Syracuse (212 B.C.) by some such means. In 1747 Buffon by a combination of mirrors burned wood at the distance of 200 feet and melted tin at the distance of 150 feet.

BURNISHER. A blunt, smooth tool, used for smoothing and polishing a rough surface by rubbing. Agates, tempered steel, and dogs' teeth are used for burnishing.

BURN′LEY. A parliamentary, municipal, and county borough of England, in Lancashire, about 22 miles N. of Manchester. The town presents a modern appearance, and is well built, mostly of stone. The staple manufacture is cotton goods, and there are large cotton-mills and several extensive foundries and machine-shops, with collieries and other works, in the vicinity. Burnley was made a parliamentary borough with one member in 1867. Pop. (1931), 98,259.

BURNOOSE, or **BURNOUS** (bėr-nös′). A large kind of mantle in use among the Bedouin Arabs and the Berbers of Northern Africa, commonly made of white wool, but sometimes also of red, blue, green, or some other colour, and having a hood which may be drawn over the head in case of rain.

BURNOUF (bůr-nöf), **Eugène.** French scholar, born at Paris in 1801, died 1852. He devoted himself to the study of Oriental languages, particularly those of Persia and India. In 1826 he attracted the attention of men of learning throughout Europe by publishing, in conjunction with his friend Christian Lassen, an *Essai sur le Pâli.* But his fame is chiefly due to his having, so to speak, restored to life an entire language, the Zend or old Persian language in which the Zoroastrian writings were composed. Burnouf also distinguished himself by his labours on Buddhism, publishing *Introduction a l'Histoire du Bouddhisme Indien* (1844).

BURNS, Rt. Hon. John, M.P. English politician, born in London, 20th Oct., 1858. He worked in a candle factory at Battersea and then as an engineer. Soon he became known as a forceful speaker at Socialist and trade union meetings, and in 1885, as a Social Democrat, he stood for Parliament (W. Nottingham). In 1886 he was sent to prison for his share in a riot of the London unemployed. In 1889, the year in which he took a prominent part in the strike of the dock labourers, he was elected to the L.C.C. In 1892 he entered Parliament as M.P. for Battersea. Gradually his opinions became less extreme and in 1905, as President of the Local Government Board, he entered the Liberal Cabinet. In 1914 he was transferred to the Board of Trade, but on the outbreak of the Great War he resigned. He kept his seat in Parliament until 1918.

Robert Burns

BURNS, Robert. Scottish poet. He was born near Ayr on 25th Jan., 1759, and died on 21st July, 1796. His father was William Burness (so he preferred to spell his name), a farmer on a small scale. Burns was employed on the farm at a very early age, and was largely self-educated, but he acquired a considerable amount of learning and a good general acquaintance with English literature.

Of the details of Burns's short and unhappy life too much has perhaps been already said by biographers who were only too willing to thank God that they were not as other men. The name of Burns, which should be revered beyond most names, was used by nineteenth-century moralists to point a moral and adorn a tale. He that is without sin, let him first cast a stone. Wordsworth, who owed a deep debt to Burns, and who was himself one of the most righteous of men, has finely ended his fine poem on Burns with the lines :

The best of what we do and are,
Just God, forgive.

The chief facts of the life of Burns are as follows. His farming ventures with his brothers failed so totally that he thought of leaving Scotland for the West Indies. To defray the cost of his passage he published a collection of his poems in what is known as the Kilmarnock edition (1786). He at once became famous; the first edition only brought him in £20 in cash, but it introduced him to the best society in Edinburgh, where he was entertained and fêted and to some extent spoiled for a humdrum farmer's life.

After spending two winters in Edinburgh he returned to the country with about £500 which he had realised by the second edition of his poems. He took a considerable farm (Ellisland) near Dumfries, and afterwards became an exciseman. He chivalrously but unwisely married Jean Armour, an uneducated girl quite unfitted to be his wife. After a while he gave up his farming and relied for a livelihood upon his employment as an exciseman alone. At this time he wrote many beautiful songs adapted to old Scottish tunes. But his health, which had been impoverished by dissipation and misfortunes, began to break up, and he died of the effects of rheumatic fever in July, 1796, in the thirty-eighth year of his age.

During his life-time Burns was his own worst enemy, but since his death that position has been filled by several of his biographers. Burns was often foolish and misguided, but he was totally free from all cold vices such as meanness or duplicity. He was a fearlessly proud man and was honest and independent almost to a fault. But it is his intense sympathy with everything, bird, beast, or fellow-mortal, that sets him among the greatest of writers and makes him near akin to Shakespeare. He is one of the greatest lyric poets of the world, and in several respects is not unlike Catullus. When Catullus imitated Callimachus and the Alexandrians, and when Burns reclined on the bosom of Gray and Shenstone, they did not either of them produce anything that was memorable. But Catullus's spontaneous hendecasyllables and Burns's Doric songs and poems spring straight from the heart, and therefore go straight to the hearts of those who hear them. Catullus's poem on the death of Lesbia's sparrow and Burns's *To a Field-mouse* have much in common. Both poets in touching the little get in touch with the permanent and universal.

While Burns can hardly be called a better lyric poet than Catullus (for what can be better than the best?) he has a wider range. His poems range from the greatest of war-songs to the most pathetic of laments (*To Mary in Heaven*), and he has complete mastery over every tone and semitone of humour and pathos. It is difficult to pick out any poems for special mention when all are so good, but the following are considered by competent critics as among his most remarkable productions: *Tam o' Shanter*, the most famous of his narrative poems; *The Jolly Beggars*, a glorification of careless vagabond jollity; *The Twa Dogs*, a humorous comparison between the rich and poor; *The Cottar's Saturday Night*, a eulogy of a quiet, sincerely devout home; *The Holy Fair*, a fierce satire; *Hallowe'en*, which deals with rustic fortune-telling; and *Address to the Deil*, a masterpiece of whimsical drollery. Burns's poems have become part of Scotland; it is hardly too much to say that they *are* Scotland. Every phase of Scottish life is mirrored in them; and he is the national poet of his country in an even more intimate sense than Homer is the national poet of Greece.—BIBLIOGRAPHY: J. Gibson Lockhart, *Life of Burns*; Prof. J. Campbell Shairp, *Burns* (in English Men of Letters Series); Sir Leslie Stephen, article in *Dictionary of National Biography*; Auguste Angellier, *Robert Burns: la vie et les œuvres*; T. F. Henderson, *Robert Burns*; W. A. Craigie, *Primer of Burns*.

BURNS AND SCALDS. Injuries produced by the application of excessive heat, in some form, to the human body. They are dangerous according to the extent of surface involved, and when widespread produce most serious consequences from shock. The mortality from them is high during the first twenty-four hours, especially in children. To combat the shock there should be a minimum of exposure and handling. The patient should be put to bed immediately, kept warm, and allowed to drink as much cooling liquid as desired. In cases of great suffering morphia should be administered to lessen the pain. When required, stimulants and oxygen may be given, and saline solution injected intravenously where the pulse is weak. A subsequent danger is that of septic absorption from the large sloughing surface leading to septic pneumonia, duodenal ulceration, meningitis, thrombosis, etc. In its final stages much trouble may arise from scars, causing deformity and disability.

The immediate local treatment for a burn or scald is the application of either an oily dressing, e.g. eucalyptus oil and vaseline, or a weak antiseptic dressing, e.g. picric acid or carbolic acid. This first dressing should be allowed to remain, if possible, till the shock is over. As most burns become septic, frequent changes of dressings must be made, or, where possible, the injured part should be bathed in a weak solution of some antiseptic.

BURNT'ISLAND. A royal municipal and police burgh of Scotland, in Fife, on the estuary of the Forth, a favourite summer residence and bathing-place as well as a busy port. Shale-oil, vegetable oil, and oil-cake are made, and there are railway repairing works. Pop. (1931), 5389.

BURNT-OFFERING. Something offered and burnt on an altar as an atonement for sin; a sacrifice. The burnt-offerings of the Jews were either some clean animal, as an ox, a sheep, a pigeon; or some species of vegetable substance, as bread, flour, ears of wheat or barley.

BURNT-SIENNA. A fine orange-brown pigment produced by calcining raw sienna, a natural ochreous earth (*Terra di Sienna*). *See* OCHRES.

BURNT-UMBER. A pigment of reddish-brown colour obtained by burning umber, a soft earthy mixture of the peroxides of iron and manganese, deriving its name from Umbria in Italy. *See* PIGMENTS.

BURO. *See* BOORO.

BURR. Botanical name for the prickly covering of some fruits, such as the horse-chestnut. The heads of the burdock and the rough minute fruits of the goose grass are other examples.

In geology, burr stone is a siliceous rock used for millstones. The rough edge left on metal after cutting with a tool is termed a burr, and it is also the name of a small circular saw.

BURR, Aaron. Third Vice-President of the United States, born in New Jersey in 1756. After serving with honour in the Revolutionary army he became a lawyer, and finally leader of the Democratic party and Vice-President 1801. His duel with Alexander Hamilton, which ended fatally for the latter, drove him from New York to settle farther west, where he conceived an audacious and grandiose scheme of founding an empire in the south-west. He was tried for treason, and, though acquitted, sank into obscurity. He died in 1836.

BURRARD INLET. An inlet of British Columbia, forming a fine harbour, and having Vancouver, the terminus of the Canadian Pacific Railway, at its entrance.

BURRIA'NA. A town of S. Spain, province of Castellar de la Plana, not far from the sea, in a district producing great quantities of oranges. Pop. 14,243.

BUR'RITT, Elihu. The "learned blacksmith", as he was called, was born at New Britain, Connecticut, 8th Dec., 1810. He was apprenticed to a blacksmith, but, conceiving a strong desire for knowledge, he began to read English literature, and with great diligence and perseverance at length acquired proficiency not only in the ancient, but also most of the modern languages of Europe. He afterwards came into public notice as a lecturer on behalf of temperance, the abolition of slavery and war, etc., and founded papers, missions, and organisations to further these ends. In 1848 the first International Peace Congress was held under his guidance at Brussels. In 1865 he was consular agent at Birmingham. In 1868 he returned to live on his farm in America, and died 7th March, 1879. His best-known writings are: *Sparks from the Anvil, Thoughts and Things at Home and Abroad, Chips from Many Blocks*, etc.

BURROWING-OWL. An American owl, the *Speotyto cunicularia*, which dwells in holes in the ground either made by itself or by some other animal, as the prairie-dog or marmot. It feeds on insects and seeks its food by day.

BURRSTONE. *See* BUHRSTONE.

BUR'SARY. An endowment in one of the Scottish universities, corresponding to an exhibition in an English university, and intended for the support of a student during his ordinary course, and before he has taken a degree in the faculty in which he holds the bursary. This circumstance, according to the usage prevailing in Scotland, distinguishes bursaries from scholarships and fellowships, both of which are bestowed after the student has taken a degree. Each of the four universities of Scotland has a greater or smaller number of bursaries. Of late years most bursaries are awarded after competitive examination, and only a few are now given by the patrons for special reasons.

BURSCHEID (bųr'shīt). A manufacturing town of Prussia, some 20 miles from Düsseldorf. Pop. 6310.

BURSERACEÆ. *See* AMYRIDACEÆ.

BURS'LEM. A town of England, in Staffordshire, within the municipal borough of Stoke-upon-Trent, and in the centre of "The Potteries". Here is the Wedgwood Memorial Institute, comprising a free library, a museum, and a school of art, erected in honour of Josiah Wedgwood, who was born at Burslem in 1730. There are extensive manufactures of china and earthenware, in which and coal-mining the inhabitants are chiefly employed. Burslem gives its name to one of the parliamentary divisions of Stoke-upon-Trent.

BUR'TON, John Hill. Historian of Scotland, born at Aberdeen 1809, died near Edinburgh 1881. He graduated at Marischal College, Aberdeen, adopted law as a profession, and became an advocate in Edinburgh, but literature was really the business of his life. He early contributed to the *Westminster Review*, as afterwards to the *Edinburgh* and *North British*, to *Blackwood's Magazine*, and to the *Scotsman*. His first book was *The Life and Correspondence of David Hume* (1846), followed by lives of Lord Lovat and Duncan Forbes of Culloden, and other works. His chief work was his *History of Scotland from the Earliest Times to 1746* (2nd edition, 8 vols., 1873); others equally well known were *The Scot Abroad* and *The Bookhunter*. He was appointed secretary to the Scottish Prison Board in 1854, and was connected with this department till his death.

BURTON, Sir Richard Francis, K.C.M.G. English traveller and linguist, born in 1821, died 1890. He joined the Indian army in 1842, and showed a remarkable facility in acquiring the languages and manners of the natives. In 1853 he went to Arabia, and visited Mecca and Medina disguised as a Mohammedan pilgrim—a sufficiently dangerous journey. After serving in the Crimean War he made a journey to East Africa along with Captain Speke, which led to the discovery of the great Lake Tanganyika. He was British Consul at Fernando Po, at Santos in Brazil, and from 1872 at Trieste. He visited many countries and published many works, among which are: *Sindh and the Races that inhabit India*; *Personal Narrative of a Pilgrimage to El Medinah and Mecca*; *The Lake Regions of Central Africa*; *The City of the Saints and across the Rocky Mountains to California*; *The Nile Basin*; *The Highlands of Brazil*; *Ultima Thule, or a Summer in Iceland*; *The Gold Mines of Midian*; *The Book of the Sword*; translations of Camoens' *Lusiads* and an unbowdlerised version of the *Arabian Nights*.

BURTON, Robert. An English writer, born at Lindley, in Leicestershire, in 1577, died in 1640. He studied at Christ Church, Oxford, where he seems to have lived all his life. His vast out-of-the-way learning is curiously displayed in his book *The Anatomy of Melancholy*, which he published in 1621. He was a man of integrity and benevolence, though of eccentric habits and subject to fits of hypochondriac melancholy.

BURTON-UPON-TRENT. A county borough of England, in Staffordshire, on the N. bank of the Trent, in a low, level situation. It is chiefly celebrated for its excellent ale, manufactured in numerous breweries, which employ upwards of 10,000 men and boys, the largest establishments being those of Messrs. Bass & Co. and Messrs. Allsopp. Pop. (1931), 49,485. Burton gives its name to a parliamentary division of the county.

BURTSCHEID (burt'shīt). A town in Rhenish Prussia, which was united with Aix-la-Chapelle in 1897. It has extensive manufactures, particularly of woollens, and celebrated thermal springs. Pop. 15,950.

BURU. One of the Molucca Islands in the Indian Archipelago, west of Ceram and Amboyna, belonging to the Dutch. It is oval in shape, 90 miles long and 50 miles broad. Though mountainous and thickly covered with wood, it is productive, yielding rice, dye-woods, etc. Pop. 19,631.

BURUJIRD. A town, Persia, province of Luristan, in a fertile and well-cultivated valley. Pop. 21,000.

BURWOOD. A town of New South Wales, 7 miles west of Sydney, of which it forms a residential suburb. Pop. 8280.

BURY (be'ri). A municipal, county, and parliamentary borough (with one member) of England, in Lancashire, 8 miles N.N.W. of Manchester, well situated on a rising ground between the Irwell and the Roch. The staple manufacture is that of cotton, and there are also large woollen factories, bleaching, and printing works, dye-works, foundries, etc. Sir Robert Peel was born near Bury in 1788. A bronze statue was erected in the town in memory of him. Pop. (1931), 56,186.

Burying-beetle burying a Dead Vole. (*Necrophorus humator* and *Necrophorus vespillo*)

BURY, John Bagnell. Scholar and historian, born in Ireland in 1861, educated at Dublin University, graduated with distinction and was elected a Fellow in 1885. He also studied in Germany, and had a wide acquaintance with languages, including Russian. He held the chair of modern history in Dublin University from 1893 to 1902, and from 1898 was also regius professor of Greek. In 1902 he was appointed professor of modern history in Cambridge University. Besides annotated editions of Pindar's *Nemean* and *Isthmian Odes*, and an edition of Gibbon's *Decline and Fall*, with many learned notes (7 vols., 1896-1900), his works include: *History of the Later Roman Empire from Arcadius to Irene* (1889), *Student's History of the Roman Empire from Augustus to Marcus Aurelius* (1893), *History of Greece to the Death of Alexander the Great* (1900, published in a library edition two years later—2 vols.), *Life of St. Patrick and his Place in History* (1905), *Imperial Administration in the Ninth Century*, *History of the Eastern Roman Empire*, *History of Free Thought*; with many articles in periodicals such as the *Classical Review*. He died in 1927.

BURYING-BEETLE (Necrophŏrus). The name of a genus of insects belonging to the order Coleoptera, or beetles, and the tribe of the Silphidæ, or carrion beetles. They have a very keen scent, which guides them to the dead bodies of rats, mice, etc., which form their food. Several beetles will unite to cover such animals, burying them sometimes more than 6 inches in the earth. They deposit their eggs on the carrion, and in less than a fortnight the larvæ issue. The species is common everywhere.

BURY ST. EDMUND'S, or ST. EDMUNDSBURY. A market town and municipal borough in Suffolk, England, well built and delightfully situated on the Larke, 26 miles from Ipswich. Agricultural implements are manufactured, and there is a large trade in agricultural produce. A parliamentary borough until 1918, Bury St. Edmund's now gives its name to a parliamentary division of W. Suffolk. It is an ancient place and derived its name from St. Edmund, a king of the East Angles, slain by the heathen Danes in 870 and buried there in 903. It contains the remains of an abbey, built in the eleventh century, once the most wealthy and magnificent in Britain. Pop. (1931), 16,708.

BUSA'CO. A mountain ridge in the province of Beira, Portugal. It was here that Wellington repulsed Massena (27th Sept., 1810) and continued his retreat to the lines of Torres Vedras.

BUS-BARS. *See* ELECTRICITY.

BUSBY (buz'bi). A military head-dress worn by hussars, artillerymen, and engineers, consisting of a fur hat with a bag, of the same colour as the facings of the regiment, hanging from the top over the right side. The bag appears to be a relic of a Hungarian head-dress from which a long padded bag hung over, and was attached to the right shoulder as a defence against sword-cuts.

BUSH-BUCK. A name given to several species of antelopes, especially

Bush-buck

to *Tragelăphus sylvatica,* an antelope of S. Africa, 4 feet long and 2½ feet high, with triangular sub-spiral horns. The male is dark sepia-brown and the female reddish-brown above; both are white below. The *white-backed bush-buck* is the *Cephalŏphus sylvicultrix,* a white-backed antelope of Sierra Leone, with black, shining, pointed, and nearly straight horns, short slender limbs, sleek, glossy, deep-brown hair.

BUSHEL. An English dry measure, containing 8 gallons or 4 pecks. The British imperial bushel introduced in 1826 has a capacity of 2218·192 cu. inches, and holds 80 lb. avoirdupois of distilled water at the temperature of 62° F. with the barometer at 30 inches. Previous to this the Winchester bushel had been the standard measure. Its capacity was 2150·42 cu. inches. The bushel frequently varies locally with the article measured: thus the bushel is equal to 60 lb. wheat, 50 lb. barley, 39 lb. oats, 60 lb. rye and maize in England; 62 lb. wheat, 38 lb. barley, 40 lb. oats, 60 lb. rye and maize on the Continent; 60 lb. wheat, 48 lb. barley, 32 lb. oats, 56 lb. flax seed, 48 lb. buckwheat, 44 lb. hemp seed in the United States. *See* WEIGHTS AND MEASURES.

BUSHEY. Urban district of Hertfordshire. It adjoins Watford, and is 16 miles from London, on the L.M.S. railway. Pop. (1931), 11,243.

BUSHIRE (bö'shēr; properly, **ABU SHEHR,** the father of cities). The principal seaport of Persia, on the Persian Gulf, 188½ miles W.S.W. of Shiraz. It lies on the edge of a desert, and is a mean, unhealthy, and dirty place. It carries on a considerable traffic with India and Britain, importing rice, indigo, sugar, cotton goods, etc., and exporting shawls, dates, tobacco, carpets, wool, drugs, etc. The anchorage is indifferent, but is the best on the coast. Pop. perhaps 20,000.

BUSHMEN, or **BOSJESMEN.** A race of people who dwell in the western part of South Africa, in the immense plains bordering on the north side of the province of the Cape of Good Hope. They are the most degraded of the races who inhabit this part of the country, although the cruelty attributed to them is much exaggerated. They do not form societies, but unite only for defence or pillage. They have no huts, and do not cultivate the land, but support themselves by hunting. Their language is exceedingly poor, consisting only of a certain clicking with the tongue and harsh gurgling tones, for which we have no letters.

BUSH'RANGERS. The name for desperadoes in Australia who, taking to the bush, supported themselves by levying contributions on the property of all and sundry within their reach. Considerable gangs of these lawless characters have sometimes collected, a body of fifty holding part of New South Wales in terror about 1830. A gang of four (one of whom was "Ned" Kelly), fell victims to justice in 1880, after having robbed a bank and committed other outrages—the last bushrangers known.

BUSH-SHRIKES. American birds of the shrike family, forming the group Thamniphilinæ.

BUSINESS. Word meaning much the same as trade or commerce. In English law certain statutes make it illegal to carry on certain businesses, such as pawnbroking and money-lending, without licence or registration.

By law it is necessary for all persons who trade in names that are not their own to register such names at Somerset House, London. These names must be shown on the firm's note-paper.

Business day is a term used in the Bills of Exchange Act, 1882. Every day is a business day except Sunday, Christmas day, Good Friday, and days set apart as public holidays under the Bank Holidays Act, 1878, and days appointed by royal proclamation as days of fast or thanksgiving.

BUSI'RIS. A town of ancient Egypt, in the Delta, the chief place where the rites of Isis were celebrated. The name is also given as that of a mythical Egyptian king.

BUS'KIN (the usual translation of the Lat. *cothurnus*). A kind of high shoe worn upon the stage by the ancient actors of tragedy, in order to give them a more heroic appearance: often used figuratively for tragedy, like "sock" for comedy.

BUSS. A small vessel from 50 to 70 tons burden, carrying two masts, and with two sheds or cabins, one at either end, used in herring-fishing.

BUSS'ORAH. *See* BASRA.

BUSSU-PALM. The *Manicaria saccifĕra*, found in the swamps of the Amazon, whose stem is only 10 to 15 feet high, but whose leaves are often 30 feet long by 4 to 5 feet in breadth, and split from end to end form thatch for houses. The spathes are used by the Indians as bags, or for cloth-making.

BUST (Fr. *buste*, It. *busto*). In sculpture, the representation of that portion of the human figure which comprises the head and the upper part of the body. During the great age of Greece the portrait busts of the learned formed an important branch of art, and in this way we come to possess faithful likenesses of Socrates, Plato, and Demosthenes, in which the artists show great power of expressing the character of those represented. The number of busts belonging to the time of the Roman Empire is very considerable, but those of the Roman poets and men of letters have not been preserved in nearly so large numbers as those of the Greeks. The first bust that can be depended upon as giving a correct likeness is that of Scipio Africanus the elder.

Indian Bustard

Above: Head of great Bustard (*Otis tarda*)

BUS'TARD. A bird belonging to the ord. Alectorides, which also includes the cranes. The great bustard (*Otis tarda*) is the largest European bird, the male often weighing 30 lb., with a breadth of wing of 6 or 7 feet. The bustard is now extremely rare in Britain, but abounds in the south and east of Europe and the steppes of Tartary, feeding on green corn and other vegetables, and on earth-worms. Its flesh is esteemed. All the species run fast, although they vary in their liking for flight. The little bustard (*O. Tetrax*) occasionally visits Britain. *O. nigriceps* is an Asiatic and *O. Cœrulescens* an African species. The Australian species (*O. Australis*) is a magnificent bird highly prized as food.

BUSTO-ARSIZIO. A town of N. Italy, 20 miles N.W. of Milan. Pop. 25,992.

BUTCHER-BIRD. *See* SHRIKE.

BUTCHER'S BROOM (Ruscus). A genus of plants, nat. ord. Liliaceæ.

The flowers are diœcious and of a green colour, and rise from branchlets dilated in the form of leaves, and the fruit is a bright-red berry. *Ruscus aculeātus*, or the common butcher's broom, a shrubby evergreen, with angular stems, is a British plant, and takes its name from being used by butchers to sweep their blocks.

BUTE (būt). An island of Scotland in the estuary of the Clyde, with an area of 30,000 acres, belonging principally to the Marquess of Bute. It is about 15 miles long, and the average breadth is 3½ miles. In Kames Hill it rises to the height of 875 feet; it has several pretty lakes, the principal of which is Loch Fad, 2½ miles long. Agriculture is in an advanced state, and there are about 20,000 acres under cultivation. The herring-fishery is also a source of considerable profit. The only town is Rothesay, whose ancient castle is one of the interesting antiquities of the island. The climate of Bute is very mild. Population of the island (1931), 12,125. The *county* of Bute comprises the islands of Bute, Arran, Great Cumbrae, Little Cumbrae, Inchmarnock, and Pladda, with a total area of 139,432 acres, but only a small part is under cultivation. Arran is about double the size of Bute, but the other islands belonging to the county are small. Ayr and Bute return three members to Parliament. Pop. (1931), 18,822.

BUTE, John Stuart, Earl of. A British statesman, born in 1713 in Scotland. He acquired great influence over Frederick, Prince of Wales, and was appointed chamberlain to his son, afterwards George III., through whose favour he became Secretary of State, and ultimately, in 1762, Prime Minister. For a time Pitt and Newcastle alike had to give way to his influence; but though possessing the full confidence of the king he was unpopular with the people, and in 1763 he suddenly resigned his office, and retired from public affairs to spend his leisure in literary and scientific pursuits, particularly in botany. He died in 1792. His son was created marquess in 1796. The third Marquess, John Patrick Crichton Stuart, born 1847, died 1900, was a writer on archæological subjects, a patron of learning, and a prominent Roman Catholic. Among his works are: *The Roman Breviary translated into English*; *David, Duke of Rothesay*; etc.

BU'TEA. A genus of plants, nat. ord. Leguminosæ, tribe Papilionaceæ, natives of the East Indies. They are trees having pinnately trifoliate leaves, with racemes of deep scarlet flowers. *B. frondōsa* yields an astringent red juice known as butea-gum or Bengal kino; it also produces lac (q.v.).

BUTLER, Alban. English Roman Catholic writer, born 1710, died 1773. He was educated at the English (R.C.) College, Douai, where he became professor first of philosophy and then of divinity; afterwards he was president of the English college, St. Omer. His *Lives of the Saints* (1756-59) is a monument of erudition which cost him thirty years' labour.

BUTLER, Benjamin Franklin. An American lawyer, general, and politician, born at Deerfield, New Hampshire, 5th Nov., 1818. He became noted as a criminal lawyer; in 1853 commenced to take a prominent part in politics on the Democratic side; in 1861, on the outbreak of the war, held a commission as brigadier-general of militia, and took service with his brigade on the Union side. In his field operations he was not a successful general, and as Governor of New Orleans, which had been taken by Admiral Farragut, he made his rule memorable by its severity. In 1866 he was elected member of Congress for Massachusetts and acquired great influence in the legislature. In 1882 General Butler was elected Governor of Massachusetts. Died 11th Jan., 1893.

BUTLER, James, Duke of Ormonde. An eminent statesman in the reigns of Charles I. and II. He was born at London in 1610, was a steady adherent of the royal cause, on the ruin of which he retired to France. At the Restoration he returned with the king, was created a duke, and appointed Lord-Lieutenant of Ireland. After losing his office and the royal favour for some years, principally through the intrigues of Buckingham, he was again appointed Lord-Lieutenant of Ireland, and retained the post till the death of Charles, when he resigned, his principles not suiting the policy of James. He died in 1688.

BUTLER, Joseph. An English prelate and celebrated writer on ethics and theology, born in Berkshire in 1692. He was brought up a dissenter, but after examining the points of controversy between the Established Church and the dissenters, he decided to become a member of the former, and accordingly removed to Oxford in 1714, where he took orders. The sermons which he delivered as preacher at the Rolls Chapel, an appointment he occupied from 1718 to 1726, still hold a high place in ethical literature. But his great work is the *Analogy of Religion, Natural and Revealed, to the Constitution and Course of Nature,* which was published in 1736, and acquired for him a great reputation. In 1738 he was made Bishop of Bristol, and in 1750 translated to the see of Durham. He died in 1752.

BUTLER, Josephine Elizabeth. English social reformer, born on 12th April, 1828. She was a zealous promoter of the higher education of women and of the Married Women's Property act of 1882. Her name is chiefly associated with her leadership of the agitation for the repeal of the Contagious Diseases Acts, and her courageous attack on the evils of prostitution. She died 30th Dec., 1906.

BUTLER, Lady. English painter. A daughter of J. T. Thompson. She was born in Switzerland in 1850, and studied art in Rome. In 1874 she made a reputation with a battle picture, *The Roll Call.* This was the first of several military scenes, including *Floreat Etona* and *The Dawn of Waterloo.* Engravings of these and others of her pictures became very popular. In 1877 Miss Thompson was married to an Irish soldier, who afterwards became Sir W. F. Butler (1838-1910).

BUTLER, Samuel. English satirical poet. He was the son of a farmer in Worcestershire, where he was born in 1612. He was educated at Worcester free school, and held various situations as clerk or amanuensis to persons of position, among them being Sir Samuel Luke, " the valiant Mamaluke ", a Puritan colonel of Bedfordshire, who is caricatured in the celebrated knight Hudibras. Butler published the first part of *Hudibras* after the Restoration, in 1663. It became immensely popular, and Charles II. himself was perpetually quoting the poem, but did nothing for the author, who seems to have passed the latter part of his life dependent on the support of friends, and died in poverty in London in 1680. A second part of *Hudibras* appeared in 1664, a third in 1678. The poem is a sort of burlesque epic ridiculing Puritanism and fanaticism and hypocrisy generally. Butler was author of various other pieces, including a satire on the Royal Society entitled *The Elephant in the Moon.*

BUTLER, Samuel. Author, born 1835, died 1902. He was educated at Shrewsbury, and at St. John's College, Cambridge. He was placed in the first class of the classical tripos in 1858, and was intended for the Church, but preferred to go sheep-farming in New Zealand. After about five years he returned to England with a moderate competence, much of which he subsequently lost in unlucky speculations. His monetary misfortunes inspired him to write a Stock Exchange oratorio, called *Narcissus.*

Butler was a man of great versatility, and could paint and compose music in a competent manner ; but he is best known as an author, where he covered a wide field. He published several scientific books, in which he joined issue with Darwin about some minor points of the evolution theory ; he wrote several highly-unorthodox books of religious speculation ; he translated Homer into colloquial English for the benefit of the working-classes, and he endeavoured in his *Authoress of the Odyssey* to prove that the *Odyssey* was written by a woman, and that she lived at Trapani in Sicily. His best-known works, however, are his two satirical romances, *Erewhon* (anagram of " nowhere "), published in 1872, and its sequel *Erewhon Revisited* (1901). These books expose many of the social and religious shams which characterised Butler's contemporaries, and are written in a lively and amusing manner. A powerful if somewhat disagreeable novel, *The Way of all Flesh,* was published in 1903, after Butler's death.

BUTLER, Sir William Francis. Lieutenant-general and writer, born in Ireland in 1838, died in 1910. He joined the army in 1858, reached the rank of major in 1874, having previously served in the Red River (Canada) Expedition ; accompanied the Ashanti expedition, 1874 ; and in 1879 acted as staff-officer in Natal. He served in Egypt in 1892 ; held important commands under Lord Wolseley in the Sudan in 1884-5 ; from 1890 till 1893 was in command at Alexandria ; attained the rank of major-general in 1892 ; subsequently held commands at Aldershot and at Dover. In 1898-9 he was in chief command, also acting as High Commissioner, in Cape Province, but came home before the war, and was put in command of the western district. He retired from the army in 1905.

Besides an *Autobiography,* his chief works are : *The Great Lone Land, The Wild North Land* (both dealing with experiences in Northern Canada), and biographies of Charles George Gordon (" Chinese " Gordon), Sir Charles Napier, and Sir George Colley. He was made K.C.B. in 1886. In 1877 he married Miss Elizabeth **Thompson.** who had by this time become well known as a painter, her *Roll Call* in particular having made a great sensation when exhibited in 1874. She has painted a number of well-known pictures since, her subjects being almost exclusively military, and including *Balaclava, Inkermann, Scotland for Ever, Defence of Rorke's Drift, Dawn of Waterloo,* and others.

BU'TOMUS. A genus of monocotyledons, nat. ord. Butomaceæ. The only species, *B. umbellatus*, the Flowering Rush, is the most elegant and beautiful of British marsh-plants; it was once abundant in the Fen country and elsewhere, but is now much scarcer.

BUTTE, or BUTTE CITY. A city of the United States, Montana, 50 miles south-west of Helena, the State capital, in a mountainous region, with rich copper-mines and extensive smelting-works, also an important railway centre. Population, 42,000.

BUTTER. A fatty substance produced from milk, especially cow's milk. When the milk is first drawn, this fatty matter is disseminated through it in minute clear globules enclosed in membranous sacs or bags which in a short time rise to the surface and form cream. The cream is then skimmed off to undergo the operation of churning, which by rupturing the sacs effects a separation of the cream into a solid called *butter* and a liquid called *butter-milk*, the latter consisting of whey and other caseous matter. In many cases, however, in order to save time, the churning is done before the cream has separated from the milk, and machines for effecting the process of separation are now frequently used. The quality of the butter depends much upon the treatment of the cream at this stage. Its temperature in warm weather ought to be between 53° and 55°; in colder weather several degrees higher. If too cold, the fat is hard and does not coalesce, and if too warm, it becomes semi-liquid. The butter, being formed into lumps, is washed well in cold water, and kneaded till all the butter-milk has been expelled.

Butter of good quality has a faint sweet odour and a soft delicate flavour. Its composition varies somewhat according to the way in which it is made. It has usually from 80 to 90 per cent of pure fat, the rest consisting of casein, water (13·05 per cent), and salt (1·02) per cent). The water should not amount to more than 16 per cent, nor the salt to more than 2 per cent of the whole weight, but butter is frequently adulterated by the excess of these two elements. Butter containing about 13 per cent water has the best flavour as a general rule. Where the butter is to be preserved only for a short time, keeping it in a cool place and covering it with pure water daily will perhaps be sufficient. More certain methods are to use water mixed slightly with tartaric acid or vinegar, or to salt it lightly, thus making what is known as "powdered" butter. Butter which is to be thoroughly "cured", so as to keep for some length of time, is usually prepared with from 5 to 8 per cent of common salt. In preserving butter it is important to exclude the air as much as possible. When exported to warm climates it may be packed in 1-lb. or 2-lb. bottles, with mouths about 2 inches across, and fitted with glass stoppers and cemented so as to be air-tight. Hermetically sealed tins may also be used.

The United Kingdom, Denmark, Holland, parts of France, Russia, Sweden, Belgium, Australia, New Zealand, the United States, and Canada are large producers of butter. Large quantities (to the value of about £20,000,000 yearly) are imported into Great Britain from Denmark, Ireland, Australian colonies, Canada, etc. Butter factories are now common—large establishments which receive the milk produced at many neighbouring farms. In the warmer countries olive or other oil is more used than butter. The butter, beer, and animal food of the north of Europe give way to oil, wine, and bread in the southern regions.—The name of *mineral butters* was given by the old chemists to certain substances which are of the consistence of butter when recently prepared. *Vegetable butters* are fixed vegetable oils which are solid at common temperatures, such as palm-oil, coconut oil, shea, nutmeg-oil, etc. *See* BUTTERINE; DAIRY FARMING.

BUTTER-BUR (*Petasītes vulgāris*). A British composite plant, with large rhubarb-like leaves and purplish flowers, growing by the side of streams; allied to colt's-foot. Although it is called butter-bur there are no burs about it; the name is said to refer to the fact that the large leaves were formerly used for wrapping up butter.

BUTTERCUP. The popular name of two or three species of the Ranunculus, namely, *R. acris, R. bulbōsus*, and *R. repens*. They are common British plants with brilliant yellow flowers. *See* RANUNCULUS. See illus. p. 322.

BUTTERFLY. The common name of all diurnal lepidopterous insects, corresponding to the original Linnæan genus Papilio. The family of the butterflies or diurnal Lepidoptera (so called to distinguish them from nocturnal or crepuscular Lepidoptera, such as moths) is a very extensive one, and naturalists differ much as to the manner of subdividing it.

One of the most remarkable and interesting circumstances connected

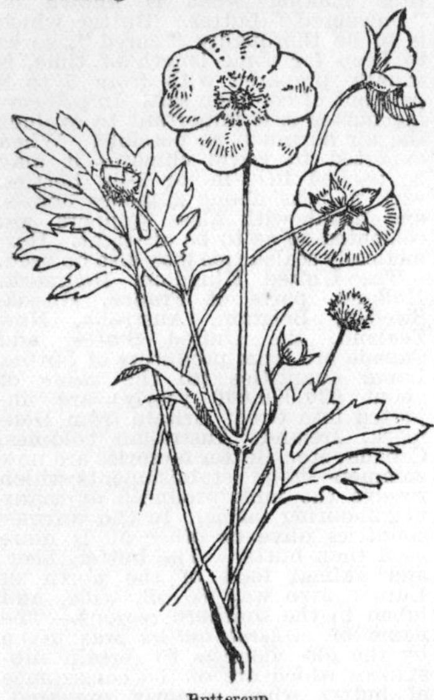

Buttercup

with these beautiful insects is their series of transformations before reaching a perfect state. The female butterfly lays a great quantity of eggs, which produce larvæ, commonly called caterpillars. After a short life these assume a new form, and become chrysalids or pupæ. These chrysalids are attached to other bodies in various ways, and are of various forms; they often have brilliant golden or argentine spots. Within its covering the insect develops, to emerge as the active and brilliant butterfly. These insects in their perfect form suck the nectar of plants, but take little food, and are all believed to be short-lived, their work in the perfect state being almost confined to the propagation of the species.

Butterflies vary greatly in size and colouring, but most of them are very beautiful. The largest are found in tropical countries, where some measure nearly a foot across the wings. They may generally be distinguished from moths by having their wings erect when sitting, the moths having theirs horizontal; also by the possession of knobbed antennæ. Some of them have great powers of flight. Among the most remarkable butterflies are those that present an extraordinary likeness to other objects—leaves, green or withered, flowers, bark, etc., a feature that serves greatly to protect them from enemies. *See Lepidoptera.*

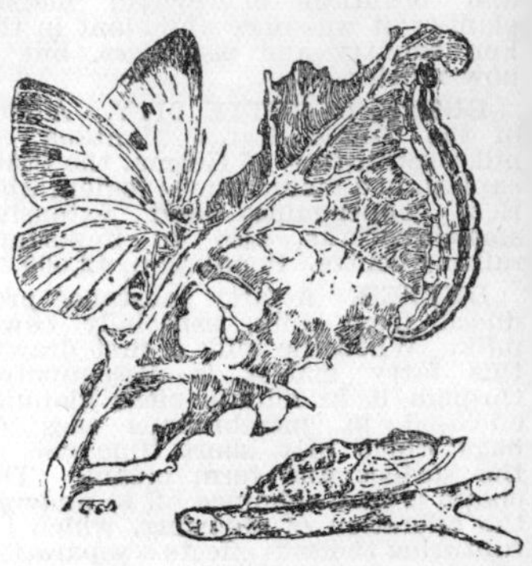

The Development of a Butterfly

BUTTERFLY-FISH. *See* BLENNY.

BUT'TERINE (-ĕn). An artificial butter, prepared from beef-suet, milk, butter, and vegetable oil, and now largely made in Britain, the United States, Holland, etc. By the use of colouring-matters it can be made to resemble butter of any given brand; but although quite wholesome when well made, it has not the delicate flavour and aroma of the highest-class butters. In Britain, by an Act passed in 1887, butterine and all artificial butters must be sold under the name of *margarine*, and stringent regulations are in force to prevent their fraudulent substitution for real butter. *See* MARGARINE.

BUTTER-NUT. The fruit of *Juglans cinĕrea*, or white walnut, an American tree, so called from the oil it contains. The tree bears a resemblance in its general appearance to the black walnut, but the wood is not so dark in colour. The same name is given to the nut of *Caryocar nucifĕrum* of South America, also known as *Suwarrow* or *Souari nut.*

BUTTER-TREE. A name of several

ees yielding oily or fatty substances ›mewhat resembling butter. *See* ASSIA.

BUTTERWORT (*Pinguicŭla vul-ăris*). Order Lentibulariaceæ; a lant growing in bogs or soft grounds Europe, Canada, etc. The leaves re covered with soft, pellucid, glan-ular hairs, which secrete a glutinous quor that catches small insects. he edges of the leaf roll over on ne insect and retain it, and the isect, when digested by the secretion, erves as food for the plant. In the orth of Sweden the leaves, acting ke rennet, are employed to curdle ilk.

BUTTMANN (bṳt'mȧn), **Philip Karl.** German philologist, born in 1764. Ie spent most of his life at Berlin, where he taught in the Joachimsthal University. His best-known works re his *Greek Grammar* and *Lexilogus or Homer and Hesiod.* He died in 829.

BUTTONS are of almost all forms nd materials—wood, horn, bone, vory, steel, copper, silver, and brass —which are either left uncovered or re covered with silk or some other naterial. The material of buttons has varied much with times and fashions. In the last century gilt, brass, or copper buttons were almost universal. Birmingham was the great seat of manufacture, as it yet is of metallic and other buttons.

The introduction of cloth-covered buttons early in the last century made a great revolution in the trade, and led to great varieties in the style of making up. The metal buttons now used are commonly made of brass or a mixture of tin and brass. They are usually made from sheets of metal by punching and stamping. Such buttons are generally used for trousers. A substance now very commonly used for buttons is vegetable ivory (seeds of the ivory-nut palm), which may be coloured according to taste. Mother-of-pearl buttons are another common kind. Of late years the making of porcelain buttons has developed into a remarkable industry. These buttons are both strong and cheap. Besides these kinds there are also glass buttons, made by softening the glass by heat and pressing it into a mould; buttons of vulcanite, marble, and many other materials; but these are fancy articles in the trade.

BUTTONWOOD. A name often given to the N. American plane (*Platănus occidentālis*).

BUT'TRESSES. In architecture, especially Gothic, projections on the outside of the walls of an edifice, extending from the bottom to the top, or nearly, and intended to give additional support to the walls and prevent them from spreading under the weight of the roof. *Flying buttresses,* of a somewhat arched form often spring from the top of the ordinary buttresses, leaning inwards so as to abut against and support a higher portion of the building, such as the wall of a clear-story, thus receiving part of the pressure from the weight of the roof of the central pile. See illustration, p. 324.

BUTTRESS-ROOT. A plank-like prop-root developed above ground at the base of the trunk. Such plank-buttresses are not uncommon among tropical trees of certain families, especially Sterculiaceæ.

BUTYR'IC ACID, $C_4H_8O_2$. An acid originally obtained from butter, and also present in perspiration. It is a colourless liquid, having a smell like that of rancid butter, and is usually prepared by the butyric fermentation of certain sugars, e.g glucose.

BUTYR'IC ETHER. A substance obtained from butyric acid with the flavour of pine-apples, used in flavouring confectionery, and as an ingredient in perfumes.

BUXAR'. A town of Bengal, on the Ganges, 350 miles N.W. of Calcutta. Pop. 10,000.

BUXBAUMIA. A genus of humus-loving mosses, interesting because of their extremely simple structure. Apart from the well-developed green protonema, they have no vegetative organs. The ♂ plant consists of a single concave leaf, devoid of chlorophyll, enclosing an antheridium; the ♀ of a tuft of leaves, likewise colourless, surrounding an archegonium. The sporogonium is relatively large, and, as in other mosses, contains abundant green tissue. The protonema is probably more or less saprophytic. There are two British species.

BUXTON. A municipal borough of county Derby, England, situated in a valley celebrated for its mineral waters. Many visitors come to drink the waters in the "season", and the resident population is kept busy catering for their needs. The surrounding scenery is fine, and there is a vast stalactite cavern called Poole's Hole in the neighbourhood. Pop. (1931), 15,353.

BUXTON, Sir Thomas Fowell. English philanthropist, born in 1786, and educated at Trinity College, Dublin. In 1811 he joined the firm of the celebrated brewers, Truman, Hanbury, & Co., and took an active share in the business. The Spitalfields distress in 1816 was the occasion of his turning his attention to philanthropic efforts, and along with his sister-in-law, the celebrated Mrs. Fry, he made inquiries which directed public attention to the system of prison discipline. In 1818 he was elected member of Parliament for Weymouth, and was long the able coadjutor of Wilberforce in his efforts to abolish slavery. He was created a baronet in 1840, and died in 1845.

BUXTON, Sydney Charles Buxton, first Earl. English statesman, born in 1853. Educated at Trinity College, Cambridge, he entered Parliament in 1883, and was a member for Poplar 1886-1914. He was Under Secretary for the Colonies 1892-5, Postmaster-General 1905-10, President of the Board of Trade 1910-14, and Governor-General of South Africa 1914-20. He was created a viscount in 1914 and an earl in Oct., 1920. His works include: *Handbook to Political Questions, The Fiscal Question*, etc.

BUXTORF, Johann. A German Orientalist. He was born in 1564, and became professor at Basel where he died in 1629. His chief work is *Lexicon Chaldaicum Talmudicum et Rabbinicum*. He has been called "Master of the Rabbins." His son Johann, born at Basel, was equally eminent as a Hebrew scholar, and succeeded to his father's chair. He died in 1664.

BUXUS. *See* BOX-TREE.

Buttresses
Left: Ordinary buttress, Northleach, Gloucestershire. Right: Flying buttress, New Shoreham, Sussex

BUYUK′DEREH. A town of Thrace on the Bosporus, a few miles from Constantinople. It is famous for its scenery, and is a favourite residence of the Christian ambassadors.

BUZ′ZARD. The name of raptorial birds which form one of the subfamilies of the diurnal birds of prey; characteristics: a moderate-sized beak, hooked from the base, long wings, long tarsi, and short weak toes. The common buzzard (*Butĕo vulgāris*) is distributed over the whole of Europe as well as the north of Africa and America. Its food is very miscellaneous, and consists of moles, mice, frogs, toads, worms, insects, etc. It is sluggish in its habits. Its length is from 20 to 22 inches. The rough-legged buzzard (*B. lagŏpus*), so called from having its legs feathered to the toes, is also a native of Britain. Its habits resemble those of the common buzzard. The red-tailed hawk of the United States is a buzzard (*B. borealis*). It is also called hen-hawk, from its

Buzzard

raids on the poultry-yard. The genus Pernis, to which the honey-buzzard (*P. apivŏrus*) belongs, has the beak rather weaker than Buteo, but does not differ much from that genus. The honey-buzzard is so called because it feeds specially on bees and wasps.

BYB'LOS, now called **JEBAIL.** An ancient maritime city of Phœnicia, a little north of Beyrout. It is a mere village with about 1000 inhabitants, most of whom are Christians. It was the chief seat of the worship of Adonis or Thammuz.

BY-LAW, or **BYE-LAW** (from the Scand. *by*, a town). A law made by an incorporated or other body for the regulation of its own affairs, or the affairs entrusted to its care. Town councils, railway companies, etc., enact by-laws which are binding upon all coming within the sphere of the operations of such bodies. By-laws must of course be within the meaning of the charter of incorporation and in accordance with the law of the land.

BYLINI. The epic songs of Russian popular poetry. Their heroes, bogatyri, or paladins, are either historical or mythical personages, or personifications of the forces of nature. These songs, the majority of which deal with historical figures, such as St. Vladimir, Boris Godunov, and Ivan the Terrible, were first handed down orally and afterwards collected from bards in the governments of Archangel, Olonetz, and Tomsk. They are divided into several cycles: cycles of Kiev, Novgorod, Moscow, etc. The central figure in the Kiev period is Ilya Muromets. The chief collections are those of Rybnikov (1860-71), Kireievsky (1868-74), and Sobolensky.

BYNG, John. British admiral, born 1704, entered the navy in 1727, and served under his father, Admiral George Byng. He was sent to relieve Minorca, blockaded by a French fleet, but failed, it was thought, through hesitation in engaging the enemy. The public odium of the failure was such that the ministry allowed Byng, who was condemned by a court martial, to be shot at Portsmouth, 14th March, 1757.

BYNG OF VIMY, GENERAL LORD. Julian Hedworth George Byng, G.C.B., G.C.M.G., M.V.O., born in 1862. In the European War he commanded successively a cavalry division, a cavalry corps, the Canadian Expeditionary Force, and the Third Army. He was responsible for the operations at Vimy Ridge (April, 1917) and at Cambrai (Nov., 1917). He was created a baron in 1919, and received a grant of £30,000. In 1919 he retired from the army. He was made a Viscount in 1926, and was Commissioner of the Metropolitan Police, 1928-1931.

BY'ROM, John. English poet and stenographer, born 1692, died 1763. He was educated at Merchant Taylors' School and Trinity College, Cambridge, and for some time studied medicine, but his chief means of livelihood for many years, till he inherited the family estates in 1740, was teaching shorthand on a system invented by himself. He was on friendly terms with many of the eminent men of his time. His earliest writings were a few papers to the *Spectator*; his poems (collected in 1773) were chiefly humorous and satirical, and show remarkable facility in rhyming.

BY'RON, George Gordon Noel, Lord Byron. A great English poet, born in Holles Street, London, 22nd Jan., 1788. He was the grandson of Admiral John Byron (q.v.) and son of the admiral's only son, Captain John Byron, of the Guards, so notorious for his gallantries and reckless dissipation that he was known as "Mad Jack Byron". His mother was Catherine Gordon of Gight, in Aberdeenshire, who was

Lord Byron

left a widow in 1791. Mrs. Byron retired with the infant poet to Aberdeen, where she lived in seclusion on the ruins of her fortune. Till the age of seven he was entirely under the care of his mother, and to her injudicious indulgence the waywardness that marked his after career has been partly attributed. On reaching his seventh year he was sent to the grammar-school at Aberdeen, and four years after, in 1798, the death of his grand-uncle gave him the titles and estates of the family. Mother and son then removed to Newstead Abbey, the family seat, near Nottingham. Soon after Byron was sent to Harrow, where he distinguished himself by his love of manly sports and his undaunted spirit. While yet at school he fell deeply in love with Mary Anne Chaworth, a distant cousin of his own. But the lady slighted the homage of the Harrow schoolboy, her junior by two years, and married another and more mature suitor. In *The Dream* Byron alludes finely to their parting interview.

Early Works. In 1805 he was entered at Trinity College, Cambridge. Two years after, in 1807, appeared his first poetic volume, *Hours of Idleness*, which, though indeed containing nothing of much merit, was castigated with much severity by Brougham in the *Edinburgh Review*. This caustic critique roused the slumbering energy in Byron, and drew from him his first really notable effort, the celebrated satire *English Bards and Scotch Reviewers*.

Childe Harold's Pilgrimage. In 1809, in company with a friend, he visited the southern provinces of Spain, and voyaged along the shores of the Mediterranean. The fruit of these travels was the fine poem of *Childe Harold's Pilgrimage*, the first two cantos of which were published on his return in 1812. The poem was an immense success, and Byron "awoke one morning and found himself famous." His acquaintance was now much courted, and his first entry on the stage of public life may be dated from this era.

During the next two years (1813-14) *The Giaour*, *The Bride of Abydos*, *The Corsair*, *Lara*, and *The Siege of Corinth* showed the brilliant work of which the new poet was capable.

Marriage. On 2nd Jan., 1815, Byron married Anna Isabella, only daughter of Sir Ralph Milbanke, but the marriage turned out unfortunate, and in about a year, Lady Byron, having gone on a visit to her parents, refused to return, and a formal separation took place. This rupture produced a considerable sensation, and the real cause of it has never been satisfactorily explained. It gave rise to much popular indignation against Byron, who left England with an expressed resolution never to return.

Journeyings. He visited France, the field of Waterloo and Brussels, the Rhine, Switzerland, and the north of Italy, and for some time took up his abode at Venice, and subsequently at Rome, where he completed his third canto of *Childe Harold*. Not long after appeared *The Prisoner of Chillon*; *The Dream, and other Poems*; and in 1817 *Manfred*, a tragedy, and *The Lament of Tasso*. From Italy he made occasional excursions to the islands of Greece, and at length visited Athens where he sketched many of the scenes of the fourth and last canto of *Childe Harold*. In 1819 was published the romantic tale of *Mazeppa*, and the same year was marked by the commencement of *Don Juan*. In 1820 appeared *Marino Faliero, Doge of Venice*, a tragedy; the drama of *Sardanapalus*; *The Two Foscari*, a tragedy; and *Cain*, a mystery.

After leaving Venice, Byron resided for some time at Ravenna, then at Pisa, and lastly at Genoa. At Ravenna he became intimate with the Countess Guiccioli, a married woman; and when he removed to Pisa, in 1822, she followed him. There he continued to occupy himself with literature and poetry, sustained for a time by the companionship of Shelley, one of the few men whom he entirely respected and with whom he was quite confidential. Besides his contributions to *The Liberal*, a periodical established at this time in conjunction with Leigh Hunt and Shelley, he completed the later cantos of *Don Juan*, with *Werner*, a tragedy, and *The Deformed Transformed*, a fragment. These are the last of Byron's poetical writings.

Last Years. In 1823, troubled perhaps by the consciousness that his life had too long been unworthy of him, he conceived the idea of throwing himself into the struggle for the independence of Greece. In Jan., 1824, he arrived at Missolonghi, was received with the greatest enthusiasm, and immediately took into his pay a body of 500 Suliotes. The disorderly temper of these troops, and the difficulties of his situation, together with the malarious air of Missolonghi, began to affect his health. On 9th April, 1824, while riding out in the rain, he caught a fever, which ten days later ended fatally. Thus, in his thirty-seventh year, died prematurely a man whose natural force and genius were perhaps superior to those of any Englishman of his time, and, largely undisciplined as they were, and wasted by an irregular life, they acquired for him a name second, in the opinion of continental Europe at least, to that of no other Englishman of his time. The body of Byron was brought to England and interred near Newstead Abbey. —BIBLIOGRAPHY: Leigh Hunt, *Lord Byron and his Contemporaries*; Thomas Moore, *Letters and Journals of Byron, with Notices of his Life*; Nichol, *Life of Lord Byron* (in English Men of Letters Series); Matthew Arnold, *Essays in Criticism*; Countess Guiccioli, *Lord Byron jugé par les temoins de sa vie*; J. C. Jeaffreson, *The Real Lord Byron*; J. Churton Collins, *Studies in Poetry and Criticism*; G. Brandes, *Main Currents in Nineteenth Century Literature*; Ethel Mayne, *Byron*. The best edition of Byron's works is that of G. E. Prothero and E. H. Coleridge.

BYRON, Henry James. English dramatist and actor, born 1834, died 1884. He wrote an immense number of pieces, including a great many farces, burlesques, and extravanganzas, besides comedies or domestic dramas, such as *Cyril's Success, Dearer than Life, Blow for Blow, Uncle Dick's Darling, The Prompter's Box, Partners for Life*, and *Our Boys*, which had an extraordinary success.

BYRON, John. An English admiral, grandfather of the poet Lord Byron, born in 1723. Embarking as midshipman in one of the ships of Lord Anson, which was wrecked on the Pacific coast (1741), north of the Straits of Magellan, he published a narrative of his adventures amongst the Indians, which is extremely interesting, and which was utilized by his grandson in *Don Juan*. In 1758 he commanded three ships of the line, and distinguished himself in the war against France. In June, 1764, he set out in a frigate to circumnavigate the globe, returning to England in May, 1766. From 1769 to 1775 he was Governor of Newfoundland. He was made vice-admiral of the white in 1779, and died in 1786.

BYSHOTTLES. *See* BRANDON.

BYSSUS. A name given to the hair or thread-like substance (called also *beard*) with which the different kinds of sea-mussels fasten themselves to the rocks. The *Pinna nobilis*, particularly, is distinguished by the length and the silky fineness of its beard, from which cloths, gloves, and stockings are still manufactured (mainly as curiosities) in Sicily and Calabria. *See* LAMELLIBRANCHIA; MUSSEL.

BYTTNERIA'CEÆ. *See* STERCULIACEÆ.

BYZAN'TINE ART. A style which arose in South-Eastern Europe after Constantine the Great had made Byzantium the capital of the Roman Empire (A.D. 330), and ornamented that city, which was called after him, with all the treasures of Grecian art. (*See* BYZANTINE EMPIRE.) One of the chief influences in Byzantine art was Christianity, and to a certain extent Byzantine art may be recognised as the endeavour to give expression to the new elements which Christianity had brought into the life of men. The tendency towards Oriental luxuriance and splendour of ornament now quite supplanted the simplicity of ancient taste. Richness of material and decoration was the aim of the artist rather than purity of conception. Yet the classical ideals of art, and in particular the traditions of technical processes and methods carried to Byzantium by the artists of the Western Empire, held their ground long enough, and produced work pure and powerful enough, to kindle the new artistic life which began in Italy with Cimabue and Giotto. It is a distinguishing characteristic of Constantinople (Byzantium) that it was able to maintain a uniform classical tradition in the face of manifold Oriental influences.

Sculpture. With regard to *sculpture* the statues no longer displayed the freedom and dignity of ancient art. The true proportion of parts, the correctness of the outlines, and in general the severe beauty of the naked figure, or of simple drapery in Greek art, were neglected for extravagant costume and ornamentation and petty details. Yet in the best period of Byzantine art, from the sixth to the eleventh century, there is considerable spiritual dignity in the general conception of the figures. But sculpture was of second-rate importance at Byzantium, the taste of those times inclining more to mosaic work with the costliness and brilliant colours of its stones.

Pictures. The first germ of a Christian style of art was developed in the Byzantine *pictures*. The artists, who appear to have seldom employed the living model, and had nothing real and material before them, but were obliged to find, in their own imaginations, conceptions of the external appearance of sacred persons, such as the mother of Christ, or the apostles, could give but feeble renderings of their ideas. As they cared but little for a faithful imitation of nature, but were satisfied with repeating what was once acknowledged as successful, it is not strange that certain forms, approved by the taste of the time, should be made, by convention, and without regard to truth and beauty, general models of the human figure, and be transmitted as such to succeeding times. In this way the artists in the later periods did not even aim at accuracy of representation, but were contented with stiff general outlines, lavishing their labour on ornamental parts.

Architecture. Byzantine *architecture* may be said to have assumed its distinctive features in the church of St. Sophia, built by Justinian in the sixth century, and still existing as the chief mosque in Constantinople (" Hagia Sophia " or " Divine Wisdom "). It is more especially the style associated with the Greek Church as distinguished from the Roman. The leading forms of the Byzantine style are the round arch, the circle, and in particular the dome. The last is the most conspicuous and characteristic object in Byzantine buildings, and the free and full employment of it was arrived at when, by the use of pendentives, the architects were enabled to place it on a square apartment instead of a

Byzantine Architecture

Part of the Nave of the Palatine Chapel, Palermo

circular or polygonal. In this style of building, encrustation, the encrustation of brick with more precious materials, was largely in use. It depended much on colour and surface ornament for its effect, and with this intent mosaics wrought on ground of gold or of positive colour are profusely introduced, while coloured marbles and stones of various kinds are greatly made use of. The capitals are of peculiar and original design, the most characteristic being square and tapering downwards, and they are very varied in their decorations.

Byzantine architecture may be vided into an older and a newer neo-Byzantine) style. The most stinctive feature of the latter is at the dome is raised on a perpen-cular circular or polygonal piece of asonry (technically the *drum*) con-ining windows for lighting the terior, while in the older style the ht was admitted by openings in e dome itself. The Cathedral of hens is an example of the neo-yzantine style. The Byzantine style d a great influence on the archi-cture of Western Europe, especially Italy, where St. Mark's in Venice a magnificent example, as also in cily. It had also material influence Southern France and Western ermany. Byzantine influence made self felt also in the minor arts, of hich the East had been the home om ancient times. In Constanti-ople there flourished, along with e art of decorative sculpture, the ts of stone carving, of working in etal and ivory, of ornamental ronze-work, of enamelling, of weav-ng, and the art of miniature-paint-ng.—BIBLIOGRAPHY: C. Errard and . Gayet, *L'Art byzantin*; C. Diehl, *Manuel d'art byzantin*; O. M. Dalton, *Byzantine Art and Archæology*; C. Bayet, *L'Art Byzantin*; T. G. Jack-on, *Byzantine and Romanesque Architecture.*

BYZANTINE EMPIRE. The Eastern Roman Empire, so called from its capital Byzantium or Con-stantinople. The Byzantine Empire was founded in A.D. 395, when Theodosius at his death divided the Roman Empire between his sons Arcadius and Honorius. In this empire the Greek language and civi-lisation were prevalent; but the rulers claimed still to be Roman emperors, and under their sway the laws and official forms of Rome were maintained. It lasted for about a thousand years after the downfall of the Western Empire. It is also known as the *Greek Empire* or *Lower Empire.* Its capital was naturally Constantinople, a city established by Constantine in 330 as the new capital of the whole Roman Empire.

History. The Eastern Empire, then comprising Asia Minor, Syria, Egypt, Greece, Thrace, Mœsia, Mace-donia, and Crete, fell to Theodosius's elder son Arcadius, through whose weakness and that of several of his immediate successors it suffered severely from the encroachments of Huns, Goths, Bulgarians, and Per-sians. In 527 the celebrated Justinian succeeded, whose reign is famous for the codification of Roman law, and the victories of his generals Belisarius and Narses over the Vandals in Africa, and the Goths in Italy, which was henceforth governed for the Eastern Empire by an *exarch* residing at Ravenna. But his energy could not revive the decaying strength of the empire, and Justin II., his successor (565-578), a weak and avaricious prince, lost his reason by the reverses encountered in his conflicts with plundering Lombards, Avars, and Persians.

Tiberius, a captain of the guard, succeeded in 578, and in 582 Mauri-cius; both were men of ability. In 608 Phocas, proclaimed emperor by the army, succeeded, and produced by his incapacity the greatest dis-order in the empire. Heraclius, son of the Governor of Africa, who headed a conspiracy, conquered Constantinople, and caused Phocas to be executed (610). He was an excellent general, and finally suc-ceeded in repressing the Avars and recovering the provinces lost to the Persians, whose power, indeed, he overthrew. But a far more dangerous enemy to the Byzantine Empire now appeared in the Muslim power, founded amongst the Arabians by Mahomet and the caliphs, which gradually extended its conquests over Phœnicia, the countries on the Eu-phrates, Judea, Syria, and Egypt (635-641). In 641 Heraclius died, and his descendants were not capable of stemming the tide of Muslim inva-sion. The Arabians took part of Africa, Cyprus, and Rhodes (653), inundated Africa and Sicily, pene-trated into Thrace, and attacked Constantinople by sea.

The empire was in sore straits when Leo the Isaurian (Leo III.), general of the army of the East, ascended the throne (717), and a new period of comparative prosperity began. Numerous reforms, civil and military, were now introduced, and the wor-ship of images was prohibited. Leo repelled the Arabians or Saracens from Constantinople, but allowed the Lombards to seize the Italian provinces, while the Arabians plun-dered the Eastern ones. Constantine V. (741) recovered part of Syria and Armenia from the Arabians; and the struggle was carried on not un-successfully by his son Leo IV. Under his grandson, Constantine VI., Irene, the ambitious mother of the latter, raised a large faction by the restoration of image worship, and, in conjunction with her paramour Stauratius, disposed her son, and had his eyes put out (797).

A revolt of the patricians placed one of their order, Nicephorus, on the throne, who fell in the war against the Bulgarians (811). Stau-ratius, Michael, Leo V., and Michael

II. (820) ascended the throne in rapid succession. During the reign of Michael II. the Arabians conquered Sicily, Lower Italy, Crete, and other countries. The long dispute as to image worship was brought to a close in 842, when the practice was finally sanctioned at the council of Nicæa, under Michael III. He was put to death by Basil the Macedonian, who came to the throne as Basil I. in 867, and whose reign formed a period of great glory in the history of the Byzantine Empire. He founded a dynasty (the *Macedonian*) which lasted till 1056. Among the greatest of his successors were Nicephorus II. (Phocas), and John Zimisces (969), who carried on successful wars against the Mahommedans, Bulgarians, and Russians.

Basil II. succeeded this prince in 976. He vanquished the Bulgarians and the Arabians. His brother, Constantine IX. (1025), was succeeded by Romanus III. (1028), who married Zoe, daughter of Constantine. This dissolute but able princess caused her husband to be executed, and successively raised to the throne Michael IV. (1034), Michael V. (1041), and Constantine X. (1042). Russians and Mahommedans meanwhile devastated the empire. Zoe's sister Theodora succeeded her on the throne (1054).

After the short reign of Michael VI. (1054-7) Isaac Comnenus, the first of the Comnenian dynasty, ascended the throne, but soon after became a monk. The three chief emperors of this dynasty were Alexius, John, and Manuel Comnenus. During the reign of Alexius I. (1081-1118) the Crusades commenced. His son, John II., and grandson, Manuel I., fought with success against the Turks, whose progress also was considerably checked by the Crusades. The Latins, the name given to the French, Venetian, etc., crusaders, now forced their way to Constantinople (1204), conquered the city, and retained it, together with most of the European territories of the empire. Baldwin, Count of Flanders, was made emperor; Boniface, Marquis of Montferrat, obtained Thessalonica as a kingdom, and the Venetians acquired a large extent of territory. Theodore Lascaris seized on the Asiatic provinces, in 1206 made Nice (Nicæa) the capital of the empire, and was at first more powerful than Baldwin. Neither Baldwin nor his successors, Henry, Peter, and Robert of Courtenay, were able to secure the tottering throne. John, Emperor of Nice, conquered all the remaining Byzantine territory except Co[nstantinople], and at last, in 12[61] Michael Palæologus, King of Ni[cæa] conquered Constantinople, and th[us] overthrew the Latin dynasty.

Thus again the vast but exhaust[ed] Byzantine Empire was united und[er] Michael *Palæologus*, founder of t[he] last Byzantine dynasty. Intern[al] disturbances and wars with t[he] Turks disturbed the reigns of [his] descendants Andronicus II. a[nd] Andronicus III. For a time t[he] Cantacuzenes shared the crown wi[th] John Palæologus, son of Andronic[us] III.; but in 1355 John again b[e]came sole emperor. In his reign t[he] Turks first obtained a firm footing [in] Europe and conquered Gallipo[li] (1357).

In 1361 Sultan Amurath too[k] Adrianople. Bajazet conquere[d] almost all the European province[s] except Constantinople, and wa[s] pressing it hard when Timur['s] invasion of the Turkish province[s] saved Constantinople for this tim[e] (1402). Manuel then recovered h[is] throne, and regained some of th[e] lost provinces from the contendin[g] sons of Bajazet. To him succeede[d] his son John, Palæologus II. (1425[)] whom Amurath II stripped of a[ll] his territories except Constantinople and laid under tribute (1444).

To the Emperor John succeeded his brother Constantine Palæologus. With the assistance of his genera[l] Giustiniani, a Genoese, he withstood the superior forces of the enemy with fruitless courage, and fell in the defence of Constantinople, by the conquest of which (29th May, 1453) Mahomet II. put an end to the Greek or Byzantine Empire. The Byzantine Empire, which thus lasted for over a thousand years, was of immense service to the world in stemming the tide of Mahommedan advance, in spreading Christianity and civilisation, and in maintaining a regular system of government, law, and policy in the midst of surrounding barbarism.—BIBLIOGRAPHY: E. Gibbon, *Decline and Fall of the Roman Empire*; J. B. Bury, *History of the Eastern Roman Empire*; C. W. C. Oman, *Byzantine Empire*; A. Rambaud, *Etudes sur l'histoire byzantine*.

BYZAN'TIUM. The original name of the city of Constantinople. It was founded by Greek colonists in 657 B.C., and owing to its favourable position for commerce it attained great prosperity, and survived the decay of most of the other Greek cities. In A.D. 330 a new era began for it when Constantine the Great made it the capital of the Roman Empire.

C

C. The third letter in the English alphabet and the second of the consonants. In English it serves to represent two perfectly distinct sounds, namely, the guttural sound pertaining to *k* and the hard or thin sound of *s*, the former being that which historically belongs to it; while it also forms with *h* the digraph *ch.* The former sound it has before the vowels, *a, o,* and *u,* the latter before *e, i,* and *y.* The digraph *ch* has three different sounds, as in *church, chaise,* and *chord.* To these the Scottish add a fourth, heard in the word *loch.*

C. In music, (*a*) after the clef, the mark of common time, in which each measure is a semi-breve or four minims, corresponding to $\frac{4}{4}$ or $\frac{2}{2}$; and when a bar is perpendicularly drawn through it *alla-breve* time or a quicker movement is indicated. (*b*) The name of the first or key-note of the modern normal scale, answering to the *do* of the Italians and the *ut* of the French.

CAABA (kä'à-bà). *See* Kaaba.

CAAING WHALE (kä'ing; Scottish name, meaning " driving whale," whale that may be driven.) The round-headed porpoise (*Globicephălus deductor, Delphīnus melas,* or *D. globiceps*), a cetaceous animal of the dolphin family, characterised by a rounded muzzle and a convex head, attaining a size of 16 to 24 feet. It frequents the shores of Orkney, Shetland, the Faroe Islands, and Iceland, appearing in herds from 200 to 1000, and numbers are often caught. They live on cod, ling, and other large fish, and also on molluscs, especially the cuttle-fishes.

CAAMA (kä'mà). *See* Hartebeest.

CAB (short for the original name *cabriolet*). A kind of hackney-carriage with two or four wheels drawn by one horse. The original cab was for only one passenger besides the driver, and was a kind of hooded chaise. In the United Kingdom cabs are regulated by a variety of statutes. In London the principal Acts are those of 1831-53, 1869, 1896, and 1907 (London Cab and Stage Carriage Act).

CABAL'. In English history applied to the ministry under Charles II., which consisted of Sir Thomas, afterwards Lord *C*lifford, Lord *A*shley, afterwards Earl of Shaftesbury, George Villiers, Duke of *B*uckingham, Henry, Lord *A*rlington, and John, Duke of *L*auderdale; the initials of whose names happened to compose the word *cabal.* This term (which existed long before, and was derived from *cabala*) is applied to any junto united in some close design, usually to promote their private ends by intrigue.

CAB'ALA, or CAB'BALA. A mysterious kind of science or knowledge among Jewish rabbins, supposed to have been delivered to the ancient Jews by revelation—specifically to Moses on Sinai—and transmitted by oral tradition, serving for the interpretation of difficult passages of Scripture. This science consists chiefly in understanding the combination of certain letters, words, and numbers which are alleged to be significant. Every letter, word, number, and accent of the law is supposed to contain a mystery, and the Cabalists claim to be able to foretell future events by the study of this science. The two written sources recognised by the Cabalists are: The *Sefer Jezirah* (Book of Creation), and the *Zohar* (Book of Light). *See* Gnosticism.

CABALLERO (kà-bà-lyer'ō), **Fernan.** Pseudonym of Cecilia Böhl von Faber, the chief modern Spanish novelist, daughter of a German settled in Spain and married to a Spanish lady, born 1796, died 1877. Her first novel, *La Gaviota,* appeared in 1849, and was followed by *Elia, Clemencia, La Familia de Alvareda,* etc., as well as by many shorter stories. The chief charm of her writings lies in her descriptions of life and nature in Andalusia. She was three times left a widow; her last husband's name was Arrón.—Cf. A. Morel-Fatio, *Fernan Caballero, d'après sa correspondance avec Antoine de Latour,* in *Bulletin Hispanique* (vol. iii. 1901).

CAB'ANIS, Pierre Jean Georges. French physician, philosopher, and *littérateur,* born 1757, died 1808. He became acquainted with Madame Helvetius, and through her with Holbach, Franklin, and Jefferson, and became the friend of Condillac, Turgot, and Thomas. He professed the principles of the Revolution, and was intimately connected with Mirabeau. His *Rapports du Physique et du Moral de l'Homme* is his most important work. It displays considerable power of analysis, and advocates the most extreme materialistic doctrines. He afterwards changed his opinions and adopted theistic views.—Cf. F. Labrousse, *Quelques Notes sur Cabanis* (1903).

CABATUAN'. A town on the Island of Panay, one of the Philippines. Pop. 20,000.

CABAZE'RA. A town in the Island of Luzon, Philippines. Pop. 15,000.

CABBAGE. The popular name of

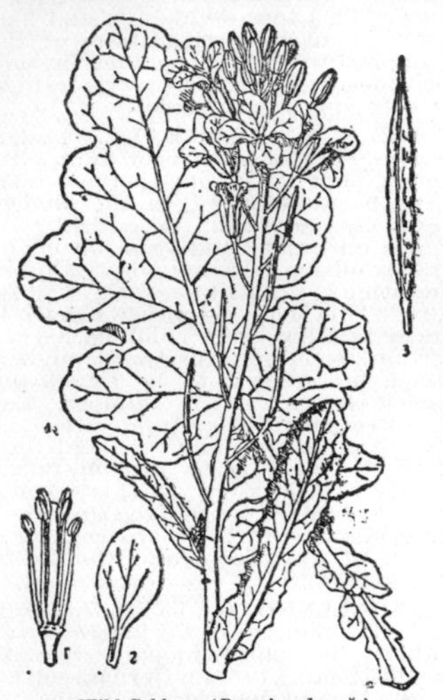

Wild Cabbage (*Brassica oleracĕa*)

1, Stamens and pistil. 2, Petal. 3, Fruit (*Siliqua*)

various species of cruciferous plants of the genus Brassica, and especially applied to the plain-leaved, hearting, garden varieties of *B. oleracĕa*, cultivated for food. The wild cabbage is a native of the coasts of Britain, but is much more common on other European shores. The kinds most cultivated are the common cabbage, the savoy, the broccoli, and the cauliflower. The common cabbage forms its leaves into heads or bolls, the inner leaves being blanched. Its varieties are the white, the red or purple, the tree or cow cabbage for cattle (branching and growing when in flower to the height of 10 feet), and the very delicate Portugal cabbage. The garden sorts form valuable culinary vegetables, and are used at table in various ways. In Germany pickled cabbage forms a sort of national dish, known as *sauerkraut*.

CABBAGE-BARK. *See* ANDIRA.

CABBAGE-BUTTERFLY. A name given to several species of butterfly, especially *Pieris brassicæ*, a large white butterfly, the larvæ of which destroy cruciferous plants, particularly of the cabbage tribe.

CABBAGE-FLY (*Anthomyia brassicæ*). A fly belonging to the same family (Muscidæ) as the house-fly and the same genus as the turnip- and potato-flies. Its larvæ or maggots are destructive to cabbages by producing disease in the roots, on which they feed.

CABBAGE-MOTH. The *Mamestra brassicæ*, a moth measuring about 1¾ inches across the open fore-wings, which are dusky brown, clouded with darker shades, and marked with dark spots, as also various streaks and spots of a yellowish or white colour. The caterpillar is greenish-black, and is found in autumn feeding on the hearts of cabbages.

CABBAGE-PALM (*Oreodoxa oleracĕa*). A native of the West Indies, the simple unbranched stem of which grows to a height of 150 or even 200 feet. The unopened bud of young leaves is much prized as a vegetable, but the removal of it completely destroys the tree, as it is unable to produce lateral buds.

CABBAGE-ROSE. A species of rose (*Rosa centifolia*) of many varieties, supposed to have been cultivated from ancient times, and eminently fitted for the manufacture of rose-water and attar from its fragrance. It has a large, rounded, and compact flower. Called also *Provence Rose*.

CAB'BALA. *See* CABALA.

CABEIRI. *See* CABIRI.

CA'BER. The undressed stem of a small tree, about 16 to 20 feet—occasionally more—in length, used in the Highland feat of "tossing the caber". The tosser holds it upright by the smaller end, and, running forward, hurls it from him in such a way that it strikes the ground with the larger end and then turns completely over.

CA'BES, or **QA'BES.** A town and port of Tunis, with a small trade. The Gulf of Qabes (*Syrtis Minor*), at the head of which the town is situated, lies between the Islands of Kerkenna and Jerba.

CABIN'DA. A seaport town of Portuguese West Africa, north of the Congo mouth, bounded by the Atlantic, the Belgian Congo, and the French Congo territory. The town carries on a considerable trade, and its people are noted for their shipbuilding and handicrafts. Pop. 10,000.

CAB'INET. The collective body of ministers who direct the government of a country. In Britain, though the Executive Government is vested nominally in the Crown, it resides practically in a committee of ministers called the *Cabinet.* Every Cabinet includes the First Lord of the Treasury, who is usually (not always) the Prime Minister, or chief of the ministry, and therefore of the Cabinet; the Lord Chancellor, the Lord President of the Council, the Chancellor of the Exchequer, the First Lord of the Admiralty, and the five Secretaries of State. A number of other ministerial functionaries, varying from two to eight, have usually seats in the Cabinet, and its members belong to both Houses of Parliament, but usually adhere to that political party which predominates for the time being in the House of Commons. Its meetings are secret, but records of its proceedings have been kept since 1916. Although the Cabinet is regarded as an essential part of the institutions of Great Britain, it has never been recognised by Act of Parliament. It began to take its present form in the reign of William III. The term is similarly used in the British colonies and in the United States, where, however, the members are not members of Congress. In the constitutional Governments of the continent of Europe, and in Japan, the model of the English Cabinet has usually been followed. In these countries, however, with the exception of France and Switzerland, there is no opportunity for the popular will to express itself directly in the choice of the chief executive.—Cf. W. Bagehot, *The English Constitution*; A. V. Dicey, *Introduction to the Study of the Law of the Constitution.*

CABI'RI, or **CABEI'RI.** Deities or deified heroes worshipped in the ancient Greek Islands of Lemnos, Imbros, and Samothrace, and also on the neighbouring coast of Troy in Asia Minor.

CABLE. A large strong rope or chain, such as is used to retain a vessel at anchor. It is made usually of hemp or steel, but may be made of other materials. A hemp-cable

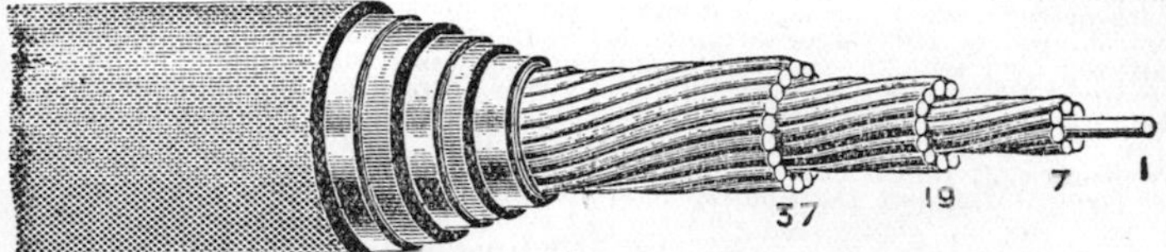

Arrangement of Strands in a 1-, 7-, 19-, and 37-stranded Cable

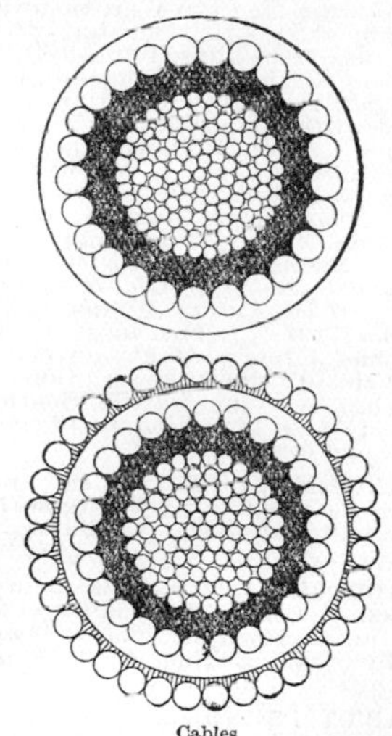
Cables

Top: Section of unarmoured concentric lead-sheathed cable. Bottom: Section of armoured concentric lead-sheathed cable.

is composed of three strands, each strand of three ropes, and each rope of three twists. A ship's cable is usually 120 fathoms or 720 feet in length; hence the expression *a cable's length.* Chain-cables have now almost superseded rope-cables. Although heavier and more difficult to manage, yet their immunity from chafing and rotting, their greater compactness for stowage, and their greater strength more than counterbalance these drawbacks.—An *electric cable* is composed of one or more copper wires enclosed in a compound of gutta-percha and resinous substances, or in specially-prepared paper. This cover is called *the insulation*. A lead covering is often superimposed on the insulation to keep out moisture and other substances. Outside the lead, again, is a layer of spirally-wound steel wire or tape when special protection is required. This steel armour is covered over with layers of jute and compound to prevent its corroding.—BIBLIOGRAPHY: Alexander Russell, *The Theory of Electric Cables and Networks*; J. R. Dick and F. Fernie, *Electric Mains and Distributing Systems*.

CABLE, George Washington. American writer, born in 1844, died in 1925. He served in the Confederate army during the Civil War, then took a commercial situation, but about 1879 devoted himself entirely to literature. His first important book was *Old Creole Days* (1879); among others written since are: *The Grandissimes*, *Madame Delphine*, *The Creoles of Louisiana* (a history), *Dr. Sevier*, *The Silent South* (a plea for the negro), *The Negro Question*, *Strange True Stories of Louisiana*, *John March*, *Strong Hearts*, *The Cavalier*, *Kincaid's Battery*, *Gideon's Band* (1914), *The Flower of the Chapdelaines* (1918). For most readers the chief interest of his novels lies in their excellent descriptions of French creole life in the Southern States; and his pictures of negro life are no less effective.

CABLE-MOULDING. In architecture, a moulding with its surface cut in imitation of the twisted strands of a rope.

CABOOSE'. The cook-room or kitchen of a ship. In smaller vessels it is an enclosed fire-place, hearth, or stove for cooking on the main deck.

CAB'OT, Sebastian. Navigator, born at Bristol about 1475, died about 1557. He was the son of John Cabot, a Venetian pilot, who resided at Bristol, and was highly esteemed for his skill in navigation. John Cabot appears to have settled in Bristol about 1472, and to have died there about 1498, after having lived again for some time at Venice. In 1496 John Cabot received from Henry VII. a commission giving him and his sons authority to sail for the purpose of discovering islands and countries then unknown; and in 1497, in company with Sebastian and two other sons, he discovered the mainland of N. America, having visited Nova Scotia and Cape Breton Island. In another voyage soon after, Sebastian is said to have visited Labrador and Newfoundland. He subsequently entered the service of King Ferdinand of Spain, and in 1516 was to make an attempt to discover the north-west passage, an attempt relinquished owing to the king's death. In 1526, when in the Spanish service, he was put in charge of an expedition which visited Brazil and the River Plata. He now held the office of Examiner of Pilots under Charles V., and while in this post he compiled a famous map of the world (1544). In 1547 he again settled in England, and received a pension from Edward VI. He became life-governor of the Company of Merchant Adventurers, who under his advice made an attempt to discover a way to Cathay (China) by the north-east, an attempt having important results for English trade with Russia and Asia. He was prime mover in organising the expedition of Willoughby and Chancellor in 1553, and that of Stephen Burrough in 1556. He was among the first who noticed and investigated the variations of the compass. — BIBLIOGRAPHY: Nicholls, *Remarkable Life of Sebastian Cabot*; Henry Harrisse, *John Cabot and his son Sebastian*; G. P. Winship, *Cabot Bibliography*.

CABOURG (kà-bör). A French sea-bathing resort, department of Calvados, not far from Caen, and near the entrance of the Dives into the English Channel. Pop. 1650.

CAB'RA. A town of Spain, Andalusia, in the province of Cordova, in a valley almost surrounded by mountains. The neighbouring region produces excellent wine and olive-oil. Pop. 12,420.

CABRAL', Pedro Alvarez. The discoverer (or second discoverer) of Brazil, a Portuguese, born about 1460, died about 1526. In 1500 he received command of a fleet bound for the East Indies, and sailed from Lisbon; but having taken a course too far to the west he was carried by the South American current to the coast of Brazil, of which he took possession in the name of Portugal. Continuing his voyage, but losing half his fleet, and among others the famous navigator Bartholomew Diaz, he visited Mozambique, and at last reached India, where he made important commercial treaties with native princes, and then returned to

Europe. Nothing further is known of the incidents of his life.

CABRE'RA. A small Spanish island, one of the Balearic Isles, south of Majorca, used as a place for receiving convicts.

CABUL, or CABOOL. *See* KABUL.

CACA'O, or CO'COA. The chocolate tree (*Theobrōma Cacāo*), nat. ord. Sterculiaceæ, and also the powder prepared from the fruit of this tree, and the beverage made with it. It is more especially to the powder and beverage that the form *cocoa* is

Cacao Plant

A, Old shoot bearing clusters of small flowers, and fruits in all stages of growth. B, Young leaf shoot. C, Ripe fruit, showing warted ridges. D, Seed, showing crumpled seed-leaves. E, Flower.

applied, this being a corruption of *cacao*, a word of native Mexican origin. The tree is 16 to 20 feet high, a native of tropical America, and much cultivated in the tropics of both hemispheres, especially in the West India Islands, Central and South America. The leaves are about 4 inches in length, smooth but not glossy, and of a dull-green colour; the flowers are saffron-coloured, and very beautiful. The fruit consists of pointed, oval, ribbed pods 6 to 10 inches long. The cultivated trees bear fruit all the year round, but the gathering is chiefly in June and December. The pods are removed by knives attached to the ends of poles. The pods are at first green, but as they ripen they change to a fine bluish-red, or almost purple colour, and in some varieties to a yellow or lemon colour. Each pod encloses fifty or more seeds in a white, sweetish pulp; and the seeds or "beans" have each a parchment-like covering enclosing a whitish pulp. These are very nutritive, containing 50 per cent of fat (about 22 per cent being starch, gum, etc., and 17 per cent being gluten and albumen), are of an agreeable flavour, and used, both in their fresh state and when dried, as an article of diet.

Cocoa and chocolate are made from them, the former being a powder obtained by grinding the slightly-fermented and undried seeds, and often mixed with other substances when prepared for sale, the latter being this powder mixed with sugar and various flavouring-matters and formed into solid cakes. Cacao is now cultivated in many tropical countries, the European supply coming mainly from Venezuela, Ecuador, Brazil, Trinidad, Ceylon, Jamaica, and West Africa. The annual consumption of cacao is upward of 100,000,000 pounds. The seeds when roasted and divested of their husks and crushed are known as *cocoa nibs*. The seeds yield also a fat called cacao-butter, used in pomatum and for making candles, soap, etc. *Coconuts* are obtained from an entirely different tree. The Spanish invaders of South America during 1513-23 found the seeds of cacao being used in place of money, and their great dietary value was investigated by Benzoni in 1550. They are first mentioned in connection with England in 1659.

CÁCERES (kä'the-res). A town of Western Spain, Estremadura, capital of a province of the same name, with an episcopal palace, an old castle, and the largest bull-ring in Spain. Pop. 17,500. Pop. of province, 415,790; area, 7667 sq. miles.

CACHALOT (kash'a-lot). *See* SPERM-WHALE.

CACHAR'. An East Indian district in Assam; area, 3769 sq. miles. Pop. 500,000, entirely engaged either in rice cultivation or on the tea plantations.

CACHE (French origin). A word in use by Canadian and Western hunters, Arctic explorers, and others, to describe a hole dug in the ground for the storing of food, game, or temporarily-abandoned stores.

CACHET (kä-shā), **LETTRES DE.** A name given especially to letters proceeding from and signed by the Kings of France, and countersigned by a Secretary of State. They were at first made use of occasionally as a means of delaying the course of justice, but they appear to have been rarely employed before the seventeenth century as warrants for the detention of private citizens, and for depriving them of their personal liberty. During the reign of Louis XIV. their use became very common, and by means of them persons were imprisoned for life or for a long period on the most frivolous pretexts. They were abolished at the Revolution.

CACHEXY (ka-kek′si), or **CACHEXIA** (Gr., "evil habit of body"), A depraved condition of nutrition. It is a sign of disturbance of the normal balance of the nutrition of the body. It is not a disease, but is the result of various diseases, e.g. cancer, malaria, Hodgkin's disease, myxedema, exophthalmic goitre.

CACHOEIRA (kä-sho-ā′i-rȧ). A town of Brazil, in the state of Bahia, and 62 miles N.W. of the town of Bahia. Pop. 15,000.

CACHOLONG. An opaque opal, commonly bluish-white, known also as pearl-opal. It derives its name from *Cach*, a river of Bokhara, where it was originally found, and the Kalmuck word *chalong*, meaning *stone*.

CACHOU (ka-shö′). A sweetmeat in the form of a pill, made from the extract of liquorice, cashew-nut, gum, etc., used by smokers to sweeten the breath.

CACHUCA (kȧ-chö′kȧ). A Spanish dance performed by a man and woman to a lively, graceful air in triple time and with a strongly-marked accent. It was introduced on the stage by Fanny Eissler, in the ballet of *Le Diable Boiteux*.

CACIQUE (ka-sēk′). In some parts of America the title of the native chiefs at the time of the conquest by the Spaniards.

CAC′ODYLE. *See* KAKODYLE.

CAC′OLET. A contrivance somewhat resembling a double arm-chair, or in other cases like a bed, fixed on the back of a mule or horse for carrying sick persons or travellers in mountainous countries.

CACOMISTLE. A species of North American carnivora (*Basariscus astutus*) related to and resembling the raccoon.

CACON′DA. A town of Angola, West Africa, about 140 miles south-east of Benguella, in a healthy district.

CACTACEÆ. *See* CACTUS.

CACTUS. A Linnæan genus of plants, now used as a name for any of the Cactaceæ, a nat. ord. of dicotyledons, otherwise called the Indian fig order. The species are succulent shrubs, with minute scale-like leaves (except in the genus Pereskia, tree-cactus, with large leaves), and with clusters of spines on the stems. They have fleshy stems, with sweetish watery or milky juice, and they assume many peculiar forms. The juice in some species affords a refreshing beverage where water is not to be got. All the plants of this order, except a single species are natives of America. They are generally found in very dry localities, being xerophytes of an extreme type, with reduced surface, very thick cuticle, and water-storing tissue. Some are epiphytes. Several have been introduced into the Old World, and in many places they have become naturalised. The fruits of some species are edible, as the prickly-pear and the Indian fig, cultivated throughout the Mediterranean region. The flowers are usually large and beautifully coloured, and many members of the order are cultivated in hot-houses. The principal genera are Melocactus, Echinocactus, Opuntia, Cereus, and Mammillaria.

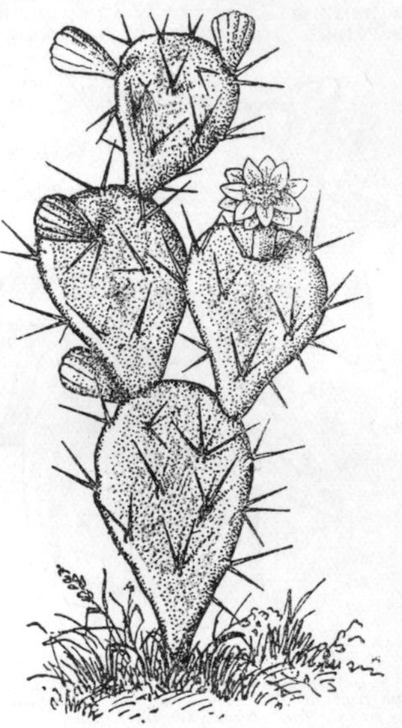

Cactus. Prickly Pear (*Opuntia Dillenii*)

CADAMOSTO, Alois da. An early navigator. Born at Venice about

1432, died 1464. He explored the west coast of Africa as far south as the Gambia. His *Book of the First Voyage over the Ocean to the Land of Negroes in Lower Ethiopia* was published in 1507.

CADAS'TRAL SURVEY. A term sometimes loosely applied to the Ordnance Survey. In its strict sense a cadastral survey includes not only the extent, divisions, and subdivisions of a country or district, but also the nature of the produce, crops, etc. It thus supplies a ground upon which land taxation can be based.

CADBURY. An English family of chocolate manufacturers. The business dates from 1794, when it was started in Birmingham by a Somerset man, Richard Tapper Cadbury. The business grew enormously, and a garden city called Bourneville was built for the works and workers.

CADDIS-FLY. An insect of the genus Phryganea, ord. Neuroptera, called also the *May-fly*, the larva or grub of which (caddis or case worm) forms for itself a case of small stones,

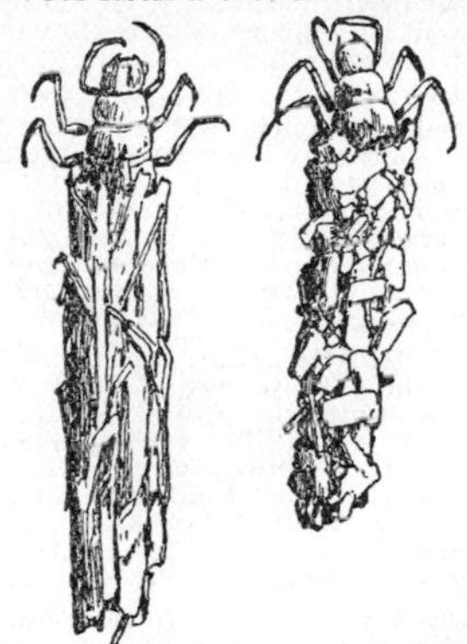

Caddis Grubs

1, In case of grass stalks. 2, In case of small stones

grass-roots, shells, etc., lives under water till ready to emerge from the pupa state, and is used as bait by anglers. This grub is very rapacious, and devours large quantities of fish-spawn.

CADE, John (better known as *Jack Cade*). A popular agitator of the fifteenth century, leader of an insurrection of the common people of Kent (1450) in the reign of Henry VI. Having defeated a force sent against him he advanced to London which he ruled for two days. On a promise of pardon being given the rebels soon dispersed, but Cade himself was killed by a gentleman of Kent named Iden.—Cf. Joseph Clayton, *True Story of Jack Cade* (1909).

CA'DENCE. The concluding notes of a musical composition or of any well-defined section of it. A cadence is *perfect, full*, or *authentic* when the last chord is the tonic preceded by the dominant; it is *imperfect* when the chord of the tonic precedes that of the dominant; it is *plagal* when the closing tonic chord is preceded by that of the sub-dominant; and it is *interrupted, false*, or *deceptive* when the bass rises a second, instead of falling fifth. Cadence, or *cadenza*, is the name also given to a running passage which a performer may introduce at the close of a movement.

CA'DENCY, Marks of. In heraldry, marks intended to show the descent of a younger branch of a family from the main stock.

CADEN'ZA. *See* CADENCE.

CADER IDRIS. A mountain mass about 10 miles long in Merionethshire, Wales. The highest peak is 2914 feet above the level of the sea.

CADET' (Fr.). A younger or youngest son; a junior male member of a noble family. Also the name or title given to a young man in training for the rank of an officer in the army or navy, or in a military school. In Britain cadets are trained for the army by a course of military discip-

Cadet

line, at the Royal Military Academy at Woolwich, or the Royal Military College at Sandhurst, previous to obtaining a commission. A naval cadet is one who holds the first or lowest grade as a candidate for a commission in the Royal Navy, the cadets being generally admitted by competition.—The *Cadets* (K.D., abbreviation for Constitutional Democrats), is the name of a modern political party in Russia, constituted in 1905.

CADET'S FUMING LIQUOR. *See* ALKARSIN.

CA'DI, or **KADI.** In Arabic, a judge or jurist. Among the Turks *cadi* signifies an inferior judge, as distinguished from the mollah, or superior judge. They belong to the higher priesthood, as the Turks derive their law from their prophet.

CADIZ (kä'*d*ēth ; ancient, **Gades**). A seaport of South-Western Spain, situated at the extremity of a long tongue of land projecting from the Island of Leon, which is separated by a narrow (bridged) channel from the coast of Andalusia. It is well built, well paved, and very clean, and is strongly fortified. The chief buildings are the great hospital, the custom-house, the old and new cathedrals, the theatres, the bull-ring, capable of accommodating 12,000 spectators, and the lighthouse of St. Sebastian. It has a medical school affiliated to the University of Seville. The bay of Cadiz is a large basin enclosed by the mainland on one side and the projecting tongue of land on the other, with good anchorage, and protected by the neighbouring hills. It has four forts, two of which form the defence of the grand arsenal, La Carraca (4 miles from Cadiz), at which are large basins and docks. Cadiz has long been the principal Spanish naval station. Its trade is large, its principal exports being wine and fruit. Cadiz was founded by the Phœnicians about 1100 B.C., and was one of the chief seats of their commerce in the west of Europe. Pop. 77,896.—The province of Cadiz is the most southerly in Spain ; area, 2834 sq. miles ; pop. 556,429.

CAD'MIUM. A metal which resembles tin in colour and lustre, but which is a little harder. It is very ductile and malleable ; has a specific gravity of 8·6 ; and fuses a little below a red heat, viz. 320° C. In its chemical character it resembles zinc. It occurs in the form of carbonate, as an ingredient in various kinds of calamine, or carbonate of zinc. Pure cadmium is not found in a natural state, but it occurs in the form of a sulphide, as the rare mineral greenockite, found in Hungary. It is used as a constituent of fusible alloys. Its symbol is Cd, its atomic weight 112. Cadmium was discovered by Stromeyer in 1817.

CADMIUM YELLOW. A pigment prepared from the sulphide of cadmium. It is of an intense yellow colour, and possesses much body.

CADMUS. In Greek legend, the son of Agenor and grandson of Poseidon (Neptune). He was said to have come from Phœnicia to Greece about 1550 B.C., and to have built the city of Cadmea or Thebes, in Bœotia. Herodotus and other writers ascribe the introduction of the Phœnician alphabet into Greece to Cadmus. The solar mythists identify him with the sun-god.

CADORE (kȧ-dō'rā). A small town of North Italy, 22 miles N.N.E. of Belluno, the native place of Titian, who was born there in 1477.

CADORNA, Count Luigi. Italian soldier, born 1850. He entered the Italian army in 1868, and was appointed Chief of the General Staff in 1914. When Italy entered the war in 1915, he was appointed Commander-in-Chief, a position which he retained until after the battle of Caporetto in 1917, when he was superseded by General Diaz. He died in 1928.

CADRE (kä'dr). The permanent establishment of officers and other ranks forming the framework of a regiment, etc. ; it is filled up by enlistment when required. The word is also used in the sense of the complement of officers of a regiment, or a list of such officers.

CADU'CEUS. Mercury's rod ; a winged rod entwisted by two serpents, borne by Mercury as an ensign of quality and office. In modern times it is used as a symbol of commerce, Mercury being the god of commerce. The rod represents power ; the serpents, wisdom ; and the two wings, diligence and activity.

CÆCILIANS (Lat. *cæcus*, blind, from the minuteness of their eyes). An amphibian order, embracing tropical worm-like forms, entirely destitute of limbs, and with very small eyes almost hidden in the skin. They burrow in the ground, and are usually 1 to 2 feet in length, but often much longer.

CÆCUM. A blind process or sac in the alimentary canal of various animals. In fishes they are often numerous and long ; and birds have generally two near the termination of the intestine. Mammals have commonly only one *cæcum*. In man the " blind-gut " is small and situated at the beginning of the colon.

CÆDMON (kad'mon). The first English poet of note who wrote in his own language, flourished about the end of the seventh century. According to Bede, in his *Ecclesiastical History*, Cædmon was originally a tenant (or perhaps only a cow-herd) on the abbey lands at Whitby, but afterwards was received into the monastery. His chief work (if it can all be attributed to him) consists of paraphrases of portions of the Scriptures, in alliterative verse, the first part of which bears striking resemblances to Milton's narrative in *Paradise Lost*.—Cf. S. H. Gurteen, *Epic of the Fall of Man*.

CAEN (käṇ). A town of France, in Normandy, chief place in the department of Calvados, 125 miles north-west of Paris, and about 9 miles from the mouth of the Orne, which is here navigable. There is a dock connected with the sea by a canal as well as by the river. It is the centre of an important trade, the market of a rich agricultural district, and carries on extensive manufactures. It is well built, with wide streets, and possesses many old buildings. One of the finest churches is that of St. Pierre, whose tower, terminated by a spire, is exceedingly graceful, and was built in 1308. Two other remarkable churches are St. Etienne or Church of the Abbaye-aux-Hommes, built by William the Conqueror, who was buried in it, and La Ste. Trinité or Church of the Abbaye-aux-Dames, founded by the Conqueror's wife. The buildings of the former abbaye are now used as a college, of the latter as a hospital. Other buildings are the castle and the hôtel de ville. There is a university, a museum, a public library with over 100,000 volumes, and a botanic garden. Lace is largely made there. Valuable building-stone is quarried. (*See* next article.) Pop. (1931), 57,528.

CAEN-STONE. The French equivalent for the Bath oolite of England, a cream-coloured building-stone of excellent quality, got near Caen in Normandy. Winchester and Canterbury Cathedrals, Henry VII.'s Chapel at Westminster, and many churches are built of it.

CAER'LEON. A small town in Monmouthshire, 26 miles from Bristol, on the River Usk. It was the site of the *Isca Silurum*, the chief Roman station in the country of the Silures, and Roman coins, statues, and sepulchral monuments are yet found. There are also the vestiges of an amphitheatre. Pop. (1931), 2326.

CAERNARVONSHIRE. County in North Wales, almost surrounded by sea. The county covers 572 sq. miles. The chief town is Caernarvon. The rivers include the Conway and the Ogwen. Pop. (1931), 120,810.

CAERPHILLY. An ancient market town of S. Wales, Glamorganshire, 7 miles north by west of Cardiff, with manufactures of woollens, ironworks, and collieries. It gives its name to one of the seven parliamentary divisions of the county. There are extensive ruins of an ancient castle. Pop. (1931), 35,760.

CÆSALPINIEÆ. A sub-division of the nat. ord. Leguminosæ, containing numerous, mainly tropical genera. The typical genus is Cæsalpinia, to which belong the Brazil-wood, sapan-wood, Nicaragua-wood, etc. The Cæsalpinieæ include also among their number senna, the carob, tamarind, logwood, etc.

CÆ'SAR. A title, originally a surname of the Julian family at Rome, which, after being dignified in the person of the dictator Gaius Julius Cæsar, was adopted by the successive Roman emperors, and afterwards came to be applied to the heir-presumptive to the throne. The title was perpetuated in the *Kaiser* of the Holy Roman Empire, and in the *Tsar* of the former Russian Empire.

CÆ'SAR, Gaius Julius. A great Roman general, statesman, and historian, born 100 B.C., died 44 B.C. He was the son of the prætor Gaius Julius Cæsar, and of Aurelia, a daughter of Aurelius Cotta. At the age of sixteen he lost his father, and shortly after he married Cornelia, the daughter of Lucius Cinna, the friend of Marius. This connection gave great offence to Sulla, the dictator, who proscribed him for refusing to put away his wife. His friends obtained his pardon with difficulty, and Cæsar withdrew from Rome and went to Asia, serving his first campaign under M. Minucius Thermus, the prætor in Asia. On the death of Sulla, Cæsar returned to Rome, where he distinguished himself as an orator. He afterwards visited Rhodes, when he was taken by pirates, and compelled to pay fifty talents for his release. To revenge himself, he fitted out some vessels at Miletus, overtook the pirates, made the greater number of them prisoners, and had them crucified before Pergamus. He now returned to Rome, where his eloquence and liberality made him very popular. He was pontifex maximus in 63 B.C., prætor in 62 B.C., and Governor of Spain in 61 B.C.

On his return to Rome, having united Pompey and Crassus in the memorable coalition called "the first triumvirate," he became consul, and then obtained the government of Gaul with the command of four legions. His military career was rapid and brilliant. He compelled the Helvetii, who had invaded Gaul, to retreat to their native country, subdued Ariovistus, who at the head of a German tribe had attempted to settle in the country of the Ædui, and conquered the Belgæ. In nine years he reduced all Gaul, crossed the Rhine twice (55 B.C. and 53), and twice passed over to Britain, defeated the natives of this island in several battles, and compelled them to give him hostages. The Senate had continued his government in Gaul for another period of five years, while Pompey was to have the command of Spain, and Crassus that of Syria, Egypt, and Macedonia for five years also. But the death of Crassus in his campaign against the Parthians dissolved the triumvirate; and about

Gaius Julius Cæsar

the same time the friendship between Cæsar and Pompey cooled. The Senate, influenced by Pompey, ordered that Cæsar should resign his offices and command within a certain time, or be proclaimed an enemy to the State, and appointed Pompey general of the army of the Republic. Upon this Cæsar urged his soldiers to defend the honour of their leader, passed the Rubicon (49 B.C.), and made himself master of Italy without striking a blow, Pompey retiring into Greece. Cæsar then levied an army with the treasures of the State, and hastened into Spain, which he reduced to submission without coming to a pitched battle with Pompey's generals.

He next conquered Massilia (now Marseilles), and returned to Rome, where he was appointed dictator. He then followed Pompey into Greece, and defeated him at Pharsalia, from which Pompey escaped only to be assassinated in Egypt. In Rome the Senate and the people strove eagerly to gain the favour of the victor. They appointed him consul for five years, dictator for a year, and tribune of the people for life. When his dictatorship had expired he caused himself to be chosen consul again, and, without changing the ancient forms of government, ruled with almost unlimited power. In 46 B.C. he crossed to Africa, defeated the Pompeians Scipio and Cato at Thapsus, and returning to Rome he was received with the most striking marks of honour. The term of his dictatorship was prolonged to ten years, the office of censor conferred on him alone; his person was declared inviolable, and his statue placed beside that of Jupiter in the Capitol. He soon after was honoured with four several triumphs, made perpetual dictator, and received the title of *imperator* with full powers of sovereignty. In Feb., 44, he declined the diadem which Antony publicly offered him, and next morning his statues were decked with diadems. His glory, however, was short-lived, for a conspiracy was set on foot by his enemy Cassius, and joined by many of his own friends, including M. Brutus; and, although dark hints had been given to him of his danger, he attended a meeting of the Senate on 15th (Ides) March, 44 B.C., and fell beneath the daggers of the conspirators.

Of his writings, we still possess the history of his wars with the Gauls and with Pompey. Cæsar was undoubtedly "the foremost man of all this world," being great as a statesman, a general, an orator, a historian, and an architect and engineer, and his assassination was brought about more by jealousy and envy than by real patriotism. — BIBLIOGRAPHY: W. Warde Fowler, *Julius Cæsar*; T. Mommsen, *History of Rome*; J. A. Froude, *Cæsar: a Sketch*; G. Ferrero, *Greatness and Decline of Rome*; Napoleon III., *Histoire de Jules César*; F. Scott, *Portraitures of Julius Cæsar*; E. G. Sihler, *Annals of Cæsar*.

CÆSARE'A. The ancient name of many cities, such as: (1) *Cæsarea Philippi* in Palestine, north of the Sea of Galilee, rebuilt by Philip, tetrarch of Galilee, son of Herod the Great.—(2) *Cæsarea*, on the shores of the Mediterranean, about 55 miles N.W. of Jerusalem, enlarged and beautified by Herod the Great, and named in honour of Cæsar Augustus; the place where St. Paul was imprisoned two years (Acts xxiii.-xxv.)—

(3) The capital of Cappadocia, in Asia Minor.

CÆSA'REAN OPERATION. A surgical operation for the delivery of a live child by means of an incision through the walls of the abdomen and womb. This operation is necessary when the pelvis of the mother is too narrow to allow of delivery of the child by natural means, or when there are other causes of obstruction. It is said to be so named because Julius Cæsar was delivered in this manner from the womb of his dead mother. Pliny mentions that Scipio Africanus was born in this way, and the names of Æsculapius, Macduff, and Edward VI. are also connected with this operation—incorrectly in the case of the last named. *See* OBSTETRICS; SURGERY.

CÆSA'RION. Son of Julius Cæsar and Cleopatra, put to death by order of Augustus.

CÆSIUM. A rare metal, first discovered by Bunsen and Kirchhoff by spectrum analysis in 1860; symbol, Cs; atomic weight, 133. It is soft, and of a silver-white colour. It is always found in connection with rubidium. It belongs to the same group of elements with lithium, sodium, potassium, and rubidium, viz. the group of the alkali-metals.

CÆS'TUS. The boxing-glove of the Grecian and Roman pugilists. It was loaded with metal to increase the weight of the blow.

CÆSU'RA (Lat., a cutting). In Latin verse the separation of the last syllable of any word from those which precede it, by making it part of the following foot. In English poetry it is equivalent to a pause.

CAF, or KAF. In Mahommedan mythology, a mountain, which surrounds the whole earth as a hedge encloses a field. Its foundation is the stone Sakhral, which is an emerald, whose reflection gives the sky its tints.

CAFFA, Strait of. *See* YENIKALE.

CAFF'EÏNE, or THE'ÏNE. The active principle of tea and coffee, a slightly-bitter, highly-azotised substance, crystallising in slender, silk-like needles, found in coffee-beans, tea-leaves, Paraguay tea, guarana, etc. The stimulating action of tea and coffee is largely due to the presence of this substance, commercial coffee containing 1·5, and tea from 2 to 4 per cent of caffeine. Doses of 2 to 10 grains induce violent nervous and vascular excitement.

CAFFRARIA. *See* KAFFRARIA.

CAFFRE-CORN. A variety of millet (*Sorghum vulgāre*). *See* DURRA.

CAFFRES. *See* KAFFIRS.

CAFTAN. *See* KAFTAN.

CAGLI (kȧl'yē.) A town of Central Italy, 13 miles S. of Urbino, with a cathedral which contains a great fresco by the father of Raphael, Giovanni Santi. Pop. (commune), 12,964.

CAGLIARI (kȧl'yȧ-rē). The capital of the Island of Sardinia, at the head of a fine bay on the south coast. It is the residence of the viceroy and of an archbishop, and the seat of a university founded in 1624. It has some manufactures, and is the chief emporium of all the Sardinian trade. Its spacious and safe harbour is defended by several forts. Pop. 61,175.

CAGLIARI, Paulo. *See* VERONESE, PAUL.

CAGLIOSTRO (kȧl-yos'trō), **Count Alessandro** (real name *Guiseppe* [*Joseph*] *Balsamo*). A celebrated charlatan, born in 1743 at Palermo. He was the son of poor parents, and entered the order of the Brothers of Mercy, where he acquired a knowledge of the elements of chemistry and physic. He left, or had to leave, the order, and committed so many crimes in Palermo that he was obliged to abscond. He subsequently formed a connection with Lorenza Feliciani, whose beauty, ability, and want of principle made her a valuable accomplice in his frauds. With her he travelled through many countries, assuming other names besides that of Count Cagliostro, claiming to have supernatural powers, and wringing considerable sums from those who became his dupes.

In England he established an order of what he called Egyptian Masonry, in which, as *grand kophta*, he pretended to reveal the secrets of futurity, and made many dupes among the higher classes. In Paris he was implicated in the affair of the diamond necklace which caused so great a scandal in the reign of Louis XVI., and was imprisoned in the Bastille, but escaped by means of his matchless impudence. He afterwards visited England, but met with little success. In 1789 he revisited Rome, where he busied himself about freemasonry; but being discovered, and committed to the Castle of St. Angelo, he was condemned by a decree of the Pope to imprisonment for life as a freemason, an arch-heretic, and a very dangerous foe to religion. He died in prison in 1795.—Cf. W. R. H. Trowbridge, *Cagliostro: the Splendour and Misery of a Master of Magic.*

CAGOTS (kä'gōz). A peculiar race of men inhabiting France, in the Western Pyrenees. In the Middle Ages they were believed to be cannibals and heretics, and treated with the greatest ignominy. Legally they are now on a level with other Frenchmen, but socially they are still regarded as degraded. The name is probably derived from the Armorican *cacouz*, leprous, the Cagots being supposed to be descended from lepers.

CAHIR (kā'ėr). An inland town, Ireland, County Tipperary, on the Suir, about 10 miles W. by N. of Clonmel, with an old picturesque castle on the summit of a rock. Pop. (1931), 1707.

CAHORS (kä-ōr). A town in Southern France, department of Lot, on the River Lot, 60 miles north of Toulouse. Under the Romans it was adorned with a temple, theatre, baths, an immense aqueduct, and forum, remains of which are still to be seen. Among the principal buildings are the cathedral, and an episcopal palace, now converted into the prefecture. It was the birthplace of Gambetta. Pop. 13,650.

CAHUECITE. An explosive invented by R. Cahue in 1875. *See* EXPLOSIVES.

CAI'APHAS. A Jew, the high-priest at the time when the crucifixion took place. He was deposed A.D. 35, and Jonathan, the son of Annas, appointed in his stead.

CAICOS, CAYOS (kī'kōz, kī'ōz), or **THE KEYS** (Sp. *cayo*, a rock or islet). One of the island groups comprehended under the general name of the Bahamas, consisting of six islands besides some uninhabited rocks. The largest, called the Great Key, is about 30 miles long. The inhabitants are few in number, and mostly engaged in fishing and the preparation of salt. In 1873 the Turks Islands and the Caicos were united into a commissionership under the governor of Jamaica. Pop. 5615, of whom 286 are white.

CAILLAUX, Joseph. French statesman, born at Mans in 1863. He studied law, but entered politics in 1888, and was appointed professor in the Ecole des Sciences Politiques in 1892. He was elected to the Chamber of Deputies in 1898, and was three times Minister of Finance between 1899 and 1911. He became Prime Minister in 1911, but was compelled to resign in 1912, having been violently attacked for his secret negotiations with Germany on the question of Morocco. He again became Minister of Finance in 1913, but Gaston Calmette, the editor of the *Figaro*, started a campaign with a view to driving him from office. On 16th March, 1914, Mme Caillaux shot Calmette in his office, and Caillaux immediately resigned. During the European War he took no active part in the Chamber of Deputies, where he made his first reappearance in the summer of 1917.

The attacks upon his pacifist policy, which had been made from time to time, now increased, and he was openly accused of being a pro-German, a traitor to his country, and of intriguing in Italy on behalf of a German peace. He was accused of being at the head of the *défaitist* elements in France. On 11th Dec., 1917, a demand for his trial was made, and his parliamentary immunity was suspended on 22nd Dec. On 14th Jan., 1918, he was arrested by order of M. Bouchardon, the examining magistrate, and confined to prison, awaiting trial before the High Court. He was tried in Feb., 1920, and was acquitted of treason, but found guilty of holding relations with the enemy likely to harm the Allies' cause. He was sentenced to three years' imprisonment (most of which he had already served) and to loss of civil rights for ten years. In 1924 both political and civil rights were restored to M. Caillaux, and in 1925 he was asked to join the Government as Minister of Finance, though later in the year he resigned. Again in 1926 he held the same office.

CAIN. The eldest son of Adam and Eve; the first murderer, who slew his brother Abel. For the Biblical history of Cain and his descendants see Gen. iv.-vii. A Gnostic sect of the second century, called *Cainites*, held that Cain was the offspring of a superior power and Eve, and Abel of an inferior power—the Jewish God—and that the killing of Abel symbolised the defeat of the inferior by the superior power.

CAINE, Sir Thomas Henry Hall. Novelist and miscellaneous writer, born in 1853 of Manx and English parents. Educated in the Isle of Man and at Liverpool, he was trained as an architect, but early gave up architecture for journalism and literature. Among his earliest writings were: *Sonnets of Three Centuries*, *Recollections of Rossetti*, and *Cobwebs of Criticism* (1883); followed by a *Life of Coleridge* in the Great Writers Series (1887). His first novels were: *The Shadow of a Crime* (1885), and *A Son of Hagar* (1886), but *The Deemster* (1887, dramatised as *Ben-my-Chree*) first brought him into prominent notice.

His other novels include: *The Bondsman, The Scapegoat, The Prophet, The Manxman, The Christian, The Eternal City, The Prodigal Son, Pete, The Woman Thou Gavest Me*—all popular, though meeting with severe criticism at the hands of critics. His most successful novels deal with Manx life, with which he made himself familiar during a long residence in the island. He travelled in Iceland, Morocco, Russia, and N. America. During the European War, Sir Hall Caine devoted himself almost exclusively to British propaganda in the United States. He was created a K.B.E. in 1918, and made a Companion of Honour in 1922. He died 31st Aug., 1931.

CAINOZO'IC. A geological name (from Gr. *kainos*, recent, and *zōē*, life) for the third great group into which systems of strata have been arranged, with reference to the age of the fossils that they include, and for the corresponding era of time. The *Tertiary* group and era of many geologists corresponds generally with the Cainozoic; but the latter term is sometimes extended to include the Quaternary group also. The Cainozoic, beginning with the Eocene period, is essentially the "age of mammals." It is written also Kainozoic. The appearance of man in Postpliocene times is usually held to end the Cainozoic era, and to open the Quaternary era, in which we still are living.

ÇA-IRA (sä-ē-rä: "It [the revolution] shall go on"). The burden or refrain of a French revolutionary song of 1790, the words by Ladré, a street singer. The air was a favourite one with Marie Antoinette. It was banned by the Directoire in 1797.

CAIRD, Edward. Born in 1835, educated at Glasgow and Oxford; was professor of moral philosophy at Glasgow 1866-93, then master of Balliol College, Oxford. He published *Account of the Philosophy of Kant, Social Philosophy and Religion of Comte, Essays on Literature and Philosophy, The Evolution of Religion, The Evolution of Theology in the Greek Philosophers*, etc. He died in 1908.

CAIRD, John, D.D. Scottish divine, brother of the above, born 1820; was professor of divinity in Glasgow University 1862, principal 1873-98; died 1898. He published sermons (*The Religion of Common Life, etc.*), *Introduction to the Philosophy of Religion*, etc.

CAIRN (kärn). A heap of stones; especially one of those large heaps of stones common in parts of the British Isles, particularly in Scotland, Ireland, and Wales, and generally of a conical form. They are of various sizes and forms, however, and were doubtless constructed for different objects. Some are evidently sepulchral, containing urns, stone chests, bones, etc. Many of this class date from prehistoric times, and they often cover a considerable area, and enclose a chamber or chambers entered by a long covered passage. The oldest British cairns belong to the

Cairn

Stone Age, the later to the Bronze Age, these latter being without an internal chamber. Some cairns were erected to commemorate some great event, others appear to have been intended for religious rites, while the modern cairn is generally set up as a landmark. Barrows are much the same as sepulchral cairns, but are chiefly composed of earth heaped up.

CAIRNES (kernz), **John Elliot.** Political economist, born at Drogheda 1823, died 1875. He graduated at Trinity College, Dublin, and became successively professor of political economy in Dublin, Galway, and University College, London. Chief works: *Character and Logical Method of Political Economy*; *Political Essays*; *Leading Principles of Political Economy*; *Essays on Political Economy, Theoretical and Applied.* He was on the whole a follower of J. S. Mill, but held very independent opinions.

CAIRNGORM. A Scottish mountain forming one of a great group of the Grampians on the borders of Aberdeen, Banff, and Inverness shires, and rising to the height of 4084 feet above sea-level. It is particularly celebrated for the brownish or yellowish quartz crystals found on it, or in its neighbourhood, called *cairngorms*, and found also in many other localities. They are much used for brooches, seals, and other ornaments. *Smoky quartz* is a name given to some of the darker-coloured varieties.

CAIRNS, Hugh M'Calmont. First Earl Cairns and Lord Chancellor, born in Ireland 1819, died 1885. He graduated with distinction at Dublin University, came to London to study law, was called to the Bar in 1844, and was made Q.C. in 1856. In 1858, Lord Derby, being Premier, he was appointed Solicitor-General, and received a knighthood, having been member of Parliament for Belfast since 1852. He now took a prominent position in Parliament, was made Attorney-General by Lord Derby in 1866, and also Lord Justice of Appeal, and the following year was raised to the Upper House as Baron Cairns. In 1868 he became Lord Chancellor under Disraeli, retiring with the fall of the Government the same year. He strongly opposed the disestablishment of the Irish Church, and the Irish land legislation that immediately followed. In 1874 he again became Lord Chancellor under Disraeli, and held this position during the six years that the administration lasted, being created Viscount Garmoyle and Earl Cairns in 1878. After 1880 he took less part in public affairs.

CAIRNS. A seaport on the east coast of Northern Queensland, the port of a district which produces large quantities of sugar, and in or near which gold-mining and tin-mining are also carried on. A railway runs some distance inland. Pop. 5193.

CAIRN TERRIER. Small dog of the terrier breed. In colour it varies from grey to black, or sandy or brindled. Its hair is wiry and its tail and legs short. It is a good house-dog and useful in sport.

CAIRO (kī'rō; Ar. *Kahira*, the Victorious). The capital of Modern Egypt, situated on the right bank of the Nile, 12 miles above the apex of its delta, and 150 miles by rail from Alexandria. The character of the town is still mainly Arabic, though in modern times the European style in architecture and other matters has become more and more prevalent. The city is partly surrounded by a fortified wall, and is intersected by seven or eight great streets, from which runs a labyrinth of narrow crooked streets and lanes. There are several large squares or places, the principal being the Ezbekīyeh. To the south-east of the town is the citadel, on the last spur of the Mokattam Hills, overlooking the city. It contains the fine mosque of Mohammed Ali, a well 270 feet deep, called Joseph's Well, cut in the rock, the palace of the Viceroy, etc. There are upwards of 400 mosques. The finest is that of Sultan Hassan. The principal seat of Koranic learning at Cairo is the mosque and University of El-Azhar, founded in the year 361 of the Hegira (A.D. 972). It has about 400 professors and 10,000 students of Islam. There are also some forty Christian churches, Jewish synagogues, etc. The tombs in the burying-grounds outside the city also deserve mention, especially those known as the tombs of the Caliphs. Cairo has a Court of Appeal, about half of its members being European. The trade of Cairo is large, and the bazaars and markets are numerous. Of these the Khan el Khalili, in the north-east of the town, consists of a series of covered streets and courts in which all kinds of Eastern merchandise are displayed. Pop. of administrative division of 42 sq. miles in 1927, 1,059,824.

CAIRO (kā'ro). A river-port of the United States, in Illinois, at the junction of the Ohio and Mississippi. Pop. 15,000.

CAIS'SON (Fr. *caisse*, a chest or case). In civil engineering, (*a*) a water-tight rectangular box, usually constructed of mild steel, for closing the entrance to docks. It may be either of the type which is floated in and out of position against the sill

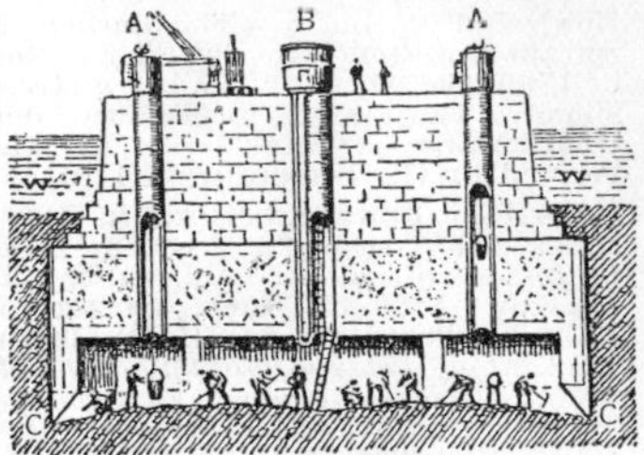

Caisson and Pier—Sectional View

A, Material locks. B, Workmen's air-lock. C, Cutting edge. W, Water.

of the dock, or of the sliding type, which is carried across the dock-mouth on rollers. (*b*) An apparatus on which vessels may be raised and floated, especially a kind of floating dock, which may be partly immersed and floated under a vessel's keel, used for their docking and repair. (*c*) A rectangular iron or steel box, used in the construction of foundations in water of quays and bridges. One type is floated into position, carrying the masonry or concrete built in, and there sunk, the sides being afterwards detached and floated away. Another form is shaped like a rectangular diving-bell, with a cutting-edge on its lower sides. This is placed in position, loaded, and sunk. An air-shaft, with air-lock, is carried to above water-level, by means of which compressed air is used to drive out the water, and permit of access to build the foundation.—Cf. *Kempe's Year Book*.

CAISSON DISEASE. Workers in caissons are exposed to atmospheric pressure two to three and a half times greater than normal. To enable them to work at such pressure, men are subjected to gradual rises of pressure, called "compression," in adjoining air-locks. After work, men returning to the normal atmosphere undergo "decompression" in the air-lock, and it is only after the man has left the air-lock that the symptoms of caisson disease appear. These are severe pains in the muscles and paralysis of the lower extremities, with the accompanying minor ones of headache, vomiting, and nose-bleeding. Rest in bed is all that is required for mild cases, but for severer attacks the sufferer must be placed back in the air-lock and accustomed gradually to the change from the abnormal to the normal atmosphere. The disease can be avoided altogether if slow and gradual "decompression" is carried out thoroughly and carefully.

CAITH'NESS. A county occupying the extreme north-east of the mainland of Scotland; area, 438,878 acres, of which about a fourth is under crop. The surface is generally moory and bare; it is watered by numerous small streams. The coast is rocky, and remarkable for bays and promontories, including among the latter Dunnet Head, Duncansby Head, and Noss Head. Fishing, together with the rearing of sheep and cattle, forms the principal employment of the inhabitants. Flagstones (Caithness flags) for pavement are extensively quarried. The towns are Wick, the county town, and Thurso. Caithness gives the title of earl to the head of the Sinclair family. Caithness-shire and Sutherlandshire unite in returning one member to Parliament. Pop. (1931), 25,656.

CAIUS (kēz), **KEY,** or **KAYE, Dr. John.** English physician, born at Norwich in 1510, died 1573. He was successively first physician to Edward VI., Mary, and Elizabeth. Having obtained permission to enlarge Gonville Hall, at Cambridge, into the college which still bears his name (Gonville and Caius College), he accepted the mastership and retired from public life, when he appears to have assiduously devoted himself to literary labours connected with his profession. His books include critical, antiquarian, and scientific works, the most famous being *A Boke of Counseill against the Sweat and Sweating Sickness* (1552).

CAIVANO (kī-vä'nō). A town of S. Italy, about 9 miles north of Naples. Pop. 12,986.

CAIX. Village of France, department of Somme, on the River Luce. Captured by the Germans in March, 1918, it was retaken by the French in August.

CAJAMARCA (kä-*hȧ*-mär'kȧ). *See* CAXAMARCA.

CAJANUS. A genus of Leguminosæ, sub-ord. Papilionaceæ. The only species, *C. indicus*, is a valuable pulse of the tropics (Congo Pea or Dhal).

CAJ'EPUT, CAJUPUT. The name of several trees, genus Melaleuca, ord. Myrtaceæ, natives of the East Indies and Australia.

CAJ'EPUT OIL. A volatile oil distilled from the leaves of the cajeput tree, found in the Indian Archipelago. It is a pale bluish-green liquid with a strong penetrating odour, and it has a close connection with eucalyptus oil, which it resembles in many characteristics. It is applied externally as a counter irritant for chilblains, myalgia, and rheumatism, and is used internally as a carminative for gastro-intestinal troubles.

CAJ'ETAN (ka'ye-tan), **Thomas da Vio, Cardinal.** Born 1469, died 1534; took his name of Cajetan from the Italian town of Gaeta, in which he was born. When only fifteen years of age he became a Dominican monk, and in 1508 general of his order. In 1517 he was made a cardinal by Leo X., who, in the following year, sent him as his legate into Germany, the principal object of his mission being to endeavour to bring Luther back to the old faith. He was author of a *Commentary on the Bible*, a *Commentary on the Summa of Thomas Aquinas*, a *Treatise on the Authority of the Pope*, etc.

CAJ'UPUT *See* CAJEPUT.

CAKILE. *See* SEA-ROCKET.

CALABAR'. A name given to a district of West Africa, in Southern Nigeria, intersected by two rivers, called respectively Old and New

Calabar. The former enters the estuary of the Cross River, opening into the Bight of Biafra, and near its mouth is the trading-town and mission-station of Calabar or Duke Town, capital of S. Nigeria. The New Calabar enters the Bight of Biafra farther west, and is believed to be one of the numerous branches of the Niger. The seaport of Bonny is near its mouth. There are several stations of British missionaries here. A large portion of the population is employed in the palm-oil trade.

CALABAR BEAN. The seed of *Physostigma venenōsum*, a leguminous African plant nearly allied to the kidney bean. It is a powerful narcotic poison, operating also as a purgative and emetic, and in virtue of these last qualities is the famous "ordeal bean" of Africa, administered to persons suspected of witchcraft. If it causes purging it indicates crime; if vomiting, innocence. It is employed in medicine, chiefly (externally) as an agent for producing contraction of the pupil of the eye in certain cases; sometimes also (internally) in tetanus, strychnine poisoning, and locomotor ataxy.

CAL'ABASH. A vessel made of a dried gourd-shell or of a calabash shell, used in some parts of America and Africa. They are so close-grained and hard that when they contain any liquid they may be put many times on the fire as kettles.

CALABASH TREE. The popular name of the tropical American trees or shrubs belonging to the genus Crescentia, given to them because of their large gourd-like fruits, the hard shells of which are made into numerous domestic utensils, as basins, cups, spoons, bottles, etc.

CALABOZO (-bō'thō). A town of Venezuela, in a plain between the Rivers Guarico and Urituco. The neighbouring ponds abound in electric eels. Pop. 6000.

CALA'BRIA. A name anciently given to the peninsula at the south-eastern extremity of Italy, but now applied to the S.W. peninsula in which Italy terminates, from about lat. 40° N. to the Strait of Messina; area, 5819 sq. miles; pop. 1,503,201. It is divided into three provinces—Cosenza, Reggio, and Catanzaro. The central region is occupied by the great Apennine ridge, to which whole colonies with their cattle migrate in the summer. The flats near the coast are marshy and unhealthy, but the valleys at the foot of the mountains are rich with the most luxuriant vegetation. The country is subject to earthquakes. Wheat, rice, saffron, anise, liquorice, madder, flax, hemp, olives, almonds, and cotton are raised in abundance. Sheep, horned cattle, and horses are numerous. Silkworms are extensively raised. The minerals include alabaster, marble, gypsum, alum, chalk, rock-salt, lapis-lazuli, etc. The fisheries are valuable.

CALA'DIUM. A genus of plants, ord. Araceæ, natives of tropical S. America, often cultivated in hot-houses on account of their large finely-coloured leaves. There are about a dozen species.

CALAHORRA (kȧ-lȧ-or'rȧ; ancient, **Calagurris**). A town of Spain, near the south side of the Ebro, province of Logroño. Birthplace of Quintilian. Wine, grain, oil, and flax are produced in the neighbourhood. Pop. 9871.

CALAIS (kä-lā). A fortified seaport town of France, department of Pas-de-Calais, on the Straits of, and 25 miles S.E. of, Dover, and distant 184 miles by rail from Paris. The Old Town or Calais proper has a citadel, and was till recently surrounded by fortifications; but the modern suburb of St. Pierre les Calais having been amalgamated with Calais proper, both are now surrounded with forts and other works, to which morasses lend additional strength. The harbour, which was formerly shallow, has been greatly improved, and has a lighthouse 190 feet high. Calais has considerable exports of grain, wine and spirits, eggs, fruit and vegetables. The town is important as being the chief landing-place for English travellers to the Continent. It has manufactures of cotton and silk bobbin-net lace. In 1347 Calais was taken by Edward III. of England, after a siege of eleven months. In 1558 it was retaken by the Duke of Guise, being the last relic of the French dominions of the Plantagenets, which at one time had comprehended the half of France. The town received the Croix de Guerre for its participation in the Great War. Pop. 73,001.

CALAIS. A town of the United States, in Maine, on the River St. Croix, a centre of the lumber trade. Pop. 6116.

CALAIS, Straits of. *See* DOVER, STRAITS OF.

CALAMAN'CO. A glossy woollen stuff chequered in the warp, and either ribbed or plain.

CALAMAN'DER WOOD (supposed to be a corruption of *Coromandel wood*). A beautiful species of wood, the product of *Diospy̆ros quæsita*, nat. ord. Ebenaceæ, a native of

Ceylon. It resembles rosewood, but is so hard that it is worked with great difficulty. It takes a very high polish, and is wrought into chairs and tables, and yields veneers of almost unequalled beauty.

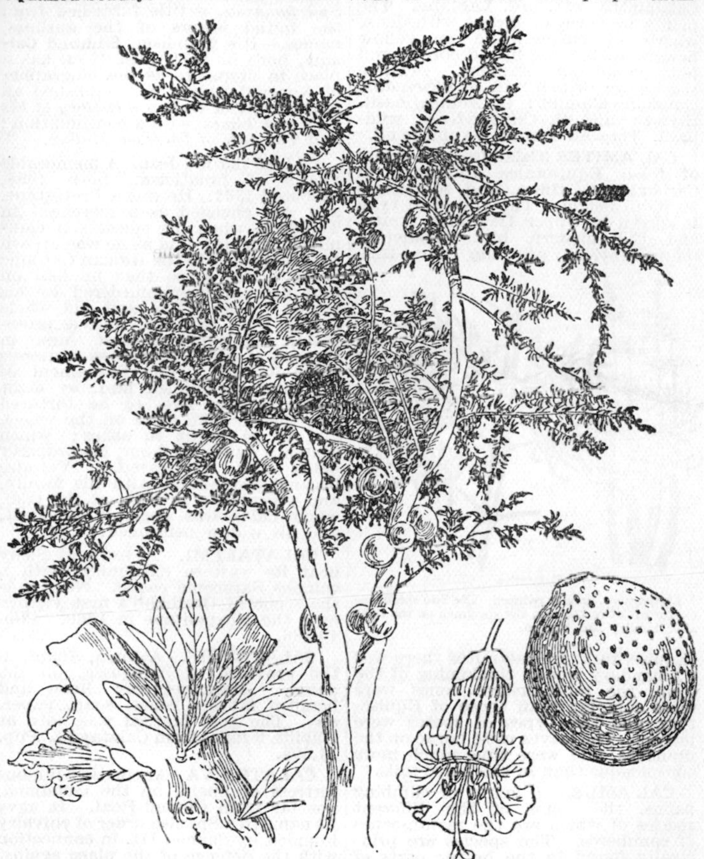

Calabash Tree (*Crescentia ciyete*) with Flower and Fruit

CAL'AMARY. The general name for two-gilled decapod cuttle-fishes of the family Teuthidæ, but properly used to designate those of the genus Loligo. The body is oblong, soft, fleshy, tapering, and flanked behind by two triangular fins, and contains a pen-shaped gladius or internal horny flexible shell. They have the power of discharging, when alarmed or pursued, a black fluid from an ink-bag. The species are found in all seas, and furnish food for dolphins and whales. Some species can dash out of the water and propel themselves through the air for 80 or 100 yards. *Loligo vulgāris* occasionally grows to the length of 2½ feet. Called also *Squid*.

CALAMIANES (-ä'nez). A cluster of islands in the Indian Sea, among the Philippines, midway between the Islands of Mindoro and Palawan.

One of them is 36 miles long and 17 miles broad.

CAL'AMINE. An ore of zinc. *See* ZINC.

CAL'AMINT. A plant of the genus Calamintha, nat. ord. Labiatæ. The plants are herbs or shrubs with dense whorls of purple-white or yellow flowers, with a two-lipped corolla and four conniving stamens. Three species are British, viz. *C. officinālis*, common calamint; *C. Acĭnos*, basil-thyme; and *C. Clinopodium*, wild-basil. They all contain a volatile oil.

CAL'AMITES (Calamītes). A group of fossil Equisetales abundant in Carboniferous times, and sometimes 50 ft. in height. The ancestral type is known in Upper Devonian strata, and the modern but degenerate representatives are the horse-tails

Calamites

Restorations, greatly reduced. The two specimens on the left after Dawson, the specimen on the right after Lindley and Hutton.

(Equisetum). In Calamites there was a secondary woody thickening of the stem, the reproductive cones were more complex than those of Equisetum, and two types of spores were present. The leaves were borne on the branches, and were thus much more conspicuous than in the horse-tails.

CAL'AMUS. A genus of climbing palms, the stems of the different species of which are the rattan-canes of commerce. The species are principally found in the hotter parts of the East Indies.

CAL'AMUS. In Scripture the word used to translate a Hebrew term which is believed to mean an aromatic substance obtained from some kind of reed or cane, probably *Andropōgon Schœnanthus* or *A. Calamus aromaticus* (sweet-scented lemon-grass). The name is also given to the root of the sweet-flag or sweet-rush (*Acŏrus Calamus*). *See* SWEET-FLAG.

CAL'AMY, Edmund. A Presbyterian divine, born in London in 1600, died 1666. He engaged warmly in the religious disputes of the day, and was one of the writers of the famous treatise against Episcopacy, entitled *Smectymnuus*, a title furnished from the initial letters of the authors' names.—His grandson, **Edmund Calamy,** born in 1671, died 1732, has a place in literature as the biographer of Nonconformity. He published an abridgment of Baxter's *History of his Life and Times*, with a continuation; and *The Life of Increase Mather*.

CALAS (kä-lä), **Jean.** A memorable victim of fanaticism, born 1698, executed 1762. He was a Protestant, and was engaged as a merchant in Toulouse, when his eldest son committed suicide; and as he was known to be attached to the Roman Catholic faith, a cry arose that he had on that account been murdered by his father. Jean Calas and his whole family were arrested, and a prosecution instituted against him, in support of which numerous witnesses came forward. The Parliament of Toulouse condemned him, by eight voices against five, to be tortured and then broken alive on the wheel, and to be burnt to ashes; which sentence was carried out, his property being also confiscated. Voltaire became acquainted with his family, and procured a revision of the trial, when Calas was declared innocent, and his widow pensioned.

CALATAFI'MI. A town of Sicily near its western extremity, with a ruinous Saracenic castle. Near it is the scene of Garibaldi's first victory over the Neapolitans in 1860. Pop. 10,486.

CALATAYÚD'. A town, Spain, in the province of Saragossa, on the Jalon. Manufactures: linen and hempen fabrics, ropes, soap, paper, etc. The poet Martial was born at Bilbilis, 2 miles from Calatayúd. Pop. 11,594.

CALATRA'VA. Anciently a famous fortress of Spain, on the Guadiana, not far from Ciudad-Real. It gave its name to a Spanish order of chivalry founded by Sancho III. in connection with the defence of the place against the Moors, 1158. For a long period the war with the Moors was carried on mainly by the knights of Calatrava, who acquired great riches. In 1808 their possessions were confiscated, and the order became merely an order of merit.

CALCA'REOUS. A term applied to substances partaking of the nature of lime, or containing quantities of lime. Thus we speak of calcareous waters, calcareous rocks, calcareous soils.—*Calcareous spar*, crystallised carbonate of lime. It is found crystallised in more than seven hundred different forms, all having for their primitive form an obtuse rhomboid. The rarest and most beautiful crystals are found in Derbyshire.—*Calcareous tufa*, an alluvial deposit of carbonate of lime, formed generally by springs, which, issuing through limestone strata, hold in solution a portion of calcareous earth; this they deposit on coming in contact with air and light. Calc-sinter is a variety of it.

CALCEOLA'RIA (Lat. *calceŏlus*, a slipper, from the shape of the inflated corolla resembling a shoe or slipper). Slipperwort, a genus of ornamental herbaceous or shrubby plants, nat. ord. Scrophulariaceæ. All the species are South American; several have been long known in British gardens. Most of them have yellow flowers. The greater number in cultivation are hybrids and not true species; many of these have very large, brilliantly-coloured flowers.

CALCINA'TION. The operation of roasting a substance or subjecting it to heat, generally with the purpose of driving off some volatile ingredient, and so rendering the substance suitable for further operations. The term was formerly also applied to the operation of converting a metal into an oxide or metallic calx: now called *oxidation*.

CALCI'PHILOUS PLANTS. Those which grow preferably on a calcareous soil or in water rich in lime. Examples from the British flora are: Chalk Milkwort (*Polygala calcarea*), Lady's Fingers (*Anthyllis vulneraria*), Bee Orchis (*Ophrys apifera*), and, among Algæ, the Desmids. *See* Calciphobous Plants.

CALCIPH'OBOUS PLANTS. Those which shun calcareous soil or water. Examples from the British flora are: Heather (Calluna), Foxglove, and Sphagnum mosses. The problem of the relation of plants to lime is a complex one, involving the physical as well as the chemical character of the soil, and the factor of competition between allied species.—Cf. Schimper, *Plant Geography* (chap. v.).

CAL'CITE, or **CALCA'REOUS SPAR.** The commonest form of calcium carbonate (carbonate of lime), crystallising in the trigonal system in a great variety of forms. All these, however, on fracture yield the same characteristic cleavage form, a rhombohedron with angles between its faces of 105° 5′ and 74° 55′; and this form was used by Haüy (1743-1822) as the basis for his discovery of the fundamental law of crystallography. Iceland spar is a transparent variety used for optical experiments and polariscopes, on account of its strong double refraction. Very many marine organisms make their shells of calcite. Aragonite, the rhombic form of calcium carbonate, occurring in coral skeletons and most molluscan shells, passes into calcite in geological time. Calcite is also deposited from water in veins and cold mineral springs, and as stalactites in caves, the majority of limestones and marbles are formed of calcite, impurities giving them various colours. Chalk (q.v.) is a pure limestone, consisting almost entirely of calcite.

CAL'CIUM. A lustrous, silver-white brittle metal. It is not so malleable as sodium and potassium, and shows a crystalline fracture. It can be cut with a knife, and will scratch lead. Its symbol is Ca, its atomic weight is 40, and its oxide occurs widely in nature as lime. Calcium combines directly with ammonia-gas, giving *calcium ammonium*, a bronze-coloured substance that catches fire on exposure to the air.

CALCIUM CARBIDE (CaC_2). A substance obtained by heating quicklime and carbon in an electric furnace. This substance is made in large quantity for the generation of acetylene. Calcium carbide is a greyish crystalline substance which decomposes immediately on coming in contact with water, generating acetylene.

CALCIUM CYANAMIDE. *See* Nitrolim.

CALC-SINTER. A deposit of calcium carbonate (calcite or aragonite) from dropping waters (stalactites and stalagmites), or as terraces and basins from mineral springs.

CALCULATING MACHINES. Instruments for counting mechanically, now much used in banks, insurance offices, and large mercantile establishments. In a common type of machine, the sums to be worked are set by means of keys like typewriter keys, and the machine adds columns of numbers, or of pounds, shillings, and pence, and prints the result. The British mathematician Babbage (1792-1871) planned many machines for more difficult operations. One, in unfinished form, may be seen in the South Kensington Museum.

CALCULUS. In pathology, a general term for the various inorganic concretions which are sometimes formed in the hollow organs of the body. Such are *biliary calculi* or gall-stones, formed in the gall bladder; *urinary calculi*, formed by a morbid deposition from the urine in the kidney or bladder; and various others known as *salivary*, *arthritic*, *pancreatic*, *lachrymal*, etc. Urinary and biliary calculi are the most common. The former, when the particles are comparatively small in size, are known as *gravel*, when larger as *stone*. All varieties of calculi may cause painful and dangerous symptoms, and it is usually necessary to have these stones removed by a surgical operation. For stones in the bladder the operation lithotomy or lithotrity (q.v.) may be performed.

CAL'CULUS, THE INFINITESIMAL. A branch of mathematical analysis. If one variable quantity y depends upon another x in such a way that it changes continuously as x changes and can be found from x when x is given, y is called a function of the independent variable x. The relation between x and y is conveniently represented by a graph.

Let P, Q be two points on the graph, the co-ordinates of P being x, y and those of Q, $x + \delta x$, $y + \delta y$; where the symbol δx is to be taken as a whole, in the sense of "the difference in the value of x."

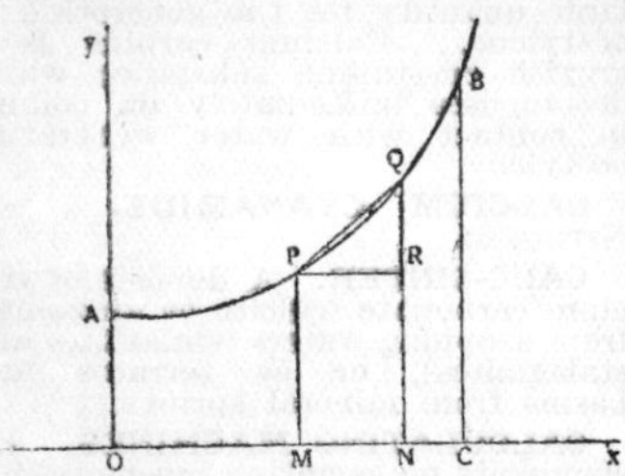

In the figure PR = δx, RQ = δy, and $\frac{\delta y}{\delta x}$ is the trigonometrical tangent of the angle QPR, or the gradient of the secant PQ. Now suppose the point Q to move gradually up towards P. Usually the secant PQ will tend to coincidence with a certain definite line, namely the tangent to the graph at P. The fraction $\frac{\delta y}{\delta x}$ will therefore tend to a definite limiting value, which measures the gradient of the graph at P; this limiting value is called the *differential coefficient*, or *derivative*, of y with respect to x, and is written $\frac{dy}{dx}$. Hence $\frac{dy}{dx}$ represents the rate of change of y per unit change of x. y and x can stand for quantities of different kinds; for example, if y represented distance gone in time x, then $\frac{dy}{dx}$ would represent the rate of change of distance with time, i.e. velocity. As y passes through a maximum or minimum value, $\frac{dy}{dx}$, the rate of change is zero. The *differential calculus* treats firstly of methods for finding differential coefficients, and afterwards deals with their uses in determining maximum and minimum values, geometrical properties of curves, expansion in series, etc. The *integral calculus* may be considered the inverse of the differential. In the differential calculus, given y as a function of x, $\frac{dy}{dx}$ has to be found; in the integral calculus, given $\frac{dy}{dx}$, y is to be found as a function of x. This process is called *integration*. To illustrate its use, let the area AOMP in the figure be denoted by z. Then z is a function of x, and its derivative is easily found. For if δx = MN, then δz = area PMNQ, which lies between $y\delta x$ and $(y + \delta y)\delta x$; so that $\frac{\delta z}{\delta x}$ lies between y and $y + \delta y$, and therefore $\frac{dz}{dx} = y$. Thus to find z we have to integrate y; that is, we have to find a function the derivative of which is y.

There is another view of integration, which is very important. Suppose the area AOCB divided into strips like PMNQ; then the area may be regarded as the limiting value of the sum of such rectangles as MNRP. Hence the limiting value of a sum of terms of the form $f(x)\delta x$, when δx tends to zero, may be found by integration. By this process of integration (or summation) areas, volumes, centres of mass, moments of inertia, etc., are determined.

The name "infinitesimal" was applied to the calculus because the quantities δx which have appeared above and which tend to the limit zero, were regarded as "infinitely small," that is, as neither zero nor finite, but in some intermediate evanescent condition. There was no necessity for this confused conception, and it was gradually discarded for the precise notion of a limit. Leibnitz disputed with Newton the honour of discovering the principles of the calculus, but investigation has supported Newton's claim to priority.

The notation used is that of Leibnitz. Higher branches of the calculus are *differential equations, calculus of variations, calculus of finite differences.*—BIBLIOGRAPHY: W. M. Baker, *The Calculus for Beginners* (Cambridge Mathematical Series); H. Lamb, *An Elementary Treatise on the Infinitesimal Calculus*; G. A. Gibson, *A Treatise on the Calculus*; G. H. Hardy, *Pure Mathematics*; I. Todhunter, *The Calculus of Variations*; A. R. Forsyth, *Differential Equations.*

CALCUTTA (*Kâli Ghattah*, the ghaut or landing-place of the goddess Kâli). A city of India, capital of Bengal, situated about 80 miles from the sea, on the left bank of the Hooghly (Húglí), a branch of the Ganges, navigable up to the city for large vessels. The river opposite the city varies in breadth from about 2 furlongs to three-quarters of a mile. Calcutta extends along the river for about 5 miles from north to south, stretching eastward for nearly 2 miles in the south, and in the north narrowing to half a mile. Adjacent to the city proper are extensive suburbs, which include the large town of Howrah on the opposite side of the Hooghly, connected with Calcutta by a pontoon bridge. The south-western portion of the city area is occupied by the Maidan, a great park lying along the river bank for about 1¾ miles, and having in the south a breadth of 1½. It is a grassy and tree-studded area, intersected by fine drives and partly occupied by a race-course, cricket-ground, public gardens, etc., and partly by Fort William, which rises from the river bank. The fashionable European residential quarter lies east of the Maidan, the European business quarter on the north of it.

Along the river bank runs a fine drive and promenade, the Strand Road; while a spacious way, the Circular Road, forms nominally the eastern boundary of Calcutta. In the European quarters are many fine buildings, and numerous residences of almost palatial character; while in the north and east are great suburban areas occupied by the natives, and consisting mainly of mud huts, where, notwithstanding recent efforts, sanitation is still very defective. The celebrated Fort William is a magnificent octagonal work, said to have cost altogether £2,000,000 sterling. It was begun by Clive after the battle of Plassey, and was completed about 1773. Government House, or the palace of the Governor-General, built by the Marquess Wellesley at an expense of £1,000,000 sterling, stands on the Esplanade, a street or road running along the north side of the Maidan. Here also are the High Court and the town hall, other buildings in this quarter being the currency office, post office, Bank of Bengal, mint, etc. The churches include the cathedral, St. John's (the old cathedral), St. Andrew's Scottish church, Roman Catholic cathedral, etc. A tolerably good supply of filtered water from the Hooghly is furnished to the inhabitants; and a complete system of drainage has been constructed. Calcutta has an extensive system of internal navigation through the Ganges and its connections, as also by the railways (the chief of which start from Howrah), and it almost monopolises the external commerce of this part of India.

Industries. The principal exports are opium, cotton, rice, wheat, jute, gunny-bags, tea, indigo, seeds, raw silk, etc. Of the imports the most important in respect of value are cotton goods. The jute manufacture is extensively carried on, as also that of cottons. Bengal coal is in demand throughout India. The maritime trade is of the annual value of fully £95,000,000; the inland trade is as large or larger. The port extends for about 10 miles along the river, and there are several docks. The educational institutions comprise the Presidency College, the Mohammedan College, the Sanskrit College, and the Bethune Girls' School, all Government colleges, besides others mainly supported by missionary or native efforts, there being five of the former class. Other educational institutions are Calcutta Medical College, Campbell Vernacular Medical College, Government school of art, a school of engineering (at Howrah), and Calcutta University, an examining and degree-conferring institution.

The principal literary and scientific societies of Calcutta are the Bengal Asiatic Society, founded in 1784 by Sir William Jones, the Bethune Society, the Dalhousie Institute, etc. Among the hospitals are the general hospital, the Mayo Hospital (for natives), the Eden Hospital (for women and children), and the hospital connected with the Medical College. The Martinière (named from its founder, General Martin, a Frenchman in the Company's service) is an institution for the board and education of Christian children. The East India Company's first factory in Bengal was established at Hooghly, some distance above Calcutta, in 1644, but being driven from this in 1686, the English occupied part of the present site of Calcutta, which in 1689-90 became the headquarters of the Company's commercial enterprises in Bengal.

The original Fort William, named

after William III., was built in 1696, on a site considerably to the north of the present fort. Calcutta was taken and plundered by Suraj-ud-Dowlah in 1756, and retaken by Clive next year. To the capture by Suraj-ud-Dowlah belongs the famous episode of the "Black Hole" (*see* BLACK HOLE OF CALCUTTA and CLIVE). The town had then to be rebuilt, the new Fort William being constructed between 1757 and 1773. In 1773 Calcutta became the seat of the British government for the whole of India. Since then the history of the city has been an almost unbroken record of progress and prosperity. In 1912, however, the capital of the empire and the seat of government was moved from Calcutta to Delhi. Pop. (with suburbs), in 1891, 741,144; in 1901, 1,026,987; in 1911, 1,222,213; in 1921, 1,132,256.

CALDA'RA, Polidoro (called also **CARAVAGGIO**). An Italian painter, born in 1495 at Caravaggio, in the Milanese. In his youth he carried bricks for the masons in the Vatican, and, envying the artists at work there, devoted himself to painting. He was employed by Raphael on the friezes of the Vatican. *Christ on the way to Calvary* is his chief work. In 1543 he was murdered by his servant.

CALDAS (from Lat. *calidas* (*aquas*), warm waters). A name of various places with warm springs in Spain, Portugal, and S. America. *Caldas de Reyes*, in the Spanish province of Pontevedra, on the Umia, is a place of 7500 inhabitants. *Caldas da Rainha*, a popular Portuguese bathing-place in the province of Estremadura, has a bathing-establishment founded in 1485.

CAL'DECOTT, Randolph. Artist, born at Chester, 1846. He entered a bank, but gave up banking for art. His first success was the publication, in 1875, of his illustrations of a volume of selections from Washington Irving's *Sketch-book*, under the title of *Old Christmas*. It was followed by his illustrations of *Bracebridge Hall* (1876), of Mrs. Carr's *North Italian Folk* (1877), of Blackburn's *Breton Folk* (1879), of *Æsop's Fables with Modern Instances* (1883). His most popular work was a series of children's coloured books, including *John Gilpin*, the *Elegy on the Death of a Mad Dog*, and *The Great Panjandrum Himself*. He died at St. Augustine, Florida, in 1886.

CALDE'RA. A seaport, Chile, 50 miles N.W. of Copiapó, an outlet for the produce of the copper-mines in the interior. Pop. 3500.

CALDERON, Philip Hermogenes. Painter, born in 1833, died 1898, son of a Spaniard settled in London; studied art as a lad, and in 1853 exhibited at the Academy his picture *By the Waters of Babylon*. He was elected A.R.A. in 1864, R.A. in 1867. Among his more notable pictures are: *Broken Vows*; *The Gaoler's Daughter Liberating Prisoners on the Young Heir's Birthday*; *After the Battle*; *The English Embassy at Paris on St. Bartholomew's Day*; *Her Most High, Noble, and Puissant Grace* (a little princess with attendants); *Whither?* (his diploma picture); *La Gloire de Dijon*; *Home they Brought her Warrior Dead*; *Renunciation of St. Elizabeth of Hungary* (his masterpiece, which is in the National Gallery of British Art).

CALDERON' DE LA BARCA, Don Pedro. The great Spanish dramatist, born at Madrid, 1600, educated in the Jesuits' College, Madrid, and at Salamanca. Before his fourteenth year he had written his third play. Leaving Salamanca in 1625, he entered the army and served with distinction for ten years in Italy and the Netherlands. In 1636 he was recalled by Philip IV., who gave him the direction of the Court entertainments. The next year he was made knight of the order of Santiago, and he served in 1640 in the campaign in Catalonia. In 1651 he entered the clerical profession, and in 1653 obtained a chaplain's office in the archiepiscopal church at Toledo. But as this situation removed him too far from Court, he received, in 1663, another at the king's Court chapel; and at the same time a pension was assigned him from the Sicilian revenue. His fame greatly increased his income, as he was solicited by the principal cities of Spain to compose their *autos sacramentales*, for which he was liberally paid, and on which he specially prided himself. Besides heroic comedies and historical plays, some of which merit the name of tragedies, Calderon has left 95 *autos sacramentales*, 200 *loas* (preludes), and 100 *saynètes* (farces). He wrote his last play in the eightieth year of his age. His smaller poems are now forgotten; but his plays have maintained their place on the stage even more than those of Lope de Vega. Their number amounts to 128. He wrote, however, many more, some of which were never published. English translations of his plays have been published by D. F. MacCarthy and Edward Fitzgerald. He died 25th May, 1681.—Cf. Archbishop Trench, *Essay on the Life and Genius of Calderon*.

CAL'DERWOOD, David. Scottish divine and ecclesiastical historian, born 1575, and in 1604 ordained minister of Crailing, Roxburghshire, where he distinguished himself by his opposition to the introduction of prelacy. In 1617 he was banished for contumacy, and went to Holland. In 1625 he returned to Scotland, and in 1640 became minister of the church of Pencaitland, near Edinburgh. He then engaged in writing the *History of the Church of Scotland*, a work published by the Wodrow Society (in 8 vols., 1842-9). He died in 1650.

CALEDO'NIA, CALEDONIANS. The names by which the northern portion of Scotland and its inhabitants first became known to the Romans, when in the year A.D. 80 Agricola occupied the country up to the line of the Firths of Clyde and Forth. He defeated the Caledonians in 83, and again at Mons Graupius in 84, a battle of which a detailed description is given by Tacitus. In the early part of the third century they maintained a brave resistance to Severus, but the name then lost its historic importance. Caledonia is now used as a poetical name for Scotland.

CALEDONIAN CANAL. A waterway passing through Glenmore or the Great Glen of Scotland, and allowing vessels of 500 or 600 tons to sail from the Moray Firth to Loch Eil and the sea on the west. The route passes through Lochs Ness, Oich, and Lochy, the whole distance from sea to sea being about 60 miles, of which only 22 consist of canal proper. There are twenty-eight locks, the highest being about 95 feet above the sea. Constructed between 1803 and 1822, it cost £1,350,000, and has never been a paying concern.

CAL'ENDAR (Lat. *calendarium*, from *calendæ*, the first day of the month). A record or marking out of time as systematically divided into years, months, weeks, and days. The periodical occurrence of certain natural phenomena gave rise to the first division of time, the division into weeks being the only purely arbitrary partition. The year of the ancient Egyptians was based on the changes of the seasons alone, without reference to the lunar month, and contained 365 days divided into twelve months of thirty days each, with five supplementary days at the end of the year. The Jewish year consisted of lunar months, of which they reckoned twelve in the year, intercalating a thirteenth when necessary to maintain the correspondence of the particular months with the regular recurrence of the seasons.

The Greeks in the earliest period also reckoned by lunar and intercalary months, but after one or two changes adopted the plan of Meton and Euctemon, who took account of the fact that in a period of nineteen years the new moons return upon the same days of the year as before. This period of nineteen years was found, however, to be about six hours too long, and subsequent calculators still failed to make the beginning of the seasons return on the same fixed day of the year. Each month was divided into three decads.

The Romans at first divided the year into ten months, but they early adopted the Greek method of lunar and intercalary months, making the lunar year consist of 354, and afterwards of 355 days, leaving ten or eleven days and a fraction to be supplied by the intercalary division. This arrangement continued till the time of Julius Cæsar. The first day of the month was called the *calends*. In March, May, July, and October, the 15th, in other months the 13th, was called the *ides*. The ninth day before the ides (reckoning inclusive) was called the *nones*, being therefore either the 7th or the 5th of the month. From the inaccuracy of the Roman method of reckoning, the calendar came to represent the vernal equinox nearly two months after the event, and at the request of Julius Cæsar the Greek astronomer Sosigenes, with the assistance of Marcus Fabius, contrived the so-called *Julian calendar*. The chief improvement consisted in restoring the equinox to its proper place by inserting two months between November and December, so that the year 707 (46 B.C.), called the *year of confusion*, contained fourteen months. In the number of days the Greek computation was adopted, which made it 365¼. To dispose of the quarter of a day it was determined to intercalate a day every fourth year between the 23rd and 24th of February. This calendar continued in use among the Romans until the fall of the empire, and throughout Christendom till 1582.

By this time, owing to the cumulative error of eleven minutes, the vernal equinox really took place ten days earlier than its date in the calendar, and accordingly Pope Gregory XIII. issued a brief abolishing the Julian calendar in all Catholic countries, and introducing in its stead the one now in use, the *Gregorian* or *reformed calendar*. In this way began the *new style*, as opposed to the other or *old style*. Ten days were to be dropped; every hundredth year, which by the old style was to have been a leap year, was now to be a common year, the fourth excepted; and the length of the solar year was taken to be 365 days, 5 hours, 49 minutes, and 12 seconds, the difference between which and subsequent observations is immaterial. The new calendar was adopted in Spain, Portugal, and France in 1582; in Catholic Switzerland, Germany, and the Netherlands in 1583; in Poland in 1586; in Hungary in 1587; in Protestant Germany, Holland, and Denmark in 1700; in Switzerland in 1701; in England in 1752; and in Sweden, 1753. In the English calendar of 1752, also, the 1st of January was now adopted as the beginning of the legal year, and it was customary for some time to give two dates for the period intervening between 1st January and 25th March, that of the old and that of the new year, as January 175⅔. Russia and the Greek Church generally still retain the old style, which now differs thirteen days from the new. In 1913 the Chinese Republic adopted the calendar of Western Europe.

In France, during the Revolution, a new calendar was introduced by a decree of the National Convention, 24th Nov., 1793. The time from which the new reckoning was to commence was the autumnal equinox of 1792, which fell upon the 22nd of Sept., when the first decree of the new republic had been promulgated. The year was made to consist of twelve months of three *decades* each, and, to complete the full number, five *fête* days or *sansculotides* (in leap years six) were added to the end of the year. The seasons and months were as follows: Autumn—22nd Sept. to 22nd Dec.: *Vendémiaire*, vintage month; *Brumaire*, foggy month; *Frimaire*, sleet month. Winter—22nd Dec. to 22nd March: *Nivôse*, snowy month; *Pluviôse*, rainy month; *Ventôse*, windy month. Spring—22nd March to 22nd June: *Germinal*, bud month; *Floréal*, flower month; *Prairial*, meadow month. Summer—22nd June to 22nd Sept.: *Messidor*, harvest month; *Thermidor*, hot month; *Fructidor*, fruit month. The common Christian or Gregorian calendar was re-established in France on the 1st Jan., 1806, by Napoleon. For the Mahommedan calendar see HEJRA. The reform of the calendar has been a problem of international discussion for some time, and by 1922 the matter was brought before the League of Nations for consideration. By 1929 the Committee on Communications and Transit had recommended that national committees should be formed.

CAL'ENDER. A machine consisting of two or more cylinders (calenders) revolving so nearly in contact with each other that cloth or paper passed between them is smoothed and glazed by their pressure, or some other kind of finish is imparted to the surface.

CAL'ENDERS. A sect of dervishe[s] in Turkey and Persia. They preach i[n] the market-places, and live upon alm[s].

CAL'ENDS (Lat. *calendæ*). The firs[t] day of the month among the Roman[s]. See CALENDAR.—*The Greek calends*, an imaginary date, equivalent t[o] "never," originating in the fact tha[t] the Greeks had nothing correspondin[g] to the Roman calends.

CAL'GARY. A rising town o[f] Canada, province of Alberta, on th[e] Canadian Pacific Railway, where othe[r] lines meet, near the eastern base o[f] the Rocky Mountains, the centre of a[n] important stock-raising and grain growing district, and now a centre o[f] trade, industry, and other activities. Pop. 63,305.

CALHOUN (kal-hön'), **John Caldwell.** An American statesman, born in 1782, died 1850. A lawyer by profession, he distinguished himself in Congress, and in 1817 was made Secretary of War under President Munroe; in 1825 he became Vice-President of the United States; in 1831, a Senator; in 1843, Secretary of State, and in 1845, again a Senator. He continued till his death an advocate of extreme State rights, and of the policy of the slave-holding States.—Cf. H. T. Peck, *American Party Leaders*.

CALI (kä'lē). A town of S. America, Colombia, State of Cauca, with a good trade. Pop. 27,747.

CAL'IBRE. A technical term for the diameter of the bore of a fire-arm, measured across the *lands* or the portions of the bore left between the grooves of the rifling.

CAL'ICO (from *Calicut* in India). A general term for any plain white cotton cloth; in America it is usually applied to printed cottons.

CALICO-PRINTING. The art of applying colours to fabric after it has come from the hand of the weaver in such a manner as to form patterns or figures. This art, originally brought from India, is sometimes practised on linen, wool, and silk, but most frequently on that species of cotton fabric called calico. The process was first introduced into Britain in 1676, and was originally accomplished by means of hand-blocks made of wood on which patterns, or parts of patterns, for each different colour were cut. These blocks were of various dimensions, according to the nature of the work, and, where several colours were employed in one pattern, a block for each colour was necessary. As an improvement in the method of printing from wooden blocks, especially where delicacy of outline is required, engraved copper-plates were introduced out 1760; but the greatest improve- ent was effected by the introduction cylinder-printing about 1783, which s almost superseded the other ethods, except for particular styles. The machinery now generally used nsists of various modifications of the linder printing-machine, in which a umber of separate engraved cylinders e mounted, corresponding to the umber of colours to be printed. For- erly the fabric had to pass once rough the machine for every colour; ut now, by an arrangement of ma- inery equally ingenious and effec- ve, any number of cylinders are fitted n one machine, and act on the cloth ne after the other, and by this means ne pattern is finished with a corre- ponding number of colours in the ame time as was formerly employed give one. A great variety of meth- ds is employed in calico-printing, ut they all fall under the general eads of *dye-colours* and *steam-colours*. Under the first head are included all he styles in which the pattern is rinted on the fabric by a mordant— substance of no colour itself, but which has an affinity for the fibre on he one hand, and for the colouring- natter on the other—the dye-stuff eing subsequently fixed by dyeing on uch parts of the cloth as have been mpregnated with the mordant, and hus bringing out the pattern. In steam-colour printing the dye-stuff is applied to the fabric direct from the printing-cylinder, and subsequently fixed by steaming. In steam-colours there is no limit to the number and variety of shades which may be pro- duced, each colour-box on the cylinder printing-machine containing all the ingredients essential to the production and the fixation of a separate and distinct shade.

The agents chiefly employed for fixing the dye-stuffs are aluminium, tin, chromium, and iron mordants, tannic acid, etc., which are mixed with the dye-stuffs and then printed. The effects in calico-printing are varied by other operations, such as the *discharging*, in which the fabric is first dyed all over, then printed in a certain pattern with discharge-chemi- cals, which either produce a pattern of some other colour, or one purely white, as in the Turkey-red bandanna handkerchiefs. The *resist-style*, in some respects, is the reverse of the discharge-style; the process being to print a pattern in certain chemicals, which will enable those parts to resist the action of the dye-stuff subse- quently applied to all other parts of the fabric. After the printing process the fabrics are submitted to a series of finishing operations, the object of which is to impart to them a pleasing appearance to the eye.—BIBLIOGRAPHY: Sir W. Crookes, *Dyeing and Calico Printing*; C. F. S. Rothwell, *The Printing of Textile Fabrics*; *Cyclopædia of Textile Work*; E. Knecht and J. B. Fothergill, *The Principles and Practice of Textile Printing*.

CAL'ICUT. A seaport of India, presidency of Madras, on the Malabar coast, which was ceded to the British in 1792. It was the first port in India visited by Europeans, the Portuguese adventurer, Pedro da Covilham having landed here about 1486, and Vasco da Gama in 1498. It has a considerable trade, and manufactures cotton cloth, to which it has given the name *calico*. Pop. 82,334.

CALIF and **CALIFATE.** *See* CALIPH.

CALIFOR'NIA. One of the United States of America, on the Pacific Ocean; area, 158,297 sq. miles. The coast extends the full length of the State, measuring about 700 miles, following the indentations. On the south part of the coast are a few islands. The State may be divided into three distinct portions—the central being much the most densely populated. This central portion is embraced between the parallels 35° and 40°, and has on its E. side the Sierra Nevada, and on its W. the Coast Ranges. Between these two mountain chains lies the Great Central Valley of the Sacramento and San Joaquin, renowned for its beauty and fertility. It is this valley, which is about 450 miles in length by about 40 in breadth, to which the State now owes its principal wealth, and which has made it famous for its wheat, its wool, its fruits (including sub-tropical fruits in the S.), and the produce of its vineyards. North of the parallel of 40°, where the Coast Ranges and the Sierra unite, the country is extremely rough and thinly inhabited. That portion of the State which lies to the S. and E. of the southern junction of the Coast Ranges and the Sierra is also thinly inhabited, with the exception of a narrow strip along the coast.

The principal river is the Sacramento, which flows S. for upwards of 300 miles, receiving numerous affluents from the Sierra Nevada, and falls into the Bay of Suisun. The San Joaquin rises in the Sierra Nevada, flows N. for about 250 miles, and joins the Sacramento about 15 miles above Suisun Bay. It receives the waters of Lake Tulé or Tulares, and has numerous tributaries. The Bay of San Francisco, forming the most capacious harbour on the Pacific coast, is about 60 miles in length, 11 miles broad, and with a coast-line of 275 miles. It is connected with the ocean by a strait about 2 miles wide, and from 5 to 7 miles long, called the Golden Gate. The city of San Francisco stands on the N.W. shore of the southern arm.

Mountains. The peaks of the Sierra Nevada—Mount Shasta, Lassen's Butte, Spanish Peak, Pyramid Peak, Mounts Dana, Lyell, Brewer, Tyndall, Whitney, and others—reach from 10,000 to nearly 15,000 feet above the sea (Mount Whitney is 14,886). The volcanic character of the State is manifested by the mountain formations; and earthquakes are frequent. California is celebrated for its many wonderful natural objects and remarkable scenery. Noteworthy are the Yosemite Valley (q.v.) and the "big tree groves," containing groups of giant redwood trees—*Sequoia gigantēa*—some of which reach the height of nearly 400 feet.

Minerals. The mineral resources of California are of great importance. Gold is found in abundance, the quantity obtained in 1926 being valued at about 11,922,481 dollars. It was first discovered in 1848, and brought a great rush of settlers to this part of the world. Among other minerals found in the State are silver, quicksilver, copper, coal, lead, tin, antimony, cobalt, etc.

Temperature. California, being intersected by the isothermal line of 60°, has the same mean annual temperature as the north of Spain and the centre of Italy, and may, generally speaking, be esteemed genial and mild. The year may be divided into a dry and a wet season. On the lower slopes of the Sierra Nevada the climate is said to be that of constant spring. Wheat, barley, oats, maize, and other cereals, the root-crops and vegetables of temperate climates are very largely grown. Fruits are most varied, including olives, grapes, apples, pears, plums, figs, oranges, peaches, pomegranates, plantains, bananas, and coconuts; the indigo-plant also, and the sugar-cane and tobacco, yield abundant returns. The cultivation of the vine is rapidly extending, and the production of wine and brandy and raisins is increasingly large. Irrigation is practised in many localities.

The principal town and port is San Francisco; the capital is Sacramento. Of the other towns the most important are Oakland and Los Angeles. The extensive foreign export trade, consisting chiefly in wheat, flour, wool, wine, etc., is carried on almost exclusively at San Francisco; but the State also sends eastwards large quantities of produce by rail, including raisins and dried fruits, honey, timber, and furs. Much of the foreign trade is with Britain, China, and Japan. Railways have been built to the extent of 13,033 miles (1926). San Francisco now the terminus of three tran continental railways. Ocean steame run regularly between San Francisc and Australia, Panama, Mexico, Chin and Japan.

California (a much larger area tha the present State) was ceded b Mexico to the United States on 2n Feb., 1849, and in 1850 was admitte into the Union. The State Senat consists of 40, and the Assembly of 8 members. It sends 2 Senators and 1 representatives to Congress. Wome have been eligible for election sinc 1911. Education is well provided fo It is compulsory for children betwee 8 and 15 years of age for at least fiv months in the year. The State spend on education about 30,000,000 dollar annually. The State library contain about 300,000 volumes. The Stat university (established in 1868) is a Berkeley, near Oakland. The pop. i 1860 was 379,994; in 1920, 3,426,861 including over 17,000 Indians an 34,075 Chinese. There are abou 40,000 negroes.—BIBLIOGRAPHY: T H. Hittell, *History of California*; J Royce, *History of California*.

CALIFORNIA, Gulf of. A gulf on the W. coast of North America, in Mexico, lying between the peninsula of Lower California and the mainland. It is about 700 miles long, and through most of its length is less than 100 miles wide. It has long had a pearl fishery.

CALIFORNIA, LOWER. A territory of Mexico, comprising a peninsula jutting into the Pacific Ocean, and separated from the mainland throughout its entire length by the Gulf of California. It is over 750 miles in length, and in different places from 30 to 140 miles wide; area, 58,343 sq. miles. It is largely mountainous and arid, but is said to possess valuable agricultural and mineral resources. The chief towns are Loretto and La Paz, the capital. Pop. 52,244, of whom perhaps one half are Indians.

CALIFORNIAN POPPY. A perennial herb of the poppy order, from the Californian coast. It is cultivated in Great Britain as an annual, and has finely-cut leaves and bright-yellow, saffron-eyed, four-petalled blooms.

CALIFORNIAN PROCESS. *See* MERCURY; METALLURGY.

CALIG'ULA, Gaius Cæsar Augustus Germanicus. Roman emperor, son of Germanicus and Agrippina, was born A.D. 12, in the camp at Antium; assassinated by conspirators A.D. 41. He received from the soldiers the surname of Caligula, on account of his wearing the *caligæ*, the Roman equivalent of ammunition boots. He succeeded Tiberius, A.D. 37, and made himself very popular by his mildness and ostentatious generosity; but at the end of eight months he was seized with a disorder, caused by his irregular mode of living, which appears to have permanently deranged his intellect. After his recovery, he suddenly showed himself the most cruel and unnatural of tyrants—a monster of debauchery and prodigality, a perpetrator of the greatest crimes and follies. The most exquisite tortures inflicted on the innocent served him for enjoyments. In the madness of his arrogance he even considered himself a god, and caused sacrifices to be offered to himself. One of his greatest follies was the building of a bridge between Baiæ and Puteoli (Puzzuoli), in order that he might be able to boast of marching over the sea on dry land. He projected expeditions to Gaul, Germany, and Britain, and having reached the sea, he bade his soldiers gather shells for spoils, and then led them back to Rome. At last a band of conspirators put an end to his career in the twenty-ninth year of his age.—Cf. S. Baring-Gould, *The Tragedy of the Cæsars.*

CAL'IPER COMPASSES. Compasses made either with arched legs to measure the diameters of cylinders or globular bodies, or with straight legs and points turned outwards to measure the interior diameter of holes. *See* VERNIER; GAUGE.

CAL'IPH, CALIF, or **KHALIF** (*vicegerent*). The name assumed by the successors of Mahomet in the government of the faithful and in the high-priesthood. *Caliphate* is therefore the name given to the empire of these princes which the Arabs founded in Asia, and enlarged, within a few centuries, to a dominion exceeding even the Roman Empire in extent. The appellation of caliph has long ago been swallowed up in *Shah, Sultan, Emir*, and other titles peculiar to the East. Mahomet having died without naming his successor, three rival parties appeared immediately after his death. The first was headed by Omar, a kinsman of the prophet, who demanded the election of Abu Bekr, Mahomet's father-in-law. The second party was headed by Ali, the husband of Fatima, the prophet's daughter, who declared for himself. The third party consisted of people of Medina, who demanded the election of one of themselves. Abu Bekr was chosen (A.D. 632), and prosecuting the conquest of Syria, he defeated the Byzantine Emperor Heraclius and took Damascus.

His successor, Omar, completed the conquest of Syria, took Jerusalem, subjugated Egypt, and defeated the Persians. He is said to have erected over 1500 mosques. He was succeeded by Othman, or Osman, who completed the conquest of Persia and other Eastern countries, extended his dominion in Africa, and took Cyprus and Rhodes. Othman was succeeded by Ali, who is regarded as the first legitimate possessor of the dignity by a numerous sect of Mahommedans, which gives him and his son, Hassan, almost equal honour with the prophet. During his reign a great schism divided the Mahommedans into two sects called the Sunnites and the Shiites, the former acknowledging the authority of all the caliphs, the latter acknowledging only Ali and his descendants. Ali was murdered in A.D. 660, and his son Hassan in 661, when Moawiyah, the founder of the dynasty of the Ommiyades, became caliph, and transferred his capital from Medina to Damascus.

His army continued the conquest of Northern Africa, and twice unsuccessfully attacked Constantinople. Carthage was taken in 698, after which the Mahommedans encountered no serious opposition in Northern Africa. From the union of the Arabic and Berber races of Africa sprang the Moors of Saracenic history. The conquest of Spain immediately followed, Tarik, the lieutenant of the Saracen general, Musa, having totally defeated the King of the Goths. The caliphate now extended from the Oxus and Indus to the Atlantic. In 732 a great host of Muslim soldiery crossed the Pyrenees and invaded France, but were totally defeated at Tours by Charles Martel. In 755 the Mahommedan dominion split up into the *Eastern* and *Western Caliphates*, the western caliph having Spain, with his capital at Cordova; and the eastern including Northern Africa, with the capital at Bagdad. The former was ruled by a series of Ommiyade caliphs; the latter by the dynasty of the Abbasides.

Haroun al Raschid. The most celebrated of the Abbaside caliphs of Bagdad was Haroun al Raschid (Aaron the Just), 786-808, under whom learning, science, and art were in a flourishing state. Subsequently the Muslim kingdom lost province after province, and the temporal authority of the caliph of Bagdad was destroyed. Numerous independent dynasties were set up, the most important of which was that of the Fatimites, founded by an African Saracen who claimed descent from Fatima, the daughter of the prophet. This dynasty conquered Sicily and several parts of Italy, Egypt, and Palestine. It came to an end in 1171. In 1031 the Western Caliphate ceased, and the Saracenic dominions in Spain were broken up into several small States. The most brilliant period of the Western Caliphate was in the ninth and tenth centuries, when literature, science, and art were in more flourishing condition than anywhere else in Europe. The Eastern Caliphate lingered on till 1258, when Bagdad was taken and sacked by the Mongols.—BIBLIOGRAPHY: S. Lane Poole, *The Mohammedan Dynasties*; Sir William Muir, *The Caliphate: its Rise, Fall, and Decline.*

CALISA'YA BARK. A variety of Peruvian or cinchona bark, namely, that of *Cinchŏna calisāya.*

CALISTHENICS. Physical exercises designed and practised to give grace and strength to the body. The term is usually employed to describe systems of physical culture for women.

CAL'IVER. An early form of handgun, musket, or arquebuse, lighter and shorter than the musket, which had the advantage of the latter in being fired without a rest, and much more rapidly. It was introduced in the sixteenth century, but seems to have been superseded by the musket about 1600.

CALIX'TINES, or UTRAQUISTS. A sect of Hussites in Bohemia, who published their confession in 1421, the leading article of which was a demand to partake of the cup (*calix*) as well as of the bread in the Lord's Supper, from which they received their name of *Utraquists* (Lat. *uterque*, both). Their tenets were conceded by the articles of Basel in 1433, and they became the predominant party in Bohemia. The name Calixtine is also given to a follower of Georg Calixtus.

CALIX'TUS. The name of three Popes.—**Calixtus I.** was a Roman bishop from 217 to 224, when he suffered martyrdom.—**Calixtus II.** was elected in 1119, in the monastery of Clugny, successor of the expelled Pope, Gelasius II., who had been driven from Italy by the Emperor Henry V., and had died in this monastery. He excommunicated the Emperor Henry V. on account of a dispute respecting the right of investiture; as also the anti-Pope Gregory VIII., whom he drove from Rome. He availed himself of the troubles of the emperor to force him, in 1122, to agree to the Concordat of Worms. He died in 1124.—**Calixtus III.**, chosen in 1168 in Rome, as anti-Pope to Paschal III., and confirmed by the Emperor Frederick I., in 1178, was obliged to submit to Pope Alexander III. As he was not counted among the legal Popes, a subsequent Pope, Alfonso Borgia, made Pope in 1455, was called *Calixtus III.* He died in 1458.

CALIXTUS (properly CALLISEN), Georg. An able and enlightened German theologian of the Lutheran Church in the seventeenth century, was born in 1586 in Schleswig, died 1656. In 1614 he became professor of theology in Helmstedt. He wrote against the celibacy of the clergy, and proposed a reunion of Catholics and Protestants upon the basis of the Apostles' creed.

CALL. A term used in various senses; as, (1) in reference to joint stock companies, and the like, a demand for payment of the whole or a portion of the amount which a person has undertaken to contribute to any scheme; (2) in Presbyterian churches, the written document signed by the members of a congregation calling on or inviting a clergyman to become their pastor, and presented to him after he has been duly elected.—*Call to the Bar*, the formal admission of a person to the rank of barrister.

CALLA. A genus of plants, nat. ord. Araceæ. The only species, *C. palustris*, occurs in the north of Europe and America. It has a creeping rootstock extremely acrid in taste, but which, when deprived of its causticity by maceration and boiling, is made by the Lapps into bread. The beautiful *Richardia ethiopica* (Arum lily) was formerly included in this genus, and is still sometimes called *Calla ethiopica.*

CALLANDER. Burgh and market town of Perthshire, on the river Teith, 16 miles from Stirling. It is in the midst of beautiful scenery near the Trossachs.

CALLAO (kȧl-yä'ō). A seaport town of Peru, the port of Lima, from which it is 6 miles distant, and with which it is connected by a railway; pop. 52,843. The roadstead is one of the best in the Pacific, and there is a dock, with an area of nearly 52 acres, constructed at a cost of £1,700,000, besides a floating iron dock. A wireless office was opened at Callao in 1913. Callao is the emporium of the whole of the trade of Peru, importing manufactured goods, and exporting guano, copper-ore, cubic nitre, wool, bark, etc. In 1746 the old town was destroyed by an earthquake, with much loss of life and damage to shipping.

CALLCOTT, Sir Augustus Wall. English landscape painter, born at Kensington in 1779, died 1844. He studied portrait-painting under Hoppner, but distinguished himself specially in landscape-painting. In 1837 he was knighted, and in 1843 was appointed keeper of the royal collections of pictures.

CALLCOTT, John Wall. An eminent composer, born at Kensington in 1766, died 1821. He studied under Handel; obtained the D.Mus. degree at Oxford; was the author of a *Musical Grammar*, and was especially noted for his glee compositions.

CALL'ERNISH. A village and district of Scotland, Isle of Lewis, 16 miles west of Stornoway, famous for its circles of standing-stones. The main circle is 40 feet in diameter, formed of twelve unhewn blocks of gneiss from 10 to 13 feet high, with a larger block in the centre. From this circle rows of stones project to the east, west, and south. There are upwards of forty blocks altogether.

CALLICHTHYS (-ik'this). A genus of fishes belonging to the abdominal malacopterygians, and family Siluridæ or cat-fishes. They are natives of hot climates, and are said to make their way over land in search of water during dry seasons.

CALLI'GONUM. A genus of desert and steppe shrubs, nat. ord. Polygonaceæ, natives of Northern Africa, Western Asia, and Southern Europe; they are sand-tolerating switch-plants, and have been planted along railway lines in deserts, to act as a living screen against sand-drifts.

CALLIM'ACHUS. 1. A Greek poet and grammarian, born at Cyrene, in Libya, of a noble family; flourished between 310 and 240 B.C. He taught at Alexandria, and was appointed by Ptolemy Philadelphus librarian of the Alexandrine Museum. He wrote an epic poem called *Galatea*, several prose works, and tragedies, elegies, comedies, etc., but only some seventy-two epigrams and six hymns remain. One of the most famous of his elegies was *Coma Berenices* (Berenice's Lock), written in 240 B.C., in honour of Queen Berenice. We only know this poem from Catullus's imitation of it (*Carmen* 66). Callimachus is the author of an Epigram on the death of Heraclitus, which has been translated by W. J. Cory in a famous rendering which commences "They told me, Heraclitus."—2. A Greek architect and sculptor, flourished about 400 B.C., the reputed originator of the Corinthian column.

CALL'INGER. *See* KALINJAR.

CALLI'NUS, of Ephesus. The earliest Greek elegiac poet, flourished about 730 B.C. Only a few fragments of his elegies are extant.

CALLIOPE (kal-ī'o-pē). One of the Muses. She presided over eloquence and heroic poetry, and is said to have been the mother of Orpheus by Apollo.

CALLIS'THENES (-ēz). A Greek philosopher and historian, a native of Olynthus, was appointed to attend Alexander in his expedition against Persia. His expressed disapprobation of the conduct of Alexander incurred the displeasure of the courtiers and royal favourites, and he was put to death on a pretended charge of treason, 328 B.C. He wrote a *History of the Actions of Alexander*, and other historical works.

CALLISTHEN'ICS (Gr. *kalli*, stem of *kallos*, beauty, and *sthenos*, strength). The art of exercising the body so that the muscular system may be strengthened, and at the same time grace given to the carriage. The term is therefore usually applied rather to the physical exercises as practised by girls than to boys' gymnastics.

CALLOS'ITY. Any thickened or hardened part of the human skin caused by pressure and friction. Also the natural cutaneous thickenings on the buttocks of monkeys.

CALLOT (kál-ō), **Jacques.** A French engraver, born about 1593, died in 1635. He distinguished himself in Italy and France, and was patronised by the Grand-Duke of Tuscany and by Louis XIII. He preferred etching, probably because his active and fertile genius could in that way express itself more rapidly. In the space of twenty years he designed and executed about 1600 pieces, the characteristics of which are freedom, variety, and *naïveté*.

CALLU'NA. *See* HEATHER.

CAL'LUS. A callosity; also a new growth of osseous matter between the extremities of fractured bones, serving to unite them.

CALLUS. In botany, a term used in two senses: (1) for the tissue first formed as the result of an injury, e.g. at the end of a cut stem; it closes the wound, and often gives rise to new organs, such as roots or buds; (2) for the carbo-hydrate substance deposited on sieve-plates so as to close the pores (better called *callose*).

CAL'MAR, or KALMAR. The principal city of a province of the same name in Sweden, is situated opposite to Oeland, on the Island of Quarnholm, and has some manufactures and a good trade. It derives celebrity from the treaty of 1397, called the Union of Calmar, by which the three Scandinavian kingdoms Denmark, Norway, and Sweden were united under Margaret, hereditary Queen of Denmark, and widow of Haco, King of Norway. Pop. 16,678.

CALMET (kȧl-mā), **Augustin.** A distinguished French exegetical and historical writer, born in Lorraine in 1672, died at Paris 1757. He early entered the order of St. Benedict, and became the head of several abbeys in succession. He was an industrious compiler of voluminous works, such as *Commentaire sur tous les Livres de l'Ancien et du Nouveau Testament* (Paris, 1707-16), *Dictionnaire Historique et Critique de la Bible* (4 vols., 1722-8, translated into English, German, and other languages), *Histoire Ecclésiastique et Civile de la Lorraine* (1745-7), etc.

CALMS, Regions of. Those ocean tracts of the Atlantic and Pacific on the confines of the trade-winds, and immediately (from 1° to 3°) north of the Equator, in which, owing to the general pressure of the air being vertically upwards, wind is often totally absent. The northern limit of these regions varies from 5° north at the winter solstice to 12° in summer.

CALMUCKS. *See* KALMUCKS.

CALNE (kän). A municipal and, until 1885, a parliamentary borough in Wiltshire, England, 31 miles N.N.W. of Salisbury. It is the centre of the manufacture of the famous Wiltshire bacon. Pop. of municipal borough (1931), 3463.

CALOCHORTUS. A genus of Liliaceæ, natives of North America. *Calochortus venustus* and other species are the Mariposa lilies, among the most beautiful and easily cultivated of ornamental bulbs.

CAL'OMEL (Hg_2Cl_2). Mercurous chloride, a preparation of mercury much used in medicine. It is prepared by subliming a mixture of mercury and mercuric chloride, or by grinding in a mortar mercuric sulphate with as much mercury as it already contains, and heating the mixture with common salt in a retort until the mercury sublimes. The calomel is thus produced as a white powder. It is used in a variety of ailments, as a purgative, a vermifuge, etc.

CALONNE (kȧ-lon), **Charles Alexandre de.** A French statesman, born in 1734 at Douai, died at Paris 1802. He studied at Paris, and devoted himself to the duties of an advocate. In 1783 he succeeded Maurepas as Minister of Finance; but after four years of incessant endeavours at financial reform he could do nothing but advise an assembly of the notables, which accordingly met in 1787. The financial statement which he then made led to his dismissal, and he retired to England. On the breaking out of the Revolution he supported the Royalist party with much zeal.

CALOPHYL'LUM. A genus of plants, nat. ord. Guttiferæ, consisting of large timber trees, with shining leaves which have numerous transverse parallel veins. *C. Inophyllum* yields a medical resin, the tacamahac of the East Indies. The seeds afford an oil which is used for burning, for making ointment, etc.

CALORES'CENCE. The transmutation of heat rays into light rays; a peculiar transmutation of the invisible calorific rays, observable beyond the red rays of the spectrum of solar and electric light, into visible luminous rays, by passing them through a solution of iodine in bisulphide of carbon, which intercepts the luminous rays and transmits the calorific. The latter, when brought to a focus, produce a heat strong enough to ignite combustible substances, and to heat up metals to incandescence; the less refrangible calorific rays being converted into rays of higher refrangibility, whereby they become luminous.

CALOR'IC. The name given to a supposed subtle imponderable fluid to which the sensation and phenomena of heat were formerly attributed.—*Caloric engine*, an air-engine (q.v.).

CALORIE. In physics, a heat unit. It is the amount of heat required to raise 1 gram of water 1° C. The interval of 1° C. is usually taken by experimenters as from 4° to 5° C., or from 15° to 16° C. Another unit, called the large calorie, is sometimes used. It contains 1000 ordinary, or small, calories.

CALORIM'ETER. An apparatus for measuring quantities of heat. In its simplest form, viz. a copper can containing water, the rise of temperature caused by the immersion of a hot body in the water is employed to measure specific and latent heats. A more complicated apparatus is necessary in determining the calorific values of fuels. Vessels made of platinum or silver, and containing water or air, are used.

CALORIM'ETRY. Deals with the measurement of quantities of heat. The heat to be measured may be that of a body undergoing change of temperature, change of physical state, or of chemical composition; it may be heat liberated by a transformation of energy, as when heat is produced by friction or by the flow of an electric current. The units of heat most frequently employed are two in number. The *calorie* measures the heat taken in by 1 gramme of pure water when raised from 15° to 16° C. The *British* *thermal unit* is that quantity which will raise 1 lb. of water 1° F. Equal masses of different substances require, as a rule, unequal quantities of heat to raise them through the same range of temperature. This difference of thermal property is expressed by saying that the substances have different specific heats; the latter term denotes the quantity of heat required to raise the unit mass of the substance through 1° C. It thus follows that when a body of known mass in grammes undergoes a given change of temperature, its gain or loss of heat in calories may be computed from the product: mass in grammes, specific heat and change of temperature C. By the aid of this principle, the specific heats of solids, liquids, and gases are determined, and also the latent heats of melting and of vaporisation. It is further applied in determining the heat equivalents of quantities of mechanical and electrical energy.—BIBLIOGRAPHY: C. H. Draper, *Heat and the Principles of Thermodynamics*; J. Clerk Maxwell, *Theory of Heat.*

CALOT'ROPIS. A genus of shrubs or small trees, ord. Asclepiadaceæ, one species of which yields the Indian fibre called *mudar* (q.v.). For another species *see* APPLE OF SODOM.

CALOTTE (ka-lot'). A skull-cap worn by ecclesiastics in Catholic countries; formerly used for the coif of a serjeant-at-law in England.

CALOT'TISTS, or the **REGIMENT DE LA CALOTTE.** A society which sprang up at Paris in the last years of the reign of Louis XIV., and was named from the word *calotte* (a skull-cap), which was the symbol of the society. All were admitted whose ridiculous behaviour, odd character, foolish opinions, etc., had exposed them to public criticism.—Cf. *Mémoires pour servir à l'histoire de la Calotte* (1725).

CAL'OTYPE. The name given to the process, invented by Dr. Fox Talbot about 1840, of producing photographs by the action of light upon paper impregnated with nitrate of silver. *See* PHOTOGRAPHY.

CAL'OYERS (Gr. *kalos*, beautiful, and *-gĕros*, in comb., old, i.e. good in old age, venerable). Greek monks, belonging to the order of St. Basil, who lead a very austere life. Their most celebrated monastery in Asia is at Mount Sinai; in Europe at Mount Athos. They do not all agree as to their mode of life. Some of them are cenobites: that is, they live in common. Others are anchorites, living alone, or with only one or two companions; and others again are recluses, who live in grottoes or caverns in the greatest retirement, and are supported by alms supplied to them by the monasteries.

CALPEE', or **KALPI.** A town, India, United Provinces, on the right bank of the Jumna, about 50 miles S.S.W. of Cawnpore. During the sepoy mutiny Calpee became a principal rendezvous of the revolted Gwalior contingent, which was signally defeated, first by Sir Colin Campbell, in the vicinity of Cawnpore, and afterwards at Calpee itself by Sir Hugh Rose, 26th May, 1858. Pop. 10,568.

CALPUR'NIA. The wife of Julius Cæsar, married to him 59 B.C. She was a daughter of L. Calpurnius Piso, who was consul in 58 B.C.

CALPUR'NIUS, Titus. A Latin pastoral poet, born in Sicily about the end of the third century. Seven eclogues composed by him were translated by E. J. L. Scott (1890).

CALTABELLO'TA. A town of Sicily, province of Girgenti. Pop. 7000.

CALTAGIRONE (-jē-rō'nā). A town of Sicily, 34 miles S.W. of Catania; the see of a bishop. It is noted for the manufacture of terra-cotta figures and pottery. Pop. 43,169.

CALTANISSET'TA. A town, Sicily, capital of the province of the same name, on the right bank of the Salso, 62 miles S.E. of Palermo. In the vicinity are springs of petroleum and of hydrogen-gas, a mud-volcano, and important sulphur-mines. Pop. 60,086 (1921).—The province has an area of 1271 sq. miles, with a pop. of 391,482.

CALTHA. The genus of ranunculaceous plants to which the marsh-marigold (*C. palustris*) belongs. The plant is acrid and poisonous.

CALTON HILL. A hill overlooking Edinburgh. It is 350 feet high, and has on it an observatory and several memorials.

CAL'TROP. A military instrument with four iron points disposed in such a manner that three of them being on the ground the other points upward, formerly scattered on the ground to impede the progress of an enemy's cavalry.—Also the common name of *Centaurĕa Calcitrăpa* (the star-thistle), found in waste places in the south of England. The heads are covered with long yellow spines. The water caltrop is *Trapa natans*, the fruit of which has several horns formed of the indurated lobes of the calyx.

CALUM'BA, or **COLOMBO.** A plant, *Jateorhīza calumba*, indigenous to the forests of Mozambique, nat. ord. Menispermaceæ. The large roots are much used as a bitter tonic in cases of indigestion. American or false calumba is the bitter root of *Frasēra Carolinensis*, a gentianaceous herb found in North America.

CAL'UMET. A kind of pipe used by the American Indians for smoking tobacco. Its bowl is usually of soft red soapstone, and the tube a long reed, ornamented with feathers. The calumet was used in the ratification of all solemn engagements, both of war and peace. To accept the calumet is to agree to the terms of peace, and to refuse it is to reject them. The calumet of peace is differently made from the calumet of war.

CALUMET. A town of the United States, Houghton County, Michigan, famous for its output of copper. It includes the villages of Red Jacket and Laurium, west of which is the celebrated Calumet and Hecla mine. Pop. 32,345.

CALVADOS (kȧl-vȧ-dos). A French department, part of the old province of Normandy, bounded on the N. by the English Channel, and E., W., and S. by the departments of Eure, La Manche, and Orne. Area, 2197 sq. miles. It is named from a dangerous ridge of rocks which extends along the coast for 10 or 12 miles. The department is undulating and picturesque, and possesses rich pastures. Chief town, Caen. Pop. (1926), 390,492.

CALVAERT (kȧl-värt'), **Dionys.** A painter, born at Antwerp in 1555, died at Bologna 1619. He went very young to Italy, and ultimately opened a school at Bologna, from which proceeded 137 masters, and among these Albano, Guido Reni, and Domenichino.

CAL'VARY (from Lat. *calvaria*, a skull). Used in the *Vulgate* to translate the Heb. *golgotha* (a skull), and applied to the place outside Jerusalem where Christ was crucified, usually identified with a small eminence on the north side of the city. The term is also applied in Roman Catholic countries to a kind of chapel, sometimes erected on a hill near a city and sometimes on the exterior of a church, as a place of devotion, in memory of the place where our Saviour suffered; as also to a rocky mound or hill on which three crosses are erected, an adjunct to religious houses.

CALVÉ, Emma (Emma de Roquer). French singer, born in 1864. She studied under Rosine Laborde, and made her debut at Brussels in 1882. She has sung in England, Italy, Spain, Russia, and the United States, and her rich soprano voice and dramatic power have been greatly admired. She has won fame as Carmen, and created the leading parts in De Lara's *Messaline* (1900), Massenet's *Navarraise* (1895), and in *Sapho*.

CAL'VERLEY, Charles Stuart. English poet, born 1831, died 1884. He was educated at Harrow, Balliol College, Oxford, and Christ's College, Cambridge. He showed great skill in Latin and Greek composition both at school and college, taking his degree as second classic in 1856—a high position considering that he did not read energetically. Afterwards he made himself famous as a writer of humorous English verse, and also for serious poetical efforts, both in original poetry and translation. He was called to the Bar, but his promising legal career was cut short by a serious accident which befell him. He has few equals as a parodist and writer of light verse, and his translations from Homer, Theocritus, and Horace are of great merit. An edition of his writings in one volume was published in 1901, with a short memoir.

CAL'VERT, George. The first Baron Baltimore (q.v.).

CAL'VI. A fortified seaport of France, on the N.W. side of Corsica. It was taken by the English in 1794, but abandoned in the following year. Pop. 2269.

CALVIN, John (so called from *Calvinus*, the Latinised form of his family name, *Cauvin* or *Chauvin*). Reformer and Protestant theological writer, born at Noyon, in Picardy, 1509, died at Geneva 1564. His father, Gérard Cauvin, *procureur-fiscal* and diocesan secretary, dedicated him early to the Church, and he was presented with a benefice at the age of twelve. The income derived from this nominal office enabled him to proceed to Paris and enter on a course of regular study. He was soon led to entertain doubts respecting the priesthood, and became dissatisfied with the teaching of the Roman Catholic Church; in consequence he gave up his cure, and took to the study of the law in Orleans. In 1532 he returned to Paris a decided convert to the reformed faith, and was soon compelled to fly, when, after various wanderings, he found a protector in Margaret of Navarre. In 1534 he returned to Paris; but, finding that the persecution against those who were inclined to the doctrines of the reformers was still raging, he retired to Basel in the autumn of the same year.

At Basel he completed and published his great work, *The Institutes of the Christian Religion* (Christianæ Religionis Institutio; 1536). Having gone to Italy, after a short stay at Ferrara he went to Geneva, where reform had just been established. A spirit of rebellion, however, broke out against the rule of Calvin and Farel, who had introduced a reign of extreme strictness. As they refused to yield to the wishes of a party animated by a more liberal spirit than themselves, both Calvin and Farel were expelled from the city in April, 1538. Calvin removed to Berne and then to Strassburg. Here he married a widow, Idelette de Burie, and had one son, who died early.

John Calvin

In 1541 his friends in Geneva succeeded in effecting his recall, when he laid before the council the draft of his ordinances respecting Church discipline, which were immediately accepted and published. His college of pastors and doctors and his consistorial court of discipline formed a theocracy, with himself at the head of it, which aimed virtually at the management of all municipal matters and the control of the social and individual life of the people. A magistrate was deposed and condemned to two months' imprisonment " because his life was irregular, and he was connected with the enemies of Calvin." James Gruet was beheaded " because he had written profane letters and obscene verses, and endeavoured to overthrow the ordinances of the Church." Michael Servetus, passing through Geneva in 1553, was arrested, and through Calvin's instrumentality was burnt alive because he had attacked the mystery of the Trinity in a book which was neither written nor printed at Geneva. This was the great blot on Calvin's career, though approved of by many others of the reformers.

His energy and industry were enormous : he preached almost daily, delivered theological lectures three times a week, attended all deliberations of the consistory, all sittings of the associations of ministers, and was the soul of all the councils. He was consulted, too, upon points of law as well as of theology. Besides this, he found time to attend to political affairs in the name of the Republic, to publish a multitude of writings in defence of his opinions, and to maintain a correspondence through all Europe. Up to 1561 the Lutherans and the Calvinists were as one, but in that year the latter expressly rejected the tenth article of the Confession of Augsburg, besides some others, and hence arose the name of *Calvinists*.

Calvin retained his personal influence to the last ; but a year or two before his death his health had broken down. As a theologian Calvin was equal to any of his contemporaries in profound knowledge, acuteness of mind, and in the art of making good a point in question. As an author he merits great praise. His Latin works are written with much method, dignity, and correctness. He was also a great jurist and an able politician. Besides the *Institutes*, the most important of Calvin's works are the *De Necessitate Reformandæ Ecclesiæ, In Novum Testamentum Commentarii*, and *In Librum Geneseos Commentarii*. The first complete edition of Calvin's works is that of Amsterdam, 1671, in 9 vols., superseded, however, by the critical edition of Baum, Cunitz, Reuss, Lobstein, and Erichson, in 59 vols. (1863-1900). The collected works of Calvin have been published in English by the Calvin Translation Society of Edinburgh in 52 vols. 8vo (1843-55).—BIBLIOGRAPHY : T. de Beza, *Vie de Calvin* ; T. H. Dyer, *Life of John Calvin* ; E. Doumergue, *Jean Calvin* ; A. Erichson, *Biographia Calviniana* ; P. E. Henry, *Life and Times of Calvin* ; A. Menzies, *Study of Calvin*.

CALVINISM. The theological tenets or doctrines of John Calvin, including a belief in predestination, election, total depravity, original sin, effectual calling, and the final perseverance of the saints. These doctrines were received before Calvin's days, though he is doubtless amongst the most learned and copious writers in their propagation and defence. The system also includes several other points of controversy, such as that of free-will, the Sonship of the Second Person of the Trinity, and other differences in doctrine as between Calvinists and Arminians. Calvinism is the theological system expounded in the Westminster Confession of Faith, and is therefore the faith officially held by the Presbyterian Churches generally; it is also substantially identical with what is known as "evangelicalism" in any of the Churches or religious bodies.—BIBLIOGRAPHY: A. Kuyper, *Calvinism*; Philip Schaff, *History of the Christian Church*; T. M. Lindsay, *History of the Reformation.*

CALX (Lat., lime or chalk). A term formerly applied to the *residuum* of a metal or mineral which has been subjected to violent heat, burning, or calcination.

CALYCAN'THUS. A genus of hardy American shrubs (related to Magnolia), of which one species, Florida allspice (*C. floridus*), has yellow flowers, and is sweet-scented.

CALYCIFLORÆ. In Bentham and Hooker's system, the second subdivision of polypetalous dicotyledons, distinguished by their perigynous or epigynous flowers.

CAL'YDON. An ancient city of Northern Greece, in Ætolia, celebrated in Greek mythology on account of the ravages of a terrible boar. All the princes of the age assembled at the famous Hunt of the Calydonian Boar, which was finally killed by Meleager.

CALYP'SO. In Greek mythology, a nymph who inhabited the island Ogygia, on the shores of which Ulysses was shipwrecked. She promised him immortality if he would consent to marry her, but after a seven years' stay she was ordered by the gods to permit his departure.

CALYP'TRA. The hood or cap covering the capsule of mosses. It consists of the upper part of the archegonium wall, torn away from the lower portion and raised aloft by the elongating sporogonium. It falls off when the capsule is quite ripe. The presence of a calyptra in all mosses (except Sphagnum and Archidium), and its absence in liverworts, is one of the most constant distinctions between these two great subdivisions of the Bryophyta.

CALYPTRÆ'IDÆ. A family of gasteropodous molluscs, known as bonnet or chambered limpets. The typical genus Calyptræa includes the cup-and-saucer limpet.

CALYSTEGIA. *See* BINDWEED.

CA'LYX. In botany, the name given to the exterior covering of a flower, that is, the floral envelope consisting of a circle or whorl of leaves external to the corolla, which it encloses and supports. The parts or leaves which belong to it are called *sepals*; they may be united by their margins, or distinct, and are usually of a green colour and of less delicate texture than the corolla. In many flowers, however (especially monocotyledons), there is little or no difference in character between calyx and corolla, in which case the whole gets the name of *perianth.* When the calyx leaves are distinct, the calyx is called *polysepalous* (*a a a* in accompanying cut); when united, *gamosepalous* or *monosepalous* (*b b*). The principal function of the calyx is to enclose and protect the other parts of the flower while in bud. It is, accordingly, very much reduced or abortive where this duty is assumed by bracts, as in the massed inflorescences of Compositæ and Umbelliferæ. The calyx frequently plays a part in connection with fruit-dispersal. *See* DISPERSAL OF SEEDS AND FRUITS; WATER-CALYX.

Forms of Calyx

CAM, or GRANTA. An English river which rises in Essex, flows N.E. through Cambridgeshire, and falls into the Ouse after a course of about 40 miles.

CAM. In machinery, a revolving disc (commonly heart-shaped), curved surface, or cylinder with grooves used to give a variable or reciprocating motion to other bodies, which slide or roll in contact with it. Any desired motion may be transmitted by suitably shaping the periphery of the cam. In many machines the cam revolves at a uniform rate, and produces a reciprocating motion of the body in contact with it. A well-known example of a cam is to be found in the long and short cam-grooves in the rear of the bolt of a rifle; when the bolt-lever is raised, the bolt rotates to the left, and forces the stud on the cocking-piece to move backward from the long to the short cam-groove; this action withdraws the striker about one-eighth of an inch.

CAMAIEU (ka-mā'ū). Monochrome painting or painting with a single colour, varied only by gradations of the single colour, by light and shade, etc. Drawings in Indian-ink, sepia, etc., are classed as works *en camaieu.* The term is also applied to wood-engravings imitating pencil or pen-and-ink drawings.

CAMAL'DOLITES, CAMALDULIANS, or **CAMALDUNIANS.** A nearly extinct fraternity of monks founded in the Vale of *Camaldoli* in the Apennines, in 1018, by St. Romuald, a Benedictine monk. They were originally hermits, but as their wealth increased they associated in convents. They have always been distinguished for their extreme asceticism: their rules in regard to fasting, silence, and penances being most severe. Pope Gregory XVI. (1831-46) belonged to the order of the Camaldolites. Like the Benedictines, they wear white habits.

CAMALODUNUM. A Roman town in England, situated where Colchester now stands. It was one of the largest Roman settlements in the country. Boadicea captured it in A.D. 62. Remains of many Roman buildings have been unearthed.

CAMARGUE (kȧ-märg), **LA.** The delta of the Rhône, in S. France, department of Bouches-du-Rhône. It is protected from the inundations of the river by dikes, and is mostly an unhealthy tract of pools and marshes, only a small portion of it being cultivated.

CAMARIL'LA. A word first used in Spain, but now in other countries also, for a company of secret counsellors or advisers to a ruler; a cabal; a clique.

CAMAYEU. *See* CAMAIEU.

CAMBACÉRÈS (käŋ-bȧ-sā-rā), **Jean Jacques Régis de, Duke of Parma.** Born in 1753 at Montpellier, died at Paris 1824. He was trained a lawyer, and by his talents soon attracted the notice of the Convention, and was appointed to various judicial offices. In the discussion about the king he declared Louis guilty, but disputed the right of the Convention to judge him, and voted for his provisory arrest, and in case of a hostile invasion, death. For a time he had the management of foreign affairs; and when Bonaparte was First Consul, Cambacérès was chosen second. After the establishment of the empire, Cambacérès was created Arch-chancellor, Grand Officer of the Legion of Honour, and ultimately Duke of Parma. He was banished on the second restoration of Louis XVIII., but was subsequently permitted to return.

CAM'BALUC, or **CAM'BALU.** The name by which the city which we now know as Peking became known to Europe during the Middle Ages.

CAM'BAY. A feudatory State in India, Bombay Presidency, lying at the head of the gulf of the same name in the western part of Gujrát. Area, 350 sq. miles; pop. 75,225. Also, chief town of above State, situated at the head of the Gulf of Cambay, formerly a flourishing port, but now less so. Pop. 31,395.—The gulf separates the peninsula of Kathiawar from the northern coast of Bombay, having a length of about 80 miles, and an average breadth of 25 miles.

CAM'BERWELL. A metropolitan and parliamentary borough of London, south side of the Thames. It returns 4 members to Parliament. Pop. (metropolitan borough), 251,373 (1931).

CAM'BERWELL BEAUTY. A rare British butterfly, *Vanessa Antiŏpa,* so named from having been sometimes found at Camberwell when it was more rural than now, and from its great beauty. It is called in the United States " mourning cloak ". The wings are deep, rich, velvety brown, with a band of black, containing a row of large blue spots around the brown, and an outer band or margin of pale yellow dappled with black spots. The caterpillar feeds on the willow.

CAM'BIUM. The secondary meristem of stems and roots, which by its continued active division gives rise to new xylem (wood) on its inner and to new phloem (bast) on its outer side, thus producing the secondary growth in thickness of the organ. It is typically developed in conifers and woody dicotyledons among living plants, but was also present in many extinct types of pteridophyta. The *phellogen,* or bark-forming secondary meristem, is often called the *cork-cambium. See* MERISTEM; SECONDARY THICKENING.

CAMBO'DIA, or **CAMBO'JA.** A country in the Indo-Chinese peninsula bounded N. by Siam, E. by Annam, S. by French Cochin-China and the Gulf of Siam, and W. by the Gulf of Siam. The greater part of it is low and flat with numerous streams, the chief being the Mekong (q.v.). The soil is very fertile, producing large quantities of rice, and the vegetation generally is marked by tropical luxuriance. Cattle are exceedingly numerous; among wild animals are the elephant and tiger; gold and precious stones are found. The exports comprise salt fish, cotton, tobacco; the imports salt, wine, and textiles. In early times Cambodia was a powerful State exacting tribute even from Siam, but it gradually fell into decay, and in the eighteenth and early in the nineteenth century lost a large part of its dominions to Siam. Magnificent ruins, bridges, etc., attest the former prosperity of the country. Since 1863 it has been a protectorate of France, and since 1884 practically a French colony, though nominally ruled by a king of its own. King Norodom, who recognised the French protectorate, was succeeded by his brother, Sisowath, in 1904. The chief town is Pnom-Penh on an arm of the Mekong; the port is Kampot, on the Gulf of Siam. Its area was increased in 1907 by the cession to it by Siam of the provinces of Battambong and Siamrap. Area, 67,550 sq. miles; pop. estimated at 2,465,581, partly Cambodians proper, partly Siamese, Annamese, etc.

CAMBON, Pierre Paul. French legislator and diplomatist, born in Paris, 1843. He was chief of the cabinet of the Prefecture de Seine when Ferry was prefect, and after holding several prefectures entered the diplomatic service in 1882. He was French ambassador at Madrid (1886), Constantinople (1891), and in 1898 came to London. Here he had many opportunities to display his diplomatic tact. He was among those most responsible for the Anglo-French *entente*. He died in 1924.

CAM'BORNE. A town and parliamentary division of England, county of Cornwall, 11 miles N.W. of Falmouth. Being in the vicinity of productive tin and copper-mines, it has risen of late to be a place of some importance. Pop. of urban district (1931), 14,157.

CAM'BRAI (the Roman Camaracum). A French town 37 miles south-east of Lille. It is traversed by three arms of the Schelde, called in French territory the Escaut. In the fifteenth century Baptiste Coutaing, who was born and lived at Cambrai, invented a fine muslin, or linen cloth, which is known as "cambric" all the world over—although the French call it *batiste*, after the inventor's name. In 1508 the famous League of Cambrai was formed against Venice, comprising Maximilian, Louis XII., Pope Julius II., and Ferdinand of Argon. In 1528 the *Paix des Dames* was signed at Cambrai. The town has belonged to France since 1679. It is the birth-place of Fénelon, the famous French author. The old fortifications of Cambrai had been levelled before the outbreak of the European War, but, as the city possessed military importance as the converging point of numerous highways and four railways, both the Allies and the Germans were anxious to hold it. After their retreat from the Marne in 1914 the Germans made Cambrai one of their distributing-centres. The town received the Legion of Honour in 1919, and a part of the town was adopted by Birkenhead in Sept., 1920.

CAM'BRAI, BATTLES OF. The first battle of Cambrai opened on 20th Nov., 1917; the capture of the town was not Haig's object; that might or might not happen, but his advance was intended to secure his right flank. The main objective was towards the N.E. Bourlon, and the Arras-Cambrai road. General Byng's surprise victory before Cambrai broke into the supposed impregnable Hindenburg line. The attack of the Third Army under General Byng was renewed in the late summer of 1918, and the second battle of Cambrai lasted from 30th Sept. to 9th Oct., when the town was captured.

CAM'BRIA. The Latin name of Wales, derived from Cymri, the name of the branch of the Celts to which the Welsh belong.

CAMBRIAN SYSTEM. In geology, a group of strata first named by Adam Sedgwick from the area studied by him in Wales (Cambria). Comparison with strata of the same age, in N. America and elsewhere, has led to a classification by the prevalent trilobites (antique crustacea), three series being now established, marked respectively, and in upward succession, by Olenellus, Paradoxides, and Olenus. The faunas associated with these forms serve in assigning a relative age, even when the trilobites named are absent. The Olenellus series is represented in Britain in the north-west highlands of Scotland, where there is a considerable mass of folded limestone at Assynt; in the Llanberis states; and on the east flank of the Longmynd on the Welsh border. Since any strata older than this series are classed as pre-Cambrian, and are therefore older than the Palæozoic era (q.v.), great interest is attached to the determination of the "Olenellus zone" in any country.

These lowest Cambrian strata are

best styled Taconic, following Emmons and Lapworth; above them in Britain come the Menevian (Paradoxides series) and the Lingula Flags and the overlying Tremadoc beds, forming the Olenus series. The Cambrian of N.W. Scotland has a fauna allied to that in N. America rather than to that in Wales. The Cambrian fauna of the north-eastern United States is particularly rich in forms; traces even of jelly-fish occur, with abundant brachiopods, limpet-like gastropods, and a few bivalve molluscs. Except for some small crustaceans of higher groups, the trilobites are the most highly-developed forms of life. No traces of vertebrates are known. The beds in Central Bohemia studied by Barrande have yielded a large number of well-preserved fossil forms. The paucity of animal remains in strata older than the Olenellus series makes it probable that the power of using calcium salts in sea-water for the construction of hard parts was introduced as a feature of the organic world in Cambrian times.

Owing to their great antiquity the Cambrian strata are commonly altered and compacted. The sandstones overlying the Torridon beds in Scotland are now white quartzites, that cap the mountains as if they were fields of snow. The shales are often changed by pressure into slates. For Bibliography, *see* article GEOLOGY.

CAM'BRIC. The name of a fine kind of linen which was originally manufactured principally at Cambrai (Fl. *Kambryk*) in French Flanders, whence the name. It is also applied to a cotton fabric, which is very extensively manufactured in imitation of the true cambric, and which is in reality a kind of muslin.

CAMBRIDGE (kām'brij). An inland county of England, bounded by the counties of Lincoln, Northampton, Huntingdon, Bedford, Hertford, Essex, Suffolk, and Norfolk; area, 315,168 acres. The soil is diversified and generally fertile; a large part belongs to the Fen country. The principal rivers are the Cam or Granta, and the Ouse. By drainage much of the fen land (including the Bedford Level) has been converted into good arable land and into excellent pastures, and about nine-tenths of the county is under cultivation. The county abounds in dairy farms, celebrated for the production of excellent butter and cheese. The S.E. of the county, extending from Gogmagog Hills to Newmarket, being bare and heathy, is used chiefly as pasture land for sheep; on the south the ground produces fine wheat, barley, and oats. Since 1918 this county returns one member to Parliament.

The county town is Cambridge; other towns are Ely, Wisbech, Newmarket, and March. Pop. (1931), 140,004. — *Cambridge*, the county town, is situated on the River Cam, 50 miles N. of London. It is an ancient place, and was a Roman station (Granta). It occupies a perfect level encompassed by the colleges, and their beautiful grounds and gardens, on both sides of the Cam. Several of the streets are narrow and winding, but some are spacious and airy, and much improvement has taken place of late years. The town is important mainly on account of the university, but has some manufactures. It sends one member to Parliament. Pop. (1931), 66,803.

CAMBRIDGE. A city of Massachusetts, United States, separated from Boston by Charles River. It is well laid out with fine broad streets and avenues, and many open spaces adorned with shrubs and trees. The most important institution it contains is Harvard University (q.v.). Pop. in 1925, 119,669. Though distinct from Boston it really forms part of it.

CAMBRIDGE, UNIVERSITY OF. One of the two great English universities, as old at least as the thirteenth century. The following list contains the names of the colleges or distinct corporate bodies comprised in the university, with the date when each was founded:—

	College	Founded
1.	St. Peter's College, or Peterhouse	1284
2.	Clare College, formerly Clare Hall	1326
3.	Pembroke College	1347
4.	Gonville and Caius College	1348
5.	Trinity Hall	1350
6.	Corpus Christi College	1352
7.	King's College	1441
8.	Queens' College	1448
9.	St. Catharine's College, or Catharine Hall	1473
10.	Jesus College	1496
11.	Christ's College	1505
12.	St. John's College	1511
13.	Magdalene College	1542
14.	Trinity College	1546
15.	Emmanuel College	1584
16.	Sidney Sussex College	1596
17.	Downing College	1800

There is also Selwyn College (or hostel), founded in 1882, for Church of England students only. Each of the colleges is a separate corporation, which is governed by laws and usages of its own, although subject to the paramount laws of the university. At the head of each is an official who is styled the Master of the college, except at King's College, where he is called Provost, and Queens', where he is called President. Next in rank come the Fellows (in number about 400), who are graduates and have formerly been distinguished students, and who receive an annual allowance from the college funds, varying from about £150 to £250.

The students (undergraduates) are of several classes, namely: *scholars*, who are elected by examination or otherwise, and receive an annual allowance from the college funds; *pensioners*, who form the great body of the students and pay ordinary fees; and *sizars*, students of limited means, who receive various emoluments. There is also a certain number of non-collegiate students. The head of each college and the fellows together form the governing body of the college. The university is composed of a chancellor, vice-chancellor, the masters or heads of colleges, fellows of colleges, and students, and is incorporated as a society for the study of all the liberal arts and sciences. The senate, which is composed of all who have taken the degree of Doctor or Master and kept their names on the books, is the great legislative assembly of the university. The chief executive power is vested in the chancellor, the high-steward, and the vice-chancellor, who is the head of some college. Two proctors superintend the discipline of all persons *in statu pupillari*.

Terms. There are three terms: Michaelmas, or October term, which lasts from the 1st of October to the 19th of December; Lent, or January term, which begins on the 8th of January and lasts till within a few days of Easter; and Easter, or Midsummer term, beginning three weeks after the end of the Lent term, and ending on the 24th of June. Every student must have completed nine terms' residence during three-fourths of each term before he can take the degree of B.A., LL.B., M.B., or B.Ch., for which, accordingly, a residence of three years is required. The degree of M.A. is obtained four years after that of B.A. without examination. Bachelors of Arts may obtain "honours" in the following subjects — Mathematics, Classics, Moral Sciences, Natural Sciences, Law, History, Theology, Oriental Languages, Modern and Mediæval Languages, Mechanical Sciences, Economics, Anthropology, Geography, and English. The candidates in each of these subjects are arranged in a *tripos* in three grades. In the mathematical tripos (Part 2) these three grades are called respectively Wranglers, Senior Optimes, and Junior Optimes; in the other triposes they are called first, second, and third class. The last mathematical tripos under the old regulations was held in 1909, when Mr. P. J. Daniell of Trinity was the last Senior Wrangler. The other degrees conferred are: Doctor and Bachelor of Divinity, Doctors of Letters, Science, Laws, and Medicine, Doctor and Bachelor of Music, and Ph.D., M.Litt., and M.Sc.

Since 1913 Divinity degrees are no longer limited to clergymen of the Church of England, but only the latter may be appointed Regius and Lady Margaret Professors of Divinity. Women who have fulfilled the conditions of residence and standing are admitted to the tripos examinations. Those who pass are placed in the published lists, and receive degrees, but are not members of the senate after proceeding M.A., etc. Two colleges (Girton and Newnham) have been established for women, but they are not part of the university, though the university lectures are open to students of these colleges. The annual income of the university in 1920 was about £300,000, arising from various sources, including the produce of fees at matriculations, for degrees, etc.

The number of undergraduate students in 1922 was 5960. There are 160 professors, etc., in the various departments. A botanic garden, an anatomical school, an observatory, and a valuable library containing more than 900,000 printed volumes, besides many manuscripts, are attached to the university. The new museums and laboratories for the study of science are among the most complete in the country. The university sends two members to the House of Commons. The right of election is vested in the members of the senate.—BIBLIOGRAPHY: *Cambridge University Calendar*; J. Bass Mullinger, *History of the University of Cambridge*; C. W. Stubbs, *Cambridge*; J. W. Clark, *Cambridge: Historical and Picturesque*; A. H. Thompson, *Cambridge and its Colleges*.

CAMBRITE. *See* EXPLOSIVES.

CAMBUSKEN'NETH. An ancient abbey of Scotland, now in ruins, near Stirling, founded in 1147 by David I.

CAMBUSLANG'. A town of Scotland, Lanarkshire, 3¾ miles S.E. of Glasgow, with collieries adjacent. A revival, known as the "Camb'slang Wark", was held here, under Whitefield, in 1741. Pop. (parish, 1931), 27,128.

CAMBY'SES. (1) A Persian of noble blood, to whom King Astyages gave his daughter Mandane in marriage. Astyages was dethroned by Cyrus, the offspring of this union. (2) The son of Cyrus the Great, and grandson of the preceding, became, after the death of his father, King of the Medes and Persians, 529 B.C. In the fifth year of his reign he invaded Egypt, conquering the whole kingdom within six months. But his expeditions against the Ammonites and Ethiopians having failed, his violent and vindictive nature broke out in cruel treatment of his subjects, his brother Smerdis and his own wife being among his victims. He died in 521 B.C.

CAMDEN. A town of New Jersey, United States. It is on the left bank of the Delaware, and connected with Philadelphia, on the opposite side, by a steamboat service. There are manufactories of various kinds, foundries, saw-mills, etc. Pop. in 1920, 116,309.

CAMDEN TOWN. District of London in the borough of St. Pancras and Islington to the N.W. of the city. It has many factories and warehouses.

CAMDEN, William. A celebrated antiquary and historian, was born in London in 1551. Appointed second master of Westminster School, he devoted all his leisure to the study of British antiquities, and began to collect matter for his great work, the *Britannia*, which gives a topographical and historical account of the British Isles from the earliest ages. In 1586 the first edition was published, and procured the author a high reputation. Later editions were considerably enlarged and improved. In 1593 Camden became head master of Westminster, and four years afterwards Clarencieux king-at-arms. Besides the *Britannia*, Camden published a narrative of the Gunpowder Plot (*Actio in Henricum Garnetum*), and a history of the reign of Queen Elizabeth (*Annales Rerum Anglicarum regnante Elizabetha*), and an account of the monuments and inscriptions in Westminster Abbey. He died 9th Nov., 1623, at Chislehurst in Kent, in the house which was afterwards that of Napoleon III.

CAMEL (Camēlus). A genus of ruminant quadrupeds, characterised by the absence of horns; the possession of incisor, canine, and molar teeth; a fissure in the upper lip; a long and arched neck; one or two humps or protuberances on the back; and a broad elastic foot, with pads on its under surface, which does not sink readily in the sand of the desert. The native country of the camel is said to extend from Morocco to China, within a zone of 900 or 1000 miles in breadth. The common camel (*Camēlus Bactriānus*), having two humps, is only found in the northern part of this region, and exclusively from the ancient Bactria, now Turkestan, to China. The dromedary, or single-hump camel (*Camēlus dromedarius*, or Arabian camel), is found throughout the entire length of this zone, on its southern side, as far as Africa and India. The Bactrian species, found in a wild state in parts of the desert of Gobi, is the larger, more robust, and more fitted for carrying heavy burdens. The dromedary has been called the race-horse of its species.

To people residing in the vicinity of the great deserts the camel is an invaluable mode of conveyance. It will travel three days under a load, and five days under a rider, without drinking. The stronger varieties carry from 700 to 1000 lb. burden. The camel's power of enduring thirst is partly due to the peculiar structure of its stomach, the lining of which is folded into little pouches capable of straining off and storing up water for future use, when journeying across the desert. It can live on little food, and of the coarsest kind, leaves of trees, nettles, shrubs, twigs, etc. In this it is helped by the fact that its humps are mere accumulations of fat (the backbone of the animal being quite straight) and form a store upon which the system can draw when the outside supply is defective. Hence the camel-driver who is about to start on a journey takes care to see that the humps of his animal present a full and healthy appearance.

Camel (*Camēlus Bactriānus*)

Camels which carry heavy burdens will do about 25 miles a day, those which are used for speed alone, from 60 to 90 miles a day. The camel is rather passive than docile, showing less intelligent co-operation with its master than the horse or elephant; but it is very vindictive when injured. It lives from forty to fifty years. Its flesh is esteemed by the Arab, and its milk is his common food. The hair of the camel serves in the East for making cloth for tents, carpets, and wearing apparel. It is imported into European countries for the manufacture of fine pencils for painting and for other purposes. The South American members of the family Camelidæ constitute the genus Lama, to which the llama and alpaca belong; they have no humps.

CAMEL. A water-tight box or caisson used to raise a sunken vessel, or to float a vessel over a shoal or bar. It is let down with water in it, and is attached to the vessel, after which the water is pumped out, and the camel rises owing to its buoyancy.

CAMELFORD. A village, and, previous to 1832, a parliamentary borough of England (with two members), county of Cornwall, on the Camel, 28 miles N.W. of Plymouth. Camelford is the Camelot of the Arthurian romance, and four miles to the N.W. of Camelford are the ruins of King Arthur's castle of Tintagel.

CAMELLIA (ka-mel'ya). A genus of plants, ord. Ternstrœmiaceæ (the tea order), with showy flowers and elegant, dark-green, shining, laurel-

Camellia

like leaves, nearly allied to the plants which yield tea, and named from George Joseph Kamel, a Moravian Jesuit. The *C. japonica*, in Japan and China, is a lofty tree of beautiful proportions. It is the origin of many double varieties of our gardens. Other species are also cultivated in Europe.

CAMEL'OPARD. A name given to the giraffe (*Giraffa camelopardălis*), originally from the notion that it was

Camelopard

a kind of hybrid between a camel and a leopard. It constitutes the only species of its genus (Camelopardalidæ). *See* GIRAFFE.

CAMELOT. The name given to King Arthur's capital. Though its locality is uncertain, it has been identified with Caerleon.

CAMEL'S THORN (genus *Alhagi*). A name of several plants belonging to the nat. ord. Leguminosæ, and the sub-order Papilionaceæ. They are herbaceous or half-shrubby plants growing in the deserts of Egypt and the East, and derive their name from the fact that they afford a food relished by camels. Some of the species yield a manna-like exudation from the leaves and branches.

CAM'EO. A general name for all gems cut in relief, in contradistinction to those hollowed out, or *intaglios*. More particularly, a cameo is a gem composed of several different-coloured layers having a subject in relief cut upon one or more of the upper layers, an under layer of a different colour forming the ground. For this purpose the ancients used the onyx, sardonyx, agate, etc. The shells of various molluscs are now much used for making cameos; and they are also imitated on glass.

CAM'ERA LU'CIDA (Lat., "clear chamber"). An optical instrument employed to facilitate the sketching of objects from nature by producing a reflected picture of them upon

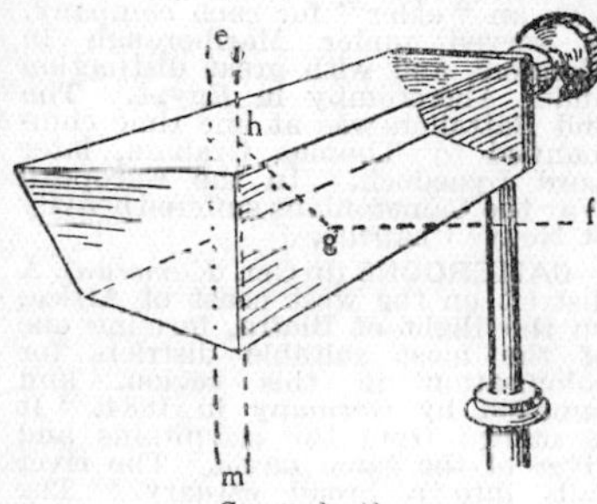

Camera Lucida

paper. Dr. W. H. Wollaston's apparatus is one of the commonest. The essential part is a totally-reflecting prism with four angles, one of which is 90°, the opposite one 135°, and the other two each 67° 30'. One of the two faces which contain the right angle is turned towards the object to be sketched. Rays falling normally on this face, as from *f*, are totally reflected at *g* from the face *cb* to the next face at *h*, whence they are again totally reflected to emerge normally from the fourth face. An eye (*e*) placed so as to receive the emergent rays, will see an image of the object in the direction *m*, and by placing the sketching-paper below, in this place, the image may be traced with a pencil. As the paper, for convenience of drawing, must be at a distance of about a foot, a concave lens, with a focal length of something more than a foot, is placed close in front of the prism in drawing distant objects. By raising or lowering the prism in its stand, the image of the object to be sketched may be made to coincide with the plane of the paper. The prism is mounted in such a way that it can be rotated either about a horizontal or a vertical axis; and its top is usually covered with a movable plate of blackened metal, having a semicircular notch at one edge, for the observer to look through. This form of camera, of which the prism was invented by Wollaston in 1807, was very convenient on account of its portability. It was largely used by draughtsmen for copying, reducing, and enlarging purposes; the process has now been superseded by photography. *See* OPTICS.

CAM'ERA OBSCU'RA (Lat., "dark chamber"). An optical instrument employed for exhibiting the images of objects in their forms and colours, so that they may be delineated by means of a tracing or represented by photography. A simple camera obscura is presented by a darkened chamber into which no light is permitted to enter excepting by a small hole in the window-shutter. This forms the basis of the "pinhole" camera. An inverted picture of the objects opposite the hole will then be seen on the wall, or on a white screen placed opposite the opening. A simple camera obscura is shown in the figure; the rays of light passing through a convex lens at A are reflected from the mirror M (which is at a slope of 45°) to the glass plate N, where they form an image that may be traced. Another arrangement is a kind of tent surrounded by opaque curtains, and having at its top a revolving lantern,

Camera Obscura

containing a lens with its axis horizontal, and a mirror placed behind it at a slope of 45°, to reflect the transmitted light downwards on the paper. It is still better to combine lens and mirror in one by using a glass of peculiar shape, in which rays from external objects are first refracted at a convex surface, then totally reflected at the back of the lens, which is plane, and finally emerge through the bottom of the lens, which is concave, but with a larger radius of curvature than the first surface. The camera obscura was first applied to photography about 1794 by Thomas Wedgwood. The modern development of this instrument is found in the periscope of the trenches and of the submarine. The camera obscura employed by photographers is commonly a box of adjustable length with a tube in front containing a photographic lens. This lens is capable of forming an image of the object to be photographed, on a screen or slide of ground glass at the back of the camera. Focusing having been performed by the motion of the screen or of the lens, a sensitive plate or film is substituted for the ground glass, and is exposed for a suitable time to light from the object. Subsequent development and fixing produces a negative of the picture. *See* OPTICS; PHOTOGRAPHY.

CAMERI'NO. A town of Central Italy, province of Macerata, 41 miles S.W. of Ancona, seat of an archbishopric, with archiepiscopal palace and a spacious cathedral. Its university was founded in 1727. Pop. 11,689.

CAMERLENGO, or **CARDINALE CAMERLENGO.** The chamberlain or highest officer in the papal household, and formerly also the head of the Government.

CAM'ERON, Sir David Young. A Scottish artist, born in Glasgow in 1865. In 1911 he was made A.R.A., in 1920 R.A., and in 1924 he was knighted. He has published *Paris Etchings* and *Etchings in Belgium.*

CAM'ERON, Richard. A Scottish Covenanter, born at Falkland, in Fife. Becoming an enthusiastic votary of the pure Presbyterian system, on the 20th of June, 1680, at the head of a small band of followers, he entered Sanquhar, and formally renounced allegiance to the king (Charles II.) on account of his misgovernment. The little band kept in arms for a month in the mountainous country between Nithsdale and Ayrshire, but were at length surprised by a much superior force at Aird's Moss, and after a stubborn fight overcome. Cameron was amongst the slain. *See* CAMERONIANS.

CAMERON HIGHLANDERS, THE (Queen's Own). A Highland regiment raised by Alan Cameron (1793), greatly distinguished itself in the Peninsula, routing the Imperial Guard at Fuentes d'Oñoro. First to leave Brussels on the morning of 16th June, 1815, the Camerons were publicly praised by Wellington for their behaviour at Quatre Bras. They suffered heavy losses at the Aisne in 1914.

CAMERONIANS. The name applied to the small but zealous sect of Presbyterians which Richard Cameron (q.v.) led, and extended to the small body of Presbyterians who, after the revolution of 1688, continued to insist on the fulfilment of the stipulations in the Solemn League and Covenant against prelacy, schism, etc.—Cf. J. Cunningham, *Church History of Scotland,* 1883.

CAMERONIANS (Scottish Rifles), **THE.** A regiment recruited from the Cameronian sect in 1688, and given a chaplain of its own persuasion, with an "elder" for each company. It served under Marlborough in Flanders, and with great distinction under Abercromby in Egypt. The 2nd Battalion was at one time commanded by Thomas Graham, later Lord Lynedoch. In the European War the Cameronians suffered heavily at Neuve Chapelle.

CAMEROONS (in Ger. *Kamerun*). A district on the west coast of Africa, on the Bight of Biafra, forming one of the most suitable districts for colonisation in this region, and annexed by Germany in 1884. It is named from the mountains and river of the same name. The river falls into a broad estuary. The mountain range is volcanic in character and has a peak over 13,000 feet high. A British Expeditionary Force occupied the Cameroons in 1915-16, and in 1919 France annexed to French Equatorial Africa the territory ceded to Germany in 1911. Of the remainder, 166,489 sq. miles were mandated to France, and the remaining 31,000 sq. miles, a strip stretching along the Nigerian border from the sea to Lake Chad, to Britain. The country is bounded by Nigeria, French Equatorial Africa, the Congo, and the South Atlantic. It is generally mountainous, but there is much rich agricultural land, and the ports on the Cameroon estuary export oil, rubber, cocoa, cotton, and ivory. The principal port is Duala. The climate is hot, disease, particularly leprosy, malaria, and sleeping sickness, is on the increase, and it is not a white man's country. Victoria is the chief town in the British area. The population of the French mandate is 1,500,000, and of the British 550,000. There are about 1900 Europeans.—BIBLIOGRAPHY: A. F. Calvert, *The Cameroons*; F. W. H. Migeod, *Through British Cameroons.*

CAMIL'LUS, Marcus Furius. A Roman patrician, famous as the deliverer of the city of Rome from the Gauls. In 396 B.C. he was made dictator during the Veientine War, and captured the town of Veii by mining, after it had defied the Roman power for ten years. In 394 B.C. Camillus besieged the Falerii, and by an act of generosity induced them to surrender. Three years after, the envy and jealousy of enemies caused him to exile himself for a time, and he was living in retirement when the Gauls under Brennus invaded and captured Rome, with the exception of the Capitol. Camillus was now appointed dictator a second time, and was successful in repelling the invaders. After having been four times appointed dictator, a new invasion of the Gauls called Camillus, now eighty years old, again to the front, and for the fifth and last time, being appointed dictator, he defeated and dispersed the barbarians. He died in 365 B.C.

CAM'ISARDS. Calvinists in France (in the Cévennes), who, in the beginning of the eighteenth century, in consequence of the persecution to which they were exposed after the revocation of the Edict of Nantes in 1685, rose against the royal deputies. A large army was required to put them down (1702-5), and great numbers were massacred, the French Government considering it a laudable work to suppress the Protestant heresy in this manner. The name is from *camisa*, a provincial form of Fr. *chemise*, a shirt, because their ordinary outer garment was a kind of shirt or blouse, and also on account of an incident at the siege of Montauban in 1629, when such a blouse was used as a signal. The word *camisade* is the equivalent of night-attack.—Cf. De la Baume, *Relation de la révolte des Camisards.*

CAMLET. A fabric made of long wool, hand spun, sometimes mixed with cotton, silk, or linen: originally made of camel's hair or of the hair of the Angora goat.

CAM'OENS, Luiz Vaz de. The most celebrated poet of the Portuguese, born at Lisbon of a good family, probably in 1524 or 1525. Disappointed in love, he became a soldier, and served in the fleet which the Portuguese sent against Morocco, losing his right eye in a naval engagement before Ceuta. An affray into which he was drawn was the cause of his embarking in 1553 for India. He landed at Goa, but, being unfavourably impressed with the life led by the ruling Portuguese there, wrote a satire which caused his banishment to Macao (1556). Here, however, he was appointed to an honourable position as administrator of the property of absentee and deceased Portuguese, and here, too, in what were the quietest and most prosperous years of his life, he wrote the earlier cantos of his great poem, *The Lusiads*. Returning to Goa in 1561, he was shipwrecked and lost all his property except his precious manuscript. After much misfortune Camoens in 1570 arrived once more in his native land, poor and without influence, as he had left it. *The Lusiads* was now printed at Lisbon (1572), and celebrating, as it did, the glories of the Portuguese conquests in India, acquired at once a wide popularity.

The king himself accepted the dedication of the poem, but the only reward Camoens obtained was a pittance insufficient to save him from poverty; and it is said that his faithful Javanese servant had often to beg food for them both in the streets. He died on 18th June, 1579. Fifteen years after his death a magnificent monument was erected to his memory, with an inscription on it which called him the prince of poets. *The Lusiads* is an epic poem in ten cantos. Its subject is the voyage of Vasco da Gama to the East Indies; but many other events in the history of Portugal are also introduced. The other works of Camoens consist of sonnets, songs, epigrams, and dramas. The best editions of his works are those of the Visconde de Juromenha and of Theophile Braga. *The Lusiads* has been translated into English by William J. Mickle and Sir R. F. Burton, as well as by others.—BIBLIOGRAPHY: J. Adamson, *Memoirs of the Life and Writings of Luiz de Camoens*; Sir R. Burton, *Camoens: his Life and his Lusiads.*

CAMOMILE. *See* CHAMOMILE.

CAMOR'RA. A well-organised secret society, once spread throughout all parts of the kingdom of Naples. At one time the *Camorristi* were all-powerful, levying a kind of blackmail at all markets, fairs, and public gatherings, claiming the right of deciding disputes, hiring themselves out for any criminal service from the passing of contraband goods to assassination. The society had central stations in all the large provincial towns, and a regular staff of recruiting officers. Though properly a secret society, it did not find it necessary under the régime of the Bourbons to conceal its operations; but under the present Government of united Italy, the society, if it has not quite ceased to exist, has lost almost all its power, except in the wilder parts of Southern Italy. In 1906 the society came again into great prominence in consequence of the murder of Gennaro Cuscolo.

In 1912 over 30 of the leading Camorrists were convicted and sentenced to various terms of imprisonment after lengthy investigations and a trial lasting over a year.

CAMOUFLAGE. The application of art to war—the strategic answer to the advent of aerial reconnaissance. The airman's camera can record a picture of the landscape from the height of 14,000 feet, in which it is possible to detect where a few men have crossed a field.

If the lessons of the war are properly digested, camouflage precautions will precede and prepare the way for the concealment of all possible military activities. Surprise is the chief element of success in war, and this can rarely under modern conditions be effected without the aid of the concealing and confusing art. That was realised by the Germans, who had perfected photography and air-craft at their disposal at pre-war manœuvres, and they devised a method of covering large areas at strategic centres, including the high roads, in imitation of the ground covered, capable of hiding during the bright daylight several divisions of men, so that no traces of activity would be exposed to the airmen.

Ludendorff brought off his "surprise offensive" in 1918 by covering areas with a network (an adaptation of our fishing-net flat top) under which, he tells us, forty or fifty divisions were crowded; that is, between dark and daylight on 21st March. The avoidance of cast shadow is the camoufleur's chief problem. There are only two known methods of effecting this, to have netting with a flat top, and to slope the sides of erections at an angle of ten to fifteen degrees.

The painting of post-impressionist patterns on air-sheds and buildings generally, which stands in the popular imagination for the art of camouflage, was actually a source of danger. It merely advertised their military character.

The hanging of canvas screens from side to side across roads, adopted by us and the French, was not comparable to the entirely-covered-in roads of the Germans, the chief object of which was to screen the come and go of traffic from kite-balloon observation. In dry weather the dust, and the moving shadows when the sun was low, would give evidence of any activity on a road not entirely tunnelled over. Tents and huts are impossible to hide, hence the covering-in of camps used by our late enemy, described by them as *Verkleidung von Lagen.*

Since all sound camouflage is a restoration in appearance of the landscape used for military purposes, an aerial photograph of a district is the best guide for the selection of a position. From that the artist can determine the possibilities of disguise, and also give attention to the existing means of communication so that no traces of its whereabouts will be left on the ground. The hard road tells no tales, and an aerial photograph will eventually test the efficiency of his work.

CAMPAGNA (kȧm-pȧn'yȧ). A town of S. Italy, province of Salerno, surrounded by high mountains. It is the seat of a bishop, and contains a superb cathedral. Pop. 9910.

CAMPAGNA DI ROMA (kȧm-pȧn'yȧ). The coast region of Middle Italy, in which Rome is situated, from 30 to 40 miles wide and 100 long, and forming the undulating mostly uncultivated plain which extends from near Civita Vecchia or Viterbo to Terracina, and includes the Pontine Marshes. The district is volcanic, and its lakes, Regillus, Albano, Nemi, etc., are evidently craters of extinct volcanoes. The soil is very fertile in the lower parts, though its cultivation is much neglected, owing to the malaria which makes residence there during midsummer very dangerous; and during the months of July, August, and September its inhabitants, chiefly herdsmen and peasants, seek refuge in Rome or the neighbouring towns. In ancient times the Campagna, though never a salubrious district, was well cultivated and populated, the villas of the Roman aristocracy being numerous here. But inundations from the Tiber, and the discouragement of agricultural industry in the midst of wars and devastations, left the stagnant waters to become a source of pestilence, and the district became little better than a desert, nothing of its former prosperity being visible but the ruins of great temples, circuses, and monuments, and long rows of crumbling aqueducts overgrown with ivy and other creeping plants. During recent years the Italian Government has taken up the problem, and much has been done to make the Pontine Marshes more fit for human habitation.

CAMPAN, Jeanne Louise Henriette. Born at Paris in 1752, died at Mantes in 1822. She became reader to the daughters of Louis XV., afterwards gained the favour of Queen Marie Antoinette, and, as lady of the bed-chamber, served that ill-fated sovereign with much fidelity till the events of the Revolution separated them. After the fall of Robespierre, Madame Campan established a boarding-school for young ladies at St. Germain, which soon acquired a wide reputation. She is chiefly remembered for her *Mémoirs sur la vie privée de Marie Antoinette*, her *Journal Anecdotique*, and her correspondence with Queen Hortense.

CAMPANEL'LA, Tommaso. A learned Italian monk, born 1568, died in Paris in 1639. He entered the order of the Dominicans and studied theology and other branches of knowledge with assiduity, but was principally attracted by philosophy. In 1591 he published at Naples a philosophical work intended to show the futility of the prevailing doctrines of the Aristotelian schools. This book procured him some admirers, and more enemies. In 1599 he was arrested on a charge of conspiracy against the Spanish Government, to which Naples was then subject, was imprisoned, and, after being repeatedly tortured, condemned to perpetual confinement. While in prison he wrote many learned works, afterwards published, one of these being his famous *City of the Sun* (Civitas Solis), translated into English by T. W. Halliday, and published in *Ideal Commonwealths* (Morley's Universal Library). At length, in 1629, Pope Urban VIII. procured his liberty and bestowed a pension on him. Dreading further persecution, he withdrew in 1634 to France, where he was honourably received. Among his other works are: *Atheismus Triumphatus, Discorsi della Libertà, Prodrmous Philosophiæ Instaurandæ, De Sensu Rerum et Magia.*—Cf. C. Dareste, *Morus and Campanella.*

CAMPANE'RO. The bell-bird (Chasmorhynchus), peculiar to the neotropical region, and distinguished by its particularly clear and resonant note.

CAMPA'NIA. The ancient name of a province of Italy, in the former kingdom of Naples, which, on account of its beauty and fertility, was a favourite resort of wealthy Romans, who built there magnificent country houses. It comprises the modern provinces of Caserta, Naples, and parts of Salerno, Benevento, and Avellino. Cumæ (the oldest Greek settlement in Italy), Puteoli, Naples, Herculaneum, Pompeii, Baiæ, Stabiæ, Salernum, and Capua (its ancient capital) were the principal cities of Campania. Even now Campania is the most beautiful and fruitful part of Italy. Area, 5276 sq. miles; pop. 3,254,440.

CAMPANILE (kam-pa-nē'lā). A bell-tower detached from the church to which it belongs, common in the church architecture of Italy. Amongst the most remarkable examples are the beautiful campanile of the cathedral at Florence, designed by Giotto, and the famous leaning tower of Pisa.

Campanile, S. Andrea, Mantua, Italy

CAMPANOL'OGY. A general name for every kind of knowledge pertaining to bells, theoretical, practical, historical, etc.; but commonly restricted to the art and practice of bell-ringing, especially the ringing of bells that are used together in sets, peals, or "rings," such sets of bells being very common in the towers or belfries of English churches. The "changes" that may be rung on even a few bells, by changing or varying the order in which they are rung, are exceedingly numerous, the possible changes on seven bells, for instance, being 5040.

CAMPAN'ULA. The bell-flower

genus, a large genus of plants which gives its name to the ord. Campanulaceæ. The species, about 230 of which are known, are herbaceous plants, with bell-shaped flowers usually of a blue or white colour. Nine species are indigenous to Britain, of which the most common and best known are the *C. rotundifolia*, bluebell of Scotland or hair-bell, a native also of Asia and N. America, and the *C. medium*, or Canterbury-bell, a well-known garden flower with double and single varieties.

CAMPANULA'CEÆ. The bellworts, an extensive nat. ord. of gamopetalous dicotyledons usually herbaceous, with an inferior two or more celled fruit, many minute seeds, regular bell-shaped showy blue or white corolla, and milky acrid juice. They are natives chiefly of northern and temperate regions. *See* CAMPANULA.

CAMPBELL, Sir Colin. *See* CLYDE (LORD).

CAMPBELL (kam'bel), **George.** A Scottish divine, born at Aberdeen in 1709, educated at Marischal College, and in 1759 appointed principal of this college. In 1763 he published a celebrated dissertation on miracles in answer to Hume, and in 1776 his *Philosophy of Rhetoric*, which established his reputation as a critic and thinker. He died in 1796.

CAMPBELL, John, Lord Campbell. Lord Chancellor of England, the son of Dr. George Campbell, minister of Cupar-Fife, and born there in 1779. He was educated at Cupar, and afterwards at the University of St. Andrews. In 1798 he went to London, and after acting some time as reporter and dramatic critic to the *Morning Chronicle*, entered himself a student of Lincoln's Inn, and in 1806 was called to the Bar. He acquired a considerable practice, was elected member for Stafford in 1830, and two years after made Solicitor-General. In 1841 he was made Lord Chancellor of Ireland and raised to the peerage as Baron Campbell of St. Andrews. Some years after he accepted a post in the Ministry of Lord John Russell; in 1850 was made Chief Justice of the Queen's Bench, and nine years after was raised to the woolsack as Lord Chancellor. He died 23rd June, 1861. He is known as the author of a considerable work, *Lives of the Chancellors*, which, with its supplementary vols., *Lives of the Chief Justices*, enjoyed great though somewhat undeserved popularity.

CAMPBELL, Thomas. A distinguished poet, born at Glasgow 27th July, 1777, and educated at its university. He resided for a short time in Edinburgh, and all at once attained the zenith of his fame by publishing, in 1799, his *Pleasures of Hope*. It produced an extraordinary sensation, and soon became a familiar book at almost every hearth throughout the kingdom. In 1803, after spending some time in Germany, Campbell published an edition of *The Pleasures of Hope* with the addition of some of the finest lyrics in the English language, including *Hohenlinden*, *Ye Mariners of England*, and *The Exile of Erin*. In 1803 he went to London, and in 1806 obtained a pension of £200 through the influence of Fox. After this he appears for a time to have given his attention less to poetry than prose, and wrote various compilations, articles for Brewster's *Edinburgh Encyclopædia*, etc. In 1809 he again made his appearance as a poet, and published *Gertrude of Wyoming*, *Lord Ullin's Daughter*, and *The Battle of the Baltic*. After publishing *Specimens of English Poets* accompanied by critical essays, he became editor in 1820 of the *New Monthly Magazine*. He took an active part in the foundation of London University, and in 1827 was elected rector of Glasgow University. After this he published his *Letters from the South*, a *Life of Mrs. Siddons*, and a *Life of Petrarch*, but these later works are not his best. He died at Boulogne, 15th June, 1844, and was interred at Poets' Corner in Westminster Abbey, close to the tomb of Addison.—BIBLIOGRAPHY: J. Logie Robertson, *Complete Works of Thomas Campbell* (Oxford Edition); *Poetical Works*, edited by Hill, with Life by Allingham.

CAMPBELL - BANNERMAN, Sir Henry. Politician, born in 1836, died in April, 1908, the son of Sir James Campbell of Stracathro, a Glasgow merchant who received the honour of knighthood, and younger brother of James Campbell, LL.D., long Conservative member of Parliament for Glasgow and Aberdeen Universities: Bannerman was the name of his maternal uncle. He was educated at Glasgow University and Trinity College, Cambridge, graduating in 1858. In 1868 he entered Parliament as member for the Stirling burghs, and henceforth he represented this constituency as an advanced Liberal. After being Financial Secretary at the War Office (1871-4) and Secretary to the Admiralty, he was Chief Secretary for Ireland (1884-5), Secretary for War twice (1886 and 1892-5), on the latter occasion being first under Gladstone (whose lead he followed on Irish Home Rule) and then under Lord Rosebery. He was made G.C.B. in 1895, and from 1899 was leader of the Liberal party in the House of Commons, strongly opposing the policy that brought on the South African War. On the resignation of the Unionist Government early in Dec., 1905, Sir Henry was called upon to form a new Government, and gained an immense majority in the general election of Jan.-Feb., 1906.

CAMPBELL ISLAND. A small uninhabited island in the S. Pacific, south-east of New Zealand, to which it belongs. It is mountainous and well wooded, and has fine harbours occasionally visited by whaling vessels.

CAMPBELL OF ARGYLE. *See* ARGYLE.

CAMPBELTOWN. A royal municipal and police burgh and seaport of Scotland in Argyllshire, near the south end of Kintyre, at the head of a bay or loch. Anciently the town was called Dalruadhain, and it was the earliest seat of the Dalriadan monarchy in Scotland. There are many whisky distilleries, and the trade consists chiefly in the export of whisky, farm produce, and herrings. Along with Ayr and other places it sends a member to Parliament. Pop. (1931), 6309.

CAM'PE, Joachim Heinrich. A German author and publisher, born in 1746, died in 1818. In 1777 he became director of the Educational Institute of Dessau, and afterwards superintendent of the schools in the duchy of Brunswick. At Brunswick he became the head of a publishing house which soon became famous over all Germany, his own works, consisting mostly of books for boys, such as *Robinson the Younger*, adapted from Defoe, *Discovery of America*, etc., contributing greatly to extend its reputation.

CAMPECHE, or **CAMPEACHY** (kam'pech-e, kam'pē-chi). A seaport of Mexico, in the state and on the bay of the same name, on the W. coast of the Peninsula of Yucatan, a mart for logwood and wax. Cigars are manufactured and ships are built, though the harbour can only admit small vessels. Pop. 20,000.—The state of Campeche has an area of 18,089 sq. miles; a pop. of 74,170.

CAMPEN. *See* KAMPEN.

CAMPER, Peter. Dutch physician and anatomist, professor of medicine, etc., successively at Franeker, Amsterdam, and Groningen, born at Leyden 1722, and died at The Hague 1789. His contributions to anatomy and physiology were valuable. He was also skilful in drawing and painting, and rendered important services to art in his work on the relations of anatomy and art. One of his doctrines is that of the facial angle. *See* FACIAL ANGLE.

CAMPERDOWN, or **CAMPERDUIN.** Sandy hills or downs on the coast of Holland, south of the Helder, off which the British, under Admiral Duncan, gained a hard-won naval victory over the Dutch, under De Winter, 11th Oct., 1797. Duncan was raised to the peerage as Viscount Duncan of Camperdown, and his son became Earl of Camperdown—still the family title.

CAM'PHENE ($C_{10}H_{16}$). One of the terpenes. It occurs in turpentine, camphor, and citronella oils. Pinene, one of the constituents of turpentine, is easily transformed into camphene. It is a white crystalline solid, very volatile, and has an odour resembling that of camphor.

CAM'PHOR ($C_{10}H_{16}O$). A crystalline substance of the terpene group, obtained by distillation from the wood or young shoots of certain trees: *Cinnamōmum Camphŏra* (Lauraceæ) yields Japan camphor, *Dryobalănops aromatica* (Dipterocarpaceæ) Borneo camphor (d-borneol). Camphor is a feeble antiseptic and insecticide, and is used in the manufacture of celluloid.

Camphor Tree (*Cinnamōmum camphora*)

CAMPI. A family of Italian artists who founded what is known in painting as the school of Cremona.

Of the four of this name, Giulio, Antonio, Vincenzo, and Bernardino, the first and the last are the best known. Giulio (1502-72), the eldest and the teacher of the others, was a pupil of Giulio Romano, and acquired from the study of Titian and Pordenone a skill in colouring which gave the school its high place. Bernardino (1525-90) was the greatest of the school. He took Romano, Titian, and Correggio in succession as his models, but without losing his own individuality as an artist.

CAM'PION. The popular name of certain plants of the chickweed order.

CAM'PION, Edmund. An English Jesuit, born 1540. He was educated at Oxford, and distinguished himself greatly. Though at first a Roman Catholic, he adopted nominally the Reformed faith, and took deacon's orders in the Church of England; but he afterwards recanted, became a Jesuit, and attacked Protestantism, especially in his work *Decem Rationes* (Ten Reasons). In 1581 he was found guilty on a false charge of conspiring to raise sedition, and was accordingly executed. Pope Leo XIII. beatified Campion in 1886.

CAMPOBAS'SO. A town of Italy, province of Campobasso, on a hillslope, 52 miles N.E. Naples; has manufactures of cutlery, and a good trade. Pop. 16,330 (1921). — The province (formerly Molise) has an area of 1692 sq. miles; pop. 343,638.

CAMPOBEL'LO. An island 8 miles long, belonging to New Brunswick, Canada, in the Bay of Fundy, with a lighthouse on its northern extremity.

CAMPO - FORMIO. A town in Italy, 66 miles N.E. of Venice, famous for the treaty of peace between Austria and France which was signed in its neighbourhood on 17th Oct., 1797. Its chief provisions were that Austria should cede the Belgian provinces and Lombardy to France, receiving in compensation the Venetian States.

CAMPO-SANTO (literally "Holy Field"). The name given to a burying-ground in Italy, best known as the appellation of the more remarkable, such as are surrounded with arcades and richly adorned. The most famous Campo-Santo is that of Pisa, which dates from the twelfth century, and has on its walls frescoes of the fourteenth century of great interest in the history of art. Amongst more modern Italian cemeteries, that of Genoa is distinguished for its magnificence.

CAMPOS SALLES, Manoel Ferraz de. South American politician and President of Brazil, born in 1846. In 1884 he became a member of the Chamber of Deputies, and did much to bring about the proclamation of the Brazilian Republic in 1889. He was elected President of Brazil in 1898, retaining his office until 1906. He died in 1913.

CAMPUS MARTIUS (called also **Campus,** merely). A large place in the suburbs of ancient Rome, consisting of the level ground between the Quirinal, Capitoline, and Pincian hills, and the River Tiber, set apart for military exercises and sacred to the god Mars. In the later period of the Republic it was a suburban pleasure-ground for the Romans, and was laid out with gardens, shady walks, baths, etc. A large part of the modern city of Rome stands on it. The district in which the old Campus was situated is now called Campo Marzo.

CAMP'VERE (now **Veere, Vere,** or **Ter-Vere**). A fortified maritime town in Holland, in the province of Zeeland, on the Island of Walcheren, 4 miles N.N.E. of Middelburg. It once had some shipping trade, building-yards, etc., but has greatly fallen off. Historically Campvere is remarkable from having been for a long period the town in which the Scottish merchants had their staple in Holland, that is, the town in which all goods sent from Scotland to the Netherlands were deposited until they were sold. The Scots living at Campvere formed in some respects a separate community, and enjoyed various privileges. They had their own church, and were governed by the law of Scotland. These privileges were abolished in 1795.

CAM'TOOS. A river of Southern Africa, in Cape Province, which falls into the sea west of Algoa Bay; length, 200 miles.

CAMUCCINI (kȧ-mụt-chē'nē), **Vincenzo.** A distinguished Italian historical painter, born at Rome about 1773, died in 1844. Among his best-known works are: *Assassination of Cæsar, Death of Virginia, The Incredulity of Thomas, Horatius Cocles, Death of Mary Magdalene.* He had a valuable collection of pictures, of which a number was purchased in 1876 by the Duke of Northumberland.

CAMWOOD. A red dye-wood imported from tropical West Africa, and obtained from the *Baphia nitida*, a leguminous tree, sub-ord. Papilionaceæ. This wood is of a very fine colour, and is used in turnery for making knife-handles and other similar articles. The dye obtained from it is brilliant, but not permanent.

CANA. A village of Palestine, in Galilee, the scene of Christ's first miracle; probably represented by Kana el Jelil, a modern village 9 miles north of Nazareth.

CANAAN (kā'nan). *See* PALESTINE.

CANAANITES. The general name for the heathen peoples (Jebusites, Hittites, Amorites, etc.) whom the Israelites found dwelling in Canaan (Palestine) west of the Jordan, and whom in the end they utterly subdued, though the subjugation was not quite complete till Solomon's time. They are believed to have been, in part at least, of kindred race with the Israelites; and some authorities find traces of their descendants among the present inhabitants of Palestine. *See* PALESTINE; PHŒNICIA; SYRIA.

CANADA, DOMINION OF. An extensive series of British territories in North America, the greatest of the constituent parts of the British Empire. It comprises nine provinces and two territories, embraces the whole of British North America, with the exception of Newfoundland and part of Labrador (which belongs to Newfoundland), and its area is estimated at 3,684,723 sq. miles, of which 3,547,230 are land and 137,493 are water. Provincial boundaries were revised in Manitoba and Eastern Canada in 1912. The following table shows the areas of the several divisions of the Dominion, with their populations, according to the census return of 1921:—

Provinces.	Area, sq. miles.	Pop. in 1921.
Prince Edward Island ..	2,184	88,615
Nova Scotia	21,428	523,837
New Brunswick	27,985	387,876
Quebec	594,434	2,361,199
Ontario	407,202	2,933,662
Manitoba	251,832	610,118
British Columbia	355,855	524,582
Alberta	255,285	588,454
Saskatchewan	251,700	757,510
Yukon	207,076	4,157
North-West Territories ..	1,309,682	7,988
Totals	3,684,723	8,787,998

Nova Scotia, New Brunswick, and Prince Edward Island are called the "Maritime Provinces," though British Columbia, being on the Pacific, is also a maritime province. From the area belonging to the North-West Territories two new provinces were formed in 1905, Alberta and Saskatchewan, each with an area of more than 250,000 sq. miles. The North-West Territories were divided in 1905 and 1920 into the districts of Mackenzie, Keewatin, and Franklin. In 1927 a long-standing dispute with Newfoundland, which has always held a coastal strip in Labrador, was settled by the Privy Council award to Newfoundland of 110,000 sq. miles in Labrador.

Coasts.—On the east the coast-line is very irregular, being marked by deep indentations and fringed by islands. The province of Nova Scotia forms an odd peninsular projection with the Bay of Fundy between it and the mainland, while north of it is the Gulf of St. Lawrence, shut in from the Atlantic by Cape Breton Island and Newfoundland. In the gulf are the Island of Anticosti and Prince Edward Island. The chief features of the north coast are the archipelago of the Arctic islands and the great opening of Hudson Bay, connected with the Atlantic by Hudson Strait, and having as its southern continuation James Bay. On the west coast are Vancouver Island, the Queen Charlotte Islands, and many others. The southern boundary is most remarkable for passing through the system of great lakes—Superior, Huron, Erie, and Ontario, between the last two of which are the Falls of Niagara, partly belonging to Canada, partly to the United States.

Surface.—The Dominion is divided naturally into five regions: (1) *The Atlantic Coast Region,* consisting of Nova Scotia, New Brunswick, Prince Edward Island, and part of Quebec, and separated from the St. Lawrence Valley by the Appalachian Mountains. Here there are important timber stands, large mixed farming areas, rich deposits of coal, gypsum, and copper, and important sea fisheries. (2) *The Eastern Plains Region,* consisting of the St. Lawrence Valley westward to the Great Lakes (i.e. the provinces of Ontario and Quebec). Here are great farming, fruit, and forest areas, and good freshwater fisheries. Petroleum, coal, cobalt, natural gas, and copper are found. In the Timiskaming District is the largest Canadian gold-field; in Ontario is 75 per cent of the world's asbestos; and Ontario and Quebec produce 80 per cent of the world's nickel. This region contains more than half the total population of the Dominion, and in it are the great manufacturing centres. The towns are Ottawa (the Dominion capital), Montreal, Quebec, Toronto, Hamilton, and London. (3) *The Laurentian Region,* consisting of the vast Laurentian Plateau stretching from Labrador to Lake Superior, and thence to the Arctic Circle. This huge area (2,000,000 sq. miles) has great but undeveloped mineral wealth. It is an important fur and timber country. (4) *The Western Plains*

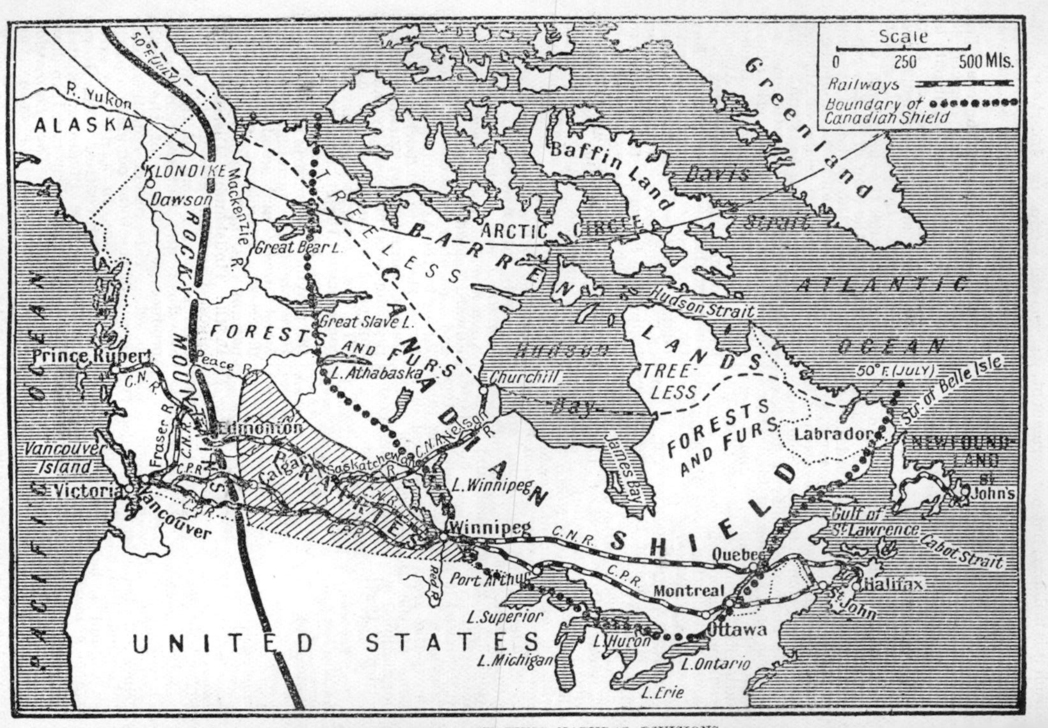

MAP OF CANADA, SHOWING NATURAL DIVISIONS

Region, extending from Lake Winnipeg to the Rockies, and including the famous Peace River District. This is the great agricultural area, and is one of the world's principal wheat reserves. In south-west Alberta are valuable coal, petroleum, and natural gas deposits. The towns are Winnipeg, Regina, Calgary, Lethbridge, Saskatoon, and Edmonton. (5) *The Pacific Coast Region*, consisting of British Columbia and part of Alberta. This is a very mountainous region, the chief range being the Rockies. Here there are fertile valleys, productive orchards, and enormous forests. The sea and river fishing (mainly salmon and halibut) are world famous. The towns are Victoria, Vancouver, and Prince Rupert.

Lakes and Rivers.—The vast lake and river systems which Canada possesses of its own, or shares with the United States, give it a unique character. Everywhere in the interior are rivers and lakes. To Hudson Bay flow the Albany, Nelson, Churchill, and many other streams; to the Arctic Ocean, the Mackenzie, Coppermine, and Back or Great Fish River; to the Pacific, the Fraser, Skeena, Stickeen, etc. The basin of the St. Lawrence, with the connected Lakes Superior, Huron, Michigan, Erie, and Ontario, affords a continuous water-way from the Atlantic to the interior of the continent. To this sytem belong the Ottawa, Gatineau, Richelieu, St. Maurice, Saguenay, and other rivers. In the prairie region and the north-west are similar great lake and river systems, formed by the Saskatchewan, Nelson, Churchill, Athabasca, and Mackenzie Rivers, and the great Lakes Winnipeg, Athabasca, Great Slave, and Great Bear. The Saskatchewan, lying in the heart of the rich wheat-growing district, must in time prove a far more important water-way than at present. The Mackenzie and its connected lakes and rivers form the most remarkable feature of the far north-west. This river, including its tributary the Peace, has a length of perhaps 2500 miles, and drains an area of 550,000 sq. miles, or almost double that of the St. Lawrence basin. Between the Mackenzie system and Hudson Bay is a great region called from its desolate character the Barren Grounds.

Geology and Minerals.—As regards the geological features of Canada, a great part of the Dominion north of the St. Lawrence and west of Hudson Bay is covered with Archæan rocks belonging to the Laurentian system, and consisting largely of granite and gneiss, with quartz-rock, schist, limestone, etc. South of the St. Lawrence, in New Brunswick and Nova Scotia, is a considerable development of Carboniferous strata. Between the Archæan rocks and the Rocky Mountains is a great area of secondary (Mesozoic) strata. In the Rocky Mountain region the Archæan, Palæozoic, Mesozoic, and Tertiary systems are represented. Canada has great mineral wealth, and the chief mineral products are coal, gold, lead, copper, nickle, silver, zinc, and asbestos. Iron-ore is abundant in Quebec, Ontario, and British Columbia. The district round Lake Superior and the upper part of Lake Huron abounds in copper and has much nickel and silver. Nova Scotia, Saskatchewan, Alberta, and British Columbia are rich in coal. In Nova Scotia there are a number of coal-mines worked; gold is also obtained in some quantity, as well as iron. Coal is worked in the north-west, and more extensively in British Columbia. Much gold is found in the Klondike, British Columbia, Ontario, and Northern Quebec (a field not discovered till 1925). Large quantities of petroleum are obtained. The chief oil district is the peninsula in the Province of Ontario formed by Lakes Erie and Huron and the River St. Clair. Other useful mineral products are asbestos, zinc, cobalt, mica, salt, gypsum, corundum, plumbago, antimony, natural gas, and building-stone.

Animals.—The chief wild animals (some of them represented by several species) are deer, the musk-ox, bear, wolf, fox, otter, beaver, squirrel, racoon, musk-rat, marten, etc. The buffalo, once plentiful in the west, has been almost exterminated. The largest of the deer kind is the moose, or elk, which is found in New Brunswick, Nova Scotia, and the northern parts of Quebec, as well as in the far west and north-west. The reindeer occurs in the north. The grizzly bear is met with in the Rocky Mountains, and the polar bear in the extreme north and north-east. Fur-bearing animals are so numerous as to have been a source of revenue to a large trading company like the Hudson Bay Company for over two centuries. Fur-farming is now a profitable occupation, especially in Prince Edward Island. Birds include the wild swan, wild turkey, geese and ducks of various kinds, partridges, quail, prairie-fowl, pigeon, woodcock, snipe, plover, etc., besides eagles, hawks, owls, and many smaller birds, among which are two species of humming-bird. Except at certain seasons game of all kinds may be shot at will. The rattlesnake and other snakes occur, but are less common than in the States. The seas, lakes, and rivers, especially the Gulf of St. Lawrence and the neighbouring waters, abound in almost all kinds of fish, and the fisheries are extremely valuable, employing over 80,000 people. The chief sea-fish caught are cod, herring, mackerel, halibut, haddock, hake, shad, salmon, etc. The rivers and lakes abound with salmon, white-fish, bass, trout, sturgeon, mas-kinonge (or maskelonge), pike, pickerel, etc. The seal and whale fisheries are also valuable. Lobsters and oysters are abundant and excellent. The total value of the produce of the fisheries of Canada is over 50,000,000 dollars.

Vegetation.—The forests are of great extent, and the timber trade is a great source of wealth, vast quantities of timber, forest products, paper and paper-pulp being shipped annually. In the forests grow more than sixty kinds of trees. Amongst the most valuable are the white and red pine, white and black spruce, maple, ash, beech, oak, walnut, butternut, chestnut, basswood, birch, cedar, etc. Over most parts of the Dominion (except in the prairie regions of the interior) good timber is found, though in the older and more closely-settled parts the forests have been largely cleared off. The forests of British Columbia produce the largest timber, the Douglas pine being the chief tree. The balsam poplar grows to an immense size on the Athabasca, Peace, and Mackenzie Rivers, and even at the mouth of the last, within the Arctic Circle, trees of some size are found. The Banksian pine grows to the height of 100 feet on the southern shores of Hudson Bay; and spruce suitable for building purposes, and the tamarac or larch, extend as far north as Fort St. George on its east and Fort Churchill on its west shore. The sugar-maple, a forest tree attaining the height of 120 feet, flourishes in the greater part of the St. Lawrence valleys up to lat. 49°, and is much valued for the sugar that is obtained from it. There are a great many varieties of wild fruits, as the wild plum, wild cherry, raspberry, service-berry, cranberry, gooseberry, straw-berry, black and red currant, wild vine, blueberry, buffalo berry, etc., and numerous wild flowers and flowering shrubs. Of the wild fruits, the raspberry, the cranberry, and the blueberry are alone important eco-nomically. There are rich pasture grasses, but they cannot be utilised in cultivation.

Climate.—The climate of a country of such vast extent and varied features as Canada naturally differs very much in different places, and in this respect British Columbia on the Pacific coast, and Nova Scotia and the other Atlantic regions, are very dissimilar to the prairie region of the centre. So different, indeed, is the climate of one portion of the Dominion from that of other portions that Canada has been said to present " climates and productions similar to those of north-west and central Europe—that is, of Russia, Norway, the British Islands, Denmark, Germany, France, Holland, Belgium, Switzerland, and Northern Italy." In Ontario and the region of the Upper St. Lawrence it may be de-scribed as temperate, although the heat in summer and the cold in winter are on the average twenty degrees greater than the correspond-ing seasons in Great Britain.

Generally the climate of the Domi-nion shows considerable extremes of heat and cold, but, except in some of the coast regions, the exceeding dryness of the Canadian atmosphere makes both extremes of temperature more pleasant and healthy than similar temperatures in Britain. Apart from the portions of the Domi-nion that fall within the Arctic Circle, Labrador and all the country east of Hudson Bay have the most severe climate. The Pacific coast region has a decidedly moist climate. The peninsula lying between Lakes Ontario, Erie, and Huron has the finest climate, allowing of fruits, shrubs, and flowers to be grown that cannot stand the winter elsewhere. The Mackenzie River district—especi-ally in the region of the Peace River, where the temperature throughout the year is remarkably genial—possesses a climate much less severe than one might expect, and would allow of agriculture almost to the Arctic Ocean.

Agriculture.—Agriculture has been called " the economic heart of Canada," for it is the chief means of livelihood within the Dominion. It is estimated that there are in Canada fully 380,000,000 acres of cultivable lands little more than a fifth of which produce field crops. It is thus clear that Canada is capable of supporting many millions more inhabitants. All branches of farming are pursued—grain-growing, dairy-farming, fruit-farming, ranching—but Canada is chiefly notable for the vast areas under wheat in the prairie provinces of Alberta, Manitoba, and Saskatchewan. In addition to wheat, oats, barley, rye, maize, potatoes, turnips, etc., are raised. Fruit-growing is extensively carried on in

Nova Scotia, Ontario, and British Columbia, apples being the most important of orchard fruits. Peaches, pears, and plums are also grown, and there is a valuable vineyard area in the Niagara Peninsula. Dairy-farming is carried on in all the provinces, but is most extensive in Ontario and Quebec. There are numerous creameries and butter and cheese factories throughout the Dominion, and there is a large export of dairy produce. Stock-raising is not of great importance except in the provinces of Alberta and Saskatchewan—elsewhere it is merely a subsidiary of mixed farming. Tobacco of good quality is grown in Ontario and Quebec. In connection with agriculture there are various subsidiary industries, such as flour-milling, fruit canning and drying, and the manufacture of butter and cheese for export. The wheat from the prairies is exported by three main routes: from Vancouver and other west coast ports; through Fort William and Port Arthur by the Great Lakes water-ways to the St. Lawrence; and by the Hudson Bay Railway to Port Nelson on Hudson Bay.

Commerce.—The trade of the Dominion is chiefly with Great Britain and the United States. About four-fifths of the whole exports are sent to these two countries, while nearly nine-tenths of the imports come from them, sometimes more than one-half being from the U.S.A. alone. Besides agricultural products, timber, paper, and animal products, the chief articles of export are fish, iron and other minerals, leather, and woollen goods. The total exports in 1928 were valued at about 1,267,573,142 dollars, the imports at 1,030,892,505 dollars. The imports chiefly consist of manufactured goods, coal, iron, tea, coffee, sugar, cotton, etc. The value of Britain's imports from Canada in 1928 was about 450,000,000 dollars. Britain receives grain and flour, timber, cattle, paper and pulp, butter, furs, fish, etc. The chief imports of British produce are iron goods, woollens, cottons, apparel and haberdashery, etc. Canada's fiscal system gives British trade some advantage over foreign trade.

Among ship-owning countries Canada holds a high place. A decimal system of coinage was established in 1871. The unit of account is the dollar of 100 cents, the value of which is declared to be on the basis of 486⅔ cents to the pound of British sterling money. The average rate of exchange makes the dollar equal to about 4*s.* The money used consists of bank bills and gold, silver, and bronze coins, besides Government notes (partly of small denominations up to 4 dollars), the bank bills being not of lower denominations than 5 dollars. There is a uniform system of weights and measures, the Canadian standards being the same as the British imperial standards. The British hundredweight of 112 lb. and ton of 2240 lb. are, however, superseded by the United States weights of 100 lb. and 2000 lb. respectively.

Railways.—The inland trade has been enormously enlarged by the making of railways, now extending to over 40,000 miles. Since 1922 these railways, except a few of the smallest lines, have been divided into two great systems, the Canadian National Railway and the Canadian Pacific Railway. The Canadian National Railway, including the Intercolonial, the Canadian Northern, the Transcontinental, the Grand Trunk, and the Grand Trunk Pacific lines, has over 22,500 miles of track, and is therefore one of the largest State-owned railways in the world. It has two transcontinental lines with termini at Halifax, Vancouver, and Prince Rupert, and it also operates in the United States with termini at Portland (Maine) and Chicago. The Canadian Pacific Railway has 14,892 miles of permanent way, and its transcontinental line from Montreal (St. John, N.B., in winter) to Vancouver is 2903 miles long. The efficiency of the Canadian Pacific service is such that the journey from Montreal to Vancouver is accomplished in 92 hours. Both these great systems have branch lines in every part of Canada, making connections with the main lines and providing transport facilities to some of the most remote districts of the Dominion. The Ontario Government now operates the Timiskaming and North Ontario Railway, which has a track length of 470 miles. The electric railway mileage is over 2500.

Canals.—Some of the canals are stupendous achievements. The most important, from a commercial point of view, are the St. Lawrence Canals and the Welland Canal. The former series of canals, with an aggregate length of about 70 miles, avoids the rapids on the St. Lawrence between Montreal and Kingston on Lake Ontario, and thus affords to vessels the means of ascending to that lake (in descending vessels of 700 tons can shoot the rapids with safety); and the latter, which has a length of 27 miles, avoids the Niagara Falls and rapids, and enables vessels to ascend from Lake Ontario to Lake Erie. Both the Welland Canal and the St. Lawrence series have been enlarged and deepened so as to accommodate the increased traffic expected as a result of the settlement of the north-western provinces, and the construction of the additional western railways. The last Canadian canal necessary to complete the navigation of the St. Lawrence to Lake Superior is St. Mary's Canal, opened in 1895 at a cost of £750,000, avoiding the St. Mary rapids (Sault Ste Marie), a tumultuous descent by which Lake Superior pours its waters into Lake Huron. Next after those mentioned, the most important of the Canadian canals is the series of locks and short artificial connections known as the Rideau Canal. It connects Lake Ontario at Kingston with the Ottawa near the city of that name. By means of these works large vessels can sail by the St. Lawrence route from the Atlantic to the head of Lake Superior.

Constitution, etc.—By the Act of Confederation of 1867 the constitution of the Dominion was required to be similar in principle to that of the United Kingdom. There is a Central Federal Government and separate Provincial Governments and Legislatures. The Central Executive Government is vested in the sovereign of Great Britain and Ireland, and is carried on in his name by a Governor-General appointed by the Crown, and a Privy Council. The Governor-General has a salary of £10,000 per annum. He is assisted by a Privy Council consisting of the Prime Minister and thirteen other ministers or heads of departments. The legislative authority rests with a Parliament consisting of two Houses, the Senate and the House of Commons. The Senate consists of ninety-six members (eighty-seven till 1917), nominated by the Governor-General. Each Senator must be a born or naturalised subject, thirty years of age, and own real or personal property to the value of 400 dollars in the province for which he is appointed. There are twenty-four Senators from the province of Ontario, twenty-four from Quebec, ten from Nova Scotia, ten from New Brunswick, six from Manitoba, six from British Columbia, four from Prince Edward Island, six from Alberta, and six from Saskatchewan. The House of Commons is elected by the people for five years. It has 245 members, 65 of whom come from Quebec, the remainder being divided proportionately among the other provinces. There is a uniform franchise, a vote being given to every male of twenty-one years of age possessed of a small property qualification. Each of the provinces has a separate parliament and administration, independent in its own sphere, at the head being a Lieutenant-Governor appointed by the Central Government.

The provinces of Quebec and Nova Scotia have each two chambers; the other provinces have only one. The administration of justice is based on the English model, except in Quebec Province, where the old French law prevails. The only court that has jurisdiction throughout the Dominion (except the Exchequer and the Maritime Court) is the Supreme Court, the ultimate court of appeal in civil and criminal cases. In certain cases an appeal may be had to His Majesty's Privy Council. The capital is Ottawa, but the largest cities are Montreal, Toronto, Winnipeg, and Vancouver. By the *National Defence Act, 1922*, the naval, military, and air forces are controlled by the Department of National Defence. The militia is classified as active (authorised strength, 10,000) and reserve (total strength about 125,000). The Royal Canadian Navy is little more than a coast-patrol and fisheries defence force, while the Air Force, with head-quarters at Camp Borden, is much used for forest fire protection, survey work, fisheries patrol, communication with isolated districts, and other similar duties. The Royal Canadian Mounted Police (strength about 1000) is a Dominion Government force charged with preserving law and order in the Yukon, the North-West Territories, and the Indian Reserves. It also assists Provincial Governments if required.

Religion and Education.—There is no State Church in the Dominion. The prevailing religion in Quebec is that of the Roman Catholic Church. In Ontario Methodists predominate, then Presbyterians, the English Church, and the Roman Catholics. Of the total population in 1921, 3,389,636 were Roman Catholics, 1,409,407 Presbyterians, 1,407,994 Anglicans, 1,159,458 Methodists. Education is well attended to, being everywhere more or less under the supervision of Government, and excellent free schools being provided. Education is under the control of the provincial governments; it is aided by local taxation, and liberally supported by grants from the several governments. In Quebec Protestant and Roman Catholic schools are under the Department of Public Instruction but are administered separately, while Roman Catholic secondary schools are independent but subsidised by the State. Minority elementary schools (whether Protestant or Roman Catholic) are, in Alberta, Ontario, and Saskatchewan, called Separate Schools, and are under the same administrative authority as the majority schools. Secondary education in these three provinces is, however, non-sectarian. There are in Canada 23 universities, 6 of which are State-controlled.

Literature.—See COLONIAL LITERATURE.

People.—The population is increasing rapidly both naturally and by means of immigration. Over 100,000 immigrants arrive in the Dominion every year. The nationality of the inhabitants is varied. Ontario is inhabited principally by emigrants from Great Britain and their descendants, with considerable numbers of Germans and Americans. In the province of Quebec the people are mostly French in origin, speech, and customs, being mainly descendants of the French colonists who inhabited the region before it became British. There are, besides, the Indian tribes and the Esquimaux, the latter in the extreme north. The Indians are estimated to number about 110,000. They are divided into various tribes as well as larger stocks or races, such as the Tinneh or Athabascan Indians, the Thlinkets and Hydahs of British Columbia and the west coast, the Algonquins, Hurons, Iroquois, etc., of the St. Lawrence region.

History.—English ships were the first to reach the shores of what is now Canada. In 1497 John Cabot, sailing from Bristol, landed on the coast of Labrador, and planted the English flag there. But it was the French navigator Jacques Cartier who first really opened up Canada for European settlers. In 1534 Cartier in a single ship sailed up the Gulf of St. Lawrence till he could see land on each side. Having returned the year following, he reached the Indian town of Hochelaga, to the height above which he gave the name of Mont Royal, now Montreal, and passed the winter at the mouth of the St. Charles, where the city of Quebec now stands. Some years later vigorous attempts at colonisation were made. The Sieur de Roberval was appointed Viceroy of New France, as the newly-discovered territory had been called, and under his leadership and that of Cartier two hundred colonists were landed, who, after struggling for two winters with the hardships of their situation, had eventually to return. For the next fifty years no further attempts were made in these regions, except that on the part of the English, Martin Frobisher, in 1576, and Sir Humphrey Gilbert, in 1583, explored and took formal possession of Newfoundland and the adjacent coasts.

In 1603 Samuel Champlain, a French naval officer, sailed up the St. Lawrence to where the city of Montreal now stands, and two years afterwards a settlement was made at Port Royal in Acadia (New Brunswick and Nova Scotia) in connection with a French fur-trading company, but it was abandoned three years afterwards. At length, in 1608, a French colony under the leadership of Champlain and Des Monts settled at Quebec. Two years later another English navigator, Henry Hudson, explored the river and the bay which bear his name. In 1627, the fur trade having made considerable development under the guidance of Champlain, Cardinal Richelieu organised the company of the Hundred Associates for the further colonisation of New France; but two years after the colony received a check in the capture of Quebec and other settlements by an English expedition under Sir David Kirk. The conquests, however, were soon restored to the French by the Treaty of St. Germain-en-Laye. The growth of the colony, however, was slow. At Champlain's death in 1635 it numbered but 250 Europeans, and in 1663 was still under 2000.

The most formidable foes of the colonists were the Iroquois Indians, who swarmed round the settlements, rooting up the mission-stations of the French Jesuits, and pursuing the fugitives to the very walls of Quebec fort. In 1663, Colbert being at the head of affairs in France, fresh supplies of emigrants and a strong body of troops were sent out to Canada. The Iroquois found it advisable to make peace, and the soldiers, turning colonists, received grants of land under a kind of feudal tenure, their seigniors being often their former officers. Under the governorship of Count de Frontenac the explorations of Jesuit missionaries, and of the adventurers Joliet and La Salle, opened up the regions of the Mississippi and the "Great West"; but the French generally preferred an adventurous life as *coureurs de bois* and trappers to the solid pursuits of agriculture. In 1682 a new war with the Iroquois broke out, in which the colonists, at first successful, afterwards suffered severely, receiving a crushing blow in the massacre of Lachine, when 1200 Iroquois descended on the Island of Montreal, fired the village of Lachine, and massacred its inhabitants.

The French colonists had scarcely recovered from this blow, which practically reduced their dominion to the military posts along the St. Lawrence, when war broke out between France and England, invol-

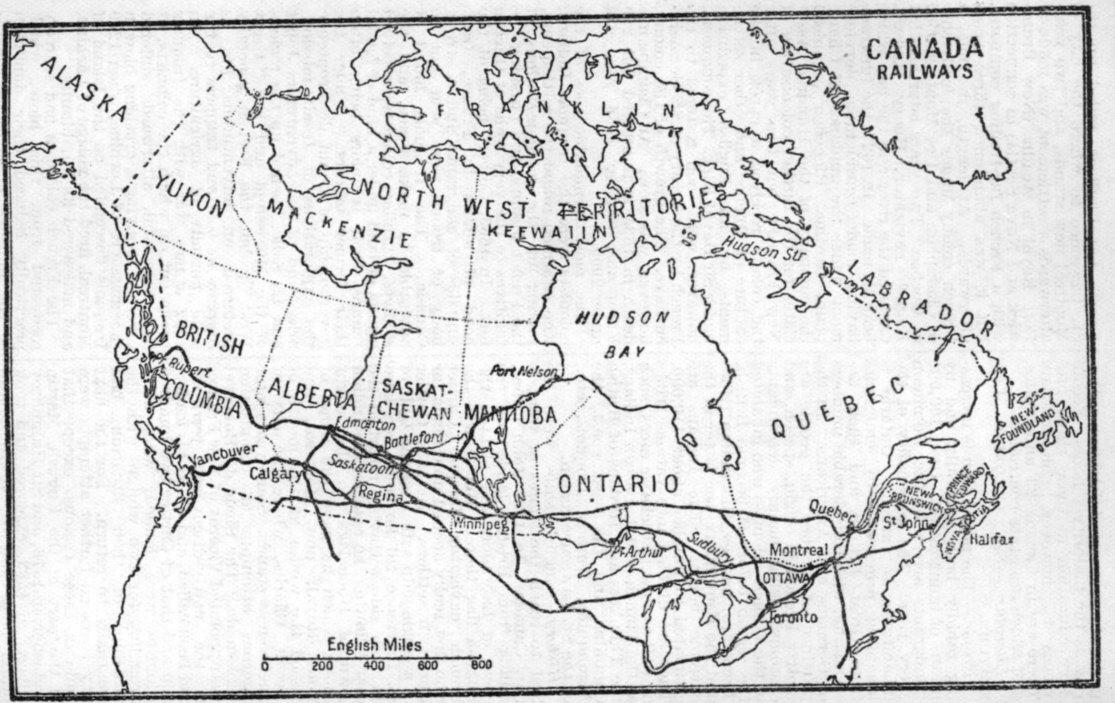
CANADA
RAILWAYS
ALASKA
FRANKLIN
YUKON
NORTH WEST TERRITORIES
MACKENZIE
KEEWATIN
Hudson Str
LABRADOR
HUDSON
BAY
BRITISH
Rupert
COLUMBIA
ALBERTA
SASKAT-
CHEWAN
MANITOBA
Port Nelson
QUEBEC
NEW-
FOUNDLAND
Edmonton
Battleford
Vancouver
Saskatoon
Calgary
Regina
ONTARIO
NEW
BRUNSWICK
PRINCE
EDWARD I
Quebec
St John
NOVA SCOTIA
Halifax
Winnipeg
Pt Arthur
Sudbury
Montreal
OTTAWA
Toronto
English Miles
0
200
400
600
800

ving them in a strife with the British settlers in New England. The French struck the first blow by the burning of the British settlement at Corlaer (now Schenectady) and the massacre of its inhabitants. The British colonists retaliated; but the Peace of Ryswick put an end to the war without altering the position of the parties. In 1702 a new conflict arose, terminating in 1713 with the Peace of Utrecht, by which the British obtained Acadia, Newfoundland, and the regions around Hudson Bay, France retaining Canada, Cape Breton, etc. The thirty years of peace which followed was virtually a testing period for the colonising capacities of the two nations. The French did not altogether neglect industrial development; they laid the foundation of shipbuilding at Quebec, encouraged the fur trade and other industries; but in general their colonists lacked the qualifications for agricultural and other settled pursuits. The British colonists, on the other hand, stuck to agriculture, and reclaimed every year great tracts of forest land.

As a natural consequence their population rapidly increased, and when the final struggle began, the British colonies in America numbered three millions of prosperous inhabitants against some sixty thousand French colonists hampered by feudal tenures, commercial monopolies, and a corrupt set of officials. In 1754 the French Governor Du Quesne, an energetic and aggressive man, established new military posts in the Ohio valley, and seized a newly-built British stockade on the spot where Pittsburg now stands. The French were already in occupation and had named the post Fort Du Quesne, when a force, dispatched by the Governor of Virginia and under the command of Colonel George Washington, arrived to take possession. They were met by a small party of French sent apparently to warn them off the ground. Washington, mistaking their intention, gave the word to fire, with the result that the French leader, Jumonville, was shot. Both sides at once prepared for war. The English Government sent out two regiments under General Braddock, a brave but incapable leader, who allowed himself to be surprised and routed near the Monongahela, while marching on Fort Du Quesne at the head of over two thousand men. But an expedition against Crown Point under the leadership of General William Johnson drove the French within their entrenched camp at Ticonderoga.

Now happened the incident of the expulsion of the Acadian peasants (described in Longfellow's *Evangeline*), of whom about seven thousand still remained in Nova Scotia, mostly on the shores of the Bay of Fundy. Although steadily refusing to take the oath of allegiance to the British Government, they were on the whole a peaceful and inoffensive community. But a few of the more turbulent spirits took a leading part in the Indian raids on the neighbouring British settlements, and were accused, besides, of intriguing with their countrymen at Louisburg, the strong fortress of Cape Breton. On these grounds the council at Halifax resolved upon the expulsion of the whole French population, and the measure was carried into effect with thoroughness. The war in America was but a portion of the great conflict in which Britain was now engaged against France—the Seven Years' War, 1756-63. The early part of the struggle was decidedly in favour of the French, whose Generals Montcalm, De Levi, and St. Veran were superior in energy and ability to their opponents Loudon and Abercrombie. But with the appointment of Pitt as colleague of Newcastle and virtual Prime Minister in 1758, the face of affairs changed. Strong reinforcements were sent out under Wolfe, Howe, and Amherst.

The fortress of Louisburg, garrisoned by over 3500 soldiers and sailors, fell before Amherst, Boscawen, and Wolfe. General Johnson took Fort Niagara; Washington planted the British flag on the ramparts of Fort Du Quesne; Amherst drove the enemy from Ticonderoga and Crown Point; and the long struggle was at length virtually ended by Wolfe's brilliant capture of Quebec on 13th Sept., 1759. The French made a stand for a year longer at Montreal; but, on 8th Sept., 1760, the appearance of 16,000 British before its walls forced a capitulation, by which Canada passed finally from the dominion of France.

Canada was now formally annexed to the British Empire, and in 1774 an Act passed in the British Parliament (the Quebec Act) extended the bounds of the province from Labrador to the Mississippi and from the Ohio to the watershed of Hudson Bay. In 1775 the war of the American Revolution broke out, and Canada became the scene of a brief struggle between the royalists and the revolted colonists of New England. The war ended with the recognition of the independence of the American colonies by the Treaty of Versailles,

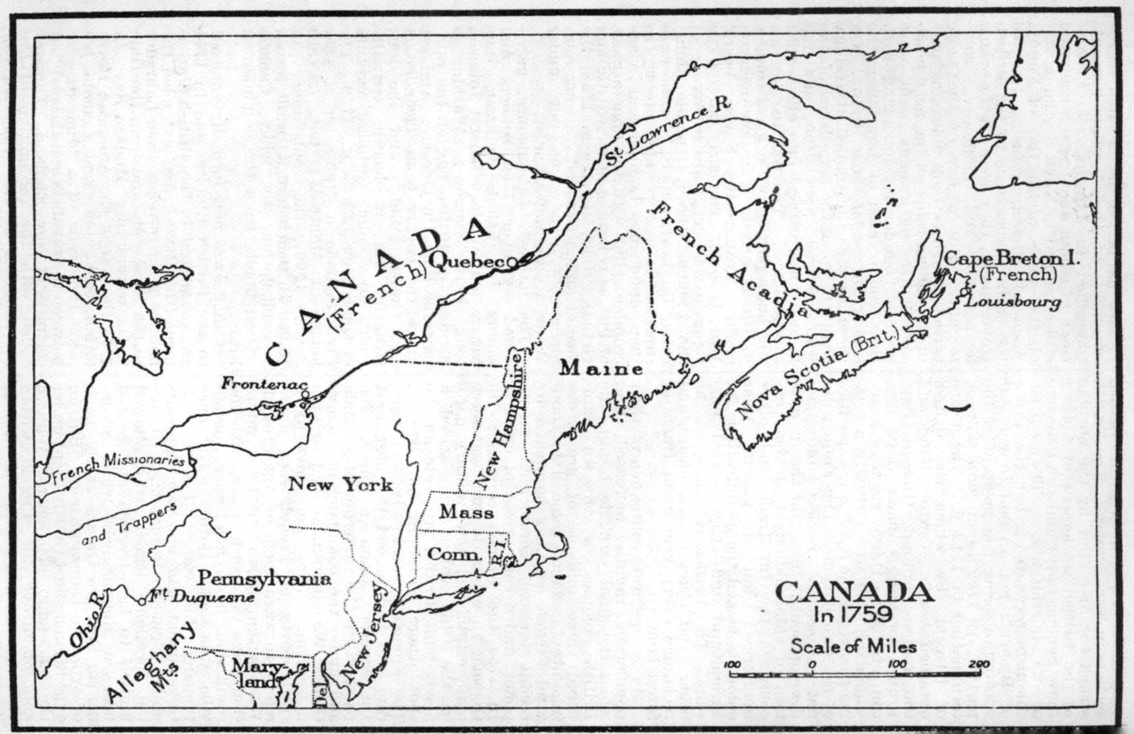
CANADA
In 1759
Scale of Miles
100 0 100 200
Cape Breton I.
(French)
Louisbourg
Nova Scotia (Brit.)
French Acadia
St. Lawrence R.
Quebec
CANADA
(French)
Frontenac
Maine
New Hampshire
Mass
R.I.
Conn.
New York
French Missionaries
and Trappers
Pennsylvania
Ft. Duquesne
Ohio R.
Allaghany Mts
Mary-land
Del
New Jersey

3rd Sept., 1783, which detached from Canada the region between the Mississippi and the Ohio. On the other hand, thousands of American loyalists sought new homes in Canada; and a large number settled on the St. John River, and had that district made into the separate province of New Brunswick. More than 10,000 settled in Ontario, where they received liberal grants of land. In 1791 Canada was divided into two provinces—Upper Canada or Ontario, and Lower Canada or Quebec—the latter still retaining its seigneurial tenure and French law in civil cases. In Upper Canada British law and freehold tenure were introduced. In both Upper and Lower Canada representative institutions, although not responsible government, were established.

From 1812 to 1815, war having broken out between Great Britain and America, Canada was again the scene of much bloodshed. Amongst the chief incidents of this fighting were Brock's victory over the Americans on the heights of Queenstown, and the battles of Chippewa, Lundy's Lane, Moravian's Town, etc. In 1837-8 the discontent of the people of Lower Canada with their system of irresponsible government took the form of a rebellion, which was repressed after a brief but sharp struggle. At the same time the failure to secure responsible government brought about an insurrection in Upper Canada under the leadership of William Lyon Mackenzie, aided subsequently by a number of American filibusters, but it was quickly suppressed by the energy of the Canadian militia. The Earl of Durham was sent out as Governor-General to settle affairs on a just and liberal basis, and made a report on the condition of Canada which is one of the historical monuments of the country.

The year 1839 was distinguished by the celebrated "Boundary Dispute" between New Brunswick and the United States. After threatening preparations on both sides the quarrel was settled in 1842 by the Ashburton Treaty, which fixed the forty-fifth parallel as the boundary-line westward from the disputed territory to the St. Lawrence, and the forty-ninth parallel, from the Lake of the Woods to the Pacific, the central line of the great lakes and their connecting rivers completing the boundary. The result of the rebellion of 1837-8, and Lord Durham's report, was the reunion in 1841 of Upper and Lower Canada as one province with equal representation in the common legislature, and the practical concession on the part of the mother country of responsible government. Kingston was selected as the new seat of government, and three years afterwards Montreal. In 1848, the Parliament House at Montreal having been burned in a riot, the seat of government was removed to Toronto and Quebec alternately every four years.

In 1854 the Reciprocity Treaty with America was concluded, according to which there was to be free exchange of the products of sea and land, with navigation of the St. Lawrence, the St. John, and the canals, and the use of the inshore fisheries in the British waters to the Americans and of Lake Michigan to the Canadians. In the same year (1854) the Bill for the secularisation of the Clergy Reserve Lands, originally amounting to one-seventh of the Crown territory, and a Bill for the abolition of seigneurial tenure in Lower Canada were passed. By the former Act the principle of religious equality was practically established in Canada. In 1858 Ottawa was finally selected as the capital of Canada, the choice having been referred to the queen. During these years the population of Upper Canada or Ontario had been rapidly increasing, and now exceeded that of Lower Canada or Quebec by nearly 300,000. Under the old constitution, however, the two provinces had equal representation in the legislature. Hence a demand arose on the part of the Upper Canadians for representation by population. This demand was practically conceded in a scheme of federation of the British North American colonies approved of by the Canadian Parliament at Quebec in 1865 and forwarded to the Imperial Government for approbation.

In 1866, the Reciprocity Treaty with the United States having expired, the Government of that country practically refused to renew it except on the most disadvantageous terms for Canada. About the same time a Fenian movement against Canada, originating in the United States, began to be heard of. Gangs of desperadoes, mostly the refuse of the Civil War, collected near the frontier, and ultimately crossed, occupying some villages and plundering the neighbourhood. But the prompt mustering of Canadian volunteers made the filibusters recross the frontier in some haste, to be ultimately disarmed and dispersed by United States troops.

In 1867 (28th March) the British North America Act for confederation of the colonies passed the Imperial

Parliament. It united Upper Canada or Ontario, Lower Canada or Quebec, New Brunswick, and Nova Scotia into one territory, to be named the Dominion of Canada. Newfoundland declared against joining the confederation, but with that exception all the British territory north of the United States was gradually included within the Dominion—the Hudson's Bay Company's territory by purchase in 1868, British Columbia in 1871, Prince Edward Island in 1873. In 1870 an insurrection of the Red River settlers, who were under apprehensions as to how their titles to their lands might be affected by the cession of the Hudson's Bay Company's rights, took place under the leadership of Louis Riel, and had to be suppressed by a military expedition under Colonel (later Viscount) Wolseley. To reassure the settlers a part of the newly-purchased territory was made into an independent province under the name of Manitoba, the unorganised territory beyond receiving the name of the North-Western Territory.

In 1871 the Washington Treaty arranged that the fisheries of both Canada and the United States should be open to each country for the next twelve years, Canada receiving a compensation, afterwards fixed at five and a half million dollars, for the superior value of its fisheries. In 1884 considerable disaffection was caused amongst the half-breeds and Indians in the Saskatchewan and Assiniboine districts on account of the difficulty of obtaining valid titles to their lands. The discontent at length took shape in an insurrection which Louis Riel was invited to head. The rebels seized the Government stores at Duck Lake and induced some of the Indian tribes to co-operate with them, with the result that a massacre of settlers took place at Frog's Lake. Within a few months an expedition under General Middleton, who had under his command several thousand volunteers, suppressed the rebellion. Only the leaders were arrested. Riel was tried and executed at Regina on 28th July, 1885.

On 7th Nov. of the same year the Canadian Pacific Railway was completed, being opened for through traffic the following year. Since 1883, when the Washington Treaty expired, disputes between the American and Canadian fishermen have again been frequent, and several American fishing-vessels have been seized on the Canadian coasts. A joint British and American commission was instituted in 1887, for the adjustment of differences, but no final settlement has yet been arrived at. The seal-fishing in Behring's Sea also caused friction with the United States, but this matter was settled in 1903, as also the boundary between Canada and Alaska. In 1905 new provinces of Saskatchewan and Alberta were created. In 1912 the boundaries of Quebec, Ontario, and Manitoba were extended.

In the same year an agreement was entered into with the West Indies for mutual trade preference, and in 1913 the preference granted to British goods was extended to the remaining parts of the empire which had not hitherto enjoyed it. During the European War, Canada gave magnificent support to the Allied cause, and hundreds of thousands of Canadians fought in France. When peace was concluded with Germany in 1919, Canadian ministers signed the Treaty on behalf of the Dominion. This was the first actual recognition of Canada's autonomy within the British Empire. She has now complete freedom of action in the management of her home affairs, and, like other British dominions, is practically an independent state.—BIBLIOGRAPHY: W. P. Greswell, *Geography of the Dominion of Canada*; Sir George Parkin, *The Great Dominion*; W. Maxwell, *Canada of Today*; Shortt and Doughty, *Canada and Its Provinces*; *The Canada Year-Book*; *The Canadian Annual Review of Public Affairs* (1902 *et seq.*).

CANADA BALSAM. A fluid oleoresin obtained from the balsam fir (*Abies balsamea*), common in Canada and the United States. It is used in medicine, in microscopy, and in making varnishes.

CANADA GOOSE (*Brenta canadensis*). An American wild goose 30 to 35 inches long, brownish above, lighter below, head, neck, bill, and feet black, a white patch on the cheek; breeds in the north of the continent, and migrates southwards when the frost becomes severe.

CANADA RICE (*Zizania aquatica*). A floating grass growing in lakes and sluggish streams in Canada and the northern United States, yielding a grain that forms part of the food of the Indians, and is eaten by whites also.

CANADIAN MOUNTED POLICE, ROYAL. Police maintained by the Dominion of Canada, for service in the Arctic, the N.W., and Yukon territories, and also in Indian reservations. The force is controlled from Ottawa and is organised in 10 divisions, its strength being about 1000 officers and men.

CANADIAN PACIFIC RAILWAY. A line of railways which traverses British North America from the St. Lawrence to the Pacific. One of the conditions upon which the province of British Columbia in 1871 entered the Dominion of Canada was the construction of such a railway. Since that time more than one Act has been passed empowering different companies to go on with the work. Eventually, however, it was completed, according to arrangement with the Canadian Government, by a syndicate of London, Paris, and American capitalists, being opened for general traffic in June, 1886. Commencing at Montreal, the line goes on to Ottawa, thence round the north of the Great Lakes to Port Arthur at the head of Lake Superior, and thence to Winnipeg, Manitoba, thence to Stephen in the Rocky Mountains, then across British Columbia to Vancouver on the Pacific. Vancouver, now a thriving town, owes its existence to this railway. The line is of great importance, not only as a means of communication between Europe and Eastern Asia and Australasia, but also as a military highway binding together the great masses of the British Empire. The length from Montreal to Vancouver is 2903 miles, from Quebec 3078 miles; the total length owned by the company in 1927 was about 14,892 miles. The fleet consists of 68 vessels. In conjunction with their services between Britain and Canada, the Canadian Pacific Railway maintains a service from Vancouver to Australian ports. Besides their lake steamers, the company also runs steamers between Vancouver and China and Japan, and also between England and Canada.

CANADIAN RIVER. A river of the United States, in New Mexico, Texas, and Indian Territory, a tributary of the Arkansas; length, 900 miles.

CANAL. An artificial watercourse for the transport of goods or passengers by boats or ships, or for purposes of drainage or irrigation. The most familiar canals are for navigation. These consist usually of a number of different sections, each on one level throughout its course, but differing in relative height from the others. From one section to another boats are transferred by means of *locks*, or it may be by *inclines* or *lifts*. The lock is a water-tight enclosure with gates at either end, constructed between two successive sections of a canal. When a vessel is descending, water is let into the lock till it is on a level with the higher water, and thus permits the vessel to enter; the upper gates are then closed, and by the lower gates being gradually opened, the water in the lock falls to the level of the lower water, and the vessel passes out.

In ascending, the operation is reversed. The *incline* conveys the vessel from one reach to another, generally on a specially-constructed carriage running on rails, by means of drums and cables. The *lift* consists of two counter-balancing troughs, one going up as the other descends, carrying the vessel from the higher to the lower level, or vice versa. Works of great magnitude in the way of cuttings, embankments, aqueducts, bridges, tunnels, reservoirs for water-supply, are often necessary in constructing canals. Canals have been known from remote times, Egypt being intersected at an early period by canals branching off from the Nile to distant parts of the country, for purposes of irrigation and navigation. Under the Ptolemies, before the Christian era, there existed a canal between the Red Sea and the Nile. In China, also, canals were early made on a very large scale. In Holland, where the country is flat and water abundant, canals were constructed as early as the twelfth century. The lock, however, was not invented until the fifteenth century, both the Dutch and the Italians claiming to have invented it.

Since then Europe has been provided with numerous canals, which, being connected usually with navigable rivers, give access by water to most parts of its interior. Among the numerous canals of Holland, the largest is now the North Holland Ship Canal, from 200 to 300 feet wide and 26 feet deep, which connects Amsterdam with the North Sea. In France there are many canals and canalised rivers, the principal being the Canal du Midi, branching off from the Garonne at Toulouse, and falling into the Gulf of Lyons at Narbonne, thus connecting the Bay of Biscay and Mediterranean, and three canals connecting the basins of the Rhone, Loire, Seine, and Rhine.

The canals of France have a total length of 3104 miles, of which 3052 miles are actually navigated, besides canalised rivers making 2000 miles. The Marseilles-Rhone Canal, begun in 1904, would have been finished in 1918 but for the European War. In Belgium there are the Bruges Ship Canal, and the Ghent-Terneuzen Canal, to Ghent from the Scheldt estuary. The chief canal in Germany is the great North Sea and Baltic Canal for sea-going vessels, constructed at a cost of £8,000,000, starting near the mouth of the Elbe and reaching the Baltic near Kiel. Another German canal is the Ludwigs-Canal in Bavaria, connecting (through the Main and Regnitz) the Rhine and the Danube. On 17th June, 1914, the Hohenzollern Canal, between Berlin and Hohensaaten, was opened. In Russia there is canal and river communication between the Caspian and the Baltic, a large part of the route consisting of the Volga. In Britain one of the earliest and most celebrated is the Bridgewater Canal (1761-5), in Lancashire and Cheshire, with a length of 38 miles.

In Scotland there are the Forth and Clyde Canal, 35 miles long, joining these two rivers; and the Caledonian, 60½ miles (including lakes), from the Moray Firth on the E. coast to Loch Eil on the W., passing through Loch Ness, Loch Oich, and Loch Lochy. The greatest British canal is the Manchester Canal, a waterway for ocean-going vessels from the estuary of the Mersey, near Runcorn, to Manchester, through a few locks and partly in the beds of the Mersey and the Irwell, begun in 1887, opened in 1894; total cost, about £15,000,000. In the British Islands there is a total length of canal of 4673 miles, 3641 being in England and Wales, 184 in Scotland, and 848 in Ireland. In 1917 the Government appointed the Canal Control Committee to manage the principal canals. In the United States the most extensive undertaking of this kind is the canal connecting the Hudson with Lake Erie. It is 363 miles in length, and carries an immense traffic. In Canada, besides the Welland Canal, uniting Lakes Erie and Ontario, and avoiding the Niagara River and its falls, there are several other important canals. The Suez Canal (q.v.) is 100 miles long. It is an example of a ship canal without locks, open at both ends to the sea. A similar but not important canal is that of Corinth.

The great Panama Canal (q.v.), completed in 1914, is about 49 miles in length. In Sept., 1919, a Congress of International Waterways was held at Strassburg, and it was proposed to construct a canal between the Rhine and the Marne, and another from Dieppe to Rouen, thus bringing Dieppe into direct waterway communication with Paris. In 1926 different new schemes for the construction of new canals were under consideration. It was proposed to connect the Danube with the Adriatic, the Don with the Volga, the Forth with the Clyde, and Lake Huron with the St. Lawrence.—BIBLIOGRAPHY: J. Priestley, *History of Navigable Rivers, Canals, etc., in Great Britain*; L. F. Vernon-Harcourt, *Rivers and Canals*; P. Berthot, *Traité des routes, rivières, canaux*; A. B. Hepburn, *Artificial Waterways of the World*; G. Bradshaw, *Canals and Navigable Rivers of England and Wales.*

CANALETTO (whose true name was **ANTONIO CANALE,** or **DA CANAL**). A Venetian painter, born in 1697, died in 1768. He is chiefly celebrated for his pictures of Venice, and is said to have been the first to use the camera obscura for perspective. He went to England in 1746 and painted English landscapes, with views of Whitehall and of Eton College.

CANALETTO, Bernardo Belotti. Nephew of above, born in 1724; was likewise a good artist, lived in Dresden, where he was a member of the Academy of Painters, and died at Warsaw in 1780. The Canaletti especially excelled at painting ancient ruins and buildings.

CANANDAI'GUA. A beautiful lake in New York State, 15 miles long and nearly 2 miles wide, with a small town of the same name on its banks. Pop. 7541.

CAN'ANORE. A seaport town, India, Malabar district, Presidency of Madras, chief military station of the British in Malabar. Pop. 27,418.

CAN'ARA. A maritime region of India, now partly in the Madras Presidency (South Canara), and partly in the Bombay Presidency (North Canara), extending along the Indian Ocean for 180 miles, with a mean breadth of 40 miles. The Bombay portion has an area of 3910 sq. miles and a pop. of 454,230; the Madras portion 3902 sq. miles and 1,134,600 inhabitants.

CANA'RIUM. A genus of trees, ord. Amyridaceæ, natives of S.E. Asia, one species of which yields black damar resin.

CANARY, GRAND, or **GRAN CANARIA.** An island in the Atlantic Ocean, about 180 miles from the coast of Africa. It is the most fertile and important of the Canary Islands, to which it gives its name. Area, 531 sq. miles; pop. 162,601. Canary, or Cividad de Palmas, is the capital.

CANARY-BIRD. An insessorial singing bird, a kind of finch from the Canary Islands, the *Serinus canarius*. They were introduced into Europe in the latter part of the fifteenth or early in the sixteenth century. Many of the cage canaries are really mules, produced by the interbreeding of canaries with allied species, such as the goldfinch, siskin, linnet, etc.

Canary

CANARY-FLOWER (*Tropæolum peregrinum*). An annual climbing plant of the Indian cress family, a native of New Granada, cultivated in Europe for its showy yellow flowers.

CANARY ISLANDS, or **CANARIES.** A cluster of islands in the Atlantic, about 60 miles from the N.W. coast of Africa, and belonging to Spain. They are thirteen in number, seven of which are considerable, viz. Palma, Ferro, Gomera, Teneriffe, Grand Canary, Fuerteventura, and Lancerota. The other six are very small: Graciosa, Roca or Rocca, Allegranza, Sta Clara, Inferno, and Lobos. All are volcanic, rugged, and mountainous, frequently presenting precipitous cliffs to the sea. The principal peak is that of Teneriffe, 12,182 feet; El Cumbre in Gran Canaria is 6650 feet. The area of the whole has been estimated at 2810 sq. miles. Their fine climate and their fertility, which owes little to cultivation, justified their ancient name of *Fortunate Islands*. Fresh water is not very abundant. The islands furnish good wine, especially Palma and Teneriffe. The exports to the United Kingdom amounted to £2,238,346 in 1916, and to £3,182,000 in 1927, and consisted of bananas, potatoes, tomatoes, and wine. Of the Guanches, who originally inhabited these islands, we know little. The islands were discovered and conquered by the Spaniards between 1316 and 1334; they then passed into the hands of the Portuguese, but were reconquered towards the end of the fifteenth century by the Spaniards. The capital is Santa Cruz, in Teneriffe; it and Las Palmas in Grand Canary are the chief ports. The islands now attract many visitors, especially in winter, and hotels and other attractions have been provided for them. The Canaries form a Spanish province; pop. 503,151.—

BIBLIOGRAPHY: G. Glas, *History of the Canary Islands*; J. Pitard and L. Proust, *Les Iles Canaries*; F. Du Cane, *The Canary Islands*; A. S. Brown, *Madeira and the Canaries*; C. F. Barker, *Two Years in the Canaries*.

CANARY-SEED. The seed of the canary-grass (*Phalăris canariensis*), ord. Graminaceæ. The seed is used as food in the Canaries, Barbary, and Italy, and is largely collected for canary-birds. It has been successfully cultivated in England and the European continent.

CANARY WOOD. Mahogany-like timber. It is procured from evergreen tree laurels, and is sometimes sold as Madeira mahogany. The trees grow in Madeira and the Azores.

CANAS'TER (canister). The rush basket in which South American tobacco was packed, and hence applied to a kind of tobacco consisting of the leaves coarsely broken for smoking.

CANBERRA. The federal capital of Australia. The federal territory of 940 sq. miles is situated in New South Wales, and is directly under the Commonwealth Government. The town, which is 190 miles from Sydney, is planned on modern methods. The Federal Parliament first met at Canberra in 1927. Pop. of territory (1931), 8789.

CANCALE (kaŋ-kal). A seaport and bathing-place, France, department of Ille-et-Vilaine, about 8 miles E.N.E. of St. Malo, celebrated for its oysters. Pop. 3760.

CANCER (L., a crab). In astronomy, the fourth sign in the zodiac, marked thus ♋; entered by the sun on or about the 21st of June, and quitted about the 22nd of July. The constellation Cancer is no longer in the sign of Cancer, but at present occupies the place of the sign Leo.

CANCER. The term is now applied to any malignant growth, and includes the two large groups of *Carcinoma* and *Sarcoma*.

Carcinoma are divided into (1) *medullary*, where the tumour is soft, cellular, and of rapid growth; (2) *scirrhous*, where the tumour is compressed, hard, and of slower growth; (3) *simplex* stands intermediate between the two first named; (4) *epithelial*, where the disease attacks the skin and mucous membranes, appearing in hard nodules, which in the later stages form ulcers; (5) *colloid*, where the digestive organs are affected, extensive mucoid degeneration is present; (6) *rodent*, a localised form in which a slow-growing ulcer is found on the part affected. Carcinoma usually attacks persons of over forty years of age.

Sarcoma is of more rapid growth, and is a more malignant form of cancer. It frequently attacks quite young persons, but may occur at any period. There are many types of sarcoma. The rapidity with which a malignant tumour becomes fatal depends naturally first of all on its rate of growth, and secondly on the amount of harm done by its spreading through the blood or lymph to other parts of the body. It is in each case a proliferation of the tumour cells at the expense of the normal body cells, and as there is no limiting membrane this continues indefinitely. As well as the local irritation caused by the disease, there are also marked symptoms of anæmia and increasing cachexia.

Treatment.—Operation, to be successful, requires not only the complete removal of the tumours and surrounding parts, but also of the glands in the region to which the tumour cells may have been carried. In cases treated in time this may be possible, but too often the infection has already been spread and the disease recurs.

CANCER, TROPIC OF. *See* TROPICS.

CANDELA'BRUM. An ornamental candlestick or lamp-holder, often of a branched form. Ancient candelabra frequently displayed much ingenious and artistic treatment in the design, and the branches were often numerous. Marble and other materials, as well as metal, were employed. Many bronze candelabra have been found in Etruria, Pompeii, and Herculaneum.

CANDIA. A town of Crete, formerly the capital of the island. For a long time the entire island was known in Western Europe under the name of Candia. It stands on the north coast of the island, north of Mount Ida. The town, founded in the ninth century by the Saracens, was taken by the Turks in 1669. Pop. 33,400. *See* CRETE.

CAN'DIDATE. A term taken from the Lat. *candidatus*, a candidate, literally a person dressed in white, because, among the Romans, a man who solicited an office, such as the prætorship or consulship, appeared in a bright white garment—*toga candida.*

CANDLE. A solid cylindrical rod of some fatty substance, with a small bundle of loosely-twisted threads placed longitudinally in its centre, used for a portable light. The chief material used for making candles is tallow, either in a pure state or in mixture with other fatty substances, as palm-oil, spermaceti or wax (which came into use at the beginning of the eighteenth century). Paraffin candles, which came into general use about 1850, are now made in considerable quantities also. Ordinary tallow candles are either *dipped* or *moulded.* The former, generally composed of the coarser tallow, are made by attaching a number of separate wicks to a frame and dipping the whole into a cistern of melted tallow as often as may be necessary to give the candle the required thickness. Moulded candles, as their name implies, are formed in moulds. These, made generally of pewter, are hollow cylinders of the length of the candle, and open at both ends, but provided at the upper end with a conical cap, in which there is a hole for the wick. A number of these moulds are inserted in a wooden frame or trough with their heads downwards; the wick is then drawn in through the top hole by means of a wire, and kept stretched while the moulds are filled by running melted tallow from a boiler into the trough.

Considerable modern improvements have been made in the manufacture of candles. One of the most important of these consists in not employing the whole of the fatty or oily substances, but in decomposing them, and then using only the *stearine* of the former and the *palmitin* of the latter class of substances. Wax cannot be formed into candles by melting it and then running it into moulds. Instead, the wicks, properly cut and twisted, are suspended by a ring over a basin of liquid wax, which is poured on the tops of the wicks until a sufficient thickness is obtained, when the candles, still hot, are placed on a smooth walnut table, kept constantly wet, and rolled upon it by means of a flat piece of boxwood. The large wax candles used in Roman Catholic churches are merely plates of wax bent round a wick and then rolled.—BIBLIOGRAPHY: W. L. Carpenter, *Soaps and Candles*; L. L. Lamborn, *Modern Soaps, Candles, and Glycerine.*

CANDLEBERRY, CANDLEBERRY MYRTLE, WAX MYRTLE, etc. (*Myrica cerifĕra*). A shrub, nat. ord. Myricaceæ, growing from 4 to 18 feet high, and common in North America, where candles are made from its drupes or berries, which are about the size of peppercorns, and covered with a greenish-white wax popularly known as Blayberry tallow. The wax is collected by boiling the drupes in water and skimming off the surface. A bushel of berries yields from 4 to 5 lb. of wax.

CANDLE-FISH. A sea-fish of the salmon family, the *Thaleichthys pacificus*, frequenting the north-western shores of America, of about the size of the smelt. It is a favourite article of food in British Columbia. It is converted by the Indians into a candle simply by passing the pith of a rush or a strip of the bark of the cypress tree though it as a wick, when its extreme oiliness keeps the wick blazing. It is called also *Oulachon.*

CAN'DLEMAS. A Church feast, instituted, according to Baronius, by Pope Gelasius I. (492-496), in commemoration of the presentation of Christ in the temple and of the purification of Mary. It falls on 2nd Feb., and on this day among Roman Catholics lighted candles are carried about in procession, and all candles and tapers which are to be used in the churches during the entire year are consecrated. The event, i.e. the first solemn introduction of Christ into the house of God, was celebrated in the Church of Jerusalem in the earliest times, but the feast then had no proper name, and was observed on 14th Feb. In Scotland Candlemas is one of the four term-days. — BIBLIOGRAPHY: Duchesne, *Christian Worship*; Brand, *Popular Antiquities.*

CANDLE-NUT. The nut of *Aleurītes trilŏba*, a tree of India, the Moluccas, Pacific Islands, etc., nat. ord. Euphorbiaceæ. It is about the size of a walnut, and yields an oil used for food and for lamps, while the oily kernels are also strung together and lighted as torches.

CANDLE STANDARD. The unit of light in terms of which the luminous intensity of a source of light is expressed, as when we speak of a 32-candle-power glow-lamp. Originally the standard candle was of sperm wax, weighing six to the pound, and burning at the rate of 120 grains per hour. Afterwards, standard lamps came into use, e.g., in Britain, the pentane lamp, of 10 candle power (c.p.); and, in France, the Carcel lamp, which burns colza oil and is of 9·62 c.p. Great Britain, France, the United States, and Russia have now agreed on a common standard unit of roughly 1 c.p., called the international candle. Germany still uses the Hefner lamp, which burns amyl acetate and has a power of about 0·9 candle.

CANDLE TREE (*Parmentiera cerifera*). A middle-sized South American tree, nat. ord. Bignoniaceæ, so called from the long fleshy cylindrical yellow fruits, which hang in great numbers from the trunk and older branches like candles in a chandler's shop. The flower has a water-calyx.

CANDLISH, Robert Smith, D.D. A Scottish divine, born at Edinburgh in 1807, died in 1873; educated at Glasgow University. In 1828 he was licensed, and in 1834 transferred from Bonhill to St. George's, Edinburgh. In 1839 he threw himself into the conflict with the civil courts in the matter of congregational right of election and independent Church jurisdiction in matters spiritual, and soon became, next to Chalmers, the most prominent leader of the "non-intrusion" party and disruptionists of 1843. From the death of Chalmers till his own death, Candlish was the ruling spirit in the Free Church. In 1862 he was made principal of the New College, Edinburgh. He was the author of *Reason and Revelation*, *The Two Great Commandments* (1860), and several other popular books on religious subjects.

CANDY, or KANDY. A city, near the centre of Ceylon, and former capital of the island, 72 miles N.E. of Colombo (with which it is connected by railway), in a fertile valley surrounded by finely-wooded hills. The residence of the Governor at the N.E. extremity is among the finest structures in Ceylon. Other noteworthy places are the Buddhist temple called "the palace of the tooth" (Daladá Malagawá), the most sacred in the Buddhist world, the old royal cemetery, the military magazine in the centre of a lake, the Government brickworks, etc. Pop. 32,562.

CANDY. An Eastern measure of weight, varying from 560 up to above 800 lb.

CAN'DYTUFT. The popular name of several flowers of the genus Ibēris, ord. Cruciferæ, common in gardens: said to be named from Candia.

CANE. *See* BAMBOO; RATTAN; SUGAR-CANE.

CANE'A, or KHANIA. Chief commercial town of Crete and capital of a province, on the north coast, the principal mart for the commerce of the island in wax, soap, oil, silk, fruit, wool, and provisions. Pop. 26,600; the pop. of the province is 99,736.

CANEL'LA, WHITE (*C. alba*). A tree belonging to the West Indies, growing to the height of 10 to 50 feet, with a straight stem branched only at the top. It is covered with a whitish bark, which is freed from its outward covering, dried in the shade, and brought to Europe in long quills, somewhat thicker than those of cinnamon. It is moderately warm to the taste, and is esteemed as a pleasing and aromatic bitter.

CANE'PHORUS. One of the bearers of the baskets containing the implements of sacrifice in the processions of the Dionysia, Panathenea, and other ancient Grecian festivals, an office of honour much coveted by Athenian maidens. The term is applied to architectural figures bearing baskets on their head, sometimes improperly confounded with Caryatides.

CANES VENATICI (kā'nēz vē-nat'i-sī; "the hunting dogs"). A northern constellation, within the limits of which several remarkable nebulæ occur. Cor Caroli (the Heart of Charles II.) is the name which Halley gave to the principal star of this constellation.

CANG, CANGUE, or **KEA.** The wooden collar, weighing from 50 to 60 lb. and fitting closely round the neck, imposed upon criminals in China.

CANICAT'TI. A town in Sicily, province of Girgenti, well built, and with a population of 25,000, mostly engaged in agriculture.

CANIC'ULA. The dog-star or Sirius; hence *Canicular days*, the dog-days.

CANI'NO, PRINCE OF. *See* BONAPARTE (LUCIEN).

CANIS MAJOR ("the greater dog"). A constellation of the southern hemisphere, remarkable as containing *Sirius*, the brightest star. —**Canis Minor** ("the lesser dog") is a constellation in the northern hemisphere, immediately above Canis Major, the chief star in which is *Procyon*.

CANISTER SHOT. *See* CASE-SHOT.

CANKER. (1) In medicine, a collection of small sloughing ulcers in the mouth, especially of children; called also water canker. (2) In botany, a diseased condition of trees, caused by parasitic fungi, in which the bark and cambium are gradually destroyed, so that a continually enlarging, gaping wound results. The most important canker-fungi are *Dasyscypha Willkommi* (larch canker) and *Nectria ditissima* (canker of apple, ash, and many other trees). Most canker-fungi start as wound parasites, and their attacks can be prevented by prompt disinfection and tarring of wounds due to storms, hail, frost, pruning, etc. (3) In farriery, a disease in horses' feet causing a discharge of fetid matter from the cleft in the middle of the frog, generally originating in thrush.

CANKER-WORM. A worm or larva destructive to trees or plants; in America specifically applied to moths and larvæ of the genus Anisopteryx.

CANNA. A genus of plants, ord. Marantaceæ, some species of which have fine flowers, and from their black, hard, heavy seeds are called Indian shot. Many of the cultivated forms now met with in Europe came from Peru and Brazil.

CANNABIS. *See* HEMP.

CANNÆ. A town of S. Italy, province of Bari, near the mouth of the Ofanto, formerly the Aufidus, famous as the scene of the great battle in which the Romans were defeated by Hannibal (216 B.C.) with immense slaughter.

CAN'NANORE. *See* CANANORE.

CANNEL COAL. A dull black coal which breaks with a conchoidal fracture, and does not soil the fingers when handled. In some aspects it resembles jet. It is easily cut, and will take a high polish. It burns with a large white flame (this is indicated by the name, which is a corruption of *candle coal*), and contains a large proportion of volatile constituents, which make it extremely suitable for gas manufacture. The average composition is: carbon, 66 to 84 per cent; hydrogen, 5·5 to 9 per cent; oxygen and nitrogen, 5 to 10·5 per cent; ash, 2 to 6 per cent. The calorific value is from 13,000 to 14,000 B.T.U.'s, and it usually gives about 11,000 cu. feet of gas per ton. There are several British varieties of cannel, e.g. splint coal, parrot, the once famous Lesmahagow gas-coal, and torbanite. Ribs of cannel often occur in seams of ordinary bituminous coal. Geologists look upon cannel coal as a mass of fossil sapropel, derived from vegetable material, particularly Algæ and spores. Cannel coal is also found in Kentucky, Ohio, and Indiana.

CANNES (kån). A seaport of France, on the shore of the Mediterranean, department of Alpes-Maritimes; famous as a winter residence, and as the place where Napoleon landed when he returned from Elba, 1st March, 1815. Pop. 47,259.

CANNIBALISM, or **ANTHROPOPHAGY.** The eating of human flesh as food, a practice that has been known from the earliest times, and in the most widely spread localities. The word is derived from Caniba, a variant of Carib, a West Indian tribe among whom the Spanish discoverers first noticed the custom. Cannibalism has been ascribed to economic reasons, but it may be safely asserted that originally the custom was almost a religious ceremonial, having its origin in the belief that the qualities of the person eaten might be acquired by the eater. *See* ANTHROPOPHAGI.—BIBLIOGRAPHY: E. B. Tylor, *Early History of Mankind*; Sir J. G. Frazer, *The Golden Bough*.

CANNING, Charles John, Earl. Son of George Canning, born in 1812, died in 1862; educated at Eton and Oxford. In 1841 he was appointed Under-Secretary of State for Foreign Affairs in Peel's Government, and in 1846 Commissioner of Woods and Forests. In the Aberdeen ministry of 1853, and under Palmerston in 1855, he held the postmaster-generalship, and in 1856 went out to India as Governor-General. Throughout the mutiny he showed a fine coolness and clear-headedness, and though his carefully-pondered decisions were sometimes lacking in promptness, yet his admirable moderation did much to re-establish the British Empire in India. He was raised to the rank of earl and made viceroy, but returned to England with shattered health in 1862, dying in the same year.

CANNING, George. A distinguished orator and statesman, born in London in 1770, died 1827; educated at Eton and at Oxford. He was first brought into Parliament by Pitt in 1793, and in 1796 became Under-Secretary of State. In 1797 he projected, with some friends, the *Anti-Jacobin*, of which Gifford was appointed editor, and to which Canning contributed the *Needy Knife-grinder* and other poems and articles. In 1798 he supported Wilberforce's motion for the abolition of the slave-trade. In 1807 he was appointed Secretary of State for Foreign Affairs in the Portland administration, and was slightly wounded in a duel with Lord Castlereagh arising out of the dispute which occasioned the dissolution of the ministry. In 1810 he opposed the reference of the Catholic claims to the committee of the whole House, on the ground that no security or engagement had been offered by the Catholics, but supported in 1812 and 1813 the motion which he had opposed in 1810.

In 1814 he was appointed minister to Portugal, and remained abroad about two years. He refused to take any part in the proceedings against the queen, and in 1822, having been nominated Governor-General of India, he was on the point of embarking when the death of Castlereagh called him to the Cabinet as Foreign Secretary. One of his earliest acts in this capacity was to check the French influence in Spain. He continued to support the propositions in favour of Catholic emancipation, arranged the Triple Alliance for the preservation of Greece, but opposed parliamentary reform and the Test and Corporation Acts. On 12th April, 1827, his appointment to be Prime Minister was announced, but his administration was terminated by his death on the 8th of August following. On all the leading political questions of his day, with two exceptions—the emancipation of the Catholics and the recognition of the South American republics—he took the high Tory side. His collected poems were issued in 1823, and his speeches in 1828.—BIBLIOGRAPHY: R. Bell, *Life of Canning*; A. G. Stapleton, *Canning and His Times*; J. S. R. Marriot, *George Canning and His Times*; W. Alison Phillips, *George Canning*.

CANNING, Stratford. Viscount Stratford de Redcliffe, an English diplomatist, son of a London merchant and cousin of George Canning, born in 1786, died in 1880. He entered the diplomatic service in 1807 and in 1820 became plenipotentiary at Washington. In 1824 he went as Ambassador Extraordinary to St. Petersburg, and afterwards to Constantinople about the Greek difficulty; but negotiations were broken off by the battle of Navarino. He was sent again to Constantinople in 1831, and to Spain in 1832, and from 1834 to 1841 sat in Parliament for King's Lynn. In 1842 he became Ambassador at Constantinople, a post held by him for sixteen years, under varying ministries, with high honour. In 1852 he was raised to the peerage, and in 1869 created Knight of the Garter. He retired from diplomatic work in 1858, but exercised no small influence in the House of Lords, and as late as 1880 drew up a paper on the Greek claims. He died in August of that year, having done more than any one man to establish British prestige in the East. His works include, besides a few volumes of poetry, such as *Shadows of the Past, The Exile of Calauria*, and *Alfred the Great in Athelnay*, the devotional treatises, *Why I am a Christian* (1873) and *The Greatest of Miracles* (1876).

CANNING TOWN. A district of London in the borough of West Ham. It lies along the north of the Thames, and is a busy industrial area. It includes the Victoria and Royal Albert Docks.

CAN'NOCK. A town of England, in Staffordshire, 7½ miles N.W. of Walsall, with coal-mines, etc. It gives its name to one of the parliamentary divisions of the county. Pop. (1931), 34,588. Near it is Cannock Chase, a tract of 3600 acres.

CANNON. A big gun or piece of ordnance. The precise period at which engines for projecting missiles by mechanical force (catapults, etc.) were supplanted by those utilising explosive materials is a matter of controversy, the invention of cannon being even attributed to the Chinese, from whom the Saracens may have acquired the knowledge.

Gunpowder was probably invented by Friar Roger Bacon in 1248. The *Origin of Artillery* attributes the invention of cannon to an unknown German monk in 1313, and dates their introduction into England as the year following. Case-shot was used at the siege of Belgrade in 1439; single shot the size of the bore began to be used about 1495, and explosive shells were used in large numbers and with good effect at Bergen-op-Zoom and Wachtendonck in 1588. A rifled 1-pounder gun with telescopic sights was constructed by Dr. Lind of Edinburgh in 1776, and marked success with breech-loading rifled guns was first achieved by Lord Armstrong in 1859. In 1866 muzzle-loading rifled guns displaced breech-loaders, but in 1886 breech-loaders again came into use, and in the same year the invention of cordite brought the gunpowder period to a close.

Cannon were at first made of wood, well secured by iron hoops, or sometimes of leather. The earliest shape was somewhat conical, with wide muzzles, and afterwards cylindrical. They were then made of iron bars firmly bound together with iron hoops like casks, "Mons Meg" at Edinburgh Castle being a good example. Bronze was used in the construction of the "Twelve Peers of France" (1461-83), and cast-iron ordnance was first made in England at Buckestead, in Sussex, by Hoge and Baude in 1543.

Cannon formerly received the following distinctive names: cannon royal, or carthoun, carrying 48 lb.; culverin, 18 lb.; demi-culverin, 9 lb.; falcon, 6 lb.; basilisk, 48 lb.; siren, 60 lb.; etc. They were afterwards named from the weight of the balls which they carried: 6-pounders, 12-pounders, etc., and later by their weight, as a 25-ton gun, a 67-ton gun, an 80-ton gun, etc. They are now generally designated by their calibre (or diameter of bore), as a 6-inch gun, 9·2-inch howitzer, etc. Pieces of the same calibre are distinguished by adding the weight of the piece, as a 6-inch howitzer, 26 cwt.; and a 6-inch howitzer, 30 cwt. Modern weapons may be divided into three main classes, viz. guns, howitzers, and trench-mortars. Guns have a flat trajectory and a high muzzle velocity, and are comparatively long and heavy weapons. Howitzers have a high trajectory and a low muzzle velocity, and the piece is shorter and lighter than a gun of corresponding calibre. Trench-mortars are generally smooth-bore muzzle-loading pieces, firing a heavy bomb at high angles for short ranges; they are very

"Mons Meg", Edinburgh Castle

effective against earthworks and fortifications, owing to their steep angle of descent and great shell-power.

Great improvements and changes in the manufacture of cannon have been introduced in recent years. The introduction of rifling, in 1859, enabled an elongated projectile (called the *shell*) to be used. The increased weight of these projectiles, their rapid rotation, and the increased rate of fire due to the introduction of breech-loading, try the piece so severely that iron, brass, and gun-metal are now entirely superseded in modern weapons by steel low in carbon. The construction and connected mechanism of artillery is now somewhat complicated, so that to turn out a large gun of modern type is a long and expensive process. Field-guns and most howitzers are generally made in two or more layers, each layer shrunk on to the one inside it. Heavier guns are made by winding steel ribbons, $\frac{1}{16}$ inch thick and $\frac{1}{4}$ inch wide, round and round the inner tube with gradually decreasing tension, so as to get an equal resistance throughout. A jacket or outer tube is then shrunk on over the wire. Wire-wound guns are much lighter for the same strength than built-up guns. When corroded or worn out from frequent firing, the inner tube of a piece made by either method can be removed and replaced by a new one. Various Governments have gun-factories of their own, such as the British factory at Woolwich; but there are also some famous private firms that turn out ordnance according to order, such as the Armstrong-Whitworth firm (Elswick), the Coventry Ordnance Works, the Schneider-Canet firm at Creusot (France), and until lately the firm of Krupp at Essen.

It is highly important that the mechanism for closing the breech should be as simple and as easily worked as possible, while also sufficiently strong and tight enough to prevent any escape of gas. The earlier Armstrong breech-loading guns had the breech closed by a separate movable steel stopper, put in loosely by hand through a slot, and kept tight against the end of the bore by a screw that required a number of turns. All modern guns and howitzers are breech-loading. The breech is closed either by a swinging block with an interrupted screw (e.g. British field-gun), or by a wedge of slight taper which slides in a slot across the breech (e.g. German field-gun and British field-howitzer), or else by an eccentric screw (e.g. French field-gun).

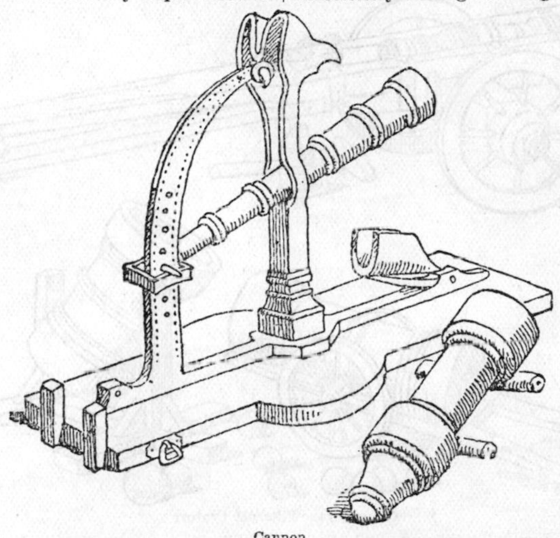

Cannon

The interrupted-screw system is used in most British guns. In it the screw surface of the breech-block is broken by four to six strips, while there are corresponding screwed and smooth strips in the interior of the bore at the breech. By placing the screwed relief portions of the one opposite the smooth sunk portions of the other, the breech-screw is locked in the gun by an eighth or a twelfth of a turn. Till the breech-block is locked fully home, and the lock placed in the firing position—which is done automatically—the gun cannot be fired. All modern breech actions have safety devices which prevent the gun from being fired till the breech is closed and locked. Various special arrangements are provided to prevent the least escape of gas to the rear on firing, the provision for this being called obturation. When a cartridge-case is used, it expands against the sides of the bore on firing and so seals the breech.

Cannon of the Fifteenth Century

For heavy guns and howitzers the weight of the cartridge-case becomes excessive, and an obturator is used. In British weapons this consists of a pad of asbestos and grease fixed to the front of the breech-screw and covered by a mushroom head. On discharge the soft pad is compressed, and swells out so tightly against the surface of the bore as to prevent any gas escaping past it. In a gun-carriage or gun-mounting, provision has to be made for checking the recoil, for running up the gun to firing-position after recoil, elevating it, and traversing laterally. These were formerly provided for by simple means, but somewhat complicated arrangements have of late been introduced, especially as regards the recoil, which the use of a high charge has greatly increased, and which requires to be speedily dealt with in quick-firing arrangements.

The principle of the hydraulic buffer is now commonly employed to deal with the recoil, the gun being connected with a piston which slides in a metal cylinder, filled with liquid, mineral oil, compressed air, etc., and fixed to the carriage. The energy of recoil is absorbed by forcing the liquid through holes in the piston-head or partly by the compression of air. The piece itself has longitudinal projections fitting in featherways cut in a top carriage or " cradle." It can freely recoil in the cradle, to which the cylinder of the buffer is fixed. After recoil the piece is run up to the firing-position by strong springs or compressed air, which have been compressed by the action of recoil. In guns and howitzers not on fixed mountings the carriage is anchored by brakes and a so-called " spade " on the end of the trail. The heavy guns of modern battleships require a powerful system of hydraulic or electric appliances to work them. Quick-firing guns are exceedingly powerful in proportion to their size, owing to the rapidity with which they can bring to bear a great weight of metal against an enemy, and they are of the utmost value in naval warfare.

In nearly all gun-equipments, elevation is usually given by an elevating-screw under the breech end of the cradle. Howitzers usually have a tooth-arc attached to the cradle, gearing into a pinion on the carriage. The means of traversing are usually very simple. In our own equipment it consists of an endless screw, gearing into a toothed arc at the rear of the upper carriage. In German field-guns a screw on the traversing-bed engages with a nut at the rear

Howitzer (Austrian) and Crew

end of the cradle. All French guns are traversed on the axle-tree.

The first sight used was a tangent-sight, consisting of a pointed fore-sight and a V-shaped back-sight mounted on a vertical scale which could be raised or lowered according to the range. This was later superseded by an arc-sight working on the same principle. Modern weapons in the field now carry in addition a dial-sight, which enables them to be layed from behind cover. This consists of a short telescope bent at right angles and surmounted by a movable head. The head is fixed on a horizontal graduated table, and is capable of being turned in any direction.

The projectiles for rifled guns, as already stated, are elongated, their length being three or four times their diameter; and they require to be so constructed that they may take hold of the grooves of the bore and thus get the required rotation to send them at high speed, point first, through the air. For this purpose they used to have rows of studs projecting and fitting into the grooves (which were wide and few in number), or a coating of lead, which served the same purpose; afterwards the projectile had a flanged copper disc fitted on to the base, and the pressure of the gas when the charge was exploded forced out the flanges into the grooves. The necessary spin is nowadays imparted to the projectile by one or more bands of soft copper, called the "driving-bands," secured round the shell, generally near the base. On discharge the ribs of the rifling cut into the soft copper, and force the shell to follow their helical course and to rotate. The driving-band also prevents escape of gas past the shell.

Guns are now rifled by having a considerable number of shallow grooves cut spirally round the interior of the bore, with a rib or "land" left between each two grooves. The rifling is done after the guns are built up, a special apparatus being employed. *See* ARTILLERY; ORDNANCE.

CANNON-BALL TREE (*Couroupita guianensis*). A tree of the ord. Lecythidaceæ, a native of Guiana, with a hard globular fruit. The flowers and fruits are borne on special leafless branches near the base of the trunk (cauliflory).

CANNSTADT (kȧn'stȧt), or **CANSTATT.** An old town in Würtemberg, on the Neckar, 2 miles north-east of Stuttgart and incorporated with it in 1905. It has manufactures of woollens, cottons, steel, machines, etc., and extensive dyeworks. Pop. 26,497.

CA'NO, Alonzo. A painter, sculptor, and architect, born in 1601 at Granada, died in 1667. He first made himself known by his statues for the great church of Lebrija, and was in 1638 appointed painter to the king. His wife having been murdered by a servant or pupil, he was suspected and put to torture; but his right arm was spared, from respect for his talents. He afterwards became a priest. Among his pictures is *The Seven Joys of the Virgin.*

CANOE (ka-nö'; through the Sp. *canoa*, from the native West Indian name). A light boat, narrow in the beam, and adapted to be propelled by paddles, often in conjunction with sails. The name was originally given to the boats of uncivilised races, but its application has been considerably extended, and canoes of home make may be seen on the waters of the most civilised countries. They are of the most diverse materials and construction. Canoes are often hollowed out of a single log. The Indian canoes of Canada are of bark on a wooden frame. The Esquimaux *kaiaks* consist of a light wooden frame, covered with seal-skins sewed together with sinews, and having only one opening to admit the boatman to his seat. In the Pacific the natives have double canoes, united by a strong platform, serving in this way as one vessel. (*See* PROA, OUTRIGGER). Modern canoeing as a sport owes its popularity to two men in England, who built canoes and took long pleasure journeys in them: John Macgregor in the *Rob Roy*,

Fijian Sailing-canoe with Outrigger

between 1866 and 1869, and Baden-Powell in the *Nautilus*.—BIBLIOGRAPHY: J. Macgregor, *A Thousand Miles in the* Rob Roy; W. Baden-Powell, *Canoe Travelling*.

CAN'ON (Gr. *kanōn*, a rule, measure, or standard). A term given collectively to the books of the Holy Scriptures received as genuine by Christian Churches. Some books accepted as canonical by the Roman Catholics are generally rejected by Protestants.

CAN'ON. A Church dignitary who possesses a prebend, or revenue allotted for the performance of divine service in a cathedral or collegiate church. Canons were formerly divided into canons *regular*, or those living a monastic life, and canons *secular*, those not so living. In England, besides the ordinary canons—who with the dean form the *chapter*—there are honorary canons and minor canons; the latter assist in the daily choral service of the cathedral. Of course these are all secular.

CAN'ON. In music, a composition in which several voices (or instruments) begin at fixed intervals, one after the other, and in which each successive voice sings the strain of the preceding one. Finite canons, like ordinary compositions, end with a cadence, while infinite canons are so contrived that the theme is begun again before the parts which follow are concluded.

CAÑON (sometimes spelt *canyon*, the Spanish word for tube or funnel). A word introduced into America from Spain, and now generally applied, particularly in the Western States, to long, deep, narrow river gorges or ravines. Such, due to fluvial action, are of frequent occurrence in the Rocky Mountains; magnificent cañons are found on the Colorado and Snake Rivers, the most notable being the Grand Cañon of the Colorado, which is more than 300 miles long.

CANONICAL BOOKS. The books of Scripture belonging to the *canon*. *See* CANON.

CANONICAL HOURS. Certain stated times of the day appropriated by ecclesiastical law to the offices of prayer and devotion in the Roman Catholic Church, viz. matins with lauds, prime, tierce, sext, nones, evensong or vespers, and compline. In England the term is also applied to the hours within which marriages may be lawfully celebrated in a parish church, i.e. from 8 a.m. to 3 p.m.

CANONISATION. A ceremony in the Roman Church, by which deceased persons are declared saints. The Pope institutes a formal investigation of the miraculous and other qualifications of the deceased person recommended for canonisation; and an *advocate of the devil*, as he is called, is appointed to oppose the canonisation and submit evidence. If the examination is satisfactory, the Pope declares the prospective saint a "venerable servant of God" and pronounces his beatification, the actual canonisation generally taking place some years afterwards, when a day is dedicated to his honour, his name inserted in the calendar of the Saints, a solemn mass is celebrated by the Pope, and his remains preserved as holy relics. In the Greek Church the right to perform the ceremony of canonisation is vested in the Patriarch of Constantinople, but it is rarely exercised. In the Russian Church the authority rests with the Holy Synod.—Cf. F. W. Faber, *Essay on Beatification and Canonization*.

CANON LAW. A collection of ecclesiastical constitutions for the regulation of the Church of Rome, consisting for the most part of ordinances of general and provincial councils, decrees promulgated by the Popes with the sanction of the cardinals, and decretal epistles and bulls of the Popes. There is also a canon law for the regulation of the Church of England, which under certain restrictions is used in ecclesiastical courts and in the courts of the two universities. In the Roman

Church these collections came into use in the fifth and sixth centuries. The chief basis of them was a translation of the decrees of the four first general councils, to which other decrees of particular synods and decretals of the Popes were added. In the time of Charlemagne the collection of Dionysius the Little acquired almost the authority of laws. Equal authority, also, was allowed to the spurious ninth-century collection of decretals falsely ascribed to Isidore, Bishop of Seville.

After the tenth century systematical compendiums of ecclesiastical law began to be drawn from these canons, the most important being that of the Benedictine Gratian of Chiusi, finished in 1151. Within ten years after its appearance the Universities of Bologna and Paris had their professors of canon law, who taught from Gratian's work, which superseded all former chronological collections. After the appearance of the *Decretum Gratiani*, new decrees of councils and new decretals were promulgated, which were collected by Raymond of Pennaforte, under the name of *Decretales Gregorii Noni* (1234); and the later decretals, etc., collected by Boniface VIII., were published as the sixth book of the Gregorian Decretals in 1298, all these having the authority of laws. Pope Clement V. published a collection of his decrees in 1313. About the year 1340 the decretals of John XXII. were published (*Extravagantes Johannis XXII*); and at a later period the subsequent decretals, to the time of Sextus IV. (*Extravagantes Communes*) appeared. These *Extravagantes* have not altogether the authority of law.

Under Pope Pius IV. a commission was appointed to revise the *Decretum Gratiani*, the work being completed under Gregory XIII., and sanctioned by bull in 1589. The authority of the canon law in England, since the Reformation, depends upon the statute 25th Henry VIII., according to which such ecclesiastical laws as were not repugnant to the laws of the realm and the king's prerogative were to remain in force till revised. This revision was never made. A body of 141 canons was drawn up for the English Church in 1603-4, and these are still partially in force, so far as concerns the clergy. In Scotland the Roman canon law still prevails to a certain extent. Cf. R. S. Mylne, *Canon Law*.

CANOP'IC VASES. Vessels found in Egypt, which were placed in tombs, and contained the entrails of embalmed bodies.

CANO'PUS. An ancient Egyptian city, between Alexandria and the western mouth of the Nile, once the chief harbour of the Delta. It had a popular temple of Serapis.—In Egyptian mythology, a water-god, whose worship was superseded under the first Ptolemy by that of Serapis.—In astronomy, Canopis, or Alpha Argus, is, next to Sirius, the brightest of fixed stars. Though its distance has not been determined, it is known to be many times more distant than Sirius. Its intrinsic luminosity must therefore be much greater, and is estimated to be at least 40,000 times the sun's. Some have suggested that this gigantic star is a central governing body to the sidereal system, as our sun is to the planetary system, but there is little ground for such a belief.

CAN'OPY. A raised and ornamental covering above a throne, a bed, or the like; in architecture, a decorative structure serving as a hood or cover above an altar, pulpit, or niche.

CANO'SA (the ancient **CANUSIUM**). A city of South Italy, province of Bari delle Puglie, famous for the rock-cut tombs in its vicinity, from which many rare antiquities have been obtained, vases, weapons, ornaments, etc. Near by is the battleground of Cannæ. Pop. 24,700.

CANOSSA. A ruined castle in Italy, 12 miles S.W. of Reggio. It is famous as the place where the Emperor Henry IV. obtained absolution from Pope Gregory VII. in 1077. The expression "Go to Canossa" used to denote a surrender to the claims of the Church.

CANO'VA, Antonio. An Italian sculptor, born in 1757 at Possagno, in Venetian territory, died at Venice in 1822. He was first an apprentice to a statuary in Bassano, from whom he went to the Academy of Venice, where he had a brilliant career. In 1779 he was sent by the Senate of Venice to Rome with a salary of 300 ducats, and there produced his *Theseus and the Slain Minotaur*, which marked a new era in modern sculpture. In 1783 Canova undertook the execution of the tomb of Pope Clement XIV. in the Church of the Apostles, a work in the Bernini manner, and inferior to his second public monument, the tomb of Pope Clement XIII. (1792) in St. Peter's. From 1783 his fame rapidly increased. He established a school for the benefit of young Venetians, and amongst other works produced his group of *Venus and Adonis*, a *Psyche and Butterfly*, a *Repentant Magdalene*, the well-known *Hebe*, the colossal *Hercules hurling Lichas into the Sea*,

The Pugilists, and the group of *Cupid and Psyche* (in the Louvre). In 1796 and 1797 Canova finished the model of the celebrated tomb of the Archduchess Christina of Austria, and in 1797 made the colossal model of a statue of the King of Naples executed in marble in 1803. He afterwards executed in Rome his *Perseus with the Head of Medusa*, which, when the *Belvedere Apollo* was carried to France, was thought not unworthy of its place and pedestal. In 1802 he was invited by Bonaparte to Paris to make the model of his colossal statue. Among the later works of the artist are a colossal *Washington*, the tombs of the Cardinal of York and of Pius VII.; a *Venus rising from the Bath*; the colossal group of *Theseus killing the Minotaur*; the tomb of Alfieri; the *Graces rising from the Bath*; a *Dancing Girl*; a colossal *Hector*; and a *Paris*. After the second fall of Napoleon, in 1815, Canova was commissioned by the Pope to demand the restoration of the works of art carried from Rome. He went from Paris to London, and returned to Rome in 1816, where he was made Marquis of Ischia, with a pension of 3000 scudi. —BIBLIOGRAPHY: Quatremère de Quincey, *Canova et ses Ouvrages*; A. G. Meyer, *Canova*.

CANROBERT (kåṇ-ro-bār), **François Certain.** French marshal, born 1809, died in 1895. He commanded in the Crimean War under St. Arnaud, and after his death received the chief command, but could not work in harmony with the British and made way for Pélissier. In the Italian War (1859) he commanded the 3rd Division and distinguished himself at Magenta. In the Franco-Prussian War he belonged to the force that was shut up in Metz and had to capitulate. He became a member of the Senate in 1876, and was returned in 1879 and in 1885.

CAN'SO, GUT or **STRAIT OF.** A narrow strait or channel, about 17 miles long, separating Nova Scotia from Cape Breton Island.

CANTABILE (kan-tab'i-le). In music, a term applied to movements intended to be performed in a graceful, elegant, and melodious style.

CAN'TABRI. The least civilised and most valiant of all the old Iberian tribes anciently inhabiting the northern mountains of Spain.

CANTA'BRIAN MOUNTAINS. The general name of the various mountain ranges extending from the Western Pyrenees along the north coast of Spain to Cape Finisterre.

CANTACUZE'NUS, John. A Byzantine emperor and historian, born about 1292, died about 1380. He was minister of Andronicus III., on whose death he became regent during the minority of John Palæologus. He defeated the Bulgarians and Turks, assumed the diadem, and entered Constantinople in triumph in 1346. After an honourable reign he retired to a monastery (1355), where he employed himself in composing a Byzantine history and other works, chiefly theological.

CANTAL'. A central department in France, area 2229 sq. miles; capital, Aurillac. This department, formerly part of Upper Auvergne, is named from its highest mountain, the Plomb du Cantal, 6094 feet in height. The greater part of it, occupied by the Cantal Mountains and high lands, furnishes only timber, archil, and pasture. It is watered by numerous rivers, the principal of which are the Dordogne, Cère, and Lot. The principal crops are rye, buckwheat, potatoes, and chestnuts, hemp and flax. Cattle, sheep, pigs, horses, and mules are reared in large numbers. Large quantities of cheese ("Auvergne cheese") are made. Hot mineral springs are abundant. Pop. 193,505.

CAN'TALOUPE (-löp). A small round variety of musk-melon, globular, ribbed, of pale-green or yellow colour, and of delicate flavour; first grown in Europe at the castle of Cantaloupe.

CAN'TARO. A measure of weight and capacity; in Turkey, 125 lb.; in Egypt, 99 lb.; in Malta, 175 lb. The Spanish wine-measure cantaro is about 3½ gallons.

CANTATA (kan-tä'ta). A vocal composition, consisting of an intermixture of air, recitative, duet, trio, quartette, and chorus, often taking the form of a short oratorio or unacted opera.

CANTEEN' (It., *cantina*, a wine-cellar). In military language, a regimental establishment managed by a committee of officers, in every British post, barracks, and standing camp, for the sale of liquors, tobacco, groceries, etc., to the soldiers at reasonable prices. The profits are employed for the benefit of the soldiers themselves.

CAN'TERBURY. A county of a city of England, in Kent, 54¾ miles S.E. of London, giving name to an archiepiscopal see, the occupant of which is Primate of all England. The Roman name was *Durovernum*, and the place was of early importance. Its present name is a modification of the Saxon *Cant-wara-byrig*, the

Kentishmen's city. The foundation of the archiepiscopal see took place soon after the arrival of St. Augustine in 596. In the eighth, ninth, tenth, and eleventh centuries the city was dreadfully ravaged by the Danes, but at the Conquest its buildings exceeded in extent those of London. The ecclesiastical importance of the place was added to by the murder of Thomas à Becket in the cathedral, the priory and see benefiting by the offerings of devotees and pilgrims at his shrine. Henry VIII. dissolved the priory in 1539, and ordered the bones of Becket to be burned; and the troopers of Oliver Cromwell made a stable of the cathedral.—The town is beautifully situated in a fertile vale, on the River Stour. Small portions of the old walls and one of the old gates still remain.

Buildings. The cathedral, one of the finest ecclesiastical structures in England, 530 feet in length and 154 feet in breadth, has been built in different ages, the oldest part dating from about 1174. The great tower, 235 feet in height, is a splendid specimen of the Pointed style. Other ecclesiastical buildings are St. Augustine's monastery, now a Church missionary college, St. Margaret's church, and the church dedicated to St. Martin, believed to be one of the oldest existing Christian churches. The church of St. Dunstan contains the burial vault of the Roper family, in which the head of Sir Thomas More is said to have been placed by his daughter. The old archiepiscopal palace is now represented by a mere fragment, and the archbishops have long resided at Lambeth. Canterbury has a royal grammar-school, founded by Henry VIII., numerous other schools, art gallery, etc. There are breweries and malting establishments; and the principal articles of trade are corn and hops. There are extensive barracks for cavalry and infantry. A parliamentary borough till 1918, Canterbury now gives its name to one of the eleven Parliamentary divisions of the county. Pop. (1931), 24,450.—BIBLIOGRAPHY: J. Brent, *Canterbury in the Olden Times*; A. P. Stanley, *Historical Memoirs of Canterbury*; G. R. S. Taylor, *The Story of Canterbury*.

CANTERBURY. A district occupying most of the centre of South Island, New Zealand, with a coast-line of 200 miles, and a greatest breadth of about 150 miles. The western part is traversed by mountains, from which a fertile plain of 2,500,000 acres slopes gradually down to the sea. Banks' Peninsula is a projection on the east coast, consisting of an assemblage of densely-wooded hills, and containing several harbours. The famous "Canterbury Plains," extending along the coast, are admirably adapted for agriculture, while the interior is fine pastoral country, though, except near the highlands, very destitute of trees. Its considerable mineral resources are as yet not well developed, though some coal—of which there are large beds—is raised. The chief places in the province are Christchurch, the capital; and Lyttelton, the port town, 8 miles from Christchurch. Area, 13,940 sq. miles; pop. 213,890.

CANTERBURY-BELL. A name given to species of Campanŭla, *C. medium* and *C. trachelium*. In varieties the colour may be white, rose, or pure blue. *See* CAMPANULA.

CANTHAR′IDES, or **SPANISH FLY** (*Canthăris* or *Lytta vesicatoria*). A kind of beetle common in Spain, Italy, and France, having the body from 6 to 10 lines long, and of a golden-green colour. It lives on trees, the leaves of which it eats. When bruised, these insects are extensively used as the active element in vesicatory or blistering plasters, and internally in certain cases. Their use is very dangerous, and care must be exercised even in collecting them. Their active properties they owe to *cantharidin*, a powerful poison.

CANTICLES. *See* SOLOMON, THE SONG OF.

CANTILEVER. Engineering term used for a beam or girder which projects from a wall or other structure, and is supported only at one end. It is the essential feature in certain types of bridge where two or more cantilevers are used, and in modern concrete architecture, where solid overhanging and projecting slabs are used.

CANTO FERMO. Plain-song or choral song in unison or octave, with the notes all of one length; the grave measured chant of the ancient Church.

CANTO FIGURA′TO. A term applied by the old ecclesiastics to the chant in its more florid forms, in which more than one note was sung to a syllable.

CANTON′ (Chin. *Quang-chow-foo*). A large and important city of Southern China, 80 miles from the sea, on the Pearl River (here about the width of the Thames at London Bridge), in the province of Quang-tung (of which name *Canton* is a corruption). The city proper is enclosed by walls 25 feet high and 20 feet thick, forming a circuit of 6 miles, with twelve gates; and it is divided into two parts by a wall running east and west, the larger portion north of this wall being called the old, that on the south of it the new city. The streets are long, straight, and in general paved, but very narrow, and gaudy with painted signs. The houses of the poorer classes are mere mud hovels; those of the shop-keeping class are commonly of two stories, the lower serving as the shop. The foreign mercantile houses, and the British, French, and American consulates, have as their special quarter an area in the suburbs in the south-west of the city, with water on two sides of it. In the European quarter are churches, schools, and other buildings in the European style. The river opposite the city for the space of 4 or 5 miles is crowded with boats, a large number of which—as many it is said as 40,000—are fixed residences, containing a population of 200,000.

Industries. The industries of Canton are varied and important, embracing silk, cotton, porcelain, glass, paper, sugar, lacquered ware, ivory-carving, metal goods, etc. The first attempt by European Powers to open commercial relations with Canton was made in 1517, when a Portuguese ambassador was sent to China with such an object in view. The Dutch began to trade with Canton later in the century, but were soon superseded by the British, who established a factory at Canton in 1684. Canton remained the chief foreign emporium in China until 1850, when Shanghai began to surpass and other ports to compete with it; but its exports and imports together sometimes amount in value to £15,000,000. There are now waterworks and a supply of electric light and power. River steamers ply daily between Canton, Hong-Kong, and Macao. In 1856 the foreign factories were pillaged and destroyed by the Chinese, and about a year after this Canton was taken by an English force, and occupied by an English and French garrison until 1861, since when Canton has been practically open to foreign trade and residence. Pop. estimated at 812,241.

CANTON′. A town of the United States, in Ohio, with various industrial establishments. Pop. 104,906.

CAN′TON. A small division of territory constituting a distinct State or government, as in Switzerland.

CANTON′MENTS. The places in which troops are quartered when they are detached and distributed over a number of towns and villages, with facilities for concentration. In India the permanent military stations erected in the neighbourhood of the principal cities are so called.

CAN′TOR. The leader of the singing in a cathedral; a precentor.

CANTYRE. *See* KINTYRE.

CANUTE, or CNUT (ka-nūt′, knųt). King of England and Denmark, born about 994 (?), died in 1035. He succeeded his father Swegen or Sweyn on his death in England in A.D. 1014, and confirmed the Danish power in England. He began by devastating the eastern coast, and extended his ravages in the south, where, however, he failed to establish himself until after the assassination of Edmund Ironside, when he was accepted king of the whole of England (1017). Canute, who began his reign with barbarity and crime, afterwards became a humane and wise monarch. He restored the English customs at a general assembly, and ensured to the Danes and English equal rights and equal protection of person and property, and even preferred English subjects to the most important posts. His power was confirmed by his marriage with Emma, Ethelred's widow. At Harold's death in 1018 he gained Denmark; in 1028 he conquered Norway; and in 1031 he made an invasion of Scotland. Sweden also was vassal to him. He died at Shaftesbury, leaving Norway to his eldest son, Sweyn; to the second, Harold, England; to the third, Hardicanute, Denmark.—BIBLIOGRAPHY: E. A. Freeman, *Norman Conquest*; Dr. Steenstrup, *Normannerne*; L. M. Lawson, *Canute the Great and the Rise of Danish Imperialism*; and the article on Canute in the *Dictionary of National Biography*.

CAN′VAS. A coarse and strong cloth, made of flax or hemp, and used for sails, tents, etc. When prepared for portrait-painting it is classed as *kit-cat*, 28 by 36 inches; *three-quarters*, 25 by 30 inches; *half-length*, 40 by 50 inches; *bishop's half-length*, 44 or 45 by 56 inches; *bishop's whole length*, 58 by 94 inches.

CANVAS-BACK DUCK (*Fuligŭla vallisneria* or *Nyrŏca vallisneria*). A bird peculiar to N. America, and considered the finest of the water-fowl for the table. They arrive in the United States from the north in November, sometimes assembling in immense numbers. The plumage is black, white, chestnut-brown, and slate colour; length about 20 inches.

CANYON. Deep gorge or ravine between steep rocks. Ravines are usually made by rivers cutting their way through the rocks. The most famous in the world are in the western part of the United States. The Grand Canyon of the Colorado in

Arizona has walls of 6000 ft. high.

CANZONE (kan-tsō′nā). A kind of lyric poem in several stanzas, of Provençal origin, reduced to method in the Italian poetry of the thirteenth century. There are several varieties of it. The canzone was used by Dante, Petrarch, Leopardi, and D. G. Rossetti.

CAN′ZONET, or CANZONETTA. In Italian poetry a canzone with short verses, much used in the fifteenth century. In music, *canzonet* originally signified a short song in parts, but has often been loosely applied to any trifling air.

CAOLIN. *See* KAOLIN.

CAOUTCHOUC (kö′chök or kou′-chök). *See* RUBBER.

CAP. In ships, a strong piece of timber placed over the head or upper end of a mast, having in it a round hole to receive the top or top-gallant masts, which are thus kept steady and firm.

CAP. A covering for the head, usually of softer materials and less definite form than a hat. *Cap of maintenance*, a cap formerly worn by dukes and commanders in token of their dignity, now an ornament of state carried before the sovereigns of England at their coronation, and also before the mayors of some cities.

CAPE BRETON. An island of the Dominion of Canada, separated from Nova Scotia, to which province it belongs (since 1819), by the narrow Gut or Strait of Canso; area, 3125 sq. miles. It is of very irregular shape, the Bras d'Or, an almost landlocked arm of the sea, penetrating its interior in various directions, and dividing it into two peninsulas connected by an isthmus across which a canal has been cut. The surface is rather rugged, and only small portions are suited for agriculture; but it possesses much timber, valuable minerals (several coal-mines being worked), and the coast abounds in fish. Timber, fish, and coal are exported. The island belonged to France from 1632 to 1763, and Louisburg, its capital, was long an important military post. It was separate from Nova Scotia from 1784 until 1819. Chief town, Sydney. There is a wireless station near Glace Bay. Pop. of Cape Breton, 130,000.

CAPE COAST CASTLE. A town with a fort in West Africa, largest town in the British colony of the Gold Coast. The fortress stands on a rock close to the sea; the town chiefly consists of mud huts. The climate is unhealthy. Steamers regularly call here; principal exports, gold-dust, ivory, and palm-oil. Pop. 17,685.

CAPE COD. A large peninsula of the United States on the south side of Massachusetts Bay; 65 miles long and from 1 to 20 broad. It is mostly sandy and barren, but populous.

CAPE COLONY. *See* CAPE PROVINCE.

CAPEFIGUE (kȧp-fēg), **Baptiste Honoré Raymond.** French historian and biographer, born 1802, died in 1872. He held various journalistic posts in connection with the *Temps*, the *Messager*, etc., his royalist articles winning him a temporary appointment in the Foreign Office under the Bourbons. His numerous works include biographies and histories extending over the whole field of French history from the time of Hugh Capet to that of the Empire. His best work is perhaps *Histoire de la réforme, de la ligue, et du régne de Henri IV*. (8 vols., 1834-5).

CAPE GOOSEBERRY. Shrub grown in S. Africa and other warm countries. It bears whitish flowers and purple berries which are acid to the taste.

CAPE HAT′TERAS. A dangerous cape on the coast of North Carolina, the projecting point of a long reef of sand.

CAPE HAY′TIEN. A town on the N. coast of Hayti. It has an excellent harbour, but has declined in importance since the last century. Pop. about 20,000.

CAPE HORN, or THE HORN. The southern extremity of an island of the same name, forming the most southerly point of South America. It is a dark, precipitous headland, 500 to 600 feet high, running far into the sea. Navigation round it is dangerous on account of frequent tempests. The cape was first doubled in 1616 by Schouten, a native of Hoorn, in Holland, whence its name.

CAP′ELIN (*Mallōtus villōsus*). A small fish of the salmon family abundant on North American coasts, and used as bait for cod and also as food.

CAP′ELL, Arthur. First Baron Capell, son of Sir Henry Capell, born about 1600; raised to the peerage by Charles I. During the revolutionary war he fought bravely as one of the Royalist generals in the west in the engagements at Bristol, Exeter, and Taunton. Having been at length forced to surrender at Colchester to General Fairfax, he was imprisoned, and, after some vicissitudes, executed on 9th March, 1649. His *Daily Observations or Meditations* was published posthumously with a memoir.

CAPEL'LA, Martianus Minneus Felix. A Latin writer of the fourth century whose work, the *Satiricon*, was in high repute in the Middle Ages as an encyclopedia of the liberal culture of the time. The *Satiricon* consists of nine books, the first two of which constitute an allegory, *The Nuptials of Philology and Mercury* (De Nuptiis Philologiæ et Mercurii). His statement of the heliocentric system of astronomy may possibly have given hints to Copernicus.

CAPELLA, or **ALPHA AURIGÆ.** In astronomy, one of the three most conspicuous, and almost equally bright, stars in the northern hemisphere. It is always above the horizon to places in Great Britain. It belongs to the solar type of star, its spectrum being almost identical with that of the sun, but it is probably much larger, its light output having been estimated as about 190 times the sun's.

CAPE OF GOOD HOPE. A celebrated promontory near the southern extremity of Africa, at the termination of a small peninsula extending south from Table Mountain which overlooks Cape Town. This peninsula forms the west side of False Bay, and on its inner coast is Simon's Bay and Simon's Town, where there is a safe anchorage and a British naval station. Bartholomew Diaz, who discovered the Cape in 1487, called it Cape of Storms; but John II. of Portugal changed this to its present designation. It was first doubled by Vasco da Gama in 1497.

CAPE PROVINCE. The most southern province of the Union of South Africa, being one of the four original provinces, and formerly known as Cape Colony. It is bounded by Bechuanaland Protectorate, the Orange Free State, Basutoland, and Natal on the north, the Indian Ocean on the east and south, and the Atlantic on the west. Area, 276,536 sq. miles; pop. 3,163,700 (748,455 being European). It consists of the original colony, Bechuanaland, East Griqualand, Tembuland, Pondoland, Transkei, and Walvis Bay. The coast is not much indented; the principal bays are St. Helena, Saldanha, Table, False, Walker, Mossel, and Algoa. In the interior almost every variety of soil and surface is found, but a great part of the province is arid and uninviting in appearance.

Several ranges of mountains, running nearly parallel to the southern coast, divide the country into successive terraces, rising as they recede inland, between which lie belts of fertile land, or vast barren-looking plains, one of them, the Great Karroo, being 300 miles long and 100 miles broad. These plains make valuable sheep-walks, and the soil, where there is a sufficiency of water, is generally fertile. Irrigation, however, is greatly required, and large reservoirs are now being constructed. The principal and farthest inland mountain terrace, averaging 6000 or 7000 feet in height, commences in Namaqualand and runs to the north-east frontier. The culminating point is the Compass Berg, over 8000 feet. The Table Mountain at Cape Town rises almost perpendicularly about 3556 feet in height.

Rivers. The province is deficient in navigable rivers, and many of the streams are dry or almost so in the warm weather. The Orange is the largest, the other principal streams being Olifants River, flowing west; the Breede, Groote, Gamtoos, emptying themselves on the S.; the Great Fish and Great Kei, on the S.E.; and the Hartebeest and the Vaal, tributaries of the Orange.

The climate is very healthy and generally pleasant. Except along the coast, especially the south-east coast district, where there are extensive forests, timber is scarce, but with irrigation trees can be grown anywhere. The quadrupeds of the province comprise the African elephant (still found in the forests of the south-east coast region), buffalo, wild boar, leopard, hyena, jackal, several species of antelope, baboon, armadillo, etc. The birds include vultures, eagles, the serpent-eater, pelicans, flamingos, and, most important of all, the ostrich, now bred in farms for the sake of its feathers. The cobra and other reptiles are found.

Industries. The principal minerals are copper-ore, coal, iron-ore, manganese, and diamonds, amethysts, agates, etc. Coal and copper are worked, and the diamonds have brought a great amount of money into the province since 1869, and have given rise to the town of Kimberley, the centre of the diamond-fields. Wheat, maize, and other cereals can be grown almost everywhere, if there is sufficient moisture, in some years yielding a surplus for exportation. All kinds of European vegetables, pot-herbs, and fruits thrive excellently, and fruits dried and preserved are exported. The vine is cultivated, and excellent wines are made. Sheep-rearing, especially that of pure merinoes, is the most important industry, and wool the chief export. Ostrich feathers, hides, and skins are also exported. Both native and Angora goats are bred, and the export of mohair is important. Cattle-breeding is also carried on to some extent. In the present century irrigation development has made rapid strides, and technical and financial assistance has been given by the State under the Irrigation Laws of 1906 and 1912.

There are as yet few manufactures of importance. In May, 1910, the Government lines were merged into one system, the South African Railways, and the total open mileage of this system in the Cape Province at the end of March, 1926, was 4950 miles. British money, weights, and measures are alone in use, except that the general land measure is the Dutch *morgen* = 2·116 acres. The total imports from the United Kingdom in 1927 were in value £14,239,807, the total exports to the United Kingdom £15,082,404. Diamonds and gold figure largely in the exports, the latter chiefly from the Transvaal. Wool, goats' hair, and ostrich feathers are valuable exports. The total value of diamonds produced has been some £190,000,000.

The European inhabitants consist in part of English and Scottish settlers and their descendants, but, notwithstanding the recent influx of settlers from Britain, the majority are still probably of Dutch origin. The coloured people are chiefly Hottentots, Kaffirs, Basutos, Griquas, Malays, and a mixed race. The labourers are chiefly Hottentots and Kaffirs. Education is compulsory for children of European extraction, and is supported by grants from the general revenue. For the higher education there are five colleges, besides the three Universities of Cape Town, Stellenbosch, and South Africa, established in 1918, in place of the University of Cape of Good Hope, dissolved in 1916. The Dutch first colonised the Cape in 1652, and till the end of the eighteenth century the colony was under the Dutch East India Company. It was held by the British from 1795 to 1801, and it came finally into British possession in 1806.

The progress of the colony was long retarded by a series of Kaffir wars, the last of which was from 1851 to 1853. Responsible government was possessed by the former colony from 1872, the executive being vested in the Governor (appointed by the Crown) and an Executive Council of office-bearers appointed by the Crown, while the legislature consisted of a Council of twenty-six members (the Upper House), and a representative House of Assembly of 107 members (the Lower House). On the 31st May, 1910, the colony was merged into the Union of South Africa, forming an original province of the Union, being known officially as the province of the Cape of Good Hope. As such it is under an Administrator and a Provincial Council of 51, elected for three years. Cape Town, the capital of the province, is the seat of the Provincial Administration; and other important towns are Port Elizabeth, East London, Graham's Town, Kimberley, and Paarl. *See* SOUTH AFRICA, UNION OF.—BIBLIOGRAPHY: Sir H. H. Johnston, *History of the Colonisation of Africa by Alien Races*; E. F. Knight, *South Africa after the War*; A. F. Trotter, *Old Cape Colony;* S. Playne, *Cape Colony: Its History, Commerce, Industries, and Resources*; G. M. Theal, *History of South Africa.*

CA'PER. The unopened flower-bud of a low trailing shrub (*Cappăris spinōsa*, ord. Capparidaceæ) which grows in the crevices of rocks and walls, and among rubbish, in the countries bordering the Mediterranean. Picked and pickled in vinegar and salt they are much used as a condiment. Caper-sauce has been the accompaniment of boiled mutton since the time of Shakespeare ta least. (See *Twelfth Night*, i., 3, 129, 130.) The plant was introduced into Britain as early as about 1490, but has never been grown on a large scale. The flower-buds of the marsh marigold (*Caltha palustris*) and nasturtium are frequently pickled and eaten as a substitute for capers.

CAPERCAIL'ZIE, CAPERCAIL'LIE, or COCK OF THE WOOD. The wood-grouse (*Tetrāo urogallus*), the largest of the gallinaceous birds of Europe, weighing from 9 to 12 lb. In the male the neck and head are ashy black, the wings and shoulders brown with small black dots, the breast variable green, the belly black with white spots, the rump and flanks black with zigzag lines of an ashy colour, and the tail-feathers black with small white spots near their extremities. The female, about one-third less than the male, is striped and spotted with red or bay, black and white, and has the feathers of the head, breast, and tail of a more or less ruddy hue. The capercailzie inhabits pine-forests in various parts of Europe, over a range extending from Lapland to Spain, Italy, and Greece. It was once indigenous to Great Britain and Ireland, but disappeared with the pine-forest, lingering latest in Scotland, where it became extinct in the latter half of the eighteenth century. The laird of Glenorchy sent one as a present to Charles II. in 1651. It was successfully reintroduced in 1838 in many districts in Scotland where suitable woods exist.

Capercailzie (*Tetrão urogallus*)

CAPERNAUM (ka-per′nā-um). A village in ancient Palestine, on the west side of the Sea of Tiberias. Nothing of it now remains, but the site is identified with Tel Hum and Khan Minyeh.

CAPE ST. VINCENT. The S.W. point of Portugal; noted for the victory over a Spanish fleet gained off it by Sir John Jervis (Earl St. Vincent) on the 14th Feb., 1797.

CA′PET. The name of the French race of kings which has given 118 sovereigns to Europe, viz. 36 kings of France, 22 kings of Portugal, 11 of Naples and Sicily, 5 of Spain, 3 of Hungary, 3 emperors of Constantinople, 3 kings of Navarre, 17 dukes of Burgundy, 12 dukes of Brittany, 2 dukes of Lorraine, and 4 dukes of Parma. The first of the Capets known in history was Robert the Strong, a Saxon, made Count of Anjou by Charles the Bold, and afterwards Duke of the Ile de France. His descendant, Hugh, son of Hugh the Great, was in 987 elected King of France in place of the Carlovingians. On the failure of the direct line at the death of Charles IV., the French throne was kept in the family by the accession of the indirect line of Valois, and in 1589 by that of Bourbon. Capet being thus regarded as the family name of the kings of France, Louis XVI. was arraigned before the National Convention under the name of Louis Capet.

CAPE TOWN. Capital of the Cape Province, Union of South Africa, at the head of Table Bay, and at the base of Table Mountain, 30 miles from the Cape of Good Hope. It is the seat of legislature of the South African Union. It is regularly laid out and furnished with most of the institutions and conveniences of a European town, has a fine public library (50,000 vols.) and museum, a Roman Catholic and an Anglican cathedral, new and handsome Houses of Parliament, Government offices, a university (incorporated originally in 1873, reorganised in 1918), a botanic garden, an observatory, town house, exchange, railway station, etc. The port has a breakwater 3640 feet long, two docks (water area, 75½ acres), a large graving dock, etc. Besides the railway going inland, a railway connects the town with Simon's Town on False Bay. Pop. in 1875, 33,239; in 1891, 51,251; in 1921 the white population was 112,059, and the coloured 93,807; total, 205,866. The white population was 149,236 in 1931.

CAPE VERDE. The extreme west point of Africa, between the Senegal and the Gambia, discovered by Fernandez, 1445.

CAPE VERDE ISLANDS. A group of fourteen volcanic islands and rocks in the Atlantic, 320 miles west of Cape Verde (see above), belonging to Portugal. They are, in general, mountainous, and the lower hills are in many places covered with verdure; but water is scarce, and the failure of the annual rains has sometimes caused severe famines. They produce rice, maize, coffee, tobacco, the sugar-cane, physic-nuts, and various fruits. Coffee, hides, archil, physic-nuts, etc., are exported. Most of the inhabitant are negroes or of mixed race. The chief town is Praia, a seaport on São Thiago (Santiago), the largest island. Porto Grande, on São Vicente, is a coaling station for steamers. The population according to the 1928 census was 150,160, of whom about 5000 were Europeans.

CAPE WRATH. The north-west extremity of Scotland, County Sutherland. It is a pyramid of gneiss bearing a lighthouse, the light of which is 400 feet above sea-level.

CAPGRAVE, John. English historian, born at Lynn, Norfolk, in 1393. Most of his life was passed in the Augustinian friary of his native place, where he died in 1464. He was one of the most learned men of his day, and wrote numerous commentaries, sermons, and lives of the saints. His most important work was his *Chronicle of England from the Creation to A.D. 1417*. Other works were a *Liber de Illustribus Henricis* and a *Life of St. Katherine* (in English verse).

CA'PIAS (Lat., take, or you may take). In English law, a writ of two sorts: one before judgment, called a *capias ad respondendum*, to take the defendant and make him answer to the plaintiff; the other, which issues after judgment, of divers kinds; as, a *capias ad satisfaciendum*, or writ of execution.

CAP'ILLARIES. In Anatomy, the fine blood-vessels which form the links of connection between the extremities of the arteries and the beginnings of the veins. *See* ARTERIES; VEINS; HEART.

CAPILLAR'ITY. The general name applied to certain phenomena exhibited by the surfaces of liquids, because of the rise of liquids in narrow or capillary tubes. The

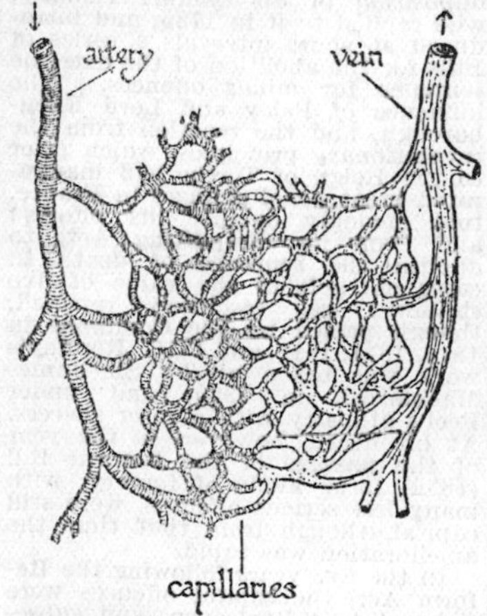

surface film of a liquid behaves as if it were stretched equally in all directions. This is exemplified by the soap-bubble. Also, a small drop of mercury on a table, or a drop of water which falls on a dry, dusty road, assumes a spherical shape for the same reason. This surface property is sometimes employed when it is desired to pour a liquid into a narrow-necked bottle without spilling. The liquid, when poured down a glass rod in contact with the bottle, appears to cling to the rod, and can thus be made to enter the bottle in a narrow stream. That the surface tension has different values in different liquids may be demonstrated in various ways, e.g. by the difference in the sizes of drops of the liquids when falling from tubes of the same diameter.

There is a notable difference in the behaviour of liquids in contact with solids, according as they do or do not wet the solid. Thus, if an open glass tube of small bore be inserted in water, it will be noted that the liquid rises within it, above its former level, to a height varying inversely as the diameter of the bore, and that the surface of this column is more or less concave in form. The same phenomenon occurs in any fluid which will wet the tube; but in the case of a fluid like mercury, which does not wet the glass, the converse phenomenon appears, the liquid being depressed in the tube below its former level, and the portion within the tube exhibiting a convex surface. Similarly, round the sides of the respective vessels, and round the outsides of the inserted tubes, we find in the first case an ascension, and in the second a depression of the liquid, with a corresponding concavity or convexity at its extreme edge. Two parallel plates immersed in the liquids give kindred results. As these phenomena occur as readily in air as *in vacuo*, they cannot be attributed to the action of the atmosphere, but depend upon molecular actions taking place between the particles of the liquid itself, and between the liquid and the solid, these actions being confined to a very thin layer forming the superficial boundary of the fluid. The part which capillarity plays among natural phenomena is a very varied one. By it the fluids circulate in the porous tissues of animal bodies; the sap rises in plants, and moisture is absorbed from the air and soil by the foliage and roots. For the same reason a sponge or lump of sugar or a piece of blotting-paper soaks in moisture, and the oil rises in the wick of a lamp.—BIBLIOGRAPHY: Lord Rayleigh, *Collected Scientific Papers*; F. Bashforth, *An Attempt to test the Theories of Capillary Action*; H. Poincaré, *Capillarité*.

CAP'ITAL. In trade, the term applied to the money, or property convertible into money, used by a producer or trader for carrying on his business and intended to yield a revenue; in economics, that portion of the produce of former labour which is reserved from consumption for employment in the further production of wealth—the apparatus of production; in social discussion, sometimes applied to the employing class as opposed to *labour*. It is sometimes classified under two main heads—circulating capital and fixed capital. Circulating capital comprises those forms of capital which require renewal after every use in production, being consumed (absorbed or transformed) in the single use, e.g. raw materials and wages. Fixed capital, on the other hand, comprises every form of capital which is capable of use in a series of similar productive acts, e.g. machinery, tools, etc.

Modern theory does not regard this distinction as particularly useful, since the only difference between the two kinds of capital is the length of time elapsing between the outlay of the capital and its return. For the purposes of trade and theory it is convenient to limit the term capital to material objects directly employed in the reproduction of material wealth, but from the social point of view many things less immediately concerned in productive work may be regarded as capital. Thus, Adam Smith includes in the fixed capital of a country, "the acquired and useful abilities of all the inhabitants"; and the wealth sunk in prisons, educational institutions, etc., plays ultimately a scarcely less important part in production than that invested in directly productive machinery. Socialistic writers apply the term *capital* to any form of wealth that yields an income independently of the work and exertions of the owner. The tools of the artisan, therefore, are not *capital* in this sense. *See* ECONOMICS; WEALTH. — BIBLIOGRAPHY: J. S. Mill, *Principles of Political Economy*; Sir L. Chiozza Money, *Riches and Poverty*; W. Sombart, *The Quintessence of Capitalism*; H. Cahn, *Capital To-day*.

CAPITAL. An architectural term, usually restricted to the upper portion of a column, the part resting immediately on the shaft. In classic architecture each order has its distinctive capital, but in Egyptian, Indian, Saracenic, Norman, and Gothic they are much diversified. *See* COLUMN.

CAPITAL PUNISHMENT. In criminal law, the punishment by death. Formerly in Great Britain, as in many other countries, it was the ordinary form of punishment for felonies of all kinds; but a more accurate knowledge of the nature and remedies of crime, a more discriminating sense of degrees in criminality, and an increased regard for human life have all combined to restrict, if not to abolish, the employment of the penalty of death. The improvement in the penal laws of Europe in this respect may be traced in large part to the publication of Becaria's *Treatise on Crimes and Punishments* (Dei Delitti e delle Pene) in 1764. At that time in England, as Blackstone a year later pointed out with some amount of feeling, there were 160 capital offences in the statute book. The work of practical reform was initiated in 1770 by Sir William Meredith, who moved for a committee of inquiry into the state of the criminal laws; but the modifications secured by it were few, owing to the opposition of the House of Lords, which continued down to 1832 to oppose systematically all attempts at criminal law reform.

The publication of Madan's *Thoughts on Executive Justice*, in 1784, urging the stricter administration of the law as it then stood, brought out the opposition of Sir Samuel Romilly, who replied to it in 1785, and introduced at short intervals a series of Bills for the abolition of the extreme sentence for minor offences. The influence of Paley and Lord Ellenborough, and the reaction from the revolutionary principles, which prior to the Reign of Terror had inaugurated great penal changes in France, told strongly against his efforts; and even his Shoplifting Act, to abolish the sentence of death in cases of theft to the value of five shillings, was resolutely rejected, though passed by the Commons in 1810, 1811, 1813, and 1816. Romilly's work was taken up by Sir James Mackintosh in 1820, and under Peel's Ministry with greater success. At his death, however, in the year of the passage of the Reform Bill (1832) forty kinds of forgery, with many less serious offences, were still capital, though from that time the amelioration was rapid.

In the five years following the Reform Act, the capital offences were reduced to thirty-seven, and subsequent changes left in 1861 only four capital charges—setting fire to H.M. dockyards or arsenals, piracy with violence, treason, and murder. At the present time the last two of these may be regarded as the only capital crimes; and the statement holds good for Scotland also, though robbery, rape, incest, and wilful fire-raising are still capital crimes in Scottish common law. In several other European countries—Sweden, Denmark, North Germany, Bavaria, Austria—there is even a greater unwillingness to enforce capital punishment than is found in Great Britain, though the penalty remains upon the statute books.

Capital punishment has been done away with in Italy, Portugal, Rumania (1864), and Holland (1870). In Russia capital punishment was abolished in 1917, but was reintroduced by the Government of the Soviets. In Belgium there has been no execution since 1863. In Switzerland capital punishment was abolished in 1874, and though the right of restoring it was allowed to each canton in consequence of an increase of murders, only seven out of a total of twenty-two have availed themselves of it. In several of the States of America—Michigan, Wisconsin, Rhode Island, and Maine—imprisonment for life has been substituted for murder in the first degree; in the remainder, capital punishment is retained, though the experiment of its abolition was made for a short time in New York and Iowa.

The manner of inflicting the punishment of death has varied greatly. Barbarous nations are generally inclined to severe and vindictive punishments; and even in civilised countries, in cases of a political nature, or of very great atrocity, the punishment has been sometimes inflicted with many horrible accompaniments, such as tearing the criminal to pieces, starving him to death, breaking his limbs upon the wheel, pressing him to death in a slow and lingering manner, burning him at the stake, crucifixion, etc. In modern times, amongst civilised nations, public opinion is strongly disposed to discountenance the punishment of death by any but simple means; and even in governments where torture is still countenanced by the laws it is rarely or never resorted to.

In Great Britain the method of execution is by hanging. In Germany and France the sword and the guillotine are the usual means; in Spain, strangulation by means of the *garrote*, a sort of iron collar tightened by a screw. In modern times the tendency, as shown in various countries, is to give the preference to electricity as the means of death, and in the United States this method has been generally adopted. Since 1868 the law of the United Kingdom has required all executions to take place privately within the prison walls, and this system was adopted in 1877 by Germany. Capital punishment cannot be inflicted, by the general humanity of the laws of modern nations, upon persons who are insane or who are pregnant, until the latter are delivered and the former become sane. In military law, sentence of death may be passed for various offences, such as sedition, violence, and gross neglect of duty, desertion, assault upon superior officers, disobedience to lawful commands, etc.—BIBLIOGRAPHY: Andrews, *Old Time Punishments*; *A Century of Law Reform*; H. Oppenheimer, *The Rationale of Punishment*.

CAPITALS. The large letters used in writing and printing, most commonly as the initial letters of certain words. As among the ancient Greeks and Romans, so also in the early part of the Middle Ages, all books were written without any distinction in the kind of letters, large letters (capitals) being the only ones used; gradually the practice became common of beginning a book, subsequently, also, the chief divisions and sections of a book, with a large capital letter, usually illuminated and otherwise richly ornamented. All names of the Deity, and frequently personal pronouns referring to God and Christ, begin with capitals.

CAPITA'NIS. The hereditary chieftains of certain bands of Christian warriors who, about the beginning of the sixteenth century, retired to the mountain fastnesses of Northern Greece, where they maintained a kind of independence of the Turkish Government, and supported themselves by predatory incursions on the neighbouring provinces. The Turks tried to organise them as a paid police, but with imperfect success; and in the struggle for Greek independence they not only formed an insurgent body of about 12,000 men, but furnished most of the Greek generals of that period—Odysseus, Karatasso, and Marko Bozzaris.

CAPITATION-GRANT. A grant of so much per head; specifically applied to grants from Government or governing bodies to schools according to the number of scholars in attendance, or to the number of those passing a certain test examination.

CAPITATION-TAX. A tax or impost upon each head or person. A tax of this kind existed among the Romans, but was first levied in England in 1377 and in 1380, the tax levied in the latter year occasioning the rebellion under Wat Tyler. It was again levied in 1513, and by Charles II, in 1667, after which it remained in force till abolished by William III. in 1608. In France a capitation-tax was first imposed in 1695. It was abolished in 1697, but renewed again in 1701.

it became a regular source of income until the Revolution.

CAP'ITOL, now **CAMPIDOGLIO.** The citadel of ancient Rome, standing on the Capitoline Hill, the smallest of the seven hills of Rome. It was planned by Tarquinius Priscus, but not completed till after the expulsion of the kings. At the time of the civil commotions under Sulla it was burned down, and rebuilt by the Senate. It suffered the same fate twice afterwards, and was restored by Vespasian and by Domitian, who instituted there the Capitoline games. The present capitol (Campidoglio), standing partly on the site of the old one, is a modern building, begun in 1536 after the design of Michael Angelo. It is used as a *hôtel de ville*, museum, etc., contains some fine statues and paintings, and commands a superb view of the Campagna.—The name of *capitol* is also given to the edifice in Washington where Congress assembles. Some of the States of North America also call their State-houses *capitols*.

CAPIT'ULARIES. A term particularly applied to the laws promulgated by the Frankish kings, with the advice of the nobles and bishops. Those of Charlemagne were specially famous. The capitularies regulated equally the spiritual and temporal administration of the kingdom; and the execution of them was entrusted to the bishops, the courts, and the *missi regii*, the king's dispensers of law in the provinces.

CAPITULA'TION. The making of terms for surrender of a fortress, territory, or body of troops; the action of surrendering to an enemy upon stipulated terms, in opposition to surrendering at discretion. The terms usually include freedom of religion and security of property on the one hand, and disarmament upon the other. When a place can no longer be held against the enemy, it is customary to hoist a white flag as a sign that the governor is willing to capitulate. The terms of capitulation are severe in proportion to the danger in which the fortress was placed. A capitulation on easy terms is called a *convention*; and one concluded by an officer who has not the proper authority so to do is known as a *sponsion*, and must be ratified in order to be binding.

CAPITULUM. *See* COMPOSITÆ.

CAP MARTIN. Pleasure resort of France. It is on the Riviera and is best reached from Mentone. It is a popular winter resort.

CAP'NOMANCY. Divination (practised from the Greek days onward) by the ascent or motion of the smoke either of a sacrifice or of burning vervain, or seeds of jasmine or poppy. If the smoke was thin and ascended in a vertical line, instead of being blown back by the breeze, the augury was good.

CAPO D'ISTRIA. A seaport, formerly belonging to Austria, on the Gulf of Trieste, 9 miles S. of Trieste, with a cathedral. Pop. 12,490.

CAPO D'ISTRIA, John Antony, Count. Greek statesman, born at Corfu in 1776. In 1809 he entered the service of Russia, and obtained an appointment in the department of Foreign Affairs. As Imperial Russian Plenipotentiary he subscribed the Treaty of Paris, 20th Nov., 1815. In 1828 he became President of the Greek Republic, in which office he was very unpopular, and in 1831 he was assassinated by Constantine and George Mavromichales.—Cf. Phillips, *The War of Greek Independence*.

CAPONIERE, or **CAPONNIÈRE** (kap-o-neer'). In fortification, a passage from one part of a work to the other, protected on the right and left by a wall or parapet, and sometimes covered overhead. When there is a parapet on one side only, it is called a *demi-caponiere*. In recent works on field fortifications caponieres are also known as *tambours*.

CAPORETTO, BATTLE OF. Fought in Oct., 1917, between the Italians and the German-Austrians, and ending in the overwhelming defeat of the former.

CAPPADO'CIA. In antiquity, one of the most important provinces in Asia Minor, the greater part of which is included in the modern province of Karaman. Its boundaries varied greatly at different times. It was conquered by Cyrus, and was ruled by independent kings from the time of Alexander the Great until A.D. 17, when it became a Roman province. It was traversed by the River Halys, and among its chief towns were Comana, Ariarathia, and Tyana.

CAPPAGH BROWN (kap'a*h*). A bituminous earth, coloured by oxide of manganese and iron, which yields pigments of various rich brown colours: called also *manganese brown*. It derives its name from Cappagh, near Cork, in Ireland.

CAPPARIDA'CEÆ. A nat. ord. of dicotyledonous, polypetalous, herbaceous plants, shrubs and trees, having four petals and sepals, a great number of stamens, and an ovary elevated upon a long stalk. All of them appear to be more or less acrid. Some are very poisonous, others act as vesicatories, and a few are merely stimulant, as the *Cappăris spinōsa*, or caper-bush, the flower-buds of which constitute the capers of the shops.

CAPRAJA (kȧ-prä'yȧ). A small volcanic island belonging to Italy, about 15 miles in circumference, situated between the north point of Corsica and the coast of Tuscany. Its principal product is wine.

CAP'REÆ. *See* CAPRI.

CAPRE'RA. A small rocky and barren Italian island, on the N.E. of Sardinia, and separated from it by a narrow strait. Area about 15 sq. miles. It was for many years the place of retirement of Garibaldi, who died there in 1882. The island was purchased from his heirs by the Italian Government in 1885.

CAPRI (ancient, Caprĕæ). An island belonging to Italy, in the Gulf of Naples, 5 miles long and 2 miles broad, rising to the height of about 1900 feet, everywhere well cultivated. The inhabitants, amounting to 7500, are occupied in the production of oil and wine, in fishing, and in catching quails at the seasons of their migrations. Capri is visited yearly by over 30,000 strangers. It contains the towns of Capri in the east, and Anacapri in the west, situated on the summit of a rock, and accessible by a stair of 522 steps. The Emperor Tiberius spent here the last seven years of his life in degrading voluptuousness and infamous cruelty. The ruins of his palaces are still extant, and other ruins are scattered over the island. The island has several stalactitic caverns or grottoes in its steep rocky coast, which are famed for the wondrous colours reflected on the rocks, the Blue Grotto (*Grotta Azurra*) being the most famous.—BIBLIOGRAPHY: G. N. Douglas, *Siren Land*; E. Petraccone, *L'Isola di Capri*.

CAPRICCIO (ka-prich'i-o). A musical composition, the form of which is left very much to the composer's fancy.

CAPRICORN, or CAP'RICORNUS. A constellation of the southern hemisphere, and one of the twelve signs of the zodiac, the one to which belongs the winter solstice, represented by the figure of a goat or a figure having the fore-part like a goat and the hind-part like a fish. Its symbol is ♑.

CAPRICORN, TROPIC OF. *See* TROPICS.

CAP'RIDÆ (Lat. *caper*, a goat). The goat tribe, a sub-family of ruminating animals, in which horns are directed upwards and backwards and have a bony core.

CAPRIFICA'TION. A horticultural operation performed since early times upon figs. It consists in suspending above the cultivated figs branches of the wild fig covered with a species of gall insect, which carries the pollen of the male flowers to fertilise the female flowers of the cultivated fig. The term is also applied to the fecundation of the female date-palms by shedding over them the pollen from the male plant. *See* FIG.

CAPRIFOLIA'CEÆ. A nat. ord. of gamopetalous dicotyledons. It includes a number of erect or twining shrubs and herbaceous plants, comprising the honeysuckle, elder, viburnum, and snowberry. The characteristics of the order are opposite leaves without stipules, free anthers, epipetalous stamens, and fruit, generally a berry, sometimes dry, but not splitting open when ripe.

CAPRIMUL'GIDÆ. The goat-suckers, or night-jars, a family of insessorial, fissirostral birds, nearly allied to the Hirundinidæ or swallow tribe.

CAPRIVI, Georg Leo, Count von. German statesman, born 24th Feb., 1831, died on his estate, Skyren, in Brandenburg, 6th Feb., 1899. After his studies in Berlin he entered the German army in 1849, and was made a major in 1866, during the campaign in Bohemia. He distinguished himself during the Franco-Prussian War, and in 1883 Bismarck selected him to succeed Admiral Stosch as Chief of the Admiralty. He resigned in 1888, and in 1890 succeeded Bismarck as Chancellor of the German Empire and President of the Prussian Ministry. He was made a count in 1891. As Chancellor of the Empire, and successor of Bismarck, his position was a rather difficult one, but he displayed great ability and talent for administration, carrying through the Reichstag several important Bills, notably one for an increase in the army. He was responsible for the so-called Anglo-German partition of East Africa, which he arranged with Lord Salisbury in July, 1890. Caprivi resigned the Chancellorship in 1894.

CAPSELLA. *See* SHEPHERD'S PURSE.

CAP'SICIN. An alkaloid, the active principle of the capsules of *Capsicum annuum*, or Guinea pepper. It has a resinous aspect and a burning taste.

CAP'SICUM. A genus of annual plants, ord. Solanaceæ, with a wheel-shaped corolla, projecting and converging stamens, and a many-seeded berry. They are chiefly natives of the East and West Indies, China, Brazil, and Egypt, but have spread to various other tropical or sub-tropical countries, being cultivated for their fruit, which in some reaches the size of an orange, is fleshy and variously coloured, and contains a pungent principle, Capsicin,

Capsicum Plant
Single flowers shown on larger scale

which is present also and more largely in the seed. The fruit or pod is used for pickles, sauces, etc., and also medicinally. Several of them, as *C. annuum*, *C. frutescens*, and *C. baccā-tum*, yield Cayenne pepper, and the first (called often Guinea pepper, though originally a native of South America) also yields chillies. *C. baccātum* is called bird-pepper. *See* CAYENNE PEPPER.

CAP'STAN. A strong upright column of timber, movable round a strong iron spindle, and having its

Capstan

upper extremity pierced to receive bars or levers, for winding a rope round it to raise weights, such as the anchors of a vessel, or to perform other work that requires great power. It is distinguished from a windlass by the axis, and consequently the barrel, being vertical.

CAP'SULE. In botany, a dry fruit containing many cells and seeds, opening when ripe by valves or otherwise.

CAPTAIN (from Lat. *caput*, head). One who is at the head or has authority over others, especially : (1) The military officer who commands a company of infantry, or is second-in-command of a six-gun battery of artillery, or second-in-command of a squadron of cavalry. Since the introduction of the double-company system, in 1914, a company is commanded by a major or mounted captain, and the company second-in-command is also a captain. (2) An officer in the navy commanding a ship of war. The naval captain is next in rank above the commander, and in Britain ranks with a lieutenant-colonel in the army, but after three years from the date of his commission he ranks with a full colonel. Captains of ships were formerly designated *post-captains*. Captain of the fleet, a flag-officer temporarily appointed by the Admiralty, who acts as adjutant-general of the force, sees to the carrying out of the orders of the commander-in-chief, and to proper discipline being maintained in the fleet. (3) The master of a merchant vessel.

CAPTION. In law, a certificate stating the time and place of executing a commission in chancery, or of taking a deposition, or of the finding of an indictment, and the court or authority before which such act was performed, and such other particulars as are necessary to render it legal and valid.

CAP'UA. A fortified city of Italy, province of Caserta, in a plain 17 miles N. of Naples, on the Volturno, which is crossed by a handsome bridge. It is the residence of an archbishop, and has a cathedral. The city was stormed in 1501 by Cæsar Borgia, and the Cappella de' Morti, outside the town, commemorates this event. Pop. 13,220. The ancient city was situated 3½ miles S.E. of the modern town. The site is now occupied by a small town, called Santa-Maria-di-Capua Vetere. The ancient Capua was of such extent as to be compared to Rome and Carthage. It was a favourite place of resort of the Romans on account of its agreeable situation and its healthy climate, and many existing ruins (including an amphitheatre) attest its ancient splendour.

CAPUCHIN MONKEY (kap-ụ-shēn'). A name given to various species of South American monkeys of the genus Cebus. The hair of their heads is so arranged that it has the appearance of a capuchin's cowl, hence the name. The name is most frequently given to the Sai (*Cebus*

Capucinus), the Horned Sapajou (*C. fatuellus*), as well as to *Pithecia chiropotes*, a monkey belonging to an allied genus.

Capuchin Monkey (*Cebus Capucinus*)

CAPUCHINS (kap-ų-shēnz'). Monks of the order of St. Francis, so called from the *capuchon* or *capuce*, a stuff cap or cowl, the distinguishing badge of the order. They are clothed in brown or grey, go barefooted, and never shave their beard. *See* FRANCISCANS.

CAPUS, Alfred. French author, born at Aix in 1858. Trained as an engineer, he soon turned his attention to journalism, contributed to the French paper *Le Figaro*, and made his reputation as dramatist and novel-writer. His best novels are: *Monsieur veut rire, Faux Départ, Années d'Aventures*; his principal plays, *Brignol et sa Fille, Innocent, Rosine, La Veine, L'Adversaire, Les Deux Ecoles*, and *Monsieur Piégois*. He was elected a member of the Académie Française in Feb., 1915. He died 1922.

CAPUT MOR'TUUM (Lat.). Literally, a dead head; a fanciful term much used by the old chemists to denote the residuum of chemicals when all their volatile matters had escaped; hence, anything from which all that rendered it valuable has been taken away.

CAPYBA'RA (*Hydrochœrus capybāra*). A species of aquatic rodent, sometimes known by the name of the water-hog or water-horse (from the Du. *waterhaas*), and of the family Caviidæ (guinea-pig). It attains the length of about 4 feet, and has a very large and thick head, a thick body covered with long, coarse, brown hair, and short legs, with long feet, which are webbed and fit it for an aquatic life. It has no tail. It is common in several parts of South America, where it is called *carpincho*, and particularly in Brazil. It feeds on vegetables and fish, which it catches somewhat in the manner of the otter.

CARAB'IDÆ, or **GROUND-BEETLES.** A family of carnivorous beetles usually large, adorned with brilliant metallic colours, and either wingless or having wings not adapted for flying. They include very numerous species, of almost world-wide distribution.

CAR'ABINE, or **CARBINE.** The name given to a short rifle, such as is carried by the Royal Irish Constabulary. The name of carabineers is given to the 6th Dragoon Guards, probably because they were the first regiment of cavalry to be armed with this weapon. A carbine is in some respects slightly more convenient than a rifle, but it is very much less accurate, and it is accordingly little used.

CARABO'BO. A state of Venezuela, washed on the north by the Caribbean Sea. Area about 2984 sq. miles; pop. 147,204. The capital is Valencia, the chief port Puerto Cabello.

CAR'ABUS. A genus of beetles, type of the family Carabidæ (q.v.).

CAR'ACAL. A species of lynx (*Felis caracal*), a native of Northern Africa and South-Western Asia. It is about the size of a fox, and mostly of a deep-brown colour, having tufts of long black hair which terminate the ears. It possesses great strength and fierceness.

Capybara (*Hydrochœrus capybāra*)

CARACAL'LA, Marcus Aurelius Antoninus. Eldest son of the Emperor Severus, born at Lyons A.D. 188, died 217. On the death of his father he succeeded to the throne with his brother Antoninus Geta, whom he speedily murdered. To effect his own security upwards of 20,000 other victims were butchered. He was himself assassinated on the road to Carrhæ, in Mesopotamia, at the instigation of Macrinus, the prætorian prefect, who succeeded him.

CARACA'RA (from its hoarse cry). The popular name for *Polybŏrus Braziliensis* (the Brazilian caracara) and several other raptorial birds of the sub-family Polyborinæ, family Falconidæ. They are of considerable size, natives of South America, and are characterised by having the bill hooked at the tip only, the wings long, and the orbits, cheeks, and part of the throat more or less denuded of feathers.

CARAC'AS. A city of South America, capital of Venezuela, situated in a fine valley about 3000 feet above the Caribbean Sea, connected by railway with the port La Guayra, about 10 miles distant. It is regularly laid out, and has some good buildings, including a cathedral, university, federal palace, and other Government buildings. In 1812 it was in great part destroyed by an earthquake, and nearly 12,000 persons buried in the ruins. Another serious earthquake occurred in 1900. Pop. 135,253.

CARACCI (kȧ-răch'ē). *See* Carracci.

CARACCIOLI (kȧ-răch'o-lē), **Francesco.** Neapolitan admiral, born at Naples about 1748, died 1799. In 1798 he entered the service of the Parthenopean Republic, and repelled, with a few vessels, an attempt of the Sicilian-English fleet to effect a landing. When Ruffo took Naples in 1799 Caraccioli was arrested, and, contrary to the terms of capitulation, was condemned to death, and hanged at the yard-arm of a Neapolitan frigate, Lord Nelson consenting to his execution.

CARAC'TACUS (Latinised form of the Welsh *Caradawg*, often spelt *Caradoc*). A king of the ancient British people called Silures, inhabiting South Wales. He defended his country with great perseverance against the Romans, but was at last defeated, and led in triumph to Rome, A.D. 51, after the war. His noble bearing and pathetic speech before the Emperor Claudius procured his pardon, and he and his relatives appear to have remained in Italy.

CARADOC SERIES. In geology, an upper division of the lower Silurian rocks, consisting of red, purple, green, and white micaceous and sometimes quartzose grits and limestones containing corals, mollusca, and trilobites. Named after the hilly range of *Caer-Caradoc* in Shropshire.

CAR'AGEEN. *See* Carrageen.

CA'RAITES. *See* Karaites.

CAR'AMAN. *See* Karaman.

CARAMA'NIA. *See* Karamania.

CARAM'BOLA. The fruit of an East Indian tree, the *Averrhŏa Carambŏla*, ord. Oxalidaceæ. It is of the size and shape of a duck's egg, of an agreeably acid flavour, and is used in making sherberts, tarts, and preserves.

CAR'AMEL. The brown mass which cane-sugar becomes at 220° C., used in cookery as a colouring and flavouring ingredient, and in distilling to give a brown colour to spirits.

CARA'PA. A genus of tropical plants, nat. ord. Meliaceæ. A South American species, *C. guianensis*, is a fine large tree, whose bark is in repute as a febrifuge. Oil made from its seeds (called carap-oil or crab-oil) is used for lamps, and masts of ships are made from its trunk. The wood is called crab-wood. The oil of the African species, *C. guineensis*, called Coondi, Kundah, or Tallicoona oil, is used by the negroes for making soap and anointing their bodies. The oil of the South American carapa is used for the same purpose also.

CAR'APACE. The upper part of the hard shell or case of chelonian reptiles, as the tortoise or turtle, the lower part being called *plastron.* It consists of bony plates covered by horny shields, the latter being the source of natural "tortoise-shell." The term is also applied in some of the higher Crustacea to the hard covering of the head and thorax, and in some of the lower members of that class to a shield-like investment that grows back from the head and may form a bivalve shell.

CAR'AT. A weight of 3·16 grains troy, used by jewellers in weighing precious stones and pearls. The term is also used to express the proportionate fineness of gold. The whole mass of gold is divided into twenty-four equal parts, and it is called gold of so many carats as it contains twenty-fourth parts of pure metal. Thus if a mass contain twenty-two parts of pure gold out of every twenty-four, it is gold of twenty-two *carats.* The word is derived from the Ar. *qirat*, pod, husk; compare the Gr. *keration*, fruit of the locust tree. It is the name given to the seeds of the Abyssinian coral tree. These seeds, small and uniform in size and weight, were first used for weighing gold, jewels, and diamonds. For many years the carat varied in different countries of Europe and Asia, but in 1905 a suggestion was made for the introduction of an international carat based on the metric system, and equal to 200 milligrams, or one-fifth of a gramme (3·086 grains). This suggestion was at once adopted by several European countries, and by an order in council was adopted in England as from 1st April, 1914.

CARAU'SIUS. A Roman general, a native of Batavia. He was sent by the Emperor Maximian to defend the Atlantic coasts against the Franks and Saxons; but, foreseeing impending disgrace, he landed in Britain and got himself proclaimed emperor by his legions (A.D. 287). In this province he was able to maintain himself six years, when he was assassinated at York by one of his officers named Allectus (A.D. 293).

CARAVA'CA. A town, Spain, province of Murcia, and 43 miles W. by N. of the town of Murcia. It has manufactures of woollen and hempen goods, paper, soap, and earthenware. Pop. 16,500.

CARAVAGGIO (kȧ-rȧ-vȧj'ō). A town of North Italy, province of Bergamo, 24 miles E. of Milan, on the Gera d'Adda. It is celebrated as the birthplace of the two great painters Polidoro Caldara (q.v.) and Michel Angelo Merighi, both called *Caravaggio*. Pop. 9000.

CARAVAGGIO, Michel Angelo Amerighi, or Merighi da. A celebrated painter, born at Caravaggio 1569, died 1609. He attained distinction as a colourist of the Neapolitan school, being considered the head of the so-called *Naturalisti* school. He was coarse and violent in his character and habits, and was in continual trouble through his quarrelsome disposition. Among his chief pictures are: *The Card Player* (at Dresden), *The Burial of Christ*, *St. Sebastian*, *Supper at Emmaus*, and a *Holy Family*.

CAR'AVAN. A Persian word used to denote large companies which travel together in Asia and Africa for the sake of security from robbers, having in view, principally, trade or pilgrimages. In Mohammedan countries caravans of pilgrims are annually formed to make the journey to Mecca. The most important are those which annually set out from Damascus and Cairo. Camels are used as a means of conveyance on account of their remarkable powers of endurance.

CARAVAN'SERAI, or CARAVANSARY. In the East, a place appointed for receiving and lodging caravans; a kind of inn where the caravans rest at night, being a large square building with a spacious court in the middle. Though caravanserais in the East serve in place of inns, there is this radical difference between them, that, generally speaking, the traveller finds nothing in a caravanserai for the use either of himself or his cattle. He must carry all his provisions and necessaries along with him. Those built in towns serve not only as inns, but contain shops, warehouses, and even exchanges.

CAR'AVEL. The name of different kinds of vessels, particularly a small ship used by the Spaniards and Portuguese in the fifteenth and sixteenth centuries for long voyages. It was narrow at the poop, wide at the bow, and carried a double tower at its stern and a single one at its bow. It had four masts and a bowsprit, and the principal sails were lateen sails. It was in command of three such caravels that Columbus crossed the Atlantic and discovered America.

CARAVEL'LAS. A seaport of Brazil, State of Bahia, the principal port of the surrounding country, and the head-quarters of the Abrolhos Islands whale-fishery. Pop. about 8000.

CAR'AWAY (*Carum Carui*). An umbelliferous biennial plant, with a tapering fleshy root, a striated furrowed stem, and white or pinkish flowers. It produces a well-known seed used in confectionery, and from which a carminative oil is extracted and the liqueur called *kümmel* prepared. The white or true caraway is largely grown in Essex and Kent, also in Holland, Prussia, Northern Russia, and occasionally in Upper India.

CARBAZOT'IC ACID. *See* PICRIC ACID.

CAR'BERRY HILL. A piece of rising ground in Midlothian, about 7 miles to the S.E. of Edinburgh, where Mary Queen of Scots surrendered herself to the confederate nobles of the kingdom, 15th June, 1567.

CAR'BIDE. A compound of a metal with carbon, usually harder and more brittle than the metal itself. These carbides are produced at high temperatures usually by means of an electric furnace. From calcium carbide acetylene gas is prepared. *See* ACETYLENE.

CAR'BINE. *See* CARABINE.

CARBOHY'DRATE. A generic name in chemistry applied to compounds like glucose, cane-sugar, cellulose, starch, etc.

CARBOLIC ACID (phenol, phenic acid, or hydroxybenzene, C_6H_5OH). A derivative of benzene and obtained from coal-tar. The fraction boiling between 150° and 200° C. contains phenol. This is allowed to cool and then shaken with a solution of caustic soda; phenol dissolves in the caustic soda, forming sodium phenate, C_6H_5ONa, and thus is separated from the lighter hydrocarbons. The phenate is decomposed by sulphuric acid and crude carbolic oil, separated as a dark oily substance containing 40 per cent of phenol. This is then fractionally distilled between 175° and 185° C. until it crystallises at ordinary temperature. When pure, phenol is a colourless crystalline substance possessing a strong odour and a burning taste, and is soluble in water. It is usually slightly coloured and tends to become more coloured when kept, owing to oxidation of traces of impurities in it. Carbolic acid is poisonous, blisters the skin, and arrests fermentation and putrefaction, hence it is much used as a disinfectant in medicine and surgery. *Calvert's disinfecting powder* consists of fine clay with 12 to 16 per cent of phenol. "Liquefied phenol," used in medicine, is 90 per cent phenol and 10 per cent water.

CARBON (chemical symbol, C; atomic weight, 12). An element existing uncombined in three forms: charcoal or amorphous carbon, graphite or plumbago, and diamond. These are different forms of one chemical element, and are called *allotropic* modifications; they are built up of the same element, but differ in physical properties and carry different amounts of available energy. The diamond is the purest form of naturally-occurring carbon. Of the different varieties of amorphous carbon, lamp-black is the purest form; charcoal, coal, anthracite are more or less mixed with other substances. Charcoal is a black, brittle, light, inodorous substance; the crystalline form diamond is colourless and the hardest known substance, and graphite crystallises in flat plates which are soapy to the touch.

Carbon may be obtained from most organic substances, animal or vegetable, by distillation out of contact with air, when volatile substances distil off, leaving a residue of carbon. The compounds of this element are more numerous than those of all the other elements taken together, and are classified under the name *organic compounds*. With hydrogen it forms a large number of compounds called *hydrocarbons*, some of which are of great economic importance. With oxygen, carbon forms two compounds: *carbon dioxide*, if burnt in air; *carbon monoxide*, if the supply of air be limited. It is a regular constituent of all animal and vegetable tissues in combination with hydrogen, oxygen, and many other elements.

CARBONADO. *See* BORT.

CARBONA'RI (literally, "charcoal-burners"). The name of an Italian political secret society, which appears to have been formed by the Neapolitan republicans during the reign of Joachim Murat, and had for its object the expulsion of the strangers and the establishment of a democratic government. The ritual of the Carbonari was taken from the trade of the charcoal-burner. A lodge was *baracca* (a hut); a meeting was *vendita* (a sale); an important meeting *alta vendita*. There were four grades in the society; and the ceremonies of initiation were characterised by many mystic rites. The language of religion was much used to express their purposes. Christ was the lamb torn by the wolf, whom they were sworn to avenge. Clearing the wood of wolves (opposition to tyranny) became the symbolic expression of their aim. By this they are said to have meant at first only deliverance from foreign dominion; but in later times democratical and antimonarchical principles sprang up, which were discussed chiefly among the higher degrees. The order, soon after its foundation, contained from 24,000 to 30,000 members, and increased so rapidly that it spread through all Italy. In 1820, in the month of March alone, about 650,000 new members are said to have been admitted. After the suppression of the Neapolitan and Piedmontese revolution in 1821, the Carbonari, throughout Italy, were declared guilty of high treason, and punished as such by the laws. Expelled from Italy, the Carbonari began to take root in France, and Lafayette became their chief. Societies of a similar kind were formed in France, with which the Italian Carbonari amalgamated; and Paris became the head-quarters of Carbonarism. After the July revolution the Charbonnerie Démocratique was founded, based on the principles of Babeuf. The organisation took on more of a French character, and gradually alienated the sympathies of the Italian members, a number of whom dissolved connection with it, in order to form the party of "Young Italy."—BIBLIOGRAPHY: Saint-Edme, *Constitution et organisation des Carbonari*; R. M. Johnston, *Napoleonic Empire in Southern Italy, and the Rise of the Secret Societies*; B. King, *A History of Italian Unity*; A. Baron, *Les Sociétés secrètes*.

CARBON ASSIMILATION, or **PHOTO-SYNTHESIS.** The building up of organic material from atmospheric carbon dioxide which takes place in green parts of plants. This important process, which is ultimately the source of the food-supply of the entire living world, is carried out in the chloroplasts or chromatophores coloured green by chlorophyll, the energy required for breaking up the carbon dioxide and for the synthesis of sugars, etc., being derived from sunlight absorbed by this colouring matter; it involves liberation of oxygen, which can be seen escaping in bubbles from the surface of water-plants if these are brightly illuminated. The first visible product of photosynthesis is usually starch; this is easily demonstrated by exposing a green leaf, covered with a stencil plate, to sunlight for a few hours, and then applying the iodine test for starch, when only those parts to which light could gain access will be found to stain dark-purple or black.

CAR'BONATES. The salts of carbonic acid, e.g. $CaCO_3$, calcium carbonate; Na_2CO_3, sodium carbonate; $BaCO_3$, barium carbonate; $NaHCO_3$, sodium bicarbonate. Many of the carbonates are extensively used in the arts and in medicine.

CAR'BONDALE. An American city, State of Pennsylvania, about 110 miles N.N.W. of Philadelphia. It is the centre of a rich coal-field. Pop. 20,061.

CARBON DIOXIDE, or **CARBONIC ANHYDRIDE,** also incorrectly called **CARBONIC ACID** (CO_2). A colourless, poisonous heavy gas composed of carbon and oxygen. It is the final product of the complete combustion of carbon, hence it is produced when carbonaceous substances, coal, wood, etc., burn. *Choke-damp* or *after-damp* of coal-mines is carbon dioxide formed during the explosion of carbon compounds liberated from the coal-seams. Large quantities are produced during fermentation and decomposition of organic matter. Carbon dioxide is also produced during the process of respiration, expired air containing 4 to 5 per cent of carbon dioxide, so that air in crowded, badly-ventilated rooms becomes polluted with carbon dioxide. Plants, on the other hand, absorb carbon dioxide present in the atmosphere in presence of sunlight, utilise the carbon to build up their structure, and return the oxygen to the air. Carbon dioxide is found free in many volcanic regions, and the valley of the Upas, Java, is dangerous because of the presence of this gas. It is also generated wherever organic matter is decaying, and owing to its weight it tends to accumulate in caves, cellars, and underground passages where ventilation is bad.

It is also present dissolved in water in many mineral springs, and, combined with the oxides of metals, it occurs as carbonates in many minerals, e.g. combined with magnesium oxide and calcium oxide it forms whole mountain ranges of dolomite and limestone; the latter is used as a source of carbon dioxide. It is not an active poison; but air containing even 0·5 per cent has an injurious effect, larger proportions cause insensibility, and above 20 per cent causes death due to suffocation. It is soluble in water, yielding a slightly acid solution regarded as containing *carbonic acid*, H_2CO_3; this imparts to the water a pleasant acidulous taste, and aerated beverages of all kinds, beer, champagne, soda-water, and carbonated mineral waters owe their refreshing quality to its presence, for, though poisonous if inhaled, it has no such effect when swallowed. Carbon dioxide is easily liquefied and solidified, and is manufactured in large quantity for various industrial purposes. The gas is used in sugar-refining, white-lead manufacture, and in the manufacture of sodium bicarbonate. In the liquid form it is also used for aerating beverages, in some types of ice-machine, for hardening steel, for the production of extreme cold, and in certain types of fire-extinguishers.

CARBON DISULPHIDE (CS_2). A compound formed by burning carbon in sulphur vapour. It is a colourless, extremely volatile liquid, boiling at 46° C., non-miscible with water, and both the liquid and its vapour are highly inflammable. It is largely used as a solvent for sulphur, phosphorus, iodine, etc., and as a fat extractor.

CARBONIC ACID. *See* CARBON DIOXIDE.

CARBONIC OXIDE. *See* CARBON MONOXIDE.

CARBONIF'EROUS FLORA. The vegetation that flourished in the Carboniferous period, of which very rich and varied remains have come down to us, often in a marvellous state of preservation. It consists mainly of the plants which inhabited the immense and widely-distributed swamp-forests of that time, and which formed the source of coal. Among the leading types are the huge Calamites and Lepidodendra, allied to the insignificant horse-tails and club-mosses of our own times. Seed-bearing trees, such as Cordaites and the remarkable Pteridosperms—intermediate in some respects between Ferns and Gymnosperms—were also prominent, as well as genuine ferns like Botryopteris.

CARBONIF'EROUS SYSTEM. In geology, the great group of strata which lies between the Old Red Sandstone below and the Permian or Dyas formation above, named from the quantities of coal and carbonaceous shale contained in them in many areas. They include, in England, the coal-measures, millstone grit, and a lower series consisting largely of marine limestone. The coal-measures include the most productive seams of our coal-fields. Iron-ore, limestone, clay, and building-stone are also yielded abundantly by the Carboniferous strata which are found in many parts of the world, often covering large areas. (*See* COAL.) As coal consists essentially of altered vegetable matter, fossil plants are very numerous in the Carboniferous rocks. The trees include large lycopods and horse-tails, and a highly-interesting series known as Pteridosperms, which have fern-like characteristics combined with a reproductive system foreshadowing that of the flowering plants. Some conifers and cycads also occur. The animal life on land includes insects, scorpions, and amphibians, and the marine fauna furnishes numerous corals, crinoids, and brachiopods, with cephalopods prominent among the molluscs. The fish are mainly sharks and ganoids, some of the latter being preserved in an entire condition. For bibliography *see* GEOLOGY.

CARBON MONOXIDE, or **CARBONIC OXIDE** (CO). This is produced when carbon is burned in a limited supply of air or when carbon dioxide is passed over red-hot coke; hence the blue flame playing over the surface of a glowing coke or coal fire is burning carbon monoxide. It is a colourless, tasteless, odourless gas, and is extremely poisonous, as it combines with the hæmoglobin of the blood, thus causing the loss of power to absorb oxygen. Unlike carbon dioxide, it is combustible, and burns with a pale-blue flame, producing carbon dioxide. When steam is passed over incandescent carbon at 1000° C., a mixture of carbon monoxide and hydrogen is produced; the product is known as *water-gas*, and is used as a gaseous fuel. *Producer gas* is obtained by partial burning of coke in air, and is a mixture of carbon monoxide and nitrogen. Both these gases are used as a source of heat and power in industry, and owe their valuable properties to the heat produced when carbon monoxide burns. Carbon monoxide is a reducing agent on account of the readiness with which it unites with oxygen, and is used in many metallurgical processes. It is also a valuable reagent in the metallurgy of nickel.

CARBON POINTS. In electric lighting, two pieces of very hard, compact carbon, between which the electric current is broken, so that the resistance which they offer to the passage of the current produces a light of extraordinary brilliancy. *See* ELECTRIC LIGHT.

CARBON TETRACHLORIDE, CCl_4. A substance resembling chloroform in odour, and prepared by the action of chlorine on carbon disulphide. It is a colourless liquid boiling at 77° C., with a pleasant odour, non-miscible with water, and used as a solvent for many organic substances. On account of its non-inflammable nature it is used as a substitute for benzene in degreasing woollen goods, dry cleaning, etc. It has the disadvantage of attacking most metals in presence of moisture, so that extractors must be lead-lined or tinned, tin and lead being very little attacked. It is a valuable solvent for shellacs, gums, and resins, and has been used in some types of fire-extinguishers. Carbon tetrachloride is registered under the trade name *benzinoform*.

CARBORUNDUM. A compound of silicon and carbon (silicon carbide) formed by the action of carbon (graphite) on sand in an electric furnace. It is crystalline, dark and lustrous, and its hardness, between that of emery and diamond, makes it important as an abrasive material. It is worked up as grinding-wheels, hones, etc. Since its accidental production in 1891 (by Acheson in America), a natural mineral with the same composition has been discovered.

CAR'BOY. A large and somewhat globular bottle of green glass protected by an outside covering of wickerwork or other material, for carrying vitriol or other corrosive liquid.

CARBUN'CLE. A beautiful gem of a deep-red colour with a mixture of scarlet, found in the East Indies. When held up to the sun it loses its deep tinge, and becomes exactly of the colour of a burning coal. The carbuncle of the ancients is supposed to have been a garnet.

CARBUN'CLE. In surgery, an inflammation of the true skin and tissue beneath it akin to that occurring in boils. It is more extensive than the latter, and instead of one has several cores. It is associated with a bad state of general health, from which condition its danger arises, for it may threaten life by exhaustion or blood-poisoning. With regard to the local treatment, the principal thing to be done is to make a free incision into the tumour; as much of the contents as possible should then be pressed out, and a poultice applied. The patient's strength should be supported by nourishing and easily-digested food, and tonics and cordials should be administered.

CAR'BURETTED HYDROGEN. *See* METHANE.

CARBURETTER. Apparatus used

in motor-cars and gas-engines for converting petrol or other hydrocarbons into a gaseous or finely divided state to form with the air an explosive mixture.

CARCAGENTE (kȧr-kȧ-*h*en'tā). A town, Spain, province of Valencia, on the Jucar, well built, with delightful promenades and gardens. Trade in grain, fruits, and silk. Pop. 14,040.

CAR'CAJOU. A species of badger found in N. America, *Meles labradorica.*

CAR'CANET. A necklace or collar of jewels. They were manufactured in Venice in the fifteenth century.

CAR'CASS. In gunnery, an iron case, with several apertures, filled with combustible materials, which used to be discharged from a mortar, howitzer, or gun, and which was intended to set fire to buildings, ships, and wooden defences.

CARCASSONNE. Capital of the department of Aude, France, on the Aude and a branch of the Canal du Midi, 53 miles S. of Toulouse. It consists of an old and a new town, which communicate by a bridge spanning the river. The old town is surrounded by a double wall, part of it so ancient as to be attributed to the Visigoths. The new town is regularly built, and has many handsome modern houses. The staple manufacture is woollen cloth. Pop. 34,921.

CARD. An instrument for combing, opening, and breaking wool, flax, etc., freeing it from the coarser parts and from extraneous matter. It is made by inserting bent teeth of wire in a thick piece of leather, and nailing this to a piece of oblong board to which a handle is attached. But wool and cotton are now generally carded in mills by teeth fixed on a wheel moved by machinery. The word is derived through the Fr. *carde*, a teasel, from Lat. *carduus*, a thistle, teasels having been used for cards.

CARD. An oblong piece of thick paper or pasteboard prepared for various purposes. (1) A piece of cardboard with one's name written or printed on it, used in visiting, and generally for indicating the name of the person presenting it. (2) A piece of cardboard on which are printed certain coloured devices or figures, forming one of a *pack*, and used in playing games. *See* CARDS, PLAYING.

CARDAMINE (kar - da - mī ' nē). Called Lady's Smock, a genus of plants, nat. ord. Cruciferæ. *See* CUCKOO-FLOWER.

CAR'DAMOMS. The aromatic capsules of different species of plants of the nat. ord. Scitamineæ (gingers), employed in medicine as well as an ingredient in sauces and curries. The true Cardamom is indigenous to Western and Southern India, and is cultivated in places from 500 to 5000 feet in altitude in Kanara, Mysore, Coorg, Ceylon, Java, etc. The cardamoms known in the shops are the large, produced by *Amōmum angustifolium*, a Madagascar plant; the middle-sized and the small, both the produce of *A. Cardamōmum*, a native of Sumatra and other Eastern islands. Those recognised in the British pharmacopœia, called *true* or *officinal cardamoms* and known in commerce as *Malabar cardamoms*, are the produce of *Elettaria Cardamōmum*, a native of the mountains of Malabar and Canara. Grain of Paradise is the fruit of *A. grana-paradisi.*

CARDAN, or CARDA'NO, Geronimo (*Hieronymus Cardānus*). Italian philosopher, physician, and mathematician, born in 1501 at Pavia, died about 1576. He held successively the chairs of mathematics or medicine at Pavia, Milan, and Bologna, and ultimately went to Rome. Here he was received into the medical college, and was allowed a pension by the Pope. He acquired extraordinary reputation as a physician, and was invited to Scotland to attend Archbishop Hamilton of St. Andrews, who had been sick for ten years, and who was restored to health by his prescriptions. He made some important discoveries in algebra, studied astrology, pretended to a gift of prophecy, and wrote a large number of books. His chief works are: *De Vita Propria*, an account of himself; *Ars Magna*, a treatise on Algebra; *De Rerum Varietate*; and *De Rerum Subtilitate.*

CARD'BOARD. A kind of stiff paper or pasteboard for cards, etc., usually made by sticking together several sheets of paper.

CARDE'NAS. A seaport on the north coast of Cuba, 103 miles E. of Havana, with which it is connected by rail. One of the principal commercial centres of the island; chief exports, sugar, molasses, and coffee. Pop. 32,513.

CARDI, Ludovico. Surnamed *Civoli* or *Cigoli*. Italian painter and architect, born in 1559, died 1631. He studied painting, and afterwards formed his style on the works of Andrea del Sarto, Correggio, and Baroccio. His architectural works possess considerable merit. Among his pictures are: *The Conversion of St. Paul* at Rome, *The Martyrdom of Stephen*, *The Trinity*, *Mary Magdalene*, and *Ecce Homo* at Florence. He painted many altar-pieces, excelled to some degree as an engraver, and wrote a treatise on perspective.

CAR'DIFF ("the city on the *Taff*"). A city, also a county and parliamentary borough and seaport, the county town of Glamorganshire, Wales, situated at the mouth of the Taff on the estuary of the Severn. It is a rapidly increasing town, and the principal outlet for the mineral produce and manufactures of South Wales. Iron shipbuilding is carried on, and there are iron and other works on a large scale. Among the chief buildings are the county buildings, town hall, infirmary, university college (for S. Wales and Monmouthshire), law courts, free library, and a museum. The docks are extensive and well constructed (total area about 200 acres). As regards tonnage entered and cleared, Cardiff is now the third port in the United Kingdom; in respect of coal exported it is the first, more than 11,200,000 tons being sent abroad in 1918.

There is here a castle which dates from 1080. It is the property of the Marquess of Bute, and has been modernised and part of it converted into a residence. The development of Cardiff has been greatly furthered by those in charge of the Bute property, which embraces most of the town. Since 1918 the town returns three members to the House of Commons. Since 1905 the Mayor is called Lord Mayor. Pop. in 1861, 32,954; in 1911, 182,280; in 1921, 200,262; in 1931, 223,648.

CAR'DIGAN. The county town of Cardiganshire, South Wales, on the River Teifi, about 3 miles from its mouth in Cardigan Bay. Vessels of light tonnage come up to the wharves. The ruins of Cardigan Castle, famous in Welsh history, are in the vicinity. The salmon-fishery is extensively carried on. Previous to 1885 it was one of a group of parliamentary boroughs. Pop. (1931), 3309.

CARDIGAN, COUNTY OF. Has an area of 443,189 acres, of which two-thirds is under crops or pasture. The surface of the northern and eastern parts is mountainous, but interspersed with fertile valleys; while the southern and western districts are more level and produce abundance of corn. The county has an extensive coastline, and many of the male population are sailors and fishermen. It is rich in metalliferous lodes, particularly lead. The principal town is Aberystwyth. The county returns one member to Parliament. Pop. (1931), 55,164.

CARDIGAN BAY. A large open expanse of sea on the west coast of Wales, having Cardiganshire on the east and Carnarvon on the north.

CARDIIDÆ. A family of bivalve molluscs, including the cockles and their allies.

CAR'DINAL. An ecclesiastical prince and the highest dignitary in the Roman Catholic Church, who has a voice in the conclave at the election of a Pope, who is chosen by the cardinals. The cardinals are appointed by the Pope, and are divided into three classes or orders, comprising six bishops, fifty priests, and fourteen deacons, making seventy at most. There are generally, however, from ten to fifteen vacancies, and in 1914 there were but fifty-four cardinals. These constitute the Sacred College and compose the Pope's council.

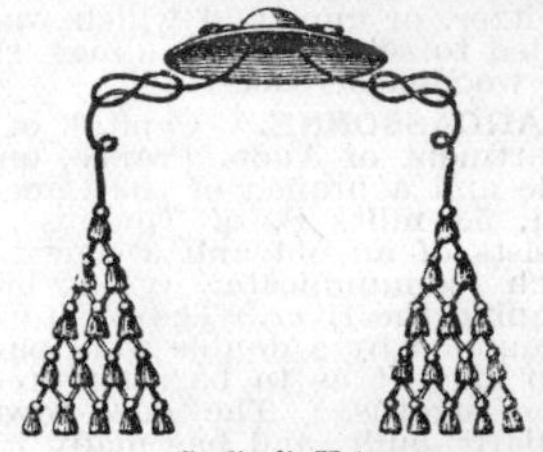

Cardinal's Hat

Originally they were subordinate in rank to bishops; but they now have the precedence. The chief symbol of the dignity of cardinal is a low-crowned, broad-brimmed red hat, with two cords depending from it, one from either side, each having fifteen tassels at its extremity. This hat is always presented by the Pope in person, and is then laid aside until the funeral obsequies, when it is placed on the catafalque of the cardinal. Other insignia are a red biretta, a scarlet cassock, a sapphire ring, etc. —BIBLIOGRAPHY: Aubéry, *Histoire générale des Cardinaux*; Du Peyrat, *Traité de l'origine des Cardinaux*; Muratori, *De Cardinalium Institutione*, in *Antiquitates Italicæ*.

CARDINAL BIRD (*Cardinālis virginiānus*). A North American bird of the finch family, with a fine red plumage, and a crest on the head. Its song resembles that of the nightingale, hence one of its common names, *Virginian Nightingale*. In size it is about equal to the starling. Called also *Scarlet Grosbeak* or *Cardinal Grosbeak* and *Redbird*.

CARDINAL-FLOWER. The name commonly given to *Lobēlia cardinālis*, because of its large, very showy, and intensely red flowers;

it is a native of North America, but is much cultivated in gardens in Britain.

CARDINAL POINTS. The four chief points of the horizon, as marked on the mariner's compass N., S., E., W. They are the four intersections of the horizon with the meridian and the prime vertical circle.

CARDING. The process wool, cotton, flax, etc., undergo previous to spinning, to lay the fibres all in one direction, and remove all foreign substances. *See* CARD.

CAR'DIOGRAPH. An instrument which, when applied to the chest, produces a waved line traced on a revolving cylinder, showing the character of the heart's beats. It is used for medical and physiological purposes, the tracing produced being called a *cardiogram.*

CARDI'TIS. Inflammation of the heart substance. Inflammation of the lining membrane is *endocarditis,* of the external membrane *pericarditis.*

CARDO'NA. A Spanish town, province of Barcelona. In its vicinity is a hill of rock-salt 500 feet high, which has a dazzling appearance in the sunlight. Pop. 4200.

CARDOON'. The *Cynăra Carduncŭlus,* a perennial plant belonging to the same genus as the artichoke, and somewhat resembling it. It is a native of the countries bordering the Mediterranean. The thick fleshy stalks and ribs of its leaves are blanched and eaten in Spain and France as an esculent vegetable. The flowers have the property of curdling milk.

CARDS, PLAYING. A modern pack of playing cards numbers fifty-two, and consists of four *suits,* two red (hearts and diamonds) and two black (spades and clubs), each suit comprising thirteen cards—three picture-cards (*court*-cards), the king, queen, and knave; and ten other cards numbered from one, the ace, to ten, according to the pips or marks belonging to the respective suits printed on them. They are of Eastern origin, and there is evidence that they were in use in Egypt. They were known in Europe in the fourteenth century, but were not commonly used until the beginning of the fifteenth. The manufacture of playing cards, from the enormous numbers of them used, is now one of some importance, and they are produced in a rather artistic and effective style, the backs often being very ornamental. In Britain since 1862 there has been a Government duty of 3*d.* on each pack. The import duty levied upon one dozen packs was 3*s.* 9*d.*, according to the tariff in operation in 1920.—BIBLIOGRAPHY: W. A. Chatto, *Facts and Speculations on the Origin and History of Playing Cards*; E. S. Taylor, *History of Playing Cards*; Allemagne, *Les Cartes à Jouer du XIV au XX Siècle*; E. Lanes, *Nouveau Manuel Complet des Jeux des Cartes.*

CARDUCCI, Giosue. Italian poet, born 1835, died 1907. He is not only the greatest Italian lyric poet of the nineteenth century, but represents the highest ideals of the new Italian spirit, standing not only for sincerity in art, but also for free thought and individualism under a just government. Among his works are: *Juvenilia* (1850-60), *Levia Gravia* (1860-71), *Giambi ed epodi* (1867-79), *Odi barbari* and *Rime e ritmi* (1880-1900).

CAR'DUUS. *See* THISTLE.

CARDWELL, Edward, Viscount Cardwell. English politician, son of a Liverpool merchant, born 1813, died 1886. He entered Parliament in 1842, became a follower of Peel, and was Secretary to the Treasury from 1845 to 1846. Under Lord Aberdeen he became President of the Board of Trade in 1853, and was the chief agent in carrying the great Merchant Shipping Act of 1854. In Palmerston's Cabinet of 1859 he became Secretary for Ireland, and under Palmerston and Russell he was Colonial Secretary from 1864 to 1866. As War Secretary under Gladstone, from 1868 to 1874, he introduced great reforms in the army, including the short service and reserve system, and abolition of the purchase of commissions. He was created a peer in 1874, and henceforth took no great part in public affairs. He was one of the four editors of the *Peel Memoirs.*

CAREENING. A nautical term for heaving or bringing a ship to lie on one side for the purpose of caulking, repairing, cleansing, paying with pitch, or the like.

CA'RET (Lat., "there is something wanting"). In writing, a mark made thus, ʌ, which shows that something, omitted in the line, is interlined above or inserted in the margin, and should be read in that place.

CAREW (kā'ri), **Thomas.** An English poet, born of a Gloucestershire family in 1595 or 1598, died 1639 or 1645. Educated at Oxford, he wrote much polished verse, and was the subject of much eulogy by Ben Jonson, Davenant, and other writers of the period. His works are masques, lyrics, and sonnets, and were first printed in 1640. Carew is coupled with Waller as a reformer of English metre.

CA'REX. A large genus of plants, nat. ord. Cyperaceæ; the sedges. They are perennial grass-like herbs, with unisexual flowers aggregated in spikelets. There are more than a thousand species distributed all over the world, about sixty being indigenous to Britain. *C. arenaria*, as a sand-binder, is second only to Marram grass. Sedges may be distinguished at sight from grasses by their three-sided stems and three-ranked leaves.

CA'REY, Henry. A composer, dramatist, and poet, born at London in 1696, a natural son of George Saville, Marquess of Halifax. He composed the words and music of many popular songs, including *Sally in Our Alley* and *God Save the King*. He also wrote farces and other works. He is said to have committed suicide, 1743.

CAREY, Henry Charles. American economist, born in Philadelphia 1793, died 1879. He was the eldest son of Matthew Carey, and in 1814 became a partner in his father's bookselling and publishing firm, where he continued until 1836. In that year he published an essay on the Rate of Wages, which he afterwards expanded into *Principles of Political Economy*. His other important works are: *The Credit System*; *The Past, the Present, and the Future*; *The Principles of Social Science*; *Review of the Decade 1857-67*; *The Unity of Law*. Originally a free-trader, he became an advocate for protection; held that the growth of population was self-regulating; and was opposed to the theories of Ricardo and others on the law of diminished returns from the soil and on rent. He was also opposed to any arrangement on the subject of international copyright.

CAREY, William, D.D. An English Oriental scholar and Christian missionary, born in 1761, died at Serampore 1834. He was early apprenticed to a shoemaker, but his natural turn for languages, and his zeal for the spread of the gospel, were too strong to be overcome. With the little assistance he could procure he acquired Latin, Greek, and Hebrew, and likewise studied theology. In 1786 he became pastor of a Baptist congregation at Moulton, and in 1787 was appointed to a similar situation in Leicester. In 1793 he sailed for the East Indies as a Baptist missionary, and in 1800, in conjunction with Marshman, Ward, and others, he founded the missionary college at Serampore. Here he had a printing-press, and issued various translations of the Scriptures. His first work was a *Bengali Grammar*. It was followed by the *Hitopadesha*, in the Mahratta tongue, a *Grammar of the Telinga and Carnatic*, and a *Bengali Lexicon*. Under his direction the mission issued 200,000 Bibles, or portions thereof, in about forty Oriental languages or dialects. He was professor of Sanskrit, Mahratta, and Bengali in Calcutta from 1800 to 1830.—His son, **Felix Carey**, born in 1786, died 1822, was the author of a *Burmese Grammar*, and translated several English works into Bengali, Sanskrit, and Burmese.

CARGILL (-gil'), **Donald.** A Scottish covenanting preacher, born about 1610, died 1681. He studied at Aberdeen, and became minister of the Barony Church in Glasgow in 1650. In 1679 he took part in the battle of Bothwell Bridge, where he was wounded. He had a principal hand in the Queensferry and Sanquhar Declarations. For formally excommunicating Charles II., the Duke of York, and others, he was executed at Edinburgh for high treason.

CARGO. The goods or merchandise carried by a trading vessel from one place to another. When part of the cargo is on deck, it is called the *deck cargo*, as distinguished from the *inboard cargo*.

CARHAM. A village in Northumberland, situated on the Tweed, 19 miles from Berwick. In 1018 the Scots, under Malcolm II., defeated the English here.

CA'RIA. An ancient country, forming the south-western corner of Asia Minor, and partly settled in early times by Greek colonists chiefly of the Dorian race. It was included in the dominions of Crœsus, King of Lydia, and on his overthrow by Cyrus was transferred to the Persian monarchy, under whose protection a dynasty of Carian princes was established. About 129 B.C. it was incorporated in the Roman province of Asia. Cnidus, Halicarnassus, and Miletus were among the chief towns.

CARIA'CO. A seaport town, Venezuela, situated to the east of the Gulf of Cariaco, near the mouth of a river of the same name. Pop. 7000. The Gulf of Cariaco is 38 miles long, from 5 to 10 broad, from 80 to 100 fathoms deep, surrounded by lofty mountains.

CAR'IACOU. The Virginian deer (*Cervus virginiānus*), found in all parts of North America up to 43° N. lat. It is smaller than the common stag, and its colour varies with the season. In spring it is reddish-brown, in autumn slaty-blue, and in winter dull-brown.

CARIBBE'AN SEA. That portion of the North Atlantic Ocean lying between the coasts of Central and South America, and the West India Islands. It communicates with the Gulf of Mexico by the Yucatan Channel.

CAR'IBBEES, or **LESSER ANTILLES.** Usually divided into the Windward and Leeward Islands, a section of the West India Islands.

CARIBOU. The name of two American species of reindeer, sometimes regarded as specifically identical with the Old World reindeer. They rank in size next to the moose and elk. They have never been brought under the sway of man, but

Caribou

are a great object of chase for the sake of their flesh and skins. The woodland caribou (*Rangifer caribou*) most nearly resembles the common reindeer. It is found over considerable tracts of Canada, as also in Newfoundland and Labrador, and is migratory in its habits. The Barren Ground caribou (*Rangifer grœnlandicus*) is much smaller, but has larger horns. It inhabits the Barren Grounds north-west of Hudson Bay, and also extends into Greenland. It is migratory, going north to the Arctic Ocean in summer, and returning in autumn.

CAR'IBS. The original inhabitants of the W. India Islands, and, when Europeans became acquainted with America, also found in certain portions of Central America and the north of South America. At present only a few remain on Trinidad, Dominica, and St. Vincent. Owing to intermarriage with the negroes, some of them are distinguished as Black Caribs.

CAR'ICATURE (It. *caricatura*, from *caricare*, to load, to overcharge). A representation of the qualities and peculiarities of an object, but in such a way that beauties are concealed and peculiarities or defects exaggerated, so as to make the person or thing ridiculous, while a general likeness is retained. Though a degenerate form of art, it is one of the oldest. Egyptian art has numerous specimens of caricature, and it has an important place in Greek and Roman art. It flourished in every European nation during the Middle Ages, and in the present day it is the chief feature in the so-called comic papers. The chief masters of caricature in Britain are Hogarth, Gillray, Rowlandson, Bunbury, John Doyle (" H.B."), Leech, Richard Doyle, Cruickshank, Tenniel, etc. *Punch* and *Vanity Fair* contain some of the best examples of caricature in contemporary British art. Among more recent artists mention should be made of Harry Furniss and Sir F. C. Gould, both of whom died in 1925. Max Beerbohm, though a clever and witty writer, is perhaps more famous as a caricaturist. His portraits of celebrities of all kinds are extraordinarily lifelike, while remaining caricatures, and in some cases the legends are the perfection of subtle irony.

" Poy," " Strube," Low, and other cartoonists of the British and foreign press are also masters of caricature.—BIBLIOGRAPHY: Champfleury (Jules Fleury), *Histoire générale de la Caricature*; Thomas Wright, *History of Caricature and Grotesque in Literature and Art*; Graham Everitt, *English Caricaturists and Graphic Humorists of the 19th Century*; T. Gaultier, *Le Rire et la Caricature*.

CA'RIES (kā'ri-ēz; Lat., " rottenness "). A disease of bone analogous to ulceration in soft tissues. The bone breaks down, or may be said to melt down into unhealthy matter, which works its way to the surface and bursts. Excision of the carious portion of the bone is often effected with good results, but the disease often results in death. *Caries of the teeth* is decay of the enamel, that extends into the dentine or body of the tooth.

CARIGNANO (kȧ-rē-nyä'nō). A town of Italy, 11 miles S. of Turin, left bank of the Po. From this town is named a branch of the House of Savoy. Pop. 7170.

CAR'ILLON. A set of bells in a tower or belfry on which tunes may be played. It differs from chimes as the bells are fixed instead of swinging and are struck on the outside by hammers.

CARIMA'TA. An island about 50 miles from the coast of Borneo. It is about 10 miles long, and rises to a height of 2000 feet. It is visited by Malays, who collect tortoise-shell, trepang, and edible birds' nests.

CARINA'RIA. A genus of marine snails belonging to the ord. Heteropoda, and possessing a small conical glassy shell by which the most important organs are protected. The animal itself is about 2 inches long, and lives in the open sea, swimming upside down by means of a laterally flattened fin or foot. Like many other forms of like habit, it is so transparent that the internal organs are easily seen with a microscope.

CARINA'TÆ (from Lat. *carīna*, a keel). Huxley's second order of the class Aves or birds, the other two being Saururæ and Ratitæ. The Carinatæ include all the living flying birds, that is, all existing birds except those of the ostrich kind, and are characterised by the fact that the sternum or breastbone is furnished with a prominent median ridge or keel, whence the name. The keel is for the attachment of the well-developed muscles of flight which make up the flesh of the breast.

CARI'NI. A town of Sicily, 11 miles W.N.W. of Palermo, beautifully situated on a river of the same name. Pop. 14,300.

CARINTH'IA (Ger. *Kärnthen*). Formerly a western duchy or province of Austria, on the borders of Italy; area, 3688 sq. miles. It is extremely mountainous, generally sterile, and very thinly populated. The principal river is the Drave. The iron, lead, and calamine mines are the main sources of its wealth, though there are several manufactories of woollens, cottons, silk stuffs, etc., most of which are in Klagenfurt, the capital. Pop. 370,817. By the Peace Treaty of 1919 Carinthia remained Austrian, except the south-eastern corner.

CAR'ISBROOKE. A village near the centre of the Isle of Wight, and overlooked by the ruins of its ancient castle, where Charles I. was imprisoned for thirteen months previous to his trial and execution.

CARIS'SIMI, Giovanni Giacomo. An Italian musical composer, born about 1604, died at Rome about 1674. He wrote many oratorios, cantatas, and motets, and occupies an important place in the history of music.

CAR'JACOU. *See* CARIACOU.

CARLEN', Emilie. Swedish novelist, born in 1807, died in 1892. She was married to Johan Gabriel Carlen (1814-75), a lawyer and miscellaneous writer. Her graphic pictures of every-day life have secured her a place among the great novelists of the day. Many of her novels have been translated into Danish, French, German, and English. *Gustav Lindorm*, *The Rose of Tistelön*, and *The Maiden's Tower* are among them.

CARLETON, William. Irish novelist, born in 1794 at Prillisk, in the county of Tyrone, died at Sandford, near Dublin, 1869. His education commenced at a hedge-school, and terminated with two years' training in an academy kept by a relation, a priest, at Glasslough. Thence he went to Dublin to try his fortune in the walks of literature. There, in 1830-2, were published his *Traits and Stories of the Irish Peasantry*. Among his other publications are: *Fardorougha, the Miser*; *The Misfortunes of Barney Branagan*; *Valentine M'Clutchy*; *The Black Prophet*; *The Tithe Proctor*; *Willy Reilly*; and *The Evil Eye*; this last novel appearing in 1860. He enjoyed a Government allowance of £200 per annum several years before his death.

CAR'LINE-THISTLE (*Carlīna vulgāris*). A thistle common in dry fields and pastures throughout Britain and the European continent, about a foot in height, with prickly, somewhat hoary leaves, and a purple head of flowers with a straw-coloured involucre, the inner bracts of which spread outwards in dry and fold inwards in damp weather.

CARLISLE (kär-līl'). A parliamentary and municipal borough of England, county town of Cumberland. It stands at the confluence of the Eden, Caldew, and Petteril, and has been identified with the *Luguvallum* of Antoninus from which was derived the British name *Caer-Luel*. Sacked by the Danes, it was rebuilt by William Rufus. It was held by the Scots during their tenure of Cumberland, and the Church of St. Mary's was founded by David I., who died here. During the border wars Carlisle underwent many sieges. It surrendered to Charles Edward in 1745. It is a bishop's see. The cathedral, begun in the reign of William Rufus, was partly destroyed by Cromwell in 1648. In the various improvements of the city all the walls, gates, and fortifications have been removed, except a portion of the west wall, and the castle.

The town is somewhat irregularly built, but its principal streets are spacious and well paved. The municipal buildings are the town hall and guildhall. The courts of justice and the county jail were erected after a design by Smirke, at a cost exceeding £100,000. It has also an agricultural college. Carlisle is the seat of various manufactures, of which cotton is the principal. It was formerly connected by canal with Port-Carlisle, on the Solway Firth, a distance of about 11 miles; but this canal is replaced by a railway to Port-Carlisle, which is extended to Silloth, where an extensive dock has been constructed. Communicating in this way with the sea, Carlisle is still classed as a port. The Citadel Station is the terminus of seven different lines of railway. The city sends one member to Parliament. Pop. (1931), 57,107.

CARLISLE. A town, United States, in Pennsylvania, 114 miles W. of Philadelphia. Dickinson Methodist College, which was founded in 1783, is there. Pop. 12,497.

CAR'LISTS. The name given to the followers of Don Carlos of Bourbon and his descendants. *See* CARLOS DE BOURBON.

CARLOS', Don, Prince of Asturias. Son of Philip II., born 1545, died 1568. He was deformed in person, of a violent and vindictive disposition, and though originally declared heir to the throne, he was afterwards passed over in favour of his cousins Rodolph and Ernest. In consequence of this he is supposed to have entered into a plot against the king and the Duke of Alva. Tried on the charge of conspiring against the life of the king, he was found guilty, and imprisoned, waiting sentence from the king. He died shortly after, and King Philip's enemies asserted that he had been killed at the king's own orders, but modern authorities are now agreed that he died as a result of his own maniacal practices. The story of Don Carlos has furnished the subject of several tragedies, viz. by Thomas Otway (English), Schiller (German), and Alfieri (Italian).—BIBLIOGRAPHY: M. Hume, *The Spanish People*; Dr. A. S. Rappoport, *Mad Majesties* (1913, complete bibliography).

CARLOS DE BOURBON, Don Maria Isidor. The second son of Charles IV. of Spain and brother of Ferdinand VII., born 1788, died 1855. He was heir presumptive to the throne until the birth of Maria Isabella in 1830. On the death of his brother he claimed the throne as legitimate king of Spain, and was recognised as such by a considerable party, who excited a civil war in his favour, and thenceforward were designated by the title of *Carlists*. After several years' fighting, he found himself obliged in 1839 to take shelter in France. In the meantime he and his descendants had been formally excluded from the succession by a vote of the Cortes in 1836. In 1845 he resigned his claims in favour of his eldest son, and in 1847 was permitted to take up his abode in Trieste, where he died. His eldest son, Don Carlos (1818-61), married Maria Carolina Ferdinanda, a sister of Ferdinand II., King of Naples. On more than one occasion he endeavoured to excite an insurrection in his favour in his native country, but these attempts were always frustrated. His nephew, Don Carlos, Duke of Madrid, born 1848, died 1909, was the next representative of the Carlists. He married the sister of the Count of Chambord. In 1873 he instigated a rising in the north of Spain, and continued the struggle till after Alfonso XII. came to the throne, when he was defeated and withdrew. In 1876 he went to France, but was expelled in 1881 for supporting the claims of the Count of Chambord to the French throne. A short time before his death he abdicated in favour of his son, Don Jaime de Bourbon (born in 1870), who is the present representative of the Carlists.—Cf. H. Butler Clarke, *Modern Spain*.

CARLOS I., King of Portugal. Son of Luiz I., born 28th Sept., 1863. He ascended the throne on the death of his father on 19th Oct., 1889, and reigned peacefully for a number of years. He translated Shakespeare into Portuguese, and encouraged literature and art. Owing, however, to the policy of his minister, Franco, whom he appointed dictator in 1907, a revolution broke out in Portugal. On the 1st Feb., 1908, the king and his eldest son, Luiz, were both assassinated in Lisbon, and Manoel, the only surviving son of King Carlos, ascended the throne of Portugal.

CARLOVIN'GIANS. The second dynasty of the French or Frankish kings, which supplanted the Merovingians, deriving the name from Charles Martel or his grandson Charlemagne (that is, Karl or Charles the Great). Charles Martel (715-741) and his son Pepin (741-768) were succeeded by Charlemagne and his brother Carloman (768-771). Charlemagne became sole king in 771, and was succeeded in the Empire of the West by his son Louis le Debonnaire (814). He divided his empire among his sons, and at his death (840) his son Charles the Bald became King of France. He died in 877, and was succeeded by a number of feeble princes. The dynasty came to an end with Louis V., who died in 987. —BIBLIOGRAPHY: Gerard and Warkönig, *Histoire des Carolingiens*; F. Lot, *Les Derniers Carolingiens.*

CAR'LOW. A county of Leinster, Irish Free State, surrounded by Kildare, Wicklow, Wexford, Kilkenny, and Leix (Queen's County). Area, 346 sq. miles, or 221,485 acres. The chief rivers are the Slaney and Barrow. From the remarkable fertility of its soil it is altogether an agricultural county, producing a great deal of butter, corn, flour, and other agricultural produce for exportation. The population was shown by the 1926 census to be 34,504.—**Carlow,** the county town, is on the left bank of the Barrow, 34 miles S.W. of Dublin. It is the principal mart for the agricultural produce of the surrounding country, and has flour-mills. There is a Roman Catholic cathedral and divinity college. On a rising ground stand the ruins of the ancient castle of Carlow, still presenting an imposing appearance. Pop. (1926), 7175.

CARLOWITZ (kår'lo-vits). A town of Yugoslavia on the Danube, 7 miles S.E. of Peterwardein; the centre of a famous wine-growing district. A peace was concluded here in 1699 between Austria, Russia, and Poland, and the Turks. Pop. 5800.

CARLSBAD (kårls'bát; "Charles's Bath"), or **KARLOVY VARY.** A town now belonging to Czechoslovakia, in Bohemia, famous for its hot mineral springs, and much frequented by visitors from all parts of the world. Its waters are useful in diabetes, gout, and biliary diseases. Permanent pop. about 24,029.

CARLS'BURG ("Charles's Castle"), or **ALBA JULIA.** A town and fortress of Transylvania, Rumania, 33 miles N.W. of Hermannstadt, with a fine Roman Catholic cathedral. Pop. 11,616.

CARLSCRO'NA ("Charles's Crown"), or **KARLSKRONA.** A fortified seaport at the southern extremity of Sweden, on the Baltic, capital of the län or province of Blekinge or Carlscrona. It stands on several rocky islets connected with one another and with the mainland by bridges. It is the chief Swedish naval station, the harbour being safe and spacious, with fine dock, shipyards, arsenal, etc. It has a considerable export trade in timber, tar, potash, and tallow. The town was founded by Charles XI. in 1680. Pop. 25,492.

CARLSHAMN (kårls'håm; "Charles's Haven"). A seaport town, Sweden, 27 miles W. of Carlscrona, exporting timber and articles of timber. Pop. 7120.

CARLSRUHE (kärls'rö; "Charles's Rest"). The capital of the late Grand-duchy of Baden, 3 miles from the Rhine, laid out in 1715. The fine castle of the former grand-duke stands as a centre, and from this point a number of streets radiate at regular distances, thus forming a kind of fan. There are many fine buildings. The former Grand-ducal library contains 100,000 vols.; there are also a large public library, several valuable museums and art collections, a botanic garden, polytechnic school, etc. The industries are active and varied. Pop. 148,043.

CARL'STAD. A town, Sweden, on an island in Lake Wener, connected with the mainland by two bridges. Pop. 20,911.

CARLSTADT (kårl'ståt), or **ANDREAS RUDOLF BODENSTEIN.** German reformer, born 1480, died 1541. He was appointed professor of theology at Wittenberg in 1513. About 1517 he became one of Luther's warmest supporters. He was excommunicated by the bull against Luther, and was the first to appeal from the Pope to a general council. Whilst Luther was at the Wartburg, Carlstadt incited the people and students to destroy the altars and the images of the saints, greatly to the displeasure of Luther. In 1524 he declared himself publicly the opponent of Luther, and commenced the controversy respecting the sacrament, denying the bodily presence of Christ in the sacramental elements. This controversy ended in the separation of the Calvinists and Lutherans. After many misfortunes, he settled as vicar and professor of theology at Basel, where he died.

CARLTON. A town and urban district of England, 3 miles northeast of Nottingham, with manufactures of lace and hosiery. Pop. (1931), 22,336.

CARLTON CLUB. A famous political club in Pall Mall, London, the recognised head-quarters of the Conservative party. It was founded by the Duke of Wellington in 1832, and held its first meeting in Charles Street, St. James's; removed to Carlton Gardens in 1832; built a club-house in Pall Mall, 1836; and the present house in 1854. It has about 2000 members.

CARLTON PLACE. A town of Canada, province of Ontario, about 30 miles south-west of Ottawa, on a tributary of that river called the Mississippi (which here forms a small lake), and at an important railway junction; with saw-mills, railway and other workshops. Pop. 4059.

CARLUDOVICA. A genus of palm-like monocotyledons, natives of tropical America. Genuine Panama hats are made from the dried and bleached leaves of *C. palmata*.

CARLUKE (kår-lök′). A town of Scotland, in Lanarkshire, 18 miles south-east of Glasgow, and 4½ miles north-west of Lanark, in a populous district in which coal and iron are worked. Pop. (parish, 1931), 10,507.

CARLYLE (kår-līl′), **Alexander, D.D.** Generally known as "Jupiter" Carlyle, a Scottish Presbyterian minister, born in Dumfriesshire 1722, died at Inveresk 1805. He was one of the leaders of the Moderate party in the Church. He was present at the Porteous riots, served as a volunteer in the '45 rebellion, and was present at the battle of Prestonpans. He was intimate with all the most eminent Scotsmen of the day, and got into trouble with the presbytery for assisting at the production of Home's *Douglas*. In his old age he wrote an *Autobiography*, which was not published till 1860. It is a singularly interesting production, both from the vigour and sprightliness of its style and the pictures which it presents of Scottish society in the eighteenth century.

CARLYLE, Thomas. British essayist, historian, and philosopher, born 4th Dec., 1795, at Ecclefechan, Dumfriesshire, died at Chelsea, 5th Feb., 1881. He was the eldest son of James Carlyle, a mason, afterwards a farmer, and was intended for the Church, with which object he was carefully educated at the parish school and afterwards at the burgh school of Annan. In his fifteenth year (in 1810) he was sent to the University of Edinburgh, where he developed a strong taste for mathematics. Having renounced the idea of becoming a minister, after finishing his curriculum (in 1814) he became a teacher for about four years, first at Annan, afterwards at Kirkcaldy. In 1818 he removed to Edinburgh, where he supported himself by literary work, devoted much time to the study of German, and went through a varied and extensive course of reading in history, poetry, romance, and other fields. His first literary productions were short biographies and other articles for the *Edinburgh Encyclopædia*. His career as an author may be said to have begun with the issue in monthly portions of his *Life of Schiller* in the *London Magazine*, in 1823, this work being enlarged and published separately in 1825. In 1824 he published a translation of Legendre's *Geometry*, with an essay on proportion by himself prefixed. The same year appeared his translation of Goethe's *Wilhelm Meister's Apprenticeship*. He was next engaged in translating specimens of

Thomas Carlyle

the German romance writers, published in 4 vols. in 1827.

In 1826 he married Miss Jane Baillie Welsh, daughter of a doctor at Haddington, and a lineal descendant of John Knox. After his marriage he resided for a time in Edinburgh, and then withdrew to Craigenputtock, a farm in Dumfriesshire belonging to his wife, about 15 miles from the town of Dumfries. Here he wrote a number of critical and biographical articles for various periodicals; and here was written *Sartor Resartus*. The writing of *Sartor Resartus* seems to have been finished in 1831, but the publishers were shy of it, and it was not given to the public till 1833-4, through the medium of *Fraser's Magazine*. The publication of *Sartor Resartus* soon made Carlyle famous, and on his removal to London early in 1834 he became a prominent member of a brilliant literary circle embracing John Stuart Mill, Leigh

Hunt, John Sterling, Julius Charles and Augustus William Hare, F. D. Maurice, and others. He fixed his abode at Cheyne Row, Chelsea, where his life henceforth was mainly spent. His next work of importance was *The French Revolution*, published in 1837. About this time, and in one or two subsequent years, he delivered several series of lectures, the most important of these, *On Heroes and Hero-worship*, being published in 1840. *Chartism*, published in 1839, and *Past and Present*, in 1843, were small works bearing more or less on the affairs of the time. In 1845 appeared his *Oliver Cromwell's Letters and Speeches, with Elucidations*, a work of great research, and brilliantly successful in vindicating the character of the great Protector. In 1850 came out his *Latter-day Pamphlets*. This work was very repulsive to many from the exaggeration of its language, and its advocacy of harsh and coercive measures. He next wrote a life of his friend John Sterling, published in 1851, and regarded as a finished and artistic performance. The largest and most laborious work of his life, *The History of Friedrich II. of Prussia, called Frederick the Great*, next appeared, the first two volumes in 1858, the second two in 1862, and the last two in 1865, and after this time little came from his pen.

In 1866, having been elected Lord Rector of Edinburgh University, he delivered an installation address to the students on the Choice of Books. While still in Scotland the sad news reached him that his wife had died suddenly in London. This was a severe blow to Carlyle. Mrs. Carlyle, besides being a woman of exceptional intellect, was a most devoted and affectionate wife. From this time his productions were mostly articles or letters on topics of the day, including *Shooting Niagara; and After?* in which he gave vent to his serious misgivings as to the result of the Reform Bill of 1867. An unimportant historical sketch, *The Early Kings of Norway*, appeared in 1874, but was written long before. Towards the end of his life he was offered a Government pension and the Grand Cross of the Bath, but declined both. He left the estate of Craigenputtock to the University of Edinburgh, settling that the income from it should form ten bursaries to be annually competed for—five for proficiency in mathematics and five for classics (including English).

He had appointed James Anthony Froude his literary executor, who, in conformity with his trust, published *Reminiscences of Thomas Carlyle* (1881); *Thomas Carlyle: the First Forty Years of his Life* (1882); *Letters of Jane Welsh Carlyle* (1883); and *Thomas Carlyle: Life in London* (1884). The character of Carlyle presented in these volumes gave an unexpected shock to the public, and a bitter controversy raged regarding Froude's conduct in the matter. Meantime the reputation of Carlyle has suffered somewhat. Other works are: *Early Letters of Thomas Carlyle*, edited by Charles E. Norton (1886); *Correspondence between Goethe and Carlyle* (1887); *New Letters and Memorials of Jane Welsh Carlyle*, edited by Alexander Carlyle (1903); *The Love Letters of Thomas Carlyle and Jane Welsh*, same editor (1909). A statue was erected to Carlyle's memory on the Chelsea embankment in 1882, and in 1895 his house in Cheyne Row was purchased and opened to the public.—BIBLIOGRAPHY: A. S. Arnold, *Story of Thomas Carlyle*; R. S. Craig, *The Making of Carlyle*; F. W. Roe, *Carlyle as Critic of Literature*; and article in *Dictionary of National Biography*.

CARMAGNOLA (kȧr-mȧ-nyō′lȧ). A town of N. Italy, 18 miles S.S.E. of Turin. It has the remains of a strong castle, and is noted for its annual silk fairs. Pop. 12,050.

CARMAGNOLE (kȧr-mȧ-nyōl). A name applied in the early times of the French Republic (1792-3) to a highly-popular song (author and composer unknown), and a dance by which it was accompanied. The appellation afterwards became a sort of generic term for revolutionary songs. It first became well known on 10th Aug., 1792, after the storming of the Tuileries.

CARMAR′THEN, or CAERMAR′THEN. A maritime county, South Wales, the largest of the Welsh counties; area, 588,472 acres, of which about 440,000 are under tillage or permanent pasture. It is of a mountainous character generally, and its valleys are noted for the beauty of their scenery. The principal river is the Tywi or Towy. The mineral products of the county are iron, lead, coal, and limestone. The chief towns are Carmarthen and Llanelly. The county returns two members to Parliament. Pop. (1931), 179,063.—**Carmarthen**, the county town, is situated 9 miles from the sea, on the Towy, which is navigable to its outlet in Carmarthen Bay. There are some tin and lead works, cloth manufactories, and iron-foundries, and the salmon-fishery is extensive. A parliamentary borough till 1918, it still gives its name to a parliamentary division. It is a county of a town. Pop. (1931), 10,310.

CARMARTHEN BAY. A bay of South Wales, opening from the Bristol Channel between Giltar Point and Worms Head; 17 miles across the entrance, and 9 miles from the line of entrance to the Towy's mouth.

CARMAUX (kär-mō). A town of Southern France, department of Tarn, about 10 miles north of Albi, in a district which yields considerable quantities of coal; the chief manufacture is glass. Pop. 11,600.

CARMEL. A range of hills in Palestine, extending from the Plain of Esdraelon to the Mediterranean, and terminating in a steep promontory on the south of the Bay of Acre. It has a length of about 16 miles, and its highest point is 1850 feet above the sea.—**Carmel, Knights of Mount,** an order of 100 knights, each of whom could prove at least four descents of nobility by both father and mother, instituted by Henry IV. of France.

CAR'MELITES. Mendicant friars of the order of Our Lady of Mount Carmel. From probably the fourth century holy men took up their abode as hermits on Mount Carmel in Syria, but it was not till about the year 1150 that pilgrims established an association for the purpose of leading a secluded life on this mountain, and so laid the foundation of the order. Being driven by the Saracens to Europe in 1247, they adopted all the forms of monastic life and a somewhat milder rule. In time they became divided into several branches, one of them distinguished by walking barefooted. They are still to be seen in Roman Catholic countries. The habit of the order is of a dark-brown colour, and over it when out of doors they wear a white cloak, with a hood to cover the head.—BIBLIOGRAPHY: Helyot, *Histoire des Ordres religieux*; *Monumenta Historica Carmelitana*; and article in *Catholic Encyclopædia*.

CAR'MINATIVES. Medicines obtained chiefly from the vegetable kingdom, and used as remedies for flatulence, and spasmodic pains. They include peppermint, ginger, cardamoms, anise, and caraway.

CAR'MINE. The fine red colouring-matter or principle of cochineal, from which it is prepared in several ways, the result being the precipitation of the carmine. It was first prepared by a Franciscan monk at Pisa, and began to be manufactured in 1650. It is used to some extent in dyeing, in water-colour painting, to colour artificial flowers, confectionery, etc. Other preparations get the same name.

CARMO'NA. A town of Spain, in Andalusia, 20 miles E.N.E. of Seville. Among its edifices are a ruined fortress, a Gothic church with a lofty spire, a fine Moorish gateway, etc. Near the town a number of ancient rock-cut tombs have been opened up. Pop. 21,500.

CARNAC. A village in Brittany, France, department of Morbihan, on a height near the coast, 15 miles S.E. of Lorient, and remarkable for the so-called Druidical monuments in its vicinity. These consist of eleven rows of unhewn stones, which differ greatly both in size and height, the largest being 22 feet above ground, while some are quite small. These avenues originally extended for several miles, but many of the stones have been cleared away for agricultural improvements. They are evidently of very ancient date, but their origin is unknown. Pop. (commune), 3160.

CAR'NALLITE. A hydrated chloride of potassium and magnesium (potassium 14·1 per cent, commercially stated as potash 17 per cent), one of the most important "potash salts" of the Stassfurt district in Prussia; though carnallite is sometimes sold crude as a fertilizer, the potassium is usually extracted as potassium sulphate.

CARNAR'VON, now **CAERNARVON.** A maritime county of North Wales, forming the N.W. extremity of the mainland; area, 364,108 acres. It is traversed by lofty mountains, including the Snowdon range, whose highest peak is 3571 feet, and the highest mountain in South Britain. There are other summits varying from 1500 feet to more than 3000 feet. Lakes are numerous, but the only river of importance is the Conway, which separates the county from Denbighshire. The chief mineral is slate, large quantities of which are exported. Although the most mountainous county in Wales, there are many tracts of low and fertile land, but the arable area is small. It sends one member to Parliament. Pop. (1931), 120,810. — **Carnarvon,** the county town, is a seaport and parliamentary borough (joining with Conway, Bangor, Pwllheli, Nevin, and Criccieth), on the S.E. side of the Menai Strait. The old part of the town is surrounded by an ancient wall. The magnificent castle or palace of Edward I., and in which Edward II. was born, stands at the W. end of the town, almost overhanging the sea, and is still externally entire. Carnarvon is a sea-bathing resort, and the shipping trade is considerable. Pop. (1931), 8469. The Carnarvon boroughs send one member to Parliament.

CARNAT'IC. The district in South-Eastern India extending from Cape Comorin to the Northern Circars, lying east of the Ghats, and reaching to the sea on the Coromandel coast. It is now included in the Presidency of Madras. It was annexed by the British in 1801.

CARNA'TION (from Lat. *caro, carnis*, flesh). In the fine arts, flesh colour; the parts of a picture which are naked or without drapery, exhibiting the natural colour of the flesh.

CARNATION. The popular name of varieties of *Dianthus Caryophyllus*, the clove-pink. Rabbits greedily eat carnations, as also do many birds. The carnations of the florists are much

Carnation

prized for the beautiful colours of their sweet-scented double flowers. They are arranged into three classes according to colour, viz. *bizarres*, *flakes*, and *picotees*.

CARNAUBA (kår-nȧ-ö'bȧ). The Brazilian name of the palm *Copernicia cerifĕra*, which has its leaves coated with waxy scales, yielding a useful wax. The wood is used in building.

CARNE'ADES (-dēz). An ancient Greek philosopher, founder of the third or new academy, is supposed to have been born in 213 B.C., died at Athens 129 B.C. Carneades held that although man has no infallible criterion of truth, yet we infer appearances of truth, which, as far as the conduct of life goes, are a sufficient guide. Carneades, along with Diogenes and Critolaus, went as an envoy from the Athenians to Rome to beg the mitigation of a fine, and so captivated the Roman people by his eloquence, delivering the one day a harangue in praise of justice, and on the next proving it to be an odious institution, that Cato, alarmed at the effect of such clever sophistry persuaded the Senate to send the philosophers back without delay.

CARNEGIE (kär-neg'i), **Andrew.** Multi-millionaire and philanthropist, born at Dunfermline, Scotland, 15th Nov., 1835, died 11th Aug., 1919. He went to America with his parents in 1848, held one or two unimportant situations, and was for a number of years a superintendent on the Pennsylvania Railroad; he subsequently made an immense fortune in connection with iron and steel works at Pittsburg. During his latter years he resided chiefly in Scotland, having purchased the estate of Skibo in Sutherlandshire. He gave away immense sums of money for useful objects, both in Britain and America, especially for the building of libraries and the advancement of education. One of his greatest single gifts was that of £2,000,000 to the Scottish universities, the annual income to be spent partly in paying the fees of deserving and needy students, partly in increasing the efficiency of the universities generally.

Andrew Carnegie

His native town of Dunfermline also benefited by the gift of a park and recreation-grounds, and £500,000. He was elected Lord Rector of the University of St. Andrews in 1901, 1902, and 1906, and of Aberdeen University in 1912. In 1902 he received the honorary degree of LL.D. from the University of St. Andrews. He built a Palace of Peace for the International Court of Arbitration at the Hague, and created the Carnegie Endowment for International Peace (1910). His publications include: *An American Four-in-hand in Britain*; *Triumphant Democracy, or Fifty Years' March of the Republic*; *The Gospel of Wealth*; *The Empire of Business*; and *Problems of To-day*. —Cf. B. Alderson, *Andrew Carnegie: the Man and his Work*.

CARNE'LIAN. A clear red chalcedony used for seals and jewellery. It is found in India, Brazil, and Siberia.

CARNFORTH. A town of England, N. Lancashire, about 6 miles north by east of Lancaster, an important junction on the London and North-Western Railway, with large ironworks. Pop. (1931), 3193.

CARNIO'LA (Ger. *Krain*). Formerly a duchy or province of Austria (bounded by Carinthia, Styria, Croatia, and Italy), but now belonging to Yugoslavia; area, 3845 sq. miles. It is covered with lofty mountains, and, generally speaking, was one of the most barren regions of the former Dual Monarchy. It is remarkable for its underground rivers, winter lakes, and stalactite caverns. There are iron, lead, and quicksilver mines, and abundance of coal, marble, and valuable stone. Pop. 530,189. The capital is Laibach.

CAR'NIVAL. The feast or season of rejoicing before Lent, observed in Catholic countries with much revelry and merriment. The name comes from L.Lat. *carnelevāmen*, for *carnis levāmen*, solace of the flesh or body, feasting permitted in anticipation of any fast. Another explanation is that which derives *carnival* from *carne vale*, i.e. flesh farewell, an apt appellation for the day on which the indulgence of the senses was permitted for the last time before the great Lenten fast. Carnival observances have much declined, but in some of the cities of Italy, especially Rome, Milan, and Naples, it is still a great popular festival, as well as in the Catholic cities of the Rhine valley, Mayence, Bonn, but above all Cologne. The feast of Carnival is not observed to any extent in Protestant countries. In Spain the carnival festivities last four days, whilst in France they are restricted to Shrove Tuesday, or *mardi gras*. Some have thought the carnival mainly a survival of the pagan Saturnalia of the Romans, which it much resembles in many of the usages, and in the tricks and mummeries with which it abounds.—BIBLIOGRAPHY: S. Reinach, *Cultes, Mythes, et Religions*; and article in Hasting's *Encyclopædia of Ethics and Religion*.

CARNIV'ORA. A term applicable to any creatures that feed on flesh or animal substances, but now applied specially to an order of mammals which prey upon other animals. The head is small, the jaws powerful, and the skin is well covered with hair. Two sets of teeth, deciduous or milk and permanent, are always developed in succession, and in both sets incisors, canines, and molars are distinguishable. The stomach is simple and the alimentary canal short, thus making the body as light and slender as possible for the purpose of hunting and springing on its prey. The muscular activity of the Carnivora is very great, their respiration and circulation very active, and their demand for food is consequently constant. Carnivora are often divided into Plantigrada, comprising the bears, badgers, raccoons, etc.; Digitigrada, comprising lions, tigers, cats, dogs; and Pinnipedia or Pinnigrada, comprising the seals and walruses. The two former divisions are also classed together as Fissipedia. The typical Plantigrada are distinguished by their putting the whole sole of the foot to the ground in walking, while the Digitigrada walk on the tips of their toes. The Plantigrada are also less decidedly carnivorous, and feed much on roots, honey, and fruits. In the Pinnigrada the body is long and of a fish shape, the fore- and hind-limbs are short and form broad webbed swimming-paddles. The hind-feet are placed far back, and more or less tied down to the tail by the integuments.

CARNIVOROUS PLANTS. Plants which derive nourishment directly from the bodies of insects or other small creatures entrapped by them in various ways. Such plants, of which there are several hundred kinds, mostly belong to the nat. ords. Sarraceniaceæ or Pitcher-plants (genera Sarracenia, Darlingtonia, etc.), Droseraceæ (genera Drosera, Dionæa, Aldrovanda, etc., Lentibulariaceæ (genera Pinguicula, Utricularia, etc.), and Nepenthaceæ (genus Nepenthes). In all these the apparatus for catching insects consists of a modified leaf or portion of a leaf, and in some the modifications are so curious and the adaptation so perfect that the plant seems almost endowed with intelligence. In the Pitcher-plant order the leaf consists of a longer or shorter tube, ventrally winged, and sometimes crowned by a sort of hood. Insects are enticed to the leaves by means of a sugary secretion produced near the mouth, and sometimes also continued down the edge of the wing, so as to form what has been described as a "saccharine trail" from near the ground up to the orifice. The tube when not hooded may contain rain, in addition to the secreted juice, but in the hooded forms rain is excluded.

In Nepenthes the sessile leaf-blade is continued as a twining tendril, which bears on its summit a pitcher closed in the younger plants by a hinged lid. The species of Drosera or Sun-dew, of which some are common in British bogs, have their leaves provided with stalked glands, which exude a clear sticky juice. When an insect alights on any of these glands, those in the neighbourhood bend towards it in order to secure it more effectively. In the allied *Dionœa muscipula* or Venus's Fly-trap of Carolina, the leaf-blade bears on its apex a sort of trap, consisting of two pieces hinged together. These have a few sensitive bristles on their inner faces, and if an insect touches either these or the hinge, the trap closes and secures it. The common Butterwort of Britain (*Pinguicula vulgaris*) also has leaves which catch and digest insects by means of glandular hairs; and the Bladderworts (Utricularia) bear tiny submerged pitchers provided with a curious trap-door device. The chief English work on this subject is Darwin's *Insectivorous Plants* (1875). Consult also Kerner's *Natural History of Plants*, and the articles on the plants mentioned.

CARNOT (kär-nō). **Lazare Nicolas Marguerite.** A French statesman, general, and strategist, born in 1753, and died in 1823. When the Revolution broke out he was captain in the corps of engineers. In 1791 he was appointed deputy to the Constituent Assembly. In the following March he was sent to the Army of the North, where he took command and successfully repulsed the enemy. On his return he was made member of the Committee of Public Safety, and directed and organised the French armies with great ability and success. In 1797 Carnot, having unsuccessfully opposed Barras, had to escape to Germany, but returned, and was appointed Minister of War by Napoleon (1800). But he remained in principle an inflexible Republican, voted against the consulship for life, and protested against Napoleon's assumption of the imperial dignity. For seven years after this Carnot remained in retirement, publishing several valuable military works. In 1814 Napoleon gave him the chief command at Antwerp, and in 1815 the post of Minister of the Interior. After the emperor's second fall he retired from France.—A grandson of his, *Marie François Sadi*, born in 1837, was elected President of the French Republic in 1887, and assassinated in 1894.

CARNOUSTIE (kär-nös'ti). A burgh of Scotland, on the coast of Forfarshire, 7 miles south-west of Arbroath; carries on the jute manufacture, boot and shoe making, iron-founding, and other industries; and its bathing facilities and golf-links attract many visitors. Pop. (1931), 4806.

CARO, Annibāle. One of the most celebrated Italian authors of the sixteenth century, born 1507, died 1566. He was secretary to several members of the great Farnese family. He devoted himself to numismatics and the Tuscan language, and became famous for the elegance of his style. Among his works are a translation of the *Æneid* and of Aristotle's *Rhetoric*.

CAROB TREE, or **ALGAROBA-BEAN** (*Ceratonia siliqua*). A leguminous plant of the sub-ord. Cæsalpinieæ, growing wild in all the countries on the Mediterranean. It has a dark-green foliage, and produces pods in which the seeds are embedded in a dry nutritious pulp of a sweet taste. The names *locust-beans* and *St. John's bread* have been given to the legumes of this plant, from an idea that they were the food eaten, along with wild honey, by the Baptist in the wilderness. In the south of Europe they are principally used as food for horses, and they are imported into Britain as a food for cattle.

CAR'OL. A song, especially one expressive of joy. It often signifies, specifically, a religious song or ballad in celebration of Christmas, such as are sung about Christmas-tide in English churches or by "waits" out-of-doors. Some of the most famous early carols are contained in a MS. of the fifteenth century in the British Museum.—BIBLIOGRAPHY: E. Duncan, *The Story of the Carol*; W. Sandys, *Christmas-tide: its History, Festivities, and Carols.*

CAROLI'NA, NORTH. One of the United States, bounded N. by Virginia, E. by the Atlantic, S. by South Carolina and Georgia, and W. by Tennessee; area, 52, 426 sq. miles. The principal rivers are the Roanoke and Chowan, Neuse, Pamlico or Tar, and Cape Fear and Yadkin. The coast is generally difficult of access, being fringed by a line of narrow sandy islands, between which and the mainland the passages are mostly shallow and dangerous. There are three noted capes on the coast, viz. Cape Hatteras, Cape Look-out, and Cape Fear, all dangerous to seamen. North Carolina is generally a dead level for 40 to 60 miles inland, this part largely consisting of cypress swamps; next comes a fine undulating country largely under cultivation or clothed with deciduous trees; lastly comes the region of the Appalachians, with Mt. Mitchell (6707 feet) the highest of all: fine fruits and picturesque scenery are here the characteristics.

The mineral resources are highly valuable, including coal and iron in abundance, silver, lead, zinc, emery, etc. In the level parts the soil generally is but indifferent. On the banks of some of the rivers, however, and particularly the Roanoke, it is remarkably fertile. The more elevated grounds are also for the most part highly fertile. Cotton is grown in large quantities in the sandy isles and the flat country; rice is grown largely among the swamps. The chief staples, however, are Indian corn, tobacco, wheat, oats, and sweet-potatoes. The pitch-pine, which grows abundantly in the low districts, is one of the most valuable productions, affording the pitch, tar, turpentine, and various kinds of lumber which together constitute about one-half of the exports of North Carolina. There is considerable diversity of climate, as in all the southern states. Intermittent fevers are frequent in the low-lying parts of the country, but the western and hilly parts are very healthy. School attendance is compulsory, and there are separate schools for white and for coloured children. Higher instruction is given in fifteen university and college institutions. The university of North Carolina, at Chapel Hill, was founded in 1795, and the agricultural and engineering college at West Raleigh, in 1889. The chief religious denominations are the Baptist and Methodist. The largest towns are Charlotte, with a pop. of 82,675; Winston-Salem, pop. 75,274; Wilmington, pop. 32,270; Greensboro, 53,569. Raleigh is the capital. The first attempt to colonise in this part by the English was made in 1587, but the colony was never again heard of. In 1650 emigrants from Virginia, and in 1661 an English colony from Massachusetts, made settlements. In 1720 the two Carolinas were separated into North and South Carolina. In 1861 the state seceded from the Union, and it was not formally restored till 1868. Pop. in 1900, 1,891,992; in 1910, 2,206,287; estimated at 3,170,276 in 1930.—BIBLIOGRAPHY: S. A. Ashe, *History of North Carolina*; H. G. Connor and J. B. Cheshire, *The Constitution of North Carolina*; W. S. Wilson, *North Carolina Blue Book*; R. O. W. Connor, *North Carolina Manual.*

CAROLINA, SOUTH. One of the United States, bounded N. by North Carolina, E. by the Atlantic, S.W. and W. by Georgia; area, 30,989 sq. miles, of which 494 is water. Columbia is the seat of government, but Charleston is much the largest town. The chief rivers are the Great Pedee and the Congaree and Wateree, which unite to form the Santee, together with the Savannah forming the boundary between South Carolina and Georgia. These and other streams, flowing generally in a S.E. direction, afford an inland navigation to the extent of 2400 miles. There is now also a considerable network of railways, the total mileage being 3890 in 1925. The principal harbour is that of Charleston. Numerous small islands along the coast supply the famous Sea-island cotton.

In physical constitution South Carolina resembles its northern neighbour, a great level plain of forest and swamp extending westward from the sea, till it begins 100 miles inland to rise in ranges of sand-hills, and finally reaches ranges of 4000 feet in the Appalachians. In this western district the land is fertile, well cultivated, and watered by considerable streams. The staple products of the state are cotton and rice, of which great quantities are annually exported. The cultivation of wheat, barley, oats, and other crops has been comparatively neglected. The rice-lands of South Carolina give employment to thousands of coloured people. The low country is subject to fevers, but the upper country enjoys as salubrious a climate as any part of the United States. South Carolina is rich in minerals, including gold, iron, manganese, copper, lead, granite, limestone, and valuable phosphate-marls. The commerce is considerable, the chief exports being cotton, rice, timber, and naval stores. School attendance is not compulsory, but there are restrictions on the employment of illiterate children in mines or factories.

The University of South Carolina was founded at Columbia in 1805. The Baptists and Methodists are the most numerous of the religious denominations. The first settlement of South Carolina was made by whites at Port Royal about 1670, but a permanent establishment was formed only ten years later by the congregation of a few settlers at Charleston. In 1695 the cultivation of rice was introduced by Governor Smith; that of cotton followed; and on these two staples the colony soon began to flourish. South Carolina was the first of the states to secede from the Union, and it suffered severely in the civil war between North and South. Pop. in 1900, 1,340,312; in 1910, 1,575,400; it was estimated to be 1,738,765 in 1930.—BIBLIOGRAPHY: E. M'Crady, *The History of South Carolina*; E. J. Watson, *Handbook of South Carolina*.

CAROLINE. British queen. She was a daughter of the Duke of Brunswick-Wolfenbüttel, born 17th May, 1768, died 7th Aug., 1821. In 1795 she was married to the Prince of Wales, afterwards George IV. The marriage was not to his liking, and after the birth of the Princess Charlotte he separated from her. Many reports

Queen Caroline

were circulated against her honour, and a ministerial committee was formed to inquire into her conduct. But the people in general sympathised with her, regarding her as an ill-treated wife. In 1814 she made a journey through Germany, Italy, Greece, to Jerusalem, in which an Italian, Bergami, was her confidant and attendant. When the Prince of Wales ascended the throne in 1820, he offered her an income of £50,000 on condition that she would never return to England. She refused, and in the June of same year entered London amid public demonstrations of welcome. The Government now instituted proceedings against her for adultery but the public feeling and the splendid defence of Brougham obliged the ministry to give up the Divorce Bill after it had passed the Lords. Though banished from the court, the queen now assumed a style suitable to her rank. She was refused admittance to Westminster Abbey when George IV was crowned, 19th July, 1821, and her disappointment at this treatment hastened her death.

CAROLINE ISLANDS, or NEW PHILIPPINES. A large archipelago, North Pacific Ocean, between lat. 3° and 12° N. and long. 132° and 163° 6′ E., and between the Philippines and the Marshall Isles, first discovered by the Spaniards in 1543, if not by the Portuguese in 1525. Many of the islands are mere coral reefs little elevated above the ocean. They form many groups, the most important being the Pelews, and those to which the largest islands of all, Yap and Ponape, respectively belong. The population is estimated at 23,414, made up of inhabitants of different races and stages of civilisation. The most important vegetable productions are palms, bread-fruit trees, and bananas. The natives show great skill in constructing their canoes and building their houses. There is an American Protestant and a Roman Catholic mission. Some trade is carried on at Yap and Ponape. The islands were long in the possession of Spain, but in 1899, after the conclusion of the war between that power and the United States, they were sold to Germany. They were occupied by a Japanese force in 1914, were for a time in British military occupation, and were mandated to Japan in 1922.—BIBLIOGRAPHY: F. W. Christian, *Caroline Islands*; W. H. Furness, *The Island of Stone Money*.

CAROLINGIAN. *See* CARLOVINGIAN.

CAR'OLUS. A gold coin struck in the reign of Charles I., and originally 20*s.* in value, afterwards 23*s.* The name was given also to various other coins.

CAROLUS-DURAN, Emile Auguste. French painter and teacher, born at Lille, 4th July, 1838, died in Paris 18th Feb., 1917. He studied in Lille under Phidias de Beaupré and Souchon, and later went to Paris. In 1860 he won the Wicar prize with his picture *Visite au Convalescent*, which enabled him to travel in Italy and continue his studies.

He first attracted attention by his two pictures *The Evening Prayer* and *The Victim of Assassination*, bought by the town of Lille for 5000 francs. He then went to Spain, where he became an ardent disciple of Velasquez. He became famous in 1869 through his painting *Lady with the Glove*, a portrait of his wife, which is now at the Luxembourg Museum. Carolus-Duran, although famous as a portraitist, was also active in painting historical and religious subjects, such as *L'Ultima ora di Cristo*. One of his most notable works is a mural painting on a ceiling in the Louvre called *Gloria Mariae Medici*, wherein the influence of the Venetian and Flemish painters, Tiepolo and Paul Veronese, Rubens and Van Dyck, is noticeable. He was a grand officer of the Legion of Honour, a member of the Académie des Beaux-Arts, and director of the French Academy in Rome from 1904 to 1913. He also wrote novels and short stories under the name of *Charles Durand*, his original name.

CARO'TID ARTERIES. The two great arteries which convey the blood from the aorta to the head and the brain. The *common carotids*, one on either side of the neck, divide each into an external and an internal branch. The *external carotid* passes up to the level of the angle of the lower jaw, where it ends in branches to the neck, face, and outer parts of the head. The *internal carotid* passes deeply into the neck, and through an opening in the skull near the ear enters the brain, supplying it and the eye with blood. Wounds of the carotid trunks cause almost immediate death.

CAROUGE (kà-rözh). A town of Switzerland, on the Arve, near Geneva, with which it is connected by a bridge. Pop. 7890.

CARP (Cyprinus). A genus of soft-finned fishes (type of the family Cyprinidæ), distinguished by the small mouth, toothless jaws, and gills of three flat rays. They have but one dorsal fin, and the scales are generally of large size. They frequent fresh and quiet waters, feeding chiefly on vegetable matters, also on worms and molluscs. The common carp (*C. carpio*) is olive-green above and yellowish below, and in many parts is bred in ponds for the use of the table. It sometimes weighs many pounds, is of quick growth, and spawns thrice a year. It is said to live to the great age of 100 or even 200 years. The well-known gold-fish is *C. aurātus*, believed to be originally from China.

CARPACCIO (kår-pàch'ō), **Vittore.** Italian painter, one of the most celebrated masters of the old Venetian school, was born probably at Venice about 1450-5, and died there after 1521. His distinguishing characteristics are natural expression, vivid conception, correct arrangement, and great variety of figures and costumes. He also excelled as an architectural and landscape painter. His favourite employment was the dramatic representation of sacred subjects, several of which he has illustrated by a series of paintings.

CARPA'THIAN MOUNTAINS (Ger. *Karpathen*). A range of mountains in Southern Europe, forming a great semicircular belt of nearly 800 miles in length. The Carpathian chain may be divided into two great sections—the West Carpathians, in Hungary, to the north-west, and the East Carpathians, in Transylvania, to the south-east, with lower ranges stretching between. To the Western Carpathians belongs the remarkable group of the Tatra, in which is situated the culminating summit of the system, the Gerlsdorf peak, namely, rising to the height of 8721 feet; several other peaks have an elevation of over 8000 feet. The outer bend of the Carpathians is much steeper than that which descends towards the valleys of Transylvania and Hungary. The only important rivers which actually rise in the chain are the Vistula, the Dniester, and the Theiss. The Carpathian range is rich in minerals, including gold, silver, quicksilver, copper, and iron. Salt occurs in beds, which have sometimes a thickness of 600 or 700 feet. On the plateaux corn and fruit are grown, to the height of 1500 feet. Higher up the mountain steeps are covered with forests of pine. The scenery is magnificent. During the European War fighting took place in the Carpathians, between Russia and Austria, in 1914, 1915, and 1916.—Cf. L. Phillimore, *In the Carpathians*.

CAR'PEL. In botany, a single-celled ovary or seed-vessel, or a single cell of an ovary or seed-vessel, together with what belongs to that cell, as in many cases a separate style and stigma of the pistil. The pistil or fruit often consists of only one carpel, in which case it is called *simple*; when either consists of more than one carpel it is called *compound*. A carpel is regarded as a modified leaf.

CARPENTA'RIA, GULF OF. A large gulf on the north coast of Australia, having Cape York Peninsula, the northern extremity of

Queensland, on the east, and Arnhem Land on the west.

CARPENTER, William Benjamin, M.D., LL.D. An English physiologist, born 1813, died 1885. He studied medicine at University College, London, and at Edinburgh University, subsequently held several lectureships in London, and ultimately became registrar at London University (1856-79). He wrote several well-known works on physiology: *Principles of General and Comparative Physiology*, *Principles of Mental Physiology*, *Principles of Human Physiology*, *A Manual of Zoology*, etc. He took a leading part in the expeditions sent out by Government between 1868 and 1870 for deep-sea exploration in the North Atlantic. He was chosen president of the British Association at Brighton in 1872.

CARPENTER-BEE. The common name of the different species of hymenopterous insects of the genus Xylocŏpa. The species are numerous in Asia, Africa, and America, and one species inhabits the south of Europe. They are generally of a dark violet-blue, and of considerable size. They usually form their nests in pieces of half-rotten wood, each nest consisting of a series of compartments or cells in which the eggs are deposited.

CARPENTIER, Georges. French boxer, born at Lens, 12th Jan., 1894. Beginning his boxing career quite early, he gained different weight championships in France. In 1913 he defeated Wells, the English heavy-weight champion, and on 16th July, 1914, he gained the world's white heavy-weight championship against Gunboat Smith. On 4th Dec., 1919, he defeated J. Beckett, but was himself defeated by Dempsey at Jersey City on 2nd July, 1921.—BIBLIOGRAPHY: Georges Carpentier, *My Fighting Life*; F. H. Lucas, *From Pit Boy to Champion Boxer*.

CARPENTRAS (kȧr-pȧn̦-trä). A town, Southern France, department of Vaucluse, 14 miles N.E. of Avignon, surrounded by walls flanked with towers. It is an ancient town, and has a Roman triumphal arch, an aqueduct, etc. Pop. 11,800.

CAR'PENTRY. The art of combining pieces of timber to support a weight or sustain pressure. The work of the carpenter is intended to give stability to a structure, that of the joiner is applied to finishing and decoration. An explanation of some of the terms employed in carpentry may be useful. The term *frame* is applied to any assemblage of pieces of timber firmly connected together. The points of meeting of the pieces of timber in a frame are called *joints*. *Lengthening* a beam is uniting pieces of timber into one length by joining their extremities. When neatness is not required, this is done by *fishing*, that is, placing a piece of timber on each side of where the beams meet and securing it by bolts passed through the whole. When the width of the beam must be kept the same throughout, *scarfing* is employed. This is cutting from each beam a part of the thickness of the timber, and on opposite sides, so that the pieces may be jointed together and bolted or hooped. When greater strength is required than can be produced by a single beam, *building* and *trussing* beams are resorted to. Building beams is combining two or more beams in depth so as to have the effect of one. In trussing the beam is cut in two in the direction of its length, and supported with cross-beams, as in roofing. *Mortise* and *tenon* is a mode of jointing timber. An excavation called the mortise is made in one piece, and a projecting tongue to fit in it called the tenon in the other. The timber framework of floors is called *naked flooring*, and is *single* if there be but a single series of joists, *double* if there are cross-binding joists, and *framed* if there are girders or beams in addition to the joists. The *roof* is the framework by which the covering of a building is supported. It may consist of a series of sloping pieces of timber, with one end resting on one wall and the other end meeting in a point with a corresponding piece resting on the opposite wall: these are called *rafters*. There is usually a third piece, which connects the lower extremities of the rafters and prevents them from spreading. This is called a *tie*, and the whole frame a *couple*. The principal instruments used in carpentry are saws, as the circular-, band-, and tenon-saws; planes, as the jack-plane, smoothing-plane, moulding-plane, etc.; chisels, gouges, brad-awls, gimlets, descriptions of which will be found in their places.—BIBLIOGRAPHY: J. Barnard. *Every Man his own Mechanic*; B. F. Fletcher, *Carpentry and Joinery*; G. Ellis, *Modern Practical Carpentry*.

CARPET. A thick fabric, generally composed wholly or principally of wool, for covering the floors of apartments, staircases, and passages in the interior of a house. Carpets were originally introduced from the East, where they were fabricated in pieces, like the modern rugs, for sitting on—

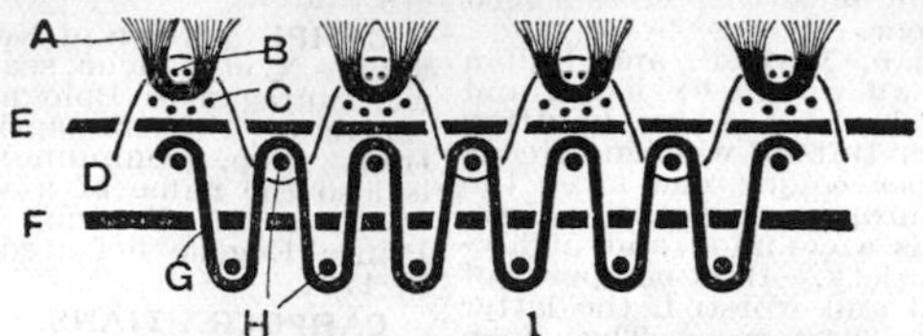

Section of Chenille Axminster Carpet with single shed or tapestry back

A, Fur or chenille. B, C, Fur wefts. D, Small chain binding the fur to the base. E, Flout warp. F, Stuffer warp. G, Smal. chain or ground warp of the base structure. H, Filling weft.

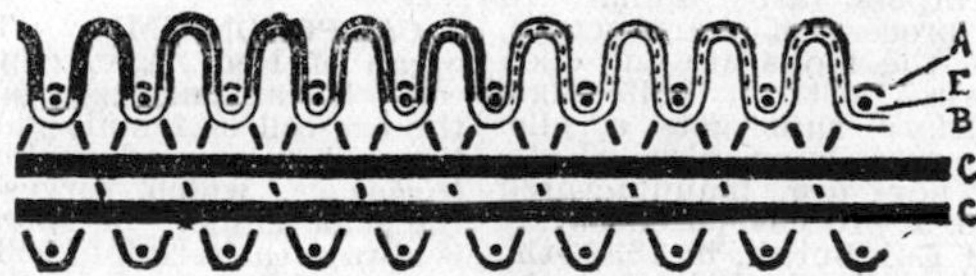

Section of Medium Tapestry Carpet.

A, Ground warp. B, Pile Warp. C C, Stuffer warp. E, Weft.

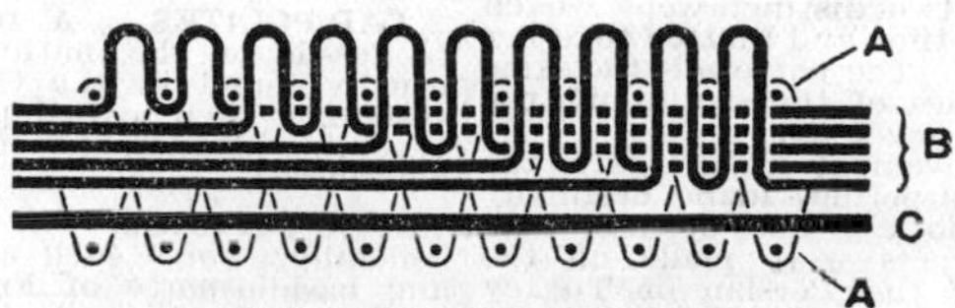

Section of Five-frame Brussels Carpet

A, A, Small chain. B, Pile warp. C, Stuffer warp.

Section of Wilton Carpet

A, A, Small chain. B, Pile Warp. C, Stuffer Warp.

Section of Two-ply Scotch Carpet

a use obviously suggested by the Eastern habit of sitting cross-legged upon the floor.

The Persian, Turkish, and Indian carpets are all woven by hand, and the design is formed by knotting into the warp tufts of woollen threads of the proper colour one after the other. Of European carpets the *Brussels* carpet is a common and highly-esteemed variety. It is composed of linen thread and worsted, the latter forming the pattern. The linen basis does not appear on the surface, being concealed by the worsted, which is drawn through the reticulations and looped over wires that are afterwards withdrawn, giving the surface a ribbed appearance.

Wilton carpets are similar to Brussels in process of manufacture, but in them the loops are cut open by using wires with a knife-edge, and the surface thus gets a pile. *Tapestry* carpets have also a pile surface. They are manufactured according to a process patented by Whytock, of Edinburgh, in 1832, the great speciality of which is that the threads are particoloured by printing in the proper manner for each design before being woven up. The *Kidderminster* or *Scotch* carpet consists of two distinct webs woven at the same time and knitted together by the woof. The pattern is the same on both sides of the cloth, but the colours are reversed.

An improvement upon this is the three-ply carpeting, made originally at Kilmarnock. The original *Axminster* carpets were made on the principle of the Persian or Turkey carpets. Patent Axminster carpets (invented by Templeton, of Glasgow, 1839) have a fine pile, which is produced by using chenille as the weft, the projecting threads of which form the pile, which is dyed before being used. Carpets of felted wool, with designs printed on them, are also used, and are very cheap. Cheap jute carpets are also made.—BIBLIOGRAPHY: Christopher Fresser, *Carpets*; T. H. Hendley, *Asian Carpets*; F. R. Martin, *History of the Oriental Carpets before 1800*; S. Humphries, *Oriental Carpets and Rugs*; G. Lewis, *The Practical Book of Oriental Rugs.*

CARPET-BAGGER. A needy political adventurer who goes about the country pandering to the prejudices of the ignorant, with the view of getting into place or power, so called because regarded as having no more property than might fill a *carpet-bag*. Originally applied to needy adventurers of the Northern States of America who tried in this way to gain the votes of the negroes of the Southern States.

CARPI. A town of Northern Italy, 9 miles N. of Modena, seat of a bishopric, suffragan to Bologna. It is the centre of a fertile agricultural district. Pop. (commune), 30,730.—It is also the name of a village in the province of Verona, near which Prince Eugène defeated the French in 1701.

CARPOCRA'TIANS. A sect of Gnostics of the second century, so called from *Carpocrates*, a prominent teacher of gnosticism. They maintained that only the soul of Christ went to heaven, that his body would have no resurrection, and that the world was made by angels.

CARPOGONIUM. The female organ of Red Algæ, consisting of a cell with an enlarged base enclosing the egg-cell or female gamete, and a thread-like upward prolongation, the *trichogyne*, which serves to receive the male gamete or *spermatium*. It is always the terminal cell of a special carpogonial branch. The term is sometimes also applied to the female organ which occurs in certain Ascomycetous Fungi, but this is more properly called an *ascogonium*.

CAR'POLITES. A term applied to fossils of the nature of fruits, usually found in the Carboniferous system. Their exact place in the vegetable kingdom has not yet been determined.

CARPOSPORES. In plants: (1) generally, spores such as ascospores and basidiospores of Fungi, formed as the result of a reduction division, tetraspores of Red Algæ, and the asexual spores of all higher plants; (2) in Red Algæ, the spores formed directly or indirectly from the fertilised carpogonium. The second usage conflicts with (1), and should be discontinued. *See* REDUCTION DIVISION, and groups mentioned.

CARPUS. In anatomy, the bones between the forearm and hand, the wrist in man, or corresponding part in other animals.

CARRACCI (kȧr-rȧch'ē), **Ludovico, Agostino,** and **Annibale.** The three founders of the Bologna, or, as it has been called, the eclectic school of painting.—Ludovico (lŏ-do-vē'kō) was born in 1555 at Bologna. At Florence he studied under Andrea del Sarto, and afterwards went to Parma for the purpose of studying Correggio, who was then imitated by almost all the Florentine painters. He then set up a studio in Bologna, and established a school of painting characterised particularly by its attention to composition and its principle of eclecticism, or endeavour to imitate and unite the chief excellences of different great masters, the drawing of Raphael, the colouring of Titian, etc.

To assist him Ludovico had his two younger cousins, Agostino and Annibale, educated as artists; and after the completion of their studies all three by their able work soon made a high reputation for the academy of the Carracci at Bologna. Ludovico has left many works, the finest of which, such as *The Transfiguration* and *The Birth of St. John the Baptist*, are in the Pinacoteca at Bologna. *Susannah and the Elders* is at the National Gallery, London. He died in 1619.—Agostino (à-gos-tē'nō) was born in 1558 at Bologna; he died at Parma in 1601. He engraved more pieces than he painted, though some of his pictures were admired by contemporaries even more than those of his brother Annibale.—Annibale (àn-nib'à-lā) was born in 1560 at Bologna. In 1600 he was invited by Cardinal Farnese to Rome, where the influence of Raphael and Michael Angelo's work tempered the characteristics he had acquired from the Lombard and Venetian schools. His chief work is the series of frescoes for the Farnese Palace at Rome, which occupied him for eight years. He is generally considered the greatest of the Carracci. He died at Rome in 1609.

CARRAGEEN, or CARRAGHEEN (kar'ra-gēn). *Chondrus crispus*, a Red Sea-weed very common on rocks and stones on every part of the coast of Britain. It is a very variable weed, with a flat branching frond usually of a deep purple-brown colour. When dried it becomes whitish, and in this condition is known as Irish-moss, and is used for making soups, jellies, size, etc. The name comes from Carragaheen, near Waterford, Ireland, where it abounds.

CARRANZA, Venustiano. Mexican general and statesman, born in Coahuila, 1859. He studied law, but retired to his estate on account of ill-health. In 1893 he joined a revolt against President Diaz, and in 1910 became Secretary for War in the Government of Madero. When the latter was assassinated in 1913, Carranza opposed the new President, Huerta, and organised revolution, with the help of Villa and Obregon, proclaiming himself chief of the Mexican army. In Oct., 1915, Carranza was recognised by President Wilson, and soon afterwards by Great Britain and other European Powers, as President of Mexico. In April, 1920, a revolution broke out in Mexico, and Carranza was killed on 20th May.

CARRA'RA. A city of Northern Italy, 59 miles S.W. of Modena, a few miles from the coast, with some interesting buildings, including an old church, an academy of sculpture, etc. It is surrounded by hills which contain fine white statuary marble, in the preparation of which and commoner sorts most of the inhabitants are occupied. Pop. (commune) 52,700.—The Carrara marble is the variety generally employed by statuaries. It was formerly supposed to be a primitive limestone, but is now considered an altered limestone of the Oolitic period. Although the Carrara quarries have been worked for 2000 years, having furnished the material for the Pantheon at Rome, the supply is still practically inexhaustible. They employ 6000 or 7000 men.

CAR'REL, Armand. French Republican writer. He was born in 1800. For some years he was an officer in the army, but afterwards settled in Paris, and acquired a reputation as an essayist and contributor to the leading opposition papers. In 1827 he published a history of the English Revolution of 1688, and in 1830 united with Thiers and Mignet in editing the *National*, which soon rose to be the leading newspaper in opposition to the Government of Charles X. After the Revolution his colleagues joined the Government of Louis Philippe, and he was left with the chief direction of the paper, which still continued in opposition. In 1832 the *National* became openly Republican, and enjoyed great popularity. Carrel was killed in 1836 in a duel with Emile de Girardin.

CARRHÆ. The site of an ancient city in North-Western Mesopotamia, the Haran of the Bible, famous as the scene of the defeat and death of the Roman triumvir Crassus while fighting the Parthians, 9th June, 53 B.C.

CARRIAGE. A general name for a vehicle, but more especially for one of the lighter and more ornamental kind. *See* COACH, where the chief kinds are referred to.

CARRICK. The southern district of the county of Ayr, Scotland. The Prince of Wales bears the title of Earl of Carrick.

CARRICKFER'GUS. A seaport of Ireland, County Antrim, a parliamentary borough till 1885, 11 miles by railway N.E. of Belfast. It is memorable as the landing-place of King William III., 14th June, 1690. The castle stands upon a rock projecting into the bay, and is still maintained as a fortress, and used as an army ordnance store. There are manufactures, principally linen, and extensive fisheries. Pop. (1926), 4751.

CARRICK-ON-SUIR. A town, Irish Free State, County Tipperary, 85 miles S.W. of Dublin, on the left bank of the Suir, navigable here by small vessels; it has a considerable trade in agricultural produce. Pop. 5236.

CAR'RIER. A person who undertakes to transport the goods of other persons from place to place for them. Persons who undertake this as a systematic business are called *common carriers,* and come under special legal regulations, such as that they shall be responsible for the goods entrusted to them so long as in their custody. Three centuries ago, one Thomas Pickford took up the business of conveying goods on pack-horses between London and the surrounding towns. He appears to have been a pioneer, for he was among the first to use the covered wagon instead of the pack-horse for short journeys. By his foresight and energy the trade of the firm grew, and extended its operations far north of the capital.

CARRIER (kȧr-yā), **Jean Baptiste.** An infamous character of the first French Revolution, born 1746, executed 1794. Though an obscure attorney at the beginning of the Revolution, he was chosen, in 1792, member of the National Convention. In Oct., 1793, he was sent to Nantes to suppress the civil war and the uprising of La Vendée. The prisons were full; there was dearth of provisions, and Carrier determined to lessen the "useless mouths" by summary measures. He first caused ninety-four priests to be conveyed to a boat with a perforated bottom, under pretence of transporting them, but instead they were drowned by night.

This artifice was repeated a number of times, while Carrier also caused multitudes of prisoners to be shot without any pretence of trial. The executioners, it is said, sometimes amused themselves by tying together a young man and woman, and then drowning them; and they called these murders "republican marriages." Some months before the fall of Robespierre, Carrier was recalled. On the 9th Thermidor (27th July), 1794, he was apprehended and brought before the revolutionary tribunal, which condemned him to death, and the guillotine did its work.

CARRIER PIGEON. A variety of the common domestic pigeon used for the purpose of carrying messages. Several varieties are thus employed but what is distinctively called the carrier pigeon is a large bird with long wings, a large tuberculated mass of naked skin at the base of the beak, and with a circle of naked skin round the eyes. This variety, however, is rather a bird for show than use, and the variety generally employed to

Carrier Pigeon

carry messages more resembles an ordinary pigeon.

The practice of sending letters by pigeons belongs originally to Eastern countries, though in other countries it has often been adopted, more especially before the invention of the electric telegraph. An actual post-system in which pigeons were the messengers was established at Bagdad by the Sultan Nureddin Mahmud, who died in 1174, and lasted till 1258, when Bagdad fell into the hands of the Mongols, and was destroyed by them.

These birds can be utilised in this way only in virtue of what is called their "homing" faculty, or instinct which enables them to find their way back home from surprising distances. But if they are taken to the place from which the message is to be sent and kept there too long, say over a fortnight, they will forget their home and not return to it. They are better to get some training by trying them first with short distances, which are then gradually increased.

The missive may be fastened to the wing or the tail, and must be quite small and attached so as not to interfere with the bird's flight. By the use of microphotography a long message may be conveyed in this way, and such were received by the besieged residents in Paris during the Franco-Prussian War of 1870-1, the birds being conveyed out of the city in balloons.

Seventy-two miles in two and a half hours, a hundred and eighty in four and a half, have been accomplished by carrier pigeons. Large numbers of these birds are now kept in England, Belgium, France, etc., there being numerous pigeon clubs which hold pigeon races to test the speed of the birds. During the European War, 1914-18, pigeons were employed to some extent by all sides with considerable success.

CARRINGTON, Richard Christopher. British astronomer, born 1826, died 1875. Educated at Trinity College, Cambridge, he held the post of astronomical observer at the University of Durham from 1849 to 1852. In 1853 he erected an observatory at Redhill, Surrey, where he conducted valuable private investigations. Secretary of the Royal Astronomical Society from 1857 to 1862, he was elected a Fellow of the Royal Society in 1860. His contributions to science, and especially to solar physics, were very valuable, and his works include: *Catalogue of 3735 Circumpolar Stars* (1857) and *Observations on the Spots on the Sun.*

CARRION-CROW. In Britain the common crow (*Corvus corōnē*), so called because it often feeds on

Carrion-crow (*Corvus corōnē*)

carrion. The name is often incorrectly applied to the gregarious rook (*C. frugilegus*). In America the name is given to a small species of vulture called the Black Vulture.

CARRION-FLOWERS. A common name for species of the genus Stapelia (nat. ord. Asclepiadaceæ), so called because of their putrid odour, which, though nauseous to us, is highly attractive to the flies that effect cross-pollination. Similar flowers, recalling carrion not only by their smell, but also by their colouring, recur in other genera and nat. ord., e.g. Aristolochia, Rafflesia, Araceæ.

CARROLL, Lewis. Pen-name of the Rev. Charles Lutwidge Dodgson, poet, mathematician, and general writer. He was born in 1832, and received his academical education at

Lewis Carroll

Christ Church, Oxford, where he had a distinguished career. He took deacon's orders in 1861, though he never proceeded to priest's orders, and held a mathematical lectureship at his college for more than twenty years, ending in 1881.

His earliest publications were: *A Syllabus of Plane Algebraical Geometry* (1860), *Formulæ of Plane Trigonometry* (1861), and *A Guide to the Mathematical Student* (1864). He did not, however, become known to the public at large until 1865, when he leapt into fame as the author of *Alice's Adventures in Wonderland*. Equally delightful is the continuation of Alice's adventures narrated in *Through the Looking Glass and What Alice Found There* (1871), both books admirably illustrated by Tenniel. *The Hunting of the Snark: an Agony in Eight Fits* (1876), a fantastic narrative in verse, had, however, by no means an equal popularity.

Among his other works are: *An Elementary Treatise on Determinants, Phantasmagoria and other Poems, Euclid and his Modern Rivals, Rhyme? and Reason?, A Tangled Tale, The Game of Logic, Curiosa Mathematica, Sylvie and Bruno,* and *Symbolic Logic* (1896). He died at Guildford on 14th Jan., 1898.

CAR'RON. A village of Scotland, in Stirlingshire, 2 miles from Falkirk, celebrated for its extensive ironworks, begun in 1760. Pop. 1940.—The river of the same name falls into the Forth at Grangemouth after an easterly course of about 17 miles.

CARRONADE. An iron gun introduced in 1779 by the director of the Carron Foundry, from which it took its name. They were of large calibre, but short and much lighter than common cannon. They were of great service in close naval engagements, but they had a very short range, and have been long ago superseded by more modern inventions.

CARRON-OIL. A term for a liniment composed of linseed-oil and lime-water, so called from being much used in the case of burns at the Carron Ironworks.

CARROT (*Daucus Carōta*). A biennial umbelliferous plant, a native of Britain and other parts of Europe. The leaves are tripinnate, of a handsome feathery appearance. The plant rises to the height of 2 feet, and produces white flowers. The root, in its wild state, is small, tapering, of a white colour, and strong-flavoured; but that of the cultivated variety is large, succulent, and of a red, yellow, or pale straw-colour, and shows remarkably the improvement which may be effected by cultivation. It is cultivated for the table and as a food for cattle. Carrots contain a large proportion of saccharine matter, and attempts have been made to extract sugar from them. The Peruvian carrot is *Aracācha esculenta*.

CARROT-FLY. A minute fly which lays its eggs on the plant close to the ground. The maggots that hatch out attack the roots, causing them to become "rusty" carrots.

CARROUSEL (kȧr'ö-zel). A name given in the Middle Ages to a tilting match or other occasion when knightly exercises, such as riding at the ring or throwing the lance, were publicly engaged in. They were superseded by tournaments, but were again revived when the latter had fallen out of use, and were frequent at the court of Louis XIV.

CARRYING-TRADE. That department of trade or commerce which consists in the carriage of commodities from one place or country to another; generally applied to the carrying of merchandise from one country to another by sea, especially when the vessels conveying the goods belong to a different country from either of the other two.

CARSE. A word of uncertain origin, applied in Scotland to a tract of fertile alluvial land along the side of a stream, the "Carse of Gowrie" being a well-known example. Such tracts are usually, though not invariably, highly fertile.

CARSON OF DUNCAIRN, Edward, Lord. A Lord of Appeal since 1921, born at Dublin 1854. Educated at Portarlington School and Trinity College, Dublin, he entered Parliament in 1892, representing his University. He acted as Solicitor-General for Ireland in 1892, was appointed Queen's Counsel in 1894, and became Solicitor-General for England in 1900, which position he retained until 1906. He was knighted in 1900, and made a Privy Councillor in 1905.

Throughout the land troubles in Ireland he was one of the most ardent advocates of Unionist principles in the House of Commons, so that on the retirement of Mr. Balfour he was looked upon as the future leader of the Unionist party. A strong anti-Home Ruler, Sir Edward became the head of the Ulster resistance to the Home Rule Bill for Ireland in 1912. He presided over a huge meeting in Ulster, where about 100,000 men paraded in military array, and when the Home Rule Bill was introduced into Parliament he organised the Signing of the Covenant (28th Sept., 1912), pledging resistance to the Bill.

In 1913 a Provisional Government for Ulster was determined upon, and Carson became the head of the Executive Committee. He also played the most prominent part in organising the Ulster Volunteer Force, but when war broke out he urged the members of this force to join the army, which most of them did, forming the celebrated 36th (Ulster) Division. During the Great War he was Attorney-General (1915), First Lord of the Admiralty (1917), and Minister without Portfolio (1917-18). In 1921 he was made a life peer and a Lord of Appeal, a post he resigned in 1929.

CARSON CITY. A town, United States, capital of the state of Nevada, picturesquely situated near the foot of the Sierra Nevada, 3 miles from Carson River; founded in 1858. Pop. 1600.

CARSTAIRS, or CARSTARES, William. A Scottish divine of political eminence, born in 1649 near Glasgow, died 1715. He studied at the University of Edinburgh, and afterwards at Utrecht. He was introduced to the Prince of Orange, on whom he made a favourable impression. In 1672 he came to London, and two years after he was arrested on account of his connection with the exiles in Holland,

and was kept five years a prisoner in Edinburgh Castle.

He was released in 1679, and afterwards played a part of some importance in the schemes of those who were working in favour of William of Orange. Though he did not approve of it, he became privy to the Rye-house plot, in consequence of which he was apprehended and subjected to the torture, which he endured with great firmness. Being released, he returned to Holland, and was received by the Prince of Orange as a sufferer in his cause. His scholarship, sagacity, and political information won for him the confidence of William, who planned the invasion of 1688 mainly by his advice.

When William was settled on the throne, Carstairs was constantly consulted by him on Scottish affairs. He was the chief agent between the Church of Scotland and the court, and was instrumental in the establishment of Presbyterianism, to which William was averse. Owing to his authority in Church matters, he was nick-named *Cardinal Carstairs.* On the death of William he was no longer employed on public business, but Anne retained him as her chaplain royal, and made him principal of the University of Edinburgh. When the union of the two kingdoms was agitated, he took a decided part in its favour. He was repeatedly moderator of the General Assembly of the Church.—Cf. Rev. R. H. Story, *Character and Career of William Carstairs.*

CARTAGENA (kår-tå-*hā'*nå), or **CARTHAGENA** (kår-thă-jē'na). A fortified town and seaport of Spain, in the province of and 31 miles S.S.E. of Murcia, with a harbour which is one of the largest and safest in the Mediterranean, sheltered by lofty hills. The town is surrounded by a wall; the principal streets are spacious and regular. It is a naval and military station, with an arsenal, dockyards, etc. Lead-smelting is largely carried on; and there are in the neighbourhood rich mines of excellent iron. Esparto grass, lead, iron-ore, oranges, etc., are exported. Formerly very unhealthy, it has been greatly improved by draining. There is now a wireless station at Cartagena.

Cartagena was founded by the Carthaginians under Hasdrubal about 243 B.C., and was called New Carthage. It was taken by Scipio Africanus 210 B.C., and was long an important Roman town. It was ruined by the Goths, and revived in the time of Philip II. It was held by some communist rebels from July, 1873, to Jan., 1874. Pop. 96,891.

CARTAGENA (kår-tå-*hā'*nå), or **CARTHAGENA** (kår-thă-jē'na). A city and seaport, Republic of Colombia, on the Caribbean Sea, capital of the state of Bolivar, well laid out, with well-paved streets and a naval arsenal. The exports are coffee, cotton, ivory-nuts, rubber, hides, etc. The trade, which had partly gone to Sabanilla and Santa Marta, is being again recovered since the reopening of the canal to the River Magdalena. The town was founded by Dom Pedro de Heredia in 1533, was burned by Drake in 1585, but resisted an assault by the English in 1741. Pop. 92,000.

CARTA'GO. A town of Central America, in Costa Rica. It formerly had a population of about 37,000, but was utterly ruined by an earthquake in connection with an eruption of a neighbouring volcano in 1841, so that its population had decreased to 14,833 in 1927. Present pop. 16,000.

CAR'TAGO. A town in Colombia, in the valley of the Cauca, in a well-cultivated district and with a good trade. Pop. 10,000.

CARTE, Thomas. An English historian, born in Warwickshire in 1686, died in 1754. He studied at Oxford and Cambridge, took the degree of M.A. at the latter, and entered the Church. Having incurred the suspicion of having been concerned in plots against the Government, he fled to France and remained abroad for some years, returning in 1728. In 1736 he published *Life of James, Duke of Ormonde* (2 vols. folio), and between 1747 and 1752 three vols. of his voluminous *History of England*, a fourth being published in 1755. His work is distinguished by careful and elaborate research, and has supplied Hume and other historians with much material.

CARTE-BLANCHE (kårt-blånsh; literally *white* or *blank paper*). A blank paper, duly signed, entrusted to a person to fill up as he pleases, and thus giving unlimited power to decide.

CARTE-DE-VISITE (kårt-dė-vi-zēt'). Literally a visiting-card, a name applied to a size of photographs somewhat larger than a visiting-card, and usually inserted in a photographic album. Cartes-de-visite were introduced by Disdéri in 1854.

CAR'TEL. An agreement for the delivery of prisoners or deserters; also, a written challenge to a duel. **Cartel-ship.** A ship commissioned in time of war to exchange prisoners.

CARTER, Elizabeth. An English lady of great learning, the daughter of Dr. Nicholas Carter, a clergyman in Kent. Born in 1717, died in 1806. She was educated by her father, and learned Latin, Greek, French, and German, to which she afterwards added Italian, Spanish, Portuguese, Hebrew, and Arabic. She wrote poems, contributed two papers to the *Rambler*; translated the critique of Crousaz on Pope's *Essay on Man*; Algarotti's *Neutonianismo per le donne*; and Epictetus; and was a friend of Johnson, Reynolds, Burke, and other eminent men of the time.

CARTERET, Baron. English politician, born April 22nd, 1690, John Carteret was educated at Westminster and Christ Church, Oxford, and took his seat in the House of Lords among the Whigs in 1711. After a period as ambassador to Sweden, he was made a secretary of state. He was Lord Lieutenant of Ireland, 1724-30, and from 1742 to 1744 was again a secretary of state. In 1751 he was appointed Lord President of the Council. He died Jan. 22nd, 1763.

In 1744, on his mother's death, he became Earl Granville, a title which became extinct when his son, Robert, died in 1776, but was later revived.

CARTE'SIAN DIVER. A hydrostatic toy consisting of a little hollow glass figure, which has a small opening some distance below the top, and is rather lighter than an equal column of water, so as to be able to float. The figure is placed in a bottle or cylindrical vessel of water closed with a piece of bladder or india-rubber so as to exclude air. On pressing this with the finger the air inside the figure is compressed, it sinks down, and from the introduction of a small quantity of water becomes specifically heavier. By removing the pressure the water is expelled, and the figure, thus lightened, again rises to the surface.

CARTESIAN PHILOSOPHY. *See* DESCARTES.

CARTESIAN VORTICES. *See* DESCARTES.

CAR'THAGE (Lat. *Carthago*, Gr. *Karchēdōn*). The most famous city of Africa in antiquity, capital of a rich and powerful commercial republic, situated in the territory now belonging to Tunis. Carthage was the latest of the Phœnician colonies in this district, and is supposed to have been founded by settlers from Tyre and from the neighbouring Utica about the middle of the ninth century before Christ. The story of Dido and the foundation of Carthage is mere legend or invention. The history of Carthage falls naturally into three epochs. The first, from the foundation to 410 B.C., comprises the rise and culmination of Carthaginian power; the second, from 410 to 265 B.C., is the period of the wars with the Sicilian Greeks; the third, from 265 to 146 B.C., the period of the wars with Rome, ending with the fall of Carthage.

History. The rise of Carthage may be attributed to the superiority of her site for commercial purposes, and the enterprise of her inhabitants, which soon acquired for her an ascendancy over the earlier Tyrian colonies in the district, Utica, Tunis, Hippo, Septis, and Hadrumetum. Her relations with the native populations, Libyans and nomads, were those of a superior with inferior races. Some of them were directly subject to Carthage, others contributed large sums as tribute, and Libyans formed the main body of infantry as nomads did of cavalry in the Carthaginian army. Besides these there were native Carthaginian colonies, small centres and supports for her great commercial system, sprinkled along the whole northern coast of Africa, from Cyrenaica on the east to the Straits of Gibraltar on the west.

In extending her commerce Carthage was naturally led to the conquest of the various islands which from their position might serve as entrepôts for traffic with the northern shores of the Mediterranean. Sardinia was the first conquest of the Carthaginians, and its capital, Caralis, now Cagliari, was founded by them. Soon after they occupied Corsica, the Balearic, and many smaller islands in the Mediterranean. When the Persians under Xerxes invaded Greece, the Carthaginians, who had already several settlements in the west of Sicily, co-operated by organising a great expedition of 300,000 men against the Greek cities in Sicily. But the defeat of the Carthaginians at Himera by the Greeks under Gelon of Syracuse effectually checked their further progress (480 B.C.).

The war with the Greeks in Sicily was not renewed till 410. Hannibal, the son of Gisco, invaded Sicily, reduced first Selinus and Himera, and then Agrigentum. Syracuse itself was only saved a little later by a pestilence which enfeebled the army of Himilco (396). The struggle between the Greeks and the Carthaginians continued at intervals with varying success, its most remarkable events being the military successes of the Corinthian Timoleon (345-340) at Syracuse, and the invasion of the Carthaginian territory in Africa by Agathocles 310 B.C. After the death of Agathocles the Greeks called in

Pyrrhus, King of Epirus, to their aid, but notwithstanding numerous defeats (277-5 B.C.), the Carthaginians seemed, after the departure of Pyrrhus, to have the conquest of all Sicily at length within their power.

The intervention of the Romans was now invoked, and with their invasion, 264 B.C., the third period of Carthaginian history begins. The first Punic War (Lat. *Punicus*, Phœnician), in which Rome and Carthage contended for the dominion of Sicily, was prolonged for twenty-three years, 264 to 241 B.C., and ended, through the exhaustion of the resources of Carthage, in her expulsion from the island.

The loss of Sicily led to the acquisition of Spain for Carthage, which was almost solely the work of Hamilcar and Hasdrubal. The second Punic War, arising out of incidents connected with the Carthaginian conquests in Spain, and conducted on the side of the Carthaginians by the genius of Hannibal, and distinguished by his great march on Rome and the victories of Lake Trasimene, Trebia, and Cannæ, lasted seventeen years, 218 to 201 B.C., and after just missing the overthrow of Rome, ended in the complete humiliation of Carthage. (*See* ROME; HANNIBAL.) The policy of Rome in encouraging the African enemies of Carthage occasioned the third Punic War, in which Rome was the aggressor. This war, begun 149 B.C., ended 146 B.C. in the total destruction of Carthage.

Constitution. The constitution of Carthage, like her history, remains in many points obscure. The name of king occurs in the Greek accounts of it, but the monarchical constitution, as commonly understood, never appears to have existed in Carthage. The officers called kings by the Greeks were two in number, the heads of an oligarchical republic, and were otherwise called Suffetes, the original name being considered identical with the Heb. *Shofetim*, judges. These officers were chosen from the principal families, and were elected annually. There was a Senate of 300, and a smaller body of thirty chosen from the Senate, sometimes another smaller council of ten.

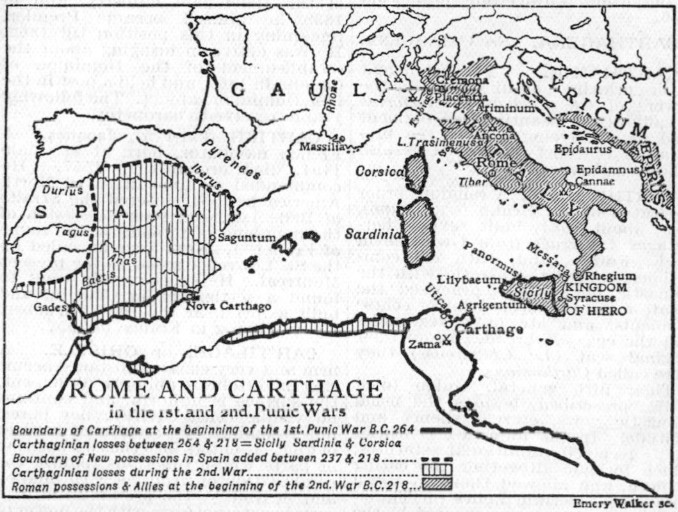

ROME AND CARTHAGE
in the 1st. and 2nd. Punic Wars

Boundary of Carthage at the beginning of the 1st. Punic War B.C. 264
Carthaginian losses between 264 & 218 = Sicily Sardinia & Corsica
Boundary of New possessions in Spain added between 237 & 218
Carthaginian losses during the 2nd. War
Roman possessions & Allies at the beginning of the 2nd. War B.C. 218

In its later ages the state was divided by bitter factions, and liable to violent popular tumults. After the destruction of Carthage her territory became the Roman province of Africa. Twenty-four years after her fall an unsuccessful attempt was made to rebuild Carthage by Gaius Gracchus. This was finally accomplished by Augustus, and Roman Carthage became one of the most important cities of the Empire. It was taken and destroyed by the Arabs in 638.

The religion of the Carthaginians was that of their Phœnician ancestors. They worshipped Moloch or Baal, to whom they offered human sacrifices; Melkart, the patron deity of Tyre; Astarte, the Phœnician Venus; and other deities, who were mostly propitiated by cruel or lascivious rites.—BIBLIOGRAPHY: N. Davis, *Carthage and her Remains*; R. B. Smith, *Carthage and the Carthaginians*; E. Babelon, *Carthage*; Mabel Moore, *Carthage of the Phœnicians in the Light of Modern Excavation.*

CARTHAGE. A town of the United States, in the south-west of Missouri, in a region rich in lead and zinc; an important railway junction. Pop. 9736.

CARTHAGENA. *See* CARTAGENA.

CAR'THAMIN. An astringent bitter principle obtained from the flowers of the *Carthămus tinctorius* or safflower, a beautiful red pigment used in silk-dyeing and in the preparation of toilet-rouge. It is also called *Carthamic Acid.*

CARTHU'SIANS. A religious order instituted by St. Bruno (*see Bruno*), who, about 1084, built several hermitages 4 leagues from Grenoble in S. E. France, and, with six companions, united the ascetic with the monastic life. They practised the greatest abstinence, wore coarse garments, and ate only vegetables and the coarsest bread. From their original seat (*La Chartreuse*) they were called *Carthusians.*

Their fifth general, Guigo (died 1137), prescribed, besides the usual monastic vows, eternal silence and solitude. In the following centuries they received additional statutes, which forbade altogether the eating of flesh, and allowed them to speak only during certain hours on Thursdays and the days on which the chapter met. With increasing wealth some modifications were introduced in their silent and solitary life. Their habit is a hair-cloth shirt, a white tunic, a black cloak, and a cowl.

The Carthusians came into England about 1178, and built the Charterhouse (a name corrupted from *Chartreuse*) in 1370. Their chief house was long La Grande Chartreuse. In 1900 the monks possessed eleven monasteries in France and nine in other parts of Europe. The French houses are now empty, in consequence of the expulsion of the Carthusians from France under the Association Laws of 1901. In England there is now one Charterhouse, established at Parkminster, in Sussex, in 1883. It is the largest Charterhouse in the world, with 36 cells, and contains the community of Nôtre-Dame des Près Montreuil, as well as its own.—Cf. article in *Catholic Encyclopœdia.*

CARTIER, Sir George Étienne. Canadian statesman, born at St. Antoine, Quebec, in 1814, died in England in 1873. He was admitted to the Bar in 1835, took part in the rebellion of 1837, and had for a time to leave Canada. In 1848 he entered the Canadian Parliament, and in 1855 became Provincial Secretary. Next year he became Attorney-General for Lower Canada, in which post he interested himself in legal reforms. In 1857 he was a member of the Macdonald ministry, and in 1858 he himself became Premier, remaining in this position till 1862. He was active in bringing about the establishment of the Dominion of Canada in 1867, and held a post in the first Dominion cabinet. The following year he received a baronetcy.

CARTIER (kär-tyā), **Jacques.** A French navigator, born at St. Malo 1494, died probably in 1557. He commanded an expedition to North America in 1534, entered the Straits of Belle Isle, and took possession of the mainland of Canada in the name of Francis I. Next year he sailed up the St. Lawrence as far as the present Montreal. He subsequently went to found a settlement in Canada, and built a fort near the site of Quebec. He was living in France in 1552.

CAR'TILAGE, or GRISTLE. A firm and very elastic substance occurring in vertebrate animals. When cut, the surface is uniform, and contains no visible cells, cavities, nor pores, but resembles the section of a piece of glue. It enters into the composition of parts whose functions require the combination of firmness with pliancy and flexibility, the preservation of a certain external form with the power of yielding to external force or pressure. The ends of bones entering into the formation of a joint are always coated with cartilage. *Temporary cartilages* are those from which bones are formed by ossification. The *permanent cartilages* are of various kinds. They are found in the external ear, and aid in forming the nose, the larynx, etc.

CARTILAGINOUS FISHES (laj'i-nus). A general designation for those fishes whose internal skeleton consists of cartilage instead of bone. They comprise sharks and rays (*see* ELASMOBRANCHII, CHIMÆRAS, and HOLOCEPHALI) and sturgeons (*see* STURGEON and GANOIDEI).

CARTOGRAPHY. The constructing of maps of the globe's surface, or portions thereof. Maps are of different kinds, according to the purpose in view, e.g. *political* maps, where countries, towns, etc., are shown; *physical*, representing natural features; *orographical*, exhibiting specially the diversities of surface level. Variation of level may be depicted in relief, on a scale much larger than that adopted for the horizontal lengths, or may be indicated by different tints or shading, by hatching or "hachures," or by curves (contour-lines) connecting places of certain definite altitudes.

The position of places for laying down on a map are found by operations of surveying, whereby the whole country concerned is divided into a network of triangles, and the lengths of their sides determined step by step through trigonometrical processes, from one or more original base-lines, measured with extreme accuracy. Astronomical determinations of latitude and longitude are also utilised.—BIBLIOGRAPHY: A. Germain, *Traité des projections des cartes géographiques*; P. T. E. Goedseels, *Leçons sur la cartographie*; A. R. Hinks, *Map Projections*; P. B. Phillips, *A List of Works relating to Cartography.*

CARTOON'. In painting, a drawing on stout paper or other material, intended to be used as a model for a large picture in fresco, a process in which it is necessary to complete the picture portion by portion and in which a fault cannot afterwards be easily corrected. The cartoon is made exactly the size of the picture intended, and the design is transferred to the surface to be ornamented by tracing or other processes.

Cartoons executed in colour, like paintings, are used for designs in tapestries, mosaics, etc. The most famous are those painted by Raphael for the Vatican tapestries, seven of which are still preserved in the South Kensington Museum, London. They were purchased by Rubens for Charles I., saved by Cromwell, and preserved from neglect by William III. The subjects of the seven are: *Paul Preaching at Athens, The Death of Ananias, Elymas the Sorcerer struck with Blindness, Christ's Charge to Peter, The Sacrifice at Lystra, Peter and John Healing the Cripple at the Beautiful Gate of the Temple, The Miraculous Draught of Fishes.*

In modern times the term is also applied to a pictorial sketch relating to some notable character or events of the day, and generally published in a daily or weekly paper. Those in *Punch* are the most finished of their kind, but those in the London daily papers, by Sir F. C. Gould, and later by Tom Webster, Low and Strube, are also celebrated. Cartoons of this kind are humorous or satirical.

CARTOUCHE (kär'tösh). (1) In architecture, a sculptured ornament in the form of a scroll unrolled, often appearing on the cornices of columns, used as a field for inscriptions, etc.—(2) In heraldry, a sort of oval shield, much used by the Popes and secular princes in Italy, and others, both clergy and laity, for painting or engraving their arms on.—(3) The name given to that oval ring or border which includes, in the Egyptian hieroglyphics, the names of persons of high distinction.

CAR'TRIDGE. The term given to the compact form of ammunition now invariably used in modern small-arms, quick-firing guns, and sporting weapons. The two main portions of a military cartridge are the case and the projectile. The "case" is of brass, and contains the explosive material; in its base is the "cap," consisting of a composition of fulminate of mercury, which, being operated on by the "striker," explodes the "charge." The case is rather less in diameter at its forward end than it is at the base, the reason being that in all rifles the "chamber," which receives the cartridge in the rifle, is larger than the actual bore of the rifle. In this forward end of the case is inserted the bullet, which is held in its place by means of indents in the case fitting into a groove cut in the base of the bullet. Between the charge and the bullet is a cardboard wad, which helps to prevent escape of gas and the consequent waste of power at the moment of ignition.

Cartridges for quick-firing guns are made on the same principle, while those for use in shot guns are slightly different in that both charge and shot are completely enclosed in the case, which is a perfect cylinder closed with a wad. Such cases are made either of brass or of thick paper with a brass base. Blank cartridge is a cartridge without ball or shot, and is used on field-days and by firing-parties at military funerals.

CARTRIDGE-PAPER. A thick sort of paper originally manufactured for soldiers' cartridges, but extensively used in the arts—its rough surface giving it an advantage for drawing upon—and for other purposes.

CARTWRIGHT, Edmund. The inventor of the power-loom. He was born in 1743 in Nottinghamshire, died in 1823. He was educated at Oxford, and took orders in the Church. In 1785 he brought his first power-loom into action. Although much opposed both by manufacturers and workmen, it made its way, and in a developed and improved form is now in universal use. Cartwright spent much of his means in similar inventions, and fell into straitened circumstances, from which a parliamentary grant of £10,000 relieved him.

CARTWRIGHT, Thomas. One of the eminent Puritan divines of the sixteeenth century, born in Hertfordshire in 1535, died in 1603. He suffered imprisonment and exile more than once for his nonconformist opinions. He was a learned man and at one time professor of divinity at Cambridge.

CAR'UCATE. Formerly as much land as one team could plough in the year. The size varied according to the nature of the soil and practice of husbandry in different districts.

CA'RUM. *See* CARAWAY.

CAR'UNCLE. A fleshy excrescence on the head of a fowl, as the comb of a cock, the wattles of a turkey.

CARUNCLE. A small hard outgrowth from the apical end of a seed, connected, as a rule, with seed-dispersal; well seen in the castor-oil seed.

CARU'PANO. A seaport of Venezuela, on the peninsula of Paria. Pop. 13,500.

CARUS (kä'rụs), **Julius Victor.** German zoologist, born in 1823, died in 1903. He studied at Leipzig, Würzburg, and Freiburg; was for a time keeper of the Oxford museum of comparative anatomy; in 1853 was appointed professor of comparative anatomy and Director of the Zoological Institute at Leipzig. In 1873-4 he lectured on zoology at Edinburgh, taking the place of Professor Wyville Thomson, then absent on the *Challenger* Expedition. One of his principal works was a *Handbook of Zoology*. He translated most of Darwin's works into German, also Lewes's *Physiology of Common Life*, and his work on Aristotle.

CARUS (kä'rụs), **Karl Gustav.** German physician and physiologist, born at Leipzig 1789, died at Dresden 1869. He became professor of midwifery at the Medical Academy, and then royal physician, being afterwards a Privy Councillor. He published a great number of writings covering a wide field of science, including medicine, physiology, anatomy, psychology, physics, painting, besides memoirs of his life.

CARUSO, Enrico. Famous Italian singer, born at Naples 25th Feb., 1873. He obtained his first great success in *La Traviata* (Naples, 1896). In 1898 he appeared at Milan in *La Bohême*, and he has since established his reputation as one of the leading operatic singers, his principal rôles being Des Grieux in

Enrico Caruso

Manon Lescaut, the Duke in *Rigoletto*, etc. He appeared at Covent Garden in 1903. He died 2nd Aug., 1921.

CARVEL-BUILT. A term applied to a ship or boat the planks of which are all flush and not overlapping, as in clinker-built boats.

CARVIN (kär-vaṇ), or **CARVIN EPINAY.** A town of France, department of Pas de Calais; industries: coal-mining, iron-founding, distilling, beetroot sugar, and flax-spinning. Pop. 16,650.

CARVING. As a branch of art, the process of cutting a hard body by means of a sharp instrument into some particular shape, and a term generally employed in speaking of figures cut out in ivory or wood, in contradistinction to sculpture, or figures produced in stone or metal. The art of carving is of the highest antiquity. Even among the most uncivilised tribes, rudely-carved representations in wood are common. In the early and Middle Ages wood-carving became general for the decoration of Christian churches and altars.

A more recent development of the art of carving is the modern invention of carving by machinery. A machine patented in 1845 by Jordan is capable of copying any carved design that can be produced, so far as that is possible, by revolving tools; the finish is afterwards given by hand-labour.

CARY, Rev. Henry Francis. The translator of Dante. Born in 1772 and educated at Oxford. In 1797 he received the vicarage of Abbot's Bromley, Staffordshire. In 1805 appeared his translation of Dante in English blank verse. He subsequently translated the *Birds* of Aristophanes and the *Odes* of Pindar. He also wrote a series of memoirs in continuation of Dr. Johnson's *Lives of the Poets*. In 1826 he was appointed assistant librarian in the British Museum, and retired in 1837 on a pension of £200 a year. He died in London 14th Aug., 1844.

CARY, Lucius. *See* FALKLAND.

CA'RYA. The hickory genus of plants.

CARYAT'IDES (-dēz), or **CAR'YATIDS.** In architecture, figures of women dressed in long robes, serving to support entablatures. Vitruvius relates that the city Caryæ sided with the Persians after the battle of Thermopylæ, and that it was on that account sacked by the other Greeks, who took their wives captive, and to perpetuate this event erected trophies in which figures of women dressed in the Caryatic manner were used to support entablatures. This story is, however, believed to be unworthy of credit, as such figures are already found in ancient Egypt as supporters of thrones. But it is not improbable that the name of the Caryatides was derived from this city. Corresponding male figures are called *Atlantes*.

CAR'YOCAR. A genus of plants, nat. ord. Caryocaraceæ, consisting of lofty trees, natives of tropical America, which produce good timber, and also *souari* or butter-nuts.

CARYOPHYLLA'CEÆ. An order of plants, of which the pink, named formerly Caryophyllus, and now Dianthus, may be considered as the type. The plants have opposite undivided leaves, without stipules, tumid articulations of the stems, and seeds disposed upon a free central placenta, surrounded by several carpellary leaves. The great proportion of the species are inconspicuous weeds, like chick-weed, sandwort, etc., but many are found as favourite plants in our gardens, as the carnation, sweet-william, etc.

CARYOP'SIS. In botany, a small one-seeded, dry, indehiscent fruit in which the seed adheres to the thin pericarp throughout, as in wheat and other grains.

CARYO'TA. A genus of palms, with doubly-pinnate leaves, the best-known species of which (*C. urens*) is a native of most of tropical Asia; it supplies an inferior kind of sago, and from its sap is made toddy or palm-wine and palm-sugar.

CASABIANCA, Louis de. French naval officer. A Corsican by birth, he entered the French Navy, and helped to convoy French troops to America during the War of Independence. He was appointed to the ship *Orient*, and at the Battle of the Nile off Aboukir, when defeated, safeguarded the crew and perished with the ship, with his ten-year-old son, Giacomo Jocante, Aug. 1, 1798. Their heroism is commemorated in Mrs. Hemans' poem.

Caryatides, Erechtheum, Acropolis, Athens

CASA BLANCA. *See* DAR-AL-BEIDA.

CASALE (kȧ-sä'lā). A city of Northern Italy, province of Alessandria, on the Po, 18 miles N.N.W. of Alessandria. Its citadel, founded in 1590, was one of the strongest in Italy, and its fortifications have been greatly strengthened and extended in recent years. It has a cathedral, consecrated in 1107. Silk is the chief industry. Pop. 34,000.

CASALPUSTERLENGO. A town of Northern Italy, in the province of Milan; trade in Parmesan cheese. Pop. 6380.

CASALS, Pablo. Spanish 'cellist. Born in 1878, he studied music in the Conservatoire at Barcelona and soon won fame as an executive musician. He played in London and other European capitals, and in 1912 won the medal of the Royal Philharmonic Society.

CASAMICCIOLA (kå-så-mich'o-lå). A village on the Italian island of Ischia, frequented for sea-bathing and the use of its warm springs; restored after being destroyed by earthquake in 1883. Pop. 3630.

CASANO'VA, Giovanni Jacopo, de Seingalt. Born at Venice, 1725, known by his *Memoirs* as an adventurer who acted a prominent part in all situations, amongst all classes of society, and in all the large cities of Europe, by turns acting the part of diplomatist, preacher, abbot, lawyer, and charlatan. Among others with whom he came in contact were Rousseau, Voltaire, Suvarov, Frederick the Great, and Catherine II. He died in Bohemia in 1798. His celebrated *Memoirs* are a lively picture of the manners of his times, but probably not very veracious.—BIBLIOGRAPHY: Ottmann, *Jacob Casanova*; E. Maynial, *Casanova et son temps*; J. D. Rolleston, *Medical Interest in Casanova's Memoirs*.

CASAS, Bartolomeo de las. *See* LAS CASAS.

CASAU'BON, Isaac de. Classical scholar, born 18th Feb., 1559, at Geneva. Educated by his father, a clergyman. In his ninth year he spoke Latin fluently. In 1582 he became professor of the Greek language at Geneva. Henry IV. invited him to Paris and made him royal librarian. After the death of Henry IV. he followed Sir Henry Wotton, envoy extraordinary from James I., to England, where he was received with distinction, had two benefices and a pension conferred on him, and died at London, 1st July, 1614. He was buried in Westminster Abbey.

Casaubon was a liberal theologian, a man of extensive learning, a good translator, and an excellent critic of the ancient classics, many of which he edited. He wrote also an excellent treatise on Greek and Roman satire. His *Life* was written by M. Pattison (1875), revised edition by Nettleship (1892).—Cf. L. J. Nazelle, *Isaac Casaubon et son temps*.—His son, *Meric*, born at Geneva, 1599, likewise distinguished himself by his learning, publishing commentaries on Terence, Marcus Aurelius, etc. He died in England in 1671.

CAS'BIN or **KAZVIN.** *See* KAZVIN.

CASCADE RANGE. A range of mountains in North America, near the Pacific coast, to which they are parallel, extending from the Sierra Nevada in California northwards to Alaska. It contains several active volcanoes, Highest peak, Mount St. Elias, 18,017 feet. The highest peaks in the United States portion of it are in Washington territory, where Mount Rainier or Tacoma reaches 14,408 feet, St. Helens 10,000 feet, and Mount Adams, 12,307.

CAS'CARA SAGRA'DA (Sp. *cascăra*, bark, *sagrado*, sacred). The bark of a kind of N. American buckthorn, and an aperient medicine prepared from it now in common use as a mild remedy.

CASCARIL'LA. The aromatic bitter bark of *Croton Eleutheria*, a small tree of that nat. ord. Euphorbiaceæ.

CASCO BAY. A bay of America, in Maine, United States, between Cape Elizabeth on W.S.W. and Cape Small Point on E.N.E. Within these capes are more than 300 small islands, most of them very productive.

CASE. In grammar, a term indicating certain relationships in which nouns and pronouns may stand as regards other words, and which are often marked by special forms or inflections. A word that is the subject of a verb is generally said to be in the *nominative* case, one that is an object in the *objective* or *accusative* case. In English these two cases are alike except in pronouns, the only inflected noun-case in English being the *possessive*. English pronouns have three cases—nominative, possessive, and objective, as *he*, *his*, *him*. In Sanskrit there are eight cases. In Russian there are seven cases. In French, Italian, Spanish, and Portuguese there are no case-forms. In German there are four cases, nominative, gentitive, dative, accusative.

CASE-HARDENING. A process by which mild steel is superficially converted into hard steel, in such articles as require the toughness of the former as well as the hardness of the latter substance. The articles intended for case-hardening are first manufactured in mild steel, and are then placed in an iron box, with carbonaceous matter, and heated to redness. After cooling, the articles are reheated and quenched in water in order to harden the case.

CASEIN (kā′sē-in; from Lat. *caseus*, cheese). That ingredient in milk which is neither coagulated spontaneously, like fibrin, nor by heat, like albumen, but by the action of acids alone, and constituting the chief part of the nitrogenised matter contained in it. Cheese made from skimmed milk and well pressed is fully half casein. Casein is one of the most important elements of animal food as found in milk and leguminous plants. It consists of carbon, 53·13 per cent; hydrogen, 7·06; nitrogen, 15·78; oxygen, 22·40; sulphur, 0·77; and phosphorus, 0·86. Casein is used in making biscuits, also as casein gum or *lacterin*, and in a number of industries.

CASE′MATES (from the Sp. *casa*, a house, and *matare*, to kill). In fortification, vaults which are proof against bombs, and which may serve as a place for keeping ordnance, ammunition, etc., and in case of necessity as habitations for the garrison.

CASEMENT, Sir Roger. An Irish conspirator, born 1st Sept., 1864. He was engaged in the British consular service from 1895 to 1913, and was given the Queen's medal for special services in Cape Town (1899 and 1900) during the South African War. He was knighted in 1909, and in 1912, while Consul-General at Rio de Janeiro, he became quite famous for his investigations of the cruelties practised on natives in Putumayo by a British rubber company. In 1913 Casement retired on a pension. During the European War he went over to Germany and tried to persuade the Irish prisoners of war to join the German armies. Having met with very little success, he attempted to get back to Ireland to take part in the Sinn Fein rebellion which broke out in Dublin in April, 1916.

During the night of 20th April, 1916, an attempt was made to land arms and ammunition in Ireland by a vessel disguised as a neutral merchant ship, in reality, however, a German auxiliary. The vessel was sunk and many prisoners were made; among these was Sir Roger. He was degraded from the rank of knight-bachelor, and his name was removed from the rolls of the Order of St. Michael and St. George. He was placed upon his trial in the civil courts on a charge of high treason, was committed for trial on 17th May, and a week later a grand jury found a *true bill*, and the prisoner was convicted of high treason and sentenced to death. The indictment charged him with "adhering to the King's enemies elsewhere than in the King's Realm, to wit, in the Empire of Germany." He appealed against his conviction, but the appeal was dismissed, and he was hanged in Pentonville Jail on 3rd Aug., 1916.

CASER′TA, or CASERTA NUOVA. The capital of the province of Caserta, South Italy, in a plain, 7 miles E.S.E. of Capua and 18 miles from Naples. The principal edifice is the royal palace, a large and richly-decorated structure, commenced in 1752 by Charles III. of Spain. Pop. 35,172.—The province has an area of 2034 square miles and a population of 823,985.

CASE-SHOT, or CANISTER-SHOT. An obsolete form of ammunition. Formed by putting a quantity of small iron balls into a cylindrical tin box, called a *canister*, that just fitted the bore of the gun. This kind of shot was very injurious to an enemy within a short distance. The shrapnel-shell is a modern variety of case-shot.

CASHAN. A town, Persia. *See* KASHAN.

CASH CREDIT, or CASH ACCOUNT. A mode of advancing funds originated by the Scottish banks, and since adopted by others. A cash credit is an account which the trader may overdraw to a certain amount as he may require, paying cash in and taking it out according to his needs within that limit. Heritable property, two sureties, or some other form of security is usually demanded by the bank.

CASH′EL. A town, Ireland, County Tipperary, 88 miles S.W. of Dublin; with a spacious cathedral, a handsome episcopal palace (now the deanery-house), barracks, etc., and several interesting ruins. Cashel was the seat of the ancient kings of Munster. Here Henry II. received the homage of the King of Limerick in 1172. Pop. (1926), 2945.

CASHEW′ (*Anacardium occidentāle*). A tree of the ord. Anacardiaceæ, common in the West Indies. Its fruit is called the cashew-nut. The nut is small, kidney-shaped, ash-grey, and contains an acrid juice, but its noxious property is destroyed by roasting, after which it is esteemed a great delicacy. It is used to flavour Madeira wine, and is eaten cooked in various ways. The fumes it gives off when roasting are so acrid as sometimes to cause inflammation. The stalk or receptacle of the nut is large and fleshy, and has an agreeable acid flavour.

CASHGAR′. *See* KASHGAR.

CASHMERE. *See* KASHMIR.

CASH ON DELIVERY. System of selling through an agent to customers at a distance, payment being made on delivery. The Post Office, often working in conjunction with the railway companies, is the agent usually employed. The Swiss Post Office started the system in 1849, and in 1885 regulations for the service were laid down by the Postal Congress at Lisbon.

After the Great War, a C.O.D. system was introduced into Great Britain, and in 1930 extended to include perishable goods. The Post Office will collect any sum up to £40 when delivering a parcel. A small fee is charged. In 1929 the number of parcels dealt with under this system was 2,290,000. There is a C.O.D. service between Great Britain and other parts of the Empire and with certain foreign countries.

CASH REGISTER. Machine invented by James Ritty in 1879 for retail traders. A common modern type has keys representing particular sums, which, when operated like those of a typewriter, record the amount of the purchase, register the total amount passed through the machine, and raise an indicator to show the customer the purchase amount. The drawers containing the cash cannot be opened without a record being made in the machine.

CASIMIR III. THE GREAT. King of Poland, born in 1309, died in 1370. He ascended the throne in 1333, conquered Little Russia, Silesia, and repelled the Tartars. He protected the peasants with much energy, and, in order to please one of his mistresses, who was a Jewess, conferred valuable privileges on the Jews. After his death the crown of Poland was recognised as elective.

CASIMIR-PÉRIER, Jean Paul Pierre. President of the French Republic, born 8th Nov., 1847, died 1907. He served in the Franco-Prussian War, and was elected to the Chamber of Deputies in 1874. Although regarded as an Orleanist, Casimir-Périer always acted as a staunch Republican. In 1893 he became President of the Chamber of Deputies, and on 3rd Dec., President of the Council and Prime Minister. On 22nd May, 1894, after the assassination of President Carnot, he was elected President of the Republic. He resigned, however, on 15th Jan., 1895, either on account of complications with Germany arising out of the Dreyfus case, or because he was unable to cope with factional politics.

CASI'NO (It., a summer house). A name generally given to a kind of club-house or place of amusement, containing rooms for dancing, playing billiards, etc.

CASKET LETTERS. Debatable collection of documents attributed to Mary Queen of Scots, which, if genuine, prove her complicity in the murder of her husband, Darnley. The Earl of Morton professed to have found them in June, 1567, three months after their alleged date, in a silver casket. There were eight letters and some sonnets in French. They disappeared after the execution of the Earl of Gowrie in 1584. On examination Mary maintained that the letters were a forgery.

CASO'RIA. A town of Italy, 6 miles N.N.E. of Naples. Pop. 16,500.

CAS'PE. A town, Spain, Aragon, province of Saragossa, 12 miles N.N.E. of Alcañiz, near the Ebro. Pop. 8878.

CASPIAN SEA. A large lake or inland sea between Europe and Asia, 730 miles in length from N. to S., and from 130 to 270 miles in breadth; area, 170,000 sq. miles; the largest isolated sheet of water on the globe. Its surface is 85 feet below that of the Sea of Azov; greatest depth about 3250 feet. Russian territory surrounds it on three sides, Persia on the fourth. It abounds in shallows, making navigation difficult. Among the rivers which flow into it are the Volga, Ural, Terek, and Kur. It has no outlet. The water is less salt than that of the ocean, of a bitter taste, and of an ochre colour, without ebb or flow. The fisheries are valuable, including those sturgeon, sterlet, roach, bream, perch, carp, and porpoises. The only ports at all worthy the name on or near the Caspian are Astrakhan, Derbend, Baku, Krasnovodsk, and Astrabad. Steam vessels have long been plying on it. The Russians have also a naphtha flotilla in the Caspian. By the Volga and canals there is water communication with the Baltic.

CASS, Lewis. An American politician, born in Exeter, New Hampshire, in 1782, died in June, 1866. In 1813, having entered the army, he rose to the rank of general. He was Governor of Michigan from 1814 to 1830, Minister of War in 1831, a candidate for the presidency several times, a Senator, and from 1857 to 1860 Secretary of State. He wrote *Inquiries concerning the History, Traditions, and Languages of Indians Living within the United States.*

CASSAGNAC (kȧs-ȧn-yȧk), **Adolphe Bernard Granier de.** A French journalist and politician, born 1806, died 1880. He began his career at

Paris as contributor of literary criticisms to the *Journal des Débats*, and soon made himself known, and afterwards notorious, as editor of various papers, the *Globe*, the *Pouvoir*, the *Pays*, etc., and as being involved in many controversies and duels. He published various books, chiefly historical. Amongst the principal are: *Portraits Littéraires*, *Histoire des Causes de la Révolution Française*, *Histoire des Girondins*, *L'Empereur et la Démocratie moderne*.

CASSAGNAC, Paul de. Son of above, born 1842, died 1904. He had a career and a reputation not dissimilar to those of his father. Like his father he was a devoted Bonapartist.

CASSAN'DER. A king of Macedonia, born about 354 B.C. He displaced his brother Polysperchon in the regency, removed in succession the mother, the wife, and the son of Alexander the Great to make way for himself to the throne. He married Thessalonica, Alexander's half-sister, and founded the city of that name in her honour. In company with Seleucus, Ptolemy, and Lysimachus he defeated and slew Antigonus, King of Asia, whose dominions were divided amongst the conquerors. He died in 297 B.C.

CASSAN'DRA. In Greek legend, a daughter of Priam and Hecuba. She is fabled to have been endowed by Apollo with the gift of prophecy, coupled with this disadvantage, that her prophecies should never be believed. She frequently foretold the fall of Troy, and warned her countrymen in vain against the stratagem of the horse. When Troy was taken, she fell, as part of his share of the booty, to Agamemnon, who, in spite of her warnings, carried her with him as his slave to Mycenæ, where they were both murdered by Clytemnestra.

CASSA'NO. Two towns in Italy.—(1) A town, province of and 32 miles N.N.E. of Cosenza, the seat of a bishopric. It has hot sulphurous springs. Pop. 8552.—(2) **Cassano d'Adda,** a town 16 miles N.N.E. of Milan, where Prince Eugène was defeated in 1705 by the Duc de Vendôme, and the French, under Moreau, by Suvarov in 1799. Pop. (commune), 9150.

CAS'SAREEP. The concentrated juice of the roots of the common or bitter cassava (*Manihot utilissima*; *see* CASSAVA), flavoured by aromatics and deprived of its poisonous properties by boiling. It is used to give a relish to soups and other dishes, and forms the basis of the West Indian "pepper-pot." It has antiseptic properties, and is very useful in keeping meat fresh in a tropical climate.

CASSA'TION. A term used in the courts on the continent of Europe, signifying the annulling of any act or decision, if the forms prescribed by law have been neglected, or if anything is contained in it contrary to law.

Court of Cassation. One of the most important institutions of modern France, established by the first National Assembly in 1790. In 1814 the number of its members was fixed at forty-nine, a first president, three sectional presidents, and forty-five councillors or *conseillers*, at which it still remains. The members are appointed for life. The sphere of this court is to decide on the competency of the other courts, and on the petitions to have their decisions reviewed or annulled. Its decisions are not only recorded in the journals of the courts the decisions of which are reversed, but published likewise in an official bulletin. It has enjoyed from its commencement the respect and confidence of France.

CASSA'VA (*Manihot utilissima*). A South American shrub, about 8 feet in height, with broad, shining, and somewhat hand-shaped leaves, and beautiful white and rose-coloured flowers, belonging to the nat. ord. Euphorbiaceæ, sub-ord. Crotoneæ. A nutritious starch is obtained from the white soft root of the plant, and is called by the same name. It is prepared in the West Indies, tropical America, and in Africa in the following manner: The roots are washed, stripped of their rind, and grated down to a pulp, which is put into coarse, strong canvas bags, and submitted to powerful pressure to express the juice, which is highly poisonous in its natural state. The flour that remains after pressing is formed into cakes, and baked on a hot iron plate. In this state it forms a valuable article of food, upon which many of the inhabitants of Southern America live almost entirely. From cassava the tapioca of commerce is prepared.

Another species (*M. Aipi*), the sweet cassava, has roots the juice of which is not poisonous, and which are an agreeable and nutritive food. *Piwarri* is an intoxicating drink prepared from cassava cakes partially masticated by women, then expectorated into wooden vessels, and retained until fermentation takes place. It is then boiled, filtered, and in some cases distilled. The cassava is also called *Manioc* or *Mandioc.*

CAS'SEL, or KASSEL. Formerly the residence of the Elector of Hesse-Cassel, it is now the chief town in the province of Hesse-Nassau, Germany, on the Fulda, 91 miles N.N.E. of Frankfort-on-the-Main. The Old and New Town are connected by a bridge over the Fulda. There are several fine squares, in the principal of which, the Friedrichsplatz, the largest in any town in Germany, stands the palace of the ex-elector, an indifferent structure. There is a museum and library (160,000 vols.), and a valuable picture-gallery. The city has manufactures of machinery, mathematical instruments, gold and silver wares, chemicals, knives, gloves, leather, porcelain, etc. There are many fine walks and public gardens in the vicinity; amongst the latter are the gardens of Wilhelmshöhe, in which is situated the ex-elector's summer palace, the residence of the late Emperor Napoleon III., after his being taken prisoner at Sedan, from 5th Sept., 1870, to 19th March, 1871. Pop. 177,661.

CAS'SEL (ancient **Castellum Menapiorum**). A town, France, department of Nord, on an isolated hill in the centre of a large and fertile plain, dating from the time of Julius Cæsar.

CAS'SIA. A large tropical genus of Leguminosæ, sub-ord. Cæsalpineæ. The species consist of trees, shrubs, or herbs; the leaves are abruptly pinnated, and usually bear glands on their stalks. The leaflets of several species constitute the well-known drug called senna. That imported from Alexandria is obtained from *C. acutifolia* and *C. obovāta.* East Indian senna consists of the lance-shaped leaflets of *C. angustifolia*; and other species supply smaller quantities in commerce. *C. Fistŭla* is found wild in India, and has been introduced into other tropical countries. Its legumes contain a quantity of thick-pulp, which is a mild laxative, and enters into the composition of the confection of cassia and the confection of senna. The leaves and flowers are also purgative. The bark and roots of several of the Indian species are much used in medicine.

Cassia bark is a common name for the bark of an entirely different plant, *Cinnamōmum cassia*, belonging to the laurel family. It is much imported into Europe, mostly from China, and is also called *Cassia lignĕa.* Its flavour somewhat resembles that of cinnamon, and as it is cheaper it is often substituted for it, but more particularly for the preparation of what is called oil of cinnamon. The cassia of the Bible was probably cassia bark. *Cassia buds*, which are similar in flavour are obtained from allied trees.

CAS'SICUS. An American genus of insessorial birds, the Cassicans, family Icteridæ (American orioles), allied to the starlings, remarkable for the ingenuity with which they weave their nests. *C. cristātus* sometimes called the crested oriole, a South American bird, constructs a pouch-shaped nest of the length of 30 inches.

CASSI'NI. A name famous in astronomy and physics for three generations:—(1) Giovanni Domenico, born in 1625 near Nice, became professor of astronomy at the University of Bologna, but afterwards settled in France. He discovered four new satellites of Saturn and the zodiacal light, proved that the axis of the moon is not perpendicular to the plane of the ecliptic, and showed the causes of her liberation. He died in 1712.—(2) Jacques, his son, born at Paris in 1677. After several essays on subjects in natural philosophy, etc., he completed his great work on Saturn's satellites and ring. His labours to determine the figure of the earth are well known. He died in 1756.—(3) Cassini de Thury, César François, son of the preceding, born in 1714, member of the Academy from his twenty-second year, undertook a geometrical survey of the whole of France, which was completed by his son. He died in 1784.—(4) Cassini, Jean Dominique, Comte de Thury, son of the preceding, born at Paris 1748, was a statesman of ability as well as a mathematician. In 1787 he completed the topographical work which was begun by his father, and which in its complete state consists of 180 sheets. He died in 1845.

CASSI'NO. A game at cards somewhat resembling whist, in which two, three, or four players can take part. The cards have a special value, and the players' object is to secure as many cards as possible.

CASSINO (kȧs-sē'nō). A town of Italy, province of Caserta, on the railway from Rome to Naples, formerly called San Germano, with remains of the ancient town Casinum (including an amphitheatre), and the famous ancient monastery Monte-Cassino (q.v.) on a neighbouring hill. Pop. 19,000.

CASSIODO'RUS, or CASSIODORIUS, Magnus Aurelius. A Roman writer, born in the latter half of the fifth century A.D. He became chief minister of the Ostrogoth King Theodoric, and wrote a collection of letters, *Variarum Epistolarum Libri XII.*, which contain most valuable information with regard to the Ostrogothic rule in Italy. He wrote also *Historia Gothorum.*

CASSIOPEIA (-pē'ya). A conspicuous constellation in the northern hemisphere, situated next to Cephus, and often called the *Lady in her Chair.* It contains fifty-five stars, five of which arranged in the form of a w, are of the third magnitude.

CASSIQUIARI (kȧ-sik-i-ä'rē), or **CASSIQUIARE.** A large river of South America, in Venezuela, which branches off from the Orinoco and joins the Rio Negro, a tributary of the Amazon. By means of this river water communication is established for canoes over an immense tract of South America, it being practicable to sail from the interior of Brazil to the mouth of the Orinoco.

CASSITERIDES (-dez). A name derived from the Gr. *kassiteros*, tin, and applied by classical writers to a group of islands situated, according to Strabo, who says they were ten in number, " in the open sea."

Certain modern antiquaries think the Cassiterides were " fabulous ;" some, believing otherwise, differ as to their location, and suggest the Balearic Islands, a group of islands off the north-west coast of Spain, or the Scilly Isles and Cornwall. M. Reinach struck at the heart of the problem when he asked: " In what Western European islands is tin found?" The Spanish group has yielded no traces of tin. According to Strabo, the distance to the Cassiterides, which were visited by Crassus, was greater than that from the Continent to Britain. A definite statement of this kind cannot be ignored.

Another important point is that the tin-ore was not mined, but found on the surface of the islands. The earliest reference to tin being mined in Cornwall was made by Posidonius, who is believed to have visited England in the first century of our era. Prior to that period surface tin was found on Dartmoor, round Tavistock, St. Austell, and in valleys " looking towards the southern coast of Cornwall " (Rhys). Surface tin has been traced on the Scilly Islands. Traces of surface tin have also been found in the Hebrides as far north as Lewis. Tin has been discovered in small quantities at Ardross, in Ross-shire, and near Alloa, in Clackmannan. In Ireland " tinstone occurs in several parts, such as Wicklow, Dublin, and Killarney " (Joyce). The Cassiterides were probably identical with the Œstrymnides referred to in the fourth-century metrical rendering by Rufus Festus Avienus of the lost work of Himilco, the Carthagenian explorer who reached Britain about 500 B.C. The poem states that Œstrymnides " raise their heads, lie scattered, and are rich in tin and lead."

When Pytheas visited Britain in the fourth century B.C., he found that tin was brought from an island situated " inwards " at a distance of " six days' sail from Britain." "Inwards" signifies " northwards." The reference may have been to one of the islands of the Hebrides. Julius Cæsar stated (*De Bello Gallico*, v., 12) that tin came from the middle region (*in mediterraneis regionibus*) of Britain. Festus Avienus gives a definite location to the tin islands. He says that they were distant " two days' voyage from the Sacred Isle " (Ireland), and that near them lay " the broad isle of the Albiones." Scotland was known to the Irish Gaels as " Alba," of which the genitive is " Alban." Before the time of Festus Avienus, England became known as Britain.

The Phœnicians carried tin from the Cassiterides direct to the Spanish port of Corbillo, in the estuary of the Loire. They kept secret their knowledge of the places where the rare metal was found. In one of the prehistoric canoes found in Glasgow silt was a cork-plug which could have come only from the Mediterranean coast (Geikie). According to Pliny, the Cassiterides were discovered by Midacritus, who appears to have been a predecessor of Himilco.

The Hebridean claim is strengthened by the fact that, as Rice Holmes says, " the ancient geographers distinguished the Cassiterides from the British Isles." There are Gaelic tin place-names in Western Scotland. Ancient Scottish bronze artifacts contain more lead than the English bronze artifacts. It has been suggested that the Cornish miners sent inferior tin to Scotland, but this is not very convincing, especially in view of the evidence summarised above.

CASSIT'ERITE. A hard mineral, usually dark-brown and almost black, with a high lustre, composed of tin dioxide (tin, 79 per cent). It is the one important ore of the metal, and occurs mostly in veins in granites that have been altered by subterranean vapours. Its resistance to decay and its high specific gravity (6·8) cause it to accumulate in alluvial gravels, from which, as *stream-tin*, it is often mined.

CAS'SIUS. Full name Gaius Cassius Longinus, a distinguished Roman, one of the assassins of Julius Cæsar. In the civil war that broke out between Pompey and Cæsar he espoused the cause of the former, and, as commander of his naval forces, rendered him important services. After the battle of Pharsalia he was apparently reconciled with Cæsar, but later was amongst the more active of the conspirators who assassinated him 44 B.C. He then, together with Brutus, raised an army, but they were met by Octavianus and Antony at Philippi. The wing which Cassius commanded being defeated, he imagined that all was lost, and killed himself, 42 B.C.

CAS'SIUS, PURPLE OF (named from its discoverer, a German physician). A purple pigment used in porcelain and glass painting, prepared from the muriate of gold by adding to it a mixture of the protochloride and perchloride of tin.

CASSIVELLAU'NUS. A British chief who, when Cæsar invaded Britain, held sway over the tribes living north of the Thames, and who, on account of his valour, was appointed leader of the British forces which opposed Cæsar. He had at first some slight successes, but Cæsar ultimately forced a passage across the Thames and put the enemy to flight. In the end Cassivellaunus sued for peace, which was granted on condition that he should pay a yearly tribute and give hostages.

CAS'SOCK. A tight-fitting coat worn under the gown or surplice by the clergy. The cassock is generally black; but in the Church of Rome only priests wear black cassocks, those of bishops being purple, of cardinals scarlet, and that of the Pope white.

CAS'SOWARY. One of the running birds (Ratitæ) belonging to the Australian region. The shortness of their wings totally unfits them for flying, and, like others of their order, the pectoral or wing muscles are comparatively slight and weak, while those of their posterior limbs are very robust and powerful.

The cassowary family (Casuariidæ) includes two genera—Casuarius, or cassowary proper, and Dromæus, the emu. The former has a long compressed bill, a crest on the head, and stiff featherless quills on the wings; the latter has a broader and shorter bill, feathers on the head, and no rudiment of the wing visible externally. They all have three toes. Several species of both genera are known, and of these the most familiar is the helmeted cassowary (*C. gelelātus*), so called from its head being surmounted by an osseous prominence, covered with a sort of horny helmet.

The cassowary feeds on fruits, eggs of birds, etc., and bolts its food with great voracity. It is a native of the Island of Ceram. The skin of the head and superior part of the neck is naked, of a deep-blue and fiery-red tint, with pendent wattles similar to those of the turkey-cock. It is about 5½ feet long. Of the other nine species one inhabits Australia and five New Guinea, the rest the adjacent islands. The Australian species is very similar to that of Ceram; indeed, they all

Helmeted Cassowary (*Casuarius galeātus*)

resemble each other. They inhabit thick forests and scrub, and run with great rapidity. In self-defence they can kick with great force. *See* EMU and RATITÆ.

CASSY'THA. A tropical genus of Lauraceæ, parasites with the aspect and mode of life of dodder (Cuscuta), which, however, belongs to quite a different nat. ord.

CAST. In the fine arts, an impression taken by means of wax or plaster of Paris from a statue, bust, bas-relief, or any other model, animate or inanimate. When plaster casts are to be exposed to the weather, their durability is greatly increased by saturating them with linseed-oil, with which wax or resin may be combined.

CASTA'LIA. A celebrated fountain in Greece sacred to Apollo and the Muses, and fabled to have the power of inspiring those who drank its waters. It flows from a fissure between two peaked cliffs adjoining Mount Parnassus.

CAS'TANETS. An instrument composed of two small concave shells of ivory or hardwood, shaped like spoons,

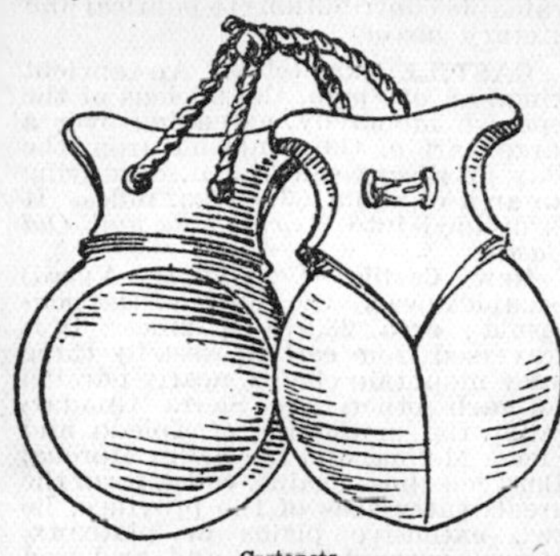
Castanets

placed together, fastened to the thumb, and struck against each other by the other fingers. This instrument is used by the Spaniards and Moors as an accompaniment to their dances and guitars.

CASTE. A term applied to a distinct class or section of a people marked off from others by certain restrictions, and whose burdens or privileges are hereditary. The word is derived from the Port. *casta*, a breed or race, and was originally applied to the classes in India whose occupations, customs, privileges, and duties are hereditary.

It is probable that wherever caste exists it was originally grounded on a difference of descent and mode of living, and that the separate castes were originally separate races. It now prevails principally in India, but it is known to exist or have existed in many other regions. Some maintain that it was prevalent in ancient Egypt, but this seems uncertain.

Social distinctions exist amongst all nations, even in ultra-democratic countries, such as Russia under Bolshevik government, but nowhere are they so rigidly observed as amongst the Hindus. All Hindus are divided into four castes: the Brahmans or sacerdotal class, the Kshatriyas or military class, the Vaisyas or mercantile class, and the Sudras or servile class. But this fourfold division is rather a theory than according to the facts, the Hindus being actually divided into a great number of special castes, distinguished by their trades and other social considerations. "The effect of the caste system is," as the *Cyclopædia of India* says, "that no man may lawfully eat with any individual of any other caste, or partake of food cooked by him, or marry into another caste family; but he may be his friend, his master, his servant, his partner." Those that are outside of any caste are known as *pariahs*.—BIBLIOGRAPHY: Sir H. H. Risley, *Tribes and Castes of Bengal*; A. C. Lyall, *Asiatic Studies*; E. Sevort, *Les Castes dans l'Inde*; *Indian Census Report*; W. Crooke, *Things Indian*; C. Bonglé, *Essais sur le régime des Castes*; Sir Sidney Low, *Vision of India*.

CASTELAR', Emilio. A Spanish politician and author, born in 1833, died in 1899. In 1856 he was made professor of history in the University of Madrid, but becoming involved in the republican disturbances of 1866, he had to take refuge in Switzerland. Having gone back to Spain in 1868, he was returned to the Cortes in the following year. In 1873 he was elected president of the republican Cortes, but resigned in Jan., 1874, in consequence of the vote of confidence being defeated. After the *pronunciamiento* in favour of Alphonso XII., 13th Dec., 1874, Castelar retired from Spain, but in a year or two returned, and again sat in the Cortes. He published many novels, poems, and popular works.

CASTEL - FRANCO. A fortified town in North Italy, in the province and 15 miles W. of Treviso; the birthplace of the painter Giorgione. Pop. 17,302.

CASTEL'LAMMARE. 1. A seaport of Italy, on the Gulf of Naples. It is fortified, and has a royal dockyard, manufactories of cottons and silk. Pop. 39,200.—2. A seaport on the north coast of Sicily, 20 miles E. of Trapani. Wine, fruit, grain, and oil are exported. Pop. 17,367.

CASTEL'LAN, or CHÂ'TELAIN. Properly the owner or commander of a castle. In Flanders and France the title went with the possession of certain districts, and in Normandy and Burgundy châtelains ranked next after bailiffs, with both civil and military authority. In Germany the châtelains were imperial officers with military and civil jurisdiction in fortified places.

CASTELLA'NA. A town of S. Italy, province of Bari. Pop. 11,510.

CASTELLANE'TA. A cathedral town of Southern Italy, 18 miles N.W. of Tarentum. Cotton is extensively grown in the vicinity. Pop. 11,533.

CASTELLEO'NE. A town of North Italy, 12 miles N.W. of Cremona. Pop. 8970.

CASTELLO BRANCO. An episcopal city of Portugal, province of Beira,

120 miles north-east of Lisbon, with a trade in wine, oil, and cork. Pop. 10,486.

CASTELLON-DE-LA-PLANA (kȧs-tel-yon′). A town, Spain, capital of the province of Castellon, 40 miles N.N.E. of Valencia, in a large and fertile plain, with manufactures of sailcloth, woollen and hempen fabrics, ropes, paper, soap, etc., and some trade in hemp, grain, and fruit. Pop. of town, 37,227 (1930); of province, 318,126 (1930); area of latter, 2495 sq. miles.

CASTELNAU, Marie Joseph Edouard de Curières de. French soldier, born 24th Dec., 1851, at Saint Affrique, Aveyron. He entered the French army in 1870, and fought during the Franco-German War. He became a brigadier-general in 1906, and a member of the Superior War Council in 1913. In 1914 he commanded the Second French Army, became chief of the general staff in 1915, and went to Salonica in December of the same year. In 1917 he was in command of the French armies at Verdun, and in 1918 he commanded an army in Lorraine. He was elected to the Chamber of Deputies in 1919.

CASTELNAU′DARY (the **Sostomagus** of the Romans). A town of Southern France, department of Aude, 22 miles W.N.W. of Carcassone, with manufactures of cloth, linen, and earthenware, distilleries and tanneries, and a good trade. It suffered greatly in the crusade against the Albigenses, and was captured by the Black Prince in 1355. Pop. 7900.

CASTEL-VETRA′NO. A town, Sicily, province of Trapani, on a rocky hill; industries: silk, linen, and cotton. The white wine produced in the neighbourhood is esteemed the best in Sicily. Pop. 24,860.

CASTI, Giambatista. A poet, born in 1721 at Prato, in the vicinity of Florence. His writings are of a lively and graceful but almost always licentious character. The *Novelle Galanti*, a series of tales; the *Animali Parlanti*, an epic poem; and his comic operas are amongst his chief works. He died at Paris in 1803.

CASTIGLIONE (kȧs-tēl-yō′nā). A small town of North Italy, 17 miles S.E. of Brescia, where the French obtained a decisive victory over the Austrians in 1796, which gave to Marshal Augereau his title of Duc de Castiglione. In the vicinity is Solferino. Pop. 6000. There is a larger town of the same name in Sicily, province of Catania; pop. 18,189.

CASTIGLIONE (kȧs - tēl - yō′nā), **Baldassare.** One of the most elegant of the older Italian writers, born 1478, died 1529. Among his works the *Libro del Cortegiano* (Book of the Courtier) is the most celebrated. His letters are valuable contributions to political and literary history.

CASTILE (kas-tēl′). An ancient kingdom of Spain, the nucleus of the Spanish monarchy, extending over a large part of the peninsula from the Bay of Biscay southward, occupying an area of about 53,500 sq. miles. It is divided into *New Castile* and *Old Castile*.

New Castile (*Castilla la Nueva*) occupies nearly the centre of the peninsula; area, 28,016 sq. miles. It is traversed from east to west by three lofty mountain chains, nearly parallel to each other—the Sierra Guadarrama, the mountains of Toledo and Sierra Molina, and the Sierra Morena. Between those chains, which form the great watersheds of the province, lie two extensive plains or plateaux, almost without wood, and arid and barren in appearance. Dryness, indeed, is the curse of the whole country, and there is a great deficiency of method alike in agriculture and industries. The inhabitants are of a grave, manly character, with much of the old Spanish pride and probity, but devoid of enterprise, and content to live on from day to day as their fathers did before them. This ancient province now forms the five provinces of Madrid, Ciudad-Real, Cuenca, Guadalajara, and Toledo. Pop. 2,593,227.

Old Castile (*Castilla la Vieja*) stretches from the Bay of Biscay to New Castile; area, 25,408 sq. miles. It is traversed by three mountain chains—the Sierra de Guadarrama, the Sierra de Deza, and the Cantabrian Mountains. It is less dry than New Castile, and grain, particularly wheat, is raised in great abundance. The pastures both of the mountains and the plains are excellent, and much merino wool is produced. Old Castile now forms the provinces of Burgos, Logroño, Santander, Soria, Segovia, Avila, Palencia, and Valladolid. Pop. 2,481,583. *See* SPAIN.

CASTILLEJO (kȧs-til-yā′*h*ō), **Cristo′val de.** A Spanish poet, born in 1494, died 1556. His works possess great originality, and his language is pure and manly, yet sparkling with wit and satire. He was the last representative of the old Spanish court poetry, and strenuously opposed Boscan and Garcilaso in introducing the classical Italian forms of literature.

CASTILLOA. *See* RUBBER.

CASTING. The running of melted metal into a mould prepared for the purpose, so as to produce an article of a certain shape. Iron-casting (or iron-

founding) is the most important branch. Dry sand mould and green sand mould, which are used in a damp state, and chilled moulds, in which pieces of metal are embedded in order to cause local chilling and thus hasten solidification, are all used in foundries.

In general an exact pattern, usually of wood, is employed by the iron-founder. The floor of every foundry is composed, for several feet deep, of a loamy sand, in which deep pits may be sunk to bury large moulds. The wooden pattern is pressed firmly down into this, the sand being shovelled up all around, level with the top of the pattern, and well rammed down. The pattern is then lifted out of the sand, all small pieces of sand which may have fallen into the mould carefully blown away, and some finely-powdered charcoal sifted over the surface. The molten metal is then poured into the mould until it is full. The whole is then covered with sand to keep the air from it while it cools.

An open horizontal bed of sand is sufficient for casting many articles, but with articles of a more complex form and not too large, a frame or box, called a *flask*, is generally employed to hold together the sand used in casting, the number of flasks varying according to the form and parts of the mould.

In ordinary operations the pattern is laid on a board known as the turnover board, and the flask placed over it, the sand being carefully rammed into the flask till it is full. Another board, known as the bottom-board, is then laid upon it. The flask is then turned over, the first or turn-over board taken off, the one side of the pattern uncovered, a fine facing of sand spread upon the surface to prevent adhesion, after which a second flask, called the *cope*, sometimes made with crossbars to strengthen it and help to hold the sand, is placed upon it and sand carefully rammed in.

The cope or second flask is then lifted off, the sand which it contains carrying the impression of the upper side of the pattern; the pattern in the lower part of the flask, or *drag*, is then carefully drawn out, and any injuries which the mould receives during the operation repaired. Holes or passages are then cut into the sand for pouring in the metal, all loose sand carefully removed, the cope replaced and secured to the drag by clamps. The mould is now ready for the molten metal. It is only in lighter castings that sand, of the proper degree of dryness, porosity, and adhesiveness, is used. In heavy castings the mould is usually made of loam, which is more adhesive, and in complicated articles the making of the mould is often a difficult process.

Small articles of simple form and of easily-fusible alloys, such as bullets, printing types, etc., are often cast in metal moulds. Articles of sculpture are usually cast in plaster of Paris, which, when mixed with water, runs into the finest lines of a mould and takes a most exact impression. The variety of articles made by casting is very great: cylinders, pumps, railings, grates, cooking-utensils, and many objects of decorative art.

CASTING-VOTE. The vote of a presiding officer in an assembly or council which decides a question when the votes of the assembly or house are equally divided between the affirmative and negative.

CAST IRON. The name given to the iron obtained from the blast-furnace after melting it in a suitable furnace and pouring into moulds. Pigs of iron obtained by running iron from blast-furnaces into long narrow channels 3 to 4 feet long and 3 to 4 inches broad are frequently called cast iron.

CASTLE. An edifice serving at once as a residence and as a place of defence, especially such an edifice belonging to feudal times. Castles differed somewhat at different times and in different places, but they had all several features of similarity. The first defence of a castle was usually the moat or ditch, that sometimes comprised several acres; and behind it was the outer wall, generally of great height and thickness, strengthened with towers at regular distances, and pierced with loopholes through which missiles could be discharged at the assailants. The main entrance through the outer wall was protected by the *barbican*, with its narrow archway, and strong gates and *portcullis*, and inside there were usually an outer and an inner court, and the strong more or less detached building known as the *keep*, which formed the residence of the owner and his family. This was the most strongly constructed of all the buildings, to which the defenders retreated only in the last extremity.

The drawing shows the castle of the Sires de Coucy, France, built in the thirteenth century. In the foreground is the outer bailey or esplanade, fortified, and containing a chapel, stables, and other buildings. The outer entrance to this was formed by the barbican. *a* is the fosse, 20 yards broad; *b*, the gateway, approached by two swing-bridges, defended by two guard-rooms, and having a double portcullis within, giving entrance to vaulted guard-rooms, with sleeping apartments, etc., above, *c*; *d*, inner bailey or courtyard; *e*, covered buildings for the men defending the walls or curtains; *f*, apartments for the family, entered by the grand staircase, *g*; *h*, great hall, with storerooms and vaults below; *i*, donjon or keep (the

Castle of the Sires de Coucy

chapel is seen behind it), the strongest part of the castle, with walls of immense thickness. At *k* was a postern leading from the donjon and communicating with an outer postern, drawbridge, etc.; *l, m, n, o*, towers or bastions flanking the walls.

In English Edwardian castles (so named from Edward III.) the solid keep becomes developed into an open quadrangle, defended at the sides and angles by gatehouses and towers, and containing the hall and state apartments ranged along one side of the court. Around this inner court two or three lines of defence are disposed concentrically. Such castles frequently enclose many acres, and present an imposing appearance.

The parts of a perfect Edwardian castle are—the *inner bailey* or inner court; the *walls of the enceinte*, single, double, or triple; the *middle* and *outer baileys*, contained between the walls; the *gatehouses* and *posterns*, or small doors in the wall; and the *moat* or *ditch*, which was usually filled with water. The walls were all strengthened by towers, either circular, square, oblong, or multangular, projecting both outwards and inwards. Such towers were capable of being defended independently of the castle. The gatehouses are distinct works covering the entrance; they contain gates, one or two portcullises, and loopholes raking the passage. From the front of these gatehouses the drawbridge was lowered over the ditch. The gateways had frequently a barbican attached. This was a passage between high walls, in advance of the main gate, and having an outer gate of entrance, which was defended by towers and the parapet connected with the main gateway. The top of the wall was defended by a battlemented parapet, and frequently pierced by cruciform loopholes.—BIBLIOGRAPHY: G. T. Clark, *Mediæval Military Architecture*; J. O. Mackenzie, *The Castles of England*; E. B. d'Auvergne, *Castles of England*; F. R. Fraprie, *Castles and Keeps of Scotland*; H. C. Shelley, *Royal Castles of England*.

CASTLEBAR'. A town, Ireland, county town of County Mayo, with some trade in grain and other agricultural produce. Pop. (1926), 4256.

CASTLE-DOUGLAS. A town (police burgh) of Scotland, Kirkcudbrightshire, 18½ miles south-west of Dumfries, at the north end of a small sheet of water called Carlinwark Loch, a railway junction, with important sales of sheep and cattle. Pop. (1931), 3008.

CASTLEFORD. A town of Yorkshire, W. Riding, 10 miles S.E. of Leeds, with large glassworks. Pop. (1931), 21,781.

CASTLEMAINE. A municipal town in Talbot County, Victoria, Australia, 64 miles north-west of Melbourne, pleasantly situated and well built and laid out. It owes its importance to the gold-mining and agriculture carried on in its neighbourhood. Pop. 7170.

CASTLEREAGH (kas'l-rā), **Lord.** *See* LONDONDERRY.

CASTLETOWN. A small town and seaport near the southern extremity of the Isle of Man, long the capital of the island. In the centre is Castle Rushen, originally a Danish fortress of the tenth century, afterwards much extended, and now partly used as a prison and public offices. Pop. 1713.

CAS'TOR, or **CASTO'REUM.** A reddish-brown substance, of a strong penetrating smell, secreted by two glandular sacs connected with the organs of reproduction of the beaver, and used by perfumers.

CASTOR AND POLLUX. In Greek mythology, twin divinities, sons of Tyndareus, King of Lacedæmon, and Leda, or, according to a later tradition, the sons of Zeus (Jupiter) and Leda, also called Dioscūri (sons of Zeus). Castor was mortal, but Pollux was immortal. The former was particularly skilled in breaking horses, the latter in boxing and wrestling. They were the patron deities of mariners. In the heavens they appear as one of the twelve constellations of the zodiac, with the name of *Gemini* (the Twins).

CASTOR AND POLLUX. Two minerals which are found together in granite in the Island of Elba. Castor is a silicate of aluminium and lithium; pollux is a silicate of aluminium and the rare element cæsium.

CASTOR'IDÆ. A family of rodent animals comprising the beaver, etc.

CASTOR-OIL. The oil obtained from the seeds of *Ricinus commūnis*, or *Palma christi*, a native of India, but now distributed over all the warmer regions of the globe. The oil is obtained from the seeds by bruising and pressing. The oil that first comes away, called cold-drawn castor-oil, is reckoned the best, an inferior quality being obtained by heating or steaming the pressed seeds, and again subjecting them to pressure. The oil is afterwards heated to the boiling-point, which coagulates and separates the albumen and impurities.

Castor-oil is used medicinally as a mild but efficient purgative. Castor-oil is also often used for burning, and gives a cooler and brighter light than any other vegetable oil. It is chiefly imported from India. The plant is often cultivated as an ornamental plant.

CASTRATION. The act of depriving a male animal of the testicles. It is practised on domestic animals (as oxen and horses) with the object of rendering them more submissive and docile. Men who are castrated are known as eunuchs. Pigs are the easiest of animals to castrate.

CASTRÉN, Matthias Alexander. A philologist and distinguished student of the Finnish languages, born 1813 at Tervola, Finland, died 1852 at Helsingfors. Educated at the University of Helsingfors, his attention was turned to the language of his native country. He travelled much among the nations of the Arctic regions, both in Europe and Asia, including the Norwegian and Russian Lapps, and the Samoyeds of Siberia and the coasts of the White Sea. He was appointed in 1851 professor of the Finnish and old Scandinavian languages in the University of Helsingfors, but he died next year. Among his works are a Swedish translation of the great Finnish epic, *The Kalevala*. He also wrote: *Elementa Grammatices Syrjænæ, Elementa Grammatices Tscheremissæ, De affixis personalibus linguarum Altaicarum*, besides travels and other works.

CASTRES (kästr). A town of Southern France, department of Tarn, 46 miles east of Toulouse, on the Agout, which divides it into two parts. There are tanneries, paper-mills, foundries, etc., and manufactures of woollen goods, linen, glue, etc. It suffered during the wars of religion in the sixteenth century, and Louis XIII. razed its fortifications in 1629. Pop. 28,084.

CAS'TRIES. A town of the W. Indies, capital of the British island St. Lucia. Pop. 5899.

CASTRO, Cipriani. Ex-President of Venezuela, born in the Andean province of Tachira in 1861. He was elected a Senator for his state, and supported Crespo's rebellion against President Andueza Palacio. In 1899 he became the leader of an insurrection against President Andrade. When the latter fled to Curaçao, Castro was chosen provisional President, and in 1902 formally elected President for six years. He involved his country in dangerous quarrels and disputes with European nations, the United States, Colombia, and France. Re-elected in 1905, he was compelled to resign the presidency in 1908.

CASTRO, Inez de. A lady of noble birth, secretly married to Pedro, son of Alphonso IV., King of Portugal, after the death of his wife Constantia (1345). The old King Alphonso, fearful that this marriage would injure the interests of his grandson Ferdinand (the son of Pedro by his deceased wife), resolved to put Inez to death. Three noblemen, Diego Lopez Pacheco, Pedro Coelho, and Alvarez Gonsalvez, were his counsellors in this scheme, and carried it out themselves by stabbing Inez within the convent where she lived (1355).

Two years after King Alphonso died, and Pedro, inducing the King of Castile to give up to him two of the murderers, who had taken refuge there (the third, Diego Lopez, managed to escape), put them to death with cruel tortures. The king then made public declaration of the marriage that had taken place between him and the deceased Inez; and had her corpse disinterred and placed on a throne, adorned with the diadem and royal robes, to receive the homage of the nobility. The body was then conveyed to Alcobaça and buried with great honours. The history of the unhappy Inez has furnished many poets of different nations with materials for tragedies, and her story is one of the finest episodes in the *Lusiads* of Camoens.—Cf. Ferdinand Denis, *Chroniques Chevaleresques de l'Espagne et du Portugal*.

CASTRO-DEL-RIO. A town, Spain, Andalusia, in the province and 16 miles S.E. of Cordova, on the Guadajoz. There are manufactures of linen, woollen goods, and earthenware. Pop. 15,000.

CASTROGIOVANNI (-jo-vȧn'nē). A town, Sicily, province of Caltanissetta, near the centre of the island, on a high tableland more than 4000 feet above the sea-level. The site of ancient Enna, in ancient times it was adorned with the groves and temples of Ceres (Demeter). Sulphur is obtained in the district. Pop. 26,500.

CASTRO URDIALES (ụr-di-ä'lez). A seaport of Northern Spain, province of Santander, a place of export for iron-ore, sardines, etc. Pop. 11,800.

CASTROVIL'LARI. A town of S. Italy, province of Cosenza. Pop. 10,000.

CAST STEEL. Steel made by fusing the materials and running the product into moulds.

CASTUERA (kȧs-tụ-ā'rȧ). A town, Spain, province of Badajoz, and 67 miles E. by S. of the town of that name. Pop. 7100.

CASUALTIES. Mishaps or accidents of any kind, particularly wartime losses in battle, and by sickness.

Various attempts at a final estimate of the casualties in the Great War have been given from time to time. An authoritative statement was made in the House of Commons in May, 1921, as follows:

	Dead	Wounded
British Empire		
Great Britain	743,702	1,693,262
Canada	56,625	149,732
Australia	59,330	152,171
New Zealand	16,136	40,729
India	61,398	70,859
Elsewhere	8,832	15,153
	946,023	2,121,906
Allied Countries		
France	1,385,300	?
Belgium	38,172	44,686
Italy	460,000	947,000
Portugal	7,222	13,751
Rumania	335,706	?
Serbia	127,535	133,148
United States	115,660	205,690
Enemy Countries		
Germany	2,050,466	4,202,028
Austria-Hungary	1,200,000	3,620,000
Bulgaria	101,224	152,400
Turkey	300,000	570,000

No figures were given for Russia.

CASUALTY. Term used in Scots law. It refers to a payment to be made by a tenant to a landlord upon the happening of a certain specified contingency. One such case occurred in 1929 when the Duchess of Norfolk, under an Act of 1914, demanded casualties from her tenants in Maxwelltown.

CASUAL WARD. Poor law institution at which the casual poor are sheltered. Vagrants and tramps are admitted and provided with cocoa and bread and a compulsory bath. Before discharge some work must usually be done, such as wood chopping or stone breaking, but oakum picking, formerly a common task, has been abolished.

CASUARI'NA, or BOTANY-BAY OAK. The single genus of the nat. ord. of Casuarinaceæ, or cassowary trees. There are about thirty species, natives chiefly of Australia. They are jointed leafless trees or shrubs, related to the birches, having their male flowers in whorled catkins and their fruits in indurated cones. Some of them produce timber called *Beefwood* from its colour. *C. quadrivalvis* is called the she-oak, *C. equisetifolia* the swamp-oak. They are chalazogamic, and show other primitive features.

CAS'UISTRY (from the Lat. *casus*, a point of law, a case). That part of the old theology and morals which relates to the principles by which difficult cases of conscience (especially where there is a collision of different duties) are to be settled. Hence a casuist is a moralist who endeavours to solve such doubtful questions. Casuistry has been rightly defined as "a particular development of accommodation in religious matters."

There have been many celebrated casuists among the Jesuits—for example, Escobar y Mendoza (1589-1669), Sanchez, Hermann Busenbaum, Paul Laymann, and V. Figliucci (1566-1622)—famous for their ingenuity and the fine-spun sophistry of their solutions. The Reformation was a violent protest against the moral theology of the Jesuits, but even within the Catholic Church protests were raised. In his famous *Lettres Provinciales*, Pascal dealt with the Casuists and the artificiality of their methods. By the middle of the eighteenth century the very name of casuistry became a synonym for moral laxity.

CAT (*Felis domesticus*). A well-known domesticated quadruped, ord. Carnivora, the same name being also given to allied forms of the same order. It is believed that the cat was originally domesticated in Egypt, and the gloved cat (*F. maniculāta*) of Egypt and Nubia has by some been considered the original stock of the domestic cat, though more probably it was the Egyptian cat (*F. caligāta*). The Egyptians regarded the cat as a sacred animal, the mummified remains of many of these animals being still in existence. It was seldom, if at all, kept by the Greeks and Romans, and till long after the Christian era was rare in many parts of Europe.

Some have thought that the domestic breed owed its origin to the wild cat; but there are considerable differences between them, the latter being larger, and having a shorter and thicker tail, which also does not taper.

Cat's Foot, showing the Claws

The domestic cat belongs to a genus—that which contains the lion and tiger—better armed for the destruction of animal life than any other quadrupeds. The short and powerful jaws, trenchant teeth, cunning disposition, combined with nocturnal habits (for which their eyesight is naturally adapted) and much patience in pursuit, give these animals great advantages over their prey.

The cat in a degree partakes of all the attributes of her race. Its food in a state of domestication is necessarily very various, but always of flesh or fish if it can be obtained. Instances of it catching the latter are known, though usually the cat is extremely averse to wetting itself. It is a very cleanly animal, avoiding to step in any sort of filth, and preserving its fur in a very neat condition. Its fur is very easily injured by water on account of the want of oil in it, and it can be rendered highly electric by friction. The cat goes with young for sixty-

CATS

Manx Smoke Persian Silver Tabby Blue Persian
Siamese Persian Common Domestic Chinchilla

three days, and brings forth usually from three to six at a litter, which remain blind for nine days. It is usually regarded as less intelligent than the dog, but this is by no means certain. It has a singular power of finding its way home when taken to a distance and covered up by the way.

Among the various breeds or races of cat may be mentioned the tortoise-shell, with its colour a mixture of black, white, and brownish or fawn colour; the large Angora or Persian cat, with its long silky fur; the blue or Carthusain, with long soft greyish-blue fur; and the tailless cat of the Isle of Man (the Manx), which even half a century ago was becoming scarce. The mere absence of a tail, however, does not necessarily indicate that the cat is a Manx cat, as a large number have had their tails removed in order to deceive unwary purchasers. The Manx cats were formerly known in England as "Cornish cats."

The **wild cat** (*Felis catus*) is still found in Scotland and in various other parts of Europe and Western Asia, chiefly in forest regions, making its lair in hollow trees or clefts of rocks. It is a very fierce animal. There are a number of other animals of similar size and habits known as cats, such as the fishing-cat (*F. viverrīna*) of Bengal and Eastern Asia, the leopard cat (*F. bengalensis*) of Northern India and South-Eastern Asia, the marbled cat (*F. marmorāta*) of the same region, the rusty-spotted cat (*F. robiginōsa*), a small Indian species, etc. The ocelot, serval, and margay may also be called cats.—BIBLIOGRAPHY: E. Hamilton, *The Wild Cat of Europe*; F. Simpson, *The Book of the Cat*; M. L. Williams, *The Cat: its Care and Management.*

CATACHRESIS (-krē-sis). A figure in rhetoric, when a word is too far wrested from its true signification; as, to speak of tones being made more *palatable* for "agreeable to the ear." Also, in philology, the employment of a word under a false form through misapprehension in regard to its origin; thus *crayfish* or *crawfish* (Fr. *écrevisse*) has its form by *catachresis.*

CAT'ACLYSM. In geology, a physical catastrophe of great extent, supposed to have occurred at different periods, and to have been the cause of sudden changes in the earth's surface.

CAT'ACOMBS (Gr. *kata*, down, and *kumbē*, a hollow or recess). Caves or subterranean places for the burial of the dead, the bodies being placed in graves or recesses hollowed out in the sides of the cave. Caves of this kind were common amongst the Phœnicians, Greeks, Persians, and many Oriental nations. There is a considerable number of catacombs in Egypt, Northern Africa, Sicily (Syracuse, Palermo), Malta, etc. In Asia Minor numerous excavations have been discovered containing sepulchres, and the catacombs near Naples are remarkably extensive. Those of Rome, however, are the most important.

The term *catacumbæ* is said to have been originally applied to the district near Rome which contains the chapel of St. Sebastian, in the vaults of which, according to tradition, the body of St. Peter was first deposited; but (besides its general application) it is now applied in a special way to all the extensive subterranean burial-places in the neighbourhood of Rome, which extend underneath the town itself as well as the neighbouring country, and are said to contain not less than 6,000,000 tombs. They consist of long narrow galleries usually about 8 feet high and 5 feet wide, which branch off in all directions, forming a perfect maze of corridors. Different stories of galleries lie one below the other. Vertical shafts run up to the outer air, thus introducing light and air, though in small quantity.

The graves or *loculi* lie longwise in the galleries. They are closed laterally by a slab, on which there is occasionally a brief inscription or a symbol, such as a dove, an anchor, or a palm-branch. These inscriptions and paintings constitute precious monuments of early Christian epigraphy. The earliest that can be dated with any certainty belongs to the year A.D. 111.

It is now regarded as certain that in times of persecution the early Christians frequently took refuge in the catacombs, in order to celebrate there in secret the ceremonies of their religion; but it is not less certain that the catacombs served also as ordinary places of burial to the early Christians, and were for the most part excavated by the Christians themselves. In early times rich Christians constructed underground burying-places for themselves and their brethren, which they held as private property under the protection of the law. But in course of time, partly by their coming under the control of the Church and partly by accidents of proprietorship, these private burying-grounds were connected with each other, and became the property, not of particular individuals, but of the Christian community. In the third century A.D. there were already several such common burying-places belonging to the Christian congregations, and their number went on increasing till the time of Constantine, when the catacombs ceased to be used as burying-places.

From the time of Constantine down

to the eighth century they were used only as places of devotion and worship. But their use as formal places of worship can only have been occasional, for the limited dimensions even of the largest rooms, and the extreme narrowness of the passages, must have made it impossible for any large number to take efficient part in the services at one time. But though the idea of the catacombs as regular places of worship may be carried too far, there is no doubt, from the episcopal chairs, altars, basins, etc., found within them, and from the subjects of the mosaics and carvings on the walls, that the rites of the Church, and particularly the eucharist and the sacrament of baptism, were often celebrated there. They could never have served as dwelling-places for any length of time to the Christians, residence in most of them for more than a short time being very dangerous to the health.

Catacomb of St. Cornelius, Rome

During the siege of Rome by the Lombards in the eighth century the catacombs were in part destroyed, and soon became entirely inaccessible, so that by the twelfth century they were forgotten. In 1578 a catacomb on the Via Salaria was accidentally rediscovered, but it was not until the publication of *Roma Sotterranea Cristiana* by A. Bosio (1632) that attention was called to the catacombs.

The real discoverer of the catacombs, however, was Giovanni Battista de Rossi. He and Parker, by their careful and laborious investigations, have thrown much light on the origin and history of the catacombs. There are extensive catacombs at Paris, consisting of old quarries from which has been obtained much of the material for the building of the city. In them are accumulated bones removed from cemeteries now built over. —BIBLIOGRAPHY: G. B. de Rossi, *Roma Sotterranea*; Bosio, *Roma Sotterranea*; Perret, *Les Catacombes de Rome*; Northcote and Brownlow, *Roma Sotterranea*; J. H. Parker, *The Archæology of Rome: the Catacombs*; M. Besnier, *Les Catacombes de Rome*; T. B. Englefield, *The Catacombs of St. Callixtus, St. Sebastian, St. Domitilla.*

CATAFALQUE (derived from the It. *catafalco*, a scaffold, or elevation). A temporary and ornamental structure, representing a tomb placed over the coffin of a distinguished person or over a grave. A very famous catafalque was that erected to the memory of Michel Angelo by his brother artists.

CAT'ALAN. A native of Catalonia, or North-Eastern Spain, or the language of Catalonia, which holds a position similar to the Provençal, having been early cultivated and boasting a considerable literature. It was established as a literary language by the close of the thirteenth century, and is still to some extent used as such in its own region.

CATALAN GRAND COMPANY. The name given to a troop of adventurers raised by Roger di Flor about the beginning of the fourteenth century. They numbered about 8000 men of different nationalities, Catalans, Sicilians, Arragonese, and were led by Roger to the East to aid Emperor Andronicus II. in his struggle with the Turks. They fought well and did good service, but their habits of plunder and rapine made them as formidable to their friends as to their foes. The company was broken up in 1315, some twelve years after its formation, and the Catalans disappeared before the end of the fourteenth century.

CATALA'NI, Angelica. One of the most celebrated of Italian opera singers, born in 1779 at Sinigaglia, died in 1849. Family misfortunes compelled her to turn her remarkable voice to account, and in her sixteenth year she made her first appearance on the stage at Venice. After filling the chief soprano parts in the best opera-houses of Italy, she visited successively Madrid, Paris, and London, where she enjoyed great professional triumphs, as she continued to do in similar tours which she repeatedly made afterwards. In 1830 she retired.

CATALAUNIAN PLAIN. The wide plain around Châlons-sur-Marne, famous as the field where Aëtius, the Roman general, and Theodoric, king of the West Goths, gained a complete victory over Attila, A.D. 451.

CATALEP'SY. A spasmodic nervous disorder in which there is a sudden suspension of sensation and volition, with statue-like fixedness of the body and limbs in the attitude immediately preceding the attack. The rigidity then gives place to an equally remarkable state of unconscious flexibility; the limbs are maintained in any position or attitude in which the observer may place them. It is generally the consequence of some emotional disturbance, and most often occurs in hysterical young women.—BIBLIOGRAPHY: A. Binet and C. Féré, *Animal Magnetism*; Richer, *Études cliniques sur la grande hystérie*; Gilles de la Tourette, *Traité clinique et thérapeutique de l'hystérie.*

CATALO'NIA (ancient **Hispania Tarraconensis**). An old province of Spain, bounded N. by France, E. and S.E. by the Mediterranean, S. by Valencia, and W. by Arragon. The country in general is mountainous, but intersected with fertile valleys, while the mountains themselves are covered with valuable woods and fruit trees, the slopes being cut in terraces and plentifully supplied with water by an artificial system of irrigation. Wheat, wine, oil, flax, hemp, vegetables, and almost every kind of fruit are abundant. There are mines of lead, iron, alum, etc. On the coast is a coral-fishery. Catalonia, though less fertile than most of Spain, stands pre-eminent for the industry of its inhabitants, who speak the Catalan dialect. Pop. 2,490,889; area, 12,427 sq. miles. It comprises the modern provinces of Tarragona, Gerona, Lerida, and Barcelona.—Cf. A. F. Calvert, *Catalonia and the Balearic Isles.*

CATAL'PA. A genus of plants, ord. Bignoniaceæ. The species are trees with simple leaves and large, gay, trumpet-shaped flowers. *C. bignonioides*, a North American species, is well adapted for large shrubberies, and has been introduced into England and other parts of Europe.

CATALYSIS. The speed at which a chemical reaction takes place is often appreciably affected by the addition of some extraneous material, which, since it emerges from the reaction unchanged, apparently conduces by its mere presence to the alteration in the reaction velocity. Such a body is called a *catalyst* in respect of that particular reaction. Though the effect of the addition may be either positive or negative, the number of bodies which retard a reaction is so small, comparatively speaking, that the term *catalyst* may be taken to relate only to those substances which accelerate the reaction.

Of course other means are available for increasing the velocity of a reaction, e.g. raising the temperature or pressure, or increasing the concentration of the reacting materials, but their employment, if not actually undesirable, usually entails the expenditure of energy. By the use of a catalyst, however, many reactions which under ordinary conditions are impracticably slow can be accelerated to the point of economic success with the minimum expenditure of energy. For this reason catalysis has found extensive practical application, as, for instance, in the synthesis and oxidation of ammonia, the hardening of fats, and the manufacture of sulphuric acid.

It should be noticed that the final state of equilibrium of a reaction is not affected by the presence of the catalyst, nor yet by its nature and amount, since the catalyst, by emerging unchanged from the reaction, introduces no energy into it. And as the final state of equilibrium depends upon the ratio of the velocities of the forward and reverse reactions, it follows that the catalyst affects these two reaction velocities to the same extent. The influence of a catalyst is sharply differentiated thereby from that of other factors, such as temperature, pressure, and concentration.

Theoretically, only a trace of the foreign material should be sufficient to effect the transformation of indefinitely large quantities of the reacting materials. In practice it is found necessary to renew the catalytic material at intervals, largely owing to the deleterious influence of certain impurities which act as *poisons*, even though they be present in relatively minute amounts. Strangely enough, there are other substances, termed *promoters*, which increase the activity of a catalyst, a small quantity often producing an astonishing effect. Each catalyst appears to possess its own individual list of poisons and promoters.

No comprehensive theory has yet been put forward in explanation of the activity of a catalyst. In the majority of cases there is reason to believe that it participates in the reaction, that is to say, the catalyst functions as a "carrier" by temporarily combining with one reaction component to form an unstable body which is immediately decomposed by the other component, liberating the catalyst to repeat the process indefinitely. On the other hand, instances are common in which the rôle of the catalyst is obviously a physical one, being dependent upon surface phenomena only.

CATAMARAN'. A sort of raft used in the East Indies, Brazil, and elsewhere. Those of the Island of Ceylon, like those of Madras and other parts of that coast, are formed of three logs lashed together. Their length is from 20 to 25 feet, and breadth 2½ to 3½ feet. The centre log is much the largest, and is pointed at the fore-end. These floats are navigated with great skill by one or two men in a kneeling posture. They think nothing of passing through the surf which lashes the beach at Madras when boats of the best construction would be swamped.

CATAMAR'CA. A province of the Argentine Republic, South America; area, about 36,800 sq. miles; mountainous in all directions except the south. Pop. 128,422 (1931). The capital is Catamarca, or more fully San Fernando de Catamarca. Pop. 13,262.

CATAME'NIA. *See* MENSTRUATION.

CAT'AMOUNT, or **CATAMOUNTAIN.** The wild cat. In America the name is also given to the lynx or the puma.

CATA'NIA (ancient **Catăna**). A city on the east coast of Sicily, capital of the province of Catania, at the foot of Mount Etna. Ancient Catăna was founded by Greeks from Chalcis. It has been repeatedly visited by tremendous earthquakes, one of the worst of which was in 1693, and has been partially laid in ruins by lava from eruptions of Mount Etna. The ancient ruins were excavated by Prince Biscari in the eighteenth century, and his collection is in the Museo Biscari in the town.

Catania has always recovered from these earthquakes, however, and has much more the features of a metropolis than Palermo. The streets are broad and straight, and most of the edifices have an air of magnificence unknown in other parts of the island. The cathedral of St. Agatha, founded by Count Roger in 1091, is a fine building. The other noteworthy buildings comprise the former Benedictine monastery of San Nicola, now partly used as a museum and library; the Castel l'Ursino, erected in 1232 by Frederick II.; the church of San Carcere, with a fine eleventh-century marble portal; and the university, founded in 1434. The church has an organ, built by Donato del Piano, with 72 stops and 2916 pipes.

The Piazza del Duomo, the principal square, is adorned with a fountain surmounted by an antique elephant in lava bearing an Egyptian obelisk of granite. In the Piazza Stesicoro (named after the poet Stesichoros, who died in 556 B.C.) there is a monument to Bellini, the composer, who was a native of the town. The grounds of the Villa Bellini are a picturesque and pleasant place of resort. There are ruins of an ancient theatre and of other ancient buildings.

The manufactures include silk, sulphur, tobacco, soap, matches, Portland cement, and articles in amber and lava. The harbour was choked up by the eruption of 1669, but was greatly improved afterwards. The trade is of some importance, the chief exports being sulphur, oranges and lemons, wine, oil, liquorice, and lemon juice. Pop. 263,030. The area of the province is 1907 sq. miles; pop. 892,032.

CATANZA'RO. A cathedral city of Calabria, South Italy, capital of province of same name, on a height 5 miles from the Gulf of Squillace, with manufactures of silk and velvet, etc. There are ruins of a castle founded by Robert Guiscard. On 13th Oct., 1914, the province of Catanzaro was devastated by a cyclone. Pop. of town, 34,300; of province, 570,047 (area, 2034 sq. miles).

CAT'APULT. A machine of the ancients for projecting missiles, chiefly arrows. *Ballistæ* were engines somewhat similarly constructed, but were chiefly confined to the shooting of stones.

CAT'ARACT. A disease of the eye, consisting in opacity of the crystalline lens. Its earliest approach is marked by a loss of the natural colour of the pupil, and when developed it causes the pupil to have a milk-white or pearly colour. A large proportion of the cases of cataract are found in elderly persons, but accidental injury to the eye may produce it. Children are sometimes born with cataract. Even when a cataract has "ripened," and the patient is blind for all practical purposes, he can still distinguish between light and darkness.

Treatment. Cataract is treated by different surgical operations. In *couching*, the lens is depressed, removed downwards, and kept from rising by the vitreous humour; but this method is now entirely given up in favour of removal of the lens by extraction. *Extraction* consists in making an incision in the cornea and in the capsule of the lens, by which the lens may be brought forward and through the cut in the cornea, so as to be altogether removed. The third operation is by *absorption*. This consists in wounding the capsule, breaking down the crystalline, and bringing the fragments into the anterior chamber of the eye, where they are exposed to the action of the aqueous humour, and are at length absorbed and disappear. Extraction is now the regular method, and after it is effected a special kind of spectacles is required. In children the lens is soft, and accordingly the method of absorption is preferred for them.

CATARACT, or WATERFALL. The name given to the sudden and perpendicular fall of the water of a stream over a ledge or precipice occurring in its course; it is thus distinct from "rapids," where the water flows swiftly over a steeply-sloping and often rock-strewn portion of the bed; while "cascades" are formed by a succession of waterfalls. Cataracts are due to rock erosion at the points where they occur, and are more usually found in the upper reaches of rivers.

One of the finest cataracts in Britain is the double fall of Foyers, in Inverness-shire, in which the lower of the two falls has a drop of 165 feet. Little less striking are the three falls of the Clyde near Lanark —Bonnington, 30 feet; Corra Linn, 84 feet; and Stonebyres, 80 feet. The cascades of the Grey Mare's Tail on the Tailburn, where it leaves Loch Skene, in Dumfriesshire, have a total fall of 350 feet. There are many highly-picturesque falls, locally called *forces*, in the Lake District of England.

Generally considered unsurpassed for grandeur in the whole of Europe is the magnificent Rjukanfos waterfall (800 feet) in Norway, on the River Maan, 80 miles west of the capital; but the loftiest is the Fall of Gavarnie in the Pyrenees, where the water drops 1380 feet into the corrie or *cirque*, reaching the bottom in a cloud of spray. The Trollhättan Falls, on the Swedish river Göta, near its exit from Lake Wener, are 100 feet in height. At Schaffhausen the Rhine falls 100 feet in three leaps, which form a cascade of imposing grandeur.

The Staubbach Fall, near Lauterbrunnen, Switzerland, has a single drop of 870 feet, but the water is rarely sufficiently plentiful to do more than form a lace-like veil of exquisite beauty on the rock face. In Italy the three falls on the Velino, near Terni, have a combined drop of some 600 feet.

Among the most famous cataracts of Asia are the twin falls on the Cauvery, India, which drop 300 feet on either side of an island. The most magnificent of African waterfalls are the Victoria Falls, on the Zambezi, with a height of about 400 feet. On the Congo are the Stanley Falls, which have a total descent of 200 feet. The "cataracts" of the Nile are misnamed, being in reality "rapids".

America possesses the most famous of all cataracts in the Niagara Falls, a celebrated spectacle. (*See* NIAGARA.) The great falls in the Yosemite Valley, California, are formed of three cascades—Upper, 1436 feet; Middle, 626 feet; Lower, 400 feet, or a total of 2462 feet. In the same valley is the Bridal Veil Fall (630 feet), so named from its fluttering like a white veil in the wind. The Yellowstone National Park possesses several splendid falls. Canada has those on the Montmorency, near Quebec, and, in Labrador, the Grand Falls on the Hamilton River.

In South America the most important falls occur on the Funza, a tributary of the Magdalena, where, near Bogota, the Tequendama Falls have a drop of 475 feet; the Kaleteur Fall, in Guiana (741 feet); and the Brazilian cataract called the Paulo Affonso Falls (300 feet), on the Sao Francisco River. In the South Island of New Zealand the Sutherland Falls descend 1900 feet in three leaps. Several of the more important of the falls alluded to above are found described in separate articles.

Cataracts present to the engineer obvious opportunities for their utilisation as water-power; among the many instances where this is taken advantage of may be named the Falls of Foyers, where aluminium works were established at the close of the last century.

CATARRH. The general term for inflammation of a mucous membrane, but specially applied to the inflammation of the mucous membrane of the nose, throat, and bronchial tubes; in short, it is the medical term for a common cold. In the earliest stage, when the patient has a burning dry sensation in the nose and throat, and is feverish, various remedies are used with varying success.

Any of the following drugs are to be recommended: (1) Dover's powders (10 grains); (2) quinine (5 grains); (3) ammoniated tincture of quinine, followed by a hot bath and twenty-four hours in bed. In the second stage, when the "cold" has started, many household remedies are of use, e.g. a hot bath in a warm room and the immediate retiral of the patient to bed; the administration of plenty of hot drinks, either lemon or whisky. To relieve local discomfort, steam inhalations of benzoin, menthol, etc., are good; as is also the application of some soothing ointment to the nose.

Where the patient is very young or very old, greater importance is attached to a cold owing to the danger of its becoming bronchitis. Cocaine in any form must on no account be used. In the third stage, when the profuse watery discharge tends to become sticky and mucopurulent, alkaline nasal lotions should be applied, either by snuffing up from the palm or by nasal irrigator. A nasal douche should *not* be used.

Much can be done to prevent catarrh, especially in children: the use of warm yet light clothing; plenty of fresh air; sleeping with windows open; avoidance of overheated rooms; good nourishing, wholesome food; a daily bath. Should a child be troubled with repeated catarrhal attacks, it is advisable to have the nose examined for obstruction, adenoids, polypus, thickening or deviation of septum.

CATAW'BA. A river, United States, in the Carolinas, giving its name to a light wine of rich Muscadine flavour, which has acquired some celebrity in America, and the praises of which have been sung by Longfellow.

CAT - BIRD (*Galeoscoptes carolinensis*). A well-known species of American thrush, which during the summer is found throughout the Middle and New England States; so named from its cry of alarm. It is about 9 inches in length, the plumage being of a deep slate-colour above and lighter below. In habit it is lively, familiar, and unsuspicious; the song is largely imitative of those of other birds.

CATCH. A short piece of music, frequently of a humorous and bacchanalian character, written generally in three or four parts. It is a sort of short canon, the second voice taking up the theme when the first has completed the first phrase, the third following the second in the same manner. In 1761 a Catch Club was founded in London.

CATCHFLY. A popular name of several plants of the genus Silēnē (q.v.). *Dionæa muscipula* and *Lychnis Viscaria* are also so called.

CATCHMENT AREA. Defined space of land made by its rainfall into a self-contained drainage basin. The catchment area of the Amazon is 2,722,000 sq. miles, of the Thames 5924 sq. miles. The term is also used in hydraulic engineering for the area available for furnishing water at a specific point for a public water supply.

CATCH THE TEN. A game of cards, played with a pack of thirty-six cards, and sometimes called Scotch whist.

CÂTEAU - CAMBRÉSIS (kä-tō-kaŋ-brā-sis), or **LE CATEAU.** A town, France, department of Nord, on the right bank of the Selle, famous for a treaty between England, France, and Spain, signed in 1559. It has various textile manufactures. Pop. 10,212.

The Battle of Le Câteau was fought on Wednesday, 26th Aug., 1914, by the British under General Sir Horace Smith-Dorrien against the Germans under von Kluck.

CATECHET'ICAL SCHOOLS. Institutions for the education of Christian teachers, of which there were many in the Eastern Church from the second to the fifth century. The first and most renowned were those formed at Alexandria (A.D. 160-400) on the model of the famous schools of Grecian learning in that place, Pantænus, Clement, and Origen being their most famous teachers. The schools at Antioch were also in high repute from about 290 till the fifth century. The Arian controversy broke up the Alexandrian, and the Nestorian and Eutychian controversies the Antioch schools. They were succeeded at a later date by the cathedral and monastic schools.

CATECHISM (kat'e-kizm; from Gr. *katēchein*, to sound down, utter, instruct orally). An elementary book containing a summary of principles in any science or art, but particularly in religion, reduced to the form of questions and answers. To *catechise* means generally to give oral instruction, as distinct from instruction through the medium of books. The first regular catechisms, which have grown out of the usual oral teaching of catechumens, appear to have been compiled in the eighth and ninth centuries, those by Kero of St. Gall and Otfried of Weissenburg being most famous.

In the Roman Catholic Church each bishop has the right to make a catechism for his diocese. But in modern times Roman Catholic catechisms are generally a close copy of the one drawn up by the Council of Trent (published 1566), of which an English translation was issued in London (1687) under the patronage of James II. Among Protestants the catechisms of Luther (1518, 1520, and 1529) acquired great celebrity, and continue to be used in Germany, though not exclusively. Calvin's smaller and larger catechisms (1536-39) never gained the popularity of those of Luther.

The catechism of the Church of England is contained in the *Book of Common Prayer*. In the *First Book of Edward VI.*, 1549, it contained merely the baptismal vow, the creed, the ten commandments, and the Lord's prayer, with explanations, the part relative to the sacraments being subjoined during the reign of James I.

The catechism of the Church of Scotland is that agreed upon by the Assembly of Divines at Westminster, with the assistance of commissioners from the Church of Scotland, and approved of by the General Assembly in the year 1648. What is called the *Shorter Catechism* is merely an abridgment of the *Larger*, and is the one in most common use. The best-known catechism among English Protestant Dissenters was that of Dr. Watts; but the use of catechisms is far from usual amongst them.—BIBLIOGRAPHY: P. Schaff, *History of the Creeds of Christendom* (3 vols.); Mitchell, *Catechisms of the Second Reformation*; H. A. Lester and E. G. Wainwright, *Catechism: the Life of Faith and Action*; J. A. Rivington, *How to Teach and Catechize*; H. Lee, *The Way of Worship: Lessons introductory to the Church Catechism.*

CAT'ECHU (-shö). A name common to several astringent extracts prepared from the wood, bark, and fruits of various plants, especially by decoction and evaporation from the wood of *Acacia Catechu* (black catechu), as well as from the *Uncaria Gambir* (pale catechu or gambier). Catechu is one of the best astringents in the materia medica. It consists mainly of tannin, and is used in tanning, in the manufacture of fishing-lines and nets, and in calico-printing. It is chiefly obtained from Burmah. Called also *Terra Japonica* and *Cutch.* The original khaki was cloth dyed and shrunk with Acacia cutch.

CATECHUMENS (-kū'menz; literally, persons receiving instruction). A name originally applied to those converted Jews and heathens in the first ages of the Church who were to receive baptism and had a particular place in the Church, but were not permitted to share the sacrament. Afterwards it was applied to young Christians who, for the first time, wished to partake of this ordinance, and for this purpose went through a preparatory course of instruction. Several references to this systematic instruction in Christian doctrine, with a view to being admitted into the body of the Church, occur in the New Testament (Luke, i. 4; Acts, xviii. 24; etc.). At the beginning the duty was undertaken by the Apostles themselves, and the instruction was given *after* baptism.

CAT'EGORY, or **PREDICAMENT** (Gr. *categoria*, accusation, attribution). In logic, an assemblage of all the beings contained under any genus or kind ranged in order. The term was transferred by Aristotle from its forensic meaning, i.e. procedure in legal accusation, to its logical use as attribution of a subject. Its technical significance is suggested by its Latin equivalent *prædicamentum*, employed by Boethius.

The ancients, following Aristotle, held that all beings or objects of thought may be referred to ten categories, viz. *substance, quantity, quality, relation, action, passion, time, place, situation*, and *possession*. Plato admits only five: *substance, identity, diversity, motion*, and *rest*; the Stoics four: *subjects, qualities, independent circumstances, relative circumstances*. Descartes suggested seven divisions: *spirit, matter, quantity, substance, figure, motion*, and *rest*. Others make but two categories, *substance* and *attribute*, or *subject* and *accident*; or three, accident being divided into the *inherent* and *circumstantial*.

In the philosophy of Kant the term categories is applied to the primitive conceptions originating in the understanding independently of all experience (hence called pure conceptions), though incapable of being realised in thought except in their application to experience. These he divides into four classes, quantity, quality, relation, and modality, placing under the first class the conceptions of unity, plurality, and totality; under the second, reality, negation, and limitation; under the third, inherence and subsistence, causality and dependence, and community (mutual action); and under the fourth, possibility and impossibility, existence and non-existence, necessity and contingency.

J. S. Mill applies the term categories to the most general heads under which everything that may be asserted of any subject may be arranged. Of these he makes five, existence, co-existence, sequence, causation, and resemblance, or, considering causation as a peculiar case of sequence, four.—BIBLIOGRAPHY: B. Bosanquet, *Knowledge and Reality*; H. W. B. Joseph, *Introduction to Logic*.

CATE'NARY CURVE (Lat. *catena*, a chain). That curve which is formed by a cord or chain of uniform density and thickness when allowed to hang freely between two points. It is of interest as bearing on the theory of arches and domes, and as the curve assumed by the chains of a suspension bridge.

CA'TERHAM. A town of England, in Surrey, near Croydon, with barracks for the foot guards, and in the neighbourhood the metropolitan district lunatic asylum. Pop. (Caterham and Warlingham urban district), 19,503 (1931).

CATERPILLAR. Larva of a butterfly, moth, or sand-fly. Its head bears strong biting mandibles for nipping leaves or gnawing timber, with three simple eyes, three thoracic segments each with a pair of true joined legs, and ten abdominal segments variably endowed with tubular hooked prolegs, the last two being claspers. Their function is to store food for the pupal or resting stage, and their voracity frequently causes serious loss to farmers.

CAT-FISH. One of the Siluroids, a widely-distributed family of freshwater bony fishes. The name has reference to the presence of long sensitive feelers (barbels) in the neighbourhood of the mouth. Catfishes are represented by a large number of temperate and tropical species, and some of them enter estuaries or even the sea. The only European species is the Wels (*Silurus glanis*), found in the rivers east of the Rhine, and attaining a length of 13 feet and a weight of 400 lb.

CAT'GUT. A cord made from the intestines of sheep, and sometimes from those of the horse, ass, and mule, but not from those of cats. The manufacture is chiefly carried on in Italy and France by a tedious process. Catgut for stringed instruments, as violins and harps, is made principally in Milan and Naples, the latter having a high reputation for treble strings.

CATHA. A genus of plants, nat. ord. Celastraceæ, mostly natives of Africa. The leaves and twigs of *C. edūlis*, known as *khat* or *cafta*, possess properties akin to those of tea and coffee, and the plant is much cultivated by the Arabs. The use of khat is of greater antiquity than that of coffee.

CATH'ARI (Gr. *kathăros*, pure). A name akin to "Puritans," applied at different times to various sects of Christians. The Novatians of the third century were frequently known as Cathari. It became a common appellation of several sects which first appeared in the eleventh century in Lombardy and afterwards in other countries of the West, and which were violently persecuted for their alleged Manichæan tenets and usages. They had many other local names. Thus from their relation to the Bulgarian Paulicians they were sometimes termed *Bulgarians*. They were also known as *Piphili*, *Arians*, *Manichæans*, and *Textores* (Weavers), from the trade which many of the members followed. Corrupted forms of Cathari are *Cazzari* and *Gazzari* in Italy, and *Ketzer* in Germany. In Southern France, when they were mostly prosperous, they were confounded with the Albigenses, and were exterminated with them.

The Cathari proper were dualists, of a type closely related to the older Gnostics, held a community of goods, abstained from war, marriage, and the killing of animals, and rejected water-baptism. They professed to strive after a higher life than that embodied in the ordinary religious ideals.—Cf. C. Schmidt, *Histoire et doctrine de la secte des Cathares*.

CATHAR'TES. *See* TURKEY-BUZZARD.

CATHAR'TICS. A general name for purgative medicines; strictly a medicine which is capable of producing the second grade of purgation, of which laxative is the first and drastic the third.

CATHAY'. An old name of China.

CATHCART, Charles Murray, second Earl of. Son of the first earl, born in 1783; served under Wellington in the Peninsula and at Waterloo, was in 1830 created a major-general, and in 1851 commander-in-chief in Canada; died in 1859.

CATHCART, Sir George. Son of the first earl, born in 1794; entered the Life Guards in 1810, accompanied his father as attaché to Russia, and subsequently acted as aide-de-camp to the Duke of Wellington at Waterloo. He served in Nova Scotia and the West Indies, quelled the rebellion in Canada in 1837, and was appointed in 1852 Governor at the Cape of Good Hope, where he showed ability in subduing the Kaffir insurrection. On the outbreak of the Crimean War great things were expected of him, but he fell as divisional commander at Inkerman in 1854.

CATHCART, William Schaw, Earl of. British general, son of Baron Cathcart of Cathcart, Renfrew, born in 1755, died in 1843. He served in the American War and against the French Republic in Flanders and Germany, and in 1807 commanded the land forces in the expedition against Copenhagen, being then created viscount. In 1812 he went to Russia as minister-plenipotentiary, and in 1814 was created an earl. Subsequently he was for several years Ambassador to the Russian court.

CATHE'DRAL (Gr. *kathedra*, a seat). The principal church of a diocese. The word was used of the throne of the bishop in the apse of his church, and hence the episcopal church possessing the episcopal chair was called a cathedral church, *ecclesia cathedralis*. This is really what distinguishes a cathedral from other churches, though most cathedrals are also larger and more elaborate structures than ordinary churches, and have various dignitaries and functionaries connected with them.

The cathedral establishments in England regularly consist of a dean and chapter, presided over by the bishop, the chapter being composed of a certain number of canons. The dean and chapter meet in the chapter-house of the cathedral; in them the property of the cathedral is vested, and they nominally elect the bishop on a *congé d'élire* from the Crown. There are often a certain number of honorary canons, also "minor canons" who assist in the performance of the choral services, choristers, etc.

As regards architecture, cathedrals naturally vary much. Those in England are almost all in the Gothic style, cruciform or cross-shaped in arrangement, and having connected with them a chapter-house, side chapels (varying in number and position), cloisters, crypt, etc. This style and arrangement are also common on the continent of Europe, and in most modern cathedrals; but the Romanesque, Renaissance, and Byzantine styles of architecture are also employed.

Many cathedrals furnish the most magnificent examples of the architecture of the Middle Ages; and as they were intended to accommodate great numbers of people, and to exhibit imposing religious services, they are often of great size (St. Peter's, Rome, is 613 feet long and 450 feet across the transepts). Among the most notable cathedrals are St. Peter's, the largest of all, founded 1450; the cathedral at Milan, founded in 1386, built of white marble; the cathedral at Florence, begun about 1294, one of the finest specimens of the Italian-Gothic style; Cologne Cathedral, commenced in 1248 (and only finished recently); Nôtre-Dame, at Paris,

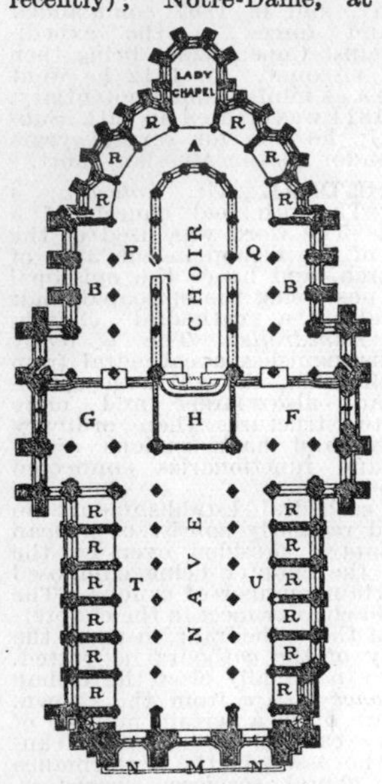

Plan of Amiens Cathedral

A, Apsidal aisle. B B, Outer aisles of choir. F G, Transepts. H, Central tower. I J, Western Turrets. M, Principal or western doorway. N N, Western side doors. P Q, North and south aisles of choir. R R R, Chapels. T U, North and south aisles of nave.

begun 1163; and those of Amiens, Chartres, and Rheims.

The most noteworthy English cathedrals are St. Paul's, London (1675-1711), in the Renaissance style, and those of Canterbury, Ely, Exeter, Lichfield, Lincoln, Norwich, Salisbury, Wells, Westminster, and York. The cathedrals of Glasgow and Kirkwall are the only entire cathedrals in Scotland, exclusive of modern edifices. — BIBLIOGRAPHY: *Cathedrals of England and Wales* (Cassell); A. Fairbairns, *Cathedrals of England and Wales*; T. F. Bumpus, *Cathedrals of N, Italy, Cathedrals of N. France*; J. A. Gade, *Cathedrals of Spain.*

CATHERINE I. Empress of Russia, and wife of Peter the Great, born in 1683, died in 1727. She was a woman of humble origin, who, having become mistress to Prince Menschikov, was relinquished by him to the Tsar.

Plan of Wells Cathedral

A, Apse or apsis. B, Altar, altar-platform, and altar-steps. D F, Eastern or lesser transept. F G, Western or greater transept. H, Central tower. I J, Western towers. K, North porch. L, Library or register. M, Principal or western doorway. N N, Western side doors. O, Cloister yard or garth. P Q, North and south aisles of choir. R S, East and west aisles of transept. T U, North and south aisles of nave. R R, Chapels. V, Rood screen or organ loft. W, Altar of Lady chapel.

In 1708 and 1709 she bore the emperor the Princesses Anna and Elizabeth, the first of whom became the Duchess of Holstein by marriage, and mother of Peter III. The second became Empress of Russia. In 1711 the emperor publicly acknowledged Catherine as his wife, and she was subsequently proclaimed empress, and crowned in Moscow in 1724. When Peter with his army seemed irreparably lost on the Pruth in 1711, Catherine secured the relief of her husband by bribing the Turkish general. At Peter's death in 1725 Catherine was proclaimed Empress and autocrat of all the Russias, and the oath of allegiance to her was taken anew. Catherine died suddenly in 1727, her death having been hastened by dissipation.—Cf. R. N. Bain, *The First Romanovs.*

CATHERINE II. Empress of Russia, born in 1729, her father being Christian Augustus, Prince of Anhalt-Zerbst, died in 1796. In 1745 she was married to Peter, nephew and successor of the Russian Empress Elizabeth, on whose death in 1762 her husband succeeded as Peter III. In danger of being supplanted by his mistress, the Countess Woronzov, Catherine, with the assistance of her lover, Gregory Orlov, and others, won over the guards and was proclaimed monarch (July, 1762). Peter attempted no resistance, abdicated almost immediately, and was strangled in prison a few days later, apparently without Catherine's knowledge. By bribes and threats she readily secured her position, and at once entered upon the administration with great and far-seeing activity.

On the death of Augustus III. of Poland she caused her old lover, Poniatowski, to be placed on the throne with a view to the extension of her influence in Poland, by which she profited in the partition of that country in the successive dismemberments of 1772, 1793, and 1795. By the war with the Turks, which occupied a considerable part of her reign, she conquered the Crimea and opened the Black Sea to the Russian navy. Her dream, however, of driving the Turks from Europe and restoring the Byzantine Empire was not to be fulfilled Her relations with Poland and with other European powers induced her to make peace with Turkey in 1792, and accept the Dniester as the boundary line between the two countries.

She appears to have been successful in improving the administration of justice, ameliorated the condition of the serfs, constructed canals, founded the Russian Academy, and in a variety of ways contributed to the enlightenment and prosperity of the country. Her enthusiasm for reform, however, was summarily checked by the events of the French Revolution; and the dissipation and extravagance of her court were such that there was even a danger of its exhausting the empire. Of her many lovers Potemkin was longest in favour, retaining his influence from 1775 till his death in 1791, directing Russian politics throughout that period in all essential matters.—Cf. Waliszewski, *Autour d'un Trône.*

CATHERINE, ST. In the Roman hagiology there are six saints of this name, of whom only two are of importance: (1) St. Catherine, a virgin of Alexandria who suffered martyrdom in the fourth century. She is represented with a wheel; and the legend of her marriage with Christ has been painted by several of the first masters. (2) St. Catherine of Siena, born in 1347, died 1380. She was preternaturally pious from her birth, and at six years of age was given to self-castigation and other penances. Urban VI. and Gregory XI. sought her advice, and in 1460 —80 years after her death—she was canonised. Her poems and letters have been published.—Cf. E. G. Gardner, *Saint Catherine of Siena.*

CATHERINE, ST., ORDERS OF. The knights of St. Catherine on Mount Sinai are an ancient military order, instituted for the protection of the pilgrims who came to visit the tomb of St. Catherine on this mountain. In Russia the order of St. Catherine, was a distinction for ladies, instituted by Catherine, wife of Peter the Great, in memory of his signal escape from the Turks in 1711.

CATHERINE DE' MEDICI (dā-med'i-chē). Wife of Henry II., King of France, born at Florence in 1519, died in 1589. She was the only daughter of Lorenzo de' Medici, Duke of Urbino, and the niece of Pope Clement VII. In 1533 she was married to the Duke of Orleans, afterwards Henry II., but had little or no influence at the French court during the reign of her husband, who was under the influence of his mistress Diana de Poitiers.

Her political power really began on the death of Henry II., 10th July, 1559, and during the reign of her eldest son, Francis II., who, in consequence of his marriage with Mary Stuart, was devoted to the party of the Guises. The death of Francis placed the reins of government, during the minority of her son Charles IX., in her hands. Wavering between the Guises on one side, who had put themselves at the head of the Catholics, and Condé and Coligny on the other, who had become very powerful by the aid of the Protestants, she played off one faction against the other in the hope of increasing her own power; and the thirty years of civil war which followed were mainly due to her. Her influence with Charles IX. was throughout of the worst kind, and the massacre of St. Bartholomew's Day was largely her work.

After the death of Charles IX., in 1574, her third son succeeded as Henry III., and her mischievous influence continued. She died shortly before the assassination of Henry III. Of her two daughters, Elizabeth married Philip II. of Spain, and Margaret of Valois married Henry of Navarre, afterwards Henry IV.—Cf. E. Sichel, *Catherine de' Medici and the French Reformation*; *The Later Years of Catherine de' Medici*.

CATHERINE HOWARD. Queen of England, fifth wife of Henry VIII., daughter of Lord Edmund Howard, son of the Duke of Norfolk, born 1522. Her beauty and vivacity induced the king to marry her in 1540, but her conduct appears to have been of a dubious kind both before and after marriage, and she was charged in 1541 with adultery. Her paramours Derham and Culpepper were beheaded, and two months later (Feb., 1542) she shared the same fate.

CATHERINE OF ARAGON. Queen of England, the youngest daughter of Ferdinand of Aragon and Isabella of Castile, born in 1485. In 1501 she was married to Arthur, Prince of Wales, son of Henry VII. Her husband dying about five months after, the king, unwilling to return her dowry, caused her to be contracted to his remaining son, Henry, and a dispensation was procured from the Pope for that purpose.

On his accession to the throne as Henry VIII. in 1509 she was crowned with him, and despite the inequality of their ages retained her ascendancy with the king for nearly twenty years. Her children, however, all died in infancy, excepting Mary, and, having fallen in love with Anne Boleyn, Henry pretended to doubt the legality of his union with Catherine. He applied therefore to Rome for a divorce, but the attitude of the papal court ultimately provoked him to throw off his submission to it, and declare himself head of the English Church.

In 1532 he married Anne Boleyn; upon which Catherine, no longer considered Queen of England, retired to Ampthill in Bedfordshire. Cranmer, now raised to the primacy, pronounced the sentence of divorce, notwithstanding which, Catherine still persisted in maintaining her claims, showing from first to last a firm and dignified spirit. She died in Jan., 1536.

CATHERINE OF BRAGANZA. Wife of Charles II., King of England, and daughter of John IV., King of Portugal, born in 1638. In 1662 she married Charles II., but her husband's infidelities and neglect, and her childlessness, were a source of mortification to her. In 1693 she returned to Portugal, where, in 1704, she was made regent, and in the conduct of affairs during the war with Spain showed marked ability. She died in 1705.

CATHERINE PARR. Sixth and last wife of Henry VIII. of England, born in 1512, and had had two husbands before she became Henry's queen in 1543. Her attachment to the reformed religion brought her into some danger, but from this she was released by the king's death in 1547. After the death of the king she espoused the Lord-Admiral Lord Thomas Seymour, uncle to Edward VI.; but the union was an unhappy one, and she died in childbed in 1548. She was the author of a volume of Prayers or Meditations, and a tract and letters published posthumously.

CATH'ETER. A term applied in surgery to a tube, usually of silver or india-rubber, which is introduced into the bladder through the urethra, for the purpose of drawing off the urine when it cannot be discharged in the natural way. The term is also applied to other tubes designed for introduction into other cavities. For example, the Eustachian catheter is used in certain kinds of deafness for opening the passage that leads from the pharynx into the middle ear.

CATHETOM'ETER (Gr. *kathetos*, vertical, and *metron*, measure). An instrument for measuring small differences of level between two points; in its simplest form a vertical graduated rod, upon which slides a horizontal telescope. With the telescope the observer sights the two objects under examination, and the distance on the graduated rod moved over by the telescope is the measure of the distance of height between the two objects.

CATHODE. *See* ANODE.

CATH'OLIC APOSTOLIC CHURCH. *See* IRVINGITES.

CATHOLIC CHURCH. The universal Church, the whole body of true believers in Christ; but the term is often used as equivalent to the Roman or Western Church.

CATHOLIC EMANCIPATION. The abolition of those civil and ecclesiastical restraints to which the Roman Catholics of Great Britain, and particularly of Ireland, were once subjected. By the statutes of William III. Roman Catholics were forbidden to hold property in land, and their spiritual instructors were open to the penalties of felony; and although these restrictions were not enforced for some years while still in the statute book, they remained unrepealed in England until 1778. The proposal to repeal similar enactments on the Scottish statute books was delayed by the strenuous opposition of the Protestant associations, in connection with which the Lord George Gordon riots occurred. In 1791, however, a Bill was passed allowing Roman Catholics who took the oath of allegiance to hold landed property, enter the legal profession, and enjoy freedom of education.

In Ireland the Roman Catholics had been even more severely treated. Their public worship was proscribed, all offices and the learned professions were closed against them, they were deprived of the guardianship of their children, and if they had landed estates they were forbidden to marry Protestants. Burke and a strong body of followers took up their cause, and in 1792 and 1793 the worst of the disabilities were removed by the Irish Parliament. Restraints on worship, education, and disposition of property were removed; they were admitted to the franchise, and to some of the higher civil and military offices, and to the honours and endowments of Dublin University. They continued to be excluded, however, from thirty public offices, and from Parliament—an arrangement which could not be changed without a repeal of the Corporation and Test Acts.

It was part of Pitt's scheme when the union with Ireland was formulated in 1799 to admit Irish Roman Catholics to the Parliament of the United Kingdom and to offices of State. To this proposal, however, George III. was strongly hostile, and in 1801 Pitt was compelled to resign. Between that year and 1828 numerous attempts were made to abolish remaining disabilities, but without success, the Lords throwing out the Bills passed in the Commons, and George IV. proving not less unyielding than his father.

At length, in 1829 (10th April), an Emancipation Bill was carried through the Commons by Peel, and through the Lords by the Duke of Wellington. By this Act Catholics are eligible for all offices of State excepting the Lord Chancellorships of England and Ireland, the Lord-Lieutenancy of Ireland, the office of Regent or Guardian of the United Kingdom, and that of High Commissioner to the Church of Scotland. They are still excluded from the right of presentation to livings, and all places connected with the ecclesiastical courts and establishment. The Church patronage attached to any office in the hands of a Catholic is vested in the Archbishop of Canterbury. Attached to the Bill is a clause for the gradual suppression of the Jesuits and monastic orders (religious establishments of women excepted).

CATHOLIC EPISTLES. A name given to seven epistles of the New Testament—one of James, two of Peter, the first three of John, and one of Jude—because, unlike the epistles of St. Paul, they were written to Christians in general, and not to those in some particular place.

CATHOLIC MAJESTY. A title which Pope Alexander VI. gave to the Kings of Spain, in memory of the complete expulsion of the Moors from Spain in 1491 by Ferdinand of Aragon. But even before that time, and especially after the Council at Toledo in 589, several Spanish kings are said to have borne this title.

CATHOL'ICOS. The title of the Nestorian and Armenian patriarchs.

CAT'ILINE (Lucius Sergius Catilina). A Roman conspirator, of patrician rank, born about 108 B.C. In his youth he attached himself to the party of Sulla, but his physical strength, passionate nature, and unscrupulous daring soon gained him an independent reputation. Despite the charges of having killed his brother-in-law and murdered his wife and son, he was elected prætor in 68 B.C., and Governor of Africa in 67 B.C. In 66 B.C. he returned to Rome to contest the consulship, but was disqualified by an impeachment for maladministration in his province.

Urged on by his necessities as well as his ambition, he entered into a conspiracy with other disaffected nobles. The plot, however, was revealed to Cicero, and measures were at once taken to defeat it. Thwarted by Cicero at every turn, and driven from the Senate by the orator's bold denunciations, Catiline fled, and put himself at the head of a large but ill-armed following. The news of the suppression of the conspiracy and execution of the ringleaders at Rome diminished his forces, and he led the rest towards Gaul. Metellus Celer threw himself between the rebels and their goal, while Antonius pressed upon their rear, and, driven to bay, Catiline turned upon the pursuing army and perished fighting (62 B.C.).—BIBLIOGRAPHY: Prosper Merimée, *Études sur la guerre sociale et la conjuration de Catiline*; J. L. Strachan Davidson, *Cicero*; G. Boissier, *Cicero and his Friends*.

CATINAT (kȧ-ti-nä), **Nicholas.** Marshal of France, born at Paris 1637, died in 1712. He attracted the notice of Louis XIV. at the storming of Lille (1667), and by his conduct, especially at the battle of Senef, gained the friendship of Condé. He was sent as lieutenant-general against the Duke of Savoy, gained the battles of Staffardo (1690), and Marsaglia (1693), occupied Savoy and part of Piedmont, and was made marshal in 1693. In Flanders he displayed the same activity, and took Ath in 1697. In 1701 he received the command of the army of Italy against Prince Eugène; but his ill-furnished forces were defeated at Carpi, and he was disgraced.

CATIN'GA. The local name for the thorn-scrub found in the dry interior of Brazil, which contains many remarkable plant-forms, mostly drought-resisting types, such as Barrel trees (Cavanillesia), Cacti, and Bromeliaceæ.

CAT ISLAND. One of the Bahama Islands, about 46 miles in length from north to south, and 3 to 7 in its mean breadth. Pop. 3000. It was long thought that it, and not Watling Island, was the Guanahani, or San Salvador, where Columbus first touched the New World in 1492.

CATKIN, or **AMENTUM.** A spike of apetalous unisexual flowers, usually pendulous; examples: birch, hazel, poplar.

CATLIN, George. A writer on the American Indians, born in Pennsylvania 1796, died 1872. After practising as a lawyer for two years, he set up at New York as a portrait-painter, and in 1832 commenced special studies of Indian types, residing many years amongst them both in North and South America. In 1840 he came to Europe, and subsequently introduced three parties of American Indians to European courts. His finely-illustrated works are: *Manners, Customs, and Condition of the North American Indians* (1841); *North American Portfolio* (1844); *Eight Years' Travels and Residence in Europe* (1848); *Last Rambles amongst the Indians, etc.* (1868). Most of his portraits came into the possession of the Government, and now constitute the Catlin Gallery of the National Museum.

CATO, Dionysius. The reputed author of the small collection of moral apophthegms entitled, *Dionysii Catonis Disticha de Moribus ad Filium* (Moral Couplets addressed to his son). The real author of the book is unknown, but it is believed to date from the fourth century A.D. The book contained a great deal of the proverbial philosophy of the ancient world. It had an established reputation in the Middle Ages, and is referred to by Chaucer.

CATO, Marcus Porcius. The Censor, surnamed *Priscus,* also *Sapiens* and *Major* (the Wise and the Elder). A celebrated Roman, born 234 B.C. at Tusculum. He inherited from his father, a plebeian, a small estate in the territory of the Sabines, which he cultivated with his own hands. He served his first campaign, at the age of seventeen, under Fabius Maximus, was present at the siege of Capua in 214 B.C., and five years after fought under the same commander at the siege of Tarentum.

After the war was ended he returned to his farm, but by the advice of Valerius Flaccus removed to Rome, where his forensic abilities had free scope. He rose rapidly, accompanied Scipio to Sicily as quæstor in 204 B.C., became an ædile in 199 B.C., and in 198 B.C. was chosen prætor, and appointed to the province of Sardinia. Three years later he gained the consulship, and in 194 B.C. for his brilliant campaign in Spain obtained the honour of a triumph. In 191 B.C. he served as military tribune against Antiochus, and then, having abundantly proved his soldierly qualities, returned to Rome. For some years he exercised a practical censorship, scrutinising the characters of candidates for office, and denouncing false claims, peculations, etc. His election to the censorship in 184 B.C. set an official seal to his efforts, the unsparing severity of which has made his name proverbial.

From that year until his death, in 149 B.C., he held no public office, though zealously continuing his unofficial labours for the state. His hostility to Carthage, the destruction of which he advocated in every speech made by him in the forum, was the most striking feature of his closing years. His incessant "Delenda est Carthago" (Carthage must be destroyed) did much to further the third Punic War. Of his works his *De Agricultura* or *De Re Rustica* (edited by H. Kiel, 1884-91) alone survives, though there exist in quotation fragments of his history and speeches.—Cf. Warde Fowler, *Social Life at Rome.*

CATO, Marcus Porcius (called **Cato of Utica,** the place of his death, to distinguish him from the Censor, his great-grandfather). A distinguished Roman, born 95 B.C. He formed an intimacy with the Stoic Antipater of Tyre, and ever remained true to the principles of the Stoic philosophy. He distinguished himself as a volunteer in the war against Spartacus, served as military tribune in Macedonia in 67 B.C., and was made quæstor in 65 B.C. His rigorous reforms won him general respect, and in 63 B.C. he was chosen tribune of the people.

During the troubles with Catiline, Cato gave Cicero important aid both by his eloquence and sagacity, and

Marcus Porcius Cato (of Utica), from a bust in the Vatican

at the same time set himself to thwart the ambitious projects of Pompey, Cæsar, and Crassus. Such success as he had, however, was only temporary, and he failed to prevent the formation of the triumvirate. To get rid of him they sent him to take possession of Cyprus, but, having successfully accomplished his mission, he returned, opposed the Tribonian law for conferring extraordinary powers on the triumvirs, and in 54 B.C. enforced, as prætor, an obnoxious law against bribery. On the breach between Pompey and Cæsar he threw in his lot with Pompey, and guarded the stores at Dyrrhachium, while Pompey pushed on to Pharsalia.

After receiving news of Pompey's defeat, he sailed to Cyrene and effected a junction with Metellus Scipio at Utica, in 47 B.C. He took command of that city, but its defence appearing hopeless after the defeat of Scipio at Thapsus, he determined on suicide, and, after spending some time in the perusal of the *Phædo* of Plato, stabbed himself with his sword. His wounds were bound up by his attendants, but he tore off the bandages and died, 46 B.C.—Cf. C. W. Oman, *Seven Roman Statesmen of the Later Republic.*

CATOP'TRICS (from Gr. *katoptron*, a mirror). That branch of optics which explains the properties of incident and reflected light, and particularly that which is reflected from mirrors or polished surfaces. The whole doctrine of catoptrics rests on the principle that the angle of incidence is equal to the angle of reflection and in the same plane.

CATOPTROMANCY (from the Gr. *katoptron*, mirror, and *manteia*, prophecy). Divination or prophecy by means of a looking-glass or mirror. The superstitious practice originated in Greece, where a mirror was let down by a thread until it touched the water in a fountain before the temple of Demeter. By means of this mirror the recovery or death of the sick was foretold. If the face of the person appeared healthy in the mirror, he or she would recover, if it looked ill, death would follow. The modern superstition attaching ill-luck to the breaking of a looking-glass is a relic of Greek catoptromancy.

CATO STREET CONSPIRACY. Plot to murder British ministers in 1820. Arthur Thistlewood, who had already been mixed up with revolutionary projects, conceived a plan for assassinating Lord Castlereagh and his ministerial colleagues at a dinner in Grosvenor Square, London, on Feb. 23rd. Arms were collected in a hired rendezvous in the neighbouring Cato Street. The plot was discovered, Thistlewood and his colleagues were arrested, and he and four others were executed.

CATS, Jacob. One of the fathers of the Dutch language and poetry, born in 1577, died in 1660. He studied at Leyden, Orleans, and Paris, and settled at Middelburg, where he produced his *Emblems of Fancy and Love, Galateu, The Mirror of Past and Present*, etc. In 1627 and 1631 he was ambassador to England, where he was knighted by Charles I., and from 1636 to 1652 he was grand-pensioner of Holland. He represents the best side of the prosaic Flemish genius of the period, and his many works had a wide and prolonged popularity. His autobiography, *Eighty-two Years of my Life*, was first printed in 1734.

CAT'S-EYE. A variety of quartz including fibres of asbestos, which give it opalescence. When cut *en cabochon*, that is, with a spherical or ellipsoidal surface, it resembles a cat's eye.

CATSKILL MOUNTAINS. A fine range of mountains in New York State. They lie on the west side of and nearly parallel to the Hudson, from which their base is, at the nearest point, 8 miles distant. The two most elevated peaks are Round Top and High Peak; the former 3804 feet, the latter 3718 feet high.

CAT'TARO. A fortified seaport of Yugoslavia in Dalmatia at the foot of the Gulf of Cattaro, on the east side of the Adriatic. The cathedral and the castle are its chief buildings. Pop. 6040.

CAT'TEGAT. A large gulf of the North Sea, between Denmark on the W., Sweden on the E., and the Danish islands of Zealand, Funen, etc., on the S.; about 150 miles from N. to S.; greatest breadth, about 90 miles. It is noted for its herring-fishery, but is difficult of navigation. It contains the islands Samsöe, Anholt, Lessöe, and Hertzholm.

CAT'TERMOLE, George. English painter, born 1800 in Norfolk, died in 1868. He was employed as a draughtsman on Britton's *English Cathedrals* when only sixteen, drew admirable illustrations for various works (*Waverley Novels, Historical Annual*, etc.), and exhibited both at the Academy and the Water-Colour Society. He long painted chiefly in water-colours, but after 1857 took up oil-painting. Among his works are: *The Murder of the Bishop of Liège, The Armourer relating the Story of the Sword*, etc. He was intimate with many literary and other celebrities, such as Dickens, Thackeray, and Browning.

CATTI, or CHATTI. One of the most renowned of the ancient German tribes. They inhabited what is now Hesse, also part of Franconia and Westphalia.

CATTLE. This is the popular name of the ruminants, otherwise known as the "true" oxen, which belong to the genus Bos, and are included in the family Bovidæ, together with sheep, goats, and antelopes. In all these forms it is usual for both sexes to possess a pair of hollow horns actually composed of horny substance and supported on bony "cores." Oxen are further distinguished by their massive build, broad naked muzzle, and simply curved, not twisted, horns with a smooth surface. They have a very wide geographical distribution, but none of them are indigenous to South America, Madagascar, or the Australian region.

The genus Bos embraces a considerable number of species, to some of which belong the African and Indian buffaloes, the bisons of Europe and America, and the yak of Tibet; but "cattle," with which we are here concerned, appear to have diverged along two different lines, one now represented by the humped oxen of South Asia, and the other by the humpless European breeds familiar in this country. The former have probably descended from the extinct *Bos indicus*, while the origin of the others is more obscure.

In the case of British cattle one suggested ancestor is the great ox or urus (*Bos primigenius*), which had a wide range in Europe during prehistoric times, long before the Western races of mankind had learnt the use of metals, and which was contemporaneous in Britain with the mammoth, woolly rhinoceros, and cave lion. But satisfactory evidence for this is lacking. We only know that the bovine populations of Britain arrived in successive waves, differing in kind, much as in the case of the human population. From these have arisen the eighteen or nineteen British breeds now recognised, many of which are due to the intermixture of two or more original varieties, largely as the result of artificial selection exercised by man.

Black Cattle. The earliest farmers of Britain were men of Iberian stock, users of polished and neatly-chipped stone implements, and the owners of small black cattle derived from the extinct *Bos longifrons* or Celtic Shorthorn. These prehistoric men came into our country from the Continent, driving out still more primitive races, and bringing their black cattle with them. They were subsequently largely supplanted by metal-using Celts, who were the dominant race at the time of the Roman invasion, when it is probable that all our native cattle were still of the small black type. It is likely that the Welsh and Kerry breeds, among existing races, are most nearly allied to the small black cattle of pre-Roman Britain.

Welsh Cattle. Of several varieties, which all possess long horns, while black is the predominant colour. They represent a great improvement on the original stock, and are noted for beef-production, while some strains have been specialised for dairy purposes. The **Kerry** breed, native to South and West Ireland, is a small and active type, with short up-standing horns, and is a notable milk-producer. The short-

CATTLE
Top: Jersey and Shorthorn.
Centre: Highland Cow.
Bottom: Ayrshire and Kerry.

legged **Dexter** has been derived from this, but is a useful dual-purpose breed, and may be either black or red.

White Cattle. The Romans brought white cattle into Britain, and from these the "wild white cattle" of Chillingham, Chartley, etc., have probably descended. Their white colour and long upwardly-curving horns appear to have had some influence in the shaping of some of the existing domesticated breeds. The Anglo-Saxon invaders introduced a red breed, and this has undoubtedly played a great part in the evolution of Lincoln, Red Poll, Sussex, Devon, and Hereford cattle.

Lincoln Reds, an excellent dual-purpose breed, closely allied to the Shorthorns, began to be selected as a special strain about the end of the seventeenth century. **Red Polls** are also dual-purpose cattle, and their chief characteristics have been acquired by the intermixture of two earlier types, the Norfolk and Suffolk. The **Sussex** breed is large and brownish-red in colour, with short horns curving forwards and upwards. As a beef producer it is greatly esteemed.

The **North Devons** are also a beef breed, smaller and more graceful than the Sussex type, and making the most of poor hill pastures. The thick horns of the bull project straight out at the side, while those of the cow are slender, with a neat upward and backward curve, in typical cases. **South Devons** (Hams) are red or orange in colour, with white spreading horns. They attain a very large size, and, though mainly of repute for beef-production, present great possibilities as dairy cattle, for they yield a large quantity of very rich milk.

Herefords are greatly esteemed as a beef breed, and are of large size. Red is the prevailing colour, but the face, upper side of the neck, and under side of the body are white. The horns are wax-coloured, those of the bull projecting laterally and drooping a little at the end, while those of the cow project forwards and upwards.

Polled Cattle. Another factor in the fashioning of British breeds was contributed by Norse invaders and settlers, who introduced their hornless (polled) dun cattle into this country. Colour and hornlessness have both been handed down in certain cases. The old Norfolk polled breed, for example, was essentially of Scandinavian type, and its hornlessness has been inherited by the Red Polls. At a much later time black-and-white Dutch cattle were brought into this country, and some of our breeds, distinguished by broken colours, attest their influence. This was long prior to the introduction of **British Friesian,** the most recent of our recognised breeds, distinguished by their black-and-white colour, and noted as a milk-producer, though the abundant milk is not very rich.

We have seen that Herefords are of broken colour, being red and white; and the important and widely-distributed breed of **Shorthorns** is another example of colour mixture, white and red being present in varying proportions, while pure red and pure white are not unknown. The closely-allied Lincoln Reds have already been mentioned. Shorthorns have a great and well-deserved reputation as dual-purpose cattle, while milking characters are being increased in the sub-breed known as Dairy Shorthorns. The breed is a mixture of various strains, and in the latter part of the eighteenth century Charles and Robert Colling played a great part in its establishment. Other notable breeders who took part in its improvement were Thomas Booth, Thomas Bates, Amos Cruickshank, and Anthony Cruickshank.

Channel Island Breeds. There further appears to have been another ancestral race, blackish-brown or mulberry in colour, and of unknown origin, which, crossed with black or red, has given rise to brindles, i.e. cattle with dark spots or streaks on a grey or tawny background. To this race the Channel Islands breeds most nearly approximate. **Jerseys** are dairy cattle pure and simple, and their colours are fawn, silver-grey, and mulberry, to which a certain amount of white may be added. The muzzle is dark, surrounded by a light band. **Guernseys** are larger and less shapely, but equally esteemed as producers of rich milk. They are typically fawn-coloured, often with white markings, while the muzzle is never dark.

Longhorns. Brindles, indicating the presence of blood from the last-named ancestral type, are common among Longhorns and Highland cattle. *Longhorns* are a large dual-purpose breed, possessed of widely-curving horns, and their chief colours are brown, mulberry, and brindle, with a certain amount of white, especially along the back. The breed was established during the second half of the eighteenth century by Robert Bakewell of Dishley, Leicestershire, and his success was due to his adoption of a system of close inbreeding, in those days a novelty. **Highland** cattle are small

CATTLE

Top: Long-horned and Red Poll.
Centre: Hereford Bull.
Bottom: British Frisian and Galloway.

and hardy, with well-developed horns, and are classed among the beef breeds. The hair is very abundant, and the colours are black, red, yellow, dun, and brindle. They appear to have been built up on the black Celtic type by crossing with the blackish-brown strain, Norse duns, and English reds.

Three other breeds require mention all of them Scottish, i.e. Ayrshire, Galloway, and Aberdeen-Angus.

Ayrshires are a wedge-shaped dairy breed, already well established in West Scotland by the end of the seventeenth century. In colour they are a mixture of white and red, the former predominating. The shortish horns are directed upwards and forwards, curving back a little at the tip. The broken-coloured Dutch type has undoubtedly played an important part in the formation of the breed.

Galloways are a small black-polled breed, noted for the quality of their beef. Red, dun, and brindled individuals were once common, and they are obviously a composite stock, which has been formed by crossing the old black Celtic type with other strains, especially the hornless Norse duns. As indicated by their name, Galloways were evolved in the south-west of Scotland.

Aberdeen-Angus cattle, native to the north-east of Scotland, resemble Galloways in being hornless and black in colour, and also in being a noted beef breed, but they are of larger size. Duns and brindles were at one time common, but these colours have been for the most part eliminated. The race has been built up in similar fashion to the Galloways, but the larger size marks the embodiment of one or more southern strains. —BIBLIOGRAPHY: Rev. J. Storer, *The Wild White Cattle of Great Britain*; R. Wallace, *Farm Live Stock of Great Britain*; R. Bruce, *Fifty Years among Shorthorns*; W. A. Henry, *Feeds and Feeding*; H. W. Mumford, *Beef Production.*

CATTLE-DISEASES include *foot-and-mouth disease, pleuropneumonia, rinderpest, black-quarter, red-water,* etc. See the articles, also CONTAGIOUS DISEASES (ANIMALS); VETERINARY SCIENCE.

CATT'LEYA. A genus of orchids, natives of tropical America, growing on trees and rocks, with showy flowers, coloured and marked in the most diverse manner, and much cultivated in green-houses. A number of hybrids have been produced by orchid-growers. The varieties of *C. labiata* have large rose and crimson flowers.

CATTY. In China and the Malayan Archipelago, a weight of 1⅓ lb.

CATUL'LUS, Gaius Valerius. The greatest lyric poet of Rome. He was probably born in 84 B.C., and died, in the thirtieth year of his age, in 54 B.C. Almost all that we know about his life is derived from inference from his works. He was of good family, and was himself well-to-do, though he humorously complains of poverty. He owned a yacht, a country house at Benacus, and a Tiburtine farm. He went to Rome probably in 63-62 B.C., and there he met the notorious Clodia, a woman eleven years older than himself. He fell passionately in love with her, and has immortalised her under the name of Lesbia. In his poems we can trace the whole history of the unfortunate entanglement; the first poems are all love and trust (*Carm.* 3, 5, 7, etc.); then Catullus begins to doubt Lesbia; the rift widens and widens; he is torn by conflicting emotions (as in the famous *Odi et amo* of *Carm.* 85); finally, in *Carm.* 11, he says farewell to her with studied insults.

Catullus went to Bithynia in 57 B.C. with the prætor Memmius, and his songs of travel (31 and 46) are among the most charming of his poems. The last dated event in Catullus's life is the prosecution of Vatinius (Aug. 54 B.C.), and it is probable that Catullus died towards the end of that year. He may have died of consumption (*Carm.* 38 refers to an illness, *Carm.* 44 to a hacking cough, and *Carm.* 76 to his morbid listlessness). Catullus was a friend of Cicero, of Plancus, Cinna, and Cornelius Nepos; to the last he dedicated a collection of his poems. He was a bitter opponent of Julius Cæsar, whom he attacked with keen invective (*Carm.* 29, 57, 93).

The poems of Catullus consist of 116 pieces, varying in length from two to four hundred and eight lines. According to present arrangement, the non-dactylic poems come first; then comes the beautiful epithalamium written for the wedding of Junia and Mallius, the marriage song (*Vesper adest, iuvenes*), the *Attis*, the long poem on the marriage of Peleus and Thetis, and, finally, a collection of poems of all kinds in the elegiac metre. Catullus was an admirer of Callimachus and of the Alexandrian school of poetry, and some of his elegiac pieces are forced and artificial (e.g. 66, and to some extent 68). In *Carm.* 68 he implies that he cannot write without his library.

His Alexandrian poems are not of

much account; but his spontaneous lyric poems do count; they spring straight from his passionate heart, and set him alone with Sappho and Shelley. He is the greatest of all Latin poets in poetic gifts and musical language. No love poems yet written are more exquisite than his, and in other kinds of poetry, in bantering his friends (14) or himself (10, 13, 44), in attacking his enemies (23, 29, 39), in a beautiful poem like the Sirmio one (31), in a poem of consolation like 96, or of mourning for his brother (101), he has the pre-eminence over all Roman poets.

He has a style of imperious lucidity, which, when we try to follow it, "makes mouths at our speech", as Swinburne happily said of it. A writer in the *North British Review* (vol. xxxvi) has succinctly summed up the supreme merit of Catullus: "He is one of the very few writers in the world who, on one or two occasions, speaks directly from the heart. The great number even of great poets speak only from the imagination . . . but this one speaks as nature bids him, the joys and sorrows of his own heart."—BIBLIOGRAPHY: Robinson Ellis, *Commentary on Catullus*; H. A. J. Munro, *Criticisms and Elucidations of Catullus*; W. Y. Sellar, *The Roman Poets of the Republic*.

CAUCA (kou'kà). A South American river in Colombia, an important tributary of the Magdalena; length, 600 to 700 miles. It gives its name to a department or state of Colombia; area, 10,917 sq. miles; pop. 317,782.

CAUCASIAN RACE. A term introduced into ethnology by Blumenbach, in whose classification of mankind it was applied to one of the five great races into which all the different nations of the world were divided. Blumenbach believed this to be the original race from which the others were derived, and he gave it the epithet of Caucasian because he believed that its most typical form—which was also that of man in his highest physical perfection—was to be met with among the mountaineers of the Caucasus.

In later classifications, or ethnologic speculations, *Caucasic* or *Caucasian* is often applied to all peoples of the fair or white type, as opposed to Mongols and others. Recognition of the fact that several distinct races enter into the composition of the white population of Europe has led to the disuse of the term *Caucasian* in scientific literature, except in America, where it is still employed as a convenient expression to distinguish the white races from the negro. Keane divided the Caucasian peoples into: *Homo Europæus, Homo Alpinus*, and *Homo Mediterranensis*.—BIBLIOGRAPHY: A. H. Keane, *Ethnology*; *Man Past and Present*; Sergi, *Mediterranean Race*.

CAU'CASUS. A chain of mountains which, until the revolution of 1917, gave name to a lieutenancy under Russian government lying to the south-east of Russia Proper, between the Black Sea and the Caspian. It was divided into Ciscaucasia and Transcaucasia. The total area of the lieutenancy (including Russian Armenia, acquired in 1878) was 181,173 sq. miles, and the population about 13,500,000. The Caucasus chain of mountains traversed the former lieutenancy from north-west to south-east through a length of 700 miles. It does not form a single chain, but is divided, at least for part of its length, into two, three, or even four chains, which sometimes run parallel to one another, and sometimes meet and form mountain ganglions. The heights of the chief summits are: Elbruz, 18,572 feet; Kosh-tan-tau, 17,123 feet; Dych-tau, 16,928 feet; Kasbek, 16,546 feet. Those mountains, as they lie north of the Caucasian watershed, are to be looked upon as European. The chief rivers are the Terek and Kur, flowing into the Caspian, and the Kuban and Rion (ancient *Phasis*) into the Black Sea.

The northern part of the country produces little but grass; but the slopes and valleys on the south, and especially those nearest the Black Sea, produce various kinds of fruits, grain of every description, rice, cotton, hemp, etc. The minerals are valuable. At Baku on the Caspian immense quantities of petroleum are obtained. The inhabitants consist of small tribes of various origin and language—Georgians, Abassians, Lesghians, Ossetes, Circassians, Tatars, Armenians. Some of them are Greek and Armenian Christians, others are Mahommedans and Jews.

The Caucasian tribes, especially the Circassians, attracted much attention for over half a century by their stubborn resistance to the arms of Russia. This resistance came to an end in 1859 by the capture of Shamyl, their most distinguished leader.

CAU'CUS. A term, originally American, for a private meeting of citizens to agree upon candidates to be proposed for election to offices or to concert measures for supporting a party. In Britain the term is applied to the system of political organisation of which the Birmingham

Liberal Association is a type, where all electioneering business is managed by a representative committee of voters. Its origin is supposed to refer to a fray between some British soldiers and Boston rope-makers in 1770, which resulted in democratic meetings of rope-makers and *caulkers*, called by the Tories (or Loyalists) *caucus* meetings. Others derive the term from an Algonquin word *kaw-kaw-was*, meaning to talk. A political club, called the " Caucus " or " Caucas " Club, seems to have existed in Massachusetts as early as 1724.

CAUDEBEC (kōd-bek). A picturesque little French town, department of Seine-Inférieure, on the Seine, with a fine Gothic church. Pop. 2180.

CAUDEBEC-LES-ELBEUF (kōd-bek-lā-zel-beuf). A manufacturing town of France, department of Seine-Inférieure, adjoining Elbeuf, of which it really forms part. Pop. 9080.

CAUDINE FORKS. A pass of S. Italy, in the form of two lofty fork-shaped defiles, in the Apennines (now called the valley of Arpaia), into which a Roman army was enticed by the Samnites, 321 B.C., and being hemmed in was forced to surrender.

CAUDRY (kō-drē). A town of Northern France, department of Nord, arrondissement Cambrai, with manufactures of tulle, lace, and woollens. Pop. 12,460.

CAUL (O.Eng. *calle*, Fr. *cale*, a cap). A popular name for a membrane investing the viscera, such as the peritoneum or part of it, or the pericardium; also a portion of the amnion or membrane enveloping the fetus, sometimes encompassing the head of a child when born. This caul was supposed to predict great prosperity to the person born with it, and to be an infallible preservative against drowning, as well as to convey the gift of eloquence. During the last century seamen often gave from £10 to £30 for a caul. These practices and beliefs are probably survivals of a very ancient idea that the placenta or after-birth was endowed with special life-giving and death-averting properties and was able to bring good luck and prosperity.

CAULER'PA. A large genus of marine green Algæ, natives of warm, still waters. The thallus is varied in form, and often mimics the shoots of higher plants; like all members of the group Siphoneæ, it is non-septate (cœnocytic), but this genus is strengthened by numerous rods of cellulose which traverse the internal cavity.

CAULFIELD. A town of Australia, state of Victoria, a short distance south-east of Melbourne, with fine residences, and an excellent race-course. Pop. 40,693.

CAULIFLORY. The production of flowers and fruit on the older branches or main trunk, a feature of many tropical trees; examples: cacao, cannon-ball tree, jack tree, species of Ficus.

CAU'LIFLOWER. A garden variety of cabbage, in which cultivation has caused the inflorescence to assume when young the form of a compact fleshy head, which is highly esteemed as a table vegetable. It is the tenderest of all the cabbage tribe. Broccoli is a coarser and hardier form of the cauliflower.

CAULKING (kạk'ing) of a ship, driving a quantity of oakum into the seams of the planks in the ship's decks or sides in order to prevent the entrance of water. After the oakum is driven very hard into these seams, it is covered with hot melted pitch to keep the water from rotting it. The term is also applied to tightening joints formed by overlapping metal plates, as in a boiler or ship's hull. This is done by driving the edge of one plate hard down on to the surface of the other with a caulking-iron, which is sometimes pneumatically operated.

CAULOP'TERIS. A genus of fossil tree-ferns found in the coal-measures.

CAUSALITY. The necessary connection of events in the time series. It is the relation in which cause stands to effect and effect to cause. Causality is both opposed to mere logical necessity, in which *time* is not involved, and to chance in which the connection is not a necessary one.

CAUSE. That which produces an effect; that from which anything proceeds and without which it would not exist. In the system of Aristotle the word rendered by cause and its equivalents in modern language has a more extensive signification. He divides causes into four kinds: efficient, formal, material, and final. The efficient or first cause is the force or agency by which a result is produced; the formal, the means or instrument by whch it is produced; the material, the substance from which it is produced; the final, the purpose or end for which it is produced. In a general sense the term is used for the reason or motive that urges, moves, or impels the mind to act or decide.

CAUSTIC (Gr. *kaustikos*, burning, from *kaiō*, I burn). A name given to various substances which burn or corrode the skin or other tissues. As a rule they disintegrate and destroy the structure of all organic substances, for example, cotton-wool, etc.—*Lunar caustic*, a name given to nitrate of silver when cast into sticks for the use of surgeons and others.—*Caustic potash* is potassium hydrate, KOH.—*Caustic soda* is sodium hydroxide, NaOH.

CAUSTIC. In optics, the name given to the curve to which the rays of light, reflected or refracted by another curve, are tangents. The caustic formed by reflection may be observed in a full teacup, being formed on the surface of the liquid by rays reflected from the inner edge of the cup.

CAUTERETS (kōt-rā). A celebrated bathing locality in France, department of Hautes-Pyrénées.

CAU'TERY. In surgery, the searing or burning of living flesh by a hot iron (*actual* cautery) or a caustic substance, as powerful acids or alkalis, (*potential* cautery).

CAUTION. A legal term signifying much the same as guarantee or security, now mostly used in Scots law.

CAU'VERY. *See* CAVERY.

CA'VA. A town, South Italy, 3 miles N.W. of Salerno, with manufactures of silk, cotton, and linen. About 1 mile from Cava is a magnificent Benedictine convent, La Trinita della Cava, founded in 1025. Pop. (Commune) 26,580.

CAVAIGNAC (kȧ-vān-yȧk), **Louis Eugène.** French general, born 1802, died 1857. His father, Jean Baptiste Cavaignac, was an ardent revolutionist and member of the Council of Five Hundred. Young Cavaignac in 1824 joined the 2nd Regiment of Engineers, and being at Arras on the outbreak of the revolution of 1830, he was the first officer in his regiment to declare for the new order of things. In 1832 he was sent to Africa, where he remained for several years, and greatly distinguished himself.

When the revolution of 1848 broke out, Cavaignac was appointed Governor-General of Algeria; but on being elected a member of the Constituent Assembly, he returned to Paris and was appointed Minister of War. At the outbreak of the June insurrection Cavaignac was appointed dictator with unlimited powers. For three days Paris presented a dreadful scene of tumult and bloodshed. About 15,000 persons perished, and property was destroyed to the value of upwards of £200,000. By the energy of Cavaignac, aided by the loyalty of the army and the National Guard, the insurrection was suppressed, and France saved from a threatened dissolution of all the bonds of society.

Towards the close of the year he became a candidate for the presidency of the Republic, but was defeated, and Louis Napoleon was preferred to the office. On 20th Dec. he resigned his dictatorship. After the *coup d'état* of 2nd Dec., 1851, he was arrested and conveyed to the fortress of Ham, but was liberated after about a month's detention. In 1852 and 1857 he was elected member for Paris of the legislative body, but on both occasions was incapacitated from taking his seat by refusing to take the oath of allegiance to the emperor.

CAVAILLON (kȧ-vȧ-yōn). A town of Southern France, department of Vaucluse, 14 miles S.E. of Avignon, an important railway junction. Pop. 10,450.

CAVALCAN'TI, Guido. A Florentine philosopher and poet, born in the early part of the thirteenth century, died 1300. He was the friend of Dante (who dedicated to him his *Vita nuova*), and, like him, a zealous Ghibelline. His *Canzone d'Amore* have gained him the most fame.

CAVALIER. In fortification, a work commonly situated within the bastion, but sometimes placed in the gorges or on the middle of the curtain. It is 10 or 12 feet higher than the rest of the works, and is used to command all the adjacent works and the surrounding country.

CAVALIER (kȧ-vȧ-lyā), **Jean.** Leader of the Camisards in the war of the Cevennes, son of a peasant, born in 1679 near Anduse (department of Gard), died at Chelsea 1740. He was engaged in agricultural labours at Geneva when the cruel persecutions of the Protestants of the Cevennes by Louis XIV. induced him to return home. He became their leader, and, led by him, they forced Marshal Villars to make a treaty with them. Cavalier then accepted a commission in the king's service, but, fearing treachery, he retired to England, and took service under the Earl of Peterborough and Sir Cloudesley Shovel in Spain. He commanded a regiment of refugee Camisards, and distinguished himself greatly at the battle of Almanza, in New Castile, in 1707, where he was severely wounded. He was afterwards appointed Governor of Jersey.

CAVALRY. Troops which fight on horseback and depend for their full effect on shock-action and the *arme blanche*. They are also armed with rifles and machine-guns, which enable them to employ fire-action when dismounted, though this fire-effect when so employed is less than that of an equal number of infantry owing to the necessity of detaching a proportion of men to act as horse-holders.

In mediæval times mounted men were the principal and more considerable portion of an army, and looked on themselves as a race apart, even to the extent of, on occasions, refusing to serve with infantry; but at a somewhat earlier period the heavier-armed principal troops, though provided with horses, invariably dismounted to fight, thus turning themselves into what was afterwards known as *mounted infantry*. The chief duties of cavalry, according to modern ideas, are the service of security, reconnoitring, and pursuit. Further, being provided with machine-guns and accompanied by horse artillery, cavalry is enabled to make rapid dashes to seize important places in advance of the main army, and to hold them until relieved.

In the British service cavalry is organised in regiments of three squadrons, each commanded by a major or senior captain; four troops, each commanded by a captain or subaltern, make a squadron; and troops are again subdivided into sections, each under a non-commissioned officer. There are three regiments of Household Cavalry, the 1st and 2nd Life Guards (uniform scarlet), and the Royal Horse Guards (The Blues), all dating from the Restoration (1662); seven dragoon guards (uniform scarlet, except the 6th, which is blue); three dragoons (all scarlet); twelve hussars (all blue, the 11th Hussars having crimson overalls); and six lancers (blue with the exception of the 16th Lancers, which is scarlet).—BIBLIOGRAPHY: G. T. Denison, *A History of Cavalry*; E. Nolan, *Cavalry: its History and Tactics*; Earl Haig, *Cavalry Studies*; E. Childers, *War and the Arme Blanche*; von Bernhardi, *Cavalry*; M. F. Rimington, *Our Cavalry*.

CAV'AN. An inland county, Irish Free State; area, 467,162 acres, of which three-fourths are arable. The north-western part is hilly; the remaining surface, which is undulating and irregular, is pervaded by bog and interspersed with many lakes; the soil is generally poor. Oats, flax, and potatoes are the chief crops. The principal towns are Cavan, Cootehill, and Belturbet. The population by the census of 1926 was returned at 82,452.—**Cavan,** the county town, 57 miles N.W. of Dublin, has a court-house, endowed school founded by Charles I., a Roman Catholic college. It has a considerable trade in farm produce. Pop. (1926), 3056.

CAVAN, Frederick Rudolph Lambart, tenth Earl of. British soldier, born 16th Oct., 1865. Educated at Eton, he entered the Grenadier Guards and saw active service in South Africa (1889-1902). During the European War he commanded the 14th Corps, and went to Italy in Nov., 1917. When General Sir Herbert Plumer returned to France, Cavan became head of the British forces in Italy. He was created a Knight of St. Patrick in 1916, G.C.B. in 1926, and was Chief of the Imperial General Staff from 1922 to 1926.

CAVATI'NA. In music, a melody of simpler character than the *aria*, and without a second part and a *da capo* or return part. The term is occasionally applied, however, to short simple airs of any kind.

CAVE, or **CAVERN.** An opening of some size in the solid crust of the earth beneath the surface. Caves are principally met with in limestone rocks, sometimes in sandstone and in volcanic rocks. Some of them have a very grand or picturesque appearance, such as Fingal's Cave in Staffa; others, such as the Mammoth Cave of Kentucky, which encloses an extent of about 40 miles of subterranean windings, are celebrated for their great size and subterranean waters; others for their gorgeous stalactites and stalagmites; others are of interest to the geologist and archæologist from the occurrence in them of osseous remains of animals no longer found in the same region, perhaps altogether extinct, or for the evidence their clay floors and rudely-sculptured walls, and the prehistoric implements and human bones found in them, offer of the presence of early man.

Caves in which the bones of extinct animals are found owe their origin, for the most part, to the action of rain-water on limestone rocks. The deposit contained in them usually consists of clay, sand, and gravel combined. In this are embedded the animal remains, and stones either angular or rounded. Some of the remains found in European caverns belong to animals now found only in the tropical or subtropical regions, and others are the remains of animals now living in more northerly areas;

others, again, are the relics of extinct animals. Among the latter class of animals are the cave bear and lion, the mammoth and mastodon, and species of rhinoceros. Of others that have only migrated may be mentioned the reindeer, which is no longer found in Southern Europe; and the *Hyæna crocuta*, found in the Gibraltar caves, which now lives in South Africa. The ibex, the chamois, and a species of ground squirrel are shown to have once lived in the Dordogne, but are now found only on the heights of the Alps and Pyrenees.

Thus it is evident that the geographical conditions of the country must have been very different from what they are now. Man's relation to these extinct animals, and his existence at the time these changes took place, are demonstrated by such discoveries as those of human bones and worked flints beneath layers of hyena droppings, as in Wookey Hole, near Wells, England; mixed up indiscriminately, as in Kent's Hole, near Torquay, with bones of elephant, rhinoceros, hyena, etc.; and by the fact that many bones of the extinct animals are split up, evidently for the sake of the marrow.

In the Dordogne and Savigné caves fragments of horn have been found bearing carved, or rather deeply-scratched, outline figures of ibex, reindeer, and mammoth. Among the most remarkable bone-caves are those of Kirkdale, in Yorkshire; Kent's Hole, Wookey Hole; of Franconia, in Bavaria; the banks of the Meuse, near Liège; and the south of France. In the cave of La Colombière, on the River Ain in France, a series of paleolithic sketches engraved on smoothed stones and bone was unearthed in 1913.—BIBLIOGRAPHY: Boyd Dawkins, *Cave-hunting*; E. A. Martel, *Les Abîmes, les Cavernes, etc.*; S. Baring-Gould, *Cliff Castles and Cave-dwellings of Europe*.

CAVE, Edward. An English printer, the founder of the *Gentleman's Magazine*, was born in 1691, died 1754. The first number of the *Gentleman's Magazine*, which, in a considerably modified form, continued for a century and a half, was published in Jan., 1731. Cave is also remembered as the first to give literary work to Samuel Johnson.

CA'VEAT (Lat. *cavere*, to beware, let him beware). In law, a process in a court to stay proceedings until the party entering the caveat has had an opportunity of putting forward his objection, as in proceedings about to be taken under a disputed will; to prevent the patenting of an invention, or the enrolment of a decree in chancery, in order to gain time to present a petition of appeal to the Lord Chancellor.

CAVE-DWELLERS. This term has no exact significance, as there have been men in almost every age and in

Cave-dweller

many countries who have made natural caves their home. But during the Stone Age in Europe, and probably during the early history of the human race in every country, caves were the usual place of retreat and the dwelling-place of men; and most of the remains of early man, his tools, and the evidences of his customs have been recovered from caves.

The best-known dwellings of ancient man in Britain are Kent's Cavern, near Torquay; Brixham

Cave, in the same neighbourhood; Paviland Cave, in South Wales; Kirkdale Cavern, in Yorkshire; Victoria Cave, near Settle in Yorkshire; Cresswell Crags Cave, in Derbyshire; and many others in the same county; others in the Mendips and in the Vale of Clwyd and elsewhere. These caves have been inhabited by man at various epochs during the so-called Old Stone and New Stone Ages, as well as in more recent times, and some of them contain remarkable collections of the bones of animals used by man as food, and flint implements used in killing and carving his prey.

Many other famous caves have been explored in Belgium, Germany, Switzerland, Italy, Croatia, and in other parts of the world; but none of them have yielded so much information concerning early types of men, their implements, their manner of life, the animals they hunted, and their artistic ability as the caves of France and Northern Spain. Cave exploration has been carried on in France for many years with great skill and devotion, and most of our information concerning the sequence of human types and industries has been recovered by the investigations of such scholars as Rivière, Boule, Catailhac, de Villeneuve, Capitan, Breuil, and others.

The most famous of these caves are situated in the Dordogne valley, in the neighbourhood of the Pyrenees, and at Grimaldi, near Mentone. In the caves of Le Moustier, La Chapelle-aux-Saints, La Ferassie, and La Quina, in the region of Dordogne and Perigord, remains of the brutal Neanderthal race of the Old Stone Age have been found, with their implements and the remains of the now extinct animals they hunted.

In the Pyrenees and Northern Spain were discovered the marvellous frescoes and clay models of animals wrought by the men of the later phases of the Old Stone Age—men quite unlike their predecessors of the Neanderthal race, and conforming definitely to the modern type of *homo sapiens*. In one of the Grimaldi caves, known as the Grotte des Enfants, were found the remains of a series of occupations by man ranging in time from the early part of the Old Stone Age until the New Stone Age. Near the top of the strata of the Old Stone Age was found a thick layer of ashes and the skeletons of an old woman and two children, wearing necklaces and armlets of shells. In an adjoining cave was a man's skeleton, with artifacts of stone, bone, and horn, and a vast collection of animal bones (cave-bear, brown bear, lion, hyena, marmot, woolly rhinoceros, wild horse, urus, elk, red deer, etc.).

In Paris the Prince of Monaco has founded a special museum of human palæontology devoted to the study of these cave-dwellers.

A concise summary of our knowledge of the subject is given by James Geikie (*Antiquity of Man in Europe*, Edinburgh, 1914.)

CAVELL, Edith. English nurse, born 4th Dec., 1865, the daughter of the Rev. Frederick Cavell, Vicar of Swardeston, Norfolk. Trained as a nurse, she was appointed matron of the École Belge d'Infirmières Diplomées, at Brussels, in 1907. Here the European War found her. She refused to return to England, and remained in Brussels during the German invasion. On 23rd March, 1915, seventeen Belgians were shot at Ghent Barracks, and during October a much larger number of death sentences were pronounced.

Among these was one upon Miss Cavell, who was arrested on 5th Aug., 1915, condemned to death on 11th Oct., and shot in the early morning on the 12th. The charge upon which she was condemned was that of having harboured in her house French and British soldiers as well as Belgians of military age, and of having facilitated their escape from Belgium. There was no doubt of the truth of these charges, for Miss Cavell freely confessed to them. The execution of the sentence led to an outburst of horror and indignation throughout the civilised world. The secretary of the American Legation pleaded for leniency, but Baron von Bissing, the German Military Governor, could not be moved, and Nurse Cavell was shot at two o'clock in the morning. She displayed great fortitude and resignation. A statue to her memory was erected in London, between St. Martin's Church and the National Gallery, and was unveiled by Queen Alexandra in March, 1920.

CAV'ENDISH. Tobacco which has been softened and pressed into quadrangular cakes, so called from Thomas Cavendish, the Elizabethan circumnavigator.

CAV'ENDISH, Henry. English physicist and chemist, born at Nice in 1731, died in London 1810. He was the son of Lord Charles Cavendish, and grandson of the second Duke of Devonshire. He devoted himself exclusively to science, and greatly contributed to the progress of chemistry, having discovered the peculiar properties of hydrogen and the composition of water. He also wrote on electricity, and determined the mean density of the earth. He lived in great retirement, and though very wealthy (he left a fortune of £1,175,000) his habits were extremely simple. His writings consist of treatises in the *Philosophical Transactions*.

CAVENDISH, Spencer Compton. *See* DEVONSHIRE, EIGHTH DUKE OF.

CAVENDISH, or CANDISH, Thomas. An English circumnavigator in the reign of Elizabeth, born about 1555, died 1592. Having collected three small vessels for the purpose of making a predatory voyage to the Spanish colonies, he sailed from Plymouth in 1586, took and destroyed many vessels, ravaged the coasts of Chile, Peru, and New Spain, and returned by the Cape of Good Hope, having circumnavigated the globe in two years and forty-nine days, the shortest period in which it had then been effected. In 1591 he set sail on a similar expedition, during which he died.

CAVENDISH, William. *See* DEVONSHIRE, FIRST DUKE OF.

CAVENDISH, William. *See* NEWCASTLE, DUKE OF.

CAVENDISH EXPERIMENT. An important scientific experiment first made by the celebrated Henry Cavendish, for the purpose of ascertaining the mean density of the earth by means of the torsion balance.

CAVERSHAM. A town (urban district of England) in the south of Oxfordshire, on the opposite bank of the Thames from Reading. Pop. 9870.

CA'VERY, or CAUVERY. A river of Southern India, which, after a winding S.E. course of about 470 miles, falls into the Bay of Bengal by numerous mouths, forming in its course two magnificent cataracts. It is known to devout Hindus as the Ganges of the South, and is largely utilised for irrigation purposes.

CAVERYPAUK. A town, India, North Arcot district, Madras Presidency, where Clive gained a victory over the French in 1752. Pop. 5478.

CAVE-TEMPLE. A cave used as a temple; but the name is especially applied to temples excavated in the solid rock, such as exist in considerable numbers in India. *See* ELEPHANTA, ELLORA.

CAVIARE (kav'i-är). The roes of certain large fish prepared and salted. The best is made from the roes of the sterlet and sturgeon, caught in the lakes or rivers of Russia. Botargo is a relish made of the salted roe of the tunny.

CAVICOR'NIA, or CAVICORNS (Lat. *cavus*, hollow, and *cornu*, a horn). A family of ruminants, characterised by persistent horns (thus differing from the deer) consisting of a bony core and a horny sheath or case covering the bone, in both sexes or in males only. They comprise the antelopes, goats, and oxen. In various species, as the antelopes, the bony nucleus has no internal cavity; in others, as the ox and goat, it is hollow. The first horny case sheds off in the second year, after which the horns become smoother.

CAVITE (kȧ-vē'tā). A town in the Island of Luzon, one of the Philippines; situated on the Bay of Manila, about 11 miles S.W. of Manila. It is a naval station with docks and arsenal. It gives its name to a province with a pop. of 157,347. Pop. of town about 13,000.

CAVO-RILIEVO (It.; kä'vō-ri-li-ā'vō). In sculpture, a kind of relief

Cavo-rilievo.—Wall Sculpture, Great Temple of Philæ, Egypt

in which the highest surface is only level with that of the original stone, giving an effect like the impression of a seal in wax. It is also called *intaglio rilievato*.

CAVOUR (kȧ-vör'), **Count Camillo Benso di.** A distinguished Italian statesman. Born at Turin in 1810, died in 1861. He was educated in the military academy at Turin, and after completing his studies he made a journey to England, where he remained for several years, making himself acquainted with the principles and working of the British constitution, and forming friendships with some of the most distinguished men. He became a member of the Sardinian Chamber of Deputies in 1849, and the following year Minister of Commerce and Agriculture. In 1852 he became Premier, and not long afterwards took an active part in cementing an alliance with Great Britain and France, and making common cause with these powers against Russia during the Crimean War.

The attitude, however, thus taken by Sardinia could not fail to prove

Count Cavour

offensive to Austria. A collision, therefore, was inevitable, resulting in the campaign of 1859. The intimate connection formed at that time with France, who lent her powerful assistance in the prosecution of the war, was mainly due to the agency of Cavour, who was accused by some on this occasion of having purchased the assistance of Napoleon III. by unduly countenancing his ambitious projects; and Metternich is reported to have said: "There is only one diplomatist in Europe, M. de Cavour, but, unfortunately, he is against us". In 1860 Garibaldi's expedition to Sicily took place; but towards this and the subsequent movements of the Italian liberator Count Cavour was forced to maintain an apparent coldness. He lived to see the meeting of the first Italian Parliament, which decreed Victor Emmanuel King of Italy.

Cavour's political writings and speeches have been published as *Opere politico economiche del Conte Camillo di Cavour*.—BIBLIOGRAPHY: Countess E. M. Cesaresco, *Cavour*; W. de la Rive, *Le Comte de Cavour*; E. Dicey, *A Memoir of Cavour*; W. R. Thayer, *Life and Times of Cavour*.

CA'VY. The popular name for a genus of rodent animals (Cavia), family Caviidæ, characterised by molars without roots, fore-feet with five toes, hinder with three, and the absence of a tail and clavicles. They are natives of tropical America, the most familiar example of this genus being the guinea-pig.

CAWNPORE'. A town, India, United Provinces, on the right bank of the Ganges, which is here about a mile wide, 130 miles N.W. of Allahabad, 628 miles N.W. of Calcutta, and 266 miles S.E. of Delhi. It is a modern town with nothing specially noteworthy about it as regards site or buildings. It has manufactures of leather and cotton goods and a large trade. Including the native city, cantonments, and civil station, it had in 1931 a pop. of 243,755.

In 1857 the native regiments stationed there mutinied and marched off, placing themselves under the command of the Rajah of Bithoor, the notorious Nana Sahib. General Wheeler, the commander of the European forces, defended his position for some days with great gallantry, but, pressed by famine and loss of men, was at length induced to surrender to the rebels on condition of his party being allowed to quit the place uninjured. This was agreed to; but after the European troops, with the women and children, had been embarked in boats on the Ganges, they were treacherously fired on by the rebels; many were killed, and the remainder conveyed back to the city, where the men were massacred and the women and children placed in confinement. The approach of General Havelock to Cawnpore roused the brutal instincts of the Nana, and he ordered his hapless prisoners to be slaughtered, and their bodies to be thrown into a well. The following day he was obliged by the victorious progress of Havelock, to retreat to Bithoor.

A memorial has since been erected over the scene of his atrocities, and fine public gardens now surround the well. The district of Cawnpore, in the Allahabad division, has an area of 12,384 sq. miles and a pop. of 1,142,286.

CAXAMARCA, or CAJAMARCA (kȧ-*h*ȧ-mȧr′-kȧ). A mountainous interior department of Northern Peru, with a capital of the same name. The products of the department include maize, wheat, tobacco, and wool; and silver is mined. Area, 12,538 sq. miles; pop. 450,000. The town, situated at a great elevation on a small tributary of the Marañon or Upper Amazon, is connected by rail with the Pacific coast.

It has manufactures of arms, straw hats, woollens, and cottons. It was the scene of the imprisonment and murder of Atahualpa, the last of the Incas. Pop. about 30,000.

CAXIAS (kȧ-shē'ȧs). A town of Brazil, in the state of Maranhão, on the Itapicuru, which here is navigable. Rice and cotton are cultivated here. Pop. about 25,000.

CAXTON, William. The introducer of the art of printing into Britain. He was born in the Weald of Kent about 1422, died at Westminster 1491. He served an apprenticeship to Robert Large, a London mercer. On the death of his master Caxton went into business for himself at Bruges. He was appointed about 1463 Governor at Bruges to the London Association of Merchant Adventurers. About 1471 he entered the service of Margaret, Duchess of Burgundy, sister of Edward IV.

He now learned the newly-discovered art of printing, probably at Cologne; and his *Recuyell of the Historyes of Troye*, the translation of a popular mediæval romance (from the French of Raoul le Fèvre) was printed about 1474, probably at Bruges, and is the earliest specimen of typography in the English language. His *Game and Playe of the Chesse* (Bruges, 1475) is the second English book printed. In 1476 he returned to England, and in 1477 printed at Westminster Lord Rivers's translation of *The Dictes and Sayengis of the Philosophres*, the first book printed in England.

In fourteen years he printed nearly eighty separate books, nearly all of folio size, some of which passed through two editions, and a few through three. He translated twenty-one books, mainly romances, from the French, and one (*Reynard the Fox*) from the Dutch, helping materially to fix the literary language. He was patronised by Edward IV., Richard III., and Henry VII.; and he was on intimate terms with Earl Rivers, the Earl of Worcester, and others of the nobility, the two noblemen named having even translated works for his press.

Thenne beganne agayne the bataylle of the one par te/And of the other Eneas ascryed to theym and sayd. Lordes why doo ye fyghte/ Ye knowe well that the couenaunte ys deuysed and made/ That Tur: nus and I shall fyghte for you alle/

Thenne beganne agayne the batayllo of the one parte / And of the other Eneas ascryed to theym and sayd. Lordes why doo ye fyghte / Ye knowe well that the couuenante ys deuysed and made / That Turnus and I shall fyghte for you alle /

Then began again the battle on the one part. And on the other, Aeneas cried to them and said: "Lords, why do ye fight? Ye know well that the covenant is devised and made, that Turnus and I shall fight for you all."

Facsimile of part of Caxton's Aeneid (reduced), with the same in modern type and in modern spelling

Besides the works named above, he printed Chaucer's *Canterbury Tales*, *Troylus and Creside*, *House of Fame*, and translation of Boethius; Gower's *Confessio Amantis*; works by Lydgate; Malory's *Morte d'Arthur*; *The Golden Legend*; *The Fables of Æsop*. His books have no title-pages, but are frequently provided with prologues and colophons. His types are in the Gothic character, and copied so closely from the handwriting of his time that many of his books have been mistaken for manuscript. In some no punctuation is used; in others the full point and colon only; commas are represented by a long or short upright line.

Copies of some of his books now fetch extraordinary prices. A unique copy of the *Morte d'Arthur* has brought £1950, the *Recuyell* £1820, and *The Royal Book* £2225 (in 1902). He was buried in the church of St. Margaret's, Westminster. A typographical exhibition, commemorating Caxton and his work, was held in London in 1877.—BIBLIOGRAPHY: William Blades, *Life and Typography of William Caxton*; E. Gordon Duff, *William Caxton*.

CAYENNE (kī-en'). The capital of the colony of French Guiana. It is a seaport on an island of same name at the mouth of the Cayenne River. It is a noted penal settlement, has a large but shallow harbour, and contains about 13,900 inhabitants.

Printing in Caxton's day

CAYENNE PEPPER, or **CAPSICUM.** The name given to the powder formed of the dried and ground fruits, and more especially the seeds, of various species of Capsicum, and especially of *C. frutescens*. It is employed as a condiment to improve the flavour of food, aid digestion, and prevent flatulence. In medicine it is used as a stimulant, and is a valuable gargle for a relaxed throat. *See* CAPSICUM.

CAYLEY, Arthur. A distinguished mathematician, born at Richmond in 1821, died at Cambridge in 1895. He entered Trinity College, Cambridge, in 1838, and in 1842 graduated as senior wrangler, gaining the Smith's prize in the following year. He was called to the Bar at Lincoln's Inn in 1849, and after fourteen years' practice as a conveyancer, was appointed, in 1863, to the newly-established Sadleirian professorship of pure mathematics at Cambridge, a post which he held till his death. He was president of the British Association in 1883, and received many honours, both in his own country and from abroad.

Cayley was a mathematician of marvellous power and range, and modern mathematics owes him much. His papers, more than nine hundred in number, have been published in 13 vols. (1889-99) by the University of Cambridge under the title of *Collected Mathematical Papers*.

CAYLUS (kā-lüs), **Anne Claude Philippe de Tubières, Count.** French archæologist, born 1692 at Paris, died there 1765. After having served in the army, he travelled extensively in Europe and the East. He left numerous works, tales as well as antiquarian researches. Among the latter is his *Recueil d' Antiquités Égyptiennes, Étrusques, Grecques, Romaines et Gauloises* (Paris, 1752-67, 7 vols.). His *Œuvres badines complètes* were published at Amsterdam in 1787, and his *Contes Orientaux* were translated into English in 1817, and published under the title *Oriental Tales* in Gueulette's *Chinese Tales*.

Caylus was also an industrious and skilful engraver, after the first masters. His mother, Marquise de Caylus (1673-1729), niece of Madame de Maintenon, made herself known by a spirited little work, *Mes Souvenirs*, first edited by Voltaire in 1770.

CAYMAN, or **CAIMAN**. The name given to several species of tropical American alligators, differing from typical alligators in certain minor details of structure. They are found in greatest numbers on the banks of the Amazon, where they are known as *jacare* or *yacare*.

CAYMAN ISLANDS. Three islands situated about 140 miles N.W. of Jamaica, of which they are dependencies. Grand Cayman, the largest, is 17 miles long and from 4 to 7 miles broad, and has two towns or villages. The inhabitants, 3945 in number, partly descendants of the buccaneers, are chiefly employed in catching turtle. The other two islands are Little Cayman (pop. 95, all whites) and Cayman Brac (pop. 1213).

CAYU'GA LAKE. A lake in the state of New York, 38 miles long and from 1 to 3½ miles wide. It is much frequented by pleasure parties. The Cayuga duck, which was first found near the lake, has never become popular in Britain.

CAZALLA-DE-LA-SIERRA (kȧ-thȧl'yȧ). A town, Spain, Andalusia, in the province and 36 miles N. by E. of Seville, on a declivity of the Sierra Morena, which is here rich in timber and metals. Pop. 10,000.

CAZEMBE'S (kȧ-zem'be) **DOMINION.** Formerly a native state of Central South Africa, lying to the south of Lake Tanganyika, in the region of which Lakes Moero and Bangweulu are important features. It now belongs partly to Rhodesia, partly to the Belgian Congo. It was visited by Dr. Livingstone in 1868, but had then greatly declined in importance. It is a land of forest-covered sandstone ridges and grassy plains, intersected by streams generally flowing northwards.

CAZORLA (kȧ-thor'lȧ). A town, Spain, Andalusia, in the province of Jaen, and 41 miles E. of the town of that name, with 8000 inhabitants.

CAZOTTE (kȧ-zot), **Jacques.** French writer, born in 1719, executed by the revolutionists 1792. He became first known by *Tout au beau milieu des Ardennes*, but especially by a romance of chivalry, *Ollivier*, published in 1763; and subsequently his *Le Diable Amoureux*, the *Lord Impromptu*, and *Œuvres Morales et Badines*, gave proof of his rich imagination. With the assistance of an Arabian monk he translated four volumes of *Arabian Tales*—a continuation of the *Arabian Nights*.

CEARÁ (sā-ȧ-rä'). A state on the northern coast of Brazil; area, 40,241 sq. miles. Among its productions are numerous medicinal plants, gums, balsams, and resins; cotton, coffee, sugar-cane, etc., are cultivated. The first Portuguese colony in Ceará was founded in 1610, in the neighbourhood of Ceará, or Fortaleza, the present capital. This town is situated on the coast, and carries on a considerable trade in rubber, coffee, sugar, etc. Pop. of state, 1,626,025 (1926); of town Ceará, 99,000.

CEBU (thā-bö'). One of the Philippine Islands, lying between Luzon and Mindanao, 135 miles long, with an extreme width of 30 miles. Sugar cultivation and the manufacture of abaca are the chief industries. Pop. 1,066,000. The town of Cebu, on the eastern coast of the island, the oldest Spanish settlement on the Philippines, is a place of considerable trade, and has a cathedral and several churches; pop. 86,000.

CE'BUS. A genus of monkeys. *See* CAPUCHIN and SAPAJOU.

CECCO D'ASCOLI (chek-o-dȧs'ko-lē). Proper name **FRANCESCO DEGLI STABILI.** Italian poet, born at Ascoli 1257, burned at Florence 1327. His chief work, *L'Acerba*, a kind of poetic cyclopædia, passed through many editions. He adversely criticised the writings of Dante and Cavalcante, and suffered death at the hands of the Inquisition for alleged heterodoxy.

CECIDOMY'IA. A genus of gall-gnats, to which belong two destructive insect-pests, the Hessian fly and the wheat midge.

CECIL, Lord Hugh. English politician. Hugh Richard Heathcote Gascoyne Cecil, youngest son of the Marquess of Salisbury, was born 14th Oct., 1869. Educated at Eton and University College, Oxford, in 1895 he entered Parliament and was M.P. for Greenwich from 1895 to 1906. In 1910 he was elected M.P. for the University of Oxford, and was re-elected at succeeding elections, including 1931. He was made a privy councillor in 1918. Although never in office, Lord Hugh Cecil has dominated the House of Commons as an orator.

CECIL (ses'il), **Robert, Earl of Salisbury.** English statesman, second son of William Cecil, Lord Burleigh, born about 1563, died in 1612. He was of a weak constitution, on which account he was educated at home till his removal to the University of Cambridge. Having received the honour of knighthood, he went to France as assistant to the English ambassador. On the death of Sir Francis Walsingham he succeeded him as principal secretary, and continued to be a confidential minister of Queen Elizabeth until the end of her reign. Having secretly supported the interests of James I. previous to his accession to the crown, he was continued in office under the new sovereign and raised to the peerage. In 1603 he was created a baron, in 1604 Viscount Cranborne, and in 1605 Earl of Salisbury. In 1608 Lord Salisbury was made Lord High-Treasurer, an office which he held till his death.

CECIL OF CHELWOOD, Edgar Algernon Robert Cecil, 1st Viscount. British politician, third son of the third Marquess of Salisbury. He was born in 1864, and educated at Eton and University College, Oxford. From 1886 to 1888 he was private secretary to his father, was called to the Bar in 1887, and made K.C. in 1900. He entered Parliament in 1906. During the European War he was Parliamentary Under-Secretary for Foreign Affairs (1915-6) and Minister of Blockade (1916-8). He resigned office in November, 1918. At the Peace Conference in Paris he was appointed British delegate to the League of Nations. In 1922 he was raised to the peerage, and in 1924 his work for the League of Nations was given practical recognition when he received the annual award of the Woodrow Wilson Peace Prize. In 1924 he became Chancellor of the Duchy of Lancaster, but resigned from office in August, 1927.

CECIL, William, Lord Burleigh. Eminent English statesman. He was the son of Richard Cecil, Master of the Robes to Henry VIII., and was born at Bourne, in Lincolnshire, in 1520, died 1598. He studied at St. John's College, Cambridge, whence he removed to Gray's Inn, with a view to preparing himself for the practice of the law, but an introduction to the court of Henry VIII. changed his aims. On the accession of Edward VI. his interests were advanced by the Protector Somerset, whom he accompanied in the expedition to Scotland.

He held no public office during the reign of Mary, and by extraordinary caution managed to escape persecution. On the accession of Elizabeth he was appointed Privy Councillor and Secretary of State, and during all the rest of his life he was at the helm of affairs. One of the first acts of her reign was the settlement of religion, which Cecil conducted with great skill and prudence, considering the difficulties to be encountered.

The general tenor of Cecil's policy was cautious, and rested upon an avoidance of open hostilities, and a reliance on secret negotiation and intrigues with opposing parties in the neighbouring countries, with a view to averting the dangers which threatened his own. On the suppression of the northern rebellion in 1571 Elizabeth raised him to the peerage by the title of Baron Burleigh, and created him Knight of the Garter and Lord High-Treasurer. Much of the glory of the reign of Elizabeth is due to the counsels and measures of Cecil.

CECIL'IA, Saint. The patron saint of music, who had been falsely regarded as the inventress of the organ, and who is said to have suffered martyrdom A.D. 230, although other dates are given. In the Roman Catholic Church her festival (22nd Nov.) is made the occasion of splendid music. Her church in the Trastevere quarter of Rome was rebuilt by Pope Paschal I. about 820, and again restored by Cardinal Sfondrati in 1599. Her story forms one of Chaucer's *Canterbury Tales*, and Dryden in his *Alexander's Feast*, and Pope in his *Ode on St. Cecilia's Day*, have sung her praises. Raphael, Domenichino Dolce, and Mignard have represented her in celebrated paintings.

CECRO'PIA. A genus of beautiful South American trees, nat. ord. Moraceæ. *C. peltāta*, or trumpet-wood, is remarkable for its hollow stem and branches, the former being made by the Indians into a kind of drum, and the latter into wind-instruments. The light porous wood is used for procuring fire by friction, and for floats. Many species harbour fierce protective ants; these insects live in the hollow stems, to which they gain access by boring through pre-formed thin places. Food-bodies are abundantly produced on the leaf-bases. In the case of other species, leaf-cutting ants are unable to climb up the stem, owing to the presence of a slippery coating of wax; in these there are neither food-bodies nor thin places, and "police-ants" are lacking. *See* BULL'S HORN THORN; MYRMECOPHILOUS PLANTS.

CECROPIA MOTH (*Platysamia cecropia*). The largest moth of the United States. It belongs to the silk-worm family, and its caterpillar spins a large cocoon from which a coarse silk may be prepared.

CE'CROPS. According to tradition, the founder of Athens and the first King of Attica. He was said to have taught the savage inhabitants religion and morals, and made them acquainted with the advantages of social life. By the later Greeks he was represented as having led a colony to Attica from Egypt about 1400 or 1500 B.C., but modern critics do not look upon this event nor on the life of Cecrops at all as historical.

CE'DAR (*Cedrus Libăni*). A coniferous tree which forms fine woods on the mountains of Syria and Asia Minor. It is an evergreen, grows to a great size, and is remarkable for its durability. Three species, all highly ornamental trees, are recognised and have been introduced into Britain.

Cedar of Lebanon

Of the famous cedars of Lebanon comparatively few now remain, and the tree does not grow in any other part of Palestine. The most celebrated group is situated not far from the village of Tripoli, at an elevation of about 6000 feet above the sea. The circumference of the twelve largest trees here varies from about 18 to 47 feet. The first specimens in Scotland were planted in 1683. The most interesting group of Lebanon cedars is the avenue of 170 on the Dropmore estate (Bucks), planted 100 years ago. Cedar timber was formerly much prized, but in modern times is not regarded as of much value, perhaps from the trees not being of sufficient age.

The name is given also to the deodar (*C. Deodāra*), which is indeed regarded by many botanists as a mere variety of the cedar of Lebanon, and which produces excellent timber. It is a native of India, and is a large and handsome tree, growing in the Himalayas to the height of 150 feet, with a circumference of 30 feet. It has wide-spreading branches, which droop a little at the extremities. The leaves are tufted or solitary, larger than those of the cedar of Lebanon, and very numerous, of a dark-bluish green, and covered with a glaucous bloom. The cones are rather larger than those of the Lebanon cedar, and very resinous. The wood is well adapted for building purposes, being compact and very enduring. The deodar was introduced into Great Britain in 1882, and is now common in lawns and parks.

The Mount Atlas cedar (*C. atlantica*), as its name implies, is a native of the mountains of North Africa, and was introduced into Britain in 1843. This cedar, though differing in habit and minor features, is regarded by some botanists as specifically identical with the other two. The name is also applied to many trees which have no relation to the true cedar, as the Bermuda cedar (*Junipĕrus bermudiāna*), used for making pencils, the red cedar (*J. virginiāna*), the Honduras, or bastard Barbadoes cedar (*Cedrēla odorāta*), and the red cedar of Australia (*C. austrālis*). *See* CEDRELA.—BIBLIOGRAPHY: Loiseleur-Deslongchamps, *Histoire du cèdre du Liban*; H. C. Baker, *Illustrations of Conifers*.

CEDAR-BIRD. A name given to the American wax-wing (*Ampĕlis americānus* or *Bombycilla carolinensis*), from its fondness for the berries of the red cedar. It is a handsome and lively bird, found throughout the whole of the United States, but has no song.

CEDAR CREEK. A stream in Shenandoah County, Virginia, near which General Sheridan converted a defeat of the Federals by the Confederates into a complete victory, Oct., 1864.

CEDAR LAKE. A lake in Canada, an expansion of the Saskatchewan before it enters Lake Winnipeg; nearly 30 miles long, and where widest 25 miles broad.

CEDAR OIL. An aromatic oil obtained from the American red cedar (*Junipĕrus virginiāna*).

CEDAR RAPIDS. A flourishing town of the United States, in Iowa, on Red Cedar River, with large railway machine-shops and numerous industrial establishments. Pop. 56,097.

CEDIL'LA. A mark used under the letter *c*, especially in French (thus ç), to indicate that it is to be pronounced like the English *s*.

CEDRE'LA. A genus of large timber trees, natives of the tropics of both hemispheres, ord. Meliaceæ. *C. odorāta* of Honduras and the W. Indies yields bastard cedar; *C. austrālis* is a valuable Australian timber tree; one or two E. Indian species have febrifugal properties.

CEDRELA'CEÆ. *See* MELIACEÆ.

CEFALU (chef'ā-lö). A seaport and bishop's see on the north coast of

Sicily. The trade is small, but a productive fishery is carried on. Pop. 13,200.

CEILING. Interior overhead surface of an apartment. Some ceilings are boarded; others utilise the roof beams and joists to emphasise panelled patterns. The concealment of the roof timbers by horizontal or coved surfaces found expression in the painted ceilings of the Italian Renaissance, introduced into France, and into England by Verrio and others. This principle, facilitated by the use of plaster, was especially utilised in the eighteenth-century low-relief classical mouldings of the Adam brothers. Painted ceilings are also a striking feature of some modern architectural work. Plaster mouldings, notably in reinforced construction, have been replaced by fire-resisting sheet steel stampings.

CEL'ANDINE. A name given to two British plants, the greater celandine and the lesser celandine; also called *swallow-worts*, because the plants were believed to flower when the swallow arrived, and to die when it departed. The former is *Chelidonium majus*, and the latter *Ficaria ranunculoides* or *Ranunculus Ficaria*. This latter is a favourite wild flower from its being one of the earliest British plants to come into blossom, having petals of a fine golden-yellow colour. Its root consists of small fleshy tubers. It is often called pilewort, being a reputed cure for piles. The greater celandine belongs to the poppy family; it is full of a yellow juice of a poisonous acrid nature.

CELANO (che-lä'nō), **LAKE OF.** *See* FUCINO.

CELANO (che-lä'nō), **Tommaso da.** One of the reputed authors of the Latin hymn *Dies Iræ*. Born towards the end of the twelfth or about the beginning of the thirteenth century at Celano, in the Abruzzi, and died in Italy after 1250. He was one of the most devoted adherents of St. Francis of Assisi, whose life he wrote.

CELASTRA'CEÆ. An order of polypetalous dicotyledons, consisting of shrubs and small trees, natives of S. Europe, Asia, America, and Australia, most of them of no great importance. *See* SPINDLE TREE.

CELAYA (se-lä'yȧ). A town of Mexico, state of Guanajuato, on the Rio Laja, with manufactures of leather, saddlery, woollens, and cottons. Pop. 26,000.

CELEBES (sel'e-bēz). One of the larger islands of the Dutch East Indies, between Borneo on the W. and the Moluccas on the E. It consists mainly of four large peninsulas stretching to the E. and S., and separated by three deep gulfs; total area, 73,160 sq. miles (including the dependent islands). No part of it is more than 70 miles from the sea. Celebes is mountainous chiefly in the centre and the north, where there are several active volcanoes. It has also broad grassy plains and extensive forests. Gold is found in all the valleys of the north peninsula, which abounds in sulphur. Copper occurs at various points, and in Macassar tin also. Diamonds and other precious stones are found.

The island is entirely destitute of feline or canine animals, insectivora, the elephant, rhinoceros, and tapir (though these are found in Borneo); but it has the antelopean buffalo (Anoa), and the spiral-tusked pig (Babyroussa). Among domesticated animals are small but vigorous horses, buffaloes, goats, sheep, and pigs. Trepang and turtle are caught in abundance. Marsupial animals are represented by the cuscus, an opossum-like animal with a prehensile tail. Among the trees are the oak, teak, cedar, upas, and bamboo. Among cultivated plants are the coffee tree, indigo, cacao, sugar-cane, manioc root, and tobacco.

The maritime districts are inhabited by Malays; the Peninsula of Macassar is occupied by Bugis and Macassars. Mandhars dwell in the W. of the island, and the mountainous regions in the interior, especially in the N., are inhabited by Alfuros. The inhabitants may be classed into two groups: the Mahommedan semi-civilised tribes, and the pagans, who are more or less savages. The capital is Macassar, in the S.W. of the island. The trade in trepang is very important, Macassar being the chief staple place for this article of commerce.

The three great languages of the island, not reckoning the dialects of the savage tribes, are those of the Bugis, the Macassars, and the Mandhars. The ancient Bugi is the language of science and religion. The Bugis have a considerable body of literature.

Celebes was first visited by the Portuguese in 1512, but no factory was established by them there till a few years later. In 1660 Macassar was taken by the Dutch, the southern portion of the island put under Dutch rule, and the Portuguese expelled. In 1683 the northern part likewise fell into their hands. The island was conquered by the British in 1811, but a few years later it was again given up to the Dutch, in whose possession it has remained ever since. Pop. estimated at 3,678,815.—BIBLIOGRAPHY: A. S. Walcott, *Java and her Neighbours*; *A Traveller's Notes in Java and Celebes*.

CEL'ERES. In Roman antiquity, a body of 300 horsemen, formed by Romulus from the wealthier citizens. Their number was afterwards augmented, and they are thought to have been the origin of the *equites*.

CELER'IAC. Turnip-rooted celery, a variety of celery in which the root resembles a turnip and may weigh 3 or 4 lb. It is much cultivated on the continent of Europe, less so in Britain, and is eaten either in salads or cooked.

CEL'ERY. An umbelliferous plant (*Apium gravĕolens*) indigenous to the ditches and marshy places near the sea-coast in England and Ireland, and elsewhere in Europe, and long cultivated in gardens as a salad and culinary vegetable. There are two varieties in cultivation, viz. red and white stalked, and of these many sub-varieties. Celery is commonly blanched by heaping up the soil about the plants.

CELERY FLY (*Acadia heraclei*). A small two-winged fly, the larvæ of which are destructive to the leaves of celery and parsnip.

CELESTIAL PHOTOGRAPHY. *See* PHOTOGRAPHY.

CELESTINE. The name of five Popes. **Celestine I.** was elected Pope in 422, died in 432, and is recognised by the Church as a saint.—**Celestine II.**, a native of Tuscany, who had studied under Abelard, filled the papal chair for five months (8th Oct., 1143, to 8th March, 1144). He granted absolution to Louis VII. of France, and removed the interdict which for three years was laid upon that country.—**Celestine III.**, one of the Orsini family, born 1106, died 1198. He was elected Pope in 1191, when about eighty-four years of age. He crowned the Emperor Henry VI., but afterwards excommunicated both Henry and Leopold, Duke of Austria, on account of the captivity of Richard Cœur de Lion.—**Celestine IV.**, a Milanese, who, when a monk, wrote a history of Scotland, was elected Pope in 1241, but reigned only seventeen days.—**Celestine V.** was chosen Pope 5th July, 1294, but abdicated his dignity 13th Dec., 1294, and died 19th May, 1296. He is the founder of the Celestines, and was canonised in 1313 by Clement V.

CEL'ESTINES (from their founder Pope Celestine V.). A religious order, instituted about the middle of the thirteenth century in Italy, who followed the rule of St. Benedict, and were devoted entirely to a contemplative life. Very few priories of this once-numerous order now exist.

CEL'ESTITE ($SrSO_4$). Native strontium sulphate occurring associated with sulphur as fine crystals in the Sicilian sulphur-deposits. Clear crystals are found in hollow nodules in Permian marls near Bristol. It is transparent and colourless, but sometimes reddish or a delicate blue; the name is derived from the blue variety.

CEL'IBACY. The state of being celibate or unmarried; specially applied to the voluntary life of abstinence from marriage followed by many religious devotees and by some orders of clergy, as those of the Roman Catholic Church. The ancient Egyptian priests preserved a rigid chastity; the priestesses of ancient Greece and Rome were pledged to perpetual virginity; and celibacy is the rule with the Buddhist priests of the East.

Among Christians the earliest aspirants to the spiritual perfection supposed to be attainable through celibacy were not ecclesiastics as such, but hermits and anchorites who aimed at superior sanctity. The Christian advocates of religious celibacy sought a basis for it in the New Testament, and maintained that the words "There are eunuchs, which made themselves eunuchs for the kingdom of heaven's sake" countenanced a voluntary celibacy. During the first three centuries the marriage of the clergy was freely permitted, but by the Council of Elvira in Spain (305) continence was enjoined on all who served at the altar. For centuries this subject led to many struggles in the Church, but was finally settled by Gregory VII. positively forbidding the marriage of the clergy. The Council of Trent (1593) confirmed this rule.

In the Greek Church celibacy is not compulsory on the ordinary clergy. The Protestants denounced clerical celibacy, and all the great creeds and confessions of the time reflect their feelings on the question. Protestants hold that there is no moral superiority in celibacy over marriage, and that the Church has no right to impose such an obligation on any class of her ministers.—BIBLIOGRAPHY: A. Vassal, *Le Célibat ecclesiastique au 1er siècle de l'église*; F. Chavard, *Le Célibat, le prêtre et la femme*; H. C. Lea, *History of Sacerdotal Celibacy* (2 vols.).

CELL. A term of various applications. **Ecclesiastically** it was sometimes applied to a lesser or subordinate religious house, dependent upon a greater. The apartments or private dormitories of monks and nuns are also called *cells*. The term *cell* is applied also to the part of the interior of a temple where the image of a god stood.

In electricity the cell is the unit from which batteries are made up. Each cell contains a positive and a negative element (originally copper and zinc in Volta's cell) immersed in a conducting liquid. There are various types of cell, such as the Leclanché and its modern form the dry-cell, but in all of them the negative element is zinc. In the storage-cell lead is the chief constituent of the plates, and this type requires to be charged before it will give a current.

In biology a *cell* is a microscopically small semi-fluid portion of matter, consisting of a soft mass of living, contractile, jelly-like matter, and a central structure, consisting of a small, roundish body, called the *nucleus*, generally more solid than the rest of the cell, and which may have within it a still more minute body, the *nucleŏlus*. The cell substance or protoplasm (q.v.) which surrounds the nucleus is an albuminous substance possessing fundamental vital properties, and believed to be the starting-point of all animal and vegetable organisms. The cell-wall when present consists of an alteration of the external portion of the cell body, and is not a separate structure. All cells have but a very limited duration, so the tissues are being constantly renewed.

CELLARDYKE. A part of the royal burgh of Kilrenny and Anstruther. *See* ANSTRUTHER.

CELLE (tsel'le). A town in the Prussian province of Hanover, Germany, 23 miles N.E. of the town of Hanover, in the midst of a sandy plain, at the confluence of the Fuse with the Aller, which is navigable. The manufactures are varied, and the trade is extensive. Pop. 25,545.

CELLINI (chel-lē'nē), **Benvenu'to.** A sculptor, engraver, and goldsmith, born at Florence in 1500, died there in 1571. Of a bold, honest, and open character, but vain and quarrelsome, he was often entangled in disputes which frequently cost his antagonists their lives. At the siege of Rome (if we believe his own account, given in his autobiography) he killed the Constable of Bourbon and the Prince of Orange. In 1537 he was imprisoned in the castle of Sant' Angelo on the charge (probably false) of having stolen the jewels of the Papal crown, and only escaped execution through the intercession of Cardinal Ferrara. He then visited the court of Francis I. of France.

He afterwards returned to Florence and under the patronage of Cosimo de' Medici made a *Perseus with the head of Medusa* in bronze, which is still an ornament of one of the public squares; also a statue of Christ, in the chapel of the Pitti Palace, besides many excellent dies for coins and medals. Nearly all his masterpieces have unfortunately been melted down. One of his greatest productions, the salt-cellar of Francis I., is in the Museum of Vienna.

His works may be divided into two classes. The first, for which he is most celebrated, comprises his smaller productions in metal, the embossed decorations of shields, cups, salvers, ornamented sword and dagger hilts, clasps, medals, and coins. The second includes his larger works as a sculptor, such as the *Perseus* mentioned above; a colossal *Mars* for a fountain at Fontainebleau; a marble *Christ* in the Escurial Palace; a life-size statue of *Jupiter* in silver; etc. His *Autobiography*, translated into English by J. A. Symonds (1896), is very racy and animated.—BIBLIOGRAPHY: E. Plon, *Cellini: orfèvre, médailleur*; R. H. H. Cust, *The Life of Benvenuto Cellini*.

CELL THEORY. A theory elaborated by Schleiden (1838) and Schwann (1839), that takes the cell as the unit of structure and function in organisms.

CELLULA'RES. In botany, that division of plants which are altogether composed of cellular tissue, without fibres or vessels. They form the greater portion of the acotyledonous or cryptogamic plants.

CELLULAR TISSUE. In physiology, a plant or animal tissue mostly or entirely composed of obvious cells. In botany, the term is applied to the soft substance of plants, composed of elementary vesicles or cells without woody or vascular tissues.

CELLULITIS. A disease characterised by the existence of a spreading inflammation of the tissues underlying the skin. It is caused by organisms, and leads to suppuration, sloughing, or even extensive gangrene. The treatment is by incisions and dressing of the affected part.

CELL'ULOID. An artificial substance extensively used as a substitute for ivory, bone, hard rubber, and coral, having a close resemblance to these substances in hardness, elasticity, and texture. It is composed of gun-cotton (cellulose nitrate) and camphor, and is moulded by heat and pressure to the desired shape. It is used for buttons, handles for knives, forks, and umbrellas, billiard-balls, piano keys, napkin-rings, backs to brushes, etc. It can be variously coloured and is dangerous on account of the readiness with which it takes fire. *See* CELLULOSE.

CELL'ULOSE. A generic name for the substances of which cell-membranes of plants are composed. Cellulose ($C_6H_{10}O_5$) belongs to the class of substances known as carbohydrates, and is allied to starch; thus when treated with dilute mineral acids it yields sugar, just as starch does. Cellulose has been found in a few invertebrate animals, but the source of the substance is from plant tissues. Cotton-wool is almost pure cellulose, and wood-pulp for paper-making consists mainly of cellulose; paper itself is impure cellulose. Pure cellulose is a white amorphous substance, odourless and tasteless; it is not dissolved by ordinary solvents, but its character may be very much modified by treatment with various chemical reagents; thus if paper be dipped in sulphuric acid, diluted with half its volume of water, and then washed free from acid and dried, the paper is gelatinised and toughened, forming *parchment paper*.

If cellulose in any of its forms be treated with a cold concentrated solution of caustic soda, it swells up and becomes semi-transparent; this is the basis of *mercerised cotton*. Various methods of artificial silk manufacture are also based on the changes which cellulose undergoes on treating with chemicals. "Viscose," used largely in photographic-film manufacture, is also specially-prepared cellulose. Many important derivatives of cellulose are used; for example, *collodion* and *gun cotton* are prepared by treating cellulose with nitric acid.

Celluloid or artificial ivory is also prepared from cellulose by first forming collodion and then mixing it with certain proportions of camphor and zinc oxide.

CEL'SIUS. The name of a Swedish family, several members of which attained celebrity in science and literature. The best known is *Anders Celsius*, born 1701, died 1744. After being appointed professor of astronomy at the University of Upsala, he travelled in Germany, England, France, and Italy; and in 1736 he took part in the expedition of Maupertuis and others for the purpose of measuring a degree of the meridian in Lapland. He is best known as the constructor of the Centigrade thermometer, the first idea of which he presented in his monograph *On the Measurement of Heat*.

CELSIUS SCALE. Another name for the Centigrade thermometric scale, from that of the inventor, Anders Celsius. *See* THERMOMETER.

CEL'SUS. An Epicurean philosopher of the second century after Christ, who is usually said to have been the author of an attack on Christianity entitled *Logos Alēthēs* (True Word), which is now lost, but is mostly preserved in the extracts contained in the more celebrated work *Contra Celsum*, in which it was answered by Origen.

CELSUS, Aurelius (or perhaps Aulus) **Cornelius.** A celebrated Latin writer on medicine who lived, probably, under the Roman Emperors Augustus and Tiberius, or in the beginning of the Christian era. He also wrote on rhetoric, the art of war, and agriculture. He is, however, best known by his *De Medicina*, long one of the chief manuals on medicine.

CELTIBE'RI, or CELTIBERIANS. Inhabitants of Celtiberia, now known as Old and New Castile. They originated from Iberians mixed with Celts. After a long resistance to the Romans, they were at last subjected to their sovereignty, adopted their manners, language, dress, etc.

CELTIC CIVILISATIONS. Ethnologists do not favour the idea that there was a distinct Celtic race. Early classical references depict the Celts as a tall and fair people who occupied Central and Western Europe. In the West they fused with the aboriginal Iberians, a darker people, and formed the Celtiberian confederacy. According to Posiedonius of Apamea (born *c.* 135 B.C.), the Iberians and Celts waged wars for possession of land, and at length, entering into an understanding, held the country in common and intermarried. The Celtiberians wore black cloaks of heavy texture, and had iron weapons and bronze helmets. They fought on foot and on horseback. On the other hand, the Celts wore tunics dyed in many colours and with variegated diamond-shaped patterns—apparently tartan cloth. "Their leg-wear they call 'breeches'."

The Celtiberians had round shields, but the Celtic shield was "the height of a man," and the bronze head-gear had large projections, either horns or figures of birds and quadrupeds. Some warriors wore breast-plates; others fought naked. The sword was short and double-edged; the Celts also used iron-tipped lances and javelins, some of which were straight and some twisted spirally.

Poseidonius says the appearance of the Celts was awe-inspiring; their voices were deep and gruff; they spared their words and expressed themselves in cryptic sentences, leaving most of their meaning to be inferred. They had bards who accompanied their songs on the harp, and Druids who were revered and obeyed.

Human beings were sacrificed to their gods. The Celts kept herds of sheep and swine, and supplied salted mutton and pork to theRomans, and imported great quantities of Italian wine. They also traded in precious and other metals.

Philologists have divided the Celtic languages into the " P " and " Q " groups. In these islands the P-Celtic dialects are represented by Welsh and Cornish, and the Q-Celtic by Gaelic. The ancient Britons of England and Scotland were P-Celts; the Q-Celts appear to have entered Scotland from Ireland. Language being no sure indication of racial origin or affinities, the term " Celtic " is nowadays applied to indicate peoples who speak, or recently spoke, a Celtic dialect.

The modern view regarding the ethnics of Great Britain and Ireland is that the Celtic intruders of pre-Roman times formed military aristocracies among the earlier peoples, as they had previously done on the Continent. Groups of Celts invaded Greece, and, having mixed with the natives, became known as Galle-Grecians. There were settlements of Celts in Northern Italy. The Galatians of Asia Minor were Celts who had formed a military aristocracy after invasion and conquest.

Little or nothing is known regarding the early relations of the Celts and Germans. Apparently the Teutons (" strangers ") had Celtic overlords in some areas, but they shook off the Celtic yoke before Cæsar conquered Gaul. After Rome grew weak the Celts suffered greatly from Teutonic aggression on the Continent and in England, where the Anglo-Saxons achieved wide conquests and subjected the Romanised Britons.

Ireland appears to have been a refuge for the continental Celts during the Roman period, as Brittany was for the Celts of England during the early Anglo-Saxon age. At any rate a brilliant Celtic civilisation flourished in Ireland during and after the Roman age, and a good deal of its heroic and religious literature has survived.

The Scottish problem is more obscure. During the latter part of the Roman period the Scots from North Ireland and the mysterious Picts came into prominence. According to Bede and others, the latter were seafarers who had established themselves in Orkney and pressed southward. Some think they were, like the later Vikings, pirates and traders, and that they came originally from Poitiers (Poictiers), where they were rivals of the sea-faring Veneti. There were also Britons in prehistoric Scotland. The Gaelic Q-Celts rendered the racial name " Prydyn " as " Cruithne." In Ireland the " Cruithne " are by some writers referred to as " Picts," but the Irish Gaels never used the term Pict. Their rendering of it would have been " Cicht."

It is possible that in Scotland the Picts were overlords of the Britons (Cruithne), as well as of other peoples of non-Celtic speech, including those who did not understand the language of St. Columba when he went beyond Inverness to Christianise them. In Ptolemy's map there are tribal names in Scotland that survive in some place-names. The Selgovæ of Galloway, for instance, gave their name to the Solway Firth, and names like Crinan and Carron (Loch Carron) are reminiscent of Ptolemy's Western tribal names Creones, Cerones, Carini or Carnonacæ. In names like Forteviot and Fortingal philologists trace the root " Ver " (surviving as " For ") of the Vernicomes, a tribe placed by the ancient geographer in Eastern and Central Scotland. The personal name Vortigern is of interest in this connection. The Caledonian tribal name survives in Dunkeld (Gael. *Duncelden* or *Dunchallan,* " stronghold of the Caledonians "), and Schiehallion (Gael. *Sith-Chaillinn,* " fairy-hill of the Caledonians ").

That a non-Celtic and non-Teutonic element persisted in Scotland is evident by the fact that pork was tabooed in ancient times; this taboo, once prevalent in the Lowlands, as Sir Walter Scott testifies, still obtains in parts of the Highlands. The ancient Irish, like the continental Celts, reared pigs and ate pork.

CELTIC LITERATURE. The Celtic literature of ancient Gaul perished long centuries ago. That of Brittany did not become distinctively national until last century; its mediæval mysteries and miracle plays imitated French models. It may be that much was carried from Gaul to Ireland during the Roman period.

At any rate, the Gaelic literature of the Green Isle has archaic features and contains legends and references of respectable antiquity. Its most notable saga (or epical narrative) is the *Tain Bo Cualnge* (The Kine Raid of Cooley), which deals with events dating back to the first century of our era. Although it has survived in prose form, interspersed with lyrics and ballads, the original form may have been metrical. The internal evidence of the saga, or group of sagas, is of particular interest. Vivid descriptions are given of costumes, arms, houses, customs, etc., and the mythological references are of value to historians as well as to students of comparative religion. The warriors are quite Homeric. They have weapons of bronze and iron, fight in chariots, and deliver orations. All observe laws of chivalry.

The Cuchullin Cycle. The chief hero is Cuchullin, the Gaelic Achilles, who, like the Homeric warrior, terrifies his opponents by his battle-roar, and occasionally displays on his forehead the " light of valour." Ulster, in this tale, defends itself against the combined forces of the rest of Ireland, which are under the leadership of Queen Meave of Connaught, who raids the northern province to obtain possession of a famous bull. Cuchullin holds up her army, by fighting single combats at a ford, until the Red Branch army of Ulster comes to his relief. The narrative is preserved in the *Book of the Dun Cow*, the *Book of Leinster*, the *Yellow Book of Lecan*, and other manuscript works in Gaelic dating from the twelfth till the nineteenth centuries. Some of these are copies of older works dating back, as the linguistic evidence shows, to the seventh century. The archæological evidence suggests a greater antiquity.

To this group, also referred to as the " Cuchullin sagas," belongs the Deirdre story, in which the heroine takes flight to Scotland. In the ancient manuscripts survive, too, the fragments of a wonderfully complete system of mythology (*see* CELTIC MYTHOLOGY). Native Irish literature is voluminous and varied. It was fostered by the Celtic Church, and has of late been revived. Welsh literature is also rich and important. From the Middle Ages survive the literary relics of more ancient times contained in the *Black Book of Carmarthen*, the *Book of Aneurin*, the *Book of Taliessen*, and the *Red Book of Hergest*. The most notable of the epic poems, called *Gododin*, and attributed to Aneurin, refers to the wars waged in Southern Scotland when the Gaels of Dalriada and the Britons of Strathclyde were opposed to the Picts and the Saxons of the eastern counties.

The Mabinogion. In the heroic poems and the prose romances of the twelfth and thirteenth centuries are mythological and historical references. A student-bard was in ancient Wales called a " Mabinog," and the lore and literature he had to memorise was referred to as " Mabinogi." The plural, " Mabinogion," is in modern treatises applied to a wide group of old narratives translated and edited by Lady Charlotte Guest. Several of these tales, such as *Kulhwch and Olwen*, belong to the Arthurian cycle. A famous Welsh bard was Dafydd ab Gwilym, who lived in the fourteenth century. He is still a popular poet. As in Ireland, the Celtic Revival has fostered a modern literature.

Scotland is particularly rich in Gaelic folk-literature. In consequence, perhaps, of the linguistic changes of the past—Gaelic having supplanted Pictish and other languages or dialects—the ancient manuscripts are scanty. The *Book of Deer* (Aberdeenshire) contains the Gospels in Latin, with notes in Gaelic as well as in Latin, and references to grants and privileges awarded to the monastery of Deer. The *Book of the Dean of Lismore* is of sixteenth-century date, and contains Gaelic ballads, etc., collected by Sir James Macgregor, Dean of Lismore. The *Book of Fernaig* and the *Red and Black Books of Clanranald* are not older than the seventeenth century. Famous eighteenth-century bards include Iain Lom (John Macdonald), Duncan Ban MacIntyre, and Rob Donn. The accomplished Mary MacLeod was born in the seventeenth century. Manx Gaelic literature is, like most of the ancient Scottish, of the traditional order, and therefore of uncertain age.

CELTIC MYTHOLOGY. There were local systems of mythology in Gaul, Britain, and Ireland, suggesting culture-mixing and development in isolation. The Romans identified a number of Gaulish and British deities with their own. On the Roman wall between the Forth and Clyde appears the name of Mars-Camulus. Camulus, a Celtic war-god, gave his name to Colchester (originally Camulodunum).

The Celtic Pantheon. The Celtic Lud's name lingers in London and Lydney. A goddess, called Sulis-Minerva, was associated with Bath. The war-god Belatucadros, also identified with Mars, is referred to in fourteen Roman inscriptions in England and Scotland ; other Celtic Mars are Cocidius, Albiorix (world-king), Caturix (battle-king), Dunatis (fort god), Leŭcetiŭs (god of lightning), Mulo (mule god), etc. The Gaulish gods Taranucus (thunderer), Uxellimus (the highest), and Aramo (the gentle) were identified with Jupiter. With Apollo were linked Borvo (whose name lingers in Bourbon), Grannos, Mogons, and Maponos (the supreme youth).

The rivers named Dee, Devon, Avon, etc., bear the name of the ancient Celtic goddess Deva. Groups of goddesses include Mairæ or Matrona (the mothers), whose name clings to the River Marne. Apollo-Grannos was associated with Sirona (the long-lived), probably an earth goddess. Cæsar tells that the Gauls claimed to be descended from Dis, god of death, who may have been the Celtic Beli. Animal deities included Epŏna (the mare), Moccus (the pig), Artio (the bear), and Damona (the sheep). The Celtic Hermes or Mercury appears to be represented in Irish mythology by Lugh (pronounced *loo*), whom some connect with Lud of London, although others think Lud is the Irish Nuada (Welsh Nudd).

Tuatha de Danann. The Irish deities are in two opposing groups, the Tuatha de Danann (pronounced *too'a de dan'-an*), " the tribe of the goddess Danu," and the fierce deities whose name is Englished as Fomorians. The Dananns invaded Ireland and overcame the Fomorians. The leader of the defenders, Balor (perhaps the Irish Dis), was slain by Lugh. Danu (or Anu), the mother of the gods, was, as Buanann, the "nurse of heroes." She is believed to be identical with Brigit (not to be confused with the Christian saint of that name) and with Brigantia, the mother goddess of the Brigantes of North-Eastern England and South-Eastern Scotland, referred to by Roman writers. Prominent Danann gods included Dagda (the Irish Odin), Angus (the love-god), and Lugh (a Hermes or Apollo), whose human incarnation was Cuchullin. Neit was a god of battle, and Diancecht a god of healing. The great sea-god was Manannan mac lyr, whose name lingers in Isle of Man (Manannan's Isle).

The Scottish Fomorians. There is no evidence that the Irish Danann myths obtained in Scotland, but the Fomorians are well known in folk-stories associated with the grants of certain headlands and glens. The Scottish Fomorians are continually fighting duels by throwing boulders. All are children of a nameless mother goddess whose chief seat is Ben Nevis. She is credited with having, assisted by her creel-carrying sisters, formed the mountains, rivers, and lochs. During winter she keeps a fair maid a prisoner. When her son elopes with this maid, she raises storms to keep them apart, and these are named in the Gaelic Calendar. The son attacks her and she takes flight. In the end, like Morgan le Fay, when pursued by Arthur, she transforms herself into a stone.

The Irish Morrigan is believed to be the same goddess. In Irish tales she appears sometimes as an old woman, sometimes as a comely maiden, and sometimes as a scald-crow, an eel, a heifer, or a wolf. She is also one of a group of three goddesses, as is also Brigit. In Scotland, Brigit is known as Bride, and is welcomed on 1st Feb. (old style), " Bride's day," when the serpent " comes from its hole."

Welsh Deities. In Wales the sea-god is Llyr, the same deity as the Irish Manannan-mac-lir; Shakespeare's Lear is a memory. A goddess Caridwen links with the Scottish mother goddess; both have " cauldrons of wisdom." The Welsh " children of Don " appear to be similar to the Irish Dananns. Llyr's daughter, Cordelia, has two lovers—Gwynn, son of Nudd, and Gwythyr, son of Griedwal. The rivals fight for her on 1st May each year, and will continue to do so until the day of doom, when the victor will marry her. Cordelia's sister, Branwen (the Welsh Venus), marries a king of Ireland, who is cruel to her. Her brother Bran crosses the sea to avenge her and is slain. The best popular account of Celtic mythology is C. Squire's *Celtic Myth and Legend, Poetry, and Romance.*

CELTIS. A genus of trees. *See* NETTLE TREE.

CELTS, THE. The references to the Celts by early Greek writers are somewhat vague, but it can be gathered that they occupied the Danube valley and were extending their sphere of influence westward towards Spain about the fifth century B.C. Strabo, quoting Ptolemy, son of Lagus, says that Alexander the Great received envoys from Celts of high stature who came from the Danube, the Adriatic, and the Ionian Gulf. Hieronymus of Cardia (born *c.* 370 B.C.) says the Galati of the remotest parts of Europe " on the shore of a great sea " were originally called Celts, and that they raided Greece, were repulsed in the neighbourhood of Parnassus, and afterwards crossed to Asia Minor in ships and plundered its sea-coast. They then occupied the country which became known as Galatia.

The Celts of Gaul are most frequently referred to by ancient writers. Poseidonius of Apamea (born *c.* 135 B.C.), who visited Western Europe, and speaks of the tin trade from Britain, refers to the Galati as blondes of high stature who wore tunics and breeches dyed in many colours ; their cloaks with floral patterns (? tartan) were fastened at their shoulders with brooches. They were great warriors and of awe-inspiring appearance, and in conversation " left much to be inferred." Human sacrifices were offered up by the Druids, and the bards celebrated their military achievements. Those Celts who had mingled with the Greeks were called Gallogræcians, and those who had mingled with the Iberians of the west were called Celtiberians. The Celts of Gaul exported much salted pork to Italy. The Roman conquest of Gaul broke up the Celtic confederacies. It is uncertain when the Celts first invaded Britain.

The Celtic dialects, like the Italic,

were divided into "P" and "Q" groups. Apparently the P-Celts came first. Archæological evidence tends to show that about 300 B.C. the Iron Age culture of Gaul reached and began to spread in Britain. Prior to the Roman invasion the Britons were excellent metal-workers and expert in the art of enamelling on bronze. In Southern England Celtic gold and silver coins were in circulation, and trade with the Continent was brisk. The Celts probably formed military aristocracies in Britain.

The term "Celtic" is now used by scholars in reference to peoples who spoke Celtic dialects in historic times. In Ireland, Scotland, and the Isle of Man the Q-Celts are represented linguistically by Gaelic; the P-Celts are represented by Welsh, Cornish (now extinct), and Breton. The ancient Britons were P-Celts. The oldest form of Britain used by the Romans was "Britannia;" the Welsh is "Prydyn," believed to be connected with *brethyn*, cloth, and signifying a cloth-wearing people. The Q-Celts changed P to C, and rendered the racial name as Cruithne (as if a name like "Pritten" became "Critten").

P-Celtic place-names in Scotland are most numerous south of the Grampians, but there are survivals in the north-east. The Gaelic language spread into Scotland from Ireland, especially in early Christian times, displacing the Old British of the P-Celts, and apparently other languages or dialects. In Scotland the Picts were also called "Cruithne;" in Ireland we meet with "Cruithne" only; the name "Pict" was never applied to the Irish Cruithne. It may be the Picts were a military aristocracy in Scotland and of different origin from the Cruithne (Britons), as were, undoubtedly, the Silures (probably Iberians) of Wales.

CELTS (L.Lat. *celtis*, a chisel). The name given to certain prehistoric weapons or other implements of stone or bronze which have been found over nearly the whole surface of the earth. Stone celts are found in the form of hatchets, adzes, chisels, etc. In size they vary, some being found only about 1 inch in length, and others approaching 2 feet; but the most common length is from 6 to 8 inches, and the breadth is usually about a half or one-third of the length.

The materials of which they are made are flint, chert, clay-slate, porphyry, various kinds of greenstone and of metamorphic rocks, and, in short, any very hard and durable stone. Bronze celts belong to a later period than stone ones, and are not so numerous. Some stone celts, however, have been found along with bronze celts in such a manner as to show that stone celts were still used when the method of working bronze had been discovered, a circumstance that need not be wondered at. Bronze celts are not found so large as the largest stone celts, the largest bronze celt being under 1 foot; but the average size of a bronze celt is about the same as that of a stone one, namely about 6 inches.

CEMBRA PINE (*Pinus Cembra*). A fine conifer of Central Europe and Siberia, having edible seeds and yielding a turpentine called Carpathian balsam. Arolla pine and Siberian pine are also names given to it.

CEMENTA'TION. The conversion of iron into steel by heating the iron in a mass of ground charcoal, and thus causing it to absorb a certain quantity of the charcoal. The term is also applied to describe the method of closing the fissures and solidifying water-bearing strata in advance of sinking operations by the injection of Portland-cement grout. It was first used in France in 1882, and has rapidly gained favour.

Two methods are employed. In the deep-hole method a number of holes is bored round the site of the shaft, and grouted for some depth in one operation. The short hole method fills the fissures as they are reached through a series of holes 10 or 12 feet in advance of the sinking. In both cases the holes are pumped to remove all sand, then plugged, and cement grout forced in at a pressure of several hundred pounds per square inch. The cement sets in the fissures, and keeps the water back until the shaft has been fitted with a water-tight lining.

CEMENT DISEASE, or **CEMENT ITCH.** A form of dermatitis produced by dust in cement-works. It causes considerable irritation of the skin, and may last so long that the patient is forced to change his occupation. The action of dust on the lining membrane of the nose is especially irritating, and may lead to ulceration of the nasal septum.

CEMENTS. The general name for any material which causes adhesion between two surfaces, or forms a matrix to unite particles. There are three main divisions: (*a*) *Building cements.*—These all contain lime, and include Portland cement, hydraulic lime, and plaster of Paris. (*b*) *Bituminous cements.*—These are largely composed of natural asphalt and pitch, and are used for damp courses and waterproofing to reservoirs and roads. (*c*) *Adhesives.*—These comprise a large class including resinous cements (marine glue, shellac), oleaginous (linseed oil), and gelatinous (gum-arabic and the gelatin glues).

CENCI (chen'chē), **Beatrice.** Called the *beautiful parricide*; the daughter of Francesco Cenci, a noble and wealthy Roman (1527-98), who, according to the common story, after his second marriage, behaved towards the children of his first marriage in the most shocking manner, procured the assassination of two of his sons on their return from Spain, and debauched his youngest daughter Beatrice. She failed in an appeal for protection to the Pope, and planned and executed the murder of her father. She was beheaded in 1599 and the Cenci estates confiscated. She is the alleged subject of an admired painting by Guido, and is the heroine of one of Shelley's most powerful plays, *The Cenci.*

Recent researches have deprived the story of most of its romantic elements, and have shown Beatrice to be a very commonplace criminal, whatever the evil deeds of her father may have been. Her stepmother and brother, who were equally guilty with her, were also executed. The portrait by Guido in the Barberini Palace, Rome, is now believed not to represent her at all.

CENIS (sė-nē'), **MONT.** A mountain belonging to the Graian Alps, between Savoy and Piedmont, 11,755 feet high. It is famous for the winding road constructed by Napoleon I. which leads over it from France to Italy, and for an immense railway tunnel, which, after nearly fourteen years' labour, was finished in 1871. The tunnel does not actually pass through the mountain, but through the Col de Fréjus, about 15 miles to the S.W., where it was found possible to construct it at a lower level. The Mont Cenis Pass is 6765 feet above the level of the sea, whereas the elevation of the entrance to the tunnel on the side of Savoy is only 3801 feet, and that on the side of Piedmont 4246 feet. The total length of the tunnel is 12,849 metres (42,145 feet, or nearly 8 miles). The total cost amounted to £2,600,000, which was borne partly by the French and Italian Governments and partly by the Northern Railway Company of Italy. The tunnel superseded a grip railway which was constructed over the mountain by Fell, an English engineer, 1864-8.

CEN'OBITE (Gr. *koinos*, common, and *bios*, life). One of a religious order living in a convent or in community: in opposition to an anchorite or hermit, who lives in solitude.

CEN'OTAPH (Gr. *kĕnos*, empty, and *taphos*, a tomb). A monument erected in honour of a deceased person, but not containing his body, as is implied from the derivation. The Greeks erected cenotaphs, and a number were built after the Great War. The chief is that in Whitehall, London. It was

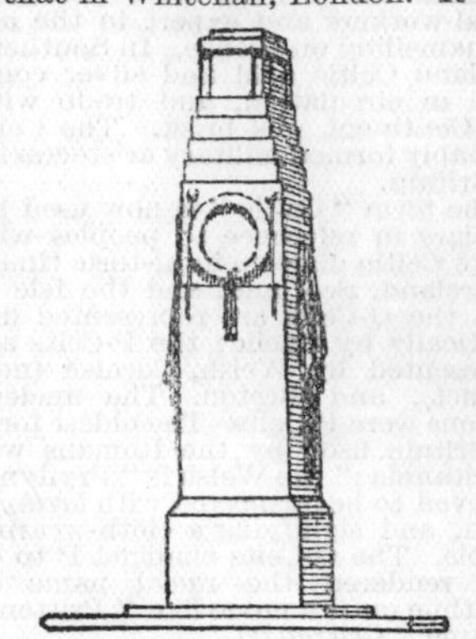

Cenotaph, Whitehall, London

designed by Sir E. Luytens and unveiled by the King on Armistice Day (11th Nov., 1920). It bears the inscription "The glorious dead."

CEN'SER. A vase or pan in which incense is burned; a vessel for burning and wafting incense. Among the ancient Jews the censer was used to offer perfumes in sacrifices. Censers, called also thuribles, are still used in the Roman Catholic Church at mass, vespers, and other offices, as well as in some Anglican and other churches. They are of various forms. In Shakespeare's time the term was applied to a bottle perforated and ornamented at the top, used for sprinkling perfume, or to a pan for burning any odoriferous substance.

CEN'SORS. Two officers in ancient Rome who held office for eighteen months, and whose business was to draw up a register of the citizens and the amount of their property, for the purposes of taxation; to keep watch over the morals of the citizens, for which purpose they had power to censure vice and immorality by inflicting a public mark of ignominy on the offender; and to superintend the finance administration and the keeping up of public buildings. The office was the highest in the state next to the dictatorship, and was invested with a kind of sacred character. The term is now applied to an officer empowered to examine books before publication. *See* BOOKS, CENSORSHIP OF.

CEN'SUS. With the Romans a registered statement of the particulars of a person's property for taxation purposes; an enumeration and register of the Roman citizens and their property, introduced by King Servius Tullius 577 B.C. In modern times a census is an enumeration of the inhabitants of a country, accompanied by any other information that may be deemed useful. In most civilised countries such enumerations now take place at fixed intervals.

In Great Britain the first census was taken in 1801, and a census was taken every ten years from that date till 1931. In 1920 an Act was passed empowering the taking of a census every five years, but it was subsequently decided to adopt this course after 1931. The first census that was attempted in Ireland was that of 1811, but the census of that country taken in 1831 is regarded as the first on which reliance can be placed. The first census of the entire British Empire was not taken till 1871.

The first authentic census in France appears to have been that of 1700; since 1822 it has been taken every five years. The first census in Russia was taken by order of Peter the Great in 1723, and it was decreed that it should be repeated every twenty years. It now takes place more frequently. In Prussia the practice of taking a census of the population dates from the time of Frederick the Great. The first census of the German Empire was taken in 1871, since when there has been a census every five years in Germany. In the United States of America, Switzerland, Sweden, Norway, Holland, Belgium, and Portugal, a census is taken every ten years. The facts brought out by the census differ in different countries. In Ireland religious statistics are tabulated—not in Britain. In the United States the census inquiry is very complete.

CENT, or **CENTIME** (sån-tēm). The name of a small coin in various countries, so called as being equal to a hundredth part of some other coin. In the United States and in Canada the cent is the hundredth part of a dollar. In France the *centime* is the hundredth part of a franc. Similar coins are the *centavo* of Chile; and the *centesimo* of Italy, Peru, etc. Cents or centimes are written as decimals of the unit.

CENTAL. A weight of 100 lb., originally used in the corn trade; now more general.

CENTAU'REA. A genus of composite plants. The species are annual or perennial herbs, with alternate leaves and single heads, all the florets of which are tubular. They are found in Europe, Western Asia, and North Africa. The annuals, *C. Cyănus* (bluebottle), *C. moschāta* (purple or white sultan), and *C. suaveōlens* (yellow sultan), are sometimes cultivated in gardens, but the species in general are of very little importance, and many are mere weeds, such as *C. nigra* and *C. Scabiōsa*, the knapweed of meadows and pastures.

CEN'TAURS. In Greek mythology, fabulous beings represented as half man, half horse. The earliest notices of them, however, merely represent them as a race of wild and savage men inhabiting the mountains and forests

Centaur.—From the Metope of the Parthenon, among the Elgin Marbles in the British Museum

of Thessaly. Mythology relates the combats of the Centaurs with Hercules, Theseus, and Peirithoüs. The Centaurs Nessus, Chiron, and others are famous in ancient fable. Chiron and Pholus are the good Centaurs, whilst the others are represented as lustful and savage.

CENTAU'RUS. A constellation of the southern hemisphere, near the south pole, E. and N. of the Southern Cross.

CEN'TAURY. The *Erythræa Centaurium*, an annual herb of the gentian family with pretty red flowers. It is common throughout Europe, and is extolled for its medicinal properties by the old herbalists. It is common in England, especially on dry, sandy, or chalky soils.

CEN'TENARY. The commemoration of any event, as the birth of a great man, which occurred 100 years before.

CEN'TERING. The framing of timber by which the arch of a bridge or other arched structure is supported during its erection. The same name is given to the woodwork or framing on which any vaulted work is constructed. The centering of a bridge has to keep the stones or *voussoirs* in position till they are keyed in, that is, fixed by the insertion of the requisite number of stones in the centre.

CENTIARE (sàn̦-tyär). A French measure, the hundredth part of an *are*; a square metre, equal to 1·19 sq. yards.

CEN'TIPEDE. A term applied to various air-breathing arthropods having many pairs of legs and a body consisting of numerous similar rings or segments (*somites*), all belonging

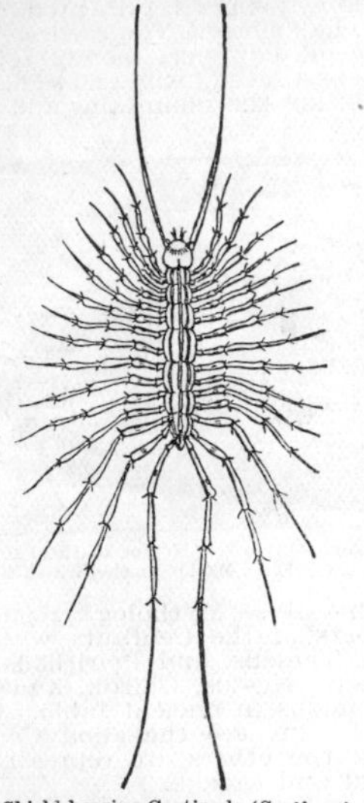

Shield-bearing Centipede (*Scutigera*)

to the ord. Cheilopoda, class Myriapoda. The most common British centipede, *Lithobius forficātus*, is quite harmless, but those of tropical countries belonging to the genus Scolopendra inflict severe and often dangerous bites. They sometimes grow to a foot in length.

CENT'LIVRE, Susanna. Dramatic writer, daughter of a Lincolnshire gentleman named Freeman, born in Ireland about 1667, died 1723. After being twice left a widow within a short time of her marriage, she took for a third husband Joseph Centlivre, chief cook to Queen Anne.

She had some success as an actress, but her fame rests on *The Busybody*, *The Wonder* (in which Garrick found perhaps one of his best parts), *A Bold Stroke for a Wife*, and fourteen other plays, all of which were published in a collected edition, 1761. Mrs. Centlivre enjoyed the friendship of Steele, Farquhar, Rowe, and other wits of the day.

CENT'NER. A common name on the continent of Europe for a hundredweight. In Switzerland it is equal to 110 lb.; in Austria, 110½ lb.; in Sweden, 112·06 lb.; in Germany, 110·25 lb.

CEN'TO (Lat., a patchwork). A poem formed out of verses taken from one or more poets, so arranged as to form a distinct poem. Specimens of this form of perverted ingenuity may be found in the works of Ausonius.

CENTRAL AFRICA. A term of which the application is somewhat vague, geographers and map-makers still differing widely as to the exact extent of country so to be defined. Some regard it as extending from 5° N. to 10° S. of the equator, bounded on the east by a line drawn from the mouth of the Nile to that of the Zambesi, and on the west by the coastal belt. Others, including Sir Harry Johnston, would apply the term to practically the whole portion of Africa lying south of a line connecting the Cameroons and Mombasa, excluding only the Hottentot-peopled district of the extreme south-west. This definition is based largely on the presence of a Bantu-speaking population and on the explorations of Livingstone.

Physical Features. If, however, either of these limits be accepted, or a middle course between the two extremes, Central Africa will be found to contain some of the most striking features of the continent, including the Central Plateau with the Congo Basin, the great lakes of Victoria Nyanza, Tanganyika, and Nyassa, and the mountain mass of Ruwenzori (16,815 feet). A line drawn north and south through the middle of the district will divide it into portions differing markedly from each other in regard to characteristic features. To the east are high mountains, extensive lakes, and a rolling savannah-like country which affords excellent grazing-ground and is often well-timbered; the rivers have continuous woods upon their banks. The west is largely covered by forests, and watered by countless rivers and streams.

Flora and Fauna. Here exist many animals of peculiar interest, including some species of anthropoid apes closely akin in structure to the human form; remarkable lemurs and civets, and a red tiger-cat; many birds of special interest, and several genera of snakes not found elsewhere. The flora is less notable for any striking peculiarity of character than for the flourishing growth, due largely to moist climate and a fertile soil. The eastern section of the district is, however, far superior in respect of fauna generally, and in especial with regard to "game;" possessing, among other creatures not found west of the imagined line, the rhinoceros, giraffe, lion, cheetah, larger buffalo, kudu, eland, zebra, many antelopes, and numerous rodents; with the ostrich, secretary-bird, bustard, sand-grouse, and lark.

People. The native inhabitants live chiefly by hunting, a very elementary cultivation of the soil, and pastoral pursuits. The earliest human population of Central Africa was probably supplied by immigrants from Asia, direct ancestors of the bushmen and of such pigmy tribes as the Akka and others, still surviving in some parts to-day. These were gradually absorbed or replaced by arrivals of the true negro type, which overran the southern half of the great continent about two thousand years ago.

The coasts of Central Africa, if we allow the district to include a coastal line, were explored at an early period by the Phœnicians, and later, to some extent, by the Greeks and Persians. Still more recently arrived the Arabs and the Portuguese, followed, towards the close of the eighteenth century, by the British.

CENTRAL AMERICA. A geographical division, including the stretch of territory from the Isthmus of Panama to the Isthmus of Tehuantepec, but by political arrangements the limits most generally assigned to it include the five republican states of Guatemala, Honduras, San Salvador, Nicaragua, and Costa Rica, with British Honduras and the Mosquito Coast. It thus has Mexico on the N.W., Panama on the S.E., and the Pacific Ocean and Caribbean Sea on either side. Its entire length may be about 800 miles, with a breadth varying from between 20 and 30 to 350 miles. It is generally mountainous, contains a number of active volcanoes, and on the whole is a rich and fertile but almost totally undeveloped region. The area is about 188,999 sq. miles; the pop. 6,000,000.

CENTRAL ASIA. *See* ASIA, CENTRAL.

CENTRAL CRIMINAL COURT. London court of law. It is in the Old Bailey on the site of old Newgate Prison, and was set up in 1834. Here serious criminal cases from the London and surrounding districts are heard. It thus corresponds to the assizes held outside the London area. The judges are the lord mayor, recorder, common serjeant, city aldermen, and judges of the city court, but usually a judge of the high court presides. The present building was completed in 1905 at a cost of £250,000.

CENTRAL FALLS. A town of the United States, Rhode Island, about 4½ miles north of Providence and adjoining Pawtucket, with cotton and other manufactures. Pop. 25,898.

CENTRAL FORCES. In dynamics, treats of forces whose directions always pass through a fixed point called the *centre*. The force may be one of attraction or repulsion. Under the former is included the study of planetary motion, in which the sun is taken as the centre of force. Under certain conditions, the path of a body moving under the action of a central force will be respectively a hyperbola, a parabola, or an ellipse. Thus the planets move in ellipses round the sun. This statement is from one of Kepler's laws, all of which have been verified by the principles of central forces.

CENTRAL INDIA AGENCY includes 87 native states all of which are in various ways related to the Government of India. The Governor-General has an Agent at Indore, and there are Political Agents for Baghelkhand, Bundelkhand, Bhopal, and in the Southern States of Central India and Malwa. The total area of the Agency is 51,505 sq. miles, and the pop. is 6,615,120.

CENTRALISATION. A term in a specific sense applied to a system of government where the tendency is to administer by the central government matters which had been previously, or might very well be, under the management of local authorities.

CENTRAL POWERS. Name given during the Great War to Germany and Austria, and their allies.

CENTRAL PROVINCES AND BERAR. An extensive British territory in India. They became a separate administration in 1861, and are under the authority of a chief commissioner. Their total area is 131,052 sq. miles, of which 99,876 sq. miles are British territory, and 31,176 the territory of native protected states, fifteen in number. In 1891 the total population was 15,842,296; in 1901, 14,627,045; in 1921, 15,979,660. The province is divided into five commissionerships, Jabalpur (Jubbulpore), Nagpur, Narbada (Nerbudda), Chhattisgarh, and

Berar, the last till 1905 a separate province.

CENTRE-BOARD, or **DROP-KEEL.** A sort of moving keel used especially in American yachts, and capable of being raised and lowered in a well extending longitudinally amidships. It tends to prevent lee-way, and gives the vessel greater stability when under a press of canvas.

CENTRES. In mechanics, points which occupy a unique position in a body with regard to forces acting upon it.—*Centre of attraction*, the point towards which the attracting force is directed.—*Centre of buoyancy*, that point in a floating body through which the resultant upthrust of the water on it acts; it is the centre of gravity of the water displaced.—*Centre of friction*, that point on the base of a rapidly-revolving body about which it rotates.—*Centre of gravity*, that point of a body through which the line of action of the resultant of the weights of the particles composing the body passes, provided they can be considered as a set of parallel forces.—*Centre of gyration*, the point at which, if the whole mass of a revolving body were collected, the rotatory effect would remain unaltered.—*Centre of inertia*, or mass of a body. Its position is determined by multiplying each separate mass by its distance from a fixed line or plane and dividing the total by the sum of the masses.—*Centre of motion*, that point which remains at rest relative to the other points moving. —*Centre of oscillation*, that point of a body suspended by an axis, at which, if all the matter were concentrated, the oscillations would be performed in the same time.—*Centre of percussion*, that point of a body rotating about a fixed axis which can be struck without causing any instantaneous pressure on the axis. —*Centre of pressure*, in hydrostatics, that point of an immersed area through which the resultant of all the water-pressures at each point of the area acts.

CENTRIF'UGAL and **CENTRIP'ETAL.** In botany, terms applied to two kinds of inflorescence, the former being that in which the terminal or central flower is the first to expand, as in a true cyme (examples, elder and valerian), the latter being that kind in which the lower or outer flower is the first to expand, as in spikes, racemes, umbels, and corymbs. The laburnum, hemlock, and daisy are examples. *See* INFLORESCENCE; CYME; RACEME.

CENTRIFUGAL FORCE, and **CENTRIPETAL FORCE.** It is a fundamental principle of dynamics that a body which is not subjected to the action of force moves with uniform velocity in a straight line. If, therefore, we observe a body moving in a curved path, even though its speed is uniform, we infer that some force is acting on it. Take the simple case of a small mass moving with uniform speed in a circle, a case which may be realised practically by whirling a stone at the end of a string. We note that the force acting on the stone, namely the tension of the string, is directed towards the centre of the circle, or is *centripetal*. The force which the stone exerts on the string, and through it on the hand, is equal and opposite to this, and tends to pull the string away from the centre. The force exerted *by the stone* on the string is therefore correctly described as *centrifugal*.

But it does not follow, as is sometimes erroneously supposed, that if the string were cut the stone would fly off in the direction of the force which it is exerting, that is radially. It would continue to move in the straight line which it is following at the moment of release, that is to say, in the tangent to its circular path.

The actual value of the force on a mass m moving with uniform velocity v in a circle of radius r is mv^2/r absolute units.

It is often convenient, when discussing problems of rotation, to deal with centrifugal rather than centripetal forces. The root idea of this method is that, since the applied forces supply the necessary centripetal force, they will be in statical equilibrium with the centrifugal force. For example, the proper amount of elevation of the outer rail of a railway curve, or the proper angle of banking of a cycle-track, is found from the consideration that the resultant of centrifugal force and weight must be at right angles to the plane of the rails or track. Again, the form of the free surface of a rotating liquid is given by the condition that the resultant of the centrifugal force and weight of a particle of liquid is at right angles to the free surface.

As a last example, we may take the apparent loss of weight of a body due to the rotation of the earth. If the body is resting on the ground at the equator, the upward pressure of the ground and the upward centrifugal force together balance the attraction of the earth on the body, so that the pressure of the body on the ground, which is its *apparent* weight, is less than its real weight by the amount of the centrifugal force. It is easy to prove that the apparent loss of weight at the Equator is about 1/289 of the real weight.

CENTRIFUGAL MACHINES. Machines in which centrifugal force produced by rapid revolution is utilised. They may be used for drying articles, clothes, for instance, the articles being placed in the inside of a hollow cylinder made of wire-gauze or having many perforations in its walls, the moisture being driven off when the cylinder is made to revolve rapidly. Sugar is often separated from molasses by a centrifugal machine, the impure sugar being placed in a cylinder which is contained within a larger cylinder, the latter receiving the molasses which is removed by the rapid revolution of the inside cylinder. Cream is now commonly separated from milk in large dairies by this method, which can also be employed in the clarification of liquids, such as beer.

CENTROBARIC BODY. A body which attracts gravitating matter as if its whole mass were concentrated at the centre.

CENTROID. In mechanics, a name given by some writers to centre of mass or inertia. In geometry, the point whose distance from a line or plane is the mean of the distances of several other points from that line or plane.

CENTU'RION. In the ancient Roman army, the commander of a century, or body of 100 men, but afterwards an indefinite number, the sixtieth part of a legion. The rank of a centurion corresponded more or less to that of a captain in modern armies.

CENTURIPE (chen-tö'ri-pā; ancient **Centuripa**), also called **CENTORBI.** A town of Sicily, province of Catania, situated in a fertile district yielding soda, sulphur, and marble. The ancient city, of which considerable remains exist, was one of the most flourishing in Sicily. Pop. 13,100.

CEN'TURY (Lat. *centuria*, from *centum*, a hundred). One of the divisions or companies into which the Roman legions were divided, originally 100 men. This name was also given to the divisions of the six classes of the people introduced by Servius Tullius. According to Livy, the first class contained eighty-two, to which were added the eighteen centuries of the knights; the three following classes had each twenty centuries; the fifth, thirty-four; and the sixth only one century.

CENTURY-PLANT. A popular name of the *Agāve americāna*, or American aloe.

CEPHA'ËLIS. *See* IPECACUANHA.

CEPHALAS'PIS (Gr. *kephalē*, the head, and *aspis*, a shield). A genus of fossil fishes occurring in the Old Red Sandstone. The vertebræ remained unossified, and the somewhat narrow body and tail were protected by rows of bony scales of the same structure as the large semicircular head-shield that covered the front portion. The nearest living allies of these primitive fishes are the freshwater Polypterus and Lepidosteus (the bony pike of the United States).

Centurion

CEPHALEUROS. A genus of Green Algæ, group Ulotrichales, half-parasites living in the leaves of various flowering plants. *C. virescens* is the cause of the "red rust" of tea in India, the most serious disease to which the tea-plant is liable in that country. *C. coffeæ* produces a similar disease in Liberian coffee.

CEPHALIC INDEX. Term used to denote the size and class of human skulls. It is anthropometric ratio of breadth to length of head. Retzius devised it, about 1842, by multiplying by 100 the number representing the greatest breadth above the ear level, ascertained by calipers, and dividing this by the greatest length from the glabella, or point above root of nose, to the back of the occiput. The cranial index of the skull is one or two units less than the cephalic index of the living head. Persons from 75 to 80 are medium-headed, below long-headed, and above broad-headed.

CEPHALISA'TION. In biology, a term proposed to denote a tendency in the development of animals towards a localisation of important parts

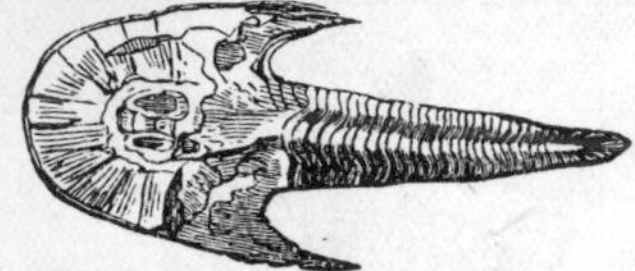

Cephalaspis Lyellii

in the neighbourhood of the head, as by the transfer of locomotive members or limbs to the head (in the Cephalopoda, for example). The term is also used to indicate the degree in which the brain dominates over the other parts of the animal structure.

CEPHALO'NIA (ancient **Kephallenia**). An island of Greece, the largest of the Ionian Islands, west of the Morea, at the entrance of the Gulf of Patras, about 31 miles in length, and from 5 to 12 in breadth; area, 256 sq. miles; pop. 71,186. The coast-line is very irregular and deeply marked with indentations, and the surface is rugged and mountainous, rising in Monte Negro, the ancient Ænos, to a height of 5380 feet. There is rather a deficiency of water on the island. The principal towns are Argostoli (8293 inhabitants) and Lixuri (6000). The chief exports are currants, oil, and grain; wine, cheese, etc., are also exported. The manufactures are inconsiderable. Earthquakes are not infrequent. One of the most destructive was that of the year 1867.

CEPHALOP'ODA, or **CEPH'ALOPODS** (Gr. *kephalē*, head, *pous*, *podos*, foot). A class of the mollusca characterised by having the organs of prehension and locomotion, called tentacles or arms, attached to the head. The arms are furnished with numerous suckers, and enable them to cling to and entangle their prey; and they have a pair of well-developed jaws and eyes.

They are divided into two sections, Tetrabranchiata (four-gilled) and Dibranchiata (two-gilled). The nautilus and the fossil genera Orthoceras, Ammonites, Goniatites, etc., belong to the Tetrabranchiata, in which the animal has an external shell. The dibranchiate group includes the argonaut, the octopus or eight-armed cuttle-fishes, and the ten-armed forms, as the calamaries, and the fossil belemnites. The chambered shell is in all these internal (being known as the "pen" and the "cuttle-bone"), in some rudimentary. The fossil Cephalopoda are multitudinous. *See* NAUTILUS, SEPIA.

CEPHALOTHO'RAX. The anterior part of the body in spiders, scorpions,

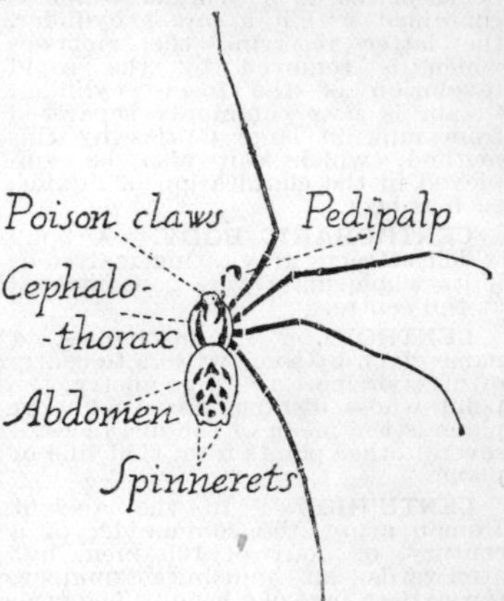

Diagram of a Spider showing the Cephalothorax, legs of left side omitted

and crustaceans, consisting of the head and thorax combined.

CEPHALOTUS. The sole genus of Cephalotaceæ, a nat. ord. of polypetalous dicotyledons, allied to Saxifragaceæ. The only species, *C. follicularis*, is a small rosette-plant growing in swamps at King George's Sound, W. Australia. The lower leaves of the rosette are transformed into pitchers very like those of Nepenthes in structure and mode of action.

CEPHEUS (kē'fūs). A king of Ethiopia and husband of Cassiopeia, father of Andromeda, and father-in-law of Perseus; his name was given to a constellation of stars in the northern hemisphere surrounded by Cassiopeia, Ursa Major, Draco, and Cygnus.

CERAM'. An island in the Moluccas, lying west of New Guinea; area about 6800 sq. miles; pop. estimated at 98,744. It is about 200 miles long with an average width of 35 miles. Its interior is traversed by mountain ranges from 6000 to 8000 feet high, but is little known. The vegetation is luxuriant, the sago-palm supplying the chief food of the inhabitants as well as an article of trade. The inhabitants of the coast are of Malay origin, the interior being peopled by Alfuros. It is under the Dutch.

CERAMIA'CEÆ. A family of Red Algæ, small richly-branched plants, including some of the most elegant of British seaweeds, such as the species of Callithamnion, Ceramium, Griffithsia, and Ptilota.

CERAMICS. *See* POTTERY.

CERAS'TES (Gr., from *keras*, a horn). A genus of African vipers, remarkable for their fatal venom,

Cerastes Cornutus

and for two little horns formed by the scales above the eyes. Hence they have received the name of horned vipers. The tail is very distinct from the body. *C. cornutus* is the horned viper of Northern Africa and Arabia, a species known to the ancients. There are several other species.

CE'RATE. The name of an external medicament, more or less liquid, having for its basis wax and oil. Simple cerate consists of 8 oz. of lard and 4 oz. of white wax melted together and stirred till cold.

CERATITES. One of the best-known types of early ammonites in Europe, occurring in the marine middle Triassic beds in Germany.

CERAT'ODUS (Gr. *kĕras, kĕratŏs*, a horn, *ŏdous, ŏdŏntŏs*, a tooth). A genus of the Dipnoi or lung-fishes, and named from the numerous cusps on the edges of its large teeth. Its remains are found in the Triassic rocks. The barra-munda or Burnet salmon (Neoceratodus) of the Burnet and Mary Rivers in Queensland is nearly related. This fish breathes not only by gills but also by a lung-like swim-bladder. It is 4 or 5 feet in length. *See* DIPNOI.

CERATOPTERIS. A genus of Leptosporangiate Ferns. *C. thalictroides*, a common tropical fern, is one of the few water-plants among genuine ferns.

CERAUNOGRAPHY (Gr. *keraunos*, thunder-bolt, *graphe*, drawing). The photography of lightning. A lightning flash is so momentary that the human eye is unable to give a correct presentment of it. Important information has, however, been gained through photography. By a side to side motion of the camera analytic records are obtained, which show that the so-called forked lightning is an illusion, and also that a flash which seems to flicker represents a quick succession of flashes traversing a common path.

CER'BERUS. In classical mythology, the dog-monster of Hades, variously described as having a

Cerberus

hundred, fifty, and three heads, with a serpent's tail, and a mane consisting of the heads of various snakes. Homer mentions him simply as the dog of Hades. He was subdued by Heracles (Hercules), who, as the last test of his strength, snatched Cerberus from the halls of Hades. The conception of a monster like Cerberus is to be met with in the *Rigveda*.

CERCA'RIA (Gr. *kerkos*, a tail). In flukes or trematodes, the final larval stage, resembling a minute tadpole. *See* LIVER-FLUKE.

CERCOPITHE'CUS. A genus of African monkeys, including the Guenons, one being the Diana monkey (*C. diana*), and another the Green Guenon (*C. sabæus*).

CERDIC (ker'dik). King of the West Saxons; invaded England about the end of the fifth century, and established the kingdom of Wessex about 516. At his death in 534 his kingdom included the present counties of Berks, Wilts, Dorset, and Hants (including the Isle of Wight).

CERE (sēr) (Lat. *cera*, wax). The naked skin that covers the base of the bill in some birds.

CE'REALS. A term derived from Ceres, the goddess of corn, though sometimes extended to leguminous plants, as beans, lentils, etc., is more usually and properly confined to the Gramineæ, as wheat, barley, rye, oats, and other grasses, cultivated for the sake of their seed as food. The true fruit of the cereals is a caryopsis, or nut-like structure, containing an embryo and a store of food for it—the endosperm—which consists largely of starch (57 to 70 per cent) and proteids (7 to 13 per cent).

CEREBRATION. Action of the brain. Physiologists hold that molecular changes in the brain substance attend all mental processes in consciousness. In 1853 Dr. W. B. Carpenter, believing that these changes also continue automatically called "unconscious cerebration" what Sir W. Hamilton had previously called "latent thought." It accounts, for example, for the sudden recollection of forgotten facts.

CEREBRO-SPINAL FEVER (epidemic cerebro-spinal meningitis). Known popularly as "spotted fever." An infectious fever found throughout Europe and America in sporadic form, but periodically breaking out in limited areas as an epidemic. These epidemics are most common in spring, and are particularly severe where the patients are children under ten. Overcrowding and insanitary conditions foster their appearance. Fatigue, exposure, or injury to the head are predisposing causes in individual cases. In epidemics the mortality is as high as from 50 to 70 per cent. The disease may be very acute (fulminant type), when death occurs within forty-eight hours after the onset, or it may be the more common and less severe form. The chief symptoms are vomiting, intense headache, stiffness of neck, convulsions, delirium, fever, insomnia, resentment of all handling, hæmorrhagic rash giving the skin a mottled appearance (hence the name "spotted fever.") It has to be distinguished from other forms of meningitis, also pneumonia, typhus, and influenza.

Treatment.—Sedatives should be given freely, and in all cases serum should be injected into the spinal canal. The more general treatment is the same as for other acute fevers.

CEREBRUM and CEREBELLUM. *See* BRAIN.

CEREOP'SIS. A genus of birds allied to the geese, the only species being *C. Novæ Hollandiæ*, called New Holland or Australian goose.

CERES (sē'rēz). A Roman goddess, corresponding to the Greek Dēmētēr; she was the daughter of Kronos and Rhea, and the mother of Proserpine and Bacchus. She was the goddess of the earth in its capacity of bringing forth fruits, especially watching over the growth of grain and other plants. The Romans celebrated in her honour the festival of the Cerealia (12th to 19th April) with games in the circus. Ceres was always represented in full attire, her attributes being ears of corn and poppies, and her sacrifices consisted of pigs and cows.

Ceres is also the name of a planet discovered by M. Piazzi at Palermo, in Sicily, in 1801. It was the first discovered of the asteroids. Its size is less than that of the moon.

CE'REUS. A genus of cactuses, natives of tropical America, with large funnel-shaped flowers. Many are night-flowering plants, like *C. grandiflōra* of the W. Indies, well known in hot-houses.

CERIA'MA. *See* SERIEMA.

CERIGNOLA (cher-ē-nyō'lȧ). A town of South Italy, in the province of Foggia, and 24 miles S.E. of the town of that name. It has linen manufactures and a trade in almonds and cotton. Pop. 36,000.

CERIGO (cher-ē'gō; ancient **KYTHÊRA**). A Greek island in the Mediterranean, south of the Morea, from which it is separated by a narrow strait; area about 116 sq. miles. It is mountainous and barren, though some of the valleys are fertile, producing corn, wine, and olives. Excellent honey is produced. Sheep, hares, and quails are abundant. In Greek mythology ancient Kythēra is mentioned as the sacred abode of Aphrodite (Venus). Pop. 16,100.—On its west coast is the town of Cerigo; pop. 1200. It is the see of a Greek bishop.

CERIN'THUS. The founder of a Gnostic-Ebionite heretical sect of the first century whose doctrines were a mixture of Judaism and Gnosticism. The Apostle St. John is supposed to have written the Fourth Gospel against Cerinthus.

CE'RITE. *See* CERIUM.

CERITH'IUM. The typical genus of a family of aquatic snails, containing numerous species, both marine and freshwater, and having spiral, elongated, and many-whorled shells.

CE'RIUM. A rare metal discovered in the mineral *cerite* by Klaproth in 1804. Its value lies in the fact that its oxide ceria, in the proportion of 1 per cent to 99 per cent of thoria, greatly increases the glow of incandescent gas-mantles. Cerium is commercially extracted from the mineral *monazite* (q.v.), cerite being practically confined to the gneissic rocks of Bastna, in Westmanland, Southern Sweden.

CERNAVODA. Village in Rumania. Situated on the Danube's right bank, almost directly between Bukarest and the Black Sea port of Constanza, it was chosen for the site of the Caro Bridge, built in 1896 for the railway connecting the capital and the port. This double bridge was strategically important because it was the only bridge across the Danube between Belgrade and the Black Sea. It was seized by Germano-Bulgarian forces in Oct., 1916.

CEROGRAPHY (Gr. *kērographia*, encaustic painting). The art of painting or engraving with wax, was known at an early period by the Greeks and Romans. The painting-matter was applied either with a stylus, spatula, or brush, the last-named method proving most satisfactory for the decoration of ships. In the Munich Residenz is some fine modern cerographic work by Schnorr.

CEROX'YLON. A genus of South American palms; the wax-palm of the Andes.

CERRETO (cher-rā'tō). A town in South Italy, province of Benevento, on the slope of Mount Matese, a pleasant town with a handsome cathedral. Pop. 5650.

CERRO DE PASCO. A town of Peru, capital of the department of Junin, 14,275 feet above the level of the sea. The town came into existence in 1630, in consequence of the discovery of veins of silver there. The climate is trying and the whole place uninviting, though it still contains the most productive of the Peruvian mines. Pop. about 25,000.

CERTALDO (cher-tȧl'dō). A small town of North Italy, 15 miles S.W. of Florence. It is the birthplace, was long the home, and now contains the ashes of Boccaccio, and many interesting relics. His house was restored in 1823. Pop. 10,600.

CER'THIA. A genus of perching birds, type of the family Certhiidæ or Creepers.

CERTIFICATE. Document for attesting or certifying facts. Any signed attestation of facts is a certificate, but the word is now almost invariably applied to official or semi-official documents, e.g., medical certificates, examination certificates and certificates by auditors of accounts.

Other certificates are those issued by registrars to prove births, marriages and deaths. Copies of these can be obtained from Somerset House London, or the General Register Office, Edinburgh.

Still another kind is the Savings Certificate (q.v.) first issued during the Great War.

CERTIORA'RI. In law, a writ issuing out of a superior court to call up the records of an inferior court or remove a cause there depending, that it may be tried in the superior court. This writ is obtained upon the complaint of a party that he has not received justice, or that he cannot have an impartial trial in the inferior court.

CERTOSA DI PAVIA (cher-tō'sȧ). A celebrated Italian monastery near Pavia, founded in 1396 by Galeazzo Visconti, Duke of Milan. The church is a splendid building.

CERU'LEUM. A blue pigment, consisting of stannate of protoxide of cobalt mixed with stannic acid and sulphate of lime.

CERU'MINOUS GLANDS. The glands of the ear which secrete the cerumen or wax which passes into the passage to the tympanum and helps to prevent the entrance of foreign matter.

CERUSE (sē'rụs). White-lead, much used in painting and also as a cosmetic. It consists of lead carbonate and lead hydroxide, and is usually produced by the action of acetic acid on metallic lead in the presence of air rich in carbon dioxide. Although highly poisonous, it is valued for the "body" that it possesses as a pigment.

CE'RUSSITE (called *cerussa nativa*, native white-lead, in the sixteenth century. A mineral lead carbonate ($PbCO_3$), common with galena in almost all lead-mines. Specific gravity, 6·5. It is readily reduced to lead before the blow-pipe.

CERVANTES SAAVEDRA (thervȧn'tes sȧ-ȧ-vā'-*drȧ*), **Miguel de.** Spanish poet, playwright, and novelist, born at Alcalá de Henares in 1547, died at Madrid in 1616. At the age of seven he removed to Madrid, and commenced writing verses at an early age. His pastoral *Filena* attracted the notice of Cardinal Acquaviva, whom he accompanied to Italy as page. In 1570 he served under Colonna in the war against the Turks and African corsairs, and in the battle of Lepanto (1571) he lost the use of his left hand and received two gunshot wounds in the chest. After this he joined the troops at Naples, in the service of the Spanish

Cervantes

king, winning the highest reputation as a soldier.

In 1575, while returning to his country, he was taken by the corsair Arnaut Mami, and sold in Algiers as a slave—a condition in which he remained for seven years, displaying great fortitude. In 1580 his friends and relations at length ransomed him, and, rejoining his old regiment, he fought in the naval battle and subsequent storming of Terceira. In 1583, however, he retired from service, and recommenced his literary work, publishing in 1584 his pastoral *Galatea*. In the same year he married, and lived for a long time by writing for the stage, to which he contributed between twenty and thirty plays, of which two only have survived. From 1588 to 1599 he lived in retirement at Seville, where he held a small office.

He did not appear again as an author till 1605, when he produced the first part of *Don Quixote*, a work having as its immediate aim the satirical treatment of the novels of chivalry then popular, but embodying at the same time human types of cosmopolitan interest, and having a profounder bearing upon life than its express object covered. In 1613 his twelve *Exemplary Novels* (his best work after *Don Quixote*), in 1614 his *Journey to Parnassus*, and in 1615 eight new dramas, with intermezzos, were published. In 1614 an unknown writer published, under the name of Alonzo Fernandez de Avellaneda, a continuation of *Don Quixote*, full of abuse of Cervantes, who thereupon published the real continuation, which was the last work of his issued during his lifetime. His novel *Persiles and Sigismunda* was published after his death, which took place at Madrid on the same day as that of Shakespeare, 23rd April, 1616.—BIBLIOGRAPHY: James Fitzmaurice-Kelly, *Cervantes in England*; *Miguel de Cervantes Saavedra: a Memoir*; R. Smith, *Life of Cervantes*.

CERVETRI (cher-vā′trē). A small place in Italy, province of Rome, where formerly stood the ancient Etruscan city of Cære. It has yielded many artistic and other objects of Etruscan manufacture.

CERVIN (ser-van), **Mont** (Ger. *Matterhorn*; It. *Monte Silvio*). A mountain, Switzerland, Pennine Alps, on the southern frontiers of canton Valais, about 6 miles W.S.W. of Zermatt. It is an almost inaccessible obelisk of rock, starting up from an immense glacier to a height of 14,837 feet. The peak was first ascended by a party of four English travellers and three guides in July, 1865, but three of the party and a guide perished in the descent.

CERVUS. The genus of deer to which the red deer, wapiti, and fallow deer belong, forming the type of the deer family Cervidæ.

CESAREVITCH. Name used in Russia before 1917 for the eldest son of the tsar. It is also the name of a race run at Newmarket in October. This was started in 1839 and was named after Alexander III., the Cesarevitch, who was then in England.

CESAROTTI (che-sȧ-rot′tē), **Melchiore.** One of the most celebrated of the Italian literati of the eighteenth century, born at Padua in 1730, where he became professor of rhetoric, and subsequently professor of the Greek and Hebrew languages. Besides his own poems, his works include translations of Voltaire's tragedies, Ossian, Demosthenes, and the *Iliad*, and essays on the *Philosophy of Languages*, on *Studies*, etc. He died in 1808.

CESENA (che-sā′nȧ). A town of Central Italy, province of Forli, on the right bank of the Savio, at the foot of a mountain. It has a handsome town house, a cathedral, and some silk-mills. Pop. 54,000.

CESPEDES (thes′pe-*des*), **Pablo de.** Spanish painter, sculptor, architect, poet, and man of letters, born at Cordova in 1538, died in 1608. He entered the university of Alcalá de Henares in 1556, and finally went to Rome, where he studied under Zucchero and Michael Angelo, and became renowned both for frescoes and sculptures. In 1577 he obtained a prebend in the cathedral of Cordova, and from that time resided alternately in his native town and in Seville.

His best pictures are Cordova, Seville, Madrid, and several towns of Andalusia. He was the head of the then Andalusian school of painting, and numbered among his pupils some painters of distinction.

CESSIO BONO′RUM. In Scots law, a yielding or surrender of property or goods—a legal proceeding by which a debtor surrenders his whole means and estate to his creditors. *See* BANKRUPT.

CESTODA. Cestode, or cestoid worms (Gr. *kĕstŏs*, girdle, *eidos*, resemblance). The group of tape-worms, of which the genus Tænia is most typical.

CESTRA′CION. A genus of sharks, of which the best-known living type is the Port Jackson shark (*C. Philippi*), which ranges from Japan to Australia and New Zealand. It possesses several rows of blunt hind teeth, adapted for crushing the shells of molluscs.

CESTUS. In classical mythology, a girdle worn by Aphroditē or Venus, endowed with the power of exciting love towards the wearer.

CESTUS, or CÆSTUS. A leathern thong or bandage often covered with knots and loaded with lead and iron,

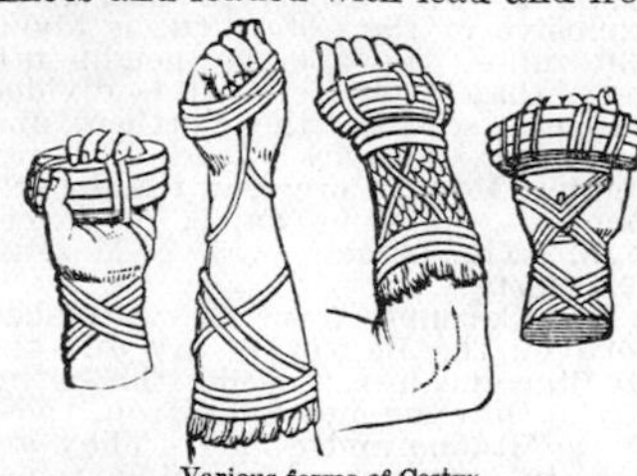

Various forms of Cestus

anciently worn by Roman pugilists to increase the force of the blow.

CETA′CEA. An order of marine animals, surpassing in size all others in existence. They are true mammals, since they suckle their young, have warm blood, and respire by means of lungs, for which purpose they come to the surface of the water to take in fresh supplies of air. The body is fish-like in form, but ends in a bilobate tail, which is placed horizontally, not, as in the fishes, vertically. The posterior limbs are represented only by small internal vestiges, and the anterior are converted into broad paddles or flippers, consisting of a continuous sheath of the thick integument, within which are present representatives of all the bones usually found in the fore-limb of mammals. The fish-like aspect is further increased by the presence of a dorsal fin, but this is a simple fold of integument, and does not contain bony spines.

The right whale and its allies have no teeth in the adult state, their place being taken by the triangular plates of *baleen* or whalebone which are developed on transverse ridges of the palate, but the fœtal whales possess minute teeth, which are very soon lost. The nostrils open directly upwards on the top of the head, and are closed by valvular folds of integument which are under the control of the animal. When it comes to the surface to breathe, it expels the air violently (popularly known as " blowing " or " spouting "), and the vapour it contains becomes condensed into a cloud, which resembles a column of water and spray; the top of the windpipe is prolonged into a sort of cone that fits into the back of the nasal passages, and enables the animal to swim rapidly through the water with its mouth open, for the purpose of securing prey, without risk of suffocation. The blood-vessels in these animals break up into extensive plexuses or networks, in which a large amount of oxygenated blood is delayed, and they are thus enabled to remain a considerable time under water. Injury to these dilated vessels leads to profuse hemorrhage, and hence the whale is killed by the comparatively trifling wound of the harpoon.

The Cetacea (which are grouped broadly as Mysticeti, or toothless whales; and Odontoceti, Denticeti, or toothed whales) are commonly divided into five families: (1) Balænidæ, or whalebone whales, divided into two sections: smooth whales, with smooth skin and no dorsal fin, and furrowed whales, with furrowed skin and a dorsal fin; (2) Physeteridæ, sperm-whales or cachalots, the palates of which have no baleen-plates, and which are furnished with teeth, developed in the lower jaw only; (3) Delphinidæ, a family possessing teeth in both jaws, and including the dolphins, porpoises, and narwhal; (4) Rhynchoceti, a family allied to the sperm-whales, but having only a pair or two pairs of teeth in the lower jaw, a pointed snout or beak, a single blow-hole, etc.; (5) Zeuglodontidæ, an extinct family, distinguished from all the tooth-bearing whales by the possession of molar teeth implanted by two distinct fangs, etc.

The last family is exclusively confined to the Eocene, Miocene, and Pliocene periods. The genus Protocetus from the Eocene strata of Egypt is particularly interesting, as it forms a connecting link with the primitive extinct Carnivora (Creodonta) from which the Cetacea have undoubtedly taken origin. *See* WHALE.

CETEOSAURUS. Extinct dinosaurian reptile. Its fossil remains, found in the Jurassic oolites, persist into the Wealden beds of the cretaceous period. Examples found at Peterborough and elsewhere show it as a gigantic, small-headed, long-necked reptile, sometimes nearly 70 ft. long and 10 ft. high.

CETERACH (set'ėr-ak). A genus of ferns, subord. Polypodiaceæ, chiefly known by the reticulated veins, the simple sori, with scarcely any indusium, and the abundance of chaffy scales which clothe the under surface of the leaf. One species, *C. officinārum* (the scale-fern or miltwaste), is indigenous to Britain, and common on rocks and walls.

CETEWAYO (kech-wā'ō). A Kaffir chief or king, son of Panda, King of the Zulus. Disturbances as to the succession having arisen in Zululand, Theophilus Shepstone, representative of the Natal Government, secured the recognition of Cetewayo as king in 1873. The latter, however, in spite of the obligations into which he had entered, proved a tyrannical ruler, and maintained a large army. A dispute which had arisen regarding lands on the frontier was settled by arbitration in favour of the Zulus; but on the refusal of Cetewayo to comply with the conditions imposed, war was declared against him by the British, and the king made prisoner soon after the battle of Ulundi (July, 1879). In 1882 he was conditionally restored to part of his dominions. In the following year he was driven from power by the chief Usibepu, and remained under the protection of the British until his death in 1884.

CETINJE. Formerly capital of Montenegro, which is now part of Yugoslavia. It is situated in a valley, and commands a good strategic position about 10 miles inland from the Adriatic. During the European War (1914-8) Cetinje was occupied by the Austrian troops on 13th Jan., 1916. It was occupied by the Serbians on 4th Nov., 1918. Pop. 5500.

CETIOSAU'RUS. The whale-lizard, a genus of gigantic fossil reptiles, some 40 feet long, belonging to the ord. Dinosauria, so named from its supposed resemblance to a whale. It is found in Jurassic strata, and is interesting as a primitive and British type of the still more gigantic Sauropoda of the United States.

CETTE (set). A fortified seaport, France, department of Hérault, upon a peninsula between the Mediterranean and Lake Thau, into which the great canal of Languedoc enters. After Marseilles, Cette is the principal trading port in the south of France, and it is much resorted to as a watering-place. Pop. 35,400.

CET'YL. An alcoholic radical supposed to exist in a series of compounds obtained from spermaceti.

CEUTA (sū'ta). A strongly fortified seaport in Morocco, possessed by the Spaniards, on a peninsula of the African coast opposite Gibraltar, the seat of a bishop. Ceuta is used as a place of transportation for criminals. Pop. 35,219.

CEVADIL'LA. *See* SABADILLA.

CEVENNES (sė-venz'; Lat. *Cebennæ*). A chain of mountains in the south-east of France, in the widest sense extending from the Pyrenees in the south-west to the Vosges in the north-east, the Côte d'Or being sometimes considered as a part of it, sometimes as a part of the Vosges system. The length of the chain, exclusive of the Côte d'Or, is about 330 miles, the average height not more than 3000 feet. It is divided into two sections, the Northern and Southern Cevennes; the dividing-point is Mount Lozère, in the department of the same name, 5582 feet high. The highest peak is Mezenc, 5755 feet.

The Cevennes form the watershed between the Bay of Biscay and the Mediterranean, separating the basins of the Garonne and Loire from those of the Rhone and Saône. They are rich in minerals, containing mines of copper, iron, lead, and coal, and quarries of granite, porphyry, marble, and plaster. The Cevennes were the scene of persecutions of the Albigenses, Waldenses, and others holding opinions opposed to those of the Roman Church.

CEYLON (sē-lon′; native name, **Singlaha,** ancient **Taprobănē**). An island belonging to Great Britain in the Indian Ocean, 50 to 60 miles S.E. of the southern extremity of India, from which it is separated by the Gulf of Manaar and Palk Strait, and by a chain of sand-banks, called Adam's Bridge, impassable by any but very small vessels. Length, about 270 miles north to south; average breadth, 100 miles; area, 25,332 sq. miles, or a sixth less than Scotland. The island is pear-shaped —the small end to the north. There are few important indentations. At Trincomalee, on the north-east coast, there is one of the finest natural harbours in the world. Galle, a seaport on the south coast, is a common place of call for vessels; but by far the chief seaport, now provided with a safe and commodious harbour, is Colombo the capital (on the west coast). The north and north-west coasts are flat and monotonous, those on the south and east bold, rocky, and picturesque, with exuberant vegetation. The mountainous regions are confined to the centre of the south and broader part of the island. Their average height is about 2000 feet, but several summits are upwards of 7000 and one over 8000 feet high, the culminating point being Pidurutallagalla, 8296 feet. Adam's Peak, reaching 7420 feet, is the most remarkable from its conical form, the distance from which it is visible from the sea, and from the legend that thence Buddha ascended to heaven, leaving in evidence a gigantic footprint.

Rivers.—The rivers, though numerous, especially on the south and south-west, are merely mountain streams, navigable only by canoes, and that but for a short distance from their mouths. The most important, the Mahawelliganga, which rises near Adam's Peak, and falls into the sea by a number of branches near Trincomalee, has a course of 134 miles, and drains upwards of 4000 sq. miles. There are a few extensive lagoons in the island yielding large quantities of salt, but no lakes worth noticing.

Climate.—In respect of climate, it is found that where the jungle has been cleared away, and the land drained and cultivated, the country is perfectly healthy; but where low wooded tracts and flat marshy lands abound it is malarial and insalubrious. The east part of the island, being exposed to the north-east monsoon, has a hot and dry climate, resembling that of the coast of Coromandel; while the west division, being open to the south-west monsoon, has a temperate and humid climate like that of the Malabar coast. The quantity of rain that falls annually is estimated at three times that of England, the rains being less frequent, but much heavier.

Fauna.—Most of the animals found in India are native to this island, excepting the tiger. Elephants are numerous, especially in the north and east provinces, and licences for their capture and exportation are issued by Government. The wild life of the island includes bears, buffaloes, leopards, hyenas, jackals, monkeys, wild hogs, several species of deer, porcupines, armadilloes, mongooses, the pangolin or scaly ant-eater, the loris or Ceylon sloth, flying-foxes, crocodiles, numerous snakes, partly poisonous, and a great variety of birds of brilliant plumage.

Products.—In the luxuriance of its vegetable productions Ceylon rivals the islands of the Indian Archipelago, and in some respects bears a strong resemblance to them. Its most valuable products are tea and coco-nuts, with rice, cinnamon (which is found almost exclusively in the south-west), cacao, areca-nuts, rubber, timber. Codee used to be very extensively cultivated, but disease has reduced the produce to a mere fraction of its former amount, and tea cultivation has taken its place, tea being now by far the chief export.

The south parts of the island produce the jaggery-palm, the sap of which yields a coarse sugar, and its fruit a substitute for rice-flour. The taliput-palm, the jack and bread-fruit trees are abundant, and the Ceylon areca-nut, celebrated for its superior qualities, is exported in large quantities. Excellent tobacco is raised in the north district. The island abounds with timber of various descriptions, including ebony, satin, rose, sapan, iron, jack, and other beautiful woods adapted for cabinet work. Attention has been directed with success to the cultivation of rubber trees.

The chief mineral products are plumbago or graphite (there being about 2800 mines), and a variety of gems, including sapphires, rubies, etc. The pearl-fisheries are famous, but, for some unexplained reason, sometimes fail for years, having been unproductive between 1837 and 1854, and between 1863 and 1874. When the pearl-fishery is in existence it is confined to the Gulf of Manaar. In Jan., 1906, the fisheries were leased to an English company for twenty years, conditional upon the expenditure of stipulated sums for improvements; but the lease was

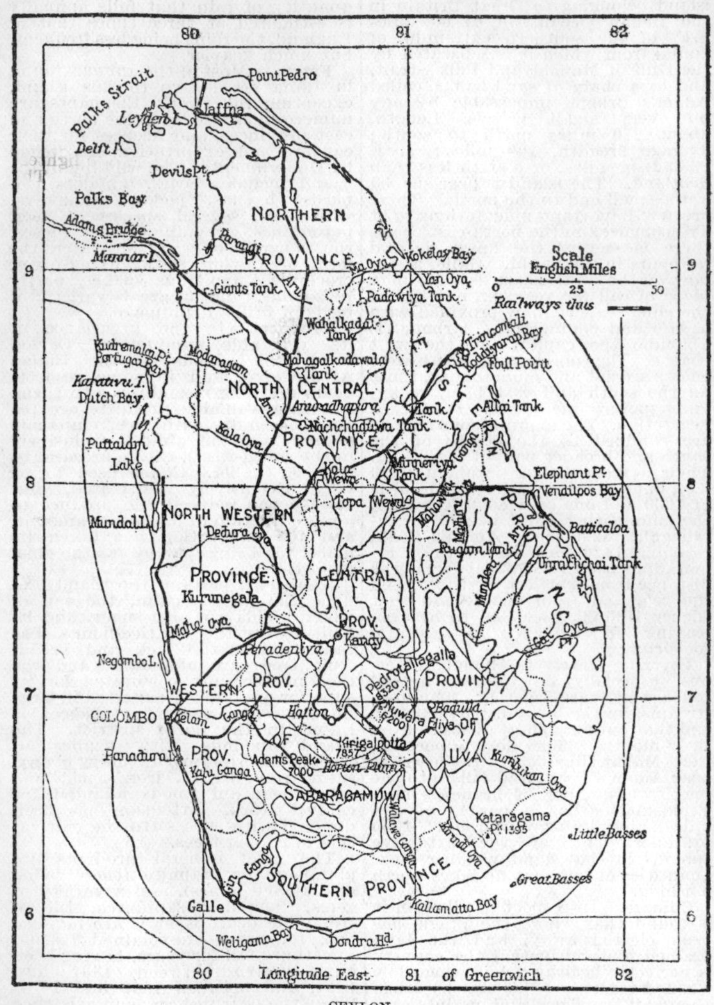
80
81
82
Palks Strait
Point Pedro
Jaffna
Leyden I.
Delft I.
Devils Pt.
Palks Bay
Adams Bridge
Mannar I.
NORTHERN
PROVINCE
Parangi
Aru
Ma Oya
Kokelay Bay
Yan Oya
Scale
English Miles
0
25
50
Railways thus
9
Giants Tank
Padawiya Tank
Wahalkadai Tank
Trincomali
Koddiyarab Bay
Foul Point
Kudremalai Pt.
Portugal Bay
Modaragam
Aru
Mahagalkadawala Tank
Karativu I.
Dutch Bay
NORTH CENTRAL
Anuradhapura
Tank
Allai Tank
Nachchaduwa Tank
PROVINCE
Kala Oya
Puttalam
Lake
Minneriya Tank
Kala Wewa
Elephant Pt.
Vendilpos Bay
8
Topa Wewa
NORTH WESTERN
Mundal L.
Deduru Oya
Batticaloa
Pugam Tank
Unnichchai Tank
PROVINCE
Kurunegala
CENTRAL
PROV.
Kandy
Maha Oya
Peradeniya
Negombo L.
Pedrotallagalla
8320
PROVINCE
WESTERN
PROV.
7
COLOMBO
Kelani Ganga
Hatton
Nuwara Eliya
6200
Badulla
OF
Kirigalpotta
7857
Panadura
PROV.
Adams Peak
7000
Horton Plains
UVA
Kumbukan Oya
Kalu Ganga
SABARAGAMUWA
Walawe Ganga
Katagarama
Pt. 1395
Little Basses
Great Basses
SOUTHERN PROVINCE
Galle
Kallamatta Bay
6
Weligama Bay
Dondra Hd.
80
Longitude East
81
of Greenwich
82

CEYLON

later terminated, and the fishery is now a Government monopoly.

Commerce.—The commerce of Ceylon is now important. The total value of exports in recent years has been about £30,000,000 annually (over £16,000,000 to Britain); the value of imports is about £25,000,000 (over £5,000,000 from the United Kingdom). The exports comprise tea, plumbago, areca-nuts, coco-nut oil, fibre, and kernels (copra), cinnamon, rubber, cacao, coffee, etc. The principal articles of import are manufactured goods chiefly from Great Britain, as cotton manufactures, apparel and haberdashery, iron and steel manufactures, machinery, etc.; from other countries dried fish, rice, wheat, sugar, tea, cowries, etc. The island is provided with a system of excellent roads, and the railways had a length of about 951 miles (in 1929), since then several new lines have been surveyed. The chief industry is agriculture; manufactures (coir-matting, baskets, cotton cloth, etc.) are unimportant. The Ceylon currency consists of rupees (present value about 1*s.* 6*d.*) and cents. The weights and measures are those of Britain.

Government.—Ceylon is one of the British Crown colonies, the Government being conducted by a Governor and two Councils, executive and legislative, of both of which the Governor is president. The first is composed of nine members, excluding the Governor; the other of forty-nine members, exclusive of the Governor. The powers of the Councils are limited, being wholly subordinate to the Governor, who can carry into effect any law without their concurrence. All laws, before being acted on, must be approved of by the Secretary of State. Any individual properly qualified may be appointed to the most responsible situation, without reference to service, nation, or religion.

The island is divided into nine provinces—the Eastern, Western, Northern, Southern, Central, North-Central, North-Western, Uva, Sabaragamuwa, which again are subdivided into districts. The chief sources of revenue are the customs duties, railway receipts, land-rents and sales, licences and salt-farms. The revenue and expenditure for 1929–30 are £9,371,836 and£8,882,656 respectively. The public debt for public works alone amounted in 1930 to £15,639,693, but sinking funds for their redemption were accumulated amounting to £4,889,026.

Population.—The present population of Ceylon is composed of Singhalese or Cingalese, who are the Ceylonese proper, Tamils (from India), Moormen or Moors, Malays, Veddahs, a small proportion of Europeans and their descendants, and negroes. The Singhalese are in stature rather below the middle size; their limbs slender, but well-shaped; eyes dark; finely-cut features; hair long, smooth, and black, turned up and fixed with a tortoise-shell comb on the top of the head; colour varying from brown to black, or rather from the lightest to the darkest tints of bronze. The general population of the island was decreasing for several centuries. It is now, however, on the increase, and recently this increase has been rapid. In 1911 the population was 4,110.367; the census population in 1921 was 4,504,549, of whom 8099 were Europeans. In 1921 the Singhalese numbered 3,015,970, the Tamils 1,119,699. The present population is 5,312,548 (est.).

Religion.—Buddhism prevails in the interior, and generally among the Singhalese of the sea-coasts. The Singhalese have a colloquial language peculiar to themselves, but their classic and sacred writings are either in Pali or Sanskrit. The Hindu religion (Brahmanism) prevails among the Tamils or population of Indian extraction, which forms a large proportion of the inhabitants of the north and north-east districts. The Tamils speak their own Tamil tongue. The Government has a department of public instruction, and the total number of scholars in Government and other schools is about 410,000. On the west and south-west coast numbers of the Singhalese are Roman Catholics, and there are various Protestant churches and chapels. The total number of Christians in 1920 was 443,400, of whom over 200,000 are Roman Catholics.

History.—The Singhalese possess a native chronicle, the *Mahawansa* (translated by Turnour and Wijesinha), which records the history of the island from 543 B.C. to A.D. 1818, under a long series of kings reigning most frequently at the ancient capital Anuradhapura, the earliest of these being leader of an invading host from India. Buddhism was introduced 307 B.C. These incomers brought with them the civilisation of India; great part of the country became covered with towns and villages having temples and dagobas, agriculture flourished, and the aborigines (represented by the Veddahs of to-day) were compelled to construct artificial lakes, tanks, and other irrigation works. The capital, Anuradhapura, as its ruins still testify, was a place of great extent and magnificence.

The island was not known to Europeans till the time of Alexander the Great, and their knowledge of it was long vague and meagre. By the time of Pliny it had become better known, and he gained much additional information from Ceylonese envoys that were sent to Rome. In the Middle Ages the country was much troubled by invasions of the Malabars, and for a time it was even tributary to China. It had greatly declined in prosperity when visited by Europeans, the first of whom was Marco Polo in the end of the thirteenth century. At its most flourishing period its population was probably ten times as great as at present.

Little, however, was known in Europe regarding the island until 1505, when the Portuguese established a regular intercourse with it, and subsequently made themselves masters of it. When they arrived, the Malabars were in possession of the north, the Moors or Arabs held all the seaports, the rest was under petty kings and chiefs. The Portuguese, who were cruel and oppressive rulers, were subsequently expelled by the Dutch in 1658, after a twenty years' struggle. The Dutch in turn were driven from the island by the British in 1796, though a part of the island remained independent under native princes. The King of Kandy, nominally the sovereign of the island, was deposed in 1815 on account of his cruelties, and the island was then finally annexed by Britain, though a rebellion had to be put down in 1817. The principal towns are Colombo (the capital and chief port), Kandy, Galle, Jaffna, and Trincomalee.—BIBLIOGRAPHY: E. Carpenter, *Ceylon*; Constance F. Gordon-Cumming, *Two Happy Years in Ceylon*; S. M. Burrows, *The Buried Cities of Ceylon*; G. E. Mitton, *The Lost Cities of Ceylon*; *Oxford Survey of British Empire* (vol. ii): R. Knox, *An Historical Relation of Ceylon*; J. C. W. Pereira, *The Laws of Ceylon*.

CÉZANNE, Paul. French painter. Born Jan. 19, 1839, his earlier work was influenced by Poussin and El Greco. Swayed by the contemporary tendencies represented by Manet and Pissarro, he sought to portray nature in the presence of subtle manifestations of light. Some of his choicest work is now in the Louvre. He died Oct. 23, 1906.

CHABAZITE. A mineral hydrous aluminium calcium silicate with some potassium and sodium, of the Zeolite group, crystallizing in forms that are very nearly cubes. It is colourless, and is common as a product of hydrothermal action in the cavities of basaltic lavas.

CHABLAIS (shȧ-blā). A district of France, in Savoy, south of the Lake of Geneva. In the eleventh century Chablais passed from the possession of the House of Burgundy to that of Savoy, and was finally ceded to France with the rest of Savoy in 1860.

CHABLIS (shȧ-blē). A town, France, department of Yonne, famous for white wines of a beautifully clear and limpid colour, good body, and extreme delicacy of flavour. Pop. 2300.

CHABOT (shȧ-bō), **François.** One of the leading Jacobins of the French Revolution, born in 1759. Being chosen Deputy to the National Convention, he displayed the greatest zeal in the propagation of revolutionary ideas, and in denouncing the court. The conversion of the cathedral of Notre-Dame into the Temple of Reason is said to have originated with Chabot. He at last became suspected by his party, appealed in vain to Robespierre, and attempted to poison himself, but was guillotined in 1794.

CHACO. *See* GRAN CHACO.

CHAD. *See* TCHAD.

CHÆRONEA (kē-ro-nē′a). An ancient Greek town in Bœotia, famous as the scene of a battle fought 338 B.C., when Philip of Macedon crushed the liberties of Greece. Plutarch was born at Chæronea.

CHÆTODONTIDÆ. *See* SQUAMIPENNES.

CHA′FER. A term loosely applied to certain insects of the beetle order, especially those which feed on leaves in the adult state.

CHAFF-CUTTER. An agricultural instrument for chopping hay or straw into short lengths to be used as food for animals. The economical advantage of the chaff-cutter does not depend on its rendering the chopped food more digestible, but on permitting it to be more thoroughly mixed with the more nutritive and palatable food, and preventing the animal from rejecting any part of it. By the use of the chaff-cutter animals are therefore induced to consume a much larger proportion of fodder with their food, which not only improves the condition of the stock, but saves time in feeding, thus allowing the animal more time for digestion. The best type of chaff-cutter now in use is the radial wheel-knife. By the Chaff-cutting Machines Act,

1897, it is provided that a machine worked by motive-power must be fitted with a contrivance to prevent accidents.

CHAFF'INCH (*Fringilla cœlebs*). A lively and handsome bird of the finch family, very common in Britain, where its haunts are chiefly gardens

Male Chaffinch

and shrubberies, hedgerows, plantations, etc. The eggs are usually five in number, and are greenish in colour with purple blotches. The male is 6 or 7 inches in length, and is very

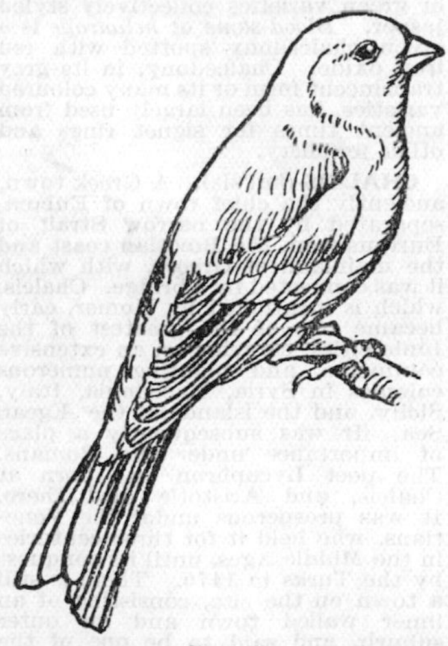

Chaffinch

agreeably coloured, having a chestnut back, reddish-pink breast and throat, and a yellowish-white bar on the wings. The food consists of seeds and of insects and their larvæ. The nest, which is generally placed in the fork of a tree, is often covered with moss and lichens.

CHAGOS (chā'gōs) **ISLANDS.** A group of islands in the Indian Ocean belonging to Britain; a southward extension of the Maldive Islands. The largest, called Diego Garcia or Great Chagos, 100 miles S. of the main group, is about 15 miles long by 3 miles broad. They are scantily peopled, and the chief product is coco-nut oil. Pop. about 2000.

CHAGOS. Group of coral atolls south of the Maldives in the Indian Ocean. On the direct route from the Red Sea to Australia, the group is administered from Mauritius. Total area 76 sq. miles. Pop. about 1000.

CHAGRES (chă'gres). A seaport of America, on the north coast of the Isthmus of Panama, at the mouth of the Chagres River, formerly of some importance.

CHAILLU, Paul Belloni Du. French explorer. Born 31st July, 1835, he led an expedition into Central Africa, where he spent four years. His book, translated into English as *Explorations and Adventures in Equatorial Africa*, 1861, was regarded by some as fiction owing to its accounts of the strange men and animals encountered, but later it was admitted as true. After another expedition he wrote *A Journey to Ashango Land*, 1867. Chaillu then turned his attention to Russia and a series of journeys there produced several books, including *The Viking Age*, 1889. He died in St. Petersburg, 29th April, 1903.

CHAIN. In surveying, a measure of length 22 yards or 66 feet (the length of a cricket-pitch), subdivided into 100 equal parts called *links*. 10 chains=1 furlong; 10 sq. chains =1 acre. It is now a common unit in elementary arithmetic.

CHAIN-ARMOUR. Coats and other pieces of mail, formed of hammered iron links, constituting a flexible garment which fitted to the person. See illustration, p. 528.

CHAINS. Strong links or plates of iron, the lower ends of which are bolted to a ship's side, used to contain the blocks called *dead-eyes*, by which the shrouds of the masts are fastened.

CHAIN-SHOT. An obsolete form of ammunition consisting of two cannon-balls connected by a chain, which, when discharged, revolved upon their shorter axis, and mowed down masts, rigging, etc.

CHAIR OF ST. PETER. At Rome, a wooden chair overlaid with ivory-work and gold, first mentioned by Ennodius in A.D. 500, and in honour of which a feast was instituted by Paul IV. in 1658.

Fourteenth-Century Chain-Armour

CHALAZOGAMY. In seed-plants, the condition in which the pollen-tube enters the ovule through the basal end of chalaza, instead of, as is normally the case, through the micropyle (porogamy); it is found in many primitive dicotyledons, e.g. Casuarina, elm, walnut, *Betulaceæ*, *Fagaceæ*.

CHALCE'DON (kalsē'don). A Greek city of ancient Bithynia, opposite Byzantium (Constantinople), at the entrance of the Black Sea, about 2 miles S. of the modern Scutari. It was a flourishing town when it came into the possession of the Romans, under the testament of Nicomedes, 74 B.C., as included in the kingdom of Bithynia. It was finally destroyed by the Turks, by whom it was taken about 1075. In ecclesiastical history it is important as the place at which, in 451, Marcian held the fourth general council for destroying the influence of Dioscuros and the Monophysites by formulating the belief in the existence of two natures in Christ.

CHALCEDONY (kal-sed'ō-ni). A mineral form of silica composed of minute crystalline particles or fibres, commonly filling or partially filling cracks and cavities in rocks, and often showing a mammillated surface. It has clearly been deposited from solution, under more rapid conditions than those that promote the growth of quartz. Sometimes it forms nodules replacing limestone and fossil shells. In hardness and specific gravity it resembles quartz, of which it is probably only a minutely crystalline variety.

Its colour is grey and milky; but it is often stained by impurities, as in the fine apple-green *chrysoprase*, the red *sard*, and the dull-red, brown, or green varieties collectively styled jasper. *Blood-stone* or *heliotrope* is a green chalcedony spotted with red iron oxide. Chalcedony, in its grey translucent form or its many coloured varieties, has been largely used from ancient times for signet rings and other jewellery.

CHALCIS (kal'sis). A Greek town, anciently the chief town of Eubœa, separated by the narrow Strait of Euripus from the Bœotian coast and the mainland of Greece, with which it was connected by a bridge. Chalcis, which is mentioned by Homer, early became one of the greatest of the Ionic cities, carrying on an extensive commerce, and planting numerous colonies in Syria, Macedonia, Italy, Sicily, and the islands of the Ægean Sea. It was subsequently a place of importance under the Romans. The poet Lycophron was born at Chalcis, and Aristotle died there. It was prosperous under the Venetians, who held it for three centuries in the Middle Ages, until its conquest by the Turks in 1470. There is still a town on the site, consisting of an inner walled town and an outer suburb, and said to be one of the prettiest and most attractive of Greek provincial towns. A bridge, so constructed as to let vessels pass through, connects it with the mainland. In 1894 the town suffered from an earthquake. Pop. about 13,466.

CHALCOCITE. More correctly *chalcosine*, a deep lead-grey ore of copper, containing 79·85 per cent of the metal. It can be cut with a knife. Excellent crystals have been obtained from Cornish mines.

CHALCONDYLAS (kal-kon′di-las), **Demetrius.** A Greek grammarian, born at Athens about 1424. On the taking of Constantinople by the Turks he came to Italy, was invited to Florence by Lorenzo de' Medici about 1479, and afterwards by Ludovico Sforza to Milan, where he died in 1510 or 1511. He did much to further the study of the Greek language and literature in the west of Europe.

CHALCOPYRITE, or **COPPER PYRITES.** The commonest ore of copper in most mining districts, a joint sulphide of copper and iron, $CuFeS_2$, with 33 per cent of copper. Brass yellow, with a faint greenish tinge, it can be distinguished from iron pyrites by its being easily scratched with a knife, and by its tetrahedral crystal form. Sometimes brilliantly iridescent on the surface (peacock ore).

CHALDÆA. In ancient geography, the southerly part of Babylonia, or in a wider sense corresponding to Babylonia itself. The name Chaldæans was especially applied to a portion of the Babylonian Magi, who were devoted to the pursuit of astronomy and magical science.

CHALDÆAN CHRISTIANS. A branch of the Nestorians, in communion with the Roman Church.

CHALDEE LANGUAGE. A name often given to the Aramaic language (or a dialect of it), one of the principal varieties of the ancient Semitic. Chaldee literature is usually arranged in two divisions: the Biblical Chaldee, or those portions of the Old Testament which are written in Chaldee, namely, Daniel from ii. 4 to vii. 28; Ezra iv. 8 to vi. 18, and vii. 12–26; and Jer. x. 11; and the Chaldee of the Targums and other later Jewish writings.

CHAL′DER. An obsolete Scottish dry measure containing 16 bolls or 12 imperial quarters.

CHAL′DRON. An old English measure of 36 bushels, used chiefly in measuring coal.

CHÂLET (Lat. *castellum*, fort, castle). French-Swiss name for the wooden summer huts of the Swiss herdsmen on the mountains. Picturesque villas built in imitation of Swiss houses are also called châlets.

CHALEUR BAY (sha-lör′). An inlet of the Gulf of St. Lawrence, between Quebec and New Brunswick. The French fleet was here defeated by the British in 1760.

Swiss Châlet

CHALIAPIN. *See* CHALYAPIN.

CHAL′ICE. A term generally applied to a communion cup for the wine in the Eucharist, often of artistic and highly ornamental character. The chalice is the symbol of St. John the Evangelist.

Chalice

CHALK. A pure soft limestone, opaque white, and usually formed by the accumulation of the shells of foraminifera, together with those of larger marine organisms. Occasionally, through the action of pressure or igneous contact, harder forms occur; but the rock does not take a polish. It is one of the purest forms of calcium carbonate in a massive state, and in Europe constitutes thick beds in the Upper Cretaceous series. The white cliffs of southern England and north-western France, the North and South Downs, and Salisbury Plain afford notable examples of its effect on landscape. Chalk is also a name for other substances, natural or artificial, used in drawing, such as coloured "chalks," *French chalk* (steatite), ordinary *crayons*, and even *black chalk*, which is a soft black slate.

CHALL'ENGE. To jurors, is an objection either to the whole panel or array, that is, the whole body of jurors returned, or to the *polls*, that is, to the jurors individually; and it is either *peremptory*, that is, without assigning any reason, or *for cause* assigned. *See* JURY.

CHALLENGER EXPEDITION. A circumnavigating voyage for scientific purposes, organised in 1872 by the British Government on the lines of those carried out by the *Lightning* in 1868, and the *Porcupine* in 1870. On 7th Dec., 1872, the corvette *Challenger* (2306 tons) started from Sheerness, and after a voyage of 68,900 nautical miles, and investigations carried out at 362 stations, reached Spithead on 24th May, 1876. Those on board included Captain Nares as head of a nautical surveying staff, and Professor (later Sir) Wyville Thomson, with scientific assistants. The ship carried every necessary appliance for her work of taking soundings, examining the ocean bed, recording temperatures, currents and atmospheric conditions, and for collecting specimens of the fauna.

The voyage was via Madeira, Canary Islands, West Indies, Nova Scotia, the Azores, Cape Verde, Fernando Noronha, Bahia, Tristan d'Acunha, Cape of Good Hope. Kerguelen, Melbourne, Chinese Sea, Hong-Kong, Japan, Valparaiso, Magellan's Strait, Monte Video, and Vigo. The deepest sounding made was 4575 fathoms, taken between Japan and the Admiralty Isles. The results of the expedition were fully recorded in the *Reports on the Scientific Results of the Voyage of H.M.S. Challenger*, which, edited by Sir Wyville Thomson and Sir John Murray, filled 50 vols.—Cf. H. N. Moseley, *A Naturalist on the Challenger*.

CHALMERS (chä'mėrz), **Alexander.** A British journalist, editor, and miscellaneous writer, born at Aberdeen in 1759, where his father, the founder of the first Aberdeen newspaper, was a printer. About 1777 Chalmers went to London, was employed as journalist, and edited the *British Essayist* (from the *Tatler* to the *Observer*), published 1803. He also issued an edition of Shakespeare, with notes, in 1809; and the works of the English poets from Chaucer to Cowper, with Johnson's *Lives*, and additional *Lives* in 1810. His most extensive work was the *General Biographical Dictionary*, 32 vols., 1812–17. He died in London in 1834.

CHALMERS, George. A Scottish antiquary, born in 1742, studied law at Edinburgh, and removed to America, where he practised for upwards of ten years. On his return he was appointed in 1786 clerk to the Board of Trade, an office held by him till his death in 1825. He published various political and statistical works, but afterwards turned his attention in a great measure from political science to literature. In 1790 he published his life of Daniel Defoe, and in 1794 his life of Thomas Ruddiman. In 1800 he edited the works of Allan Ramsay, and in 1806 the writings of Sir David Lindsay; but his chief work was his *Caledonia*, of which the first volume was published in 1807, a laborious historical and topographical account of North Britain from the most ancient to recent times. Only three volumes were published during Chalmers's lifetime, but he left the remainder of the work nearly ready for the press, and the complete work was published in 7 vols., 1888–93.

CHALMERS, Thomas, D.D. An eminent Scottish divine, born in 1780, at Anstruther Easter, Fife. At the age of twelve he was sent from the parish school to the University of St. Andrews, and after studying there seven years, was licensed as a preacher in July, 1799. During the two following years he studied mathematics and chemistry in Edinburgh, and then became assistant to the professor of mathematics at St. Andrews. In 1803 he was presented to the parish of Kilmany, in Fife, where he made a high reputation as a preacher. In 1804 he was unsuccessful in his application for the chair of natural philosophy at St. Andrews, and in 1805 failed to obtain the same chair in Edinburgh University. In 1808 he published an *Inquiry into the Extent and Stability of National Resources*. In 1813 his article on Christianity appeared in the *Edinburgh Encyclopædia*, and shortly afterwards his review of Cuvier's *Theory of the Earth*, in the *Christian Instructor*.

His fame as a preacher had by this time extended itself throughout Scotland, and in 1815 he was inducted to the Tron Church of Glasgow. His astronomical discourses delivered there in the following winter produced a sensation not only in the city but throughout the country, 20,000 copies selling in the first year of their publication.

It was while pastor of this church that he developed his scheme for the reorganization of the parochial system with a view to more efficient work among the destitute and outcast classes, his influence leading to a considerable extension of the means of popular instruction, both religious and secular.

In 1819 he was transferred from the Tron to St. John's, a church built and endowed expressly for him by the Town Council of Glasgow, but his health having been tried by overwork he accepted, in 1823, the chair of moral philosophy at St. Andrews. In 1827 he was elected to the divinity chair in the University of Edinburgh, an appointment which he continued to hold till the disruption from the Scottish Church in 1843.

In 1832 he published his *Political Economy*, and shortly afterwards his Bridgewater Treatise *On the Adaptation of External Nature to the Moral and Intellectual Constitution of Man*. During this period he was occupied with the subject of church extension on the voluntary principle, but it was in the great non-intrusion movement in the Scottish Church that his name became most prominent. Throughout the whole contest to the disruption in 1843, he acted as the leader of the party that then separated from the Establishment, and may be regarded as the founder of the Free Church of Scotland, of the first assembly of which he was moderator. Having vacated his professorial chair in Edinburgh University, he was appointed principal and primarius professor of divinity in the new college of the Free Church.

In addition to his duties in these posts, he continued in Edinburgh his zealous labours for the elevation of the "home-heathen," giving a practical exemplification of his schemes by the establishment of a successful mission in the West Port. His death took place suddenly, and apparently during sleep, in the night preceding 31st May, 1847. He was a D.D. of Glasgow University and a D.C.L. of Oxford.—BIBLIOGRAPHY: Mrs. Oliphant, *Thomas Chalmers: Philosopher and Statesman*; Blaikie, *Thomas Chalmers*; Fraser, *Thomas Chalmers*; Dr. W. Hanna, *Memoirs*.

CHALON-SUR-SAÔNE (shä-lõṇ-sůr-sõn). A town of France, department of Saône-et-Loir, on the right bank of the Saône, which here becomes navigable for steamboats, and at the commencement of the Canal du Centre. It has a cathedral of the thirteenth century, a fine river quay, an exchange, communal college, etc. There are foundries, dyeworks, etc., and a flourishing trade. Pop. 32,533.

CHÂLONS-SUR-MARNE (shä-lõṇ-sůr-mȧrn). A city of France, capital of the department Marne (Champagne), on the right bank of the River Marne. The principal public buildings are the cathedral, a fine edifice in the Gothic style; three other interesting Gothic churches; the Hotel de Ville, built in 1772; the Hotel de la Prefecture, built in 1764, one of the finest buildings of the kind in France. There are manufactures of woollen and cotton goods; also cotton mills, tanneries, etc. It was known to the Romans as *Catalauni*, and in 451 Attila was defeated before the walls of Châlons (Catalaunian Fields). From the tenth century it flourished as an independent state under counts-bishops, having about 60,000 inhabitants. After being united to the French Crown in 1360, it declined. A celebrated camp was established by Napoleon III., in 1856, about 18 miles from Châlons for the purpose of training the French troops, still to some extent employed. Pop. 32,307.

CHALYAPIN, Fyodor Ivanovitsh. Famous Russian singer, born at Kazan in 1873. The son of peasants, Chalyapin was a shoemaker in his early youth until he was admitted into the cathedral choir of his native town. In 1890, whilst already singing in an opera company, he was obliged to work as a railway porter, his emoluments not being sufficient to support him. He sang at Tiflis in 1892 and at Petrograd in 1894, and has established his reputation since. In 1913 and 1914 he was a member of the Beecham Opera Company, and appeared at Drury Lane in *Boris Godunov* and *Ivan the Terrible*. He has appeared successfully in many rôles. In 1927 he was deprived by the Soviet of his title "People's Artist."

CHALYBEATE WATERS (ka-lib′ē-ȧt). Waters holding iron in solution, either as a carbonate or as a sulphate with or without other salts. All waters containing iron are distinguished by their styptic, inky taste.

CHALYBITE. Native iron carbonate ($FeCO_3$), also called *siderite*. It is a common ore, crystallizing like calcite, with more frequent occurrence of rhombohedra as the crystal form. The cleavage breaks it up easily into rhombohedral blocks; specific gravity, 3·8. An argillaceous concretionary variety is called *clay-ironstone*, and occurs frequently in the coal-measures as an important ore of iron. *Blackband* is a carbonaceous clay-ironstone.

CHAMA kā'ma). The gaping cockle, a genus of large marine bivalves. The giant clam (*Chama gigas*) is the largest shell yet discovered, sometimes measuring 4 feet across. It is found in the Indian Ocean.

CHAMÆROPS (ka-mē'rops). A genus of palms belonging to the northern hemisphere, and consisting of dwarf trees with fan-shaped leaves borne on prickly petioles, and a small berry-like fruit with one seed. The *C. humilis* is the only native European palm. It does not extend farther north than Nice. The fibres of its leaves form an article of commerce under the name of *crin végétal* (vegetable hair). A Chinese species, *C. Fortunei*, is quite hardy in the south of England.

CHAM'ALARI, or CHAM'ALHARI. A peak of the Himalaya Mountains, at the western extremity of the boundary line between Bhutan and Tibet. Height, 23,929 feet.

CHAMBER. A word used in many countries to designate a branch of Government whose members assemble in a common apartment, as the *Chamber* of Deputies in France, or applied to bodies of various kinds meeting for various purposes. The *imperial chamber* (in Ger. *Reichskammergericht*) of the old German Empire was a court established at Wetzlar, near the Rhine, by Maximilian I. in 1495, to adjust the disputes between the different independent members of the German Empire, and also such as arose between them and the emperor.—*Chambers of Commerce* are associations of the mercantile men of towns for the purpose of protecting and furthering the interests of the commercial community.

CHAMBERLAIN (chām'bėr-lin). An officer charged with the direction and management of the private apartments of a monarch or nobleman. The *lord chamberlain* or *lord great-chamberlain* of Great Britain is the sixth officer of the Crown. His functions, always important, have varied in different reigns. Among them are the dressing and attending on the king at his coronation; the care of the palace of Westminster (Houses of Parliament); and attending upon peers at their creation. The office of *Lord Chamberlain of the Household* is quite distinct from that of the Great-Chamberlain, and is changed with the administration. This officer has the control of all parts of the household (except the Ladies of the Queen's bed-chamber) which are not under the direction of the Lord Steward, the groom of the stole, or the Master of the Horse. The king's (queen's) chaplains, physicians, surgeons, etc., as well as the royal tradesmen, are appointed by him; the companies of actors at the royal theatres are under

Chamberlain

his regulation; and he is also the licenser of plays. He has under him a vice chamberlain.—Cf. W.R. Anson, *Law and Custom of the Constitution.*

CHAMBERLAIN, Arthur Neville. Born in Birmingham, March 18, 1869; he was the younger son of Joseph Chamberlain and half-brother of Sir Austen Chamberlain. Educated at Rugby, he was in business in the West Indies, afterwards taking part in the public life of Birmingham. In 1915 he was lord mayor of the city. In 1916 he was appointed Director of National Service, and in 1918 he entered Parliament as M.P. for a Birmingham division. He was Postmaster-General, Minister of

Health, and then Chancellor of the Exchequer in the Unionist ministry of 1922–24, and throughout the ministry of 1924–29 was a most energetic and successful Minister of Health. Chairman of the Conservative party organisation, 1930–31, he then became Chancellor again.

CHAMBERLAIN, Sir Austen. British politician, eldest son of Rt. Hon. Joseph Chamberlain, born in 1863, and educated at Rugby and Trinity College, Cambridge. He entered Parliament as Liberal-Unionist member for East Worcestershire in 1892, and was Civil Lord of the Admiralty from 1895 to 1900. In 1900 he became Financial Secretary to the Treasury, in 1902 Postmaster-General, and in 1903 Chancellor of the Exchequer. He was Secretary of State for India, 1915–17 ; a member of the War Cabinet, 1918–19 ; Chancellor of the Exchequer, 1919–21 ; and became Lord Privy Seal and Leader of the House of Commons in March, 1921. He became Secretary of State for Foreign Affairs and Deputy Leader of the House of Commons in Nov., 1924. He was largely responsible for the signing of the Locarno Pact, and was made K.G. in 1925. He was Foreign Secretary until 1929.

In 1926 he was awarded the Nobel Prize.

CHAMBERLAIN, Joseph. British statesman, born in London in 1836, and educated at University College School, London. He became a member of a firm of screw-makers at Birmingham, but gave up active connection with the business in 1874. He early became prominent in Birmingham both in connection with civic and political affairs, being an advanced Radical and an able speaker, was chairman of the school board, and thrice in succession mayor of the city (1874–76). In 1876 he entered Parliament as a representative of Birmingham, and at the general election of 1880 he was chosen for the same city along with Bright and Muntz. Under Gladstone's premiership he now became President of the Board of Trade, and a Cabinet Minister, and was able to pass the Bankruptcy Act now in force, though he failed with his Merchant Shipping Bill.

In the Gladstone Government of 1886 he was President of the Local Government Board; but his leader's Irish policy caused him to resign, and afterwards, as member for West Birmingham, he was one of the most pronounced members of the Liberal-Unionist party. As Colonial Secretary from 1895 to 1903, he was one of the first to perceive the importance for Great Britain of a closer bond uniting the dominions to the mother-country. In order to counteract German and American competition in the domains of commerce and industry, he conceived the idea of creating an imperial federation by means of a solidarity of economic interests.

He resigned in 1903 from the Balfour Cabinet, in order to be able to advocate more freely his policy of fiscal changes and tariff reform. A tariff union, Chamberlain maintained, was sure to lead to a political union, and would prove the best means to make the colonies interested in the defence of the empire. He failed, however, in his endeavours, as protection did not appeal to the majority of the nation. He was seized by serious illness in 1906, and from that time till his death on 2nd July, 1914, was unable to take any active part in public life.—BIBLIOGRAPHY: Jeyes, *Mr. Chamberlain: his Life and Public Career* ; Creswicke, *Life of Joseph Chamberlain* ; Mackintosh, *Joseph Chamberlain.*

CHAMBERS. Term used for rooms in which barristers do their work before appearing in court. In London, the buildings in the Temple, Lincoln's Inn, and Gray's Inn are given up to chambers.

Another kind of chambers are those in the courts of law in London. In these questions preliminary to trials are decided, and applications of all kinds in connection with forthcoming trials are made. Questions of costs are often settled in chambers. In the chancery division the cases in chambers are heard by masters. In the King's Bench division, one of the judges sits in chambers.

CHAMBERS (chām'bėrz), **Ephraim.** A miscellaneous writer, and compiler of a popular *Dictionary of Arts and Sciences,* born at Kendal, in Westmorland, in the latter part of the seventeenth century. During his apprenticeship to a mathematical instrument and globe maker in London, he formed the design of compiling a *Cyclopædia,* and even wrote some of the articles for it behind his master's counter. The first edition was published in 1728. Several subsequent editions appeared previously to his death in 1740, and it was the basis of the *Cyclopædia* of Dr. Abraham Rees.

CHAMBERS, Robert. Historical and miscellaneous writer, the younger of two brothers originally composing the publishing firm of W. & R. Chambers, born at Peebles in 1802, his father being a muslin weaver. Along with his brother William, who was his senior by two years, he received his education at the Peebles parish school and in the High School of Edinburgh. His family experiencing a reverse of fortune, he got together all the books belonging to his mother and himself, their value being about £2, and at the age of sixteen commenced business as a bookseller in Edinburgh. His elder brother William established himself in the neighbourhood as a printer, and they united in projecting and issuing a short-lived periodical called the *Kaleidoscope*, Robert being editor and chief contributor, and William printer. Robert's *Illustrations of the Author of Waverley* and his *Traditions of Edinburgh* (1823) won a ready popularity, and various other works followed in quick succession from this period till 1832: *Popular Rhymes of Scotland* (1827), *Picture of Scotland* (1827), *Histories of the Scottish Rebellions*, and a *Life of James I*.

He next edited *Scottish Ballads and Songs*, a *Biographical Dictionary of Eminent Scotsmen*, and on the 4th of Feb., 1832, the brothers commenced *Chambers's Edinburgh Journal*, which achieved an immense success. From this time W. & R. Chambers united in the publishing business, and issued a series of works for the entertainment and instruction of "the people." Robert Chambers contributed numerous essays to the *Journal*, besides editing or compiling many instructive works of a high class, including the *Cyclopœdia of English Literature*, the *Domestic Annals of Scotland*, *Ancient Sea-Margins*, and the *Book of Days*. He also edited a valuable edition of Burns. He died at St. Andrews in 1871. His name was long associated with the authorship of the famous *Vestiges of Creation*, and it was not known to be really his till years after his death.—Cf. William Chambers, *The Story of a Long and Busy Life*.

CHAMBERS, William. Wrote *Things as they are in America*; *History of Peeblesshire*; *France: its History and Revolutions*; *Memoir of Robert Chambers, with Autobiographic Reminiscences*; etc. He was twice Lord Provost of Edinburgh, and bore the expense of restoring the old church of St. Giles, Edinburgh. He also presented the town of Peebles with an institution embracing a library, reading-room, museum, etc. He died in 1883, just as a baronetcy was to be conferred on him.

CHAMBERSBURG. A town, United States, Pennsylvania, in a fertile and populous district. Pop. 13,788.

CHAMBERTIN (shäṇ-ber-taṇ). A superior kind of red Burgundy wine, named after the place where it is produced. This wine was a favourite both with Louis XIV. and Napoleon.

CHAMBÉRY (shäṇ-bā-ri). A town of south-east France, capital of department of Savoie. It is an archbishop's see, and contains a cathedral, a castle, now the prefecture, the palace of justice, barracks, etc. The old ramparts have been converted into public walks. In its vicinity are excellent baths, much frequented in summer. It has manufactures and distilleries. Pop. 26,407.

CHAMBORD (shäṇ-bōr). A castle, park, and village near Blois, department of Loir-et-Cher, in France. The splendid castle, in the Renaissance style, was mainly built by Francis I., being begun in 1526, and was completed under Louis XIV. In 1745 it was given by Louis XV. to Marshal Saxe, who died there in 1750. Napoleon gave it to Berthier, and in 1821 a company of Legitimists bought it and gave it to the Duke of Bordeaux. In 1883 the castle passed on to the Parma dynasty, but it was sequestered by the French Government during the European War.

CHAMBORD (shäṇ-bōr), **Henri Charles Ferdinand Marie Dieudonné, Comte de, Duke of Bordeaux.** The last representative of the elder branch of the French Bourbon dynasty, called by his partisans Henry V. of France. He was born in 1820, seven months after the assassination of his father, Prince Charles Ferdinand d'Artois, Duc de Berry. Charles X., after the revolutionary outbreak of 1830, abdicated in his favour; but the young count was compelled to leave the country with the royal title unrecognised by the nation. He lived successively in Scotland, Austria, Italy, and London, keeping a species of court, and occasionally issuing manifestoes.

In 1846 he married the Princess Maria-Theresa, eldest daughter of the Duke of Modena; and in 1851 inherited the domain of Frohsdorf, near Vienna, where for the most part he subsequently resided. While abstaining from violent attempts to seize the crown, he let slip no opportunity of urging his claims, especially after Sedan; but his belief in divine right, his devotion to the see of Rome, and his failure to recognise accomplished facts and modern tendencies, destroyed all chance of his succession. He died at Frohsdorf, in Austria, in 1883, leaving no heir.—Cf. H. de Pène, *Le Comte de Chambord: étudié dans ses voyages et sa correspondance*.

CHAMBRE ARDENTE (shäṇ-br-ȧr-däṇt; *fiery chamber*). The name formerly given in France to an apartment, hung with black and lighted with tapers, in which sentence of death was pronounced on heinous offenders. The name was afterwards more especially given to those extraordinary tribunals which, from the time of Francis I., ferreted out heretics by means of a system of espionage, directed the proceedings against them, pronounced sentence, and also saw it carried into execution. The Chambre Ardente ceased its activity in 1680.—Cf. N. Weiss, *La Chambre Ardente.*

CHAME'LEON (ka-mē'li-on). A genus of reptiles belonging to the Saurian or lizard order, a native of parts of Asia, Africa, and the south of Europe. The best-known species, *Chamæleo africānus* or *C. vulgāris,* has a naked body 6 or 7 inches long, with a prehensile tail of about 5 inches, and feet suitable for grasping branches. The skin is cold to the touch, and con-

Chameleon

tains small grains or eminences of a bluish-grey colour in the shade, but in the light of the sun all parts of the body become of a greyish-brown or tawny colour. It possesses the curious faculty, however, of changing its colour, either in accordance with its environment, or with its temper when disturbed, the change being due to the presence of clear or pigment-bearing contractile cells placed at various depths in the skin, their contractions and dilatations being under the influence of the nervous system. Their power of fasting and habit of inflating themselves gave rise to the fable that they lived on air, but they are in reality insectivorous, taking their prey by rapid movements of a long viscid tongue. In general habit they are dull and torpid.

CHAMELEON MINERAL. A name given to manganate of potassium, because a solution of it changes from green, through a succession of colours, to a rich purple.

CHAMFORT (shaṉ-fōr), **Sebastien-Roch Nicolas.** A French man of letters, wit, and revolutionist, born in 1741. By his success as dramatist, critic, and conversationalist he obtained a place in the French Academy, a pension, and a post at court. An intimate friend of Mirabeau, he threw himself heartily into the Revolution, was secretary to the club of the Jacobins, was one of the first of the storming-party in the attack on the Bastille, and having been employed by Roland in the Bibliothèque Nationale, published the first twenty-six *Tableaux Historiques de la Révolution.* His cynical wit could not, however, restrain itself, and he was denounced and threatened with imprisonment. Rather than undergo it he inflicted fatal injuries upon himself, dying in 1794. He is seen at his best in the collection of *bon mots* published under the title of *Chamfortiana.*

CHAMIER (sham'i-ėr), **Frederick.** An English writer of fiction, born in 1796, died in 1870. He entered the navy, took part in the last campaigns against the French, and distinguished himself in the American War of 1812. He retired in 1833 with the rank of captain. His principal works are: *The Life of a Sailor, Ben Brace, The Arethusa, Jack Adams, Tom Bowline, Jack Malcolm's Log.*

CHAMISSO (shá-mis'ō), **Adelbert de.** German poet, French by birth, born at the castle of Boncourt, in Champagne, in 1781. His family being driven to Berlin by the Revolution, he became, from 1796 to 1798, page to the queen-mother, and afterwards entered the Prussian service, where he remained till 1808. He then revisited France; but shortly after returned to Prussia, and for three years devoted himself to the study of natural science at Berlin. In 1815 he accompanied as naturalist an expedition for the discovery of the north-west passage, and on his return took up his residence at Berlin, where he was appointed superintendent of the botanic garden. He died at Berlin in 1838.

He wrote several works on natural history and botany, and an account of his voyage, but his reputation as a naturalist has been somewhat eclipsed by that which he acquired as a poet. Between 1804 and 1806, in concert with Varnhagen von Ense, he published a collection of poems, under the name of the *Muses' Almanac*; and in 1813 appeared his famous tale, *Peter Schlemihl*, the man who sold his shadow, the plot suggested by a casual question of Fouqué's. Many of his ballads and songs are masterpieces in their way and still maintain their popularity. His collected works, containing his biography by Hitzig and his letters, appeared at Leipzig in 6 vols. (1836–39).

CHAMOIS (sham'wä; *Rupicapra tragus*). A species of goat-like antelope inhabiting high inaccessible mountains in Europe and Western Asia. Its horns, which are about 6 or 7 inches long, are round, almost smooth, perpendicular and straight

Chamois (*Rupicapra tragus*)

until near the tip, where they suddenly terminate in a hook directed backwards and downwards. Its hair is brown in winter, brown-fawn colour in summer, and greyish in spring. The head is of a pale-yellow colour, with a black band from the nose to the ears and surrounding the eyes. The tail is black. Its agility, the nature of its haunts, and its powers of smell render its pursuit an exceedingly difficult and hazardous occupation. The skin of the animal when dressed is extremely soft and supple; but what is commercially known as chamois or "shammy" leather is generally prepared from the skins of goats, sheep, or deer.

CHAMOMILE, or **CAMOMILE** (kam'o-mīl; *Anthĕmis nobilis*). A well-known European plant belonging to the nat. ord. Compositæ. It is perennial, and has slender, trailing, hairy, and branched stems. The flower is white, with a yellow centre. Both

Chamomile
a, Ray floret. *b*, Disc floret.

leaves and flowers are bitter and aromatic. The fragrance is due to the presence of an essential oil, called oil of chamomile, of a light-blue colour when first extracted, and used in the preparation of certain medicines. Both the leaves and the flowers are employed in fomentations and poultices, and also in the form of an infusion as a stimulant or anti-spasmodic. The plant is very abundant in Cornwall and some other parts of England.—Wild chamomile (*Matricaria chamomilla*) is now out of use in

England: but its medicinal properties resemble those of common chamomile, and it is still used in some parts of Europe.—Stinking chamomile (*Anthemis cotula*) is an erect and bare annual weed with a fœtid odour, which grows among corn and on waste ground.

CHAMOND (chä-mōn̦), **St.** A manufacturing town of France, department of Loire, on the railway from St. Etienne to Lyons. It is well built, has an old castle and a handsome parish church; and has silk-factories, large iron-foundries, dye-works, etc. Pop. 15,246.

CHAMOUNI (shȧ-mö-nē), or **Chamonix** (shȧ-mo-nē). A celebrated valley in France, department of Haute-Savoie, in the Pennine Alps, over 3000 feet above sea-level. It is about 12 miles long, by 1 to 6 miles broad, its east side formed by Mont Blanc and other lofty mountains of the same range, and it is traversed by the Arve. The mountains on the east side are always snow-clad, and from these proceed numerous glaciers, such as the Glacier de Bossons and the Mer de Glace. The village of Chamouni (pop. 1500), which owes its origin to the Benedictine convent founded between 1088 and 1099, is much frequented by tourists, and is one of the points from which they visit Mont Blanc.

CHAMPAGNE. An ancient province of France, which before the Revolution formed one of the twelve great military governments of the kingdom. It forms at present the departments of Marne, Haute-Marne, Aube, Ardennes, and part of those of Yonne, Aisne, Seine-et-Marne, and Meuse. Troyes was the capital. Fierce fighting took place in the Champagne during the European War.

CHAMPAGNE (sham-pān′). A French wine, white or red, which is made chiefly in the department of Marne, in the former province of Champagne, and is generally characterized by the property of creaming, frothing, or effervescing when poured from the bottle, though there are also *still* Champagne wines. The creaming or slightly sparkling Champagne wines are more highly valued by connoisseurs, and fetch greater prices than the full-frothing wines, in which the small quantity of alcohol they contain escapes from the froth as it rises to the surface, carrying with it the aroma and leaving the liquor nearly vapid. The property of creaming or frothing possessed by these wines is due to the fact that they are partly fermented in the bottle, carbonic acid being thereby produced. Wine of a similar kind can, of course, be made elsewhere, and some of the German champagnes are hardly to be distinguished from the French.

CHAM′PARTY, or **CHAMPERTY** (Lat. *campi partitio*, a dividing of land). In *law*, a bargain with the plaintiff or defendant in any suit to have part of the land, debt, or other thing sued for, if the party that undertakes it prevails therein; the champertor meanwhile furnishing means to carry on the suit. Such bargains are illegal.

CHAMP-DE-MARS. That is, Field of Mars, an extensive piece of ground in Paris, used as a place of military exercise. It was here that Louis XVI. swore to defend the new constitution in 1790, and it was the site of the exhibitions of 1867, 1878, 1889, and 1900. At one end of the Champ the Eiffel Tower was built for the exhibition of 1889.

CHAMPERICO (chȧm-pā′ri-kō). A seaport of Guatemala, on the Pacific, connected with the interior by railway. Pop. 2000.

CHAMPIGNON (sham-pin′yon). A name given to the common mushroom of Britain (*Agaricus campestris*), also to the edible fairy-ring fungus *Marasmius oreades*.

CHAM′PION OF THE KING. A person whose office it was at the coronation of English monarchs to ride armed into Westminster Hall, and make challenge that if any man should deny the king's title to the crown he was ready to defend it in single combat. The custom dates back to William the Conqueror, and in the time of Richard III. it became hereditary in the Dymoke family. It was last observed at the coronation of George IV.

CHAMPLAIN (shän̦-plan̦), **Samuel.** A French naval officer and maritime explorer, born about 1570. His exploits in the maritime war against Spain in 1595 attracted the attention of Henry IV., who commissioned him in 1603 to found establishments in North America. After three voyages for that purpose, in the last of which he founded Quebec, he was in 1620 appointed Governor of Canada. He wrote an account of his voyages, and died in 1635.

CHAMPLAIN (sham-plān′), **LAKE.** A lake, chiefly in the United States, between the states of New York and Vermont, but having the north end of it in Canada; extreme length, north to south, about 120 miles; breadth, from half a mile to 15 miles; area, about 600 sq. miles. It is connected by canal with the Hudson River, and has for outlet the River

Richelieu, or Sorel, flowing north to the St. Lawrence. Its scenery is beautiful, and attracts many visitors. The naval battle of Lake Champlain was fought on 11th Sept., 1814, between a British fleet and an American squadron.

CHAMPOLLION (shäṇ-pol-yōṇ), **Jean François.** French Egyptologist, born at Figeac, department of Lot, in 1790. At an early age he devoted himself to the study of Hebrew, Arabic, Coptic, etc., and in 1809 became professor of history at Grenoble. He soon, however, retired to Paris, where, with the aid of the trilingual inscription of the Rosetta Stone and the suggestions thrown out by Dr. Thomas Young, he at length discovered the key to the graphic system of the Egyptians, the three elements of which—figurative, ideographic, and alphabetic—he expounded before the Institute in a series of memoirs in 1823.

These were published in 1824 at the expense of the State, under the title of *Précis du Système Hiéroglyphique des Anciens Égyptiens.* In 1826 Charles X. appointed him to superintend the department of Egyptian antiquities in the Louvre; in 1828 he went as director of a scientific expedition to Egypt; and in 1831 the chair of Egyptian archæology was created for him in the Collège de France. He died at Paris in 1832. Other works are his *Grammaire Égyptienne, Dictionnaire Hiéroglyphique,* and *Panthéon Égyptien.*—Cf. A. Champollion, *Les deux Champollion: leur vie et leurs œuvres.*

CHAMPOLLION-FIGEAC, Jacques Joseph. The elder brother of the preceding, born at Figeac in 1778, died in 1867. His principal works are: *Antiquités de Grenoble* (1807), *Paléographie Universelle, Annales des Lagides* (1819), *Traité élémentaire d'Archéologie* (1843), *Écriture démotique Égyptienne* (1843), *L'Égypte Ancienne.*

CHAMPS ÉLYSÉES. The fashionable promenade of Paris, an avenue leading from the Place de la Concorde to the Arc de Triomphe, Place de l'Étoile. It was laid out by Marie de' Medici in 1616.

CHANCELLOR. The Lord High Chancellor of Great Britain, who is also Keeper of the Great Seal, is the first judicial officer of the Crown, and ranks as first *lay* person of the State after the Blood Royal. Originally the sole administrator of equity, he was subsequently assisted as a judge in Chancery by the Master of the Rolls, and latterly also by three Vice-Chancellors, down to the creation of the Supreme Court of Judicature of which he is the head. A Cabinet Minister and a Privy Councillor in virtue of his office, he is Prolocutor of the House of Lords by prescription with a total salary of £10,000 a year, and he is entitled to a pension of £5000 a year. He vacates his office with the Ministry which appoints him and of which he is a member. He has the nomination of all judges of the High Court of Justice and (except in the County Palatine of Lancaster) appoints all judges of county courts and justices of the peace. He is Keeper of the King's Conscience, visitor in the King's right of all royal foundations, guardian of all charitable uses and of lunatics and infants, and exercises considerable ecclesiastical patronage.

The Chancellorship of Scotland was abolished by the Act of Union, and contrariwise that of Ireland by the Act of 1922 creating the Free State. The Chancellor of the Duchy of Lancaster exercises there generally similar privileges and duties except judicial. He is a Cabinet Minister, not necessarily a lawyer, and a very considerable and important business of the Chancery Palatine Court with sittings at Manchester and Liverpool is conducted by the Vice-Chancellor, who must be a barrister.

The Chancellor of the County Palatine of Durham is a barrister who is necessarily a leading member of the north-eastern circuit. He has unlimited Chancery jurisdiction within the County Palatine and his duties are judicial merely, there being no appointment in his gift other than of the officers of the court.

The Chancellor of the Exchequer has one judicial appearance in each year, when he sits at the Royal Court of Justice in London to settle the list of persons who are able and qualified to fill the costly office of High Sheriff for the counties of England and Wales.

The Chancellor of the Duchy of Lancaster presides in the court of the duchy chamber, to decide questions relating to lands held of the king as Duke of Lancaster.

The Chancellor of the Order of the Garter, and other orders of knighthood, is an officer who seals the commissions and the mandates of the chapter and assembly of the knights of the order, keeps the register of their proceedings, and delivers their acts under the seal of their order.

Chancellor of a university, the highest honorary official in the university, from whom the degrees are regarded as proceeding. The post in Britain is usually occupied by a person of rank.

CHAN'CELLORSVILLE. The site of one of the greatest battles of the

American Civil War, in which, on the 2nd, 3rd, and 4th of May, 1863, a nominal victory was gained by the Confederates under Generals Lee and Jackson over the Federal troops commanded by General Hooker. The Federal troops, though compelled to retreat across the Rappahannock, carried with them some thousands of prisoners and one more gun than they had lost, while the Confederates lost from 15,000 to 18,000 men and their brilliant leader Jackson.

CHANCE-MEDLEY. In law, homicide happening either in self-defence, on a sudden quarrel, or in the commission of an unlawful act without any deliberate intention of doing mischief. The term is now almost obsolete, having been superseded by the term "manslaughter."

CHAN'CERY. Formerly the highest court of justice in England next to Parliament, but since 1873 a division of the High Court of Justice, which is itself one of the two departments of the Supreme Court of Judicature (q.v.). Formerly it embraced six superior courts called high courts of chancery, viz. the court of the Lord High-Chancellor, the court of the Master of the Rolls, the court of appeal in chancery, and the courts of the three vice-chancellors, with various inferior courts. The jurisdiction of the court was both ordinary and extraordinary, the former as a court of common law, the latter a court of equity.

The extraordinary court, or court of equity, proceeded upon rules of equity and conscience, moderating the rigour of the common law, and giving relief in cases where there was no remedy in the common law courts. The Chancery Division now consists of the Lord Chancellor as president and five justices. The matters of which it specially takes cognizance are such as the administration of the estates of deceased persons, partnerships, mortgages, trust estates, rectification or setting aside of deeds, contracts in regard to real estates and wardship of infants and care of their estates.—Cf. Kerly, *Historical Sketch of the Equitable Jurisdiction of the Court of Chancery.*

CHANDA (chân-dă). A town of India, Central Provinces, surrounded by a wall 5½ miles long, with manufactures and a considerable trade. Pop. 22,981.—The *District* has an area of 10,785 sq. miles, a pop. of 677,544.

CHANDAUSI (chan-dou-sē). A town of India, United Provinces, Moradabad district. Pop. 25,164.

CHANDERI (chan-dā'rē), or **CHANDHAIREE.** A town in Central India, Scindia's Dominions, in a hilly and jungly tract, 103 miles S. of Gwalior, formerly of considerable extent and splendour, but now an insignificant place. There is a fort which figured much in the wars of the Mogul dynasty.

CHAN'DERNAGORE, or **CHAN'-DARNAGAR** ("city of sandalwood"). A town in Hindustan, belonging to France, on the right bank of the Hooghly, 16 miles N.N.W. of Calcutta. The French established a factory in it in 1676, and in 1688 obtained a formal cession of it, together with its territory of 3½ sq. miles, from Aurangzib. It was three times occupied by the British, but was finally restored to the French in 1816. Pop. of town and territory, 27,262.

CHANDOS, Duke of. English title borne from 1719 to 1789 by the family of Brydges. Sir John Brydges was made Baron Chandos of Sudeley in 1554 and his descendant, James, the 9th baron, was made a duke in 1719. He built a magnificent house at Canons, Middlesex. He died in 1744, and the title became extinct when the 3rd duke died in 1789.

Sir John Chandos was a noted soldier in the time of Edward III. and one of the first of the Knights of the Garter.

CHANDPUR'. A town of India, Bijnaur district, United Provinces; thriving, well paved and drained. Pop. 12,255.

CHANG-CHOW-FOO. A city, China, province of Fukien, 28 miles S.W. of Amoy, which is its port. It is the centre of the silk manufacture of the province. Pop. about 1,000,000.

CHANGELING. Child substituted for another, usually at birth. There was formerly a belief that babies, before christening, were in danger of being stolen by fairies and that any weakly or peevish child was a changeling.

CH'ANGSHA. A city of China, province of Hunan. Pop. 606,972.

CHANG TSO LIN. Chinese politician. Born in Manchuria, he became Governor of Fengtien and later of other provinces, and was, when civil war began, the most powerful man in the northern part of the country. In 1925 he entered Pekin and remained supreme there until 1928, when he was driven out by the Nationalist force from Nanking. He was fatally wounded by a bomb on June 21, when returning to Manchuria.

CHANK-SHELL. The common conch-shell (*Turbinella pyrum*), of a spiral form, worn as an ornament by the Hindu women. A shell with its spires or whorls turning to the right is held in peculiar estimation and fetches a high price. The chank is one of the gasteropodous mollusca.

CHANNEL ISLANDS. A group islands in the English Channel, off the west coast of department of La Manche, in France. They belong to Britain, and consist of Jersey, Guernsey, Alderney, and Sark, with some dependent islets. They are not bound by Acts of the Imperial Parliament unless specially named in them. They are almost exempt from taxation, and their inhabitants enjoy besides all the privileges of British subjects. The government is in the hands of bodies called the "states," some members of which are named by the Crown, while others are chosen by the people, and others sit *ex officio*. The islands have been fortified at great expense. They form the only remains of the Norman provinces once subject to England. Area, 75 sq. miles; pop. (1931), 93,061. (See the separate articles.) — BIBLIOGRAPHY: E. E. Bicknell, *The Channel Islands*: J. E. Morris, *The Channel Islands*; Wimbush and Carey, *The Channel Islands*.

CHANNELS, or CHAIN-WALES, of a ship. Broad and thick planks projecting horizontally from the ship's outside, abreast of the masts. They are meant to keep the shrouds clear of the gunwale.

CHANNING (chan'ing), **William Ellery.** American preacher and writer, born at Newport, Rhode Island, in 1780, died 1842. He studied at Harvard College, became a decided Unitarian, and propagated Unitarian tenets with great zeal and success. His first appointment as a pastor was in 1803, when he obtained the charge of a congregation in Boston, and ere long he became known as one of the most popular preachers of America. His reputation was still farther increased by the publication of writings, chiefly sermons and reviews on popular subjects.

CHANNING, William Henry. Nephew of the former, born 1810, died 1884, a Unitarian preacher (for some time at Liverpool). He was a supporter of the socialistic movement, wrote a *Memoir of William Ellery Channing* (his uncle) and other works.

CHANT. A short musical composition consisting generally of a long reciting note, on which an indefinite number of words may be intoned, and a melodic phrase or cadence. A single chant consists of two strains, the first of three and the second of four bars in length. A double chant has the length of two single ones.

CHAN'TABUN. A seaport of Siam, on the Gulf of Siam, with exports of timber and other articles. There are ruby and sapphire mines in the neighbourhood. It was held by the French for years, but was restored in 1904. Pop. 7000.

CHANTERELLE. A British edible mushroom (*Cantharellus cibarius*) of a bright orange colour, with a pleasant fruity smell.

CHANTILLY. A town, France, department of the Oise, 25 miles N.N.E. of Paris, celebrated for a variety of lace made here and in the neighbourhood; for the splendid château, built by the great Condé, but levelled by the mob at the Revolution; and also for another palace built by the Duc d'Aumale after the estate came into his possession in 1850, which, along with the fine domain, was presented by the duke to the French Institute in 1887. It is a horse-racing centre, noted for the three annual race-meetings held there. Pop. 5765.

CHANT'REY, Sir Francis. An English sculptor, born in 1781 near Sheffield, died in 1842. He was the son of a well-to-do carpenter. Even in boyhood his chief amusement was in drawing and modelling figures, and he was apprenticed in 1797 to a carver and gilder. In 1802 he commenced work for himself at Sheffield by taking portraits in crayons. After studying at the Royal Academy in London, he eventually settled in the metropolis, where he presented numerous busts at the exhibitions of the Royal Academy. One of these, in 1811, attracted the admiration of Nollekens, who had the generosity to exclaim: "There's a fine, a very fine *busto*; let the man who made it be known; remove one of my busts and put this one in its place, for it well deserves it."

This was the commencement of his career of fame and fortune, and he soon came to be regarded as the first monumental sculptor of his time. In 1816 he was chosen an associate and in 1818 a member of the Royal Academy. He was knighted in 1835. His most celebrated works are the *Sleeping Children*, in Lichfield Cathedral; the statue of Lady Louisa Russell, in Woburn Abbey; the bronze statue of William Pitt, in Hanover Square, London; a statue of Washington, in the States House, Boston; statues of Horner, Canning, and Sir J. Malcolm, in Westminster Abbey, and the statues of George III., in the Guildhall, and of George IV., in Trafalgar Square. His best works are his busts; his full-length figures betray an insufficient acquaintance with anatomy, and several of his equestrian statues are still more defective. He left a fund of £105,000 to the Royal Academy "for the purchase of British works of art" (Chantrey bequest).

CHANT'RY. An endowment to provide for the singing of masses; also the chapel where the masses are chanted. Chantry chapels were frequently endowed by the will of the founders in order to have mass sung for the repose of their souls.

CHAO-CHOW. A city, China, province of Kwangtung, on the River Han, 195 miles N.E. of Hong-Kong, the centre of an important maritime division of the province. Pop. 200,000.

CHAOS (kā'os). In old theories of the earth, the void out of which sprang all things or in which they existed in a confused, unformed shape before they were separated into kinds.

CHAPALA (chå-pä'å). A picturesque lake of Mexico, states of Xalisco and Michoacan. Area, 1400 sq. miles.

CHAP-BOOKS. A species of cheap literature which preceded the popular periodicals of the present day. They usually consisted of coarsely printed (and often coarsely written) publications sold for a copper or two, and were so called because they were prepared by the popular publishers expressly for sale by the chapmen or pedlars, who hawked them from district to district. They included lives of heroes and wonderful personages, tales of roguery and broad humour, witch and ghost stories, etc. They were issued in London, Edinburgh, Newcastle-on-Tyne, Glasgow, Falkirk, and Paisley.—BIBLIOGRAPHY: J. Ashton, *A History of the Chap-books of the Eighteenth Century*; C. Nisard, *Histoire des livres populaires.*

CHAP'EL. A term applied to buildings of various kinds erected for some sort of religious service. Thus it may mean a subordinate place of worship attached to a large church, and especially to a cathedral, separately dedicated and devoted to special services. Or it may mean a building subsidiary to a parish church and intended to accommodate persons residing at a distance from the latter; or a place of worship connected with a palace, castle, university, etc.

CHAPEL-EN-LE-FRITH. A market town of England, in North Derbyshire, about 6 miles north of Buxton, with manufactures of cotton, paper, etc.; a centre for tourists visiting the Peak country. Pop. (rural district), 17,758 (1931).

CHAPEL ROYAL. Place of worship attached to the royal court. The chief chapel royal is in St. James's Palace, London. The chapels royal have a dean, sub-dean, priests in ordinary, and gentlemen and children of the choir. The Savoy Chapel, London, is still called a chapel royal. There is a chapel royal at Holyrood. St. George's Chaple, Windsor, is a chapel royal.

CHAPLAIN (chap'lin). Literally a person who is appointed to a chapel, as a clergyman not having a parish or similar charge, but connected with a court, the household of a nobleman, an army, a prison, a ship, or the like. Forty-eight clergymen of the Church of England and six clergymen of the Church of Scotland hold office as royal chaplains.

CHAPLAIN-GENERAL. The head of the chaplains attached to the staff of the British army. He assists the War Office in selecting the chaplains and regulating their duties. He has a salary of £1000 a year.

CHAPLET. A string of beads used by Roman Catholics to count the number of their prayers. A chaplet is the third of a rosary, and usually consists of fifty-five beads. In heraldry it means a garland of leaves, with four flowers amongst them at equal distances; in architecture, a small moulding carved into beads, pearls, etc.

CHAPLIN, Charles Spencer. American film artiste. Born in Camberwell, London, in 1889, he was a son of Charles Chaplin, a variety comedian. He started work early in life in the variety business and eventually played leading parts in Fred. Karno's companies in many of the music-halls and variety theatres of England. From 1910 till the end of 1913 he interpreted comic sketches in the United States. For the next four years he appeared in moving pictures of the Keystone Comedy Co., made at Los Angeles, California. Early in 1918 he formed his own company for producing such pictures and erected large studios at Hollywood. Among the most successful films which he has released are *Shoulder Arms, The Kid, The Gold Rush, The Circus,* and *City Lights.*

CHAPMAN. In general a merchant or trader, but in modern times more specifically a hawker or one who has a travelling booth. The word is derived from *chap,* equivalent to *cheap,* which originally signified a market or place for trading.

CHAPMAN, George. An English poet, the earliest, and perhaps the best, translator of Homer. Born about the year 1559, and died in 1634. He was educated at Oxford, and in 1576 proceeded to London; but little is known of his personal history. His translation of the *Iliad* was published in three separate portions, in 1598, 1600, and 1603. It has been highly commended by Pope, Keats, Coleridge, and Lamb. Keats's sonnet *On First Looking into Chapman's Homer* ("Then felt I like some watcher of the skies," etc.) is well known. In 1614 appeared his translation of the *Odyssey*, followed in the same year by that of the *Battle of the Frogs and Mice* and the Homeric hymns. He also translated Hesiod's *Works and Days* and portions of various classic poets. He wrote numerous plays, almost all now forgotten, though containing some fine passages. His complete works, edited by Shepherd, with an essay by Swinburne, appeared in 1874.

CHAPOO. A seaport, China, province of Chekiang, on the north side of a large bay, 35 miles N. from Ningpo. It carries on a considerable trade with Japan.

CHAPTAL (shap-tȧl), **Jean Antaine Claude.** Comte de Chanteloup, peer of France, born in 1756, died in 1832. He devoted himself to the study of medicine and the natural sciences, and especially chemistry. A supporter of the Revolution, he was appointed in 1799 Counsellor of State, and in 1800 Minister of the Interior, in which post he encouraged the study of the arts and established a chemical manufactory in the neighbourhood of Paris. In 1805 he was made a member of the Senate. On the Restoration he was obliged to retire to private life, but in 1816 the king nominated him a member of the Academy of Sciences, and subsequently made him a peer. Chaptal's works on national industry, chemistry, and the cultivation of the vine were highly thought of, especially his *Chimie Appliquée aux Arts* (Paris, 1807, 4 vols.), his *Chimie Appliquée à l'Agriculture* (Paris, 1823, 2 vols.), and *De l'Industrie Française* (Paris, 1819, 2 vols.).

CHAPTER. One of the chief divisions of a book. As the rules and statutes of ecclesiastical establishments were arranged in chapters, so also the assembly of the members of a religious order, and of canons, was called a *chapter*. The orders of knights use this expression for the meetings of their members, and some societies and corporations call their assemblies *chapters*.

CHAPTER-HOUSE. The building attached to a cathedral or religious house in which the chapter meets for the transaction of business. They are of different forms, but are often polygonal in plan. Some chapter-houses, such as those at York, Southwell, and Wells, exhibit the most elaborate architectural adornment. The stained-glass windows at York are of exquisite beauty. Sometimes chapter-houses were the burying-place of clerical dignitaries. *See* CATHEDRAL.

CHAR, or CHARR (*Salmo salvelinus*; Gael. *ceara*, blood-coloured). A European freshwater fish of the salmon genus, found plentifully in the deeper lakes of England, Wales, and Ireland, more rarely in those of Scotland. The chars inhabit the colder regions of deep waters, where the temperature is less liable to vary. The body somewhat resembles that of a trout, but is longer and more slender, as well as more brilliant in colouring, with crimson, rose, and white spots; weight sometimes 2 lb., but generally under 1 lb. Char is much esteemed for the table.

CHARA'CEÆ, Charophyta, or **Stoneworts.** A family of cryptogams, related to Green Algæ, but with many

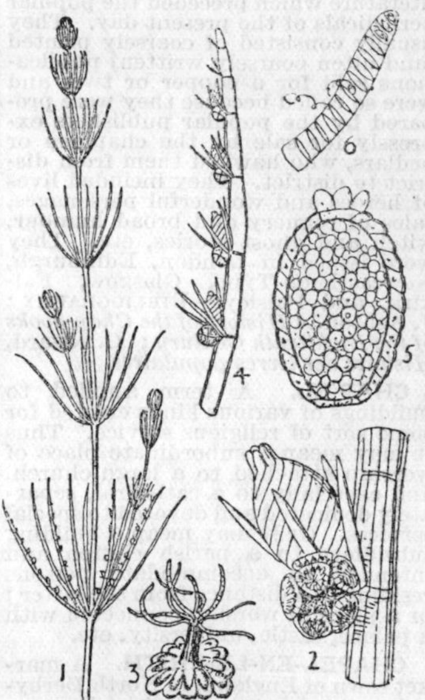

Stonewort (*Chara fragilis*)

1, Plant. 2, Sporangium and antheridium. 4, Enlarged branch. 5, Section of sporangium. 6, End of a filament.

peculiar features. The chief genera are Chara and Nitella. They are submerged plants, rooting in the mud of fresh or brackish waters, varying in size from a few inches to 2 or 3 feet. The thallus is filamentous in type and very regular in construction. The main axis in Nitella is composed of long internodes, each consisting of a single huge cylindrical cell, alternating with disc-shaped nodes made up of several flattened cells. Each node bears a whorl of short branches (" leaves "), and also one or two long branches, which repeat the structure of the main shoot. The base of the shoot bears colourless rhizoids, which ramify in the mud.

The reproductive organs are antheridia and oogonia of very complex structure. Chara resembles Nitella in essential features, but the internodal cells are covered by " cortical filaments," which grow up and down from the adjoining nodes. In many species of Chara all parts of the plant are encrusted with a thick coating of lime, which makes the thallus hard and brittle, and harsh to the touch (hence the name " Stoneworts ") ; it is owing to this property that oospores of Chara often occur as well-preserved fossils.

CHARADE. A species of riddle, in which a word proposed for discovery is divided into several syllables, each of which is taken separately as an individual and significant word, forming a portion of the final " whole." When the meaning of the separate syllables and of the " whole " is indicated by means of dramatic representation, an " acting charade " is constituted.

CHARA'DRIUS (ka-). The genus to which the plover belongs, forming the type of the family Charadriadæ, which includes also the lapwings, pratincoles, oyster-catchers, turnstones, sanderlings, etc.

CHAR'COAL. A term applied to an impure variety of carbon, especially such as is produced by charring wood. One kind of it is obtained from bones (*see* BONE BLACK) ; lampblack and coke are also varieties. Wood-charcoal is manufactured by the partial combustion of wood piled in heaps, with air-spaces between, and covered with turf. Water and various combustible materials are driven off, and impure carbon retaining the original structure of the wood is left. The more modern method is to heat the wood in closed retorts, when, in addition to the charcoal which is left behind, various volatile products of importance are obtained ; among these are a combustible gas, wood-spirit, pyroligneous acid, and wood-tar.

Charcoal can be made from any kind of wood, but the finest quality, used for making gunpowder, is that furnished by the alder-buckthorn and dogwood shrubs, and by alder. Wood-charcoal, well prepared, is of a deep-black colour, brittle and porous, tasteless and inodorous. It is combustible at high temperatures, cannot be fused in any flame or furnace, but is volatilised at the high temperature of the electric arc, presenting a surface with a distinct appearance of having undergone fusion.

Charcoal is insoluble in water, and is not affected by it at low temperatures ; hence, wooden stakes which are to be immersed in water are often charred to preserve them, and the ends of posts stuck in the ground are also thus treated. Owing to its peculiarly porous texture, charcoal possesses the property of absorbing considerable volumes of air or other gases at ordinary temperatures, and of yielding the greater part of them when heated. Charcoal likewise absorbs the odoriferous and colouring principles of most animal and vegetable substances, and hence is a valuable deodoriser, disinfectant, and decoloriser. Water which, from having been long kept in wooden vessels, as during long voyages, has acquired an offensive smell, is deprived of it by filtration through charcoal powder. It can also prevent the decay of animal and vegetable matter.

It is used as a smokeless fuel in stoves, etc., as a reducing agent in metallurgical operations, e.g. for obtaining metals from their oxides, and for converting wrought iron into steel by the process of cementation. It is an important component of ordinary gunpowder, and is used in domestic filters. In its finer state of aggregation, under the form of ivory-black, lamp-black, etc., it is the basis of black paint ; and mixed with fat oils and resinous matter, to give a due consistence, it constitutes printing-ink.

Charcoal-burning is one of the most ancient of British industries. The last of charcoal iron-furnaces was shut down in 1800 at Ashburnham, Sussex. Nowadays charcoal-burning is only practised extensively in the Forest of Dean (in Gloucestershire) and in some parts of the Midlands.

CHARCOT, Jean Baptiste Etienne Auguste. French Antarctic explorer, born at Neuilly-sur-Seine in 1867. He is a son of Jean Martin Charcot, the famous neurologist. He studied medicine, was investigator in the

Pasteur Institute, and from 1896 to 1898 head of the clinical department in the school of medicine at the University of Paris. He conducted Antarctic expeditions from 1903 to 1905, and from 1908 to 1910, which took him as far as Adelaide Island, and he saw the inaccessible coast of Alexander I. Land. He has published *Anthropodes* (1907), *expedition antarctique française, 1903–1905* (1908), *Deuxième expedition antarçtique française, 1908–1910* (1911), *Pourquoi pas dans l'Antarctique* (1911).

CHARCOT, Jean Martin. French physician, born in Paris 1825, died at Morvan 1893. In 1856 he was appointed physician to the Central Bureau of Hospitals, in 1873 professor of pathological anatomy in the faculty of medicine in Paris, and in 1882 professor of diseases of the nervous system. In 1862 he began his work at the Salpêtrière, chiefly in connection with nervous diseases, and his researches in hypnotic suggestion were very remarkable. He was elected a member of the Academy of Medicine in 1873, and of the Institute in 1883. His works include: *Leçons sur les maladies du système nerveaux, Leçons sur les maladies du foie, des voies biliaires et des reins*, etc.

CHARCOT LAND. District of the Antarctic Ocean. It lies to the south of Graham Land and is named after the French explorer, Jean Baptiste Etienne Auguste Charcot, who did valuable surveying work in this region in 1903, 1909, and 1910.

CHARD. A municipal borough of England, Somersetshire, on an eminence near the southern border of the county, with manufactures of lace, woollens, etc. Pop. (1931), 4053.

CHARD. The leaves of artichoke covered with straw in order to blanch them and make them less bitter.—*Beet chards*, the leaf stalks and midribs of a variety of white beet in which these parts are greatly developed, dressed for the table.

CHARDIN (shår-daṇ), **John.** Son of a jeweller in Paris, and a jeweller himself, born in 1643, died in 1713. Sent by his father to the East Indies to buy diamonds, Chardin resided a number of years in Persia and India, and subsequently published an account of his travels. He settled in London in 1681, was knighted by Charles II., and was envoy to Holland for several years.

CHARENTE (shȧ-rȧṇt). A river in Western France, rising in the department of Haute-Vienne, and falling into the sea about 8 miles below Rochefort, opposite to the Isle of Oleron, after a course of about 200 miles. It gives its name to two departments.

CHARENTE. An inland department of France, formed chiefly out of the ancient province of Angoumois, and traversed by the River Charente; area, 2305 sq. miles; capital, Angoulême. Soil generally thin, dry, and arid; one-third devoted to tillage, a third to vineyards, and the remainder meadows, woods, and waste lands. The wines are of inferior quality, but they yield the best brandy in Europe, the celebrated cognac brandy being made in Cognac and other districts. Pop. (1931), 310,489.

CHARENTÉ-INFÉRIEURE (aṇ-fā-ri-*eur*; "Lower Charente"). A maritime department of France, comprises parts of the former provinces of Angoumois and Poitou; area, 2791 sq. miles. Surface in general flat; soil chalky and sandy, fertile, and well cultivated; a considerable portion planted with vines; salt marshes along the coast. The pastures are good, and well stocked with cattle, horses, and sheep. The wine is of common quality, and chiefly used for making brandy. Oysters and sardines abound on the coast. Capital, La Rochelle. Pop. (1931), 415,249.

CHARENTON-LE-PONT (shȧ-rȧṇ-tōṇ-l-pōṇ). A town about 5 miles east of Paris, at the confluence of the Marne with the Seine, with numerous mercantile and manufacturing establishments. Pop. 20,890.

CHARGÉ-D'AFFAIRES (shȧr-zhā-dȧf-ār). The title of an inferior rank of diplomatic agents. *See* DIPLOMATIC SERVICE.

CHARGE. Word meaning load or burden. It is applied to the ammunition in a firearm, to the electricity in a battery, and to the explosives in blasting operations.

Legally, a charge is a mortgage, i.e. an equitable transfer of a title to goods or property as security for a loan. The word is also used to denote responsibility and, in military and sporting matters, a violent advance.

CHARGE. In heraldry a device upon a coat of arms. It represents either those things which keep their own names (proper), or bear technical names such as chevron, etc. (common).

CHARIKAR. A town, Afghanistan, in the district of Kohistan, 21 miles north of Kabul. Pop. 5000.

CHA'RING-CROSS. The titular centre of London, so named from a cross which stood until 1647 at the village of Charing in memory of Eleanor, wife of Edward I. It is now a triangular piece of roadway at Trafalgar Square.

CHARIOT. A term applied to vehicles used both for pleasure and in war. Ancient chariots, such as those used among the Egyptians, Assyrians, Greeks, and Romans, were of various forms. A common form was open behind and closed in front, and had only two wheels. The chariot was strongly and even elegantly built, but not well adapted for speed. In ancient warfare chariots were of great importance thus we read of the 900 iron chariots of Sisera, as giving him a great advantage against the Israelites. The Philistines in their war against Saul had 30,000 chariots. The sculptures of ancient Egypt show that the chariots formed the strength of the Egyptian army, these vehicles being two-horsed and carrying the driver and the warrior, sometimes a third man, the shield-bearer. There is no representation of Egyptian soldiers on horseback, and consequently when Moses in his song of triumph over Pharaoh speaks of the "horse and his rider," "rider" must be understood to mean chariot-rider.

Assyrian War-Chariot

In the Egyptian chariots the framework, wheels, pole, and yoke were of wood, and the fittings of the inside, the bindings of the framework, as well as the harness were chiefly of raw hide or of tanned leather. We have also numbers of sculptures which give a clear idea of the Assyrian chariots. These resembled the Egyptian in all essential features, containing almost invariably three men—the warrior, the shield-bearer, and the charioteer. A peculiarity of both is the quiver or quivers full of arrows attached to the side.

The Assyrian war-chariot shown in the figure is drawn by three horses abreast, and all the appointments are rich and elaborate. It has, as will be noticed, two quivers crossing each other on the side, filled with arrows, and each also containing a small axe. A socket for holding the spear is also attached. From the front of the chariot a singular ornamental appendage stretches forward. War-chariots had sometimes scythe-like weapons attached to each extremity of the axle, as among the ancient Persians and Britons. Among the Greeks and Romans chariot-races were common. In Britain the name chariot was formerly given to a kind of light travelling carriage.—Cf. Daremberg and Saglio, *Dictionnaire des Antiquités*, s.v. *Currus*.

CHARITABLE TRUSTS. Property held in trust for charitable purposes. By English law all bequests for charitable purposes to be valid must be strictly for the public benefit; that is to say, in favour of institutions for the advancement of learning, science, and art, for the support of the poor, or for other objects connected with the welfare of the public. All bequests for superstitious uses or for private charity are null and void. The system of charitable trusts and the method of administering them in England is now based upon a series of statutes known as the Charitable Trusts Acts, passed in 1853, 1855, 1860, 1869, and 1888, and upon the

Mortmain and Charitable Uses Act, passed in 1891. A body of commissioners (the Charity Commissioners), under whose superintendence such benevolent trusts are placed, was established under the Charitable Trusts Act of 1853.

CHARITES (kar'i-tēz). The Greek name of the Graces. They were three in number, and named Euphrosyne (joy), Thalia (bloom), and Aglaia (brilliance). Their oldest shrine was at Orchomenus, in Bœotia, where their festival, the Charitesia, was celebrated.

CHARITY ORGANISATION SOCIETIES. Societies instituted in London and other large towns for the purpose of organising and rendering most efficient the different charitable agencies and preventing overlapping. The expressed objects of these societies are such as the following: the promotion of co-operation among charities and benevolent institutions and charitable persons, and the exchange of information, so that due investigation and fitting action may be taken in all cases; the assistance of poor persons in such a manner as may effect permanent benefit in their condition; the repression of mendicity; the exposure of imposture; and the promotion of thrift and of well-advised methods for improving the condition of the poor. Such institutions have proved a great boon to the really deserving poor, and they are a guarantee to the charitable that their contributions will be worthily employed. The Society for Organising Charitable Relief and Suppressing Mendicity was started in London, in 1869, under the leadership of Goschen, President of the Poor Law Board, the Bishop of London, and others. The first charity organisation in America was formed in 1911.

CHARLEMAGNE (shår-lė-măn'; *Carolus Magnus*, Charles the Great). King of the Franks, and subsequently Emperor of the West. Born in 742, probably at Aix-la-Chapelle. His father was Pepin the Short, King of the Franks, son of Charles Martel. On the decease of his father, in 768, he was crowned king, and divided the kingdom of the Franks with his younger brother Carloman, at whose death, in 771, Charlemagne made himself master of the whole empire, which embraced, besides France, a large part of Germany. His first great enterprise was the conquest of the Saxons, a heathen nation living between the Weser and the Elbe, which he undertook in 772; but it was not till 803 that they were finally subdued, and brought to embrace Christianity. While he was combating the Saxons, Pope Adrian implored his assistance against Desiderius, King of the Lombards. Charlemagne immediately marched with his army to Italy, took Pavia, overthrew Desiderius, and was crowned King of Lombardy with the iron crown.

In 778 he repaired to Spain to assist a Moorish prince, and while returning his troops were surprised in the valley of Roncesvalles by the Biscayans, and the rear-guard defeated; Roland, one of the most famous warriors of those times, fell in the battle. As his power increased, Charlemagne meditated more seriously the accomplishment of the plan of his ancestor, Charles Martel, to restore the Western Empire. Having gone to Italy to assist the Pope, on Christmas Day 800 he was crowned and proclaimed Cæsar and Augustus by Leo III. His son Pepin, who had been made King of Italy, died in 810, and his death was followed the next year by that of Charles, his eldest son. Thus of his legitimate sons one only remained, Louis, King of Aquitania, whom Charlemagne adopted as his colleague in 813. He died 28th Jan., 814, in the forty-seventh year of his reign, and was buried at Aix-la-Chapelle, his favourite and usual place of residence.

Charlemagne was a friend of learning, and deserves the name of restorer of the sciences and teacher of his people. He attracted by his liberality the most distinguished scholars to his court (among others, Alcuin, from England), and established an academy in his palace at Aix-la-Chapelle, the sittings of which he attended with all the scientific and literary men of his court. He invited teachers of languages and mathematics from Italy to the principal cities of the empire, and founded schools of theology and the liberal sciences in the monasteries. The school which Alcuin established at Tours was famous for centuries. Charlemagne strove to cultivate his mind by intercourse with scholars; and, to the time of his death, this intercourse remained his favourite recreation. His mother-tongue was a form of German, but he spoke several languages readily, especially Latin, and was naturally eloquent. He sought to improve the liturgy and church music, and attempted unsuccessfully to introduce uniformity of measures and weights. He built a lighthouse at Boulogne, constructed several ports, encouraged agriculture, and enacted wise laws. He convened councils and parliaments, published capitularies, wrote many letters (some of which are still extant), a grammar and several Latin poems.

His empire comprehended France, most of Catalonia, Navarre, and Aragon; the Netherlands, Germany as far as the Elbe, Saale, and Eider, Upper and Middle Italy, Istria, and a part of Slavonia. In private life Charlemagne was exceedingly amiable; a good father and generous friend. In dress and habits he was plain and economical. In person he was strong and of great stature. He was succeeded by his son Louis (le Débonnaire). — BIBLIOGRAPHY: Einhard, *Vita Karoli Magni*; E. Dümmler, *Poetae Latini Aevi Carolini*; J. I. Mombert, *History of Charles the Great*; Davis, *Charlemagne* (in Heroes of the Nations Series); *The Cambridge Mediæval History* (vol. ii.).

CHARLEROI (shärl-rwä). A town in Belgium, province of Hainaut, on both sides of the River Sambre, 20 miles E.N.E. of Mons. It has manufactures of glass, hardware, and woollen stuffs, and in the neighbourhood are extensive pits of iron and coal (the ironworks of Corvillet). Charleroi was dismantled in 1794, again fortified in 1816 under Wellington's direction, but finally dismantled in 1859. During the European War the town was the scene of many sanguinary struggles, and the great battle of Charleroi opened on 22nd Aug., 1914. The town was reoccupied by the Allies on 18th Nov., 1918. Pop. 28,069.

CHARLES I. Ex-Emperor of Austria and King of Hungary, born at Persenbeug, 17th Aug., 1887. The son of Archduke Otto and Princess Maria, and a grand-nephew of the late Emperor Francis Joseph, he became heir to the throne when the heir-presumptive, Archduke Francis Ferdinand, his uncle, was murdered with his wife at erajevo on 28th June, 1914. Charles succeeded his great-uncle Francis Joseph upon the latter's death on 21st Nov., 1916. He was married in 1911 to the Princess Zita of Bourbon-Parma, and had four sons and a daughter. The young emperor's reign was not of long duration. In Nov., 1918, a revolution broke out in Austria, and he abdicated on 11th Nov. Two attempts to return to Hungary in 1921 failed. He died 1st April, 1922.

CHARLES I., or CAROL. King of Rumania, born 20th April, 1839, died 10th Oct., 1914. The second son of Prince Karl Anton of Hohenzollern-Sigmaringen, he served in the Prussian army, and was elected Prince of Rumania, at that time nominally part of the Turkish Empire, in April, 1866. He showed tact and statesmanship, and, in spite of foreign intrigues and factions, strengthened his position as ruler of the country. In 1877 he concluded an alliance with Russia, led an army against the Turks, and rendered valuable service in the siege of Plevna. A few weeks after the outbreak of the Turkish War Rumania declared her independence, but this was accepted by the Powers only in 1881 when Prince Charles assumed the title of king and was crowned at Bucharest on 22nd May. He married Princess Elizabeth von Wied, better known as Carmen Sylva. His nephew Ferdinand succeeded him on the throne.—Cf. Whitman, *Reminiscences of the King of Roumania.*

CHARLES I. Surnamed *le Chauve*, or *the Bald*, King of France, the son of Louis le Débonnaire, was born 823, and died in 877. After his father's death in 840 he fought with his half-brother Lothaire for the empire of the Franks, and finally acquired by the Treaty of Verdun (843) all those territories between the ocean on the one part, and the Meuse, the Scheldt, the Saône, the Rhone, and the Mediterranean on the other. But he lost Southern Aquitaine to his nephew Pepin, and had to divide Lorraine with his brother Louis the German. In 875 he was crowned emperor by Pope John VIII.

CHARLES II. Surnamed *le Gros*, or *the Fat*, King of France, is also known as Charles III., Emperor of Germany, and was born about 832. He was the son of Louis the German, and ascended the French throne in 885 to the prejudice of his cousin, Charles the Simple, but was deposed in 887 and died the following year.

CHARLES III. Surnamed *the Simple*, King of France, was the son of Louis the Stammerer, and born in 879. His reign is noted for his long struggle with the piratical Northmen or Normans, to whose chief, Rollo, he eventually ceded the territory of Normandy. He died in 929.

CHARLES IV. Surnamed *le Bel*, or *the Handsome*, King of France, third son of Philippe le Bel, was born in 1294, and ascended the throne in 1322. He died in 1328, without male issue, and was the last of the direct line descended from Hugh Capet.

CHARLES V. Surnamed *the Wise*, King of France, was the son of King John, and was born in 1337. His father being taken prisoner by the English at Poitiers, the management of the kingdom devolved on him at an early age. With great skill and energy, not free, however, from duplicity, he suppressed the revolt of the Parisians and a rising of the peasants, kept the King of Navarre at bay, and deprived the English of a great part of their dominion in France. He died in 1380. He erected the Bastille for the purpose of overawing the Parisians.

CHARLES VI. Surnamed *the Silly*, King of France, son of the foregoing, was born at Paris in 1368, and died in 1422. In 1388 he took the reins of government into his own hands. Four years later he lost his reason, and one of the most disastrous periods of French history began. The kingdom was torn by the rival factions of Burgundians and Armagnacs (Orleanists). In 1415 Henry V. of England crossed over to Normandy, took Harfleur by storm, won the famous victory of Agincourt, and compelled the crazy king to acknowledge him as his successor.

CHARLES VII. King of France, was born at Paris in 1403, and died in 1461. He succeeded only to the southern provinces of the kingdom, Henry VI. of England being proclaimed King of France at Paris. The English dominon in France was under the gove.nment of the Duke of Bedford, and so skilfully did the English general conduct his operations that Charles had almost abandoned the struggle as hopeless, when the appearance of Jeanne d'Arc, the Maid of Orleans, gave, as if by a miracle, a favourable turn to his affairs, and the struggle ended in the expulsion of the English from all their possessions in France, except Calais.

CHARLES VIII. King of France, son of Louis XI., was born in 1470, and succeeded his father in 1483. In 1491 he married Anne, the heiress of Brittany, and thereby annexed that important duchy to the French Crown. The chief event in the reign of Charles VIII. is his expedition into Italy, and rapid conquest of the kingdom of Naples, a conquest as rapidly lost when a few months later Gonsalvo de Cordova re-annexed it to Spain. Charles was meditating a renewed descent into Italy when he died in 1498.

CHARLES IX. King of France, son of Henry II. and Catherine de' Medici, born in 1550, ascended the throne at the age of ten years. His haughty and ambitious mother seized the control of the State. Along with the Guises she headed the Catholic League against the Calvinists, and her tortuous and unscrupulous policy helped to embitter the religious strife of the factions. After a series of Huguenot persecutions and civil wars, a peace was made in 1570, which two years later, on 24th Aug., 1572, was treacherously broken by the Massacre of St. Bartholomew's Day. The king, who had been little more than the tool of his scheming mother, died two years afterwards, in 1574.

CHARLES X. King of France, Comte d'Artois, born at Versailles in 1757, died in 1836. He was the grandson of Louis XV., being the youngest son of the Dauphin, and brother of Louis XVI. He left France in 1789, after the first popular insurrection and destruction of the Bastille, and afterwards assuming the command of a body of emigrants, acted in concert with the Austrian and Prussian armies on the Rhine. Despairing of success, he retired to Great Britain, and resided for several years in the palace of Holyrood at Edinburgh. He entered France at the Restoration, and in 1824 succeeded his brother, Louis XVIII., as king. In a short time his reactionary policy brought him into conflict with the popular party, and in 1830 a revolution drove him from the throne. His grandson, the Comte de Chambord, claimed the French throne as his heir

CHARLES IV. Emperor of Germany, of the House of Luxemburg, was born in 1316, died at Prague in 1378. He was the son of King John of Bohemia. In 1346 he was elected emperor by five of the electoral princes, while the actual emperor, Louis the Bavarian, was still alive. On the death of the latter a part of the electors elected Coun Gunther of Schwarzburg, who soon a.ter died; and Charles at length won over his enemies, and was elected and consecrated emperor at Aix-la-Chapelle. In 1354 he went to Italy and was crowned King of Italy at Milan, and emperor at Rome the year following. On his return to Germany in 1356 Charles issued his Golden Bull (q.v.) regulating the election of the German emperors. Charles was artful, but vacillating, and careless of all interests but those of his own family and his hereditary kingdom of Bohemia. In Germany bands of robbers plundered the country, and the fiefs of the empire were alienated. In Italy Charles sold states and cities to the highest bidder, or, if they themselves offered most, made them independent republics. But Bohemia flourished during his reign. He encouraged trade, industry, and agriculture, made Prague a great city, and established there the first German university (1348).

CHARLES V. Emperor of Germany and King of Spain (in the latter capacity he is called Charles I.), the eldest son of Philip, Archduke of Austria, and of Joanna, the daughter of Ferdinand and Isabella of Spain, was born at Ghent, 24th Feb., 1500, and died 21st Sept., 1558. Charles was thus the grandson of the Emperor

Maximilian and Mary, daughter of Charles the Bold, last Duke of Burgundy, and inherited from his grandparents on both sides the fairest countries in Europe—Aragon, Naples, Sicily, Sardinia, Castile; and the colonies in the New World—Austria, Burgundy, and the Netherlands. On the death of Ferdinand, his grandfather, Charles assumed the title of King of Spain. In 1519 he was elected emperor, and was crowned at Aix-la-Chapelle with extraordinary splendour. The progress of the Reformation in Germany demanded the care of the new emperor, who held a Diet at Worms. Luther, who appeared at this Diet with a safe-conduct from Charles, defended his case with energy and boldness.

The emperor kept silent; but after Luther's departure a severe edict appeared against him in the name of Charles, who thought it his interest to declare himself the Defender of the Roman Church. A war with France, which the rival claims of Francis I. in Italy, the Netherlands, and Navarre made inevitable, broke out in 1521. Neither side had a decided success till the battle of Pavia in 1525, where Francis was totally defeated and taken prisoner. Charles treated his captive with respect, but with great rigour as regarded the conditions of his release. A league of Italian states, headed by Pope Clement VII., was now formed against the overgrown power of Charles; but their ill-directed efforts had no success. Rome itself was stormed and pillaged by the troops of the Constable of Bourbon, and the Pope made prisoner. Nor was the alliance of Henry VIII. of England with France against the emperor any more successful, the war ending in a treaty (Cambrai, 1529) of which the conditions were favourable to Charles.

A war against the Turks by which Solyman was compelled to retreat, and an expedition against the Bey of Tunis, by which 20,000 Christian slaves were released, added to the influence of Charles, and acquired for him the reputation of a chivalrous defender of the faith. In 1537 he made truce with Francis, and soon after, while on his way to the Netherlands, spent six days at the court of the latter in Paris. In 1541 another expedition against the African Moors, by which Charles hoped to crown his reputation, was unsuccessful, and he lost a part of his fleet and army before Algiers without gaining any advantage. A new war with France arose regarding the territory of Milan. The quarrel was patched up by the Peace of Crépy in 1545. The religious strife was again disturbing the emperor. Charles, who was no bigot, sought to reconcile the two parties, and with this view alternately flattered and threatened the Protestants.

At length in 1546 the Protestant princes declared war, but were driven from the field and compelled to submit. But the defection of his ally, Maurice of Saxony, whom Charles had invested with the electoral dignity, again turned the tide in favour of the Protestants. Maurice surprised the imperial camp at Innsbruck in the middle of a stormy night, and Charles with great difficulty escaped alone in a litter. The Treaty of Passau was dictated by the Protestants. It gave them equal rights with the Catholics, and was confirmed three years later by the Diet of Augsberg (1555). Foiled in his schemes and dejected by repeated failures, Charles resolved to resign the imperial dignity, and transfer his hereditary estates to his son Philip.

In 1555 he conferred on him the sovereignty of the Netherlands, and on 15th Jan., 1556, that of Spain, retiring himself to a residence beside the monastery of Yuste in Estremadura, where he amused himself by mechanical labours and the cultivation of a garden. He still took a keen interest in public affairs, though he was very much of an invalid his ill health being partly caused by his mode of living.—BIBLIOGRAPHY: W. Robertson, *History of the Emperor Charles V.*; E. Armstrong, *The Emperor Charles V.*; Sir W. Stirling-Maxwell, *The Cloister Life of the Emperor Charles V.*: C. Hare, *A Great Emperor.*

CHARLES VI. German Emperor, the second son of the Emperor Leopold I., was born 1st Oct., 1685, and died 20th Oct., 1740. He was destined, according to the ordinary rules of inheritance, to succeed his relative Charles II. on the throne of Spain. But Charles II. by his will made a French prince, Philip, Duke of Anjou, grandson of Louis XIV., heir to the Spanish monarchy. This occasioned the War of the Spanish Succession, in which England and Holland took the part of the Austrian claimant. Charles held possession of Madrid for a time, and was supported by the skill of Marlborough and Eugene, but he was eventually obliged to resign Spain to the French claimant, and content himself with the Spanish subject-lands, Milan, Mantua, Sardinia and the Netherlands (Treaty of Utrecht, 1713, and Treaty of Rastadt, 1714).

He became emperor in 1711. In a war against the Turks his armies, led by Eugene of Savoy, gained the decisive victories of Peterwardein and

Belgrade. After the death of his only son, Charles directed all his policy and energies to secure the guarantee of the various powers to the Pragmatic Sanction, settling the succession to the Austrian dominions on his daughter Maria Theresa. In 1733 a war with France and Spain regarding the succession in Poland terminated unfavourably for him, he having to surrender Sicily, Naples, and part of Milan to Spain, and Lorraine to France. In 1737 he renewed the war with the Turks, this time unsuccessfully.

CHARLES VII. Emperor of Germany, was born in 1697, and died in 1745. He was the son of Maximilian Emanuel, Elector of Bavaria. In 1726 he succeeded his father as Elector of Bavaria. He was one of the princes who protested against the Pragmatic Sanction, and after the death of Charles VI., in 1740, he refused to acknowledge Maria Theresa as heiress. In support of his own claims he invaded Austria with an army, took Prague, was crowned King of Bohemia, and in 1742 was elected emperor. But fortune soon deserted him. The armies of Maria Theresa reconquered all Upper Austria, and overwhelmed Bavaria. Charles fled to Frankfort, and returning to Munich in 1744, died there the following year.

CHARLES I. King of England, Scotland, and Ireland, was born at Dunfermline, Scotland, in the year 1600, and was the third son of James VI. and Anne of Denmark. On the 27th of March, 1625, he succeeded to the throne, receiving the kingdom embroiled in a Spanish war, and on the 1st of May he was married by proxy to Henrietta Maria, daughter of Henry IV. of France. The first Parliament which he summoned, being more disposed to state grievances than grant supplies, was dissolved. Next year (1626) a new Parliament was summoned; but the House proved no more tractable than before, and was soon dissolved.

In 1628 the king was obliged to call a new Parliament, which showed itself as much opposed to arbitrary measures as its predecessor, and after voting the supplies prepared the Petition of Right, which Charles was constrained to pass into a law. But the determined spirit with which the Parliament resisted the king's claim to levy tonnage and poundage on his own authority led to a rupture, and Charles again dissolved the Parliament, resolving to try and reign without one. In this endeavour he was supported by Strafford and Laud as his chief counsellors. With their help Charles continued eleven years without summoning a Parliament, using the arbitrary courts of High Commission and Star Chamber as a kind of cover for pure absolutism, and raising money by unconstitutional or doubtful means. He made various attempts to get estates into his possession on the pretext of invalid titles, and in May, 1635, the city of London estates were sequestered. In 1637 John Hampden began the career of resistance to the king's arbitrary measures by refusing to pay ship-money, the right to levy which, without authority of Parliament, he was determined to bring before a court of law. His cause was argued for twelve days in the Court of Exchequer; and although he lost it by the decision of eight of the judges out of twelve, the discussion of the question produced a very powerful impression on the public mind.

It was in Scotland, however, that formal warlike opposition was destined to commence. Charles was crowned in Edinburgh with full Anglican ceremonial in 1633, and this lost him the goodwill of a number of his Scottish subjects. In 1636 the new *Book of Canons* was issued by the king's authority, and this attempt of Charles to introduce an Anglican liturgy into Scotland produced violent tumults, and gave origin to the famous Covenant in 1638 to oppose the king's design. An English army was sent north, but was defeated by the army of the Covenanters, and in 1640 a Parliament was again summoned, which proved to be the famous Long Parliament. An account of the struggle between king and Parliament, the trial and execution of Strafford and Laud, etc., cannot here be given, but the result was that both king and Parliamen' made preparations for war. The king had on his side the great bulk of the gentry, while nearly all the Puritans and the inhabitants of the great trading towns sided wit the Parliament. The first action, the battle of Edgehill (23rd Oct., 1642), gave the king a slight advantage; but nothing very decisive happened till the battle of Marston Moor, in 1644, where Cromwell routed th Royalists. The loss of the battle of Naseby, the year following, completed the ruin of the king's cause. Charles at length gave himself up to the Scottish army at Newark (5th May, 1646).

After some negotiations he was surrendered to the commissioners of the Parliament. The extreme sect of the Independents, largely represented in the army and headed by Cromwell, now got the upper hand, and, coercing the Parliament and the more hesitating of the Presbyterians, brought

Charles to trial for high treason against the people, and had sentence of death pronounced against him. All interposition being vain, he was beheaded before the Banqueting House, Whitehall, on 30th Jan., 1649, meeting his fate with great dignity and composure.

Charles had many good qualities. Possessed of a highly-cultivated mind, with a fine judgment in arts and letters, he was also temperate, chaste, and religious, and, although somewhat cold in his demeanour, kind and affectionate. Nor was talent wanting to him. But these merits were counterbalanced and all but neutralized by a want of self-reliance and a habit of vacillation, which in his position came near being, if it was not altogether, a kind of insincerity. — BIBLIOGRAPHY: S. R. Gardiner, *History of England*; G. M. Trevelyan, *England under the Stuarts*; E. B. Chancellor, *Life of Charles I.*; Sir J. Skelton, *Charles I.*; A. Fea, *Memoirs of the Martyr King.*

CHARLES II. King of England, Ireland, and Scotland, son of Charles I. and Henrietta Maria of France, was born on the 29th of May, 1630. He was a refugee at the Hague at the time of the death of his father, on which he immediately assumed the royal title. Cromwell was then all-powerful in England; but Charles accepted an invitation from the Scots, who had proclaimed him their king (July, 1650), and, passing over to Scotland, was crowned at Scone (1651). Cromwell's approach made him take refuge amongst the English Royalists, who, having gathered an army, encountered Cromwell at Worcester, and were totally defeated. With great difficulty Charles escaped to France. On the death of Cromwell the Restoration, effected without a struggle by General Monk, set Charles on the throne after the Declaration of Breda, his entry into the capital (29th May, 1660) being made amidst universal acclamations.

In 1662 he married the Infanta of Portugal, Catherine of Braganza, a prudent and virtuous princess, but in no way calculated to acquire the affection of a man like Charles. For a time his measures, mainly counselled by the Chancellor Lord Clarendon, were prudent and conciliatory. But the indolence, extravagance, and licentious habits of the king soon involved the nation as well as himself in difficulties. Dunkirk was sold to the French to relieve his pecuniary embarrassment, and war broke out with Holland. A Dutch fleet entered the Thames, and burned and destroyed ships as far up as Chatham. The great plague in 1665, and the great fire of London the year following, added to the disasters of the period. In 1667 Clarendon was dismissed, and a triple alliance between England, Holland, and Sweden, for the purpose of checking the ambition of Louis XIV., followed; but the extravagance of the king made him willing to become a mere pensioner of Louis XIV., with whom he arranged a private treaty against Holland in 1670.

The *Cabal* ministry was by this time in power, and they were quite ready to break the triple alliance and bring about a rupture with the Dutch. As the king did not choose to apply to Parliament for money to carry on the projected war, he caused the exchequer to be shut up in Jan., 1672, and by several other disgraceful and arbitrary proceedings gave great disgust and alarm to the nation. The war ended in failure, and the Cabal ministry was dissolved in 1673. The year 1678 was distinguished by the pretended Popish plot of Titus Oates, which led to the exclusion of Roman Catholics from Parliament. In 1679 the Habeas Corpus Act was passed, and the temper of the Parliament was so much excited that the king dissolved it. A new Parliament which assembled in 1680 had to be dissolved for a like reason, and yet another which met the year following at Oxford. Finally, Charles, like his father, determined to govern without a Parliament, and after the suppression of the Rye House plot and the execution of Lord Russell and Algernon Sidney (Monmouth, also involved in the plot, was finally banished to the Hague), Charles became as absolute as any sovereign in Europe. He died from the consequences of an apoplectic fit in Feb., 1685, after having received the sacrament according to the rites of the Roman Church.

Charles was a man of wit, and possessed an easy good-nature, but was entirely selfish, and indifferent to anything but his own pleasure. He had no patriotism, honour, or generosity, but was not destitute of the ability to rule. He had no legitimate children. His mistresses were numerous, and several of them were raised to the highest ranks of nobility. Six of the sons he had by them were made dukes, viz. Monmouth (by Lucy Walters), St. Albans (by Nell Gwynn), Richmond (by Louise de Querouaille), and Cleveland, Grafton, and Northumberland (by Barbara Villiers). — BIBLIOGRAPHY: S. R. Gardiner, *History of the Commonwealth*; Macaulay, *History of England*; O. Airy, *Charles II.*;

E. Scott, *The King in Exile*; R. Crawford, *The Last Days of Charles II.*; Sir H. M. Imbert-Terry, *A Misjudged Monarch: Charles Stuart.*

CHARLES XII. King of Sweden, was born at Stockholm, 27th June, 1682. On the death of his father, in 1697, when he was but fifteen years old, he was declared of age by the Estates. To his jealous neighbours this seemed a favourable time to humble the pride of Sweden. Frederick IV. of Denmark, Augustus II. of Poland, and the Czar Peter I. of Russia concluded an alliance which resulted in war against Sweden. With the aid of an English and Dutch squadron the Danes were soon made to sign peace, but Augustus of Saxony and Poland and the Czar were still in the field. Rapidly transporting 20,000 men to Livonia, Charles stormed the Czar's camp at Narva, slaying 30,000 Russians and dispersing the rest (30th Nov., 1700). Crossing the Dwina he then attacked the Saxons and gained a decisive victory. Following up this advantage, he won the battle of Clissau, drove Augustus from Poland, had the crown of that country conferred on Stanislaus Lesczinsky, and dictated the conditions of peace at Altranstadt, in Saxony, in 1706. In Sept., 1707, the Swedes left Saxony, Charles taking the shortest route to Moscow. At Smolensk he altered his plan, deviated to the Ukraine to gain the help of the Cossacks, and weakened his army very seriously by difficult marches through a district extremely cold and ill supplied with provisions. In this condition Peter marched upon him with 70,000 men, and defeated him completely at Poltava.

Charles fled with a small guard, and found refuge and an honourable reception at Bender, in the Turkish territory. Here he managed to persuade the Porte to declare war against Russia. The armies met on the banks of the Pruth (1st July, 1711) and Peter seemed nearly ruined, when his wife, Catherine, succeeded in bribing the grand vizier, and procured a peace in which the interests of Charles were neglected. The attempts of Charles to rekindle a war were vain, and after having spent some years at Bender, he was forced by the Turkish Government to leave. Arrived in his own country in 1714, he set about the measures necessary to defend the kingdom, and the fortunes of Sweden were beginning to assume a favourable aspect when he was slain by a cannonball as he was besieging Frederikshall, 30th Nov., 1718. Firmness, valour, and love of justice were the great features in the character of Charles, but were disfigured by an obstinate rashness. After his death Sweden sank from the rank of a leading power. — BIBLIOGRAPHY: Voltaire, *Histoire de Charles XII.*; Lavisse et Rambaud, *Histoire générale* (vol. vi.); R. N. Bain, *Charles XII. and the Collapse of the Swedish Empire.*

CHARLES XIII. King of Sweden, was born in 1748, being the second son of King Adolphus Frederick. In the war with Russia, in 1788, he received the command of the fleet, and defeated the Russians in the Gulf of Finland. After the murder of his brother, Gustavus III., in 1792, he was placed at the head of the regency and gained universal esteem in that position. The revolution of 1809 placed him on the throne at a very critical period, but his prudent conduct procured the union of Sweden with Norway, 4th Nov., 1814. He adopted as his successor Marshal Bernadotte, who became king on the death of Charles, 5th Feb., 1818.

CHARLES XIV. *See* BERNADOTTE.

CHARLES I. King of Spain. *See* CHARLES V., EMPEROR OF GERMANY.

CHARLES IV. King of Spain, born at Naples 12th Nov., 1748, died in 1819. He succeeded his brother, Ferdinand VI., in 1788, and was all his life completely under the influence of his wife and her paramour Godoy. In 1808 Charles abdicated in favour of Napoleon.

CHARLES. Archduke of Austria, third son of the Emperor Leopold II., was born in Florence 5th Sept., 1771, died in 1847. After distinguishing himself in various campaigns, in 1796 he was appointed commander-in-chief of the Austrian army on the Rhine, and won several victories against the French. In 1805 he commanded in Italy against Masséna, and won Caldiero (31st Oct.); but in the campaign of 1809 in Germany against Napoleon he was unsuccessful, the battle of Wagram (5th and 6th July) laying Austria at the feet of the French emperor. With that event the military career of Charles closed. He published several military works of value.

CHARLES ALBERT. King of Sardinia, born 1798, was the son of Charles Emmanuel, Prince of Savoy-Carignan. In 1831 he succeeded to the throne on the death of Charles Felix, but his government at first greatly disappointed the Liberal party by its despotic tendencies. It was not till near 1848 that, seeing the growing strength of the progressive and national movement in Italy, he took up the position of its champion. As such he took the field against Austria on behalf of the Lombardo-Venetian provinces, but was crushingly defeated at Novara, 23rd March, 1849. He abdicated in favour of his son, Victor Emmanuel, and, retiring to Portugal, died 28th July, 1849.

CHARLES EDWARD STEWART. Called the *Young Pretender*, born 1720 at Rome, died 1788. He was a grandson of James II., King of England, son of James Edward (the *Old Pretender*) and Clementina, daughter of Prince Sobieski. In 1742 he went to Paris, and persuaded Louis XV. to assist him in an attempt to recover the throne of his ancestors. Fifteen thousand men were on the point of sailing from Dunkirk, when the English admiral Norris dispersed the whole fleet. Charles now determined to trust to his own exertions. Accompanied by seven officers, he landed on the west coast of Scotland, from a small ship called the *Doutelle.* Many Lowland nobles and Highland chiefs went over to his party. With a small army thus formed he marched forward, captured Perth, then Edinburgh (17th Sept., 1745), defeated an army of 4000 British under Sir John Cope at Prestonpans (22nd Sept.), and, advancing, obtained possession of Carlisle.

He now caused his father to be proclaimed king, and himself Regent of England; removed his headquarters to Manchester, and soon found himself within 100 miles of London, where many of his friends awaited his arrival. The rapid successes of the adventurer now caused a part of the British forces in Germany to be recalled. Want of support, disunion, and jealousy among the adherents of the House of Stewart, some errors, and the superior force opposed to him, compelled Prince Charles to retire in the beginning of 1746. The victory at Falkirk (28th Jan., 1746) was his last. As a final attempt he risked the battle of Culloden against the Duke of Cumberland, 16th April, 1746, in which his army was defeated and entirely dispersed. The prince now wandered about for a long time through the wilds of Scotland, often without food, and the price of £30,000 sterling was set upon his head.

At length, on 20th Sept., 1746, five months after the defeat of Culloden, he escaped in a French frigate. He received a pension of 200,000 livres yearly from France, and of 12,000 doubloons from Spain. Forced to leave France by the terms of the Peace of Aix-la-Chapelle (1748), he went to Italy, and in 1772 married a princess of Stolberg-Gedern, from whom eight years later he was separated. (*See* ALBANY.) He subsequently became an inveterate drunkard, died on 31st Jan., 1788, and was buried at Frascati. The funeral service was performed by his only surviving brother, Henry, Cardinal York, with whose death in 1807 the Stewart line ended. The cardinal received a pension from Britain of £4000 a year till his death.—BIBLIOGRAPHY: A. C. Ewald, *Life and Times of Prince Charles Stuart, Count of Albany*; Andrew Lang, *Prince Charles Edward.*

CHARLES MARTEL'. Ruler of the Franks, a son of Pepin Héristal, born about 688, died in 741. His father had governed as mayor of the palace under the weak Frankish kings with so much justice that he was enabled to make his office hereditary in his family. Chilperic II., King of the Franks, refusing to acknowledge Charles Martel as mayor of the palace, the latter deposed him, and set Clothaire IV. in his place. After the death of Clothaire he restored Chilperic, and subsequently placed Thierri on the throne. Charles Martel rendered his rule famous by the great victory which he gained in Oct., 732, over the Saracens, near Tours, from which he acquired the name of *Martel*, signifying *hammer*. Charlemagne was his grandson.

CHARLES THE BOLD. Duke of Burgundy, son of Philip the Good and Isabella of Portugal, born at Dijon, 10th Nov., 1433. While his father yet lived Charles left Burgundy, and, forming an alliance with some of the great French nobles for the purpose of preserving the power of the feudal nobility, he marched on Paris with 20,000 men, defeated Louis XI. in 1466, and won the counties of Boulogne, Guines, and Ponthieu. Succeeding his father in 1467, he commenced his reign by severe repression of the citizens of Liége and Ghent. In 1468 he married Margaret of York, sister of Edward IV. of England. Liége having rebelled, the duke stormed and sacked the town.

In 1470 the war with France was renewed, and although the duke was forced to sue for a truce he soon took up arms anew, and, crossing the Somme, stormed and fired the town of Nesle. Louis meanwhile involved him in greater embarrassments by exciting against him Austria and the Swiss. Charles, ever ready to take up a quarrel, threw herself on Germany with characteristic fury, and lost ten months in a futile siege of Neuss. He was successful, however, in conquering Lorraine from Duke

René. Charles now turned his arms against the Swiss, took the city of Granson, putting 800 men to the sword. But this cruelty was speedily avenged by the descent of a Swiss army, which at the first shock routed the duke's forces at Granson, 3rd March, 1476. Mad with rage and shame, Charles gathered another army, invaded Switzerland, and was again defeated with great loss at Morat. The Swiss, led by the Duke of Lorraine, now undertook the reconquest of Lorraine, and obtained possession of Nancy. Charles marched to recover it, but was utterly routed and himself slain.

The House of Burgundy ended with him, and his death without male heirs removed the greatest of those independent feudal lords whose power stood in the way of the growth of the French monarchy. His daughter Mary married Maximilian of Germany, but most of his French territory passed into the hands of the French king.—BIBLIOGRAPHY: J. F. Kirk, *History of Charles the Bold*; R. Putnam, *Charles the Bold.*

CHARLES THE GREAT. *See* CHARLEMAGNE.

CHARLES RIVER. A river in Massachusetts, which flows into Boston harbour, dividing Boston from Charlestown.

CHARLESTON. A city and seaport of South Carolina, on a tongue of land formed by the confluence of the Rivers Cooper and Ashley, which unite just below the city, and form a spacious and convenient harbour extending about 7 miles to the Atlantic, and defended by several forts. The city is regularly laid out, most of the principal thoroughfares being 60 to 70 feet wide and bordered with beautiful trees. It is much the largest town in the state, and is one of the leading commercial cities in the south. The staple exports are cotton, cottonseed, rice, resin and turpentine, lumber, and phosphate. The Civil War greatly damaged the trade, but there has since been marked commercial and industrial progress.

Yellow fever has made frequent ravages in Charleston, but on the whole it is considered more healthy than most other Atlantic towns in the southern states. It was the scene of the outbreak of the Civil War on 12th April, 1861, and was evacuated by the Confederates on 17th Feb., 1865. On 31st Aug., 1886, the coast region of the United States from Alabama to New York experienced a series of earthquake shocks, from which Charleston in particular suffered severely, many lives and about five million dollars worth of property being destroyed. Pop. 62,265.

CHARLESTOWN. former city and seaport of the United States, since 1874 part of the municipality of Boston, with which it is connected by bridges across Charles River. In the south-east part there is one of the chief navy-yards in the United States, occupying an area of from 70 to 80 acres. Bunker Hill, on which was fought one of the most celebrated battles of the American Revolution, is in this town, and there is on the site a commemorative monument 220 feet high.

CHARLEVILLE (the mediæval **Arcæ Remorum** and **Carolopolis**). A town, France, department of Ardennes, on the Meuse, opposite Mézières, which is joined to it by a bridge. It has wide and regular-built streets, considerable manufactures of metal goods, etc., and a large trade in coal, iron wine, etc. It was an important military station until the destruction of its fortifications in 1687. Captured by the Germans early in Aug., 1914, it was reoccupied by the French in Nov., 1918. Pop. 22,708.

CHAR'LOCK. The English name of *Sinăpis arvensis*, a common yellow weed in cornfields, also called wild mustard. Jointed or white charlock is *Raphanus Raphanistrum.* It too is a common cornfield weed, but it has white or straw-coloured flowers and jointed pods.

CHARLOTTE. A town of the United States, in North Carolina, with a college for women, a military institute, and several manufactories. Outside the city limits is Biddle University for coloured students. Pop. 82,675.

CHARLOTTE-AMALIE. A town, West Indies, capital of the Island of St. Thomas, one of the Virgin Islands, belonging to the United States, lying on the south side of the island. It has an excellent harbour, and is a considerable entrepôt for goods for the neighbouring islands. Pop. about 12,000.

CHARLOTTE AUGUSTA. Princess, daughter of Queen Caroline and George IV., was born at Carlton House, 7th Jan., 1796. She was carefully educated and highly accomplished. In 1816 she married Prince Leopold of Coburg, afterwards King of the Belgians, and died 5th Nov., 1817, after being prematurely delivered of a dead child.

CHARLOTTENBURG (shăr-lot'en-burh). A town of Germany, on the Spree, about 3 miles from Berlin.

with which it was incorporated in 1920. It contains a palace and park, great technical school or college, also a number of industrial and manufacturing establishments. Pop. 305,181.

CHARLOTTESVILLE. A town of the United States, not far from the centre of Virginia, having the State university adjacent. Pop. 15,245.

CHARLOTTETOWN. A town of British North America, capital of Prince Edward Island, on Hillsborough Bay, 110 miles N. of Halifax. It contains handsome public buildings and churches, is advantageously situated for commerce, and its harbour is one of the best in North America. Pop. 12,361.

CHARM. Anything believed to possess some occult or supernatural power, such as an amulet, spell, etc., but properly applied (as the name, derived from Lat. *carmen*, a song, indicates) to spells couched in formulas of words or verses.

CHARON (kā'ron). In Greek mythology, the son of Erebus and Night. It was his office to ferry the dead over the rivers of the infernal regions, for which office he received an obolus, or farthing, which accordingly was usually put into the mouth of the deceased. He was represented as an old man, with a gloomy aspect, matted beard, and tattered garments.

CHARPENTIER, Gustave. French musical composer, born at Dieuze, Lorraine, 1860. He studied at Lille, and under Massart and Massenet at the Paris Conservatoire. In 1887 he gained the Grand Prix de Rome with *Didon*, a lyrical drama. The most famous of his works, for which he wrote both music and libretto, is his opera *Louise*, produced at the Opéra Comique, Paris, in 1900. After taking Paris by storm the opera met with great success elsewhere on the Continent, in England, and in the United States. His other works include: *La Vie du Poète, Julien, Marie,* and *Orphée*.

CHART. A term applied chiefly to a representation of some portion of the sea, with or without adjacent coasts; as distinct from a "map" of land surfaces. The word is also given to graphical records of fluctuations in temperature, weather, population, etc. A hydrographical or marine chart displays such coasts, islands, rocks, channels, harbours, rivers, and bays as occur in the section covered; with points of the compass, soundings—that is, depth of water, etc.: every guidance needed by a vessel for her safety in the neighbourhood.

In a *plane chart* the meridians are supposed parallel to each other, the parallels of latitude at equal distances, and the degrees of latitude and longitude everywhere equal to each other. The earliest-known charts date from the beginning of the thirteenth century; contour lines were marked on charts before they were applied to terrestrial maps, owing to the comparative facility with which sea depths can be discovered by sounding as compared with the more complicated methods needed for ascertaining heights on land. Numerous excellent charts are produced by the Hydrographic Department of the British Admiralty, and sold at a low price with a view to making their use general among seamen. In the United States charts are published by the Coast Survey Department. *See also* MAP.

CHARTER. A written instrument, executed with usual forms, given as evidence of a grant, contract, or other important transaction between man and man. *Royal charters* are such as are granted by sovereigns to convey certain rights and privileges to their subjects, such as the Great Charter, granted by King John in 1215 (*see* MAGNA CHARTA), and charters granted by various sovereigns to boroughs and municipal bodies, to universities and colleges, or to colonies and foreign possessions. Somewhat similar to these are charters granted by the State or Legislature to banks and other companies or associations, etc.

CHARTERED COMPANIES. Trading companies which receive from the Government of the country to which they belong a charter granting them certain rights and privileges in a certain region or sphere of action, and also imposing upon them certain obligations or restrictions. One of the oldest, and the greatest and most celebrated of all these companies, was the East India Company, which received its first charter in 1600, and was the means of founding the British Empire in India. A Russia company was of earlier date, and maintained its existence down to 1825. The Hudson Bay Company, though late in origin, still exists in a highly flourishing condition.

Several chartered companies of recent origin have come prominently before the public, and have done much to enlarge the British Empire, though not granted by their charters such exclusive privileges as the chartered companies of early times. One of these the Imperial British East Africa Company—had a comparatively short career receiving a charter in 1888, and being finally wound up in 1897, after having resigned its charter to the Government. Its founder was Sir W. Mackinnon (died in 1893), and it was mainly through him and the company that Uganda and the region extending between it and the Indian Ocean were secured to the British Empire. The Government paid the company £250,000 on the surrender of its charter and all rights and property in the region, a sum far smaller than had been disbursed. A more fortunate company, established in West Africa, in the Niger region, and for a time known as the National African Company, received a charter in 1886, and became well known as the Royal Niger Company. At the head of it was Sir George Taubman Goldie, to whom may be ascribed the acquisition for Britain of Northern Nigeria, and parts of the territory between it and the sea. Latterly it was decided that the administrative rights and powers of the company should be transferred to the Crown, and the transfer took place in 1900.

The company then became simply a trading company—the Niger Company, Limited. In South Africa a huge tract or territory, the main portion of which is now comprised in Rhodesia, has been acquired for Britain by the British South Africa Company. The moving spirit in this company was the late Cecil Rhodes, and the charter was obtained in 1889. It expired in 1914, but was renewed for a further period of ten years. An immense amount has been spent in opening up the country, in constructing railways, telegraphs, and roads, in providing a settled government, and otherwise, and so far the expenditure has greatly exceeded the revenue. In 1920 a commission was appointed to investigate the claim of the company for repayment of its expenditure upon the administration of the territory. Another chartered company is the British North Borneo Company, which acquired its charter in 1882, and under it administers a region as large as Ireland, and rich in various tropical products.

CHARTERHOUSE. A celebrated school and charitable foundation in the city of London. In 1371 Sir Walter Manny built and endowed it as a priory for Carthusian monks (hence the name, a corruption of *Chartreuse*, the celebrated Carthusian convent). After the dissolution of the monasteries it passed through several hands till it came into the possession of Thomas Sutton, who converted it into a hospital and school, richly endowed, consisting of a master, preacher, head schoolmaster, forty-four boys and eighty decayed gentlemen, with a physician and other officers and servants. In 1872 the Charterhouse School was removed to new buildings at Godalming, in Surrey. The old premises were sold to the Merchant Taylors' School, which is now installed here in new buildings erected in 1875.

The non-academic department of the Charterhouse still remains in the old hospital buildings. Each of the "poor brethren" receives food, clothing, and lodging in the hospital, and an allowance of £36 a year. They must be over fifty years of age, and members of the Church of England. In the school there are thirty junior scholarships of £75 a year, and thirty senior of £95. The school has long had a high reputation, and many boys are educated there other than the scholars properly so called. Among famous men who have received their education at the Charterhouse are Isaac Barrow, Addison, Steele, John Wesley, Blackstone, Grote, Thirlwall, Havelock, John Leech, and Thackeray, who gave a description of the hospital and "poor brethren" in *The Newcomes*.—BIBLIOGRAPHY: L. Hendricks, *The London Charterhouse*; Wilmot and Streatfield, *Charterhouse, Old and New*.

CHARTER-PARTY. A contract executed by the freighter and the master or owner of a ship, containing the terms upon which the ship is hired to freight. The ordinary forms of charter are either for the use of a ship on a particular voyage to carry particular goods to be shipped by the charterer, or a similar charter with liberty given to the charterer to carry goods of any shippers as in a general ship, or a charter of a ship for a particular time. The masters and owners usually bind themselves that the goods shall be delivered (dangers of the sea excepted) in good condition. The charterer is bound to furnish the cargo at the place of lading, and to take delivery at the port of discharge within specified periods called *lay days*.—Cf. Sir T. E. Scrutton, *Charter-parties and Bills of Lading*.

CHARTERS TOWERS. A town of Australia, in Queensland, 82 miles S.W. by rail of the port of Townsville, on the northern spurs of the Towers Mountains, a flourishing place, with rich gold-mines, which have yielded gold to the value of £20,000,000. Pop. 9499.

CHARTIER (shär-tyā), **Alain.** A French poet and moralist, born, it is supposed, at Bayeux about 1386, died in 1449. His contemporaries considered him the father of French eloquence. His poems are often graceful and nervous, and his vigorous prose contains many fine thoughts and prudent maxims.

CHARTISM and **CHARTISTS.** Names for a political movement and its supporters that formerly caused great excitement in Britain. The Reform Bill passed in 1832 gave political enfranchisement to the middle-classes, but to the large body of the working-classes, it brought, primarily at least, no additional advantages, and this circumstance was turned to account by many demagogues, who urged on the people the idea that they had been betrayed by the middle-classes and their interests sacrificed. A period of commercial depression and a succession of bad harvests brought discontent to a head in the Chartist movement. It was founded on the general idea that the evils under which the people were labouring were due to the misconduct of the Government and a defective political representation. In 1838 the famous "Charter," or "People's Charter," was prepared by a committee of six members of Parliament and six working-men. It comprised six heads, namely:—1. Universal suffrage, or the right of voting for every male of twenty-one years of age. 2. Equal electoral districts. 3. Vote by ballot. 4. Annual Parliaments. 5. No other qualifications to be necessary for members of Parliament than the choice of the electors. 6. Members of Parliament to be paid for their services.

Immense meetings were now held throughout the country, and popular excitement mounted to the highest pitch. Physical force was advocated as the only means of obtaining satisfaction. In June, 1839, after the refusal of the House of Commons to consider a monster petition in favour of the Charter, serious riots took place. In 1848 the French Revolution of February stirred all the revolutionary elements in Europe, and a great demonstration on the part of the Chartists was organized. But the preparations taken by the Government for defence prevented outbreaks of any consequence, and Chartism then gradually declined. In London alone 200,000 special constables were enrolled, among which number was the subsequent Emperor Napoleon III. Some of the demands of the Charter have been adopted by the Liberal party and made into law; while the more advanced section of Chartism has been absorbed by Socialistic and Republican movements. — BIBLIOGRAPHY: Carlyle, *Chartism*; R. G. Gammage, *History of the Chartist Movement*; Kingsley, *Alton Locke*.

CHARTRES (shärtr). A city, France, capital of the department of Eure-et-Loire, on the Eure, 49 miles S.W. of Paris. It is a very ancient city, with many antique houses, largely built of timber. The cathedral, one of the most magnificent in Europe, partly of the twelfth century, and with much old glass, is rendered conspicuous by its two spires, and by its position surmounting the height on which the city partly stands. Manufactures: woollens, hats, machinery, leather, etc. Chartres was occupied by the Germans in 1870, and formed their base of operations against the army of the Loire. Pop. 25,357.

CHARTRES, Robert Philippe Louis Eugène Ferdinand d'Orléans, Duc d'. Born 1840, died 1910. He was the second son of the Duc d'Orléans, and a grandson of Louis Philippe. Driven into exile by the revolution of 1848, he lived in Germany and England. In 1861 he went to America, where he entered the Federal army, but soon returned to England and married his cousin, a daughter of the Prince de Joinville. After the revolution of 1870 he served for some years in the French army, but in 1886 his name was struck off the Army List in consequence of a new law which excluded the members of royal families from serving in the army or the navy. His *Souvenirs de Voyage* appeared in 1869.

CHARTREUSE (shär-treuz), or **GREAT CHARTREUSE.** A famous monastery in South-Eastern France, north-east of Grenoble, at the foot of high mountains, 3280 feet above sea-level, till recently the headquarters of the order of the Carthusians. It was founded in 1084, but the present building, a huge, plain-looking pile, dates from 1676. The monks used to make here the well-known liqueur called *Chartreuse*, according to a secret recipe; since the expulsion in 1903 it is made at Tarragona, in Spain.

CHAR'TULARY. A record or register in which the charters or title-deeds of any corporation were copied for safety and convenience of reference. They were often kept by private families.

CHARYBDIS (ka-rib'dis). An eddy or whirlpool in the Straits of Messina, celebrated in ancient times, and regarded as the more dangerous to navigators because in endeavouring to escape it they ran the risk of being wrecked upon Scylla, a rock opposite to it. There are several whirlpools in this region which may have been dangerous enough to the undecked boats of the Greeks, but none which the modern navigator with due caution may not easily pass.

CHASE. In printing, an iron frame used to confine types when made into pages.

CHASE, or CHACE. The name given in Norman times to a tract of ground stocked with wild beasts and game, and having the hunting rights thereon reserved. It differed from a "forest" by being, as to the hunting, in private rather than in royal hands; but the two terms were occasionally interchangeable, for a forest granted to a subject might become a chase, while a chase which passed to royalty became a forest in so doing.

CHASE, Salmon Portland. American politician and jurist, born in New Hampshire, 1808, died in 1873. Having adopted law as his profession, he settled at Cincinnati and acquired a practice there. He early showed himself an opponent of slavery, and was the means of founding the Free-soil party, which in time gave rise to the great Republican party—the power that brought the downfall of

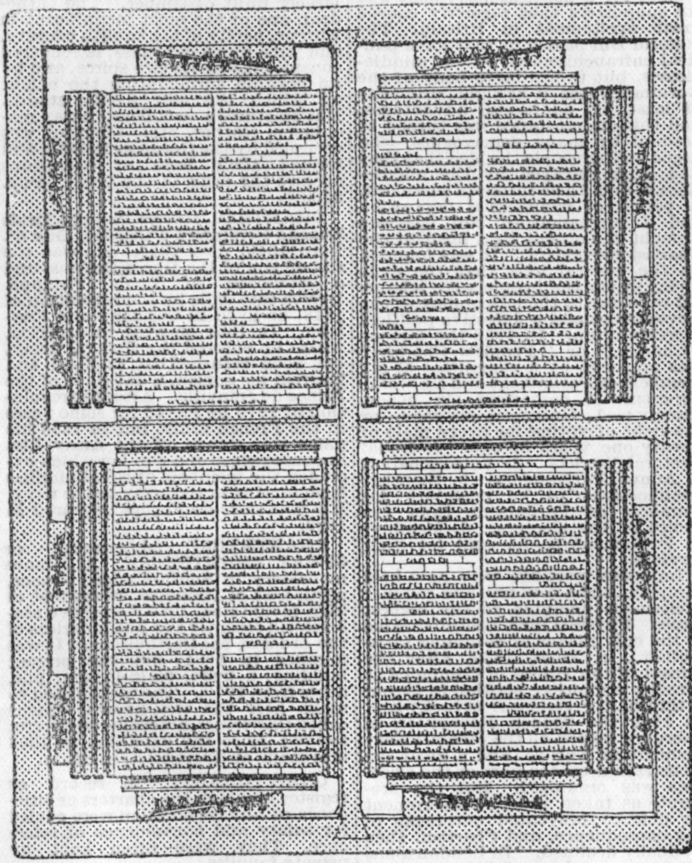

A Forme, consisting of type pages, locked up in a Chase

slavery. From 1849 to 1855 he was a member of the United States Senate, in which he vigorously opposed the extension of slavery into the new territories. In 1855 he was elected Governor of Ohio, being re-elected in 1857. In 1860 he was an unsuccessful candidate for the presidency. In 1861 he was nominated Secretary of the Treasury, and in this post was signally successful in providing funds for carrying on the Civil War. In 1864 he resigned office, and was appointed Chief Justice of the Supreme Courts.

CHASIDIM (*h*as'i-dēm), or **PIETISTS.** The name of a Jewish sect which appeared in the middle of the eighteenth century. Its adherents are strongly inclined to mysticism, and believe in extraordinary cures. They are most numerous in Russian Poland, Rumania, and some parts of Galicia and Hungary, and are regarded with great antipathy by the orthodox Jews. Chasidim is also the name given to a sect which sprang up about the second century B.C. This party is credited with the origin of the revolt of the Maccabees, with combating the erroneous notions bred among the Jews by the study of Grecian philosophy, and with being the parent stock of the Pharisees.

CHASING. The art of working decorative forms in low-relief in gold, silver, or other metals. It is generally practised in connection with repoussé work, in which the figures are punched out from behind and are then sculptured on the front or *chased* with the graver.

CHASSEPÔT RIFLE (shás-pō). A breech-loading rifle, named after its inventor, Antoine Alphonse Chassepôt, and adopted as the fire-arm of the French infantry in 1870, but since given up. It was about 4 lb. lighter than the needle-gun, and about 1 lb. lighter than the Martini-Henry rifle.

CHASSEURS (shás-*eur*; a French word signifying "hunter"). A name given to various sections of light infantry and cavalry in the French service.

CHASSIS. Originally meaning a window-frame, the word is now widely used for that portion of a motor vehicle which consists of the wheels, frame, and machinery, but excludes the body. The chassis and the body are frequently manufactured by different makers, being provinces of the engineer and coachbuilder respectively.

CHASTELARD, or **CHÂTELARD, Pierre de Bocsozel de.** A young Frenchman, celebrated for his infatuation for Mary Queen of Scots, born 1540 in Dauphiné. He was of good family, handsome, with a turn for verse-making, and possessed of all the accomplishments of a gallant of the age. He fell madly in love with Mary Stuart at the Court of Francis II., followed her to Scotland, and, being graciously received, was foolish enough to invade twice the royal bedchamber while Mary was being undressed by her maids. He was tried publicly at St. Andrews and hanged (1563), the queen resisting all appeals for pardon. She is said to have encouraged his passion more than was consistent with prudence.—Cf. Swinburne, *Chastelard: a Tragedy.*

CHAS'UBLE. The upper garment worn by a priest during the celebration of mass. It was originally circular, had a hole in the middle for the head, but no holes for the arms. In later times the sides were cut away to give a freer motion to the arms, and it has now become an oblong garment hanging down before and behind, made of rich materials, as silk, velvet, cloth of gold, and has a cross embroidered on the back. (See illustration on p. 560.)

CHAT. The popular name of birds of the genus Saxicŏla, family Sylviadæ or warblers. They are small, lively birds, moving incessantly and rapidly about in pursuit of the insects on which they chiefly live. There are three species found in Britain, the stone-chat, whin-chat, and wheat-ear. The yellow-breasted chat of the United States is a larger bird, belonging to the genus Icteria (*I. polyglotta*), family Turdidæ or thrushes.

CHATALJA. Village near Constantinople. In 1912 the Turks built fortifications through it, called Chatalja lines, to protect their capital against the Bulgarians in the first Balkan War. They were attacked in force from 17th Nov. to 19th Nov., when the Bulgarians, unable to make any progress, withdrew.

CHÂTEAU (shä-tō). The French term for a castle or mansion in the country; a country-seat.—*Château en Espagne*, literally a castle in Spain; a castle in the air: a phrase of doubtful origin.

CHATEAUBRIAND (shä-tō-bri-äṇ), **François Auguste, Vicomte de.** A celebrated author and politician, born at St. Malo, in Brittany, of a noble family, 14th Sept., 1768, died 1848. After serving in the navy and the army he travelled in North America; but the news of the flight of Louis XVI. and his arrest at Varennes brought him back to France. Shortly after he quitted France, and joined with other emigrants the Prussian army on the Rhine. After being wounded at the siege of Thionville and suffering many miseries, he made his way to London, where, friendless and penniless, he was just able to earn a subsistence by giving lessons in French and doing translations. Here he published in 1797 his *Essai Historique*, which met with but small success. At this time the death of his mother, and the accounts of her last moments transmitted to him by his sister, helped to effect a certain change in the religious opinions of Chateaubriand, and from a not very profound sceptic he became a not very profound believer.

CHASUBLES
Left, Ancient form. *Right,* Modern form.

In 1800 he returned to France, and in the following year published his romance of *Atala*, the scene of which is laid in America, and the year after his celebrated work *Le Génie du Christianisme*, which is a kind of brilliant picture of Christianity in an æsthetic and romantic aspect. Style, power of description, and eloquence are the merits of the book rather than any depth of thought; but it carried the author's reputation far and wide, and contributed much to the religious reaction of the time. After a short career as diplomatist under Napoleon, Chateaubriand made a tour in the East (1806-7), visiting Greece, Asia Minor, and the Holy Land. As the fruit of his travels he published *Les Martyrs* (1809) and *Itinéraire de Paris à Jérusalem* (1811). He hailed the restoration of Louis XVIII. with enthusiasm, was appointed ambassador to Berlin, and then to London, but in 1824 quarrelled with the Premier, M. de Villèle, and was summarily dismissed. After the revolution of 1830 he refused to take the oath of allegiance to Louis Philippe, forfeiting thus a pension of 12,000 francs. At this time his writings were chiefly political, and mostly appeared as newspaper articles, pamphlets, etc. In his later years he wrote several works, but none of the value of his earlier productions. He died 4th July, 1848, leaving memoirs (*Mémoires d'outre-tombe*) which contain severe judgments on contemporary men and things.—BIBLIOGRAPHY: Sainte Beuve, *Chateaubriand et son groupe littéraire*; E. Faguet, *Le XIX. Siècle*; J. Bedier, *Etudes critiques*; F. Gribble, *Chateaubriand and his Court of Women*.

CHÂTEAUDUN (shä-tō-dün). A town, France, department of Eure-et-Loire, 26 miles S.S.W. of Chartres, near the Loire. The old castle of the Counts of Dunois overlooks the town. Pop. 7296.

CHÂTEAU-GAILLARD (shä-tō-gā-yär). A celebrated feudal fortress in France, near Andelys (department of Eure), built by Richard Cœur de Lion. As late as the fifteenth century it was considered one of the strongest fortresses in Normandy. Its picturesque situation on a high rock overlooking the river has made it a favourite subject for artists. Turner has twice represented it.

CHÂTEAU-GONTIER (goṇ-tyā). A town, France, department of Mayenne, on the Mayenne, with linen and serge manufactories, bleachfields, tanneries. Pop. 7150.

CHÂTEAU-LAFITTE, CHÂTEAU-LATOUR, and **CHATEAU-MARGAUX** (mär-gō). Famous vineyards, all in the department of the Gironde, France, furnishing the best of the red wines of Bordeaux.

CHÂTEAUROUX (shä-tō-rö). A town, France, capital of the department of Indre, 144 miles S.S.W. of Paris, on the Indre. It has straight, broad streets, and spacious squares. Cloth, cotton, hosiery, woollen yarn, paper, etc., are made; and there are tanneries and dyeworks. Pop. 26,707.

CHÂTEAU-THIERRY (ti-ā-ri). A town, France, department of Aisne, on the Marne, 38 miles S.S.W. of Laon, with manufactures of linen and cotton twist, pottery, leather, etc. It is the birthplace of La Fontaine. In the European War Château-Thierry, occupied by the Germans, was recaptured by American and French troops in July, 1918. The town received the Legion of Honour in July, 1920. Pop. 8265.

CHÂTELET (shät-lā; diminutive of *château*). Anciently a small castle or fortress. Two such buildings at Paris gained some historical importance—the Grand and Petit Châtelet. The Grand Châtelet was the castle of the Counts of Paris, and was long the seat of certain courts of justice; but afterwards, like the Petit Châtelet, was converted into a prison. The Grand Châtelet was demolished in 1802, the Petit Châtelet in 1782.

CHÂTELET (shät-lā). A manufacturing town of Belgium, province of Hainaut, on the Sambre. Pop. 15,124.—*Châtelineau*, opposite to it, has a pop. of 17,500.

CHÂTELLERAULT (shä-tel-rō). A town, France, department of Vienne, 20 miles N.N.E. of Poitiers, on the Vienne. It is a place of some antiquity, having once been the capital of a duchy which, in 1548, was bestowed by Henry II. on the Earl of Arran, Regent of Scotland, and still gives a title to his descendant, the Duke of Hamilton. It has a Government small-arms factory, and manufactures cutlery, hardware, etc. Pop. 17,704.

CHATHAM (chat'am). Municipal borough, town, naval arsenal, and seaport, England, Kent, on the Medway, about 34½ miles by rail from London, adjoining Rochester so closely as to form one town with it. Formerly a parliamentary borough returning one member to the House of Commons, Chatham was disfranchised in 1918. The importance of Chatham is due to the naval and military establishments at Brompton in its immediate vicinity. The royal dockyard was founded by Queen Elizabeth previous to the sailing of the Armada. Since 1867 it has been greatly enlarged, and is now about

2 miles in length, with most capacious docks, in which the heaviest warships can be equipped and sent directly to sea. Building-slips, saw-mills, and metal-mills, and all the requisites of a great naval station are here on the largest scale and in the finest order. The military establishments include extensive barracks, arsenal, and park of artillery, hospital, store-houses, and magazines, etc. The town is poorly built, but is defended by a strong line of fortifications which also serve as a flank defence for the metropolis. Pop. (1931), 42,996.

CHATHAM. A town of Canada, province of Ontario, on the River Thames, 11 miles N. of Lake Erie, with manufactures of machinery, iron castings, and woollens, and a trade in lumber, etc. Pop. 14,569.

CHATHAM. A town in New Brunswick, at the mouth of the Miramichi, with a Roman Catholic cathedral and college, and a large trade in lumber. Pop. 4017.

CHATHAM, William Pitt, Earl of. One of the most illustrious statesmen of Britain, the son of Robert Pitt of Boconnoc, in Cornwall, born 15th Nov., 1708, died 11th May, 1778. He was educated at Eton and Oxford, and entered Parliament as member for the borough of Old Sarum (which was the property of his family), and soon attracted notice as a powerful opponent of Walpole. In spite of the king's dislike, Pitt was powerful enough to win a place in the administration (1746), first as Vice-Treasurer of Ireland, and afterwards as Paymaster-General. In 1756 he became Secretary of State and real head of the Government. Dismissed in 1757 on account of his opposition to the king's Hanoverian policy, no stable administration could be formed without him, and he returned to power the same year in conjunction with the Duke of Newcastle.

It was under this administration and entirely under the inspiration of Pitt that Britain rose to a place amongst the nations she had not before occupied. Wolfe and Clive, both stimulated and supported in their great designs by Pitt, won Canada and India from the French, and the support the Great Commoner gave Frederick of Prussia contributed not a little to the destruction of French predominance in Europe. The accession of George III. brought Lord Bute into power, and Pitt, disagreeing with Bute, resigned in 1761. In 1766 he strongly advocated conciliatory measures towards the American colonies, and undertook the same year to form an administration, he himself going to the House of Lords as Earl of Chatham. But the ministry was not a success, and in 1768 he resigned.

After this his principal work was his appeals for a conciliatory policy towards the colonies. But his advice was disregarded, and the colonies declared themselves independent in 1776. The character of Chatham was marked by integrity, disinterestedness, and patriotism. With great oratorical gifts and the insight of a great statesman he had liberal and elevated sentiments; but he was haughty, and showed too marked a consciousness of his own superiority. —BIBLIOGRAPHY: Rev. F. Thackeray, *History of the Right Hon. William Pitt, Earl of Chatham*; F. Harrison, *Chatham* (in *Twelve English Statesmen*); Lord Rosebery, *Lord Chatham: his Early Life and Connections*.

CHATHAM ISLANDS. A group of three islands in the South Pacific Ocean, belonging to New Zealand. The largest, or Chatham Island, lat. (S. point) 44° 7′ S.; long. 176° 49′ W., is about 350 miles E. from New Zealand, and is about 38 miles long and 25 miles broad. Pitt Island is much smaller, and Rangatira is an insignificant patch. A considerable portion of Chatham Island is occupied by a salt lagoon. The soil is in many places fertile, and crops of potatoes, wheat, and vegetables are successfully grown. Cattle and sheep are reared, and thus whaling or other vessels that call are supplied with fresh provisions as well as with water. The original inhabitants, called Morioris, differed considerably from the Maoris, by whom and a mixed race they have been supplanted. The islands were discovered in 1791, and form part of New Zealand for administrative purposes. Area, 372 sq. miles. Pop. (1926), 562.

CHATI (chä'tē). A species of small leopard found in South America, very destructive to small quadrupeds and birds, and especially to poultry-yards, but so gentle, when domesticated, as to have gained for itself the name of *Felis mitis*, or gentle leopard.

CHÂTILLON-SUR-SEINE (shä-tē-yōṇ-sûr-sen). A town, France, department of Côte d'Or, 45 miles N.W. of Dijon, on the Seine. It is chiefly notable for the congress of the Allied Powers and France held here in 1814. In 1870 (19th Nov.) the Germans suffered here a severe repulse. Pop. 4640.

CHAT MOSS. An extensive morass, area about 6000 to 7000 acres, situated chiefly in the parish of Eccles, Lancashire. It is remarkable as being the scene of operations for reclaiming bog-lands first successfully carried out on a large scale in the end of the eighteenth and beginning of the nineteenth century; also for offering one more field of triumph to George Stephenson, who in 1829 carried the Liverpool and Manchester Railway over it after all other engineers had declared the feat impossible.

CHATOY'ANT. A term applied to certain minerals that, when cut and polished, show a changeable undulating lustre when turned to the light, e.g. cat's-eye opal and Labrador felspar.

CHÂTRE (shä-tr), **LA.** An old town, France, department of Indre, 21 miles S.E. of Châteauroux, right bank of Indre. Pop. 4581.

CHATSWORTH. An estate of the Dukes of Devonshire, in Derbyshire, purchased in the reign of Elizabeth by William Cavendish, who began the building of a hall which served as one of the prisons of Mary Queen of Scots. The present building was nearly completed by the first Duke of Devonshire between 1687 and 1706, the north wing being added by the sixth duke. It forms a square, with an inner court, and is remarkable for the collections of pictures and statues it contains. The façade is 720 feet long, or with the terraces 1200 feet. The park is about 11 miles in circumference, diversified by hill and dale. The conservatory covers nearly an acre, and was designed by Paxton, forming on a small scale the forerunner of the exhibition building of 1851.

CHATTAHOO'CHEE. A river, United States, rising in the Appalachian Mountains in Georgia, and forming for a considerable distance the boundary between Georgia and Alabama. In its lower course, after the junction of the Flint River, it is named the Appalachicola, and is navigable to Columbus in Georgia for steamboats. Total course, about 550 miles.

CHATTANOO'GA. A town of the United States, in Tennessee, on the Tennessee River, near the Alabama boundary, an important centre of trade and manufactures. During the Civil War, in Oct., 1863, the Confederates suffered a great defeat there after desperate fighting. The University of Chattanooga was founded in 1867. Pop. 119,798.

CHAT'TELS. Property movable and immovable, not being freehold. The word *chattel* is originally the same word with *cattle*, formed from L.Lat. *capitalia*, meaning heads of cattle, from Lat. *caput*, head. Chattels are divided into real and personal. Chattels *real* are such as belong not to the person immediately, but dependently upon something, as an interest in a land or tenement, or a lease, or an interest in advowsons. Any interest in land or tenements, for example, is a real chattel; so also is a lease, an interest in advowsons, and so forth. Chattels *personal* are goods which belong immediately to the person of the owner, and include all movable property.

CHATTERERS. The popular name of certain insessorial birds of the family Ampelidæ, genus Ampĕlis, as the Bohemian chatterer or wax-wing (*Ampĕlis garrŭla*) and the chatterer of Carolina (*A. cedrōrum*).

CHATTERIS. An ancient market town of England, in the north of Cambridgeshire, with brewing, malting, engineering, and other establishments. Pop. 5153.

CHAT'TERTON, Thomas. A youth whose genius and melancholy fate have gained him much celebrity, born at Bristol in 1752, of poor parents, and educated at a charity school. He exhibited great precocity, became extremely devoted to reading, and was especially fond of old writings and documents. At the age of fourteen he was apprenticed to an attorney. In 1768, when the new bridge at Bristol was completed, he inserted a paper in the *Bristol Journal* entitled *A Description of the Friars' First Passing over the Old Bridge*, which he pretended he had found along with other old manuscripts in an old chest in St. Mary Redcliffe Church, Bristol. He also showed his friends several poems of similarly spurious antiquity which he attributed to one Rowley.

In 1769 he ventured to write to Horace Walpole, then engaged upon his *Anecdotes of Painters*, giving him an account of a number of old Bristol painters which was clever enough to deceive Walpole for a time. Dismissed from the attorney's office, he left with his manuscripts for London, where a favourable reception from the booksellers gave him high hopes. For them he wrote numerous pamphlets, satires, and letters, but got no substantial return, and his situation became daily more desperate. At last, after having been several days without food, he poisoned himself, 25th Aug., 1770. The most remarkable of his poems are those published under the name of Rowley (*The Rowley Poems*), spurious antiques, such as *The Tragedy of Ælla*, *The Battle of Hastings*, *The Bristow Tragedy*, etc. The poetical works of Chatterton, with an essay by W. W. Skeat, and a memoir of the poet by Edward Bell, appeared in 1871 in the Aldine Edition of the British Poets.—BIBLIOGRAPHY: D. Wilson, *Chatterton: a Biographical Study*; J. H. Ingram, *The True Chatterton.*

CHATTERTON'S COMPOUND. A mixture of Stockholm tar, resin, and gutta-percha, used in the construction of submarine telegraph cables, etc.

CHAU'CER, Geoffrey. Born in London in the year 1340 or thereabouts. It is not possible to ascertain the exact date of his birth, but in a legal document dated 1386 he is spoken of as being of the age of forty and upwards, and as having borne arms for twenty-seven years. If we reckon that he began to bear arms when aged nineteen—a reasonable supposition—this would fix the date of his birth as 1340. At any rate, this date cannot be wrong by more than a year or two.

Early Life.—Chaucer's father was John Chaucer, a well-to-do vintner of London, who must have been in favour at court, for he accompanied the king and queen to Flanders and Cologne in 1338. His influence apparently secured the appointment of Chaucer as page to Lionel, Duke of Clarence, and his wife, the Countess of Ulster, in the year 1357, when Chaucer was seventeen, according to our previous assumption. Chaucer, as is obvious to anyone reading his works, was a well-educated and well-read man, but there is no reason to suppose that he studied at either university. He was with the Clarence household both in London and Yorkshire. In 1359 Chaucer went to France as a soldier, with Edward III. and the four princes; he was taken prisoner, but was liberated in March, 1360, the king paying £16 towards his ransom, a sum worth £200 nowadays.

In the year 1366 we find mention of a certain Philippa Chaucer, who received an annual pension of ten marks from the queen; it is usually assumed for good but not conclusive reasons that this lady was Chaucer's wife. It is extremely likely that her maiden name was Roet, and that she was the sister of Catherine de Roet, who eventually became the third wife of John of Gaunt. This would account for the friendly relations between Chaucer and John of Gaunt, and John's son, Henry IV.

In 1367 Chaucer was granted a pension of twenty marks; he is referred to in the document which has been preserved as "valettus noster." In an undated document which probably belongs to 1368 Chaucer's name stands seventeenth on the list of names of thirty-seven esquires of the royal household. In 1369 Chaucer was again campaigning in France; he is spoken of as "a squire of less estate."

Diplomatic Service.—During the next ten years Chaucer was often abroad on diplomatic missions. In 1370 he went abroad, though we do not know his destination; in 1373 he went with two others to Genoa to settle a commercial treaty; we know that he was back in England by 28th April, and that he visited Florence. It is very likely that he met the great Italian poet Petrarch (1304–74) at Padua, and was told by him *The Story of Grisilde,* which afterwards Chaucer turned into *The Clerkes Tale.*

The next year, 1374, is an important one, as marking a great increase in Chaucer's material prosperity. The king granted him a pitcher of wine daily. Chaucer afterwards exchanged this gift in return for twenty marks a year. He was also appointed Comptroller of the Customs of Wool in the Port of London; he was obliged in this capacity to keep the rolls with his own hand, and to be continually present. John of Gaunt granted him an annuity of £10 for life. Finally, the Corporation of London gave him a lease for life of the dwelling-house over the city-gate of Aldgate. In 1376 Chaucer was employed on some secret mission with Sir J. Burley; the next year he went to Flanders, and later on in the year to France, where he was engaged in peace negotiations. In 1378 he was again in France, endeavouring to arrange a marriage between Richard II. and a daughter of the King of France. In the same year he went to Lombardy on a mission to the Duke of Milan.

In 1382 Chaucer was appointed to be Comptroller of Petty Customs in the Port of London, and was given permission to discharge his duties by deputy. In 1385 he was given similar permission with regard to his duties as Comptroller of Wool. In 1386 Chaucer was elected a Knight of the Shire for Kent. Later in this year, owing to public dissatisfaction with the customs department rather than any personal shortcomings, Chaucer was deprived of both his comptrollerships.

Later Career.—In 1387 Chaucer's wife died, as her pension, hitherto regularly paid, ceased in June of that year. In 1388 Chaucer sold his two pensions, as he was in pecuniary difficulties; the next year his difficulties were lightened by his being appointed Clerk of the King's Works by Richard II., who for the first time took the government into his own hands.

In 1390 Chaucer was made forester of North Petherton Park, in Somerset, by the Earl of March, who was grandson of the Duke of Clarence. He was robbed of the king's money twice in September, once at Westminster, and once at Hatcham, Surrey, near the "foul oak."

In 1391 Chaucer lost his appointment as Clerk of the Works, though we do not know for what reason. He seems to have been in need of money from this time onwards, until the usurpation of Henry IV., although Richard II. granted him an annuity of £20 in 1394. In 1398 Chaucer applied twice to the Exchequer for an advance of 6*s.* 8*d.*, so his annuity does not seem to have been paid regularly. At this time Chaucer was granted a tun of wine annually for life. In 1399 the accession of Henry IV. brought prosperity again to the poet, who was now old and in failing health. He was given forty marks a year, as well as his pension of £20. On the strength of this prosperity he leased a house in Westminster for fifty-three years. He was not to enjoy his good fortune long, for he died on 25th October, 1400, and was buried in Westminster Abbey, being the first as well as the greatest poet to be buried in what is now known as Poets' Corner.

These are the facts which we know about Chaucer's life, and though they are pitifully scanty, and we should often prefer information about other sides of his life, we may well be grateful that we know as much as we do. That we do know these facts is due entirely to the nature of Chaucer's life. He lived at court, he held responsible positions there, and was chosen to go on difficult foreign embassies. Hence it is that we know about his journeys and we possess quite full information about his grants of money and pensions.

Personal Characteristics.—We have, however, information of another kind about him which is both more interesting and on unimpeachable authority—the authority of Chaucer's own works.

In the Prologue to *Sir Thopas* we get a description of Chaucer's personal appearance. The host, Harry Bailly, addressed him as follows:

> "'What man artow,' quod he
> Thou lokest as thou woldest finde an hare,
> For ever upon the ground I see thee stare.
> Approche neer, and loke up merrily.
> Now war yow, sirs, and lat this man have place
> He in the waast is shape as wel as I;
> This were a popet in an arm t' enbrace
> For any womman, smal and fair of face.
> He semeth elvish by his countenaunce,
> For unto no wight dooth he daliaunce.'"

From this passage we can see that Chaucer frequently wore an abstracted look, that he was a man of small, slender build (for the host is obviously speaking ironically when he compares him to himself), and that he did not lightly enter into casual conversation with strangers. Occleve, a disciple of Chaucer, has preserved his master's portrait with loving care in the margin of one of his own works. His features are gentle and expressive, and even here, too, his eyes are cast down as if he would find a hare. He looks like a quiet, reflective man with just a suspicion of quaint or ironic humour. In the *House of Fame*, lines 605–660, Chaucer gives us a description of his way of life; it is too long to quote in full, but he speaks of how he set himself to make songs and books, and how he often made his head ache with writing. For when he had gone through the routine of his official duties, and had balanced his books, he used to go home and sit at a book of another kind, hearing neither this nor that; and instead of rest and recreation he used to study, as dumb as a stone, till he looked dazed.

He lived, in fact, a hermit's life, though he was by no means an ascetic. But although books had a strong claim on him, the love of nature has a stronger; and in a very delightful passage in the Prologue to the *Legend of Good Women* he tells us how spring made him desert his books:

> "And as for me, though that I can but lyte,
> On bokes for to rede I me delyte,
> And to hem yeve I feyth and ful credence,
> And in myn herte have hem in reverence,
> So hertely that there is game noon
> That fro my bokes maketh me to goon,
> But hit be seldom, on the holyday;
> Save, certeynly, whan that the month of May
> Is comen, and that I here the foulis singe,
> And that the floures ginnen for to springe,
> Farwel my book and my devocioun!"

Love of nature and love of books, then, were Chaucer's two master passions. His descriptions of Nature are among the most charming passages in all his works. They have an inimitable freshness and vivacity. Although more than five hundred years old, Chaucer's poems make most modern poems look out-of-date, stale, and unprofitable. His work is of perennial interest and permanent charm. It is plain to see that Chaucer was also a keen student of books. Yet his scholarship is not a dead thing, as scholarship and learning too often tend to become, for it is enlivened by the natural vivacity of his mind. Though fond of books, Chaucer was no mere book-worm or pedant: he was a man who had led a busy and useful life at court, who had met and mixed with many of the best and most cultured men of his day, and who had been employed in responsible diplomatic work. Last, but by no means least, he was a man who had travelled both as a soldier and as a diplomatist; he had, therefore, entirely shaken off that insular spirit which is not uncommonly the bane of English writers. He writes always in the broad-minded, tolerant manner of a thorough man of the world.

Works.—We have now got some idea of Chaucer's life and character; let us look in detail at what he wrote. His work has for long been divided into three periods—the French, the

Chaucer

Italian, and the English—and although attempts have been made to upset this method of grouping, they have not been successful, and the three-group arrangement still is the most satisfactory and most instructive. It must, of course, be understood that these periods are artificial, not natural, divisions, made by scholars for convenience in tracing the development of Chaucer's mind and art; and that the periods are not separated by impassable barriers, since there is a period of transition between the French and Italian and between the Italian and English periods.

The First, or French Period may be said to date from when Chaucer began to write until about the year 1379. During this period Chaucer was serving his apprenticeship as a poet: most of his early works, therefore, are translations from the French. The most important of these is the translation of *The Romance of the Rose*, a very famous French poem begun by William de Lorris as a romance and finished by Jean de Meung as a satire. It is usually thought that the translation of *The Romance of the Rose* which we possess is not in its entirety the work of Chaucer; it is customary on linguistic and other grounds to divide the poem into three parts, A, B, and C, and to say that Chaucer wrote A, a North of England man B, and a quite unknown man C. Some critics, on account of the intrinsic merits of the poem, claim that it is all Chaucer's work. Anyhow, Chaucer could not have found a more suitable poem to work upon when learning how to write, and the translation is not only good in itself, but is admirably faithful to the original.

In 1369 Blanche, the first wife of John of Gaunt, died, and Chaucer wrote *The Book of the Duchess* in memory of her. It is not only a very beautiful poem, but it shows great artistic power in the handling of some rather conventional devices.

In 1373, when Chaucer perhaps met Petrarch at Padua, he probably wrote *The Story of Grisilde*, afterwards introduced into the *Canterbury Tales* as *The Clerk's Tale.*

In this first or more or less French period we may place the following, though the exact dates of them are not known: *Chaucer's A.B.C.*, a prayer to the Virgin, possibly composed for Blanche, who, as we have seen, died in 1369; *The Life of Saint Cecyle*, afterwards *The Second Nun's Tale*; *The Complaint to Pity*, a piece of no great merit; *The Story of Constance*, afterwards *The Man of Law's Tale*; *The Twelve Tragedies*, afterwards *The Monk's Tale*; and *The Complaint of Mars.*

The Second, or Italian Period.—*The Parliament of Fowls* was written in 1382 for the marriage of Richard II. and Anne of Bohemia. It is a delightful poem, but, although it seems altogether English and original, it is, as a matter of fact, based upon Italian and French models. But Chaucer could assimilate his reading better now, and could select what was good and reject what was bad with great skill. *The House of Fame*, an incomplete poem with many reminiscences of Dante, was probably written in 1384.

The Legend of Good Women was written in about 1385. The Prologue of this poem is an excellent piece of work, and the poem itself is good, but the scheme which lay behind it did not admit of any variety.

Chaucer must have recognised himself that it was becoming monotonous, for he did not complete the poem. There were to have been twenty stories, but only eight were completed — *Cleopatra, Thisbe, Dido, Hypsipyle and Medea, Lucretia, Ariadne, Philomela,* and *Phyllis. Hypermnestra* was left unfinished.

The Complaint to his Lady, Anelida and Arcyte, To Adam the Scrivener, and the delightful mock-sentimental ballad *To Rosamond* are all minor poems written about this time. To this period also belongs Chaucer's *Translation of Boethius,* one of his favourite authors, whom he translated into prose. But by far the most important poem of this period is *Troilus and Cressida,* a poem based upon the *Filostrato* of Boccaccio. This is considered by some critics to be Chaucer's masterpiece, though it does not make such a universal appeal as the *Canterbury Tales. Troilus,* though indebted to Boccaccio, does not follow its model too closely. Chaucer has introduced an element of his own into the story—his own inimitable humour. Tragedy and comedy are harmoniously blended, and the characters are treated dramatically, the strong contrasts between them being deftly brought out.

Palamon and Arcite, afterwards *The Knight's Tale,* is also modelled on Boccaccio (*The Teseide*), and was also written about this time. It, too, shows how Chaucer has absorbed and in some ways improved upon his model.

The Third, or English Period contains several minor poems, the *Envoy to Scogan,* the *Envoy to Bukton,* the *Complaint to his Purse* (1399), *The Former Age, Fortune, Truth, Gentleness,* and *Lack of Steadfastness.* In 1391 he wrote a *Treatise on the Astrolabe,* a kind of hand-quadrant or sextant for observing the positions of the stars. This treatise is dedicated to his little son Lewis, a boy at that time ten years old. It is an interesting work, not only as showing what a tender, thoughtful father Chaucer must have been to his motherless son, but also as showing the versatility of the author and how he could write so as to be understood by a child.

But by far the greatest of all Chaucer's works, as well as the most typical of his final or English period, is the immortal *Canterbury Tales.* Chaucer may have conceived the idea of writing the *Tales* in about the year 1386; as we have seen, he included in his scheme several pieces that had been written previously. It has been suggested that Chaucer derived from Boccaccio the idea of a connected series of tales. This may or may not have been so; the plan of collecting different tales and linking them up by means of a central story was of great antiquity in the East. But if Chaucer owed any debt to Boccaccio, he has repaid it with interest, for the framework of the *Canterbury Tales* is far more artistic than that of the *Decameron.*

A pilgrimage upon which all sorts and conditions of men met on terms of temporary equality, and combined religion with holiday-making, was an ideal setting for a varied collection of tales. The original scheme of the tales was too much even for Chaucer to carry out; had it been adhered to we might have had some one hundred and twenty tales, as it is we have only twenty-four. Even in their incomplete condition the tales not only give us by far the best picture which we possess of life in the Middle Ages, they are also one of the greatest works in English, or for that matter in any language.

Chaucer, then, was one of the greatest Englishmen, as well as one of the greatest pioneers; a great man-of-letters and a great poet; but above all a great man, winning our love by his charm, his freshness, his tolerance, and more especially by his all-pervading humour.—BIBLIOGRAPHY: T. R. Lounsbury, *Studies in Chaucer*; A. W. Pollard, *Chaucer*; Sir A. W. Ward, *Chaucer* (English Men of Letters Series); W. W. Skeat, *The Chaucer-Canon*; T. Tyrwhitt, *Poetical Works of Chaucer*; F. J. Snell, *The Age of Chaucer.*

CHAUCI. An ancient Teutonic tribe dwelling east of the Frisians, between the Ems and Elbe on the shore of the North Sea.

CHAUDEFONTAINE (shōd-foṇ-tān). A village of Belgium, 4 miles from Liège, on the Vesdre, with hot springs much frequented in summer.

CHAUDES-AIGUES (shōd-āg). A village, France, department of Cantal, 28 miles E.S.E. of Aurillac, with thermal springs so copious that the water is used for warming the town in winter and for washing fleeces. Pop. 1675.

CHAUDET (shō-dā), **Antoine Denis.** French sculptor, born at Paris 1763, died there 1810. His first work was a bas-relief under the peristyle of the Pantheon, representing the love of glory, an excellent work, the very simplicity and grandeur of which prevented its being justly estimated by the false taste of the age. In the museums of the Luxembourg and Trianon are several of Chaudet's finest works, such as *La Sensibilité,* and the beautiful statue of Cyparissa.

CHAUDIÈRE (shōd-yār). A river of Canada, Quebec province, which rises on the borders of Maine, near the sources of the Kennebec, and flows into the St. Lawrence about 6 miles above Quebec. The banks of the river are generally steep and rocky, and about 3 miles above its junction with the St. Lawrence are the Chaudière Falls, about 120 feet high. On the Ottawa River are other two falls of lesser dimensions, known as the Great and the Little Chaudière.

CHAUL'MUGRA. A tree (*Taraktogenos Kurzii*) of S. Asia, from the seeds of which an oil is obtained that has long been known and highly valued in India and China as a remedy for leprosy and other diseases, and has been introduced into Western countries in the treatment of skin complaints.

CHAUMONT (shō-mōn̦). A town, France, capital of the department of Haute-Marne, on a height between the Marne and the Suize. The town traces its origin to a baronial castle erected in A.D. 940. Here the Allies (Great Britain, Russia, Austria, and Prussia) signed the treaty of alliance against Napoleon, 1st March, 1814. Pop. 15,941.

CHAUMONTELLE (shō-mon-tel'). A delicious dessert pear which is much grown in Jersey, Guernsey, and the south of England.

CHAUNY (shō-nē). A town, France, department of Aisne, 19 miles W. by N. of Laon, on the Oise, It has manufactures of sacking, soda, sulphuric and nitric acids; cotton-mills; bleachworks and tanneries. Pop. 10,640.

CHAUSSES (shōs). The tight covering for the legs and body, reaching to the waist, formerly worn by men of nearly all classes throughout Europe. They resembled tight pantaloons with feet to them. The name *chausses de mailles* was given to defensive armour worn on the same parts of the body.

CHAUTAU'QUA. A beautiful lake in New York State, United States, 18 miles long and 1 to 3 broad, 726 feet above Lake Erie, from which it is 8 miles distant. On its banks is the village of Chautauqua, the centre of a religious and educational movement of some interest. This originated in 1874, when the village was selected as a summer place of meeting for all interested in Sunday-schools and missions. Since then the Chautauqua Literary and Scientific Circle has taken origin here, the most prominent feature of which is to engage the members—wherever they may reside—in a regular and systematic course of reading, extending, when completed, over four years, and entitling the student to a diploma.

CHAUVINISM (shō'vin-izm). An unreflecting and fanatical devotion to any cause, so called from *Nicholas Chauvin*, a soldier so enthusiastically devoted to Napoleon I. and so demonstrative in his adoration that his comrades turned him into ridicule. A *Chauvinist* now means a man who has narrow-minded notions of patriotism and hostility towards foreign people. It is equivalent to the English *Jingo*.

CHAUX-DE- ONDS (shōd-fōn̦), **LA.** A town of Switzerland, in the canton and 9 miles N.W. of the town of Neufchâtel, in a deep valley of the Jura. The inhabitants are largely engaged in the making of watches and clocks, of which Chaux-de-Fonds and Locle are the chief centres in Switzerland, and in similar branches of industry. Pop. 37,708.

CHAVICA (chav'i-ka). A genus of plants, nat. ord. Piperaceæ, including the common long pepper, Java long pepper, and betel-pepper.

CHAVONNE. A village of France, department of Aisne. It was the scene of fighting during the European War, in Sept., 1918.

CHAY-ROOT (shā). The roots of a small biennial plant of Hindustan, the *Oldenlandia umbellata*, growing principally on dry sandy ground near the sea; and extensively cultivated, chiefly on the Coromandel coast. It yields a dye which is much used in colouring Indian cotton and chintzes.

CHEADLE. A market town of England, in the north of Staffordshire, 14 miles N.E. of Stafford, and 4 miles E. of Longtown (Potteries), with collieries and manufactures of hardware. Pop. 6747. There is another Cheadle in Cheshire, 2 miles S.W. of Stockport, forming with Gatley an urban district. Pop. (1931), 18,469.

CHEB. Official name of Eger (q.v.).

CHEBOYGAN. A town of the United States, Michigan, near the north-west end of Lake Huron, a lake port, with saw-mills, grain-mills, etc. Pop. 9859.

CHECHENSK. *See* RUSSIA (table).

CHED'DAR. A parish and thriving village, England, County Somerset, 19½ miles S.W. of Bristol. The dairies in the neighbourhood have long been famous for the excellence of their cheese, which is made from the whole milk by a highly approved method now widely practised. Cheddar cheese can be traced to the time of Camden (1551-1623). Harding of Marksbury introduced the system of cheddar-making into Scotland. Pop. 2007.

CHEDU'BA. An island in the Bay of Bengal, belonging to Burma, about 10 miles off the coast of Arracan; length and breadth, each about 15 miles; area, 220 sq. miles; pop. 30,197. The soil is fertile, and produces tobacco, rice, indigo, and pepper. Petroleum is also found.

CHEE-FOO. A town of China, in the province of Shantung, one of the last ports opened to foreign trade, which is now of considerable volume. Pop. 119,305.

CHEESE. One of the most important products of the dairy. Composed principally of *casein*—which exists in cows' milk to the extent of about 3 or 4 per cent—fat, and water. It is made from milk, skimmed wholly, partially, or not at all, the milk being curdled or coagulated, and the watery portion or whey separated from the insoluble curd, which being then worked into a uniform mass, salted (as a rule), and pressed in a vat or mould forms cheese, but requires to be *cured* or *ripened* for a time before being used. The coagulation of the milk may be effected either by adding an acid, as in Holland, or sour milk, as in Switzerland, or rennet, as usual in Britain and America.

There are a great many varieties of cheese, of which the most notable are Stilton, Cheshire, Cheddar, Wiltshire "truckles," Dunlop, amongst British; and Parmesan, Gruyère (Emmenthaler), Gorgonzola, Gouda, Roquefort, Camembert, amongst foreign ones. There are a good many cheeses, mostly made in Germany, which require that one's taste should be born to them, or that it should subsequently undergo a long, intricate, and not altogether pleasant training. In the United States cheese manufacture is carried on on a huge scale, and almost all the different European kinds, but chiefly Cheddar, are made. Large factories are there devoted to the manufacture, receiving the milk of many hundred cows. Cheese to the value of over £20,657,000 was imported by Britain in 1920, some three-fourths from Canada, much also coming from the United States, Holland, and New Zealand. Sheep's- and goat's-milk cheeses are also made.

CHEESE-FLY. A small black fly, *Piophĭla casei*, akin to the house-fly or blow-fly. It lays its eggs in the cracks of cheese. The maggot, well known as the *cheese-hopper*, is furnished with two horny claw-shaped mandibles, which it uses both for digging into the cheese and for moving itself, having no feet. It performs its leaps by a jerk, first bringing itself into a circular attitude, when it can project itself twenty to thirty times its own length.

CHEETAH. The *Cynælurus jubātus* or hunting leopard of India, a native of Arabia and Asia Minor. It has its specific name (*jubātus*, crested or maned) from a short mane-like crest at the back of the head. When used for hunting, it is hooded and placed in a car. When a herd of deer is seen, its keeper places its head in the proper direction and removes its hood. It slips from the car, and, approaching its prey in a stealthy manner, springs on it with several bounds. It is about the size of a large greyhound, has a cat-like head, but a body more like a dog's. A slightly different variety inhabits Africa.

Cheetah

CHEFOO. *See* CHEE-FOO.

CHEILANTHES. A large genus of Leptosporangiate Ferns, mostly inhabitants of dry, rocky stations; it includes the Gold and Silver Ferns, which have the lower side of the leaf covered with a resinous powder of a golden or silvery appearance, secreted by glandular hairs.

CHEILOGNATHA (Diplopoda). A plant-eating ord. of Myriapoda, including Millipedes. Body cylindrical; antennæ short; two pairs of weak legs to each segment, with their bases approximated.

CHEILOPODA (Syngnatha). A carnivorous ord. of Myriapoda, including Centipedes. Body flattened; antennæ long; one pair of strong legs to each segment, with widely separated bases.

CHEIROLEPIS (kī-rol'e-pis). A genus of fossil ganoid fishes found in the Old Red Sandstone of Orkney and Morayshire, characterised by the great development of the pectoral and ventral fins.

CHEIRON (ki'ron). *See* CHIRON.

CHEIRONECTES, or CHIRONECTES. A small aquatic opossum, the Yapock, native to Central and South America. It lives on fish, and its hind-feet are webbed.

CHEIROPTERA. *See* BAT.

CHEIROTHERIUM. A name formerly given to hand-like footprints upon the rocks of the Trias or New Red Sandstone epoch. They are now known to have been made by gigantic extinct amphibians, Labyrinthodonts, so named from the complex foldings of their conical teeth.

CHEKE, Sir John. An English scholar, born at Cambridge in 1514, died in 1557. He was educated at St. John's College, and made the first regius professor of Greek. In 1544 he was appointed tutor to the future Edward VI., and appears likewise to have assisted in the education of the Princess Elizabeth. On the accession of Edward he received substantial signs of favour, was knighted, became Secretary of State in 1553, and was also a Privy Councillor. On the king's death he supported Lady Jane Grey, and was committed to the Tower. After a few months, however, he was set at liberty, and settled in Strasburg; but his connection with the English Protestant Church there gave offence to the Catholics in England, and his estates were confiscated. He supported himself by teaching Greek, but in 1556, having been induced to visit Brussels, he was arrested by order of Philip II. and sent prisoner to England. Under threat of the stake he recanted, and received the equivalent of his forfeited estates; but he felt so keenly his degradation that he died of grief. His chief distinction was the impulse given by him to the study of Greek. He wrote *De Pronuntiatione Græcæ Linguæ.*

CHEKHOV, Anton Pavlovitsh. Russian novelist and dramatist, born 1860, died 1904. His parents, although liberated serfs and illiterate people, gave their son a good education. Chekhov studied medicine, but after finishing his studies decided to embrace the literary profession. Under the pseudonym of *Chekhonte* he at first contributed numerous sketches to popular periodicals, but soon produced more serious work, which was received very favourably. In fact some literary critics did not hesitate to point him out as a worthy successor of Turgenev. In addition to his delicate sense of humour, Chekhov is a great stylist, his mastery of words being wonderful. In depicting his characters he is strictly objective and realistic, although he is not free from a strain of pessimism, a characteristic from which none of the younger Russian writers is free. His works include: *Philosophy at Home, Sorrow, In Exile, Darling, Terrible Night, The Black Moon and other Stories, The Kiss and other Stories.* Among his plays are: *The Sea-Gull, The Cherry Garden, The Swa Song,* and *Uncle Vanya.*

CHE-KIANG. A maritime province, China, between lat. 27° and 31° N., and including the Chusan Archipelago; area, 36,680 sq. miles; pop. 24,139,766. It is traversed by the Grand Canal, and has its principal ports Ningpo and Hangchow, the capital. Staple exports: silk and tea. On 11th April, 1916, the province of Che-kiang declared its independence.

CHELLEAN. A culture stage, so called after Chelles, a town east of Paris, where the Palæolithic artifact, the *coup de poing,* or "hand axe," was found in river-drift deposits resting directly on deposits of Tertiary Age. Professor James Geikie (1914), following Penck (1910), has relegated the Chellean artifacts to the Second Interglacial epoch. Weiger (1913) agrees. On the other hand, Osborne (1916), Boule, Breuil, Obermaier, and Schmidt (1912) place the Chellean phase in the Third Interglacial epoch. The Chellean artifacts were produced by Neanderthal man, who became extinct before or during the Fourth Glacial epoch. Pre-Chellean flint artifacts are called Eolithic.

CHELMSFORD. County town of Essex (to a parliamentary division of which it gives name), England, in a valley between the Chelmer and Cann, with several handsome public buildings. There are manufactories of agricultural implements, and a considerable trade in corn and malt. Pop. (1931), 26,537.

CHELMSFORD, LORD, The Right Hon. Frederic Augustus Thesiger. Eldest son of the first Lord Chelmsford, who was twice Lorc Chancellor; born 1827, educated at Eton, served in the Crimea and through the Indian Mutiny. As Deputy Adjutant-General he served in the Abyssinian campaign, was created C.B., made aide-de-camp to Her Majesty, and Adjutant-General to the forces in India (1868–76), and in 1877 was appointed commander of the forces and Lieutenant-Governor of Cape Colony. He restored Kaffraria to tranquillity, and was given the chief command in the Zulu War of 1879. After great difficulties with the transport, and some disasters, he gained the decisive victory of Ulundi, before the arrival of Sir Garnet Wolseley, who had been sent to supersede him On his return he was made G.C.B., and from 1884 to 1889 was Lieutenant of the Tower. He died in 1905.

CHELMSFORD, Frederic John Napier Thesiger, first Viscount. British administrator, born 12th Aug., 1868. Educated at Winchester and Magdalen College, Oxford, he became a barrister. He sat on the London School Board and London County Council, was Governor of Queensland from 1905 to 1909, and Governor of New South Wales from 1909 to 1913. He was appointed Viceroy of India in 1916, and held this office until 1921. In 1932 he was appointed Warden of All Souls College, Oxford. He died on 1st April, 1933.

CHELONIANS (ke-lō′-), or **CHELONIA.** An order of reptiles including the tortoises and turtles, and distinguished by the body being enclosed in a bony case, usually covered with horny scales or plates. The toothless jaws are covered by horny sheaths with cutting edges. There are eleven families: (1) Sphargidæ, including only the huge leathery turtle or Luth, ranging through tropical seas; (2) Chelydridæ, the snapping turtles from the fresh waters of North America; (3) Dermatemydidæ, freshwater tortoises from Central America; (4) Cinosternidæ, including a few terrapins from North and Central America, and Guiana; (5) Platysternidæ, a single species of water-tortoise from south-east Asia; (6) Testudinidæ, most of the water-tortoises, including the majority of the American terrapins; and the land-tortoises, some of these living, or recently living, in various islands (Galapagos Islands, Bourbon, Mauritius, Rodriguez, Aldabra, and the Seychelles) being of very large size; (7) Chelonidæ, three widely distributed marine species, the edible or green turtle (devoured at aldermanic feasts and the source of "real" turtle soup), the hawksbill turtle (yielding "tortoise-shell"), and the loggerhead turtle; (8) Polomedusidæ, freshwater forms from Africa and South America, of which may be named the "Arrau" turtle from the latter, valuable on account of its oil-yielding eggs; (9) Chelydidæ, a few freshwater tortoises from South America and Australia; (10) Carettochelydidæ, a single freshwater species from New Guinea; (11) Trionychoidea, the mud-turtles or soft tortoises from the rivers of Asia, Africa, and North America.

CHELSEA (chel′sē). A metropolitan and parliamentary borough of London, on the Thames, opposite Battersea, and chiefly distinguished for containing a royal military hospital, originally commenced by James I. as a theological college, but converted by Charles II. for the reception of sick, maimed, and superannuated soldiers. The building was finished in 1692 by Sir Christopher Wren. Connected with the hospital is a royal military asylum, founded in 1801, for the education and maintenance of soldiers' children. The parliamentary borough returns one member. Pop. (metropolitan borough) (1931), 59,026.

CHELSEA. A city of Massachusetts, United States, forming practically a north-east suburb of Boston. Pop. 45,816.

CHELTENHAM (chel′tn-am). A municipal and parliamentary borough and fashionable watering-place in England, in the county of Gloucester, beautifully situated on the small river Chelt, within the shelter of the Cotswold Hills. It grew rapidly into a place of fashionable resort after the discovery of its saline, sulphuric, and chalybeate springs in 1716, to which, in 1788, George III. paid a visit. The town has fine squares, crescents, terraces, gardens and drives, pump-rooms, assembly-rooms, and theatre, and has become famous for its colleges and schools. The Cheltenham College for boys, founded in 1841, and incorporated in 1894, and the Ladies' College, founded in 1854, and incorporated in 1880, are both of high repute, and there is also a grammar-school (founded in 1574), and a training college for teachers. The parish church and the Roman Catholic and Congregational churches are all fine buildings. The town has little trade, but depends almost wholly on its visitors and resident families. It returns one member to Parliament. Pop. (1931), 49,385.

CHELYABINSK. *See* TCHELYABINSK.

CHELYUSKIN, CAPE. The most northerly point of Siberia, a projection of the Taimyr Peninsula, called also *North-east Cape*.

CHEMICAL RAYS. A name given to the blue and violet rays of the spectrum, and also to the non-luminous rays at the violet end, which have a peculiarly powerful chemical effect on silver compounds.

CHEMIN DES DAMES. An important road running along the crest of hills overlooking the valley of the Ailette River in Northern France. After the battle of the Aisne in 1914 the Germans retained a foothold here, and the French offensive in 1917 included an attack on the Chemin des Dames. Some of the most desperate fighting in the campaign of 1918 took place at the Chemin des Dames.

CHEMISTRY. The science which treats of the nature, laws of combination, and mutual actions of the minute particles of the different sorts of matter composing our universe, and the properties of the compounds they form. It is a modern science developed from the earlier *Alchemy* (q.v.). The alchemists in their study of minerals and metallic ores made important but isolated discoveries, and at the close of the seventeenth century the German chemist Becher threw out certain speculations regarding the cause of combustion, which were taken up and extended by Stahl in the "phlogistic theory," and constitute the first generalisation of the phenomena of chemistry, though the theory itself was diametrically opposed to the truth. About the middle of the eighteenth century Dr. Black made his great discovery of a gas differing from atmospheric air, rapidly followed by that of a number of other gases by Cavendish, Rutherford, Priestley, and Scheele.

The discovery of oxygen by the two last-named chemists afforded to Lavoisier the means of revolutionising and systematising the science. By a series of experiments he showed that all substances, when burned, absorb oxygen, and that the weight of the products of combustion is exactly equal to that of the combustible consumed and of the oxygen which has disappeared. The application of this theory to the great majority of the most important chemical phenomena was obvious, and the Stahlian hypothesis disappeared. A yet more important step was the discovery by Dalton of the laws of chemical combination. His theory was immediately taken up by Berzelius, to whose influence, and careful determination of the chemical equivalents of almost all the elements then known, its rapid adoption was mainly due. To Berzelius we owe many of the modern improvements in the methods of analysis, while Sir H. Davy laid the foundation of electro-chemistry.

Of late years every branch of the science has advanced, but the most extraordinary progress has been made in organic chemistry, or the chemistry of the carbon compounds, and in physical chemistry, a branch of chemistry which is closely allied to certain branches of physics. The investigations of chemists have shown that the great majority of the different natural substances can be broken up into substances of less complicated nature, which resist all further attempts to decompose them, and appear to consist of only one kind of matter. These substances, by union of which all the different sorts of known matter are built up, are about eighty in number, and are called the *chemical elements*. The list (given below) includes such substances as gold, iron, oxygen, hydrogen, carbon, calcium, etc.

When any two or more of these elements are brought in contact, under suitable conditions, they may unite and form chemical compounds of greater or less complexity, in which the constituents are held in union by a form of energy which has received the name of *chemical affinity*. This affinity is characterised by its acting between dissimilar particles, and producing a new kind of matter, readily distinguishable from either of the substances combining to form it, and which cannot be again separated into its elements by merely mechanical processes. In these respects, and also in the fact that union occurs in definite proportions by weight, the compounds differ from mere mixtures of elements.

Laws of Combination.—(1) Combination takes place when the substances are in actual contact, and invariably produces considerable changes, so that the compound differs entirely from the original components. The more chemically unlike substances are, the more readily do they combine. (2) When substances, elementary or compound, combine together, they do so in fixed and definite proportions by weight. (*Law of definite proportions.*) (3) When substances combine in more than one proportion, the weights of the one substance which combine with a fixed weight of the other are multiples of a common factor. (*Law of multiple proportions.*) Thus, 28 parts of nitrogen combine with 16 parts of oxygen to form nitrous oxide, while 28 parts of the former and 32 of the oxygen produce nitric oxide. (4) Gases combine in fixed and definite proportions by volume as well as by weight, and the volume relationships can be expressed by simple integral numbers. (*Gay-Lussac's Law.*) Thus one volume of hydrogen combines with one of chlorine to yield two of hydrochloric acid gas; two of hydrogen with one of oxygen to yield two of steam (water vapour); and three of hydrogen with one of nitrogen, in the presence of acid, to yield two of ammonia. In many cases, e.g. steam, contraction occurs during the combination, but in no case is the volume of the product greater than the sum of the volumes of the reacting gases.

A study of the more important laws of combination led Dalton, in 1804, to introduce his atomic theory. According to this each element consists of a number of minute particles termed *atoms.* The atoms of any one element, e.g. hydrogen, are all alike as regards weight, size, etc., but differ from those of another element, say oxygen. For many years it was thought that these atoms were indivisible, and that they were the minutest particles of matter conceivable. The recent work of Sir J. J. Thomson and others indicates that in reality these atoms are themselves complex, and are built up of positive and negative *electrons* in such a manner that the atom as a whole is electrically neutral. According to this conception the atoms of all elements are formed of the same material—these electrons—but in different quantities, and it is thus not inconceivable that one element should be transformed into another. (*See* MATTER; RADIUM; HELIUM.)

The atoms are extremely minute, and it is impossible to determine the weight of the atom of any one element in ordinary units by purely chemical means (*see* MATTER), but chemists are able to determine the relative weights of the atoms. Thus the atom of lead is 207 times as heavy as the hydrogen atom. For various reasons it has been concluded that the atoms of most elements do not exist singly, but combine together in groups of two, three, etc., to form more complex particles, which are termed *molecules.* Thus the molecules of hydrogen, oxygen, nitrogen, chlorine, etc., each contain 2 atoms, ozone 3, phosphorus and arsenic 4, sulphur 8, and the majority of metals only 1, i.e. they are monatomic elements. When elements combine together, the combination occurs between the atoms, thus one atom of hydrogen combines with one atom of chlorine to yield a molecule of hydrochloric acid gas. Two atoms of hydrogen combine with one of oxygen to form a molecule of water or steam. An atom is sometimes defined as the smallest particle of an element which can enter into a chemical reaction, and the molecule as the smallest particle of a substance which can exhibit the characteristic properties of the substance. Gay-Lussac's law of volumes has been accounted for by a conclusion drawn by Avogadro (1811), that equal volumes of all gases under the same conditions of temperature and pressure contain the same number of molecules.

Symbols and Formulæ.—The names given to certain elements indicate some characteristic property. Chlorine (Gr. *chlōros* = yellow) indicates the yellow colour of the gas. Bromine (*brōmos* = stinking) indicates the pungent odour. Cæsium (*cæsius* = sky blue) indicates the blue colour of its spectrum. Many of the newer elements, e.g. Gallium, Germanium, Scandium, and Polonium, owe their names to the nationalities of their discoverers. For the sake of convenience each element is represented by a symbol. Dalton himself used a special set of symbols, but the modern system, which is largely due to Berzelius, consists in using the initial, or, in certain cases, to avoid confusion, the first two letters, of the English or Latin name, e.g. Al for aluminium, O for oxygen, C for carbon, Fe (from *ferrum*) for iron, Ag (*argentum*) for silver, etc.

These symbols not merely stand for the different elements but for definite quantities, viz. for one atom, and since each atom has a definite relative weight each symbol represents a definite weight. In deciding the atomic weights it is necessary to select some atom as unity. For many purposes it is simpler to select the lightest atom, viz. hydrogen, as unit, and to compare all the others with this; in modern chemistry it is becoming more customary to select oxygen as the standard, to say O = 16 and to give all the others on this basis (since the majority of atomic weights are determined experimentally with reference to oxygen and not to hydrogen), then H = 1·008. The following is a list of the commoner elements with their symbols and atomic weights (to which may be added Hafnium—Hf—180·0):—

ELEMENTS AND ATOMIC WEIGHTS, O=16

Element	Symbol	Weight	Element	Symbol	Weight
Aluminium	Al	27·1	Neodymium	Nd	144·3
Antimony	Sb	121·77	Neon	Ne	20·2
Argon	A	39·9	Nickel	Ni	58·7
Arsenic	As	75·0	Nitrogen	N	14·04
Barium	Ba	137·4	Osmium	Os	190·9
Bismuth	Bi	209·0	Oxygen	O	16
Boron	B	11·0	Palladium	Pd	106·5
Bromine	Br	79·92	Phosphorus	P	31·04
Cadmium	Cd	112·4	Platinum	Pt	195·2
Cæsium	Cs	132·81	Potassium	K	39·15
Calcium	Ca	40·1	Praseodymium	Pr	140·9
Carbon	C	12·0	Radium	Ra	226·0
Cerium	Ce	140·25	Rhodium	Rh	102·9
Chlorine	Cl	35·45	Rubidium	Rb	85·5
Chromium	Cr	52·0	Ruthenium	Ru	101·7
Cobalt	Co	58·97	Samarium	Sm	150·3
Columbium	Cb	93·5	Scandium	Sc	45·1
Copper	Cu	63·57	Selenium	Se	79·2
Erbium	Er	167·7	Silicon	Si	28·4
Fluorine	F	19	Silver	Ag	107·88
Gadolinium	G	157·3	Sodium	Na	23·00
Gallium	Ga	69·9	Strontium	Sr	87·63
Germanium	Ge	72·5	Sulphur	S	32·06
Glucinium	Gl	9·1	Tantalum	Ta	181·5
Gold	Au	197·2	Tellurium	Te	127·6
Helium	He	4	Terbium	Tb	159·2
Hydrogen	H	1·008	Thallium	Tl	204·1
Indium	In	114·8	Thorium	Th	232·5
Iodine	I	126·97	Thulium	Tm	169·4
Iridium	Ir	193·0	Tin	Sn	119
Iron	Fe	55·84	Titanium	Ti	48·1
Krypton	Kr	83	Tungsten	W	184
Lanthanium	La	138·9	Uranium	U	238·5
Lead	Pb	207·20	Vanadium	V	51·0
Lithium	Li	7·00	Xenon	Xe	130·2
Magnesium	Mg	24·36	Ytterbium	Yb	173·5
Manganese	Mn	54·93	Yttrium	Y	88·7
Mercury	Hg	200·6	Zinc	Zn	65·37
Molybdenum	Mo	96·0	Zirconium	Zr	90·6

By means of these symbols we can use formulæ for different compounds, thus H_2O indicates a compound of the two elements hydrogen and oxygen, in which 2 parts by weight of the former are combined with 16 of the latter. This is the actual composition of water, and thus the formula for the compound water is H_2O. This formula further denotes one molecule of water, which is built up of two atoms of hydrogen and one of oxygen. Again, oil of vitriol is composed of H, O, and S, and the relative weights are 2 of H, 32 of S, and 64 of O; we can therefore represent it by the formula H_2SO_4 (since 1H = 1, 1S = 32, and 1O = 16). Similarly, the formula for marble or calcium carbonate is $CaCO_3$, and indicates one molecule built up of one atom of calcium, one of carbon, and three of oxygen, or 40 parts by weight of calcium, 12 of carbon, and 48 of oxygen. Slaked lime or calcium hydroxide is $Ca(OH)_2$, oxalic acid $H_2C_2O_4$. If we wish to denote more than one molecule of a compound we prefix a large number, e.g. 2HCl indicates two molecules of hydrochloric acid gas, each consisting of one atom of hydrogen and one of chlorine.

An electrical theory of the nature of atoms, based on the properties of electrons, has made great progress in recent years. According to this theory, the mass of an atom is derived from a nucleus, which is made up of some whole number of elementary nuclei, all perfectly alike. The atomic weight of an atom will on this theory be represented by a whole number. A glance at the table will show that this does actually hold good for many of the elements, e.g. carbon, fluorine, helium, and lithium. By means of the positive ray analysis of Sir J. J. Thomson, the point has been experimentally settled by F. W. Aston for all elements which can conveniently be obtained in the gaseous form. Aston's conclusion is that an element either has an integral atomic weight, or else is made up of two or more components with integral atomic weights. (*See* ISOTOPES.)

Valency.—A glance at the formula of some simple hydrogen compounds, e.g. hydrogen chloride HCl, water HO_2 ammonia NH_3, and methane CH_4, or of certain metallic chlorides, e.g. NaCl, $CaCl_2$, $AlCl_3$, $SnCl_4$, indicates that the atoms of all the elements will not combine with the same number of atoms of hydrogen or of chlorine. Thus it has become customary to divide the elements into groups according to their *valency*, or according to the number of atoms of hydrogen with which one atom of the given element can combine or which it can displace.

Monovalent Elements .	H, Cl, Br, I, Na, K, Ag.
Divalent Elements . .	O, S, Ca, Ba, Sr, Pb, Sn.
Trivalent Elements .	N, P, As, Sb, Al, B, Au.
Tetravalent Elements .	C, Si, Sn, Pb.
Pentavalent Elements .	N, P, As, Sb.
Hexavalent Elements .	O, S, Se. Cr.

The above list indicates that the valency exhibited by a certain element is not always the same, e.g. in phosphorus trichloride, PCl_3, the phosphorus atom is trivalent, and in phosphorus pentachloride, PCl_5, it is pentavalent.

Closely related to the atomic weight of an element is its *equivalent weight*; this is often defined as the weight of the element which can combine with or displace unit weight of hydrogen (or on the oxygen basis 8 parts by weight of oxygen). Now in methane it can be proved experimentally that 4 parts by weight of hydrogen are combined with 12 parts by weight of carbon, hence the equivalent of carbon is 3 and its atomic weight is known to be 12. In ammonia we have 3 parts by weight of hydrogen combined with 14 of nitrogen, hence the equivalent of nitrogen is $\frac{14}{3}$, but its atomic weight is 14. There is always a simple relationship between the equivalent and atomic weights. The atomic weight is either equal to or a simple multiple of the equivalent weight—or atomic weight = equivalent weight × valency.

Classification of Chemical Substances.—The elements themselves are usually divided into the two main groups, *Metals* and *Non-metals*. The metals, e.g. Fe, Cu, Ag, Zn, Hg, Na, with the exception of mercury, are all solid at the ordinary temperature, possess a metallic lustre, and are usually good conductors of heat and electricity. Their oxides are as a rule basic oxides, and their chlorides fairly stable in presence of water. The non-metals, H, O, N, C, S, P, Cl, Br, etc., may be gases, liquids, or solids at the ordinary temperature; very few, e.g. C and I, possess a metallic lustre; as a rule they are bad conductors of heat and electricity; their oxides are acidic (acid anhydrides), and their chlorides are as a rule readily decomposed by water. The majority form definite stable compounds with hydrogen, whereas the metals do not. It is somewhat difficult to say whether certain elements, like As and Sb, should be placed with the metals or non-metals, and hence they are sometimes placed in a special group termed *metalloids*.

The modern classification of the elements is termed the "periodic" classification. It is based on Newlands's law of octaves (1864), which has since been developed by Lothar Meyer and Mendelejeff. According to Newlands, if the elements are arranged in the order of increasing atomic weight, then the 8th element resembles the 1st, the 9th, the 2nd, and so on.

H	Li	Be	B	C	N	O
F	Na	Mg	Al	Si	P	S
Cl	K	Ca	Cr	Ti	Mg	Fe

In the time of Newlands the number of elements known was small, and the atomic weights assigned to them were often incorrect, but with increasing progress the value of the law became more marked. The table of classification drawn up by Mendelejeff was based on Newlands's law.

According to Mendelejeff, the properties of the elements, as well as those of their compounds, are periodic functions of the atomic weights of the elements. Mendelejeff was able to show that certain atomic weights, then generally accepted, were incorrect, as the old atomic weights would not bring the elements into their proper positions, e.g. he altered Indium from 76 to 114, Beryllium from 13·8 to 9·2. Mendelejeff was also enabled to predict the properties of elements then not known but since discovered; the best-known examples are scandium, gallium, and germanium. According to this classification we see that elements with similar properties fall into the same group, e.g. F, Cl, Br, and I together; N, P, As, and Sb in the same group or family; Ba, Ca, Sr, and Mg, and S, Se, and Te. Again, the elements of each group exhibit, as a rule, the same valency.

PERIODS

		I.	II.	III.	IV.	V.	VI.	VII
Even Series.	0	He	Ne	A	Kr	Xe		
	1	Li	Na	K	Rb	Ca		
	2	Be	Mg	Ca	Sr	Ba		
	3			Sc	Y	La	Yb	
	4			Ti	Zr	Ce		Th
	5			V	Nb		Ta	
	6			Cr	Mo		W	U
	7			Mn				
Transition Elements	8			Fe	Ru		Os	
				Co	Rh		Ir	
				Ni	Pd		Pt	
Odd Series.	1			Cu	Ag		Au	
	2			Zn	Cd		Hg	
	3	B	Al	Ga	In		Tl	
	4	C	Si	Ge	Sn		Pb	
	5	N	P	As	Sb		Bi	
	6	O	S	Se	Te			
	7	F	Cl	Br	I			

The compounds of the elements with oxygen are termed *oxides*, and these are usually divided into basic oxides, acidic oxides, and peroxides. The basic oxides are all metallic oxides; the majority are insoluble in water, but the few which are soluble yield solutions with strongly alkaline reaction. The basic oxides are all capable of neutralizing acids yielding metallic salts and water. Acidic oxides, or acid anhydrides, as they are termed, are either the oxides of non-metals, e.g. NO_2, SO_3, CO_2, or the oxides of metals rich in oxygen, e.g. CrO_3, Mn_2O_7; as a rule they dissolve in water to strongly acidic solutions, in fact they are the anhydrides of acids, and the majority readily combine with water to yield the corresponding acids. An acid anhydride can combine with a basic oxide to yield a salt, e.g. CaO and CO_2 give $CaCO_3$, calcium carbonate. Peroxides are all rich in oxygen, e.g. N_2O_4, PbO_2, H_2O_2. As a rule they give up part of their oxygen when heated alone or with sulphuric acid, and they yield chlorine with concentrated hydrochloric acid.

When only one oxide of an element is known, the nomenclature is simple, e.g. CaO is the only common oxide of calcium, and is termed calcium oxide. Barium gives rise to the two oxides, BaO and BaO_2, termed barium oxide and barium peroxide. Iron gives the oxides FeO, Fe_2O_3, and Fe_3O_4, termed ferrous oxide, ferric oxide, and magnetic oxide of iron. Tin gives the oxides SnO and SnO_2, termed stannous and stannic oxides. The suffixes *-ous* and *-ic* applied to oxides always indicate that the *-ous* compound contains relatively less oxygen than the *-ic*, and the prefix *per-* indicates an oxide extremely rich in oxygen. The compounds of elements with sulphur are termed sulphides, with bromine bromides, with nitrogen nitrides, etc., e.g. KI is the formula for potassium iodide, and CaC_2 for calcium carbide.

Certain elements can combine with oxygen or other elements, yielding four or five distinct compounds, e.g. the oxides of nitrogen, and then the nomenclature is somewhat more complex—N_2O, nitrous oxide; NO, nitric oxide; N_2O_3, nitrogen trioxide or nitrous anhydride; N_2O_4, nitrogen tetroxide or nitric peroxide; and N_2O_5, nitric anhydride or nitrogen pentoxide. The expression anhydride is one frequently met with in connection with oxides, and indicates that the oxide is an acid anhydride, and when combined with water yields the acid of the same name as the oxide, thus, nitric anhydride and water yield nitric acid. Sulphur dioxide, SO_2, is often termed sulphurous anhydride, since with water it yields sulphurous acid, H_2SO_3; and sulphur trioxide, SO_3, is termed sulphuric anhydride, as it yields sulphuric acid, H_2SO_4, with water.

Three extremely important groups of compounds are those known respectively as *acids, bases,* and *salts.* Boyle grouped together as acids all compounds which possessed an acid taste, and were capable of turning certain blue vegetable dyes (litmus), etc.) red, and of decomposing wood ashes. According to Lavoisier, oxygen was a necessary constituent of acids (hence name *oxygen*, or acid producer, for this element), but it is now known that hydrogen and not oxygen is the essential constituent. Acids are thus particular compounds of hydrogen, and their characteristic property is that either the whole or part of the hydrogen they contain can be replaced by metals (metallic radicles) when the acid is treated with a metal, or a metallic oxide or hydroxide.

Thus sulphuric acid, H_2SO_4, with moist cupric oxide, CuO, yields a compound in which the whole of the hydrogen of the acid is replaced by the cupric radicle, and we have $CuSO_4$, cupric sulphate. Similarly, nitric acid, HNO_3, with potassium hydroxide, yields potassium nitrate, KNO_3. Hydrochloric acid, HCl, with calcium hydroxide, yields calcium chloride, $CaCl_2$. This reaction between an acid and a metallic hydroxide is often termed neutralisation, as by this process the acid properties are destroyed, and a compound known as a salt is formed. Most acids possess the characteristic properties mentioned above, and also evolve hydrogen when mixed with metallic magnesium, or carbon dioxide when mixed with sodium carbonate.

The majority of acids which contain oxygen—the oxy-acids as they are sometimes termed—decompose into water and an acid anhydride when strongly heated, e.g. H_2SO_4 into H_2O and SO_3, carbonic acid into H_2O and CO_2, silicic acid, H_2SiO_3, into H_2O and SiO_2 (silica). The modern view of acids is that they are hydrogen compounds which in aqueous solution are dissociated or ionised into hydrogen ions, which carry a positive charge of electricity, and other ions, which carry negative charges. Thus HCl in aqueous solution is supposed to give $\overset{+}{H}$ and $\overset{-}{Cl}$ ions, hydrions, and chloride ions, H_2SO_4 gives $\overset{++}{HH}$ and $\overset{--}{SO_4}$ ions, nitric acid HNO_3 gives $\overset{+}{H}$ and $\overset{-}{NO_3}$ ions. These hydrions are not the same as hydrogen atoms. They are hydrogen atoms carrying a considerable electric charge, and this gives them properties entirely distinct from those of the ordinary hydrogen atom. Again, the chloride ion $\overset{-}{Cl}$ is quite distinct from the atom of chlorine. The characteristic acidic properties of solutions of acids are thus generally attributed to the presence of the free hydrions contained in the solution.

Ions with positive charges are usually termed *cations*, and those with negative charges *anions*. Different ions can carry one, two, three, or more charges, but in any given solution the sum of positive charges must equal the sum of negative, since the solution as a whole is electrically neutral. The expression "acid radicle" or "salt radicle" is often used for the anion when deprived of its charge, thus SO_4 (without any charge) is the sulphate radicle; NO_3, the nitrate radicle, etc. An acid is thus a compound of hydrogen with an acid radicle such that when dissolved in water the hydrogen radicles take up positive charges of electricity, and the acid radicles, negative charges.

Bases.—This expression is now generally restricted to the metallic hydroxides, which are capable of reacting with acids to form water and salts. At one time it was used indiscriminately to denote anything which would neutralise an acid, e.g. metallic oxides, metallic hydroxides, ammonia, etc. A metallic hydroxide is the hydrated oxide, e.g. calcium hydroxide, $Ca(OH)_2$, is CaO plus water; or it may be defined as the compound formed by the union of a metallic radicle with one, two, or more hydroxyl (OH) groups of radicles, e.g. KOH, NaOH, $Ba(OH)_2$, $Al(OH)_3$, etc. The majority of these hydroxides are insoluble in water, and when strongly heated decompose into the oxide and water. A few—of which caustic soda, or sodium hydroxide, NaOH, and the corresponding caustic potash, KOH, are the best-known examples—are readily soluble in water, and yield strongly alkaline solutions. Such bases are very stable, and cannot readily be decomposed into water and oxide; they are usually termed alkalis. According to the modern theory of solutions, alkalis, when dissolved in water, give rise to metallic ions with positive charges, and hydroxyl ions with negative charges, e.g. NaOH gives $\overset{+}{Na}$ and $\overset{-}{OH}$, $Ca(OH)_2$ gives $\overset{++}{Ca}$ and $2\overset{-}{OH}$, and the alkaline properties of all such solutions are attributed to the presence of these free hydroxyl ions.

Salts are often defined as the products formed by the neutralisation of an acid by a base, water being also formed. They may also be regarded as the products formed by the union of a metallic radicle with an acid. Thus common salt, sodium chloride, NaCl, according to the first view, is the product formed, together with water, by the neutralisation of hydrochloric acid with caustic soda, and according to the second view it is the compound of the sodium radicle Na with the chloride radicle Cl. Salts, like acids and bases, when dissolved in water, are supposed to undergo dissociation into positively charged ions (cations) and negatively charged ions (anions). It is the metallic radicle which takes on the +, and the acid radicle which takes the −. Thus NaCl in aqueous solution gives rise to $\overset{+}{Na}$ and Cl ions, KNO_3 gives $\overset{+}{K}$ and $\overset{-}{NO_3}$ ions, and Na_2SO_4 gives $\overset{+}{Na}\overset{+}{Na}$ and $\overset{=}{SO_4}$ ions. Many salts are practically insoluble in water, e.g. barium sulphate, $BaSO_4$, silver chloride, AgCl.

The nomenclature of salts is fairly simple, and is based on the metallic and acid radicles present. Thus salts derived from potassium hydroxide are termed potassium salts. When a metal gives rise to two distinct sets of salts, e.g. copper gives the two chlorides Cu_2Cl_2 and $CuCl_2$, and mercury the two nitrates $HgNO_3$ and $Hg(NO_3)_2$, it is usual to term these *-ous* and *-ic* salts, e.g. Cu_2Cl_2 cuprous chloride, $CuCl_2$ cupric chloride, $HgNO_3$ mercurous nitrate, and $Hg(NO_3)_2$ mercuric nitrate, since the mercurous and cuprous salts may be regarded as derived from the lower oxides, Hg_2O mercurous oxide, and Cu_2O cuprous oxide; and the mercuric and cupric from the higher oxides, HgO mercuric oxide, and CuO cupric oxide. The name for the salts also indicates the relationship of the salt to the acid from which it is derived. Thus all salts of sulphur*ic* acid are called sulph*ates*; of nitr*ic* acid, nitr*ates*; of carbon*ic* acid, carbon*ates*, etc. All salts of sulphur*ous* acid are termed sulph*ites*, of nitr*ous* acid, nitr*ites*, etc.

The formulæ H_2SO_4 sulphuric acid, Na_2SO_4 sodium sulphate, $CaSO_4$ calcium sulphate, $Al_2(SO_4)_3$ aluminium sulphate, $PbSO_4$ lead sulphate, $CuSO_4$ cupric sulphate—HNO_3 nitric acid, KNO_3 potassium nitrate, $Ba(NO_3)_2$ barium nitrate, $Bi(NO_3)_3$ bismuth nitrate—H_2SO_3 sulphurous acid, Na_2SO_3 sodium sulphite, $CaSO_3$ calcium sulphite—readily show the relationship between an acid and its salts, and also indicate the fact that an acid, and the salts derived from it, contain the same acid radicle, e.g. SO_4 in sulphates, NO_3 in nitrates, and SO_3 in sulphites.

All the salts mentioned above are termed *normal*, or sometimes *neutral*, *salts*. They are the salts derived from an acid by the replacement of the whole of its replaceable hydrogen by metallic radicles. Another group is composed of the *acid salts*, which may be regarded as derived from the molecule of an acid containing several replaceable hydrogen atoms by the replacement of only part of this hydrogen by metallic radicles. Thus sulphuric acid can give rise to the acid salts $NaHSO_4$, $KHSO_4$, sodium hydrogen sulphate and potassium hydrogen sulphate, sometimes also called sodium bisulphate and potassium bisulphate. Similarly, carbonic acid gives $NaHCO_3$, sodium bicarbonate, and $Ca(HCO_3)_2$, calcium bicarbonate. Phosphoric acid, H_3PO_4, yields the acid salts NaH_2PO_4, Na_2HPO_4, and $CaHPO_4$.

At the present time the study of chemistry is usually dealt with under the various headings Inorganic Chemistry, Physical Chemistry, Organic Chemistry, Physiological Chemistry, Analytical Chemistry.

Inorganic Chemistry deals largely with the elements and the compounds which they form with one another, with the exception of the carbon compounds, which belong to the province of organic chemistry. Reference has already been made to the fact that elements unite to form compounds, which differ in most respects from the elements of which they are constituted. Such combinations of simple substances to form more complex substances are termed *syntheses*. The reverse process, the splitting up of a complex substance into simpler substances, either compounds or elements, is a phenomenon frequently met with, and is spoken of as *decomposition* or *analysis*.

One extremely important fact which has been established experimentally with regard to the formation and decomposition of compounds is that during these operations matter is not lost; or, in other words, the weight of a compound formed is equal to the sum of the weights of the simpler substances from which the compound is formed; or in the case of a decomposition, the sum of the weights of all the products is equal to the weight of the original complex substance. The whole science of chemistry is founded on this principle, which is known as the *Law of the Conservation of Matter*. Most of the analyses and syntheses carried out in the laboratory can be represented by means of chemical equations. On the one side of such an equation we write the formulæ for the original substance or reacting substances, and on the other side the formulæ for the products, with the sign = between. Thus, in the combination of iron and sulphur to form ferrous sulphide, we write the equation $Fe+S=FeS$, or in the reaction between zinc and dilute sulphuric acid we write $Zn+H_2SO_4=H_2+ZnSO_4$. No equation can be correct unless the number of atoms of an element on one side of the equation is the same as the number of atoms of the same element on the opposite side, as otherwise the law of conservation of mass could not hold good.

The decompositions met with may be brought about by various means, the commonest being heat, electricity, and chemical reagents. As examples of substances which are decomposed when raised to a relatively high temperature, we have red oxide of mercury decomposed into metallic mercury and oxygen, $2HgO=2Hg+O_2$, a reaction of great historical importance, as it was one of the first methods employed by Priestley (1776) for the preparation of oxygen. Again, potassium chlorate, when heated, yields as final products potassium chloride and oxygen, $2KClO_3=2KCl+3O_2$, a method often used for the preparation of oxygen in the laboratory; and finally, marble or calcium carbonate, when heated, yields lime or calcium oxide and carbon dioxide, $CaCO_3=CaO+CO_2$, a reaction which is the basis of the common method for the manufacture of quicklime in lime-kilns.

Practically all acids, bases, and salts are decomposed by the electric current when in the fused state or in solution. At the present time metallic sodium is prepared by passing an electric current through fused caustic soda; aluminium is manufactured by decomposing its oxide with the electric current; and silver, in ordinary electro-plating, is deposited from solutions of its salts by the electric current. All such decompositions are termed processes of electrolysis. Examples of decompositions by chemical methods are numerous; thus iron, when introduced into dilute sulphuric acid, evolves hydrogen gas, and leaves a solution of ferrous sulphate (green vitriol), $Fe+H_2SO_4=FeSO_4+H_2$, or a solution of barium chloride added to a solution of sodium sulphate produces a precipitate of barium sulphate, $BaCl_2+Na_2SO_4=BaSO_4+2NaCl$. Such reactions as these, which, according to the equations representing them, consist in the exchange of two radicles, e.g. in the last case, Na_2 and Ba, are termed double decompositions. When two aqueous solutions are mixed together, double decomposition occurs. Thus the precipitation of barium sulphate, silver chloride, or ferric hydroxide, as represented by the equations $BaCl_2+H_2SO_4=BaSO_4+2HCl$; $NaCl+AgNO_3=AgCl+NaNO_3$ and $FeCl_3+3KOH=Fe(OH)_3+3KCl$. Many of these reactions are now written in the form of *ionic* equations, i.e. equations which represent the reaction as taking place between the ions present in the solutions; the above equations thus become $\overset{++}{Ba}+\overset{--}{SO_4}=BaSO_4$; $\overset{+}{Ag}+\overset{-}{Cl}=AgCl$ and $\overset{+++}{Fe}+3\overset{-}{OH}=Fe(OH)_3$. The products are insoluble, and therefore cannot be in the ionic state. (*See* INORGANIC CHEMISTRY.)

Physical Chemistry deals largely with the so-called physical properties of substances—such as melting-point, boiling-point, specific gravity, refractive index, optical activity—and the relationship between such properties and the chemical constitution of the compounds. It includes the various methods for determining atomic and molecular weights, the phenomena of thermo-chemistry and electro-chemistry, the laws of mass action, and the rates at which different chemical reactions proceed. Chemical reactions are always accompanied by the evolution or absorption of heat; in the former case, which is much the commoner, the reaction is said to be *exothermic* and in the latter *endothermic*. These amounts of heat may be measured accurately in a calorimeter, and the results expressed in the form of a thermochemical equation, e.g. the equation $Pb+I_2=PbI_2+398$ Cal., indicates that 398 large units of heat are produced during the formation of a gram molecule (461 grams) of lead iodide from its elements. (*See* PHYSICAL CHEMISTRY.)

Organic Chemistry, originally so named from the fact that naturally occurring carbon compounds were supposed to require a vital force for their production; it now deals with the chemistry of all carbon compounds, not merely with those found in organised (plant or animal) tissues. One main reason why this branch is separated from inorganic chemistry is on account of the enormous number of such carbon compounds. The study of these compounds is largely facilitated by the fact that they may be grouped into *homologous series.* Thus compounds which are similar in chemical properties when arranged in increasing order of complexity form a series such that any member differs both from the preceding and also the succeeding member by the definite quantity CH_2. Thus in the paraffin hydrocarbons we have CH_4, C_2H_6, C_3H_8, C_4H_{10}, etc.; in the series of fatty acids, CH_2O_2, $C_2H_4O_2$, $C_3H_6O_2$, $C_4H_8O_2$, etc.

The members of any one series resemble one another closely as regards all important chemical characteristics, and may all be prepared by similar methods. They differ largely, however, as regards physical properties. Some may be gases, some liquids, and some solids. Another phenomenon characteristic of carbon compounds is the frequent occurrence of isomerism. Thus we have two definite substances—ethyl alcohol a liquid readily acted on by sodium or acids, and dimethyl ether, a gas which does not react with sodium or acids, and both have to be represented by the same molecular formula C_2H_6O; They are isomeric. The explanation of this phenomenon is that although both compounds contain the same elements and the same number of atoms, these atoms may be arranged differently within the molecules in the two cases; thus it can be shown that in the ethyl alcohol molecule the arrangement is $CH_3 \cdot CH_2 \cdot OH$, i.e. the two carbon atoms are directly united, 5 hydrogen atoms are attached to carbon and one to oxygen, and this in its turn is united to carbon; whereas in dimethyl ether the arrangement is $CH_3 \cdot O \cdot CH_3$, i.e. all 6 hydrogens are attached to carbon, and the carbons are not directly united together, but are both attached to the atom of oxygen.

A problem which the organic chemist has to attack in addition to the analysis of carbon compounds and the determination of molecular weights, is the determination of the constitutions of the various carbon compounds, i.e. to determine in each case the manner in which the atoms are arranged within the molecule. Another problem is the synthesis by laboratory methods of the most useful natural products; this has already been accomplished in the case of benzoic acid, alizarine, indigo, and numerous other substances which are now manufactured on a large scale. Other compounds, such as starch, albumin, etc., have not been obtained artificially. (*See* ORGANIC CHEMISTRY.)

Physiological Chemistry ist the department of chemistry which deals with the composition and chemical constituents of the fluids and solids of animal origin and the changes which take place in animal bodies. Four elements are almost invariably found in animal matter, carbon, hydrogen, oxygen, and nitrogen. To these may be added many other elements occurring in small quantity, e.g. sulphur, phosphorus, calcium, sodium, potassium, chlorine, and iron. Sulphur occurs in blood and in secretions; phosphorus is found in the nerves, in the teeth as calcium phosphate, and in some fluids. Chlorine occurs throughout the body; calcium is found in bone and in the teeth. Iron occurs as hæmoglobin in blood; sodium also occurs throughout the body, and potassium in muscles and nerves. Many other elements are present, but in still smaller amounts, e.g. silicon, manganese, lead, lithium, etc. Compounds in the human organism are divided into two classes, i.e. organic and inorganic. Of *inorganic substances* water is the most abundant. About two-thirds by weight of the body is water.

Other inorganic substances are calcium phosphate, sodium and potassium chloride, etc. *Organic compounds* may be divided roughly into nitrogenous and non-nitrogenous substances. Of the former the chief are albumen, found in blood and lymph; casein, in milk; myosin, in muscle; and gelatine, in bone. Non-nitrogenous substances are usually organic acids and salts, such as formic acid, acetic acid, butyric acid, stearic acid, and starches, fats, and oils. Almost all the substances which occur in the body have been synthesized in recent years, and their properties and action on one another fully examined. The development of this branch of chemistry has been slow, on account of the difficulty of working with living matter, but solid progress has been made, and several recent advances in physiological science have originated in investigations in physiological chemistry. (*See* PHYSIOLOGICAL CHEMISTRY.)

Analytical Chemistry deals with the analysis, both qualitative and quantitative, of all kinds of materials. Thus the analytical chemist is required to analyse water in order to determine its suitability for drinking or other purposes; to examine foods and drugs for impurities; to analyse specimens of minerals, ores, and the metals obtained from them; to analyse and examine the raw materials and the finished products met with in the brewing and sugar-refining industries, in gas manufacture, iron and steel works, acid and alkali works, glass and porcelain works, etc. (*See* PRACTICAL CHEMISTRY.)

BIBLIOGRAPHY: Caven and Lander, *Inorganic Chemistry*; Roscoe and Schorlemmer, *Inorganic Chemistry*; J. Walker, *Physical Chemistry*; W. C. M'C. Lewis, *Physical Chemistry*; A. Bernthsen, *Organic Chemistry*; Richter-Anschutz, *Organic Chemistry*; F. P. Treadwell, *Analytical Chemistry*; J. N. Friend, *Theory of Valency*; R. M. Caven, *Foundations of Chemical Theory*.

CHEMISTS. Those engaged in the pursuit of any branch of pure or applied chemistry, e.g. organic chemist, physical chemist, analytical chemist, tanning chemist, dyeworks chemist, etc. The name is often given also to pharmacists or pharmaceutical chemists, who keep retail shops for the sale of drugs. In Britain pharmaceutical chemists are those who, after passing the necessary examinations, are registered by the Pharmaceutical Society, incorporated by royal charter in 1843. Apprentices must first pass a preliminary general knowledge examination, and afterwards the qualifying minor and major examinations of the society. By the Pharmacy Act of 1868 all persons who are not duly registered are forbidden under a penalty to keep open shop to retail, dispense, or compound poisons, or to use the title of chemist, druggist, pharmaceutist or pharmacist, or pharmaceutical druggist. The Act, however, does not interfere with the business of any legally qualified apothecary, nor of any member of the Royal College of Veterinary Surgeons of Great Britain, nor with the making of and dealing in patent medicines.

CHEMNITZ (kem'nits). The principal manufacturing town in the Republic (since 1918) of Saxony, on the Chemnitz, 39 miles S.W. of Dresden. It is well built, and has a castle, a lyceum, town hall, and a school of design. The principal manufactures are white and printed calicoes, ginghams, handkerchiefs, woollen and half-woollen goods. There are also extensive cotton-spinning and other mills; dyeworks, printworks, bleachworks, chemical works and large manufactures of cotton hosiery. The manufacture of machinery is also important. Pop. 335,982.

CHEMNITZ (kem'nits), **Martin.** A German Protestant theologian, born in 1522, died in 1586. Chief works: *Loci Theologici* (1591), a commentary on Melanchthon's system of dogmatics, and *Examen Consilii Tridentini* (1563-73), on the Council of Trent.

CHEMOSH (kē'mosh). Frequently referred to both in the Old Testament and on the Moabite Stone as the national god of the Moabites, who were on that account called the "people of Chemosh" (Num. xxi. 29; Jer. xlviii. 46). At an early period the same deity appears too as the national god of the Ammonites (Judges, xi. 24), though his worship seems afterwards to have given place to that of Moloch (1 Kings, xi. 5, 7), if Moloch be not merely another name for the same deity. The worship of Chemosh was even introduced among the Hebrews by Solomon, who built "an high place for Chemosh, the abomination of Moab, in the hill that is before Jerusalem" (1 Kings, xi. 7).

CHEMOSIS (kē-mō'sis). An affection of the eye, in which the conjunctiva is elevated above the transparent cornea.

CHEMOTAXIS, or **CHEMIOTAXIS.** Movement of a free-swimming cell or organism induced by a chemical stimulus, e.g. the attraction of fern spermatozoids to the archegonium by the malic acid excreted by that organ.

CHEMOTROPISM. In botany, the curvature of a plant organ, due to unequal growth induced by a chemical stimulus. The most familiar instance is the attraction of pollen-tubes towards the stigma of the same species. The active substance in this case is frequently cane-sugar, but in other instances, e.g. Narcissus, it is a protein. The curvatures termed "ærotropic" and "hydrotropic" are merely special forms of chemotropic curvature in response to the influence respectively of oxygen and water. Pollen-tubes show *negative ærotropism,* i.e. they grow away from air, and *positive hydrotropism,* i.e. they cling closely to the moist surface of the stigma, all these forms of chemotropism combining to guide them by the most direct route to the ovules which form their legitimate goal. The hyphæ of Fungi also exhibit chemotropism in a marked degree, and this property is of great importance, especially to the parasitic forms, in leading them towards their sources of food-supply.

CHEMULPO (chē-mul'pō). One of the treaty-ports of Korea, exporting beans and ginseng, and importing European and American manufactures. It is the port of Seoul, the capital, and is connected with it by railway. Pop. 53,700.

CHEMUNG FORMATION A marine Upper Devonian series of strata in New York State, corresponding in time with the lacustrine Catskill Beds of New York and Pennsylvania.

CHENAB (chen-ȧb'). A river of India, one of the five rivers of the Punjab. It rises in the Himalayan ranges of Kashmir, and, entering the Punjab near Sialkot, flows in a south-westerly direction till it unites with the Jehlam; length about 800 miles. At Wazirabad it is crossed by a great iron railway bridge more than a mile long.

CHENG. A Chinese musical instrument, consisting of a series of tubes having free reeds. It resembles a teapot filled with bamboo pipes of graduated lengths. Its introduction

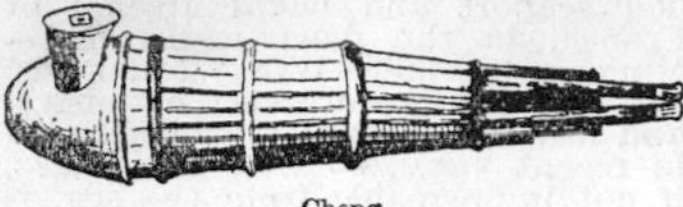
Cheng

into Europe led to the invention of the accordion, harmonium, and other free-reed instruments.

CHÉNIER (shā-nyā), **André-Marie de.** A French poet, born at Constantinople in 1762, went to France when very young, and entered the army, but left shortly after his twentieth year to devote himself to literary pursuits. In 1790 he joined the moderate section of the Republicans, and made himself offensive alike to the Royalist and Jacobinical party. Being brought before the revolutionary tribunal, he was condemned and guillotined, 25th July, 1794. The poems of Chénier give the author a high place amongst the poets of France, and include elegies, and some beautiful odes, of which *La Jeune Captive*, written in prison, is perhaps the best known. The best edition of Chénier's works is that of 1872, edited by Becq de Fouquières. In many respects Chénier resembles Shelley and Keats.—BIBLIOGRAPHY: E. Faguet, *André Chénier*; Becq de Fouquières, *Lettres critiques sur André Chénier.*

CHÉNIER, Marie Joseph Blaise de. Brother of the foregoing, born 1764, died 1811; served as an officer of dragoons, left the service, and devoted himself to literature. His dramas, *Charles IX.*; *Henri VIII.*; *Jean Calas, ou l'école des Juges*, full of wild democratic declamation, were received with great applause. He was chosen a member of the Convention, and belonged to the party of the most violent Democrats. His works comprise odes, songs, and hymns.

CHENILLE (she-nil'). A sort of ornamental fabric of cord-like form, made by weaving or twisting together warp-threads, with a transverse filling or weft, the loose ends of which project all round in the form of a pile. Chenille carpets have a weft of chenille, the loose threads of which produce a fine velvety pile.

CHÉNONCEAUX (shā-noṇ-sō). A village of Central France, department of Indre-et-Loire, famous for its castle, one of the most celebrated examples of Renaissance architecture. It was founded in 1515 by Thomas Bohier, and added to at various later dates. The gallery leading to the left bank of the Cher was built by Catherine de' Medici. Mary Queen of Scots spent her first honeymoon there. The castle was carefully restored in 1864.

CHENOPODIA'CEÆ (kē). A nat. ord. of apetalous dicotyledons, consisting of more or less succulent and halophytic herbs or shrubs, belonging to about eighty genera and 600 species. Several are employed as pot-herbs, such as spinach and beet, and others for the manufacture of soda. The genus Chenopodium consists of weedy plants, common in waste places, and known in Britain by the names of goosefoot, fat-hen, good King Henry, *C. Bonus Henricus*, *etc.* *C. anthelminticum*, wormseed, is a species well known in the United States, the seeds or the oil obtained from them being given as a remedy for worms. *C. Quinoa* is an important S. American species, having edible seeds, on account of which it is largely cultivated in Peru and Chile as a food-plant.

CHEOPS (kē'ops). The name given by Herodotus to the Egyptian despot whom the Egyptians themselves called Khufu. He belonged to the rulers who had for their capital Memphis; lived about 2800-2700 B.C. (but according to Petrie about 1000 years earlier), and built the Great Pyramid. According to Herodotus he employed 100,000 men on this work constantly for 20 years.

CHEPHREN (kef'ren), or **CEPHREN.** The successor of Cheops as King of Egypt, and the builder of the second pyramid. His name is properly Khafra.

CHEP'STOW. A town and port in England, Monmouthshire, on the Wye, 14 miles N. by W. of Bristol. The high tides of the Wye allow large ships to reach the town, which is very ancient, and has a castle, portions of which date back to the Conquest. Pop. (1931), 4303.

CHEQUE. A draft or bill on a bank payable on presentation. A cheque may be drawn payable to the bearer, or to the order of some one named; the first form is transferable without endorsation, and payable to any one who presents it; the second must be endorsed, that is the person in whose favour it is drawn must write his name on the back of it. Cheques are a very important species of mercantile currency wherever there is a well-organised system of banking. The regular use of them for all payments, except of small amount, makes the transfer of funds a mere matter of cross-entries and transferring of balances among bankers, and tends greatly to economize the use of the precious metals as a currency.

What is called a "crossed cheque" has two lines drawn across it transversely, with or without the words "& Co." between. A cheque thus marked can only be paid by the banker on whom it is drawn when presented by some other banker, and the person to whom it is sent can consequently only obtain payment of it through his own bankers. Such cheques are not used in the United States. The stamp duty on British cheques was raised in 1918 from one penny to twopence. The cheque system, which has contributed to the economic development of Great Britain and the United States, was but little known and certainly far from popular in France. In recent years, however, its vogue as a mercantile currency has increased considerably, and a new law, passed on 2nd Aug., 1917, with regard to forged cheques, has strengthened the confidence of the public in such a mode of payment.—BIBLIOGRAPHY: W. Thomson, *Dictionary of Banking*; D. Duverger, *Le Rôle économique du Chèque*; J. J. Maclaren, *Bills, Notes, and Cheques*; J. A. Slater, *Bills, Cheques, and Notes*.

CHEQUERS. An estate and mansion in Buckinghamshire, England. The estate, inherited by Lord Lee of Fareham in 1909, was presented to the nation in 1917, to serve as the official country residence of the Prime Minister. Lloyd George was the first British Prime Minister to take up his residence at Chequers, in 1921.

CHEQUY CHECKY, or CHEQUERED. In heraldry, applied to a field or charge when it is divided into squares like those of a chess-board.

CHER (shãr). A river of Central France, a tributary of the Loire, which it enters near Tours; length, 200 miles.

CHER (shãr). A department of Central France, named from the river Cher, and formed from part of the old provinces of Berry and Bourbonnais; area, 2819 sq. miles; capital, Bourges. The surface is in general flat, but is diversified in the north by chains of inconsiderable hills. Soil various, but fertile in the neighbourhood of the Loire and Allier. The forest and pastures are extensive. More grain and wine are produced than the demands of the inhabitants require. The preparation and manufacture of iron, called Berry-iron, is the principal branch of industry. The department is divided into three arrondissements. Pop. (1931), 293,918.

CHERBOURG (shãr-bör). A fortified seaport and naval arsenal of France, in the department of La Manche, 196 miles W.N.W. of Paris. The fortifications are very extensive, and have been greatly strengthened in recent years, so that Cherbourg, if not impregnable from the sea, is at least very difficult of attack. The port is divided into the commercial and naval ports, which are quite distinct. The Port Militaire is accessible at all times of tide for vessels of the largest class; there are slips for vessels of the largest dimensions, dry docks, building-sheds, masthouses, boiler-works, and, in short, everything necessary for the building and fitting out of ships of war.

There is a great *digue* or breakwater, stretching across the roadstead. which, though protected on three sides by the land, was formerly open to the heavy seas from the north. The *digue* was commenced under Louis XVI., is 4120 yards long, and is 2¼ miles from the harbour, in water varying from 42 to 62 feet deep. A fort and lighthouse occupy the centre of the *digue*, and there are circular forts at the extremities. The principal industry of the town is centred in the works of the dockyard, the commercial trade and manufactures being comparatively insignificant. Large quantities of eggs are shipped to England. Cherbourg occupies the site of a Roman station. William the Conqueror founded a hospital in it, and built the castle church. The castle, in which Henry II. frequently resided, was one of the strongholds of Normandy. The town was taken by the British in 1758. Pop. 37,461.

CHERIBON (sher'i-bon). A seaport in the Island of Java, capital of the province of the same name. The province lies on the coast towards the north-west, produces coffee, timber, areca-nuts, indigo, and sugar, and has about 770,000 inhabitants. The town lies in a deep bay on the north coast, and is the residence of a Dutch governor. Pop. 26,790.

CHERIMOY'ER (cher-). The fruit of the *Anōna Cherimolia*, a native of S. and Central America, allied to the custard-apple. It is a heart-shaped fruit with a scaly exterior, and numerous seeds buried in a delicious pulp. Both flowers and fruit emit a pleasant fragrance. This fruit is now cultivated in various tropical regions.

CHERKASY. A river-port of Ukraine, on the Dnieper, with manufactures of sugar and tobacco. It has sawmills, and has considerable trade in grain, salt, sugar, cattle, and wood. Pop. 38,500.

CHERNYSHEVSKY, Nikolai Gavrilovitsh. Russian author, born 1828, died 1889. His father, a distinguished priest, supervised the early education of his son, whom he afterwards sent to the University of St. Petersburg (Petrograd). Here the ability of the young man attracted general attention, and in 1855 he presented a dissertation, entitled *The Æsthetic Relation of Art to Reality*, which was confiscated by the authorities, as it contained subversive and revolutionary views. This treatment, not usual in the Russia of the nineteenth century, was another stimulus for young Chernyshevsky to devote himself to literary work wherein he could display his brilliant talent.

The most influential Russian review of the time, the *Contemporary* (or *Sovremennik*) placed its pages at Chernyshevsky's disposal, and in the course of two years the influence of the progressive periodical upon public opinion became so enormous that the autocratic Government grew alarmed. The *Contemporary* was suppressed, and Chernyshevsky sent to prison in 1862. It was at the fortress of St. Peter and St. Paul, whilst awaiting his trial, that Chernyshevsky wrote his famous novel *Tshto Dyelatj* (What's to be Done).

The author of *Tshto Dyelatj* was sent to Siberia and kept in exile for nearly twenty years. When he returned to Russia, he was broken in health and no longer felt strong enough to resume his previous work. He died a few months afterwards. Chernyshevsky's writings appeared in 4 vols.: *Studies in Russian Literature in the Days of Gogol, Æsthetics and Poetry, Notes on Contemporary Literature, Critical Essays.* Another collection, containing all his articles, appeared in 10 vols. in 1906. Chernyshevsky's merit consists in having awakened the Russian social consciousness, helped to rid Russian thought of Hegelian metaphysical speculation, and popularized science.

CHEROKEES'. A tribe of North American Indians in the United States, occupying an allotted region in the Indian Territory. Their old seats were in Georgia, Alabama, Mississippi, and Tennessee. The Cherokees are the most enlightened of the Indian tribes, have invented an alphabet (which they use for the composition of sacred formulæ), printed books and newspapers in their own language, live in well-built villages, and have an excellent school system. They number about 28,000, including many individuals incorporated from other tribes. Their religion is a polytheistic form of zoolatry, or animal worship, which may have had a totemic origin. As with the ancient Egyptians, with the Cherokees religion enters into every act of existence.—Cf. T. V. Parker, *The Cherokee Indians.*

CHERRY (*Prunus Cerăsus*). A very ornamental tree, and therefore much cultivated in shrubberies as well as for its fruit. The cultivated varieties are numerous, as the red or garden cherry, the red heart, the white heart, the black cherry, etc. The fruit of the wild cherry, or *gean* (*P. avium*), is often as well flavoured, if not quite so large, as that of the cultivated varieties. According to Pliny, this fruit was brought from Cerasus, in Pontus, to Italy, by Lucullus, about 70 B.C. It was introduced into England by the Romans about A.D. 46. Cultivated and improved varieties, however, do not seem to have been known in England before the time of Henry VIII., when several were introduced into Kent.

Cherry Blossom

There are now over 100 named varieties of cherries in cultivation in English gardens alone. The cherry orchards of Kent are famous. The cherry is used in making the liqueurs Kirschwasser and Maraschino. The wood of the cherry tree is hard and tough, and is very serviceable to turners and cabinetmakers. An ornamental but not edible species is the bird-cherry.

CHERRY-LAUREL. The English name of *Prunus Lauro-cerăsus*, nat. ord. Rosaceæ, an evergreen shrub, a native of Asia Minor, but now naturalised in S. Europe and common in British shrubberies. It is commonly called laurel, but must not be confounded with the sweet-bay or other true species of laurel. The leaves yield an oil nearly identical with that got from bitter almonds. The distilled water (called "laurel water") from the leaves is used in medicine in the same way as diluted hydrocyanic or prussic acid. It is poisonous in large doses. The Portugal laurel is another species.

CHERSO (ker'so). An island in the Adriatic, yielding wine, olives and other fruits, and having a pop. of 10,200. It contains a town of the same name; pop. 5000.

CHERSONESUS (ker-so-nē'sus; Gr., "a peninsula"). Anciently a name applied to several peninsulas, as the Cimbrian Chersonesus (*Chersonesus Cimbrica*), now Jutland, etc., the Tauric Chersonesus (*Ch. Taurica*), the peninsula formed by the Black Sea and the Sea of Azof—the Crimea and the Thracian Chersonesus, or modern Gallipoli Peninsula.

CHERT. A massive form of crystalline silica, practically identical with flint, though attempts have been made to discriminate between them. Flint is so well known in the white chalk of England that all flints outside this formation have been called chert, including those of Portland and the Carboniferous Limestone. Chert often cements sandstone, as in the bands found in the English Lower Greensand, where it is associated with the remains of siliceous sponges. Radiolaria are preserved in many cherts, as in those of Carboniferous and older horizons, and the material has often arisen from the solution of their siliceous shells or of sponge-spicules, and from redeposition, as in the case of ordinary flint, in a chalcedonic form.

CHERT'SEY. A town, England, in Surrey, 19¾ miles S.W. of London, on the Thames, giving name to one of the seven parliamentary divisions of the county. Bricks and tiles are made, and vegetables cultivated. Pop. (1931), 17,130.

CHERUB (cher'ub; in the plural *Cherubs* and *Cherubim*; a Hebrew word borrowed from the Assyr. *kirubu*, from *karâbu*, "to be near," hence it means "familiars," "bodyguards"). One of an order of angels variously represented at different times, but generally as winged spirits with a human countenance, and distinguished by their knowledge from the seraphs, whose distinctive quality is love.

The first mention of cherubs is in Gen. iii. 24. The cherubs in Ezekiel's vision had each four heads or faces, the hands of a man, and wings. The four faces were the face of a bull, that of a man, that of a lion, and that of an eagle. (Ezek. iv. and x.) In the celestial hierarchy cherubs are represented as spirits next in order to seraphs. In the course of time the idea of the cherub has lost the whole of its original and specific sense, and has become a term for any superhuman being who is conceived as occupied with the praising of God.—Cf. article *Cherubim* in Hastings's *Encyclopædia of Religion and Ethics*.

CHERUBINI (ke-ru̧-bē'nē), **Maria Luigi Carlo Zenobio Salvatore.** An eminent Italian composer, born at Florence in 1760. His first opera, *Quinto Fabio*, was produced in Alessandria in 1780, and in Rome (in an altered form) in 1783, with such success as to spread his fame over Italy. After visiting London, where the Philharmonic Society commissioned him to write a symphony, an overture, and a composition for chorus and orchestra, he finally settled in Paris, where he became director of the École Royale in 1822, and died in 1842.

Among his compositions are: *Iphigenia in Aulide, Lodoiska, Faniska,* and *Les Deux Journées*. In his later years he confined himself almost exclusively to the composition of sacred music, and gained a lasting fame by his *Coronation Mass*, and more especially his well-known *Requiem*. Cherubini left some 450 works, about 100 of which have appeared in print.—Cf. E. Bellasis, *Cherubini*.

CHERUSCI (ke-rus'sī). An ancient German tribe, whose territory probably was situated in that part of Germany lying between the Weser and the Elbe, and having the Harz Mountains on the north, and the Sudetic range on the south. This tribe was known to the Romans before 50 B.C., and occasionally served in the Roman armies. But when Varus attempted to subject them to the Roman laws, they formed a confederation with many smaller tribes, and, having decoyed him into the forests, destroyed his whole army in a battle (the battle of Teutoburg) which lasted three days, and in which he himself was slain (A.D. 9). Upon this the Cherusci became the chief object of the attacks of the Romans. Germanicus undertook several unsuccessful campaigns against them. Subsequently the Cherusci were overcome by the Chatti, and their territory was occupied by the Saxons.

CHER'VIL. The popular name of umbelliferous plants of the genus Chærophyllum, but especially of *C.*

temŭlum, the only British species, a hairy weed with longish grooved fruits. Garden chervil is *Anthriscus cerefolium*, an umbelliferous plant much used in soups and salads in some European countries. The parsnip chervil (*C. bulbōsum*) has a root like a small carrot, with a flavour between that of a chestnut and a potato. Sweet chervil, sweet cicely, or myrrh is *Myrrhis odorāta*, an aromatic and stimulant umbellifer formerly used as a pot-herb, growing in a semi-wild state in Britain.

CHERVONETZ. Russian monetary unit. Instituted under the U.S.S.R., in 1922 as part of the New Economic Policy. The chervonetz equalled 10 pre-war roubles, or 2*s.* 1½*d.*, and notes were issued, interchangeable 25 per cent in money, and 75 per cent in goods or securities.

CHERWELL. River of England. It rises at Charwelton in Northamptonshire. At Oxford it is called the Cher and joins the Thames. It is 30 miles long.

CHES'APEAKE BAY. A large bay of North America, in the states of Virginia and Maryland. Its entrance is between Cape Charles and Cape Henry, 16 miles wide, and it extends 180 miles to the northward. It is from 10 to 30 miles broad, and at most places as much as 9 fathoms deep, affording many commodious harbours and a safe and easy navigation. It receives the Susquehanna, Potomac, and James River. It is connected with Delaware Bay by canal.

CHE'SELDEN, William. English surgeon and anatomist, born in Leicestershire in 1688, died at Bath, 10th April, 1752. He went to London to prosecute his studies, and at the age of twenty-two began to give lectures on anatomy. In 1713 he published a treatise on *The Anatomy of the Human Body*, long considered a standard manual of the science. In 1723 he published a *Treatise on the High Operation for the Stone*, and afterwards added to his reputation by operating for the stone. In ophthalmic surgery he is famous for his operation of iridectomy. In 1733 was published his *Osteography, or Anatomy of the Bones*, folio, consisting of plates and short explanations, a splendid and accurate work.

CHESHAM. A market town and urban district of England, Buckinghamshire, 25½ miles by rail from London, with manufactures of utensils from beech, which grows abundantly in the district. Extensive watercress beds are also to be found here. Pop. (1931), 8809.

CHESHIRE (chesh'ĭr). A maritime county and county palatine of England, bounded by the counties of Lancaster, York, Derby, Stafford, Salop, Denbigh, Flint, the estuaries of the Dee and Mersey, and the Irish Sea. The area is 1056 sq. miles, of which only a sixteenth is uncultivated. The surface is generally level, the soil mostly a rich reddish loam variously clayey or sandy. There is some of the finest pasture-land in England; and cheese, the softest of our hard-pressed varieties, is made in great quantities. Extensive tracts of land are cultivated as market gardens, the produce being sent to Liverpool, Manchester, and other towns.

Industries.—Minerals abound, especially rock-salt and coal, which are extensively worked. Cotton manufacture is carried on at Stockport, Stalybridge, and the north-eastern district, shipbuilding at Birkenhead and other places. Trade is facilitated by numerous railway lines and a splendid system of canals. The chief rivers are the Mersey, the Dee, and the Weaver. Small sheets of water called *meres* are numerous. Cheshire has nine parliamentary divisions, each returning one member. Principal towns: Chester, the county town, Macclesfield, Stockport, Birkenhead, and Stalybridge. Pop. according to census return of 1931, 1,087,554.—Cf. C. E. Kelsey, *Cheshire* (Oxford County Histories), also Victoria County History, *Cheshire*.

CHESHIRE REGIMENT, The. Raised by the Duke of Norfolk in 1689. It fought at the Boyne, and later in the West Indies, America, and India, where it distinguished itself under Sir Charles Napier. It saw service in South Africa (1900-2), and suffered severely early in the European War, being later represented on the Tigris.

CHESHUNT. A town of England, in the south-east of Hertfordshire, near the Essex border and the River Lea, with an ancient church, nurseries, and market gardens, brick-fields, etc. Pop. (urban district), 14,651 (1931).

CHESS. A game of skill of very ancient origin, was probably first played in India; it passed thence in the sixth century to Persia, became known to the Arabians, and was introduced into Europe before 1100. Both the name of the game and the terms employed in play are obviously of Eastern origin; *chess* being derived, through the O.Fr. *eschecs*, from the Pers. *shâh*, a king; *rook* from *roka*, Sanskrit for ship or chariot; and *checkmate* from *shâh mât*, Persian for *the king is dead*.

The game is played by two opponents on a board divided into sixty-four squares, arranged in eight rows of eight squares each, the squares being black (or red) and white alternately. Each player has sixteen men, eight of which, called *pawns*, are of the lowest grade; the other eight, called *pieces*, are of varying value and power. The pieces include, for each player, *king* and *queen*: two *bishops*, two *knights*, and two *rooks* or *castles*. The board is placed so that each player has a white square on his right hand in the row nearest to him. The men are then set out on the two rows of squares next to the player owning them, the pieces on the row nearest him, the pawns on the next row, four rows being thus left vacant between the two opposing rows of pawns. The king and queen occupy the two central

Chess-board

squares, and face the king and queen on the opposite side. The queen, at the commencement of the game, always stands on her own colour, white queen on white square, black on black. The two bishops are placed on the squares next the king and queen, the two knights next the bishops, with the rooks in the corner squares. The pawns, all equal in value, fill the front or second row. The men standing on the king's or queen's side of the board are named respectively king's and queen's men. Thus king's bishop or knight is the bishop or knight on the king's side of the board.

The pawns are named from the pieces before which they stand—king's pawn, king's knight's pawn, queen's rook's pawn, etc. The names of the men are contracted as follows: King, K.; King's Bishop, K.B.; King's Knight, K.Kt.; King's Rook, K.R.; Queen, Q.; Queen's Bishop, Q.B.; Queen's Knight, Q.Kt.; Queen's Rook, Q.R. The pawns are contracted: K.P., Q.P., K.B.P., Q.Kt.P., etc. The board is divided, inversely from the position of each player, into eight rows and eight files. Counting from White's right hand to his left, or from Black's left to his right, each file is named from the piece which occupies its first square, and, counting inversely from the position of each player to that of the other, the rows are numbered from 1 to 8. At White's right-hand corner we thus have K.R. square; immediately above this K.R.2, and so on to K.R.8, which completes the file; the second file begins with K.Kt. square on the first row, and ends with K.Kt.8 on the eighth. White's K.R.8 and K.Kt.8 are thus Black's K.R. square and K.Kt. square, and the moves of each player are described throughout from his own position in inverse order to the moves of his opponent.

In chess all the men capture by occupying the position of the captured man, which is removed from the board, and all captures are optional. The ordinary move of a *pawn* is straight forward in the same file; it never moves backward. The first time a pawn is moved it may be played forward one square or two; afterwards one square only at a time. But in taking an adverse piece the pawn moves diagonally and occupies the position on which the captured man stood.

Thus, if White opens a game by playing P. to K.4, and Black answers with P. to K.4, the two pawns are immovable, being unable either to advance or to take each other. But if White now plays P. to K.B.4, or P. to Q.4, Black may capture the P. last advanced. Pawns have a further mode of capture peculiar to themselves and available against pawns only. If Black's P., instead of occupying K.4, stood on K.5, and White played P. to Q.4, Black could not capture it by placing his P. on the square it occupies, which would be a false move; but he is at liberty to effect the capture by placing his own P. on the square (Q.6) which White's P. has passed over. This is called taking *en passant*, and must be done, if at all, on the next move after P. to Q.4. When a P., by moving or capturing, reaches the eighth square of any file. it no longer remains a P., but is exchanged for a piece. The player may choose any piece except the king, but the queen, as the most valuable, is usually selected. This exchange is called *queening* a pawn, and a player may thus have more than one queen on the board.

The Rook.—The moves of the *pieces* are not, like those of pawns, limited to a single direction. The R.

moves in any direction, and for any distance that is open, along either the row or the file on which it stands—horizontally or perpendicularly to the player, backwards or forwards, to the right or left. It can capture any obstructing man and occupy its place.

The Bishop.—The B.s, like the R.s, are unlimited in range and can move either backward or forward; but that movement is diagonal, and thus a bishop which commenced the game on a white square never leaves that colour, and is powerless against a man on a black square.

The Queen.—The Q. combines the moves of the R. and B. She is the most powerful piece on the board, and can move to, or capture at, any distance or direction in a straight or diagonal line.

The King.—The K. is at once the weakest and the most valuable piece on the board. In point of direction he is as free as the Q., but can move only one square at a time; standing on any middle square, he commands the eight adjoining squares and those only. In addition to his ordinary move, the K. has a further privilege, shared by the R. Once in the game, provided that the squares between the K. and R. are clear, that neither K. nor R. has moved, that K. is not attacked by any hostile man, and that no attack commands the square over which K. has to pass, K. may move two squares towards either K.R. or Q.R., while R., in the same move, is placed on the square over which K. has passed. This is called *castling*, and often serves as a considerable protection to K.

The Knight.—The Kt., unlike all other pieces, never moves in a straight line. His move is limited to two squares at a time, one forwards, backwards, or sideways, and one diagonally, and he can leap over any man occupying an intervening square. He thus always changes the colour of his square after every move. The Kt., like the K., when on a central square, commands eight squares, but they are all at two squares' distance, and are in an oblique direction.

The definite aim in chess is the reduction to surrender of the opposing king. The K. is inviolable to the extent that he cannot be captured, but he can be put in such a position that he would be captured were he any other piece. Notice of any direct attack upon him must be notified by the adversary saying "Check!" and, the K. being attacked, all other moves and plans must be abandoned, and other men, if necessary, sacrificed, in order that he may be removed from danger, the attack covered by the interposition of a man—a course not possible when the attacker is a Kt.—or the assailant captured. It is also a fundamental rule of the game that the K. cannot be moved into check. When the K. can no longer be defended on being *checked* by the adversary, either by retiring from the dangerous square, by interposition of other men, or by capture of the assailing piece or pawn, the game is lost, a result announced by the victor calling "Checkmate!"

When, by inadvertence or want of skill, a player blocks up his opponent's K. so that he cannot move except into check, and no other man can be moved without the K.s being exposed, the player reduced to this extremity cannot, without violating the fundamental rule above referred to, play at all. In such a case, which is known as *stalemate*, the one player being unable to play and the other out of turn, the game is considered *drawn*, without advantage to either side. If two K.s remain alone on the board together, all other men having been captured, a similar result is arrived at, neither being unable, without assistance, to checkmate the other. The laws of the game should be studied in a special manual; one of the best codes will be found in Staunton's *Chess Praxis*. BIBLIOGRAPHY: H. Staunton, *Chess Player's Handbook*; *Chess Theory and Practice* (edited by R. T. Wormald); H. J. R. Murray, *History of Chess*; J. Mason, *The Art of Chess*; P. C. Morphy, *Morphy's Games of Chess*; E. Lasker, *Chess Strategy*.

CHEST. In man and the higher vertebrates, the cavity formed by the breastbone in front and the ribs and backbone at the sides and behind, shut off in mammals from the abdomen below the diaphragm or midriff. It contains the heart, lungs, etc., and the gullet passes through it.

CHESTER. An English episcopal city, county of a city, and municipal borough, county town of Cheshire, situated on the Dee about 16 miles from Liverpool. It is a bishop's see, and contains an old and interesting cathedral. The four principal streets have the roadways sunk considerably below the level of the footways, which run within piazzas covered by the upper portion of the houses, and in front of the ranges of shops. Flights of steps at convenient distances connect the carriage-ways with the footways or "rows." There are also shops and warehouses below the rows. These features, together with the ancient walls (now a public promenade) and the quaintly carved wooden gables of many of the houses, give an antique and picturesque appearance to Chester. Chester has manufactories of lead pipes, boots and shoes, and has iron-foundries and chemical works. The port has been improved of late years, but the shifting navigation of the Dee will never allow it to become of leading consequence. A parliamentary borough till 1918, Chester now gives its name to one of the nine parliamentary divisions of the county. Pop. (1931), 41,438.

CHESTER. A city o Pennsylvania, United States, on the Delaware, 13 miles W.S.W. of Philadelphia, founded by the Swedes in 1643. Pop. 59,164.

CHES'TERFIELD. A town, England, Derbyshire, 24 miles N. of Derby, irregularly but substantially built. Its church has a remarkable twisted spire, made of wood covered with lead. The principal manufactures are ginghams, lace, and earthenware, but a majority of the working-classes are employed in connection with the collieries, iron-mines, and blast-furnaces of the vicinity. It gives name to one of the eight parliamentary divisions of the county. Pop. (municipal borough) (1931), 64,146.

CHESTERFIELD, Philip Dormer Stanhope, Earl of. An English statesman and author, born in London in 1694, and studied at Cambridge. On the accession of George I. (1714) he became gentleman of the bedchamber to the Prince of Wales, and was returned by the borough of St. Germains, in Cornwall, to Parliament. He succeeded his father in the title in 1726, sat in the House of Lords, and acquired some distinction as a speaker. In 1728 he was ambassador to Holland, in 1744 Lord-Lieutenant of Ireland, a position which he occupied with great credit, and in 1746 Secretary of State; but in 1748 retired from public affairs. He obtained some reputation as an author by his *Letters to his Son*, first published in 1774. Chesterfield's *Letters to his Godson*, with a memoir by the Earl of Carnarvon, were published in 1890. These writings combine wit and good sense with great knowledge of society; but Dr. Johnson said that they taught the morals of a courtesan and the manners of a dancing-master. Lord Chesterfield died in 1773.—Cf. W. H. Craig, *Life of Lord Chesterfield*.

CHESTER-LE-STREET. A town of England, in the county, and 6½ miles N., of Durham, giving its name to a parliamentary division. It has coal-mines and ironworks. Pop. (1931), 16,639.

CHESTERTON. Till 1918 a parliamentary division of Cambridgeshire, so named from Chesterton, an urban district forming a suburb of Cambridge. Pop. (1931), 26,877.—Another Chesterton is in Staffordshire, in the Potteries district, about 2 miles W. of Burslem.

CHESTERTON, Gilbert Keith. British author, journalist, and critic, born at Kensington in 1874. Educated first at St. Paul's School, he entered the Slade School, where he studied art. He afterwards worked in a publisher's office, reviewing at the same time books for the *Speaker* and the *Bookman*. In 1900 he definitely took up literature as a profession, and contributed to various newspapers and periodicals. Unconventional in appearance, style, and ideas, Chesterton is a master of paradox and a brilliant satirist; he early attracted attention

G. K. Chesterton

by his piquant style, and has gained a high reputation in English letters. His works include: *The Wild Knight* (1900); *Greybeards at Play* (1900); *Browning* (English Men of Letters Series, 1903); *G. F. Watts* (1904); *The Napoleon of Notting Hill* (1904); *The Club of Queer Trades* (1905); *Dickens* (1906); *The Man Who was Thursday* (1908); *Orthodoxy* (1908); *Tremendous Trifles* (1909); *George Bernard Shaw* (1909); *What's Wrong with the World?* (1910); *The Innocence of Father Brown* (1911); *Manalive* (1912); *The Victorian Age in English Literature* (1913); *The Flying Inn* (1914); *The Crimes of England* (1915); *A Short History of England* (1917) *Irish Impressions* (1919); *The Superstition of Divorce* (1920). He became editor of *The New Witness* in 1916. In 1922 he joined the Roman Church. His *Everlasting Man* was published in 1925, the *Return of Don Quixote* in 1927, and *The Four Faultless Felons* in 1930.

CHEST-FOUNDERING. A disease in horses, a rheumatic affection of the chest and fore-legs.

CHESTNUT. A genus of plants, ord. Fagaceæ. The sweet or Spanish chestnut (*Castānea sativa*) is a stately tree, with large, handsome, serrated, dark-green leaves. The fruit consists of two or more seeds enveloped in a prickly husk. A native of Asia Minor, it has long been naturalised in Europe, and was introduced into Britain by the Romans. The tree grows freely in Britain, and may reach the age of many centuries. Its fruit ripens only in some cases, however, and the chestnuts eaten in Britain are mostly imported.

Sweet Chestnut

A, A, Male or barren catkins. B, B, Female or fertile flowers. C, Fruit.

Chestnuts form a staple article of food amongst the peasants of Spain and Italy.

The timber of the tree was formerly more in use than it is now; it is inferior to that of the oak, though very similar to it in appearance, especially when old. Two American species of chestnuts, *C. americāna* and *C. pumĭla* (the latter a shrub), have edible fruits. The former is often regarded as identical with the European tree.—The name of Cape Chestnut is given to a beautiful tree of the rue family, a native of Cape Province.—The Moreton Bay Chestnut is a leguminous tree of Australia, *Castanospermum australe*, with fruits resembling those of the chestnut.—The water-chestnut is the water-caltrop, *Trapa natans*.—The horse-chestnut (introduced into Britain about 1550) is quite a different tree from the common chestnut.

CHETAH. *See* CHEETAH.

CHET'VERT. A Russian grain-measure, equal to 0·7218 of an imperial quarter, or 5·77 bushels.

CHEVALIER, Maurice. French actor. He started as a boy with small engagements on the music hall stage in Paris. In 1913 he appeared at the Folies Bergères, but military service soon interrupted his career. In the Great War he was made prisoner by the Germans, but he escaped to reappear in Paris and to make his London debut with Elsie Janis. He then became a cinema actor.

CHEVALIER (shė-vȧ-lyā), **Michel.** A celebrated economist, born at Limoges, in France, 13th Jan., 1806, died in 1879. He was educated as an engineer in the School of Mines, joined the St. Simonians, and suffered six months' imprisonment for promulgating the free doctrines of "Père" Enfantin's party. On his liberation M. Chevalier renounced his extreme doctrines, and was sent to the United States and to England on special missions. He became a Councillor of State (1838), professor of political economy in the Collège de France (1840), member of the Chamber of Deputies (1846) and member of the Institute (1851). By this time he had written a number of works: *Lettres sur l'Amerique du Nord, Des Intérêts Matériels en France, Essais de Politique Industrielle, Cours d'Economie Politique*, and *De la Baisse Probable d'Or* (translated into English by Cobden). He was known as a strong advocate of free trade, and as a specialist on questions of currency. Along with Cobden and Bright he had a great part in the commercial treaty of 1860 between France and Britain.

CHEVAUX-DE-FRISE (shė-vō'-dė-frēz; "Friesland horses," so called because first used at the siege of Groningen, in that province, in 1658). Contrivances used in warfare, consisting of long pieces of timber or iron forming a centre, with long sharp-pointed spikes projecting all round, placed on the ground and serving to defend a passage or to stop a breach.

CHE'VIOT HILLS. A range on the borders of England and Scotland, stretching S.W. to N.E. for above 35 miles; culminating point, the Cheviot, 2688 feet. These hills are clothed for the most part with a close green sward, and are pastured by a celebrated breed of sheep.

CHEVIOT SHEEP. A breed of white-faced sheep, taking their name from the well-known Border mountain range extending along the border of Northumberland and Roxburghshire, noted for their large carcass, prime quality of mutton, and valuable wool used in the manufacture of Cheviot tweeds, which qualities, combined with a hardiness second only to that of the black-faced breed, constitute them the most valuable race of mountain sheep in the kingdom. The fleece weighs from 3 to 4 lb., and the carcass of ewes varies from 12 to 16 lb. per quarter, that of wethers from 16 to 20 lb. The Cheviot sheep has been bred on the Cheviot Hills from time immemorial. It was unknown elsewhere till near the end of the eighteenth century, when Sir John Sinclair, founder of the British Wool Society, called public attention to its admirable qualities. At the present

Cheviot Sheep

day it is only a little less popular than the black-faced breed throughout practically the whole of Scotland.

CHEVREUL (shė-vreul), **Michel Eugène.** A French chemist, born in 1786, died in 1889. In 1813 he became professor of physical science in the Charlemagne Lyçeum, in 1824 director of dyeing in the Gobelins manufactory, in 1830 professor of chemistry in the Collège de France. In 1879 he retired. His position as director of the Gobelins led to his important discoveries, both in the chemistry of dyeing and in the physics of colour. He wrote various works on chemistry and dyeing, and an important work, *The Law of Silmultaneous Contrast of Colours* (published in 1839), translated into English.

CHEV'RON. A heraldic and ornamental form, variously used. In heraldry, the chevron is an ordinary supposed to represent two rafters meeting at top. It is one of charges called honourable ordinaries. A similar form is used for the distinguishing badge worn on the arm of a non-commissioned officer in the British army, one chevron denoting a lance-corporal, two a corporal, three a sergeant, and three and a crown a company quartermaster-sergeant. During the European War (1914-18) the War Office sanctioned the issue of

Chevron

chevrons for overseas service. Anyone who had proceeded overseas was entitled to wear a chevron, with an additional one for every complete twelve months' service overseas. The chevrons were worn on the right forearm, and were blue in colour; but

Chevron Moulding

anyone who had proceeded overseas prior to 31st Dec., 1914, was entitled to a red chevron. In architecture, the *chevron moulding* consists of a variety of fret ornament of a zigzag form, common in Norman architecture.

CHEV'ROTAINS. Small hornless deer-like animals, including the Kanchils (species of Tragulus) of South and South-East Asia, and the Water Chevrotain (*Dorcatherium aquaticum*) found in the neighbourhood of streams in West Africa.

CHE'VY CHASE. The name of a celebrated British Border ballad, which is probably founded on some actual encounter which took place between its heroes, Percy and Douglas, although the incidents mentioned in it are not historical. On account of the similarity of the incidents in this ballad to those of *The Battle of Otterbourne*, the two ballads have often been confounded; but the probability is that if any historical event is celebrated at all in the ballad of *Chevy Chase*, it is different from that celebrated in *The Battle of Otterbourne*, and that the similarity between the two ballads is to be explained by supposing that many of the events of the former were borrowed from the latter.

There are two versions of the ballad bearing the name of *Chevy Chase*, an older one, originally called *The Hunt-*

ing of the Cheviot, and a more modern one. From the fact that the older version is mentioned in the *Complaynt of Scotland*, written in 1548, it is clear that it was known in Scotland before that time. The age of the more modern version is believed to be no later than the reign of Charles II. This is the version which forms the subject of the critique by Addison in Nos. 70 and 74 of the *Spectator*.

CHEWING GUM. The coagulated latex (Chicle gum) of *Achras Sapota*, a tree of tropical America, nat. ord. Sapotaceæ, impregnated with spearmint or other flavouring matter. It enjoys a great vogue in the United States, and was also popular with the British troops in the late war.

CHEYENNE (shī-yen'). A town of the United States, capital of the state of Wyoming, on the Union Pacific Railway, where it is joined by the Denver Pacific; a rising place. Pop. 17,361. The River Cheyenne, or Big Cheyenne, a tributary of the Missouri, is formed by two branches, the N. Fork and the S. Fork, which rise in this state, and have the Black Hills between them, each about 300 miles long, the Big Cheyenne being 150 miles more.

CHEYENNE. A North American Indian tribe of the Algonquian family, consisting of two divisions: the Northern Cheyenne, numbering about 1400, and the Southern Cheyenne, comprising about 1900. The great tribal ceremony of the Cheyenne is the sun-dance, a tribal recognition of the sun as their elder brother.

CHEYNE, Thomas Kelly. Biblical critic, born in London, 18th Sept., 1841, died in 1915. He took his degree at Oxford in 1862, and became Oriel Professor of Holy Scripture Interpretation in 1885. He was canon of Rochester in 1885, rector of Tendring, Essex, 1880-85, a member of the Old Testament Revision Company, and Bampton Lecturer in 1889. His publications are numerous, and include: *Commentaries on Isaiah* (1884), *Job and Solomon* (1887), *Jeremiah: his Life and Times* (1888), *The Hallowing of Criticism* (1888), *Founders of Old Testament Criticism* (1894), *Jewish Religious Life after the Exile* (1898), *Critica Biblica* (1904), *Bible Problems and the New Material for their Solution* (1904), *The Two Religions of Israel* (1910), *The Veil of Hebrew History* (1913). He also edited, together with J. S. Black, the *Encyclopædia Biblica*. His views were extremely broad and liberal.

CHIABRERA (ki-å-brā'rå), **Gabriel Lo.** Italian poet, born in 1552, died in 1637; wrote various kinds of poems, and imitated Pindar and Anacreon in odes and canzonets, not unsuccessfully.

CHIANA (ki-ä'nå; anciently Clanis). A river and valley, Italy, in Tuscany and Umbria. The river is artificially divided into two branches, the one flowing into the Arno, the other into the Paglia. By works begun in 1551, and completed only in 1823, the valley of the Chiana has been drained and brought under cultivation, being now one of the most productive portions of Italy.

CHIANG KAI-SHEK. Chinese politician. A soldier, he became a follower of Sun Yat Sen, and was made head of the military school. In 1925 he was chosen Commander-in-Chief of the forces directed from Nanking, and he led these to the capture of Pekin and to other victories over the northerners. In 1928 he was chosen President of the Republic, and in 1930 conducted, simultaneously, campaigns against the Communists in the south and the northerners who still refused to accept his rule.

CHIANTI (ki-ån'tē). A district in Italy, near Siena, where what is now the best-known red wine of Italy is produced. Chianti wine is full flavoured and astringent, with an alcoholic strength of about 20 per cent.

CHIAN TURPENTINE (kī-an). A turpentine or resin obtained from the Island of Chios (Scio), yielded by *Pistachia Terebinthus*, a native of the Mediterranean islands and shores, used in medicine. Called also Cyprus turpentine.

CHIAPAS (chi-ä'pås). A state of Mexico, on the Pacific coast; area, 27,527 sq. miles. It is in many parts mountainous, is intersected by the River Chiapas, and covered with immense forests. The valleys are fertile, and produce much maize, sugar, cacao, and cotton. But trade is quite undeveloped on account of the lack of roads. Capital, Tuxtla-Gutierrez. Pop. 521,318.

CHIARAMONTE (ki-å-rå-mon'tā). A town of Sicily, province of Syracuse, on a hill in a highly fertile neighbourhood. Pop. 15,570.

CHIARI (ki-ä'rō). A town of N. Italy, province of Brescia, and 14 miles W. of the town of that name, with manufacturing of silk. Pop. 12,489.

CHIAROSCURO, or **CHIARO-OSCURO** (ki-ä-rō-skö'rō; an Italian term, meaning "clear-obscure;" in French, *clair-obscur*). In painting, the distribution of the lights and shadows in a picture. A composition, however perfect in other respects, becomes a picture only by means of the chiaroscuro, which gives faithfulness to the representation, and therefore is of the highest importance to the painter. The drawing of a piece may be perfectly correct, the colouring may be brilliant and true, and yet the whole picture remain cold and hard. By the chiaroscuro objects are made to advance or recede from the eye, produce a mutual effect, and form a united and beautiful whole.

CHIASTOLITE. A mineral, a variety of andalusite (aluminium silicate crystallizing in nearly square prisms) formed where slaty rocks have been altered by igneous intrusions, and characterised by a regular arrangement of carbonaceous impurities within its crystals. When broken across, a central square black column appears, with thin lines (the sections of black planes) reaching from its angles to those of the crystal, where they join four other black columns which run down parallel with the long edges of the crystal. The name of this mineral variety arises from the white cross that is marked out by the black portions encroaching on the white crystal from the angles. This mineral is found in most countries along granite contacts, and on a large scale at Bimbowrie in South Australia.

CHIAVARI (ki-ä′vȧ-rē). A seaport town, Italy, in the province of Genoa, 23 miles E. by S. of Genoa, in a district productive of wine, olives, and silk. Pop. 13,700.

CHIAVENNA (ki-ȧ-ven′nȧ). A town, Italy, Lombardy, 38 miles N.N.W. of Bergamo, in the province of Sondrio, in a valley in the midst of magnificent scenery on the road to the Splügen Pass, with an important transit trade. Pop. 4810.

CHIBOUQUE (shi-bök′; French form of the Turk. *chibuk*, literally a stick). A Turkish pipe with a long stem.

CHICA (chē′kȧ). A red colouring-matter which the Indians on the upper parts of the Orinoco and the Rio Negro prepare from the leaves of a plant native to that region called *Bignonia Chica*, and with which they paint their skin, in order to be better able to resist the rays of the sun.

CHICA (chē′kȧ). A kind of beer made from maize, in general use in Chile, Peru, and elsewhere in the mountainous regions of South America.

CHICACOLE, or CHIKAKOL. A town of India, in the Ganjam district, Madras Presidency, 567 miles N.E. of Madras, notable for its fine muslin manufactures. Pop. 17,850.

CHICAGO (shi-ka̧′gō). A city, Illinois, United States, the capital of Cook County, on the south-west shore of Lake Michigan, and on both sides of Chicago River. It stands on a level plain, and is surrounded by a beautiful and fertile country. The Chicago River and its two branches

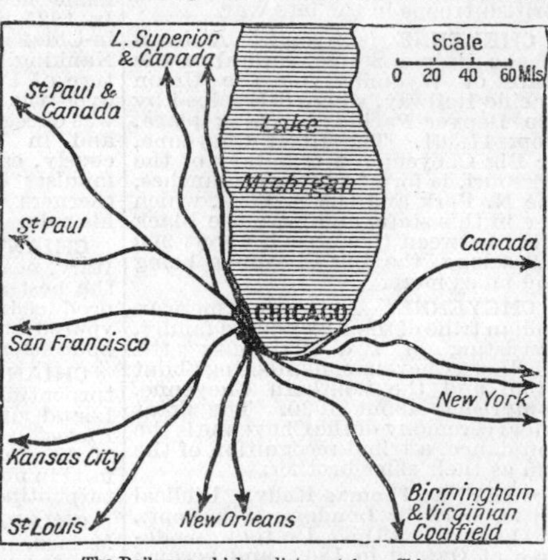

The Railways which radiate out from Chicago

separate the city into three unequal divisions, known as the North, the South, and the West, connected by numerous bridges and two tunnels under the river. The streets are wide and laid out at right angles, many of them being adorned by rows of fine forest trees. The site of the city was originally unhealthy from its lowness, but a large portion of it has been artificially heightened (even while occupied by buildings) by 8 or 10 feet. The public parks have an area of 2000 acres.

Among the chief buildings are the new city hall and court-house, the custom-house and post office, and the chamber of commerce. There is a university, opened in 1892, and a large number of higher-class colleges and seminaries. The public library, founded in 1872, contains over 500,000 vols. To supply the town with water two tunnels have been constructed which extend for 2 miles under Lake Michigan, and convey the pure water of that lake into the town, where it is pumped up to a height of 160 feet and distributed. Another tunnel 4 miles long has been constructed. There are also several artesian wells. From its position at the head of the great chain of the American lakes, and at the centre of a network of railroads communicating with all parts of the Union, Chicago has always been more a commercial than a manufacturing city. There are extensive docks, basins, and other accommodation for shipping.

Industries.—The industries include iron-founding, brewing, distilling, leather, hats, sugar, tobacco, agricultural implements, steam-engines, boots and shoes. In commerce Chicago is only second to New York. It has an enormous trade in pork-packing, and is the greatest market for grain and timber in America. Other articles for which it is a centre of trade are flour, provisions, wool, hides, soft goods, clothing. Before 1831 Chicago was a mere trading-station. Its charter is dated 4th March, 1837, its population being then 4170, but since then it has advanced at an altogether extraordinary rate. On 7th Oct., 1871, a great fire occurred which burned down a vast number of houses and rendered about 150,000 persons homeless and destitute. But the energy of its inhabitants and its favourable situation enabled it to recover in a surprisingly short time. In 1880 its population was 503,185; in 1930 it had increased to 3,376,438. In 1892-93 a great international exhibition was held in this city. A World's Fair is to be held in Chicago in 1933 to celebrate the city's centennial anniversary, and to illustrate the progress of science and culture throughout the world. It is to be called "The Century of Progress Celebration."—BIBLIOGRAPHY: A. T. Andreas, *History of Chicago*; J. Kirkland, *The Story of Chicago*; J. S. Currey, *Chicago: its History and its Builders* (5 vols.).

CHICHEN (chē-chen′), or **CHICHEN-ITZA.** An ancient ruined city of Yucatan, Central America, about 35 miles W. of Valladolid. Its ruins are very magnificent, and are in better preservation than most of the other ruined cities of the same province.

CHICH′ESTER. An episcopal and municipal city, and until 1885 a parliamentary borough, of England (now giving name to one of the two parliamentary divisions of West Sussex), near the south-west corner of the county of Sussex, well built, with wide streets. Its old wall, still in good preservation and lined with lofty elms, gives it a very picturesque appearance. Its principal building is the cathedral, an ancient Gothic structure with a most graceful spire. Chichester takes its name (Cissaceaster) from the South Saxon king Cissa, who rebuilt it. Pop. (1931), 13,911.

CHICK′ADEE. The popular name in America of the black-cap titmouse (*Parus atricapillus*) and other allied species, an imitation of their note.

CHICKAHOM′INY. A river in Virginia, rising about 20 miles N.W. of Richmond, flowing S.E. till it joins the James River. Near this river many important battles during the Civil War took place, such as the battle of Williamsburg, of the Seven Pines, of Gaines's Mill.

CHICKAMAU′GA. A small tributary of the Tennessee River, state of Tennessee, United States, where a battle took place 19th to 20th Sept., 1863, between the Federal troops under Rosecrans and the Confederates under Bragg and Longstreet, the latter gaining the victory.

CHICK′ASAW INDIANS. A tribe of American Indians of the Appalachian nation. In 1832 they gave up to the United States the last of their lands south of the Tennessee River, receiving as compensation a money indemnity and new lands on the left bank of the Red River, in the Indian Territory. The Chickasaws number about 4000. They have made considerable advances towards civilisation, have a Senate, House of Representatives, and more than a million dollars in deposit with the Union Government.

CHICKEN-POX (Varicella). An infectious disease mainly confined to children. It commences with feverishness, and an eruption of pimples, which speedily become blebs filled with clear fluid and as large as split-peas. Within a week these dry up into dark-coloured scabs, which within another week have fallen off. The disease is never fatal, and has no evil results. A little opening medicine and a mild diet is all the treatment required.

CHICK-PEA. The popular name of *Cicer arietinum*, which grows wild along the shores of the Mediterranean and in many parts of the East, producing a short puffy pod with one or generally two small wrinkled seeds. It is an important article in French and Spanish cookery under the name of *pois chiche*, or *gervance*. Gathered when quite ripe, they form the basis of the French soup called *purée aux croutons*. The plant is cultivated in Europe, Egypt, Syria, India ("gram"), Mexico, etc. When roasted it is the common *parched pulse* of the East. The herbage serves as fodder for cattle.

CHICK'WEED. The popular name of *Stellaria media*, ord. Caryophyllaceæ, one of the most common weeds in cultivated and waste ground everywhere in Britain, flowering through-

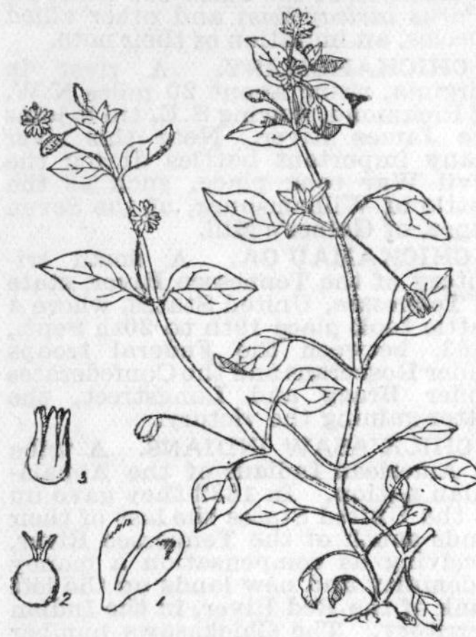

Chickweed

1, Petal. 2, Ovary. 3, Fruit (dehiscent).

out the year. It has a procumbent more or less hairy stem, with ovate pointed leaves, and many small white flowers. It is much used for feeding cage-birds, which are very fond both of its leaves and seeds.

CHICLA'NA. A town, Spain, Andalusia, 12 miles S.E. of Cadiz, built of snow-white stone; it contains a magnificent hospital, and has manufactures of linen and earthenware. The sulphur baths, temperature 60°, are good for skin-diseases, and are much frequented. Pop. 12,010.

CHIC'OPEE. A town of Massachusetts, United States, on the River Connecticut, at the mouth of the Chicopee, with manufactures of cotton, machinery, and paper. Pop. 43,930.

CHIC'ORY (Cichorium). A genus of composite plants, including the two important species of *C. Endivia* (endive) and *C. Intÿbus* (chicory or succory). The former, a native of the East, is found in the two forms—the *curled* and the *Batavian*—both forming well-known salads by the blanching of their leaves. The *C. Intÿbus* or *chicory* is a common per-

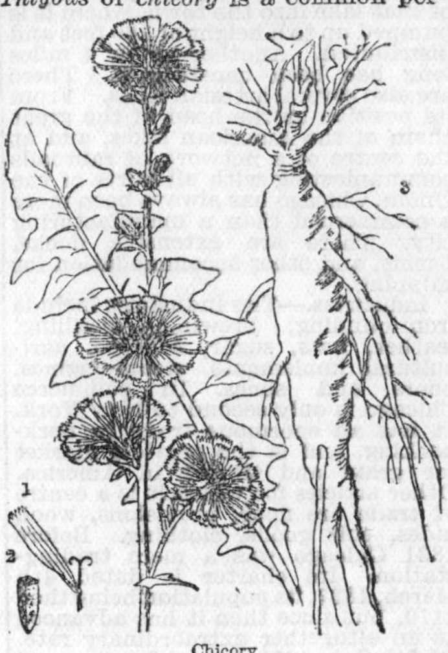

Chicory

1, Floret. 2, Seed. 3, Root.

ennial plant, from 2 to 3 feet high. The leaves are sometimes blanched, to be used as salad, in the same way as *C. Endivia*. But the most important part of the plant is its long, fleshy, and milky root, which, when roasted and ground, is now extensively used for mixing with coffee. Its presence among coffee may easily be detected by putting a spoonful of the mixture into a glass of clear cold water, when the coffee will float on the surface, and the chicory separate and discolour the water as it subsides.

CHIEF. In heraldry, the upper part of the escutcheon cut off by a horizontal line, and normally occupying a third of the shield.

CHIEF JUSTICE, or LORD CHIEF JUSTICE. In England, the presiding judge in the King's Bench division of the High Court of Justice, and, in the absence of the Lord Chancellor, president of the High Court, and also, *ex officio*, one of the judges of the Court of Appeal. The *Chief Justice of the Common Pleas*, previous to 1881, was the presiding judge in the Common Pleas division of the High Court of Justice, but the office is now merged in that of the Chief Justice of England. The title chief justice is also generally given in the various British colonies to the heads of the different judicial establishments, as in Canada and Australia. In Canada there is not only a chief justice at the head of the supreme court of the Dominion, but also chief justices in the separate provinces. Similarly, in the United States, the presiding justice of the supreme court is called chief justice, as are also similar officers in the individual states.

CHIENGMAI (chi-eng-mī'). A town of Northern Siam, capital of a semi-independent Lao state, on a tributary of the Menam, favourably situated as a centre of trade with Burmah, South-Western China, etc., the seat of a British consul and an international court. Teak is an important article of trade. Pop. 30,000.

CHIERI (ki-ā'rē). An old town of North Italy, 8 miles E.S.E. of Turin, with a very large Gothic church, and manufactures of cotton, silk, etc. It was a manufacturing centre as far back as 1422. Pop. 14,000.

CHIETI (ki-ā'tē). A town, Southern Italy, capital of province of the same name, on a hill near the right bank of the Pescara. It is well built, is the see of an archbishop, and has manufactures of woollens. Pop. 29,219.

CHIFF-CHAFF (*Phylloscopus collybita*). A bird, so called from its cry, one of the warblers, a summer visitant to England from the Continent, 4 or 5 inches long; inhabits woods and thickets, and destroys many insect larvæ.

CHIGNECTO. Bay of Canada. An area of the Bay of Fundy, it runs between Nova Scotia and New Brunswick, and forms Shepody Bay and Cumberland Basin. It is 30 miles long and about 8 wide. The piece of land uniting Nova Scotia and New Brunswick and separating two areas of the Atlantic, is called the Isthmus of Chignecto. It is about 24 miles across, and along it a railway line (C.N.R.) runs. A proposal has been made to cut a canal across the isthmus.

CHIGOE (chig'ō), or **JIGGER.** A very curious insect (*Sarcopsylla penetrans*), closely resembling the common flea, but of more minute size, found in the West Indies, S. America, Africa, etc. It burrows beneath the skin of the foot, and soon acquires the size of a pea, its abdomen becoming distended with eggs. If these eggs remain to be hatched beneath the skin, great irritation and even troublesome sores are sure to result. The insect must be extracted entire, and with great care, as soon as its presence is indicated by a slight itching or tingling.

CHIH-LI (chi-lē'), or **PE-CHI-LI.** One of the northern provinces of China, watered by the Pei-ho, containing Peiping. Area 115,830 sq. miles; pop. 38,905,695.

CHIHUAHUA (chē-wä'wä). A city, Mexican Confederation, capital of the state of the same name, generally well built, and supplied with water by a famous aqueduct. It is surrounded by silver-mines, and is an important entrepôt of trade. Pop. 44,000.—The *State* is bounded on the north by the United States and on the north-east by the Rio Grande del Norte, and is rich in silver-mines. Area, 90,036 sq. miles; pop. 491,893.

CHILAW'. A seaport town on the west coast of Ceylon, 45 miles N. by W. of Colombo, formerly a place of greater importance than it is now. Pop. 5000.

CHILBLAINS. A mild form of frost-bite, and consist of painful inflammatory swellings, of a deep purple or leaden colour, to which the fingers, toes, heels, and other extreme parts of the body are subject on being exposed to a severe degree of cold. The pain is not constant, but rather pungent and shooting at particular times, and an insupportable itching attends it. In some instances the skin remains entire, but in others it breaks and discharges a thin fluid. Compound camphor liniment is a useful application, and the parts should be kept warm.

CHILDEBERT. The name of three kings of the Merovingian dynasty, France. The first of this name was the third son of Clovis, and born about A.D. 495. On his father's death, in 511, he succeeded to the kingdom of Paris as his share of the paternal dominions. He died in 558.—**Childebert II.** was the son of Sigebert and Brunehaut, and born about 570. He died from the effects of poison in 596.—**Childebert III.**, surnamed *the Just*, son of Thierry I., King of the Franks, was born about 683, and proclaimed king in 695 on the death of his brother, Clovis III. His kingship, however, was merely nominal, the true sovereign being Pepin le Gros or d'Héristal, who, under the title of Mayor of the Palace, exercised the real authority. Childebert III. died in 711. He was thus one of those Merovingian kings who, from their incapacity, received the appellation of *rois fainéants*, or *sluggard kings*.

CHILDERMAS DAY. An old English name for Innocents' Day, a festival celebrated by the Anglican

Church and the Church of Rome on the 28th of December, in commemoration of the massacre of the Innocents.

CHILD LABOUR REGULATION. Children and labour were not unacquainted at any time of which we have record, but it was not until the beginning of the nineteenth century that the question of the regulation of the industrial employment of children was seriously considered. It has been increasingly realized how bad are the after effects of employing young children in factories and workshops. The most obviously urgent question in dealing with the protection of child labour is that of fixing a minimum age under which the child may not be employed. This point has received much attention by the International Labour Office, and a minimum age of 14 has been fixed.

In Great Britain Jonas Hanway made an attempt in 1760 to abolish the custom of employing boys and girls as chimney-sweeps, and by the Chimney-sweepers' Chimneys Regulation Act, 1840, as amended by the Acts of 1864 and 1875, it is made illegal to allow any person under 21 years of age to sweep chimneys. The first Factory Act, restricted to the protection of apprentices in cotton and other mills and factories, was passed in 1802. This legislation culminated in the Factory and Workshops Acts of 1901 to 1911, which supply the main regulations under which the labour of children in factories and workshops may be employed.

Under the Act of 1901 no child under 12 years of age may be employed in any factory or workshop. The Act provides for half-time attendance at school and half-time employment between the ages of 12 and 14. In certain cases children who have made a limited number of attendances at school and have passed an educational test may be exempted at 13, and become whole-time workers. The Act makes it illegal for children and young persons to work at night, and limits the hours of their employments, e.g. in textile factories, to ten per day exclusive of meal-times, with not more than four and a half hours' work without a break.

The Coal Mines Act (1911) prohibits the employment of any boy under the age of 14 and of any woman or girl in any mine below ground.

By the Education Act of 1921 power is given to local Education Authorities for elementary education to make by-laws regulating in certain respects the employment of children under the age of 14, and street trading by children under 16. By the same Act it is made a criminal offence to cause or allow a boy under the age of 14 or a girl under the age of 16 to be in any street, or in any premises licensed for the sale of any intoxicating liquor (other than premises licensed according to law for public entertainment), for the purpose of singing, playing, or performing, or being exhibited for profit, or offering anything for sale between 9 p.m. and 6 a.m., and in the case of a child under 14 between 8 p.m. and 6 a.m. But no child under 12 is to be allowed to perform or be exhibited for profit in similar circumstances at any hour. A certain latitude as to some of these restrictions, however, may be allowed by competent local authorities in certain circumstances. Special regulations are made in regard to children who are to be trained to acrobatic or other dangerous performances. Further measures for the protection of children were passed in 1932 and 1933.

The laws in other countries are on similar lines to those of the United Kingdom, in some particulars better, in some not so good. There is an almost universal prohibition of the employment of children in occupations considered dangerous to health, and, with few exceptions, night-work in industry is forbidden for children (and also for women).

In the United States factory legislation is a State function, and more or less stringent laws on the European model exist in nearly all states. Their variety, and a certain laxity in their execution, has led to the enactment of federal legislation for child protection, under the guise of regulating inter-state commerce. The Children's Labour Law (1917) bars from inter-state commerce the products of mines and quarries where children under 16 are employed, and the products of mills, factories, canneries, and workshops where children of 14 are employed.

In Germany, prior to the Great War, children were not permitted to be employed between the hours of 8 p.m. and 6 a.m. The age limit in factories was 13, and the hours ten per day. Persons over 13 who had not completed their school instruction were counted as children. Between the ages of 14 and 16 the hours were limited to six per day. In France the age limit is 13, and the maximum hours twelve per day. Children between the ages of 12 and 13 must have a school and health certificate. The employment between 9 p.m. and 5 a.m. of young persons under 18 is prohibited. Girls and women have at least eleven hours' consecutive rest in each twenty-four hours.

The international protection of children in industry formed an important subject of consideration at the Conference held at Washington in Oct., 1919, under the League of Nations, when recommendations were made to the several nations of the League for levelling up the legislation of the more backward nations to a common minimum standard. A further Conference was held at Genoa in 1920 dealing with the hours of work in ships. At both these Conferences certain draft conventions were adopted, and were submitted to the various nations who are represented in the League of Nations. Most of the nations have ratified these conventions and have passed, or are in process of passing, laws to limit the employment of young children.

In 1920, in Great Britain, the Women, Young Persons and Children (Employment) Act was passed. It makes it illegal for any child under the age of 14 to be employed in any industrial undertaking, other than an undertaking in which only members of the same family are employed. It also makes it compulsory for employers to keep a register of all persons under the age of 16 years employed by them, and of the dates of their births. It prohibits the employment of children under the age of 14 years on vessels other than vessels upon which only members of the same family are employed. It makes it imperative for every shipmaster to keep a register of all persons under the age of 16 years employed on board his vessel, or a list of them in the articles of agreement, and of the dates of their births. This Act does not apply to children under the age of 14 years who were at the commencement of the Act (Jan., 1921) lawfully employed in any industrial undertaking or ship. The Act does not apply to domestic service, agriculture, or transport by hand.

The Merchant Shipping Act (1894) regulated apprenticeship in the sea service and sea-fishing service. By this Act no boy under the age of 12 years may be apprenticed to the sea service unless he is of sufficient health and strength, and gives his consent to be bound. This Act gives special protection to boys in Poor Law Institutions from being sent to sea against their wish. No boy under the age of 13 years can be apprenticed to the sea-fishing service, and no boy under the age of 16 can be engaged in the sea-fishing service without being bound by an indenture of apprenticeship.—BIBLIOGRAPHY: S. and B. Webb, *Industrial Democracy*; M. E. Alden, *Child Life and Labour*; O. J. Dunlop, *English Apprenticeship and Child Labour*; F. Keeling, *Child Labour in the United Kingdom*; E. Markham, *Children in Bondage*.

CHILDREN, Cruelty to. Societies for the prevention of cruelty to children were first instituted in America, and about 1883-84 they were introduced into England. Up to the year 1889 there was no special legislation for the prevention of cruelty to children, though under the ordinary laws such cruelty could, of course, be punished, and the employment of children of tender years was forbidden or restricted in various ways, by the Factory Acts or otherwise. In 1889 a special Act was passed to prevent cruelty to children; in 1894 this was superseded by another Act; and in 1904 a fresh Act was passed and brought into operation, most of the previous enactments being re-enacted and some new ones added.

Cruelty to a child takes place if any person over the age of 16, who has the custody, care, or charge of any child under that age, wilfully assaults, ill-treats, neglects, abandons, or exposes such child (or causes any of these things) in a manner likely to produce unnecessary suffering to the child, or injury to its health, including injury to or loss of sight, hearing, limb, or bodily organ, and any mental derangement. For the more serious offences, the offender being convicted on indictment (before a jury), the punishment may be a fine not exceeding £100, or imprisonment for not more than two years, with or without hard labour; for the less serious, the offender being summarily convicted, the punishment is a fine not exceeding £25, or imprisonment for not more than six months, with or without hard labour. If the person guilty of cruelty has a pecuniary interest in the child's death, the penalty may be increased to £200, or five years' penal servitude.

It is forbidden to cause or allow boys under 14, and girls under 16, to beg or receive alms on the street or elsewhere, whether under pretence of singing, playing, performing, or otherwise; or to cause or allow children of such age to sing, play, or perform for profit, or offer articles for sale in the street or premises licensed for intoxicating liquor between 9 p.m. and 6 a.m., though such children may sing or perform for gain in places duly licensed for public entertainments; but no child under 11 is to be allowed to perform, or be exhibited, for gain in public at any hour. A certain latitude as to some of these restrictions, however, may be allowed by competent local authorities in certain circumstances.

Special regulations are made in regard to children that are to be trained to acrobatic or other dangerous performances. A constable is authorized to take into custody, without warrant, persons committing in his presence offences against the Act, when name and residence are unknown and cannot be ascertained. The court may order that the child be taken out of the custody of the person convicted or bound over to keep the peace, and handed over to the charge of a relation or some other fit person; and an offending parent may be compelled to contribute to the child's maintenance. The Act, of course, does not interfere with the right of parents, guardians, or teachers to administer due punishment. Much has been and is done to prevent cruelty to children and bring offenders to justice by the National Society for the Prevention of Cruelty to Children, having its central quarters in London. —Cf. R. J. Parr, *Prevention of Cruelty to Children Act* (1904).

CHILDRENITE. A mineral hydrous phosphate of aluminium, iron, and manganese, especially known from its occurrence in brownish crystals, sometimes an inch long, in mines in Devon and Cornwall.

CHILDREN, Laws relating to. These laws form a numerous and widely scattered collection, dealing with civil status and general welfare of children, and their amenability to criminal proceedings. The civil status, or capacity of children to acquire rights and incur obligations, whether through contract or delict, is left mainly to the common law. In England all persons under 21 are termed "infants," and most contracts made by an infant are voidable, though capable of ratification after majority. By the Infants Relief Act (1877), however, contracts for the repayment of loans or the purchase of goods are void *ab initio*.

In Scotland a distinction is drawn between persons above and those below 14 years, in the case of males, and 12 in the case of females; the former, up to 21 years of age, ar termed "minors"; the latter "pupils." Minors, whether acting alone or with their guardians (termed "curators"), may validly bind themselves by contract, but may reduce their obligations, if seriously injurious to their interests, within four years after majority (*quadriennium utile*). Pupils cannot validly contract at all; any acts necessary for administration being performed by their natural or legal guardians or "tutors." In both countries the contractual liability of persons under age is recognised in the case of "necessaries"; also where the person has held himself out as over age when contracting.

As regards damages for delict or negligence, children in both countries are in the same position as adults. They are seldom sued for such damages, however, there being no vicarious responsibility upon the parents. Actions of damages by children are common, and in these "contributory negligence" is not an effectual defence, unless the child was intelligent enough to realize the danger. The law relating to children's welfare is mainly statutory, the leading Act being the Children Act (1908), by which the practic of putting children under 7 out to nurse is restricted and controlled, and severe penalties are imposed for crrelty, including neglect, inadequate feeding and clothing, etc.; also for allowing children to beg in public, and exposing them to physical and moral dangers, including smoking. The sale of intoxicating liquor to children is forbidden under a separate Act (1901).

Many Acts restrict the employment of children both generally and in particular trades. The most important of these are the Employment of Children Act (1903), the Mines Act (1900), the Factory and Workshop Act (1901), and the Children's Dangerous Performance Act of 1879 (amended in 1897). The Education Acts also incidentally restrict employment in connection with the provisions as to compulsory education. Criminal responsibility cannot attach to a child under 7. Above that age, however, there is no essential difference between children and adults, except in the matter of punishment.

The Children Act (1908) prohibits death sentence, and also forbids imprisonment and penal servitude, except in special cases, for children under 16, and in lieu thereof provides special punishments, e.g. whipping, or detention in reformatories or industrial schools. By the Prev ntion of Crimes Act (1908), since amended by the Criminal Justice Acts of 1914 and 1925, somewhat similar provision is made for detention in Borstal Institutions of offenders between the ages of 16 and 21. *See* MINOR, CURATOR.—BIBLIOGRAPHY: W. H. S. Garnett, *Children and the Law*; R. W. Holland, *The Law relating to the Child.*

CHILDREN'S GAMES. The study of children's games is an important branch of folk-lore. These games are historically valuable on account of their derivation from the ancient ceremonies and religious rites inseparable from every great occasion in the lives of our ancestors. They are among the earliest forms of drama, and were at first probably all accompanied by words and music, but now are divided into singing and non-singing games. Non-singing games are played by boys, the words and music having been dropped as unnecessary to the action. Games of this sort usually partake of the character of a contest, typifying the meeting of hostile forces.

Singing Games.—The singing games are of a more domestic character, and have retained much of their ancient dramatic form. They are played by both sexes, and may be divided into four classes, viz. "line," "circle," "arch," and "characteristic" games. The *line games* are contestant in character, and consist of two lines of players, representing rival tribes or villages, which alternately advance and retreat before each other. "Nuts in May" is a popular example of the line game, and preserves the ancient custom of marriage by capture, the boy, or prospective husband, advancing to carry off the girl for his wife.

Circle Games are the survivals of those occasions when the people of one community met to celebrate some special local event, such as a marriage, seed-time, or harvest. "Oats and Beans and Barley" belong to this class, and depicts the ceremonies of seed-time combined with marriage customs. "Kiss in the Ring" is also a circle game representing an early form of marriage by choice.

Arch Games consist of two players joining hands and forming an arch, beneath which the remaining players run. They typify events occurring in one village or parish; but whereas in one form the players join hands and dance round after passing beneath the arch, thereby signifying agreement and goodwill, in another they celebrate a contest between rival factions. Of this latter type "Oranges and Lemons" is a favourite game. Orange and lemon probably represent the colours of rival parties. As each child is captured whilst passing under the arch, she chooses one or the other, and, according to her choice, takes up her position behind one of the leaders. Finally, when all the players have taken sides, a tug-of-war ensues. The punishment suggested by the words "Here comes a chopper to chop off your head" may refer to the fate which awaited the laggard in answering his lord's call to arms.

Characteristic Games are those in which one or more of the players perform actions and sing words different from those of the majority. "Fox and Goose" is an example of this type, and depicts an incident typical of the farmyard.

CHILE or **CHILI** (chē'lē, chē'lā). A republic of South America, extending along the Pacific coast from lat. 17° 57′ S. nearly to Cape Horn, and including Chiloé and many other islands and part of Tierra del Fuego. It is bounded on the north by Peru (the

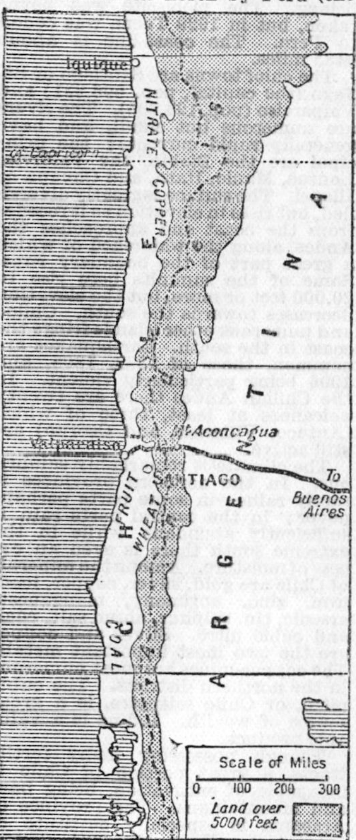

Chile, showing products

River Sama being the boundary), on the north-east and east by Bolivia and the Argentine Republic, from which it is separated by the chief range of the Cordilleras. Its length from north to south is about 2661 miles; its breadth, ranging from 58 to 273 miles; area, 285,133 sq. miles, divided into 23 provinces, subdivided into 82 departments and one territory;

pop. (1930), 4,237,445. By the war with Peru and Bolivia, which terminated in 1882, Chile gained all the seaboard of Bolivia, and annexed also the Peruvian provinces of Tarapacá, Arica, and Tacna, the two last for ten years, at the end of which period a plebiscite of the provinces was to decide to which country they should belong. The plebiscite was never taken, but in 1929 Tacna was ceded to Peru. The coast-line is about 2485 miles.

The chief towns are Santiago or St. Jago (the capital, pop. 696,231) and Valparaiso (pop. 193,205). The rivers are numerous but small, and have generally rapid currents; the principal are the Biobio, the Valdivia, Lontue, Maule, Itata, and Chuapa or Illapel. The surface is greatly diversified, but rises in elevation as it recedes from the coast and approaches the Andes, along the watershed of which a great part of the boundary runs. Some of the summits here rise to 20,000 feet or more, but the elevation decreases towards the south. Chiloé and numerous other islands fringe the coast in the south. Earthquakes are common, those of 1822, 1868, and 1906 being particularly violent. In the Chilian Andes there are twenty volcanoes at least, three of which (Antuco, Villarica, and Osorno) are still active.

The climate is remarkably salubrious. In the northern provinces it rarely rains—in some parts perhaps never; in the central parts rain is sufficiently abundant while in the extreme south there is even an excess of moisture. Among the minerals of Chile are gold, silver, copper, lead, iron, zinc, antimony, manganese, arsenic, tin, sulphur, alum, salt, coal, and cubic nitre. Silver and copper are the two most important metals. The copper-mines are most numerous in the northern districts. The cubic nitre, or Chile saltpetre, is a great source of wealth. Iodine is a valuable product.

Though possessing many fertile tracts, a great portion of Chile is incapable of cultivation, being bare and mountainous. The province of Atacama is especially destitute of vegetation. From the 29th degree of latitude southwards green valleys and fertile tracts appear, the character of the vegetation getting always richer, till in the southern provinces we find the sides of the Andes clothed with forests and with herbaceous plants and flowers of the richest and most beautiful hues. In some of the northern districts wheat and barley are the chief agricultural products. Fruits are abundant—apples, pears, apricots, peaches, figs, grapes, oranges, and water-melons. The spread of European plants has been so great in some places to as crowd out native species, and cultivation is rapidly carrying this farther.

Animals.—The wild animals include the guanaco, puma or American lion, the chinchilla, coypu, and deer. Cattle and sheep are raised in great numbers, sheep-rearing being a most important industry.

Commerce.—The manufactures are of little importance, but include cordage, soap, copper wares, leather, and brandy. The commerce is increasing rapidly. The greater part of the foreign trade is with the U.S.A and Britain. Mineral products form five-sixths of the total exports, the principal article being cubic nitre (or Chile saltpetre), of which the value was £15,460,000 in 1907 and £14,832,655 in 1931; next come copper, iodine, wool, and silver. The annual value of exports has in recent years reached as high as £46,721,497; the imports, £30,584,520; in 1931 they were £23,160,000 and £17,722,500 respectively. The total exports from Chile to the United Kingdom amounted to £4,737,002 in 1931; the imports from the United Kingdom to Chile, £2,148,696. Accounts are kept in *pesos* (12 cents), the gold peso (=100 *centavos*) being of the value of 6*d*. £1 sterling therefore equals, at par, 40 gold pesos.

There are over 5540 miles of railway, of which the State owns over 3600. The Transandine Railway has brought Santiago within 36 hours of Buenos Aires. The Arica to La Paz Railway was opened in 1912 Electrification of the railways was begun in 1921 on the line between Valparaiso and Santiago. Aviation is highly developed, and a plant for the manufacture of airplanes was established in 1930. Chile is a Republic, and is considered the best-regulated in South America. It is under a President, elected for five years, and a Council of State. The legislature is composed of a Senate, elected for six years, and a House of Deputies, elected for three years. There are 1348 miles of navigable rivers and lakes. There are well-equipped wireless stations all along the coast. The army numbers about 20,000 men (war strength, 200,000); the chief vessels of the navy are a battleship and five protected cruisers. The Chilians are mostly of Spanish or Indian descent. They are generally fond of agricultural pursuits, and possess a considerable amount of energy and enterprise. Education is free and, since 1920, compulsory.

There are a State University, a Catholic University, two Industria

Universities, and numerous colleges, lyceums, and special institutions. Roman Catholicism is the established religion of Chile. The part of Chile lying south of the River Biobio (or about lat. 38° S.) is inhabited chiefly by Indians. The Araucanians, who also call themselves Alapuche, or "children of the soil," and number about 101,118, inhabit the region lying between the Rivers Biobio and Valdivia, and long maintained their independence, till in 1882 they became subjects of the Chilian Government.

History.—Chile originally belonged to the Incas of Peru, from whom it was wrested by the Spaniards under Pizarro and Almagro in 1535. From this period Chile continued a colony of Spain till 1810, when a revolution commenced, which terminated in 1817 in the independence of Chile. Several internal commotions have since occurred; but the country has been free from these compared with other South American states. A war begun with Spain in 1865 led to the blockade of the coast by the Spanish fleet, and the bombardment of Valparaiso in 1866. Between 1879 and 1881 a war was successfully waged with Bolivia and Peru, in reference to the rights of Chile in the mineral district of Atacama. In 1891 an insurrection arose against President Balmaceda's administration, a movement which resulted in his overthrow and suicide. The Tacna-Arica dispute with Peru (q.v.) was settled in 1929 by ceding Tacna to Peru.—BIBLIOGRAPHY: D. Barros Arana, *Historia jeneral de Chile* (15 vols.); A. U. Hancock, *History of Chile*; G. F. S. Elliott, *Chile: its History and Development*; M. R. Wright, *The Republic of Chile*; W. H. Koebel, *Modern Chile*; F. J. G. Maitland, *Chile: its Land and People*.

CHILE PINE. Evergreen coniferous tree native to mountainous regions in S. Chile (*Araucaria imbricata*). Popularly called monkey puzzle, it yields durable timber; the oval cones are roasted for food. It sometimes grows to a height of 150 feet. It was introduced into Britain in 1796.

CHILE SALTPETRE. *See* SODA NITRE.

CHILHAM. Village of Kent. It is 5 miles from Canterbury and 65 from London, on the Southern Railway. It has a fine old church and a castle built in Norman times. Pop. 1232.

CHILI. *See* CHILLIES.

CHILKÁ. A shallow lagoon in India, separated by a narrow ridge from the Bay of Bengal, and mostly in Orissa.

CHILKOOT PASS. A pass on the frontier of North-West Canada and Alaska, on the route from the sea, by way of the Lynn Canal, to the Klondyke.

CHILLAN (chil-yàn′). A town, Chile, capital of the province of Nuble, in an angle between the Chillan and Nuble, connected by rail with Talcahuano and Santiago. Pop. 39,511.

CHILLED IRON. Iron cast in metal moulds called *chills*, where, on account of the rapid conducting of the heat, the iron cools more quickly on the surface than it would do if cast in sand. Chilled iron is whiter, and has a harder surface than iron cast in any other way.

CHILLIANWAL′LA. A village of India in the Punjab, near the Jhelum, famous for a well-contested battle fought in its vicinity in Jan., 1849, between the British under Lord Gough and the Sikhs, in which the latter all but gained the victory.

CHILLICOTHE (-koth′e). A beautiful and flourishing town, Ohio, United States, on the west bank of the Scioto, with manufacturing and other industries. Pop. 18,340.

CHIL′LIES. The fruits of the Capsicum, used to make cayenne pepper, pickles, and chilli vinegar. Chillies are all natives of tropical America, and were first made known to Europe by Peter Martyr the year after the discovery of America.

CHILLINGHAM. Village of Northumberland. It stands on the Till, 4 miles from Wooler. Chillingham Castle, the seat of the Earl of Tankerville, was built in the fourteenth century, but in its present form dates from the seventeenth. In the park a herd of wild cattle is still maintained, though the castle has been closed.

CHIL′LINGWORTH, William. An English divine, born at Oxford in 1602, and educated at Trinity College, Oxford, where metaphysics and theology were his favourite studies. Subtle reasoning on authority and infallibility led him for a time into the Church of Rome, but he afterwards returned to the English Church, and published in 1638 a great work in justification of himself, *The Religion of Protestants a Safe Way to Salvation*. He was made Chancellor of the bishopric of Salisbury, and on the outbreak of the Civil War supported the king's cause, and was made prisoner at the surrender of Arundel Castle. He died 30th Jan., 1644. *Sermons* and other works were also published by him, but his *Religion of Protestants* is what has given him lasting fame. A *Life*, by Rev. T. Birch, will be found in the 1742 edition of Chillingworth's *Works*.

CHILLON (shē-yōn). A castle, Switzerland, on the Lake of Geneva, 6½ miles S.E. of Vevay, once an important stronghold of the Counts of Savoy, and the prison-house of Francis Bonnivard, prior of St. Victor, Geneva, from 1530 to 1536. It has acquired interest from Byron's poem, *The Prisoner of Chillon*.

CHILOÉ (chēl-wā'). A province and island of Chile. The province comprehends the Island of Chiloé together with a number of other islands and a portion of the mainland. The Island of Chiloé is for the most part covered with dense forests, but large tracts of it are still unexplored. The chief town is San Carlos, or Ancud. The exports consist chiefly of timber from the forests of the island and the mainland. The climate is healthy but very wet. Area of the province, 12,680 sq. miles; pop. 183,499.

CHILOGNATHA, or CHILOPODA. *See* CHEI-.

CHILON (kī'lon), or **CHILO**. Son of Damagetus, one of the so-called Seven Sages of Greece. He flourished about the beginning of the sixth century B.C., and was a native of Sparta, and one of the Ephori, or chief magistrates. A collection of his sayings is extant.

CHILPERIC. The names of two Frankish kings. **Chilperic I.**, on the death of his father Clotaire I., attempted to take possession of the kingdom, but was compelled by his brothers to divide it amongst them. He was assassinated in 583. **Chilperic II.**, son of Childeric II., became king of Neustria in 715. Charles Martel made him king over the whole kingdom, soon after which he died.

CHILTERN HILLS. A range of flint and chalk hills, England, extending through Oxford, Hertford, and Buckingham shires; loftiest summit, 905 feet. These hills were anciently covered with forests, and were infested by numerous bands of robbers. To protect the inhabitants

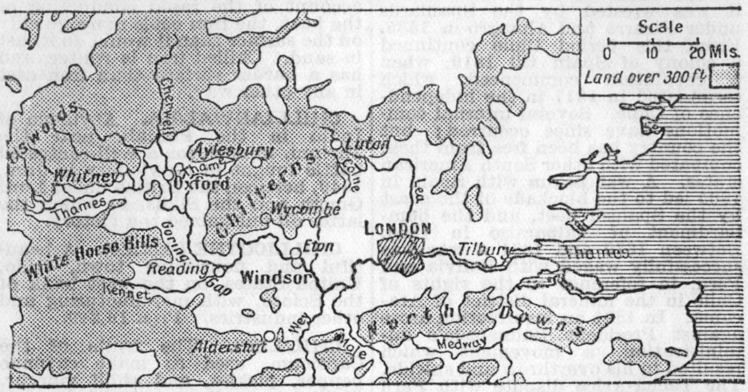

The Basin of the Thames, showing the position of the Chiltern Hills

of the neighbouring districts an officer was appointed by the Crown, called the Steward of the Chiltern Hundreds, and, although the duties and emoluments have long ceased, the office still exists, and is made use of to afford members of the House of Commons (who cannot give up their seats directly) an opportunity of resigning their seats when they desire to do so. Being regarded as an appointment of honour and profit under Government, the acceptance of it disqualifies a member from retaining his seat. The practice began about the year 1750.

CHILTERN HUNDREDS. Three hundreds in Buckinghamshire, Desborough, Burnham, and Stoke. They owe their importance to their connexion with parliamentary procedure. In the olden days stewards of the Chiltern Hundreds were appointed to keep the district free from robbers. A small salary was paid to them, but in course of time the office became a sinecure. It is still retained, however, and a member of Parliament who wishes to resign does so by accepting the office of Steward of the Chiltern Hundreds. Legally a member cannot resign his seat. If, however, he accepts a position of profit under the crown he vacates it.

CHILVERS COTON. A parish in the county of Warwick, 8 miles from Coventry. There are extensive coal-fields in the vicinity. It is served by the Coventry Canal.

CHIMÆRA, or CHIMERA (ki-mē′ra). In classical mythology, a fire-breathing monster, the foreparts of whose body were those of a lion, the middle of a goat, and the hinder of a serpent. Thus the name came to be used for an unnatural production of the fancy.

CHIMÆRA (ki-mē′ra). A genus of cartilaginous fishes, and the chief type of the ord. Holocephali, related to sharks. The best-known species is the *Chimæra monstrōsa,* which inhabits the northern seas, and is sometimes called *king of the herrings*, and, from its two pairs of large teeth, *rabbit-fish.* There is but one gill-opening, and the tail terminates in a point, the fish having altogether a singular appearance. It seldom exceeds 3 feet in length. The Holocephali also include the somewhat similar *Callorhynchus antarcticus,* which possesses a downwardly bent snout and is native to the South Pacific and Antarctic; and two species of Harriotta, deep-water forms living in the North Atlantic and North Pacific.

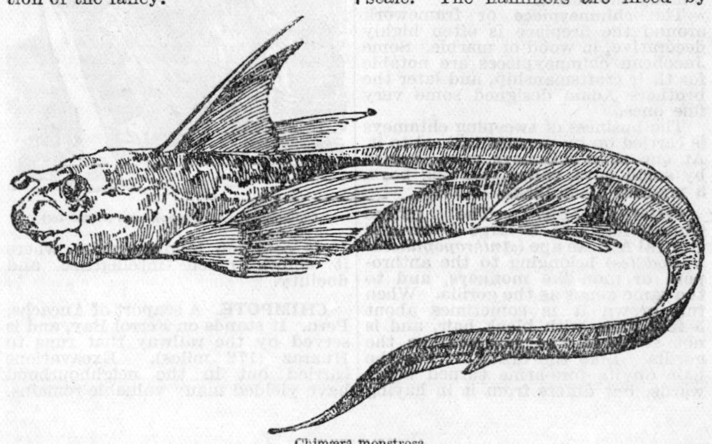

Chimæra monstrosa

CHIMBORA′ZO. A mountain of Ecuador, about 90 miles S. by W. of Quito; lat. 1° 20′ S. Though not the loftiest summit of the Andes, it rises to the height of about 20,498 feet above the level of the sea, and is covered with perpetual snow 2600 feet from the summit and upwards. In 1880 its summit was reached for the first time by E. Whymper.—*Chimborazo* is also the name of a province in Ecuador; pop. 210,000.

CHIMERE (shi-mēr′). The upper robe to which the lawn sleeves of a bishop are attached.

CHIMES. A species of music, mechanically produced by the strokes of hammers against a series of bells, tuned agreeably to a given musical scale. The hammers are lifted by levers acted upon by metallic pins, or wooden pegs, stuck into a large barrel, which is made to revolve by clockwork, and is so connected with the striking part of the clock mechanism that it is set in motion by it at certain intervals of time, usually every hour, or every quarter of an hour. The chime mechanism is sometimes so constructed that it may be played like a piano, but with the fist instead of the fingers.

CHIM′NEY. A structure, generally of stone or brick, containing passage or flue by which the smoke of a fire or furnace-gases escape to the open air. In this sense the first chimneys we read of are no earlier than the Middle Ages. The higher a chimney, the more is its draught, provided the fire is great enough properly to heat the column of air in it, because the tendency of the smoke or gases to draw upwards is in proportion to the difference in weight between the column of heated air in the chimney and a similar column of cooler external air. Smoky chimneys may be caused by the presence of adjoining buildings obstructing the wind, causing irregular currents of air, or by faulty construction of the fireplace and adjacent parts of the chimney. The first may generally be cured by fixing a chimney-pot of a particular construction, or a revolving cowl, on the chimney top to prevent the wind blowing down; in the second case the narrowing of the chimney throat and the filling in of the eddy corners will generally remedy the defect.

The **chimneypiece** or framework around the fireplace is often highly decorative, in wood or marble. Some Jacobean chimneypieces are notable for their craftsmanship, and later the brothers Adam designed some very fine ones.

The business of sweeping chimneys is carried on by persons trained to it. At one time chimneys were cleaned by small boys, called climbing boys, a practice made illegal in 1842.

CHIMPAN'ZEE. The native Guinea name of a large West and Central African ape (*Anthropopithecus troglodўtes*) belonging to the anthropoid or man-like monkeys, and to the same genus as the gorilla. When full grown it is sometimes about 5 feet high, with black hair, and is not so large and powerful as the gorilla. Like the orang, it has the hair on its fore-arms turned backwards, but differs from it in having an additional dorsal vertebra and a thirteenth pair of ribs. It walks erect better than most of the apes. It feeds on fruits, often robs the gardens of the natives, and constructs a sort of nest amongst the branches.

Chimpanzee (*Anthropopithecus troglod ies*)

It is common in menageries, where it shows much intelligence and docility.

CHIMPOTE. A seaport of Ancachs, Peru. It stands on Ferrol Bay, and is served by the railway that runs to Huaraz (172 miles). Excavations carried out in the neighbourhood have yielded many valuable remains.

END OF VOLUME II